marketing

. . . and the winner of the *Marketing* cover competition is . . .

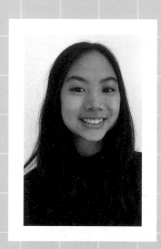

June Lin

a third year student studying Graphic Communication at the University of Reading

In 2017, Oxford University Press invited creative undergraduate and postgraduate students to enter a competition to design the front cover of the fifth edition of *Marketing*.

Our panel of judges, which included the authors and members of the Higher Education team at Oxford University Press, chose the winning entry based on the striking simplicity of the design and how well it represented marketing as a discipline.

Congratulations to June and thank you to all those who participated in our competition.

We need you!

Do you want to have your say on business textbooks?
Do you want to help us develop our textbooks to better meet your needs?
You can do this all whilst gaining credits to spend on OUP books, as well as bolstering your CV. OUP needs you to review and offer opinions on new publishing ideas, text, covers, and more. Join our business student panel today.
To find out more and join visit:

global.oup.com/ukhe/panel/business_panel

5TH EDITION

marketing

Paul Baines

Chris Fill

Sara Rosengren

Paolo Antonetti

OXFORD
UNIVERSITY PRESS

Great Clarendon Street, Oxford, OX2 6DP,
United Kingdom

Oxford University Press is a department of the University of Oxford.
It furthers the University's objective of excellence in research, scholarship,
and education by publishing worldwide. Oxford is a registered trade mark of
Oxford University Press in the UK and in certain other countries

Second edition 2011
Third edition 2014
Fourth edition 2017
Impression: 1

Published in the United States of America by Oxford University Press
198 Madison Avenue, New York, NY 10016, United States of America

British Library Cataloguing in Publication Data

Data available

Library of Congress Control Number: 2018959365

ISBN 978-0-19-880999-9

Printed in Italy by L.E.G.O. S.p.A.

To Ning, for taking us to new places
Paul Baines

To Karen, my loving companion in life
Chris Fill

To Olof, Alma, and Moa—my own dream team
Sara Rosengren

To Ermanno and Giuliana, for their example and support
Paolo Antonetti

Brief Contents

Detailed Contents

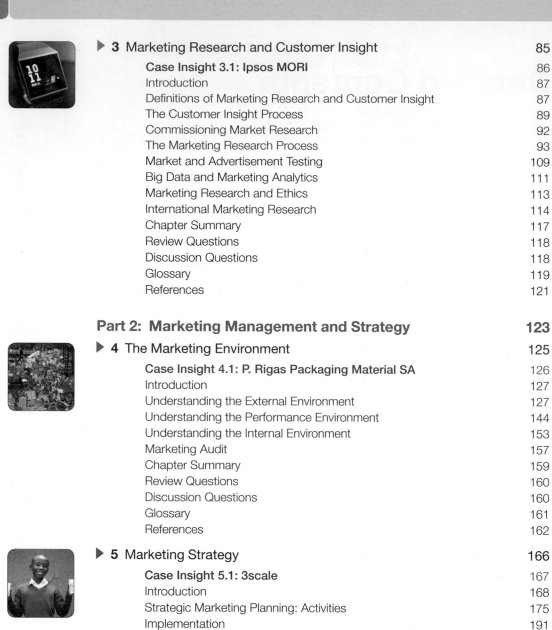
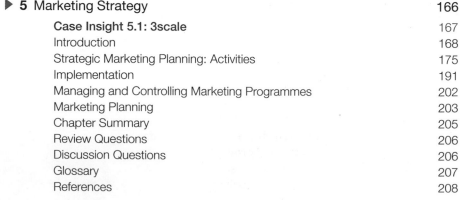

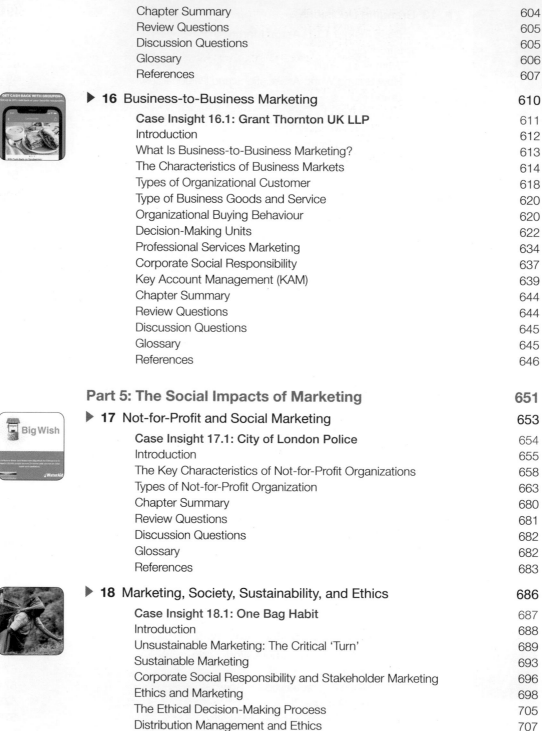

Case Insights

Chapter 1: Aldoraq Water Bottling Plant
Established in 1994 by its founder and owner Khaled A. Almaimani, Aldoraq Water Bottling Plant was one of the first water-bottling factories in Madinah, Saudi Arabia. We speak to Abdurahman Almaimani, general manager, to find out more about how the company seeks to compete with well-known international brands.

Chapter 2: Holdz®
Founded in 2000, Holdz® is an online climbing holds and accessories firm. We speak to its managing director, Steve Goodair, to find out more about how the firm meets its customers' needs.

Chapter 3: Ipsos MORI
When Unilever wanted to develop its medium-term innovation pipeline for four of its household cleaning brands, it turned to global market research firm, Ipsos. We speak to Ipsos's Billie Ing, innovation engagement lead; Leora Unsdorfer, qualitative research manager; and Alex Gilby, quantitative associate director, to find out more.

Chapter 4: P. Rigas Packaging Material SA
P. Rigas Packaging Material SA is one of the leading wholesale companies in the Greek agricultural, livestock, and industrial packaging industry, with more than 25 years of experience. We speak to Achilleas Rigas, chief executive officer (CEO) and chair of the board of directors, to find out how the company conducts its market scanning, aiming to survive in the very difficult Greek economic environment.

Chapter 5: 3scale
Through its staff and offices in Barcelona and San Francisco, 3scale helps organizations to open, manage, and use application programming interfaces (APIs). We speak to Manfred Bortenschlager, API market development director, to find out how the company competes in its marketplace.

Chapter 6: Soberana
When an international beer brand took 10 per cent of the Panamanian beer market, it was time for local brand Soberana to re-evaluate its approach. We talk to Fermin Paus, brand franchise manager, to find out how Soberana responded.

Chapter 7: Lanson International
Founded in 1760, Champagne Lanson is one of the oldest existing champagne houses in France, making some of the world's finest champagnes. We speak to Paul Beavis, managing director, Lanson International, to find out more about how the company looks to further develop its presence in international markets, including the UK.

Chapter 8: Cheil UK
Cheil is a full-service, data-driven agency network, rooted firmly in digital innovation. Cheil UK is part of the Cheil Worldwide Network, made up of more than 6,000 people in 53 offices across five continents. We speak to Manish Bhan, head of retail transformation, to find out how Cheil UK helped client Samsung to develop its retail offering.

Chapter 9: Simply Business
Founded in 2005, Simply Business is an online insurance broker. We speak to Philip Williams, director of strategy and pricing, to find out more about how the company has developed its pricing strategy.

Chapter 10: Åkestam Holst
How can marketing communications stay relevant for consumers increasingly avoiding marketing messages? We speak to Petronella Panérus, chief executive officer (CEO) at the advertising agency Åkestam Holst, to find out how the agency works with clients to ensure that the advertising they create is relevant to consumers' everyday life.

Chapter 11: Adnams

The Adnams brand, founded in 1872, in Southwold, Suffolk, England, is synonymous with beer and, since 2010, now gin, vodka, and whisky too. The company also owns and manages a number of pubs, inns, and retail stores. We speak to Emma Hibbert, marketing director, to find out how the beer at the heart of the brand has been, and continues to be, promoted.

Chapter 12: Spotify

What role do social media play and how should organizations incorporate them into their communication campaigns? We talk to Chug Abramowitz, vice president of global customer service and social media at Spotify, to find out more.

Chapter 13: Aston Martin

The Aston Martin brand, founded in 1913, is synonymous with hand-crafted luxury, peerless beauty, incredible performance, and international motorsport glory. We speak to Simon Sproule, director of global marketing and communications, to find out how the brand is promoted in China.

Chapter 14: Åhléns

As shopper behaviour turns increasingly digital, established retailers have to adapt their channel strategies. We talk to Lotta Bjurhult, business developer retail operations at Åhléns, Sweden's largest department store chain, to find out what it takes to add an online channel to an existing network of department stores.

Chapter 15: Withers Worldwide

Founded in London in 1896, Withers Worldwide has global revenues of over US$200 million, 163 partners, more than 1,000 employees, and clients in more than 80 countries, and has acted for 42 per cent of the top 100 Sunday Times Rich List and 20 per cent of the top 100 of the Forbes Rich List. We speak to Laura Boyle, head of EU marketing and business development, to explore how Withers works to improve the quality of its client relationships.

Chapter 16: Grant Thornton UK LLP

Grant Thornton UK LLP is part of Grant Thornton International Limited (GTIL), one of the world's leading independent advisory, tax, and audit firms. In the UK, Grant Thornton traces its origins to Thornton and Thornton in Oxford in 1904. It grew through many mergers and, by 1980, had formed an alliance with US firm Alexander Grant & Co. One year later, a new international organization, GTIL, was set up. We speak to Anne Blackie, head of bids and strategic accounts at Grant Thornton UK, to find out how the firm manages its client relationships.

Chapter 17: City of London Police

Founded in 1839, the City of London Police (CoLP) police London's 'Square Mile' financial district, with a national responsibility for fraud and economic crime. Because they also police many high-profile public events, they also focus on the prevention of terrorism and crime. We speak to Superintendent Helen Isaac to find out how the CoLP uses social marketing to support law enforcement.

Chapter 18: One Bag Habit

Many sustainability initiatives require new thinking and new partners. Sometimes, they require collaboration with your competitors. We talk to Anna-Karin Dahlberg (Corporate Sustainability Manager, Lindex), Felicia Reuterswärd (Sustainability Manager, H&M Sweden), and Fredrika Klarén (Sustainability Manager, KappAhl) to understand the challenges involved in working on initiatives targeted at stimulating more sustainable consumption behaviours together with your closest competitors.

Market Insights

Author Profiles

 **Paul Baines** is Professor of Political Marketing and Associate Dean (External Relations) at the University of Leicester, and Visiting Professor at Cranfield University. For more than two decades, Paul's research has particularly focused on political marketing, public opinion, and propaganda. He is a Fellow of the Market Research Society (MRS) and the Institute of Directors. Paul's work has been published, among other places, in the *Journal of the American Statistical Association*, *Psychology & Marketing*, *European Journal of Marketing*, and *Journal of Business Research*. Paul's consultancy work includes experience working with government departments on strategic communication research projects, as well as with many small, medium, and large private enterprises, including Glassolutions Saint-Gobain, IBM, 3M, and many more. Paul is director of Baines Associates Limited, a strategic marketing/research consultancy.

 Chris Fill is director of Fillassociates, which develops and delivers learning materials related to marketing and corporate communications (see https://www.chrisfill.com). Formerly principal lecturer at the University of Portsmouth, Chris now works with a variety of private and not-for-profit organizations, including several publishers. He is a Fellow of the Chartered Institute of Marketing (CIM), where he was the senior examiner responsible for the marketing communications modules and, more recently, the Professional Postgraduate Diploma module 'Managing Corporate Reputation'. In addition to numerous papers published in a range of academic journals, Chris has written or contributed to more than 40 books, including his market-leading and internationally recognized textbook, *Marketing Communications*, now in its seventh edition.

 **Sara Rosengren** is Professor of Marketing and Retailing at Stockholm School of Economics, where she is also Head of the Centre for Retailing. Sara is a board member of the European Advertising Academy (EAA). Her research on creative marketing communications has been published in leading academic journals such as the *Journal of Advertising*, *Journal of Advertising Research*, and *Journal of Brand Management*. She is especially renowned for her work on advertising equity. Sara is passionate about bridging the gap between marketing academy and practice. She is frequently invited to speak at academic institutions, industry seminars, and company get-togethers, and regularly comments on marketing- and retail-related phenomena in the Swedish media.

 Paolo Antonetti is Associate Professor of Marketing at Neoma Business School, Rouen Campus (France). He is also Visiting Professor at the School of Business and Management, Queen Mary University of London. His research focuses on the role of consumer emotions in a range of marketing and business contexts, with a specific focus on how emotions influence consumers' reactions to corporate social responsibility. Paolo's articles have appeared in several leading international publications and examine a wide range of marketing, business ethics, and general management topics. Research results have been disseminated in the *British Journal of Management*, *Journal of Service Research*, *Journal of Business Research*, *Journal of Business Ethics*, and the *European Journal of Marketing*, among others. Paolo is on the editorial board of the *European Journal of Marketing*, *International Journal of Market Research*, and *Frontiers Psychology*.

Acknowledgements

Course textbooks constitute major writing and research projects, resulting from the combined efforts of many people, not only in the design, development, and production phases, but also in the sales, marketing, and distribution phases of a 'book' writing project. I say 'book', because our endeavour really encompasses an entire learning system, with both physical and electronic elements, including the substantial online resources that accompany the (e-)book. Producing the textbook is therefore one small component of the entire endeavour.

This fifth edition builds on the work undertaken by many people who have contributed to the development of previous editions. Many more people, and some of our previous contributors, also contributed to this fifth edition and its online resources. As ever, most of those people are acknowledged below, but there are many others whose contributions deserve to be acknowledged anonymously. We thank them for their selfless help in evaluating and contributing to the development of this project.

We would like to thank our colleagues and former colleagues at our various respective universities over the years for their support and discussions, all of which have in some way made their way into the book in some form. We would also like to thank Yanjun Gao, a PhD student at Cranfield University, for her contribution to the online resources for the fifth edition.

As with any large textbook project, this work is the result of a co-production between the academic authors and Oxford University Press editors and staff. For the fifth edition, we would like to thank Nicola Hartley, our commissioning editor, for making the commissioning and development processes run so smoothly and for her constant positivity. Thanks are also due to Kate Gilks, our publishing editor, for her help in incorporating the comments of the very many reviewers, managing the development process (including the video production) so efficiently, and for her considerable help in polishing the final manuscript. Her steady guidance and wisdom have been invaluable in producing this revised edition to what has been a very challenging production cycle. We would like to thank Joe Matthews, senior production editor, for his role in shaping the final design of the book and bringing it out on schedule with the help of designers Anna Scully and Claire Dickinson. The media team at Oxford Digital Media—particularly, James Tomalin, Nikisha McIntosh, Matt Greetham, and Jose Silver—have, as ever, improved our online resources proposition with great video production work.

Unless our customers, students, and lecturers want to use this book, there's little point in writing and producing it. It's due to the efforts of the marketing team—Marianne Lightowler, head of marketing, and Jen Crawley, marketing manager—that the book hits the shops, gets clicked on, and appears in your hands. Their openness to the authors' (sometimes mad) marketing ideas is refreshing and we know, as marketers, that we cannot be the easiest people to work with (that is, too many chefs spoil the broth!).

The original ideas for the template for the book—right back to the first edition—derived from six anonymous university lecturer participants in a focus group, who kindly met with us at OUP's offices to discuss what a new marketing textbook, in an already crowded market, needed to look like. Since then, the book has become the best-selling book in the field. Our success remains attributable to the comments they made about what they really wanted in a textbook and we've tried to stay true to that formula ever since. For this edition, we have replaced many of the market insights and, as ever, we have included contributions from students, practitioners, and marketing academics.

The authors and publishers would like to thank the following people for their comments and reviews throughout the process of developing the text and the online resources over the last five editions:

David Alcock, Birmingham City University, UK
Liz Algar, University of Essex, UK
Dr Seamus Allison, Nottingham Trent University, UK
Malcolm Ash, Staffordshire University, UK
Graham Bailey, University of Chichester, UK
Dr Nina Belei, Radboud University, The Netherlands
Riccardo Benzo, Birkbeck, University of London, UK
De Laura Bradley, University of Ulster, UK
Jenny Bratherton, Regent's University London, UK
Jane Burns, University College London, UK
Dr Rahul Chawdhary, Kingston University, UK
Dr Geraldine Cohen, Brunel University, UK
Professor Joseph Coughlan, Maynooth University, Ireland
Denise Daniels, Newcastle University, UK
Dr Katherine Duffy, University of Glasgow, UK
Dr Susanne Durst, University of Skövde, Sweden
Professor John Egan, Regent's University London, UK
Dr Fiona Ellis-Chadwick, Open University Business School, UK
Dr Margaret Fletcher, University of Glasgow, UK
Mike Flynn, University of Gloucestershire, UK
Dr Mikael Gidhagen, Uppsala University, Sweden
Malcolm Goodman, Durham University, UK
Dr Charles Graham, London South Bank University, UK
Dr Catherine Groves, University of Swansea, UK
Anne Hampton, University of Buckingham, UK
Dr Michael Harker, University of Strathclyde, UK
Graham Harrison, University of Sussex, UK
David Harvey, (formerly) University of Huddersfield, UK
Jocelyn Hayes, University of York, UK
Mick Hayes, University of Portsmouth, UK
Clive Helm, University of Westminster, UK
Dr Auke Hunneman, BI Norwegian Business School, Norway
Dr Elizabeth Jackson, Curtin Business School, Australia
Nigel Jones, Sheffield Hallam University, UK
Dr Aidan Kelly, University of East London, UK
Jaya Kypuram, University of East London, UK
Dr Sotiris Lalaounis, University of Exeter, UK
Dr Margaret-Anne Lawlor, Dublin Institute of Technology, Ireland
Robert Leonardi, Södertörn University, Sweden
Joe Liddiatt, University of West England, UK
Dr Heléne Lundberg, Mid Sweden University, Sweden
Fares Lutfi, NHL Stenden University of Applied Sciences, The Netherlands
Dr Nnamdi Madichie, University of Sharjah, United Arab Emirates

Alice Maltby, University of the West of England, UK
George Masikunas, Kingston University, UK
Dawn McCartie, Newcastle University, UK
Dr Patrick McCole, Queen's University Belfast, Northern Ireland
Tony McGuinness, Aberystwyth University, Wales, UK
Richard Meek, Lancaster University, UK
Dr Nina Michaelidou, Loughborough University, UK
Dr Caroline Miller, Keele University, UK
Dr Janice Moorhouse, University of Roehampton, UK
William Mott, University of Wolverhampton, UK
Connie Nolan, Canterbury Christ Church University, UK
Pfavai Nyajeka, University of Hertfordshire, UK
Dr Winfred Onyas, University of Leicester, UK
Dr Anastasios Pagiaslis, University of Nottingham, UK
Wybe Popma, University of Brighton, UK
Nicholas Pronger, Birbeck, University of London, UK
Professor Andrea Prothero, University College Dublin, Ireland
Chris Richardson, Aston University, UK
Neil Richardson, Leeds Beckett University, UK
Professor Deborah Roberts, University of Nottingham, UK
Vicky Roberts, University of Staffordshire, UK
Chris Rock, University of Greenwich, UK
Irene Roozen, Katholieke Universiteit Leuven, Belgium
Professor Michael Saren, University of Leicester, UK
Dr Declan Scully, University of Roehampton, UK
Peter Simcock, Liverpool John Moores University, UK
Bert Smit, NHTV Breda University of Applied Sciences, The Netherlands
Dr Lorna Stevens, University of Ulster, UK
Dr Frauke Mattison Thompson, Universiteit van Amsterdam, UK
Dr Ann Torres, National University of Ireland, Galway, Ireland
Professor Paul Trott, University of Portsmouth, UK
Dr Prakash Vel, University of Wollongong, Dubai, UAE
Dr Lucia Walsh, Dublin Institute of Technology, Ireland
Dr Fatima Wang, King's Business School, UK
Peter Waterhouse, University of Bedfordshire, UK
Jennie White, University of Chichester, UK
Dr Kevan Williams, University of East Anglia, UK
Peter Williams, Leeds Beckett University, UK
Matthew Wood, University of Brighton, UK
Professor Helen Woodruffe-Burton, Edge Hill University, UK

We would particularly like to thank the following lecturers, students, and practitioners who contributed market insights to the fifth edition:

Professor Carmen Abril, IE Business School, Spain
Carl-Philip Ahlbom, PhD candidate, Stockholm School of Economics, Sweden
Claire Allison, Sherwood Forest Hospitals NHS Foundation Trust, UK

Dr Seamus Allison, Nottingham Trent University, UK
Professor Ilaria Baghi, Modena and Reggio Emilia University, Italy
Dr Ning Baines, De Montfort University, UK
Dr Isabel Carrero, Comillas University, Spain
Dr Ethel Claffey, Waterford Institute of Technology, Ireland
Dr Jonas Colliander, Stockholm School of Economics, Sweden
Professor Victoria Labajo González, Universidad Pontificia Comillas, Spain
Chris Liassides, University of Sheffield, International Faculty, CITY College, UK
Joe Liddiatt, University of the West of England, UK
Dr Karina T. Liljedal, Stockholm School of Economics, Sweden
Rachael Millard, PhD candidate, Queen Mary University of London, UK
Dr Erik Modig, Stockholm School of Economics, Sweden
Dr Paul Morrissey, Waterford Institute of Technology, Ireland
Marie O'Dwyer, Waterford Institute of Technology, Ireland
Dr Robert P. Ormrod, Aarhus University, Denmark
Dr Eleni Papaoikonomou, Rovira and Virgili University, Spain
Professor Anthony Patterson, University of Liverpool, UK
Dr Norman Peng, University of Westminster, UK
Naomi Ramage, former student, Buckinghamshire New University, UK
Dr Ian Richardson, Stockholm University, Sweden
Sofie Sagfossen, PhD candidate, Stockholm School of Economics, Sweden
Leon Savidis, Business Analyst, Damart
Tina Sendlhofer, PhD candidate, Stockholm School of Economics, Sweden
Bert Smit, NHTV University of Applied Sciences, Netherlands
Martin Söndergaard, PhD candidate, Stockholm School of Economics, Sweden
Julius Stephan, Aston University, UK
Dr Frauke Mattison Thompson, Universiteit van Amsterdam, The Netherlands
Dr Sarah Turnbull, University of Portsmouth, UK
Dr Carmen Valor, Universidad Pontificia Comillas, Spain
Dr Lucia Walsh, Dublin Institute of Technology, Ireland

As ever, we have also incorporated a series of practitioner marketing 'problems' within the text. This requires a considerable commitment from practitioners in developing the marketing 'problem' with the authors and in filming the 'solution'. Thus we would like to thank the following practitioners who contributed to the new edition for their time, effort, and commitment to this project.

Chug Abramowitz, vice president global customer service and social media, Spotify, Sweden/United States
Abdurahman Almaimani, general manager, Aldoraq Water Bottling Plant, Saudi Arabia
Paul Beavis, managing director, Champagne Lanson UK/International Markets, UK
Manish Bhan, head of retail transformation, Cheil UK, UK
Lotta Bjurhult, business developer retail operations, Åhléns, Sweden
Anne Blackie, head of bids and strategic accounts, Grant Thornton UK LLP, UK
Manfred Bortenschlager, API market development director, 3scale.net, Spain
Laura Boyle, head of EU marketing and business development, Withers Worldwide, UK
Alex Gilby, quantitative associate director, Ipsos MORI, UK

Steve Goodair, managing director, Holdz®, UK

Emma Hibbert, marketing director, Adnams, UK

Billie Ing, innovation engagement lead, Ipsos MORI, UK

Superintendent Helen Isaac, Community Policing—Uniformed Policing Directorate, City of London Police, UK

Petronella Panérus, chief executive officer, Åkestam Holst, Sweden

Fermin Paus, brand manager, Soberana, Panama

Achilleas Rigas, chief executive officer and chair of the board of directors, P. Rigas Packaging Material SA, Greece

Simon Spoule, director of marketing and communications, Aston Martin Lagonda, UK

Leora Unsdorfer, qualitative research manager, Ipsos MORI, UK

Philip Williams, director of strategy and pricing, Simply Business, UK

Other reviewers have chosen to remain anonymous, but contributed considerably to the final proposition. We would like to thank them for taking time out of their busy schedules to evaluate the various draft chapters of the book. The publishers would be pleased to clear permission with any copyright holders whom we have inadvertently failed, or been unable, to contact.

Preface

Welcome to the fifth edition of *Marketing*. You might be wondering, 'Why should I buy this marketing textbook?' The answer is that your marketing lecturers told us you need a new one! Our first edition was the first truly integrated print and electronic learning package for introductory marketing modules. For this fifth edition, we've gone even further. Before we started writing, we consulted marketing lecturers, building on our research for the previous editions, to identify how we might tailor the book and online resources to meet your learning needs better. Our aim with this edition's book and online resources is to provide an innovative learning experience and to pique readers' curiosity to inspire the next generation of marketers to excel in this amazing, exciting, and fast-moving discipline.

In our research for the book, we discovered that you needed:

- more consideration of how marketing theory links to marketing practice;
- more consideration of ethics, sustainability, and marketing's impact on society;
- updated market insights, and an updated digital and social media marketing chapter to keep pace with the changes in the marketplace;
- an increased digital presence throughout the book;
- for the book to contain even more enticing advertising images;
- for the book to contain even more student-friendly case studies; and
- for the book to contain more variety in the format of the case insight videos.

As with the first, second, third, and fourth editions, we sought to bring contemporary marketing perspectives to life for students new to the concept of marketing. We want the book to be motivational, creative, applied, and highly relevant to you.

Marketing starts with the fundamentals of marketing from classical marketing perspectives, then contrasts these with newer views from the services and societal schools of marketing, helping you to develop your knowledge and understanding of marketing. In the fifth edition, there remains extensive coverage of the societal implications of marketing and we continue to emphasize how marketing theory operates in practice. This important link element means that we have worked harder to relate our market insights to the theoretical frameworks, models, and concepts outlined in each chapter, to aid your learning.

In the online resources, we also provide you with web-based research activities, abstracts from seminal papers, study guidelines, multiple-choice questions, and a flashcard glossary to help you to broaden and reinforce your own learning.

We aim to provide powerful learning insights into marketing theory and practice through a series of 'insight' features—case, market, and research insights. *Marketing* is for life, purchased for use on first- and second-year undergraduate marketing programmes, or as reference reading on professional and postgraduate marketing courses, but to be retained and referred to throughout the course of your marketing or business degree. We sincerely hope you enjoy learning more about marketing, and that this book and its online resources pique your curiosity!

If you have any comments about any of the content in this book, please tweet them to: @DrPaulBaines and add the hashtag, #BainesetalMarketing5e. The more you tweet, the more we learn about what you want from a marketing text.

Who Should Use This Book?

The main audiences for this book are as follows:

- Undergraduate students in universities and colleges of higher and further education, who are taught in English, around the world, will find this text of use. The case material and the examples within the text are deliberately global and international in scale, so that international students can benefit from the text.

- Postgraduate students on MBA and MSc/MA courses with a strong marketing component will find this text useful for pre-course and background reading, particularly because of the real-life case problems presented at the beginning of each chapter, accompanied by audiovisual material presenting the solution available in the online resources.

- Professional students studying for marketing qualifications through the Chartered Institute of Marketing, the Direct Marketing Association, and other professional training organizations and trade bodies should find that the extensive use of examples of marketing practice from around the world make this text relevant for those working in a marketing or commercial environment.

New to This Edition

- New and updated market insights incorporate a broader range of more international, digital, and ethics-focused examples.

- More images and adverts are included, illustrating real-life campaigns, offerings, and events.

- There is new coverage of the latest phenomena in marketing seldom covered in other textbooks, including showrooming, co-creation, and demarketing.

- Brand new case insights and accompanying video interviews feature well-known companies, including Ipsos MORI, Adnams, Grant Thornton, and Åkestam Holst.

- Additional videos include top marketers talking about their routes into the industry, and offering careers advice on how to stand out at interviews and assessment days.

How to Use This Textbook

This text seeks to enhance your learning as part of an undergraduate or introductory course in marketing, or as pre-reading for your postgraduate or professional course. It can, however, also act as a 'book for life', operating as a reference book for you on all matters marketing, particularly during the initial part of your career in marketing and business.

Generally, we learn only what is meaningful to us. Dr Edward de Bono, who coined the term 'lateral thinking', talks of the human mind as a self-organizing pattern recognition system. This means that we incorporate new information by considering how that information is related to existing information already stored in our minds. In this book, we have tried to make your learning fun and meaningful by including a multitude of real-life cases. We also try to stimulate your thinking in each chapter by asking you questions at the beginning of the chapter to stir your own reflections on marketing phenomena based on your own lived experience. But it's not enough simply to rely on your own (admittedly vast) experience of consumer marketing and reflections; you also need to be ready to read beyond the book. Consequently, we recommend readings in research insight sections throughout the book. Try to get hold of the seminal articles and books highlighted in these research insights through your university's electronic library system and skim-read them. Again, if possible reflect on your own experience around the concepts you are studying. But remember that you are not on your own in your learning: you have your tutor, your classmates, this book, and the online resources to help you to learn more about marketing.

This textbook includes not only explanatory material and examples on the nature of marketing concepts, but also a holistic learning system designed to aid you, as part of your university or professional course, to develop your understanding by means of reading the text and working with the materials available in the online resources. Work through the examples in the text and the review questions; read the seminal articles that have defined a particular sub-discipline in marketing; use the learning material on the website. This textbook aims to be reader-focused, designed to help you to learn marketing for yourself.

As students, we tend to operate either a surface or a deep approach to learning. With the surface approach, we tend to memorize lists of information, whereas with a deep approach, we are actively assimilating, theorizing about, and *understanding* the information. With a surface learning approach, we run into trouble when example problems learnt are presented in different contexts. We may have simply memorized the procedure without understanding the actual problem. Deep approaches to learning are related to better-quality educational outcomes and better grades, and the process is more enjoyable. To help you to pursue a deep approach to learning, we strongly suggest that you complete the exercises, visit the web links, and conduct the Internet activities referred to throughout and at the end of each chapter, as well as the other activities available in the online resources, to improve your understanding and your course performance.

When it comes to revising for your exams, listen to the authors' chapter podcasts for an overview of the concepts in each chapter. Tackle the multiple-choice questions to identify what you do and don't know, so that you can focus your scarce time on those concepts you need to know more about. When revising, skim-read chapters to save time, but slow down your reading when you encounter material and concepts you don't properly understand. Don't be afraid to read through sentences several times if it's not sinking in. Turn off any negative 'voices' in your own mind that chastise you for not understanding and develop instead a positive, sympathetic 'voice' that supports you as you learn. In other words, be your own best friend when it comes to learning. For your assignments, use the research insights in the various chapters to identify seminal articles or books to cite. Look at the references at the back of each chapter when a particular concept is discussed and consult those original sources, and even the references within these sources, afterwards. By 'snowballing' through references in this way, you can develop a much stronger understanding of a concept, which will in turn demonstrate to your tutors and markers that you have read widely and understood the concept.

Honey and Mumford's Learning-Style Questionnaire

Honey and Mumford (1986) developed a learning-style questionnaire that divides learners into four categories based on the aspect of Kolb's learning process at which they perform best. Completion of the 40-item questionnaire, available at a reasonable price at https://www.peterhoney.com, provides you with scores on each of the following four categories to allow you to determine your dominant learning style:

1 *Activists*—Where this style is dominant, you learn better through involvement in new experiences through concrete experience. You learn better by *doing*.

2 *Reflectors*—Where this style is dominant, you are more likely to consider experiences with hindsight and from a variety of perspectives, and then to rationalize these experiences. You learn better by *reflecting*.

3 *Theorists*—Where this style is dominant, you develop understanding of situations and information by building an abstract theoretical framework for understanding. You learn better by *theorizing*.

4 *Pragmatists*—Where this style is dominant, you learn best by understanding what works best in what circumstances in practice. You learn through *practice*.

Analysis of your learning style will allow you to determine how you learn best at the moment and give you pointers as to what other approaches to learning you might adopt to balance how you develop. You may already have completed a learning-style questionnaire at the beginning of your course and so know which learning styles you need to develop.

We believe most other textbooks are designed to particularly develop the theorist learning style. Review-type questions also enhance the reflector learning style. However, in this text, we also aim to develop the pragmatist component of your learning style by providing you with case insights that highlight decisions made by real-life marketers. Finally, we ask end-of-chapter discussion questions, which require you to work in teams and on your own, as well as provide Internet activities to complete and web links to visit, to develop your activist learning style.

We aim to enhance your learning by providing an integrated marketing learning system, incorporating the key components that you need to understand core marketing principles. As a result, we hope not only that this text and its associated website will facilitate and enhance your learning, making it fun along the way, but also that you will find it useful to use this text, and refer back to it, throughout your student and life experiences of marketing.

Learning a discipline as exciting as marketing should be both fun and challenging. We hope that this textbook and its associated resources bring the discipline alive for you, piquing your curiosity about how the marketing world works. Good luck with your learning and in your career!

How to Use this Book

This book comes equipped with a range of carefully designed learning features to help you get to grips with marketing and develop the essential knowledge and skills you'll need for your future career.

IDENTIFY & REVIEW *through* Learning Outcomes

Introducing you to every chapter, Learning Outcomes outline the main concepts and themes that will be covered to clearly identify what you can expect to learn. These bullet-pointed lists can also be used to review your learning and effectively plan your revision.

Learning Outcomes

After reading this chapter, you will be able to:

▶ Define the concept of marketing

▶ Explain how marketing has developed over the twentieth century and into the twenty-first century

▶ Understand the concepts of exchange in marketing and the marketing mix

▶ Describe the three major contexts of marketing application—that is, consumer goods, business-to-

LEARN & EVALUATE *through* Case Insights

Learn from the professionals with real-life case studies from leading marketers. Discover what their businesses aim to do, what their jobs involve, and what kind of challenges they face, before evaluating your own response to tackling their marketing problem. In the online resources you can find bespoke video interviews with all these professionals, and gain an insight into how they ultimately resolved their marketing dilemmas.

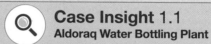

Case Insight 1.1
Aldoraq Water Bottling Plant

Established in 1994 by its founde
Almaimani, Aldoraq Water Bottlir
first water-bottling factories in M
speak to Abdurahman Almaiman
out more about how the compan
well-known international brands

ANALYSE & APPLY *through* Market Insights

Contemporary and varied examples from the business world illustrate the concepts discussed in the chapter and prompt you to analyse the marketing practices of a huge range of companies. Theory into Practice boxes will then help you apply the marketing theory to these practical examples, with accompanying questions reinforcing your learning.

Market Insight 1.1
V&D Goes Bust!

On New Year's Eve 2015, Dutch department store Vroom & Dreesman (V&D), owned by US private equity firm Sun Capital, declared itself insolvent after suffering poor sales, a loss of €49 million on sales of €604 million in 2014, and a year of conflict with unions and landlords. The company was finding it difficult to compete with new competitors and the shift to online

from its financial
of up to 70 candi
administrators inv

Sources: Anon. (201

Research Insight 1.1

To take your learning further, you might wish to read

Borden, N.H. (1964). The concept of the marketing mix. *J. Research*, 4, 2–7.

This early, easy-to-read article explains how marketing managers act as developing marketing programmes. The marketing mix, popularized as

RESEARCH & PROGRESS *through* Research Insights

Take your learning further with the key books and journal articles highlighted in Research Insights, to aid your research and progress your understanding of key topics.

Chapter Summary

To consolidate your learning, the key points from this chapter are summ

■ **Define the concept of marketing.**

Marketing is the process by which organizations anticipate and satis parties' benefit. It involves mutual exchange. Over the last 25 years, recognize the importance of long-term customer relationships to org of marketing recognize the importance of marketing's impacts on so where they are negative.

RECAP & CONSOLIDATE *through* Chapter Summaries

Recap the core themes and ideas of the chapter to consolidate and review your learning in these handy chapter summaries.

Review Questions

1 What is the process consumers go through when buying offerir

2 What is cognitive dissonance and how does it relate to consum

3 How are the psychological concepts of perception, learning, ar understanding consumer choice?

4 How are concepts of personality relevant to understanding con

5 How are concepts of motivation relevant to understanding cons

6 What is the theory of planned behaviour?

REVIEW & REVISE *through* Review Questions

Stimulating questions at the end of every chapter will review your knowledge and highlight any areas that need further revision ahead of the exam.

Discussion Questions

1 Having read Case Insight 1.1 at the beginning of this chapter, how v differentiate itself when competing against local and international b

2 Read the section on the marketing mix within the chapter, and draw following organizations and their target customers:

   A Streaming video company Netflix and its audiences

   B A wealth management company and its clientele

   C Pharmacies (for example Boots UK Ltd, Sweden's Apoteket AB, H consumers

CHALLENGE & REFLECT *through* Discussion Questions

Develop your analytical and reasoning skills by challenging the theory and reflecting on key issues with these stimulating Discussion Questions designed to create lively debate.

Glossary

advertising a form of non-personal communication, by an identified sponsor, that is transmitted through the use of paid-for media.
aggregated demand demand calculated at the population level rather than at the individual level.

American Ma membership and marketir States, opera and Canada.

LOOK UP & CHECK *through* Key Terms and Glossaries

Key Terms are highlighted in blue when they first appear and are collated into glossaries at the end of each chapter, designed for you to look up terms and check your understanding of essential definitions.

How to Use the Online Resources

www.oup.com/uk/baines5e/

There are signposts to the online resources throughout each chapter, and the following specialized resources are available:

Student Resources – Free and open-access material available for users of the book.

Case Insight Videos
Watch the authors in discussion with the leading marketing practitioners featured in the chapter-opening Case Insights as they expand on the marketing challenges they face and what strategies they used to tackle them. Transcripts of each video are also available.

Career Insight Videos
Top practitioners offer valuable career advice for those looking to work in marketing or related fields.

Library of Video Links
A bank of links to marketing videos designed to demonstrate key principles and themes in practice.

Author Audio Podcasts

Short audio summaries of each chapter from the authors, to listen to on the go and help you revise.

Multiple-Choice Questions

Test your knowledge of the chapter and receive instant results with these interactive questions. References to page numbers in the book accompany every question to help you navigate to the topics that need further study.

Flashcard Glossary

Learning the jargon associated with the range of topics in marketing can be a challenge, so this online glossary has been designed to help you understand and memorize the key terms in the book.

Internet Activities

Arranged by chapter, these Internet Activities help you develop your knowledge and improve your understanding of the topic through online research.

Research Insights

Follow the links to access the seminal academic papers suggested in the book's Research Insights.

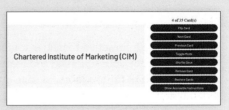

Web Links

Annotated links allow you easy access to up-to-date and reliable marketing-related sites.

Lecturer Resources – For all registered adopters of the book.

VLE Content

To make your teaching more efficient and learning more effective, import all the material available on the Online Resources into your VLE.

PowerPoint Slides

A suite of fully customizable PowerPoint slides for use in lecture presentations accompanies each chapter.

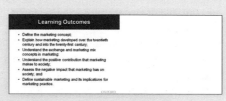

Test Bank

A ready-made interactive testing resource, fully customizable for your teaching and featuring built-in feedback for students, to save you time when creating assessments.

Essay Questions

Provided for each chapter, these stimulating essay questions are accompanied by clear and detailed answer guidance.

Tutorial Activities

Designed for use in seminars and tutorials, and to reinforce practical marketing skills, these activities are directly related to concepts and companies in the book. They offer a range of suggested ideas for easily integrating the book and its resource with your teaching.

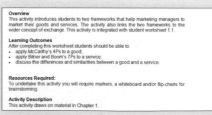

Discussion Question Pointers

Possible points for inclusion when answering the discussion questions at the end of each chapter of the textbook.

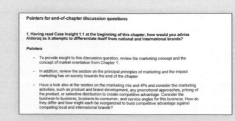

Figures and Tables from the Book

Available for downloading into presentation software or for use in assignments and exam material.

Dashboard

Simple. Informative. Mobile.

Dashboard is a cloud-based online assessment and revision tool. It comes pre-loaded with test questions for students, a homework course if your module leader has adopted Dashboard, and additional resources as listed below. If your lecturer has adopted Dashboard and you have purchased the Dashboard Edition of the book, your standalone access code should be included and will provide instructions on how to sign up for the platform. If you have not purchased the Dashboard Edition or if you have purchased a second-hand copy, you can purchase standalone access online—visit https://www.oxfordtextbooks.co.uk/dashboard for more information.

SIMPLE: With a highly intuitive design, it will take you less than 15 minutes to learn and master the system.

MOBILE: You can access Dashboard from every major platform and device connected to the Internet, whether that's a computer, tablet, or smartphone.

INFORMATIVE: Your assignment and assessment results are automatically graded, giving your instructor a clear view of the class's understanding of the course content.

Student Resources

Dashboard offers all the features of the online resources, but comes with additional questions to take your learning further.

Lecturer Resources

A pre-loaded homework course structured around the book is available, supported by a test bank containing additional multiple-choice questions. Your students can follow the pre-loaded course, or you can customize it, allowing you to add questions from the test bank or from your existing materials to meet your specific teaching needs. Dashboard's Gradebook will automatically grade the homework assignments that you set for your students. The Gradebook also provides heat maps for you to view your students' progress, which helps you to quickly identify areas of the course in which your students may need more practice, as well as the areas in which they are most confident. This feature helps you to focus your teaching time on the areas that matter.

The Gradebook also allows you to administer grading schemes, manage checklists, and administer learning objectives and competencies.

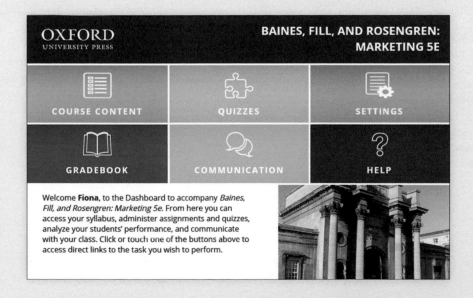

Part 1
Principles of Marketing

Part 1
Principles of Marketing

Chapter 1

Marketing Principles and Practice

Learning Outcomes

After reading this chapter, you will be able to:

▸ Define the concept of marketing

▸ Explain how marketing has developed over the twentieth century and into the twenty-first century

▸ Understand the concepts of exchange in marketing and the marketing mix

▸ Describe the three major contexts of marketing application—that is, consumer goods, business-to-business, and services marketing

▸ Understand the positive contribution marketing makes to society

Case Insight 1.1
Aldoraq Water Bottling Plant

Market Insight 1.1
V&D Goes Bust!

Market Insight 1.2
Servitization at Rolls-Royce

Market Insight 1.3
Harrods: Time for (Thai) Tea

Market Insight 1.4
Google: World-Changing Innovations

Market Insight 1.5
Where Now, Autonomous Car?

Case Insight 1.1
Aldoraq Water Bottling Plant

Established in 1994 by its founder and owner Khaled A. Almaimani, Aldoraq Water Bottling Plant was one of the first water-bottling factories in Madinah, Saudi Arabia. We speak to Abdurahman Almaimani, general manager, to find out more about how the company seeks to compete with well-known international brands.

Aldoraq, headquartered in Madinah, Saudi Arabia, distributes its natural mineral water products throughout the Kingdom, and particularly in Madinah, Makkah, and Yanbu. It is one of the biggest factories in the Middle East and a member of one of the oldest and largest family-owned businesses in Saudi Arabia. The company produces purified drinking water in different bottle sizes and capacities (from 250 ml bottles to 5 gallon containers), and was the first water company in Saudi Arabia to join the International Bottled Water Association (IBWA). The water produced by Aldoraq contains a good percentage of fluoride, is derived from natural water bore-wells, and is purified by ozone. In 2015, sales of the company's 250 ml, 375 ml, and 600 ml products had increased strongly on 2014 sales, but fallen slightly in the 2 litre, 1 gallon, 5 litre, and 5 gallon bottle categories. The 5 gallon refill category, however, had seen a slight gain.

Fast forward to the current year and the future looks bright for bottled water in the Kingdom, with population size expected to reach 39.1 million by 2030 (a 24.1 per cent increase on 2015, according to Euromonitor), growing retail infrastructure, and an increasing number of *baqalah* (small independent stores). Aldoraq's customers are mostly hypermarkets, supermarkets, and medium and small stores that distribute or sell bottled water to consumers (restaurants, fast food stores, canteens, hospitals, households, etc.). Other customers include catering companies, hotels, airport retail outlets, and corporate offices. Often, such customers are looking for price discounts, longer terms of payment, and even coolers to store the water. Distributors decide to buy bottled drinking water from Aldoraq's factory based on which products are available in time and can steadily be supplied to

customers' volume requirements, terms of deals, and consignments, including beneficial payment terms. Of particular importance to customers is the ability to buy all the products they need from one location. Because there are more than 30 water distributors in Madinah, many customers base their decision on the price they pay.

To promote awareness of its brand, Aldoraq recommends that its customers display its product prominently in their stores, in potential consumers' line of sight, and offers volume discounts to its largest distributors accordingly. In addition, Aldoraq supports its community by giving free water to charities and discounted water to the mosque, as well as other religious places. Nevertheless, more recently, some large hotels and stores have started to purchase only premium water from companies selling international brands, such as Evian, Nestlé, and Aquafina, making it hard for Aldoraq to compete. These big brands are trying to dominate the supply chain system. For example, Aquafina, owned by Pepsico, is pushing its water product alongside other products such as Pepsi-Cola. When Aquafina first entered the market, it gave away free samples of water with its Pepsi-Cola product and then pushed customers to buy its Aquafina water brand at the same time. Coca-Cola also competed in this way with its water product Arwa.

How should Aldoraq seek to differentiate itself and thereby compete against both local and international brands?

 Visit the online resources to watch a video interview with Khaled A. Almaimani, where he explains what Aldoraq did.

● ●

Introduction

How have companies marketed their offerings to you previously? Consider the last smartphone you bought, the sports teams you follow, the music you stream, and the airlines you've flown on. Why did you purchase these offerings? Each one has been promoted to you to cater for a particular need. Consider how the offering was distributed. What physical and service-based components is it made of? What societal contributions, positive or negative, do these offerings make, if any? Are substitute offerings available that meet your needs and the needs of society better? These are some of the questions that marketers should ask themselves when designing, developing, and delivering **customer** offerings.

In this chapter, we develop our understanding of marketing principles and marketing's positive impact upon society by defining marketing, comparing and contrasting American, British, and French definitions. (We consider marketing's negative impacts upon society in Chapter 18.) We consider the origins and development of marketing throughout the twentieth and into the twenty-first centuries. We explore how marketing differs in the **consumer** or business-to-consumer (B2C), business-to-business (B2B), and services marketing sectors. The core principles of marketing, incorporating the **marketing mix**, the principle of marketing exchange, **market orientation**, **relationship marketing**, and **service-dominant logic (SDL)**, are all considered. This chapter seeks to provide a thorough grounding in the principles of marketing. (Many of these concepts are considered again in detail in later chapters.)

What Is Marketing?

Consider your own vast experience of being marketed to throughout your life. You will have been subjected to millions of marketing communications messages, bought many thousands of offerings, been involved in very many customer service calls, and visited tens of thousands of shops, supermarkets, and retail outlets (on- and off-line). You're already an experienced customer. In this text, our role is to explain how professionals seek to persuade you to buy their offering, rather than a competitor's. Most customers are just like you and will be as discriminating in their buying habits.

To explain how we market offerings to customers, we first describe what marketing is. There are numerous definitions, but three are presented for easy reference in Table 1.1.

Visit the **online resources** and follow the web links to the CIM and AMA websites to read more about their views on 'What is Marketing?'

The **Chartered Institute of Marketing (CIM)** and **American Marketing Association (AMA)** definitions recognize marketing as a 'management process' and an 'activity', although many firms organize marketing as a discrete department rather than as a service across departments (Sheth and Sisodia, 2005). Nike uses a regional matrix organizational structure, enabling marketing to operate within and across departments, for example in apparel, footwear (Brenner, 2013). The CIM and AMA definitions stress the importance of determining the customer's requirements and 'delivering **value**'. Conversely, our French definition refers to developing an offer of *superior* value. The AMA and French definitions refer to an 'offer' and 'offering', recognizing that marketing can be applied equally to the marketing of goods, services, and ideas, and

Table 1.1 Definitions of marketing

Defining institution/author	Definition
The Chartered Institute of Marketing (CIM)	'The management process responsible for identifying, anticipating, and satisfying customer requirements profitably' (CIM, 2015)
The American Marketing Association (AMA)	'Marketing is the activity, set of institutions, and processes for creating communicating, delivering, and exchanging offerings that have value for customers, clients, partners, and society at large' (AMA, 2013)
A French perspective	'Stratégie d'adaptation des organisations à des marchés concurrentiels, pour influencer en leur faveur le comportement des publics dont elles dépendent, par une offre dont la valeur perçue est durablement supérieure à celle des concurrents. Dans le secteur marchand, le rôle du marketing est de créer de la valeur économique pour l'entreprise en créant de la valeur perçue par les clients.' (de Baynast, Lendrevie, and Lévy, 2017)
	[Broadly translating as: '[A] strategy of adaptation of organizations to competitive markets in order for them to influence the behaviour of the publics on which they depend, through an offering whose perceived value is durably superior to that of competitors. In the commercial sector, the role of marketing is to create economic value for the company by creating value as perceived by customers.']

in the not-for-profit sector. From here on in, except where marketing theory is developed only around products or services, we use the term 'offering' or 'proposition' to refer to the formulation of benefits a company designs to meet customers' needs, whether these are in service or product form, or a combination of the two.

The CIM definition discusses anticipating or identifying needs and the AMA discusses 'creating . . . offerings that have value for customers'. Both definitions recognize that marketers should engage in marketing research (see Chapter 3) and in **environmental scanning** (see Chapter 4) to satisfy customers and, in the long term, to anticipate customers' needs.

The French definition discusses influencing the behaviour of 'publics', rather than customers, recognizing the wider remit of marketing in society. The challenge, according to the French definition, is to develop an offering that is 'durably superior' to that of the competition. This definition recognizes explicitly the importance of the concepts of market segmentation and **positioning** (see Chapter 6).

The CIM definition presupposes that marketing has a profit motive, although it does not state what kind of profit this is, for example gain in society, gain in financial terms. The AMA definition is clearer, arguing that marketing is a process undertaken to benefit 'clients, partners, and society at large'.

What all these definitions display is how the concept of marketing is changing, from transactional concepts such as pricing, promotion, and distribution, to relationship concepts such as the importance of customer trust, risk, commitment, and co-creation.

In addition, the nature of the relationships between an organization and its customers, in its offerings and its mission, are different in not-for-profit and for-profit organizations (see Chapter 17). Nevertheless, the broad principles of how marketing is used remain the same.

 Visit the **online resources** and complete Internet Activity 1.1 to learn more about the professional marketing associations around the world.

What's the Difference between Customers and Consumers?

What is a customer? And what is the difference between a customer and a consumer? The difference is subtle, but real. A customer is a buyer, a purchaser, a patron, a client, or a shopper—someone who buys from a shop, a website, a business or, in the sharing economy, another customer (for example Airbnb or Uber).

The difference between customer and consumer is that a customer purchases or obtains an offering, but a consumer uses it (or eats it, in the case of food).

To illustrate, consider the marketing course you are enrolled on, assuming that you are using this book as an aid to learning on the course. Did you pay your course fees yourself? Or did someone else pay them? If you paid your own fees, you are the customer. If someone else paid, they are the customer—although you make use of, and study for, the course, which makes you the consumer.

Mondelez International's Dairylea Dunkers is a dairy food designed to be a good source of calcium, with each pack contributing at least 26 per cent of the daily reference intake of calcium. When purchasing this offering, the customer is typically the chief shopper (that is, the parent or guardian) and the consumer is a child. Sometimes, the customer and consumer can be the same, for example a woman buying cinema tickets for herself and her partner online.

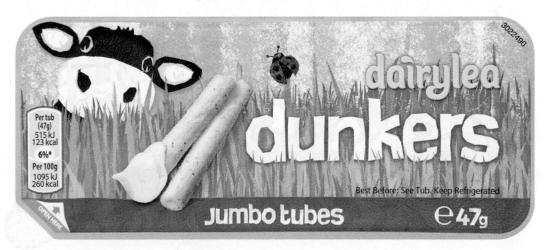

Dairylea Dunkers, the moo-vellous snack for children
Source: Reproduced with kind permission of Mondelez International.

Market Orientation

The concept of market orientation (Kohli and Jaworski, 1990) is the beating heart of marketing. Developing a market orientation is said to make organizations more profitable in both the long and short runs (Kumar et al., 2011), especially when there are limited competition, unchanging customer wants and needs, fast-paced technological change, and strong economies in operation. In a **meta-analysis** of market orientation studies, Kirca, Jayachandran, and Bearden (2005) conclude that market orientation is likely to be fundamental for survival in service firms and the source of competitive advantage in manufacturing firms.

Developing a market orientation is not the same as developing a market*ing* orientation. So, what's the difference? A company with a marketing orientation would be a company that recognizes the importance of marketing within the organization, for example by appointing a marketing person as chief executive officer (CEO), or as chair of its board of directors (or trustees, in the case of a charity), or to the executive team in a limited company or partnership.

Developing a market orientation refers to 'the organization-wide generation of market intelligence pertaining to current and future customer needs, dissemination of the intelligence across the departments, and organization-wide responsiveness to it' (Kohli and Jaworski, 1990: 6). So a market orientation not only involves the marketing function, but also involves everyone gathering and responding to market intelligence (that is, customers' verbalized needs and preferences, customer and employee survey data, sales data, and information gleaned from discussions with customers and trade partners, from websites, and from social media). Developing a market orientation means developing:

- *customer orientation*—concerned with creating superior value by continuously developing and redeveloping offerings to meet customer needs—which means that we must measure customer satisfaction on a continuous basis and train front-line service staff;

- *competitor orientation*—which requires an organization to develop an understanding of its competitors' short-term strengths and weaknesses, and its own long-term capabilities and strategies (Slater and Narver, 1994); and

- *interfunctional coordination*—which requires all functions of an organization to work together for long-term profit growth (as illustrated in Figure 1.1).

Achieving a market orientation so that an organization is internally responsive to changes in the marketplace may take organizations four years or more to develop and requires senior

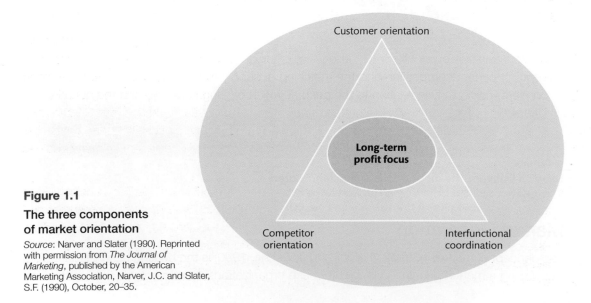

Figure 1.1

The three components of market orientation

Source: Narver and Slater (1990). Reprinted with permission from *The Journal of Marketing*, published by the American Marketing Association, Narver, J.C. and Slater, S.F. (1990), October, 20–35.

management support, the development of teams to gather the necessary market intelligence data and design appropriate market-based reward systems, and management to implement the recommendations made as a result (Kohli and Jaworski, 1990).

Developing a market orientation within a company is a capability—something that not all companies are able to do. Organizations that develop a market orientation are better at **market sensing**—that is, understanding the strategic implications of the market—and acting on the information collected through environmental scanning exercises. (This topic is covered in Chapter 4.) Surprisingly, until 2000, General Electric (GE)—the American capital, expertise, and infrastructure company—had no substantial marketing organization; instead, it had been technology-driven. To orient itself towards the market, GE organized its marketing function into two basic activities: go to market (for example segmentation) and commercial essentials (for example branding, communications). Then it organized its marketing teams across the company to ensure that they contained a mix of people with different skills, including instigators (who challenge the status quo), innovators (who develop new offerings and processes), integrators (who build bridges across organizational functions and in the marketplace), and implementers (who execute the new ideas). All this was backed with a process custom-designed to evaluate the success of the new approach (Comstock, Gulati, and Liguori, 2010).

Marketing's Intellectual Roots

Marketing typically evolves over time in organizations, just as it has throughout history. Some marketing historians regard marketing as an invention of the twentieth century (Keith, 1960), while others regard it as a process that evolved over a much longer period of time, without any production era ever having existed at all. Soap firms, for example, were **advertising** in the late nineteenth century in the UK, the United States, and Germany (Fullerton, 1988). The notion that marketing developed first in the 1950s is probably wrong, considering that self-service supermarkets operated in America from the 1930s and products were increasingly developed based on the process of 'consumer engineering', within which products were designed and redesigned, using research, to meet customer needs (Fullerton, 1988).

Marketing as a discipline has developed as a result of the influence of its practitioners, but also developments in several related disciplines, including the areas of industrial economics, psychology, sociology, and anthropology, as follows:

- *Industrial economics influences*—Our knowledge of the matching of supply and demand within industries owes much to the development of microeconomics. The economic concepts of perfect competition and the matching of supply to demand underlie the marketing concept, particularly in relation to the price at which offerings are sold and the quantity distributed (see Chapter 9) and the nature of business-to-business marketing (see Chapter 16). Theories of income distribution, scale of operation, monopoly, competition, and finance all come from economics (Bartels, 1951), although the influence of economics on marketing has declined (Howard et al., 1991).

- *Psychological influences*—Our understanding of consumer behaviour derives principally from psychology—especially from motivation research (see Chapter 3) in relation to consumer attitudes, perceptions, motivations, and information processing (Holden and Holden, 1998), and our understanding of persuasion, consumer personality, and customer satisfaction (Bartels, 1951). Understanding buyer psychology is fundamental to the marketing function. Because marketing is about understanding customers' needs, empathy with customers is a prerequisite.

- *Sociological influences*—Our knowledge of how groups of people behave derives from sociology, with insights into how people from similar gender and age groups behave (demographics), how people in different social positions within society behave (class), why we do things in the way that we do (motivation), general ways in which groups behave (customs), and culture (Bartels, 1951, 1959). What society thinks as a whole (that is, public opinion) and how communications pass through opinion leaders (Katz, 1957), as well as how we influence the way people think, for example propaganda research (Lee, 1945; Doob, 1948), have all informed marketing practice.

- *Anthropological influences*—Our debt to **social anthropology** is increasing as we use qualitative approaches such as **ethnography**, **netnography**, and **observation** in researching consumer behaviour (see Chapter 3)—particularly the behaviour of subgroups and cultures (for example **tweenagers**, **haul girls**).

- *Computer science influences*—Marketing's debt to advances in computer science is substantial in the digital age, but is set to be greater still in the next few decades. For example, this has influenced the algorithms that are used to make recommendations in the entertainment choices you make (such as Netflix) and to determine a supermarket group's retail site location decisions. Advances in our understanding of human–computer interaction have allowed the development of better (that is, easier to navigate) website pages and the use of artificially intelligent customer service chatbots. For example, Spotify's Facebook Messenger app bot allows customers to search for, listen to, and share music.

Differences between Sales and Marketing

When someone is new to marketing, they might ask themselves: how do sales and marketing differ? A comprehensive answer is that sales emphasizes the process of 'product push' by creating distribution incentives for both salespeople and customers to make exchanges, whereas marketing focuses on creating 'product pull', by stoking demand among customers and consumers. In marketing, the offering is designed and redesigned through customer insight and co-creation to meet customers' long-term needs. However, the differences are blurring as companies employ **key account management** approaches (see Chapter 16), which interface between sales and marketing functions. Marketing activity is geared around understanding and communicating with the customer to help in the design, development, delivery, and determination of the value inherent in the offering, whereas sales is organized principally around enhancing the distribution and solicitation of the companies' offerings once those offerings have already been designed. Sales departments are particularly concerned with the delivery part of the value creation process. However, sales as a function does and should have inputs into the design phase (through information from sales representatives), the development phase (particularly in test marketing—see Chapter 3), and the determination phase, in which salespeople's informal knowledge of customers' needs is critical to the marketing process.

Whereas marketing activities are designed to estimate and stimulate demand, sales activities are designed to promote customer purchase of an offering (AMA, 2015). However, the two functions should be integrated to coexist in an organization, rather than clash, since both are important in achieving a market orientation and concomitant improvement in business performance (Le Meunier-Fitzhugh and Piercy, 2011). Table 1.2 provides a summary of the basic differences.

Table 1.2 Differences between marketing and sales

Marketing	Sales
Tends towards long-term satisfaction of customer needs; part of the design and development of customer value processes	Tends towards short-term satisfaction of customer needs; part of the value delivery process
Tends towards greater customer input into design of offering (co-creation)	Tends towards lesser customer input into design of offering
Tends towards high focus on stimulation of demand	Tends towards low focus on stimulation of demand; more focused on meeting existing demand

---

What Do Marketers Do?

To answer the question 'What do marketers do?', the UK's Chartered Institute of Marketing (CIM) developed a framework of marketing abilities to guide the skills and behaviours of professional marketers at different levels of proficiency and seniority (CIM, 2016). The proficiency levels vary as follows:

1 aware;

2 active learner;

3 able;

4 accomplished; and

5 authoritative.

The core competencies of the marketer are to generate customer insights (see Chapter 3), champion the customer and hence customer focus (covered further later in this chapter), and develop marketing strategy (see Chapter 5). Technical competencies include:

- risk and reputation management (see Chapter 11);

- **brand** (see Chapter 12);

- integrated marketing communications (see Chapter 11);

- digital integration (see Chapter 12);

- product management (see Chapter 8);

- monitoring and measuring effectiveness (see Chapter 5);

- customer experience (see Chapter 15); and

- partnership marketing including managing channel partners (see Chapter 14).

The CIM also defines a set of behavioural competencies. These include influencing (other employees, customers, stakeholders), being collaborative (for example with channel partners), being responsible (for one's actions and acting ethically), and being financially literate, inspiring,

Figure 1.2

A functional map for professional marketing competencies

Source: © The Chartered Institute of Marketing 2018. Reproduced with the kind permission.

innovative, challenging, entrepreneurial, commercially aware, and creative. The framework is illustrated in Figure 1.2.

 Visit the **online resources** and follow the web link to the CIM's Professional Marketing Standards Framework to learn more about occupational standards for marketing in the UK.

Because society constantly changes, so too does the marketing profession. Marketing's place within the business profession—and within society more generally—is often criticized. Whereas doctors, teachers, and judges are generally held in high esteem (Worcester et al., 2011: 136), marketing practitioners can sometimes be held in low regard (Kotler, 2006). Sheth and Sisodia (2015) have recommended that marketers might reform their reputation by:

- showing more integrity, gratitude, recognition, and humility towards, and building real trust with, customers;

- building a true dialogue with customers and respecting their privacy;

- striving for authenticity by really personalizing customer offerings rather than only appearing to do so;

- asking for forgiveness in the occasional instance in which their judgement lapses and they treat customers badly;

- having the courage to stop over-promising and under-delivering; and

- showing respect for customers, competitors, and suppliers.

Marketing has some way to go in terms of developing its relations with customers and in terms of the power it wields inside companies. However, there are signs that major public companies are beginning to bring sales-and-marketing experience to their boards. In 2015, 21 per cent of FTSE 100 CEOs came from a sales-and-marketing background (Hobbs, 2015). Marketing functions can, however, be divorced from a strategic role in some companies. This is likely to change only if marketers demonstrate the value of marketing to their organizations. (For a more detailed consideration of how companies structure the marketing function, see Chapter 5.)

This lack of strategic input may arise because marketers do not control all elements of the marketing mix. For example, marketers do not always control pricing, distribution, product development, and even promotion, given that this is often outsourced to agencies (O'Malley and Patterson, 1998), although marketers usually exercise some influence over all these activities. Marketing is not always organized as a separate department, but the ethos and influence of marketing philosophy should nonetheless be apparent and impact upon an organization's decision-making (Harris and Ogbonna, 2003). Marketing is present in all aspects of an organization, since all departments have some role to play with respect to creating, delivering, and satisfying customers. Employees in the research and development (R&D) department, designing new products to meet existing customer needs, are performing a marketing role. Similarly, members of the **procurement** department buying components for a new offering must purchase those components at a specific quality and cost that will meet customer needs. In fact, we can go through all departments of a company and discover that, in each department, there is a marketing role to be played to some extent. In other words, marketing is distributed throughout the organization and all employees can be considered part-time marketers (Gummesson, 1990).

Marketing's Principal Principles

Despite having been studied for nearly 100 years, there are few truly scientific principles in marketing (Bartels, 1944). By 'scientific principles', we mean natural rules of law around which a theory can be developed to explain observations (and to predict future observations), which cannot be subsequently disproved. Relatively early on in marketing's history, however, Bartels (1951) modified two well-known economic 'laws' to argue that only the following marketing generalizations exist.

1 *Engels' Law*—As a consumer's income increases, the percentage of income spent for food decreases; for rent, fuel, and light remains the same; for clothing remains the same; and for miscellaneous items increases.

2 *Reilly's Law of Retail Gravitation*—Two cities attract retail trade from an intermediary city or town in the vicinity of the breaking point (the 50 per cent point) approximately in direct proportion to the populations of the two cities and in inverse proportion to the square of the distance from these two cities to the intermediate town.

Clearly, things have changed since statistician Ernst Engels produced his law in 1857, especially since populations are more mobile than they were in the nineteenth century and food is less expensive than it was 70–80 years ago, so it is debatable as to whether or not Engels' Law still applies.

The impact of Reilly's Law, first posited in 1931, is that site location specialists for a major supermarket should locate stores near the larger of two major population centres. Again, this might sound self-evident as a general principle, but Reilly's Law allows retailers to determine with some degree of precision exactly where that location might be. Nowadays, multiple retail grocers, such as Carrefour in France, Sainsbury's in the UK, Coop in Denmark, Albert Hejn in the Netherlands, and Tesco Lotus in Thailand, use complex mathematical formulae (for example algorithms) to determine site location decisions, purchasing land and developing suitable properties, in addition to converting existing business premises, in suitable locations as a result.

Despite the fact that there are no clear 'laws of marketing', several prominent academics have argued for the need to develop a 'general theory of marketing' (Bartels, 1968; Hunt, 1971, 1983). This search continues to the present day, but we are no closer to defining such a thing (Hunt, 2013). To move towards such a general theory, we would need to understand the phenomenon of marketing more completely in terms of:

■ the behaviour of buyers—that is, why which buyers purchase what they do, where they do, when they do, and in the way that they do;

■ the behaviour of sellers—that is, why which sellers price, promote, and distribute what they do, where they do, when they do, and in the way that they do;

■ the institutional framework (for example government, society, and so on) around selling and buying—that is, why which kinds of institutions develop to engage in what kinds of functions or activities to consummate and/or facilitate exchanges, when these institutions will develop, where they will develop, and how they will develop; and

■ the consequences for society of buying and selling—that is, why which kinds of buyers, buyer behaviour, seller behaviour, and institutions have what kinds of consequences on society, when, where, and how (Hunt, 1983).

The listing indicates how marketing involves a series of highly complex interactions between individuals, organizations, society, and government. We have only a limited understanding of how marketing works in theory and practice. However, although we have no 'laws' of marketing with which to construct a general theory, we can make some law-like generalizations. They may not hold all of the time, but they do hold much of the time.

According to Leone and Shultz (1980), these law-like generalizations are as follows:

■ *Generalization 1*—Advertising has a direct and positive influence on total industry (market) sales—that is, all advertising done at industry level serves to increase sales within that industry.

■ *Generalization 2*—Selective advertising has a direct and positive influence on individual company (brand) sales—that is, advertising undertaken by a company tends to increase the sales of the particular brand for which it was spent.

■ *Generalization 3*—The **elasticity** of selective advertising on company (brand) sales is low (inelastic)—that is, for frequently purchased goods, advertising has only a very limited effect in raising sales.

■ *Generalization 4*—Increasing store shelf space (display) has a positive impact on sales of **non-staple** grocery items, such as products bought on impulse (for example ice cream, chocolate bars) rather than those that are planned purchases, which are less important, but perhaps more luxurious types of good (for example gravy mixes, cooking sauces). For instance, for impulse goods, the more shelf space you give an item, the more likely you are to sell it.

Research Insight 1.1

To take your learning further, you might wish to read this influential paper:

Borden, N.H. (1964). The concept of the marketing mix. *Journal of Advertising Research*, **4, 2–7.**

This early, easy-to-read article explains how marketing managers act as 'mixers of ingredients' when developing marketing programmes. The marketing mix, popularized as the 4Ps, remains popular today, although the advent of relationship marketing has challenged the impersonal notion of marketers as manipulators of marketing policies and focused more on the need to develop long-term interpersonal relationships with customers.

 Visit the online resources to read the abstract and access the full paper.

- *Generalization 5*—Distribution, defined by the number of outlets, has a positive influence on company sales (market share)—that is, setting up more retail locations has a positive influence on sales.

(For a more detailed consideration of law-like generalizations, see Hanssens, 2009.)

As we can see, marketing techniques are still developing in a scientific sense, but in the age of social media and 'big data' analytics, companies are more able to describe—and predict—the behaviour of their consumers, customers, and producers according to some predefined formulae. Nevertheless, marketers still have to make use of trial and error, and experimentation and readjustment processes. Gordon and Perrey (2015) argue that we are entering a golden age in marketing—that advances in data analysis and statistical modelling are increasingly allowing us to measure the returns made on marketing investments, and to assess and predict customer behaviour more accurately than ever.

Marketing practice is, however, informed by managerial concepts and frameworks, as well as by general theoretical principles. Important concepts include the notion of exchange in marketing, the marketing mix for products (the 4Ps—see Research Insight 1.1) and services (the 7Ps), market orientation, and relationship marketing and service-dominant logic for marketing.

Marketing as Exchange

Marketing is a two-way exchange process. It's not solely about the marketing organization doing the work; the customer also inputs—sometimes extensively. Customers specify how we might satisfy their needs, because marketers cannot read their minds. Customers must then pay for the offering. In the mid-1970s, there was an increasing belief that marketing centred on the exchange process between buyers and sellers and associated supply chain intermediaries. Exchange relationships were seen to be economic (for example a consumer buying groceries) and social (for example the service provided by the police on behalf of society paid for by government) (Bagozzi, 1975). This recognition of the underlying exchange relationship within marketing led to the 'broadening' of marketing and the relationship marketing school of marketing.

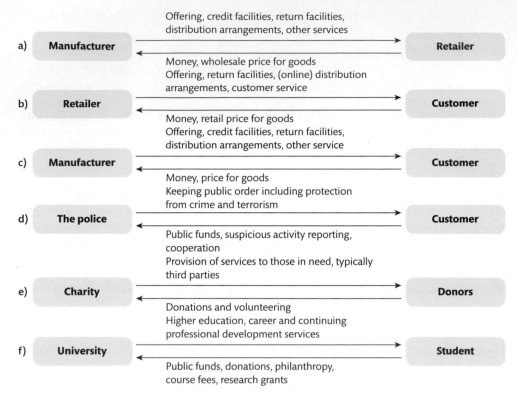

Figure 1.3

Examples of marketing exchange processes

(see Chapter 15). There are numerous types of buyer–seller exchange in marketing. Figure 1.3 illustrates some examples of two-way (**dyadic**) exchanges, as follows:

1 In the first exchange type, we have a manufacturer and a retailer. Here, the retailer (for example Harvey Nichols) purchases goods from the manufacturer (for example Burberry) through a credit facility (for example payment in 30 days), expects any damaged goods to be returnable, and wants the goods delivered in a certain way within a particular time limit. In return, the retailer undertakes to pay a wholesale (that is, trade-discounted) price.

2 In the second exchange type, we have a retailer and a customer, perhaps entering a shop (for example Jumbo—the Dutch supermarket retailer) to purchase groceries and paying for these with cash or by credit or debit card (see Chapter 14).

3 In the third type of exchange, we have a manufacturer dealing directly with its customers. An example here would be Dell, the computer manufacturer, selling directly from its website and via the telephone.

4 In the fourth exchange type, the exchange takes place between the police, who are tasked with protecting the general public from crime and terrorism, and public disorder more generally, and the public who support them, perhaps by signing petitions to keep police stations in service in a particular locale, and especially through their national and local taxes, depending on the country concerned. (See Chapter 17 for a more detailed discussion of the use of marketing by the City of London Police.)

5 In the fifth exchange type, the exchange takes place between a charity and its donors, whereby the donors provide funds (by legacy or by regular or one-off donation) and the charity makes products and services available to third parties. An example is Barnens Regnskog (meaning 'Children's Rainforest'), a Swedish not-for-profit organization that supports the preservation of rainforests in Thailand, Guatemala, Belize, Costa Rica, and Ecuador.

6 In the sixth type of exchange, we see a university, which may be a public or private organization, or some mixture of two, providing a range of educational services designed to educate its audiences and to advance their careers in return for payment.

Few marketing exchanges are really this simple. They might involve other individual transactions and multiple combinations. For example, the first and second types of exchange can be combined to indicate a simple supply chain for, say, an insurance company providing underwriting services to insurance companies selling home insurance policies directly to the general public. Other mechanisms also exist in this market: banks and brokers also sell home insurance policies directly to the general public. By understanding how exchanges take place between members of the supply chain, we can determine where to add value to the customer experience.

The Marketing Mix and the 4Ps

Neil Borden originally developed the concept of the marketing mix in his teaching at Harvard University in the 1950s. His idea was that marketing managers were 'mixers of ingredients'—chefs who concoct a unique marketing recipe to fit customers' needs at any particular time. The emphasis was on the creative fashioning of a mix of marketing procedures and policies to produce the profitable enterprise.

Borden (1964) composed a 12-item list of elements (with sub-items, not reproduced here), which the manufacturer should consider when developing marketing mix policies and procedures:

1 product planning;

2 pricing;

3 branding;

4 channels of distribution;

5 personal selling;

6 advertising;

7 promotions;

8 packaging;

9 display;

10 servicing;

11 physical handling; and

12 fact finding and analysis.

This list was simplified and amended by Eugene McCarthy (1960) to become the more memorable, but rigid, 4Ps:

1 **product**—that is, the offering and how it meets the customer's need, its packaging, and its labelling (see Chapter 8);

2 **place** (distribution channels)—that is, the way in which the offering is delivered to the customer (see Chapter 14);

3 **price**—that is, the cost to the customer and the cost plus profit to the seller (see Chapter 9); and

4 **promotion**—that is, how the offering's benefits and features are communicated to the potential buyer (see Chapters 10 and 11).

The intention was to create a simpler framework for managers to develop their planning. Although there was recognition that all of these elements might be interlinked (for example promotion based on the price paid by the consumer), such interplay between these mix components was not taken

Market Insight 1.1
V&D Goes Bust!

On New Year's Eve 2015, Dutch department store Vroom & Dreesman (V&D), owned by US private equity firm Sun Capital, declared itself insolvent after suffering poor sales, a loss of €49 million on sales of €604 million in 2014, and a year of conflict with unions and landlords. The company was finding it difficult to compete with new competitors and the shift to online purchasing. The company, first established in 1887, had more than 10,000 staff and 62 stores across the Netherlands, selling items such as designer clothing and shoes, jewellery, home electric appliances, furniture, china, stationery, books and CDs, and much more. It also owned the La Place restaurant chain in 250 locations. In early 2016, bankruptcy administrators began trying to find a buyer for parts of the business.

The V&D works council (that is, the employees) wrote to the bankruptcy administrators, Kees van de Meent and Hanneke de Coninck-Smolders, to request that the owners Sun Capital not be allowed involvement in the future activities of the company, should it emerge

from its financial difficulties. However, after suggestions of up to 70 candidate buyers for the business, the administrators invited 10 candidates to submit bids.

Sources: Anon. (2015a, 2015b); Pieters (2015).

Iconic Dutch department store V&D shuts its doors after 128 years of service
Source: iStock.com/Poulssen.

Theory into Practice

This market insight describes how a Dutch department store retailer, aimed firmly at middle-class customers, failed after a spell of annual losses that its US owner was no longer prepared to bear. As a result, the company called in the bankruptcy administrators. The market insight demonstrates that not all businesses succeed—even those that have been running with a

previously successful model for more than 100 years. The case underlines the importance of staying in touch with customers' needs if a company is to survive in the long term. It also provides an opportunity to understand how marketing strategy might be redesigned using the 4Ps, particularly in relation to **multichannel marketing** (see Chapter 14).

Market Insight 1.1
continued

Related Topics

retail marketing; marketing mix; market orientation; multichannel management; distribution

1 If you were a senior executive at a company that acquired the V&D business from bankruptcy specialists Kees van de Meent and Hanneke de Coninck-Smolders, how would you seek to use the 4Ps to revive the company's marketing to appeal to more consumers? Why might its marketing mix strategy have failed?

2 Why do you think V&D has found it so difficult to alter its business model?

3 What other companies can you think of that need to revive their marketing mixes?

into account in McCarthy's framework. (See Market Insight 1.1 for an example of why the V&D department store offering in Holland and the marketing mix more generally needs redeveloping.)

Some commentators have argued that the 4Ps framework is of limited use; however, we include it here because managers continue to use it extensively when devising their marketing plans.

The Extended Marketing Mix

It might be that exchanges in a service context (for example when purchasing a holiday) are different from those in a goods context (for example when buying a car). By the end of the 1970s, it was recognized that the traditional 4Ps approach to marketing planning (see Chapter 5 for a detailed discussion) based on physical products (for example salt, houses, alcoholic drinks) was not particularly useful for either a physical product offering with a strong service component (for example tablet computers with an extended warranty) or services with little or no physical component (for example spa and massage, hairdressing, sports spectatorship) (see Chapter 15).

Two American scholars, Booms and Bitner (1981), incorporated a further three Ps into the marketing mix to reflect the need to market services differently:

5 *Physical evidence*—This emphasizes that the tangible components of services are strategically important. For example, potential university students might assess whether or not they want to attend a university and a particular course by requesting a copy of brochures or by visiting the campus to assess the **servicescape** for themselves.

6 *Process*—This emphasizes the importance of the service delivery. When processes are standardized, it is easier to manage customer expectations. For example, DHL International GmbH, the German international express, transport, and air freight company, is a master at producing a standardized menu of service options, such as track-and-trace delivery services, which are remarkably consistent around the world.

7 *People*—This emphasizes the importance of customer service personnel, who are sometimes experts and often professionals, interacting with the customer. How they interact with customers,

and how satisfied customers are as a result of their experiences, is of strategic importance. For example, McKinsey & Company (2017) prides itself on the quality of its more than 12,000 consultants and its 2,000 research and information specialists as an integral part of its offering.

Consider how the extended marketing mix is used in the airline industry. For instance, the process component of the services marketing mix has been revolutionized through digital technologies, for example web check-in and app ticketing services. Previous intermediaries, such as travel agencies, have had to radically alter their customer proposition now that the major national carriers (for example Air France, KLM, British Airways) are offering their services directly through digital channels to compete with low-cost airlines, who are also offering their services through digital channels often at substantially lower prices. Consequently, travel agencies (such as TUI and Thomas Cook) have also put their own services online, customizing holiday offerings to differentiate themselves from the airlines and to add value for the customer, offering better deals on insurance, identifying the best flight connections, providing advice on the best airlines, and offering affiliate hotel deals (Saren, 2006). Two of the top three travel agents are online-only firms—that is, Expedia (including Trivago, hotels.com, Hotwire) and Priceline (including booking.com).

The *people*, *process*, and *physical evidence* components of the airline service marketing mix are fundamental in positioning the offering. Airlines do not offer everyone exactly the same level of service and sometimes service levels fall well below customer expectations. Consider the incident in 2017 when United Airlines dragged a passenger off an airplane for failing to give up his seat to an affiliate airline employee after United Airlines overbooked the flight. This resulted in widespread condemnation, reduced bookings, and the payment of an undisclosed, but probably large, sum in damages to the affected passenger (Associated Press, 2017).

Most airlines offer an economy service, an economy plus service (with slightly more seating space), a business class service (with even more seating space, a better meal, a personalized cabin crew service, fast-track service through passport control, and often a limousine service to and from the airport), and a first-class service (with personalized menus, luxury transport to and from the airport, and luxurious in-flight seating). From 2017, Norwegian decided to offer low-cost *long-haul* services between Norway and the United States and Asia (Anon., 2017a). Table 1.3 summarizes the marketing mix for the airline industry.

Relationship Marketing, Service-Dominant Logic, and Co-creation

The extended marketing mix was developed after recognition that the 4Ps were inadequate to describe how the marketing of services should be undertaken. But the extended marketing mix also came to be seen as overly transactional and product-focused, even for services. The question arose that if marketing was about exchange, shouldn't marketing also be concerned with relationships between those parties that are exchanging value and not only what was exchanged? This was the principal idea behind the development of relationship marketing in the 1990s. The relationship marketing concept spawned the further evolution of marketing's conceptual foundations. There was a shift from the need to engage in transactions towards the need to develop long-term customer relationships, including relationships with other stakeholders (Christopher, Payne, and Ballantyne, 2002; see Chapter 15), including:

- suppliers;
- potential employees;
- recruiters;

Table 1.3 The marketing mix: the airline industry

Marketing aspect	Airline industry
Basic customer need	Safe long- and short-haul transportation; domestic and international
Target market	Mass consumer market (economy class); the discerning traveller (economy plus); businesspeople (business class); high-net-worth individuals (first class)
Offering	Typically, differentiated based on class of passenger, with seat size increasing, check-in and boarding times reducing, quality of food increasing, and levels of ancillary services (e.g. limousine service) increasing as we move from economy through business to first class Some carriers focus on 'no-frills' basic services (e.g. EasyJet, Ryanair, Air Asia) Some carriers offer low-cost long-haul services (e.g. Norwegian)
Price	Substantial difference depending on class of service, type of carrier, and purchasing approach (e.g. cheaper via Internet)
Principal promotional tools	(1) Banner ads, paid search, search engine optimization; (2) press and magazine advertising; (3) billboards
Distribution	Increasingly purchased via mobile apps and the Internet, including third-party brokerages such as Expedia, as well as (to a lesser degree in many countries) through physical travel agents
Process	Self-service via smartphone or Internet, or aided by travel agent in retail location Travel options increasingly customized to customer's needs, including size of baggage allowance, class of travel, and increasing availability of alternative and multicentre locations Customer and organization use of social media to air and resolve problems now very important
Physical evidence	Airline loyalty cards and souvenirs, in-flight magazines, in-flight entertainment services, food and snack meals, grooming and toiletry products provided On some flights, depending on class purchased, suites, bars, and shower facilities offered
People	Combination of check-in staff, customer service personnel, baggage handlers, and cabin crew/pilot teams, all of whom interface with customer or their belongings at different points in the experience

- referral markets—where they exist, for example retail banks partly relying on professional services organizations, including estate agents, for mortgage referrals;

- influence markets—for example regulatory authorities, politicians, and civil servants (see also Viney and Baines, 2012); and

- internal markets—for example existing employees.

Hult and colleagues (2011) added shareholders and the local community to this list. For them, the definition of marketing provided by the AMA (see Table 1.1) is inadequate because it fails to consider a sufficiently wide set of stakeholders. The concept of relationship marketing was concerned with integrating customer service, quality assurance, and marketing activity (Payne, 1993). Companies employing a relationship marketing approach stressed customer retention over customer acquisition. Customer retention is an important activity in marketing, because research has demonstrated that when a company retains loyal customers, it is more likely to be profitable compared with competitors who do not, because loyal customers:

- will increase their purchases over time;

- are cheaper to promote to;

- who are happy with their relationship with a company refer it to others; and

- are prepared to pay a (small) price premium if they are loyal (Reichheld and Sasser, 1990).

The idea of developing stronger relationships with existing customers is particularly important in mature industries in which markets are saturated, such as utilities and telecommunications, the travel industry, and retail banking, as well as in service-based industries, such as banking and corporate legal services. Retention programmes are developed to focus marketing activity on enhancing customer service satisfaction and rewarding loyalty, building **customer relationship management (CRM) systems**, and undertaking sales promotion activities. Companies have previously been urged to develop long-term interactive relationships (Gummesson, 1987). However, relationship marketing moved the concept away from simply adopting the 4Ps towards adopting an **interactive marketing** approach, paying more attention to the customer base rather than being preoccupied with building market share (Grönroos, 1994).

In the 2000s, there was a realization that marketing needed to shift beyond a goods-based paradigm towards a service-dominant logic (Vargo and Lusch, 2004). This relatively new marketing paradigm sees service as *the* fundamental basis of exchange (see Research Insight 1.2). In that sense, for physical goods offerings, the good is simply the distribution mechanism.

Research Insight 1.2

To take your learning further, you might wish to read this influential paper:

Vargo, S.L., and Lusch, R.F. (2008). Service-dominant logic: continuing the evolution. *Journal of the Academy of Marketing Science*, **36(1), 1–10.**

This article builds on, and updates, the authors' original ground-breaking article (Vargo and Lusch, 2004), which redefined how marketers should think about offerings, arguing that it was necessary to move beyond the idea of tangible versus intangible goods, embedded value and transactions, and other outmoded concepts derived from economics towards the notion of intangible resources and the co-creation of value and relationships. The article asserts that service is the fundamental basis of all exchanges in marketing and that value is always determined by the beneficiary.

 Visit the online resources to read the abstract and access the full paper.

To understand this concept better, consider the difference between purchasing a book from a shop (for example Waterstones) versus reading an e-book purchased from Amazon. The knowledge and technologies that the company embeds in the offering to meet the customer's needs are the source of competitive advantage. Because offerings are inherently service-based, customers become co-creators of the service experience; hence the value-in-use of the offering is specified by the customer, often after the sale has taken place. (See Market Insight 1.2 for an example of how Rolls Royce has transformed its product–service offering through servitization.)

Market Insight 1.2
Servitization at Rolls-Royce

Rolls-Royce is a global provider of integrated power systems and services to the civil and defence aerospace, marine, nuclear, and power systems markets. However, Rolls-Royce plc (which no longer owns the Rolls-Royce motor car brand) has completely redefined itself since the early 1970s, when it was nationalized by the then Conservative government after running into financial problems. In 2016, it had underlying revenues of £13.8 billion, up 3.2 per cent on 2015, with an order book of £79.8 billion. Product–service revenue ratios in 2016 were 48:52 per cent in civil aerospace, 40:60 per cent in defence aerospace, 57:43 per cent in the marine sector, 68:32 per cent in power systems, and 46:54 per cent in the nuclear business. By comparison, after-market sales, as they were then known, were only 20 per cent of the civil aerospace division's revenues in 1981.

Since then, Rolls-Royce has transformed its business model from selling engines and aftercare (to ensure that the engines work properly and are maintained) to selling its customers 'power by the hour', recognizing that it is not in the engine-manufacturing business, but in the power-generation integrated solutions business. In the civil aerospace sector, Rolls-Royce sells its engines with TotalCare®. With TotalCare, a customer enters an overall agreement with Rolls-Royce that provides visibility of cost and a guarantee of product reliability.

Rolls Royce wins contract to supply IAG with Trent XWB engines and long-term TotalCare® service support

Source: © Airbus S.A.S 2011—photo by e*m company/H. Goussé.

TotalCare was first introduced in the 1990s and charges airline customers based on the total number of hours flown. By collecting data from aircraft engines in flight worldwide on a continuous basis, Rolls-Royce can maintain those engines better, predict engine failures, optimize engine maintenance programmes, and improve future engine design. Service looks set to become more important than ever with Rolls-Royce's product market opportunities likely to be worth around £1.79 trillion and the services market opportunities worth £1.38 trillion between 2012 and 2032.

Sources: Ryals and Rackham (2012); Rolls-Royce (2016).

Theory into Practice

This market insight describes how a major UK manufacturer enhanced its customer offering by shifting from a conventional engineering product to a product–service mix that includes a servitized offering—that is, by offering its product as a service either by selling engines with service contracts or by leasing thrust capacity rather than purely selling an engine.

Market Insight 1.2
continued

Related Topics
product–service mix; servitization; customer needs; customer value

1 Why do you think Rolls-Royce has been so successful in selling the service concept?

2 Check out the websites of competitors Pratt & Whitney and GE. How do their service offerings in their civil aerospace divisions compare with those of Rolls-Royce?

3 Do you think that all manufacturers' products can be servitized?

Organizations should use co-creation to differentiate their offerings, given that value is tied up inside the customer's experience with the organization (Prahalad and Ramaswamy, 2004a, 2004b). The co-creation experience is about the *joint* creation of value, in which customers take part in an active dialogue and co-construct personalized experiences. Organizations wishing to enhance customer input to co-creation should map supplier and customer processes to identify how to design their services accordingly (Payne, Storbacka, and Frow, 2008). The process of co-creation potentially shifts value creation from value-in-exchange, at the point of purchase, to value-in-use, after purchase (Grönroos and Voima, 2013). For example, airplane manufacturer Boeing incorporated feedback from both airline companies and passengers into its Dreamliner plane design before final production (see Chapter 8).

Marketing in Context

Does marketing practice change if we are marketing goods compared with services and to consumers compared with businesses? To some degree, the answer is 'yes'. We've known since the 1960s, for example, that services were making important contributions to the US economy (Regan, 1963). Although the product has previously been the focus of marketing practice and theory, it shouldn't continue to be. Figure 1.4 shows how important services are to a wide variety of economies around the world, including those in the developed world (for example Sweden, Netherlands, the UK), the developing world (for example Thailand, Brazil), and the less-developed countries (for example Namibia, Nigeria). Even in China and the United Arab Emirates (UAE), services make up more than 40 per cent of the economy.

Marketing techniques need to be adapted to the specific sector in which they are used (Blois, 1974). The context—whether it is industrial (for example business-to-business), consumer-based (for example retail), or services-based (for example business-to-business services such as accountancy or business-to-business products such as component manufacturers), and profit or not-for-profit—has an impact on the marketing tools and techniques that we use. Sometimes, these differences are overplayed because marketing activities in these areas share more similarities than differences (Fern and Brown, 1984; Cova and Salle, 2007). Nevertheless,

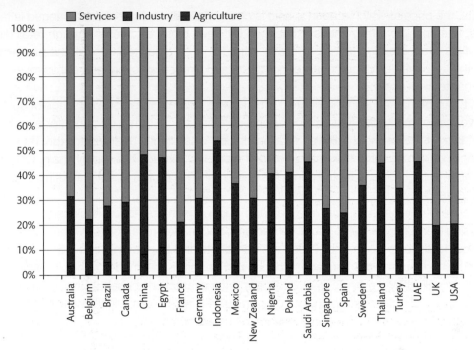

Figure 1.4

Estimated GDP composition by sector for selected countries (%, 2016)

Note: GDP = gross domestic product. All data are estimated for 2016.

Source: Data taken from CIA World Factbook (http://www.cia.gov). Reproduced with kind permission of CIA World Factbook.

whether products are business-to-business or business-to-consumer, they may be either product or service, and all offerings combine some elements of the two. (We discuss the intangible nature of services further in Chapter 15 and we discuss not-for-profit marketing in Chapter 17.)

Having identified three unique contexts of marketing—consumer goods, industrial (business-to-business), and services—we now briefly discuss how each of these contexts affects how we might undertake marketing activities. You might consider digital marketing as a separate context, but our view is that digital marketing is present in all three key environments and relates to all aspects of the 4Ps marketing mix (that is, product, place, price, promotion). We consider digital marketing in detail in Chapter 13 and throughout the book in individual chapters.

The Consumer Goods Perspective

Consumer goods are convenience goods (purchased frequently, with minimum effort), shopping goods (purchased selectively), or speciality goods (purchased highly selectively) (Bucklin, 1963). Examples of consumer goods industries include the retail car market, the luxury goods market, and multiple retail groceries. Companies operating in these industries include German car manufacturer Audi, French fashion house Louis Vuitton Moët Hennessey (LVMH), and Unilever, the Anglo-Dutch fast-moving consumer goods company.

The consumer goods perspective has dominated marketing's history. This perspective gave birth to ideas such as 'marketing mix' and the 4Ps. The consumer goods perspective, borrowing heavily from neoclassical economics, assumes that there are comparatively few suppliers within a particular industry and that all are rivals for **aggregated demand** (that is, demand totalled at population rather than individual level). In fast-moving consumer goods (FMCG) markets, the price at which a good is sold is clearly defined. The offering exchanged is tangible (that is, has physical form), and is exchanged between buyer and seller through retail distribution outlets. Consumption takes place later, with demand stimulated through the **promotional mix**—that is, advertising, personal selling, digital and direct marketing, and public relations (PR) (see Chapters 11 and 12).

The focus of marketing in this context is on how to facilitate the rapid exchange of goods, the effectiveness of marketing in matching supplier offering to customer demand (for example, see Market Insight 1.3 on how a British retail institution was slightly adapted for the Thai market), and efficiency in managing the distribution of the product through the supply chain. Of particular importance in this context are the principles and practice of multichannel marketing and retailing (see Chapter 14).

Because of the need to stimulate demand from consumers, focus is placed on the use of advertising (see Chapter 10) to stimulate demand, and market research (see Chapter 3) to determine how to develop appropriate consumer products and to determine how they are received once launched into the marketplace. Most buying decisions are made by individual customers, but occasionally they are made by several people (for example a household including children for a new car, or a friendship group choosing a particular friend's outfit). Digital marketing techniques have greatly increased the amount of information that customers receive, and online procurement approaches now dictate how retailers reorder goods and services from suppliers. (See Chapter 12 for more on digital and social media marketing.)

The Services Perspective

The services marketing perspective was developed in the late 1970s and early 1980s to recognize that the goods-centric marketing approach was ill-suited to the marketing of services. Services marketing thinkers suggested that the intangible performance-dependent nature of services substantially affected how they should be marketed (Shostack, 1977). There was a focus on the quality of service offered (Grönroos, 1984), as well as a focus on the difference between customer perceptions of service quality and their expectations of service quality (Parasuraman, Berry, and Zeithaml, 1985).

Some commentators have questioned the use of the product analogy altogether in services marketing (Grönroos, 1998; Vargo and Lusch, 2004). In relation to the debate about whether product and services marketing is different, it is worth noting that services:

- cannot be protected by patent (although services can be protected by **copyright** and **trademarks**);

- do not make use of physical packaging;

- lack a physical display; and

- cannot be demonstrated in the same way as can products (although 'taster' experiences are sometimes offered).

Others have argued that there are major similarities (Judd, 1968), including the need to:

- work at full capacity;

- develop trademarks and service marks;

- use promotional media (including digital and social media);

Market Insight 1.3
Harrods: Time for (Thai) Tea

How do companies develop their offerings to meet local consumers' needs in emerging markets? Many global brands sell their offerings using their internationally renowned images without changing their positioning too significantly when internationalizing. But just how do they pull off this delicate balancing act and still achieve sales success? This was the task facing Boonchai Kongpakpaisarn, president and CEO of LME, a Thai fashion marketing firm, who brought quintessential English retail brand Harrods to Thailand in late 2013.

Harrods, owner of one of the world's most famous department stores, has been the epitome of English luxury and fashion since its inception in 1849, serving 15 million customers per year. In addition to its department store interests, it owns Harrods Bank, Harrods Estates, Harrods Aviation, and Air Harrods. The business, employing more than 4,000 people and owned by Qatar Holdings, is probably best known for its distinctive green shopping bags, its expansive luxury goods range, and its food hall and tea rooms.

It was, in fact, Harrods' afternoon tea concept that Boonchai considered bringing to Thailand after visiting the Harrods Tea Rooms in Ginza, Japan, owned by

Mitsubishi Corporation Japan. The idea gained further ground in his mind after he found out that Thais formed one of Harrod's top five overseas customer groups.

Since setting up Harrods' Tea Rooms (with Japan's Mitsubishi Corporation as a partner), Boonchai has worked hard to ensure that the Harrods Tea Rooms concept in Thailand remains true to the English parent, partly by sending his staff to be trained in the UK (rather than getting trainers over from the UK) and by offering English dishes, including the 'Chelsea Set' of tea, scones, and clotted cream, the 'London Metro' fish and chips, and even roast beef and Yorkshire pudding. But there is also an adaptation to cater for Thai preferences, with dishes containing foie gras and truffles, including eggs Benedict foie gras, truffle omelette, and truffle cappuccino soup. Cleverly, the Harrods Tea Rooms are located in or near major shopping destinations, including in the Siam Paragon and opposite the Central department store in Bangkok. Given its apparent popularity, other stores have been planned.

Sources: Anon. (2010); Narataruksa (2014); Pholdhampalit (2014); Ruddick (2014).

Theory into Practice

This market insight describes how a Thai entrepreneur has brought a world-renowned retail brand to the Thai market. It illustrates how a famous foreign international brand can be adapted slightly to cater for local tastes without falling away from the original parent concept.

Related Topics

market entry method; marketing channels; culture; international marketing; standardization–adaptation; marketing implementation

1 **How important is it that the Harrods Tea Rooms sells a Thai-oriented food range?**

2 **Would you define the Harrods Tea Rooms food offering in Thailand as a convenience, shopping, or specialty good?**

3 **Is the Harrods Tea Rooms retail offer purely a consumer good? Why do you say this?**

- use personal selling techniques; and

- use an approach to pricing based on cost and value.

We consider services marketing in more detail in Chapter 14.

The Business-to-Business Perspective

Many marketing textbooks overemphasize consumer goods marketing, paying inadequate attention to industrial/organizational/business-to-business (B2B) marketing. Business-to-business marketing is different from consumer marketing because the customer focus is a professional buyer within a business rather than an individual. It requires that marketers deal with more sophisticated customers buying in volume and often as part of a decision-making unit (alongside other buyers and technicians), who are trained to buy (or 'procure') professionally and who are rewarded for buying the right propositions at the right price (see Chapter 16).

Much B2B marketing activity revolves around the need to develop strong prospects for a company's offerings, to ensure effective **supply chain management** operations to develop the market for a B2B offering, and to ensure that it is delivered appropriately. Because buyers purchase large volumes of products or complex 'bundles' of services (for example customized IT software solutions sold by German company SAP), tight specifications are produced with which suppliers must comply. Buyers try to ensure that they obtain the best supplier possible by offering suppliers a contract to supply for a set period of time and encouraging a bidding process.

In public sector markets, the procurement process is bound by strict legal guidelines for contracts valued over a set financial amount. This process creates substantial rivalry, with firms often submitting bids they cannot fulfil, either because they've under-priced themselves, or because they've over-promised what they can deliver—a phenomenon known as the **winner's curse** because the winning company ends up servicing an unprofitable contract (Thaler, 2012).

The emphasis in B2B markets is strongly focused on the development and building of mutually satisfying relationships based on commitment and trust (Morgan and Hunt, 1994), both to win the contract in the first instance and to deliver it to the customer's specifications. Whether or not a firm meets these specifications is in part linked to the **logistics** function (that is, warehousing, inventory management, delivery) of the firm. Consequently, B2B marketers can create a competitive advantage if they develop a strong linkage between the marketing and logistics functions, developing a strong customer service proposition by means of:

- reductions of order cycle times;

- accurate invoicing procedures;

- reliable delivery;

- effective claims procedures;

- readily available inventory;

- goods delivered in good condition or effective service delivery;

- few order size constraints or the limited customization of services;

- effective and planned visits from a salesperson;

- convenient ordering systems and the provision of order status information;

- flexible delivery times; and

- strong aftersales support (Christopher, 1986).

Marketing's Impact on Society

So far, we've considered how marketing can be characterized as operating in the consumer, business-to-business, or services domains. What is common to all contexts is that the marketer works to satisfy customers. However, more recently, there has been a realization that marketing impacts both positively and negatively on society. The study of the effect that marketing processes, activities, and institutions have on the economy and society of a nation is known as **macromarketing**.

Let's consider first how much the marketing industry contributes positively to society. (We consider the negative societal impacts and sustainable marketing considerations in Chapter 18.) For example, Wilkie and Moore (1999) describe the complexities of what they call the 'aggregate marketing system'. We can use the example of how marketing brings together the ingredients of an average European 'continental' breakfast. Consider the individual ingredients—for example coffee or tea, together with Danish pastries, cold cuts of meat, salad and cheese, muesli and cereals, various fruits, the cups/plates and glasses, the oven to cook the pastries, etc. The distributive capacity of the aggregate marketing system is amazing when we consider that there were around 516 million people in the European Union in 2017, each of whom selects their own unique mixture of breakfast offerings each morning (CIA, 2017). Broadly, the aggregate marketing system in most countries works well, but there are parts of the world in which these systems have weaknesses. Some countries experience imperfections in supply and demand because of political circumstances (such as war, dictatorship) or environmental circumstances (for example drought, famine). Therefore marketing plays an important role in developing and transforming society (see Research Insight 1.3 and Market Insight 1.4). Melinda Gates, co-chair of the Bill and Melinda Gates Foundation, has argued that not-for-profits such as charities have much to learn from for-profit companies such as Coca Cola (Gates, 2010).

Research Insight 1.3

To take your learning further, you might wish to read this influential paper:

Wilkie, W.L., and Moore, E.S. (2011). Expanding our understanding of marketing in society. *Journal of the Academy of Marketing Science*, 40(1), 53–73.

This article, building on a previous ground-breaking article (Wilkie and Moore, 1999), charts 100 years of marketing thought and the extent to which marketing in society was a key consideration in scholarship during that time. It continues to expand the idea of the 'aggregate marketing system' within society, and it maps the field of marketing in society by outlining extant research groups and a research agenda.

 Visit the online resources to read the abstract and access the full paper.

Market Insight 1.4
Google: World-Changing Innovations

In 1996, Google began life as a research project developing what became its acclaimed search engine and PageRank algorithm. Since those heady early days, Google has completely transformed society—by changing the way in which we acquire information. Many of Google's other innovations have become part of peoples' daily lives—for example Google Books, which has digitized millions of books so that people can preview a snippet of their contents prior to making purchase decisions, or Google Maps, which allows people to plan and pursue their travel routes on foot, or by car, bicycle, or public transport, wherever they have a mobile Internet connection.

So what is the company's secret to achieving innovation success? Part of the answer is that Google has been renowned for its policy of allowing its engineers and developers to spend 20 per cent of their time on independent projects; '20 per cent time' projects have included Gmail, Google News, and AdSense. Its corporate principle for innovation is referred to as the '8 Pillars of Innovation'. These highlight important ideas for building innovation capacity, such as having a mission, thinking big, but starting small, striving for continual innovation, and being willing to fail. But Google's innovation success does not derive only from corporate policy; it is generated from an understanding of what customers and users are thinking. Google champions and capitalizes on ideas gained from customer insight. Customers or users are deemed as an open source for creativity and inspiration on the basis of which Google can create something novel.

Google[x], a semi-secret R&D facility, manifests Google's innovation practices. The facility follows in the footsteps of such classic research labs as the Manhattan Project (the US site of the development of the A-bomb during the Second World War) or Bletchley Park (the British code-breaking facility where Nazi Germany's U-boat codes were cracked). Google[x]'s mandate is to invent new technologies or ways of fixing anything that presents a significant problem for mankind.

Since its inception in 2010, Google[x] has been home to many avant-garde innovations, including the self-driving car initiative and Internet-connected spectacles, known as Google Glass, among other incredible projects. Apart from the Google[x] lab located in its Googleplex headquarters in Mountain View, Santa Clara, California, Google has also based its innovation labs in other locations, such as New York and Sydney.

In 2014, Google funded a science, technology, engineering, and maths (STEM) laboratory in an educational venture in Ras Al Khaimah, UAE. The aim of the facility is to give students and teachers training in cutting-edge technologies, including robotics, 3D printing, drone building, and software coding, in areas in which resources are relatively scarce. In 2015, Belfast, Northern Ireland, was selected as the European location for a new innovation lab facility for Google. This facility is designed for collaboration with firms across the UK and Europe based on digital technology. It will generate more than 1,300 jobs for Belfast. Google prides itself on not being a conventional company. In August 2015, Google created a new parent holding company, Alphabet, ostensibly to separate 'moon shot' projects from its day-to-day business.

Sources: Bort (2014); D'Onfro (2015); George (2015); McDonnell (2015); Scott (2015); Tait (2015).

The origin of world-changing innovations: the quirky Googleplex in California
Source: © Asif Islam/Shutterstock.com.

Market Insight 1.4
continued

Theory into Practice

This market insight describes how one of the world's most innovative companies approaches the development of new offerings and how those new offerings impact upon society. A secondary insight from the case is how Google has sought to 'derisk' the day-to-day business of Google from its inspirational and aspirational world-changing projects by developing a new parent holding company, Alphabet.

Related Topics

innovation; marketing in society; new product development; marketing organization

1 Why are the innovations created by companies such as Google so important to local communities and society in general?

2 Do futuristic innovations, such as Google Glass or the self-driving car, really help society or do they simply generate profit for the developers?

3 What other companies are you aware of that have had a big impact on society? With what offerings?

This market insight was kindly contributed by Dr Ning Baines, De Montfort University, UK.

Another element of marketing's positive contribution to society is the role it plays in bringing innovations to the marketplace (see Chapter 8). For instance, some of the world's most important inventions have come to us through the aggregate marketing system.

Consider how some of the offerings outlined in Table 1.4 have affected your own life. What would we do without these inventions today? Imagine if the Internet, social media, or mobile phones did not exist. We enjoy them because innovative individuals and companies brought us these. The cardboard carton for storing milk is ubiquitous, but was invented in 1951 in Sweden. And could you imagine ketchup not existing? It was brought to us by Heinz, based on an ancient Chinese recipe for a fish sauce called *ketsiap*.

In each case, the invention outlined has been an extraordinary success. But the aggregate marketing system not only serves to bring consumers those offerings that truly meet their needs; it also stops failures from getting through (see Chapter 8). For example, Coca-Cola withdrew its mid-calorie Coca-Cola Life variant from UK shelves in 2017, having first introduced it in 2014 (Anon., 2017b). Electric cars will become the dominant form of car as opposed to petrol or diesel engine cars, particularly as countries have started banning diesel engines. The diffusion of these innovations depends on the aggregate marketing system and the marketers that exist within it, as well as on government regulation (see Market Insight 1.5 on autonomous vehicles). The system impedes offerings that don't meet consumer needs. (For more on the

Table 1.4 Some modern consumer products and the dates of their invention

Consumer product	Product attribute	Consumer need	Inventor(s)/ pioneer(s) [a]	Year of invention
Chocolate bar	Cocoa-based food	Allows chocolate to be eaten, as opposed to drunk, as had traditionally been the case	J.S. Fry & Sons, UK	1847
Ketchup (from Chinese *ketsiap*)	A food condiment, derived from the Chinese fish-based sauce *ketsiap*, but adapted to Western tastes, to use tomatoes instead	Can enhance the consumer's enjoyment of their food by modifying the taste and reducing the dryness of some foodstuffs	F. & J. Heinz Co., United States	1876
Television	Transmits moving images	Delivers information, entertainment, and education	Baird Television Development Co., UK; Telefunken, Germany	1929; 1932
Tampons (with applicator)	Feminine hygiene product	Allows girls and women to maintain more active lifestyles	Tampax, United States	1936
Carton	Cardboard liquid storage device	Allows liquid foodstuffs to be stored, packaged, and distributed in an environmentally friendly way	TetraPak, Sweden	1951
Artificial sweeteners	Xylitol, as the sweetener is known, is used to sweeten food products such as sugar-free chewing gum and toothpastes	Sweetens food products without damaging our teeth	Cultor, Finland	1969
Bar code scanners	Automatic identification and classification of products	Speeds up the pricing and checkout process at retailers	Monarch Marking, United States; Plessey Telecommunications, UK	1970
Personal computer	Allows users to play electronic games, to perform calculations, and to process documents, as well as other applications	Simplifies complex writing/arithmetic tasks and offers recreational possibilities, i.e. gaming	IBM, United States	1980

Table 1.4 (*Continued*)

Consumer product	Product attribute	Consumer need	Inventor(s)/ pioneer(s) [a]	Year of invention
Mobile phone	Handheld device for making telephone calls whilst in motion	Allows users to stay in telephone contact with others regardless of location	NTT, Japan	1979
World Wide Web/web server	System for linking hypertext documents (i.e. documents linked to other documents) via the Internet; by using a web browser, users can read web pages	Allows users with access to the Internet to read and share information across large distances	Tim Berners-Lee, UK; Robert Cailliau, Belgium; CERN,[b] EU	1990
Bluetooth	A wireless technology standard allowing data exchange over ultra-high frequency radio waves	Allows low-power wire-free communications for radios, telephone, and industrial applications	Ericsson, Sweden	1994
Social networking	Website designed for personal interaction between friends and acquaintances	Provides easy and instantaneous communication between two or more people in multiple locations around the world	Facebook Inc., United States	2004
App-based-transportation and food delivery services	Transportation system linking own-account drivers and riders via a smartphone app, using a dynamic pricing model	Allows users to obtain transportation quickly, on demand, and to pay automatically via an app on their smartphones	Uber Technologies, Inc., United States	2009

[a] The named companies are not always the inventors per se; they often acquired the patents from the inventor, and were licensed to produce and distribute the invention.

[b] Conseil Européen pour la Recherche Nucléaire.

Sources: Various, including https://www.thoughtco.com/inventions-4133303 and manufacturers' websites.

new proposition development process, see Chapter 8.) It also provides a number of benefits to society, including:

- the promotion and delivery of desired offerings;

- the provision of a forum for market learning (we can see what does and what doesn't get through the system);

- the stimulation of market demand;

- the provision of a wide scope of choice of offerings by providing a close or customized fit with consumer needs;

- the facilitation of purchases (or acquisitions generally, for example if no payment is made directly, as in the case of public services);

- time savings and the promotion of efficiency in customer requirement matching;

- the bringing of new offerings, and improvements, to market to meet latent and unserved needs; and

- the seeking of customer satisfaction for repeat purchases (Wilkie and Moore, 1999).

Market Insight 1.5
Where Now, Autonomous Car?

Over the past few years, a number of car manufacturers have announced innovative plans to develop autonomous cars, for example Tesla's development of an autopilot system and Audi's 'Level 3' autonomy technology. By using various technologies, including radar, lasers, geographical positioning systems (GPS), and computer vision, an autonomous vehicle (also known as the driverless car, self-driving car, or robotic car) has the ability to sense and navigate its surroundings without the need for human control. Even though autonomous vehicles haven't fully made an appearance on public roads, test programmes have been scheduled in many countries worldwide. For example, as part of the pilot scheme in the UK, small autonomous vehicles have moved people around the city centre of Milton Keynes. In Sweden, Volvo has launched its autonomous driving trial programme in Gothenburg, with a plan to expand it to London in early 2018.

Autonomous vehicles could introduce an improvement to transportation and society, including a reduction in car accidents, more effective transportation, and an increase in road capacity. With autonomous vehicles, customers may come to see it as a service rather than a product they must own, because customers will be able to call for a car via a click on their mobile app, just as they do with Uber now, but without a driver. In the future, the desire to own a car could become passé; hence this development would influence the marketing of cars generally. It would mean appealing to consumers on

The Tesla Model 3—Tesla's first mass-market electric vehicle—in autopilot mode
Source: © TierneyMJ/Shutterstock.com.

the basis of the quality of the features of the mobility service, rather than the traditional selling of the benefits of vehicle ownership.

However, several questions in relation to implementing the concept successfully in wider society remain unanswered. How will autonomous cars make ethical decisions? How will such a care safely navigate, especially when driving alongside normal cars controlled by humans? How will cities, streets, and parking need to change to accommodate autonomous vehicles? What will happen to car insurance and car tax as courts grapple with who is to blame in the event of an accident? What will happen to the millions of people who make a living from driving—that is, taxi, bus, or truck drivers? How will society as a whole adjust to the loss of service jobs resulting from autonomous

Market Insight 1.5

continued

vehicles? Are there any new roles that would fill these employment gaps? How should policymakers ease the transition from human controlled vehicles to autonomous vehicles? Since autonomous vehicles are no longer the stuff of science fiction films such as *I, Robot*, such questions have forced business executives, governments, and administrators to think ahead in a bid to stay on top of the coming transportation transformation.

Sources: Navigant Research (2013); Beckwith (2016); Khanna and Barrett (2017); Mercer (2017); Somaseger and Li (2017).

Theory into Practice

This market insight describes the innovative technology used in autonomous vehicle development, and the obvious improvements it will bring to transportation, customer convenience, and road accident reduction. On the flip side, this new innovation will have an impact on society as a whole. This market insight therefore considers macromarketing issues—that is, the effect that marketing strategies have on the economy and society—by reflecting on the likely impact of innovation developments on individual macro-environmental elements (that is, from ethical, legal, business, and policy perspectives) and how the national marketing system is shaped as a consequence.

Related Topics

consumer buying behaviour; marketing environment; macromarketing; innovation adoption

1 **What difficulties might manufacturers have when marketing autonomous vehicles to new customers?**

2 **Are we most likely to own our own autonomous vehicle or will we simply hire one in the future?**

3 **Who will be the biggest sellers of autonomous vehicles in your view? Will it be existing car manufacturers, consumer electronics companies, or Internet technology companies?**

This market insight was kindly contributed by Dr Ning Baines, De Montfort University, UK.

 Visit the **online resources** and complete Internet Activity 1.2 to learn more about how marketing innovation impacts upon society.

However, the aggregate marketing system, or marketing more generally, does not always serve the common good. Marketing is frequently criticized for the opposite—for being unethical in nature, manipulative, and creating wants or needs where none previously existed (Packard, 1960). Whilst this chapter has focused on the principles and practice of marketing, as well as the positive power of marketing in society, there is also a negative impact of marketing on society. This occurs both as a result of unethical marketing practice and because of structural inequalities in the aggregate marketing system. (For a detailed critique of the marketing concept, see Chapter 18.)

Chapter Summary

To consolidate your learning, the key points from this chapter are summarized here:

- **Define the concept of marketing.**

  Marketing is the process by which organizations anticipate and satisfy their customers' needs to both parties' benefit. It involves mutual exchange. Over the last 25 years, the marketing concept has changed to recognize the importance of long-term customer relationships to organizations. In addition, most definitions of marketing recognize the importance of marketing's impacts on society and the need to curtail these where they are negative.

- **Explain how marketing has developed over the twentieth century and into the twenty-first century.**

  Whereas some writers have suggested a simple timeline from production era, through sales era, to marketing era over the twentieth century, others recognize that marketing has existed in different forms in different countries at different times. Nevertheless, there is increasing recognition that marketing is a more systematic organizational activity, as a result of market research and sophisticated promotional activity, than before. There is also a move to recognize the need for companies and organizations to behave responsibly in relation to society.

- **Understand the concepts of exchange in marketing and marketing mix.**

  The concept of exchange is important and has been considered by some to be the key to uncovering the elusive 'general theory of marketing'. Empathizing with customers to understand what they want and determining how sellers seek to provide what buyers want is a central concept in marketing. The means by which organizations deploy their marketing programmes is via the marketing mix, which comprises *product* (the offering), *place* (the distribution mechanism), *price* (the value placed on the offering), and *promotion* (how the company communicates that value). For services marketing, because of the intangible nature of the service, marketers consider an extra 3Ps, including *physical evidence* (how cues are developed for customers to recognize quality), *process* (how the experience is designed to meet customers' needs), and *people* (the training and development of those delivering the customer experience).

- **Describe the three major contexts of marketing application—that is, consumer goods, business-to-business, and services marketing.**

  Marketing activity divides into three types, recognizing that marketing activities are designed based on the context in which an organization operates. The consumer goods marketing approach has been dominant, stressing the 4Ps and the marketing mix. Business-to-business marketing focuses on the principles of relationship marketing—particularly those required in coordinating supply chain members. Services marketing stresses the intangible nature of an offering, including the need to manage customer expectations levels of service quality and customer experience.

- **Understand the positive contribution that marketing makes to society.**

  The aggregate marketing system delivers to us a wide array of offerings, either directly or indirectly, through business markets, to serve our wants and needs. There is much that is positive about the aggregate marketing system and it has served to improve the standard of living for many people around the world.

Review Questions

1 How do we define the concept of marketing?
2 How do the AMA's and the CIM's definitions of marketing differ?

3 How has marketing developed historically?

4 What is the difference between sales and marketing?

5 What is a marketing exchange?

6 What is the marketing mix?

7 What is the services marketing mix?

8 What are the three major contexts of marketing application?

9 What is the winner's curse?

10 What positive contributions does marketing make to society?

 # Discussion Questions

1 Having read Case Insight 1.1 at the beginning of this chapter, how would you advise Aldoraq Water to differentiate itself when competing against local and international brands?

2 Read the section on the marketing mix within the chapter, and draw up marketing mixes for the following organizations and their target customers:

   A Streaming video company Netflix and its audiences

   B A wealth management company and its clientele

   C Pharmacies (for example Boots UK Ltd, Sweden's Apoteket AB, Holland's Etos BV) and their consumers

   D A company supplying lifts to construction companies

3 What are the attributes of the offer, and customer needs associated with those attributes, for the following?

   A Bank business accounts (for example those offered by Britain's Lloyds Bank plc)

   B A university (for example Aarhus University in Denmark) offering places to students on Masters programmes

   C Jimmy Choo Romy 100 mm glitter pumps

   D A company such as Withers Worldwide, selling legal services to businesses

   E Watching a football match live on MUTV from Old Trafford, Manchester, England in Shanghai, China

 Visit the online resources and complete the Multiple-Choice Questions to assess your knowledge of Chapter 1.

 # Glossary

advertising a form of non-personal communication, by an identified sponsor, that is transmitted through the use of paid-for media.

aggregated demand demand calculated at the population level rather than at the individual level.

American Marketing Association (AMA) a membership body for marketing professionals and marketing educators based in the United States, operating principally in the United States and Canada.

brand a name, symbol or design developed to position and differentiate an offering, particularly through promotions means and customer experience, so that the offering appeals to customers and other stakeholders.

Chartered Institute of Marketing (CIM) a membership body for marketing professionals based in the UK, with study centres and members around the world.

consumer the user of a product, service, or other form of offering.

copyright the legal, exclusive right granted to a creator to exploit the use and distribution of literary, musical and artistic work; usually denoted by the symbol ©.

customer the person who purchases and pays for (or initially requests and specifies, in the case of a non-financial transaction) a product, service or other form of offering from a company or organization.

customer relationship management (CRM) systems software systems that provide all staff with a complete view of the history and status of each customer.

dyadic essentially means two-way; a dyadic commercial relationship is an exchange between two people—typically, a buyer and a seller.

elasticity an economic concept associated with the extent to which changes in one variable are related to changes in another; if a price increase in a good causes a decline in volume of sales of that good, we say the good is price elastic and specify by how much; if it causes no change or very little change, we say it is inelastic.

environmental scanning the management process internal to an organization designed to identify the external issues, situations, and threats that may impinge on an organization's future and its strategic decision-making.

ethnography a sub-discipline derived from cultural anthropology as an approach to research that emphasizes the collection of data through participant observation of members of a specific subcultural grouping and observation of participation of members of a specific subcultural grouping.

haul girls women who shop for clothes or beauty products and then make a YouTube video showing viewers what they have bought, item by item.

interactive marketing more accurately described as creating a situation or mechanism through which a marketer and a customer (or stakeholders) interact, usually in real time.

key account management a systematic approach to managing the relationships between an organization and a selected group of its most important customers to maximize value for both parties.

logistics the process of transporting the initial components of goods, services, and other forms of offering, and their finished products, from the producer to the customer and then on to the consumer.

macromarketing refers to the impact that marketing has, when its effects are aggregated, on economic and societal systems.

market orientation refers to the development of a whole-organization approach to the generation, collection, and dissemination of market intelligence across different departments and the organization's responsiveness to that intelligence.

market sensing an organization's ability to gather, interpret, and act on strategic information from customers and competitors.

marketing mix the list of items a marketing manager should consider when devising plans for marketing products, including *product* decisions, *place* (distribution) decisions, *pricing* decisions, and *promotion* decisions; later extended to include *physical evidence*, *process*, and *people* decisions to account for the lack of physical nature in service products.

meta-analysis a research method whereby the results of multiple studies are examined and combined to identify trends more precisely.

multichannel marketing the use of multiple, usually synchronized, platforms through which to interact with customers to communicate with them and distribute an offering.

netnography the branch of ethnography that seeks to analyse Internet users' behaviour.

non-staple in the grocery context, grocery products that are not a main or important food.

observation a research method that requires a researcher to watch and record how consumers or employees behave—typically, in relation to either purchasing or selling activities.

place (distribution) essentially about how to place the optimum amount of goods and/ or services before the maximum number of members of a target market, at times and locations that optimize the marketing outcome— that is, sales.

positioning the way in which an audience of consumers or buyers perceives a product or service, particularly as a result of the marketing communications process aimed at a target audience.

price the amount the customer has to pay to receive a good or service.

procurement the purchasing (buying) process within a firm or organization.

product anything that is capable of satisfying customer needs.

promotion the use of communications to persuade individuals, groups, or organizations to purchase products and services.

promotional mix the combination of five key communication tools: advertising, sales promotions, public relations, direct marketing, and personal selling.

relationship marketing the development and management of long-term relationships with customers, influencers, referrers, suppliers, recruiters, and employees.

service-dominant logic (SDL) asserts that organizations, markets, and society are concerned fundamentally with exchange of service, based on the application of knowledge and skills; rejects the notion of dualism between goods and services marketing, arguing that all offerings provide a service.

servicescape the physical environment in which a service takes place, for example a stadium for a football game.

social anthropology the scientific discipline of observing and recording the way in which humans behave within their different social groupings.

supply chain management the management and coordination of supply-side activities (including planning, sourcing, making, and delivering), from production to consumption, to enhance customer value.

trademark A distinctive symbol, design (for example the McDonald's 'Golden Arches') or word(s) that uniquely identifies a company, or its offerings; usually denoted by the symbol ™.

tweenagers pre-adolescent children, typically taken to be between the ages of 9 and 12, who are hence about to enter their teenage years.

value the regard that something is held to be worth—typically, although not always, in financial terms.

winner's curse terminology associated with the bidding process in commercial markets where a company ends up submitting a bid at a price that is unprofitable or not very profitable simply to win the contract.

References

AMA (American Marketing Association) (2013). About AMA: definition of marketing. Retrieve from: https://www.ama.org/AboutAMA/Pages/Definition-of-Marketing.aspx (accessed 13 October 2018).

AMA (2015). Dictionary: sales. Retrieve from: https://www.ama.org/resources/Pages/Dictionary.aspx?dLetter=S (accessed 13 October 2018).

Anon. (2010). History of Harrods department stores. *BBC News*, 8 May. Retrieve from: https://www.bbc.com/news/10103783 (accessed 13 October 2018).

Anon. (2015a). Dutch V&D department store business goes bust. *BBC News*, 31 December. Retrieve from: https://www.bbc.co.uk/news/business-35208209 (accessed 13 October 2018).

Anon. (2015b). V&D on brink of bankruptcy as warm winter hits sales. *DutchNews.nl*, 23 December. Retrieve from: https://www.dutchnews.nl/news/archives/2015/12/vd-on-brink-of-bankruptcy-as-warm-winter-hits-sales/ (accessed 13 October 2018).

Anon. (2017a). The little airline that could. *The Economist*, 15 July, 54.

Anon. (2017b). Need to know. *Campaign*, 14 April, 3.

Associated Press (2017). Doctor dragged off United Airlines flight receives undisclosed settlement. *The Guardian*, 27 April. Retrieve from: https://www.theguardian.com/business/2017/apr/27/united-doctor-dragged-flight-settlement-david-dao (accessed 13 October 2018).

Bagozzi, R.P. (1975). Marketing as exchange. *Journal of Marketing*, 3(4), 32–9.

Bartels, R.D.W. (1944). Marketing principles. *Journal of Marketing*, 9(2), 151–8.

Bartels, R.D.W. (1951). Can marketing be a science? *Journal of Marketing*, 15(3), 319–28.

Bartels, R.D.W. (1959). Sociologists and marketologists. *Journal of Marketing*, 24(2), 37–40.

Bartels, R.D.W. (1968). The general theory of marketing. *Journal of Marketing*, 32(1), 29–33.

Beckwith, J. (2016). Volvo launches autonomous driving programme. *Autocar*, 12 September. Retrieve from: https://www.autocar.co.uk/car-news/industry/volvo-launches-autonomous-driving-programme (accessed 13 October 2018).

Blois, K.J. (1974). The marketing of services: an approach. *European Journal of Marketing*, 8(2), 137–45.

Booms, B.H., and Bitner, M.J. (1981). Marketing strategies and organisation structures for service firms. In: J.H. Donnelly and W.R. George (eds), *Marketing of Services*, Chicago, IL: AMA Proceedings Series, 47–52.

Borden, N.H. (1964). The concept of the marketing mix. *Journal of Advertising Research*, 4, 2–7.

Bort, J. (2014). A rare look inside Google's secret labs where they invent amazing new things. *Business Insider*, 20 April. Retrieve from: https://www.businessinsider.com/inside-googles-secret-google-x-labs-2014-4?IR=T (accessed 13 October 2018).

Brenner, B. (2013). Inside the NIKE matrix. Wirtschafts Universität Wien Case Series, Case 0001/2013. Retrieve from: http://epub.wu.ac.at/3791/1/Nike__WU-CaseSeries.pdf (accessed 13 October 2018).

Bucklin, L.P. (1963). Retail strategy and the classification of consumer goods. *Journal of Marketing*, 27(1), 51–6.

Christopher, M. (1986). Reaching the customer: strategies for marketing and customer service. *Journal of Marketing Management*, 2(1), 63–71.

Christopher, M., Payne, A., and Ballantyne, D. (2002). *Relationship Marketing: Creating Stakeholder Value* (2nd edn). Oxford: Butterworth Heinemann.

CIA (Central Intelligence Agency) (2017). *The World Factbook: European Union*, Washington, DC: CIA. Retrieve from: https://www.cia.gov/library/publications/the-world-factbook/geos/ee.html (accessed 13 October 2018).

CIM (Chartered Institute of Marketing) (2015). Marketing and the 7Ps. Retrieve from: https://www.cim.co.uk/files/7ps.pdf (accessed 13 October 2018).

CIM (2016). Professional marketing competencies. Retrieve from: https://www.cim.co.uk/media/1918/professional-marketing-competencies-2016-interactive.pdf (accessed 13 October 2018).

Comstock, B., Gulati, R., and Liguori, S. (2010). Unleashing the power of marketing. *Harvard Business Review*, 88(10), 90–8.

Cova, B., and Salle, R. (2007). The industrial/consumer marketing dichotomy revisited: a case of outdated justification? *Journal of Business and Industrial Marketing*, 23(1), 3–11.

de Baynast, A., Lendrevie, J., and Lévy, J. (2017). Lexique du marketing: marketing. Retrieve from https://www.mercator-publicitor.fr/lexique-marketing-definition-marketing (accessed 13 October 2018).

D'Onfro, J. (2015). The truth about Google's famous '20% time' policy. *Business Insider UK*, 17 April. Retrieve from: http://uk.businessinsider.com/google-20-percent-time-policy-2015-4?r=US&IR=T (accessed 13 October 2018).

Doob, L.W. (1948). *Public Opinion and Propaganda*. Oxford: Henry Holt.

Fern, E.F., and Brown, J.R. (1984). The industrial/consumer marketing dichotomy: a case of insufficient justification. *Journal of Marketing*, 48(2), 68–77.

Fullerton, R.A. (1988). How modern is modern marketing? Marketing's evolution and the myth of the 'Production Era'. *Journal of Marketing*, 52(1), 108–25.

Gates, M. (2010). What nonprofits can learn from Coca-Cola. *TED*, September. Retrieve from: https://www.ted.com/talks/melinda_french_gates_what_nonprofits_can_learn_from_coca_cola?language=en (accessed 13 October 2018).

George, B. (2015). The world's most innovative company. *Huffington Post*, 28 October. Retrieve from: https://www.huffingtonpost.com/bill-george/the-worlds-most-innovativ_b_8406556.html (accessed 13 October 2018).

Gordon, J., and Perrey, J. (2015). The dawn of marketing's new golden age. *McKinsey Quarterly*, February. Retrieve from: https://www.mckinsey.com/business-functions/marketing-and-sales/our-insights/the-dawn-of-marketings-new-golden-age (accessed 13 October 2018).

Grönroos, C. (1984). A service quality model and its marketing implications. *European Journal of Marketing*, 18(4), 36–44.

Grönroos, C. (1994). From marketing mix to relationship marketing: towards a paradigm shift in marketing. *Management Decision*, 32(2), 4–20.

Grönroos, C. (1998). Marketing services: a case of a missing product. *Journal of Business and Industrial Marketing*, 13(4–5), 322–38.

Grönroos, C., and Voima, P. (2013). Critical service logic: making sense of value creation and co-creation. *Journal of the Academy of Marketing Science*, 41(2), 133–50.

Gummesson, E. (1987). The new marketing: developing long-term interactive relationships. *Long Range Planning*, 20(4), 10–20.

Gummesson, E. (1990). Marketing orientation revisited: the crucial role of the part-time marketer. *European Journal of Marketing*, 25(2), 60–75.

Hanssens, D.M. (ed.) (2009). *Empirical Generalizations about Marketing Impact: What We Have Learned from Academic Research*. Cambridge, MA: Marketing Science Institute.

Harris, L.C., and Ogbonna, E. (2003). The organisation of marketing: a study of decentralised, devolved and dispersed marketing activity. *Journal of Management Studies*, 40(2), 483–512.

Hobbs, T. (2015). Over 20% of FTSE 100 CEOs now come from a marketing background. *Marketing Week*, 23 October. Retrieve from: https://www.marketingweek.com/2015/10/23/over-20-of-ftse-100-ceos-now-come-from-a-marketing-background/ (accessed 13 October 2018).

Holden, A.C., and Holden, L. (1998). Marketing history: illuminating marketing's clandestine subdiscipline. *Psychology and Marketing*, 15(2), 117–23.

Howard, D.G., Savins, D.M., Howell, W., and Ryans, J.K., Jr (1991). The evolution of marketing theory in the United States and Europe. *European Journal of Marketing*, 25(2), 7–16.

Hult, G.T.M., Mena, J.A., Ferrell, O.C., and Ferrell, L. (2011). Stakeholder marketing: a definition and conceptual framework. *AMS Review*, 1(1), 44–65.

Hunt, S.D. (1971). The morphology of theory and the general theory of marketing. *Journal of Marketing*, 35(2), 65–8.

Hunt, S.D. (1983). General theories and fundamental explananda of marketing. *Journal of Marketing*, 47(4), 9–17.

Hunt, S.D. (2013). A general theory of business marketing: RA theory, Alderson, the ISBM framework, and the IMP theoretical structure. *Industrial Marketing Management*, 42(3), 283–93.

Judd, R.C. (1968). Similarities and differences in product and service retailing. *Journal of Retailing*, 43(4), 1–9.

Katz, E. (1957). The two-step flow of communication: an up-to-date report on an hypothesis. *Public Opinion Quarterly*, 21(1), 61–78.

Keith, R.J. (1960). The marketing revolution. *Journal of Marketing*, 24(3), 35–8.

Khanna, A., and Barrett, S. (2017). Hard questions on our transition to driverless cars. *Harvard Business Review*, 11 April. Retrieve from: https://hbr.org/2017/04/hard-questions-on-our-transition-to-driverless-cars (accessed 13 October 2018).

Kirca, A.H., Jayachandran, S., and Bearden, W.O. (2005). Market orientation: a meta-analytic review and assessment of its antecedents and impact on performance. *Journal of Marketing*, 69(2), 24–41.

Kohli, A.K., and Jaworski, B.J. (1990). Market orientation: the construct, research propositions and managerial implications. *Journal of Marketing*, 54(2), 1–18.

Kotler, P. (2006). Ethical lapses of marketers. In: J.N. Sheth and R.J. Sisodia (eds), *Does Marketing Need Reform: Fresh Perspectives on the Future*. Armonk, NY: M.E. Sharpe, 153–7.

Kumar, V., Jones, E., Venkatesan, R., and Leone, R.P. (2011). Is market orientation a source of sustainable competitive advantage or simply the cost of competing? *Journal of Marketing*, 75(1), 16–30.

Le Meunier-FitzHugh, K., and Piercy, N.F. (2011). Exploring the relationship between market orientation and sales and marketing collaboration. *Journal of Personal Selling and Sales Management*, 31(3), 287–96.

Lee, A.M. (1945). The analysis of propaganda: a clinical summary. *American Journal of Sociology*, 51(2), 126–35.

Leone, R.P., and Shultz, R.L. (1980). A study of marketing generalisations. *Journal of Marketing*, 44(1), 10–18.

McCarthy, E.J. (1960). *Basic Marketing*. Homewood, IL: Irwin.

McDonnell, F. (2015). New PwC and Google innovation lab will be located in Belfast. *The Irish Times*, 24 November. Retrieve from: https://www.irishtimes.com/business/new-pwc-and-google-innovation-lab-will-be-located-in-belfast-1.2442406 (accessed 13 October 2018).

McKinsey&Company (2017). About us. Retrieve from: https://www.mckinsey.com/about-us/who-we-are (accessed 13 October 2018).

Mercer, C. (2017). 12 companies working on driverless cars: what companies are making driverless cars? *Techword*, 17 August. Retrieve from: https://www.techworld.com/picture-gallery/data/-companies-working-on-driverless-cars-3641537/ (accessed 13 October 2018).

Morgan, R.M., and Hunt, S.D. (1994). The commitment–trust theory of relationship marketing. *Journal of Marketing*, 58(3), 20–38.

Narataruksa, S. (2014). A cup of joy. *Thailand Tatler*, June, 44–5.

Narver, J.C., and Slater, S.F. (1990). The effect of a market orientation on business profitability. *Journal of Marketing*, 54(4), 20–35.

Navigant Research (2013). How self-driving cars will change the world. *Forbes*, 13 November. Retrieve from: https://www.forbes.com/sites/pikeresearch/2013/11/13/how-self-driving-cars-will-change-the-world/#2fed3dcf6384 (accessed 13 October 2018).

O'Malley, L., and Patterson, M. (1998). Vanishing point: the mix management paradigm re-viewed. *Journal of Marketing Management*, 14(8), 829–51.

Packard, V.O. (1960). *The Hidden Persuaders*. Harmondsworth: Penguin Books.

Parasuraman, A., Berry, L.L., and Zeithaml, V.A. (1985). A conceptual model of service quality and its implications for further research. *Journal of Marketing*, 49(4), 41–50.

Payne, A. (1993). *The Essence of Services Marketing*. Hemel Hempstead: Prentice-Hall.

Payne, A., Storbacka, K., and Frow, P. (2008). Managing the co-creation of value. *Journal of the Academy of Marketing Science*, 36(1), 83–96.

Pholdhampalit, K. (2014). Tea with the most elegant of flavours. *The Sunday Nation*, 5 January. Retrieve from: https://www.pressreader.com/thailand/the-nation/20140105/282265253270367 (accessed 13 October 2018).

Pieters, J. (2015). Dutch department store V&D declared bankrupt: some 10,000 job losses. *NLtimes*, 31 December. Retrieve from: https://nltimes.nl/2015/12/31/dutch-department-store-vd-declared-bankrupt-10000-job-losses (accessed 13 October 2018).

Prahalad, C.K., and Ramaswamy, V. (2004a). Co-creation experiences: the next practice in value creation. *Journal of Interactive Marketing*, 18(3), 5–14.

Prahalad, C.K., and Ramaswamy, V. (2004b). Co-creating unique value with customers. *Strategy and Leadership*, 32(3), 4–9.

Regan, W.J. (1963). The service revolution. *Journal of Marketing*, 27(3), 57–62.

Reichheld, F.F., and Sasser, W.E., Jr (1990). Zero defections: quality comes to services. *Harvard Business Review*, 68(5), 105–11.

Rolls-Royce (2016). *Annual Report 2016*. Retrieve from: https://www.rolls-royce.com/investors/annual-report-2016.aspx#/ (accessed 13 October 2018).

Ruddick, G. (2014). Harrods pays £118m dividend to Qatar after profits surge. *The Telegraph*, 30 October. Retrieve from: https://www.telegraph.co.uk/finance/newsbysector/retailandconsumer/11198059/Harrods-pays-118m-dividend-to-Qatar-after-surge-in-profitsh.html (accessed 13 October 2018).

Ryals, L., and Rackham, N. (2012). Sales implications of servitization. Presentation to the Key Account Management Best Practice Club, Cranfield School of Management, February. Retrieve from: http://www.som.cranfield.ac.uk/som/dinamic-content/media/Sales%20Implications%20of%20Servitization%20White%20Paper%20Feb%202012%20v2.pdf (accessed 13 October 2018).

Saren, M. (2006). *Marketing Graffiti: The View from the Street*. Oxford: Butterworth Heinemann.

Scott, A. (2015). Google-backed lab brings robotics and other technologies to RAK and Northern Emirates. *The National*, 9 April. Retrieve from: https://www.thenational.ae/business/technology/google-backed-lab-brings-robotics-and-other-technologies-to-rak-and-northern-emirates (accessed 13 October 2018).

Sheth, J.N., and Sisodia, R.S. (2005). A dangerous divergence: marketing and society. *Journal of Public Policy and Marketing*, 24(1), 160–2.

Sheth, J.N., and Sisodia, R.S. (2015). *Does Marketing Need Reform? Fresh Perspectives on the Future*. Oxford: Routledge.

Shostack, G.L. (1977). Breaking free from product marketing. *Journal of Marketing*, 41(2), 73–8.

Slater, S.F., and Narver, J.C. (1994). Market orientation, customer value and superior performance. *Business Horizons*, 37(2), 22–7.

Somaseger, S., and Li, D. (2017). Business models will drive the future of autonomous vehicles. *TechCrunch*, 25 August. Retrieve from: https://techcrunch.com/2017/08/25/business-models-will-drive-the-future-of-autonomous-vehicles/ (accessed 13 October 2018).

Tait, S. (2015). Interview with Google's head of marketing innovation APAC. *Marketing*, 24 September. Retrieve from: https://www.marketingmag.com.au/hubs-c/interview-googles-head-marketing-innovation-apac/ (accessed 13 October 2018).

Thaler, R. (2012). *The Winner's Curse: Paradoxes and Anomalies of Economic Life*. New York: Simon & Schuster.

Vargo, S.L., and Lusch, R.F. (2004). Evolving to a new service-dominant logic for marketing. *Journal of Marketing*, 68(1), 1–17.

Vargo, S.L., and Lusch, R.F. (2008). Service-dominant logic: continuing the evolution. *Journal of the Academy of Marketing Science*, 36(1), 1–10.

Viney, H., and Baines, P. (2012). Engaging government: why it's necessary and how to do it. *European Business Review*, September–October, 9–13.

Wilkie, W.L., and Moore, E.S. (1999). Marketing's contributions to society. *Journal of Marketing*, 63(3–4), 198–218.

Wilkie, W.L., and Moore, E.S. (2011). Expanding our understanding of marketing in society. *Journal of the Academy of Marketing Science*, 40(1), 53–73.

Worcester, R.M., Mortimore, R., Baines, P., and Gill, M. (2011). *Explaining Cameron's Coalition*. London: Biteback.

Chapter 2
Consumer Buying Behaviour

What guests are saying about homes in United Kingdom
☆ United Kingdom homes were rated 4.7 out of 5 stars with 6,000,000+ reviews

★★★★★
Great apartment with brilliant location. On reflection, probably a bit small for 4 (2 adults and 2 kids) - but would heartily recommend for

John
Sweden

★★★★★
Zoe's flat must be one of the best I have ever seen in UK. She made us feel very welcome and we had a really good experience in her

Alex
United Kingdom

Learning Outcomes

After reading this chapter, you will be able to:

▸ Explain the consumer product acquisition process

▸ Explain the processes involved in human perception, learning, and memory in relation to consumer choice

▸ Understand the importance of personality and motivation in consumer behaviour

▸ Describe opinions, attitudes, and values, and how they relate to consumer behaviour

▸ Explain how reference groups and cultural differences influence consumer behaviour

Case Insight 2.1
Holdz®

Market Insight 2.1
The Threat of Showrooming for Brick-and-Mortar Retailers

Market Insight 2.2
Helping Consumers to Turn Electric

Market Insight 2.3
Jameson: A Cut above the Rest

Market Insight 2.4
On Yer Bike!

Market Insight 2.5
The Iftar Market

Case Insight 2.1
Holdz®

Founded in 2000, Holdz® is an online climbing holds and accessories firm. We speak to its managing director, Steve Goodair, to find out more about how the firm meets its customers' needs.

Holdz® is a small-to-medium-sized enterprise specializing in making the polyurethane resin holds that screw onto climbing walls to allow climbers to practise indoors in a safe, but natural-looking, environment. Our holds are expertly crafted in all shapes and sizes to resemble real rock features, from cracks to crimpz and sloperz to smoothies. We also produce bouldering mats, chalk bags, and clothing.

Typical customers include climbing centres (which simulate climbing on rock faces), bouldering centres (which simulate climbing on large boulders), and serious individual climbers who have built climbing walls in their own houses to allow them to train even harder. Where climbing walls are owned by local councils, they tend to try to buy in volume because they are interested less in the shape of hold they are getting and more in obtaining a volume discount. I sometimes have to point out to them that I can make holds for low prices, but the holds would be so small that they'd be useless! So, we sometimes have to educate our customers about product and typical industry prices. Top route-setters (the people who put the holds on the wall) buy based on the shapes of the holds. This is so that they can make specific climbing route 'problems' requiring climbers to ascend a route in a certain way to different degrees of difficulty, from 'easy' through to 'hard' and 'very severe' through to 11 grades of 'extremely severe' (grades 1–11). Home wall users tend to buy a pack of holds to get them started, but they also tend to return for more after a few months, for variety and because they have mastered those holds and got stronger.

Because climbers sometimes fall when they ascend difficult routes, we produce heavy duty matting, which allows climbers to fall more safely and with less likelihood of injury. We have manufactured our matting for 15 years and it has become an industry bestseller. We have such

confidence in its quality that we offer a five-year quality guarantee. Overall, we cater for serious climbers, keen on the high product quality that we provide. We have a lot of repeat customers, especially with home walls, and we work hard to look after them. We know they that find holds quite expensive, so we put one or two free holds in with their order as a surprise. Lots of our customers share images of their purchases on social media—a great way of spreading positive word of mouth for us.

To raise awareness of the Holdz® brand, we have in the past sponsored climbing and bouldering competitions, including the International Federation of Sport Climbing World Cup. Whenever they hold a competition, they brand the wall and competitors' vests with sponsors' logos. We engage with our customers mainly by social media and face to face when we're on the road selling to climbing centres or installing our holds. But we also engage with customers in another unique way: all our products display our logo, and climbers subconsciously remember the Holdz® name and the hold's product type name when they're hanging onto it for dear life! So they recall these details when they are looking for the same type of hold when setting their own routes.

In 2006, there were no bouldering centres anywhere in the world. There were only climbing centres with a small bouldering wall. A friend opened the world's first bouldering-only centre in Sheffield and asked us to provide the crash mats. No one knew how many visitors it would receive per day or if a bouldering-only venue would take off, but it did. For our crash mats, we used foam and PVC (polyvinyl chloride), but the sheer amount of traffic this centre was receiving was phenomenal and it became very popular.

If 150 climbers were doing an average of 30 climbing 'problems' a session, the mats were being hammered 4,500 times per day. Multiply that by a

Case Insight 2.1
continued

year and that's 1.64 million feet-first landings onto the matting. Over time, our customers noticed that this force was damaging the matting as the seams and materials became stressed from the landings, requiring its constant replacement. Our customers did not want to continually have to replace the crash matting because this was expensive in materials and labour.

The problem Holdz® faced was: how could it develop a matting solution for its customers that was both durable and affordable, but still allowed the company to generate a reasonable profit?

 Visit the online resources to watch a video interview with Steve Goodair, where he explains what Holdz® did.

Introduction

What process did you go through when deciding which university course to study? How do you decide which restaurants to go to or which lipstick to buy? After reading this chapter, you will understand why consumers think and behave as they do. World-class marketers have a profound understanding of customers' needs/wants and behaviour. In this chapter, we explore consumer behaviour (for business-to-business buying behaviour, see Chapter 16). We consider **cognitions** (thoughts), **perceptions** (how we see things), and learning (how we memorize techniques and knowledge). These are processes that are fundamental in explaining how consumers think and learn about offerings. As consumers, we constantly perceive and learn new things. Learning about offerings is no different from learning about concepts in general. Consider how we find out about the launch of a new offering, for example the iPhone 8 or the Samsung Galaxy Note 8. Knowledge about these products will come from a range of sources, and will allow us to compare their benefits and prices with a range of alternatives.

We discuss **personality** and motivation to illustrate how these psychological concepts affect how we buy. These are important, because offerings are often designed to appeal to particular types of person. Banks target us for personal accounts and investment products based on our personalities and motivations, for example how financially risk-averse we might be or our attitudes to taking out credit. We also discuss **opinions**, **attitudes**, and **values** to give an understanding of how we are persuaded by **reference groups**—that is, groups that have an influence over our decision-making. Fast-moving consumer goods (FMCG) companies constantly bombard us with images of celebrity endorsers, who act as our reference groups for a wide variety of offerings. Because marketing comes alive when it is interlinked into the fabric of our social lives, we consider how **social class**, life cycles, lifestyles, and culture influence consumer behaviour.

Consumer Behaviour: Rational or Emotional?

Consumption rose particularly after the 1950s, as citizens in the Western world began to prosper in relative peace after the Second World War, and industrial companies turned their attention from producing military equipment and supplies to producing consumer and industrial goods. The growth in consumption led to the emergence of consumer research (see Research Insight 2.1).

Research Insight 2.1

To take your learning further, you might wish to read this influential paper:

Simonson, I., Carmon, Z., Dhar, R., Drolet, A., and Nowlis, S. M. (2001). Consumer research: in search of identity. *Annual Review of Psychology*, 52, 249–75.

The study of how consumers behave as individuals and groups in the marketplace has been a dominant component of marketing research. This influential review paper, written by leading researchers in the field, summarizes important controversies in the field and explains the main streams of thought. It is a useful tool with which to navigate the intricate set of theories, frameworks, and models that comprise modern research about consumers. It sheds light on the importance of basic disciplines such as philosophy, psychology, economics, sociology, and ethnography to our understanding of consumer behaviour. It summarizes important unresolved challenges that characterize current research debates.

 Visit the **online resources** to read the abstract and access the full paper.

Initially, consumers were generally thought to act rationally, according to **neoclassical economics** theory, individually maximizing their satisfaction (what economists call **utility**) based on a cost–benefit analysis of price and product scarcity (or availability). The consumer was thought to measure whether or not the functional benefits of an offering outweighed its costs. Such rational purchasing decisions are considered to be based on the offering's physical performance (Udell, 1964).

However, consider an example from the Soviet Union (that is, Russia before 1990). In such a strictly regulated planned economy, offerings were designed to meet basic functional needs. Nevertheless, consumers sought out televisions produced in certain factories in certain regions or countries because they thought that they were more reliable and produced better pictures. So, even when a country's government attempts to squeeze out human desires, the desire to possess the best of what is available remains.

Nowadays, people—at least those living in advanced economies—are more likely to indulge socio-psychological buying or emotional buying motives. This focus on consumption experiences that go beyond the satisfaction of material needs is explored further in Research Insight 2.2. Purchase motivation can thus be seen to stem from a buyer's social and psychological interpretation of the offering and its performance. One of the most popular songs of 2017 was 'Despacito', by Luis Fonsi and Daddy Yankee (featuring Justin Bieber). The song was the most streamed on Spotify, reaching an astonishing 786 million streams in July alone (Aswad, 2017). Consider now the motivations of those who might have streamed the track. In all likelihood, they were primarily interested in how the music made them feel (for example excited, elated, happy, amused). Certainly, they did not stream the track because it was useful to them or because it performed some kind of functional purpose.

Visit the **online resources** and follow the **web link** to the Psychology Matters website to learn more about the application and value of psychology in our everyday lives.

Research Insight 2.2

To take your learning further, you might wish to read this influential paper:

Carù, A., and Cova, B. (2003). Revisiting consumption experience: a more humble but complete view of the concept. *Marketing Theory*, 3(2), 267–86.

This highly cited article builds upon, and moves forward, the idea developed originally by Holbrook and Hirschman (1982) that marketing is based upon consumption experiences. The idea advises marketers to distinguish between consumer experience (experience of the process of consumption) and consumption experience (experience of the usage of the proposition), and between ordinary and extraordinary experiences, and in so doing recognize that not all marketing experiences need to be perpetually extraordinary.

The article will help you to become familiar with the concept of consumer experience, which is fundamental in current marketing practice and which will be discussed further in Chapter 15.

 Visit the **online resources** to read the abstract and access the full paper.

Proposition Acquisition

What are consumers thinking when they decide whether or not to buy a particular offering? To answer this question, we need to know how offerings move from organizations to consumers. For example, consider the electric car Tesla Model 3. Delivery of the new model started in the summer of 2017 and the company expected to deliver 20,000 cars per month by December 2017. The most affordable Tesla to date, it offers a 220-mile range (about 355 kilometres) at a starting price of US$35,000 (Anon., 2017). The car is assembled at the Tesla factory in Fremont, California. However, the batteries are manufactured at a separate facility in the state of Nevada. Furthermore, other components come from a range of supply-chain partners, some located outside the United States. Once the car is assembled, it will be distributed in different ways. Partly, Tesla sells directly to its customers through its network of showrooms (Valdes-Dapena, 2013). In some locations, however, this is legally not possible and the cars will be sold to car dealers, which manage the retailing to the final consumers (see Chapter 14).

In this process, there are transactions between various buyers and sellers as raw materials are transformed into a car, and this car is then moved forward in the supply chain—what Alderson and Martin (1965) called **transvections**. Understanding transactions and transvections is important because they chart how propositions are developed and move from suppliers, through companies, to their end users. Next, we consider the end-user component of the buyer–seller relationship—that is, the perspective of the consumer. (We consider the buyer–seller relationship again in Chapters 15 and 16.)

The consumer proposition acquisition process consists of six distinct stages (see Figure 2.1). The process model is useful because it highlights the importance and distinctiveness of

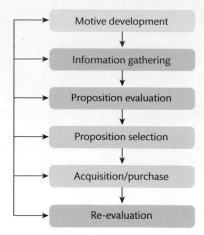

Figure 2.1
The consumer proposition acquisition process

proposition selection and re-evaluation phases in the process. In Figure 2.1, the buying process is iterative—that is, each stage can lead back to previous stages or move forward to the next stage.

Motive Development

The process begins when we decide that we wish to obtain an offering. This involves the initial recognition that we need to solve a problem—and if we are to recognize the need to solve the problem, we must first become aware of it. For example, imagine the decision a couple makes before booking a summer holiday. The decision to go on holiday might be a routine activity (perhaps they go on holiday in August every year), or might be dictated by a unique event such as a promotion or the celebration of a special occasion. They might also decide to go on holiday after an especially stressful period in their personal lives or at work. Becoming aware of the need to buy a holiday starts the acquisition process—although, of course, the specific motive driving that need will also influence the nature of this process.

Information Gathering

In the next stage, we seek alternative ways of solving our problems. Our couple planning to go on holiday might decide to start by brainstorming different alternatives, by reading travel magazines such as *Traveler* and *Afar*, or by talking with friends about their recent holiday experiences (in person or online). Online travel blogs or travel websites, such as Expedia or Booking.com, are additional sources of information that might be useful for the couple. Our search for a solution may be active—that is, an **overt search**—or passive. In other words, we are open to ways of solving our problem, but we are not actively looking for information to help us (Howard and Sheth, 1969). The search for information may be internal—that is, we might consider what we already know about the problem and the offerings we might buy to solve our problem, as in the case of the couple brainstorming holiday ideas. Alternatively, it might be external—that is, we realize that we don't know enough about our problem and so we seek advice or supplementary information. At this stage, we build our awareness by increasing our knowledge of both an offering and the competitors making that offering available.

Customers may consult popular travel blogs such as One Mile at a Time before making a purchase
Source: © One Mile at a Time.

Proposition Evaluation

Once we have all the information necessary to make a decision, we evaluate alternative propositions—but, first, we must determine the criteria used to rank the various offerings. These might be rational (for example based on cost) or irrational (for example based on desire or intuition). For example, the couple might choose the destination that meets their holiday budget—or they might opt for the destination that is more exciting or perceived as socially desirable. A consumer is said to have an **evoked set** of products in mind when they come to evaluate which particular product, brand, or service they want to solve a particular problem. In the case of a holiday, an evoked set could be the range of destinations (whether these are countries or specific localities) that come to mind when considering a holiday. A couple interested in a short break in a European capital might include Rome, Barcelona, and Paris in their evoked set. When considering a Caribbean holiday, The Bahamas, Jamaica, and St. Lucia might be in the evoked set. This stage might also be termed the 'consideration' stage.

Proposition Selection

Typically, the offering we eventually select is the one we evaluate as fitting our needs most closely. However, we might select a particular offering away from where we actually buy or acquire it. For example, a consumer buying an electronic device might go to a shop to see the item and gather information, but they might ultimately buy it online (potentially an example of showrooming—a phenomenon described in more detail in Market Insight 2.1). Therefore proposition selection is a separate stage in the proposition acquisition process, distinct from proposition evaluation, because there are times when we must re-evaluate what we buy or acquire because what we want is not available, for example buying a cinema ticket for one film because the seats for another are sold out. In the case of complex experiences like a holiday, consumers do not choose only one item, but they might select different items. For example, they might book a hotel separately from the purchase of their flight tickets. There is, of course, the possibility of purchasing an entire bundle in the form of a holiday package in which all these elements of the service experience have been selected and arranged together by a different service provider.

Market Insight 2.1
The Threat of Showrooming for Brick-and-Mortar Retailers

In the current technological environment, most companies adopt multichannel marketing strategies (see Chapter 14) in which information about the products and the possibility to purchase them is available in both online and physical stores. This leaves traditional retailers, with an extensive and costly network of physical stores, at risk of 'showrooming'. This word describes a specific type of consumer behaviour: people will go to a physical store to familiarize themselves with the product and to gather direct information, but then will complete the purchase online, often in search of a cheaper price. Showrooming can also happen while in the store as customers browse the relevant online shopping site of competitors to check whether there are price differences. There is no doubt that showrooming has been costly for retailers, with one report estimating more than US$200 billion in lost sales, with almost 50 per cent of consumers in the United States admitting to be showrooming regularly. Showrooming also devalues the role of the salesperson because it diminishes the importance of in-store customer service.

What can retailers do to counteract showrooming? A theory of planned behaviour approach would suggest changing consumers' attitudes towards showrooming. Retailers have been acting on this dimension mostly by improving the in-store customer experience and also by offering online incentives to reduce the intention to showroom. For example, while checking for the same product on the Internet, you might be provided with a voucher that incentivizes you to actually shop in-store. The theory of planned behaviour also suggests that retailer could try to make the behaviour socially unacceptable by changing perceived social norms. However, showrooming is obviously not illegal and retailers have not attempted this strategy. It is also possible to influence perceived behavioural control—that is, consumers' perceived ability to carry out the behaviour. Recently, Amazon has obtained a patent that would allow retailers to know whether you are showrooming online using the Wi-Fi offered by the shop. It is unclear how Amazon plans to use this tool, but potentially this type of technology could be used to send messages to users telling them that showrooming won't help them because, for example, all prices have been matched with those of online competitors. This could potentially affect customers' perceived ability to showroom successfully.

There is evidence that many retailers are responding effectively to the challenge of showrooming by providing customers with superior value in their physical stores. This has led to the development and prevalence of an opposite phenomenon: webrooming. More than 60 per cent of customers now admit to be regularly searching for information online while already knowing that they will make a final evaluation and purchase in the physical store.

How can retailers counteract showrooming?
Source: © gpointstudio/Shutterstock.com.

Sources: Rapp et al. (2015); Khan (2016); Dawson (2017).

Market Insight 2.1
continued

Theory into Practice

This market insight describes the phenomenon of showrooming and some of the tactics employed by retailers to deal with this issue. Showrooming simply represents a change in customers' preferences that companies need to confront by improving their offering and better integrating their online and offline communications.

Related Topics

marketing communications; distribution; retailing; consumer behaviour

1 **What kind of retailers are best suited to face showrooming successfully? Can you think of categories or products for which showrooming should be less of a concern?**

2 **Have you ever showroomed? Think about your own experience and how the retailer might have addressed the motivation for showrooming in your case.**

3 **What kind of retailers are most likely to be negatively affected by showrooming?**

Acquisition/Purchase

Once selection has taken place, different approaches to purchasing might exist. For example, the couple from our example might go regularly on holiday to the same seaside resort. Because they go there regularly, this can be considered a routine purchase. When a purchase is regular, we don't get too involved in the decision-making process; we simply buy the offering again that we bought previously, unless new circumstances have arisen. Alternatively, the purchase may be specialized, conducted on a one-off or infrequent basis, for example a gown for a formal event. In this case, we may become much more involved in the decision-making process to ensure that we understand what we are buying and that we are happy that it will satisfy our needs (relaxing by the beach for a couple of weeks). For routine purchases, we might use cash, or even payment apps such as Apple Pay, whereas for infrequent purchases, we might use a credit or store card. With infrequent purchases, the marketer might ease the pain of payment by offering credit or generous warranties. The couple might decide to travel to an exotic location for a long period of time. If they plan several legs for their journey, with different hotels and several flights, the cost and complexity of the purchase increases. As part of their holiday package, the marketer might offer a travel insurance to help them to deal with the anxiety of such a significant investment. Cancellation policies might also be more generous to entice the couple to book a certain hotel.

Acquisition also differs by channel and the prevalence of any promotional offers. Over recent years, the publishing industry has been transformed by the advent of e-books and e-book readers such as Kindle. Consumers do not need to buy and read through physical books anymore.

Despite this technological innovation, sales of physical units in the UK actually grew by 5.7 per cent in the period 2012–16, reaching 202.3 million units (Statista, 2017). Over the same period, e-book sales in the UK decreased by 7.3 per cent (Statista, 2017); suggesting that consumers enjoy reading books on different devices. The resurgence of print books also means that consumers in the UK still buy through bookshops: over the last three years, the share of revenues from different channels has remained stable, with bookshops controlling about 45 per cent of the market and Internet retailers, such as Amazon, capturing about 35 per cent of sales (Statista, 2017). Because the consumer acquires the offering at this stage, it might also be termed the 'conversion' stage.

Re-evaluation

The theory of **cognitive dissonance** (Festinger, 1957) suggests that we are motivated to re-evaluate our beliefs, attitudes, opinions, or values if the position we hold on them at one time is not the same as the position we held at an earlier period owing to some intervening event, circumstance, or action. This difference in evaluations, termed cognitive dissonance, is psychologically uncomfortable (that is, it causes anxiety). For example, we may feel foolish or regretful about a purchasing decision (perhaps we spent too much on a night out or on a meal at a slightly too fancy restaurant). Thus we are motivated to reduce our anxiety by redefining our beliefs, attitudes, opinions, or values to make them consistent with our circumstances (perhaps by not going to that particular bar as often or to that particular restaurant again). We will also actively avoid situations that might increase our feeling of dissonance. In Market Insight 2.2, we consider how marketers are helping to reduce the anxiety and potential for cognitive dissonance in the purchase of electric vehicles.

To reduce dissonance, we might try to neutralize it by:

- selectively forgetting information;

- minimizing the importance of an issue, decision, or act;

- selectively exposing ourselves only to new information that is consonant with our existing view (rather than information that isn't); and/or

- reversing a purchase decision, for example by taking an offering back or selling it for what it was worth.

The holidaying couple in our example might be disappointed by the destination that they chose or by the hotel, which might be less comfortable than anticipated. Nonetheless, to reduce cognitive dissonance, they might decide to ignore their dissatisfaction with the hotel and to focus on the more pleasurable elements of the holiday experience.

The concept of cognitive dissonance has significant application in marketing. Industrial or consumer purchasers are likely to feel cognitive dissonance if their expectations of proposition performance are not met in practice. This feeling of dissonance may be particularly acute in a high-involvement purchase, for example of a car, a house, a holiday, a high-value investment product. We are also likely to search out information to reinforce our choice of offering.

However, if we are happy with our purchase, we might decide to repurchase it, thereby displaying some degree of behavioural loyalty to a particular brand. This stage is termed the loyalty stage. One popular model developed by Dick and Basu (1994) differentiates between behavioural loyalty demonstrated by repeat purchase and loyalty in terms of relative attitude, which is a preference for the product or brand above other relevant competitors. This differentiation is

Market Insight 2.2
Helping Consumers to Turn Electric

Most car manufacturers have been investing heavily in electric vehicles (EVs). The main advantages of EVs are a reduction in air and noise pollution, savings in terms of running costs because of the cheaper cost of fuel, and the lower maintenance requirements of electric engines. However, the technology is new and cars are still relatively expensive (although costs are decreasing over time). Many motorists might be anxious about changing the type of vehicle they drive. Main concerns are the range of miles for which the cars can last, the availability of recharging points, and the potential risks of battery replacement. These concerns could cause cognitive dissonance after the purchase. In reality, the industry is improving constantly on all these issues and new models tend to have a range of more than 200 miles, while batteries last up to ten years.

Nonetheless, car manufacturers need to develop strategies to quell consumers' concerns and to make EVs more affordable and appealing. A mix of different promotional strategies has been deployed to this end. Since EVs are better from a social perspective, because they would help to deal with the harm caused by air pollution in urban areas, governments have introduced grants to support motorists who are considering buying electric cars. Depending on the model, at the time of writing, drivers in UK can qualify for a grant of up to £4,500. Several US states have also introduced incentives to promote the most efficient cars.

Manufacturers themselves have introduced a range of schemes. Nissan has invested heavily in electric models and the Nissan Leaf is one of the most popular models in the category. Nissan has heavily promoted the Leaf by targeting employees and customers of

certain energy providers with special cash discounts. Campaigns running in the summer of 2017 in several US states promised cash savings of US$10,000 on the selling price (not including additional savings available through government schemes). Considering that the Nissan Leaf starting price in the United States is $29,990, this is a very heavy promotion and should certainly reduce consumers' anxiety.

The ground-breaking Nissan Leaf
Source: © 2018 Nissan. Nissan, Nissan model names and the Nissan logo are registered trademarks of Nissan.

Another common promotion used by manufacturers of EVs consists of offering a number of years of free charging at designated charging points. The most expensive Tesla models, the Model S and the Model X, offer customers complimentary use of Tesla's network of charging points. Nissan Leaf is now also promising two years of free charging through its campaign 'No Charge to Charge', launched to promote the vehicle in several US states.

Sources: Gibbs (2014); Lelinwalla (2016); Lambert (2017).

Theory into Practice

This market insight described initiatives by car manufacturers and governments aiming to reduce consumers' anxiety when adopting a new technology in relation to a high-involvement purchase. Although the

techniques described are specific to the car industry, similar considerations apply to all cases of radical product innovation adoption.

Market Insight 2.2
continued

Related Topics

pricing; sales promotion; post-purchase anxiety; consumer behaviour; product innovation

1. **What else could Nissan do to reduce the anxiety its customers feel when considering whether or not to switch to purchasing an EV as opposed to a petrol- or diesel-powered car?**

2. **What factors could cause cognitive dissonance after purchasing an EV?**

3. **Why do you think did Nissan decide to target energy companies' employees and customers as part of its promotional effort? What is the rationale behind this choice?**

important because even consumers disappointed with a brand might continue to purchase it if they have no choice, for example because there are no alternatives available or no alternatives that they can afford. The goal of marketers is to build loyalty on the basis of both repeat purchase and superior relative attitude.

If we really like our purchase, we might also encourage others to buy the brand—the so-called advocacy stage. Such advocacy is common in the user-generated content (UGC) developed online by consumers in relation to everything from films they've watched, through houses they've stayed in (for example through Airbnb), to the holidays they've bought (for example through Expedia). Evaluating UGC is an important element of contemporary marketing research (Campbell et al., 2011), sometimes referred to as **social media listening**. Consumers who engage in positive word of mouth are a great asset to a firm. We discuss this phenomenon in more depth later in the chapter, when we consider the role of group influences on consumer behaviour.

What guests are saying about homes in United Kingdom

☆ United Kingdom homes were rated **4.7 out of 5 stars** with **6,000,000+ reviews**

★ ★ ★ ★ ★

Great apartment with brilliant location. On reflection, probably a bit small for 4 (2 adults and 2 kids) - but would heartily recommend for

 John
Sweden

★ ★ ★ ★ ★

Zoe's flat must be one of the best I have ever seen in UK. She made us feel very welcome and we had a really good experience in her

 Alex
United Kingdom

★ ★ ★ ★ ★

Great location! We enjoyed to stay at Francine's home with my son.

 Ulas
Turkey

Online reviews are one example of the advocacy stage

Source: © Airbnb, Inc. All rights reserved.

● ● ● ● ● ● ● ● ● ● ● ● ● ● ● ● ● ● ● ●

In Figure 2.1, the buying process is iterative (that is, it occurs in steps)—particularly at the re-evaluation phase of the acquisition process. This is because the re-evaluation of the offering leads us back to any or all of the previous phases in the proposition acquisition process as a result of our experiencing cognitive dissonance. For example, we may have bought a games console (an Xbox One), but not be completely happy with it (for example thinking that it has poor picture or sound). If it is covered under warranty, this might lead us to the acquisition phase, whereby the retailer should provide a new perfect product. If the product was delivered in perfect working order, but we simply didn't enjoy using it, we might go back to the original alternatives we selected (for example PS4, Wii U) and pick another purchase from among them (for example one that might offer a larger variety of games). If we are really not sure about which games console to buy after this initial purchase, we might re-evaluate the alternatives we originally selected and then decide. If we really dislike our original purchase and this has shaken our faith in what is important in selecting a games console, we might go back to the information-gathering phase to get more of an idea about the offerings available. Finally, if we are extremely disappointed, we might decide that our original motive—the need to play, to relax, and to have fun—can best be solved by purchasing something other than a games console that will still meet the same need (for example participation in sport).

Research by marketing agency Razorfish identified three categories of influencer at different stages of the proposition acquisition process:

■ key influencers (with their own blogs and huge numbers of Twitter followers, but who are unlikely to know the consumer personally);

■ social influencers (people within the consumer's social network, whom they might know personally, commenting in Twitter feeds and on blogs/forums); and

■ known peer influencers (for example family members or part of the consumer's 'inner circle').

Of all three types, known peer influencers were the most persuasive (see 'Group Influence' later in this chapter), but the three groups were differentially important at different points in the proposition acquisition process. For example, close family and friends exert the most influence at the motive development and information-gathering phases (the 'awareness' phase), YouTube and anonymous peer reviewers exert most influence at the proposition evaluation and selection phases (the 'consideration' phase), and close family and friends exert the most influence in the proposition selection and acquisition phases (the 'action' phase) (Sheldrake, 2011). For example, think about the process you went through when choosing your undergraduate degree: who were the key influencers, the social influencers, and the peer influencers in your case?

Our purchase decisions also depend on the specific **cognitive** system that is dominant at the time of choice. Researchers differentiate between two main cognitive processes: **System 1 thinking** leads to fast, instantaneous, and intuitive reactions; **System 2 thinking** is responsible for deliberate thought processes and analytical thinking (Kahneman, 2011). System 1 will ensure that you react appropriately to instant danger, but it also causes impulse purchases that sometimes might prove unnecessary or—as in the case of a chocolate treat—unhealthy. System 2 will help you to solve a maths problem or decide which car model you want to buy. Importantly, the two models demand the same mental energy to work appropriately. This means that when our attention is occupied or when we are tired, System 1 tends to kick in to save energy and System 2 is less engaged (Kahneman, 2011). This is one of the reasons why it is very difficult to control our diet when we are stressed or tired: self-control requires the ability of System 2 to monitor our behaviour, but this is not possible if we don't have the 'mental space' to do so. Research on the different cognitive systems has a key consequence for the model of proposition acquisition reviewed here: the different stages imply that the choice is being driven by the analytical System 2. However, if System 1 is in charge instead, the process will be shorter, and minimal cognitive attention will be devoted to information gathering and proposition evaluation.

Perceptions, Learning, and Memory

Often, consumers do not understand the messages marketers convey because they have not received, comprehended, or remembered those messages, or because the messages were unclear. Consumer understanding depends on how effectively the message is transmitted and perceived. In this section, we discuss how messages are perceived and remembered. (We consider how messages are communicated in Chapters 6 and Chapters 10–12.)

In any one day, consumers receive thousands of messages. Consider, for example, a typical working woman in Paris, France, who might well be awoken by her clock radio, blaring out adverts for *Galeries Lafayette*. While eating her breakfast, she checks her smartphone and encounters advertisements on Facebook or on some other websites she visits. She could also pick up visual advertisements in the *Paris Match* magazine to which she subscribes and when she opens her post, which includes direct mail from charities (for example Médecins Sans Frontières) and financial service organizations (for example BNP Paribas). On her way to the Métro station, she might encounter billboards advertising, among other things, L'Oréal. On the Métro, she will probably encounter more visual adverts. When she arrives at work, and after being further bombarded with online ads and sponsored Internet search ads, she has been subjected to hundreds of auditory, visual, and audiovisual advertising messages demanding her attention. By the time she retires to bed, this could have extended to thousands. If we also consider that consumers are recipients of social and interpersonal messages as well—through word of mouth and social media (for example Facebook and Twitter)—we begin to realize how sophisticated human perception, learning, and memory processes must be to attend to, filter, and store so many messages.

Perceptions

The American Marketing Association (AMA, 2016) defines perceptions as follows:

> . . . based on prior attitudes, beliefs, needs, stimulus factors, and situational determinants, individuals perceive objects, events, or people in the world about them. Perception is the cognitive impression that is formed of 'reality' which in turn influences the individual's actions and behaviour toward that object.

If we were to pay attention to all the messages we receive, rather than filter out all those we don't find meaningful, we would probably become overloaded—just like a computer when it crashes. The process of distinguishing meaningful from non-meaningful information is known as **selective exposure** (Dubois, 2000).

As consumers, we are interested in certain types of offering that are relevant to us when we receive marketing messages. So teetotallers would not usually be interested in adverts about champagne—unless they were to want to buy a bottle as a gift to celebrate a special occasion. Equally, young people are not usually interested in advertising messages for pensions. If you were looking to book a flight, you would become interested in messages from airline companies and travel agents, especially if these include sales promotions. Even washing machine adverts become interesting if your washing machine has broken down! The messages we choose to ignore and forget are removed from our perception, enabling us to process those messages that we wish to consider more effectively. So we avoid exposure to certain messages and actively seek out others. We may also expose ourselves selectively to particular messages through the **media** we choose to read (for example certain newspapers, magazines, e-zines, Facebook pages, Twitter feeds) or watch (for example certain terrestrial, cable, satellite, or Internet television channels). Many people do not read a daily newspaper and therefore will not see press advertisements, although they may see sponsored search ads on websites, or read, respond, and interact with Twitter posts or companies' Facebook pages. Some people do not listen to the radio often or at all. It is therefore important to determine which media channels customers use.

Advertisers label this concept of the personal importance a person attaches to a given communication message as **involvement**. This is important because it explains a person's receptivity to communications, and people can therefore be segmented into high-, medium-, and low-involvement groups (Michaelidou and Dibb, 2008). We are interested in consumers' receptivity because we are interested in changing or altering their perceptions of particular offerings. We know, from earlier in the chapter, that offerings can be characterized on the basis of whether consumers use rational or emotional thinking to evaluate their relative appeal. Figure 2.2 illustrates a variety of common products and how they are generally perceived by US consumers.

We should note that the position for a particular offering is an average of all consumers and may not represent a particular individual's decision-making well. So, for example, the purchase of life insurance is regarded as being in the high-involvement/thinking quadrant, as illustrated in Figure 2.2. The positioning of this type of offering indicates the need for more informative advertising/promotion. An expensive watch, positioned in the high-involvement/feeling quadrant, suggests a need for emotional advertising. Offerings in the low-involvement/thinking quadrant (for example liquid bleach) indicate the use of advertising/promotion to create and reinforce habitual buying. Finally, offerings in the low-involvement/feeling quadrant (for example magazines) should be promoted on the basis of personal satisfaction (Ratchford, 1987).

Another way of displaying how people think about particular offerings is **perceptual mapping**, a technique that has been in use since at least the early 1960s (Mindak, 1961). People view champagne brands differently in the UK, using (brand) personality keywords such as 'zesty' or 'mellow' and 'fresh fruit' or 'baked fruit'. Lanson is associated with zesty and fresh fruit, whilst Moët et Chandon is associated with mellow and baked fruit. (We consider brand differentiation in more detail in Chapters 6 and 13.) Organizations deliberately seek to position themselves in the minds of specific target audience groups. To do this properly, they must understand the nature of the group's subculture. However, organizations risk causing offence if they position a brand on the basis of particular dimensions that are misperceived or perceived correctly, but negatively. For example, Heinz was forced to withdraw an advert in the UK market after consumers complained that it promoted unsafe practices (Anon., 2016). The ads showed consumers using an empty can of beans as a drum to play a tune (Heinz used the catchline 'Learn the #CanSong'), with the objective of presenting the product as upbeat and friendly. There was even

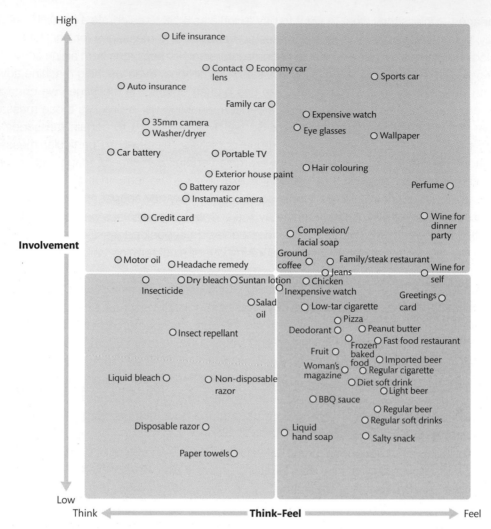

Figure 2.2

Involvement/think–feel dimension plot for common products

Source: Ratchford, B.T. (1987), 'New insights about the FCB grid', *Journal of Advertising Research*, 27(4), 24–38.

an online tutorial on how to prepare the cans for best effect. However, using cans in this way can be dangerous, especially for children, so the entire campaign was banned. The attempt at revitalizing the brand clashed with some obvious product expectations in terms of safety.

Brands can thrive or die based on how their customers perceive them. Sometimes, companies fail to position their offerings appropriately. In 2016, Thai company Seoul Secret was forced to pull an advert and apologize for its content. The campaign, promoting a skin-lightening product, used the tagline 'You just need to be white to win', and presented a woman who, to her evident dismay, suddenly becomes dark-skinned (Nudd, 2016). The issue of associating whiteness with social status is very controversial in Thailand and the company apologized through a Facebook post that denied discriminatory intent behind the campaign (Nudd, 2016).

Companies sometimes also need to change how their brands are perceived because they have developed negative associations (see Market Insight 2.3). Barilla, one of the world's largest pasta manufacturers, faced consumer backlash after its chairman, Guido Barilla, said in a radio show that the company would never feature an advert with same-sex couples because the

Market Insight 2.3
Jameson: A Cut above the Rest

Jameson Irish Whiskey is among the most popular Irish whiskeys in the world, selling almost 7 million litres globally in 2017. Produced at the Jameson Distillery in Middleton, County Cork, it is the flagship whisky of Irish Distillers. Today, it is distributed in 122 countries worldwide and accounts for the largest share of the global Irish whiskey market. It is also the fastest growing international whiskey brand.

The Jameson brand originates from 1780 and, as such, has a strong brand heritage. It is a high-end premium whiskey brand and is triple-distilled, contributing to its smooth and distinctive taste. The green bottle helps to distinguish it from the competition and reinforces its Irish heritage. The brand's motto 'Sine Metu' (meaning 'without fear, confident, and independent') is clearly indicated on the bottle's label and encapsulates the brand's fearless personality. Jameson Whiskey is viewed as 'a serious whiskey that doesn't take itself too seriously' and knows how to have fun. It has been described as a brand that is serious in the making, but not in the drinking.

Jameson is currently trying to break the age-old notion that whiskey is only for old men by targeting younger people, including women, aged 25–35. This is reflected in its use of advertising and social media to connect with this coveted age cohort. Jameson has been heavily involved in sponsorship of film, through its association with the 'Jameson Dublin International Film Festival', 'Jameson First Shot', and 'Jameson Empire Done in 60 Seconds'. Since 2003, Jameson has been title sponsor of the Dublin International Film Festival, which has fast become Ireland's premier feature film festival, playing host to a plethora of Irish and Hollywood stars, from Colin Farrell to Danny DeVito and Richard Dreyfuss. Each year, 130 films are presented over the 11-day festival, many of them Irish premieres of films originating all over the globe.

'Jameson First Shot' is an international competition that offers film-makers the chance to direct their own script, with a Hollywood actor mentoring and acting in the lead role. In the past, these actors have included

Jameson, the most popular Irish whiskey in the world
Source: Image courtesy of Irish Distillers Limited.

Adrien Brody, Uma Thurman, Willem Dafoe, and Maggie Gyllenhaal.

Finally, 'The Jameson Empire Done in 60 Seconds' competition has also raised the profile of the Jameson brand internationally. It challenges up-and-coming film-makers worldwide to write and shoot their own 60-second remake of a classic movie.

These three sponsorship opportunities have helped to promote the Jameson brand's deep heritage within film and allowed it to connect with its target audience in a meaningful way.

The whiskey's popularity among celebrities is well noted, with Lady Gaga and Rihanna among those extolling its virtues. Lady Gaga has described Jameson as her 'long-term boyfriend', while Rihanna even mentions the brand in her song 'Cheers (Drink to That)'. Such promotion by two of the world's hottest pop stars is an incredible boost for the Jameson brand, which continues to grow in popularity.

Sources: Anon. (2012a); Russell (2012); Flanagan (2014); Statista (2018); http://www.jamesonfirstshot.com; http://www.thewhiskyexchange.com; https://www.empireonline.com/movies/news/done-60-seconds/

Market Insight 2.3

continued

Theory into Practice

This market insight describes how an Irish whiskey distiller has sought to reposition itself from a brand drunk by old men to one drunk by younger people, including women, using Hollywood celebrities, an association with cinema, and sponsorship.

Related Topics

celebrity endorsement; repositioning; sponsorship

1 **Describe the personality traits of the Jameson Whiskey brand. How have these personality traits been established?**

2 **How has the brand's association with film impacted on the public's perception of the brand? What is the brand's main motivation for engaging in arts/film sponsorship?**

3 **Lady Gaga and Rihanna are only two of the many well-known celebrities who have publicly expressed their love for the Jameson Whiskey brand. How do these celebrities exert group influence and contribute to social learning?**

This market insight was kindly contributed by Marie O'Dwyer, Waterford Institute of Technology, Republic of Ireland.

brand supports a 'classic family' (Anon., 2013). Gay rights activists promoted a boycott in the United States, one of Barilla's key markets, which led to serious repercussions. The company has since changed its stance in an effort to restore its image and has introduced very advanced diversity policies for its staff members (Somashekhar, 2014). Conversely, organizations sometimes position their offerings well, as did Toyota when developing the Lexus brand for the premium car market.

Learning and Memory

Consumers continually learn about new offerings, their relative performance, and new trends through a process by which we acquire new knowledge and skills, attitudes, and values by studying, experiencing, or modelling others' behaviour. Theories of human learning include **classical conditioning**, **operant conditioning**, and **social learning**:

- *Classical conditioning*—Russian Nobel Laureate Ivan Pavlov investigated the digestive and nervous system of dogs by measuring the amount of saliva produced in response to food under certain conditions. He realized that his dog salivated before food was served and set out to ascertain why. By carrying out a series of experiments and manipulating stimuli before the food was presented, he realized that if, for example, he were to ring a bell before serving food, the dogs would associate the sound of the bell (the conditioned stimulus) with the presentation of food (the unconditioned stimulus) and begin salivating. So classical conditioning occurs when the unconditioned stimulus becomes associated with the conditioned stimulus. In other words, we learn by associating one thing with another—in this case, the sound of the bell with the arrival of food. This approach to learning is frequently used in marketing, for example in jingles in advertising, such as Danone's 'mmm, Danone' sonic logo to indicate the lip-smacking 'goodness' of its offerings, or when supermarkets include bakery sections to cause consumers to buy more because they associate the smell of warm bread with eating it, and when perfume and aftershave manufacturers (such as L'Oréal) place free samples of products in sachets in magazines, so that when readers see an advert for a particular brand of perfume or aftershave, they associate the image they see with the smell and so may be more likely to purchase the product when they see its image in the future.

■ *Operant conditioning*—B.F. Skinner (1954) was one of the pioneers of the behaviourist school of learning. He argued that learning was the result of operant conditioning whereby subjects would act on a stimulus from the environment. The resulting behaviour was more likely to occur if this behaviour was reinforced. In other words, operant conditioning is learning through behavioural reinforcement. Skinner termed this 'reinforcement' because the behaviour would occur more readily in connection with a particular stimulus if the required resulting behaviour had been reinforced through punishment or reward. In marketing, we might look to the typical in-store sales promotion as an example—perhaps a new yoghurt brand offered in a supermarket. If we don't normally eat this brand and we're curious, we might taste it because there are no costs to us in terms of time, effort, or money. The sales promotion provides the stimulus, the trial behaviour occurs, and if the consumer likes the yoghurt and is rewarded with a money-off coupon, the behaviour of purchasing that particular yoghurt brand is reinforced. (For more on sales promotion, see Chapter 11.) Supermarkets reinforce our loyalty by providing reward cards and points for purchasing particular items (for example the Nectar card in the UK or the stamps system used by retailer 7-Eleven in its convenience stores worldwide).

■ *Social learning*—This theory was proposed by psychologist Albert Bandura (1977), who suggested that humans are less animalistic than Skinner suggests. Bandura argued that we can delay gratification and dispense our own rewards or punishment. As a result, we have more choice over how to react to stimuli than proposed by Skinner, who felt that we blindly followed our instinctual drives. Bandura suggests instead that we can reflect on our own actions and change our future behaviour. This led to the idea that we learn not only from how we respond to situations, but also from how *others* respond to situations. Bandura called this modelling. In social learning, we learn by observing others' behaviour. The implications for marketers are profound. For adolescents, role models include parents, athletes, and entertainers, of whom parents are the most influential (Martin and Bush, 2000). Parents socialize their children into purchasing and consuming the same brands that they buy, actively teaching them consumer skills—materialistic values and consumption attitudes—in their teenage years. Interaction with peers also makes adolescents more aware of different offerings (Moschis and Churchill, 1978). Companies have long recognized the power of peers—particularly in the social media world, encouraging purchasers to leave reviews of products that they have previously bought, to 'like' their Facebook pages, and to retweet their messages. Research indicates that those who read reviews are twice as likely to select a product compared with those who do not (Senecal and Nantal, 2004).

But what happens once consumers have learned information? How do they retain it in their memories and what stops them from forgetting it? Consumers do not necessarily have the same experience, and therefore knowledge, of particular offerings. Knowledge develops with familiarity, repetition of marketing messages, and a consumer's acquisition of product/service information. Marketing messages need to be repeated often because people forget them over time—particularly the specific arguments or message presented. The general substance or conclusion of the message is marginally more likely to be remembered (Bettinghaus and Cody, 1994: 67).

We enhance memorization through the use of symbols, such as corporate identity logos, badges, and signs. Shapes, creatures, and people carry significant meanings, as seen in badges, trademarks, and logos. Airlines around the world have adopted symbols, for example the kangaroo of Australian airline Qantas. Well-recognized symbols worldwide include the KFC 'Colonel' symbol, Intel's symbol, Apple's 'bitten apple' logo, Coca-Cola's ubiquitous script logo, and Google's multicoloured script symbol.

Five of the world's most iconic logos
Sources: © 2018 YouTube; © 2018 Coca-Cola; © 2018 Google; © 2018 McDonald's; © 2018 Twitter, Inc.

Our memories, as a system for storing perceptions, experience, and knowledge, are highly complex (Bettman, 1979). A variety of memorization processes affect consumer choice, including the following:

- *Factors affecting* **recognition** *and* **recall**—Less frequently used words in advertising are recognized more and recalled less. The information-processing task in transferring data from short-term to long-term memory differs for recognition (2–5 seconds) and recall (5–10 seconds). Under high states of arousal, for example where the consumer is subject to time pressure, recognition speeds are increased, whereas recall speeds are hindered. In practical terms, the more unique a campaign's message, the better it is recognized, but the worse it is recalled.

- *The importance of context*—Memorization is strongly associated with the context of the stimulus, so information available in memory will be inaccessible in the wrong context. For example, vacuum cleaner manufacturers advertising in sports magazines are unlikely to be remembered.

- *Form of object coding and storage*—We store information in the form it is presented to us, either by object (brand) or dimension (offering attribute), but there is no evidence that one form is organized into memory more quickly or more accurately than the other (Johnson and Russo, 1978).

- *Load-processing effects*—We find it more difficult to process information into our short- and long-term memories when we are presented with a great deal of information at once.

- *Input mode effects*—Short-term recall of sound input is stronger than short-term recall of visual input where the two compete for attention, for example in television and YouTube advertising.

- *Repetition effects*—Recall and recognition of marketing messages/information increase the more a consumer is exposed to them, although later exposures add less and less to memory performance.

Evidence suggests that where consumers have little experience or knowledge of an offering, provision of in-store point-of-purchase information is more successful than general advertising (Bettman, 1979). This is why brand manufacturers frequently conduct product trials in-store, offering consumers the opportunity to try the offering without expending time, money, and effort in purchasing it. (See Chapter 11 for more on sales promotion.) This approach places the brand in the consumer's evoked set, and helps them to contextualize the particular product and remember it when they shop next time. Consumer knowledge of offerings can be incomplete and/or inaccurate, because consumers frequently think that they know something about an offering that is not in fact true, but they nonetheless believe this strongly (Alba and Hutchinson, 2000).

Personality

How and what we buy is also based on our personalities. Personality is that aspect of our psyche which determines how we respond to our environment in a relatively stable way over time. The theory of personality originates from Sigmund Freud's ground-breaking work on motivation. Freud believed that subconscious drives can explain much of our behaviour and his views were influential in the origins of marketing research. Modern theories of personality, however, have moved beyond Freud's view and have developed ways of assessing the different components of individual personality and their impact on behaviour.

Here, we consider two main approaches to the study of personality: trait theory, which stresses the classification of personality types; and the self-concept approach, which concerns how we perceive ourselves as consumers.

The Trait Approach

The trait approach to personality categorizes people into different personality types or so-called traits (pronounced 'trays'). Researchers characterize personalities using bipolar scales, including the following traits:

- sociable–timid;

- action-oriented–reflection-oriented;

- stable–nervous;

- serious–frivolous;

- tolerant–suspicious;

- dominant–submissive;

- friendly–hostile;

- hard–sensitive;

- quick–slow; and

- masculine–feminine.

Researchers frequently talk about the 'big five' personality dimensions:

- extraversion (sociable, fun-loving, affectionate, friendly, talkative);

- openness (original, imaginative, creative, daring);

- conscientiousness (careful, reliable, well-organized, hard-working);

- neuroticism (worrying, nervous, highly strung, self-conscious, vulnerable); and

- agreeableness (soft-hearted, sympathetic, forgiving, acquiescent) (McRae and Costa, 1987).

Certain types of personality prefer certain brands. For example, 'conscientious' people prefer 'trusted' brands, while 'extroverts' prefer 'sociable' brands. Gender differences have also been observed: 'neurotic' males and 'conscientious' females prefer 'trusted brands' (Mulyanegara, Tsarenko, and Anderson, 2009). An understanding of personality types therefore helps marketers to segment customer groups using personality dimensions (see Chapter 6). This is possible because psychologists have developed questions that reliably assess to what extent an individual's personality matches the different traits described above.

Various companies use personality as a segmentation criterion, for example car manufacturers, which link personality to particular car attributes such as safety features, aesthetics, and handling. Makers of running shoes and mobile phones are interested in two personality traits in particular, extraversion and openness to experience, because these traits link to attitudinal and purchase loyalty displayed towards those brands (Matzler, Bidmon, and Grabner-Kräuter, 2006).

 Visit the **online resources** and complete Internet Activity 2.1, an online quiz, to learn more about your own personality across a number of key personality traits.

Self-Concept Approach

People also buy offerings because of what the brand represents to them and its relation to the buyers' perception of their own self-concept or personality. This relates not only to the proposition itself, but also to values, socially responsible behaviour, and opportunities for networking (Bhattacharya and Sen, 2003), both online and offline. So we buy brands that resemble how we perceive ourselves, but marketers can also shape customer behaviour by reinforcing particular identities and redefining what it means to have that identity or creating new, highly desirable identities (Champniss, Wilson, and Macdonald, 2015).

In the luxury goods market, buyers typically divide into one of two categories:

- those who made their purchases based on product quality, aesthetic design, and excellence of service, who are motivated by the desire to impress others, their ability to pay high prices, and the ostentatious display of their wealth; and

- those who bought luxury goods based on what they symbolize—that is, purchasing luxury goods represented an extreme form of the expression of their own values (Dubois and Duquesne, 1993).

Consumers buy products based on self-concept through self-giving behaviour (Mick and DeMoss, 1990). Gift-giving is a common phenomenon, particularly among family, friends, and work colleagues. It is highly symbolic, connoting love (for example Valentine's and anniversary gifts), congratulations (for example wedding presents), regret (for example a card saying 'sorry' to a loved one), and dominance (for example clothes bought to 'improve' a partner's style). Self-giving arises from different motivations, for example to reward ourselves, to be nice to ourselves, to cheer ourselves up, to fulfil a need, and to celebrate. There is a link between the purchase of clothing as a self-gift—that is, a special purchase rather than a typical purchase—and a consumer's self-concept. An extreme example of when people purchase products to build their self-concept (although it tends to work in the short term and damages longer-term self-concept perceptions) occurs in compulsive consumer behaviour (for example gambling, excessive drinking). Compulsive shoppers are motivated in part to change their mood and improve their self-esteem (Furnham, 2014).

Visit the **online resources** and complete Internet Activity 2.2 to take a test on compulsive shopping and to learn more about the disorder.

Motivation

Abraham Maslow (1943) suggested a hierarchical order of human needs, as outlined in Figure 2.3. According to Maslow, we satisfy lower-order physiological needs first, then move on to safety needs, belongingness needs, and esteem needs, and finally the need for self-actualization. There is little research evidence to confirm Maslow's hierarchy, but the concept possesses logical simplicity, making it a useful tool for understanding how we prioritize our own needs and therefore why we might buy what we buy. In contemporary societies, offerings focus on solving consumer needs in the esteem and self-actualization categories, because needs in other categories are already provided for. However, in the poorer parts of sub-Saharan Africa, for example, offerings operate for some citizens at the level of solving safety and belongingness needs. The implications for marketers are that offerings aimed at the mass market in sub-Saharan Africa

Figure 2.3

Maslow's hierarchy of needs

Source: Adapted from Maslow (1943). This content is in the public domain.

in the self-actualization category (for example higher education, long-haul travel) are likely to fail. This does not mean that there are no market segments with this need. There are groups of people in sub-Saharan Africa whose income allows them to enjoy such offerings.

There is still debate about whether consumers are motivated by rational—as outlined by Howard and Sheth (1969)—or irrational motives. Holbrook, Lehmann, and O'Shaughnessy (1986) started to consider irrational motives when they suggested that our wants might be latent, passive, or active, and are related to both intrinsic and extrinsic reasons:

- latent needs are hidden—that is, our subject is unaware of their need;

- passive needs are such that the costs of acquisition exceed, for the moment, the expected satisfaction derived from acquisition; and

- active needs are such that the subject is both aware of their needs and expects the perceived benefits to exceed the likely costs of acquisition.

According to Holbrook and colleagues (1986), when our needs are active, they can arise either through **habit** or through the brand selection process, which the authors call **picking**. Picking is the deliberative selection of an offering from among a repertoire of acceptable alternatives, even though the consumer believes the alternatives to be essentially identical in terms of ability to satisfy their needs. It can be motivated by intrinsic or extrinsic evaluations, or both. Intrinsic evaluation occurs because a consumer likes a product—perhaps because of anticipated pleasure from using it—while an extrinsic evaluation might occur because a friend mentioned that it was a great product. Extrinsic evaluations can also entail explicit cost–benefit analyses.

Extrinsic reasons for purchase can be subdivided into five categories:

- *Economic*—This is concerned with expenditure of money, time, and effort in purchasing and consuming an offering. Economists refer to the concept of **price elasticity** of demand to explain how demand is affected when price is increased or decreased.

- *Technical*—This is concerned with the offering's perceived quality of performance in the anticipated usage situation.

- *Social*—This is concerned with the extent to which a purchase will enhance a person's feelings of self-esteem or personal worth in relation to others (see Maslow's hierarchy), as well as general adherence to group norms and effects (see 'Theory of Planned Behaviour' below).

- *Legalistic*—This is concerned with what are perceived to be the legitimate demands of others (for example buying on behalf of a company, or for a child or spouse).

- *Adaptive*—A form of social learning, this is concerned with imitating others, seeking expert advice (for example from blogs, social networking sites, or industry and consumer magazines), or relying on the reputation of a particular company or brand in the event of uncertain or limited purchasing information.

Theory of Planned Behaviour

Theories of motivation in marketing help us to understand why people behave as they do. The theory of planned behaviour explains that behaviour is brought about by our **intention** to act in a certain way (see Research Insight 2.3). This intention to act is affected by the attitude a subject has towards a particular behaviour, encompassing the degree to which a person has favourable or unfavourable evaluations or appraisals of the behaviour in question. Intention to act is also affected

Research Insight 2.3

To take your learning further, you might wish to read this influential paper:

Azjen, I. (1991). The theory of planned behaviour. *Organisational Behaviour and Human Decision Processes*, **50(2), 179–211.**

In this seminal article, the author outlines how behaviour and behavioural intention to act in a certain way are affected by the attitude the subject has towards a particular behaviour, the subjective norm, and perceived behavioural control. The author developed our understanding of the fact that how humans intend to act may not be how they end up acting in a given situation. Intention, perception of behavioural control, attitude toward the behaviour, and subjective norm all reveal different aspects of the target behaviour and serve as possible directions for attack in attempts to alter particular behaviours, making this a powerful motivational theory in marketing. Read the paper to understand how the theory can be applied in practice to understand and predict individual behaviour in different circumstances.

 Visit the online resources to read the abstract and access the full paper.

by the subjective norm, which is perceived social pressure to perform or not perform a particular behaviour (see 'Group Influence' later in the chapter). Finally, intention to act is affected by perceived behavioural control, referring to the perceived ease or difficulty of performing the behaviour, based on a reflection on past experience and future obstacles. Figure 2.4 provides a graphical illustration.

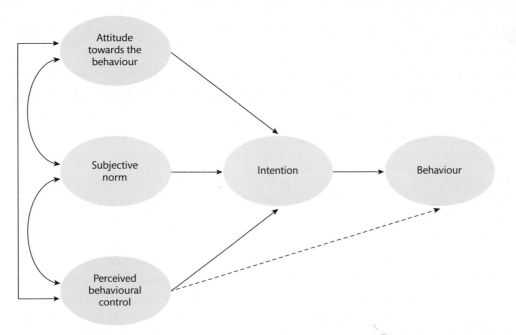

Figure 2.4
Theory of planned behaviour
Source: Azjen (1991).

For example, if we consider cigarette use, we might have different attitudes towards smoking based on our geographical location, for example whether we live in France or China versus the UK or New Zealand. We might think we can't give up smoking because we need a cigarette to calm our nerves (perhaps we have a stressful job). Equally, we may also consider the opinions that significant others have towards smoking cigarettes (for example our spouses, children, or friends). If we place ourselves in the minds of government (de)marketers, the key elements of the theory of planned behaviour (that is, attitudes, subjective norms, and perceived behavioural control) can help us to understand how to discourage smoking. For example, we could try to (a) alter subjects' attitudes towards smoking, (b) change their views on how others see them as smokers, or (c) change their perceptions of how they perceive their own ability to give up. (See Chapter 17 for a wider discussion of social marketing.) Public Health England's advertising campaign entitled 'Smokefree', which ran in late 2015, actively discouraged smoking by showing 'disgusting' images of 'rotting' entrails in roll-up cigarettes. The idea was to make people realize that smoking roll-ups is just as dangerous as smoking manufactured cigarettes (Siciliano, 2014).

Public Health England uses a 'disgust' appeal to discourage 'roll-up' smoking
Source: Image courtesy of DARE and Public Health England. Photography by Nick Georghiou.

Despite its popularity, the theory of planned behaviour has been also criticized for some of its inherent limitations. First, the theory assumes that we always have formed attitudes about a certain behaviour. Often, however, our attitudes are developed only when we are required to have an opinion or view on a certain action (that is, we don't always hold attitudes towards all relevant behaviours) (Schwarz, 2007). Second, the link between intentions and behaviour is not always very strong because there are many reasons why we might not be able to carry out our plans and this limits the applicability of the theory in some contexts. For example, while many consumers claim that they would want to buy environmentally friendly products to protect the environment, only a very small minority do so because of the higher price, reduced availability, and concerns in terms of product quality (Carrington, Neville, and Whitwell, 2010).

The Importance of Social Contexts

Although our own personality and other characteristics impact on how we consider and consume offerings, the opinions, attitudes, and values of others also affect how we consume, as we discovered with the theory of planned behaviour. Our internal perspective is determined not only by our own thoughts and personality structures, but also by the input of others. Other people have an effect on our opinions, attitudes, and values, as considered further in the next section.

Opinions, Attitudes, and Values

Opinions are quick responses given to opinion poll questions about current issues or instant responses to questions from friends. They are held with limited conviction because we have often not yet formed or fully developed an underlying attitude on an issue. An opinion might be what we think of the latest advertising campaign for a high-profile brand. Attitudes, by comparison, are held with a greater degree of conviction, over a longer duration, and are more likely to influence behaviour. Values are held even more strongly than attitudes, underpinning our attitudinal and behavioural systems. Values are linked to our conscience, developed through the familial socialization process, through cultures and subcultures, and through our religious influences, and are frequently formed in early childhood.

Opinions are cognitive—that is, based on thoughts. Attitudes are what psychologists term **affective**—that is, linked to our emotional states. Values are **conative**—that is, they are linked to our motivations and behaviour. Although we may have a specific attitude towards something, we do not always follow it in terms of our behaviour. In other words, we may want to be more fashionable in our dress sense, but we don't bother trying new styles! VALs™ (derived from 'values and lifestyles') is a psychographic framework that is used to segment consumers into differing types based on their opinions, attitudes, values, and behaviours. (See Chapter 6 for more on psychographic segmentation.)

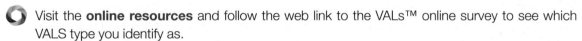 Visit the **online resources** and follow the web link to the VALs™ online survey to see which VALS type you identify as.

Group Influence

Consumers learn through imitation—that is, social learning. We've learned, for instance, by observing and copying our parents and friends. As consumers, we may compare our opinions, attitudes, values, and behaviour patterns with those of specific reference groups. A reference group is:

> . . . one that the individual tends to use as an anchor point for evaluating his/her own beliefs and attitudes. One may or may not be a member and may or may not aspire to membership in a reference group. It can have great influence on one's values, opinions, attitudes, and behaviour patterns.

> (AMA, 2016)

Group membership can exert a positive effect with the group—that is, one's individual patterns of behaviour are congruent with the group. For example, die-hard fans of the *Twilight* franchise have had themselves fitted with fang-like teeth (Roderick, 2015). Group membership can also exert a negative effect. A church, political party, or trade union, for example, can be the focus of both positive (congruent) and negative (incongruous) behaviour for its members. If a consumer feels that their freedom to choose is being threatened, they may react against this intervention. A consumer whose decision alternative is blocked, partially or wholly, can become increasingly motivated to go against that specific decision alternative by demonstrating rebellious behaviour (Clee and Wicklund, 1980). Such rebellious behaviour might include the creation of **spoof adverts**, poking fun at and caricaturing a brand. Such parodies can seriously damage a brand if they are credible (Sabri and Michel, 2014), and when there is a gap between the image the firm is trying to project and the reality of the firm's actions, as experienced by the public (Berthon and Pitt, 2012).

Children who are told that they cannot have particular offerings desire them more as a result (Rummell et al., 2000). For example, the 'tweenage' daughter (aged between 10 and 12) told by her parent not to wear make-up may do so, while the rebellious teenage son may drink too much alcohol despite his parents' advice otherwise. This form of negative group influence occurs because of **psychological reactance**.

Consumers' assumptions about an individual's behaviour, based on identifying group membership, become automated if they are frequently and consistently made (Bargh and Chartrand, 1999). This represents a form of social learning. For instance, a Swedish male consumer might purchase Abba-branded herring because this was the brand his parents ate at the breakfast table, whereas a French female beverage consumer might drink Orangina almost exclusively because that is what her parents provided for her as a child. The link between a consumer and a particular reference group depends on how closely the consumer associates with a particular reference group. Where we do associate closely, the attachment to the brand is often assumed. For example, consumers identifying with the 'biker' genre might ride Harley-Davidson motorcycles because bikers who buy big cruisers generally buy Harley-Davidson bikes.

Message receipt is also affected by peer group pressure, delivered by word of mouth, online and offline, and whether intended or not. Members of groups tend to conform to a group norm, enhancing the self-image of the recipient and increasing their feeling of group identity and belongingness. Therefore consumers may have their own cultures and sub-cultures that impact on how a particular marketing message may be received. Some marketing messages might incorporate **celebrity endorsement** appeals, for example by enlisting the endorsement of popular role models who have influence over the target consumer group. H&M, the Swedish fashion retailer, has made use of renowned pop artists over the years, including American singer Katy Perry, as well as British sports personality David Beckham, to advertise its brands, particularly to young people. (See Market Insight 2.4 on the power of celebrity endorsement for a sports participation campaign in Ireland.) Marketing campaigns frequently leverage the persuasive power of reference group membership through word-of-mouth campaigns, for example when consumers discuss their experiences on Twitter and Facebook. Increasingly brands are hosting brand communities of users (see Chapter 13) in which consumers can share useful information and help each other to improve their consumption experience (Fournier and Lee, 2009). Software company EA Sports has developed a community for its bestselling football video game FIFA, which has garnered almost 10 million posts from users (Anon., 2010). The website is integrated with Facebook, Twitter, and other networking sites, and allows fans to share tips on how to play the game and to get access to updates and trailers.

Word-of-mouth communication is powerful because we trust the opinions of our friends and colleagues. For example, in the beauty and personal care market (Mintel, 2011, 2012), different influences include (in order of importance): the opinions of family and friends; the company/product website; shop assistants; passively reading articles in magazines or newspapers; proactively looking up reviews online or in magazines; actively researching using forums and chatrooms; or reading about a company/product on Twitter. Men are more likely to gain product updates in a news format and women are more likely to visit online stores. Mums are particularly likely to share beauty content. Of those who said something positive about a product online, 45 per cent bought the product based on the recommendation of a vlogger (wvideo blogger) (Mintel, 2015).

In the next section, we consider how consumer behaviour is affected by social class, lifestyle, and life cycle.

Market Insight 2.4
On Yer Bike!

In the 1980s, Irishman Sean Kelly was one of the most feared cyclists in the world. He was the first rider to be assigned World Number 1 status when rankings were introduced in 1984 and he held this position for a record six years. An astonishing career saw Kelly record 193 professional victories—most notably, in the 1988 Vuelta De España. In recent times, the legendary cyclist has become involved in an annual initiative in his home region that has helped to revolutionize cycling participation rates in Ireland. The inaugural Sean Kelly Tour of Waterford was held on 19 August 2007, with the principal aim of stimulating interest in cycling as an exercise activity amongst a wide cross-section of society. Kelly himself was one of the 600 enthusiastic participants who took to the scenic roads of County Waterford. The branding of the event, utilizing the name of such a renowned and popular athlete, has been critical in the growth of the Kelly Tour. Innovative public relations (PR), online, and social media campaigns have also inspired growth in participation rates to 6,500 for the 2015 version of the Tour. The event showcases the benefits of cross-agency cooperation in social marketing drives. Waterford Sports Partnership and Waterford County Council operate seamlessly, in tandem with the local cycling community, to provide a varied offering that caters for the serious cyclist, casual participants, and families alike. Support from the central government Irish Sports Council and commercial sponsor An Post has also been essential in growing the Tour. Indeed, An

Post saw the opportunity to complement and replicate the success of the Kelly Tour by rolling out a series of four other similar events around Ireland. This 'An Post Cycle Series' commenced in 2009 and has also seen considerable incremental year-on-year growth in participation rates.

These events have proved to be a significant catalyst in the growth of cycling as an exercise activity. In 2007, there were 5,600 cyclists affiliated to 174 clubs in Ireland. This figure has grown dramatically in the intervening years, with Cycling Ireland reporting a membership in excess of 23,000 people across 398 clubs in 2014, of whom 64 per cent are categorized as leisure/non-competitive cyclists, while the proportion of female membership has grown from 8 per cent to 18 per cent in this time period. These figures do not include the growing numbers of recreational cyclists who are not affiliated to a club—a trend that is quite apparent on a daily basis on Irish roads. Government-led initiatives, such as the increased provision of cycle lanes and tax breaks for people purchasing bikes as a means of commuting to work, have complemented the success of the organized mass-participation events in raising the popularity of cycling to levels not seen in generations.

Sources: Ipsos MRBI/Irish Sports Council (2013); Cycling Ireland (2014); Kelly (2015).

Market Insight 2.4
continued

Theory into Practice

This market insight indicates how two civic organizations worked in partnership to promote (a) the cycling participation (particularly to the benefit of Waterford Sports Partnership) and (b) the tourism (particularly to the benefit of Waterford County Council) that a cycling event would generate. To generate the kind of mass participation needed for an event of this kind, they engaged a credible sports personality: an Irish champion cyclist.

Related Topics

social marketing; sports sponsorship; reference groups; celebrity endorsement

1 **What are the factors that you deem essential to translate the success of a mass-participation event into increased ongoing exercise participation?**

2 **How can non-profit-making events such as this maximize their exposure through the suite of marketing communications channels available to them?**

3 **Discuss examples of how the 'brand name' of iconic sports personalities could be used to support initiatives/interventions that stimulate regular exercise engagement in your country.**

This market insight was kindly contributed by Dr Paul Morrissey, Waterford Institute of Technology, Republic of Ireland.

Social Grade

In marketing, the term **social grade** refers to a system of classification of consumers based on their socio-economic grouping. Social grade was originally developed for the IPA National Readership Survey (NRS) in the 1950s and was subsequently adopted by the Joint Industry Committee for National Readership Surveys (JICNARS) on its formation in 1968. Social grade is a means of classifying the population by the type of work they do based on the occupation of the chief income earner—that is, the member of the household with the largest income. NRS Ltd (the successor to JICNARS) provides social grade population estimates not only for the National Readership Survey, but also for a number of other major industry surveys. These population estimates are obtained from the Survey's interviews with a representative sample of some 36,000 adults every year (see Table 2.1). There is a widely held belief that consumers make purchases based on their socio-economic position within society and that different social classes have different self-images, social horizons, and consumption goals (Coleman, 1983). Such variations in attitudes, motivations, and value orientations reflect differences in occupational opportunities and demands, childhood socialization patterns, and educational influences, leading consumers to vary in their purchase behaviours across social classes (Williams, 2002).

Table 2.1 Social grading scale

Social grade	Social status	Occupational status	Population estimate, Great Britain, age 15+ (Jan 2016–Dec 2016) (%)
A	Upper middle class	Higher managerial, administrative, and professional	4
B	Middle class	Intermediate managerial, administrative, and professional	23
C1	Lower middle class	Supervisory, clerical, and junior managerial, administrative, and professional	28
C2	Skilled working class	Skilled manual workers	20
D	Working class	Semi- and unskilled manual workers	15
E	Those at lowest levels of subsistence	State pensioners, casual and lowest grade workers, unemployed with state benefits only	10

Source: National Readership Survey. Reproduced with the kind permission of the National Readership Survey.

Lifestyle

Marketers increasingly target consumers on the basis of their lifestyles (see also Chapter 6). The AMA (2016) defines lifestyle as 'the manner in which the individual copes and deals with [their] psychological and physical environment on a day-to-day basis', 'as a phrase describing the values, attitudes, opinions, and behaviour patterns of the consumer', and 'the manner in which people conduct their lives, including their activities, interests, and opinions'. For example, a segmentation of the South Australian wine market reveals the following lifestyle types (Bruwer and Li, 2007):

■ *Conservative, knowledgeable wine drinkers*—Comprising 19.2 per cent of the population and more likely to be male (57 per cent), well educated, and well remunerated, this segment drinks wine frequently (particularly red), displaying connoisseur qualities when buying wine.

■ *Enjoyment-oriented social wine drinkers*—Comprising 16.2 per cent of the population, and more likely to be female and younger, this segment likes white and sparkling wine, and has an eye for value for money.

■ *Basic wine drinkers*—Comprising 23.5 per cent of the population, this is a predominantly male segment, as happy drinking beer as wine, depending on what's available.

■ *Mature time-rich wine drinkers*—Comprising 18.2 per cent of the population, this older, male segment displays connoisseur tendencies and is interested in the provenance of the wine.

- *Young professional wine drinkers*—Comprising 22.9 per cent of the population, and predominantly female and employed in the professions, this segment tends to drink red wine, mainly at business functions.

To generate clusters of consumers according to different lifestyle types, marketers typically ask consumers questions around their activities, interests, and opinions (AIO). If marketers fit around a consumer's lifestyle, consumers are more likely to benefit from, and appreciate, the proposition offered. (We cover lifestyle segmentation further in Chapter 6.)

Life stage

Marketers frequently hypothesize that people at certain stages of life purchase and consume similar kinds of offerings. In research undertaken in the United States in the 1960s, Wells and Gubar (1966) determined that there were nine stages in a consumer's life, from leaving home to living as a solitary survivor without a spouse. In contemporary society, the life-stage concept needs a degree of readjustment to take into account that fewer people get married and that those who do are doing so at a later age than they were in the 1960s, that there are more singles with children, and that increasingly couples are cohabiting. (See Chapter 6 for more on current life-stage segmentation approaches.)

 Visit the **online resources** and complete Internet Activity 2.3 to learn more about how Volkswagen uses the family life cycle to communicate its brand values to its target audience.

Most market research agencies routinely measure attitudes and purchasing patterns based on life stage to determine differences among groups. Table 2.2 indicates that there is a difference in the types of offering purchased as a result, with solitary survivors far more likely to purchase funeral plans, nursing home care, and cruise holidays, and singles more likely to spend their income on package and long-haul holidays and educational service products, for instance. Diesel, the Italian denim brand, has become the first mainstream clothing retailer to advertise, controversially, on a pornographic website Pornhub (one of the world's top 100 most visited websites), as well as on dating apps Grindr and Tinder, to project a young, sexy image (Croft, 2016). Tour operators, such as Saga, also target particular demographic groups—specifically, the older traveller—typically with more sedate appeals.

Culture and Ethnic Groups

In a globalized society, marketers are increasingly attuned to recognizing cultural differences between and within societies. Culture can be defined as the overall set of beliefs, values, and norms that are inherited or learned by members of a group and which regulate behaviour. An example of the importance of culture is how marketers are increasingly interested in marketing offerings to ethnic groups within particular populations. Such groups can be large, with their own specific customs. They can represent an opportunity either to build a niche market or to consolidate an existing market—that is, by appealing to a new set of consumers in addition to the old. For example, in the United States, the Hispanic, Latino, and Black American populations together represent a sizeable proportion of the total population. European countries also have sizeable ethnic populations. In France, for example, there is a large Black African population; in Germany, a large Turkish community. France and the UK both have large Muslim populations. In Sweden, there are large groups of Finns, former Yugoslavs, Iraqis, and Iranians. These groups within a country represent a potential opportunity for the marketer, if they are sizeable enough

Table 2.2 The life stages

Stage	Bachelor stage: young single people not living with parents/guardians	Newly married or long-term cohabiting: young, no children	Full nest I: youngest children aged <6	Full nest II: youngest children aged 6 or over	Full nest III: older married couples with dependent children	Empty nest I: older married couples, no children living at home, chief income earner or both in work	Empty nest II: older married couples, no children living at home, chief income earner or both retired	Solitary survivor, in work	Solitary survivor, retired
Characteristics	Few financial burdens. Fashion opinion leaders. Recreation-oriented	Better off financially because of dual wages. High purchase rate of consumer durables	Home purchasing at peak. Low level of savings	Financial position better. Both parents may be in work	Financial position better still. Both parents more likely to be in work. Some children will have part-time jobs. High average purchase of consumer durables	Home ownership at peak. Most satisfied with savings and financial position. Interested in travel, recreation, self-education. More likely to give gifts and make charitable contributions. Less interested in new products	Drastic cut in household income. More likely to stay at home	Medical needs will depend on age	Same medical needs as other retired group. Drastic cut in income
Likely purchases	Buy: basic kitchen equipment; basic furniture; cars; package and long-haul holidays; education	Buy: cars; refrigerators; package holidays	Buy: washer-dryer; television; baby food and related products; vitamins; toys	Buy: larger-sized family food packages; cleaning materials; pianos; childminding services	Buy: better homeware and furniture products; magazines; non-essential home appliances	Buy: luxurious holidays; eating out; home improvements	Buy: medical appliances and private health care; sleep and digestion aids	Buy: financial; healthcare and retirement plans; meals for one	Buy: household staples; cruise holidays; nursing home services; funeral plans

Source: Adapted from Wells and Gubar (1966). Published by the American Marketing Association.

to be profitable and demonstrate similar needs across the group that are different from those the rest of the population. For example, multicultural consumers spent some US$3.4 trillion in the United States in 2015 and, importantly, ethnic groups behave differently (Gil and Rosenberg, 2015). For example, in the United States, Asian Americans purchase organic foods at an above-average rate and social causes are particularly important to Hispanic Americans. Cui (1997) proposes that, in any country, where there are ethnic marketing opportunities, a company has four main strategic options, as follows:

- *Total standardization*—Use the existing marketing mix (see Chapter 1) without modifying it to the ethnic market. This is very difficult to do. Even Coca-Cola, well known for its ardent approach to standardization, adapts its cola around the world (for example by adding pineapple in Indonesia to cater for local tastes).

- *Product adaptation*—Use the existing marketing mix, but adapt the product to the ethnic market in question, for example Nestlé's selling of green-tea-flavoured KitKats in Thailand.

- *Advertising adaptation*—Use the current marketing mix, but adapt the advertising—particularly the use of foreign languages—to the target ethnic market by promoting the product using different associations that are more resonant with ethnic audiences. For example, stores in some parts of Finland advertise in Swedish and Finnish to cater for the minority Swedish population, and stores in the United States commonly advertise in Spanish.

- *Ethnic marketing*—Use a totally new marketing mix, for example Bollywood films aimed at audiences in the Indian subcontinent and in the Indian diaspora around the world, using strong love and ethical themes, and a musical format

Have a break, have a green tea KitKat!
Source: © Paul Baines.

Which of these four approaches marketers should adopt will also depend on how new communities interact with existing cultures. For example, Mexican immigrants living in the United States can react to the new consumer culture by (a) assimilating entirely to the new culture, (b) maintaining aspects of both cultures at the same time, (c) privileging Mexican heritage and resisting US culture, or (d) segregating the two cultures to specific areas of their lives that fulfil specific needs (Peñaloza, 1994). (See also Market Insight 2.5.)

Market Insight 2.5
The Iftar Market

Each year, around the world, many of the 1.6 billion-strong **Ummah** ('worldwide community of Muslims') come together to observe the holy month of Ramadan. Ramadan is the celebration of the first revelation of the Qu'ran to the Prophet Muhammad (*pbuh*), by fasting (no food, drink, sex, or cigarettes) from sunrise to sunset, by giving to charity, and doing good deeds for others. Only children, the elderly, travellers, the sick, and breastfeeding or pregnant women are exempt from the daytime fasting. Come sunset, the fast is broken with the communal *iftar* meal for Sunnis (Shi'a pray first before any food is consumed). The typical iftar might first comprise dates with water or a yoghurt drink and then, after the Mahgrib prayer at sunset, soup, salad, appetizers, and main dishes (with halal meat, rice, and fruit being the staples). Before sunrise, *suhoor* can be eaten, a typically lighter meal, washed down with a couple of glasses of water.

There were around 2.8 million Muslims in the UK in 2011, according to the 2011 Census. Given this relatively large number (about 5 per cent of the population), Ramadan is now the third most important religious event for supermarkets in sales terms, preceded only by Christmas and Easter. Other festivals that supermarkets cater for include Diwali (celebrated by Sikhs, Hindus, and Jains), and Rosh Hashanah and Passover (the Jewish New Year and Jewish Spring liberation festival, respectively), with Tesco, Sainsbury's, and Waitrose all offering enhanced kosher ranges at these times of the year.

In 2015, the UK's supermarkets enjoyed a Ramadan sales uplift of around £100 million. Tesco, Sainsbury's, Asda Walmart, and Morrisons all ran Ramadan promotions and reaped the benefits. Morrisons expected to sell 2 million tons of rice and 80,000 boxes of dates, and Tesco expected to turn over £30 million from its Ramadan product range.

There are difficulties, however: both Morrisons and Tesco found themselves in hot water after selling pork products (or, in Tesco's case, Smokey Bacon Pringles) under Ramadan promotional signage, causing outrage in some quarters. Overeating after sundown also poses health risks, prompting the UK's National Health Service (NHS) to warn against breaking the fast with a feast, with dedicated content on the NHS Choices website. In Dubai, in the United Arab Emirates (UAE), government officials have also warned against overbuying and wastage (hinting that Ramadan is supposed to be about **ascetic** observance) and have provided information screens in retail outlets on good shopping practice habits during Ramadan. Supermarkets have also responded by offering food baskets containing essential items at affordable prices in the period leading up to Ramadan.

Sources: Bingham (2015); Botros (2015); Burman (2015); Duell (2015); Gani (2015); MCB (2015).

Theory into Practice

This market insight indicates the significant market opportunities that can exist in developing offerings for particular ethnic groups who demonstrate unique consumption behaviour based around their different **cultural mores**. It also indicates some of the difficulties inherent in targeting a niche market—particularly in getting the offering right for the targeted ethnic group without offending them.

Related Topics

reference group; multicultural marketing; segmentation; targeting; positioning; international marketing

Market Insight 2.5
continued

1 **How would supermarkets decide which stores will offer their Ramadan product ranges?**

2 **Besides the type of food eaten and the timing of when the food is eaten, how else might the shopping behaviour of Muslims differ from that of non-Muslims?**

3 **Is it appropriate for supermarkets to be targeting Muslim customers at Ramadan with food and drink offers? Why do you say this?**

Chapter Summary

To consolidate your learning, the key points from this chapter are summarized here:

■ **Explain the consumer product acquisition process.**

Consumer buying behaviour has rational and irrational components, although rational theories tend to dominate the marketing literature. There are a variety of models of consumer buying behaviour, but the consumer product acquisition model is perhaps the simplest to understand, stressing that the consumer goes through six key stages in the product acquisition process, including motive development, information gathering, product evaluation, product selection, acquisition, and re-evaluation.

■ **Explain the processes involved in human perception, learning, and memory in relation to consumer choice.**

The human perception, learning, and memory processes involved in consumer decision-making are complex. When designing advertising, developing distribution strategies, designing new offerings, and implementing other marketing tactics, marketers should (repeatedly) explain the information associated with these actions to consumers. Such an approach is necessary to encourage consumers to engage with, remember, and learn about different offerings, which in turn influences consumers' buying decisions.

■ **Understand the importance of personality and motivation in consumer behaviour.**

Consumers are motivated differently in their purchasing behaviour depending on their personalities and social identities, and, to some extent, how they feel that their personality or social identity fits with particular offerings. Maslow's (1943) seminal work on human needs helps us to understand how we are motivated to satisfy five key human desires. From the theory of planned behaviour (Azjen, 1991), we know that how we intend to behave is not always how we actually behave, because this is affected by our attitudes towards the behaviour in question, subjective norms (how we think others perceive that behaviour), and our own perceptions of how we can control our behaviour.

■ **Describe opinions, attitudes, and values, and how they relate to consumer behaviour.**

Opinions are relatively unstable positions that people take in relation to an issue or assessment of something. Attitudes are more strongly held and are more likely to be linked to our behaviour. Values are more strongly held still and are linked to our conscience. Marketers are interested in all three because they help us to understand consumers better and to develop marketing approaches, particularly when it comes to positioning and repositioning an offering.

■ **Explain how reference groups influence consumer behaviour.**

Reference groups, including such role models as parents, entertainers, and athletes, have an important socializing influence on consumption behaviour, particularly, but not solely, in our adolescence. However, where we live, what social class we come from, what lifestyle we lead, what stage of the life cycle we are at, and our culture, learned as part of specific social groups, also has an impact on our behaviour as consumers. Celebrity endorsers are powerful influencers in this regard, particularly when they project a particular lifestyle that others seek to emulate.

 # Review Questions

1   What is the process consumers go through when buying offerings?
2   What is cognitive dissonance and how does it relate to consumer behaviour?
3   How are the psychological concepts of perception, learning, and memory relevant to understanding consumer choice?
4   How are concepts of personality relevant to understanding consumer behaviour?
5   How are concepts of motivation relevant to understanding consumer behaviour?
6   What is the theory of planned behaviour?
7   What are opinions, attitudes, and values, and how do they relate to consumer behaviour?
8   How do reference groups influence how we behave?
9   What is celebrity endorsement?
10 How does lifestyle and ethnicity influence how we buy?

 # Discussion Questions

1   Having read Case Insight 2.1 at the beginning of this chapter, how do you think Holdz® should develop its matting solution for its bouldering-centre corporate customers to take account of the considerable volumes of feet-first falls from climbers, but still allow Holdz to generate a reasonable profit?

2   Describe the purchasing process you might use to purchase the following using the consumer product acquisition model shown in Figure 2.1:

   A   A chocolate bar (for example Snickers or Cadbury's Dairy Milk in the UK, Plopp in Sweden, or Droste in the Netherlands)
   B   An electric car
   C   A tablet computer to help you to write essays and in group work for your marketing course
   D   A dishwasher

3   Use the theory of planned behaviour to explain consumer motivations to pursue the following behaviours:

   A   The purchase of a room at Raffles Hotel, Singapore
   B   A visit to the Abba Museum in Stockholm, Sweden
   C   Voting during an election in France

4 What kinds of celebrity endorsers have you noticed companies using in their advertising to persuade you to adopt the following?

A Make-up (for example L'Oréal, Lancôme)

B Beer (for example Heineken)

C Beverages (for example Coca-Cola or Pepsi)

Visit the online resources and complete the Multiple-Choice Questions to assess your knowledge of Chapter 2.

Glossary

affective a psychological term referring to our emotional state of mind; values are affective because they are linked to our feelings about things.

ascetic someone or something that practises or promotes self-discipline, self-denial, and abstention from sensual pleasure for religious reasons.

attitudes mental states that underlie the structuring of perceptions and guide behavioural response.

celebrity endorsement usually famous or respected members of the public, used by advertisers to market specific goods and services because they are perceived to be expert or knowledgeable or because of their ability to display particular attractive qualities.

classical conditioning a theory of learning propounded by Russian physiologist Ivan Pavlov, who carried out a series of experiments with his dogs when he realized that if he were to ring a bell before serving food, the dogs would automatically associate the sound of the bell (conditioned stimulus) with the presentation of the food (unconditioned stimulus), and begin salivating; occurs when the unconditioned stimulus becomes associated with the conditioned stimulus.

cognitions mental structures that an individual forms about something.

cognitive a psychological term relating to the action of thinking about something; opinions are cognitive.

cognitive dissonance a psychological theory proposed by Leon Festinger in 1957, which states that we are motivated to re-evaluate our beliefs, attitudes, opinions, or values if the position we hold on them at one point in time

does not concur with the position held at an earlier period owing to some intervening event, circumstance, or action.

conative a psychological term relating to our motivations to do something; attitudes are conative because they are linked to our motivations to do things.

cultural mores the customs and manners of a social group.

evoked set a group of goods, brands, or services for a specific item brought up in a person's mind in a particular purchasing situation and from which they make a decision as to which product, brand, or service to buy.

habit a repetitive form of behaviour, often performed without conscious rational thought in a routine way.

intention in the consumer context, this is linked to whether or not we intend or are motivated to purchase a good or service.

involvement the greater the personal importance a person attaches to a given communication message, the more involvement they are said to have with that communication.

media (plural of medium) facilities used by companies to convey or deliver messages to target audiences.

neoclassical economics a meta-theory of economics predicated on delineating supply and demand based on rational individuals or agents, each seeking to maximize their individual utility by making choices with a given amount of information.

operant conditioning a learning theory developed by B.F. Skinner which suggests that when a subject acts on a stimulus from the environment (antecedents), this is more likely to result in a particular behaviour (behaviour) if that behaviour is reinforced (consequence) through reward or punishment.

opinions observable verbal responses given by individuals to an issue or question; easily affected by current affairs and discussions with significant others.

overt search the point in the buying process at which a consumer seeks further information in relation to a product or buying situation, according to the Howard–Sheth model of buyer behaviour.

perceptions mental pictures based on existing attitudes, beliefs, needs, stimulus factors, and factors specific to our situation, which govern the way we view objects, events, or people in the world about us; govern our attitudes and behaviour towards whatever we perceive.

perceptual mapping a technique used to present visually the relative perception, in comparison to its competitors, of different marketing stimuli such as products, product lines, and brands.

personality that aspect of our psyche which determines the way in which we respond to our environment in a relatively stable way over time.

picking in the context of consumer behaviour, the process of deliberative selection of a product or service from among a repertoire of acceptable alternatives, even though the consumer believes the alternatives to be essentially identical in terms of ability to satisfy their need.

price elasticity the percentage change in volume demanded as a proportion of the percentage change in price, usually expressed as a negative number; a score close to 0 indicates that a product or service price change has little impact on quantity demanded, whereas a score of −1 indicates that a product or service price change effects an equal percentage quantity change; a value above −1 indicates a disproportionately high change in quantity demanded as a result of a percentage price change.

psychological reactance when a consumer perceives their freedom to pursue a particular decision alternative to be blocked, wholly or partially, they become more motivated to pursue that decision alternative.

recall a measure of advertising effectiveness based on what an individual is able to remember about an ad.

recognition when new images and words presented are compared with existing images and words in memory and a match is found.

reference groups groups that an individual uses to form their own beliefs and attitudes; can be positive, whereby we align our opinions, attitudes, values, or behaviour with theirs, or negative, whereby we are repelled by their behaviour and seek to dissociate our opinions, attitudes, values, and behaviour from theirs.

selective exposure the process associated with how consumers screen out information that is not considered meaningful or interesting.

social class a system of classification of consumers or citizens, based on the socio-economic status of the chief income earner in a household, typically into various subgroupings of middle- and working-class categories.

social grade a system of classification of people based on their socio-economic group, usually based on the household's chief income earner.

social learning a learning theory, advocated by Albert Bandura (1977), that suggests that we can learn from observing the experiences of others and that, in contrast with operant conditioning, we can delay gratification and even administer our own rewards or punishment.

social media listening the process of obtaining and evaluating what is being said about a company, its offerings, or individual employees on social networking sites such as Facebook, Instagram, and Twitter.

spoof adverts negative advertising—often, but not always, generated by amateurs—parodying an original campaign using humour, caricature, and ridicule appeals.

System 1 thinking a decision-making cognitive function that is fast, automatic, frequent, emotional, stereotypic, and subconscious (Kahneman, 2011); cf. **System 2 thinking**

System 2 thinking decision-making cognitive function that is slow, effortful, infrequent, logical, calculating, and conscious (Kahneman, 2011); cf. **System 1 thinking**

transvections a term proposed by Alderson and Martin (1965) to denote the relationships (transactions) that occur in the development of a product or service that crosses between company (that is, product/service) ownership boundaries to produce a finished product or service; now considered, from the perspective of supply chain management, to be vertical integration or cooperation.

Ummah the worldwide community of Muslims.

utility a measure of satisfaction or happiness obtained from the consumption of a specific good or a service in economic thought; typically measured as an aggregate.

values deeply held beliefs about principles and norms of behaviour that are considered very important in life.

 # References

Alba, J.W., and Hutchinson, J.W. (2000). Knowledge calibration: what consumers know and what they think they know. *Journal of Consumer Research*, 27, 123–56.

Alderson, W., and Martin, M.W. (1965). Toward a formal theory of transactions and transvections. *Journal of Marketing Research*, 2(2), 117–27.

AMA (American Marketing Association) (2016). Dictionary. Retrieve from https://www.ama.org/resources/Pages/Dictionary.aspx? (accessed 13 October 2018).

Anon. (2010). 15 examples of thriving online communities. *Feverbee*, 4 November. Retrieve from: https://www.feverbee.com/15-examples-of-thriving-online-communities/ (accessed 13 October 2018).

Anon. (2012). Jameson renews Dublin film festival sponsorship to 2015. *ShelfLife*, 30 January. Retrieve from: https://www.shelflife.ie/jameson-renews-dublin-film-festival-sponsorship-to-2015/ (accessed 13 October 2018).

Anon. (2013). Italian pasta baron's anti-gay comment prompts boycott call. *Reuters*, 26 September. Retrieve from: https://www.reuters.com/article/italy-gay-pasta/italian-pasta-barons-anti-gay-comment-prompts-boycott-call-idUSL5N0HM2O120130926 (accessed 13 October 2018).

Anon. (2016). Heinz beans ad banned: Six more canned campaigns. *BBC News*, 23 November. Retrieve from: https://www.bbc.co.uk/news/uk-38076464 (accessed 13 October 2018).

Anon. (2017). Tesla Model 3: everything you want to know. *Consumer Reports*, 7 August. Retrieve from: https://www.consumerreports.org/tesla/tesla-model-3-faq-everything-you-want-to-know/ (accessed 13 October 2018).

Aswad, J. (2017). 'Despacito' tops Spotify's songs of the summer chart. *Variety*, 31 August. Retrieve from: https://variety.com/2017/music/news/despacito-tops-spotifys-songs-of-the-summer-chart-see-the-full-lists-1202543829/ (accessed 13 October 2018).

Azjen, I. (1991). The theory of planned behaviour. *Organisational Behaviour and Human Decision Processes*, 50(2), 179–211.

Bandura, A. (1977). *Social Learning Theory*. Englewood Cliffs, NJ: Prentice-Hall.

Bargh, J.A., and Chartrand, T.L. (1999). The unbearable automaticity of being. *American Psychologist*, 57(7), 462–79.

Berthon, P.R., and Pitt, L. (2012). Brands and burlesque: toward a theory of spoof advertising. *AMS Review*, 2(2–4), 88–98.

Bettinghaus, E.P., and Cody, M.J. (1994). *Persuasive Communication* (5th edn). London: Harcourt Brace.

Bettman, J.R. (1979). Memory factors in consumer choice: a review. *Journal of Marketing*, 43(2), 37–53.

Bhattacharya, C.B., and Sen, S. (2003). Consumer–company identification: a framework for understanding consumers' relationships with companies. *Journal of Marketing*, 67(2), 76–88.

Bingham, J. (2015). What is Ramadan and why does it matter? Why Muslims fast, when to fast and what to avoid. *The Telegraph*, 18 June. Retrieve from: https://www.telegraph.co.uk/news/religion/11682139/What-is-Ramadan-and-why-does-it-matter.html (accessed 13 October 2018).

Botros, M. (2015). Stocking up on groceries for Ramadan an 'incorrect approach': official. *Gulf News*, 18 June. Retrieve from: https://gulfnews.com/news/uae/society/stocking-up-on-groceries-for-ramadan-an-incorrect-approach-official-1.1537169 (accessed 13 October 2018).

Bruwer, J., and Li, E. (2007). Wine-related lifestyle (WRL) market segmentation: demographic and behavior factors. *Journal of Wine Research*, 18(1), 19–34.

Burman, J. (2015). More Muslim outrage after supermarket sells pork next to Ramadan sticker. *Express*, 26 June. Retrieve from: https://www.express.co.uk/news/uk/587010/Muslim-Ramadan-pork-Morrisons-Tesco-London (accessed 13 October 2018).

Campbell, C., Pitt, L.F., Parent, M., and Berthon, P. (2011). Tracking back-talk in consumer-generated advertising: an analysis of two interpretative approaches. *Journal of Advertising Research*, 51(1), 224–38.

Carrington, M.J., Neville, B.A., and Whitwell, G.J. (2010). Why ethical consumers don't walk their talk: towards a framework for understanding the gap between the ethical purchase intentions and actual buying behaviour of ethically minded consumers. *Journal of Business Ethics*, 97(1), 139–58.

Carù, A., and Cova, B. (2003). Revisiting consumption experience: a more humble but complete view of the concept. *Marketing Theory*, 3(2), 267–86.

Champniss, G., Wilson, H.N., and Macdonald, E. (2015). Why your customers' social identities matter. *Harvard Business Review*, January–February. Retrieve from: https://hbr.org/2015/01/why-your-customers-social-identities-matter (accessed 13 October 2018).

Clee, M.A., and Wicklund, R.A. (1980). Consumer behaviour and psychological reactance. *Journal of Consumer Research*, 6(4), 389–405.

Coleman, R.P. (1983). The continuing significance of social class to marketing. *Journal of Consumer Research*, 10(3), 265–80.

Croft, C. (2016). Diesel underwear gets dirty with porn site ads. *Sunday Times*, 17 January. Retrieve from: https://www.thetimes.co.uk/article/diesel-underwear-gets-dirty-with-porn-site-ads-m708qh90skj (accessed 13 October 2018).

Cui, G. (1997). Marketing strategies in a multi-ethnic environment. *Journal of Marketing Theory and Practice*, 5(1), 122–35.

Cycling Ireland (2014). *Cycling Ireland Strategic Plan: A Pathway for Cycling Excellence 2015–2019*. Retrieve from: http://www.cyclingireland.ie/downloads/cycling%20ireland%20-%20strategy.pdf (accessed 13 October 2018).

Dawson, C. (2017). Amazon wins patent to stop consumers showrooming. *Tamebay*, 25 June. Retrieve from: https://tamebay.com/2017/06/amazon-wins-patent-stop-consumers-showrooming.html (accessed 13 October 2018).

Dick, A.S., and Basu, K. (1994). Customer loyalty: toward an integrated conceptual framework. *Journal of the Academy of Marketing Science*, 22(2), 99–113.

Dubois, B. (2000). *Understanding the Consumer: A European Perspective*. London: FT/Prentice Hall.

Dubois, B., and Duquesne, P. (1993). The market for luxury goods: income versus culture. *European Journal of Marketing*, 27(1), 35–44.

Duell, M. (2015). Ramadan boosts Britain's big supermarkets with £100m sales uplift as Muslims prepare lavish sundown meals. *Mail Online*, 23 June. Retrieve from: https://www.dailymail.co.uk/news/article-3135796/Ramadan-boosts-Britain-s-big-supermarkets-100million-sales-uplift-Muslims-prepare-lavish-sundown-meals.html (accessed 13 October 2018).

Festinger, L. (1957). *A Theory of Cognitive Dissonance*. Palo Alto, CA: Stanford University Press.

Flanagan, P. (2014). Rihanna and Lady Gaga help put Irish whiskey in high spirits. *Irish Mirror*, 24 September. Retrieve from: https://www.irishmirror.ie/news/irish-news/rihanna-lady-gaga-help-put-4317956 (accessed 13 October 2018).

Fournier, S., and Lee, L. (2009). Getting brand communities right. *Harvard Business Review*, 87(4), 105–11.

Furnham, A. (2014). Compulsive buying. *Psychology Today*, 5 December. Retrieve from: https://www.psychologytoday.com/blog/sideways-view/201412/compulsive-buying (accessed 13 October 2018).

Gani, A. (2015). Muslim population in England and Wales nearly doubles in ten years. *The Guardian*, 11 February. Retrieve from: https://www.theguardian.com/world/2015/feb/11/muslim-population-england-wales-nearly-doubles-10-years (accessed 13 October 2018).

Gibbs, N. (2014). Government commits to electric cars. *The Telegraph*, 31 January. Retrieve from: https://www.telegraph.co.uk/motoring/green-motoring/10607357/Government-commits-to-electric-cars.html (accessed 13 October 2018).

Gil, M., and Rosenberg, S. (2015). The multicultural edge: rising super consumers. *Nielsen Company*, March. Retrieve from: https://www.nielsen.com/content/dam/corporate/us/en/reports-downloads/2015-reports/the-multicultural-edge-rising-super-consumers-march-2015.pdf (accessed 13 October 2018).

Holbrook, M.B., and Hirschman, E.C. (1982). The experiential aspects of consumption: consumer fantasies, feelings and fun. *Journal of Consumer Research*, 9(2), 132–40.

Holbrook, M.B., Lehmann, D.R., and O'Shaughnessy, J. (1986). Using versus choosing: the relationship of the consumption experience to reasons for purchasing. *European Journal of Marketing*, 20(8), 49–62.

Howard, J.A., and Sheth, J.N. (1969). *The Theory of Buyer Behavior*. New York: John Wiley.

Ipsos MRBI/Irish Sports Council (2013). *The Irish Sports Monitor 2013 Annual Report*. Retrieve from: https://www.sportireland.ie/Research/Irish-Sports-Monitor-Annual-Report-2013/ (accessed 13 October 2018).

Johnson, E.J., and Russo, J.E. (1978). The organisation of product information in memory identified by recall times. In: K. Hunt (ed.), *Advances in Consumer Research*, Vol. 5. Chicago, IL: Association for Consumer Research, 79–86.

Kahneman, D. (2011). *Thinking, Fast and Slow*. London: Penguin.

Kelly, S. (2015). *Hunger: Sean Kelly—The Autobiography*. Hemel Hempstead: Peloton.

Khan, H. (2016). Consumers are showrooming and webrooming your business, here's what that means and what you can do about it. *Shopify Blogs*, 2 May. Retrieve from: https://www.shopify.com/retail/119920451-consumers-are-showrooming-and-webrooming-your-business-heres-what-that-means-and-what-you-can-do-about-it (accessed 13 October 2018).

Lambert, F. (2017). Nissan is heavily discounting the LEAF with special deals for just $13,000 ahead of next-generation. *Electrek*, 14 April. Retrieve from: https://electrek.co/2017/04/14/nissan-leaf-discounting/ (accessed 13 October 2018).

Lelinwalla, M. (2016). Nissan expands its free charging promotion as electric car competition from Tesla and others heats up. *Techcrunch*, 5 July. Retrieve from: https://techcrunch.com/2016/07/05/nissan-expands-its-free-charging-promotion-as-electric-car-competition-from-tesla-and-others-heats-up/ (accessed 13 October 2018).

Martin, C.A., and Bush, A.J. (2000). Do role models influence teenagers' purchase intentions and behavior? *Journal of Consumer Marketing*, 17(5), 441–54.

Maslow, A.H. (1943). A theory of motivation. *Psychological Review*, 50(4), 370–96.

Matzler, K., Bidmon, S., and Grabner-Kräuter, S. (2006). Individual determinants of brand affect: the role of the personality traits of extraversion and openness to experience. *Journal of Product and Brand Management*, 15(7), 427–34.

MCB (Muslim Council of Great Britain) (2015). *British Muslims in Numbers*. Retrieve from: https://www.mcb.org.uk/wp-content/uploads/2015/02/MCBCensusReport_2015.pdf (accessed 13 October 2018).

McRae, R.R., and Costa, P.T. (1987). Validation of the five-factor model of personality across instruments and observers. *Journal of Personality and Social Psychology*, 52(1), 81–90.

Michaelidou, N., and Dibb, S. (2008). Consumer involvement: a new perspective. *Marketing Review*, 8(1), 83–99.

Mick, D.G., and DeMoss, M. (1990). To me from me: a descriptive phenomenology of self-gifts. *Advances in Consumer Research*, 17, 677–82.

Mindak, W.A. (1961). Fitting the semantic differential to the marketing problem. *Journal of Marketing*, 25(4), 29–33.

Mintel (2011). Men's grooming and shaving products—UK, October. Retrieve from: http://www.mintel.com (accessed 13 October 2018).

Mintel (2012). Social media: beauty and personal care—UK, April. Retrieve from: http://www.mintel.com (accessed 13 October 2018).

Mintel (2015). Social media: BPC—UK, June. Retrieve from: http://www.mintel.com (accessed 13 October 2018).

Moschis, G.P., and Churchill, G.A., Jr (1978). Consumer socialisation: a theoretical and empirical analysis. *Journal of Marketing Research*, 15(4), 599–609.

Mulyanegara, R.C., Tsarenko, Y., and Anderson, A. (2009). The Big Five and brand personality: investigating the impact of consumer personality on preferences towards particular brand personality. *Journal of Brand Management*, 16(4), 234–47.

Nudd, T. (2016). Thai brand apologizes for blackface ad that said 'you just need to be white to win'. *AdWeek*, 8 January. Retrieve from: https://www.adweek.com/creativity/thai-brand-apologizes-blackface-ad-said-you-just-need-be-white-win-168926 (accessed 13 October 2018).

Peñaloza, L. (1994). Atravesando fronteras/border crossings: A critical ethnographic exploration of the consumer acculturation of Mexican immigrants. *Journal of Consumer Research*, 21(1), 32–54.

Rapp, A., Baker, T.L., Bachrach, D.G., Ogilvie, J., and Beitelspacher, L.S. (2015). Perceived customer showrooming behavior and the effect on retail salesperson self-efficacy and performance. *Journal of Retailing*, 91(2), 358–69.

Ratchford, B.T. (1987). New insights about the FCB grid. *Journal of Advertising Research*, 27(4), 24–38.

Roderick, L. (2015). Cult creation. *The Marketer*, March/April, 30–3.

Rummell, A., Howard, J., Swinton, J.M., and Seymour, D.B. (2000). You can't have that! A study of reactance effects and children's consumer behaviour. *Journal of Marketing Theory and Practice*, 8(1), 38–45.

Russell, M. (2012). Irish fog: 9 myths about whiskey mogul John Jameson. *Business Insider*, 16 March. Retrieve from: https://www.businessinsider.com/meet-john-jameson-2012-3?IR=T (accessed 13 October 2018).

Sabri, O., and Michel, G. (2014). When do advertising parodies hurt? The power of humor and credibility in viral spoof advertisements. *Journal of Advertising Research*, 54(2), 233–47.

Schwarz, N. (2007). Attitude construction: evaluation in context. *Social Cognition*, 25(5), 638–56.

Senecal, S., and Nantal, J. (2004). The influence of online product recommendations on consumers' online choices. *Journal of Retailing*, 80, 159–69.

Sheldrake, P. (2011). *The Business of Influence: Reframing Marketing and PR for the Digital Age*. Chichester: John Wiley.

Siciliano, L. (2014). Watch: graphic anti-smoking ad shows father rolling and smoking rotting flesh. *The Telegraph*, 29 December. Retrieve from: https://www.telegraph.co.uk/news/health/11315959/Watch-Graphic-anti-smoking-ad-shows-father-rolling-and-smoking-rotting-flesh.html (accessed 13 October 2018).

Simonson, I., Carmon, Z., Dhar, R., Drolet, A., and Nowlis, S.M. (1976). Consumer research: in search of identity. *Annual Review of Psychology*, 52, 249–75.

Skinner, B.F. (1954). The science of learning and the art of teaching. *Harvard Educational Review*, 24(2), 88–97.

Somashekhar, S. (2014). Human Rights Campaign says Barilla has turned around its policies on LGBT. *Washington Post*, 19 November. Retrieve from: https://www.washingtonpost.com/politics/human-rights-campaign-says-barilla-has-turned-around-its-policies-on-lgbt/2014/11/18/9866efde-6e92-11e4-8808-afaa1e3a33ef_story.html?utm_term=.c6292e480a77 (accessed 13 October 2018).

Statista (2017). Physical book unit sales in the United Kingdom. Retrieve from: https://www.statista.com/statistics/305693/physical-book-unit-sales-by-category-in-the-uk/ (accessed 13 October 2018).

Statista (2018). Sales volume of Jameson whisky worldwide from 2009 to 2017 (in million 9 litre cases). Retrieve from: https://www.statista.com/statistics/308828/jameson-whiskey-global-sales-volume/ (accessed 13 October 2018).

Udell, J.G. (1964). A new approach to consumer motivation. *Journal of Retailing*, Winter, 6–10.

Valdes-Dapena, P. (2013). Tesla's fight with America's car dealers. *CNN Money*, 20 May. Retrieve from: https://money.cnn.com/2013/05/20/autos/telsa-car-dealers/ (accessed 13 October 2018).

Wells, W.D., and Gubar, G. (1966). Life cycle concept in marketing research. *Journal of Marketing Research*, 3(4), 355–63.

Williams, T.G. (2002). Social class influences on purchase evaluation criteria. *Journal of Consumer Marketing*, 19(3), 249–76.

Chapter 3
Marketing Research and Customer Insight

Learning Outcomes

After reading this chapter, you will be able to:

▶ Define the terms 'market research', 'marketing research', and 'customer insight'

▶ Describe the customer insight process and the role of marketing research within it

▶ Explain the role of marketing research and list the range of possible research approaches

▶ Define the term 'big data' and describe its role in marketing

▶ Discuss the importance of ethics and of the adoption of a code of conduct in marketing research

Case Insight 3.1
Ipsos MORI

Market Insight 3.1
Using Marketing Metrics in a State Monopoly

Market Insight 3.2
Circularity Customer Insight: The Brief

Market Insight 3.3
Circularity Customer Insight: The Proposal

Market Insight 3.4
Research Biases: Don't Kid Yourself

Market Insight 3.5
Why Ask?

Case Insight 3.1
Ipsos MORI

When Unilever wanted to develop its medium-term innovation pipeline for four of its household cleaning brands, it turned to global market research firm, Ipsos. We speak to Ipsos's Billie Ing, innovation engagement lead, Leora Unsdorfer, qualitative research manager, and Alex Gilby, quantitative associate director, to find out more.

Unilever's household cleaning business had a need to inject more innovation into its pipeline. With gaps in the innovation funnel, Unilever's challenge was to create global product and communications propositions for four global brands. To do so, Unilever knew they had to get back to the needs of the people they serve. This is when Unilever hired us at Ipsos to help them tackle the challenge.

Unilever wanted to create robust innovation ideas that would test well, so it was essential to connect with the daily needs of consumers in six of its key markets (India, Brazil, Italy, UK, Turkey, and Russia). Dawn Farren, Global Consumer Market Insight Director at Unilever, encapsulated the innovation challenge: 'Sometimes we are so stuck in tweaking concepts, testing and retesting; we have to stop and get back down to basics and remind our teams what it is like for real people tackling their cleaning challenge.'

But just understanding consumers and their cleaning requirements wasn't going to be enough. Unilever wanted cross-disciplinary teams across the global business to learn more about the cleaning rituals of families around the world and to empathize with their circumstances so they could create better product and communication propositions.

At Ipsos, we determined that the research brief had a specific challenge. We hypothesized that culture would play a large role in cleaning rituals, but that the habitual and automatic nature of housework would lead to poor participant recall, ruling out

traditional survey-style and self-completion research approaches. We also wanted to help Unilever to develop a process for developing and testing new proposition ideas, so they could move straight into commercialization development phases shortly after our project.

At Ipsos, we believe the best proposition development ideas result from strong innovation principles: bringing in diverse perspectives, leveraging collective intelligence of teams, and delivering stimuli via a range of media to engage all five senses. But, often, the creative innovation process can become so removed from the insight itself that ideas lose their original meaning. To avoid this pitfall, Unilever wanted us to quantitatively test the new ideas against innovation metrics, among a sample of consumers in each of the six markets, and to obtain immediate feedback on the potential success of the ideas.

The question for Ipsos was: how was it to design a research programme that would provide insights into cultural cleaning rituals and practices in a diverse set of countries, embed that knowledge inside Unilever, and help Unilever to develop and test innovation ideas based on those insights?

 Visit the **online resources** to watch a video interview with Billie Ing, Leora Unsdorfer, and Alex Gilby in which they explain what Ipsos did.

Introduction

Most of us take it for granted that great companies make great offerings. But how do companies develop successful offerings? More often than not, companies develop propositions using research programmes designed to identify customers' changing needs. They are based on the knowledge that market research and customer insight can bring. Along with marketing communications, **marketing research** is a key sub-discipline of marketing practice and a fundamental component of the marketing philosophy.

Contemporary marketing research is very much affected by technology. Digitalization has led to a proliferation of information and data available to marketers. This shift in data availability, often referred to as **big data**, is currently transforming the market research industry. Traditional market research companies, such as Gallup and A.C. Nielsen, are under pressure from large tech firms (for example IBM and Adobe), as well as fast-growing analytic companies (for example BrainJuicer and Qualtrics) offering a wide range of tools to track customer behaviours in real time (ESOMAR, 2015).

We begin this chapter by defining the difference between 'marketing research' and 'market research'. Whereas market research is conducted to understand markets—customers, competitors, and industries—marketing research also investigates the impact of marketing strategies and tactics. Marketing research thus subsumes market research. 'Customer insight' refers to actionable knowledge about customers gained through research. We then introduce the different steps that marketers need to go through when conducting research. We also introduce big data and marketing analytics, which are increasingly being used to generate insights that lead to strategic marketing decisions. Finally, we consider the challenges of conducting international marketing research.

Definitions of Marketing Research and Customer Insight

Marketing research generates information to provide management with sufficient insight to make informed decisions. It follows the philosophical marketing premise that organizations must understand the motivations, desires, and behaviours of their customers and consumers if they are to survive and thrive. We speak of marketing research, market research, and customer insight, but these terms are not interchangeable, although they are related. In addition, 'marketing analytics' is often used to denote the analytical procedures used to analyse information collected from a range of different sources, often referred to as big data. We outline the definitions of these concepts in Table 3.1.

Market research is work undertaken to determine the structural characteristics of the industry of concern (for example demand, market share, market volumes, customer characteristics, and segmentation), whereas marketing research is work undertaken to understand how to make specific marketing strategy decisions (for example for pricing, sales forecasting, proposition testing, and promotion research). Marketing research is further characterized by being systematic, meaning that the procedures followed in each step of the research process are methodologically sound, well documented, and (as far as possible) planned in advance (Malhotra, 2010).

Table 3.1 Definitions in marketing research

Term	Originator	Definition
Big data	Original, adapted from various definitions, e.g. McAfee and Brynjolfsson (2012); Press (2014)	The systematic gathering and interpretation of high-volume, high-velocity, and/or high-variety information using cost-effective innovative forms of information processing to enable enhanced insight, decision-making, and process automation
Customer insight	Said et al. (2015: 1159)	'Knowledge about the customer that is valuable for the firm'
Market research	European Society for Opinion and Market Research (ESOMAR, 2016: 5)	'Market research, which includes social and opinion research, is the systematic gathering and interpretation of information about individuals or organisations using the statistical and analytical methods and techniques of the applied social sciences to gain insight or support decision making.'
Marketing analytics	American Marketing Association (AMA, 2016)	'Marketing analytics involves the discovery and communication of meaningful patterns in data from metrics like traffic, leads, sales, advertising, promotions, web activity, social media, and any other relevant marketing activity or financial data. Marketing analytics can be defined by their use of mathematical distributions, statistical sources, or analytical techniques (e.g., regression) for their construction'
Marketing research	American Marketing Association (AMA, 2015)	'Marketing research is the function that links the consumer, customer, and public to the marketer through information—information used to identify and define marketing opportunities and problems; generate, refine, and evaluate marketing actions; monitor marketing performance; and improve understanding of marketing as a process. Marketing research specifies the information required to address these issues, designs the method for collecting information, manages and implements the data collection process, analyses the results, and communicates the findings and their implications.'

In contrast, customer insights are generated based on the knowledge gained by different research activities. Information requires transformation to generate insight. Customer insights are thus distinct from customer information because they encompass a deeper understanding of what drives customers' behaviours. Marketing analytics refers to the mathematical and statistical analytical procedures used to distil insights out of high-volume, high-velocity, and/or high-variety information, typically denoted as big data. We will discuss this further in the section on big data, but before that we will look at different steps in the insight-generation and market-research processes, respectively. According to the 2018 Chief Marketing Officer (CMO) survey, marketers are looking to increase the share of marketing budgets spent on marketing analytics from around 6 per cent in 2017 to 17 per cent in 2020 (Moorman, 2018).

Visit the **online resources** and follow the web links to the Market Research Society (MRS) and the European Society for Opinion and Market Research (ESOMAR) to learn more about these professional marketing research associations.

The Customer Insight Process

Understanding customers is at the core of the marketing concept and the basic idea is that timely, continuous marketing information should be used to support decision-making. Research is thus a foundational element of marketing practice, but some companies and sectors value it more than others. In the 2018 CMO survey, 42 per cent of the surveyed CMOs used marketing analytics in their decision-making and the proportion was higher in business-to-consumer (B2C) companies than in business-to-business (B2B) companies (Moorman, 2018).

Customer insight is typically derived by fusing knowledge generated from a range of sources, including industry reports, sales force data, **competitive intelligence**, customer relationship management (CRM) systems data, employee feedback, social media analysis data, and managerial intuition. (See also 'Big Data and Marketing Analytics' later in chapter.) Barwise and Meehan (2011) distinguish between the high-tech and low-tech sources that can be used to generate insights. High-tech sources include quantitative marketing research, customer database analysis, and big data, while low-tech sources include qualitative market research, but also casual observations, mystery shoppers, and employee feedback. Typically, both high- and low-tech sources are used to generate insights.

Visit the **online resources** and follow the web links to learn more about how Procter & Gamble combines high- and low-tech sources in its market research.

A customer insight can be said to be of value if it is rare, difficult to imitate, and of potential use to formulate management decisions (Said et al., 2015). Cowan (2008) suggests that if organizations are to genuinely make use of insights, chief executive officers (CEOs) and CMOs, researchers, and insight managers need to do the following:

■ Chief executive officers and CMOs should recognize the importance of supporting the insight process, ask 'helicopter' (that is, wide-scoping) questions, not try to guess the answers to strategic problems, demand evidence-based answers, and provide the necessary resources.

■ Researchers should view themselves as problem-solvers, not reporters, and should focus on trying to gain a causal understanding, not on describing attitudes, and on changing the marketing situation.

- Insight managers should challenge strategic assumptions that the organization is making, challenge the 'obvious' solution since it is often wrong, analyse and combine all existing relevant data, and devote greater resources to extracting insight.

The information obtained through marketing research, competitive intelligence, and internal sources is typically integrated into a marketing information system (MIS). Such systems provide a formalized set of procedures for generating, analysing, sorting, and distributing information to decision-makers on an ongoing basis (Malhotra, 2010).

The kind of information marketers need includes:

- aggregated marketing information in quarterly annual summaries;

- aggregated marketing information around offerings or markets (for example sales data);

- analytical information for decision models (for example SWOT, segmentation analyses);

- internally focused marketing information (for example sales, costs, marketing performance indicators);

- externally focused marketing information (for example macro and industry trends);

- historical information (for example sales, profitability, market trends);

- future-oriented marketing information (for example horizon scanning information);

- quantitative marketing information (for example costs, profit, market share, customer satisfaction, **net promoter score**); and

- qualitative marketing information (for example buyer behaviour, competitor strategy information) (Ashill and Jobber, 2001).

This information could be provided on a continuous and/or ad hoc basis. Continuous industry trend information is gleaned from industry reports and secondary data sources, whereas ad hoc research typically involves some kind of primary data collection (that is, data that is collected specifically for that purpose). The main difficulty for the marketing manager is to obtain and customize the MIS to fit the company's specific need, and to ensure that the data are input on a timely and continuous basis. (For an illustration, see Market Insight 3.1.)

Recently, companies have been starting to invest in specific insight teams to ensure that they have the innovative organizational capabilities that help to build customer insights. According to Van Den Driest, Sthanunathan, and Weed (2016), an independent insights and analytics function should be set up to participate fully in business planning and strategy (see Research Insight 3.1). Such an insights function should be responsible for synthesizing data from different sources within and outside the organization. The team should be in charge of integrating, interpreting, and disseminating the large sets of both structured and unstructured data (for example product sales figures, advertising spending, customer service records, and social media monitoring) that are typically owned by different teams within the organization. The insights team should work independently from different functions (such as marketing) and support the top management team directly. Whereas a traditional marketing research function would provide insights based on research needs, the insight team will take on a role that emphasizes shared goals and partnership. It should be forward-looking with an affinity for action, meaning that the insight team will be proactive and help to drive implementation and action within the organization.

Market Insight 3.1
Using Marketing Metrics in a State Monopoly

Systembolaget was the world's first alcohol monopoly and remains the only retailer of alcohol in Sweden. In the past decade, it has become a leader in customer satisfaction in the retail industry.

The Swedish government has given Systembolaget the task of selling alcohol in a responsible manner, thereby contributing to reducing the harmful effects of alcohol in society. In other words, and in contrast with most privately owned companies, the goal is not to make a profit or to sell as much as possible, but rather to reduce the harmful effects of the products it sells. In addition, to be able to keep the monopoly, Systembolaget needs to ensure that the general public supports the monopoly.

Marketing research is an important tool for ensuring that Systembolaget stays true to its task.

Systembolaget continuously measures customer satisfaction across all of its more than 400 stores. These studies allow the company to see what kind of shops provide customers with most satisfaction. It can also identify the key drivers of satisfaction, which it turns out are the service staff and social responsibility (that is, reducing the harmful effects of alcohol).

Systembolaget also measures the work satisfaction and motivation of its employees. Since the service staff are an important driver of customer satisfaction, the staff receive training to be able to answer questions related to all products for sale. They are also trained to communicate in a responsible manner with regard to the products.

To track public support, Systembolaget measures support for the existence of a monopoly among the general public. This tracking includes both customers and non-customers of Systembolaget. The tracking shows a high level of support from the general public: four out of five say they would vote to keep the monopoly, if there were a referendum today. The level of customer satisfaction also contributes to this support. As long as customers are satisfied, they will support the existence of the monopoly.

Systembolaget cannot use sales to evaluate the appropriateness of its strategy. Therefore the insights gained from customer, employee, and the general public surveys are very important. In fact, guided by market research, some major changes have taken place over the past decade, such as the change of all stores from over-the-counter to self-service and the introduction of home deliveries.

Theory into Practice

Marketing research generates information to provide management with sufficient insight to make informed decisions. This information can be used to devise new offers, but also to evaluate what is currently being done. To use marketing research to assess what is being done, continuity is important because this allows decision-makers to compare key metrics over time, as well as before and after certain changes. For Systembolaget, continuously measuring customer and employee satisfaction, as well as public support for the monopoly, provides direct feedback on how well it is fulfilling the task given to it by the Swedish government.

Related Topics

customer satisfaction; employee satisfaction; customer service; service encounters; retailing

1 **What functions of a company should be measured?**

2 **Data collection can be expensive. Is it necessary to measure customers', employees', and general opinions?**

3 **How can a company keep up to date even if there is no competition?**

This market insight was kindly contributed by Sofie Sagfossen, PhD candidate at Stockholm School of Economics, Sweden.

Research Insight 3.1

To take your learning further, you might wish to read this influential article:

Van Den Driest, F., Sthanunathan, S., and Weed, K. (2016). Building an insights engine. *Harvard Business Review*, **94(9), 64–74.**

In this article, the authors discuss the capabilities that distinguish high-performing, customer-centric companies. More specifically, they argue that an independent insights and analytics function that participates in business planning and strategy is a key characteristic of such firms. Using Unilever's Consumer and Market Insights (CMI) group as a case study, the authors argue that expertise in synthesizing data, close collaboration with other functions, and innovative use of new technologies are vital if an insight team is to succeed. Furthermore, they point out the skill sets needed by team members in terms of a 'whole brain' mindset that balances creative and analytical thinking.

 Visit the online resources to read the abstract and access the full paper.

Commissioning Market Research

Much market research is not conducted in-house by marketers. When commissioning research, a client determines whether or not it wants to commission an agency, a consultant, a field and tabulation (tab) agency, or a data preparation and analysis agency. Typically, a consultant might do a job that does not require extensive fieldwork; a field and tab agency is used when the organization can design its own research, but not undertake the data collection; a data preparation and analysis agency, when the organization can both design and collect the data, but does not have the expertise to analyse it; and a **full-service agency** when the organization does not have the expertise to design the research and collect or analyse the data.

Agencies are shortlisted according to some criteria and asked to make a presentation of their services. Visits are made to their premises to check the quality of their staff and facilities, and previous reports are considered to assess the quality of their work. Permission to interview or obtain references from their clients is usually requested. Each agency is evaluated on its ability to undertake work of an acceptable quality at an appropriate price. The criteria used to evaluate an agency's suitability (after proposal submission) includes:

- the agency's reputation;
- the agency's perceived expertise;
- whether the study offers value for money;
- the time taken to complete the study; and
- the likelihood that the research design will provide insights into the **management problem**.

Shortlisted agencies are given a preliminary outline of the client's needs in a **research brief** and asked to provide proposals on research methodology, timing, and costs. After this, an agency is selected to undertake the work required. In the long term, clients are most satisfied with flexible agencies that avoid rigid research solutions and demonstrate professional knowledge of the industry, have an ability to focus on the management problem and to provide solutions, and consistent service quality (Cater and Zabkar, 2009).

The Marketing Research Brief

The marketing research brief is a formal document prepared by a marketer (client) and submitted to the marketing research agency. When marketing research is conducted in-house, the manager requiring the research prepares a brief for the market research manager. The brief outlines a management problem to be investigated (see Market Insight 3.2 for an example). The typical contents of a research brief include the following:

- A *background summary* provides a brief introduction and details about the company and its offerings.

- The *management problem* is a clear statement of why the research is needed and what business decisions depend upon its outcome.

- The *marketing research questions* comprise a detailed list of the information necessary to make the decisions outlined.

- The *intended scope of the research* outlines the areas to be covered, which industries, type of customer, etc. The brief should give an indication of when the information is required and why that date is important (for example pricing research required for a sales forecast meeting).

- The client organization should also outline how agencies will be selected—that is, its *tendering procedures*. Specific information may be required, such as CVs from agency personnel involved in the study and reference contact addresses. The number of copies of the report required, and preferences with regard to layout and format, are also outlined.

The Marketing Research Process

There are numerous basic stages that guide a marketing research project (see Figure 3.1). The first, and most crucial, stage involves problem definition and establishing the information needs of the decision-makers. The client organization explains the basis of the problem(s) it faces to the market researcher. This might be the need to understand market volumes in a potential new market or the reason for an unexpected sudden increase in uptake of an offering. Indeed, problem definition does not always imply that the organization faces a threat. The initial stage allows the organization to assess its current position, to define its information needs, and to make informed decisions about its future.

Market Insight 3.2
Circularity Customer Insight: The Brief

Mika Laurin is the director of Circularity, a start-up looking to help restaurants to reduce waste and increase profits. Circularity offers a digital platform that matches unsold food and unreserved tables with consumers looking for deals. The company has recently received venture capital funding from an investor to allow it to take the next steps in launching the platform nationally.

Mika decides that the company should invest some of these funds in concept testing research to determine the market potential for the offering, and to help to determine a launch plan to give the venture capital company and other potential investors the confidence to invest further in the full commercialization of the platform. Mika and her backers expect that the market for matching platforms will grow very quickly. Her competitive intelligence indicates that several other similar projects are being undertaken by rival start-ups by established actors such as Karma and Book a Table. She predicts that such actors will take the lion's share of the mass market. Accordingly, Mika has decided to focus on students as the target consumers. Now, she (and her financial backers) would like to know whether the concept is acceptable to restaurants and students in university cities around the country, what the likely market potential is for this offering, and what features are important to the two target groups.

Mika invites proposals from four market research agencies and provides them with the following information concerning Circularity research objectives:

1 Indicate how (a) restaurants and (b) students perceive this offering and its expected performance.

2 Compare the Circularity prototype with existing alternative offerings available in each market to determine which offerings customers perceive to be best.

3 Determine what decision factors will be at play for (a) restaurants and (b) students when it comes to signing up for such a platform.

4 Evaluate the market potential of different university cities and provide an indication of the existing competition.

Mika spends two hours meeting with each of four bidding organizations, briefing them on the background to the company and outlining why she wants to conduct the research requested. Of the four companies who each submit a proposal, Mika is most impressed with the proposal submitted by Insights International. She decides to meet its research director to discuss the agency's proposal.

Theory into Practice

A market research brief typically includes a summary of the company and its offerings, a statement of why the research is needed, and what management decisions the research will inform. It also includes a detailed list of the information necessary and the intended scope of the research, as well as information about important deadlines and tendering procedures.

Related Topics

new product development; innovation; marketing environment; B2C/B2B

1 Do you think that this brief has clear research objectives? Why, or why not?

2 Does the research brief indicate or imply that a specific methodology should be used? If so, which method does it imply?

3 What other types of research might be conducted to tackle the given research objectives?

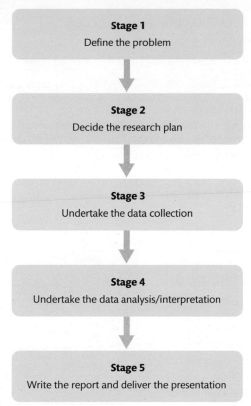

Figure 3.1

Marketing research process

Source: Baines and Chansarkar (2002). © John Wiley & Sons. Reproduced with permission.

Stage 1 Problem Definition

The first step in a market research project is defining the management problem and writing the research brief. Often, the problem is described in vague terms, because organizations are not always sure what information they require. An example might be Carrefour, the supermarket chain, explaining that sales are not as strong as expected in its Romanian stores and wondering whether or not this is a result of the emergence of a competitor supermarket (see Figure 3.2). The problem description provides the researcher with relatively little depth of understanding of the situation in which the supermarket finds itself, so the researcher needs to discuss the problem with the staff commissioning the study to investigate further. This allows the researcher to translate the management problem into a marketing research question. Typically, this question may include a number of sub-questions for further exploration. An example of a marketing research question, as well as a number of more specific sub-questions, is shown in Figure 3.3.

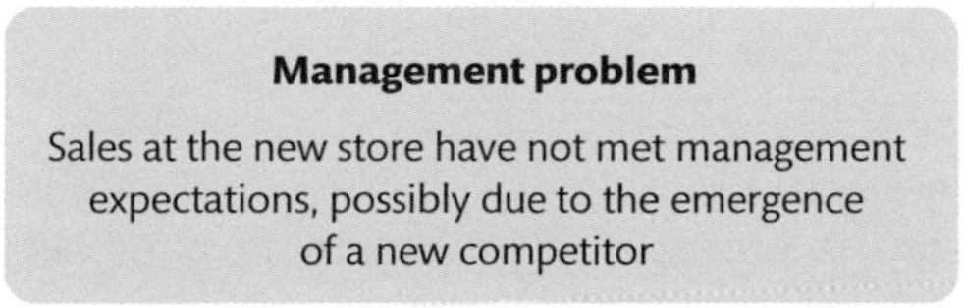

> **Management problem**
>
> Sales at the new store have not met management expectations, possibly due to the emergence of a new competitor

Figure 3.2

Example of a management problem

> **MARKETING RESEARCH QUESTION**
>
> Why are sales levels not meeting management expectations?
>
> 1. Sub-question: Has customer disposable income in the area declined over the last six months?
> 2. Sub-question: Is a new competitor, Tesco, taking away customers?
> 3. Sub-question: Are customers tired/bored of the current product range in the existing supermarket?
> 4. Sub-question: Are customers conducting more of their shopping online?
> 5. Sub-question: Were management expectations set too high and/or market potential overestimated?

Figure 3.3

Example of a marketing research question

French supermarket chain Carrefour operates globally

Source: © PhotoStock10/Shutterstock.com.

The marketing research question transforms the management problem into a question while trying to remove any assumptions made by the organization's management. Sometimes, the management problem is clear: the organization needs a customer profile, an industry profile, an understanding of buyer behaviour, or to test advertising concepts for its next campaign. The more clearly the commissioning organization defines the management problem, the easier it is to design the research to solve that problem.

Once the agency discusses the brief with the client, the agency provides a detailed outline of how it will investigate the problem. This document is called the **research proposal**. Table 3.2 briefly outlines a typical marketing research proposal and Market Insight 3.3 provides an example.

Table 3.2 Outline of a marketing research proposal

Element	Description of content
Executive summary	A brief summary of the research project, including the major outcomes and findings; rarely more than one page in length; allows the reader to obtain a summary of the main points of the project without having to read the full report.
Background	An outline of the problem or situation and the issues surrounding this problem; demonstrates the researcher's understanding of the management problem
Objectives	An outline of the objectives of the research project, including the data to be generated and how this will be used to address the management problem
Design	A clear, non-technical description of the research type adopted and the specific techniques to be used to gather the required information; includes details of data-collection instruments, sampling procedures, and analytical techniques.
Personnel specification	The details of the people involved in the collection and analysis of the data, providing a named liaison person and outlining the company's credibility in undertaking the work.
Schedule	An outline of the time requirements, with dates for the various stages to completion and presentation of results.
Costs	A detailed analysis of the costs involved in the project for large projects or simply a total cost for the project.
References	Typically, three references are outlined, so that a client can be sure that an agency has the requisite capability to do the job in hand.

Stage 2 Decide the Research Plan

Once the marketing research question(s) have been decided, it is time to develop a research plan. At this stage, the framework for conducting the project is developed. In developing this framework, marketing researchers need to consider what type of research is needed. The market research need can be specified based on objective (**exploratory research**, **descriptive research**, **causal research**), as well as source (primary versus secondary data) and methodology (qualitative versus quantitative). The research need will have implications for the design of the research plan.

Type of Marketing Research: Objectives

Generally speaking, we define three types of research objective: exploratory; descriptive; and causal. These categories specify the type of management problem that the research should solve:

- *Exploratory research* is used when little is known about a particular management problem and it needs to be explored further. Exploratory designs enable the development of hypotheses or new concepts.

Market Insight 3.3
Circularity Customer Insight: The Proposal

Client's Information Needs

The client Circularity, a start-up company, is looking to launch a new platform that helps restaurants to reduce waste and increase profits by matching unsold dishes and available seating with consumers looking for cheap meals. The offering is to be specialized for students, and sets out to provide tasty, cheap, and sustainable meals to people living on a relatively limited budget. Circularity wishes to commission concept testing and market potential research to understand whether or not it is acceptable to both restaurant owners and student consumers, how the platform compares with existing systems available in the marketplace, and the market potential in different university towns around the country.

Research Objectives

The research will answer the following questions.

1   What is the size of the marketplace for the platform for (a) restaurants and (b) students in key university towns?

2   What existing competitors (if any) are currently serving university towns and what are those competitors' relative market shares?

3   What criteria (if any) do (a) restaurants and (b) students use to evaluate the perceived value of such platforms?

4   How do (a) restaurants and (b) students rate Circularity's prototype platform and those of its competitors in relation to the attributes listed in research question 3? (Attributes are likely to include assortment, price, service, etc.)

5   What is the decision-making process used by (a) restaurants and (b) students when selecting from among different platforms?

Research Programme Proposed

Initially, a three-stage research programme is recommended, involving desk research, qualitative research, and quantitative research. We recommend that desk research is carried out initially, to map the structure of this market offering for the ten largest university towns in the country. Qualitative research will be carried

out before the quantitative stage to provide a stronger understanding of how (a) restaurants and (b) students perceive this new offering and the decision-making processes they go through to use it. This will provide a stronger understanding of how the samples should be determined in the quantitative research. Finally, quantitative research will be used to provide a stronger understanding of the market potential for the offering and a representative overview of how (a) restaurants and (b) students rate the prototype and those of its competitors on various dimensions.

Desk Research Phase

A desk research phase will involve the systematic search of market intelligence databases, industry reports, and census data on the different university towns. The intention of this research is to pull together a market map of the towns, assessing the potential market on both sides of the platform (that is, restaurants and students). Therefore the analysis aims to provide answers to the research questions 1 and 2.

Qualitative Research Phase

Sampling

Given the need to cover both restaurant and student markets, we recommend conducting a series of 15 in-depth interviews across a variety of restaurants (identified in the desk research phase) and a total of 10 discussion groups with students in different university towns (towns selected based on desk research results). The groups will incorporate a mix of gender/gender identity, as well as a mix of previous experience of using a similar platform. The in-depth interviews with potential restaurants will be conducted in person on-site using an interview of approximately 45 minutes' duration. The discussion groups will last between 60 and 90 minutes, and will be held at a central location within each of the towns listed.

Data Analysis

The qualitative data will be fully transcribed before analysis. All verbatim quotes obtained from in-depth interviews and discussion groups for the first set of interviews will be reviewed to ensure that our

Market Insight 3.3
continued

interviewers are questioning correctly before they proceed further. The analysis will use a thematic analytic approach based on research questions 3–5.

Quantitative Research Phase

For this stage, we propose using a **computer-assisted web-interviewing (CAWI)** methodology for both the restaurants and students, which will allow us to use complex question routing and skip patterns, and to undertake more efficient sample management. We aim to interview approximately 200 restaurants using a judgemental sampling method, identifying appropriate companies and respondents in conjunction with Circularity. For the student customer research, we would aim to purchase six questions on a standard omnibus survey through a subcontracted research agency.

Sampling

In the restaurant survey, respondents will be screened to ensure that they are the appropriate person. To determine the correct number of interviews to conduct in a given research study, we need to consider several factors, including the overall objective, requirements for subset analysis, and, in this case, the overall size of the target universe. We recommend using an overall sample size of 200 interviews. Using standard industrial classification (SIC) codes and company size, we will draw the sample proportionally to Circularity's key intended target markets using a judgemental sampling methodology. To facilitate the selection of the sample, we will purchase lists of client companies from Dun & Bradstreet and/or other reputable list providers.

In the student survey, we will use a subcontracted omnibus survey provider specializing in youth/student panels. Respondents will be screened to ensure that they are in the target audience. The subcontracted agency typically uses a sample size of *c.*1,000 respondents and aims to ensure that the sample is representative of the population by questioning panels constructed using a combination of gender/gender identity, location, and ethnicity. The survey uses a random sampling methodology and weighting to ensure a representative sample within this target group.

Data Analysis

On finalization of the fieldwork, collected data will be processed and tabulated. Data will be tested for statistical significance (at the 95 per cent confidence level). Cluster analysis will be employed to determine whether or not any segments emerge from either the residential or the industrial samples. Multiple regressions will be undertaken to determine the key drivers of both the residential and industrial customers' perceptions of the prototype offering. An Insights International executive will talk through the results and answer any questions. Topline survey results are checked regularly and a response analysis is produced. This regular check allows us to identify errors as quickly as possible. The analysis aims to answer research questions 1, 3, and 4.

Reporting

We will work in partnership with Circularity to ensure that the results from the research are actionable. The report will be produced in PowerPoint and structured in line with the research objectives to include all aspects of the methodology and sampling. The report will be designed to include charts and tables to best depict the main findings, together with clear and concise commentary. In addition to digital copies, two hard copies of the report, with accompanying tables, will be delivered to Circularity.

Costing and Schedule

Desk research	£5,000
Qualitative in-depth interviews	£8,000
Discussion group interviews	£20,000
CAWI set-up, sample incentives, and project management	£8,000
Omnibus survey	£4,000
Quantitative data analysis	£5,000
Qualitative analysis, data interpretation and reporting	£9,000
Total	**£59,000**

We suggest that the study is undertaken in the period from November 2019 until the end of May 2020.

Market Insight 3.3
continued

Theory into Practice

After receiving a brief, the research company (or in-house research team) transforms the management problem into a research question, while trying to remove any assumptions made by the organization's management. Sometimes, this requires a lot of thought because management might have formulated the problem very precisely. Having specified the objectives of the research, the company then moves on to plan how it will get the information needed. The plan provides a detailed outline of how it will approach the research problem, which is typically referred to as a research proposal.

Related Topics

new product development; innovation; marketing environment; B2C/B2B

1 How does the proposal compare with the brief in Market Insight 3.2?

2 Do you think that a face-to-face survey might be a more appropriate way of reaching restaurants? What other approaches might you select?

3 Do you think the research objectives are feasible, given the budget requirements? Why, or why not?

- *Descriptive research* focuses on accurately describing the variables being considered, such as market characteristics or spending patterns, in key customer groups. Examples of descriptive research are consumer profile studies, usage studies, price surveys, attitude surveys, sales analyses, and media research.

- *Causal research* is used to determine whether one variable causes an effect in another variable. To determine causality, experimental or longitudinal studies are needed. Experiments are characterized by the marketing researchers manipulating a specific variable (cause) thought to influence important outcomes (effect), thereby allowing them to carefully test causation. By contrast, longitudinal studies track the effect of a certain variable (cause) over time. Examples of causal research are studies of customer satisfaction and advertising effectiveness, which typically set out to understand what factors of an offer or an ad impacts on consumer evaluations.

Type of Marketing Research: Source

When conducting research we can either use what is already known or devise research that creates new knowledge. **Primary research** is research conducted for the first time, involving the collection of data for the purpose of a particular project. Secondary data is second-hand data, collected for someone else's purposes. **Desk research** (also known as secondary research) involves gaining access to the results of previous research projects. This method can be a cheaper and more efficient process of data collection.

We can do a large amount of secondary research for free by visiting a business library or searching the Internet. Other sources of secondary data include:

- government sources, including export databases, government statistical offices, social trend databases, and other resources;

- the Internet, including sources identified using search engines, blogs and microblogs, and discussion groups;

- company internal records, including information housed in a marketing information or CRM system (see Chapter 14) or published reports (where no formal marketing information system exists, we would identify sales reports, marketing plans, and research reports commissioned previously);

- professional bodies and trade associations, which frequently have databases available online for research purposes, and which may include industry magazine articles and research reports; and

- market research companies, for example Mintel, Euromonitor, ICC Keynote, and Google, which frequently undertake research into industry sectors or specific product groups and can be highly specialized.

We would usually undertake secondary research initially to see whether someone has undertaken similar research previously. For example, if an entertainment company had recently bought a new cinema property and wanted to know who lived in the local area, it could consult secondary data sources to ascertain the characteristics of people living in the area (for example gender, age, population size). However, if it were to want to know what film genres customers prefer, it might survey a sample of the population.

 Visit the **online resources** and follow the web links to learn more about these market research organizations.

In practice, most research projects involve both secondary and primary research, with desk research occurring initially to ensure that the company doesn't waste money. Primary research is undertaken to cover the gaps in the company's knowledge once all available secondary data has been evaluated. Once this initial insight is gleaned, we determine whether or not to commission a primary data study. Assuming that primary research needs to be undertaken, researchers usually design their research by considering what type of research to employ. Marketing directors should understand what types of study can be conducted because this impacts on the type of information collected and hence the data they receive to help them to solve their management problem.

Type of Marketing Research: Methodology

At the outset of a research project, we might consider whether to use **qualitative research** or **quantitative research**, or a combination of the two. Qualitative research denotes research methodologies relying on small samples, using open and probing questions that set out to uncover underlying motives and feelings. The data gathered is then interpreted focusing on meanings and is usually quite hard to replicate. Typically, qualitative research is intended to provide insights and understanding of the problem setting, and thus it is frequently used in exploratory market research. The main methods for collecting qualitative data are individual interviews, focus groups, and observations.

Quantitative research methods are used to elicit responses to predetermined standardized questions from many respondents. This involves collecting information, quantifying the responses as frequencies or percentages, and analysing them statistically. Quantitative research is thus commonly used in descriptive and causal marketing research, and replication is a highly desirable property of the outcome of such research. Thus quantitative data collection methods are much more structured than qualitative data collection methods. Common methods include different types of survey (online, offline), face-to-face or telephone interview, and longitudinal study.

Table 3.3 summarizes the key differences between qualitative and quantitative research methods. Although qualitative research methods are typically characterized as being exploratory and quantitative methods as being descriptive or causal, methods are not intrinsically associated with one kind of research purpose or another. The key concern is not which methods are used to generate data, but how they are used and for what purpose. There are also several ways of combining qualitative and quantitative research. What's more, many methods can be used qualitatively or quantitatively depending on purpose. For example, open and participative observations (for example ethnography) are typically used in qualitative research, whereas structured observations (for example mystery shopping) are used in quantitative research. Another example is content or sentiment analysis, which often starts out by qualitatively assessing different exemplars (for example ads, or comments on social media) and then gradually builds a vast amount of such observations, which are analysed quantitatively. For example, user-generated content (UGC) in social media can be mined for meaning to better understand consumer quality perceptions for different brands without having to ask questions (Tirunillai and Tellis, 2014).

Table 3.3 Qualitative and quantitative research methods compared

Characteristic	Qualitative	Quantitative
Purpose	Oriented towards discovery and exploration	Oriented towards cause and effect
Procedure	Emerging design; merges data collection and analysis	Predetermined design; separates data collection and analysis
Emphasis	Meaning and interpretation	What can be measured
Role of researcher	Involved; used as a 'research instrument'	Detached; uses standardized research instruments
Unit of analysis	A holistic system	Specific variables
Size of sample	Involves a small number of respondents, typically <30	Involves a large number of respondents, >30
Sampling approach	Uses purposively selected samples	Uses probability sampling techniques

The client (or in-house research client) may also have specific budget constraints or know which particular approach it intends to adopt. However, the choice primarily depends on the circumstances of the research project and its objectives. If much is known about the management problem based on past research or experience, it may be appropriate to use quantitative research to understand the problem further. If there is little pre-understanding of the management problem, it would be better to explore the problem using qualitative research to gather insights. Globally, 73 per cent of marketing research investment is spent on quantitative research (ESOMAR, 2015). Industry surveys also indicate that marketers increasingly combine both qualitative and quantitative methods, but that quantitative approaches tend to be used in 59 per cent of research projects and qualitative approaches in 35 per cent, with the remaining 6 per cent belonging to other forms of research (Murphy, 2018).

Designing the Research Project

Once we know what type of research to conduct, we should consider:

- who to question and how (the sampling plan and procedures to be used);
- what methods to use (for example discussion groups or an experiment);
- which types of question are required (whether open questions for qualitative research or closed questions for a survey); and
- how the data should be analysed and interpreted (what approach to data analysis should be undertaken).

Research methods describe the techniques and procedures that will be used to obtain the necessary information. We could use a survey or a series of in-depth interviews. We might use observation (that is, mystery shopping) to see how consumers purchase goods online or how employees greet consumers when they enter a particular shop. We could use consumer panels in which respondents record their weekly purchases or their television viewing habits over a specified time period. Nielsen Homescan is a service whereby consumers use specially developed barcode readers to record their supermarket purchases in return for points, which are redeemed for household goods. Table 3.4 summarizes the most commonly used qualitative and quantitative methods used by marketers in 2015. As can be seen, companies increasingly use online methods (see Research Insight 3.2).

Table 3.4 Top five qualitative and quantitative data collection methods, 2017

Rank	Qualitative	Quantitative
1	Focus groups (in person)	Online surveys
2	In-depth interviews (in person)	Mobile surveys
3	In-depth interview (telephone)	Face-to-face surveys
4	Discussions using online communities	Computer-assisted telephone interviews (CATI)
5	Mobile (diaries, image collection, etc . . .)	Computer-assisted personal interviews (CAPI)

Source: Murphy (2018).

Research Insight 3.2

To take your learning further, you might wish to read this influential paper:

Steward, D.W., and Shamdasani, P. (2017). Online focus groups. *Journal of Advertising*, 46(1), 48–60.

Focus groups are the most common qualitative data collection method in marketing research practice. Typically, focus groups are conducted in person, but the authors of this article discuss different types of online focus group (asynchronous, synchronous, and virtual worlds) and their pros and cons. The authors conclude that online focus-group research and face-to-face focus-group research are complementary.

 Visit the online resources to read the abstract and access the full paper.

Figure 3.4 indicates the key considerations when designing qualitative and quantitative research projects. The design of marketing research projects involves determining how each of the following components interrelates with the others:

- research objectives;
- sampling method;
- the interviewing method to be used;
- research type and methods undertaken;
- question and questionnaire design; and
- data analysis.

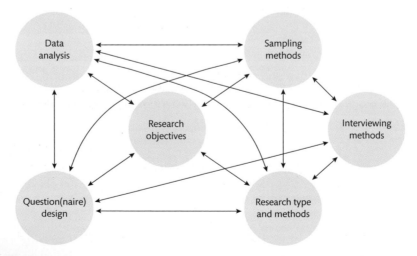

Figure 3.4

The major components of research design

Source: Baines and Chansarkar (2002). © John Wiley & Sons Limited. Reproduced with permission.

When designing research projects, we must first determine the type of approach to use for a given management problem (for example exploratory, descriptive, or causal). Then we determine which techniques are most capable of producing the desired data at the least cost and in the minimum time period.

To determine whether or not we've got the 'right' data, we must determine its **validity** (do the data correctly describe the phenomenon they measure?) and **reliability** (would the data be replicated in a future repeat study of the same type?). Generally, certain types of research use certain methods or techniques. For instance, exploratory research studies use qualitative research methods, non-probability sampling methods, and non-statistical data analysis methods. Descriptive research projects often adopt survey interviews using quota or random sampling methods, and statistical analysis techniques. Causal researchers employ experimental research designs using convenience or **probability sampling** methods and statistical data analysis procedures.

Stage 3 Data Collection and Sampling

This stage involves the conduct of fieldwork and the collection of data. At this stage, we send out questionnaires, or run online focus group sessions, or conduct a netnographic study, depending on the decisions taken in the first design stage of the fieldwork. The procedures undertaken when conducting the fieldwork might relate to how to ask the questions of the respondents—whether using the telephone, mail, or in person—and how to select an appropriate sample, as well as how to **pre-code** the answers to a questionnaire (quantitative research) or how to code the answers arising out of open-ended questions (particularly with qualitative research).

The research manager might be concerned about whether or not to conduct the research in-house or to commission a field and tab agency. Other issues concern how to ensure high data quality. When market research companies undertake shopping mall intercept interviews, they usually re-contact a proportion of the respondents to check their answers to ensure that the interviews have been conducted properly.

In qualitative research, samples are often selected on a convenience or judgemental basis. In quantitative research, we might use either probability or non-probability methods, including:

- *simple random sampling*, where the population elements are accorded a number and a sample is selected by generating random numbers that correspond to the individual population elements;

- *systematic random sampling*, where population elements are known and the first sample unit is selected using random number generation, but after that each of the succeeding sample units is selected systematically on the basis of an *n*th number, where *n* is determined by dividing the population size by the sample size; and

- *stratified random sampling*, where a specific characteristic(s) is used (for example gender, age) to design homogeneous subgroups from which a representative sample is drawn.

Non-random methods include:

- *quota sampling*, where criteria such as gender, ethnicity, or some other customer characteristic are used to restrict the sample, but the selection of the sample unit is left to the judgement of the researcher;

- *convenience sampling*, where no such restrictions are placed on the selection of the respondents and anybody can be selected; and

■ *snowball sampling*, where respondents are selected from rare populations (for example high-performance car buyers), perhaps initially from among responses to newspaper adverts and then later using referrals from the initial respondents, thereby 'snowballing' the sample.

With the growth of online market research, the reliance on Internet panels has become increasingly common. Two types of panel are used in online research (Miles, 2004). Access panels, which provide samples for survey-style information, are made up of targets especially invited by email to take part, with a link to a web survey. Proprietary panels, set up or commissioned by a client firm, are usually made up of that company's customers. To encourage survey participation, the researchers use incentives (for example a prize draw). However, there are pros and cons associated with undertaking online research (see Table 3.5).

 Visit the **online resources** and complete Internet Activity 3.1 to learn more about the Market Research Portal, a useful source of online research resources.

Stage 4 Data Analysis and Interpretation

This stage comprises data input, analysis, and interpretation. At this stage, it is important to be aware of and to counter different biases that might affect the conclusions drawn (see Market Insight 3.4). How the data are input depends on the type of data collected. Qualitative data—usually alphanumeric (that is, words and numbers)—is often entered into computer software applications (for example NVivo) as word-processed documents, or as video or sound files, for content analysis. Quantitative data analysis uses statistical analysis packages (for example **IBM SPSS**). In these cases, data are numeric and entered into spreadsheet packages (for example Microsoft Excel) or directly into the statistical computer application. Online questionnaires are

---

Table 3.5 Advantages and disadvantages of online research

Pros of online research	Cons of online research
1 Clients and analysts can see results compiled in real time	1 Demographic profile of online panels can differ from that of the general population
2 Online surveys save time and money compared with face-to-face interviews	2 If questionnaires take longer than 20 minutes to fill in, quality can suffer and they may be uncompleted
3 Consumers welcome surveys that they can fill in when they want to and often need no incentive to do so	3 Poor recruitment and badly managed panels can damage the data
4 A more relaxed environment leads to better quality, honest, and reasoned responses	4 Technical problems, such as browser incompatibility, can mean that panellists fail to complete the survey
5 Panellist background data allows immediate access to key target audiences unrestricted by geography	5 Programming costs are higher than for offline questionnaires
6 Programming facilitates question order; allowing skipping and randomization of questions more easily	6 Survey questionnaires can sometimes be perceived as junk mail

Sources: Miles (2004: 40); Evans and Mathur (2005).

useful because the data are automatically entered into a database, saving time and ensuring a higher level of data quality. If **computer-assisted personal interviewing (CAPI)** or **computer-assisted telephone interviewing (CATI)** methods are used, analysis can occur

Market Insight 3.4
Research Biases: Don't Kid Yourself

Marketing research should be a way of gaining new insights into important business decisions. Sometimes, however, marketers tend to miss out on this opportunity. The reason usually has to do with faults made in setting up the research design, including sampling errors or problems with leading questions—but missing out on insights can also be a consequence of cognitive biases leading the researcher or decision-maker astray.

Consider, for example, confirmation bias. Confirmation bias is a tendency to interpret information in light of previous assumptions rather than to let the data speak for itself. It has its roots in the fact that people tend to deliberately search for confirming evidence that corresponds with their own preconceptions, even when the data says the opposite. When interviewing consumers about a new offering, a researcher might interpret their comments in a positive light, because this kind of interpretation fits better with the researcher's own positive view of the offering. Likewise, a manager might believe that a newly developed offering has a large market potential despite the research showing the opposite.

Another common pitfall is the 'sunk-cost' fallacy. The sunk-cost fallacy is a tendency to continue to invest money in a project because of decisions made in the past, even if its future prospects are not as promising as initially thought. The idea is that you've already spent money on a project and that this money spent should not be wasted by disinvesting in the project. This fallacy can also lead people to dismiss or ignore new insights from marketing research if they happen to go against or undermine a decision that has already been made. Once the decision has been made and a product has been launched, research that highlights problems with the offering might be challenged or dismissed.

To get the most out of marketing research, it is important to be aware of, and actively work against, cognitive biases, such as confirmation bias and the sunk-cost fallacy. Without objective and accurate analyses, any investments in marketing research may be wasted.

Sources: Kahneman (2011); DeMers (2015).

Theory into Practice

When setting up a research project, great care is taken to ensure that the results are unbiased. This is why it is important to be systematic. By clearly specifying the procedures to be followed in each step of the research process and ensuring that that each of these steps is methodologically sound, well documented, and planned in advance, the risk of confirmation bias and sunk-cost fallacy can be reduced.

Related Topics

consumer buying behaviour; information processing, strategic decision-making

1 **Come up with three specific recommendations on how confirmation bias can be avoided.**

2 **Come up with three specific recommendations on how sunk-cost fallacy can be avoided.**

3 **What other cognitive biases do you know of?**

instantaneously as the interviews are undertaken. Computer-assisted web interviewing (CAWI) techniques allow the researcher to read the questions from a computer screen and to directly enter the responses of the respondents. These techniques are also commonly applied using the Internet, allowing the playback of video and audio files.

Because market research methods are aids to managerial decision-making, the information obtained needs to be valid and reliable, because company resources will be deployed on the basis of that information. Validity and reliability are important concepts in quantitative market research. They help researchers to understand the extent to which the data obtained from the study represent reality, or 'truth'. Quantitative research methods rely on the degree to which the data elicited might be reproduced in a later study (that is, reliability) and the extent to which the data generated are free from bias (that is, valid). Validity can be defined as 'a criterion for evaluating measurement scales; it represents the extent to which a scale is a true reflection of the underlying variable or construct it is attempting to measure' (Parasuraman, 1991: 441). One way of measuring validity is simply the researcher exercising their subjective judgement to ascertain whether or not an instrument is measuring what it is supposed to measure (content validity). For example, a question asked about job satisfaction does not necessarily infer loyalty to the organization.

Reliability can be defined as 'a criterion for evaluating measurement scales; it represents how consistent or stable the ratings generated by a scale are' (Parasuraman, 1991: 443). Reliability is affected by concepts of time, analytical bias, and questioning error. We can also distinguish between two types of reliability: internal and external reliability (Bryman, 1989). To determine how reliable the data are, we conduct a study again over two or more time periods to evaluate the consistency of the data. This is known as the test–retest method and it measures external reliability. Another method used involves dividing the responses into two random sets and testing both sets independently using **t-tests** or **z-tests**. This would illustrate internal reliability. The two different sets of results are then correlated. This method is known as split-half reliability testing. These methods are more suited to testing the reliability of rating scales than that of data generated from qualitative research procedures.

The results of a quantitative marketing research project are reliable if we conduct a similar research project within a short time period and the same or similar results are obtained in the second study. For example, if the marketing department of a travel agency chain were to interview 500 of its customers and discover that 25 per cent were in favour of a particular resort (for example a particular Greek island), and then to repeat the study the following year and discover that only 10 per cent of the sample were interested in the same resort, the results of the first study could be said to be unreliable in comparison and the procurement department should not base its purchase of package holidays purely on the previous year's finding.

In qualitative research, concepts of validity and reliability are generally less important, because the data are not used to imply representativeness; rather, qualitative data are more about the generation of ideas and the formulation of hypotheses. Validity can be assured by sending out transcripts to respondents and/or clients for checking, to ensure that what they have said in in-depth interviews or focus groups was properly reproduced for analysis. When the analyst reads the data from a critical perspective to determine whether or not this fits with their expectations, this constitutes what is termed a **face validity** test. Reliability is often achieved by checking that similar statements are made by the range of respondents, across and within the interview transcripts. Interviewees' transcripts are checked to assess whether or not the same respondent, or other respondents, have made the discussion point. Such detailed content analysis tends to be conducted using computer applications (for example NVivo).

Stage 5 Report Preparation and Presentation

The final stage of a research project involves reporting the results and the presentation of the findings of the study to the external or in-house client. The results should be presented free from bias. Marketing research data are of little use unless translated into a format that is meaningful to the manager or client who initially demanded the data. Senior people within the commissioning organization who may or may not have been involved in commissioning the work often attend presentations. Usually, agencies and consultants prepare their reports using a basic pro-forma template.

Market and Advertisement Testing

Marketing research reveals attitudes to a campaign, brand, or some other aspect of the exchange process, whereas market testing, by comparison, measures actual behaviour. There is a difference, because attitudes do not always determine action (see Chapter 2). For example, a consumer may respond very positively to the launch of a new television set in surveys, but family circumstances or lack of funds may mean that they never purchase it. Market testing studies use **test markets** to carry out controlled experiments in specific country regions, showing specific adverts, before exposing the 'new feature' (offering, campaign, distribution, etc.) to a full national, or even international, launch. Another region or the rest of the market may act as the **control group** against which results can be measured. For example, films are often test-screened before release because of the substantial costs of producing the film in the first place.

Marketing research is used to test advertisements (see Market Insight 3.5), whether these are in print, online, or broadcast via radio or television. Research company Kantar Millward Brown International is renowned for this type of research. A variety of methods can be used to test adverts. Typically, quantitative research is undertaken to test customer attitudes before and after exposure to see whether or not the advert has had a positive impact. In addition, research occurring after exposure to the ad tests the extent to which audiences can recognize a particular advert (for example by showing customers a still taken from a television advert, a print advert, or a photo online) or recall an advert without being shown a picture (that is, unaided recall). Qualitative research identifies and tests specific themes that might be used in the adverts, and may also test **storyboards** and **cuts** of adverts (before they are properly produced). More recently, advances in technology allow us to evaluate visual imagery more objectively, without relying on respondents' opinions. For example, technology company 3M offers a 'Visual Attention Service' (3M VAS), which allows users to test communications material to see if specific sections of the communication will be noticed and in what order, using algorithms based on sophisticated eye-tracking technology. Another approach to proposition and marketing communication testing uses facial coding analysis.

Market Insight 3.5
Why Ask?

Over time, many methods have been developed to test ads, ranging from self-reported assessment of recall, liking, and purchase intent, to sophisticated statistical approaches, referred to as **market mix modelling**, to evaluate *ex post* advertising effects. One research company that has been specializing in this area for around 40 years is Kantar Millward Brown, which boasts the industry's largest advertising database to provide contextual comparisons for advertising performance.

The past decade has experienced an explosion of research in neuroscience and the use of multiple neurophysiological methods to study advertising. This growth is the result of a combination of technological advances making functional magnetic resonance imaging (fMRI), electroencephalography (EEG), eye-tracking, and other neurophysiological tools more accessible and less costly. Hollywood studios have long been using neuromarketing techniques via companies such as Sands Research to test trailers to help to market their films.

A recent study by a group of American researchers developed an experimental protocol to compare how well six commonly used methods predict real-world advertising success in terms of advertising elasticity. The methods used were as follows:

- traditional self-reports—to capture conscious reactions, typically by asking direct questions related to the ad and brand (for example ad liking, brand attitude, purchase intention);

- implicit measures—to capture the unconscious reaction, typically by using response latencies

(for example how long it takes to pair brands with positive and negative words);

- eye-tracking—to measure participants' attention when viewing ads (for example which information, in what order, for how long);

- biometrics—to measure the physiological or automatic responses to an external stimulus (for example heart rate, breathing, skin conductance);

- EEG—to measure variations in electrical signals of cortical brain regions when viewing ads and brands; and

- fMRI—to directly measure exogenous attention and endogenous attention based on tracking localized changes in blood oxygenation during cognitive tasks.

The findings show that traditional self-reported advertising measures explain the most variance in advertising elasticities. Thus they support more than 50 years of advertising research demonstrating that asking questions regarding measures such as purchase intent are indeed good predictors of advertising success. But the findings also show that fMRI measures can help to explain advertising elasticities beyond these baseline traditional measures. For practitioners, this research proves that current methods are reliable, but that measuring biological reactions, rather than relying on asking questions, can give some additional insights.

Sources: Randall (2011); Stipp (2015); Venkatraman et al. (2015).

Theory into Practice

Traditional market research focuses on asking questions. There is often, however, a discrepancy between what consumers say and what they do. This, in turn, has led the marketing research industry to adapt new innovative methodologies that do not rely on consumers' answers to questions, but rather on their actual biological reactions. Traditional advertising measures based on asking questions about consumer reactions to ads are often valid, but you can learn even more about what advertising works by adding techniques such as fMRI.

Market Insight 3.5
continued

Related Topics

advertising effectiveness; marketing communications; consumer reactions; neuromarketing

1 **How are implicit measures, eye-tracking, biometrics, EEG, and fMRI different from traditional advertising tracking methods?**

2 **Why could it be important to collect participants' unconscious responses in**

research on proposition and marketing communication testing?

3 **Can you think of other circumstances in which implicit measures, eye-tracking, biometrics, EEG, and fMRI analysis would be useful for marketers?**

Big Data and Marketing Analytics

Big data is the systematic gathering and interpretation of high-volume, high-velocity, and/or high-variety information using cost-effective innovative forms of information processing to enable enhanced insight, decision-making, and process automation. It thus refers to a more comprehensive set of data than that traditionally used to provide marketing information and customer insights.

The notion of 'big' refers primarily to the volume, velocity, and variety of data used (McAfee and Brynjolfsson, 2012; Wedel and Kannan, 2016). 'Volume' denotes the sheer amount of information used. 'Velocity' refers to the fact that data is recorded in real time. For example, using location data from smartphones, Google is able to offer up-to-date information about travelling times adjusted for traffic. 'Variety' denotes that big data analytics combines data from several different sources. For example, combining customer databases with social media and mobile data can give a more comprehensive understanding of shopper behaviours than that which was possible before.

With increasing digitization of the everyday life of business and consumers, the availability of data is growing rapidly (see Research Insight 3.3). The different sources employed in big data analysis can be divided into five categories: public data; private data; data exhaust; community data; and self-quantification data (George, Haas, and Pentland, 2014):

- *Public data* refers to the information held by governments or local communities (for example with regard to incomes, transportation, or energy use) that is accessed under certain restrictions to guard individual privacy.

- *Private data* refers to the data held by private organizations or individuals and which cannot readily be imputed from public sources. Examples are customer database information or browsing behaviours online.

- *Data exhaust* refers to data that is passively collected—that is, non-core data with limited or zero value to the original data-collection partner. When individuals adopt and use new technologies (for example smartphones), they generate ambient data as by-products of their everyday activities. These data can be recombined with other data sources to create new insights. Another source of data exhaust is information-seeking behaviour, such as online searches and call centre calls, which can be used to infer people's needs, desires, or intentions.

■ *Community data* refers to distilled unstructured data, for example consumer reviews on products or liking in social media, which is combined into dynamic networks that capture social trends.

■ *Self-quantification data* is revealed when individuals use technology to quantify their personal actions and behaviours, for example through wristbands that monitor exercise and movement.

Research Insight 3.3

To take your learning further, you might wish to read this influential paper:

Wedel, M., and Kannan, P.K. (2016). Marketing analytics for data-rich environments. *Journal of Marketing*, 80(6), 97–121.

This article introduces a theoretical framework for when and how big data can lead to sustainable competitive advantage. More specifically, it discusses how three resources—physical, human, and organizational capital—moderate the processes of (a) collecting and storing evidence of consumer activity as big data, (2) extracting consumer insight from big data, and (c) utilizing consumer insight to enhance dynamic or adaptive capabilities.

 Visit the **online resources** to read the abstract and access the full paper.

How many steps you've done might mean as much to marketers as it does to you
Source: © Dedi Grigoroiu/Shutterstock.com.

Marketing Research and Ethics

Marketing research should be carried out in an objective, unobtrusive, and honest manner. Researchers are also concerned about the public's increasing unwillingness to participate in marketing research and the problem of recruiting suitable interviewers. The apathy among interviewees is probably associated with the growing amount of research conducted, particularly through intrusive telephone interviewing, which is on the rise, and door-to-door survey interviewing, which is in decline. Marketing research is increasingly conducted online, creating its own set of ethical concerns. For example, how can we verify that someone online is who they say they are? Is it acceptable to observe and analyse customer blogs and social networking site conversations? In social media research, ethical problems include the need to be open and transparent when conducting research within communities and anonymizing and paraphrasing comments (since verbatim comments can often be tracked back to a particular user in online research). However, the ethics of conducting social media research are still in development. Consequently, key organizations such as ESOMAR and the MRS are still devising clear policies on the topic.

Marketing research neither attempts to induce sales nor attempts to influence customer attitudes, intentions, or behaviours. The key principles in the MRS code of conduct are as follows (MRS, 2014: 3):

1. Researchers shall ensure that participation in their activities is based on voluntary informed consent.

2. Researchers shall be straightforward and honest in all their professional and business relationships.

3. Researchers shall be transparent as to the subject and purpose of data collection.

4. Researchers shall respect the confidentiality of information collected in their professional activities.

5. Researchers shall respect the rights and well-being of all individuals.

6. Researchers shall ensure that participants are not harmed or adversely affected by their professional activities.

7. Researchers shall balance the needs of individuals, clients, and their professional activities.

8. Researchers shall exercise independent professional judgement in the design, conduct and reporting of their professional activities.

9. Researchers shall ensure that their professional activities are conducted by persons with appropriate training, qualifications and experience.

10. Researchers shall protect the reputation and integrity of the profession.

Research dealing with personal data in European countries is also subject to the EU General Data Protection Regulation (GDPR). Under the GDPR, 'personal data' is defined as information relating to an identified or identifiable natural person. The aim of the GDPR is to protect consumers from breaches of their privacy by giving them control over their personal data. An essential principle under the GDPR is 'data protection by design and by default' (European Commission, 2015)—that is, it sets out to incentivize companies to protect personal data to innovate and develop new ideas, methods, and technologies for security and protection of personal data. This regulation applies to all companies processing the personal data of data subjects residing within the European Union, meaning that large corporations such as Facebook or Google must follow the Regulation when offering goods or services to EU citizens regardless of whether their actual data processing takes place within the EU or not. The GDPR also includes a set of sanctions for organizations that do not follow the rules, ranging from a warning to fines of up to €20 million or 4 per cent of the business's annual worldwide turnover.

 Visit the **online resources** to find out more about what market researchers must do to comply with the GDPR.

International Marketing Research

Marketing researchers find it challenging to understand how culture operates in international markets and how it affects research design. Complexity in the international business environment makes international marketing research more difficult because it affects the research process and design. Key decisions include whether to customize the research to each of the separate countries in a study using differing scales, sampling methods, and sizes, or to try to use a single method for all countries, adopting an international **sampling frame**. In many ways, this debate mirrors the standardization–customization dilemma common in international marketing generally (see Chapter 7).

International researchers try to ensure that comparable data are collected despite differences in sampling frames, technological developments, availability of interviewers, and the acceptability of public questioning. Western approaches to marketing research, data collection, and culture might be inappropriate in some research environments because of variations in economic development and consumption patterns. How comparable are the data related to the consumption of Burger King's offerings collected through personal interviews in the United Arab Emirates (UAE), telephone interviews in France, and shopping mall intercept questionnaires in Sweden? Might an online panel across all countries be used instead? Ensuring comparability of data in research studies of multiple markets is not simple: concepts could be regarded differently; the same offerings could have different functions; language may be used differently, even within a country; offerings might be measured differently; the sample frames might be different; and the data collection methods adopted might differ because of variations in infrastructure.

Table 3.6 outlines three types of equivalence: **conceptual equivalence**; **functional equivalence**; and **translation equivalence**. All three types of equivalence impact on the semantics (that is, meaning) of words used in different countries, for example in developing the wording for questionnaires or in focus groups. Getting the language right is important because it affects how respondents perceive the questions and structure their answers.

When designing international research programmes, we need to consider how the meaning of common words may be different and how the data should be collected. Different cultures have different ways of measuring concepts. Populations also live their lives differently, meaning that it may be necessary to collect the same or similar data in a different way. Table 3.7 outlines how measurement, sampling, and data collection equivalence impacts on international research.

Table 3.6 Types of semantic equivalence in international marketing research		
Type of equivalence	**Explanation**	**Example**
Conceptual equivalence	Exists when interpretation of behaviour, or objects, is similar across countries	Conceptual equivalence should be considered when defining the research problem, in wording the questionnaire, and determining the sample unit. For example, there would be less need to investigate 'brand loyalty' in a country in which competition is restricted and product choice is limited.
Functional equivalence	Relates to whether a concept has a similar function in different countries	Using a bicycle in India, where it might be used for transport to and from work, or France, where it might be used for shopping, is a different concept from purchasing a bike in Norway, where it might be used for mountain biking. Functional differences can be determined using focus groups before finalizing the research design by ensuring that the constructs used in the research measure what they are supposed to measure.
Translation equivalence	An important aspect of the international research process, because words in some languages have no real equivalents in others	The meaning associated with different words is important in questionnaire design because words can connote a different meaning from that intended when directly translated into another language. To avoid translation errors of these kinds, the researcher can adopt one of the following two methods: ■ *back translation*—whereby a translator fluent in the language in which the questionnaire is to be translated is used and then another translator, whose native language is the original language, is used to translate back again—identifying and resolving differences in wording; or ■ *parallel translation*—a questionnaire is translated by two or more translators, fluent in both the languages into and from which the questionnaire is to be translated, until they agree upon a final version.

Table 3.7 Types of measurement and data collection equivalence

Type of equivalence	Explanation	Example
Measurement equivalence	The extent to which measurement scales are comparable across countries	Surveys conducted in the United States may use imperial systems of measurement, while those conducted in Europe will use the metric system. Clothing sizes adopt different measurement systems in Europe, North America, and Southeast Asia. Multi-item scales present challenges for international researchers because dissatisfaction might not be expressed in the same way in two or more countries. (Some cultures are more open in expressing opinions or describing their behaviour than others.)
Sampling equivalence	The extent to which sampling criteria are comparable across countries	The respondent profile for the same survey could vary from country to country. For example, different classification systems are in existence for censorship of films shown in the cinema in France compared with the UK.
Data collection equivalence	The extent to which data collection methods are comparable across countries	Typically, data collection methods include: email or mail; by telephone or computer-assisted telephone interviewing (CATI); and personally or computer-assisted personal interviewing (CAPI). ■ *Mail or email*—Used more where literacy or Internet access is high and where the mail or email system operates efficiently. Sampling frames are compiled from electoral registers, although it is now illegal in some countries to use these lists. European survey respondents can be targeted efficiently and accurately because international sampling frames do exist. ■ *Telephone/CATI*—In many countries, telephone penetration may be limited and CATI software, using random digit dialling, may be more limited still. ■ *Personal interviews/CAPI*—Used most widely in European countries favouring the door-to-door and shopping mall intercept variants. Shopping mall intercept interviews are not appropriate in Arab countries, where women must not be approached in the street. Here, comparability is achieved using door-to-door interviews. In countries in which it is rude to openly disagree with someone (e.g., China), it is best to use in-depth interviews.

As we can see in Table 3.7, achieving comparability of data when conducting international surveys is difficult. Usually, the more countries included in an international study, the more likely it is that errors will be introduced, and that the results and findings will be inaccurate and liable to misinterpretation. International research requires local and international input. Therefore the extent to which one can internationalize certain operations of the research process depends on the objectives of the research.

With international projects, the key decision is to determine how much to centralize and how much to delegate work to local agencies. There is, throughout this process, ample opportunity for misunderstanding, errors, and lack of cultural sensitivity. To proceed effectively, the central agency should identify a number of trusted local market research providers on a variety of continents. Typically, an international agency will have a network of trusted affiliates who are monitored on a continual basis.

 # Chapter Summary

To consolidate your learning, the key points from this chapter are summarized here:

■ **Define the terms 'market research', 'marketing research', and 'customer insight'.**

Market research is research undertaken about markets (for example customers, channels, and competitors), whilst marketing research is research undertaken to understand the efficacy of marketing activities (for example pricing, supply chain management policies). Customer insight derives from knowledge about customers, which can be turned into an organizational strength.

■ **Describe the customer insight process and the role of marketing research within it.**

Understanding customers is at the core of the marketing. Customer insight is typically derived from fusing knowledge generated from a range of sources, including industry reports, sales force data, competitive intelligence, CRM data, employee feedback, social media analysis data, and managerial intuition. A customer insight is of value if it is rare, difficult to imitate, and of potential use in formulating management decisions.

■ **Explain the role of marketing research and list the range of possible research approaches.**

Marketing research plays an important role in the decision-making process and contributes through ad hoc studies, as well as continuous data collection, through industry reports, and from secondary data sources, as well as through competitive intelligence either commissioned through agencies or conducted internally, with data gathered informally through sales forces, customers, and suppliers. What methodology is used depends on the type of research problem (exploratory, descriptive, causal); the availability of data (primary or secondary sources); and the type of insight sought (qualitative or quantitative).

■ **Define the term 'big data' and describe its role in marketing.**

Big data can be defined as the systematic gathering and interpretation of high-volume, high-velocity, and/or high-variety information using cost-effective innovative forms of information processing to enable enhanced insight, decision-making, and process automation. Big data thus refers to a more comprehensive set of data than that traditionally used to provide marketing information and customer insights.

■ **Discuss the importance of ethics and of the adoption of a code of conduct in marketing research.**

Ethics is an important consideration in marketing research because consumers and customers either provide personal information about themselves or personal information is collected from them. Their privacy needs to be protected through observance of a professional code of ethics and the relevant laws in the country in which the research is conducted.

 Review Questions

1 How do we define 'market research'?
2 How do we define 'marketing research'?
3 How do we define 'customer insight'?
4 What is 'big data'?
5 What are the different types of marketing research that can be conducted?
6 Why is a marketing research code of conduct important?
7 What is a marketing information system and how is it used in the customer insight process?
8 What is the concept of equivalence in relation to obtaining comparable data from different countries?
9 How are the different aspects of the research process affected by differences in equivalence between countries?

 Discussion Questions

1 Having read Case Insight 3.1, how would you advise Ipsos MORI to design a research programme for Unilever that will provide insights into cultural cleaning rituals and practices in a diverse set of countries, embed that knowledge inside the firm, and help the firm to develop and test innovation ideas based on those insights?

2 Telefónica, the telecommunications company, wants to conduct a market research study aimed particularly at discovering what market segments exist across Europe, and how customers and potential customers view its brand. Advise Telefónica as follows:

A Write a market research question and a number of sub-questions for the study.
B How would you go about selecting the particular countries in which to conduct the fieldwork?
C What process would you use when conducting the fieldwork for this multicountry study?

3 What type of research (that is, causal, descriptive, or exploratory) should be commissioned in the following contexts? Explain your answers.

A The management of UAE airline Etihad wants to measure passenger satisfaction with the flight experience.
B Nintendo wants new ideas for online games for a youth audience.
C Spanish fashion retailer Zara wants to know what levels of customer service are offered at its flagship stores.
D Procter & Gamble, maker of Ariel detergent, wants to test a new packaging design for six months to see if it is more effective than the existing version. Fifty supermarkets have been selected from one key P&G account. In 25 of them, the new design is to be used; in the other 25, the existing version.

4 You've recently won the research contract to evaluate customer satisfaction for Pret A Manger, the food retail chain specializing in sandwiches, soups, and coffee. Your key account manager wants to increase customer satisfaction further using the knowledge gained from the study to identify potential new food offerings. Suggest a suitable research design to accomplish the following. (*Hint*: You can advise more than one type of study.)

   A To collect information about levels of customer satisfaction
   B To decide what new food offerings customers might like to see

In addition, your account manager asks you to outline what secondary data you can find in the area, detailing market shares, market structure, and other industry information, identifying specific secondary data sources and reports.

Visit the online resources and complete the Multiple-Choice Questions to assess your knowledge of Chapter 3.

Glossary

big data the systematic gathering and interpretation of high-volume, high-velocity, and/or high-variety information using cost-effective innovative forms of information processing to enable enhanced insight, decision-making, and process automation.

causal research a technique used to investigate the relational link between two or more variables by manipulating the independent variable(s) to see the effect on the dependent variable(s) and then comparing effects with a control group for which no such manipulation takes place.

competitive intelligence the organized, professional, systematic collection of information, typically through informal mechanisms, used for the achievement of strategic and tactical organizational goals.

computer-assisted personal interviewing (CAPI) an approach to personal interviewing using a handheld computer or laptop to display questions and record the respondents' answers.

computer-assisted telephone interviewing (CATI) an approach to telephone interviewing using a laptop or desktop computer to display the questions to the interviewer, who reads them out and records the respondent's answers.

computer-assisted web interviewing (CAWI) an approach to online interviewing in which the respondent uses a laptop or desktop computer to access questions in a set location to which the respondent must go; questions are generated automatically based on the respondent's answers.

conceptual equivalence the degree to which interpretation of behaviour, or objects, is similar across countries.

control group a sample group used in causal research that is not subjected to manipulation of some sort. *See* **causal research**

cuts initial productions of ads in cartoon format, complete with dialogue, prepared before the full ads are produced, filmed, and edited.

descriptive research a research technique used to test and confirm hypotheses developed from a management problem.

desk research (also known as secondary research) a technique used to collect data that has previously been collected for a purpose other than the current research situation.

exploratory research a research technique used to generate ideas to develop hypotheses based around a management problem.

face validity the use of the researcher's or expert's subjective judgement to determine whether an instrument is measuring what it is designed to measure.

full-service agency an advertising agency that provides its clients with a full range of services, including strategy and planning, designing the advertisements, and buying the media.

functional equivalence relates to whether or not a concept has the same function in different countries.

IBM SPSS (standing for Statistical Package for the Social Sciences) a software package used for statistical analysis marketed by SPSS, a company owned by IBM.

management problem a statement that outlines a situation an organization faces that requires further investigation and subsequent organizational action.

market mix modelling a research process that uses multiple regression analysis based on customer survey data to ascertain the relative contributions of different promotional techniques on a customer-based dependent variable (for example awareness, intention to buy).

marketing research the design, collection, analysis, and interpretation of data collected for the purpose of aiding marketing decision-making.

net promoter score a system for measuring the loyalty of customer relationships by determining the extent to which customers are prepared to advocate for an organization.

pre-code in surveys, to speed up data processing, answers to questions that are assigned a unique code (for example male = 1, female = 2, non-binary = 3, prefer not to say = 4) so that they can easily be analysed.

primary research a technique used to collect data for the first time specifically tailored to the current research problem.

probability sampling a sampling method in which the probability of selection of the sample elements from the population is known, typical examples including simple random sampling, stratified random sampling, and cluster sampling.

qualitative research a type of exploratory research using small samples and unstructured data collection procedures, designed to identify hypotheses, possibly for later testing in quantitative research, popular examples including in-depth interviews, focus groups, and projective techniques.

quantitative research research designed to provide responses to predetermined standardized questions from a large number of respondents and involving the statistical analysis of the responses.

reliability the degree to which the data elicited in a study are replicated in a repeat study.

research brief a formal document prepared by the client organization and submitted to either an external market research provider (for example a market research agency or consultant) or an internal research provider (for example a marketing research department) outlining a statement of the management problem and the perceived research needs of the organization.

research proposal a formal document prepared by an agency, consultant, or in-house marketing research manager and submitted to the client to outline what procedures will be used to collect the necessary information, including timescales and costs.

sampling frame a list of population members from among whom a sample is generated, for example telephone directories, membership lists.

secondary research *See* **desk research**

storyboard outline of the story that an ad will follow, showing key themes, characters, and messages, prepared before the ad is made.

test markets regions within a country used to test the effects of the launch of a new product or service, typically with regional advertising to promote the service, as well as pre- and post-advertising market research to measure promotional effectiveness.

translation equivalence the degree to which the meaning of one language is represented in another after translation.

t-test a statistical test of difference used for small randomly selected samples with a size of less than 30.

validity the ability of a measurement instrument to measure exactly the construct it is attempting to measure.

z-test a statistical test of difference used for large randomly selected samples with a size of 30 or more.

References

AMA (American Marketing Association) (2015). About AMA: marketing research. Retrieve from: https://www.ama.org/AboutAMA/Pages/Definition-of-Marketing.aspx (accessed 13 October 2018).

AMA (American Marketing Association) (2016). Common language marketing dictionary: marketing analytics. Retrieve from: http://marketing-dictionary.org/m/marketing-analytics/ (accessed 13 October 2018).

Ashill, N.J., and Jobber, D. (2001). Defining the information needs of senior marketing executives: an exploratory study. *Qualitative Market Research*, 4(1), 52–60.

Baines, P., and Chansarkar, B. (2002). *Introducing Marketing Research*. Chichester: John Wiley.

Barwise, P., and Meehan, S. (2011). Customer insights that matter. *Journal of Advertising Research*, 51(2), 342–4.

Bryman, A. (1989). *Research Methods and Organization Studies*. London: Unwin Hyman.

Cater, B., and Zabkar, V. (2009). Antecedents and consequences of commitment in marketing research services: the client's perspective. *Industrial Marketing Management*, 38(7), 785–97.

Cowan, D. (2008). Forum: creating customer insight. *International Journal of Market Research*, 50(6), 719–29.

DeMers, J. (2015). 5 cognitive biases to avoid in your market research, *Forbes*. Retrieve from: https://www.forbes.com/sites/jaysondemers/2015/03/26/5-cognitive-biases-to-avoid-in-your-market-research/2/#4ef7501515a3 (accessed 13 October 2018).

ESOMAR (2015). *Global Market Research Report 2015: An ESOMAR Industry Report*. Retrieve from: https://www.esomar.org/uploads/public/publications-store/reports/global-market-research-2015/ESOMAR-GMR2015_Preview.pdf (accessed 13 October 2018).

ESOMAR (2016). *ICC/ESOMAR International Code on Market, Opinion and Social Research and Data Analytics*. Retrieve from: https://www.esomar.org/uploads/public/knowledge-and-standards/codes-and-guidelines/ESOMAR_ICC-ESOMAR_Code_English.pdf (accessed 13 October 2018).

European Commission (2015). Fact sheet: questions and answers—data protection reform, 21 December. Retrieve from: http://europa.eu/rapid/press-release_MEMO-15-6385_en.htm (accessed 13 October 2018).

Evans, J.R., and Mathur, A. (2005). The value of online surveys. *Internet Research*, 15(2), 195–219.

George, G., Haas, M., and Pentland, A. (2014). From the editors: big data and management. *Academy of Management Journal*, 57(2), 321–6.

Kahneman, D. (2011). *Thinking Fast and Slow*. New York: Ferrar, Straus & Giroux.

Malhotra, N.K. (2010). *Marketing Research: An Applied Orientation* (6th edn). Upper Saddle River, NJ: Pearson.

McAfee, A., and Brynjolfsson, E (2012). Big data: the management revolution. *Harvard Business Review*, October. Retrieve from: https://hbr.org/2012/10/big-data-the-management-revolution (accessed 13 October 2018).

Miles, L. (2004). Online, on tap. *Marketing*, 16 June, 39–40.

Moorman, C. (2018). *CMO Survey Report: Highlights and Insights Report*, February. Retrieve from: https://cmosurvey.org/wp-content/uploads/sites/15/2018/02/The_CMO_Survey-Highlights_and_Insights_Report-Feb-2018.pdf (accessed 13 October 2018).

MRS (Market Research Society) (2014). *Code of Conduct*. Retrieve from: https://www.mrs.org.uk/pdf/mrs%20code%20of%20conduct%202014.pdf (accessed 13 October 2018).

Murphy, L.F. (2018). *The Greenbook Research Industry Trends (GRIT) Report*. Retrieve from: https://www.greenbook.org/grit/ (accessed 13 October 2018).

Parasuraman, A. (1991). *Marketing Research* (2nd edn). Wokingham: Addison-Wesley.

Press, G. (2014). 12 big data definitions: what's yours? *Forbes*, 3 September. Retrieve from: https://www.forbes.com/sites/gilpress/2014/09/03/12-big-data-definitions-whats-yours/#6923e9821a97 (accessed 13 October 2018).

Randall, K. (2011). Rise of neurocinema: how Hollywood studios harness your brainwaves to win Oscars. *The Fast Company*, 25 February. Retrieve from: https://www.fastcompany.com/1731055/rise-neurocinema-how-hollywood-studios-harness-your-brainwaves-win-oscars (accessed 13 October 2018).

Said, E., Macdonald, E.K, Wilson, H.N., and Marcos, J. (2015). How organisations generate and use customer insight. *Journal of Marketing Management*, 31(9–10), 1158–79.

Steward, D.W., and Shamdasani, P. (2017). Online focus group. *Journal of Advertising*, 46(1), 48–60.

Stipp, H. (2015). Speaker's box: the evolution of neuromarketing research—from novelty to mainstream. *Journal of Advertising Research*, 55(2), 120–2.

Tirunillai, S., and Tellis, G. (2014). Mining marketing meaning from online chatter: strategic brand analysis of big data using latent Dirichlet allocation. *Journal of Marketing Research*, 51(4), 463–79.

Van Den Driest, F., Sthanunathan, S., and Weed, K. (2016). Building an insights engine. *Harvard Business Review*, 94(9), 64–74.

Venkatraman, V., Dimoka, A., Pavlou, P.A., Khoi Vo, Hampton, W., Bollinger, B., Hershfield, H.E., Ishihara, M., and Winer, R.S. (2015). Predicting advertising success beyond traditional measures: new insights from neurophysiological methods and market response modeling. *Journal of Marketing Research*, 52(4), 436–52.

Wedel, M., and Kannan, P.K. (2016). Marketing analytics for data-rich environments. *Journal of Marketing*, 80(6), 97–121.

Part 2

Marketing Management and Strategy

Chapter 4
The Marketing Environment

Learning Outcomes

After reading this chapter, you will be able to:

▸ Identify and define the three core areas of the marketing environment

▸ Describe the key characteristics associated with the marketing environment

▸ Explain PESTLE analysis and show how it is used to understand the external environment

▸ Explain the environmental scanning process

▸ Analyse the performance environment using the Porter's Five Forces industry analysis model

▸ Analyse an organization's product/service portfolio to aid resource planning

Case Insight 4.1
P. Rigas Packaging
Material SA

Market Insight 4.1
Changing Politics; Changing Borders: What Should Companies Do?

Market Insight 4.2
Health Issues Slim Down Product Sales

Market Insight 4.3
L'Oréal Advances Beauty through Technology

Market Insight 4.4
Tuenti: To Be or Not to Be?

Case Insight 4.1
P. Rigas Packaging Material SA

P. Rigas Packaging Material SA is one of the leading wholesale companies in the Greek agricultural, livestock, and industrial packaging industry, with more than 25 years of experience. We speak to Achilleas Rigas, chief executive officer (CEO) and chair of the board of directors, to find out how the company conducts its market scanning, aiming to survive in the very difficult Greek economic environment.

P. Rigas imports its products from a large network of suppliers in Europe, Asia, and Africa, and provides its products to a national network of more than 4,000 customers, ranging from the most northern point of Greece to the smallest island in the south. The Greek sovereign debt crisis, which began in 2009, has resulted in increased unemployment and a significant decline in household disposable income. Businesses have been hit in a number of ways, including by increased taxation, increased liquidity needs, increases in non-value-adding procedures (that is, increased bureaucracy as a result of compliance and bank capital controls), and unavailability of corporate bank loans. Consequently, insecurity has increased and trust in relationships between corporate partners is unstable, largely because of fears of credit defaults, insolvency, and non-payment of invoices.

In this environment, information from the external environment is imperative. P. Rigas generates market insight from word-of-mouth information via our nationwide team of salespeople, who visit our clients on a regular basis. We also have a network of partners in external credit, accounting, legal and transportation services, and our suppliers, who feed us information on the marketplace and our clients. Information from the local and national electronic and printed press supplements this, particularly to trigger ideas for our research programmes. We participate in at least one national/international fair in Greece itself and five or six international fairs outside Greece each year, which all provide us with valuable market intelligence.

There have been a number of important external changes in the marketplace. For instance, our international suppliers are demanding faster payment over shorter credit periods, because they no longer see Greek firms as trustworthy partners. European Union (EU) legislation on agricultural support has changed considerably and our end customers have been affected. As a result of taxation changes and capital controls, the Greek construction industry has contracted, which has in turn reduced our business with this sector. Because of legal changes, such as capital controls and the EU's General Data Protection Directive (GDPR), our working processes have had to change and this has raised our administration costs. In the ecological environment, an increase in campaigning against the use of plastic packaging materials has affected us. There has been a lot of political instability and the threat of Greek exit from the euro. During this period, some of our customers went out of business. The current management team were put in place in 2013, after the sad and sudden loss of our founder and CEO, Panagiotis Rigas.

To keep abreast of the many changes that were hitting us, we developed a yearly strategic plan and worst-case scenario strategic planning processes. These are useful up to a point. However, the business environment that we work within is so dynamic that such planning is often quickly obsolete. So, at times, we have to react to market changes and discard our strategic planning! Also, quite often, the changes in the environment that affect the business are so unpredictable that we were not able to imagine them and incorporate them into our planning. Hence we redefine the strategy formally in a mid-year review and we audit the implementation of our strategy via **key performance indicators (KPIs)** on a monthly basis.

Case Insight 4.1
continued

The question for P. Rigas was: how could it grow its sales and profits, reduce its bank loans, and still increase the size of its customer base in such a difficult trading environment?

 Visit the online resources to watch a video interview with Achilleas Rigas in which he explains what P. Rigas did.

Introduction

Have you ever wondered how organizations adapt to the changing business environment? How do companies keep up with the many changes that occur in politics, markets, and economics? What processes do they use to try to anticipate changes in technologies? We consider these and other questions in this chapter.

The operating environment for all organizations—whether that be commercial, charitable, governmental, or public sector more generally—is never static and seldom entirely predictable, and can therefore profoundly affect a company's course of action. We examine the nature of the marketing environment, determine environment-related issues, and provide a context for developing marketing strategies that are explored in Chapter 5.

Now, consider the degree to which an organization can influence the various environmental forces acting on it. The *external* environment, for example, consists of political, social, and technological influences, and organizations often have very limited influence on these. The *performance* environment consists of competitors, suppliers, and indirect service providers who shape the way and extent to which organizations achieve their objectives. Here, organizations have a much stronger level of influence. The *internal* environment concerns the resources, processes, and policies with which an organization manages to achieve its goals. An organization can influence these elements directly. Each of these three marketing environments is discussed in this chapter.

By understanding the nature and trends of the elements that make up these three interlocking environments, an organization can assert varying degrees of control, allocate scarce resources more efficiently, and move closer to achieving its goals and overall performance outcomes, in both the short term and the longer term.

Understanding the External Environment

The external environment can pose serious challenges to an organization for two reasons. First, some elements of the external environment, while not having an immediate impact on the performance of an organization, can radically change market conditions in the longer term (see Research Insight 4.1 for further discussion of this point). Second, even when managers are clear that the factors in the external environment are important, it is often not possible to control them in any way (see Market Insight 4.1 for recent examples of political events that increase environmental risks). This suggests that companies need to monitor the external environment to assess the level of risk associated with their business activities.

Research Insight 4.1

To take your learning further, you might wish to read this influential paper:

Levitt, T. (1960). Marketing myopia. *Harvard Business Review*, 38(4), 45–56.

This is perhaps the most famous and celebrated article ever written on marketing. It won the author the McKinsey Award. It has twice been reprinted in the *Harvard Business Review*. The central thesis of the article—as true today as it was in 1960—is that companies must monitor change in the external environment and keep abreast of their customers' needs or else risk decline. Levitt asks fundamental questions about the strategic orientation of a business and stresses the importance of always understanding what business a company is really in (see also Market Insight 4.4, later in the chapter, for an example of a firm's failure to appreciate this insight). For example, many oil companies today consider themselves to be energy companies—yet they still invest most of their resources in oil. This is very risky because it opens them to new competitors focusing specifically on alternative energies. Companies always need to monitor the environment to understand what market they are competing in.

  Visit the online resources to read the abstract and access the full paper.

To make sense of the external environment, we use the well-known acronym **PESTLE**. This is the easiest and one of the most popular frameworks for examining the external environment, standing for the *political*, *economic*, *socio-cultural*, *technological*, *legal*, and *ecological* environments, as shown in Figure 4.1.

Figure 4.1
The external marketing environment

Market Insight 4.1
Changing Politics; Changing Borders: What Should Companies Do?

In the past few years, Europeans have witnessed an increase in the number of referendums. Crucial votes have been held for different reasons in Greece, Italy, Spain, and the UK. In June 2016, the referendum on Britain's exit from the EU—commonly known as Brexit—saw 51.9 per cent of voters (on a 72 per cent turnout) decide that leaving the EU was the right solution for the country. In October 2017, the Catalan government offered a referendum on whether Catalonia should become independent. Voters overwhelmingly supported Catalonia's independence (albeit on a turnout of about 40 per cent). The vote, however, was considered illegal by the Spanish government because it was inadmissible according to the Spanish Constitution. This created a major political and social crisis in the region.

Remain supporters march to Parliament Square, London, to show their support for the EU in the wake of Brexit

Source: © Daniel Leal-Olivas/AP/Shutterstock.com.

The binary nature of these consultations led to profound divisions in both Spain and the UK. There are two sides who campaign to frame the vote. In such contexts, what should companies do? Some of them pick a side; others do not. For example, EasyJet and Shell signed a letter supporting the motion that the UK should stay in the EU because jobs would otherwise be threatened and investment would be deterred. Tesco, Sainsbury's, and Barclays refused to sign that same letter, claiming that the

decision was up to the British people. Unilever warned its employees that Brexit could have a negative economic impact in the form of new import duties and price increases for customers. Then, in the aftermath of the referendum, Tesco and Unilever entered in a dispute because Unilever suspended supply of products such as Marmite and the Ben & Jerry's ice cream, demanding a price rise given increasing costs and the falling value of the pound. Although the dispute was ultimately settled, it led to negative media coverage for Unilever that was depicted in some newspapers as the company taking advantage of the situation for its own profit and failing to show support for the democratic decision taken by the British electorate. Tesco, by contrast, was depicted as protecting consumers by avoiding price increases. In addition, the government tried to pressure companies to support its stance in the ongoing negotiations with the EU, in an attempt to increase its chances of getting a good deal.

In the case of Catalonia, the situation has been even more tense because of the challenge to the legality of the vote. Early on, the Barcelona football club (FC) positioned itself in favour of the independence referendum. This did not come as a surprise given that being a *culé* (a fan of FC Barcelona) is almost a given for Catalan separatists and pro-independence chants have been often heard in the Camp Nou stadium. However, such positioning creates friction and consumer blogs can be found that incite consumers to buy from or boycott companies depending on which side they have picked. Within days after the referendum was held and in expectation of a possible unilateral independence declaration from the Catalan government, companies such as La Caixa and Banc Sabadell, two of the biggest Spanish banks, moved their corporate headquarters outside of Catalonia.

Sources: Papadimas and Maltezou (2015); Butler and Kollewe (2016); Glanfield (2016); Sheffield (2016); Anon. (2017); Mason (2017).

Market Insight 4.1
continued

Theory into Practice

This market insight described recent examples of changing political and social environments and companies' respective positioning and reaction. Companies are social agents and their corporate reputation depends on various factors, including how they position themselves in such situations.

Furthermore, it is important to consider the potential impact of such positioning on different stakeholders, including employees, customers, the local community, political parties, competitors, and financial and media publics.

Related Topics

external environment; consumer behaviour; stakeholder management; corporate reputation

1 Should companies remain 'neutral' in changing political environments, such as those described above, or should they clearly position themselves? Why, or why not?

2 How should companies manage their stakeholders in a highly polarized political and social environment?

3 How do you think consumers react to companies' taking a stance on political matters? Does it affect companies in the short and long terms?

This market insight was kindly contributed by Dr Eleni Papaoikonomou, Rovira and Virgili University, Tarragona, Spain.

The Political Environment

The **political environment** relates to the interaction between business, society, and government. The legal environment, examined in more detail below, is often also linked to the political environment because political institutions such as parliaments and governments are typically responsible for debating and establishing the laws and regulations associated with consumers and business practices. An understanding of the political environment therefore helps us to evaluate the conditions that lead to the development of laws and their enactment. Political environmental analysis is important because companies can detect signals concerning potential legal and regulatory changes in their industries and thus have a chance to impede, influence, and alter that legislation.

Although the political environment is uncontrollable in many ways, there are circumstances in which an organization—or, more likely, an industry coalition—can affect legislation in its own favour. There is increasingly an understanding that business–government relations, properly undertaken, can be a source of **sustainable competitive advantage** (see also Chapter 5). In other words, organizations can outperform other organizations over time if they can manage their relationships with government and regulatory bodies better than do their competitors

(Hillman, Keim, and Schuler, 2004; Lawton and Rajwani, 2011). Any understanding of the political environment and the actions taken by constituent firms should also be considered through a legal framework and with an ethical lens.

A good example of the complex interactions between a company and its political environment can be seen in recent controversies on the role of Facebook in democratic elections (see also Chapter 6). In 2017, Facebook came under pressure from politicians and intelligence agencies in the United States and other parts of the world. Concerns were raised about the fact that hostile actors can use the platform to manipulate public opinion and influence democratic elections. It is now widely believed that Russian intelligence used Facebook to influence several elections in the West (Levin, 2017; Pullen, 2017a), to obtain outcomes that are perceived as more favourable to the Kremlin. So how should Facebook manage this situation? On one hand, it is unclear to what extent these activities are illegitimate within Facebook's current community standards (Wong, 2017). On the other hand, a failure to act might create very strong political pressure as governments try to protect the democratic process from outside interference in many countries in Europe and North America. Mark Zuckerberg, CEO of Facebook, has recognized the importance of this challenge and stepped up efforts to address these concerns. He released a video in September 2017 in which he outlined all the steps the company is taking to improve its ability to detect suspicious actors on the platform. The changes include a raft of initiatives, from increasing the number of staff dedicated to evaluating political ads and their backers, through an increase in transparency and the information provided to users on who is buying and running these ads, to closer coordination with electoral commissions in countries that are deemed to be potential targets of interference (Pullen, 2017b). For example, as a consequence of this new commitment, the company shut down thousands of 'fake' or 'suspicious' accounts during the last week of the German parliamentary elections in autumn 2017.

Companies often respond to political pressure because of a concern that otherwise legislation could be introduced to regulate their activities, at least in part. As a consequence, monitoring the political process is important if a company is to foresee and potentially anticipate regulatory changes that can significantly impact its day-to-day running.

Because legislation is such a technical area, few firms have the capability to understand and influence legislation without employing specialists. In such circumstances, special industry lobbyists are hired to represent clients before government decision-makers and regulators, and to provide advice to clients on how to design their strategic communication campaigns. Small and medium-sized firms, however, can be at a disadvantage because they lack the resources to influence regulators individually. In the UK, the Federation of Small Businesses is a not-for-profit organization that tries to address this imbalance by offering support to its members. One of the areas of this organization's activity is influencing government policy by representing the voices of hundreds of thousands of small businesses across the country.

Generally, there are several ways in which marketers might conduct business–government relations in various countries, including the following:

- Lobbyist firms, with key industry knowledge, can be engaged either permanently or as needed.

- **Public relations (PR)** consultancies (for example Weber Shandwick) can be commissioned for their political services, with members of Parliament (MPs) or others with a high degree of political influence often serving as directors and/or advisers in jurisdictions in which this is legal.

- A politician may be paid a fee to give political advice on matters of importance to an organization, where this is legal within that particular jurisdiction and where that politician is not serving directly within the government in question on the same portfolio as that on which they are advising.

- An in-house PR manager might handle government relations directly.

- An industry association might be contacted to lobby on behalf of members (for example, in the European financial services industry, the European Banking Federation).

- A politician may be invited to join the board of directors, board of trustees, or board of advisers of an organization to help the company to develop its business–government relations, where this is legal.

Organizations often collaborate to influence governments. This can be achieved through industry or trade bodies, or by working with other large companies in their industry. For example, EuropaBio is made up of three main segments of the European biotechnology industry: health care (Red Biotech); industrial (White Biotech); and agri-food (Green Biotech). Experts from member companies actively participate in working groups and taskforces that cover a wide range of issues and concerns particular to their industry in an attempt to influence key **stakeholders**, including national governments and the European legislature.

The Economic Environment

Companies and organizations must develop an understanding of the economic environment because a country's economic circumstances have an impact on what economists term factor prices within a particular industry, for a particular organization. These factors could include raw materials, labour, building and other capital costs, or any other input to a business. The economic environment of a firm is affected by the following:

- *Wage inflation*—Annual wage increases in a particular sector will depend on the supply of labour in that sector. Where there is scarcity of supply, wages usually increase (for example doctors).

- *Price inflation*—How much consumers pay for goods and services depends on the rate of supply of those goods and services. If supply is scarce, there is usually an increase in the price of that consumer good or service (for example petrol).

- ***Gross domestic product (GDP) per capita***—The combined output of goods and services in a particular nation is a useful measure for determining relative wealth between countries when comparisons are calculated per member of the population—that is, GDP per capita at **purchasing power parity (PPP)**, at which we look shortly.

- *Income, sales, and corporation taxes*—These taxes, typically operating in all countries around the world, usually at different levels, substantially affect how we market different offerings.

- *Exchange rates*—The relative value of a currency vis-à-vis another currency is an important calculation for those businesses operating in foreign markets or holding financial reserves in other currencies.

- *Export quota controls and duties*—Restrictions are often placed on the amounts (quotas) of goods and services that any particular firm or industry can import into a country, depending on which trading bloc or country a company or firm is exporting to. In addition, countries sometimes also charge a form of tax on particular items to discourage or encourage imports and to protect their own economies.

When operating in other countries, we should understand how exchange rates and living standards might affect those operations. We might also need to understand how prices or labour costs might change if we are importing our goods and services, or components of them, from another country—that is, our factor prices. This is known as the rate of price or wage inflation. Difficulties arise when comparing prices across different countries. Rather than compare costs for individual products by means of the prevailing exchange rate, economists prefer to calculate prices for a particular basket of goods—a fixed list of common items—and compare the cost of that basket in one country with its cost in another. This is known as the **purchasing power parity (PPP) exchange rate** and it allows us to compare the relative costs between two countries.

Organizations usually have little impact on the wider economic environment because they have little control over macroeconomic variables. For example, firms have no control over oil prices, which might affect their business in different ways. The challenge when examining the macroeconomic environment is to foresee changes in the environment and how they might affect the firm's activities. If a computer company in Sweden imports silicon chips from Japan and pays for them in Swedish kronor, but the exchange rate for the yen is rising against the Swedish kronor (in other words, you get more yen per kronor, perhaps because of strong Japanese export sales to Europe), then the company might decide to source its silicon chips from another country to ensure that its own prices are unaffected.

Similarly, if **inflation** drives consumer prices higher in a particular country, the price of goods might become more expensive, triggering a fall in sales. Typically, during a **recession**, consumers tend to purchase fewer goods and increase their savings, and prices fall further as producers try to stimulate demand. However, prices can increase during a recession. It is therefore important to understand the wider general economic trends in a firm's marketplace. Inflation can be affected by political factors as well: after the 2016 referendum in the UK (see Market Insight 4.1), the pound lost about 12 per cent of its value and this has affected the rate of inflation in the British economy (Elliott, 2017). Surveys of consumer expectations of inflation, forecasts of foreign exchange rates, wage forecasts, and other financial information are frequently available from government central banks. Financial institutions also conduct surveys of managers to investigate underlying trends in the economy, with the objective of forecasting future trends in economic growth.

 Visit the **online resources** and complete Internet Activity 4.1 to learn more about how the contribution of service industries to the UK's national economy has changed over the last ten years.

The Socio-cultural Environment

Lifestyles are constantly changing and, over time, consumers shift their preferences. Companies that fail to recognize changes in the socio-cultural environment and to adapt or change their offerings often fail. In the UK (and some other European countries), immigration from Poland after EU enlargement increased the UK's Polish population, with some supermarkets specifically targeting that segment using adverts in Polish and by stocking products such as borscht, meatballs, pickled vegetables, and sauerkraut soup (Anon., 2006). In the United States, there is an important segment of Hispanic millennials, numbering about 19 million consumers, who represent a specific group within the broader Hispanic community (Mizrahi, 2017). These consumers have stronger connections with Hispanic culture and tend to spend more on products such as clothing, accessories, and grooming products. (See also Market Insight 4.2 for an analysis of how companies cope with the socio-cultural trend toward healthier products.)

When considering the socio-cultural environment, firms need to consider the changing nature of households, demographics, lifestyles, and family structures, and changing values in society.

Demographics and Lifestyles

Changes in population proportions impact on an organization's marketing activity. For example, there will be significant market changes as a result of the ageing of most Western societies and significant rises in life expectancy. In many developed countries, for the first time, the percentage

Market Insight 4.2
Health Issues Slim Down Product Sales

Sales of bread have been falling steadily in the last few years. The UK's three biggest bread brands, Warburtons, Hovis, and Kingsmill, which account for 60 per cent of packaged bread sales in the UK, have collectively lost hundreds of millions in revenues. According to a recent survey, since 1975 sales of bread have fallen by 75 per cent and only a quarter of young people aged 18–24 eat white bread regularly.

The reasons for this downward shift include increasing awareness of the need for healthy eating, a consumer shift towards higher protein products and lower carbohydrates, and a renewed interest in fresh artisan variants. Television programmes, such as *The Great British Bake Off*, have spurred interest in home baking to the extent that sales of baking trays at Waitrose soared by 881 per cent and those of bakeware increased by 55 per cent, all during a single week before the 2015 series started. At the same time, sales of biscuits and cakes have fallen, in part, it is claimed, because of the influence of the show.

Food and beverage companies, like their fast food counterparts, have faced increasing pressure from governments as obesity rates have increased around the world. National governments have begun to scrutinize their public health policies. Several countries, such as Denmark, Finland, Hungary, and France, have introduced a 'fat tax', added to products with high fat content, such as confectionery (including chocolate), dairy products, and sugary foods and drinks, in a bid to reduce public consumption of high-fat foods, the obesity epidemic, and the consequent impact on public health and public healthcare budgets.

A key ethical issue arises if you are the CEO of a major food manufacturer: should you seek to circumvent the obesity issue by reducing the fat content in your offerings (and educating consumers to buy lower calorie options), or ignore the obesity issue, therefore selling the same offering (and perhaps lobbying government not to introduce the tax), or pursue some mixture of these approaches?

The UK government introduced a sugar levy in April 2018
Source: © tornadoflight/Shutterstock.com.

As part of its ten-point plan against obesity, Tesco decided that it would no longer sell high-sugar drinks targeted at children in the juice category. As a result, high-sugar drinks such as Ribena, Capri-Sun, and Rubicon fruit juice cartons were delisted, and are not available from its stores.

Sources: Green (2000); Davidson (2015); Ward (2015); Young (2015); Barrie (2016).

Market Insight 4.2
continued

Theory into Practice

There are a wide range of theories that could be used to interpret the actions of both brand managers and consumers within this scenario. Clearly, society has attempted to make consumers aware of the need to eat healthy foods. This can be interpreted through explanatory theory, which holds that the nature of a problem needs to be communicated and a range of variables then identified that can be used to influence audiences.

Lewin (1935) developed a three-stage theory of change, which can be used to understand the behavioural change that consumers experience as a result of processing messages—in this case, societal messages about the dangers of obesity. Lewin argues that change occurs by means of a three-part process—that is, *unfreezing* (understanding and searching for new healthier food and so stopping the current behaviour)—*change* (to new healthier foods)—*refreezing* (establishing the new behaviour foods as the standard diet).

Related Topics

political environment; socio-cultural environment; economic environment; competitive advantage; industry analysis

1 **What are the advantages and disadvantages to food manufacturers of producing new lower calorie or healthier versions of their existing products?**

2 **To what extent will the UK government's 'sugar tax' impact the sales of high-sugar drinks such as Ribena? Explain your reasoning.**

3 **Why do you think Tesco decided to delist high-sugar drinks, yet still sell other high-sugar and high-calorie products such as Mars bars?**

---

of the population that is aged 65 or over is already larger than that of consumers aged 15 or under. These trends will imply a significant growth in some industries—typically, medical and financial services. Other industries, however, will be negatively affected. Research predicts, for example, that manufacturers of cars will be negatively affected because older people are less likely to buy vehicles. The same applies to hospitality and education—two industries that tend to target younger customers. On the contrary, some countries and regions, such as many African and Middle Eastern countries, have a comparatively high proportion of younger citizens. These differences in the age structure in different countries give rise to different-sized markets for brand propositions.

What should companies do? The most sensible strategy is to plan ahead and aim for the best diversification strategy to minimize any potential disruption caused by these external trends.

However, people's lifestyles are also changing. In Europe, there is a trend towards marrying later in life and an increased tendency to divorce than was apparent among previous generations. The average age at which people first marry is now around 30 or even higher, such as in

Sweden, where the average age is 34 (Misachi, 2017). In some countries, there is an increasing trend towards single-person households, and where states have legalized same-sex marriage and civil partnerships, there has been an evident increase in such unions (for example in Argentina, Scandinavia, Iceland, the Netherlands, South Africa, and France). Yet, overall, marriages are less common in today's society and many argue that this in itself has important social consequences.

The Technological Environment

The emergence of new technologies has affected most businesses. Examples include technologies that impact productivity and business efficiency, such as changes in energy, transportation, and information and communication technologies (ICT). New technology also changes the way in which companies go to market. For example, companies are now compelled to use a variety of channels. These include smartphone apps, as well as traditional websites and physical stores. For example, one unusual app enables shoppers to test whether a melon is ripe. The shopper rests the microphone on a melon, presses a button, and taps the melon, and the app uses an algorithm to determine whether the melon is ready to eat.

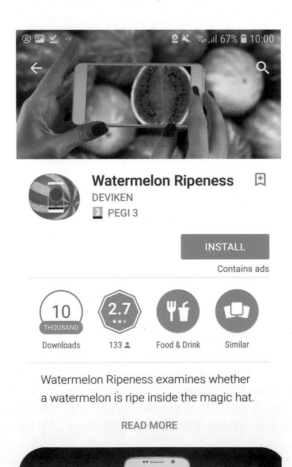

'Watermelon Ripeness' is one of several such apps available
Source: By permission of Deviken.

Changes in technology particularly affect high-tech industries, in which firms must decide whether they wish to dominate that market by pushing their own particular technology standards—especially where new technology renders existing standards obsolete. For example, cloud computing and digital music files have taken over from the cassette tape and vinyl record manufacturing industries. Customers are increasingly happy to work with companies and organizations to solve problems. Howe (2006) refers to this phenomenon as **crowdsourcing** (see also Chapter 12). Whitla (2009) suggests that the role and process of crowdsourcing is to identify a task or group of tasks currently conducted in-house and then to release the task(s) to a 'crowd' of outsiders, who are invited to perform the task(s) on behalf of the company (for a fee or prize). One of the most popular crowdsourcing platforms is Amazon Mechanical Turk (MTurk), whereby hundreds of thousands of 'workers' (as they are called by Amazon) complete small tasks in exchange for a small fee. MTurk is used by many companies and for different purposes, including conducting surveys, categorizing images, and writing short blog posts. Often, the crowdsourced work on MTurk is used to inform machine learning software. Despite its popularity, MTurk has been criticized because the average hourly rate is low (about US$8) and it is therefore seen as exploitative (Katz, 2017).

Crowdsourcing for content
Source: © 2018 Amazon Mechanical Turk, Inc. or its affiliates. All rights reserved.

When scanning the technological environment, attention has to be given to research and development (R&D) trends and the R&D efforts of competitors. Strategies to ascertain these involve regular searches of patent registration, trademarks, and copyright assignations, as well as maintaining a general interest in technological and scientific advances. For example, in the pharmaceutical and chemical industries, companies develop new compounds by modifying the compounds registered for patents by their competitors—a process referred to as **reverse engineering**.

The reverse-engineering principle can also be observed in other industries in which new propositions are based on competitor offerings, based on 'me too', or imitation marketing, strategies. This is often the result of a firm's inability to turn its own technological advances into a sustainable competitive advantage (Rao, 2005). As soon as a new offering is introduced, it is quickly copied. To overcome this, firms attempt to introduce a consistent stream of new propositions

Market Insight 4.3
L'Oréal Advances Beauty through Technology

The world of beauty and cosmetics has traditionally been based on people physically visiting a store and smelling a perfume, or trying a lipstick, prior to purchase. Advances in technology are seen by companies such as L'Oréal, the largest in the beauty sector, as an opportunity to advance their market leadership and, with it, to change consumer behaviour.

L'Oréal was an early adopter of using data and analytics to help it to identify beauty trends. For example, 'dip-dyed hair' emerged as a search term on Google Trends long before it came to the fore in popular culture. As the figures rose, L'Oréal spotted an opportunity and created a full dip-dye product called Préférence Les Ombrés. Recognizing and realizing the potential of this emerging trend resulted in sales of €50 million in the first two years following the product's launch.

L'Oréal also launched a beauty app called Makeup Genius. This works by transforming the front-facing camera of an iPhone or iPad into a virtual mirror, enabling users to 'try on' products virtually. The app uses advanced facial mapping technology that has previously only been used in Hollywood and the gaming industry to overlay products, such as lipstick and eyeliner, onto the user's face. The company is now hoping to bring out versions for hair colour, hair styling, and skincare.

L'Oréal plans to integrate the Makeup Genius technology into bathroom mirrors, giving users access to everyday coaching and advice from beauty professionals in their own homes. In addition, there will be improved sensors that will measure lifestyle habits, skin tone, sleeping patterns, stress, activity, pollution, and sun exposure, and combine all this data to offer customers personalized beauty advice.

Vichy and La Roche Posay are L'Oréal brands that focus on products designed for sensitive or problematic skin. These use live chat to guide consumers on the best products for their skin concerns. These brands also offer online skincare diagnostics and customers can consult dermatologists on their particular concerns.

L'Oréal has also been experimenting with everything that links to Instant Messaging and is very interested in video apps, such as Periscope and Twicer. The company has also investigated the use of flexible wearable electronics, designed to collect and transmit data from the body, and has partnered with a bio-printing start-up company called Organovo to look into the potential of using 3D printed skin production to test products for toxicity and efficacy.

Sources: Shayon (2014); Curtis (2015); Westcott (2015); http://www.loreal.com

Theory into Practice

This market insight demonstrates the importance of technology monitoring as an element of environmental scanning. At a macro level, Schumpeter (1934) identified that innovation can be seen as a sequence of waves that serve to restructure a market, to the advantage of those who grasp discontinuities faster. He termed this 'creative disruption'. L'Oréal's focus on technology monitoring is therefore an attempt to generate sustainable competitive advantage for itself.

From a competitive response perspective, Teece (1986) suggested that imitability and complementary assets represent two important factors that determine the success of an innovation. Imitability concerns the ease with which competitors can copy or duplicate the technology or process underpinning an innovation. Protection, in terms of intellectual property rights, procedures, and tacit knowledge, can serve to act as a barrier. Complementary assets, such as marketing channels, brand name, reputation, and positioning, gravitate around and support the core innovation. The interchange between these factors shapes the success of the innovation. So if L'Oréal's imitability is high (that is, if the technology can be accessed by competitors) and its complementary assets are strong, then the success of its innovations is likely to be high and profitable.

Market Insight 4.3
continued

Related Topics

technological environment; socio-cultural environment; competitive advantage; industry analysis; strategic analysis; portfolio analysis

1 Is a firm's external environment really uncontrollable, as theory dictates? If so, why should a firm devote resources to monitoring it?

2 To what extent might L'Oréal's use of advanced technology represent a sustainable competitive advantage over its competitors?

3 If the number of consumers who adopt these interactive technologies is relatively small, why should L'Oréal continue with this strategy?

and to stay as close to the consumer as possible. (See Market Insight 4.3 to see how L'Oréal uses technology and technology monitoring to help to maintain its dominant position in the beauty market.)

For most firms, the risk of investing in radical or cutting-edge technologies is high because the potential benefits are unsubstantiated. Fear of obsolescence is usually a strong incentive to invest in new technologies (Chandy, Prabhu, and Antia, 2003). Therefore companies have every reason to be concerned about the impact of technological changes on their product and service life cycles. However, innovation becomes a necessary condition in the strategic marketing decision-making of high-tech firms. For less technology-intensive firms, innovation (whether it is process- or product/service-focused), or at least rapid adoption of new offering variants based on competitors' offerings, is still necessary to stay ahead of the competition.

The Legal Environment

The legal environment covers every aspect of an organization's business. Laws and regulation on the transparency of pricing, the prevention of restrictive trade practices, product safety, good practice in packaging and labelling, the abuse of a dominant market position, and codes of practice in advertising, to take just a small selection, are enacted in most countries.

Product Safety, Packaging, and Labelling

In the European Union (EU), product safety is covered under the General Product Safety Directive (Directive 2001/95/EC), which aims to protect consumer health and safety both for EU member states and for importers from third-party countries to the Union or their EU agent representatives. Where products pose serious risks to consumer health, the European Commission can take action, imposing fines and criminal sentences for those contravening the Directive. The General Product Safety Directive does not, however, cover food safety; this is subject to the General Food Safety Regulation (Regulation (EC) No. 178/2002), which established a European

Food Safety Authority and a set of procedures covering food safety. Companies operating in these sectors need to keep up with changes in this and other legislation, because failure to do so might jeopardize their business.

In the pharmaceutical industry, regulations govern testing, approval, manufacturing, labelling, and the marketing of drugs. Most countries also place restrictions on the prices that pharmaceutical companies can charge for drugs. In Japan, price regulations are stipulated for individual products. Up until 2014, in the UK, strict controls were placed on the overall profitability of products supplied by a specific company to the National Health Service (NHS) under the Pharmaceutical Price Regulation Scheme. Since 2014, the Scheme has instead used a value-based pricing mechanism (DH/ABPI, 2012). (For more on value-based pricing approaches, see Chapter 9.)

Companies that develop cosmetics and fragrances are required to comply with legislative measures designed to protect users. This means that there is a need to ensure that products remain cosmetics and are not reclassified under different regulations, such as those related to medicines, which makes innovation within the cosmetic industry more difficult (Gower, 2005).

Product labelling regulation in the EU tends to relate to the recycling of packaging and waste to ensure that it complies with environmental regulations. In the United States packaging and labelling regulations are more concerned with fair practice and ensuring that packaging does not contain misleading advertising statements. Different countries around the world have different regulations, so importers and exporters should be aware of these rules from the outset.

Codes of Practice in Advertising

Advertising standards differ around the world. In the UK, advertising is self-regulated—that is, it is regulated by the advertising industry itself. In other countries, advertising is restricted by legislation. In the UK, advertising is regulated by the Advertising Standards Authority (ASA), which has a mission to apply codes of practice in advertising and to uphold advertising standards for consumers, business, and the general public. Such self-regulatory agencies operate in other countries, for example the Bureau de Vérification de la Publicité in France and the Advertising Standards Council in India. In the EU, the European Advertising Standards Alliance (EASA) oversees both statutory and self-regulatory provision in most European countries, and even in some non-European countries, including Russia, Canada, the United States, New Zealand, and Turkey. (See Chapters 10 and 11 for a more general discussion of advertising.)

Restrictions on the advertising of alcohol products exist in most parts of the world. In the UK, for broadcast advertising communications, codes of practice exist for both radio and television—typically, with specific regulations for alcohol advertising mandating that claims cannot be made in relation to sexual prowess, fitness or health, courage or strength. In Thailand, alcoholic products cannot be advertised before 10 p.m. In France, the manufacturers of alcoholic beverages are obliged to show a government health warning on all advertisements. In the UK, breweries and distillers have voluntarily placed the message 'drink responsibly' in the copy of their adverts for many years.

Government health warnings also apply to tobacco products and tobacco advertising is now virtually banned in all forms around the world. In most countries (such as Sweden, Ireland, and the UK, as well as India and Bahrain, among others), consumers are dissuaded from smoking not only by means of high taxes placed on tobacco to reduce consumption and public restrictions on where people can smoke, but also by means of legislation banning and restricting advertising and requiring the placing of government health warnings on packages. In some countries, including Canada and Australia, government health warnings provide stark information and graphic pictures. In Canada, the size of the health warning was increased to cover 75 per cent of the pack (Anon., 2012), whilst Australia was the first country to introduce plain packaging for all tobacco brands in late 2012.

Tobacco packaging using shock-based images to deter users

Source: © Newspix/REX/Shutterstock.com.

The Ecological Environment

The concept of marketing sustainability is now well established, with increasing numbers of consumers expressing concern about the impact that companies are having on ecological environments. For example, there is increased demand for 'organic' food, incorporating principles of better welfare for the animals consumed as food products and less interference with the natural processes of growing fruit and vegetables, in the form of pesticides and chemical fertilizers.

Sustainability issues embrace the sourcing of products from countries with poor and coercive labour policies. Both Nike and Apple have actively changed parts of their supply chain following investigations. Consumers are also keen to ensure that companies and their products are not damaging the environment or causing harm to consumers. This has been accompanied by a rise in the popularity of Fairtrade products.

An important question for marketers concerns the way in which an organization should embrace and incorporate the changing trend in sustainability. Orsato (2006) suggests that a company can adopt one of the following four different green marketing strategies:

- *Eco-efficiency*—It might lower costs by means of improved organizational processes, such as the promotion of resource productivity (for example energy efficiency) and better utilization of by-products. This approach should be adopted by those firms that need to focus on reducing the costs and environmental impact of their organizational processes. Supermarket chains in Norway and other Scandinavian countries have encouraged recycling for a long time.

- *Beyond compliance leadership*—This involves the adoption of a differentiation strategy through organizational processes such as certified schemes to demonstrate the company's ecological credentials or its environmental excellence, for example by adopting the UN Global Compact principles, or other environmental management system (EMS) schemes and codes. This approach should be adopted by firms that supply industrial markets, such as car manufacturers.

- *Eco-branding*—The firm might differentiate its products or services to promote environmental responsibility. Examples include Duchy Originals (the Prince of Wales' food brand), the late Thai King Bhumipol's Golden Place brand, or the Toyota Prius.

- *Environmental cost leadership*—This involves offerings that provide greater environmental benefits at a lower price. This strategy particularly suits firms operating in price-sensitive and ecologically sensitive markets, such as the packaging and chemical industries.

Whatever the company and industry, ecological trends in marketing look set to stay and further develop as the sustainability debate rages on and as companies use it to develop their own competitive strategies. It is important to assess how this movement towards greener and more sustainable marketing is affecting a particular industry to ensure that a company within that industry not only is not adversely affected by these changes (for example by non-compliance with regulatory changes in areas such as packaging), but also can take advantage of the opportunities (for example a haulage company using hybrid engine lorries to reduce energy costs).

Information about each of these sub-environments is gathered so that an organization can assess their potential impact. Organizations need to monitor all PESTLE elements, but some are more important than others. For example, pharmaceutical organizations such as GlaxoSmithKline monitor legal and regulatory developments (for example labelling, patents, testing); the Environment Agency monitors political and ecological changes (for example flood plains for housing developments); road haulage companies should watch for changes that impact on transport development (for example congestion charging, diesel duty, toll roads); and music distributors should monitor changes in technology and associated social and cultural developments (for example downloading trends and cloud computing).

Environmental Scanning

To understand how external environments change, organizations need to put in place methods and processes to inform them of developments. The process of gathering information about a company's external events and relationships to help top management in making decisions and developing a course of action is referred to as **environmental scanning** (Aguilar, 1967). It is the internal communication of external information about issues that may potentially influence an organization's decision-making process, focusing on the identification of emerging issues, situations, and potential threats in the external environment (Albright, 2004). Environmental scanning is an important component of the strategic marketing planning process that we consider in Chapter 5.

We can gather information in environmental scanning exercises using company reports, newspapers, industry reports and magazines, government reports, and marketing intelligence reports (such as those published by Datamonitor, Euromonitor, and Mintel).

Visit the **online resources** and follow the web links to learn more about the information and services provided by Datamonitor, Euromonitor, and Mintel.

'Soft' personal sources of information obtained through networking, such as contacts at trade fairs, are also important—particularly for competitive, legal, and regulatory information (see Case Insight 4.1). Such verbal personal sources of information can be crucial in fast-changing environments (May, Stewart, and Sweo, 2000), when reports from government, industry, or specific businesses have yet to be written and disseminated.

Visit the **online resources** and complete Internet Activity 4.2 to learn more about several sources that can be useful when conducting a scan of the external environment.

The process by means of which companies scan the external environment typically involves three stages (see Figure 4.2):

1 In Stage 1, the focus is principally, but not exclusively, on data gathering.

2 In Stage 2, the focus is principally, but not exclusively, on interpreting the data gathered in a process of environmental interpretation or analysis.

3 In the final stage, the focus is principally, but not exclusively, on strategy formulation.

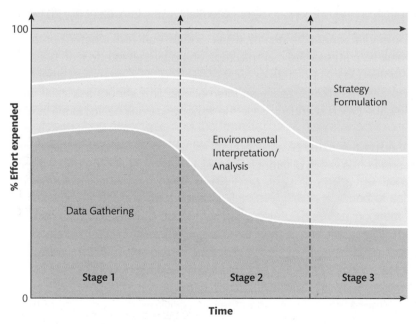

Figure 4.2

The environmental scanning process

Source: Adapted from O'Connell and Zimmerman (1979). Reproduced with the kind permission of *California Management Review*.

During each of the key scanning stages, there is also some activity in each of the other two areas, so that each of the three processes dominates at any one time, but is also ongoing in the background during the others. Although the process seems relatively straightforward and simply a matter of collecting the 'right' information, barriers to effective environmental scanning exist because it is difficult to determine what is the 'right' information. In addition, data gathering can be time-consuming. In such cases, the information gathered ceases to provide a useful input to strategic marketing decision-making. In addition, multinational corporations may see opportunities and desire organizational change, and they may collect the right data to take advantage of those opportunities, but fail actually to do so because of **switching costs** and organizational inertia related to production, sourcing, and other business operations.

Some companies, however, have developed a proactive approach by considering potential **scenarios** that their company may face in the future. Historically, companies focused on developing scenarios based on their probability and then developed different courses of action depending on the changes in the environment. For example, in its analysis of the world energy market to 2050, multinational energy company Shell identified two possible future energy scenarios based on how governments and companies might respond to the energy production and sustainability challenge. The different scenarios are based on assumptions about energy prices and environmental regulations that would impact on Shell's operations (Royal Dutch Shell, 2018).

Recent perspectives on scenario planning stress the importance of:

■ dedicating specific resources to scenario planning and to the constant updating of the scenarios developed;

■ engaging a broad range of internal and external stakeholders in the development of scenarios; and

■ challenging the assumptions in the scenario to spot potential flaws (Ramirez et al., 2017).

In this respect, it is particularly important to identify weak signals early on—that is, potential changes in the operating environment that are currently receiving only limited attention because they are not consistent with the dominant culture or 'way of thinking'. For example, rather than assuming a constant trend towards globalization, an international firm should ask itself what trends might instead reverse the process and increase the importance of local factors (Ramirez et al., 2017).

Scanning and understanding the external environment within the PESTLE framework will reveal different influences and trends within different industries and sectors. It is therefore important to realize that particular industries will focus on different issues and elements within the framework.

Understanding the Performance Environment

The **performance environment**, sometimes called the microenvironment, consists of those organizations that either directly or indirectly influence an organization's operational performance. The performance environment therefore encompasses not only competitors, but also suppliers and other organizations, such as distributors, who all contribute to an industry's value chain. There are three main types:

■ those companies that compete against the organization in the pursuit of its objectives.

■ those companies that supply raw materials, goods, and services, and those that operate as distributors, dealers, and retailers further down the marketing channel, all of which have the potential to *directly* influence the performance of the organization by adding value in the production, assembly, and distribution of products prior to their reaching the end user; and

■ those companies that have the potential to *indirectly* influence the performance of the organization in the pursuit of its objectives, which organizations often supply services, such as consultancy or financial services, or are marketing research or communication agencies.

Analysis of the performance environment is undertaken so that organizations can adopt better positions in relation to their stakeholders and those of their competitors. These adjustments are made in recognition of emerging trends, as circumstances develop, and/or in anticipation of evolving environmental and performance conditions.

Knowledge about the performance arena allows organizations to choose how and where to operate and compete, given limited resources. Knowledge allows adaptation and development in complex and increasingly turbulent markets. Conditions vary from industry to industry. Some are full of potential and growth opportunities, such as cruise holidays, Fairtrade food, and the online travel and gaming industries, whereas others are in decline or stagnating at best, for example high-street music stores and camera retailers.

Analysing Industries

An industry is composed of various organizations that market similar offerings. According to Porter (1979), we should review the 'competitive' environment within an industry to identify the major competitive forces, because this helps us to assess their impact on an organization's present and future competitive positions. Numerous variables help us to determine how attractive an industry is and shape the longer-term profitability for the different companies that make up the industry.

Think of industries such as shipbuilding, cars, coal, and steel, in which levels of profitability have been weak and unattractive to prospective new entrants. Now think of industries such as technology, fashion, airlines, and banking, in which levels of profitability have been high. Analysing an industry, however, is not important only because it helps us to determine its attractiveness; a company can also use its analysis to determine its relative competitive positioning. The competitive pressures across different markets vary quite considerably, but there are enough similarities to establish an analytical framework to gauge the nature and intensity of competition.

Porter (1979) suggests that competition in an industry is a composite of five main competitive forces: the level of threat that new competitors will enter the market; the threat posed by substitute products; the bargaining power of buyers; and the bargaining power of suppliers. These, in turn, affect the fifth force: the intensity of rivalry between the current competitors. Porter called these variables the 'Five Forces' of competitive industry analysis (see Figure 4.3).

As a general rule, the more intense the rivalry between industry players, the lower their overall performance. However, the lower the rivalry, the greater will be the performance of the industry players. Porter's model is useful because it exposes the competitive forces in operation in an industry and can lead to an assessment of their relative strengths. The collective impact determines what competition is like in the market. As a general rule, the stronger the competitive forces, the lower the profitability in a market. An organization needs to determine a competitive approach that allows it to influence the industry's competitive rules, protects it from competitive forces as much as possible, and gives it a strong position from which to compete.

New Entrants

Industries are seldom static: companies and brands enter and exit industries all the time. The entrance of a new company could be a potential threat because the new entrant might occupy a similar space in the market to the existing company. Consider the UK beverage industry, which witnessed the entrance of energy drink manufacturer, Red Bull, around 1987. Ever since then, Red Bull has been competing head-on with industry stalwarts Pepsico (which distributes Rockstar), Coca-Cola (which part-owns Monster), and GlaxoSmithKline's Lucozade, the original market-leading energy drink in the UK beverage market.

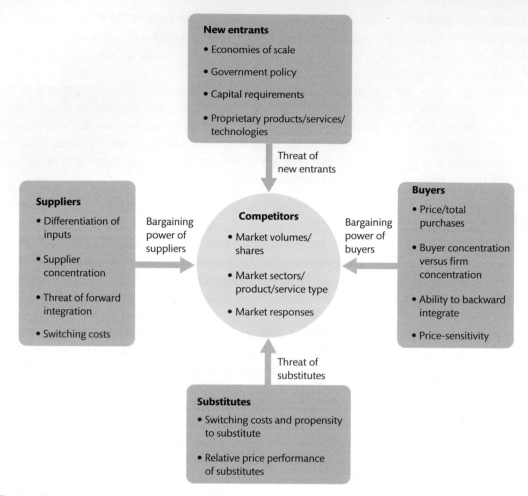

Figure 4.3

Industry analysis: Porter's Five Forces

Source: Adapted from Porter (1979). Reproduced with the kind permission of Harvard Business School Publishing.

When examining an industry, we should consider whether economies of scale are required for successful performance within it. For instance, motor manufacturing in the UK requires significant investment in plant and machinery. Unfortunately, because British labour costs are high and foreign direct investment incentives (for example government development grants) are not as lucrative as they once were, many British-based motor manufacturers have moved to Eastern Europe and the Far East. New entrants may be restricted as a consequence of government and regulatory policy, or they may be frozen out of an industry because of the capital requirement necessary to set up business. For example, in the oil and gas industry, huge sums of capital are required not only to fund exploration activities, but also to fund the extraction and refining operations.

Companies may be locked out because companies within a market are using proprietary offerings or technologies. A good example of this is the pharmaceutical industry, in which costs of developing a new drug are often prohibitive for new entrants. A recent report by the Association of the British Pharmaceutical Industry (ABPI) puts the cost of developing a single new prescription drug at £1.15 billion (Thomas, 2016). This is sufficient to ensure high concentration in the industry and to ensure that new entrants will find it extremely hard to challenge existing players.

Substitutes

In any industry, there are usually substitute offerings that perform the same function or meet similar customer needs. Substitutes are thus a threat because they could, in the long run, replace current offerings. Levitt (1960) warned that many companies fail to recognize the competitive threat from newly developing offerings. He cites the refusal of the American railroad industry to recognize the competitive threat arising from the development of the automobile and airline industries in the transport sector.

Consider the telecommunications sector in the UK. As telecommunications markets continue to converge with the development of broadband Internet services, we see a variety of different companies operating in the same competitive marketspace, for example EE, BT, Virgin Media, and many others. With the long-standing development of voice over Internet Protocol (VOIP)—the Internet telecommunication voice transmission standard—fixed-line telecommunications has become a commodity and firms operating in the area now look to develop value-added services, such as video-on-demand, streaming, interactive gaming, and web-conferencing services.

Most countries' fixed-line operators have found it difficult to hold on to their original subscribers, partly because cheaper alternatives are appearing in the market (for example cable, Internet, and fusion plans incorporating both mobile and fixed lines and television packages). It takes time for consumers to become aware of new offerings and to obtain the necessary information to allow them to make a decision over whether or not to switch. Consumers consider the switching costs associated with such a decision, which, in turn, affect their propensity to substitute the offering for another. They consider the relative price performance of one offering over another. For example, if we were to wish to travel from Amsterdam to Paris, we could fly from Amsterdam Airport Schiphol to Charles de Gaulle Airport, take the train, or drive. We would consider the relative price differences (the flight is likely to be the most expensive, but not always), and we would also factor into this decision how comfortable and convenient these different journeys are likely to be before we finally make our choice. In analysing our place within an industry, we should consider what alternative offerings exist in the marketplace that also, to a greater or lesser extent, meet our customers' needs.

Buyers

Companies should ask themselves what percentage of their sales a single buyer represents. This is an important question because if one buying company purchases a large volume of offerings from the supplying company, as car manufacturers do from steel suppliers, it is likely to be able to demand price concessions when there are a lot of competing suppliers in the marketplace relative to the proportion of buyers (that is, supplier concentration versus buyer concentration). Buyers may also decide to increase their bargaining power through what is known as **backward integration**. For example, a company is said to have integrated backwards when it moves into manufacturing the offerings it previously bought from its suppliers. Amazon offers an example of backward integration, shifting from being a bookseller at the time of its launch in 1994 to announcing it would move into other business areas beyond books in 1998 (Hansell, 1998). Since then, it has become a behemoth: the world's largest online retailer and a key player in the global cloud computing market through Amazon Web Services (AWS) (Gensler, 2017).

Tesco plc—the British multiple retail grocer, operating in 11 markets outside the UK in 2018—also sells financial services, including debit and credit services, which it previously would have purchased from Visa and MasterCard merchant operators. Because, for many years, customers have tended to pay using credit or debit cards rather than cash, Tesco has lowered its

relative strength and weakness of a particular resource; it is also important to consider how the resources compare to those of competitors, and how a company is able to manage and develop such resources going forward. Attention here is given to two main elements, products and finance, within **portfolio analysis**.

Portfolio Analysis

When managing a collection or portfolio of offerings, we should appreciate that understanding the performance of an individual offering can often fail to give appropriate insight; what is really important is an understanding of the relative performance of the offerings. By creating a balance of old, mature, established, growing, and very new offerings, there is a better chance of delivering profits now and at some point in the future, when the current offerings cease to be attractive and profitable. One of the popular methods for assessing the variety of businesses/offerings that an organization has involves the creation of a two-dimensional graphical picture of the comparative strategic positions. This technique is referred to as a portfolio matrix.

The Boston Consulting Group (BCG) developed the original idea and its matrix—the **Boston Box**, shown in Figure 4.4—is based on two key variables: market growth and relative market share (that is, market share as a percentage of the share of the product's largest competitor, expressed as a fraction). Thus a relative share of 0.8 means that the product achieves 80 per cent of the sales of the market leader's sales volume (or value, depending on which measure is used). This is not the strongest competitive position, but neither is it a weak position. A relative market share of 1 means that the company equally shares market leadership with a competitor. A relative market share of 2 means that the company has twice the market share of its nearest competitor. (Research Insight 4.3 offers more information on the history of the Boston Box.)

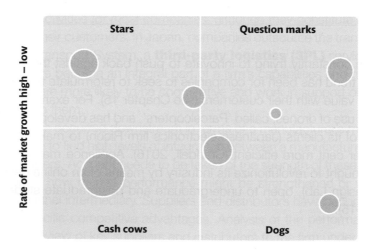

Figure 4.4

The Boston Box

Source: Reprinted from B. Hedley, 'Strategy and the business portfolio', *Long Range Planning*, 10, 1, 12. © 1977, with permission from Elsevier.

Research Insight 4.3

To take your learning further, you might wish to read this influential paper:

Morrison, A., and Wensley, R. (1991). Boxing up or boxing in: a short history of the Boston Consulting Group share/growth matrix. *Journal of Marketing Management*, 7(2), 105–29.

This highly readable and critical article outlines the history of the development of the Boston Box portfolio analysis concept from academic and practitioner perspectives. The authors conclude that the concept is useful in strategic planning, but that those using it should be aware of its limitations—namely, around the scope of the technique, the assumptions it makes, how it defines and classifies markets in terms of share and growth, its failure to consider the political dimensions of strategy development, that there are strategic implementation difficulties in real firms, and that it explains what strategy to undertake, but not how to undertake it.

See also:

Kang, W., and Montoya, M. (2014). The impact of product portfolio strategy on financial performance: the roles of product development and market entry decisions. *Journal of Product Innovation Management*, 31(3), 516–34.

 Visit the **online resources** to read the abstracts and access the papers in full.

In Figure 4.5, the vertical axis refers to the rate of market growth and the horizontal axis refers to an offering's market strength, as measured by relative market share. The size of the circles represents the sales revenue generated by the product. Relative market share is generally regarded as high when you are the market leader—that is, when the relative market share is 1 or more. Determining whether or not market growth rate is high or low is more problematic and depends on the type of industry. In some industries, a market growth rate of 5 per cent might be regarded as high, whereas in others the benchmark might be 10 per cent. The range between high and low is often taken to be 10 per cent. This lack of clarity on what is to be regarded definitively as 'high' and 'low' rates of market growth is a key criticism of the model.

The BCG typology is as follows:

- *Question marks* (also known as 'problem children') are offerings that exist in growing markets, but have low market share. As a result, there is negative cash flow and they are unprofitable.

- *Stars* are most probably market leaders, but their growth has to be financed through fairly heavy levels of investment.

- *Cash cows*, meanwhile, exist in fairly stable, low-growth markets and require little ongoing investment. Their high market share draws both positive cash flows and high levels of profitability.

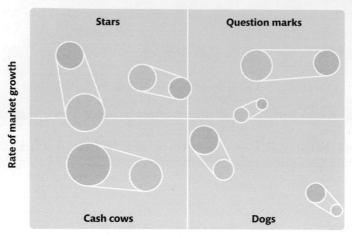

Figure 4.5

Present and future positions in the BCG matrix

Source: Reprinted from B. Hedley, 'Strategy and the business portfolio', *Long Range Planning*, 10, 1, 12. © 1977, with permission from Elsevier.

- *Dogs* experience low growth and low market share, and generate negative cash flows. These indicators suggest that many of them are operating in declining markets and they have no real long-term future.

Divestment, however, need not occur only because of low share. For example, when pharmaceutical firm Merck sold Sirna Therapeutics to Alnylam Pharmaceuticals, the sale of the drug delivery subsidiary was announced as enabling Merck to remain consistent with its strategy of reducing its emphasis on platform technologies. Merck's policy is to assess whether particular assets are core to its strategy, whether they provide competitive advantage, and whether they might generate greater value as part of Merck or outside Merck (Zhu, 2014).

From a reverse perspective, in 2009, Coca-Cola bought a minority 18 per cent stake in innocent drinks, in an attempt to give Coca-Cola access to the smoothie market, which had grown rapidly over the previous ten years and in which it had no presence whatsoever. Coca-Cola later increased its stake in innocent, by 40 per cent to 56 per cent in 2010, and then to 90 per cent in 2013. Coca-Cola thereby effectively bypassed the set-up costs of developing its own 'question mark' smoothie product, gaining a market presence at a relatively modest cost (Neate, 2013). Similarly, in 2012, Facebook controversially spent US$1 billion to acquire Instagram, which at the time had no real revenue and a relatively small (but rapidly growing) user base. However, the strategy was to increase Facebook's social networking on mobile devices and Instagram would offer new capabilities in this direction. The company now accounts for 10 per cent of the group's revenue and it is reputed to be worth $25–35 billion (Heisler, 2016).

Portfolio analysis is an important analytical tool because it draws attention to the cash flow and investment characteristics of each of a firm's offerings, and it indicates how financial resources can be manoeuvred to attain optimal strategic performance over the long term. Essentially, excess cash generated by cash cows should be utilized to develop question marks and stars, which are unable to support themselves. This enables stars to become cash cows and self-supporting. Dogs should be retained only for as long as they contribute to positive cash flow and do not restrict the use of assets and resources elsewhere in the business. Once they start to do so, they should be divested or ejected from the portfolio.

By plotting all of a company's offerings onto the Boston Box, it becomes visually easy to appreciate just how well balanced the portfolio is. An unbalanced portfolio would be one that has too many offerings clustered in one or two quadrants. Where offerings are distributed equally, or at least are not clustered in any one area, and where market shares and cash flows equate with their market position, the portfolio is financially healthy and well balanced. By analysing the portfolio in this way, it becomes possible to project possible strategies and their outcomes.

Portfolio Issues

Portfolio analysis is an important guide to strategic development, if only because it forces answers to questions such as the following:

- How fast will the market grow?

- What will be our market share?

- What investment will be required?

- How can we create a balanced portfolio from this point?

The questions posed and the answers generated through use of the Boston Box, however, do not themselves generate marketing strategies. As with all analytical tools and methodologies, the matrix provides strategic indicators, not solutions; it is management's task to consider information from a variety of sources and then make its own judgement of the best solution. The Boston Box has, however, been criticized for providing rigid solutions to product portfolio evaluation when exceptions to the rule might exist, for example proposing that 'cash cow' products should not be invested in, when a company may rely solely on its 'cash cow' products to provide profits and not necessarily have new offerings in the pipeline to replace them. Equally, the Boston Box proposes that 'dog' offerings should be divested when, in fact, they may actually be returning a profit to the company.

Finding the necessary and objective data to plot the positions of products or strategic business units (SBUs) on the two axes of relative market share and market growth rate can also be problematic. Reliable industry data may not always be available.

Finally, it is not always easy to determine what market we are concerned with. For example, if we consider the smoothie market, does this include fruit-based milkshakes, or even fruit juices more generally?

Marketing Audit

As part of the process for developing a marketing strategy, it is necessary to make sense of all the information that has been collected. This phase—referred to as the strategic market analysis part of the marketing strategy process—requires a marketing audit to be undertaken. Just as a financial audit considers the financial health of an organization, so the marketing audit considers its marketing health. In particular, it brings together views about the three environments. First, it considers the external opportunities and threats, over which management has little or no control. Second, it considers the nature, characteristics, and any changes occurring within the performance environment, over which management has partial influence. Third, it reviews the quality and potential of the organization's products, marketing systems, resources, and capabilities as part of the internal environment, over which the company has full control. The different components of a marketing audit are shown in Figure 4.6.

The audit covers the external environment, an organization's objectives and strategies, and its marketing programmes and performance, plus the organization itself and the relevant marketing systems and procedures. We undertake marketing audits because they bring together critical information, identify weaknesses so that they can be corrected, and provide a platform on which to build marketing strategy.

The marketing audit can be undertaken either by an internal team, led by a senior manager, or—if a more objective interpretation is desired—an outside consultant. Whoever conducts the audit, it should be undertaken on a regular annual basis and be regarded as a positive activity that can feed into marketing strategy. Marketing audits should not be instigated in response to a crisis.

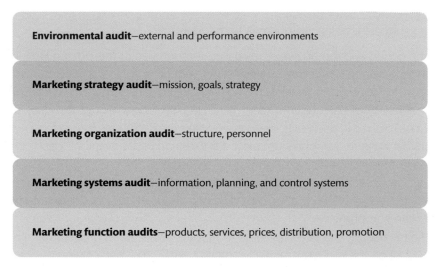

Environmental audit—external and performance environments

Marketing strategy audit—mission, goals, strategy

Marketing organization audit—structure, personnel

Marketing systems audit—information, planning, and control systems

Marketing function audits—products, services, prices, distribution, promotion

Figure 4.6
Dimensions of a marketing audit

 # Chapter Summary

To consolidate your learning, the key points from this chapter are summarized here:

■ **Identify and define the three core areas of the marketing environment.**

The marketing environment incorporates the external environment, the performance environment, and the internal environment. The external environment incorporates macroenvironmental factors, which are largely uncontrollable and which organizations generally cannot influence. The performance environment incorporates key factors within an industry that impact on strategic decision-making. The internal environment is controllable and is the principal means by which an organization influences its strategy, through its resource base.

■ **Describe the key characteristics associated with the marketing environment.**

The external environment consists of the political, social, and technological influences, and organizations have limited influence over these. The performance environment consists of the competitors, suppliers, and indirect service providers, shaping the way in which organizations achieve their objectives. Organizations have more influence over these. The internal environment concerns the resources, processes, and policies with which organizations manage to achieve their goals.

■ **Explain PESTLE analysis and show how it is used to understand the external environment.**

We considered the various components of the external marketing environment that may impact on any particular organization using the PESTLE acronym, which assesses the political, economic, socio-cultural, technological, legal, and ecological factors. Some of these factors are more important than others in any particular industry.

■ **Explain the environmental scanning process.**

The environmental scanning process consists of the data-gathering phase, the environmental interpretation/ analysis phase, and the strategy formulation phase. The three processes are interlinked, but over time more attention is focused on each one more than the others, so that, at the end of the process, greater effort is expended on using knowledge gleaned from the external and competitive environments to formulate strategy based on changes occurring and identified in the company's environment.

■ **Analyse the performance environment using the Porter's Five Forces industry analysis model.**

The most common technique used to analyse the performance environment is Porter's Five Forces model of competitive analysis. Porter (1980) concludes that the more intense the rivalry between the industry players, the lower will be their overall performance. Conversely, the lower the rivalry, the greater will be the performance of the industry players. Porter's Five Forces comprise: supplier bargaining power; buyer bargaining power; the threat of new entrants; rivalry among competitors; and the threat of substitutes.

■ **Analyse an organization's product/service portfolio to aid resource planning.**

An organization's principal resources relate to the portfolio of offerings that it carries and the financial resources at its disposal. We use portfolio analysis—specifically, the Boston Box—to determine whether different SBUs or product/service formulations are stars, dogs, question marks, or cash cows. Each of these categories suggest differing levels of cash flow and require different resources if they are to develop. It is important to undertake a marketing audit as a preliminary measure on the basis of which we can properly develop our marketing strategy.

Review Questions

1 Identify the three main marketing environments.

2 How might changes in the political environment affect marketing strategy?

3 How might changes in the economic environment affect marketing strategy?

4 How might changes in the socio-cultural environment affect marketing strategy?

5 How might changes in the technological environment affect marketing strategy?

6 How might changes in the legal environment affect marketing strategy?

7 How might changes in the ecological environment affect marketing strategy?

8 What are the three stages of the environmental scanning process?

9 What are Porter's Five Forces?

10 What is product portfolio analysis and why is it useful?

 Discussion Questions

1 Read through Case Insight 4.1. How do you think P. Rigas should grow its sales and profits, reduce its bank loans, and still increase the size of its customer base in such a difficult trading environment? (*Hint*: To help you answer the question, research—that is, scan—the current Greek macroenvironment.)

2 Read Market Insight 4.2. Search the Internet for further information on the 'healthy eating' debate on obesity and 'fat taxes', and then answer the following questions:

   A What changes have taken place in the external environment to bring about the introduction of 'fat taxes' in different countries?

   B How should firms such as Warburton's ensure that they keep up to date with trends in consumer lifestyles, government legislation, and competitors' development of new propositions?

   C What strategies, in relation to proposition development and promotion, might Ribena adopt to ensure that it does not get delisted by supermarkets other than Tesco?

3 Undertake an environmental analysis using PESTLE, by searching the Internet for appropriate information and by using available market research reports, for each of the following markets:

   A The automotive market (for example VW, Renault, BMW, Ford, or Toyota)

   B The global multiple retail grocery market (for example Walmart, Carrefour, or Tesco)

   C The beer industry (for example InBev, Carlsberg, Heineken, Miller Brands, or Budweiser Budvar)

4 Using the data in Table 4.1, identify the relative market shares of several leading manufacturer brands in the UK laundry care market. These brands are often in direct competition with each other. Use the market growth rate figure as the difference in total sales between 2011 and 2016, then draw up a Boston Box to illustrate the product portfolio for each of the key companies and its brands.

Table 4.1 UK laundry care market

	2011	2012	2013	2014	2015	2016
Persil (Unilever)	12.1%	12%	13.1%	13.5%	13.5%	13.6%
Ariel (Procter & Gamble)	11.6%	12%	12.1%	11.6%	10.4%	9.9%
Surf (Unilever Group)	6.9%	7.3%	7.3%	7.5%	7.4%	7.3%
Bold (Procter & Gamble)	8.7%	8.6%	7.7%	7.2%	7%	7%
Vanish (Reckitt Benckiser)	4.5%	4.7%	4.7%	5.4%	6.3%	6.9%
Fairy (Procter & Gamble)	6.4%	6.5%	6.6%	6.5%	6.3%	6.3%

Note: The percentages represent the share of the retail value within the laundry care market for each brand for the relevant year. The figures total about half of the value because minor brands and private labels are excluded from the analysis.
Source: Euromonitor International (2018).

Visit the online resources and complete the Multiple-Choice Questions to assess your knowledge of Chapter 4.

 # Glossary

backward integration when a company takes over one or more of its suppliers; cf. **forward integration**.

blue ocean strategy a strategic approach that focuses on the importance of reconfiguring a market space to identify uncontested new spaces that offer high potential (that is, 'blue oceans'), while avoiding those in which the company must compete on the same terms as most other organizations (that is, 'red oceans').

Boston Box a popular portfolio matrix developed by the Boston Consulting Group (BCG) and hence also sometimes known as the BCG matrix.

competitive advantage achieved when an organization has an edge over its competitors in terms of factors that are important to customers.

competitive scope the breadth of an organization's focus, as measured either horizontally (by the range of its target industries, market segments, or geographical regions) or vertically (by the extent to which it is integrated).

crowdsourcing when an organization outsources a function originally undertaken by its employees to a group ('crowd') of people, either as an open call or in a more restricted way.

environmental scanning the management process internal to an organization designed to identify those external issues, situations, and threats that may impinge on its future and its strategic decision-making.

forward integration when a company takes over one or more of its distributors; cf. **backward integration**.

gross domestic product (GDP) a measure of the output of a nation and the size of its economy; calculated as the market value of all finished goods and services produced in a country during a specified period—typically, annually or quarterly.

inflation the economic condition of rising prices.

key performance indicators (KPIs) metrics developed to measure whether or not a company is achieving its corporate goals (for example on profit margins, total revenues, market share, etc.).

niche market a small part of a market segment that has specific and specialized characteristics, which make it uneconomic for the leading competitors to enter this segment.

performance environment organizations that directly or indirectly influence an organization's ability to achieve its strategic and operational goals.

PESTLE an acronym used to identify a framework that examines the external environment in terms of political, economic, socio-cultural, technological, legal, and ecological factors.

political environment that part of the macroenvironment which is concerned with impending and potential legislation and how it may affect a particular firm.

portfolio analysis an assessment of a company's mix of products, services, investments, and other assets performed to optimize the use of resources and to assess the portfolio's suitability, level of risk, and expected financial return.

positioning the way in which an audience of consumers or buyers perceives a product or service, particularly as a result of the marketing communications process aimed at a target audience.

price-sensitivity the extent to which a company or consumer increases or lowers its purchase volumes in relation to changes in price; a customer is price-insensitive when unit volumes drop proportionately less than increases in prices.

public relations (PR) a non-personal form of communication used by companies to build trust, goodwill, interest, and ultimately relationships with a range of stakeholders.

purchasing power parity (PPP) an economic tool that seeks to demonstrate the relative value of currencies between countries, so that there is an equivalence of purchasing power.

purchasing power parity (PPP) exchange rate a measure used to determine the relative wealth of the population based on the cost of an identified basket of goods, which allows us to compare the wealth of one population with another.

recession a fall in a country's gross domestic product (GDP) for two or more successive quarters in any one year.

reverse engineering the process of developing a (competitor's) product from the finished version (for example from a competitor's prototype) by taking it back to its constituent parts rather than the usual approach of developing a (new) product by combining component parts into a finished product.

scenarios constructs of potential future events explored to assess how different outcomes may result from different strategic decisions.

stakeholders people with an interest (stake) in the levels of profit an organization achieves, its environmental impact, and its ethical conduct in society.

sustainable competitive advantage achieved when an organization is able to offer a superior product to competitors, which is not easily imitated and which enjoys significant market share as a result.

switching costs the psychological, economic, time, and effort-related costs associated with substituting one product or service for another, or changing a supplier from one to another.

third-party logistics (3PL) a firm that provides part or all of the supply chain management functions for another company—especially operational services, such as warehousing and transportation.

 # References

Aguilar, F.Y. (1967). *Scanning the Business Environment*. New York: Macmillan.

Albright, K.S. (2004). Environmental scanning: radar for success. *Information Management Journal*, 38(3), 38–45.

Anon. (2006). Supermarkets covet Polish spend, *BBC News*, 10 September. Retrieve from: http://news.bbc.co.uk/1/hi/business/5332024.stm (accessed 13 October 2018).

Anon. (2012). Larger anti-smoking warnings now on cigarette packs. *CTV News*, 19 June. Retrieve from: https://www.ctvnews.ca/health/larger-anti-smoking-warnings-now-on-cigarette-packs-1.844025 (accessed 13 October 2018).

Anon. (2017). Barcelona supports vote on Catalan independence. *USA Today*, 6 May. Retrieve from: https://www.usatoday.com/story/sports/soccer/2017/05/06/barcelona-supports-vote-on-catalan-independence/101369524/# (accessed 13 October 2018).

Barrie, J. (2015). Tesco, please don't take away my Ribena! *The Telegraph*, 27 July. Retrieve from: https://www.telegraph.co.uk/foodanddrink/healthyeating/11766006/Tesco-please-dont-take-away-my-Ribena.html (accessed 13 October 2018).

Berengueras, J.M. (2013). Tuenti supera los 15 millones de usuarios registrados. *El Periodico de Catalunya*, 21 June. Retrieve from: https://www.elperiodico.com/es/tecnologia/20130121/tuenti-supera-los-15-millones-de-usuarios-registrados-2299093 (accessed 13 October 2018).

Bhalla, G. (2016). Collaboration and co-creation: the road to creating value. *The Marketing Journal*, 25 May. Retrieve from: http://www.marketingjournal.org/collaboration-and-co-creation-the-road-to-creating-value/ (accessed 13 October 2018).

Butler, S., and Kollewe, J. (2016). Tesco and Unilever settle Marmite dispute. *The Guardian*, 13 October. Retrieve from: https://www.theguardian.com/business/2016/oct/13/tesco-unilever-resolve-marmite-dispute-price-supermarket?CMP=share_btn_tw (accessed 13 October 2018).

Buzzell, R.D., Gale, B.T., and Sultan, R.G.M (1975). Market share: a key to profitability. *Harvard Business Review*, January. Retrieve from: https://hbr.org/1975/01/market-share-a-key-to-profitability (accessed 13 October 2018).

Chandy, R.K., Prabhu, J.C., and Antia, K.D. (2003). What will the future bring? Dominance, technology expectations and radical innovation. *Journal of Marketing*, 67(3), 1–18.

Crandell, C. (2016). Customer co-creation is the secret sauce to success. *Forbes*, 10 June. Retrieve from: https://www.forbes.com/sites/christinecrandell/2016/06/10/customer_cocreation_secret_sauce/#43d366b25b6d (accessed 13 October 2018).

Curtis, S. (2015). L'Oréal: how technology is transforming beauty. *The Telegraph*, 18 July. Retrieve from: https://www.telegraph.co.uk/technology/news/11744292/LOreal-How-technology-is-transforming-beauty.html (accessed 13 October 2018).

Dans, E. (2016). Spain's Tuenti: from social network to MVNO. *Medium*, 3 February. Retrieve from: https://medium.com/enrique-dans/spain-s-tuenti-from-social-network-to-mvno-a8992dc670f9 (accessed 13 October 2018).

Davidson, L. (2015). *The Great British Bake Off* is killing packaged bread. *The Telegraph*, 12 August. Retrieve from: https://www.telegraph.co.uk/finance/newsbysector/retailandconsumer/11799225/The-Great-British-Bake-Off-is-killing-packaged-bread.html (accessed 13 October 2018).

DH/ABPI (Department of Health/Association of the British Pharmaceutical Industry) (2012). Statement on arrangements for pricing branded medicines from 2014, 3 August. Retrieve from: http://www.dh.gov.uk/health/2012/08/abpi-dh-statement/ (accessed 13 October 2018).

Elliott, L. (2017). UK inflation figures will shine light on impact of pound's Brexit slide. *The Guardian*, 18 July. Retrieve from: https://www.theguardian.com/business/2017/jul/18/uk-inflation-figures-pound-brexit-city-food-prices (accessed 13 October 2018).

Euromonitor International (2018). Laundry care in the United Kingdom. Retrieve from: https://www.euromonitor.com/laundry-care-in-the-united-kingdom/report (accessed 13 October 2018).

Gensler, L. (2017). The world's largest retailers 2017: Amazon & Alibaba are closing in on Wal-mart. *Forbes*, 24 May. Retrieve from: https://www.forbes.com/sites/laurengensler/2017/05/24/the-worlds-largest-retailers-2017-walmart-cvs-amazon/#49ec2d4e20b5 (accessed 13 October 2018).

Glanfield, E. (2016). 'Unilever would be negatively impacted if the UK were to leave the EU': ten days before Brexit, how the company's boss and his three predecessors told staff it was crucial to stay in Europe. *Daily Mail*, 13 October. Retrieve from: https://www.dailymail.co.uk/news/article-3835455/Unilever-negatively-impacted-UK-leave-EU-Ten-days-Brexit-company-s-boss-three-predecessors-told-staff-crucial-stay-Europe.html#ixzz507hfk01S (accessed 13 October 2018).

Gower, I. (ed.) (2005). *Cosmetics and Fragrances Market Report 2005*. London: Keynote.

Green, J. (2000). The role of theory in evidence-based health promotion practice. *Health Education Research*, 15(2), 125–9.

Hansell, S. (1998). Amazon.com is expanding beyond books. *New York Times*, 5 August. Retrieve from: https://www.nytimes.com/1998/08/05/business/amazoncom-is-expanding-beyond-books.html (accessed 13 October 2018).

Hedley, B. (1977). 'Strategy and the business portfolio', *Long Range Planning*, 10(1), 9–15.

Heisler, Y. (2016). Once mocked, Facebook's $1 billion acquisition of Instagram was a stroke of genius. *BGR*, 29 December. Retrieve from: http://bgr.com/2016/12/29/facebook-instagram-acquisition-1-billion-genius/ (accessed 13 October 2018).

Hillman, A., Keim, G.D., and Schuler, D. (2004). Corporate political activity: a review and research agenda. *Journal of Management*, 30(6), 837–57.

Howe, J. (2006). The rise of crowdsourcing. *Wired*, 1 June. Retrieve from: https://www.wired.com/2006/06/crowds/ (accessed 13 October 2018).

Hughes Neghaiwi, B., and Geller, M. (2015). Changing tastes churn up ice cream industry.

Reuters, 1 September. Retrieve from: https://www.reuters.com/article/2015/09/01/food-icecream-idUSL5N1134KC20150901 (accessed 13 October 2018).

Kang, W., and Montoya, M. (2014). The impact of product portfolio strategy on financial performance: the roles of product development and market entry decisions. *Journal of Product Innovation Management*, 31(3), 516–34.

Katz, M. (2017). Amazon's Turker crowd has had enough. *Wired*, 23 August. Retrieve from: https://www.wired.com/story/amazons-turker-crowd-has-had-enough/ (accessed 13 October 2018).

Kim, W.C., and Mauborgne, R. (2004). Blue ocean strategy. *Harvard Business Review*, 82(10), 76–84.

Lawton, T., and Rajwani, T. (2011). Designing lobbying capabilities: managerial choices in unpredictable environments. *European Business Review*, 23(2), 167–89.

Levin, S. (2017). Did Russia fake black activism on Facebook to sow division in the US? *The Guardian*, 30 September. Retrieve from: https://www.theguardian.com/technology/2017/sep/30/blacktivist-facebook-account-russia-us-election (accessed 13 October 2018).

Levitt, T. (1960). Marketing myopia. *Harvard Business Review*, 38(4), 45–56.

Lewin, K. (1935). *A Dynamic Theory of Personality*. New York: McGraw-Hill.

Mason, R. (2017). Government asks big companies to sign letter backing Brexit strategy. *The Guardian*, 6 September. Retrieve from: https://www.theguardian.com/politics/2017/sep/06/uk-government-asks-big-companies-sign-letter-backing-brexit-strategy (accessed 13 October 2018).

May, R.C., Stewart, W.H., Jr, and Sweo, R. (2000). Environmental scanning behaviour in a transitional economy: evidence from Russia. *Academy of Management Journal*, 43(3), 403–27.

Misachi, J. (2017). The nations of Europe by the average age at first marriage. *World Atlas*, 25 April. Retrieve from: https://www.worldatlas.com/articles/the-nations-of-europe-by-the-average-age-at-first-marriage.html (accessed 13 October 2018).

Mizrahi, I. (2017). The Hispanic market 'long tail': five hidden growth opportunities for US CMOs to win in 2017. *Forbes*, 18 January. Retrieve from: https://www.forbes.com/sites/onmarketing/2017/01/18/the-hispanic-market-long-tail-five-hidden-growth-opportunities-for-u-s-cmos-to-win-in-2017/#14ad345e22ca (accessed 13 October 2018).

Morrison, A., and Wensley, R. (1991). Boxing up or boxing in: a short history of the Boston Consulting Group share/growth matrix. *Journal of Marketing Management*, 7(2), 105–29.

Neate, R. (2013). Coca-Cola takes full control of innocent. *The Guardian*, 22 February. Retrieve from: https://www.theguardian.com/business/2013/feb/22/coca-cola-full-control-innocent (accessed 13 October 2018).

Noble, C.H., Sinha, R.K., and Kumar, A. (2002). Market orientation and alternative strategic orientations: a longitudinal assessment of performance implications. *Journal of Marketing*, 66(4), 25–40.

O'Connell, J.J., and Zimmerman, J.W. (1979). Scanning the international environment. *California Management Review*, 22(2), 15–23.

Orsato, R.J. (2006). Competitive environmental strategies: when does it pay to be green? *California Management Review*, 48(2), 127–43.

Otto, C. (2016). Tuenti cerrará su red social: sus 20 millones de usuarios no son rentables. *Confidencial*, 1 February. Retrieve from: https://www.elconfidencial.com/tecnologia/2016-02-01/tuenti-cerrara-su-red-social-sus-20-millones-de-usuarios-no-son-rentables_1141970/ (accessed 13 October 2018).

Papadimas, L., and Maltezou, R. (2015). Greeks defy Europe with overwhelming referendum 'No'. *Reuters*, 5 July. Retrieve from: https://www.reuters.com/article/us-eurozone-greece/greeks-defy-europe-with-overwhelming-referendum-no-idUSKBN0P40EO20150705 (accessed 13 October 2018).

Porter, M.E. (1979). How competitive forces shape strategy. *Harvard Business Review*, 57(2), 137–45.

Porter, M.E. (1980). *Competitive Strategy: Techniques for Analysing Industries and Competitors*. New York: Free Press.

Pullen, J.P. (2017a). Facebook removed 'tens of thousands of fake accounts' for German election. *Fortune*, 27 September. Retrieve from: http://fortune.com/2017/09/27/facebook-fake-accounts-german-election/ (accessed 13 October 2018).

Pullen, J.P. (2017b). Mark Zuckerberg outlines Facebook's plan to fight Russian election hacking. *Fortune*, 21 September. Retrieve from: http://fortune.com/2017/09/21/mark-zuckerberg-outlines-facebooks-plan-to-fight-russian-election-hacking/ (accessed 13 October 2018).

Ramirez, R., Churchhouse, S., Hoffman, J., and Palermo, A. (2017). Using scenario planning to reshape strategy. *MIT Sloan Management Review*, 58(4), 31–37.

Rao, P.M. (2005). Sustaining competitive advantage in a high-technology environment: a strategic marketing perspective. *Advances in Competitiveness Research*, 13(1), 33–47.

Royal Dutch Shell (2018). Shell scenarios. Retrieve from: https://www.shell.com/energy-and-innovation/the-energy-future/scenarios.html (accessed 13 October 2018).

Schumpeter, J.A. (1934). *The Theory of Economic Development*. Cambridge, MA: Harvard University Press.

Shayon, S. (2014). L'Oréal taps smart tech for Genius Makeup app. *Brandchannel*, 16 May. Retrieve from: https://brandchannel.com/2014/05/16/loreal-taps-smart-tech-for-genius-makeup-app/ (accessed 13 October 2018).

Sheffield, H. (2016). Why some of the biggest companies in the UK didn't sign the pro-EU letter. *The Independent*, 23 February. Retrieve from: http://www.independent.

co.uk/news/business/news/why-some-of-the-biggest-companies-in-the-uk-didnt-sign-the-pro-eu-letter-a6890841.html (accessed 13 October 2018).

Teece, D.J. (1986). Profiting from technological innovation. *Research Policy*, 15(6), 285–305.

Thomas, K. (2016). The price of health: the cost of developing new medicines. *The Guardian*, 30 March. Retrieve from: https://www.theguardian.com/healthcare-network/2016/mar/30/new-drugs-development-costs-pharma (accessed 13 October 2018).

Ward, V. (2015). Cake and biscuit sales slowdown as *Bake Off* fuels boom in home baking. *The Telegraph*, 2 September. Retrieve from: https://www.telegraph.co.uk/culture/tvandradio/great-british-bake-off/11839482/Cake-and-biscuit-sales-slow-down-as-Bake-Off-fuels-boom-in-home-baking.html (accessed 13 October 2018).

Westcott, L. (2015). L'Oréal to start printing 3-D skin with bioengineering company. *Newsweek*, 20 May. Retrieve from: https://www.newsweek.com/loreal-start-printing-3-d-skin-bioengineering-company-334204 (accessed 13 October 2018).

Whitla, P. (2009). Crowdsourcing and its application in marketing activities. *Contemporary Management Research*, 5(1), 15–28.

Wong, J.C. (2017). Russia's election ad campaign shows Facebook's biggest problem is Facebook. *The Guardian*, 22 September. Retrieve from: https://www.theguardian.com/technology/2017/sep/21/facebook-russia-advertising-mark-zuckerberg (accessed 13 October 2018).

Young, T. (2015). A fat tax is not the way to fight obesity. *The Telegraph*, 29 July. Retrieve from: http://www.telegraph.co.uk/news/health/news/11770042/A-fat-tax-is-not-the-way-to-fight-obesity.html (accessed 13 October 2018).

Zhu, K. (2014). Top 4 reasons to divest. *Axial*, 12 February. Retrieve from: https://www.axial.net/forum/top-4-reasons-divest/ (accessed 13 October 2018).

Chapter 5
Marketing Strategy

Learning Outcomes

After reading this chapter, you will be able to:

▶ Describe the strategic planning process and explain the key influences that shape marketing strategy

▶ Analyse current conditions and formulate marketing strategies

▶ Explain the different types of strategic marketing goal and associated growth strategies

▶ Describe the concepts associated with strategic market action

▶ Appreciate the main issues associated with strategy implementation, including the principles of marketing metrics

▶ Explain the key elements of a marketing plan

Case Insight 5.1
3scale

Market Insight 5.1
Making a (Values) Statement

Market Insight 5.2
KBC Bank: 'The Bank of You'

Market Insight 5.3
Targeting the Bottom of the Pyramid

Market Insight 5.4
Airlines: Fight and Flight

Market Insight 5.5
A Tale of Two Tech Companies

Case Insight 5.1
3scale

Through its staff and offices in Barcelona and San Francisco, 3scale helps organizations to open, manage, and use application programming interfaces (APIs). We speak to Manfred Bortenschlager, API market development director, to find out how the company competes in its marketplace.

Steven Willmott and Martin Tantow founded 3scale in 2007, convinced that the world would become web-enabled with APIs as a critical digital infrastructure requirement. The initial 3scale product focused on an API marketplace, providing a matchmaking service between API providers and API consumers. The company quickly shifted to a more powerful business model—providing management capabilities for API providers. Now, 3scale sells an API management product based on monthly subscriptions with different price plans, starting with a free plan in its basic form, freemium, also known as the Software-as-a-Service (SaaS) model. This model is successful because it perfectly serves customers' needs for flexibility and scale. Today, 3scale powers the APIs for close to 700 organizations.

Application programming interfaces are a software technology that provide organizations with a novel and effective way of distributing and leveraging digital assets. They represent gateways to an organization's data or services (that is, digital assets), which can be programmed and accessed by software, increasing automation, scalability, and efficiency. As an analogy, APIs can be seen as an automatic door to a building with a security mechanism (such as a pass code or a chip card). Digital transformation and digital strategies are based on APIs. The 3scale API management product provides the essential security, visibility, and control that allows organizations to define and measure their strategies when using APIs. In terms of value chain and customer requirements, our service uses a business-to-business-to-customer (B2B2C) model as follows: API provider (owning and providing digital assets) serves a developer (developing and distributing web or mobile apps), who serves the end user (the final consumer of the apps and APIs).

The most important customer requirements from the developer's perspective are, first, the value of the data or service that the API provides access to (the more unique, the higher the value) and, second, simplicity of access to the API. The most important customer requirement from an end consumer's perspective is added value to an application via additional functionality. This is often achieved via so-called API mashups, whereby a developer combines the APIs of various API providers to create something new for the end consumer. Another requirement is 'user experience', which includes ease of use, clarity, consistency, and speed.

3scale operates in a very fast-moving industry. To be successful, customer focus is essential. We need to constantly adapt our offering in terms of product features and the pricing model. To achieve that, we need to integrate engineering, marketing, and sales processes, and be able to react to change quicker than our competitors. We differentiate between 'self-service' and 'enterprise' customers. Self-service customers adopt the 3scale offer almost without any human interaction, whereas customers on enterprise plans get 24/7 phone support and/or higher guaranteed product reliability. 3scale has three main competitive differentiators:

1   The 3scale product is modular and uses cloud technologies in a unique way. Based on the customer's requirements, they can choose to host some of the product modules in 'the cloud' and some on their own IT infrastructure. This gives unmatched availability, scalability, and flexibility.

2   3scale offers the shortest time to value in the market, achieved via a comprehensive self-service

Case Insight 5.1
continued

model and detailed documentation. Customers can adopt 3scale very quickly and leverage the benefits of APIs instantly.

3 The freemium subscription model is fair and transparent with very competitive pricing. Customers appreciate the low barrier of entry and the subscription model is easy to understand, with no surprises.

One complex problem was that Amazon Web Services (AWS)—based around cloud technologies—launched the Amazon API Gateway product. This was perceived by many observers in the API management market to be a potential threat. With its size and financial resources, the expectation was that it could have a substantial impact on existing players in the market.

The question was: what strategy should 3scale develop to circumvent this competitive threat from Amazon?

 Visit the online resources to watch a video interview with Manfred Bortenschlager in which he explains what 3scale developed.

Introduction

Have you ever thought about how organizations coordinate themselves so that they can make sales, achieve profits, and keep their stakeholders satisfied? This does not happen accidentally. A great deal of thought, discussion, planning, and action needs to occur, which involves seeking answers to questions such as which markets the organization should be operating in, what resources are necessary to be successful in these markets, who the key competitors are and what strategies they are using, how we can develop and sustain a **competitive advantage**, and what is happening in the world that might affect our organization? Indeed, these are some of the key questions facing 3scale in Case Insight 5.1. You might notice that they refer to issues that represent the strategic context in which organizations operate. These contextual issues can be considered in terms of four main elements: the organization (and its resources, skills, and capabilities); the target customers; the firm's competitors; and the wider external environment. These are set out in Figure 5.1.

Figure 5.1
The four elements of the strategic context

For example, Samsung's strategic context is shaped by its communications expertise and leading-edge technology skills, customers who expect a stream of added-value communication-related products, and its main competitor, Apple. In addition, the wider environment is becoming politically more sensitive to climate-change issues, terrorism, social change, the repercussions of the economic crisis, and surges in technological development. By understanding and managing these four elements, we can develop a coherent strategic marketing plan through which offerings have a greater chance of success than if no analysis or planning is undertaken. For marketing strategy to be developed successfully, it is necessary to understand an organization's strategic context and to formulate and fit the strategy to complement the strategic context. Many organizations articulate their strategic context and their intended performance in the markets they target in terms of a framework that defines their vision, mission, **values**, **organizational goals**, and organizational strategy.

The **vision statement** sets out an organization's future. It is a statement about what an organization wants to become, giving shape and direction to its future. A vision should stretch an organization in terms of its current position and performance, yet also help employees to feel involved and motivated to want to be part of the organization's future. According to its website, Samsung Electronics' vision for the current decade is to 'Inspire the World, Create the Future'. As part of this vision, Samsung plans to create a better world full of richer digital experiences, through innovative technology and products.

The **mission statement** (often labelled 'purpose' in strategy documents) represents what the organization wishes to achieve in the long term. It should be a broad statement of intention, setting out an organization's purpose and direction, oriented towards particular markets and customers. A mission applies to all parts of an organization, binding its many elements together. Above all else, however, the mission should aid managers and employees in making investment and development decisions concerning which opportunities to pursue and which to ignore. Table 5.1 gives examples of different mission statements.

Visit the **online resources** and complete Internet Activity 5.1 to learn more about the use of mission and vision statements by different organizations and their implications for marketing activities.

Mission statements are sometimes so generic that they fail to provide sufficient guidelines or inspiration. Some stretch possibility to such an extent that they simply set a company up to fail. For example, to expect an airport such as Adelaide or Hong Kong to become the largest airport in the world would be unrealistic. Good mission statements are market-, not product-, oriented. For example, a product-oriented approach such as 'we make and sell lorries and trucks' is too general, and runs the risk of becoming outdated and redundant. By focusing on customers' needs, the mission can be more realistic and durable. So 'we transport your products quickly and safely to your customers', or 'logistical solutions for your company', provides a market approach to the mission statement. Amazon.com does not simply sell books, Kindles, and DVDs (product approach); it is much better to say that Amazon.com 'strives to be Earth's most customer-centric company where people can find and discover virtually everything they want to buy online' (Amazonjobs, n.d.).

An organization's values must coincide with its vision and mission, because they define how people should behave towards each other within the organization and help to shape how goals are achieved. Organizational values define the acceptable interpersonal and operating standards of behaviour. They govern and guide the behaviour of individuals within the organization.

Table 5.1 A selection of mission statements

Organization (country of origin)	Mission (Purpose) statement
Tesco UK	'Serving customers a little better every day'
Coca-Cola (US)	• 'To refresh the world in mind, body and spirit • To inspire moments of optimism and happiness through our brands and actions • To create value and make a difference'
Maserati (Italy)	'. . . to build ultimate luxury cars exuding timeless Italian style which have exotic interiors'
Oxfam (UK)	'. . . to help create lasting solutions to the injustice of poverty. We are part of a global movement for change, empowering people to create a future that is secure, just, and free from poverty.'
Electrolux (Sweden)	'We reinvent taste, care and wellbeing experiences for more enjoyable and sustainable living around the world. To create these experiences we focus our innovation on three areas: We help people make great tasting, healthy food for friends and family. . . . We help consumers care for their clothes by making them stay new and great looking for longer. . . . . . . Electrolux helps consumers get a better home environment through floor care, air care and water care.'
JCB (UK)	'Our mission is to grow our company by providing innovative, strong, high-performance products and solutions to meet our global customers' needs. We will support our world-class products by providing superior customer care. Our care extends to the environment and the community. We want to help build a better future for our children, where hard work and dedication are given their just reward.'

Sources: https://www.tescoplc.com/about-us/core-purpose-and-values/; https://www.coca-cola.co.uk/about-us/mission-vision-and-values; https://successstory.com/companies/maserati; https://www.oxfam.org/en/our-purpose-and-beliefs; https://www.electroluxgroup.com/en/electrolux-purpose-18919/; https://www.jcb.com/en-gb/about/careers/why-work-at-jcb

Organizations that identify and develop a clear, concise, and shared meaning of values and beliefs shape the **organizational culture** and provide strategic direction.

Organizational values are important because they can help to guide and constrain employee behaviour, as well as recruitment and selection decisions. Without them, individuals tend to pursue behaviours that are in line with their own individual value systems, which may be inappropriate and may lead to a failure to achieve corporate goals. However, values do not drive a business as such; rather, they can be used to motivate the employees within the business. For values to be useful and have meaning, they must be internalized by the organization (see Market Insight 5.1).

Market Insight 5.1
Making a (Values) Statement

IKEA, the world's largest furniture dealer, claims that its values affect its ways of working (WOWs). Its values statement is based on Ingvar Kamprad's *The Testament of a Furniture Dealer*, a guidebook written for his co-workers in the 1970s, and, for the UK division, is worded as follows.

Togetherness

Togetherness is at the heart of the IKEA culture. We are strong when we trust each other, pull in the same direction and have fun together.

Caring for people and planet

We want to be a force for positive change. We have the possibility to make a significant and lasting impact—today and for the generations to come.

Cost-consciousness

As many people as possible should be able to afford a beautiful and functional home. We constantly challenge ourselves and others to make more from less without compromising on quality.

Simplicity

A simple, straightforward and down-to-earth way of being is part of our Småland heritage. It is about being ourselves and staying close to reality. We are informal, pragmatic and see bureaucracy as our biggest enemy.

Renew and improve

We are constantly looking for new and better ways forward. Whatever we are doing today, we can do better tomorrow. Finding solutions to almost impossible challenges is part of our success and a source of inspiration to move on to the next challenge.

Different with a meaning

IKEA is not like other companies and we don't want to be. We like to question existing solutions, think in unconventional ways, experiment and dare to make mistakes—always for a good reason.

Give and take responsibility

We believe in empowering people. Giving and taking responsibility are ways to grow and develop as individuals.

Trusting each other, being positive and forward-looking inspire everyone to contribute to development.

Lead by example

We see leadership as an action, not a position. We look for people's values before competence and experience. People who 'walk the talk' and lead by example. It is about being our best self and bringing out the best in each other.

In an open statement, Samuel J. Palmisano, former chair, president, and chief executive officer (CEO) of tech company IBM, recalled the way in which IBM's current values originated. He referred to the time spent thinking, debating, and determining IBM's fundamentals. He felt that, in a time of great change, IBM needed to affirm reasons for being, for setting out how the company is different to others, and what should drive individual employee behaviour:

> Importantly, we needed to find a way to engage everyone in the company and get them to speak up on these important issues. Given the realities of a smart, global, independent-minded, 21st-century workforce like ours, I don't believe something as vital and personal as values could be dictated from the top.

Samuel J. Palmisano, IBM's former chair, president and chief executive officer, worked openly to develop an inclusive culture based on agreed values
Source: Gage Skidmore/Wikimedia Commons/CC-BY-SA-3.0.

Market Insight 5.1
continued

So, for a three-day period in 2003, for the first time in 100 years, the then 319,000 IBMers worldwide were invited to engage in an open 'ValuesJam' on the global intranet. Following much open debate, honesty, and involvement, the following values emerged:

- 'Dedication to every client's success';

- 'Innovation that matters—for our company and for the world'; and

- 'Trust and personal responsibility in all relationships'.

Palmisano's statement concludes thus:

> To me, it's also just common sense. In today's world, where everyone is so interconnected and interdependent, it is simply essential that we work for each other's success. If we're going to solve the biggest, thorniest and most widespread problems in business and society, we have to innovate in ways that truly matter. And we have to do all this by taking personal responsibility for all of our relationships—with clients, colleagues, partners, investors and the public at large. This is IBM's mission as an enterprise, and a goal toward which we hope to work with many others, in our industry and beyond.

Sources: https://www.ikea.com/gb/en/this-is-ikea/working-at-the-ikea-group/who-we-are/; https://www.ibm.com/ibm/values/us/

Theory into Practice

Whilst both values statements stress ways of working, the IBM example also supports the generally accepted idea that an organization's values should be about what an organization wants to become, by giving shape and direction to its future. The process by which organizations develop the wording of their values statements is important, because it determines the extent to which employees buy into them and follow them. By defining how all employees should behave and the importance of relationships within the organization, both IBM and IKEA seek to shape how their goals can be accomplished.

Related Topics

mission statements; corporate strategy; SWOT

1 **How do IKEA's and IBM's sets of values differ?**

2 **What might be the impact on employees of seven (IKEA), rather than three (IBM), sets of values?**

3 **Find another values statement, this time from a not-for-profit organization, and compare this with those of IKEA or IBM.**

 Visit the **online resources** and follow the web link to read Ingvar Kamprad's *The Testament of a Furniture Dealer*.

Organizational goals at the strategic level represent what should be achieved—that is, the outcomes of the organization's various activities. These may be articulated in terms of profit, market share, share value, return on investment, or numbers of customers served. In some cases, the long term may not be a viable period of focus and a focus short term is absolutely essential. For example, should an organization's financial position become precarious, it may be necessary to focus on short-term cash strategies to remain solvent and so remove any threat arising from a takeover or administrators being called in prior to bankruptcy.

Organizational strategy, or **corporate strategy**, is the means by which organizational resources are matched with the needs of the organization's operations environment. Corporate strategy involves bringing together human resources, logistics, production, operations, marketing, information technology (IT), and the financial parts of an organization into a coherent strategic plan that supports, reinforces, and accomplishes the organization's goals in the most effective and efficient way. In this chapter, we are concerned with the development of marketing strategy, and how it should support and reinforce corporate strategy.

In some very large organizations, the planning process is complicated by the fact that the organization operates in significantly different markets. In these cases, the organization creates **strategic business units (SBUs)**. Each SBU assumes the role of a separate company and creates its own strategies and plans to achieve its corporate goals. So Indian company Tata operates through seven SBUs—namely, Information Technology and Communications, Engineering, Materials, Services, Energy, Consumer Products, and Chemicals. Each of these Tata companies operates independently. Royal Philips Electronics uses four SBUs: Domestic Appliances and Personal Care; Lighting; Medical Systems; and Consumer Electronics. All of these represent significantly different markets, each with its own characteristics, customer needs, and competitors.

According to McDonald (2002: 37), a global guru of marketing planning, the strategic marketing planning process consists of a series of logical steps to be worked through to arrive at a marketing plan. These steps can be aggregated into four phases. The first phase is concerned with setting the right mission and corporate goals (that is, setting the strategic context). The second involves reviewing the current situation or context in which the organization is operating. The third phase is used to formulate strategy, and the final phase considers the allocation of resources necessary to implement and monitor the plan.

At the broad level, the strategic marketing planning process is focused around the following ten stages:

1 The organization sets out its overall vision, mission, and values at the corporate level.

2 Measurable corporate goals are established that apply to the whole organization.

3 A marketing audit is undertaken to explore the external situation in which the organization intends to operate and the resources available to be used.

4 A SWOT analysis is undertaken to explore the organization's competitive position and how external factors are impacting on the organization.

5 A set of key assumptions is drawn up to help planners to understand the basis on which the plan will be developed (for example whether inflation will continue at 2.5 per cent, whether the UK will have some form of European free trade agreement post-Brexit).

6 Marketing objectives and strategies are formulated (see Research Insight 5.1 for an overview of what strategy is).

7 The marketplace outcomes likely as a result of implementing the plan are estimated.

8 A set of alternative marketing mixes is developed (see Chapter 1) to allow planners to optimize the likely results of implementing the marketing plan.

9 Depending on the size of the organization, the range of SBUs and/or offerings is determined, and a marketing budget and other resources are allocated to help and support each one.

10 Each business and/or offering then develops detailed functional and competitive strategies and plans, such as a one-year implementation plan, the plan is implemented, and the results are measured and used to feed into the next planning cycle (McDonald, 2002).

Research Insight 5.1

To take your learning further, you might wish to read this influential paper:

Mintzberg, H. (1987). The strategy concept: five Ps for strategy. *California Management Review*, 30(1), 11–26.

Mintzberg's seminal paper made an important contribution to how we understand the concept of strategy because it argued that strategy should not simply be regarded as a linear sequential planning process. He explained that strategy can also be interpreted as a plan (what the organization intends to do); a ploy (how an organization seeks to wrong-foot its competitors); pattern (how it responds to market, environment, and competitor stimuli); perspective (how the organization sees itself and how it wants customers to see it); and position (how the organization manages its resources to appeal to its customers vis-à-vis the competition).

 Visit the **online resources** to read the abstract and access the full paper.

Marketing strategy and planning should therefore support and contribute to the overall corporate strategy (see Figure 5.2). However, note that marketing strategy and marketing plans can be written for the business, product/service, or market levels.

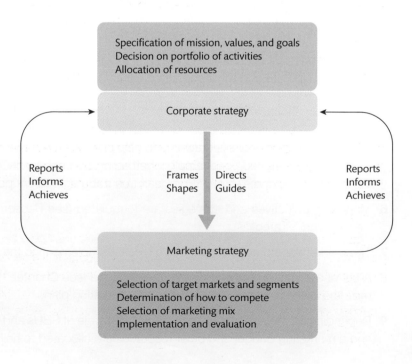

Figure 5.2

The relationship between corporate and marketing strategies

Figure 5.3
Three key activities of marketing strategy development

Strategic Marketing Planning: Activities

The development of a strategic marketing plan is a complex and involved process. It does not occur in linear logical steps, as implied earlier, but certain key aspects can be identified. These aspects concern three broad activities that are necessary when considering the development of marketing strategy and will form the framework within which we examine this topic (see Figure 5.3).

Figure 5.3 shows that it is necessary to first develop knowledge and understanding of the marketplace, referred to here as **strategic market analysis**. Second, it is necessary to determine what the marketing strategy should achieve—that is, what are the strategic marketing goals that need to be accomplished? The third decision area concerns how the goals are to be achieved. This relates directly to strategic market action—that is, how the strategies should be developed as plans and how these plans should be implemented. These three activities form the basis of this chapter and are considered next.

Strategic Market Analysis

The starting point of the marketing strategy process is the development of knowledge and understanding about the target market(s) identified as part of the corporate strategy. Different people in the organization have varying levels of market knowledge and expertise, some of it accurate and up to date, but some of it outdated and inaccurate. It is therefore crucial that all people involved in the strategy process maintain accurate, pertinent, and up-to-date information.

In Chapter 4, we saw how PESTLE and environmental scanning processes can be used to understand and make sense of the external environment. We considered Porter's (1985) 'Five Forces' model to understand industry dynamics and how firms should compete strategically if they are to be successful in the performance environment. We also learned about the key elements necessary to appreciate our competitors' actions and intentions. In addition, we gained insight into the importance of understanding the internal environment and how a firm's resources need to complement the external and performance environments. The task now is to assimilate this information—to bring it together in a form that can be easily understood.

SWOT Analysis

Perhaps the most commonly used strategic analysis tool is **SWOT analysis**—that is, the analysis of strengths, weaknesses, opportunities, and threats. It is a series of checklists deriving from the marketing audit and PESTLE analysis, and is presented as internal strengths and weaknesses (that is, relative to the competition), and external opportunities or threats. Strengths and weaknesses relate to the internal resources and capabilities of the organization, as perceived by customers (Piercy, 2002):

- A *strength* is therefore something an organization is good at doing, or something that gives it particular credibility and market advantage.

- A *weakness* is something an organization lacks or performs in an inferior way in comparison with others.

Opportunities and threats are externally oriented issues that can potentially influence the performance of an organization or offering. Information about these elements is generated through PESTLE analysis:

- An *opportunity* is the potential to advance the organization by developing and satisfying an unfulfilled market need.

- A *threat* is something that, at some time in the future, may destabilize and/or reduce the potential performance of the organization.

SWOT analysis is used to determine an organization's strategic position and is therefore an input to the strategy option formulation process. It highlights the need for a strategy to produce a strong fit between the internal capability (strengths and weaknesses) and the external situation (opportunities and threats). SWOT helps us to sort through the information generated in the audit and to identify the key issues, and it prompts thought about converting weaknesses into strengths and threats into opportunities—that is, generating conversion strategies. For example, some companies have developed and run call centres for their own internal use, but saw opportunities to leverage that strength and run call centres for other companies.

In inexperienced hands, SWOT often leads to long lists of items. Although the SWOT process may lead to the generation of these lists, the analyst should be attempting to identify the key strengths and weaknesses (which should link to the competitor analysis and Porter's Five Forces) and the key opportunities and threats (which should link to the PESTLE analysis). The individual SWOT elements should be developed because they impact on strategy; if they don't, they should not be included within the analysis. A 'strength' is not a strength if it has no strategic implications and if it not something that helps the company to compete in the marketplace.

Once the three or four elements of each part of the SWOT matrix have been derived, then a number of pertinent questions need to be asked, as follows:

1 Does the organization do something far better than its rivals? If it does, this is known as a competitive advantage (or distinctive competence, or differential advantage), and can lead to a competitive edge.

2 Which of the organization's weaknesses does the strategy need to correct and is it competitively vulnerable?

3 Which opportunities can be pursued, and are there the necessary resources and capabilities to exploit them?

4 Which strategies are necessary to defend against the key threats?

Figure 5.4 depicts a SWOT grid for a small digital media agency. The outcome of a successful SWOT analysis is a series of decisions that help the company to develop and formulate strategy and goals. Note that there are no more than four items in any one category, rather than a list of ten or so items. It is important to prioritize and make a judgement about what is really key. The actions that follow the identification of key issues should be based around matching opportunities with strengths, and weaknesses with threats. In this example, it may be possible to diversify

Strengths	Weaknesses
Quick to respond to changes in the marketing environment	Too much work from a few clients and at non-premium rates
Flat management encourages fast decision-making	Few project management skills
Use of contractors enables flexibility—lowers employment costs/finance and improves customers' perception of expertise	High office and finance costs Low customer base
Opportunities	**Threats**
Emerging markets such as professional services (e.g. dentists, lawyers, surveyors)	Larger media houses buying business
New distribution channels	Speed of technological advances
Tax incentives to encourage e-commerce	Contractors have low levels of loyalty

Figure 5.4

A SWOT analysis for a small digital media agency

into professional services, a **niche market** (an opportunity), using particular contractors who have knowledge and relevant expertise (a strength).

Weaknesses need to be addressed, not avoided. Some can be converted into strengths; others, into opportunities. In this example, entering the professional services market would probably increase the number of customers and enable premium rates to be earned. Threats, meanwhile, need to be nullified. For example, by building relationships with key contractors (suppliers) and selected larger media houses, the agency in Figure 5.4 might dissipate its threats—or even develop them into strengths. Prahalad and Hamel (1990) popularized the idea that organizations should stick to developing what they are good at—that is, focus on developing their core competences. Consequently, many companies started to divest themselves of businesses that were not profitable or which were tangential to their main purpose (see Market Insight 5.2).

 Visit the **online resources** and complete Internet Activity 5.2 to learn more about the use of SWOT analysis.

Strategic Marketing Goals

The purpose of strategic market analysis is to help managers to understand the nature of an industry, the way in which firms behave competitively within the industry, and how competition is generally undertaken. From this information, it becomes easier to determine exactly what the marketing strategy should actually achieve—that is, what the strategic marketing goals should be.

Research Insight 5.2

To take your learning further, you might wish to read this influential paper:

Prahalad, C.K., and Hamel, G. (1990). The core competence of the organisation. *Harvard Business Review*, 68(3), 79–91.

This article was ground-breaking because it provided a first important insight into core competencies as a critical means of developing superior business performance. The article led a revolution in management thinking, which moved away from aiming to develop conglomerates comprising disparate and unrelated SBUs towards aiming to develop companies with SBUs that were aligned with each other based on a common set of organizational resources and capabilities.

 Visit the online resources to read the abstract and access the full paper.

There are several types of strategic objective, but four main ones are considered briefly here: **niche**; **hold**; **harvest**; and **divest**. However, the section that follows considers a further objective—namely, growth (see Figure 5.5).

Niche objectives are often the most suitable when firms operate in a market dominated by a major competitor and financial resources are limited. A niche can be a small segment or even a small part of a segment. Niche markets arise because it is not economic for the leading competitors to enter this segment given that these customers have special needs and the leading firm does not want to devote resources to them. To be successful in niche markets, it is important to have a strongly differentiated product offering, supported by a high level of service. (See Market Insight 5.2 for an example of an Irish bank adopting a niche position in its marketplace.) The Australian government, for example, identified several niche markets when exploring the development of its tourism business. It identified sports, cycling seniors, culture and the arts, backpackers, health, people with disabilities, caravanning and camping, food, wine, and agritourism as potential niche markets.

Figure 5.5

Five types of strategic marketing goal

Market Insight 5.2
KBC Bank: 'The Bank of You'

Irish retail banking was traditionally dominated by only a few established competitors. KBC Bank Ireland, originally set up as an Irish intercontinental bank, entered domestic personal banking as a challenger brand in 2013 with a current account product. Since then, it has expanded into credit cards, personal loans, overdrafts, and other product areas. With a staff of more than 1,000, and making a commitment in 2017 to expand and grow with its 'Digital First' focus, KBC Group's €1.5 billion investment saw the establishment of an Innovation Hub in Dublin—aiming to transform the bank's digital capabilities Europe-wide. Adopting a niche strategy, KBC focused on targeting millennials, who tend to be early adopters on the cusp of making big financial decisions and who are digitally savvy.

KBC Bank positions itself as 'The Bank of You'. As a 'Digital First' challenger bank, it differentiates itself from its competitors by providing a consumer-focused brand experience. Its brand manifesto exclaims:

> We believe banking is something you should do, not just a place you visit. A bank that fits into your life as well as your pocket. That's on your terms and on your time. Our opening hours are your opening hours. We see people as people but treat them as customers. Whether it's web chat, phone chat or a face-to-face chat. At our hub or at yours. So let's start experiencing . . . the bank of you.

To live 'Digital First' requires a strong digital offering, so when Google launched Android Pay in December 2016, it was available to KBC's customers on the day of launch. KBC is the only bank in Ireland to offer digital wallets from four of the world's leading technology companies: Apple Pay; Google Pay; FitBit Pay; and Garmin Pay. Co-designed with consumers, the launch of a new instant on-boarding mobile app in 2017 was the first of its kind in the market, coming in response to growing customer demand for digital solutions that combine faster credit decision times with a seamless application and approval process. The app allows customers to open a current account and start banking in only 5 minutes. In 2018, KBC enhanced its positioning by offering overdraft and consumer finance, by lending up to €20,000 via the app, and by allowing new and existing customers to get approval and funds in no more than 60 minutes.

Although KBC is a 'Digital First' challenger bank, it has 16 non-traditional hubs around the country, recognizing that customers occasionally want personal meetings with advisers. Comfortable seats and booths, with free Wi-Fi and barista coffee, replace the traditional banking experience. With large digital screens, an open-plan layout, and greetings from a digital ambassador, KBC has broken away from the traditional banking mould—and it's paying off. KBC has grown its customer base and the average number of products that customers hold is increasing. The bank has been awarded Gold for the 'Best Technology/ Innovation Campaign' for its instant account-opening app ('five steps in five minutes') in the 2018 Smart Marketing Awards. KBC customers are highly engaged, with mobile transactions increasing by 58 per cent year on year.

Sources: KBC (2018a, 2018b, 2018c, n.d.); Nugent (2018).

Theory into Practice

This market insight illustrates how a challenger bank launched a new proposition in a new market by positioning its offering mainly around millennials. Given limited financial resources and the market advantage of incumbent banks, it developed a strongly differentiated offering by focusing on a digital-led customer strategy. Millennials in particular were drawn to the brand and its offerings as KBC Bank introduced innovative digital products with immediate access and quick decision-making, along with quirky advertising campaigns that look and feel different from those of other banks.

Market Insight 5.2
continued

Related Topics

digital marketing; segmentation; positioning; niche marketing

1 Why do you think KBC Bank Ireland was keen to target millennials?

2 Will KBC Bank be able to continue to dominate this niche market? Why, or why not?

3 What other brands can you think of that adopt a niche marketing strategy?

This market insight was kindly contributed by Dr Lucia Walsh, Dublin Institute of Technology, Ireland.

Hold objectives are concerned with defence. They are designed to prevent and fend off attack from aggressive competitors. Market leaders are the most likely to adopt a holding strategy because they are prone to attack from new entrants and their closest rivals as they strive for the most market share. Apple, with around 44 per cent of the global handset market, was pursuing this strategy when it launched the iPhone X in late 2017 with new features such as an edge-to-edge organic light-emitting diode (OLED) screen, wireless charging, facial recognition technology, and a dual-lens camera—all in the hopes of fending off arch-rival Samsung, which holds 22 per cent of the global market, and which launched the Galaxy Note 8 with similar product attributes the same week (Anon., 2017a). Market leadership is important because it generally drives positive cash flows, confers privileges such as strong bargaining positions with suppliers, and enhances image and reputation. Hold strategies can take a number of forms, varying from 'doing nothing' to maintain market equilibrium, through implementing a counter-offensive, to withdrawing from a market completely.

Harvest objectives are often employed in mature markets as firms/offerings enter a decline phase. The goal is to maximize short-term profits and stimulate a positive cash flow. By stripping out marketing communications and research and development (R&D), it becomes possible to generate cash for use elsewhere. These funds generate new offerings, support Boston Box 'stars', or turn 'question marks' into 'dogs' (see Chapter 4).

Divest objectives are necessary when offerings continue to incur losses and generate negative cash flows. Divestment can follow on naturally from a harvesting strategy. Typically, low share offerings in declining markets are prime candidates to be divested. Divestment can make companies much more profitable if they reinvest the returns in new profitable ventures (Mankins, Harding, and Weddigen, 2008). In a study by Bain & Company, companies focused on divestment significantly outperform those that are not by about 15 per cent over a ten-year period, based on **total shareholder return** (Wininger and Rujana, 2017). Divestment may be actioned by selling off the offering should a suitable buyer be available, or by simply withdrawing from the market. For example, Procter & Gamble (P&G) divested the Sunny Delight orange drink brand, General Motors sold off Saab to sports car manufacturer Spyker, and Ford sold off Jaguar to Indian company Tata. In 2014, Johnson & Johnson divested its Ortho Clinical Diagnostics unit, which makes blood-screening equipment and laboratory blood tests, to the Carlyle Group.

Growth

The vast majority of organizations consider growth to be a primary objective. However, there are different forms of growth and care needs to be taken to ensure that the right growth goals are selected. Growth can be intensive, integrated, or diversified:

- **Intensive growth** refers to concentrating activities on markets and/or offerings that are familiar. By increasing market share or introducing new offerings to an established market, growth is achieved by intensifying activities. For example, Volkswagen, the world's biggest carmaker in 2017, has said it will launch 30 new electric vehicles (EVs) by 2025, predicting that they will account for up to 25 per cent of its sales (Anon., 2017b).

- **Integrative growth** occurs where an organization continues to work with the same offerings and the same markets, but starts to perform some of the activities in the value chain that were previously undertaken by others. For example, Benetton moved from designing and manufacturing its clothing products into retailing them as well.

- Growth through **diversification** refers to developments outside the current chain of value-adding activities. This type of growth brings new value chain activities because the firm is operating with new offerings and in new markets. For example, Mars bought VCA, a veterinary services company, for US$9.1 billion, building its profile in the pet care business, alongside its manufacture of pet food products such as Whiskas, Sheba, and Pedigree (Nicolaou, 2017).

The idea that growth is allied to product–market relationships is important and Ansoff (1957) proposed that organizations should first consider whether new or established products are to be delivered in new or established markets. His product–market matrix (Figure 5.6), otherwise known as Ansoff's matrix, is an important first step in deciding what the marketing strategy should be. (The product–market matrix is examined further in Chapter 7.)

One strategy that several large corporations employ is to target new or adapted products at extremely poor people in underdeveloped countries. Referred to as 'bottom of the pyramid' (BoP) strategies (Prahalad, 2004), the approach requires firms to offer products at extremely low prices to the poorest individuals. By maintaining an extremely low cost base, they can generate low margins. Respectable profits can be achieved, however, because of the huge sales volumes. For example, Bangladesh is regarded as an attractive market because it has a population of more than 163 million. Unilever sold its Wheel brand detergent to low-income consumers in India using this strategy (Payaud, 2014).

Genuine BoP marketing strategies are considered to involve three main criteria:

- they are directed at the very poor, and feature both affordability and availability;

- they have a consumer orientation featuring adaptability and consumer education; and

- they are considered to be both fair and inclusive, so that local communities are able to participate in all stages of the value chain.

Market Insight 5.3 offers some examples.

	Present products	**New products**
Present markets	Market penetration	Product development
New markets	Market development	Diversification

Figure 5.6

Ansoff's matrix

Source: Adapted from Ansoff (1957).

Market Insight 5.3
Targeting the Bottom of the Pyramid

Nestlé's strategy involves developing a wide range of popularly positioned products (PPPs) for low-income consumers around the world. These include culinary products, beverages, and dairy and confectionery products sold under a number of major global brands, including Maggi, Nido, and Nescafé. One such PPP, developed in 2009, comprises high-quality food products that provide nutritional value to lower-income consumers. These products are sold at an affordable price and in appropriate formats to address the needs of some 3 billion lower-income consumers worldwide. The products may be fortified with micronutrients that help to address the mineral and vitamin deficiencies that are most prevalent among lower-income consumers (for example iron, zinc, iodine, and vitamin A). To help address iodine deficiency, for example, Nestlé developed its iodine-enriched Maggi products (that is, bouillons, seasonings, and noodles) using iodized salt.

Popularly positioned products are manufactured in single-serve packs that meet the needs of consumers for both affordability and convenience. Single-serves are adapted for on-the-go consumption and are very popular.

In Cameroon, consumers prefer to buy Nido, a powdered milk, in 26-gram single-serves because the quantity corresponds exactly to what is needed for a glass of milk. This avoids overconsumption and waste. Single-serves are also convenient because they avoid problems linked to conservation such as humidity, pests, and a lack of refrigeration. Products are manufactured locally using local perishable agricultural raw materials produced through Nestlé-trained local subcontractors. Cooking caravans travelling through the villages are used to inform consumers about the product benefits and how they should be used.

P&G's Children's Safe Drinking Water Program (CSDW) has provided water purification packets on a not-for-profit basis since 2004. With a range of partners, the programme supplies more than 9 billion litres of purified drinking water to more than 75 countries. P&G's goal is to be providing 15 billion litres of clean drinking water by 2020. P&G's overall marketing strategy, however, involves distributing its international brands to BoP markets, with pack sizes adapted to complement local purchasing power. This indicates that—unlike Danone, which is involved with food products—P&G is not so concerned with the environment or the inclusion of local communities in procurement, production, or distribution processes.

Sources: Payaud (2014); https://csdw.org/about-us; https://www.nestlenido.com/#aboutnido

P&G's Children's Safe Drinking Water Program provides water purification packets on a not-for-profit basis.
Source: Photo courtesy of Procter & Gamble.

Theory into Practice

The PPPs can be considered through the lens of the three main elements that are said to constitute BoP strategies. First, it is clear that PPPs are directed at the very poor (affordability and availability) and that they are consumer-oriented, because they are adaptable and help to inform or educate consumers. Evidence that the third element is present—that they are considered to be both fair and inclusive, so that local communities are able to participate in all stages of the value chain—is not entirely clear because this element is not always fully implemented.

Market Insight 5.3
continued

Related Topics

mission and values; strategic analysis; strategic goals; competitive advantage; generic strategies

1 **By means of what three criteria can BoP strategies be considered genuine? Does the P&G's CSDW Program satisfy these three criteria and can it therefore be considered a genuine BoP strategy?**

2 **Why do you believe P&G and Nestlé are involved with BoP strategies?**

3 **Find another example of a BoP strategy.**

Strategic Market Action

The final set of marketing strategy activities concerns the identification of the most appropriate way of achieving the goals and putting the plan into action: the implementation phase.

There is no proven formula or toolkit that managers can use because of the wide range of internal and external environmental factors; rather, managers tend to draw upon their own experience to know which strategies are more likely to be successful than others. We can, however, consider ideas about competitive advantage, generic strategies, competitive positioning, strategic intent, and marketing planning and implementation (see Figure 5.7).

Competitive Advantage

According to Hoffman (2000: 6), competitive advantage is 'the prolonged benefit of implementing some unique value-creating strategy not simultaneously being implemented by any current or potential competitors along with the inability to duplicate the benefits of this strategy'. In other words, sustainable competitive advantage is achieved when an organization has a significant

Figure 5.7
Strategic market action

and sustainable edge over its competitors in terms of attracting buyers. Advantage can also be secured by coping with the competitive forces better than its rivals. Advantage can be developed in many different ways. Some organizations have an advantage simply because they are the best-known organization or brand in the market. Some achieve it by producing the best-quality offering or by having attributes that other offerings do not have. For example, some pharmaceutical brands have an advantage while patent protection exists; as soon as the patent expires and competitors can produce generic versions of the drug, the advantage is lost. Some organizations have the lowest price, whereas others provide the best support and service in the industry. Whatever the advantage, the superiority has to be sustainable across time.

According to Porter (1985), the conditions necessary for the achievement of sustainable competitive advantage are as follows:

1 The customer consistently perceives a positive difference between the offerings provided by a company and its competitors.

2 The perceived difference results from the company's relatively greater capability.

3 The perceived difference persists for a reasonable period of time—that is, sustainable competitive advantage is durable only as long as it is not easily imitated.

Generic Strategies

If the importance of achieving a competitive advantage is accepted as a crucial aspect of a successful marketing strategy, then it is necessary to understand how strategies can lead to the development of sustainable competitive advantages. Porter (1985) proposed that there are two essential routes to achieving above-average performance: to become the lowest cost producer; or to differentiate the offering until it is of superior value to the customer. These strategies can be implemented in either broad (mass) or narrow (focused) markets. Porter suggested that this gives rise to three generic strategies: overall **cost leadership**; **differentiation**; and **focus**.

Cost leadership does not mean a lower price, although lower prices are often used to attract customers. By having the lowest cost structure, an organization can offer standard offerings at acceptable levels of quality, yet still generate above-average profit margins. If attacked by a competitor using lower prices, the low-cost leader has a far bigger cushion than its competitors. Charging a lower price than rivals is not the critical point; the competitive advantage is derived from *how* the organization exploits its cost/price ratio. By reinvesting the profit, for example by improving product quality, investing more in product development, or building extra capacity, it is more likely to achieve long-run superiority. One example is Chinese low-cost retailer and variety store Miniso, which has stores around the world, including in North Korea (Anon., 2017c), and offers most of its products at $2.99 in its Canadian stores (about £1.75, or €1.97, at time of writing). Another example would be the Beko brand from Turkish white goods supplier Arcelik.

A *differentiation* strategy requires that all value chain activities are geared towards the creation of offerings that are valued by, and which satisfy the needs of, particular broad segments. By identifying particular customer groups, each of which has a discrete set of needs, a product can be differentiated from its competitors. Fashion brand Zara differentiated itself by reformulating its value chain so that it became the fastest high-street brand to design, produce, distribute, and make fashion clothing available in its shops.

Customers are sometimes prepared to pay a higher price—that is, a price premium—for offerings that deliver superior or extra value. For example, the Starbucks coffee brand is strongly differentiated and valued, and consumers are willing to pay higher prices to enjoy the Starbucks

Miniso store in Sydney, Australia, advertising its $2.99 deals
Source: © Wpcpey/Wikimedia Commons (CC BY-SA 4.0).

experience. However, differentiation can be achieved by low prices, as evidenced through the success of low-cost airlines, such as the UK's easyJet and Ireland's Ryanair.

Offerings can be differentiated using a variety of criteria. Indeed, each element of the marketing mix is capable of providing the means for successful long-term differentiation. Differentiation can lead to greater levels of brand loyalty. For example, in contrast to low-cost ASDA, Waitrose provides a strongly differentiated supermarket service.

Organizations use *focus* strategies to seek gaps in broad market segments or to find gaps in competitors' ranges. In other words, focus strategies help to seek out unfulfilled market needs. The focused operator then concentrates all value chain activities on a narrow range of offerings. Focus strategies can be oriented towards being the lowest cost producer for the particular segment (for example Aldi, in the supermarket sector) or offering a differentiated offering for which the narrow target segment is willing to pay a higher price (for example Vans, in the trainer market). This means that there are two options for a company wishing to follow a focus strategy—one is low cost and the other is differentiation—but both occur within a particular narrow segment. The difference between a broad differentiator and a focused differentiator is that the former bases its strategy on attributes valued across a number of markets, whereas the latter seeks to meet the needs of particular segments within a market.

Porter (1985) argues that, to achieve competitive advantage, organizations must pursue one of these three generic strategies. He argues that a failure to be strategically explicit results in organizations being 'stuck in the middle'—that is, achieving below-average returns and having no competitive advantage. It has been observed, however, that some organizations have been able to pursue both low-cost and differentiated strategies simultaneously. For example, an organization that develops a large market share by means of differentiation and by creating very strong brands or through technological innovation may well also become the cost leader.

Competitive Positioning

Having collected industry information, analysed competitors, and considered our resources, perhaps the single most important aspect of developing marketing strategy is deciding how to compete in selected target markets. A key decision that arises is: what position do we want in the market?

The position that a product adopts in a market is a general reflection of its market share. Four positions can be identified—market leader, market challenger, market follower, and market nicher—and each has particular characteristics, as set out in Table 5.2.

There are two main reasons why we try to understand the competitive positions adopted by companies. The first is that, by establishing how various firms are positioned in the market, the company can understand where it is currently positioned itself and decide where it wants to be positioned. This shapes the nature and quantity of the resources required and the strategies to be pursued, some of which are set out in Table 5.2.

Table 5.2 Types of market position

Type	Characteristics	Prime strategies
Market leader	The market leader has the single largest share of the market. Market leadership is important because it is these offerings and brands that can shape the nature of competition in the market, and set out standards relating to price, quality, speed of innovation, and communications, as well as influence the key distribution channels. An example is Nike in the sports shoe market.	*Attack the market*: create new uses and/or users; increase frequency of use *Defend the position*: regular innovation; larger ranges; price cutting and discounts; increased promotion
Market challenger	Products that aspire to the leadership position are referred to as market challengers. These may be positioned as numbers two, three, or even four in the market. They actively seek market share and use aggressive strategies to take share from all of their rivals. An example is car-rental company Hertz.	*Attack the market leader*: pricing; new product attributes; sharp increase in advertising spend *Attack rivals*: special offers and limited editions; superior competitive advantages Maintain status quo
Market follower	Market followers have low market shares and do not have the resources to be serious competitors. They pose no threat to the market leader or challengers and often adopt 'me too' strategies when the market leader takes an initiative. An example is Morrisons in the UK supermarket sector.	Avoid hostile attacks on rivals Copy the market leader and provide good-quality products that are well differentiated Focus on differentiation and profits, not market share
Market nicher	Market nichers are specialists. They select small segments within target markets that larger companies fail to exploit. They develop specialized marketing mixes designed to meet the needs of their customers. An example is Maserati in the automotive sector.	*Provide high level of specialization*: geography; proposition; service; customer group Provide tight fit between market needs and the organization's resources

Visit the **online resources** and access Internet Activity 5.3 to learn more about business planning in the airline market.

Networks, Cooperation, and Relationships

Ideas about strategy have developed from those based on competition through attack and defence strategies, considered in Market Insight 5.4. An alternative perspective is to consider ways in which customer value can be increased by means of cooperation. By working cooperatively with other companies and their brands, relationships can evolve. These in turn provide strong opportunities to add value by means of the differentiation of brands and the development of sustainable competitive advantage.

Market Insight 5.4
Airlines: Fight and Flight

Lower fuel prices and an improving economic environment were partly responsible for the near 6.3 per cent growth in airline traffic by revenue passenger kilometres in 2016 and for the predictions of continued growth in the period up to 2020. The Middle East and Asia Pacific experienced the greatest growth, followed by Europe, Africa, Latin America, and North America.

Growth in the air travel market means that airlines have to make strategic decisions about how to grow their businesses. Airlines tend to grow by adding more frequent flights and nonstop markets to their networks, but this can lead to a fragmentation of their existing networks. The other approach is to increase airplane capacity and/or size. The evidence indicates that most of the air travel growth has been met by an increase in new non-stop markets (airport pairs) and by growth of frequency.

Airlines need to make decisions about the type of aircraft that they wish to use and this decision reflects the business model the airline decides to pursue. Low-cost carriers (LCCs) represent a fast-growing business segment. Norwegian, Southwest, easyJet, Ryanair, and Jetstar are typical low-cost carriers. They have evolved through strategies that provide customers with low seat prices, but charge fees for other services such as baggage, set seats, and food. This model has been referred to as 'pay for everything extra but a seat' model. These carriers generally operate from secondary airports and use

Norwegian is the third-largest low-cost airline in Europe, with a strategy that includes introducing new aircraft on a regular basis
Source: © DyziO/Shutterstock.com.

a single type of aircraft to increase utilization rates. For example, Southwest's entire fleet consists of Boeing 737 aircraft. Low-cost carriers rely on direct marketing, offer a single class product, do not include in-flight meals in the cost of the ticket, and do not offer frequent-flyer programmes, all of which helps to keep costs low.

Norwegian is the third-largest low-cost airline in Europe and introduces new aircraft to its fleet on a regular basis. This is because new aircraft consume less fuel and require less maintenance, which enables Norwegian to offer low fares. New aircraft offer

Market Insight 5.4
continued

improved environmental credentials and are more comfortable than their predecessors.

Low-cost carriers compete with mainstream, or legacy, airlines, which offer a tiered range of seating products, in-flight meals and entertainment, airport lounges, and frequent-flyer programmes, all at varying premium fares dependent on seat location.

What might have been a clear separation between the offerings of these two types of carrier has, however, started to become more obscure. Legacy carriers

have been uncomfortable with the growth of LCCs, and both Delta and British Airways have introduced a new type of fare that applies only to routes that compete with LCCs. Referred to as a 'budget', or 'basic economy' fare, these tickets offer no refunds, upgrades, or complimentary pre-boarding, and there is a much-reduced range of perks that a frequent flyer might experience.

Sources: Uszynski (2013); Martin (2015); IATA (2017); https://www.norwegian.com

Theory into Practice

Many early ideas about competitive marketing strategies have developed from the military and are based on approaches to warfare. Two main approaches can be identified, based on two classical works on military strategy, Sun Tzu's *The Art of War* and Clausewitz's *On War*. Fundamentally, these are **attack strategies** and **defence strategies**. Within each, there are variations, such as flanking, pre-emptive, bypass, and contraction strategies (Macdonald and Neupert, 2005).

The growth of LCCs such as Ryanair and easyJet has been based upon flanking attacks on legacy carriers, such as British Airways and Delta. BA has, in the past, served broad markets with a highly differentiated service and ignored the low-cost no-frills niche segment, but now it is seeking to compete with the LCCs on certain routes. Ryanair and other LCCs spotted the flanking opportunity early, and established themselves quickly in the market.

Related Topics

strategic analysis; strategic goals; competitive advantage; generic strategies

1 **Is the emergence of 'basic economy' fares by certain legacy carriers an example of an attack or a defence strategy? Justify your answer.**

2 **If you were the marketing director at Norwegian, how would you seek to establish a competitive advantage?**

3 **Which types of growth strategy might legacy carriers pursue?**

To develop collaborative inter-organizational relationships, it is necessary to consider an organization's whole system, or network, of stakeholder relationships. This is because networks hold together partly through 'an elaborate pattern of interdependence and reciprocity' (Achrol, 1997: 61). Indeed, it is the network of relationships that provides the context within which exchange behaviours occur.

Cooperative relationships within these networks benefit participants through shared knowledge about offerings, markets, and competitors, can lead to improvements in product and brand performance, and help to develop stronger market positions, enabling the more efficient use of resources (Harbison and Pekar, 1998). This all adds up to a unique form of differentiation that can be of significant value to customers. For example, Cisco have a Strategic Ecosystem Group, which is responsible for collaborating with partner firms such as Ericsson, Inspur (China), and Apple. The common goal is to collaborate and build next-generation offerings together, before taking them to market through Cisco's channels (Dix, 2016).

At the corporate level, cooperative relationships—sometimes referred to as alliances—can be considered a spectrum. At one end, cooperation is based around simple transactions; at the other end, cooperation can be formally established by means of a stand-alone organization within which both parties share ownership.

Outsourcing and renewable purchasing agreements are relatively short-term cooperative arrangements. Information sharing can be seen in agreements to distribute offerings; licensing and technological collaboration represents resource and asset sharing; cooperation based on share ownership is normally seen in mergers and acquisition (M&A) activity, which has a long-term perspective. In late 2016, UK supermarket group Sainsbury's bought Home Retail Group (owner of Argos, a catalogue retailer) to improve its multichannel and delivery capability and to diversify its business further into non-food items. The resulting company combined the skills and resources of both parent organizations—particularly in multichannel retailing, logistics, and procurement.

The detail concerning these various arrangements is not the focus of the strategy. What lies behind the concept of cooperation is the competitive advantage that can be developed. In particular, competitors are usually unable to determine how performance is achieved through these alliances and, even if they can, it is exceedingly difficult to replicate because they do not have the necessary or complementary resources nor do they have the same history of investments. All organizations in a cooperative arrangement—sometimes called a network alliance—have an advantage over their rival organizations outside an alliance. However, not all alliances and mergers are successful; indeed, a large number of them fail. For example, the merger between Sony and Ericsson in 2001 had begun to hit trouble by 2011 when its market share in the global mobile phone market had dropped to 2 per cent and 11th place, from a height of 9 per cent in 2007 and 4th place. In 2011, Sony eventually agreed to buy Ericsson's share of the joint venture and go it alone (Singh, 2011). At a marketing level, alliances can be developed with key distributors and retailers to control the distribution channel. Relationships with prominent or geographically important dealers provide opportunities for exclusive distribution to reach target markets. Relationships can also be developed with strategically important customers. These customers are referred to as key accounts, and significant resources are often channelled into developing and supporting these accounts (see Chapter 15). In many markets, there is little difference between offerings, so organizations try to differentiate themselves based on the services they provide to their customers both before and after a purchase has been made. Relationships between customer and supplier can be strengthened through the provision of services, because the service is perceived to offer added value.

Relationships can also be developed with consumers. Marketing strategies designed to retain customers often use loyalty schemes and customer retention programmes. These are supported by database management and marketing facilities. Relationships can also develop through branding. Some consumers develop a strong affinity with a brand to the extent that they want to share their relationship with others and talk openly about their positive brand experiences (word of mouth). Relationships with suppliers are important simply because competitive advantages can be developed through cost reduction, speed to market, and product differentiation.

Marketing strategy should be founded on developing customer value, and this can be achieved through a strategy based on building cooperative relationships with a network of suppliers, customers, distributors, and other strategically relevant stakeholders. The centrality of cooperation and relationships within marketing has become an important concept for both organizations and marketing academics. Marketing has evolved from ideas that are based solely around the 4Ps (see Chapter 1); now, marketers think and act in terms of the different types of relationship that an organization has and try to find ways of improving the right relationships with the right customers. This is referred to as relationship marketing (see Chapters 1 and 15).

Platform Strategies

The network approach not only supports the idea of collaboration and relationship development, but also its principles underpin the basis on which contemporary competitive activity is beginning to be undertaken.

Ideas about conventional strategy have been based around a linear value chain approach, which considers successive supplier/distributor participants to add value as a product moves along a chain to be consumed by end users. Van Alstyne, Parker, and Choudary (2016) refer to this as a **pipeline** effect.

Today, firms such as Apple combine the pipeline approach with a new **platform strategy**. For example, the iPhone and its operating system enable two sets of participants to be connected, creating a two-sided market. So app developers and app users both generate value through the iPhone platform. The value generated increases as the number of developers and users increases. This is referred to as network effects and is a central tenet of platform strategy (van Alstyne et al., 2016).

Uber, the world's largest taxi company, was worth around $70 billion in 2018
Source: © MikeDotta/Shutterstock.com.

Research Insight 5.3

To take your learning further, you might wish to read this influential paper:

van Alstyne, M.W., Parker, G.G., and Choudary, S.P. (2016). Pipelines, platforms, and the new rules of strategy. *Harvard Business Review***, April.**

These authors consider the way in which platform strategies (for example run by the likes of Airbnb, Uber, Alibaba, Netflix) work and compare them with pipeline (that is, classic linear value chain) models of strategy (for example those operated by Walmart). The authors argue that platform strategies change the nature of corporate strategy—and therefore, by extension, marketing strategy—in relation to the customer base and the competitive set, as well as the boundaries separating suppliers, customers, and competitors.

 Visit the **online resources** to read the abstract and access the full paper.

Companies such as Airbnb, Uber, and Alibaba all operate through platforms, and a key characteristic is their lack of ownership of any physical assets. Their use of information technology and vast amounts of data has meant that their platforms have been built quickly and relatively inexpensively. They have also disrupted the competitive landscape within their respective industries.

Platform businesses bring together producers and consumers to drive high-value exchanges. Their source of value and their competitive advantage is rooted in both information and data and the interactions that the platform generates. As the number of Uber platform participants has increased, so has the value that Uber has delivered to both sides of their market. It becomes easier for drivers to find fares and for consumers to get rides. (For more information about pipeline and platform strategies, see Research Insight 5.3.)

Implementation

For ease of explanation, the marketing planning process has been depicted as a linear sequential series of management activities. This certainly helps to simplify understanding about how strategy can be developed and it also serves to show how various activities link together. However, strategy development and planning, whether at a corporate, business, or functional level, is not linear, does not evolve in pre-set ways, and is not always subject to a regular predetermined pattern of evolution. Indeed, politics, finance, and interpersonal conflicts all shape the nature of an organization's marketing strategy. As Browne and Cuddihy (2011) point out, many have argued that there is a need for innovation, flexibility, and creativity for effective marketing planning and strategy making, particularly in the current turbulent times.

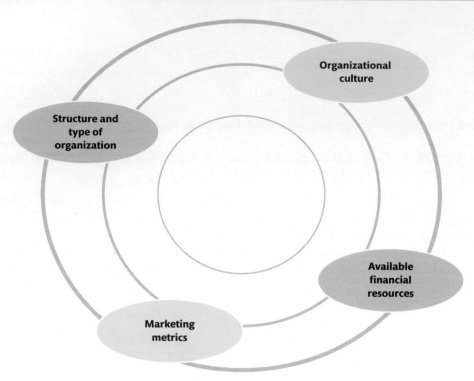

Figure 5.8

Major elements that can impact the strategy implementation process

Marketing implementation is a fundamental process in marketing because it is the action phase of the strategic marketing process. Whereas many of the concepts in this text help us to design marketing programmes, the implementation phase is about actually doing it. In reality, then, it is the most exciting part of marketing because it is the least predictable.

The implementation of any marketing plan, however, is far from straightforward owing in part to the large number of variables. Four elements that impact on the implementation of most strategic marketing plans can be identified, as depicted in Figure 5.8.

The Structure and Type of Marketing Function

The structure and type of marketing function used by an organization can influence the degree to which the implementation process is successful. How we organize ourselves to undertake the task of marketing has an impact on how effective we are.

A marketing department can be structured in many ways, but the internal alignment with the sales department, how brands are managed, and how the reporting lines involve the SBU and corporate headquarters, accompanied with varying levels of bureaucracy, can be influential.

A major problem concerns the increasing complexity associated with contemporary brand management. Mitchell (2012) refers to globalization, the growing importance of customer experience, the significance of retailer power, the role of **category management**, and the recent surge in the use and influence of social media as factors that have redefined the nature of a brand manager's job. Managing increasing amounts of information, projects, and content have added layers of complexity and responsibility.

Organizational Culture

The structural issue needs to be considered alongside the degree to which a marketing orientation prevails across an organization. Marketing is present in all aspects of an organization, because all departments have some role to play with respect to creating, delivering, and satisfying customers. For example, employees in the R&D department designing new offerings for poorly met existing customer needs are performing a marketing role. Similarly, members of the procurement department buying components for a new offering must purchase components of specific quality and at a certain cost that will meet customer needs. In fact, we can go through all the departments of a company and find that there is a marketing role to be played in each. In other words, marketing should be distributed throughout an organization and all employees should be considered to be part-time marketers (Gummesson, 1990). Marketing is not something that only people in the marketing department undertake.

Apart from the need to have a customer orientation, the extent to which the prevailing organizational culture is innovative is also important (Menon and Varadarajan, 1992). An atmosphere that promotes creativity, innovative behaviour, and a willingness to take risks can have a positive impact on employee commitment (see Market Insight 5.5).

Market Insight 5.5
A Tale of Two Tech Companies

Microsoft has a new spring in its step. The firm's share price has been on a steady trajectory upwards since 2010, reaching US$87.82 in January 2018, compared to $19.55 in May 2010. Since 2014, when Satya Nadella took over as CEO, the firm has firmly repositioned itself in cloud computing with Azure and downgraded its Windows product into a supporting role. This allowed the new CEO to change the company's culture. Remarking on the age-old strategy conundrum of whether the right culture creates the right strategy or the right strategy creates the right culture, Mr Nadella has remarked that 'culture eats strategy for breakfast'. As part of the culture change, employees are no longer assessed on a performance curve, with low performers punished with no bonus or promotion. One major change in employee engagement policy was to invite CEOs of those companies that Microsoft had recently acquired to its prestigious annual strategy retreat—usually the preserve of the company's top 150 personnel. Another change was to encourage staff to learn from failure. Microsoft's mission is 'empowering every person in every organization on the planet to achieve more' and its bet on the future is focused on cloud computing,

The Tencent booth at the 2017 Global Mobile Internet Conference
Source: © testing/Shutterstock.com.

hardware (including 3D printers, but also Xbox), and artificial intelligence. For Mr Nadella, it seems the only way is up for Microsoft and its share price.

Another large tech firm doing well is Tencent, the Chinese Internet company. It owns the WeChat and QQ apps, boasted more than 938 million active monthly users in mid-2017, and generated $23 billion in revenues in 2016. The apps offer social networking,

Market Insight 5.5
continued

payment systems, music streaming, gaming, and web searching. Tencent also holds annual retreats, typically in comfortable hotels in Japan or Silicon Valley, but in autumn 2016 CEO Pony Ma elected instead to take his team on a two-day trek through the Gobi desert. Employees, numbering around 40,000, talk of an encouraging teamwork culture, in which high performers are placed on a pedestal and rewarded accordingly, but in which criticism is also welcomed. In 2011, the company's president, Martin Lau, and CEO Pony Ma invited 72 industry experts to a series of ten closed meetings (nicknamed 'the conference of the gods') in which invitees were asked to offer blunt feedback. One issue identified was that the company needed to innovate in its own way rather than copy other companies' products.

Afterwards, Mr Ma established internal competition, famously setting up two teams without telling them about each other, and they went on to create WeChat. The company also empowers its external developers to build their own apps and services on its open platform without charging them rental fees. After acquiring Finnish mobile game maker Supercell Oy, maker of mega-game *Clash Royale*, the company is spreading its wings globally. With financial interests in everything from Tesla, through China Music Corporation, to an all-electric premium car venture, the world may not be enough.

Sources: Anon. (2017d); Lucas (2017); Stone and Chen (2017); Weinberger (2017); https://www.macrotrends.net/stocks/charts/MSFT/prices/microsoft-corp-stock-price-history

Theory into Practice

Both the Microsoft and Tencent examples demonstrate the role and strategic importance of actively involving employees in strategy development. There are numerous theories regarding employee engagement, most based on Kahn's (1990) affirmation that when individuals are engaged, they bring their cognitive, emotional, and physical elements to the performance of their work role. In addition, there are theories about job satisfaction, organizational commitment, and job involvement, plus well-known theories such as the psychological contract and even Maslow's hierarchy of needs.

These examples demonstrate the importance of organizational culture and the need for a customer orientation throughout the organization—in particular, the role of an innovative atmosphere within which to participate in the strategy process.

Related Topics

mission; values; corporate culture; strategic goals; strategy process

1 **Do you agree with Satya Nadella, Microsoft's CEO, that corporate culture is more important than strategy in achieving corporate success? Why, or why not?**

2 **How does Microsoft's strategy development approach compare and contrast with that of Tencent?**

3 **How do you think the strategy development process might differ for tech firms compared with conventional companies?**

The manner and involvement of top management in supporting the implementation process is also significant. Research shows that it is critically important that the process of marketing strategy planning occurs within a suitably positive culture. By engaging key decision-makers, such as marketing managers and in some cases all employees, in the various phases of the marketing planning process, the viability of the chosen strategy options is considerably enhanced (Ramaseshan, Ishak, and Kingshott, 2013) and, as a result, senior management is more likely to achieve above-average performance outcomes.

A final element concerns the level of freedom, or autonomy, that managers have to make meaningful decisions and to independently adjust behaviours. Managers without suitable autonomy may waste critical managerial resources or fail to respond to competitors' actions. Because the level of perceived job autonomy is positively associated with the level of perceived organizational commitment (Moon, 2000), the implementation of a marketing plan may be jeopardized if managers do not feel empowered to make changes independently of senior management.

The Available Financial Resources

The amount of financial support allocated to brands can often be contentious and can lead to considerable internal political strife. This reflects constituency-based theory, which emphasizes that internal functions, such as marketing and others, are always striving for the resources that they feel are necessary to satisfy their goals (Anderson, 1982). Once the aggregate amount is determined, however, managers should devise a marketing budget indicating how much is to be spent on marketing activities and when. Yet there are no hard-and-fast rules on how much should be allocated to marketing spend. One perspective is that many companies lack a formal and appropriate budgeting process. When marketing budgets are properly determined, they are based on pre-set tasks, numerical and timed goals, and, of course, sales forecasts. These should be produced in association with support from the finance department of an organization.

A marketing budget may be between 1 per cent and 10 per cent of sales revenues (excluding salaries), but exactly how much is spent on marketing activities is dependent on the particular industry, each firm, and the overall economic climate. Kehrer (2015) claims that companies that maintain or even increase their marketing spend during an economic downturn are very likely to recover more quickly than their competitors when the economy recovers. However, empirical work by Srinivasan, Lilien, and Sridhar (2011) suggests that investment in both R&D and advertising during a recession should be based on the actual conditions facing the firm.

Marketing Metrics

The implementation of any marketing plan is incomplete without methods to control and evaluate its performance. It is vitally important to monitor the results of the programme as it unfolds, not only when it is completed. Therefore measures need to be stated in the plan about how the results of the plan will be recorded and disseminated throughout the team. Recording the performance of the marketing plan against targets enables managers to make adjustments if it does not perform as expected, perhaps because of unforeseen market events.

The marketing budgeting process is a political process whereby scarce resources are allocated within a company. Clearly, where a department can demonstrate the effectiveness of the resources it has previously used, it is far more likely to receive an increase in the budget for the next year. Over the last 15 years or so, we have seen the rise in importance of measuring marketing effectiveness. The controls used to measure the effectiveness of the implementation process are referred to as **marketing metrics**.

There is increased recognition of the need to determine efficiency and effectiveness in organizational marketing efforts. In the past, marketing control has been achieved through the annual marketing plan, through analysis of company profitability, through some measure of efficiency (for example number of employees as a proportion of revenue or, in retailing, net profit per square metre of retail space), or in terms of market share or some other strategic measure. But, in the past, these measures have been focused on financial or human resource measures. More recently, there has been a considerable shift in thinking towards the need for customer-based measurements (Kaplan and Norton, 1992). There has been a move towards setting **key performance indicators (KPIs)**, against which companies measure their progress to determine whether or not they have improved or maintained it over a given period of time.

Research indicates that British companies are now using a variety of strategic marketing metrics as KPIs in marketing. The selection and use of KPIs depends on their relevance to what is being measured; however, KPIs should be selected in the context of strategic plans and associated higher-level goals (Lamont, 2012). ScottishPower uses software that enables it to keep track of the factors that underpin its main objective, which is customer retention. These factors include the proficiency with which customer issues are resolved and the provision of alternative interaction channels.

An organization's strategic goals should always be used to guide the way in which metrics are interpreted. For example, Lamont (2012) refers to ScottishPower, which asked its call centre agents to offer additional services, such as boiler care. As a result, call times increased by 8–10 per cent—a metric that had to be seen in terms of its retention plan rather than as a drop in the agents' productivity.

We now discuss the benefits and limitations of ten key marketing performance metrics (see Figure 5.9).

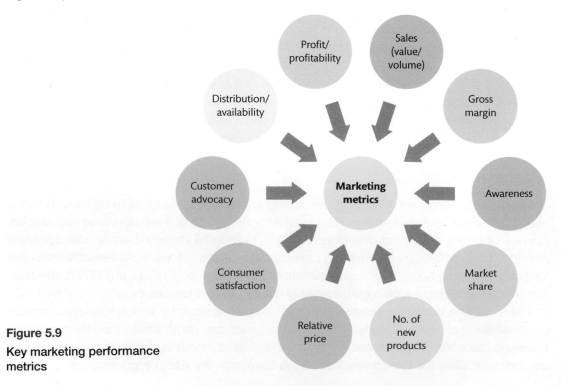

Figure 5.9
Key marketing performance metrics

Profit/Profitability

Unsurprisingly, profit and profitability is the main key performance measure, whereby profit is defined broadly how much cash there is left in the business when expenses are subtracted from revenues generated. This approach indicates the 'bottom line'. It represents what is left over either for distribution to the (private or public) shareholders of the business or for reinvestment in the business.

However, the problem with profit/profitability is that its link with marketing activity is not always clear. The process required to determine the link requires considerable input from the finance department to measure the contributions individual offerings make towards the overall profit levels of a business. Therefore it can be difficult to determine whether the marketing activity itself has led to improved levels of profitability or some other factor was responsible, such as the collapse of a competitor. Finally, we might have a very profitable business operating in the short term, for example with customers buying more of a low-value overpriced offering, but in the long term customers will defect and leave the business once they realize that they can either get better value elsewhere or they perceive manipulative intent on the part of the company from which they are buying.

Sales

Sales value or volume is a key performance measure, whereby sales value is determined by measuring how many units of an offering are sold, then multiplying this by the average unit price, and sales volume is calculated simply by determining how many units of an offering have been sold. The benefit of using this metric is that sales values and volumes can be measured directly against individual offerings. Sales values and volumes are easier to determine and require limited input from the finance department, unlike the determination of profit/profitability. Sales values and volumes may be linked to geographical sales territories, and so, when sales fall in a particular territory and efforts have been made to increase sales, it is relatively easy to determine whether or not those efforts have been successful.

The use of sales volumes as a marketing metric is more problematic because with high-volume turnover products—particularly in brokerages, which sell other companies' offerings—the profit may actually be disproportionately low. In such a situation, it would be wiser to measure profit/profitability, where the data are available. However, sales values may also hide the fact that an offering is being sold at unprofitable levels. Rewarding a sales force for selling large quantities of an offering at an unprofitable level is a recipe for disaster—the long-term decline of a company.

Operating Margin

Frequently, companies measure their performance based on the operating profit margins they can achieve in a particular industry. This metric is determined by dividing operating income by net sales. This metric is also known as return on sales. For example, the gross operating margin for supermarkets in the UK was around 1–5 per cent (Anon., 2016a), whereas in the United States operating profit margins are around 2–4 per cent (Damodaran, 2017), although they have historically been lower than those in the UK. However, supermarkets generally operate on very high-volume sales and hence they can afford to operate on low operating profit margins.

The problem with using operating margins as a marketing metric is that they do not always provide an indication of how much the customer is actually willing to pay. For example, smoothie manufacturers (such as innocent) generally operate higher operating margins (because they charge higher prices) than manufacturers in the fruit juice category (such as Del Monte, Minute Maid). However, if the smoothie manufacturers had set their initial prices based on typical fruit juice margins, they would never have been as successful as they have—especially when we consider that innocent, now 90 per cent owned by Coca-Cola, achieved sales revenue of around £100 million in its first ten years (1998–2008).

Awareness

Brand awareness is another important marketing metric—but while a customer may be aware of a brand, it does not mean they will buy that brand. As consumers we can become aware of a brand, but not particularly like it and therefore not buy it; hence building awareness may not necessarily build sales. Brands can be marketed heavily, but not achieve success, for example Strand cigarettes, Ford Edsel, and Tesco Fresh and Easy in the United States. Awareness does not necessarily lead to purchase.

Brand awareness is, however, a very useful metric for determining whether marketing communications activity is having the required impact on customer recognition. While it is true that it may take time for any increased awareness to lead to increases in sales, if it does so at all and particularly in the short term, it is generally also true that the more a target market recognizes a brand, the more likely they are to become purchasers of it.

Market Share

One of the principal measures of market performance, market share, is enshrined in many marketing strategy models, including Boston Consulting Group's growth share matrix, or Boston Box (see Chapter 4). Measuring market share is useful for determining a company's performance within the marketplace, particularly when measured relative to the market leader, because it gives an indication of how competitive a company is. Cadbury's, the confectionery company, use this metric in conjunction with other marketing metrics such as brand awareness and advertising spend (Ambler, 2000).

A company's market share is determined by measuring that company's sales revenues, incorporating the sales of all companies within the industry including itself, as a proportion of total industry sales revenues, as follows:

$$\text{market share}_{(\text{company A, \%})} = \frac{\text{sales revenue}_{(\text{company A, £})}}{\text{total industry sales revenue (£)}} \times 100$$

Relative market share is determined by measuring the company's market share against the market share of the market leader, or its nearest competitor (if the company is itself the market leader), as follows:

$$\text{relative market share}_{(\text{company A, \%})} = \frac{\text{market share}_{(\text{company A, \%})}}{\text{market share}_{(\text{market leader, \%})}}$$

If the company is itself market leader, relative market share is a value greater than one unit.

Nevertheless, a company's market share, as determined by the value of the sales, is not necessarily indicative of a profitable company. Many a company has started a price war (see Chapter 9) to try to steal market share from a competitor, only to find prices fall generally in the industry, which inevitably leads to a decline in its own profitability.

Number of New Products

Most companies pride themselves on their capacity to innovate. In many industries, innovating new offerings is vital for the prosperity of the industry. For example, pharmaceutical companies manage a pipeline of new drug compounds at various stages in the process of new proposition development. When they do finally develop a drug, they quickly patent it to protect their multibillion-dollar investments and to ensure that they can reap the financial rewards from the drug's development.

In 2006, pipeline problems occurred for global pharmaceutical manufacturers AstraZeneca and GlaxoSmithKline when various high-profile compounds failed at the clinical trial stage, sending their share prices lower as a result (Griffiths, 2006). 3M—the company behind the Post-it note, among other innovations—uses the proportion of sales attributable to new products (also known as the vitality index) as one of its marketing metrics (Ambler, 2000).

Nevertheless, simply developing new offerings without measuring or predicting their impact on the sales of existing offerings can be problematic, because the new offering can cannibalize the existing sales without adding any new business. In addition, this strategy may cause customer confusion as customers try to determine what they want from a variety of offers.

Mobile telephone companies quickly learned in the late 1990s and early 2000s that many consumers wanted a monthly charge service offering a limited range of telephone call packages, which included text message bundles and set levels of call time, or a pay-as-you-go plan with more limited options. What they didn't want was lots of different-priced telephone handset offers with many different call packages, offering different call charges for different times. Consumers wanted price transparency.

Relative Price

The price of a company's offerings can be indicative of how much it is valued in the marketplace. **Relative price** is determined by measuring the price of the company's offering against that of the offering of the market leading company, or the nearest competitor (if the company is itself the market leader), as follows:

$$\text{relative price}_{(\text{company A's offering, unit})} = \frac{\text{price}_{(\text{company A's offering, }\pounds)}}{\text{price}_{(\text{market leader's offering/nearest competitor, }\pounds)}}$$

If the company is itself the market leader, relative price is a value greater than one unit.

There is increasing recognition that a company that can charge a price premium vis-à-vis its competitors if it has a competitive advantage over them. One approach to measuring brand equity actually uses relative price premiums (Ailawadi, Lehmann, and Neslin, 2003).

The problem with measuring marketing effectiveness using relative price only is that a company may obtain only a proportion of the total revenue possible in a marketplace if the price it charges is too high. In other words, a higher relative price may lead to a smaller market share if customers do not value the company's offering more than those of its competitors.

Customer Satisfaction

Many companies operate on the principle of satisfying their customers. Companies in the travel and leisure industry (for example Hilton Hotels, TUI, and Singapore Airlines) work hard to satisfy their customers and to ensure an enjoyable experience. In the past, this meant measuring levels of service quality (see Chapter 15) to determine whether companies were providing the level of quality of service that customers expected. In some industries, customer satisfaction is notoriously low, but customers perceive the costs of switching their business to other providers to be too high. Retail banking services are a good example here because customers are reluctant to switch banks even when they are dissatisfied (Keaveney, 1995). Energy companies such as ScottishPower measure the proportion of their customers who leave and switch supplier. This is referred to as churn rate in the industry. Churn rate is a measure of disaffected customers as a proportion of new customers. Ironically, customer service is relatively poor at npower and ScottishPower—two of the UK's largest energy companies, which had 652.8 and 558.3 complaints per 100,000 customers in the first quarter of 2016 according to figures from Citizen's Advice (Anon., 2016b).

Some companies attempt to go beyond simply satisfying customers, aiming to empower their employees to provide a high level of individual and personal help for customers. For example, staff members at the Ritz-Carlton hotels are famously authorized to spend up to $2,000 to resolve a customer's problem without having to refer to a manager (Hanselman, 2012).

Nevertheless, businesses may spend too much time and effort serving customers who are neither profitable nor offer the most profit potential in the future. Generating high levels of customer satisfaction or delight may ultimately reduce shareholder value because the costs involved produce lower levels of profitability. In other words, the incremental costs of improving customer satisfaction from 95 per cent to 99.5 per cent of customers are unlikely to be worth it.

Customer Advocacy

According to Reichheld (2003), successful firms create exceptional growth by nurturing loyal customers. They invest huge amounts of time and effort in measuring customer satisfaction. However, most of the indices they have previously employed are complex, produce unclear results, and do not connect to profits or growth. The net promoter score (NPS) was developed based on measuring how likely it is that a customer would recommend a firm to a friend or a colleague. The more promoters a company can gain, the bigger its growth—that is, the inclination to promote relates to a strong degree of loyalty and growth (Reichheld, 2003).

The NPS is calculated based on the ratio of promoters to detractors. According to their responses on a 0–10 rating scale, customers are then categorized into the following groups:

1 *promoters*—those who are rated extremely likely to recommend (9–10 rating);

2 *passively satisfied*—those who are rated likely to recommend (7–8 rating); and

3 *detractors*—those who are extremely unlikely to recommend (0–6 rating).

The percentage of detractors is subtracted from the percentage of promoters to produce the NPS. Companies that earn an NPS greater than 75 per cent enjoy very strong customer loyalty. By plotting a firm's NPS against the company's revenue growth rate, Reichheld (2003) found that, in industries such as airlines or car rentals, there was a strong relationship between NPS and a company's revenue growth rate.

The advantages claimed for the NPS are said to be that:

- having the highest NPS in a business sector gives rise to growth rates, on average, 2.5 times higher than those of competitors;

- each 12-point escalation in NPS relates to a doubling of the growth rate of a firm; and

- using other metrics together with NPS provides no further predictive advantage—in other words, Reichheld claims that NPS is the only metric needed!

However, the NPS approach has drawn some criticisms. Keiningham and colleagues (2008) claimed that the results of the original study yielded different and contrasting results, and that a single-metric approach does not outperform dual- or multi-metric models.

Distribution/Availability

The extent to which an offering is distributed within the marketplace can be an important marketing metric. For example, a Hollywood blockbuster film studio will want to ensure maximum take-up of its motion pictures through many cinemas, because the more cinemas the film is shown in, the higher the box office takings will be. In other businesses, the quantity of locations within which a product is sold matter less than the quality of those locations. For example, premium fashion brands such as Burberry are sold through specialist retail outlets only, such as Selfridges in London, Siam Paragon in Bangkok, La Rinascente Womenswear in Milan, large airports (such as Heathrow, Rome, Shanghai), and its own branded shops in many other countries worldwide. Cosmetics companies (for example French cosmetics giant L'Oréal) distribute their new offerings initially through speciality cosmetics outlets and prestigious department stores, before stocking the products in supermarkets and other department stores later in the campaign.

In a wide range of diverse industry sectors, distribution is critical so that customers can readily purchase a company's offerings. For this reason, companies set up sophisticated systems to link their customers' purchasing needs with their own purchasing and distribution needs. Airline yield management systems, for example, reconcile customer pricing information with live seat availability, taking into account customers' price elasticities (see Chapter 9), to maximize total sales revenues. Measures of distribution and offering availability are critical in this and many other industries.

The use of KPIs varies considerably, but research indicates that a manager's use of KPIs is driven by a group of variables that describe the context in which the manager operates (see also Research Insight 5.4). These variables refer to 'firm strategy, metric orientation, type of marketing mix decision, firm and environmental characteristics' (Mintz and Currim, 2013: 32). Mintz and Currim (2013) also find that use of metrics is positively associated with marketing mix performance. In particular, that there is positive association between the use of marketing metrics and the performance of the marketing mix.

 Research Insight 5.4

To take your learning further, you might wish to read this influential paper:

Mintz, O., and Currim, I.S. (2013). What drives managerial use of marketing and financial metrics and does metric use affect performance of marketing-mix activities? *Journal of Marketing*, **77(2), 17–40.**

This useful article, based on an analysis of 1,287 marketing mix activities reported by 439 US firms, explains how the use of marketing metrics is positively associated with marketing mix performance. The article explains how managers can use fewer metrics, but still improve their marketing mix performance.

 Visit the online resources to read the abstract and access the full paper.

Managing and Controlling Marketing Programmes

There is increasing debate about how we measure the performance of marketing programmes to control them better. Traditionally, companies have tried to maximize marketing effectiveness—that is, they have measured market share growth, revenue growth, market position, and marketing efficiency. The last of these is a measure of sales and marketing expenses as a proportion of gross revenue. There is some evidence that companies that succeed on one dimension—that is, either marketing efficiency or effectiveness—are less successful on the other (Vorhies and Morgan, 2003). This makes sense because, to be effective at marketing, we have to spend more on marketing activity, which makes marketing inefficient! Firms that manage to be both marketing-effective and marketing-efficient probably do so by changing the 'rules of the game': they do not spend on high-cost activities such as advertising to achieve effectiveness; instead, they consider new and innovative approaches that make customers pay more attention.

One problem is that whilst marketers often consider strategy *formulation* to be problematic, they do not see strategy *implementation* as an issue. Managers frequently assume that implementation follows strategy as a sequential process. In fact, the two processes are often interlinked and run in parallel (Piercy, 1998). In other words, marketing strategy may be, and is, formulated on the basis of implementation considerations in the same way as implementation decisions are based on strategy formulation decisions.

In Figure 5.10, we can measure how effective and efficient our strategy has been by using the metrics for efficiency and effectiveness outlined earlier. Where we consider that marketing implementation has been efficient, but marketing strategy has not been effective, KPIs have not been met and we should reformulate strategy; otherwise, we are likely to reduce shareholder value in the longer term. This situation means that we have spent marketing resources well in achieving what we set out as our strategy, but that we employed the wrong strategy for what we wanted to do. The control imperative is to intervene quickly to reformulate the marketing strategy.

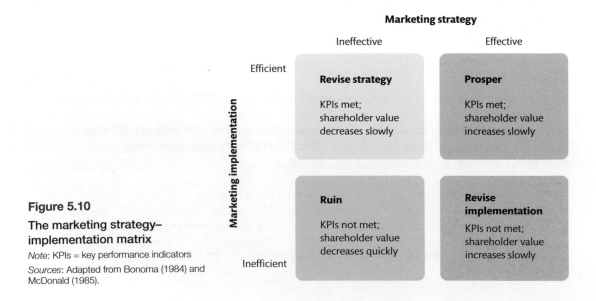

Figure 5.10

The marketing strategy–implementation matrix

Note: KPIs = key performance indicators

Sources: Adapted from Bonoma (1984) and McDonald (1985).

The dream situation is that we operate an efficient implementation plan and an effective marketing strategy. In this situation, we will prosper. There is no control imperative except to maintain a watching brief to see how competition might react, because this may force us to rethink our strategy.

Where implementation of an ineffective marketing strategy plan is inefficient, we are likely to face rapid ruin: we are spending scarce resources badly on doing the wrong things. The control imperative requires a fundamental rethink of what we are doing and how we are doing it.

Finally, where we are operating an effective marketing strategy, but implementing it inefficiently, the control imperative is to reconsider how we implement marketing programmes. Although this situation may not be disastrous in the short term, where competition is adopting a more efficient approach, it could lead to mergers, sales, or takeovers in highly competitive industry sectors.

Marketing Planning

We have considered the key activities associated with the strategic marketing planning process—essentially one of analysis, goals, and action. For organizations to be able to develop, implement, and control these activities at the offering and brand levels, marketing plans are derived. This final section considers the characteristics of the marketing planning process, identifies the key activities, and considers some of the issues associated with the process.

Marketing planning is a sequential process involving a series of activities leading to the setting of marketing objectives and the formulation of plans for achieving them (McDonald, 2002: 27). A marketing plan is the key output from the overall strategic marketing planning process. It details a company's, or brand's, intended marketing activity. Marketing plans can be developed for periods of a year, 2–5 years, or anything up to 25 years. Too many organizations, however, regard marketing plans as a development of the annual round of setting sales targets, which are then extrapolated into quasi-marketing plans. This is an incorrect approach because it fails to account for the marketplace, customer needs, and resources. The strategic appraisal and evaluation phase of the planning process should be undertaken first. This covers a 3–5-year period and provides a strategic insight into the markets, the competitors, and the organization's resources that shapes the direction and nature of the way in which the firm has decided to compete. Once agreed, this should be updated on an annual basis and modified to meet changing internal and external conditions. Only once the strategic marketing plan has been developed should detailed operational or functional marketing plans, covering a one-year period, be developed (McDonald, 2002). This makes marketing planning a continuous process, not something undertaken once a year or, worse, when a product is launched.

A marketing plan designed to support a particular offering consists of a series of activities that should be undertaken sequentially. These are presented in Table 5.3.

Many of the corporate-level goals and strategies, and internal and external environmental analyses that are established within the strategic marketing planning process, can be replicated within each of the marketing plans written for individual products, product lines, markets, or even SBUs. As a general rule, only detail concerning offerings, competitors, and related support resources need change prior to the formulation of individual marketing mixes and their implementation within functional-level marketing plans.

Table 5.3 Key activities within a marketing plan

Activity	Explanation
Executive summary	A brief one-page summary of key points and outcomes
Overall objectives	Should make reference to the organization's overall mission and corporate goals—the elements that underpin the strategy
Product/market background	A short summary of the product and/or market to clarify understanding about target markets, sales history, market trends, main competitors, and the organization's own product portfolio
Marketing analysis	Provides insight into the market, the customers, and the competition Should consider segment needs, current strategies, and key financial data Supported by the marketing audit and SWOT analysis
Marketing strategies	Should state the market(s) to be targeted, the basis on which the firm will compete, the competitive advantages to be used, and the way in which the product is to be positioned in the market
Marketing goals	Should express the desired outcomes of the strategy in terms of the volume of expected sales, the value of sales and market share gains, levels of product awareness, availability, profitability, and customer satisfaction
Marketing programmes	Should develop a marketing mix for each target market segment, along with a specification of who is responsible for the various activities and actions, as well as the resources that are to be made available
Implementation	Should set out: ■ the way in which the marketing plan is to be controlled and evaluated; ■ the financial scope of the plan; and ■ the operational implications in terms of human resources, R&D, and system and process needs
Supporting documentation	Any material too bulky to be included in the plan itself, but necessary for reference and detail, e.g. the full PESTLE and SWOT analyses, marketing research data, and other market reports and information

The strategic marketing planning process starts with a consideration of the organization's goals and resources, and an analysis of the market and environmental context in which the organization seeks to achieve its goals. It culminates in a detailed plan that, when implemented, is measured to determine how well the organization performs against the marketing plan.

 Visit the **online resources** and access Internet Activity 5.4 to read more about writing marketing plans.

 # Chapter Summary

To consolidate your learning, the key points from this chapter are summarized here:

■ **Describe the strategic planning process and explain the key influences that shape marketing strategy.**

The strategic planning process commences at the corporate level, where the organization sets out its overall mission, purpose, and values. These are then converted into measurable goals that apply to the whole organization. Then, depending upon the size of the organization, the range of strategic business units (SBUs) and/or offerings is determined and resources are allocated to support each one. Each SBU and/or offering has detailed functional and competitive strategies and plans, such as a marketing strategy and plan, developed around it.

There are three key influences on marketing strategy: strategic market analysis, which is concerned with developing knowledge and understanding about the marketplace; strategic marketing goals, which are about what the strategy is intended to achieve; and strategic market action, which is about how the strategies are to be implemented.

■ **Analyse current conditions and formulate marketing strategies.**

SWOT analysis is used to determine an overall view of the strategic position and highlights the need for a strategy to produce a strong fit between the internal capability (strengths and weaknesses) and the external situation (opportunities and threats). SWOT analysis serves to identify the key issues, and prompts thought about converting weaknesses into strengths and threats into opportunities.

■ **Explain the different types of strategic marketing goal and associated growth strategies.**

There are several types of strategic marketing goal, but the four main ones are niche, hold, harvest, and divest. However, the vast majority of organizations consider growth to be a primary objective. Although there are different ways of classifying growth, intensive, integrated, or diversified are generally accepted as the main forms.

■ **Describe the concepts associated with strategic market action.**

Strategic market action is concerned with ways of implementing marketing strategies. Various concepts and frameworks have been proposed, and, of these, we considered ideas about competitive advantage, generic strategies, and competitive positioning.

■ **Appreciate the main issues associated with strategy implementation, including the principles of marketing metrics.**

The implementation of most strategic marketing plans involves four main issues: the structure and type of marketing function; organizational culture; financial resources; and marketing metrics, or the controls used to measure the effectiveness of the implementation process.

Many companies now use various marketing metrics to monitor performance. These include metrics in the areas of: profit/profitability; sales value and volume; gross margin; (brand) awareness; market share; number of new products; relative price; number of customer complaints; consumer satisfaction; customer advocacy; distribution/availability; total number of customers; marketing spend; perceived quality/esteem; loyalty/retention; and relative perceived quality.

■ **Explain the key elements of a marketing plan.**

The key elements associated with the structure of a marketing plan are: the overall objectives; product/market background; market analysis; marketing strategy and goals; marketing programmes; implementation, evaluation, and control. Although depicted as a linear process, many organizations do not follow this process, or do not include all these elements, or undertake many of these elements simultaneously.

Review Questions

1 What is the difference between vision and mission statements?

2 Identify the four elements that make up the strategic context.

3 What are the key elements of the strategic planning process?

4 How might understanding a firm's competitors help the firm to develop its marketing strategy?

5 Identify the key characteristics of SWOT analysis. What actions should be taken once the SWOT grid is prepared?

6 What is the difference between intensive and diversified growth?

7 In what two ways does Porter (1985) argue that firms can differentiate themselves? How does each way work?

8 Name four elements that might influence strategy implementation.

9 Name the principal marketing metrics considered in this chapter.

10 List the core parts of a marketing plan.

 Discussion Questions

1 Having read Case Insight 5.1, how would you advise 3scale to develop a strategy to circumvent the competitive threat from Amazon?

2 'If the external environment is uncontrollable, and markets are changing shape increasingly quickly, there seems little point in developing a strategic marketing plan.' Discuss.

3 Explain which marketing metric(s) might be used in the following circumstances:

A A newly themed Irish pub, with a marketing objective to give customers the best pub experience in the immediate area in the first year of its operation

B A large health-and-fitness organization wanting to expand its chain of gymnasiums to other countries across Europe within a five-year timescale

C The manufacturer of a designer cosmetic, such as Gucci Pour Homme II, wishing to determine how well distributed its product is

D A pharmaceutical company wishing to find out whether its new asthma product will be better received in the marketplace in the next 12 months compared with competing brands and whether it can hold its price premium

 Visit the online resources and complete the Multiple-Choice Questions to assess your knowledge of Chapter 5.

Glossary

attack strategies derived from military origins, these strategies seek to achieve growth objectives.

category management the management of a discrete group of similar or related products whereby each category is run as a mini-business within a retailing or purchasing context.

competitive advantage achieved when an organization has an edge over its competitors on factors that are important to customers.

corporate strategy the means by which the resources of the organization are matched with the needs of the environment in which the organization decides to operate.

cost leadership a strategy involving the production of goods and services for a broad market segment, at a cost lower than that of all other competitors.

defence strategies derived from military origins, these strategies need to be deployed quickly and save time when faced with frontal or flanking attacks.

differentiation a strategy through which an organization offers products and services to broad particular customer groups, who perceive the offering to be significantly different from, and superior to, those of its competitors.

diversification a strategy that requires organizations to grow outside their current range of activities; brings new value chain activities because the firm is operating with new products and in new markets.

divest a strategic objective that involves selling or killing off a product when products continue to incur losses and generate negative cash flows.

focus (strategy) a strategy based on developing gaps in broad market segments or gaps in competitors' product ranges.

harvest a strategic objective based on maximizing short-term profits and stimulating positive cash flow; often used in mature markets as firms or products enter a decline phase.

hold a strategic objective based on defending against attacks from aggressive competitors.

integrative growth growth based on working with the same products and the same markets, but starting to perform some of the activities in

the value chain that were previously undertaken by others.

intensive growth growth that requires an organization to concentrate its activities on markets or products that are familiar.

key performance indicators (KPIs) a set of quantifiable measures used to determine and compare an organization's achievements in terms of meeting its strategic and operational goals.

marketing metrics a set of measures that senior marketers use to assess the performance of their marketing strategies and programmes.

mission statement a statement that sets out an organization's long-term intentions, describing its purpose and direction.

niche a strategic objective based on identifying a niche market.

niche market a small part of a market segment that has specific and specialized characteristics that make it uneconomic for the leading competitors to enter this segment.

organizational culture the set of systems, values, and beliefs that employees and other stakeholders share across an organization that govern how it operates, as well as the decisions that it takes and implements.

organizational goals the outcomes of the organization's various activities, often expressed as market share, share value, return on investment, or numbers of customers served.

pipeline a linear approach to value creation through a chain of interrelated organizations.

platform strategy an approach that enables organizations to connect their businesses with hosts on top of which to build products and services, and hence co-create value; sometimes referred to as plug and play, platforms are developing through digital environments.

relative price denotes the price of a company's product/service as a proportion of the price of a comparable product/service of typically the market leading company, or its nearest competitor (where the company is itself the market leader).

strategic business unit (SBU) an organizational unit that, for planning purposes, is sufficiently large to exercise control over the principal strategic factors affecting its performance; might incorporate an entire brand and/or its subcomponents, or a country region, or some other discrete unit of an organization.

strategic market analysis the starting point of the marketing strategy process, involving analysis of three main types of environment: the external environment; the performance environment; and the internal environment.

SWOT analysis a methodology used by organizations to understand their strategic position by assessing the organization's strengths, weaknesses, opportunities, and threats.

total shareholder return the return on a company's stock to an investor based on capital gain plus dividends.

values the standards of behaviour expected of an organization's employees.

vision statement a statement that sets out how an organization sees its future and what it wants to become.

References

Achrol, R.S. (1997). Changes in the theory of interorganisational relations in marketing: toward a network paradigm. *Journal of the Academy of Marketing Science*, 25(1), 56–71.

Ailawadi, K., Lehmann, D.R., and Neslin, S.A. (2003). Revenue premium as an outcome measure of brand equity. *Journal of Marketing*, 67(4), 1–17.

Amazonjobs (n.d.). We pioneer. Retrieve from: https://www.amazon.jobs/en/working/working-amazon (accessed 13 October 2018).

Ambler, T. (2000). Marketing metrics. *Business Strategy Review*, 11(2), 59–66.

Anderson, P.F. (1982). Marketing, strategic planning and the theory of the firm. *Journal of Marketing*, 46(2), 15–26.

Anon. (2016a). *UK Supermarket Investment Report*. London: MSCI/Colliers International. Retrieve from: http://www.colliers.com/-/media/files/emea/uk/services/retail/201703-colliers-msci-uk-supermarket-investment-report.pdf?la=en-gb (accessed 13 October 2018).

Anon. (2016b). The UK's best energy companies for customer service revealed. *BT*, 11 June. Retrieve from: https://home.bt.com/lifestyle/money/money-tips/the-uks-best-energy-companies-for-customer-service-revealed-11364047695615 (accessed 13 October 2018).

Anon. (2017a). Apple v Samsung: Phone tag. *The Economist*, 16 September, 64–5.

Anon. (2017b). Volts wagons. *The Economist*, 18 February, 59–60.

Anon. (2017c). Retailing in Pyongyang: minisocialist. *The Economist*, 24 June, 63.

Anon. (2017d). Microsoft: head in the cloud. *The Economist*, 18 March, 61–2.

Ansoff, I.H. (1957). Strategies for diversification. *Harvard Business Review*, 35(2), 113–24.

Bonoma, T.V. (1984). Making your marketing strategy work. *Harvard Business Review*, 62(2), 69–76.

Browne, S., and Cuddihy, L. (2011). Questioning the currency of marketing planning today. *Irish Marketing Review*, 21(1–2), 49–57.

Damodaran, A. (2017). Margins by sector (US). *NYU Stern*, January. Retrieve from: http://pages.stern.nyu.edu/~adamodar/New_Home_Page/datafile/margin.html (accessed 13 October 2018).

Dix, J. (2016). Inside the strategy team at Cisco. *Network World*, 15 February. Retrieve from: https://www.networkworld.com/article/3033153/lan-wan/inside-the-strategy-team-at-cisco.html (accessed 13 October 2018).

Griffiths, K. (2006). Pharmaceuticals: UK drug giants hit by pipeline problems. *Daily Telegraph*, 27 October, 3.

Gummesson, E. (1990). Marketing orientation revisited: the crucial role of the part-time marketer. *European Journal of Marketing*, 25(2), 60–75.

Hanselman, A. (2012). Joshie the Giraffe: a remarkable story about customer delight! *Social Media Today*, 18 May. Retrieve from: https://www.socialmediatoday.com/content/joshie-giraffe-remarkable-story-about-customer-delight-0 (accessed 13 October 2018).

Harbison, J.R., and Pekar, P. (1998). *Smart Alliances: A Practical Guide to Repeatable Success*. San Francisco, CA: Jossey-Bass.

Hoffman, N.P. (2000). An examination of the' sustainable competitive advantage' concept: past, present, and future. *Academy of Marketing Science Review*, 6. Retrieve from: https://www.ams-web.org/page/OriginalAMSRArticles? (accessed 24 September 2018).

IATA (International Air Transport Association) (2017). Another strong year for air travel demand in 2016. Press release, 2 February. Retrieve from: https://www.iata.org/pressroom/pr/Pages/2017-02-02-01.aspx (accessed 13 October 2018).

Kahn, W.A. (1990). Psychological conditions of personal engagement and disengagement at work. *Academy of Management Journal*, 33(4), 692–724.

Kaplan, R.S., and Norton, D.P. (1992). The balanced scorecard: measures that drive performance. *Harvard Business Review*, 70(1), 71–9.

KBC (2018a). KBC Bank Ireland scoops gold at An Post Smart Marketing Awards. Press releases, 4 May. Retrieve from: https://www.kbc.ie/news-and-press/latest-news-and-press-releases/kbc-bank-ireland-scoops-gold-at-an-post-smart-mark (accessed 13 October 2018).

KBC (2018b). KBC Bank Ireland PLC, financial results for Q1 2018 (to 31st March). Press release, 17 May. Retrieve from: https://www.kbc.ie/news-and-press/latest-news-and-press-releases/kbc-bank-ireland-plc,-financial-results-for-q1-(3) (accessed 13 October 2018).

KBC (2018c). KBC first Irish bank to bring Garmin Pay to customers. Press release, 19 June. Retrieve from: https://www.kbc.ie/news-and-press/latest-news-and-press-releases/kbc-first-irish-bank-to-bring-garmin-pay-to-custom (accessed 13 October 2018).

KBC (n.d.). KBC: the bank of you. Retrieve from: https://www.kbc.ie/the-bank-of-you (accessed 13 October 2018).

Keaveney, S.M. (1995). Customer switching behavior in service industries: an exploratory study. *Journal of Marketing*, 59(2), 71–82.

Kehrer, D. (2015). Precision attribution fuels marketing effectiveness. *Admap*, February, 22–4.

Keiningham, T.L., Aksoy, L., Cooil, B., and Andreassen, T.W. (2008). Linking customer loyalty to growth. *Sloan Management Review*, 49(4), 50–7.

Lamont, J. (2012). Targeting KPIs for better business performance. *KM World*, 21(8), 12–13.

Lucas, L. (2017). A global strategist with deep pockets. *Financial Times*, 6–7 January, 9.

Macdonald, J.B., and Neupert, K.E. (2005). Applying Sun Tzu's terrain and ground to the study of marketing strategy. *Journal of Strategic Marketing*, 13(4), 293–304.

Mankins, M.C., Harding, D., and Weddigen, R.M. (2008). How the best divest. *Harvard Business Review*, 86(10), 92–9.

Martin, G. (2015). When legacy airlines degrade themselves with budget fares. *Skift*, 27 April. Retrieve from: https://skift.com/2015/04/27/when-legacy-airlines-degrade-themselves-with-budget-fares/ (accessed 13 October 2018).

McDonald, M. (1985). Marketing planning and Britain's disoriented directions. *Journal of Marketing Management*, 1, 21–5.

McDonald, M. (2002). *Marketing Plans and How to Make Them* (5th edn). Oxford: Butterworth Heinemann.

Menon, A., and Varadarajan, P.R. (1992). A model of marketing knowledge use within firms. *Journal of Marketing*, 56(4), 53–71.

Mintz, O., and Currim, I.S. (2013). What drives managerial use of marketing and financial metrics and does metric use affect performance of marketing mix activities? *Journal of Marketing*, 77(2), 17–40.

Mintzberg, H. (1987). The strategy concept: five Ps for strategy. *California Management Review*, 30(1), 11–26.

Mitchell, A. (2012). Brand managers: then and now. *Marketing*, 23 May, 28–30.

Moon, M.J. (2000). Organizational commitment revisited in new public management: motivation, organizational culture, sector, and managerial level. *Public Performance and Management Review*, 24(2), 177–94.

Nicolaou, A. (2017). Mars eyes health snacks and pet food to sweeten sales. *Financial Times*, 11 September, 10.

Nugent, D. (2018). Darragh Lennon, KBC Bank Ireland director of products. *ACCA*, 1 January. Retrieve from: https://www.accaglobal.com/us/en/member/member/accounting-business/2018/01/interviews/darragh-lennon.html (accessed 13 October 2018).

Payaud, M.A. (2014). Marketing strategies at the bottom of the pyramid: examples from Nestlé, Danone, and Procter & Gamble. *Global Business and Organizational Excellence*, 33(2), 51–63.

Piercy, N. (1998). Marketing implementation: the implications of marketing paradigm weakness for the strategy execution process. *Journal of the Academy of Marketing Science*, 26(3), 222–36.

Piercy, N. (2002). *Market-Led Strategic Change: Transforming the Process of Going to Market*. Oxford: Butterworth Heinemann.

Porter, M.E. (1985). *The Competitive Advantage: Creating and Sustaining Superior Performance*. New York: Free Press.

Prahalad, C.K. (2004). *Fortune at the Bottom of the Pyramid: Eradicating Poverty through Profits*. Upper Saddle River, NJ: Pearson Education.

Prahalad, C.K., and Hamel, G. (1990). The core competence of the organisation. *Harvard Business Review*, 68(3), 79–91.

Ramaseshan, B., Ishak, A., and Kingshott, R.P.J. (2013). Interactive effects of marketing strategy formulation and implementation upon firm performance. *Journal of Marketing Management*, 29(11–12), 1224–50.

Reichheld, F.F. (2003). The one number you need to grow. *Harvard Business Review*, 81(12), 47–54.

Singh, P.P. (2011). Can Sony succeed where Sony-Ericsson partnership failed? *BBC News*, 13 October. Retrieve from: https://www.bbc.com/news/business-15285258 (accessed 13 October 2018).

Srinivasan, R., Lilien, G.L., and Sridhar, S. (2011). Should firms spend more on research and development and advertising during recessions? *Journal of Marketing*, 75(3), 49–65.

Stone, B., and Chen, L.Y. (2017). Tencent dominates in China: next challenge is the rest of the world. *Bloomberg Businessweek*, 17 June. Retrieve from: https://www.bloomberg.com/news/features/2017-06-28/tencent-rules-china-the-problem-is-the-rest-of-the-world (accessed 13 October 2018).

Uszynski, R. (2013). Southwest Airlines Marketing Strategy, *ISSUU*. Retrieve from: https://issuu.com/rainelleu/docs/southwest_airlines/3?e=6172574/1804712 (accessed 13 October 2018).

van Alstyne, M.W., Parker, G.G., and Choudary, S.P. (2016). Pipelines, platforms, and the new rules of strategy. *Harvard Business Review*, April. Retrieve from: https://hbr.org/2016/04/pipelines-platforms-and-the-new-rules-of-strategy?cm_sp=Article-_-Links-_-Top%20of%20Page%20Recirculation (accessed 13 October 2018).

Vorhies, D.W., and Morgan, N.A. (2003). A configuration theory assessment of marketing organisation fit with business strategy and its relationship with marketing performance. *Journal of Marketing*, 67(1), 100–15.

Weinberger, M. (2017). Microsoft CEO Satya Nadella explains the 'not universally loved' changes he made to a luxury executive retreat. *Business Insider UK*, 26 September. Retrieve from: https://uk.businessinsider.com/microsoft-satya-nadella-company-culture-2017-9 (accessed 13 October 2018).

Wininger, J., and Rujana, J. (2017). Good news about divestitures. *Forbes*, 26 June. Retrieve from: https://www.forbes.com/sites/baininsights/2017/06/26/good-news-about-divestitures/#385ebc6c1dfa (accessed 13 October 2018).

Chapter 6
Market Segmentation and Positioning

Learning Outcomes

After reading this chapter, you will be able to:

▶ Describe the principles of market segmentation and the STP process

▶ List the characteristics and differences between market segmentation and product differentiation

▶ Explain consumer and business-to-business market segmentation

▶ Describe different targeting strategies

▶ Discuss the concept of positioning

▶ Consider how the use of perceptual maps can assist in the positioning process

Case Insight 6.1
Soberana

Market Insight 6.1
Differentiating Medical Devices

Market Insight 6.2
Microtargeting Controversy during the US Presidential Election

Market Insight 6.3
Logistical Nightmare: Regaining Defectors

Market Insight 6.4
Positioning Premium Beer

Market Insight 6.5
Exploring C–D Maps for Strategic Positioning

Case Insight 6.1
Soberana

When an international beer brand took 10 per cent of the Panamanian beer market, it was time for local brand Soberana to re-evaluate its approach. We talk to Fermin Paus, brand franchise manager, to find out how Soberana responded.

Beer is an integral part of the Panamanian culture, mainly because of the country's tropical location and weather. Panama is almost surrounded by the Caribbean Sea and Pacific Ocean, and the temperature is above 25°C every day, all year. Not surprisingly, then, it has the highest beer consumption in Latin America and, in 2013, it had the highest consumption per capita, with 71 litres, ranking it 22nd in the world's beer consumption index.

Historically, the market has had two main players that compete with national and international brands, and which account for more than 90 per cent of the total volume: Cerveceria Nacional (part of the ABI/SabMiller group); and us, Cervecerias Baru Panama (part of the Heineken group). The rest of the market is dominated by international brands managed by trading companies. Because of its high per capita intake, market expansion opportunities in Panama are limited and slow. This means that the main growth strategies for beer players are about gaining market share at the expense of their competitors.

In 2010, Cerveceria Nacional introduced Miller Lite, after becoming the only operation outside the United States to produce and sell the brand locally. The entrance of this brand accelerated a latent consumer trend. Consumers had been shifting their flavour preferences from traditional lager beers towards soft/light options and Miller Lite matched those new preferences perfectly. Consumers were changing their behaviours and looking for beers that enabled them to extend their drinking time (more beers in more time), yet not make themselves ill or inebriated. Beers with both low alcohol and bitterness, and those with a softer taste, matched this requirement. Miller Lite was positioned as an upper mainstream option and priced a few cents above local brands.

Soberana is a soft lager sold in the Panamanian market

Source: Reproduced with kind permission of Soberana.

The intrinsic product attributes and the pricing strategy, together with an American legacy, which is an important aspirational consumption driver for Panamanians, transformed Miller Lite into one of the most important players in the market. The brand grew strongly and achieved more than 10 per cent market share. This new segment of soft/light beers now accounts for more than 70 per cent of the Panamanian beer market.

At the time of Miller's growth, we had two local brands in the market, PANAMA and Soberana. The former was the company's main national focus, while the

Case Insight 6.1

continued

latter was mainly distributed in the central region of the country and was generally neglected, in that it lacked a marketing strategy or supporting resources. These brands have different flavour profiles: PANAMA is a regular lager, while Soberana is a soft lager.

Soberana was launched in 1969 and its name, which means 'sovereign' in English, refers to a historic Panamanian moment. In the 1960s, Panama started claiming its sovereignty over territories that were in the hands of the United States, which had entered the country at the beginning of the twentieth century to finish construction of the Panama Canal.

Because Soberana was distributed mainly in the central region, its market was limited to just 25 per cent of the population. Its price strategy (a few cents below mainstream brands) and promotional/functional messages in the brand communications supported a value positioning. The brand was mostly consumed by

adults over the age of 45. This had a negative effect on the brand equity indicators and image perception. By 2011, Soberana had the lowest equity indicators in the market and a strong negative image perception. Accordingly, Soberana was not differentiated in any particular way and was not perceived to be an aspirational brand.

By the end of 2011, Miller Lite was sourcing volume from all the national brands and was the only brand in the market capitalizing on this new consumer trend.

Soberana's problem was: how could it respond to the changing market needs and challenge Miller Lite's increasingly dominant market leader position?

 Visit the online resources to watch a video interview with Fermin Paus in which he explains what Soberana did.

Introduction

Have you ever wondered how we decide to target certain market customer groups with particular marketing activities? Think about fashion retailers for a moment: how do they identify the groups of people with whom they want to communicate about new ranges? Do they base it on where those people live, their age, their gender (or gender identity), their personality, or something else? In this chapter, we consider how organizations decide on which segments of a market to concentrate their efforts. This process is known as **market segmentation** and is an integral part of marketing strategy (see Chapter 5). After first defining market segmentation, we explore the differences between market segmentation and **product differentiation** to clarify the underlying principles of segmentation. We consider consumer and **business-to-business (B2B)** market segmentation in detail.

The STP Process

The method by which whole markets are subdivided into different segments is referred to as the segmentation, targeting, and positioning process, or **STP process** (see Figure 6.1).

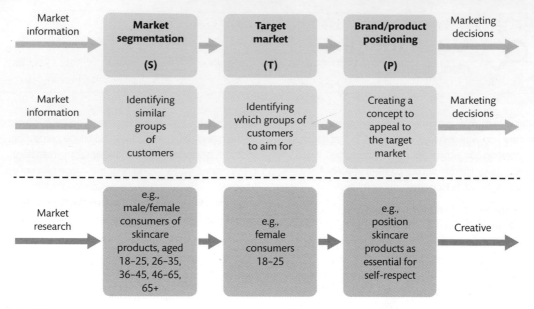

Figure 6.1
The STP process

Marketers use the STP process to identify on whom, out of all their potential customers, they should focus—that is, the most attractive and accessible groups of customers or segments. Marketers also use the STP process to identify new products and service opportunities, to develop suitable **positioning** and **communication** strategies, and to allocate scarce resources to support key marketing goals.

Organizations commission segmentation research to revise their marketing strategy, investigate a declining brand, launch a new offering, or restructure their pricing policies. When operating in highly dynamic environments, segmentation research should be conducted at regular intervals to identify changes in the marketplace. The key benefits of the STP process include:

- enhancing a company's competitive position, providing direction and focus for marketing strategies, including targeted advertising, new proposition development, and brand differentiation, such as when Coca-Cola identified that Diet Coke was perceived as 'feminine' by male consumers and hence developed Coke Zero, targeted at the health-conscious male segment of the soft drinks market;

- examining and identifying market growth opportunities in terms of new customers, growth segments, or proposition uses, such as fashion brand Burberry, once perceived as gangwear (DeMers, 2016), becoming chic and in demand around the world; and

- the effective and efficient matching of company resources to targeted market segments, promising greater return on marketing investment (ROMI), for example supermarkets such as Asda and Carrefour using data-informed segmentation strategies to target direct marketing messages (online and offline) and rewards to customers.

The Concept of Market Segmentation

Market segmentation is the division of a mass market into distinct and identifiable groups, or segments, each of which is defined by common characteristics and needs, and displays similar responses to marketing actions. For example, Lee (2013) identifies four main segments in the consumer photography market:

- The *slow photography* segment consists of consumers who share the pleasure associated with the creation and capture of an image as much as the photo itself. They like photography and the capture of a high-quality image is integral to the activity.

- The *fast photography* segment involves the speedy creation and consumption of images. Most of the images are used for immediate communication, very often shared with friends and family through social media. Mobile devices are a key device for this segment.

- The *casual photography* segment uses occasional photos to capture memories. These people rarely take photos and can be categorized as snapshot photographers.

- The *intelligent photography* segment is characterized by people who wish to blend the capture of a high-quality image with social and memory-keeping purposes. They enjoy using innovative techniques and new devices.

A selfie is an example of Lee's fast photography segment
Source: © Vladimir Gjorgiev/Shutterstock.com.

Market segmentation was first defined as 'a condition of growth when core markets have already been developed on a generalized basis to the point where additional promotional expenditures are yielding diminishing returns' (Smith, 1956: 7). It forms an important foundation for successful marketing strategies and activities (Wind, 1978).

The purpose of market segmentation is to ensure that elements of the marketing mix—namely, price, distribution, products, and promotion (and people, process, and physical evidence for service offerings)—meet the needs of different customer groups. Because companies have finite resources, it is not feasible to produce all the required offerings for all the people all the time: we can't be all things to all people. The best we can do is provide selected offerings for selected groups of people most of the time. This enables the most effective use of an organization's scarce resources.

Market segmentation is related to product differentiation as follows:

- A *product differentiation* strategy involves highlighting a product's attributes and features to emphasize the differences between it and—hence distinguishing it from—those of competitors or other product offerings.

- A *market segmentation* strategy requires a focus on particular segments or groups of customers who share similar needs or characteristics.

In fashion retailing, for example, if a traditionalist clothing firm decides to adapt its range so that its skirts are more colourful, use lightweight fabrics, and have very short hemlines, it might expect this styling to appeal more to younger women. This is product differentiation because the firm focuses first on the product offering and then sees which part of the market responds, basing its decisions on intuition. Alternatively, if the firm decides to target older women specifically as a market segment and conducts appropriate research that reveals that it ought to use darker, heavier fabrics for its skirts, with longer hemlines, this is market segmentation because the firm has focused first on researching the needs and wants of a specific market segment, and then developed the product to meet those needs (see Market Insight 6.1 and Research Insight 6.1).

Market Insight 6.1
Differentiating Medical Devices

The medical device market is segmented in many ways, but products are differentiated to meet broad customer needs. Four categories of product and service can be distinguished:

- *Premium differentiated* Innovative products and services, which drive premium prices, are usually differentiated by efficacy, outcomes, or care delivery. These are often supported by heavy selling and servicing models.

- *Premium undifferentiated* These products and services are not clinically distinguishable from competitors' offerings. They are offered by many premium companies, whose success is based on established customer relationships or strong branding.

- *Value* These products and services are designed to meet 'good enough' standards for product quality, efficacy, safety, and service standards. These customers are happy to trade innovation, quality, and service for a price that can be 20–40 per cent lower than that of premium products.

- *Basic* These rudimentary products and services compete purely on price and are often used where providers wish to supply only a basic service. This is a large, yet competitive, sector in which margins and opportunities are limited.

Source: Llewellyn, Podpolny, and Zerbi (2015).

Market Insight 6.1
continued

Theory into Practice

Theoretically, product differentiation is primarily concerned with managing supply, whereas segmentation is primarily concerned with managing demand. Where product differentiation is successful, monopolistic competition occurs.

Firms that develop a portfolio of products and distinguish them by means of key attributes are effectively practising product differentiation. They are influencing supply to manage demand. Therefore a manufacturer in the medical devices market might develop a range of products based on functionality that is different from (superior to) that of its competitors.

In contrast, the same firm might choose to segment the market's customers based on a range of factors and then develop medical devices to suit the needs of particular segment(s). This is market segmentation and is rooted in the idea of managing demand to influence supply.

A theoretical issue that arises from this is: does product differentiation lead to segmentation? In this market insight, the value category might lead a firm to identify a group of customers who prefer value products and services, and this in turn might lead to segmenting this group based on a range of needs or benefits.

Related Topics
economic theories of competition (monopolistic, oligopolistic, perfect, and imperfect); value; competitive advantage

1 Should product differentiation be regarded as an alternative to market segmentation strategies?

2 What process should companies follow in the medical device market to adopt a market segmentation approach?

3 Under what circumstances should market segmentation be used rather than product differentiation?

Market segmentation was proposed as an alternative development strategy in markets in which few competitors were selling an identical product—that is, imperfectly competitive markets. Where there are many competitors selling identical products, market segmentation and product differentiation can produce similar results, because competitors imitate each other's strategic approaches more quickly and product differentiation approaches meet market segment needs more closely. Because consumers exhibit a wider range of tastes and have greater disposable income, marketers increasingly design offerings around consumer demand—that is, market segments—rather than around their own production needs—that is, product differentiation (see Figure 6.2). Thus, globally, computer manufacturer Dell has previously structured the company around four segments, comprising consumer, big business customers, government customers, and small and medium-sized business customers (Shankland, 2009).

Research Insight 6.1

To take your learning further, you might wish to read this influential paper:

Smith, W.R. (1956). Product differentiation and market segmentation as alternative marketing strategies. *Journal of Marketing*, 21(1), 3–8.

This seminal article explained the idea that neither supply nor demand was homogeneous (that is, different groups wanted to produce *and* consume different things). A product differentiation approach concerns itself with bending demand to the will of supply, but the reverse approach—bending supply to the will of demand—also exists. This alternative marketing strategy, articulated in detail in this article for the first time, was termed market segmentation.

 Visit the online resources read the abstract and access the full paper.

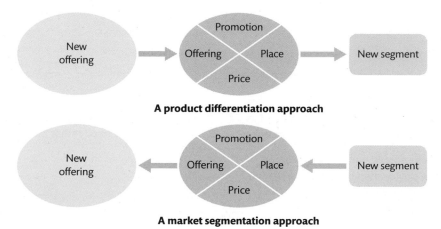

A product differentiation approach

A market segmentation approach

Figure 6.2

The difference between market segmentation and product differentiation

The Process of Market Segmentation

There are two main approaches to market segmentation. The first, known as the **build-up method**, approaches the task from the perspective of identifying markets that consist of customers who are similar; the second, known as the **breakdown method**, identifies those groups that share particular differences (Griffith and Pol, 1994).

While the breakdown method is the most established approach to segmenting consumer markets, the build-up approach seeks to move beyond the individual level, at which all customers are indeed different, to a more general level of analysis based on identifying similarities (Freytag and Clarke, 2001). In other words, the build-up method is customer-oriented, seeking

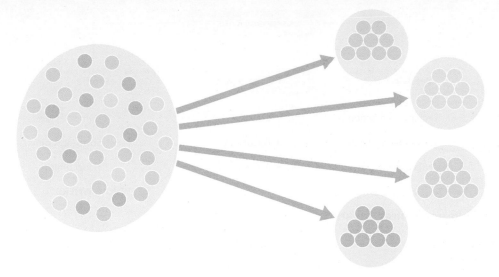

Figure 6.3
Segment heterogeneity and member homogeneity

to determine common customer needs. The aim of both methods is to identify market segments between which identifiable differences exist—segment heterogeneity—but within which similarities exist between members—member homogeneity (see Figure 6.3).

In **business markets**, segmentation should reflect the relationship needs of the organizations involved. However, problems remain concerning the practical application and implementation of business-to-business (B2B) segmentation. Managers frequently report that the analytical processes are reasonably clear, but it is unclear how they should choose and evaluate the various market segments in the first instance (Naudé and Cheng, 2003). Segmentation theory has developed in an era in which a transactional goods-centric approach to marketing has dominated rather than the service-dominant logic that exists today. Under the transactional approach, resources are allocated to achieve designated marketing mix goals. However, customers within various segments have changing needs and therefore those customers may change their segment membership (Freytag and Clarke, 2001). Consequently, market segmentation programmes should always use up-to-date customer data.

Market Segmentation in Consumer Markets

To segment consumer markets, we use market information based around key customer-, product-, or situation-related criteria. These are classified as segmentation bases and include profile criteria (for example who are my market and where are they?); behavioural criteria (for example where, when, and how does my market behave?); and psychological criteria (for example why does my market behave that way?) (see Figure 6.4). A fourth segmentation criterion is contact data—that is, a customer's name and full contact details beyond only their postcode (for example to include their postal and email addresses, and their mobile and home telephone numbers). Contact data are useful for tactical-level marketing activities, for example direct and

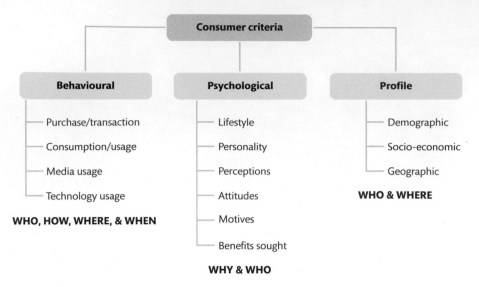

Figure 6.4
Segmentation criteria for consumer markets

digital marketing (see Chapters 11 and 12). Often, companies combine data from a variety of sources to develop a segmentation scheme. For example, in 2008 Experian segmented all adults in the UK into 19 different markets for its client, the Post Office, by fusing data from the Post Office customer insight survey, the edited electoral roll, census data, Experian lifestyle data (MOSAIC), and responses to a financial survey conducted by MORI (another market research firm) (Experian, 2008).

Table 6.1 illustrates the key characteristics associated with each of the main approaches to consumer market segmentation.

When selecting different segmentation bases, the trade-off between data acquisition costs and the ability of the data to predict customer choice behaviour should be considered. **Demographic** and **geo-demographic** data are relatively easy to measure and obtain; however, these bases suffer from low levels of accuracy in predicting consumer behaviour (see Figure 6.5). In contrast, behavioural data (for example **product usage**, purchase history, and media usage), although more costly to acquire, provide a more accurate means of predicting future behaviour: the brand of toothpaste you purchased previously is more likely to be the brand of toothpaste you purchase in future, for example. However, customer choices are also influenced by susceptibility to marketing communications. (See Research Insight 6.2 for a review of the main bases of market segmentation.)

Profile Criteria

One way of segmenting consumer markets is to use profile criteria to determine who consumers are and where they are located. To do this, we use demographic methods (for example age, gender/gender identity, race); socio-economics (for example determined by social class or income levels); and geographic location (for example using postcodes). For example, a utility company might segment households by geographical area to assess regional brand penetration, or an insurance company might segment the market by age, employment, income,

Table 6.1 Segmentation criteria

Base type	Segmentation criteria	Explanation
Profile	Demographic	Key variables concern age, sex/gender or gender identity, occupation, level of education, religion, social class, and income characteristics.
	Life stage	Based on the principle that people need different offerings at different stages in their lives (e.g. childhood, adulthood, young couples, retired).
	Geographic	The needs of potential customers in one geographic area are often different from those in another area, as a result of climate, custom, or tradition.
	Geodemographic	There is a relationship between the type of housing and location in which people live and their purchasing behaviours.
Psychological	Psychographic (lifestyles)	By analysing consumers' activities, interests, and opinions, we can understand individual lifestyles and patterns of behaviour affecting their buying behaviour and decision-making processes. We can also identify similar offering and/or media usage patterns.
	Benefits sought	The motivations customers derive from their purchases provide an insight into the benefits they seek from the use of an offering.
Behavioural	Purchase/transaction	Data about customer purchases and transactions provide scope for analysing who buys what, when, and how often, how much they spend, and through what transactional channel they purchase.
	Product usage	Segments can be derived on the basis of customer usage of the offering, brand, or product category. This may be in the form of usage frequency, time of usage, or usage situations.
	Media usage	What media channels are used, by whom, when, where, and for how long provides useful insights into the reach potential for certain market segments through differing media channels, as well as insight into the target's media lifestyle.

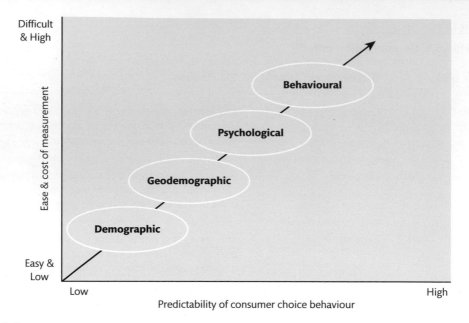

Figure 6.5

Considerations for segmentation criteria accessibility and use

Source: From Shimp. *Integrated Marketing Communications in Advertising and Promotion®*, International Edition, 7e. © 2007 South-Western, a part of Cengage Learning, Inc. Reproduced with permission.

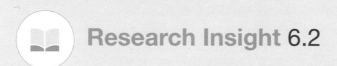

Research Insight 6.2

To take your learning further, you might wish to read this influential paper:

Beane, T.P., and Ennis, D.M. (1987). Market segmentation: a review. *European Journal of Marketing*, 32(5), 20–42.

This article provides a useful insight into the main bases of market segmentation, as well as the strengths and weaknesses of the key statistical methods used to analyse customer data to develop segmentation models. The authors suggest that there are many ways of segmenting a market and that it is important to exercise creativity when doing so.

 Visit the online resources to read the abstract and access the full paper.

and asset net worth to identify attractive market segments for a new investment portfolio. Boston Consulting Group (BCG) in Thailand has identified that more than half of Thai consumers now belong to the middle class and affluent consumers (MAC) group, presenting a specific opportunity in categories including consumer products, trade-up options, luxury goods, and experiences (Kittikachorn, 2018). These are all examples of segmentation based on profile criteria.

Demographic

Demographic variables relate to age; gender/gender identity; family size and life cycle; generation (for example baby boomers, Generation X, or millennials); income; occupation; education; ethnicity; nationality; religion; and social class. They indicate the profile of a consumer and are useful in media planning (see Chapter 11). For example, the post-millennial generation—known as Generation Z, and referring to those born between 1996 and 2010—comprise more than 27 per cent of the global population, spending US$44 billion in the United States alone. They connect with brands that express priorities of community, sustainability, and diversity (Black, Asadorian, and Dunnett, 2017), such as Vodafone and its youth sub-brand, Voxi, in the mobile category, or Converse and Vans in the trainer category.

The Chuck Taylor All Star

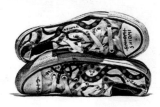

Made by Jeremy Threat

Made by Bess

Made by Sayori Wada

C NVERSE
Made by you

Converse's 'Made by You' campaign celebrates the individual experiences and self-expression embodied in a pair of Chucks
Source: © Converse Inc.

Age is a common way of segmenting consumer markets (for example children are targeted for confectionery and toys because their needs and tastes are different from those of older people). For example, Harley-Davidson is placing renewed emphasis on targeting younger riders—since the average age of a Harley owner in the United States has increased from 32 to 47 since 1990—and it has done so by setting up a 'Riding Academy'; by using younger spokespersons such as Jessica Haggett of 'The Litas', an international all-women motorcycle club; on social media; and by focusing advertising on sports such as the X Games and the Ultimate Fighting Championships (Moreno, 2017). Japanese telecoms company NTT DoComo, meanwhile, has produced a phone with larger keys and a larger display screen aiming to cater for the needs of older people (sometimes called the 'grey market') (Anon., 2016a).

Segmenting by gender has also traditionally spawned a raft of offerings targeted uniquely at women, including beauty and fragrance offerings (for example Clinique, Chanel); magazines (for example *Cosmopolitan*, *Amelia* in Sweden); hair care (for example Pantene, Clairol); and clothes (for example Monsoon, New Look). Offerings uniquely targeted at men include magazines (for example *GQ*), deodorants (for example Lynx/Axe), and beverages (for example Carlsberg,

Coke Zero). Some brands develop offerings targeted at both men and women, with fragrances (for example Versace), designer clothing (for example H&M, Next), and watches (for example Cartier). Some companies and categories are taking advantage of the trend towards a more gender-fluid world by also developing unisex offerings in their ranges, such as in kids clothing (for example Abercrombie & Fitch), perfume (for example Calvin Klein's CK2), and beauty products (for example Walmart's unisex shaving cream).

Research by Ipsos in the Middle East and North Africa (MENA) region identified that women are the chief shoppers in many households, ranging from around 94 per cent in Egypt to 46 per cent in Iraq, yet only a minority of women in the region earn their own income, with most dependent on an allowance—which has a significant impact on their purchase behaviour (Minawi, 2017).

Designer clothing targeting men and women
Source: © Richard Levine/Getty.

Income, or socio-economic status, is an important demographic variable because it determines whether or not a consumer can afford an offering (see Chapter 2). Socio-economic status comprises information about a consumer's personal income, household income, employment status, disposable income, and asset net worth. Many companies, for example those marketing luxury goods (such as Aston Martin, NetJets), target high net worth individuals (HNWIs) with high-end exclusive offerings. However, targeting low-income earners can also be profitable. German discount supermarkets (for example Aldi, Lidl) make a good profit by targeting low-income segments. Major supermarket groups such as Carrefour and Tesco use an understanding of customer socio-economics to develop their own-label offerings. For example, Tesco Finest is developed for market segments with high disposable income, in contrast with Tesco Value, which is marketed to the price-conscious, low-income segment.

Life Cycle

Life-stage analysis posits that people have varying amounts of disposable income and different needs at different times in their lives. For example, adolescents need different offerings from those required by single 26-year-olds, who need different offerings compared with 26-year-old married people with young children. Major supermarkets, such as Sainsbury's (UK), ICA Supermarket (Sweden), and Mercadona (Spain), have all invested in the development of offerings targeted at singles with high disposable incomes and busy lifestyles by offering ready meals for one, which compare with 'family value' and 'multipacks' targeted at families. As families grow and children leave home, the needs of parents change and their disposable income increases. Certain types of holiday (for example TUI's package holidays) and cars (for example people carriers) become more attractive to people in the life stage during which they have children. One modern lifecycle classification—that is, Target Group Index (TGI) from Kantar Media—classifies 12 or 13 life-stage groups based on age, marital status, household composition, and children, for example whether a person has children and the age(s) of the child(ren) (see Table 6.2). (See also Chapter 2 for a historical example of life-stage segmentation.)

 Visit the **online resources** and follow the web link to Kantar Media to learn more about the TGI.

Table 6.2 TGI life-stage segmentation groups

Group	Demographic description
Fledglings	15–34, not married and have no son or daughter; living with own parents
Flown the nest	15–34, not married, do not live with relations
Nest builders	15–34, married, do not live with son/daughter
Mid-life independents	35–54, not married, do not live with relations
Unconstrained couples	35–54, married, do not live with son/daughter
Playschool parents	Live with son/daughter and youngest child 0–4
Primary school parents	Live with son/daughter and youngest child 5–9
Secondary school parents	Live with son/daughter and youngest child 10–15
Hotel parents	Live with son/daughter and have no child 0–15
Senior sole decision-makers	55, not married and live alone
Empty nesters	55, married, and do not live with son/daughter
Non-standard families	Not married, live with relations, do not live with son/daughter, and do not live with parents if 15–34
Unclassified	Not in any group

Source: Reproduced with the kind permission of Kantar Media.

Geographics

A geographical approach is useful when there are clear locational differences in tastes, consumption, and preferences. For example, whereas the British celebrate Christmas with turkey dishes, Swedes often eat fish, and many Dutch opt for venison (and *Kerstbrood* or 'Christmas bread'). These consumption patterns provide an indication of preferences according to differing geographical regions. Markets can be considered by country or region, size of city or town, postcode, or population density such as urban, suburban, or rural. It is often said that American beer drinkers prefer lighter beers compared with their UK counterparts, whereas German beer drinkers prefer a much stronger drink than either. In contrast, Australians prefer colder, more carbonated, beer than drinkers in the UK or the United States.

In addition to proposition selection and consumption, geographical segmentation is important for retail location, advertising and media selection, and recruitment. For example, recruitment to the armed forces draws people with similar demographic attributes from a variety of geographic areas. Low-cost formats might be used for retail outlets in low-income regions. Direct sales operations (for example catalogue sales) can use census information to develop better customer segmentation and predictive models.

Geo-demographics

Geo-demographics is a natural outcome when combining demographic and geographic variables. The marriage of geographics and demographics has become an indispensable market analysis tool, because it can lead to a rich mixture of who lives where. Two of the best-known UK geo-demographic systems are A Classification of Residential Neighbourhoods (ACORN) from CACI Ltd and Experian's Mosaic.

Visit the **online resources** and complete Internet Activity 6.1 to learn more about how we use databases populated with geo-demographic data to profile market segments effectively.

ACORN breaks people into groups based on the postcodes within which they live, based on the following six categories (broken down further into 18 groups and 62 types):

1 Affluent Achievers

2 Rising Prosperity

3 Comfortable Communities

4 Financially Stretched

5 Urban Adversity

6 Not Private Households

ACORN is a geo-demographic tool used to identify the UK population and its demand for a variety of offerings to help marketers to determine where to locate operations, field sales forces, retail outlets, and so on. ACORN can also be used to determine where to plan marketing communications and social media marketing campaigns.

Visit the **online resources** and follow the web link to CACI Ltd to learn more about the ACORN system.

Mosaic is a similar geo-demographic segmentation system, developed by Experian and marketed globally. The system is based on a customer classification using more than 850 million source records and more than 450 input variables for clustering and interpretation to aggregate people into 15 groups (for example 'suburban stability', 'prestige positions') and 66 types (for example 'empty nest adventure', 'fledgling free') to create a three-tier classification that can be used at the individual, household, and postcode levels.

Visit the **online resources** and follow the web link to Experian to learn more about the Mosaic system.

Psychological Criteria

Psychological criteria used for segmenting consumer markets include the types of benefit sought by customers from brands in their consumption choices, attitudes, and perceptions (for example feelings about fast cars) and **psychographic** criteria, or the lifestyles of customers (for example 'extrovert', 'fashion conscious', 'high achiever').

Benefits Sought

The **benefits sought** approach is based on the principle that we should provide customers with exactly what they want, based on the benefits they derive from using a particular proposition (Haley, 1968). This might sound obvious, but consider the real benefits, both rational and irrational (see Chapter 2), for the different offerings that people buy (for example mobile phones and sunglasses). Major airlines often segment on the basis of the benefits passengers seek from transport by differentiating between the first-class passenger (given extra luxury benefits in their travel experience), the business-class passenger (who gets some of the luxury of the first-class passenger), and the economy-class passenger (who gets none of the luxury of the experience, but enjoys the same flight). Morrissey and Baines (2011) segmented the youth sports participation market in Ireland based on the benefits that young people seek in sport participation, creating the following four segments:

1 The *enthusiast* is a member who exercises principally for enjoyment and fitness (strength/ endurance and nimbleness) and who tends to do so regularly.

2 The *social competitor* is a member who tends to exercise regularly, be male and relatively young, and who exercises principally for interpersonal and affiliation motives. *Interpersonal motives* reflect individuals driven by the competitive and challenging aspects of exercise, in addition to peer recognition. *Affiliation motives* indicate a desire for social interaction and building of friendship through exercise.

3 The *healthy looker* is a member who exercises principally for aesthetic and health motives, and tends to be female and to exercise occasionally.

4 The *reluctant exerciser* is a member who tends to be female and to exercise occasionally, to exhibit below-average motivation for all motivational constructs, and for whom interpersonal and enjoyment motives are substantially below average.

Psychographics

Psychographic approaches rely on the analysis of consumers' activities, interests, and opinions to understand consumers' individual lifestyles and behaviour patterns. Psychographic segmentation includes understanding the values that are important to different customer types. A traditional form of lifestyle segmentation is based on customers' activities, interests, and opinions

(AIO). Taylor Nelson Sofres (TNS) developed a UK Lifestyle Typology comprising the categories 'belonger', 'survivor', 'experimentalist', 'conspicuous consumer', 'social resistor', 'self-explorer', and 'aimless'.

International Harvester undertook value-based segmentation to discover why farmers consistently rated the equipment of John Deere, its arch competitor, as 'more reliable' than its own. International Harvester had invested heavily to minimize breakdowns, but John Deere continued to lead in the reliability rankings. Surveys about repair problems revealed it was the downtime caused by breakdowns that most affected farmers because of the days of lost productivity waiting for repairs. John Deere's customers perceived reliability to be much less of a problem because of John Deere's extensive service-oriented dealer network, which stocked spare parts and offered temporary tractors, allowing a farmer to get back to work quickly. John Deere was serving a different segment of farmers: those driven by the value of a total service solution (Anon., 2013).

Behavioural Criteria

Product-related methods of segmenting consumer markets include using behavioural methods (for example product usage, purchase, and ownership) as bases for segmentation (see Market Insight 6.2). Observing consumers as they use offerings or consume services can be an important source of ideas for new uses or proposition design and development. Furthermore, new markets for existing offerings can be signalled, as well as appropriate communication themes for promotion. Purchase, ownership, and usage are three very different behavioural constructs that can be used to aid consumer market segmentation.

Market Insight 6.2
Microtargeting Controversy during the US Presidential Election

Facebook's segmentation of the US presidential election in 2016 used multiple data sources, including attitudinal data (whether people support particular political issues), behavioural data (on which parties people donate to or support), and demographic data (for example gender) and K-Means cluster analysis, to segment and profile the US electorate based on their Facebook use. This allowed them to derive five voter types based along partisanship lines, each with between one and four segments, as follows (including number of people within each segment):

■ Very Liberal

   ○ Youthful Urbanites (10.2 million)—average age 29; 40/60 per cent male/female; 1.6 million from generation AA (18 years old in 2017) and 561,000 Hispanic Americans; interested in comedy television and boxing; politics centring on women's issues, (Barack) Obama

○ Transitionals (3.4 million)—average age 26; 49/51 per cent male/female; generation of newly engaged and single; interested in sports, hip hop; politics centring on cannabis reform, (Barack) Obama, Jimmy Morales

○ Political Engaged City Dwellers (15 million)— average age 46; 47/53 per cent male/female; college educated and Protestant; interested in film festivals and opera; politics centring on women's interests, Madam President, Bernie (Sanders)

■ Liberal

   ○ Political Engaged Adults (10.2 million)—average age 50; 44/56 per cent male/female; generation of mothers and multicultural; interested in yoga, organic food; politics centring on Help Elect Women, Bernie (Sanders), Hillary (Clinton)

Market Insight 6.2
continued

- ○ Multicultural Millennials (20.1 million)—average age 28; 45/55 per cent male/female; generation of 2.3 million Hispanic Americans, 540,000 Black American, 511,000 Asian Americans; interested in football, vegan cuisine, Kardashians; politics centring on cannabis reform, Voters for Equality, Narendra Modi

- ○ Mainstream Millennials (9.3 million)—average age 33; 57/43 per cent male/female; generation of high school or less education; Catholic; no children; interested in gaming, video chat, college sports; politics centring on Voters for Equality, cannabis reform, Bernie (Sanders), (Joe) Biden, (Barack) Obama

- ■ Moderate

  - ○ Moderate (44.1 million)—average age 33; 43/57 per cent male/female; generation of mothers and Catholic; interested in football, gaming, charity, camping, boating; politics centring on Mitt Romney, Bernie (Sanders), (Barack) Obama, Hillary (Clinton), Chris Christie

- ■ Conservative

  - ○ Diverse Parents (18.4 million)—average age 42; 40/60 per cent male/female; generation of multiculturals; interested in auctions, boating; politics centring on libertarianism, American Unity Fund

  - ○ Travelling Baby Boomers (6.8 million)—average age 55; 42/58 per cent male/female; generation of parents away from families; interested in home improvement, *Duck Dynasty* (a US reality show), Paula Dean (US celebrity chef); politics centring on pro-life, Christianity

  - ○ Small Town America (5.7 million)—average age 39; 45/55 per cent male/female; generation of family householders, suburban mothers, sports utility vehicle (SUV) owners; interested in hunting, shooting, fishing; politics centring on anti-Obama, Donald Trump, Mitt Romney

  - ○ Millennial Country Culture (484,000)—average age 24; 27/73 per cent male/female; majority Western European; large proportion of jobs in military; interested in hunting, shooting, paintball, cheerleading; politics centring on no affinity for politicians

- ■ Very Conservative

  - ○ Post Grad Nest Builder (11.3 million)—average age 47; 50/50 per cent male/female; generation of parents, religious donors; interested in fishing, landscaping; politics centring on Tea Party (strictly conservative anti-establishment activists), National Republican Senate Committee (NRSC), Donald Trump, Ted Cruz

  - ○ Family Values (4.2 million)—average age 56; 38/62 per cent male/female; generation of parents, Christians; politics centring on pro-life, Heritage Action Committee for America, Rick Perry, Michelle Bachman, Mike Huckabee

  - ○ The Great Outdoors (7.3 million)—average age 41; 48/52 per cent male/female; generation of parents, donate to conservative causes; politics centring on National Rifle Association (NRA), Tea Party, Stop Obamacare

The idea behind this segmentation was for Facebook sales teams to sell the segmentation to political (and any other) advertisers using the Facebook self-serve platform during the US presidential election. The segmentation is, however, no longer available. The Trump campaign's Facebook operation is said to have targeted the 'Conservative' and 'Very Conservative' segments. One concern becoming increasingly apparent, however, is the way in which third-party organizations are using Facebook data for **microtargeting** voters, citizens, and consumers alike.

Facebook has faced questions in Congress over the purchase of US$100,000 of Facebook ads by Russian entities (for example the Internet Research Agency), aiming to sow discord before, during, and after the US presidential election, apparently reaching 126 million Americans with their messages.

If the Russian use of Facebook targeting to sow election discord wasn't enough, in 2018 the CEO of

Market Insight 6.2
continued

Facebook's Mark Zuckerberg testifying before a Senate Judiciary and Commerce Committee hearing after it was reported that Facebook users had their personal information harvested by Cambridge Analytica

Source: © Newscom/Alamy Stock Photo.

Facebook, Mark Zuckerberg, was forced to apologize after Channel 4 News and *Observer* investigation teams revealed that a Cambridge University psychology academic had harvested personal data from 50 million Facebook profiles via a 'personality questionnaire' and passed these data to Cambridge Analytica (a UK-based political consulting firm unrelated to Cambridge University) working on Donald Trump's 2016 presidential campaign. Both the US Federal Election Commission and the UK Digital, Culture, Media and Sport Select Committee are investigating. Governments around the world, including those in Israel and Australia, have demanded to know from Facebook whether their citizens' data have been harvested in the same way.

Sources: Kantrowitz (2017); Reynolds (2017); Ritson (2017); Harris (2018); Ram (2018).

Theory into Practice

The market insight illustrates the difficult line that Facebook treads in harvesting data from users and selling that data for segmentation and microtargeting purposes. The company derives much of its income from selling advertising and, more importantly, effective advertising to companies. Although the scandal has particularly focused on Cambridge Analytica's use of Facebook data, Facebook is facing the charge that it is not taking the privacy of its users sufficiently seriously, since it did not supervise third-party app developer organizations sufficiently when harvesting its data—a charge that looks particularly apposite since it also failed to pick up, or manage to stop, Russian Facebook advertising during the 2016 US presidential campaign designed to sow discord amongst the electorate.

Related Topics

segmentation; privacy; stereotyping; advertising effectiveness

1 What organizations do you think might have made use of Facebook's 2016 US presidential election segments?

2 Why do you think Facebook stopped making the segments outlined available on its self-serve platform?

3 When might a segmentation scheme lead to a breach of customer privacy?

Usage

A company may segment a market based on how often a customer uses its offerings, categorizing these into high, medium, and low users. This allows the development of service specifications or marketing mixes for each user group. For example, a bus company might target heavy users of public transport differently from heavy users of private vehicles.

Consumer usage of offerings can be investigated from three perspectives:

1 The *social interaction* perspective examines the symbolic aspects of usage and the social meanings attached to the consumption of socially conspicuous offerings, such as a car or house (Belk, Bahn, and Mayer, 1982; Solomon, 1983). For example, American animal rights organization People for the Ethical Treatment of Animals (PETA) regularly runs advertising campaigns highlighting how wearing fur products perpetuates cruelty to animals.

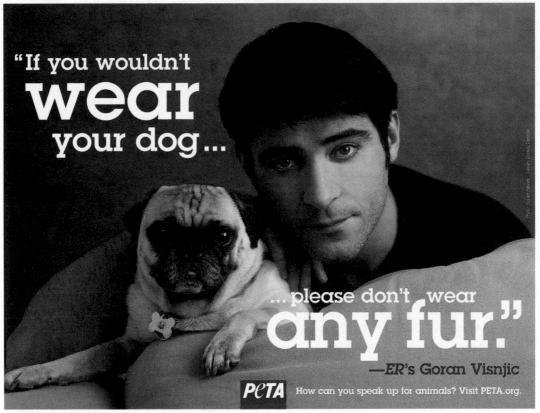

PETA targeting fur-wearing consumers
Source: © Getty Images/Handout.

2 The *experiential consumption* perspective examines the emotional and sensory experiences that result from usage—especially emotions such as satisfaction, fantasy, feelings, and fun (Holbrook and Hirschman, 1982). For example, Marmite (owned by Unilever and strangely banned in Denmark) has developed a television ad campaign around a scientific research study that found that people really *are* born 'lovers' or 'haters' of the yeast extract food product (and for £89.99 consumers can actually get their own DNA testing kit!).

Are you a lover or a hater? It may be in your DNA!
Source: © Selwyn/Alamy Stock Photo.

3 The *functional utilization* perspective assesses the functional usage of products and their attributes in different situations (Srivastava, Shocker, and Day, 1978; McAlister and Pessemier, 1982). For example, we might examine how and when bicycles are used (for example for leisure, commuting, exercise, sport), how often, and in what contexts.

Service providers often segment markets based on their customers' purchase behaviour. This might involve segmentation by loyalty to the service provider, or length of relationship, or some other mechanism.

Transaction and Purchase

The development of electronic technologies, such as electronic point of sale (EPOS) systems, standardized product codes, radio frequency identification (RFID) systems, quick response (QR) codes, and integrated purchasing systems (such as web, in-store, telephone, by app), has facilitated a rapid growth in the collection of consumer purchase and transactional data. For example, browsing and purchase data allow Amazon to make recommendations of offerings that are more likely to appeal to consumers, while EPOS systems allow retailers to track who buys what, when, for how much, in what quantities, and with what incentives (for example sales promotions). Companies have the ability to monitor purchase patterns in various geographical regions, at different times or seasons of the year, for various offerings and, increasingly, for differing market segments. Social media can also be analysed to track what people are saying once they have purchased and used particular offerings. For example, film studios track audience interest in new cinema releases via social media and use initial audience interest to allocate marketing budgets.

Transactional and purchase information is very useful for marketers to assess who are their most profitable customers. By analysing the recency, frequency, and monetary (RFM) value of purchases, marketers can identify their most profitable market segments. Customers who purchase most recently and frequently, and who spend the most—that is, customers with the highest RFM value—would be classified as profitable customers. Transactional data are records of behaviours and provide some insight into purchasing trends. Online, we can track from where someone is accessing our website. For example, if someone is coming to us from a price comparison website, they are probably price-sensitive, but if they arrive from a product review website, they have probably already decided what they want and so are less price-sensitive (Stiving, 2012).

The executional segmentation category focuses on how individual customers are treated. One approach is through 'triggers', such as commercially significant occurrences on a customer's account. In financial services, a late payment fee might indicate that a customer's needs have changed, or a customer who has just taken out cash via a credit card might need credit and be a target for a loan. Such trigger information typically needs to be combined with an assessment of the customer's credit status to ascertain whether a loan would be an appropriate offer to a customer who has just been charged a late payment fee or an overdraft extension. On the B2B side, Cisco uses the trigger information of a firm moving offices to contact those firms with offers for networking equipment (Bailey et al., 2009).

Media Usage

The logic of segmenting markets by frequency of readership, viewership, or patronage of **media vehicles** is well established. For example, heavy and light magazine readers might respond differently to ads with different creative appeals (Urban, 1976). Segmenting users by media usage frequency can provide insights into whether or not a publisher, or social networking site (for example Snapchat or Instagram), attracts and retains consumers who are more or less responsive to an advertiser's communication. This information provides input when evaluating the efficiency and effectiveness of media. Furthermore, differences in frequency may lead to differences in response to repeated passive ad exposures, competing ads of other sponsors, and prior ad exposure. For example, a study of television viewership in Mexico identified the following behavioural segments:

- *noveleros* (10 per cent of population) are family-oriented, need to watch with others and enjoy company;

- *hogareños* (26 per cent) need emotional company from the television and spend a lot of time at home;

- *rutinarios* (25 per cent) are those for whom television represents a comfort zone and an escape from a busy life;

- *pop-lovers* (15 per cent) need to be updated on the latest content, which their friends consume too; and

- *connectors* (24 per cent) are early adopters and trendsetters—the connoisseurs of television (Sanchez, 2018).

Frequency of media usage has been the predominant measure of media usage experience. However, Olney, Holbrook, and Batra (1991), and Holbrook and Gardner (1993), have identified viewing time as an important dependent variable in a model of advertising effects. On media websites, users might be segmented either by their visit frequency or by their dwell time (that is, how long they spend on a website), among other variables.

Segmentation in Business Markets

Business-to-business (B2B) market segmentation is the identification of 'a group of present or potential customers with some common characteristic which is relevant in explaining (and predicting) their response to a supplier's marketing stimuli' (Wind and Cardozo, 1974: 155). There are two main groups of interrelated variables used to segment B2B markets (see Table 6.3). The first involves organizational characteristics, such as **organizational size** and location, sometimes referred to as **firmographics**. Those seeking to segment business markets might start with these variables. The second group is based on the characteristics surrounding the decision-making process. Those organizations seeking to establish and develop customer relationships would normally expect to start with these variables.

Organizational Characteristics

Organizational characteristics concern the buying organizations that make up a business market. There are a number of criteria that can be used to cluster organizations, including size, geography, market served, value, location, industry type, usage rate, and **purchase situation**. We discuss the main three categories (see Figure 6.6).

Table 6.3 Segmentation bases used in business markets

Base type	Segmentation base	Explanation
Organizational characteristics	Organizational size	Grouping organizations by relative size (MNCs, international, large, SMEs) enables the identification of design, delivery, usage rates or order size, and other purchasing characteristics.
	Geographic location	Often, the needs of potential customers in one geographic area are different from those of potential customers in another.
	Industry type (SIC codes)	Standard industrial classification (SIC) codes are used to identify and categorize industries and businesses.
Customer characteristics	Decision-making unit (DMU) structure	Attitudes, policies, and purchasing strategies allow organizations to be clustered.
	Choice criteria	The types of offering bought and the specifications companies use when selecting and ordering offerings form the basis for clustering customers and segmenting business markets.
	Purchase situation	Buyers may be segmented by how a company structures its purchasing procedures, the type of buying situation, and whether buyers are included in an early or late stage in the purchase decision process.

Note: MNC = multinational corporation; SME = small and medium-sized enterprise

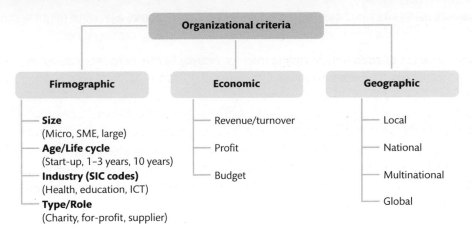

Figure 6.6
Segmentation by organizational characteristics

Organizational Size

By segmenting organizations by size, we can identify particular buying requirements. Large organizations (for example food manufacturers) may have particular delivery or design needs based on volume demand. Accordingly, supermarkets such as Denmark's Netto and Germany's Aldi would have very specific requirements of manufacturers because they pride themselves on purchasing goods in sufficiently large quantities to enable them to market their offerings at a cheaper price. A computer manufacturer such as RM Education in the UK, which specializes in providing information technology (IT) products and services to schools, colleges, universities, government departments, and educational agencies, will differ considerably in size from, say, a small local village school (with 200 pupils) or even a large civic university (with 40,000 students), and each will have considerably different IT needs.

Geographical Location

Geo-targeting is one of the more common methods used to segment B2B markets and is often used by new or small organizations attempting to establish themselves. This approach is useful because it allows sales territories to be drawn around particular locations that sales staff can service easily (for example Scotland, Scandinavia, Western Europe, the Mediterranean). Alternatively, sales territories may be based on specific regions within a country, for example, in Eastern Europe, based on individual nations (that is, Poland, Czech Republic, Romania, and Hungary). However, this approach is becoming less useful because the Internet cuts across geographic distribution channels (see Chapters 11, 13, and 14).

SIC Codes

Standard Industrial Classification (SIC) codes are used to designate different industrial markets. They are easily accessible and standardized across most Western countries (for example the UK, Europe, and the United States). However, some marketers have argued that SIC codes contain categories that are too broad to be useful. Consequently, SIC codes have received limited application, although they do provide 'some preliminary indication of the industrial segments in [a] market' (Naudé and Cheng, 2003). More commonly, companies segment

B2B markets using industry types (so-called verticals). For example, a law firm might segment its customers into financial services, utilities, transport, and retailing, among others.

Visit the **online resources** and complete Internet Activity 6.2 to learn more about how we use SIC codes to segment business markets.

Customer Characteristics

Customer characteristics concern the buyers within the organizations that make up a business market. Numerous criteria could be used to cluster organizations, including by decision-making unit, by purchasing strategies, by relationship type, attitude to risk, **choice criteria**, and purchase situation.

Decision-Making Unit

An organization's decision-making unit may have specific requirements that influence purchase decisions in a particular market, for example policy factors, purchasing strategies, the level of importance attached to these types of purchase, or attitudes towards vendors and risk. These characteristics can be used to segregate groups of organizations for particular marketing programmes. Segmentation might be based on the closeness and level of interdependence existing between organizations. Organizational attitudes towards risk and the degree to which an organization is willing to experiment through the acquisition of new industrial offerings varies. The starting point of any B2B segmentation is a good database or customer relationship management (CRM) system. It should contain customer addresses, contact details, and detailed purchase and transactional history. Ideally, it will also include the details of those buyers present in the customer company's **decision-making unit structure**. However, as Market Insight 6.3 illustrates, segmentation can also be undertaken of non-buyers (or defectors).

Market Insight 6.3
Logistical Nightmare: Regaining Defectors

Customer churn for firms such as FedEx, UPS, and XPO in the logistics industry can reach 20–25 per cent. Customers switch suppliers for a variety of reasons, but some of the more common ones concern core service failures, dissatisfactory service encounters, price, inconvenience in terms of time, location, or delays, poor response to service failure, competition, ethical problems, and involuntary switching. It is therefore important for all firms to understand these switch/defection behaviours to reduce their incidence, to retrieve lost customers, and hence to lower their long-run costs.

Segmenting B2B markets based on customers who have been lost is not necessarily the same as

segmentation to find new customers. One of the reasons for this is that 'lost customers' leave a portfolio of transactions that the sales force can use to leverage a customer's return.

Research suggests that five distinct segments of lost customers can be identified and actioned, as follows:

■ *Bought-away customers*—Often very price-oriented, these customers are attracted by competitive prices. A decision to regain this segment needs to take into account how easy and profitable it will be to retain them in the light of their price vulnerability.

■ *Pulled-away customers*—This segment is characterized by buyers seeking better overall value,

Market Insight 6.3
continued

who will collaborate with suppliers to achieve higher benefits and/or lower costs. The solution to winning back these 'lost customers' is to co-develop value propositions that are unique and sustainable.

- *Unintentionally pushed-away customers*—These customers leave because they perceive that they have been mistreated or neglected. An apology is required, but where there have been service/product failures, service recovery and reacquisition may include compensation, reimbursement, and discounts. In severe cases—often when mistakes have been repeated—customers can be retrieved only after personnel changes have been made in either or both the buying and sales centres.

- *Moved-away customers*—This segment is characterized by customers who no longer need or value the product/service offerings. They might have moved geographically or have moved into

different markets that the selling company cannot serve. Although lost for good, a positive ending to the relationship is regarded as important to secure referrals and helpful word of mouth.

- *Intentionally pushed-away customers*—These problematic or unprofitable customers are deliberately let go, perhaps as part of a deliberate customer portfolio management strategy (see Chapter 16), because the selling company no longer wants the customer's business, perhaps because they are unprofitable accounts or because they are overly demanding and expensive to serve. Allowing them to build relationships with competitors should be matched by a positive dissolution to help to maintain the company's own strong reputation and brand image.

Source: Keaveney (1995); Lopes, Alves, and Brito (2001); Liu, Leach, and Chugh (2015).

Theory into Practice

The process of segmenting customers who leave their suppliers is an important part of the relationship management process, of which sales management is an integral part. Segmentation within a relationship context requires identification of the characteristics of lost customers, which enables categorization of defection patterns. Sales staff are in a stronger position to understand customers' reasons for leaving, to reduce the level of customer churn, and thereby to retrieve 'lost customers'.

Relationship management theory is therefore a key approach underpinning our understanding this aspect of segmentation analysis. Relational factors are important antecedents to positive outcomes, and this indicates that trust, commitment, satisfaction, and other dimensions are essential elements for the development of long-run quality relationships between buyers and sellers (see Chapters 15 and 16).

Related Topics

customer life cycle; loyalty; collaboration; customer lifetime value

1 **Discuss the view that if retrieving lost customers is costly and then keeping them is problematic, there is little point in segmenting and actively trying to get them back.**

2 **To what extent is a high churn rate a function of poor customer management?**

3 **Using a different industry, try to determine how companies seek to retain customers.**

Choice Criteria

Business markets can be segmented based on the specifications of offerings they choose. For example, an accountancy practice could segment its clients by those that seek compliance-type accounting offerings, such as audits and tax submission work, companies that require management accounting services, and companies that require a complex mix of both. A computer manufacturer might segment the business market for computers by those requiring computers with strong graphical capabilities (for example educational establishments, publishing houses) and those requiring computers with strong processing capabilities (for example scientific establishments). Companies do not necessarily need to target multiple segments, however; they might successfully target a single segment, as has IT technological solutions provider RM in the UK education market.

Purchase Situation

Companies sometimes seek to segment on the basis of how organizations make purchases. Thus three questions associated with segmentation by purchase situation should be considered, as follows:

1 What is the structure of the buying organization's purchasing procedures: centralized, decentralized, flexible, or inflexible?

2 What type of buying situation is present: new task (that is, buying for the first time); modified rebuy (that is, not buying for the first time, but buying something with different specifications from previously); or straight rebuy (that is, buying the same thing again)?

3 What stage in the purchase decision process have target organizations reached? Are they buyers in early or late stages, and are they experienced or new?

For example, a large global consulting and IT services company such as Infosys in India might segment the market for IT project management services into public and private sectors. The focus might then be on fulfilling large government contracts that are put out to tender, whereby a group of selected buyers are offered the opportunity to bid for an exclusive franchise to deliver agreed services for a defined period of time.

Typically, in segmenting business markets, a service provider can use a mix of macro- and micro-industrial market segmentation approaches by defining the customers whom a company wants to target using a macro approach, such as SIC or geographic region, and then further segmenting using the choice criteria by which those customers select a provider. In other words, multistage market segmentation approaches are often adopted.

Target Markets

The second important part of the STP process is to determine which of the segments uncovered should be targeted and made the focus of a comprehensive marketing programme. Ultimately, managerial discretion and judgement determines which markets are selected and exploited. For market segmentation to be effective, the mnemonic DAMP can be applied (Kotler, 1984), comprising the following four criteria:

- *Distinct*—Is each segment clearly different from other segments? If so, different marketing mixes will be necessary.

- *Accessible*—Can buyers be reached through appropriate promotional programmes and distribution channels?

- *Measurable*—Is the segment easy to identify and measure?

- *Profitable*—Is the segment sufficiently large to provide a stream of constant future revenues and profits?

Another approach to evaluating market segments uses a rating approach for different segment attractiveness factors, such as market growth, segment profitability, segment size, competitive intensity within the segment, and the cyclical nature of the industry (for example whether or not the business is seasonal, such as retailing). Each of these segment attractiveness factors is rated on a scale of 0–10 and loosely categorized in the high, medium, or low columns, based on either set criteria or subjective criteria, depending on the availability of market and customer data and the approach adopted by the managers undertaking the segmentation programme (see Table 6.4).

Other examples of segment attractiveness factors might include segment stability (that is, stability of the segment's needs over time) and mission fit (that is, the extent to which dealing with a particular segment fits the company's mission). Once the attractiveness factors have been determined, the importance of each factor can be weighted and each segment rated on each factor. This generates a segment attractiveness evaluation matrix (see Table 6.5).

Decisions need to be made about whether a single offering is made available to a range of segments, or a range of offerings to multiple segments or a single segment, or whether one offering should be presented to a single segment. Whatever the decision, a marketing mix strategy should be developed to meet segment needs, which should reflect the organization's

---

Table 6.4 Examples of segment attractiveness factors

Segment attractiveness factors	Rating		
	High (10–7)	Medium (6–4)	Low (3–0)
Growth	>2.5%	2.5–2.0%	<2.0%
Profitability	>15%	10–15%	<10%
Size	>£5m	£1m–£5m	<£1m
Competitive intensity	Low	Medium	High
Cyclicality	Low	Medium	High

Source: McDonald and Dunbar (2004). Reproduced with permission.

Table 6.5 Example of a segment attractiveness evaluation matrix

Segment attractiveness factors	Weight	Segment 1		Segment 2		Segment 3	
		Score	Total	Score	Total	Score	Total
Growth	25	6	1.5	5	1.25	10	2.5
Profitability	25	9	2.25	4	1.0	8	2.0
Size	15	6	0.9	5	0.75	7	1.05
Competitive intensity	15	5	0.75	6	0.9	6	0.9
Cyclicality	20	2.5	0.5	8	1.6	5	1
Total	100		5.9		5.50		7.45

Source: McDonald and Dunbar (2004). Reproduced with permission.

capabilities and competitive strengths. Key questions around the development of the marketing mix include the following:

- How can the segment(s) be reached with appropriate communications?
- What is the media consumption pattern of the target audience?
- Where can they gain access to our offerings to purchase them?
- Does the offering need to be adapted for different segments and should it be priced the same or differently for all segments?

Targeting Approaches

Once segments are identified, an organization selects its preferred approach to targeting. Four differing approaches can be used (see Figure 6.7):

- The **undifferentiated approach** is used where there is no delineation between market segments and the market is viewed as one mass market with one marketing strategy for the entire market. Although expensive, this approach is used for markets in which there is limited or no segment differentiation (for example markets for petrol, housing offered by local authorities, ice cubes).

Figure 6.7
Target marketing approaches

- The **differentiated targeting approach** is used where there are several market segments to target, each being attractive to the marketing organization. To exploit them, a marketing strategy is developed for each segment. For example, HP has developed its product range and marketing strategy to target the following user segments of computing equipment: home office users; small and medium-sized businesses; large businesses; and health, education, and government departments. A disadvantage of this approach is the loss of economies of scale because of the resources required to meet the needs of multiple market segments.

- A **concentrated marketing strategy (or niche marketing strategy)** is used where there are only a few market segments. This approach is adopted by firms with limited resources to fund their marketing strategy or who prefer a very exclusive strategy towards the market. For example, Lush targets consumers interested in handmade cosmetics with ethical and pure credentials. This approach is used frequently by micro-sized and small to medium-sized organizations with limited resources (for example an electrician may focus on local residences).

One of Lush's more controversial campaigns, aiming to draw attention to the ongoing undercover policing, or 'spy cops', scandal

Source: © Mark Kerrison/Alamy Stock Photo.

- A **customized targeting strategy** involves developing marketing strategy for each customer, rather than each segment. This approach predominates in B2B markets (for example marketing research or advertising services) or consumer markets with high value and/or highly customized products (for example custom-made cars). For example, a manufacturer of industrial electronics for assembly lines might target and customize its offering differently for Nissan, Unilever, and SCA, given the differing requirements in assembly-line processes for the manufacture of cars, foodstuffs, and hygiene products (for example hand dryers). In another example, Bentley Motors made a special bullet- and bomb-proof limousine for the UK's HM Queen Elizabeth II to use for special public occasions.

Perhaps Bentley's most customized product: the Bentley State Limousine
Source: © Sebaso/Wikimedia Commons (CC0).

Segmentation Limitations

Whilst market segmentation is a useful process for organizations to divide customers into distinct groups for resource allocation purposes, it has been criticized for the following reasons:

- The process approximates offerings to the needs of customer groups, rather than individuals. Therefore there is a chance that customers' needs are not fully met. However, **customer relationship marketing (CRM)** processes and software allow companies to develop customized approaches for individual customers after a segmentation has been undertaken. Integrating CRM processes (see Chapter 15) and segmentation schemes, and key account management and segmentation schemes (see Chapter 16), requires extra planning.

- There is insufficient consideration of how market segmentation is linked to competitive advantage (Hunt and Arnett, 2004). The product differentiation concept is linked to the need

It can be seen that leading brands Lanson, Bollinger, and Moët et Chandon occupy distinct positions in their 'own' quadrants. (See Case Insight 7.1 for more information about Lanson International, a leading champagne house.)

Perceptual mapping data reveal strengths and weaknesses that can help management to make strategic decisions about how to differentiate based on the attributes that matter the most to customers.

C–D Maps

One of the issues associated with these conventional approaches to positioning is that brand performance cannot be incorporated and is measured separately to positioning in most organizations. In response to this challenge, Dawar and Bagga (2015) developed the centrality–distinctiveness (C–D) map, which incorporates performance dimensions:

- *Centrality* is concerned with the extent to which a brand, such as Coca-Cola in soft drinks and McDonald's in fast food, are most representative of their type or category. Such brands serve as reference points by which others in the category are compared and evaluated.

- *Distinctiveness* refers to a brand's individuality and the extent to which it is positioned away from the direct competition of popular central brands. The authors refer to Tesla in the car category and Corona in the beer category as examples of brands with strong distinctiveness scores.

Figure 6.9 depicts the four quadrants that a C–D map represents:

- *Aspirational* brands are highly differentiated and have wide appeal. Examples of cars include Mercedes and BMW, and for beer, Guinness and Heineken. It is quite common for highly distinctive brands to command higher prices than brands that score low on this dimension.

- *Mainstream* brands tend to be the first ones that come to mind when consumers think of the category. Their wide appeal and popularity is countered by their low distinctiveness, which in turn tends to reduce their capacity to command a premium price. Good examples are Ford or Vauxhall for cars and Miller for beer.

- *Unconventional* brands have unique distinctive characteristics that separate them from traditional products in the category. Cars such as Tesla, Mini, and the Smart car, and airlines such as Virgin and Norwegian, can be considered to be unconventional.

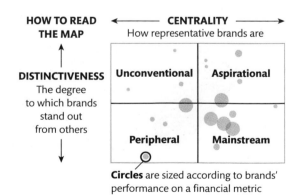

The Centrality-Distinctiveness Map
The C-D map links consumers' perceptions about brands with their business performance. Brands are positioned in quadrants according to how customers score them on two universal dimensions: **centrality** and **distinctiveness.** Each quadrant carries strategic implications for sales, pricing, risk, and profitability. The distribution of brands across the map offers insights about competitive opportunities and threats.

Figure 6.9

A C–D map

Source: Used with the kind permission of HBR.

- *Peripheral* brands are seldom recalled by consumers as a first choice and have little to distinguish them. Examples include Kia and Mitsubishi for cars and Aldi in the supermarket category. To compete, they have to carry low prices, but they can still be highly successful.

See Market Insight 6.5 for an example of how C–D maps can be used.

Market Insight 6.5
Exploring C–D Maps for Strategic Positioning

When considering the C–D maps for the US beer and car markets, research shows quite clearly that the higher a brand scores on centrality, the greater is its sales volume. This indicates that improving a brand's centrality should be a key strategic goal for many brands. Cars such as Toyota and beer brands such as Budweiser were considered to be the most central brands, with the largest sales volumes. In terms of price, however, increased centrality leads to a fall in prices

as competition intensifies. In direct contrast, research indicates that the higher a brand's distinctiveness, the lower will be its sales volume, for both cars and beer. However, these brands can charge a higher price, as demonstrated by Porsche and Guinness.

The C–D maps shown in Figure 6.10 depict brands in the US car and beer markets. Their positions across the four quadrants indicate the strategies followed

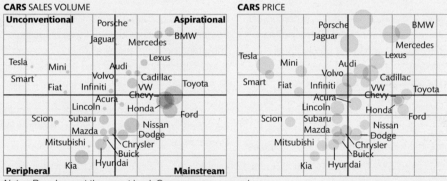

Notes: Brands are at the parent level. Cars are passenger only.

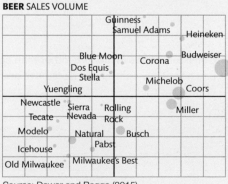
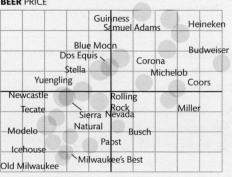

Source: Dawar and Bagga (2015)

© HBR.ORG

Figure 6.10
C–D maps for cars and beer
Source: Used with the kind permission of HBR.

Market Insight 6.5
continued

and possible directions in the future, based upon both positioning and performance.

The underlying strategic imperative is that sales volumes tend to increase, and prices fall, as a brand becomes increasingly central. In contrast, sales volumes tend to fall as distinctiveness increases, yet these brands can also increase prices.

C–D Maps for Cars and Beer

To create C–D maps, the researchers surveyed adults across the United States about their perceptions of 30 car brands and 23 beer brands, asking them to rank the brands, on a 0–10 scale, on centrality and distinctiveness. Sales volume tends to increase with centrality and prices tend to fall. The more distinctive a brand is, the lower the sales volume and higher the price. Many brands succeed by being both central and distinctive (BMW and Guinness, for example), while others compete by being neither (Kia and Old Milwaukee).

Firms can also use a C–D map to identify positioning opportunities and unexpected threats.

Source: Dawar and Bagga (2015).

Theory into Practice

Positioning maps, sometimes referred to as perceptual, brand, or spatial maps, are important techniques for measuring and evaluating consumer perceptions of a range of offerings in a market. These maps are developed according to consumers' views (perceptions) for ranking a variety of similar offerings based on specific attributes and features. Having determined the positions of competing brands on a perceptual map, individual firms can develop strategies to move and occupy a different, seemingly stronger, competitive position. Indeed, these maps have been an important tool for marketers not only because of their diagnostic capabilities, but also because of their ability to visually portray the competitive marketplace.

C–D maps represent a development of positioning maps, because they incorporate performance criteria (see also Research Insight 6.3).

Related Topics

competitive strategy; consumer perception

1 To what extent do C–D maps represent a major advance in techniques regarding how we might position brands?

2 If C–D maps encompass brand performance, what role might perceptual maps play in strategy development?

3 Consider brands in markets other than cars and beer. How central and distinctive are these brands?

Positioning and Repositioning

Understanding brand positioning helps marketers to improve a brand's performance by modifying the marketing communications used to support a brand. Through marketing communications, especially advertising, information can be conveyed about each attribute to adjust

Research Insight 6.3

To take your learning further, you might wish to read this influential paper:

Dawar, N., and Bagga, C.K. (2015). A better way to map brand strategy. *Harvard Business Review*, **June.**

Business performance metrics such as pricing and sales are excluded from conventional perceptual mapping tools. In this article, a new type of map is presented—one that links a brand's position to competitors according to its perceived 'centrality' (how representative it is of the company) and 'distinctiveness' (how much it stands out from other brands), with its business performance along a given metric.

 Visit the **online resources** to read the paper and watch a video to learn more about C–D maps.

customers' brand perceptions. Marketing communications can be used to position brands either functionally or expressively (symbolically) (see Table 6.6). Functionally positioned brands emphasize features and benefits, whereas expressive brands emphasize the ego, social, and hedonic satisfactions a brand brings (see Chapter 2). Both approaches make a promise: for example, for hair care, the promise is to deliver cleaner, shinier, and healthier hair (functional), or hair with which we feel confident because we want to be admired, or because it is important that we feel more self-assured (expressive). Different positioning approaches are likely to be more successful than others for particular offerings. For example, in the compact car market, Fuchs and Diamantopoulos (2010) found that direct benefit positioning (based on functional aspects) is likely to be more effective than indirect benefit positioning (based on experiential or symbolic dimensions) and that expressive positioning is more effective than functional approaches. User positioning can also provide a sound alternative to benefit positioning.

Technology, customer tastes, and competitors' new offerings are reasons why markets might change. For example, Disney acquired Lucasfilm in 2012 to launch the seventh *Star Wars* film in 2015 (*Star Wars: The Force Awakens*) and others in 2017 (*Star Wars: The Last Jedi*), 2018 (*Solo: A Star Wars Story*), and 2019 (*Star Wars: Episode IX*) (McCluskey, 2018). To be successful, however, Disney needed to reposition and target the new films at the generation that grew up with the *Clone Wars* cartoon and LEGO® Star Wars™ characters rather than those who watched the original trilogy in the late 1970s and 1980s (Garrahan, 2012). If the brand positioning adopted is strong, if the brand was the first to claim the position, and if the position is continually reinforced with clear simple messages, there may be little need to alter the position originally adopted. Marketers should be alert and prepared to reposition their brands because the relative positions occupied by brands in the minds of customers will be challenged on a frequent basis—especially by competing offerings. Repositioning is often difficult to accomplish because of the entrenched perceptions and attitudes held by customers towards brands and the cost of the vast (media) resources required to make these changes.

Repositioning revolves around an offering and the way in which it is communicated. It should be noted, however, that repositioning carries risks, including those of alienating the current

Table 6.6 Proposition positioning strategies

Position	Strategy	Explanation
Functional	Product features	Brand positioned on the basis of attributes, features, or benefits relative to the competition, e.g. Volvos are safe or Red Bull provides energy.
	Price quality	Price can be a strong communicator of quality. John Lewis Partnership (the UK department store) uses the tagline 'never knowingly undersold' to indicate how it will match competitors' prices on the same items to ensure its customers always get good value.
	Use	By informing when or how an offering can be used, we create a mental position in buyers' minds, e.g. Kellogg's reposition its offerings (e.g. Special K) to be consumed throughout the day, not only at breakfast.
Expressive	User	By identifying the target user, messages can be communicated clearly to the right audience. Flora margarine was initially for men and then it became 'for all the family'. Some hotels position themselves as places for weekend breaks, leisure centres, conference centres, or all three.
	Benefit	Positions can be established by proclaiming the benefits that usage confers on consumers. The benefit of using Sensodyne toothpaste is that it alleviates the pain associated with sensitive teeth.
	Heritage	Heritage and tradition are sometimes used to symbolize quality, experience, and knowledge. Kronenbourg 1664, 'Established since 1803', and the use of coats of arms by many universities are designed to convey heritage to build long-term trust.

customer base, of inaccurate forecasting and the new audience rejecting the repositioning, and of competitors closing opportunities or seizing the position vacated. Repositioning also incurs substantial costs, both internally as a result of planning and managerial time, and externally in terms of communications with both distributors and customers to inform them about the new position.

The following four methods outline ways of approaching repositioning, depending on the individual situation facing a brand. In some cases, a brand might need to be adapted before relaunch.

1. **Change the tangible attributes and then communicate the new proposition to the same market.** UBS, the financial services firm whose reputation was shattered following an estimated US$2 billion loss as a result of insider trading, spent four years transforming itself internally before relaunching and repositioning as a wealth management company (Rooney, 2015).

2. **Change the way in which a proposition is communicated to the original market.** Norwegian oil-and-gas company Statoil Hydro was repositioned globally as Statoil by communications agency Hill & Knowlton Strategies, raising its profile in key markets across Europe, including the UK.

3. **Change the target market and deliver the same proposition.** On some occasions, re-positioning can be achieved through marketing communications alone, but targeted at a new market. For example, soft drink Orangina repositioned as a premium adult drink, targeting those who remember it from childhood French holidays.

4. **Change both the proposition (attributes) and the target market.** Xerox has repositioned itself from a document company to a diversified business services company, running call centres and processing insurance claims and even toll payments (Carone, 2013).

Chapter Summary

To consolidate your learning, the key points from this chapter are summarized here:

■ **Describe the principles of market segmentation and the STP process.**

Whole markets are subdivided into different segments by means of the STP process. The abbreviation STP refers to the three activities—segmentation, targeting, and positioning—that should be undertaken sequentially if segmentation is to be successful. *Segmenting* a market means dividing it into different groups of customers with distinctly similar needs and requirements of offerings. The second part of the STP process determines which segments should be *targeted* with a comprehensive marketing mix programme. The third part of the STP process is to *position* a brand within the target market(s).

■ **List the characteristics and differences between market segmentation and product differentiation.**

Market segmentation is related to product differentiation. Given an increasing proliferation of tastes, marketers have sought to design offerings around consumer demand (market segmentation) more than around their own production needs (product differentiation).

■ **Explain consumer and business-to-business market segmentation.**

Data, based on differing consumer, user, organizational, and market characteristics, are used to segment a market. These characteristics differ for consumer and business-to-business (B2B) contexts. To segment consumer goods and service markets, market information based on certain key customer-, product-, or situation-related criteria (variables) is used. These are classified as segmentation bases and include profile, behavioural, and psychological criteria. To segment business markets, two main groups of interrelated variables are used: organizational characteristics and buyer characteristics.

■ **Describe different targeting strategies.**

Once identified, the organization selects its target marketing approach. Four different approaches exist: undifferentiated; differentiated; concentrated, or niche; and customized target marketing.

■ **Discuss the concept of positioning.**

Positioning provides the means by which offerings can be differentiated from one another and gives customers reasons to buy. It encompasses physical attributes, the way in which a brand is communicated, and how customers perceive the brand relative to competing brands.

■ **Consider how the use of perceptual maps can assist in the positioning process.**

Perceptual maps are used in the positioning process to illustrate differing attributes of a selection of brands. They also illustrate existing levels of differentiation between brands, how our brand and competing brands are perceived in the marketplace, how a market operates, and the strengths and weaknesses that can help management to make strategic decisions about how to differentiate the attributes that matter to customers and hence to compete more effectively in the market. C–D maps enable brand performance to be incorporated into the strategy positioning process.

Review Questions

1 Define 'market segmentation' and explain the STP process.

2 What is the difference between market segmentation and product differentiation?

3 Identify four different ways in which markets can be segmented.

4 How do market segmentation bases differ in consumer and B2B markets?

5 How can market segmentation bases be evaluated when target marketing?

6 What are the different approaches to selecting target markets?

7 Describe the principle of positioning and why it should be undertaken.

8 What are perceptual maps and what can they reveal?

9 Explain three ways in which brands can be positioned.

10 Make a list of four reasons why organizations need to reposition brands.

 Discussion Questions

1 Having read Case Insight 6.1, how would you advise Soberana to respond to changing consumer tastes and to the challenge of Miller Lite in Panama?

2 Consider your answers to the following questions (in groups, where appropriate):

A Using the information supplied in Table 6.7 on the champagne market and a suitable calculator, determine which segments have the greatest potential profit.

B What other data do we need to determine the size of the market (that is, its market potential)?

Table 6.7 The champagne and sparkling wine market, by segment				
Social class	Enthusiasts (%) AP = £20 F = 8/yr	Sparkling sceptics (%) AP = £10, F = 3/yr	Price-driven (%) AP = £8.50, F = 3/yr	Uneducated (%) AP = £12 F = 2/yr
AB (n = 8m)	25	31	30	14
C1 (n = 14m)	23	23	32	21
C2 (n = 8m)	27	26	33	14
DE (n = 10m)	20	26	40	14

Note: All data hypothetical; AP = average price, n = population size; F = number of bottles purchased per year; % segment sizes per socio-economic group and segment descriptions.

3 Discuss which market segmentation bases might be most applicable to the following:

A A fashion retailer segmenting the market for childrenswear

B A commercial radio station specializing in dance music and celebrity news or gossip

C A Swiss chocolate manufacturer supplying multiple retail grocers and confectionery shops across Europe (for example Godiva)

D Rakbank in Dubai, United Arab Emirates, when segmenting the market for its credit card

E The Tunisian tourist board when targeting holidaymakers in Germany

4 Write a one-sentence description of the attributes and benefits that are attractive to target consumers for an offering with which you are particularly familiar (for example Apple in the computer category, or Samsung in the mobile phone category), and in which you explain how these attributes and benefits are different from those of competitors. Your positioning statement might be as follows:

[Product A] provides [target consumers] with [one or two salient product attributes]. This distinguishes it from [one or two groups of competing product offerings] that offer [attributes/benefits of the competing products].

A Briefly describe the target market segment. This should summarize the defining characteristics of the segment (for example demographic, psychographic, geographic, or behavioural).

B Briefly explain your reasons for believing that the attributes or benefits of your positioning statement are important for your target segment.

C Draw a perceptual map that summarizes your understanding of the market and shows the relative positions of the most important competing products.

Visit the online resources and complete the Multiple-Choice Questions to assess your knowledge of Chapter 6.

 # Glossary

benefits sought by understanding the motivations that customers derive from their purchases, it is possible to have an insight into the benefits they seek from product use.

breakdown method the view that the market is considered to consist of customers who are essentially the same, so the task is to identify groups that share particular differences.

build-up method considers a market to consist of customers who are all different, so the task is to find similarities.

business markets characterized by organizations that consume products and services for use within the manufacture or production of other products, or for use in their daily operations.

business-to-business (B2B) activities undertaken by one company that are directed at another.

choice criteria the principal dimensions on the basis of which we select a particular product or service, such as price, location, range of services, level of expertise, friendliness of staff, and so on.

communication the sharing of meaning created through the transmission of information.

concentrated marketing strategy (or niche marketing strategy) a strategy that recognizes that there are segments in the market and which focuses on only one, two, or a few of those market segments.

customer relationship marketing (CRM) all marketing activities and strategies used to retain customers by providing them with relationship-enhancing products and/or services that are perceived to be of value and superior to those offered by a competitor.

customized targeting strategy a marketing strategy that is developed for each customer, as opposed to each market segment.

decision-making unit structure the attitudes, policies, and purchasing strategies on the basis of which organizations make their decisions, and which can be a way of clustering organizations into segments.

demographic data concerning age, sex/gender (or gender identity), occupation, level of education, religion, and social class, many of which determine a potential buyer's ability to purchase a product or service.

differentiated targeting approach an approach to targeting that recognizes that each of several market segments may be attractive to the marketing organization and hence a marketing strategy is developed for each.

firmographics an approach to segmentation of B2B markets using criteria such as company size, geography, standard industrial classification (SIC) codes, and other company-oriented classification data.

geo-demographic an approach to segmentation that presumes there is a relationship between the location in which people live and their purchasing behaviours.

life-stage analysis analysis based on the principle that people need different products and services at different stages in their lives (for example childhood, adulthood, young couples, retired, etc.).

market segmentation the division of customer markets into groups of customers with distinctly similar needs.

media vehicles the individual media used to carry advertising messages.

microtargeting the use of data to identify the interests and actions of specific individuals to develop predictive analytical segmentation schemes, and hence to influence their thoughts and/or actions.

organizational size a characteristic by means of which organizations can be grouped (for example multinational, international, large, small or medium-sized), which enables the marketer to identify their design, delivery, usage rates, or order size and other purchasing characteristics.

perceptual mapping a diagram, typically two-dimensional, of 'image space' derived from attitudinal market research data, which displays the differences in perceptions that customers, consumers, or the general public have of different products or services, or brands in general.

positioning the way in which an audience of consumers or buyers perceives a product or service, particularly as a result of the marketing communications process aimed at a target audience.

product differentiation a strategy by means of which companies produce offerings that are different from those of competing firms.

product usage a segmentation characteristic based on consumers' use of a product offering, brand, or product category in terms of frequency, timing, and situation.

psychographic the characteristics of consumers' activities, interests, and opinions (AIO), which allow us to understand their individual lifestyles and patterns of behaviour, which in turn affect their buying behaviour and decision-making processes, on the basis of which we can identify similar product and/or media usage patterns.

purchase situation an approach to segmentation on the basis of the way in which a buying company structures its purchasing procedures, the type of buying situation, and whether buyers are in an early or late stage in the purchase decision process.

Standard Industrial Classification (SIC) codes a typography of industries that allows for their grouping.

STP process the method by which whole markets are subdivided into different *segments* for *targeting* and *positioning*.

undifferentiated approach an approach whereby there is no delineation between market segments; rather, the market is viewed as one mass market, with one marketing strategy applied to the entire market.

 # References

Anon. (2013). Berger to reposition Sherwin Williams brand. *Chemical Business*, 27(10), 60.

Anon. (2016a). The grey market. *The Economist*, 7 April. Retrieve from: https://www.economist.com/news/business/21696539-older-consumers-will-reshape-business-landscape-grey-market (accessed 13 October 2018).

Anon. (2016b). Does Peroni's premium positioning extend to its social presence? *Campaign*, 5 April. Retrieve from: https://www.campaignlive.co.uk/article/does-peronis-premium-positioning-extend-its-social-presence/1389852 (accessed 13 October 2018).

Bailey, C., Baines, P., Wilson, H., and Clarke, M. (2009). Segmentation and customer insight in contemporary services marketing practice: why grouping customers is no longer enough. *Journal of Marketing Management*, 25(3–4), 227–52.

Beane, T.P., and Ennis, D.M. (1987). Market segmentation: a review. *European Journal of Marketing*, 32(5), 20–42.

Belk, R.W., Bahn, K.D., and Mayer, R.N. (1982). Developmental recognition of consumption symbolism. *Journal of Consumer Research*, 9(1), 4–17.

Black, A., Asadorian, D., and Dunnett, H. (2017). 8 key truths about Generation Z. *Research World* (Magazine of ESOMAR), December, 12–14.

Carone, C. (2013). Xerox's brand repositioning challenge. *Ad Age*, 12 March. Retrieve from: https://adage.com/article/cmo-strategy/xerox-s-brand-repositioning-challenge/240285/ (accessed 13 October 2018).

Dawar, N., and Bagga, C.K. (2015). A better way to map brand strategy. *Harvard Business Review*, June. Retrieve from: https://hbr.org/2015/06/a-better-way-to-map-brand-strategy (accessed 13 October 2018).

DeMers, J. (2016). 5 examples of rebranding done right. *Forbes*, 7 July. Retrieve from: https://www.forbes.com/sites/jaysondemers/2016/07/07/5-examples-of-rebranding-done-right/amp/ (accessed 13 October 2018).

Dibb, S., Simkin, L., Pride, W.M., and Ferrell, D.C. (2001). *Marketing Concepts and Strategies*. Boston, MA: Houghton Mifflin.

Experian (2008). Case study: Post Office. Retrieve from: https://www.experian.co.uk/assets/resources/case-studies/PostOffice_V4.pdf (accessed 13 October 2018).

Freytag, P.V., and Clarke, A.H. (2001). Business to business segmentation. *Industrial Marketing Management*, 30(6), 473–86.

Fuchs, C., and Diamantopoulos, A. (2010). Evaluating the effectiveness of brand-positioning strategies from a consumer perspective. *European Journal of Marketing*, 44(11–12), 1763–86.

Garrahan, M. (2012). Disney grabs a galaxy of opportunity. *Financial Times*, 1 November, 19.

Griffith, R.L., and Pol, L.A. (1994). Segmenting industrial markets. *Industrial Marketing Management*, 23(1), 39–46.

Haley, R.I. (1968). Benefit segmentation: a decision-oriented research tool. *Journal of Marketing*, 32(3), 30–5.

Harris, J. (2018). The Cambridge Analytica saga is a scandal of Facebook's own making. *The Guardian*, 21 March. Retrieve from: https://www.theguardian.com/commentisfree/2018/mar/21/cambridge-analytica-facebook-data-users-profit (accessed 13 October 2018).

Holbrook, M.B., and Gardner, M.P. (1993). An approach to investigating the emotional determinants of consumption durations: why do people consume what they consume for as long as they consume it? *Journal of Consumer Psychology*, 2(2), 123–42.

Holbrook, M.B., and Hirschman, E.C. (1982). The experiential aspects of consumer behaviour: consumer fantasies, feelings and fun. *Journal of Consumer Research*, 9(2), 132–40.

Hollis, N. (2014a). How Peroni uses images of Italy's 'Golden Age' to justify a price premium. *Millward Brown Blog*, 7 July. Retrieve from: https://www.millwardbrown.com/global-navigation/blogs/post/mb-blog/2014/07/07/how-peroni-uses-images-of-italy-s-golden-age-to-justify-a-price-premium (accessed 13 October 2018).

Hollis, N. (2014b). Beer brand Leffe taps into contemporary food trends to grow. *Millward Brown Blog*, 5 November. Retrieve from: https://www.millwardbrown.com/global-navigation/blogs/post/mb-blog/2014/11/05/beer-brand-leffe-taps-into-contemporary-food-trends-to-grow (accessed 13 October 2018).

Hunt, S.D., and Arnett, D.B. (2004). Market segmentation strategy, competitive advantage and public policy: grounding segmentation strategy in resource-advantage theory. *Australasian Marketing Journal*, 12(1), 7–25.

Kantrowitz, A. (2017). Facebook's 2016 election team gave advertisers a blueprint to a divided US. *BuzzFeedNews*, 30 October. Retrieve from: https://www.buzzfeed.com/alexkantrowitz/facebooks-2016-election-team-gave-advertisers-a-blueprint?utm_term=.kngznjPnR#.ndPoqlRqK (accessed 13 October 2018).

Keaveney, S.M. (1995). Customer switching behavior in service industries: an exploratory study. *Journal of Marketing*, 59(2), 71–82.

Kittikachorn, P. (2018). How consumers are shaping Thailand's future. *Bangkok Post*, 28 December, B5.

Kotler, P. (1984). *Marketing Management*. Upper Saddle River, NJ: Prentice Hall.

Lee, E. (2013). A new market segmentation for capture-enabled devices. *InfoTrends*, 23 September. Retrieve from: https://blog.infotrends.com/?s=A+new+market+segmentation+for+capture-enabled+devices (accessed 13 October 2018).

Leitch, L. (2018). Versace: the resurrection. *The Economist 1843*, April–May. 66–70.

Liu, A., Leach, M., and Chugh, R. (2015). A sales process framework to regain B2B customers. *Journal of Business and Industrial Marketing*, 30(8), 906–14.

Llewellyn, C., Podpolny, D., and Zerbi, C. (2015). Capturing the new 'value' segment in medical devices. *McKinsey Insights*, January. Retrieve from: http://www.mckinsey.com/insights/health_systems_and_services/capturing_the_new_value_segment_in_medical_devices (accessed 13 October 2018).

Lopes, L., Alves, H., and Brito, C. (2001). Lost customers: determinants and process of relationship dissolution. Presented at: 40th EMAC Conference, Ljubljana, Slovenia, 24–27 May.

McAlister, L., and Pessemier, E. (1982). Variety seeking behaviour: an interdisciplinary review. *Journal of Consumer Research*, 9(4), 311–22.

McCluskey, M. (2018). Here's a complete list of all the upcoming *Star Wars* Movies. *Time*, 6 February. Retrieve from: https://time.com/5045736/upcoming-star-wars-movies/ (accessed 13 October 2018).

McDonald, M., and Dunbar, I. (2004). *Market Segmentation: How to Do It; How to Profit from It*. Oxford: Elsevier.

Minawi, M. (2017). Female focus. *Impact* (Magazine of the Market Research Society), January, 13.

Moreno, I. (2017). Harley hunts for younger riders. *Bangkok Post*, 28 December, B7.

Morrissey, P., and Baines, P. (2011). Segmenting exercise participants by surface level participation motivation. Presented at: Australian and New Zealand Marketing Academy Conference, Perth, Australia, 28–30 November.

Naudé, P., and Cheng, L. (2003). Choosing between potential friends: market segmentation in a small company. Presented at: 19th IMP Conference, Lugano, Switzerland, 4–6 September.

Neal, C. (2010). Market segmentation at Dell: 7 questions with Dell's Barry Jennings. *Voices: The CMB Blog*, 13 January. Retrieve from: https://blog.cmbinfo.com/bid/29231/Market-Segmentation-at-Dell-7-Questions-with-Dell-s-Barry-Jennings (accessed 13 October 2018).

Nobel, C. (2011). Clay Christensen's milkshake marketing. *Harvard Business School Working Knowledge*, 14 February. Retrieve from: https://hbswk.hbs.edu/item/clay-christensens-milkshake-marketing (accessed 13 October 2018).

Olney, T.J., Holbrook, M.B., and Batra, R. (1991). Consumer response to advertising: the effects of ad content, emotions, and attitude toward the ad on viewing time. *Journal of Consumer Research*, 17(2), 440–53.

Poenaru, A., and Baines, P. (2011). An organizational capability model of market segmentation. Presented at: Australian and New Zealand Marketing Academy Conference, Perth, Australia, 28–30 November.

Ram, A. (2018). Cambridge academics fought man at centre of Facebook furore. *Financial Times*, 21 March. Retrieve from: https://www.ft.com/content/fe8cfa26-2d19-11e8-9b4b-bc4b9f08f381 (accessed 13 October 2018).

Reynolds, M. (2017). This is what you need to know about those Russian Facebook ads. *Wired*, 2 November. Retrieve from: https://www.wired.co.uk/article/facebook-twitter-russia-congress-fake-ads-2016-election-trump (accessed 13 October 2018).

Ries, A., and Trout, J. (1972). The positioning era cometh. *Advertising Age*, 17(24), 35–8.

Ritson, M. (2017). Facebook's segmentation abilities are depressingly impressive. *Marketing Week*, 9 November. Retrieve from: https://www.marketingweek.com/2017/11/09/mark-ritson-facebook-segmentation/ (accessed 13 October 2018).

Rooney, L. (2015). UBS unveils major brand overhaul, *Forbes*, 1 September. Retrieve from: https://www.forbes.com/sites/jenniferrooney/2015/09/01/ubs-unveils-major-brand-overhaul/#30746af04f89 (accessed 13 October 2018).

Sanchez, J.C. (2018). TVolution: the evolution of TV research in Latin America. *Research World* (Magazine of ESOMAR), February, 33–5.

Shankland, S. (2009). Dell regroups around four customer segments. *C/Net*, 2 January. Retrieve from: https://www.cnet.com/news/dell-regroups-around-four-customer-segments/ (accessed 13 October 2018).

Shimp, T. (2007). *Integrated Marketing Communications in Advertising and Promotion* (International edn, 7th edn). Mason, OH: South-Western.

Sinclair, S.A., and Stalling, E.C. (1990). Perceptual mapping: a tool for industrial marketing—a case study. *Journal of Business and Industrial Marketing*, 5(1), 55–65.

Smith, W.R. (1956). Product differentiation and market segmentation as alternative marketing strategies. *Journal of Marketing*, 21(1), 3–8.

Solomon, M.R. (1983). The role of products as social stimuli: a symbolic interactionism perspective. *Journal of Consumer Research*, 10(4), 319–29.

Srivastava, R.K., Shocker, A.D., and Day, G.S. (1978). An exploratory study of the influences of usage situations on perceptions of product markets. *Advances in Consumer Research*, 5, 32–8.

Stiving, M. (2012). Brilliant price segmentation: an example. *Pragmatic Pricing*, 4 May. Retrieve from: https://pragmaticpricing.com/2012/05/04/brilliant-price-segmentation-an-example/ (accessed 13 October 2018).

Urban, C. (1976). Correlates of magazine readership. *Journal of Advertising Research*, 19(3), 7–12.

Venter, P., Wright, A., and Dibb, S. (2015). Performing market segmentation: a performative perspective. *Journal of Marketing Management*, 31(1–2), 62–83.

Weinstein, A. (2014). Target market selection in B2B technology markets. *Journal of Marketing Analytics*, 2(1), 59–69.

Wind, Y. (1978). Issues and advances in segmentation research. *Journal of Marketing Research*, 15, 317–37.

Wind, Y., and Cardozo, R.N. (1974). Industrial market segmentation. *Industrial Marketing Management*, 3, 155–66.

Chapter 7

International Market Development

Learning Outcomes

After reading this chapter, you will be able to:

▶ Identify the key drivers for international market development

▶ Discuss how environmental factors influence the choice of international marketing strategy decisions

▶ Describe the criteria used to identify and select international markets

▶ Explore various international market entry methods

▶ Define international market development as a market growth strategy

▶ List the different forms of international marketing strategy

Case Insight 7.1
Lanson International

Market Insight 7.1
LEGO®: To Translate or Localize?

Market Insight 7.2
Dolce & Gabbana's Luxury Hijab Collection

Market Insight 7.3
Go West! Chinese Car Manufacturers Internationalize

Market Insight 7.4
Primark Extends Its Growth by Entering the US Market

Market Insight 7.5
Ad-Apt in São Paulo?

Case Insight 7.1
Lanson International

Founded in 1760, Champagne Lanson is one of the oldest existing champagne houses in France, making some of the world's finest champagnes. We speak to Paul Beavis, managing director, Lanson International, to find out more about how the company looks to further develop its presence in international markets, including the UK.

Lanson currently works in more than 30 countries around the world and this has been developed over a number of years, driven by the increase in demand for champagne in the UK, which started over 15 years ago. Generally, we believe a company should look at international markets when its appetite for growth exceeds the current in-market capacity. Obviously, general economic market conditions apply and these need to be considered before we enter any new markets. For us, a key success factor for successfully entering a new market is having data, data, and more data! Having the absolute facts about your markets is essential—it's a case of examination (of the market); diagnosis (of the entry method, what channels to use, and how to promote our brand); and prescription (of the operational approach).

Before we enter a market, we look at the current shape and size of the markets today, but also (and this is seldom easy) we try to forecast how the category will be shaped in the next three to five years. One key trend that we can see in the global economy today is a concentration of spending power across and within certain markets. To tap into those segments, internationalization has to be a core part of our strategy for the future. So we evaluate a potential market's economic conditions, searching for market data not only about current volumes, but also about consumer trends, the knowledge gap (what we know versus what we don't know about their attitudes and behaviour), other drinks categories such as spirits, and growth in wine consumption generally.

All of this insight primarily helps us to plan our route-to-market strategy. This also involves ascertaining more generally what strategy we should deploy in

terms of our market positioning—whether we use a subsidiary brand model or a distributor/agency model and considering the financial implications of each of these.

Part of the problem in the UK is that, as categories become more mature, as the UK is now, there is a real need to be able to explain why your brand is essential in the marketplace. The hardest question any business should ask itself is: what is my true competitive advantage?

In the UK market, champagne (with sales of £340 million in 2016/17) has generally seen strong competition from sparkling wine brands, particularly Prosecco (with a total market increase of 4.7 per cent expected over the period 2017–22) and especially in the off-licence trade, but Lanson enjoys the position of being the No. 1 rosé brand and the No. 2 non-vintage champagne brand. Meanwhile, Spanish Cava has seen a decline in sales.

Lanson was therefore faced with a couple of key questions in relation to its international market development strategy:

- **How should a French brand like Lanson seek to differentiate itself in a category that is dominated, in the UK, by a competitor focus on 'advertising' and the colour of the label?**

- **Once Lanson has achieved success in the UK, how might it replicate this success in other international markets?**

Visit the online resources to watch a video interview with Paul Beavis in which he explains what Lanson did.

Introduction

Have you ever considered where the products you purchase and consume are produced or manufactured? Have a look at the food products in your kitchen or the clothes in your wardrobe: are they from the UK, Scandinavia, China, or Asia? We now consume more products, read more information, and travel to more overseas countries than ever before.

In light of the increasing internationalization of world markets, increased foreign trade, changes in technology, and the economic impact of foreign markets, **international marketing** is essential for the survival of many organizations. Even organizations that compete only in domestic markets are affected, because they increasingly compete with foreign organizations. An understanding of international business, marketing, and **globalization** is essential for marketing in the twenty-first century.

This chapter explores the issues that marketers should consider when developing effective international marketing strategies and policies. This includes the drivers that often lead to internationalization, analysis of the international marketing environment, the criteria and the method used for entry in international markets, and the strategies that companies implement when managing international marketing operations. As we will see, a key strategic consideration that companies face is the choice between trying to use a common standard approach across different markets or modifying their offering to suit the local market. Marketers need to learn about dominant trends in international markets to strike the right balance.

The Drivers of International Market Development

Although international marketing is now ubiquitous, it is worth considering how it became so. The key drivers for globalization are set out in Figure 7.1. The most common are the following:

- *Historical accident*—Unplanned events can trigger international market development. In 1941, during the Second World War, Coca-Cola leader Robert Woodruff wanted to distribute a bottle of Coke to anyone in uniform anywhere in the world for 5 cents. To do so, he set up a special group of 'technical observers' to manage 64 bottling plants, producing 5 billion bottles of Coke for those in service around the world (Mooney, 2008). As a result, a wider range of people tasted the drink and an opportunity arose for Coca-Cola to build the brand through a new distribution strategy. This is said to be one of the main reasons behind the growth of Coca-Cola's international marketing operations.

- *Excess stock*—Excess stock can build up as a consequence of overproduction or insufficient sales. With limited opportunities for sales in domestic markets, organizations seek out international sales opportunities to remove excess stock. When the product is sold at a lower price in the foreign market than is charged in the domestic market, this is called dumping. Such an approach does not constitute a long-term entry strategy.

- *Limited growth in domestic markets*—One way of avoiding domestic competition when growth is limited in home markets is to enter international markets. For example, given the strong competition in the home markets of the United States and Europe, in 2015 AB InBev announced a merger after shareholders accepted its offer of US$104 billion for SAB-Miller. The strategic rationale was that the deal would give AB InBev brands access to growing markets in Africa and Latin America (where it was not strong), and that the combined entity would control a third of the world beer market (Colley, 2015).

- **Comparative advantage**—Some regions or countries develop core competencies and reputations for producing certain offerings, raw resources, or work skills. This presents an opportunity to develop comparative advantage. For example, champagne is produced by 15,800 wine growers and 320 champagne houses in the Champagne region of France, exporting about 295 million bottles in 2017 (Comité Champagne, 2017). Certain countries offer differential labour costs and specialized skills, for example China and manufacturing, or India and service process outsourcing (such as call centres). This presents an advantage not only in labour and operating costs, but also, for some industries, savings in transport and manufacturing costs.

- **Economies of scale**—For some offerings, the cost of development and production can be high. To achieve an effective return on investment, high-volume production runs are necessary and this requires large world markets. Examples include smartphones and aircraft manufacture. A high degree of standardization is evident in the manufacture of aircraft, such as the frame wings and engines, with superficial changes such as seating spacing and arrangements tailored for local markets. This enables aircraft manufacturers to achieve global economies of scale.

- *Trade liberalization*—With the creation of regional trade blocs, such as the European Union (EU), the North American Free Trade Agreement (NAFTA), and the Association of Southeast Asian Nations (ASEAN) free trade area (FTA), and the reduction of barriers to trade worldwide, many organizations engage in global competition with international firms in domestic markets and domestic organizations are increasingly moving abroad to compete overseas.

- *International product life cycle*—An opportunity for internationalization presents itself when an offering reaches different stages of its life cycle in different countries (see Chapter 8). For example, British motorcycle producer Royal Enfield ceased production in the UK in 1970, but continued production in India (where it granted a local partner a licence in 1955). The company now seeks to become the global leader in mid-sized motorcycles after investing Rs 500 crore (US$80 million) in a new factory and technology centre (Agence France-Presse, 2015).

- *Technological changes*—Advances in electronic communications (for example the Internet) have enabled international trade. Online channels are increasingly being used to sell into new markets because of open access and low costs. Changes in the technological infrastructure have provided small and medium-sized enterprises (SMEs) with a way of increasing exports with low entry costs.

- *Customer relationships*—As organizations move abroad, international marketing activities affect the whole supply chain, from end users, through intermediaries, to producers and raw material suppliers. For example, as Toyota enters new foreign markets, its product components also change, and suppliers will need to match the requirements of its new manufacturing and assembly production process. This is particularly true of service-based industries. Since services are co-produced by the interaction of customers and service providers (see Chapter 15), internationalization almost always requires transferring the service delivery abroad. For example, many universities in the UK (for example Nottingham, Liverpool,

Manchester) have opened campuses or centres in China to attract local students interested in obtaining a degree from a well-regarded British higher education institution.

- *Transnational market segments*—The growth in groups of people with similar needs, but who inhabit different countries, called transnational market segments, occurs because of migration, such as Chinese working in Singapore, similarities in demographics (for example **Generation Y**), or similarities in lifestyles (for example vegetarians). From a conceptual perspective, a truly global organization should segment markets based on similar characteristics even across national borders, because country of residence and/or birth is becoming ever less relevant as a consequence of increasing migration.

- *Organizational sustainability*—The broader the range of markets served, the less likely it is that failure in one market will result in overall organizational decline. Different markets are always at different stages of development and competitive intensity. An international market portfolio provides an organization with an increased chance of organizational sustainability. For example, McDonald's, the fast-food restaurant operator, has not suffered a strong decline in its overall reputation worldwide, despite food scandals in China and Japan (Martin and Fujikawa, 2015).

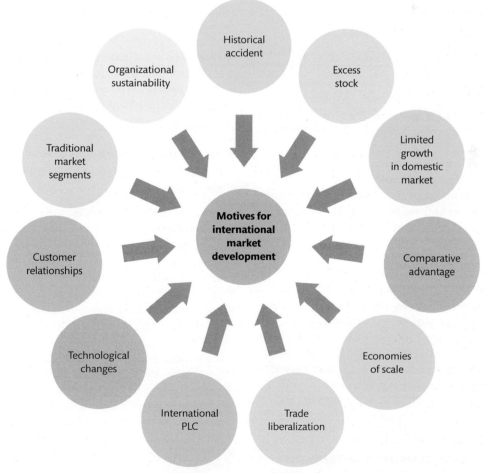

Figure 7.1
Motives for international market development

Market Insight 7.1
LEGO®: To Translate or Localize?

LEGO is known around the world
Source: © 3d_kot / Shutterstock.com

LEGO®, the Danish manufacturer of plastic building bricks, is a global toy company, with revenues of DKr28.6 billion (€3.8 billion). The company's website provides product-related content targeted at the company's core consumer segment: 5–12-year old builders, and their grandparents and parents, who typically make the purchases. The company has also expanded into emerging markets, opening offices in Malaysia, Turkey, and China. The physical product, the plastic brick, is identical around the world; the 20+ languages that are used on the LEGO website are not. So how does LEGO deal with being present in a global range of markets? Does LEGO translate the content into the local language, is the content localized, or both?

The global reach of the Internet has led LEGO to develop language-specific websites for each of its major markets. However, the challenge for marketers is to take both translation and localization into consideration, because these issues are not the same. Translating text on LEGO's website is straightforward; localizing the website for each of the major markets is a completely different story because it demands an in-depth knowledge of consumer attitudes and preferences in the individual country, together with an appreciation of cultural differences.

Many of LEGO's target consumers live outside the UK and United States, and cannot understand English; what's more, the young consumers do not necessarily share LEGO's European cultural origins. Therefore the marketing challenge for LEGO is to make sure that the company website is translated *and* localized in a way that respects these cultural differences. Translation of product descriptions is straightforward, but there are constraints on the ability of LEGO to localize its website: the global standardization of the physical product—the LEGO sets—places limits on the content that can be provided. So how can LEGO provide localized content for a globally standardized product?

Surprisingly, apart from the translated product descriptions, much of the content on the LEGO website is not actually localized. Content is developed from the outset to be seen by young consumers around the world and is structured around videos of the LEGO products with sound effects, rather than language. These videos showcase each of the products in an appropriate setting, so that LEGO's global audience can see the different functions of the products, such as opening doors, working propellers, and so on. Other content that does not need translating are games based on LEGO products, with pictorial instructions and short animated sequences.

Where localization is apparent is in country-specific marketing campaigns. Here, translation is not necessarily a factor, because there are even differences between the two largest English-speaking markets, the United States and the UK. The two markets use the same language, so no translation is necessary, but consumer preferences for different product themes and unique holiday traditions make localization a key marketing consideration. The marketing challenge that LEGO faces is to identify which elements of its online marketing need to be translated and which elements need to be localized. Translation is not the same as localization.

Sources: Anderson (2014); Anon. (2015d); https://www.lego.com/en-gb/

Market Insight 7.1
continued

Theory into Practice

This market insight illustrates that, to adapt to cultural differences, organizations use three internal processes (Mughan, 1993). The first is empathy—that is, they try to recognize a situation from the customer's perspective and adapt their behaviour accordingly. The second is to provide cultural training, particularly for employees working directly with distributors or customers. The third is to recruit direct from the local labour market—the quickest route. Successful international organizations tend to have a diverse representation of nationalities in their senior management teams. The insight also illustrates the difficulties inherent in determining the extent to which a company should standardize or adapt its offerings into new markets. This task is made particularly difficult when, like LEGO, the company operates in a large number of countries.

Related Topics

standardization–adaptation; culture; language; marketing communications; digital marketing

1 **Go to the LEGO® website and change the country by clicking on the flag icon. Choose a country with a different language from your own. Which content is translated and which is localized? Why do you think that this is the case?**

2 **Now find the 'products' page and change the country to the Chinese LEGO® website. What do you see?**

3 **Now compare the UK and the US websites. What happens to the content that you see?**

This market insight was kindly contributed by Dr Robert P. Ormrod, Aarhus University, Denmark.

However, whatever the motivation for international market development, a planned approach considerably increases the chances for success. Once international market entry has been decided as an organizational growth strategy, certain decisions have to be made to increase the chances of success. These include determining which foreign markets to pursue, which methods are the most suitable for entering new markets, and which strategy to adopt to appeal to the desired needs of foreign markets. (See Market Insight 7.1 for an example of a company deciding how to internationalize.)

International Marketing Environment

Before making investment decisions in the direction of internationalization, it is important that marketers understand the foreign marketing environment if they are to assess and select foreign markets properly. Frequently, however, firms looking to go to market internationally pay insufficient attention to aspects of the global marketing environment, including socio-cultural, economic, legal/institutional, and political developments (Young, 2001).

Social Factors

Differences in society, values, and demography can all affect the acceptability, and therefore uptake, of an offering in international markets. In some countries, such as the UK, Sweden, and Canada, there are increasing numbers of new parents returning to work, placing more reliance on grandparents, nannies, and childminders for childcare responsibilities. This contrasts with the composition of other markets and the greater level of cross-generational households, as found in China and Japan, where grandparents are a central part of the family unit and reside in the family household. Interestingly, because of house price increases in the UK, there is also an increasing trend towards multigenerational living (Davidson, 2013). Migration and the associated movement of social values can also influence social factors. In Canada, for example, immigration accounts for around 66 per cent of population growth (Martel, 2015). An awareness of these changes and transient social structures and values is imperative.

Cultural Factors

Culture is important in international market development strategy because it concerns the beliefs, norms, and values that guide the behaviour of groups of potential customers and other stakeholders. It comprises language, education, religion, lifestyle, taboos, and norms. Culture affects how people define their wants and needs through consumption and how they interact with each other (see, for example, Market Insight 7.2). For example, Unilever controls 27 per cent of global ice cream sales, but markets differently to different countries according to cultural norms. For example, portion sizes are different and there is more distribution through scoop shops in some countries compared with others (Askew, 2015). In Italy, Unilever acquired GROM to gain a foothold in the premium gelato market in addition to selling its usual brands, Carte d'Or, Algida (sold as Walls in other countries), Cucciolone, Cornetto, and Max (Watrous, 2015). Nevertheless, there are sometimes cultural behaviour changes. In France, for example, although French shoppers have tended to buy their bread as baguettes on a daily basis, they are now increasingly buying sliced bread, such as that sold by Barilla, an Italian food group (Anon., 2015c).

British–Dutch company Unilever markets its deodorant as Lynx in UK, Ireland, Australia, New Zealand, and China, but as Axe elsewhere

Source: © Paul Baines.

Market Insight 7.2
Dolce & Gabbana's Luxury Hijab Collection

Muslim consumers are a valuable market for the fashion industry

Source: © Tanya Rex/arabianEye/Getty

While growth in luxury sales in established markets such as the United States and Europe is increasingly dependent on tourism, high-end fashion is booming in the Middle East. Studies show that the global spend of Muslim consumers on only clothing and footwear is more than the total fashion spending of Japan and Italy combined. The same report said that spending was expected to reach US$484 billion by 2019. Sales of personal luxury goods in the Middle East are worth around $9 billion.

In an effort to tap into this wealthy market for luxury items, in 2016 Dolce & Gabbana launched Abaya, its first line of clothing specifically dedicated to Muslim women. The headline items of the collection were the hijab, the veil to cover women's heads, and the abaya, worn by women as a sign of modesty, usually black in colour and covering the whole body, except the face, feet, and hands.

The collection was presented on Style.com/Arabia, the most important fashion and lifestyle website in the Middle East. Stefano Gabbana, co-founder of the luxury fashion house, announced the launch of the collection on his Instagram account using the hashtag #dgabaya. The clothes presented in the first Abaya collection were made of lightweight fabrics and neutral, beige, and black colours, but featured the typical elements of the Italian fashion house: precious stones, lace, floral decorations, embroidery, and prints of lemons and daisies that chimed with the wider spring 2016 collection. Dolce & Gabbana's new line managed to be

respectful of Muslim shoppers' needs while staying true to the brand's Sicily-inspired aesthetic. The garments were to be available in Dolce & Gabbana's 13 boutiques in the United Arab Emirates (UAE) and in other locations across Bahrain, Kuwait, Qatar, and Saudi Arabia.

While other brands such as DKNY, Oscar de la Renta, Tommy Hilfiger, and Mango had produced one-off collections featuring flowing gowns and wide-leg trousers, often sold around Ramadan, Dolce & Gabbana was the first Western luxury label to create a collection specifically adapted to meet the needs of Muslim women, and including items such as the abaya and the shayla headscarf. Women from Muslim countries have long expressed their flair for fashion with expensive handbags and shoes, visible even when worn with an abaya and hijab. Many are also already consumers of designer apparel, dressing in luxury brands from head to toe underneath their modest abayas, revealed only in the privacy of their own homes or when among other women. Dolce & Gabbana's intention was to engage a young and expanding Muslim market eager for luxury goods.

If Dolce & Gabbana hijabs and abayas continue to be a hit, we can expect to see more fashion labels follow the brand's example and more retailers tailoring their operations to meet the needs of the Muslim consumer.

Sources: D'Arpizio et al. (2016); Haris (2016); Thomson Reuters (2016); Muslimin (2017).

Market Insight 7.2

continued

Theory into Practice

The market insight described how a luxury house adapted a product line to meet the specific need of an international (multi-country) consumer market. An adaptation strategy is particularly important for global companies because it ensures that the product meets local cultural and consumer needs in a different marketplace. By comparing the features that customers consider important with the current product specification, companies can identify gaps and hence opportunities to improve the product's appeal to satisfy unmet needs and target growing opportunities.

Related Topics

product adaptation in international markets; product adaptation vs product standardization; cross-cultural segmentation; intercultural marketing; consumer behaviour

1 Can you think of other markets for which Dolce & Gabbana could develop a dedicated product line? Why do you think these markets require a specific line?

2 Which other marketing mix elements should be adapted to the Middle East market by Dolce & Gabbana? Why?

3 What are the market or cultural conditions that make product adaptation necessary and unavoidable?

This market insight was kindly contributed by Professor Ilaria Baghi, Modena and Reggio Emilia University, Italy.

Culture influences the way in which we interact with each other and it affects many basic aspects of business life. Clearly, for organizations serious about international marketing, cultural sensitivity is paramount. Business conduct differs throughout the world based around:

- time, including attitudes towards punctuality, the sanctity (or otherwise) of deadlines, the time it takes to make someone's acquaintance, and the appropriate length of discussions;

- business cards, including when and how to offer them, whether to translate them or not, who gives them first, and how they should be received—for example, in China, the card should be proffered with both hands, while in India, you should use only your right hand to give and receive business cards;

- business gifts, including whether or not they are acceptable, what value of gift is reasonable, and whether or not they should be opened in the view of the giver;

- dress codes, including what should be worn for what business occasions and the relative degree of formality—for example, whether or not to wear a suit and tie to a meeting differs by country, being less common in Scandinavia than in the UK;

- entertainment for business purposes, including what type and formality of occasion are acceptable, table manners and etiquette, what type of cuisine should be served, where the event should be held, and what cultural/religious codes should be observed or are taboo—for example, in Japan, seating for business entertaining is likely to be arranged by rank; and

- body language, including greetings, for example whether to shake hands, kiss, bow or wai (a slight bow with palms pressed together); facial and hand gestures and their meaning; and the acceptability of physical proximity, touching, and different forms of posture (Mead, 1990).

Language is particularly important when considering entering into a foreign market because sellers will often need to use a customer's own language. However, English is increasingly becoming the **lingua franca** (that is, a common language between non-native speakers). Language issues also arise for the way in which brand names, slogans and taglines, and product packaging might be used. In French-speaking Quebec in Canada, a region that is hypersensitive to the use of French language in place of English, fried chicken brand KFC is known as PFK (*Poulet Frit Kentucky*). This is despite the fact that, in France, it is known as KFC. Similarly, in several Spanish-speaking areas of the United States, KFC is known as PFK (*Pollo Frito Kentucky*). The implication is that all forms of marketing communications should be translated to ensure correct interpretation and meaning. If communication is to be in Arabic, there needs to be consideration of whether or not to use local dialects such as Maghreb or Gulf Arabic. We should also consider the target audience. If the audience is business personnel, the vocabulary, grammar, and punctuation ought to reflect this; if the audience is informal or young, then a relaxed language style might be used. Getting the language style right for the target audience is important, because failures can be devastating (see Table 7.1).

Social psychologist Geert Hofstede (1983) has conducted very influential research aimed at identifying the most important dimensions that affect cultural differences globally. Four dimensions emerged as stable traits that characterize societies, and these have been used to explore cultural differences and consider their marketing implications:

- *Collectivism versus individualism*—In countries in which individualism is very high (for example the United States, the UK), there is a higher level of concern for individual freedom and the pursuit of wealth at the personal level. On the contrary, collectivist societies (such as China) value the well-being of the group and people see themselves much more as members of a clearly defined social group.

- *Power distance*—In countries with high power distance (for example China), there is a larger acceptance of inequality and autocratic styles of leadership are more common. People are less likely to challenge the leadership and authority figures are respected. Western countries tend to show lower acceptance of power distance; as a consequence, there is less obsequiousness and people prefer more horizontal leadership styles.

- *Uncertainty avoidance*—Societies vary in terms of their acceptance of risk. For example, Brazil has a much stronger tendency of uncertainty avoidance than the UK. This means that, overall, people in Brazil are more averse to taking risks and betting on the future. On the contrary, people in the UK have a higher acceptance of avoidance and feel more comfortable in investing resources now to achieve uncertain outcomes in the future.

- *Masculinity versus femininity*—Societies such as the UK, which scores highly on what Hofstede (1983) refers to as 'masculinity', place strong emphasis on achievement, success, and assertiveness as personal values. Sweden, however, is an example of a country scoring high on 'femininity', which indicates a higher preference for cooperation, care for the weak, and a focus on quality of life.

- *Long-term orientation versus short-term orientation*—Some countries, such as Japan and China, tend to have a strong respect for tradition, seeing ancient rules and institutions as still important in modern life. Other societies, such as the United States or Australia, tend to be less attached to history, and more pragmatic and open to social and cultural innovations.

Table 7.1 Examples of international brand blunders

Brand/ Company	Brand launch location	Misinterpretation
American Dairy Association	Mexico and other Spanish-speaking countries	Launched its 'Got milk?' campaign into Spanish-speaking countries, which translated as 'Are you lactating?'
Colgate	France	Introduced a toothpaste branded 'Cue', which is the name of a French pornographic magazine
Ford Pinto	Brazil	In Brazilian Portuguese, *pinto* means 'tiny male genitals'
Honda	Sweden	Was originally going to launch its Honda Fit brand, strong in Asia, into European markets as Fitta, but realized this word connoted female genitalia in Swedish and quickly changed the name to Jazz despite having already printed its brochures with the erroneous term
Mercedes Benz	China	Entered the market with the brand 'Bensi', which means 'rush to die' in Chinese
Nike	United States (and globally)	Had to recall 38,000 pairs of basketball trainers after a logo meant to look like fire was instead interpreted as the Arabic script for 'Allah'
Panos	Russia	Decided to promote its range of sandwiches using the brand name 'Panos', not realizing that this translated as 'diarrhoea' in Russian
Umbro	UK	Called a new brand of its trainers 'Zyklon', but received large numbers of complaints because this was the name of the gas used to kill millions of people in Nazi concentration camps in World War II
Vicks	Germany	German translation of the brand name, 'Ficks', connotes sexual penetration

Sources: Anon. (2007); Fromowitz (2013); James (2014).

- *Indulgence versus restraint*—Another axis that helps when differentiating cultures is the extent to which the gratification of basic human drives is accepted, or even promoted. Western European countries and the United States tend to be score highly on 'indulgence' because, in these societies, practices aimed at enjoying life and having fun are culturally accepted. In countries in the Middle East such as Iran and Saudi Arabia, however, there is in general more 'restraint'.

The dimensions outlined in Hofstede's ground-breaking research have complex, but fundamental, effects on economic behaviour. Marketers in global organizations need to consider these differences carefully and think about how to adjust their policies to fit with the specific culture of a national market.

Consumption Attitudes

Customer perceptions of a product or a company's country of origin can influence the way in which customers react. To reduce the risk of such adverse perceptions, organizations sometimes enter markets with consumption attitudes similar to those in the domestic market (that is, where the psychic distance is lower). Examples include organizations exporting from Spain to Mexico, Ireland to the UK, New Zealand to Australia, and Sweden to Norway. Entering such markets lowers the risk, because organizations can learn and develop knowledge before entering the market, and can research consumption attitudes more easily.

Technological Factors

The technological capability and rate of development in a country can have significant implications for how marketers communicate, for new proposition development, and for the overall success of a market entry strategy. In many international markets, new technology can change the way in which an organization goes to market (Sclater, 2005), for example through e-commerce or m-commerce. Nevertheless, in some developing markets, lower-level technologies such as radio remain the principal channel for marketing communications, because television diffusion is limited. In other countries (for example Nigeria), smartphone usage exceeds fixed-line Internet penetration. Therefore it is important to profile the penetration levels of different communication technologies and the supporting infrastructure when entering foreign markets.

Many customer needs and wants are constrained by the prevailing technological infrastructure. For example, whether gas or electricity is used for cooking depends on that country's energy mix and infrastructure. The type of telephone used depends on the telecommunication and economic infrastructure. Wireless telephony penetration frequently exceeds wireline (landline) penetration in developing countries. However, the needs and usage of mobile phones in developing markets differ considerably from the needs of and usage in mature markets. The Nokia phone brand, marketed by Finnish company HMD Global, has become Africa's leading phone brand by selling feature phones (that is, devices that lie between a basic phone and a smartphone in terms of offering), which are often entry-level phones offered at an inexpensive price (Anon., 2018). Nokia learned that, in hot countries, where many roads are unpaved, features such as dustproof keypads are important and of value to customers.

Economic Factors

Market potential can be affected by many different local and international economic factors. Factors that should be considered when entering a new market include basic information about per capita disposable income, consumption patterns, and unemployment trends. Typical economic measures to help a firm to assess a particular country's market potential include:

- measures of per capita income;
- ownership rates of durables (for example smartphone penetration);
- **consumer price indices (CPIs)**;
- unemployment rates;
- **gross national product (GNP)**;
- market and population sizes; and
- currency exchange rates.

When assessing a market's attractiveness, these and other measures can usually be acquired from a number of sources, including business libraries, the online resource centres of professional bodies, and market intelligence or research databases.

Political and Legal Factors

Political and legal factors might also hinder or enable international marketing opportunities. For example, governments often offer subsidies and other forms of assistance to particular organizations when entering foreign markets by, for example, setting up and covering the cost of overseas trips. The UK government, in a bid to stimulate export, developed an advertising campaign around how it supports businesses looking to export.

The British government helped Supreme Creations—the world's largest ethical manufacturer of reusable bags, eco-packaging, and giveaways—to export its wares

Source: Courtesy of BIS/UKTi.

Some governments hinder exporters by placing taxes and tariffs on certain companies and goods to deter prospective importers and to protect domestic industries. Measures invoked by governments to protect their domestic industries include:

- *quotas*, which are used to limit the amount of goods allowed into a country;

- *duties*—that is, special taxes on imports—which seek to disadvantage the importer's pricing strategy; and

- *non-tariff barriers*, which include legislation designed so that importers have to adapt their offerings, which is often expensive, before the item is legally saleable in the host country.

Governments also try to alleviate unemployment and stimulate economic activity. As such, many countries encourage foreign investment by providing tax concessions and support of various kinds to persuade international organizations to set up their manufacturing units, or service units, in depressed areas. For example, both China (the Shanghai Free Trade Zone) and the UAE (Dubai Gold and Diamond Park) have set up trade zones within their territories with favourable tax incentives to attract foreign direct investment.

Political issues can cause difficulties for international marketers, sometimes leading to their withdrawal from a market, such as Google's experience in China when it withdrew to Hong Kong after the Chinese insisted on the application of mandatory censorship filters to Google's search engine product. In some countries, a government regime change may have little effect on commercial life, but in others the change can be profound, as in Romania after the execution of former dictator Nicolai Ceausescu in 1989 and the fall of Communism. Sometimes, governments restrict foreign investment and ownership by setting up strict market entry conditions. This might involve working with a local organization as the majority shareholder and/or owner. Other restrictions include employment laws, health and safety regulations, financial laws, patent protection regulation, data protection requirements, and electronic transactions legislation.

Visit the **online resources** and complete Internet Activity 7.1 to learn more about how the international strategies of firms such as Starbucks, Apple, Google, and Primark stand up to pressures on taxation, supply, and ethics.

International Market Selection

The selection of international markets should be based on a consideration of a potential market's overall attractiveness, which can be established by examining a number of factors, some of the most important of which are as follows:

- *Market size and growth rate*—Market size refers to the number of current and potential customers. Market size can also be measured in terms of the sales value that these customers represent. Using these figures alone can be misleading, however, because some regions increase in attractiveness and others decline. Whilst the three major world markets were once what Ohmae (1985) called the Triad—Europe, the United States, and Japan—rapid growth is increasingly observed in the Pacific Rim countries (China, Singapore, South Korea, and Taiwan), the BRIC group (Brazil, Russia, India, and China), and the MINT countries (Malaysia, Indonesia, Nigeria, and Turkey), whilst growth in Western markets is anaemic. Although disposable income in these countries is unevenly distributed, the overall increasing prosperity of their populations has created demand for Western luxury brands to signal individual success and increasing personal wealth. Brands such as Burberry, Hershey, Apple, and IKEA have experienced considerable growth in recent years, whilst brands such as Prada, Nestlé, and Rolls-Royce have fared less well (Doland, 2015).

- *Market access*—Access refers to the extent to which customers can be contacted with marketing communications and can obtain an offering through distribution and sales outlets. Media availability, industry infrastructure, channel networks, and local cultural norms all potentially limit or hinder market access. For example, in many countries, former state telecommunications still maintain widespread (monopoly) market control. This results in few openings for foreign brands to enter these markets, despite there being few legal issues or import difficulties. Some countries also impose high tariffs to protect local industry.

- *Geographical proximity*—The physical distance between a potential market and the domestic market can have a direct impact on resource requirements. For example, trade between Brazil and the UK requires more resourcing than trade between Sweden and Norway.

- *Psychological proximity*—This refers to the perceived cultural and societal similarities between countries. Later in the chapter, we will look at **psychic difference**—that is, the difference between perceptions of an offering in a domestic market and perceptions of that same offering in a foreign market. Psychological proximity and psychic distance can be seen as existing at opposite ends of a perceptual similarity–difference spectrum. For example, some see greater cultural similarity between the UK and Australia than between the UK and the Netherlands. (See Market Insight 7.1, earlier in the chapter, for more on this topic.)

- *Established competitors*—When competition is intense, foreign market entrants will be received less favourably. For example, this might potentially result in price competition or in entrants finding it difficult to obtain distribution agreements with supply-chain partners.

- *Entry costs*—These can vary greatly between markets and strategies. For example, physical distribution costs can be extremely high in a country such as the United States or India, where the distances between production plants and consumers can be immense. In other countries, distances might be comparably short, but marketing channels and supply chains may be long and complex, or lack the infrastructure to support them. For example, the healthcare infrastructure in various countries in sub-Saharan Africa differs greatly from that in European countries such as the UK and Sweden.

- *Profit potential*—This refers to the number of potential customers and the profit margin that the group can generate in that market. Even though per unit profit margins might be small, a country with a large potential market might still be attractive because of the overall profit generated. For example, Indonesia and Pakistan might each offer large potential profits. Powerful buying groups, low per capita income, and strong competition are all factors that can reduce profit margins.

International market selection requires good market intelligence about the market environment and marketing opportunities. The examination of the competitive environment, discussed in Chapter 4, should therefore be developed on an international scale. At the same time, it is important to realize that market screening can be random, driven by customer enquiries or by market demand for an offering or knowledge gained through media or social networks. Visits to the potential markets are also required to gather further insights and first-hand market knowledge, and to aid the development of networks and relationships.

Questions that are useful for international market screening are detailed in Table 7.2.

Table 7.2 International market screening questions

Factor	Questions to consider
Market	▪ What is the level of market growth/decline? ▪ What is the market potential? ▪ What distribution channels exist, if any?
Proposition fit	▪ Is there a market opportunity for this offering? ▪ Is there demand or interest in an offering of this type? ▪ Will the offering require adaptation to fit into the market?
Competition	▪ Are the existing competitors in this market, if any, national and international in nature? ▪ How aggressive is the competition? ▪ What degree of power do existing competitors exercise in this market? ▪ What barriers to entry currently exist? ▪ How might the competition respond to our market entry?
Market entry	▪ What entry methods are most attractive for us to enter this market? ▪ What will market entry cost us? ▪ How might local partners support us in entering the market? ▪ How similar are the foreign culture, values, and attitudes when compared with our domestic market?
Resources	▪ How much do we need to invest to enter this market? ▪ What will the mix of local and expatriate staff be in entering this market? ▪ What development do we need to undertake to allow us to enter this market? (Examples might include acculturation, language training, and export development skills.) ▪ Can we rely on existing marketing channels for market entry or do we need to develop new ones?
Trade barriers	▪ What legal or regulatory factors could influence our market entry or operational approach? ▪ Will import tariffs or quotas be imposed on us? ▪ Can we repatriate any profits generated out of the country or are there restrictions on this? ▪ Are there any constraints on foreign organizations operating in this market, e.g. in terms of allowing foreign majority ownership structures of local firms? ▪ Will different product/manufacturing standards apply in this market?

Market Entry Selection Criteria

There are several ways in which organizations can enter foreign markets. This decision is complex and depends on the company's objectives, its type of offering, and factors associated with the target country. Six criteria to consider when selecting the market entry method are presented in Figure 7.2 (Paliwoda, 1993). The importance of each depends on the organization's international marketing objectives:

- *Speed and timing*—Some foreign market entry methods take months, whereas others can be executed immediately; hence the organization should ascertain how quickly it wishes to enter a target market.

- *Costs*—Different methods require different levels of investment; consequently, the firm should carefully consider the costs and benefits of each method.

- *Flexibility*—Some methods provide organizations with different levels of flexibility over their activities in a new market and future development opportunities. For example, some methods (such as **direct investment**) might require long-term contractual agreements or financial commitments.

- *Risk and uncertainty*—Numerous risk factors are involved with entry into new and foreign markets. Some entry methods allow for a reduction of risk and uncertainty. These include **joint ventures** and direct investment. The latter might ease political pressure, for example reducing barriers to entry, including tariffs and import quotas. However, these methods also require a larger degree of financial investment than indirect exporting or **licensing**.

- *Return on investment (ROI)*—The ROI needs to be considered alongside speed and timing, and costs. Some organizations look to achieve a rapid ROI through their market entry strategies, and thus the speed and timing of market entry is crucial. For example, it may take years to build a factory in a foreign market; it may be more suitable to develop a partnership with an existing local manufacturer who can provide this resource, thereby increasing the speed of ROI.

- *Long-term objectives*—An organization needs to review what it wants to achieve in the long term from its entry into a new foreign market, because some market entry methods will provide more flexibility and leverage for long-term opportunities than others.

Market Entry Methods

There are several approaches that an organization can adopt when entering international markets. Each offers a level of risk commensurate with the potential rewards on offer (see Figure 7.3). The higher the risk, the higher the possible rate of return. An organization's willingness and ability to commit the appropriate managerial, financial, and operational resources is crucial to realizing the potential rewards. (See Market Insight 7.3 for an analysis of the choices made by Chinese car manufacturers when entering foreign markets.)

Figure 7.2
Criteria when selecting market entry methods

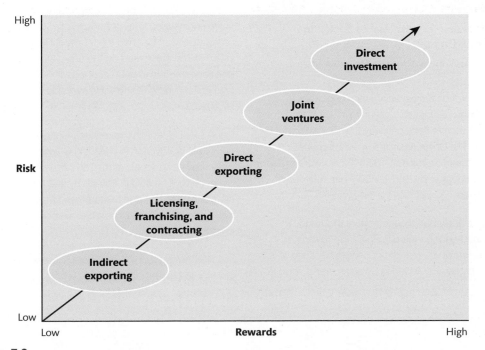

Figure 7.3
The level of potential risk and expected rewards of various market entry methods

Market Insight 7.3
Go West! Chinese Car Manufacturers Internationalize

Major exhibitions in the car industry, such as the Frankfurt Motor Show, have demonstrated the growing ambitions of Chinese brands. China's manufacturers, after years of steady expansion in the domestic market, are now targeting international expansion as a growth opportunity. Specifically, the growth of Chinese car manufacturers in international markets is seen as an important aspect of the 'One Belt, One Road' initiative—an ambitious programme of foreign investment in infrastructure supported by the Chinese government.

Geely means 'auspicious' or 'lucky' in Mandarin Chinese

Source: © Volha-Hanna Kanashyts/Shutterstock.com.

Chinese brands are especially targeting other developing countries that either have significant growth potential or can offer a gateway towards established markets. The China Association of Automobile Manufacturers claims that 190,000 cars were exported in the first quarter of 2017—a 30.7 per cent growth year on year.

Car giant Geely is at the forefront of this trend. The company, headquartered in Zhejiang Province, first became known to Western observers because of its high-profile acquisition of Swedish brand Volvo in 2010—but Geely is internationalizing in other ways too.

The company has about 10 per cent of the car market in Egypt, where it sells approximately 20,000 Geely vehicles a year. Moreover, the company is targeting the Russian market, where it aims to increase its current sales, which are of only 1,700 units. Through a joint venture with a local firm, Geely is building a new factory in Belarus, which will be able to increase production to a maximum of 60,000 vehicles each year. These plans are not without risks: previous attempts to break into the Russian market by Ford and Skoda were mostly unsuccessful.

Geely's strategy, however, is to continue growing primarily through acquisitions in foreign markets. In 2017, the firm acquired a 49.9 per cent stake in the Maylaysian car maker Proton. Analysts think that Proton will offer a good opportunity to sell Geely's own models in Malaysia. The idea is that cars manufactured in China will be slightly adapted and sold under the new brand.

At the same time, the company is also investing in new models that may be appealing to European and US consumers, primarily by leveraging Volvo engineering know-how. Lynk & Co. is a new brand that has launched the 01 model in China in 2017. The car, based on the Volvo XC40, is positioned on the idea of 'connectivity'. The goal is to make Lync & Co. models available in Europe by 2020.

Geely is not unique in this respect. Chery Automobile and Great Wall Motor, two leading Chinese brands, presented new models at the 2017 Frankfurt Motor Show that will be sold in Europe by 2021. Both firms are planning to invest in research and manufacturing facilities in Europe to support their westward expansion.

Sources: Chen (2017); Du (2017); Li (2017); Makhovsky and Stolyarov (2017); Savov (2017).

Market Insight 7.3
continued

Theory into Practice

This market insight describes how Chinese car manufacturers are internationalizing by means of a mixture of exporting and direct investment. Given the complexity of the market and the significant resources required to attempt internationalization in this industry, it is reasonable to use a variety of methods. Chinese firms are especially keen to acquire foreign firms or to build joint ventures, as demonstrated by Geely's story. It remains to be seen whether these companies will be able to challenge established European and US firms. The low-growth, saturated European market might prove particularly challenging to conquer.

Related Topics

market entry method; joint venture; acquisition; internationalization; international strategy

1 Why do you think Geely decided to acquire Swedish car maker Volvo?

2 What might prove the most challenging aspect of the European car market for Chinese manufacturers?

3 How do cultural factors influence the car industry? What cultural elements might affect the internationalization of Chinese car makers?

Some organizations use a mixture of methods, depending upon the importance of each international project. Nissan changed from indirect exporting to direct investment when it established a UK manufacturing base in the 1980s. Despite a relatively small share of the UK market at the time, the development of the European Single Market offered the potential of huge ongoing rewards. Case Insight 7.1 highlighted how Lanson uses different market entry methods in different markets, sometimes using distributors and at other times developing an overseas office (for example North America).

The entry method selected should fit the type of offering and the nature of the competition. For example, some offerings, such as fast-food restaurants and coffee houses, lend themselves to **franchising**; others, including textiles and car components, lend themselves to offshore manufacturing. Regional products, such as wine, cheese, chocolate, and luxury food items, are typically exported directly, or indirectly via distributors/agents.

Indirect Exporting

Indirect exporting refers to the situation in which production and manufacture occur in the domestic market, but an intermediary is employed to sell the offering into the foreign market. For example, New Cambridge and Hands-On are two agencies in Thailand that act on behalf of numerous British universities.

In this model, an exporting manufacturer seeks to benefit from an intermediary's knowledge, its contacts and business networks, and its experience in the target market. This reduces the producer's risk, but the size of the producer's potential rewards is reduced to compensate the intermediary. This approach is a good way for SMEs with limited resources to test a target market.

Licensing, Franchising, and Contracting

When making the decision to manufacture abroad, firms may consider entry approaches including licensing, franchising, and/or **contracting**. Licensing occurs when an organization (the licensor) grants another (the licensee) the right to manufacture goods, use patents or particular processes, or exploit trademarks in a particular market. For example, ARM Holdings licenses its microprocessor technology to **original equipment manufacturer (OEM)** companies worldwide, with regional sales teams based in the United States, Europe, China, Japan, Korea, Taiwan, and India. Licensing is relatively low risk and inexpensive, and can generate income from foreign markets by avoiding high import tariffs and the high costs of direct investment. However, this method offers limited control of the brand, and possible risks include the licensee damaging the licensor's reputation and image as a result of poor product quality and ineffective marketing. It might also create a problem in that once the licensee has obtained the necessary expertise and knowledge for manufacture of the offering, if there is insufficient legal protection in place it may be able to develop its own offering and replace the licensor. Coca-Cola and Pilkington Glass are both famous examples of companies that have used licensing to develop a global presence.

Franchising is used when the brand owner (the franchisor) authorizes another organization (the franchisee) to produce or market an offering according to certain criteria laid down by the franchisor in return for fees and/or royalties. Franchising is a way in which a company can both leverage income from its brand (because licensees pay franchise fees and royalties) and extend the brand's market coverage. The most successful franchise operations are household names, including KFC, SUBWAY®, McDonald's, and Inter IKEA systems (the owner of the IKEA trademarks).

The main benefits of franchising are managerial and financial. Financially, a firm can achieve rapid growth in market coverage, with the franchisee bearing the most risk through their investment in capital assets, such as equipment and premises, working capital, and other operating costs. However, the effectiveness of this form of market entry method relies on the strength of the franchisor–franchisee relationship, the commitment of the franchisee, the resources and support provided by the franchisor, and market interest in the franchise brand. Burger King, owned by Restaurant Brands International, had 16,767 franchises by the end of 2017, generating around US$20.1 billion of revenues (RBI, 2018). The brand has established itself in more than 100 countries, including restaurants in Brazil, Turkey, Russia, and China (RBI, 2018).

Contracting refers to situations in which a manufacturer contracts an organization in a foreign market to manufacture or assemble a product in that market. This approach avoids the costs involved in the physical distribution and supply chain issues associated with producing the offering in the home market and selling it overseas. Unlike licensing, contractors have control over all marketing activities. This method is also flexible because it avoids problems of currency fluctuations, import barriers, and the high costs and knowledge required for international distribution.

Visit the **online resources** and complete Internet Activity 7.2 to learn more about how Yum! brands uses franchising to develop its Pizza Hut, KFC, and Taco Bell brands.

M&S franchises M&S Lingerie and Beauty stores, like this one in Jeddah in Saudi Arabia, through Alhokair Fashion Retail
Source: © Paul Baines.

Direct Exporting

Direct exporting requires the manufacturing organization itself to distribute the offering directly to customers in foreign markets. Here, the organization treats its international customers in the same way as its domestic market customers. It takes responsibility for finding and selecting customers, agents, and distributors, and directly supporting their efforts. The direct exporting approach can be time-consuming and expensive. However, it gives manufacturers more control and generates higher profits than are possible when using intermediaries. Further advantages include direct access to market intelligence and the building of a clear presence in the market. For example, Spain is the world's largest exporter of wine by volume—particularly to France, where it is frequently resold as French wine (Burgen, 2015). Bulldog, a British brand of male grooming products, launches into overseas markets (for example Sweden, South Korea) by developing relationships with key retailers (Hurley, 2015).

Joint Ventures

When a foreign organization and a domestic organization join forces, either by buying into each other or by establishing a separate jointly owned enterprise, a joint venture is created. By working together, the participant organizations have enough resources to develop or enter a foreign market. For example, one partner might have the finance; the other, the know-how. Sometimes, a joint venture is the only way in which an organization can enter into or gain a foothold in a foreign market, for example because of legislation. Joint ventures tend to have a limited lifespan because the needs of each party alter and develop over time. They work best in sectors in which there is a high degree of local adaptation to the market.

Factors that contribute to a successful joint venture partnership include:

- ensuring an appropriate balance of power;
- developing strong communication channels between the partners at several points of contact and levels;
- developing a mechanism for conflict resolution (for example before an issue goes to court);
- clarity of agreed inputs and divisions of benefits;
- jointly defined goals and parameters;
- compatibility in how the two partners operate and their strategic visions;
- equal commitment from both partners; and
- complementary skills for mutual benefit.

Direct Investment

Direct investment or foreign manufacture involves some form of manufacturing or production in the target country. Advantages include a commitment to the local market, fast availability of parts, and market detection of changes in the local environment. The extent of direct investment can range from the assembly of parts through to innovation led by research and development (R&D). Another means of market entry through direct investment is the acquisition or takeover of an organization in the foreign market. Nevertheless, it is very important to monitor how effective an overseas investment is over time. Sometimes, it is necessary to exit from an investment. Tesco's exit from its US supermarket business Fresh & Easy in late 2012 was painful because it had made no profit. By 2015, Tesco was also seeking a buyer for its South Korean business Homeplus to partially pay off its debt mountain of £21.7 billion (Jung-A, Mundy, and Sender, 2015).

International Market Development

Entering international markets has been a feature of civilizations for thousands of years, ever since the first 'money'—based on metal objects—changed hands in commercial transactions around 5000BC (Bellis, 2018). However, in the last two centuries, international trade has grown enormously in scale and complexity. With this growth, different approaches to international market development have developed.

Some firms take an ad hoc approach to international marketing, responding to customer export requests only on a reactive basis. Others, such as H&M and BMW, develop an international marketing strategy proactively, to complement their domestic strategy. In the UK, for example, the Royal Mint is the world's leading exporter of circulating coin-based currency, with 15 per cent of the available market (Anon., 2015a). However, for some, international market development is their only marketing strategy and their domestic operations are considered of minor importance. Standard Chartered, a company formed as a result of the merger of two banks founded in London in the 1850s, has more than 90,000 staff in 71 countries. Much of its business comes from international markets; only 6.7 per cent of its business now comes from Europe (Standard Chartered, 2014). Regardless, the approach selected should depend on the resources available, the industry, and the type of offering. For example, some offerings, such as smartphones, airplane manufacture, and tourism, are international by nature. The high degree of investment in R&D in these industries necessitates a move into international markets because domestic markets may not provide sufficient sales and profit.

A seminal study by Johanson and Vahlne (1977) determined that companies tend to build up their commitment to international operations as they gain more knowledge about that market and gain increased confidence in their operations as their activities in that country are increased. Previously, researchers at Uppsala University in Sweden (Johanson and Wiedersheim-Paul, 1975) had identified that most firms followed a four-stage process of internationalization, starting with serving the domestic market, then penetrating foreign markets by exporting, then developing sales offices in the foreign market, and then developing foreign production facilities. This model, often referred to as the 'Uppsala Model', is based on the idea that internationalization is a slow, effortful process that happens over time as a firm acquires more knowledge about the new market in which it operates. As knowledge of the new country increases, managers feel more comfortable committing resources specifically to the new market. At this stage, managers will evaluate carefully both the specificity and amount of resources required. Very specific resources are investments that are tied very closely to a specific market. For example, a manufacturer might decide to adopt a production standard that matches the regulations of one specific country. The amount of resources relates to the size of the financial investment required to access a new market. Since knowledge of the market is critical, internationalization choices under this model

Research Insight 7.1

To take your learning further, you might wish to read this influential paper:

Chetty, S., and Campbell-Hunt, C. (2004). A strategic approach to internationalization: a traditional versus a 'born-global' approach. *Journal of International Marketing*, 12(1), 57–81.

Based on research undertaken amongst New Zealand firms, this article critiques the notion that there is a standard approach to internationalizing a brand and suggests that some brands, rather than launching from domestic markets, have to target international marketing from their very inception. The article illustrates the complex choices faced by firms that internationalize and examines how internationalizing, as a process, can in itself change an organization. The analysis of the case studies shows that most organizations do not exactly fit either the 'born global' or 'traditional' views. The authors argue that the 'born global' perspective, rather than describing a new type of company, refers to different market conditions in which rapid internationalization and global innovations force companies to internationalize faster than might have been expected in the past.

 Visit the online resources to read the abstract and access the full paper.

tend to be influenced by managers' perception of 'psychic distance' between countries. This term refers to managers' perception of difference between the characteristics of two countries. Typically, managers start internationalizing in countries with low psychic distance first.

Although the Uppsala model is often useful to understand the early stages of internationalization of firms, especially in the case of manufacturers, firms increasingly develop an international business orientation from their inception (known as **born global** firms). For example, Chetty and Campbell-Hunt (2004) found a cluster of New Zealand firms that display this tendency, principally because they cannot survive in the relatively small market that New Zealand represents (see Research Insight 7.1). They identified significant differences in how born global firms operate compared with those that internationalize traditionally, as outlined in Table 7.3.

Table 7.3 Key differences between traditional and born global approaches to internationalization

Internationalization attributes	Traditional internationalization view	Born global view
Home market	Domestic market developed first	Domestic market irrelevant because often too small
Previous internationalization experience	None expected	Founder likely to have extensive experience in relevant international markets
Extent of internationalization	Foreign markets developed sequentially	Many foreign markets developed simultaneously
Psychic distance	Markets entered in order of psychic distance	Psychic distance irrelevant
Learning to internationalize	Markets entered at a pace of learning about new markets	Learning occurs rapidly because of superior internationalization knowledge
Firm strategy	Not central to motivation to internationalize	Realization of competition requires rapid internationalization
Use of information and communication technologies	Not central to internationalization	Enabler of global market reach (e.g. the Internet, social media) and learning
Networks of business partners	Used in early stages and replaced as internal resources developed	Rapid development of global reach requires comprehensive network of partners
Time to internationalize	Not crucial to firm success; slow	Crucial to firm success; rapid

Source: Adapted from Chetty and Campbell-Hunt (2004).

Perlmutter's (1969) EPRG classification specifies four strategic orientations towards international market development: ethnocentric, polycentric, regional, and geocentric (see Figure 7.4). The first two of these assume a localized approach:

- An **ethnocentric approach** views the domestic market (home market) as the most important, with foreign markets not perceived as a serious threat.

- With a **polycentric approach**, each overseas market is seen as a separate domestic market and the organization seeks to position itself as local to that country. In some instances, each market has its own manufacturing and marketing operations, with only a limited overlap.

The last two approaches adopt a **standardized approach**:

- A **regional approach** groups countries together, usually on a geographical basis, for example Europe or Europe, Middle East, and Asia (EMEA), and provides for the specific needs of consumers within those countries. In this instance, national boundaries are respected, but do not have the same importance as cultural differences.

- A **geocentric approach** assumes that the world is a single global market, with the organization targeting global segments, for example high net worth individuals (HNWIs), and global opportunities to rationalize communications, production, and product development.

Lynch (1994) categorizes a company's strategic nature based on the size of its geographic operations using five categories, as follows.

- *Local scale*—These are organizations operating within national and local boundaries with little opportunity or desire to trade internationally (for example the local hair salon or the body repair garage working mainly for insurance companies).

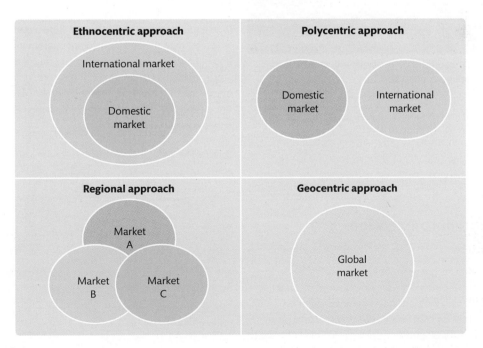

Figure 7.4

EPRG strategic orientations for international marketing

Market Insight 7.4
Primark Extends Its Growth by Entering the US Market

Primark is a fast-growing Irish retailer, operating 345 stores in 11 countries. It is owned by Associated British Foods, proprietor of such well-known brands as Allinson's, Twinings, Ovaltine, Patak's, Jordan, and Ryvita, among many others. Primark started life as Penneys in Dublin in 1969 (and now has 36 stores in Ireland), but has quickly grown from its domestic base by launching stores around the world. The company relatively quickly set up in the UK in 1973, Spain in 2006, the Netherlands in 2008, Portugal, Germany, and Belgium in 2009, Austria in 2012, France in 2013, and the United States in 2015. In 2016, the company opened its first store in Italy, in Arese Milan.

Primark's irresistible growth: will the United States prove a step too far?

Source: © Lou Jones www.fotojones.com.

Primark has enjoyed rapid growth over the last decade, with sales rising by 140 per cent. Its strategy of selling good-quality clothing at very cheap prices seems to be a hit everywhere. The company works hard to maintain its low-cost leadership by means of lean supply chain management practices, limited marketing spend, and high-volume procurement. Analysts reckoned that the company was worth up to £24 billion in 2017.

Whilst the European launches seemed an obvious next step, the US launch seemed risky. Such a move pitted the company directly against strong brands such as Ross, TJ Maxx, Marshalls, Old Navy, Forever 21, Gap, and H&M. Nonetheless, early signals seemed positive and, in 2016, the company decided to open nine more stores to add to its initial two locations in Boston and Philadelphia—and this at a time when Gap was having a tough time, announcing significant store closures in North America. Naysayers might also cite Tesco's failure in the US market after it launched Fresh & Easy in California, costing it £1.2 billion. According to a Barclay's survey, more than half of British retailers think the United States is the hardest market to enter, beating China in second place, despite sharing the same language. One reason cited for retail market entry failure in the United States is considering the market to be homogeneous, rather than a patchwork quilt of different states, each of which is characterized by different customer attitudes and behaviours. Typically, on the first day of a new store opening, customers mob the store, grabbing everything they can find. The question is: will the Americans feel the same 'Primania' as their European counterparts?

Sources: Morris (2013); Shawcross (2014); Anon. (2015b); ABF (n.d.).

Theory into Practice

This market insight describes how a retailer is developing its international markets. Primark appears to be following the traditional internationalization approach whereby it develops an international position once it has developed its own domestic market (Ireland and particularly the UK). However, the US market is often regarded as a very different market from the UK, because customer practice and the culture are significantly different.

Market Insight 7.4
continued

Related Topics
market selection; market entry method; psychic distance; psychological proximity; foreign direct investment; culture

1 Using Perlmutter's (1969) strategic orientation classification (EPRG), how would you classify the scale of Primark's operations?

2 Why do you think Primark has decided on entering the US market? (Hint: Consider what market selection criteria it used.)

3 What does Primark need to do to succeed in the US market where other European retailers have failed?

- *National scale*—This refers to those organizations that focus on the domestic market, but which find opportunities from foreign markets based on ad hoc customer enquiries.

- *Regional scale*—These are organizations focusing on specific regions within a regional trading bloc (for example the European Union or **Mercosur**), as opposed to operating throughout that trading bloc (for example all five full members of Mercosur, rather than only, say, Paraguay), and gain experience of operating abroad on a smaller scale. For example, Norwegian and Swedish organizations have a long tradition of trade relations with other Scandinavian countries as a first experience of cross-national trade.

- *European scale*—With increasing changes in the European Union and the rise in the number of member states, many organizations have turned their attention to marketing throughout Europe. Some argue that Europe is, in fact, one geographic market with a number of segments that transcend national boundaries, especially as some of the risks of international trade have been reduced or eliminated (for example currency, with the introduction of the euro). However, some differences will remain forever (for example language, culture, infrastructure), requiring differing investment in communications, product, and channel development.

- *World scale*—These organizations have a strong European base, but now operate in a range of different world markets through direct investment or joint venture, or on an exporting basis. For example, P&G, Shell, AstraZeneca, and Danone derive a significant portion of sales from outside Europe. One example is Primark, a leading Irish clothing retailer striving for world-scale operations through its market expansions into the United States (see Market Insight 7.4).

International Market Development as a Growth Strategy

Marketing strategy is about matching market opportunities to an organization's resources (what it can do) and its objectives (what management wants it to achieve). Successful strategies begin with the identification of attractive market opportunities using Ansoff's matrix (see Figure 7.5). This matrix is also referred to as the product–market matrix. It provides a useful way of considering the relationship between strategic direction and market opportunities (see Chapter 5 for a detailed consideration). This matrix provides four broad strategic options available to organizations, depending on whether the product and/or the market are considered to be new to, or existing within, an organization.

The matrix illustrates, implicitly, that risk increases the further the strategy moves away from known positions—an existing product and/or an existing market. Product development (a new proposition) and market development (a new market) typically involve greater risk than market penetration (existing offering and existing market). Diversification, a new offering in a new market, carries the greatest risk of all. Although four types of opportunity are presented, some organizations pursue more than one type simultaneously. Here, we pay specific attention to the strategy of market development, from an international perspective.

A market development strategy involves increasing sales by selling existing offerings in new markets, either by gaining new customers domestically or by entering new markets internationally. The goal is to sell more of the same things to different people. We might target different geographical markets at home and/or abroad, or target different segments—perhaps demonstrating a different behavioural profile from that of our existing customers. For example, Ryanair's airline offering was first marketed at those seeking low-cost travel, but has recently been aimed, with some service enhancements (such as priority boarding, seat choice), at business travellers. Another example is the use of military equipment repurposed for consumer purposes, such as the American Motor Corporation's Hummer, which was originally based on the high mobility multipurpose wheeled vehicle (HMMWV), or Humvee, built for the US military. We have also seen chains such as Gregg's, a British baker, expanding into new geographical locations domestically by targeting new audiences through differing retail outlets in motorway service stations, and Dixons, the British electrical group, set up Dixons Travel, an airport retail chain. These are all examples of developing new markets domestically for an existing offering.

Entering a new international market with an existing offering represents a high-risk strategy. To build brand awareness and minimize risk, organizations often rely on the reputation of their brands in domestic markets. For example, Aston Martin's foray into the Chinese market is a good example of international market development (see Case Insight 13.1).

Types of International Organization

Based on their international marketing strategies, it is possible to identify different types of organization that operate in international markets. There are several typologies that can be derived, particularly from the work of Keegan (1989), Bartlett and Ghoshal (1991), and de Mooij (1994).

	Present products	New products
Present markets	Market penetration	Product development
New markets	Market development	Diversification

Figure 7.5

Ansoff's matrix

Source: Adapted from Ansoff (1957).

Their view is that organizations can be regarded as national, international, multinational, global, or transnational (see Table 7.4), each of which has different strategic orientations towards customers and markets.

Organizations operate domestically using a marketing mix designed to meet the needs of the home market. This usually means offering a standardized proposition. Some domestic organizations evolve into international organizations as they win 'overseas' business. The first step is to use their domestically oriented marketing mix and then, at a later stage, to adapt it to the needs of the new 'overseas' market.

This adaptation phase signals the emergence of a multinational strategy and corresponding type of organization. These organizations regard the world in which they operate as comprising discrete regions, with each requiring its own marketing mix. Each country or area reports to an international head office and performance is geared to meet financial targets.

As growth occurs and more regions are brought into an organization's scope, so it transforms into a global enterprise. Global organizations are characterized by strategies founded on an understanding that the similarities across country or area markets, not the differences between

Table 7.4 Types of international organization

Type of organization	Explanation
National organizations	These organizations operate within domestic borders. The marketing policy is to serve customers with a single marketing mix. In multiple retail grocery, examples include Jumbo (the Netherlands), Morrisons (UK), and Axfood AB (Sweden), which owns the Willys and Hemköp retail outlets.
International organizations	These organizations see their overseas operations as attachments to a central domestic organization. The marketing policy is to serve customers domestically and offer these same marketing mixes in other countries (e.g. Burger King).
Multinational organizations	These organizations see their overseas activities as a portfolio of independent businesses. The policy is to serve customers with customized country-specific marketing mixes (e.g. Royal Dutch Shell).
Global organizations	These organizations regard their overseas activities as feeders or delivery tubes for a unified global market. The policy is to serve the global market with a standardized marketing mix (e.g. Nike).
Transnational organizations	These organizations regard their overseas activities as a complex process of coordination and cooperation. Decision-making is shared. The policy is to serve global business environments using flexible global resources to formulate different global marketing mixes. For example, ArcelorMittal, Vodafone, and Nestlé all hold over 90 per cent of their assets abroad.

Sources: Adapted from Bartlett and Ghoshal (1991) and de Mooij (1994); Anon. (2012)

them, are important. Customers are seen as part of a single global picture; therefore a standardized marketing mix is preferred. All decision-making is centralized.

Transnational organizations develop out of global enterprises. These are relatively sophisticated companies that establish operations in many countries around the world based on wholly or partially owned subsidiaries. The headquarters is the hub of the operations, based in one country, but managing the operations across all other countries. Transnational companies seek to serve global customers by developing efficient operations. These are based on utilizing technologies to generate synergies through the 'creation, accumulation, transferring and sharing of knowledge that exists in different locations' (de Pablos, 2006: 556).

Organizations need to be flexible and adapt to changing market conditions. As domestic markets stagnate, and technology and communication opportunities develop, opportunities come and go. In addition, organizations seek efficiency and flexibility with regard to their use of materials and resources. The use of strategic alliances and outsourcing arrangements complements this goal, and network-based organizations spanning the globe emerge. Li & Fung, based out of Hong Kong, is a case example of a multinational consumer goods design, development, sourcing, and logistics company, providing a global supply chain capability to many high-street brands.

Understanding these different types of international organization is important not only from a structural perspective, but also for the formulation and implementation of business and marketing strategies. Next, we explore ways in which organizations develop their operations, the decisions they make, and the factors and issues influencing their decision-making.

International Competitive Strategy

When entering international markets, the key competitive decision to make is to what extent the firm should standardize or adapt its marketing strategy. According to Zou and Cavusgil (2002), a firm should adapt its promotional efforts only when it needs to, to respond to customer needs, media usage, or advertising regulation. In an analysis of the rise of global competition, Hout, Porter, and Rudden (1982) suggest that, strategically, an organization can adopt different degrees of adaptation to markets based on a local or global, and a multidomestic or a global competitive approach to their international marketing strategy (see Figure 7.6). Research Insight 7.2 looks in more detail at standardization as an international marketing decision.

Multi-Domestic Competitive Strategy

With a **multi-domestic competitive strategy**, organizations pursue separate marketing strategies in each foreign market and consider how to compete on the basis of each market. This can also be referred to as an adaptive orientation because organizations adapt their operations,

Figure 7.6
The spectrum of competitive strategies

Research Insight 7.2

To take your learning further, you might wish to read this influential paper:

Katsikeas, C.S., Samiee, S., and Theodosiu, M. (2006). Strategy fit and performance consequences of international marketing standardization. *Strategic Management Journal*, **27(9), 867–90.**

This article examines under what conditions companies are more likely to opt for a standardized international strategy and explores the performance implications of standardization. The analysis is based on the study of the UK subsidiaries of German, US, and Japanese multinationals. The authors show that companies are more likely to standardize when their home market is similar to the foreign market both in relation to macroeconomic factors (for example regulatory environment, technological intensity, traditions), as well as microeconomic factors (for example customer characteristics and competitive intensity). Standardization yields superior performance under conditions of high fit between the environmental context and the choice of strategy. The article has important implications because it suggests to practitioners under what conditions strategic standardization is more likely to be successful.

 Visit the **online resources** to read the abstract and access the full paper.

procurement, and market research or insight generation to a particular country, and develop a strategy for that specific market (see also Chapter 4). Consequently, cultural, legal, language, communication, and geographical differences in each market are accounted for. For example, Malaysian casino and resorts group Gentings has adapted its London Chinatown offering to include baccarat to appeal to wealthy Chinese tourists (Blitz, 2014). Fashion is an industry with significant differences in style—particularly street style—between countries such as the United States, France, Italy, the UK, and China. There are also differences in terms of who are perceived to be influential bloggers and fashion designers in the different countries.

In any company, a central headquarters might coordinate financial controls, R&D activities, and marketing policies worldwide, but strategy and operations are often decentralized. Each subsidiary is considered to be a profit centre, and is expected to contribute earnings and growth consistent with market opportunity, with competition on a market-by-market basis (Hout et al., 1982). (See also Market Insight 7.5 for an understanding of how advertising might need to be adapted when operating in different regions.)

Global Competitive Strategy

Globalization refers to the process by which all that we experience in life is becoming standardized worldwide through the free flow of goods and services, people, capital, and information (Sirgy et al., 2007). Globalization is accompanied by the increasing consolidation of organizations within various industries, including pharmaceuticals, financial services, and airlines.

The importance and significance of global trade was first identified by Levitt (1983: 92–3), who stated that 'the global cooperation operates with resolute constancy—at low relative cost—as if the entire world (or major regions of it) were a single entity; it sells the same things in the same

Market Insight 7.5
Ad-Apt in São Paulo?

When companies internationalize, they face many strategic questions, such as: where shall we go? How shall we internationalize? Which parts of our marketing strategy should we adapt to the local market and which can we standardize across all of our markets? Whilst many of these decisions are not directly visible to the consumer, one aspect most consumers will be in direct contact with is advertising. Almost all companies, from Coca-Cola to Google, and industries, from fashion to food, adapt their advertising strategies to the local markets in which they operate. Consider Snickers, for example. The world's biggest chocolate bar produced a truly global brand idea with the slogan, 'You're not you when you're hungry', but then adapted its advertisements to feature local celebrities and symbolism to make the advertisement relevant to the target market in which the individual ad was shown. Similarly, IKEA sells an almost identical lifestyle across the globe, but adapts its advertising to local markets. Photos of its famous catalogue are adjusted to reflect the cultural values of the local target audience.

But what does a firm do when it has identified a great new potential market and it finds out that the market forbids advertising?!

In 2007, São Paulo, the world's seventh largest and Brazil's most important city, became the first city in the world to put into effect a radical near-complete ban on outdoor advertising. São Paulo introduced *Lei Cidade Limpa* (the Clean City Law). Asserting that the city needed to combat various forms of pollution, the then mayor said: 'We decided that we should start combating pollution with the most conspicuous sector—visual pollution.' The law bans the use of all outdoor advertisements, including billboards, transit, and front-of-store advertisements. Even pamphleteering in public spaces was made illegal. Imagine a city of 11 million inhabitants stripped of all its advertising!

São Paulo consumers breathe easily after the advertising ban, but advertisers choke!
Source: © Bloomberg/Getty.

Clearly, not everyone was in full support. The new law raised great concern among local and global businesses: how would they convey their advertising messages to their customers? They argued that the advertising ban would entail a revenue loss of US$133 million at 2007 prices. Consumers even argued that the loss of advertising billboards would take away from São Paulo's identity and that the city would lose the appeal of a world metropolis. Imagine London without Piccadilly Circus's neon billboards, or Times Square in New York without its neon billboards!

Yet, despite the initial uproar, the ad ban has been a success, yielding approval rates of more than 70 per cent among the city's residents. And it seems that the movement to ban ads in cities is catching on: in 2009, Chennai in India banned billboards, as did several US states, followed by Grenoble in 2014 (which banned all street advertising). The difficulty, though, is that cities earn significant revenues from their partnerships with advertising companies. Even São Paolo has seen some of its advertising return, albeit in a much more organized fashion. Nevertheless, the question remains: how do you advertise if the city pulls your ambient advertising space and what do you lose by shifting to alternative advertising forms?

Sources: Douglas and Wind (1987); Mahdawi (2015).

Market Insight 7.5
continued

Theory into Practice

This market insight describes how companies entering the Brazilian market—specifically, the city of São Paolo (and, by extension, other cities in which advertising is restricted or banned)—need to identify new ways of communicating with their customers. The example shows that companies should never take for granted how they can best communicate with their customers. It also shows that firms need to assess the regulatory and marketing environments before selecting a market and developing the entry method.

Related Topics

standardization–adaptation; market entry; culture; regulatory environment; marketing environment; marketing communications; advertising

1 **As a result of the ban, do you think São Paulo has become an unattractive market for international and global brands?**

2 **What kind of creative new advertising strategies might these companies use to overcome their inability to engage in outdoor advertising? Which advertising channels become more important?**

3 **Would you advise these companies to use adapted or standardized advertising campaigns in this particular market?**

This market insight was kindly contributed by Dr Frauke Mattison Thompson, Universiteit van Amsterdam, The Netherlands.

way everywhere'. However, there have also been detractors from this argument, who assert that whilst it was appropriate to operate a globally competitive approach to business, the key to success is to customize the offering, adapting it to local needs (Quelch and Hoff, 1986). This debate is still ongoing.

A global competitive strategy represents a standardized approach. This requires that organizations see the world as one large (global) market and that they sell the same propositions in the same way throughout the world, ignoring local, regional, and national differences. Standardization assumes that global cultures are converging and that any cultural differences are superficial (Wind and Perlmutter, 1973; Levitt, 1983; Douglas and Wind, 1987). The attractions of the standardization approach include improved operational efficiencies, enhanced customer preference, increased competitive leverage, and, importantly, substantial cost reductions (Herbig and Day, 1993). Objectors to this approach argue that cultural, legal, and national differences inhibit trade, especially when an organization assumes that differences are superficial. They argue that there might be genuine psychic difference—a difference between the people of the two countries (domestic and foreign markets) in how they perceive or use a particular offering (Evans, 2010). For example, when Carlsberg launched Somersby Cider into the Swiss market, it used a novel approach even though the brand was already on sale in 35 countries. It recruited an online consumer panel to co-create a brand awareness campaign, and then sent each member a crate of 24 bottles, as well as 2,000 bottles to friends of the panel members, and asked them all to have a party, and take pictures and post them online. This approach raised awareness of the brand from 6 per cent to 20 per cent the day before the formal product launch took place (Anon., 2015b). Communication is one of the biggest barriers to effective international marketing and is heightened when the standardization approach is used. One outcome is that advertising messages can be badly phrased or misinterpreted (see Table 7.1).

One way of evaluating the extent of psychic distance between home and target markets is to formally analyse them using the mnemonic CAGE (Ghemawat, 2001), which requires that the marketer consider a possible target market against a home market based on the dimensions of:

- *culture*—for example languages, religion, social norms;

- *administration*—for example, government policies, colonial ties;

- *geography*—for example physical remoteness, size of country, climate differences; and

- the *economy*—for example, differences in consumer incomes, cost of labour.

An effective global competitive strategy comprises two elements. The first is **selective contestability**—that is, the ability to contest successfully in any international market in which an organization chooses to compete. It is based on the core marketing principles of segmentation, targeting, and positioning—that is, the STP process (see Chapter 6). This requires that generic markets are divided into meaningful sub-markets, or segments, that the most attractive of these

Somersby Cider was launched into the Swiss market with an innovative brand awareness campaign
Source: © tofino/Alamy Stock Photo.

are then selected, and that the offering is consequently positioned appropriately. This process lies at the very heart of any competitive strategy, irrespective of whether or not the organization is competing in a regional, national, or global market.

The second element is **global capability**. This concerns an organization's ability to bring its entire worldwide resources to bear on any competitive situation, irrespective of location. A global brand goes far beyond an organization's physical presence in differing national markets, reflecting the existence of a global image. This universal recognition distinguishes an organization pursuing a focused strategy in numerous national markets. Examples include global players such as Apple (consumer electronics), Microsoft (software), Intercontinental Hotel Group (hotels), and Spar (convenience stores).

It is worth pointing out that not everyone believes globalization to be a good thing. As a consequence, an anti-globalization movement has developed to compete directly with the legitimacy and power of multinational corporations. In particular, anti-globalization protesters argue that multinationals abuse labour, particularly in developing countries, fail to pay sufficient taxes, sandblast out cultural differences with standardized products, and trample on individual liberty. (We discuss some of these issues further in Chapter 18.) Sometimes, protests can be focused on specific countries for political reasons and this can have negative implications for international brands from the targeted nation. Research Insight 7.3 discusses in more detail this phenomenon of consumer animosity towards a foreign country.

 Visit the **online resources** and complete Internet Activity 7.3 to learn more about how companies such as KFC use a 'glocal' approach by acting globally, but adapting to local differences.

 ## Research Insight 7.3

To take your learning further, you might wish to read this influential paper:

Riefler, P., and Diamantopoulos, A. (2007). Consumer animosity: a literature review and a reconsideration of its measurement. *International Marketing Review*, 27(1), 87–119.

This article offers a systematic review of an important stream of research on the determinants of foreign purchase behaviour. Scholars have noticed how international crises between countries stemming from political, economic, or military causes can lead to feelings of animosity against a target nation. These feelings of animosity can affect products originating from the target country, with consumers rejecting the foreign offerings associated with the disliked nation. For example, some Chinese consumers feel resentful towards Japan, because of past military conflicts between the two countries, and tend to avoid purchasing Japanese brands. Country animosity poses difficult challenges for marketers who need to decide how to handle this negative bias. One solution would be to avoid positioning the offering on any associations related to its country of origin. In cases in which this is not possible, firms need to consider communication campaigns and local investment to improve the perception of the company irrespective of any negative country-of-origin association.

 Visit the online resources to read the abstract and access the full paper.

Chapter Summary

To consolidate your learning, the key points from this chapter are summarized here:

- **Identify the key drivers for international market development.**

  Many factors motivate an organization to develop markets in international markets. These include historical accident, the need to move excess stock, limited growth in domestic markets, comparative advantages, economies of scale, trade liberalization, technological changes, customer relationships, the development of transnational market segments through immigration, and organizational sustainability.

- **Discuss how environmental factors influence the choice of international marketing strategy decisions.**

  The analysis of environmental forces can help to identify which countries or regions should be given priority and which market entry strategy would be best suited to that country or region. Factors to consider include social, cultural, and consumption attitudes, and technological, economic, political, and legal factors.

- **Describe the criteria used to identify and select international markets.**

  Assessing market attractiveness is very important because different markets have varying levels of attractiveness. Markets may be chosen according to various criteria, including market accessibility, market and population size, geographic proximity, psychological proximity or psychic distance, the level and quality of competition already in the market, the costs of entering the market, and the market's profit potential.

- **Explore various international market entry methods.**

  The decision regarding which method to use to enter a foreign market is based on six main factors: speed and timing; costs and the required levels of investment; flexibility; risk and uncertainty; expected return on investment (ROI); and the long-term objectives. Once reviewed, organizations use one or more of the following methods of entry: indirect exporting; licensing; franchising; contracting; direct exporting; joint ventures; and direct investment.

- **Define international market development as a market growth strategy.**

  Given the increasing internationalization of world markets, increased foreign trade, and international travel, international marketing is frequently a core activity for many organizations. A market development strategy involves increasing sales by selling existing offerings in new markets, either by targeting new audiences domestically or entering new markets internationally. International market development is growing in importance because of changes in the economic, social, and political landscape. The main considerations are the degree of risk and adjustment an organization is willing to undertake and the identification of potential opportunities within foreign markets.

- **List the different forms of international marketing strategy.**

  When entering international markets, a key competitive decision is whether the approach should be to standardize or adapt the marketing strategy. Organizations can adopt a local or global, or multi-domestic or global competitive international marketing strategy. The decision is based on the type of offering, the attitudes of the organization, and the resources available for market entry.

 # Review Questions

1 What factors influence international market development strategies?
2 Identify the key differences between multi-domestic and global competitive strategies.
3 What criteria should an organization use to assess the attractiveness of a foreign market?

4 Outline the main cultural differences that can affect international marketing.

5 What methods can an organization use to enter a foreign market?

6 What criteria should be considered when selecting an entry method to an international market?

7 When would an organization standardize, rather than adapt, its offering or promotional approach?

8 What are the key differences between indirect and direct exporting?

9 Identify the benefits of using franchises in international marketing.

10 What key success factors are associated with international joint ventures?

 # Discussion Questions

1 Having read Case Insight 7.1, how would you advise Lanson International to further differentiate itself in its category in the UK market? How would you also advise Lanson to develop its international markets?

2 Which of the following factors would have the greatest impact on a fashion retailer's assessment of the attractiveness of a foreign market: political; legal; socio-cultural; or technological? Why?

3 How do cultural factors influence a company's decision on how to enter a foreign market?

4 Marketed heavily on the basis of their country-of-origin brand image, what impact do you think joint ventures with domestic vineyards or direct investment would have on the perception of wine brands in a foreign market?

 Visit the online resources and complete the Multiple-Choice Questions to assess your knowledge of Chapter 7.

 # Glossary

born global refers to those firms that develop an international orientation to their business immediately without developing an offering within their domestic market first.

comparative advantage the ability to produce goods and/or services at a lower opportunity cost than other firms or individuals.

consumer price indices (CPIs) a measure of the current prices of a basket of goods in a particular country, usually expressed in US dollars in purchasing power parity terms (that is, allowing for comparisons between currencies).

contracting where a manufacturer contracts an organization in a foreign market to manufacture or assemble the product in that foreign market.

culture the values, beliefs, ideas, customs, actions, and symbols that are learned and shared by people within particular societies.

direct exporting where the manufacturing firm itself distributes its product offering directly to customers in foreign markets.

direct investment also known as foreign manufacture, some form of manufacture or production in the foreign or host country, which is sometimes necessary.

economies of scale the reduction in cost of each additional unit as production increases and operational efficiencies are realized.

ethnocentric approach an approach whereby the domestic market (home market) is seen to be the most important and overseas markets as inferior, with foreign imports not seen as representing a serious threat.

franchising a contractual vertical marketing system in which a franchisor licenses a franchisee to produce or market goods or services to a certain standard laid down by the franchisor in return for fees and/or royalties.

Generation Y people born in the 1980s and 1990s, regarded as being familiar with digital technologies.

geocentric approach an approach that sees the world as a single market—global—in which the organization looks for global segments (for example ageing customers) and global opportunities to rationalize communications, production, and product development.

global capability the willingness and capability to operate anywhere in the world, the direct result of which is global brand recognition.

globalization refers to increasing global connectivity, integration, and interdependence in the economic, social, technological, cultural, political, and ecological spheres.

gross national product (GNP) total domestic and foreign added value claimed by residents of a state.

indirect exporting where the production and manufacture of the product offering occurs in the domestic market and involves the services of other companies (intermediaries) to sell the product in the foreign market.

international marketing marketing activity that crosses national boundaries.

joint venture where two organizations come together to create a jointly owned third company; an example of cooperative, as opposed to competitive, operations in international marketing.

licensing a commercial process whereby the trademark of an established brand is used by another organization over a defined period of time in a defined area, in return for a fee, to develop another brand.

lingua franca a bridge, or third language—that is, a language shared by two communicators of different nationalities who speak two other languages.

Mercosur derived from the full name, Mercado Común del Sur, a regional Latin American trading bloc designed to promote free trade, and the movement of people and currency; its full members are Argentina, Bolivia, Brazil, Paraguay, Uruguay, and Venezuela; its associate members are Chile, Peru, Colombia, and Ecuador.

multi-domestic competitive strategy where an organization pursues a separate marketing strategy in each of its foreign markets while viewing the competitive challenge independently from market to market.

original equipment manufacturer (OEM) a manufacturer that sells another company's product, service, or technology, often as a component of an integrated offering, under its own name and brand.

polycentric approach an approach whereby each overseas market is seen as a separate domestic market and each country is seen as a separate entity, and the firm seeks to be seen as a local firm within that country.

psychic difference the difference that exists between how people in a home market view an offering versus the perception of those in a foreign market, based around culture, language, religion, politics, economics, and other country distinctions.

regional approach an approach that groups countries together, usually on a geographical basis (for example Europe), and provides for the specific needs of consumers within those countries.

selective contestability the ability to disaggregate generic markets into meaningful submarkets or segments, select those most attractive, and position the product offering appropriately.

standardized approach an approach whereby a firm operates as if the world were one large market (global market), ignoring regional and national differences, and simply selling the same products and services in the same way throughout the world.

References

ABF (Associated British Foods) (n.d.). Our grocery brands. Retrieve from: https://www.abf.co.uk/about_us/our_group/our_grocery_brands (accessed 13 October 2018).

Agence France-Presse (2015). India's legendary Royal Enfield motorcycle to expand production. *The Guardian*, 18 February. Retrieve from: https://www.theguardian.com/world/2015/feb/18/indias-legendary-royal-enfield-motorcycle-to-expand-production-to-uk (accessed 13 October 2018).

Anderson, E. (2014). Rebuilding Lego, brick by brick. *The Times*, 7 December, 7.

Anon. (2007). Why Honda didn't call the Fit-Jazz by its intended name. *Carscoops*, 21 September. Retrieve from: https://www.carscoops.com/2007/09/why-honda-didnt-call-fit-jazz-by-its.html (accessed 13 October 2018).

Anon. (2012). Biggest transnational companies. *The Economist*, 10 July. Retrieve from: https://www.economist.com/blogs/graphicdetail/2012/07/focus-1 (accessed 13 October 2018).

Anon. (2015a). The Royal Mint: coining it. *The Economist*, 21 February, 26.

Anon. (2015b). Support for cider drinking. *Impact*, April, 14.

Anon. (2015c). Bread in France: forget the baguette. *The Economist*, 27 June, 34.

Anon. (2015d). So everything is awesome at Lego, just as the song says. *The Times*, 26 February, 47.

Anon. (2018). Nokia seller HMD looks to smart and feature phones to grow its African business. *Reuters*, 21 June. Retrieve from: https://uk.reuters.com/article/uk-kenya-telecoms/nokia-seller-hmd-looks-to-smart-and-feature-phones-to-grow-its-african-business-idUKKBN1JH2NR (accessed 13 October 2018).

Ansoff, H.I. (1957). Strategies of diversification. *Harvard Business Review*, 25(5), 113–25.

Askew, K. (2015). Analysis: Unilever's plan to grow global ice cream sales margins. *Just-Food*, 31 July. Retrieve from: https://www.just-food.com/analysis/unilevers-plan-to-grow-global-ice-cream-sales-margins_id130732.aspx (accessed 13 October 2018).

Bartlett, C., and Ghoshal, S. (1991). *Managing across Borders: The Transnational Solution*. Cambridge, MA: Harvard Business School Press.

Bellis, M. (2018). The history of money. Retrieve from: https://www.thoughtco.com/history-of-money-1992150 (accessed 13 October 2018).

Blitz, R. (2014). The bet on Chinese gamblers. *Financial Times*, 29 May. Retrieve from: https://www.ft.com/cms/s/0/50070822-e284-11e3-89fd-00144feabdc0.html (accessed 13 October 2018).

Burgen, S. (2015). Spain becomes the world's biggest wine exporter in 2014. *The Guardian*, 6 March. Retrieve from: https://www.theguardian.com/world/2015/mar/06/spain-worlds-biggest-wine-exporter-2014-bulk-sales-spainish-wine (accessed 13 October 2018).

Chen, C. (2017). China's Geely Auto eyes expansion in overseas markets after Proton investment. *South China Morning Post*, 25 May. Retrieve from: https://www.scmp.com/business/companies/article/2095732/chinas-geely-auto-eyes-expansion-overseas-markets-after-proton (accessed 13 October 2018).

Chetty, S., and Campbell-Hunt, C. (2004). A strategic approach to internationalization: a traditional versus a 'born global' approach. *Journal of International Marketing*, 12(1), 57–81.

Colley, J. (2015). Why beer drinkers lose in the SABMiller–ABInBev merger. *Fortune*, 15 October. Retrieve from: https://fortune.com/2015/10/15/sabmiller-ab-inbev-merger-beer-drinkers-lose/ (accessed 13 October 2018).

Comité Champagne (2017). The economy of champagne: key market statistics 2017. Retrieve from: https://www.champagne.fr/en/champagne-economy/key-market-statistics (accessed 13 October 2018).

D'Arpizio, C., Levato, F., Zito, D., Kamel, M., and de Montgolfier, J. (2016). Luxury goods worldwide market study, Fall–Winter 2016: executive summary. *Bain & Company*, 27 December. Retrieve from: https://www.bain.com/publications/articles/luxury-goods-worldwide-market-study-fall-winter-2016.aspx (accessed 13 October 2018).

Davidson, M. (2013). Generation game: the return of the extended family home. *The Telegraph*, 9 May. Retrieve from: https://www.telegraph.co.uk/finance/property/buying-selling-moving/10046242/Generation-game-the-return-of-the-extended-family-home.html (accessed 13 October 2018).

de Mooij, M. (1994). *Advertising Worldwide*. Hemel Hempstead: Prentice Hall.

de Pablos, P.O. (2006). Transnational corporations and strategic challenges: an analysis of knowledge flows and competitive advantage. *Learning Organization*, 13(6), 544–59.

Doland, A. (2015). Defying tough times, these four foreign brands are successful in China. *Advertising Age*, 29 June. Retrieve from: https://adage.com/article/global-news/foreign-brands-successful-china/299242/ (accessed 13 October 2018).

Douglas, S.P., and Wind, Y. (1987). The myth of globalization. *Columbia Journal of World Business*, 22(4), 19–29.

Du, X. (2017). Chery, Great Wall rev up for global drive. *China Daily*, 16 September. Retrieve from: https://usa.chinadaily.com.cn/business/2017-09/16/content_32070328.htm (accessed 13 October 2018).

Evans, J. (2010). *Marketing Aspects of Psychic Distance*. Chichester: John Wiley.

Fromowitz, M. (2013). Cultural blunders: brands gone wrong. *Campaign*, 7 October. Retrieve from: https://www.campaignasia.com/article/cultural-blunders-brands-gone-wrong/426043 (accessed 13 October 2018).

Ghemawat, P. (2001). Distance still matters. *Harvard Business Review*, 79(8), 137–47.

Haris, R. (2016). D&G's hijab range is aimed at people like me—so why do I feel excluded? *The Guardian*, 11 January. Retrieve from: https://www.theguardian.com/commentisfree/2016/jan/11/dolce-gabbana-hijab-collection-muslim-women-western-fashion (accessed 13 October 2018).

Herbig, P.A., and Day, K. (1993). Managerial implications of the North American Free Trade Agreement. *International Marketing Review*, 10(4), 15–35.

Hofstede, G. (1983). The cultural relativity of organizational practices and theories. *Journal of International Business Studies*, 14(2), 75–89.

Hout, T., Porter, M.E., and Rudden, E. (1982). How global organizations win out! *Harvard Business Review*, September. Retrieve from: https://hbr.org/1982/09/how-global-companies-win-out (accessed 13 October 2018).

Hurley, J. (2015). Why success abroad needn't be a shaggy dog story. *The Times*, 31 August, 42–3.

James, G. (2014). 20 epic fails in global branding. Inc.com, 29 October. Retrieve from: https://www.inc.com/geoffrey-james/the-20-worst-brand-translations-of-all-time.html (accessed 13 October 2018).

Johanson, J., and Vahlne, J.E. (1977). The internationalization process of the firm: a model of knowledge development and increasing foreign market commitments. *Journal of International Business Studies*, 8(1), 23–32.

Johanson, J., and Wiedersheim-Paul, F. (1975). The internationalization of the firm: four Swedish cases. *Journal of Management Studies*, 12(3), 305–22.

Jung-A, S., Mundy, S., and Sender, H. (2015). Tesco nears the $6bn deal with MBK to offload South Korea unit. *Financial Times*, 3 September, 19.

Katsikeas, C.S., Samiee, S., and Theodosiu, M. (2006). Strategy fit and performance consequences of international marketing standardization. *Strategic Management Journal*, 27(9), 867–90.

Keegan, W.J. (1989). *Global Marketing Management*. Englewood Cliffs, NJ: Prentice Hall.

Levitt, T. (1983). The globalization of markets. *Harvard Business Review*, 61(3), 92–102.

Li, F. (2017). Automakers answer govt call to expand. *China Daily*, 22 May. Retrieve from: http://www.chinadaily.com.cn/business/motoring/2017-05/22/content_29438398.htm (accessed 13 October 2018).

Lynch, R. (1994). *European Business Strategies: The European and Global Strategies of Europe's Top Organizations*. London: Kogan Page.

Mahdawi, A. (2015). Can cities kick ads? Inside the global movement to ban urban billboards. *The Guardian*, 12 August. Retrieve from: https://www.theguardian.com/cities/2015/aug/11/can-cities-kick-ads-ban-urban-billboards (accessed 13 October 2018).

Makhovsky, A., and Stolyarov, G. (2017). China's Geely targets Russian market with new Belarus plant. *Reuters*, 17 November. Retrieve from: https://uk.reuters.com/article/china-belarus-autos/chinas-geely-targets-russian-market-with-new-belarus-plant-idUKL8N1NN496 (accessed 13 October 2018).

Martel, L. (2015). Population growth: migratory increase overtakes natural increase. *Statistics Canada*, 18 November. Retrieve from: https://www.statcan.gc.ca/pub/11-630-x/11-630-x2014001-eng.htm (accessed 13 October 2018).

Martin, A., and Fujikawa, M. (2015). Food scandals push McDonald's Japan into loss. *Wall Street Journal*, 5 February. Retrieve from: https://www.wsj.com/articles/food-scandals-push-mcdonalds-japan-into-loss-1423121899 (accessed 13 October 2018).

Mead, R. (1990). *Cross-Cultural Management Communication*. New York: John Wiley.

Mooney, P. (2008). Coke and the US troops. *Coca-Cola Company*, 11 November. Retrieve from: https://www.coca-colacompany.com/stories/2008/11/coke-and-the-us/ (accessed 13 October 2018).

Morris, R. (2013). Fresh & Easy failure: can UK firms make it in the US? *BBC News*, 17 April. Retrieve from: https://www.bbc.co.uk/news/business-22168463 (accessed 13 October 2018).

Mughan, T. (1993). Culture as an asset in international business. In: J. Preston (ed.), *International Business: Texts and Cases*, London: Pitman, 78–86.

Muslimin, A. (2017). Young Southeast Asian Muslim women are more religious yet more progressive, study finds. *Forbes*, 27 November. Retrieve from: https://www.forbes.com/sites/anismuslimin/2017/11/27/study-finds-young-southeast-asian-muslim-women-more-religious-yet-more-progressive/2/#7470831ae179 (accessed 13 October 2018).

Ohmae, K. (1985). *Triad Power*. London: Macmillan.

Paliwoda, S. (1993). *International Marketing* (2nd edn). Oxford: Butterworth Heinemann.

Perlmutter, H.V. (1969). The tortuous evolution of the multinational corporation. *Columbia Journal of World Business*, 4(1), 9–18.

Quelch, J.A., and Hoff, E.J. (1986). Customising global marketing. *Harvard Business Review*, 64(3), 59–68.

RBI (Restaurant Brands International, Inc.) (2018). Restaurant Brands International Inc. reports full year and fourth quarter results 2017. Press release, 12 February. Retrieve from: http://www.rbi.com/file/Index?KeyFile=392145069 (accessed 13 October 2018).

Riefler, P., and Diamantopoulos, A. (2007). Consumer animosity: a literature review and a reconsideration of its measurement. *International Marketing Review*, 27(1), 87–119.

Savov, V. (2017). Lynk & Co's 'shareable' 01 SUV goes on sale in China. *The Verge*, 28 November. Retrieve from: https://www.theverge.com/2017/11/28/16709932/lynk-co-01-suv-release-date-china (accessed 13 October 2018).

Sclater, I. (2005). The digital dimension. *The Marketer*, May, 22–3.

Shawcross, J. (2014). The rise and rise of Primark. *Aol Money*, 23 March. Retrieve from: https://www.aol.co.uk/2014/03/23/the-rise-and-rise-of-primark/?guccounter=1 (accessed 13 October 2018).

Sirgy, M., Lee, D.-J., Miller, C., Littlefield, J., and Atay, E. (2007). The impact of imports and exports on a country's quality of life. *Social Indicators Research*, 83(2), 245–81.

Standard Chartered (2014). *Annual Report 2014*. Retrieve from: https://www.sc.com/annual-report/2014/ (accessed 13 October 2018).

Thomson Reuters (2016). *State of the Global Islamic Economy Report 2016/17*. Retrieve from: https:// ceif.iba.edu.pk/pdf/ThomsonReuters-stateoftheGlobalIslamicEconomyReport201617.pdf (accessed 13 October 2018).

Watrous, M. (2015). Unilever acquires Italian gelato business. *Food Business News*, 10 February. Retrieve from: https://www.foodbusinessnews.net/articles/5249-unilever-acquires-italian-gelato-business (accessed 13 October 2018).

Wind, Y., and Perlmutter, H.V. (1973). Guidelines for developing international marketing strategies. *Journal of Marketing*, 37(2), 14–23.

Young, S. (2001). What do researchers know about the global business environment? *International Marketing Review*, 18(2), 120–9.

Zou, S., and Cavusgil, S.T. (2002). The GMS: a broad conceptualization of global marketing strategy performance and its effect on firm performance. *Journal of Marketing*, 66(4), 40–56.

Part 3
Managing Marketing Programmes

Part 3
Managing Marketing Programmes

Chapter 8
New Proposition Development and Innovation

Learning Outcomes

After reading this chapter, you will be able to:

▶ Explain the different levels of a proposition

▶ Identify and describe the various types of physical proposition and explain particular concepts relating to the management of products, including the product life cycle

▶ Explain the relationship between product and service offerings, and describe the product–service spectrum

▶ Explore the processes and issues associated with innovating new propositions

▶ Describe how new propositions are adopted by markets

Case Insight 8.1
Cheil UK

Market Insight 8.1
Chanel No.5: Iconic on So Many Levels

Market Insight 8.2
Battle of the Superjumbos

Market Insight 8.3
Fast Fashion: Tailoring the Life Cycle

Market Insight 8.4
Minecraft: The Gamer's Proposition

Market Insight 8.5
Streaming Wars: Apple versus Spotify

Case Insight 8.1
Cheil UK

Cheil is a full-service, data-driven agency network, rooted firmly in digital innovation. Cheil UK is part of the Cheil Worldwide Network, made up of more than 6,000 people in 53 offices across five continents. We speak to Manish Bhan, head of retail transformation, to find out how Cheil UK helped client Samsung to develop its retail offering.

Cheil was born in South Korea, a country now established as one of the world's largest economies and a leader in technological innovation. Consequently, we have been at the cutting edge of technology for over 40 years, bringing technology and creativity together to drive engagement, participation, and talkability for our clients. We redefine the way in which people connect with brands by using technology and data as a canvas for creativity, by offering brands a genuine 360-degree service, including the following elements: strategy; data and insights; retail innovation and commerce; events and experiential; social media and **content marketing**; and personalization through digital platforms.

We are a 'briefless' agency, meaning that we seek to understand the business challenges of our clients, customer barriers, and industry trends to develop a solution that overcomes barriers and enhances customer experiences. To solve a client problem, we adopt a 'rollercoaster process' whereby teams from various business functions (for example digital, social, retail, experiential, data, strategy, technology) all come together to tackle the challenge and determine how we can overcome it across all marketing channels.

The last ten years in retail have seen more change than the previous fifty and the next ten years are likely to be even more exciting. The growth of online retail and digitization has turned retail into a hothouse of innovation. New technologies, new channels, and the development of strong social media communities have transformed how shoppers make purchase decisions and the way in which brands and retailers do business. Retail is at the centre of

these innovations, with the smartphone becoming a key conduit to providing information, browsing, comparison, sales, payment, and accessing brand communities, as well as a way of engaging one-to-one with shoppers. Many retail innovations have developed in the last few years and have utilized, and will in the future utilize, mobile as a part of the retail journey. Major innovations in retail over the last ten years include: the development of **pure-play** (purely online) offerings; mobile commerce (m-commerce); on-demand delivery, retail design thinking/cognitive retail (that is, redesigning processes to focus on empathizing, and adapting to, the customer experience); social commerce (from rating and reviews to crowdsourcing); big data (to allow greater personalization, customer profiling etc.); digital and interactive screens in-store; self-service checkouts; frictionless payment via contactless payment systems; geo-locational targeting via beacons and near-field communication (NFC) in-store (which allows communication with a smartphone when a customer passes near to a retail store, particularly for advertising); and subscription services (which facilitate auto-replenishment, for example Dollar Shave Club, Netflix).

When our client Samsung wanted to develop a new digital solution to grow its retail customer base and deepen its relationships in an increasingly competitive environment, we had to consider how it would adapt to these environmental changes to better compete. But Samsung also wanted to provide a seamless experience across online and offline channels. Non-digital channel solutions (for example physical retail outlets) can increase time

Case Insight 8.1
continued

to market for new propositions, tend to have high operating costs and low customer engagement rates, and lead to fewer customer conversions. With the existing channel solution, content was silo-ed, there was no way of ensuring omni-channel delivery fulfilment, and measuring and optimizing customer experiences was difficult. Consequently, there was limited cross-channel customer engagement.

The question for Cheil UK was: what omni-channel offering did it need to develop for its client that would bring together Samsung's online and offline channels to improve its customers' experiences?

 Visit the online resources to watch a video interview with Manish Bhan in which he explains what Cheil UK did.

Introduction

An Apple smartphone, a train journey from London to Venice on the Venice Simplon-Orient-Express, a cappuccino at Starbucks in Copenhagen, the *South China Morning Post* newspaper in Hong Kong, a copy of the French magazine *20 Ans*, a haircut in Pakistan, and a manicure in Saudi Arabia are all commercial **propositions**, or **offerings**. But do they completely meet their customers' needs? Offerings can only ever be approximate solutions to customers' needs. No one can ever design a proposition to meet the needs of all people all of the time. The term 'proposition' includes an offering's tangible and intangible attributes related not only to physical goods, but also to services, ideas, people, places, experiences, and even a mix of these various elements. We use the terms 'offering' and 'proposition' to mean both physical goods and non-physical services. A proposition or offering is anything that can be offered for use and consumption in exchange for money or some other form of value. We use the terms 'product' or 'good' only when we refer to a physical offering. We use the term 'service' when we are referring to a non-physical offering.

A bottle of Adnams beer, a L'Oréal eyeliner pencil, or an Otis lift are all tangible propositions—that is, **products**. **Tangibility** therefore refers to the ability to touch an item and whether it can be stored. By comparison, a trip to the Titanic museum in Belfast, Northern Ireland, or a visit to a Zeba hair salon in Ireland cannot be touched and are incapable of being stored. These are intangible propositions—that is, **services**. However, there has also been an increasing shift, particularly in the business-to-business world, towards servitizing physical goods (that is, making products into services). We discuss this intriguing marketing phenomenon in more detail later. In this chapter, we also consider the nature of propositions, before exploring issues associated with their innovation and development. We start with a consideration of the principal characteristics associated with offerings and then discuss the notion of how all offerings are essentially services—that is, we discuss **service-dominant logic (SDL)** (see Chapter 1). The second part of the chapter examines ideas and processes related to the development of new propositions generally.

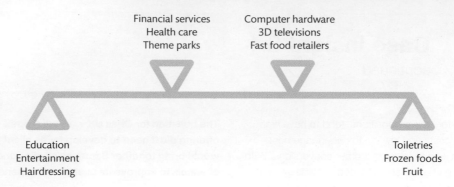

Financial services
Health care
Theme parks

Computer hardware
3D televisions
Fast food retailers

Education
Entertainment
Hairdressing

Toiletries
Frozen foods
Fruit

Figure 8.1
The product–service spectrum

The (Non-)Physical Nature of Propositions

Fruit is a purely tangible good, whereas a cinema ticket is a pure service (although you can add goods such as popcorn and a drink, of course). These propositions lie at opposite ends of a spectrum (see Figure 8.1). Inbetween the pure good and the pure service lie a host of goods–services combinations. Many offerings have intangible components. For example, fridges and houses are sold with warranties, and cars may be purchased with finance deals at 0 per cent interest. These intangible aspects are sometimes referred to as product intangibles. Many vendors develop the intangible service element of their offering to differentiate themselves in the marketplace.

This product–service spectrum and the combinations of products and services that it represents incorporate strategies designed to increase the value offered to customers through improved services. However, developing the service element to provide a point of differentiation is not always successful, because it can create price competition. As prices drop, offerings become commoditized and customers may find it difficult to see the value offered by competing firms. To avoid this, some vendors develop a third approach based around improving customer experience. The customer experience strategy is not based on either the tangible or intangible attributes of brands, but refers to the memories and fantasies that individuals retain or imagine as a result of their interaction with an offering (Tynan and McKechnie, 2009). Memories of experiences related to product usage, events, visits, or activities are internalized, unlike products and services, which are generally external to each person. Indeed, the idea that people consume emotions is recognized as an important and influential aspect of the marketing discipline (Holbrook and Hirschman, 1982). The memories and fantasies concept is best illustrated through the activities of theme and leisure parks. (For more information on managing customer experiences, see Chapter 15.)

The Three Levels of a Proposition

When people buy propositions, they are not only buying the simple functional aspect that a proposition offers; there are also other factors involved in the purchase. For example, the taste of the pralines is an important benefit arising from, say, the purchase of a box of chocolates. However, in addition to this core benefit, people are also attracted to the packaging, the price,

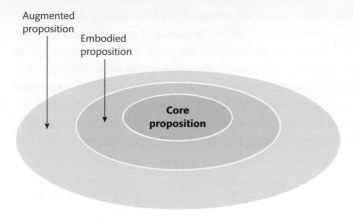

Figure 8.2
The three elements of a proposition

the flavours of the chocolate, and some of the psychosocial associations that we have learned about a brand. For example, boutique British luxury chocolatier Hotel Chocolat seeks to make chocolate exciting again and hence to provide customers with a level of psychosocial satisfaction. To understand the different elements and benefits that make up a total proposition, we refer to three different proposition components: the core proposition; the embodied proposition; and the augmented proposition (see Figure 8.2):

- The *core* proposition consists of the core benefit or service. This may be a functional benefit in terms of what the offering will enable you to do, or it may be an emotional benefit in terms of how the product or service will make you feel. Cars provide transportation and a means of self-expression. Cameras make memories by recording a scene, person, or object.

- The *embodied* proposition consists of the physical good or delivered service that provides the expected benefit. It consists of many factors, for example the features and capabilities, the durability, the design, the packaging, and the brand name. Cars are supplied with different styles, engines, seats, colours, and boot space; digital cameras are offered with a variety of picture qualities, screen sizes, pixels, zoom and telephoto features, editing, and relay facilities.

- The *augmented* proposition consists of the embodied offering plus all those other factors that are necessary to support the purchase and any post-purchase activities, such as credit and finance, training, delivery, installation, guarantees, and the overall perception of customer service.

When these levels are brought together, it is hoped that they will provide customers with a reason to buy and keep buying. Each individual combination or bundle of benefits constitutes added value and serves to differentiate, for example, one sports car from another sports car, or one disposable camera from another. Marketing strategies should be designed around the actual and augmented propositions, because it is through these that competition occurs and people are able to understand how one disposable camera differs from another.

Understanding what a brand is to its customers and how they experience the brand is vitally important. Pepsi's battle with Coca-Cola during the 1960s and 1970s saw it gradually reduce Coke's dominant market share. Famously, the battle culminated in 1985 when Coke abandoned its original recipe and introduced New Coke, a sweeter formulation designed to attract Pepsi's young market. Coke's customers boycotted New Coke, there was public outrage, and Pepsi temporarily became market leader. New Coke was soon dropped, and the original was brought back and relaunched as Classic Cola, re-establishing its credentials and retrieving the market-leading spot. The problem was that Coke had not appreciated the value that the proposition as a whole represented to its primary customers. Customers were consuming more than only the drink itself; rather, the sum of the core, embodied, and augmented propositions, encapsulated as the brand Coca-Cola, drew passion from its customers and market researchers had overlooked this when searching for a means to stop Pepsi's progress. (See Market Insight 8.1 for a discussion of the three proposition elements in relation to French perfume brand Chanel.)

Market Insight 8.1
Chanel No.5: Iconic on So Many Levels

Chanel No.5 is perhaps the most iconic fragrance of all time. Launched in 1921, the 'woman's perfume with a woman's scent', invented by Gabrielle 'Coco' Chanel, has notes of jasmine, rose, sandalwood, and vanilla. With No.5, Chanel pioneered the use of combining multiple scents into one fragrance. Coco Chanel popularized the brand by holding dinners in Parisian restaurants, inviting her high-society friends and spraying them all with it (she called them 'tastemakers'). As curious passers-by asked what the smell was, a brand was born.

A key success factor for a fragrance is how customers feel about the experience of wearing it. Consumers want a scent that is compelling, lingers on their skin, and makes them feel special. Charles Revson, founder of cosmetics firm Revlon, sums it up in his oft-quoted words: 'In the factory we make cosmetics, in the drugstore we sell hope.' Clearly, Revson understood the importance of improving the wearer's self-concept as critical to making the sale. According to psychologists, fragrances create this sense of feeling special by inspiring the imagination and evoking emotions, either by transporting the wearer into a past pleasant memory or by prompting a vision of the future for the wearer.

Another way of making the wearer feel special is via celebrity endorsement. The No.5 brand has long been associated with some of the world's most glamorous women. Marilyn Monroe gave the brand a massive unsolicited boost in 1955 when she famously responded, in an interview, that she wore only Chanel No.5 to bed. Since then, notable names advertising the brand have included French actors

Catherine Deneuve in the 1970s and Carole Bouquet in the 1980s, Australian Oscar winner Nicole Kidman in 2004, and Brazilian supermodel Gisele Bündchen in 2014. The Kidman ad—which was really more of a mini film, at 4 minutes in length—was the world's most expensive advertising campaign, costing a reputed US$18 million to make, of which Kidman was paid $2 million. Some 95 years after No.5 was launched, Chanel launched No.5 L'Eau in autumn 2016, just in time for Christmas. This time the campaign was fronted by Lily-Rose Depp, daughter of French singer and actor Vanessa Paradis, who had starred in a Chanel ad in 1990. The fragrance, aimed at extending the No.5 brand to young women, helped to increase sales of the No.5 range by around 20 per cent.

Sources: Anon. (2011); Edmond-Sargeant (2014); Anon. (2015a); Connell (2016); Ljubisavljevic (2016); Johnston (2017).

Lily-Rose Depp, daughter of Vanessa Paradis, fronts the Chanel No.5 campaign in 2016
Source: Image courtesy of The Advertising Archives.

Market Insight 8.1
continued

Theory into Practice

This market insight describes how an offering was developed and came to be perceived as one of the world's finest fragrances. We can consider the core proposition to be the benefits derived from wearing a scent, including the feeling of being special or improving one's self-concept. The embodied proposition consists of the liquid itself, its colour, its packaging, the user's association with the brand name, and the design of the bottle. The augmented proposition relates to the process of obtaining the No.5 brand, the ad campaign, the celebrity with whom it is associated, and its availability, often through exclusive retail outlets such as airport duty-free shops and department stores, as well as specialist perfumeries.

Related Topics

proposition levels; branding; word of mouth; opinion leaders; celebrity endorsement

1 **How have the offering's origins affected consumer perceptions of the No.5 brand?**

2 **Why do you think the Chanel No.5 L'Eau brand was so successful with young women and to**

what extent did the extension from the No.5 brand help or hinder this success?

3 **How might the Chanel No.5 offering be further developed?**

The development of the Internet, social media, and other digital technologies have impacted on the nature of the offering and the benefits accruing from using it. This has opened up opportunities for organizations to redefine their core and actual propositions, often by supplementing them with 'information' about the offering, such as white papers designed to engage website visitors with the brand. Another approach has been to transform current offerings into digital offerings, for example Netflix and video streaming, as opposed to DVDs or Blu-ray discs. In the software industry, the Internet has opened up the possibility of companies paying a subscription to buy centrally hosted software services—known as software as a service (SaaS)—rather than buying the software itself and hosting it on their own systems.

There are a number of ways in which **digital value** can help to augment the proposition (Chaffey et al., 2009). This can be done by coordinating activities to engage the customer through an increasingly digital purchase journey, harnessing content to empower the consumer to build their own identity, recognizing the need to think like a multimedia publisher, and plotting how to gather and use the increasing amount of digital data available (Edelman, 2010). For example, many companies provide evidence of the awards they have won, whereas others parade testimonials, case studies, white papers, endorsements, and customer comments, all as part of a content marketing strategy. These are designed to provide credibility, reduce risk, and enable people to engage with or purchase a brand. It is important at this stage to point out that most of the costs associated with the development of a new proposition are the result of the design of the proposition. In other words, getting the design of a proposition wrong at the beginning of the new proposition development process can be very costly. Joint working between marketing and research and development (R&D) is therefore important (Hise et al., 1990) (see Research Insight 8.1). There is also increasing recognition of the need for customer input into the design and development of new products (see Market Insight 8.2), sometimes referred to as **co-production**, or **co-creation**.

Visit the **online resources** and complete Internet Activity 8.1 to learn more about how HSBC approaches new product development.

Market Insight 8.2
Battle of the Superjumbos

In the global aerospace industry for large, wide-bodied passenger planes, two companies battle it out in a perpetual duopoly war for customers. But they have completely different visions of what their customers want. Boeing predicted that people would want to fly directly to a wide and growing range of destinations and developed the 787 Dreamliner, whilst Airbus predicted that people would want to fly from one major hub airport to another (for example London Heathrow to Singapore or Dubai) and developed the A380. Accordingly, the two companies developed completely different planes. The largest Airbus A380 could seat up to 840 passengers and had a range of 15,000 km, whilst the Dreamliner had an initial seat capacity of 250 (now up to 323) and a range of 15,200 km. Importantly, though, the Dreamliner has lower fuel costs, with a higher fuel efficiency (0.05–0.12 km/litre).

Boeing spent around eight years developing the 787 Dreamliner at a reputed cost of US$32 billion. It finally entered service in 2010, but analysts believe that it will not recoup its investment until 2019 or after the first 1,000 planes have been sold. Each plane sells at around $225 million (for the 787–8 version). Customers were involved at various levels of the development process. Major airlines (for example All Nippon Airways) were involved in the design and specification, major suppliers from around the world had input into plane design and production (for example Rolls-Royce, Saab, Mitsubishi, KAL-ASD), and even passengers could input their views through a dedicated website. When the first Dreamliner 787 was delivered, it was three years late. By late 2017,

Boeing had cumulative orders for 1,294 of the planes, of which it had delivered 636.

In contrast, the cost to Airbus of developing the A380, over ten years, was reputedly around $25 billion—somewhat cheaper than Boeing—and Airbus delivered the first plane to Singapore Airlines in 2007, only two years late. It used four teams of designers, one from each of its partners: France's Aérospatiale; Deutsche Aerospace; British Aerospace; and Spain's CASA. Each plane sells at $414 million and uses a double-decker design. Airbus has forecast that the market for very large planes between 2017 and 2036 will be around 1,184; By late 2017, it had cumulative orders for 539 of its A380s, of which 222 had been delivered.

In the battle for the world's most popular superjumbo, Boeing is winning, given the size of the order book (by volume and total revenue). Its bet on the popularity of point-to-point routes appears to have been correct. Although the A380 order book had been slow since 2015, an order by Emirates for six A380s per year for between nine and ten years in 2018 indicates the market for very large aircraft (with more than 450 seats) will continue. With the world's major airports becoming increasingly congested, Airbus continue to hope that airlines will shift to buying the bigger A380s rather than buying more 787s.

Sources: Ausick (2014, 2015); Armitage (2015); Hepher (2018); https://www.airbus.com/aircraft/market/orders-deliveries.html; http://investors.boeing.com/investors/financial-reports/default.aspx; https://www.airbus.com/aircraft/market/global-market-forecast.html

Market Insight 8.2
continued

Theory into Practice

This market insight describes rival proposition development for the two major companies operating in the duopolistic global aerospace market. It highlights how the two companies developed opposing ambitious visions of the future of the aerospace market and developed their products, the A380 (Airbus) and the Dreamliner 787 (Boeing), accordingly. Boeing co-created the design of its product using input from suppliers, airlines, and even passengers. Airbus initially consulted with airlines and developed its product from its supplier-partner owners. The case highlights the difficulties of, and risks associated with, managing large aerospace development projects, especially given that both companies' products were delivered late (and billions of dollars over budget).

Related Topics

new product development; co-creation; product design; time to market

1 **Why do you think it took so long for both companies to develop their rival propositions?**

2 **What customer needs did they incorporate into the design of their propositions?**

3 **What might the next generation of plane look like in 2036?**

Research Insight 8.1

To take your learning further, you might wish to read this influential paper:

Hise, R.T., O'Neal, L., Parasuraman, A., and McNeal, J.U. (1990). Marketing/R&D interaction in new product development: implications for new product success rates. *Journal of Product Innovation Management*, 7(2), 142–55.

This article explains the importance of the interaction between marketing and R&D in new product development. The authors report results of their analysis of the new product development procedures of 252 large manufacturing companies, concluding that joint working between marketing and R&D during the design stage of new products is a key factor in explaining success.

 Visit the **online resources** to read the abstract and access the full paper.

Classifying Physical Propositions

There are two main ways of classifying physical offerings: as consumer offerings; and as business-to-business (B2B) offerings. Consumers buy offerings that satisfy personal and family needs; customers buy industrial and business offerings either as a part of the business operations or to make other goods for resale. Some offerings, such as light bulbs and toilet tissue, are bought by both consumers and businesses.

Consumer Goods

The first way of classifying consumer goods is to consider them in terms of their durability. **Durable goods**, such as bicycles, music players, and refrigerators, can be used repeatedly and provide benefits each time they are used. **Non-durable goods**, such as yoghurt and newspapers, have a limited duration (that is, they are perishable) and are often used only once. Services are intangible propositions that cannot be stored (see Chapter 15).

Durable goods often require the purchaser to have high levels of involvement in the purchase decision. There is a high perceived risk in these decisions, and so consumers often spend time, care, and energy searching, formulating, and making the 'right' decision (see Chapter 2). As a result, marketers should seek to understand these patterns of behaviour, provide and make accessible sufficient amounts of appropriate information, and ensure that there is the right type of service and support necessary to meet the needs of the target market.

Non-durable goods—typically, food and grocery items—reflect low levels of involvement and buyers are seldom concerned what product they buy. Risk is seen to be low and so there is little need to shop around for the best possible price. Buyers may buy on the basis of availability, price, habit, or brand experience.

A deeper and more meaningful way of classifying consumer goods is to consider how and where consumers buy them. In Chapter 2, we considered how consumers make purchases. In particular, we looked at **extensive problem-solving**, **limited problem-solving**, and **routinized response behaviour**. Classifying products according to the behaviour consumers demonstrate when buying them enables marketing managers to develop more appropriate marketing strategies. Four main behavioural categories have been established: convenience products; shopping products; speciality products; and unsought products.

Convenience products are non-durable and are bought because the consumer does not want to put very much effort, if any, into the buying decision. Routinized response behaviour corresponds most closely to convenience products because they are bought frequently and are inexpensive. Most decisions in this category are made habitually, and if the usual brand is unavailable, an alternative brand is selected—or none at all if it is seen to be too inconvenient to visit another store.

Convenience products can be subdivided into three further categories: staples; impulse; and emergency products (see Table 8.1). All of these types of convenience product indicate that different marketing strategies might be required to make each work. However, one element common to all is distribution. If the product is not available when an emergency arises, or when a consumer is waiting to pay or walking around the supermarket, then a sale cannot be made. Pricing is also important, because customers know the expected price of convenience items and may well switch brands if price exceeds that of the competition.

Shopping products are not bought as frequently as convenience products. Consequently, consumers do not always have sufficient up-to-date information to make buying decisions. The

Table 8.1 Categories of convenience product

Type of convenience product	Explanation
Staple products	Staples are available almost everywhere. They include groceries (e.g. bread, milk, soft drinks, breakfast cereals) and petrol. They are bought frequently and habitually. For example, rice is a staple in the Far East, wheat in Europe, and corn in Latin America.
Impulse products	These are offerings that consumers may not plan to buy, but are persuaded to pick up—particularly when they see point-of-sale advertising materials for them. Typically, these items are located close to tills in supermarkets, so that customers waiting to be served are attracted to them. Chewing gum, chocolate bars, and magazines are typical impulse purchases.
Emergency products	Bought when necessary, these products represent a solution to buyers, who are hence less intent on obtaining the right quality or image-related offering. Examples might be buying a bandage when someone is cut or injured, finding a locksmith when your house key stops working, or (in a business-to-business context) purchasing new plant and machinery when the old machinery suddenly stops working.

purchase of shopping products such as furniture, electrical appliances, jewellery, and mobile phones requires some search for information, if only to explore the latest features. Consumers give time and effort to planning these purchases, because the level of risk is more substantial than that associated with convenience products. They will visit several stores, and use online and word-of-mouth communications for price comparisons, product information, and product reviews. Not surprisingly, levels of brand loyalty are quite low, because consumers switch brands to get the level of functionality and overall value they need.

The marketing strategies followed by manufacturers—and, to some extent, retailers—need to accommodate the characteristics of limited problem solving. Shopping products do not require the mass distribution strategies associated with convenience products. Here, a selective distribution strategy is required because, although the volume of purchases is lower and margins are higher, consumers frequently want the specialist advice offered by knowledgeable expert retailers.

Speciality products represent high-risk purchases, are very expensive, are bought infrequently (often only once), and correspond to extended problem-solving. People plan these purchases carefully, search intensively for information on the offering, and are often concerned only with a particular brand and in finding a way of gaining access to an outlet that can supply it. It is possible to find speciality products in many areas, for example limited-edition sports equipment (Nedstar the Dream hockey sticks), rare paintings and artwork at auction (Da Vinci, Chagall), watches (Raymond Weil), pens (Montblanc), haute couture (Chanel), Michelin-starred restaurants (Manoir Restaurant Inter Scaldes in Holland), and multi-destination holidays (TUI). All have unique characteristics—which, for buyers, means that there are few, if any, substitute offerings worth considering. Marketing strategies to support speciality products focus on a limited number of distribution outlets. Advertising seeks to establish the brand name and values. The few retailers appointed to carry the item require detailed training and support so that the buyer experiences high levels of customer service and associated prestige throughout the purchase process.

Raymond Weil watches, a speciality product
Source: © Danuta Hyniewska/age footstock.

Unsought products refer to offerings that people do not normally anticipate buying nor indeed want to buy. Very often, consumers have little knowledge or awareness of the brands in the marketplace and are motivated to find out about them only when a specific need arises. Examples include repair services for cracked car windscreens (Autoglass®) and funeral services (Cooperative Funeral Care). In a similar way, life insurance was once sold through heavily pressurized door-to-door selling because people did not see the need to buy it. That has changed with legislation, but double-glazing, home-cleaning services, and timeshare holidays are still commonly sold in this way.

Business Products

Unlike some consumer products, bought for personal and psychological rewards, business propositions are generally bought on a rational basis to meet organizational goals. These are either used to enable the organization to function smoothly or they form an integral part of the products, processes, and services supplied by the organization for resale. Like consumer goods, business propositions can also be classified according to how (organizational) customers use them. The six main categories are as follows:

- *Equipment goods* cover two main areas concerning the everyday operations of the organization: capital equipment goods and accessory equipment goods:

  - **Capital equipment goods** are buildings, heavy plant, and factory equipment required to build or assemble products. They also include major government schemes to build prisons, highways, and bridges. Whatever their nature, they require substantial investment, are subject to long planning processes, are often one-off long-term purchases, and require the involvement of many different people and groups in the procurement process.

  - **Accessory equipment goods** should support the key operational processes and activities of the organization. Typically, they include photocopiers, computers, stationery, and office furniture. These items cost less than capital equipment goods, are not expected to last as long as capital equipment goods, and are often portable, rather than fixed. Whereas a poor capital equipment purchase may put the entire organization at risk, a poor accessory purchase frustrates and slows down activities, but is unlikely to threaten the existence of the organization.

- *Raw materials* are the basic materials used to produce finished goods. Minerals, chemicals, timber, and food staples, such as grain, vegetables, fruit, meat, and fish, are extracted, grown, or farmed as necessary and transported to organizations that process them into finished or semi-finished products. They are bought in large quantities and buyers often negotiate heavily on price. However, these buying decisions can also be influenced by non-product factors, such as length of relationship, speed of delivery, service quality, and credit facilities.

- *Semi-finished goods* are raw materials that have been converted into a temporary state. For example, iron ore is converted into metal sheets that can be used by car and aircraft manufacturers, washing machines, and building contractors.

- **Maintenance, repair, and operating (MRO) goods** are those products, other than raw materials, that are necessary to ensure that the organization continues to function. Maintenance and repair goods, such as nuts and bolts, light bulbs, and cleaning supplies are used to maintain the capital and accessory equipment goods. Operating supplies are not directly involved in the production of finished goods nor are they a constituent part, but oil for lubricating machinery and office stationery (including USB drives and paperclips) are all necessary to keep the organization functioning.

- *Component parts* are finished complete parts, bought from other organizations, which components are then incorporated directly into the finished product. So, for example, Ford will buy in finished headlight assemblies and mount them directly into its Mustang, Vignale, or Transit models, as appropriate.

- *Business services* are intangible services used to enhance the operational aspects of organizations. Most commonly, these include management consultancy, finance, and accounting, including auditing, legal, marketing research, information systems, and marketing communications.

Product Range, Line, and Mix

To meet the needs of a number of different target markets, most organizations offer a variety of products and services. Although some offer an assortment based on an individual core product, it is rare that an organization offers a single product—although there are examples, including Crocs Inc. (footwear), Bogdahn International GmbH (flexi dog leashes), and the WD-40 Company Inc. (lubricant). Consumer organizations, such as Gillette, offer a range of shaving products; industrial organizations, such as Oliver Valves, offer a range of valves for the offshore and onshore petrochemical, gas, and power-generation industries. To make sense of, and understand, the relationships that one set of products have with another, a variety of terms have emerged. Table 8.2 sets out these different terms using South Korean conglomerate Samsung Electronics Co. Ltd as an example.

Visit the **online resources** and complete Internet Activity 8.2 to learn more about the terminology relating to a product range.

Table 8.2 Product terms in relation to Samsung	
Product term	**Explanation**
Product item	A distinct single product within a product line, e.g. Samsung's Galaxy S8 +
Product line	A group of closely related products—related through technical, marketing, or user considerations, e.g. all three Galaxy S8 phones
Product mix	The total number of product lines offered by an organization. At Samsung, this would mean all the mobile devices, televisions, print solutions, domestic appliances, cameras, and accessories that the company offers, as well as business-to-business products, including microchips, semiconductors, and memory and hard-drive devices.
Product line length	The number of products available in a product line, e.g. the three products available within the Samsung Galaxy S8 range (S8+, S8 + dual SIM)
Product line depth	The number of variations available within a product line, e.g. in the UK, the five trim colours (midnight black orchid grey, coral blue, arctic silver, rose pink) of the Samsung Galaxy S8 +
Product mix width	The number of product lines within a product mix

Product Life Cycles

Underpinning the concept of the **product life cycle** is the belief that offerings move through a sequential, predetermined pattern of development similar to the biological path that life forms follow. This pathway, known as the product life cycle, consists of five distinct stages—namely, development, introduction, growth, maturity, and decline. Sales and profits rise and fall across the various life stages of the product, as shown in Figure 8.3.

Products move through an overall cycle that consists of different stages. Speed of movement through the stages varies, but each product has a limited lifespan. Although the life of a product can be extended, for example by introducing new ways of using the product, finding new users, and developing new attributes, the majority of products have a finite period during which management can maximize the returns on the investment made. In Sweden, mobile phones have an overall lifespan of 9–12 months, so it is important to extend the sales period, especially through maturity. Apple and others do this through 'appstores'. The firm offers existing iPhone customers the possibility of purchasing additional applications and games (Leistén and Nilsson, 2009). There is some evidence (from Germany) that electronic goods manufacturers are deliberately shortening product life cycles, thereby adding **built-in obsolescence** (Ala-Kurikka, 2015). The average lifespan of an Android smartphone is about 21 months, because the battery deteriorates (Jones, 2017).

Just as the nature and expectations of customer groups differ by stage, so do the competitive conditions. This means that different marketing strategies, relating to the offering and its distribution, pricing, and promotion, need to be deployed at particular times so as to maximize financial returns.

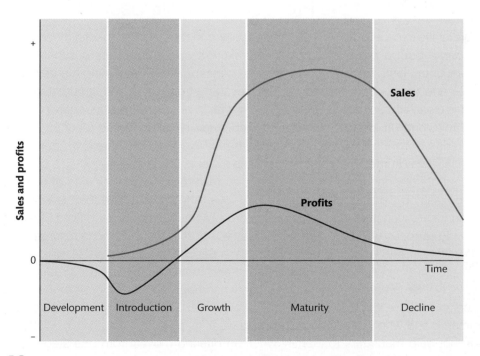

Figure 8.3
The product life cycle

The product life cycle concept does not apply to all offerings in the same way. For example, some offerings reach the end of the introduction stage and then die as it becomes clear that there is no market to sustain them. Moore (2014) termed this 'crossing the chasm'. Some products follow the path into decline and then hang around, sustained by heavy advertising and sales promotions, or they are recycled back into the growth stage by repositioning activities. Some products grow very quickly and then fade away rapidly. Examples of such fad products include the Rubik's Cube in the 1980s, the Furby furry toy in the 1990s, and low-rise jeans in the 2000s.

The brands of many fast-moving consumer goods (FMCGs) are sustained through a supermarket listing. Terminating a listed brand and losing the shelf space to a competitor is difficult to accept simply because getting the listing in the first place is so hard and because of the need to recoup the substantial investment put into the brand since its conception. Supermarkets often delist an underperforming brand unless the brand owner presents a suitable variant capable of replacing the ailing brand (Clark, 2009).

When discussing the product life cycle, care should be taken to clarify exactly what is being described. The concept can apply to a product class (computers), a product form (a tablet), or a brand (Lenovo). The shape of the curve varies, with product classes having the longest cycle because the mature stage is often extended. Product forms tend to comply most closely with the traditional cycle shape, whereas brand cycles tend to be the shortest. This is because they are subject to competitive forces and sudden change. So, whereas mid-sized coupés (product form) enjoyed a long period of success, brands such as the Alfa Brera had shorter cycles (2005–10), and have been replaced by cars that have more contemporary designs and features. For example, Alfa replaced the Brera with a derivative of the Alfa Romeo Giulia, launched in 2018 (Vellequette, 2017).

Is the Concept of the Product Life Cycle Useful?

The product life cycle is a well-known and popular concept, and is a useful means of explaining the broad path a product or brand has taken. It also clearly sets out that no product, service, or brand lasts forever. In principle, the concept allows marketing managers to adapt strategies and tactics to meet the needs of evolving conditions and circumstances. In this sense, it is clear, simple, and predictable. However, in practice, the concept is of limited use. For example, one problem is identifying which stage an offering has reached in the cycle. Some brands do not follow the classical S-shaped curve (see Figure 8.4), but rise steeply and then fall away immediately after sales reach a crest. These shapes reflect a consumer fad when rapid obsolescence occurs, or there is a craze for a particular piece of merchandise, typified by fashion clothing, skateboards, and toys. Another possible form is when demand for a brand is rejuvenated. One example is Ford's redevelopment of the Ford Mustang, now on sale in Europe, as well as in the United States. Another is the surprise resurgence of vinyl records in the UK and United States. GZ Media, a Czech firm, produced 24 million vinyl discs in 2017—about 60 per cent of global demand and nearly double what it produced in 1987 (Anon., 2017). So great care should be taken when applying the concept of the product life cycle, because while it is helpful as a general way of explaining how brands develop, its role in commerce and when developing strategy is weak (see Market Insight 8.3). Historical sales data do not help managers to identify when an offering moves from one stage to another, which means that it is difficult to forecast sales and hence determine the future shape of the lifecycle curve.

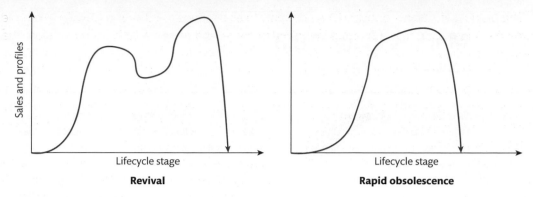

Figure 8.4
Types of product life cycle

Market Insight 8.3
Fast Fashion: Tailoring the Life Cycle

An unusual aspect of the fashion business—at least from a marketing perspective—is that, often, consumers do not stop buying items because clothes are no longer usable, but because they are no longer chic. Such artificial obsolescence drives the industry to continuously (re)create new fashions and styles. A key success factor in the fashion industry is to get a new product from the concept stage to sale more quickly than the competition—known as fast fashion. Spanish clothing retailer Zara, with more than 2,200 stores present in 94 countries, pioneered fast fashion. Whereas fashion lines had previously been based around spring/summer, autumn/winter collections, Zara developed new styles every five weeks, based on the latest fashions displayed on the world's runways. This is far ahead of, for example, H&M's six-month turnaround. But online stores such as ASOS, boohoo, and Missguided are now stealing a march, taking products from concept to sale in as little as a week.

All these companies have thousands of product items on their websites and introduce hundreds of new items each week. ASOS and Missguided offer free shipping (for orders over £20 and £30, respectively) and free returns. Zara offers free delivery for orders over £50 and free returns.

Understanding the principles underpinning the product life cycle can help these firms to forecast the length

Zara's homepage: the start of the fashion life cycle
Source: © Casimiro PT/Shutterstock.com.

of each item's sales period, to manage the stocking requirements, and to plan for the introduction of new ranges. For example, in the world of fashion, the following cycle might be evident:

- *Introduction*—A new dress is presented online, given lots of visibility, and is linked directly through newsletters and social media sites, and also from the homepage. Some fashion leaders adopt the new dress, while digital influencers (such as fashion bloggers) who have been alerted previously to the launch are given access to more detailed information and, in some cases, samples.

Market Insight 8.3
continued

- *Growth*—Offline articles, online placements, and word of mouth help sales to grow. Stock management is critical to ensure customers are not disappointed by **stock-outs**.

- *Maturity*—Competition becomes intense and it is necessary to remind audiences about the offering online. More stock may be required to ensure continuity of supply. For example, a dress from the previous collection may still be selling well. During this stage, the firm may cut the price to clear any remaining stock or sell the dresses as job lots through wholesalers, outlet malls, or auctioneers. Selling the excess stock in this way provides an opportunity to make space in the warehouse for new (more profitable) offerings.

- *Decline*—The dress ceases to be fashionable and is replaced with a new design.

Each of these specific stages of development has different characteristics, requiring different business and marketing approaches. This, in turn, has led to the development of software systems and applications that are geared to manage the individual characteristics of each stage. Importantly, ASOS also operates in the southern hemisphere where seasons are opposite to those in the UK, allowing the company to sell its products continuously. Product lifecycle management (PLM) systems are used to deal with the process of managing the life cycle of a product from its inception through design and manufacture, to service, delivery, and returns, providing marketing managers with an item's sales history and facilities to integrate order tracking, invoicing, and operations activities. It looks like fast fashion is getting even faster!

Sources: Briggs (2014); https://www.inditex.com/about-us/our-brands/zara

Theory into Practice

This market insight describes how the concept of the product life cycle operates in fashion retailing, with specific reference to both online and offline firms that dominate the European market today. The insight also illustrates how important the supply chain is in getting products to market quickly and how this critical success factor is linked to the product's life cycle more generally.

Related Topics

fashion retailing; multichannel marketing; supply chain management

1 How might, for example, ASOS's marketing activities change as it moves into the mature stage?

2 Use a search engine to find the leading online fashion companies in Australia, Canada, and another country of your choice. What do all these companies have in common?

3 How might customers' needs change over the next five years?

The product life cycle works reasonably well as a model when the environment is relatively stable and not subject to dynamic swings or short-lived customer preferences. However, contemporary marketing managers are not concerned where their brand is within the product life cycle; there are many other more meaningful ways and metrics with which they can understand the competitive strength and development of a brand (for example competitive benchmarking, brand health studies). The concept of the product life cycle has also been criticized for giving managers tunnel vision, because they assume that a brand will follow a pre-ordained advance along the curve when, in fact, a product can fail at any stage (Moon, 2005).

Service-Dominant Logic

Some researchers believe that products alone are not capable of meeting all of a customer's needs (Grönroos, 2009), particularly in B2B markets. For business customers to derive value from a product, they need to use it, and that often requires a level of integration or coordination with a supplier's processes and systems. This requirement, it is argued, suggests the need for a proposition with characteristics more like those of a service than a core product offering. There is growing recognition that satisfying a customers' needs is inherently a service—that is, selling bottled water as a physical product is really the offering of a thirst-quenching service. Since marketing is a customer management process, this entails not only proposing how an offering might be of value to customers, but also enabling and supporting customers to create the value they require through their use of the product.

This notion that all propositions really embody a service is referred to as the service-dominant logic (SDL) approach, and was first proposed by Vargo and Lusch (2004) (see Chapter 1). The traditional marketing management approach can be considered product-dominant logic. So if products alone are insufficient to meet customer needs, it is better to consider services as a more realistic means of understanding how marketing works (see Research Insight 8.2).

In more recent work, Vargo and Lusch (2016: 8) have updated their original thinking to develop 11 foundational premises (FPs) about the essentially service-based nature of marketing:

- FP1—Service is the fundamental basis of exchange.

- FP2—Indirect exchange masks the fundamental basis of exchange.

- FP3—Goods are distribution mechanisms for service provision.

 Research Insight 8.2

To take your learning further, you might wish to read this influential paper:

Vargo, S.L., and Lusch, R.F. (2004). Evolving to a new dominant logic for marketing. *Journal of Marketing*, **68(1), 1–17.**

This article introduces the ideas concerning service-dominant logic. It sets out the conceptual underpinning of the approach by tracking back and considering previous major marketing approaches, outlining eight foundational premises concerning how the proposition in marketing is inherently a service and affirming that this requires a reconsideration of how marketing should be undertaken.

 Visit the **online resources** to read the abstract and access the full paper.

- FP4—Operant resources [that is, knowledge and skills] are the fundamental source of strategic benefit.

- FP5—All economies are service economies.

- FP6—Value is cocreated by multiple actors [for example organizations], always including the beneficiary.

- FP7—Actors [that is, organizations] cannot deliver value but can participate in the creation and offering of value propositions.

- FP8—A service-centered view is inherently beneficiary oriented and relational.

- FP9—All social and economic actors [for example organizations] are resource integrators.

- FP10—Value is always uniquely and phenomenologically determined by the beneficiary.

- FP11—Value cocreation is coordinated through actor-generated [for example organization-generated] institutions and institutional arrangements.

The SDL concept has been criticized for being of little practical use to marketers (O'Shaughnessy and O'Shaughnessy, 2009), but it has generated important discussions about how organizations and their customers work together to co-create new propositions and that, regardless of the physical embodiment of those propositions, they are inherently a service offering. We turn to how new propositions are developed in the next section.

Developing New Propositions

In this section, we examine the principles and approaches used to innovate and develop new propositions for both physical (goods) and non-physical (services) propositions.

Developing New Physical Propositions

One of the key points that the concept of the product life cycle tells us is that products do not last forever; their usefulness diminishes at some point, and eventually nearly all come to an end and die. There are many reasons for this cycle: technology changes quickly, so products are developed and adopted faster; life cycles are shortening (see Market Insight 8.3, earlier in the chapter), and so new products are required faster than before. In addition to this, global competition means that if an organization is to compete successfully and survive, it needs to continually offer superior value to its customers. Consequently, a key management task is to maintain control of the organization's range or portfolio of products, and to anticipate when one product has become tired and new ones are necessary to sustain the organization and help it to grow.

The term 'new products' can be misleading. This is because there is a spectrum of newness, relevant to both the organization and to customers. Some new products might be totally new to both the organization and the market. For example, the Apple iPod revolutionized the portable media player market, which had previously been dominated by the Sony Walkman. However, some new products might be only minor adaptations that have no real impact on a market other than offering an interesting new feature (for example new colours, flavours, and pack sizes).

Unfortunately, 'new' propositions do not appear at the click of a marketer's fingers; rather, they have to be considered, planned, developed, and carefully introduced to the market. To ensure a stream of new propositions, organizations have three main options:

- buy in finished products from other suppliers, perhaps from other parts of the world, or license the use of other products for specific periods of time (for example Samsung's licensing of its processor technology);

- develop products through collaboration with suppliers or even competitors, for example as Sony tried to do, but failed, with Ericsson in the mobile phone business (Parnell, 2012); or

- develop new products internally, often through R&D departments or by adapting current products with minor design and engineering changes (for example as Dyson did with its dual-cyclone vacuum cleaner).

Whatever the preferred route, each necessitates a procedure or development pattern through which the new product can be brought to the market. There is no uniform process to new product development (Ozer, 2003); many approaches exist and the procedures an organization adopts reflect its attitude to risk, its culture, its strategy, the proposition, and the market, as well as—above all else—its approach to the development of customer relationships.

The success rate of new products is consistently poor. About 95 per cent of new products fail, according to Harvard Business School's Clay Christensen, often because firms are using inadequate segmentation approaches (Nobel, 2011). According to Drucker (1985), there are three main reasons for this:

1 No market exists for the product. For example the Sinclair C5 (a one-person electric car) famously launched in 1985 in the UK and was swiftly withdrawn nine months later when the company folded (Roberts, 2015).

2 There is a market need, but the product fails to meet customer requirements, for example Frito-Lay's WOW! fat-free crisps, made with olestra, launched in the United States in 1998, but caused gastrointestinal problems in consumers and were quietly withdrawn in 2004 (Glass, 2012).

3 The product's ability to meet the market need, although satisfactory, is not adequately communicated to the target market, for example Buckler, a very low alcohol beer in the Dutch market in the 1980s (Anon., n.d.). Ironically, low- and no-alcohol beer sales have now taken off, a record 18.2 million litres of it selling in the UK in 2017 (Woolfson, 2017).

Successful new propositions are developed on the basis of understanding customers' needs and competitors' product successes and future intentions, and partly by developing the technology to meet those identified needs. For example, when an Asian entrant to the US market for medical devices and capital equipment quickly established itself, it was thought that its lower prices were the main reason for its success. However, when a major manufacturer reviewed its own proposition, it also analysed customer needs and the nature of the competition. The results showed that the US manufacturer's products were perceived to lag slightly behind those of its competitor on several critical attributes that mattered more to customers than had previously been thought. The competitor's product also cost less to manufacture and the competitor had considerable room to lower its costs further. The US manufacturer's response was to close the cost gap by generating ideas that bridged 80 per cent of the cost disadvantage. This was all achieved without compromising those features that users valued (Narayanan, Padhi, and Williams, 2012).

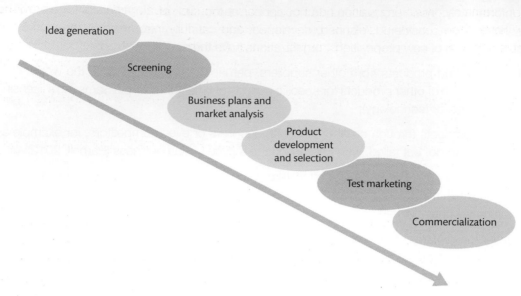

Figure 8.5

Stages within the new product development process

The development of new propositions is a complex and high-risk task, so organizations usually adopt a procedural approach. The procedure consists of several phases (stages and gates) that enable progress to be monitored, test trials to be conducted, and the results analysed before there is any commitment to the market. The most common new product development process (NPDP) is set out in Figure 8.5.

The NPDP presented in Figure 8.5 should be considered a generalization. In practice, actions can overlap, or even occur out of sequence, depending on the speed, complexity, and number of people or organizations involved in the NPDP. Apart from some minor issues, the process is the same when developing new propositions for both consumer and business markets. The process is generally perceived to be linear (but is not required to be such) in that new proposition development occurs only after managers are satisfied with progress of the development project at each stage. Therefore there is a go–no-go decision at each stage (that is, a gate). This process is often referred to as the stage–gate model.

 Visit the **online resources** and follow the web link to the Product Development and Management Association (PDMA) to learn more about the professional development, information, collaboration, and promotion of new product development and management.

Idea Generation

Ideas can be generated through customers, competitors (through website and sales literature analysis), market research data (such as reports), social media analyses, R&D, customer service employees, the sales force, project development teams, and secondary data sources such as sales records. What this means is that organizations should foster a corporate culture that encourages creativity and supports people when they bring forward new ideas for product enhancements and other improvements. 3M famously allows its engineers and scientists to spend 15 per cent of their time pursuing projects of their own choice, and

30 per cent of a division's revenue must come from products developed within the previous four years. Over the years, the company has introduced such pioneering products as the Post-it® note, Scotch™ tape, and the first electronic stethoscope with Bluetooth technology. To encourage resourcefulness in the company, 3M allows employees to bid for seed capital to form their own venture teams, and allows engineers and scientists to obtain the same level of prestige and compensation as corporate management (Govindarajan and Srinivas, 2013).

Visit the **online resources** and complete Internet Activity 8.3 to learn more about how two leading FMCG companies approach the NPDP.

Screening

All ideas need to be assessed so that only those that meet predetermined criteria are advanced. Key criteria include the fit between the proposed new idea and the overall corporate strategy and objectives. Another consideration involves the views of customers, which can be determined using concept testing. Other approaches consider how the market will react to the idea and what effort the organization will need to make if the offering is to be brought to market successfully. Whatever approaches are used, screening must be a separate activity to the idea-generation stage. If it is not, creativity might be impaired.

Business Planning and Market Analysis

The development of a business plan is crucial, simply because it will indicate the potential and relative profitability of the product. To prepare the plan, important information about the size, shape, and dynamics of the market should be determined. The resultant profitability forecasts will be significant in determining how and when the product will be developed, if at all.

Product Development and Selection

In many organizations, several product ideas are considered simultaneously. It is management's task to select those that have commercial potential and are in the best interests of the organization and its longer-term strategy, goals, and use of resources. There is a trade-off between the need to test and reduce risk, and the need to go to market and drive income to get a return on the investment committed to the new proposition. This phase is expensive, so only a limited number of projects are allowed to proceed into development. Prototypes and test versions are developed for those projects that are selected for further development. These are then subjected to functional performance tests, design revisions, manufacturing requirements analysis, distribution analysis, and a multitude of other testing procedures.

Test Marketing

Before committing a new product to a market, most organizations decide to test market the finished product (see also Chapter 3). By piloting and testing the product under controlled real-market conditions, many of the genuine issues as perceived by customers can be raised and resolved, while minimizing any damage or risk to the organization and the brand. **Test marketing** can be undertaken using a particular geographical region or specific number of customer locations. For example, Nestlé was the first company in the world to commercialize new 'ruby' chocolate (a naturally pink chocolate) in its KitKat bars, launching the product first in Japan for Valentine's Day (Rodionova, 2018).

The intention of test marketing is to evaluate the product and the whole marketing programme under real working conditions. Test marketing (including field trials) enables the product and marketing plan to be refined or adapted in the light of market reaction, but before release to the whole market. Clydesdale and Yorkshire Banking Group (CYBG) have developed what it calls the 'Studio B' concept—essentially, a 'customer lab' resembling a high-spec retail store, complete with facial recognition and robot technology. In this way, CYBG hopes to use customer interaction with these technologies to develop the next generation of banking services (Page, 2018).

It is vital for organizations to set up a system to measure the success or failure of new product development. Criteria for measuring success and failure include (but are not limited to) measures based on customer acceptance, financial performance, and product- and firm-level considerations (Griffin and Page, 1993).

- *Customer acceptance* measures include:

  - customer acceptance;

  - customer satisfaction;

  - net revenue goals;

  - net market share goals; and

  - net unit sales goals.

- *Financial performance* measures include:

  - break-even period;

  - margin goals;

  - profitability goals; and

  - internal rate of return (IRR) or return on investment (ROI).

- *Product-level* measures include:

  - development cost;

  - launched on time;

  - product performance level;

  - net quality guidelines; and

  - speed to market.

- *Firm-level* measurements include the percentage of sales attained as a proportion of new products/services.

Commercialization

To commercialize a new product, a launch plan is required. This considers the needs of **distributors**, end users, marketing communication agencies, and other relevant stakeholders. The objective is to schedule all those activities that are required to make the launch successful. These include communications (to inform audiences of the product's capabilities, and to position and persuade potential customers), training, and product support for all customer-facing employees.

Any perceived rigidity in this formal process should be disregarded. Many new offerings come to market via rather different routes, at different speeds, and at different levels of preparation.

Developing New Service Propositions

So far, the focus has been on the processes associated with developing new products, without reference to services. This is mainly because researchers have paid much more attention in the marketing literature to the development issues associated with products. This has altered in recent years because many Western economies have become heavily service-oriented.

Möller, Rajala, and Westerlund (2008) have developed ideas based on the logic that value creation is key to the development of innovative service offerings and concepts. (See Market Insight 8.4 for an example of how this was done in the gaming sector.) They distinguish three service innovation strategies:

- established services within competitive markets;

- incremental service innovation targeting value-added propositions; and

- radical service innovation, which aims to produce completely novel offerings.

Market Insight 8.4
Minecraft: The Gamer's Proposition

The name 'Minecraft', broken into its two component syllables, itself embodies the notion of destruction for creation. This popular title, based upon games such as *Dwarf Fortress* and *Dungeon Keeper*, was the brain child of Markus 'Notch' Persson. Created using the Java programming language, this sandbox game (in which gamers are free to roam and create their own virtual worlds) allows the community not only to create avatars to express themselves within the world, but also to make modifications that impact upon the gameplay itself. Popular mod packs, such as FeedTheBeast, have provided users with a whole host of free and additional content that ranges from magic and fantastical lands to technology-based systems.

The core proposition provides users with entertainment and emotional stimulation. On top of this, the embodied proposition provides users with a randomly generated world to explore and the ability to interact with other players who join, as well as various denizens such as snowmen, pigs, sheep, cows, and squids. The entire world is fully destructible and this allows players to build houses, cities, or anything that their hearts desire. Such fortifications are necessary for when the sun goes down, when enemies such as skeletons and zombies appear to wreak havoc.

Yet such innovative gameplay and freedom is not without its disadvantages: players who wish to disturb the gameplay experience of other users can do so freely. The destruction of structures built by others with explosives, throwing their items into lava, or killing them is quite commonplace. YouTube has become a popular place to upload videos of players trolling or disrupting others to the point that they quit the server. Such a display can put off potential customers and attract those who wish to replicate the acts that have been displayed—something that in turn will also drive away current users.

In response to this, the game itself has been augmented by the community in a post-purchase fashion. New modifications allow server owners to install plug-ins on their worlds, designed to protect user possessions and minimize the amount of disruption that can be caused. These do help to guarantee players some element of safety, but also reduce their freedom to interact with the world—something that impacts upon the embodied proposition put forward and advertised by the developers.

Yet, despite these setbacks, the game continues to grow in popularity (surpassing 100 million registered accounts in 2014). Microsoft purchased

Market Insight 8.4
continued

the company for US$2.5 billion in 2014; by February 2017, the game had 55 million active players—up from 40 million in June 2016. In addition, merchandise, mobile, and console versions have also appeared within the product line. Such a success story demonstrates that games developers can work with the community to enhance their original vision and improve their games without needing to retain full control.

Sources: Plé and Chumpitaz Cáceres (2010); Etherington (2014); Maiberg (2014); Makuch (2014); Anon. (2018); Statista (2018).

Theory into Practice

This market insight demonstrates how a newly launched proposition can have clear core, embodied, and augmenting propositions at the outset, and how these can change over time. This change may be driven by the developer by means of software updates, but it can also be undertaken by the consumers. Such a notion is exciting and a win–win for the provider, but can come at the cost of undermining their artistic vision and marketing campaigns if the proposition no longer exists as advertised—an intriguing problem. This market insight illustrates the importance of focusing on value co-creation and building good relationships with users. The company's approach to innovation corresponds with the radical service innovation category of Möller and colleagues (2008), which aims at producing completely novel offerings. Co-creation, as an approach to new proposition development, is becoming commonplace for many businesses, but is particularly evident in the video gaming and entertainment sector.

Related Topics

value; value co-creation; value co-destruction; new product development; product forms

1 **Plot the Minecraft game onto the three proposition components model. Is the game a product or a service?**

2 **Do you think other games developers will attempt to imitate this open-ended sandbox gameplay?**

3 **Has Minecraft's owner, Mojang, experienced its success because of a lack of direct competitors? Explain your answer.**

This market insight was kindly contributed by Joe Liddiatt, at the University of the West of England, UK.

Established services with a relatively stable value creation process are often generated under intense competition to improve operational efficiency. Dell is cited as a manufacturing business based on a simple concept, specifically selling computer systems directly to customers (rather than through retailers or other intermediaries). Dell's market leadership is the result of a constant focus on delivering positive product and service experiences to its customers.

Incremental service innovation describes a value creation strategy in which services are developed to provide extra value. Working together, the service provider and the client can produce more effective solutions. The prime example is Google, which, in addition to providing web search services for individual consumers, provides search services for corporate clients, including advertisers, content publishers, and site managers. Google continually develops new service applications based on its back-end technology and the use of linked PCs that respond immediately to each query. Google's innovation has resulted in faster response times, greater scalability, and lower costs. But Google also has a vast constellation of innovation projects, including spin-off companies investigating extending the human lifespan (Calico), Google's driverless car, drones (Project Wing), Google Fiber, Replicant (robotics projects), and many more (see Chapter 1).

Radical service innovation is concerned with value creation generated through novel or unusual service concepts. This requires new technologies, offerings, or business concepts, and involves radical system-wide changes in existing value systems. MySQL, the world's leading open-source software (OSS) database producer, uses this approach. Because the source code of the software is freely available to everybody, the software is available to everyone to use and/or modify. However, all derivative works must be made available to the original developers. As a result, MySQL has been able to increase the number of users and developers, and subsequently offer its clients improved levels of service—and this has led to increased financial performance.

Enhancing Physical Propositions through Service Development

It is helpful to view proposition innovation in the light of the product–service spectrum introduced at the start of this chapter. Services do not always need to be seen purely as an extension or add-on to a product offering; they can also be a way of creating value opportunities for clients. Shelton (2009) considers service innovation in the context of four stages of solution management maturity. The early stages of innovation maturity are characterized by a goods focus, with relatively few services used only to augment and complement those goods. The mature stages are characterized by much higher levels of service, some integrated with the products to provide solutions for customer problems:

- *Stage 1*—In this stage, services are used as aftersales support for goods (for example parts and repair services). Service innovation is framed around maintaining the good and ensuring that customers are satisfied with their purchase. As a result, customers typically view the service and goods business as distinct entities.

- *Stage 2*—This stage is characterized by aftersales services designed to complement the core element of the proposition. Here, services should improve customer satisfaction with existing goods, should increase loyalty, and may generate additional purchases. Shelton (2009) refers to Hewlett Packard's 'PC Tune-Up', which, for a fee, provides a set of diagnostics with which to assess and manage customers.

- *Stage 3*—At this stage, the portfolio includes a full line of services and goods designed to provide a clearly differentiated offering aimed at solving clients' lifecycle problems. Shelton (2009) refers to Motorola's 'Total Network Care' (TNC), which provides end-to-end support services for wireless networks. Although the service organization is often consolidated into one identifiable business, goods are still core to the company. End users see no major perceived boundaries between goods and services.

- *Stage 4*—At this stage, the highest end of innovation maturity, firms seek to integrate the services dimension as part of their total offer. Known as **servitization**, this involves the provision of an integrated bundle of goods–service solutions for the entire life cycle of their customers, 'from cradle to grave'. These solutions are developed collaboratively with clients and therefore require a deep understanding of the customer's overall business. These firms, often market leaders, generate innovative solutions through buyer–seller collaborative processes. Solutions are developed that are of mutual value.

Servitization strategies have been used to create value in a number of different industries. Robinson, Clarke-Hill, and Clarkson (2002) report their use in the chemical industry, where price-led strategies tend to dominate in a commodity context. What is noticeable is that where commodity chemical firms have implemented servitization, one of the more prominent uses has been to help to build relationships and reduce both the attitudinal and physical distance between partner organizations.

Visit the **online resources** and complete Internet Activity 8.4 to learn more about how two leading service-based organizations approach the service development process.

Service Development

As the distinctions between what is a product and what is a service blur, the traditional distinction between product development and service development is becoming increasingly artificial (Papastathopoulou and Hultink, 2012). Managers responsible for new service development should establish a system that incorporates a formal procedure for generating and evaluating new service ideas, a drawing-board approach for identifying and designing the necessary service elements and processes, and testing of new services with customers and with frontline staff to eliminate potential failure points, and a documented launch plan to ensure the proper marketing of new services (de Brentani, 1991). This process is not dissimilar to the stage–gate model outlined in Figure 8.5.

An organization developing services should have processes that become more formal as the project progresses over time, should have well-established idea-screening processes in place to determine which new ideas will be given the go-ahead by senior management, and should have a system in place to ensure that the staff are well trained and committed to selling the new service (Edgett, 1994). Services should be designed to ensure that it is easy for customers to be involved in the development of the new service and to actively contribute to the service design process. This customer involvement is often a critical success factor in the development of successful new services, perhaps even more so than in new product development projects, because of the enhanced nature of the customer–producer interaction (see Research Insight 8.3). (See also Chapter 15 for more on the simultaneous production and consumption of services and their marketing implications.)

Some services undergo **beta testing**, whereby a version of the service is made available to customers, and any imperfections are identified and removed before the final version of the service is launched. Software developers have made use of this approach extensively, as have music-streaming companies such as Google, with Google Music Key and even, allegedly, Apple with Apple Music for Android (Chenze, 2015) (see Market Insight 8.5).

Research Insight 8.3

To take your learning further, you might wish to read this influential paper:

Edvardsson, B., Kristensson, P., Magnusson, P., and Sundström, E. (2012). Customer integration within service development: a review of methods and an analysis of in situ and ex situ contributions. *Technovation*, 32(7), 419–29.

This interesting article outlines how customer feedback can be integrated into new service development. It develops a framework for categorizing customer integration methods based on whether the data are obtained in situ or ex situ and in context or ex context, creating four types of customer informant:

- the *correspondent* (in situ/in context, reporting live from the situation);

- the *reflective practitioner* (ex situ/in context, reporting from 'the armchair');

- the *tester* (in situ, ex context, reporting from 'virtual heaven'); and

- the *dreamer* (ex situ/ex context, the creative generating wild and imaginative ideas).

The article explains how it is neither sufficient to follow customer requirements in new service development nor should companies try to lead customers; rather, they should work with them to co-create new service propositions.

 Visit the online resources to read the abstract and access the full paper.

Market Insight 8.5
Streaming Wars: Apple versus Spotify

In June 2015, Apple revealed that it would offer a 'revolutionary' new music-streaming service based on the music-streaming service it had acquired after purchasing Beats, with a target of acquiring 100 million paying subscribers. Obtaining such a user base would be achievable if 20 per cent of Apple's 500 million or so iTunes users worldwide were to connect to the subscription service. But whilst Apple's music download service iTunes and its music storage and play device, the iPod, were innovative in 2001, another company had beaten Apple to the streaming market. Spotify, a Swedish company using a **freemium** business model, already had 20 million paying subscribers and 55 million users on its free ad-supported service, and has largely displaced iTunes

in the desktop and smartphone distribution channels. Spotify was the music-streaming market leader in 2017, with more than 60 million paying subscribers and 140 million active users (Reuters, 2017), although the company is not (yet) profitable, having lost US$581 million in 2016.

Despite these losses for Spotify, the music-streaming market continues to be attractive, with 97 million subscriber accounts worldwide and revenues growing by 60.4 per cent on the previous year. The question arises: what new features will Apple bring to the music-streaming party? Apple has stated that it will differentiate its service by generating playlists chosen by people rather than algorithms, offer a superior music

Market Insight 8.5
continued

search process, and provide a 24-hour radio station (Beats One), but it will not offer a free ad-supported service.

Apple are therefore seeking to cream off Spotify's most lucrative customers: the quarter of Spotify users who pay to subscribe represent three-quarters of the company's revenues. And Apple's approach might just work, because artists such as Taylor Swift (who removed herself from Spotify) are fed up with the pittance (around $0.007 per stream) that they receive when their tracks are played over the free ad-supported service (although they receive considerably more from the subscription service).

Taking the potential challenge from the world's largest brand seriously, Spotify raised $500 million, presumably to help it to further develop its own music-streaming service. But Apple are not its only competition; Google has been beta testing its Music Key service, which will shift YouTube to a freemium business model like Spotify's. And Apple has tried to enter the market before, when it unsuccessfully launched its Beats Music service in 2014. Google had also previously launched a service in 2011 that failed—Google Play Music All

Access. This is clearly a hard market to crack, not least because, until recently, music customers were happier to download music illegally and risk criminal prosecution than to pay for it. What is clear is that now that customers are shifting back to paying for their music, the battle for market leadership will continue to intensify.

Sources: Anon. (2015b); Sexton (2015); Witt (2015); Christman (2017); (IFPI, 2017).

Apple's 24-hour radio station is one of the ways it tries to differentiate its service
Source: © Hadrian / Shutterstock.com.

Theory into Practice

This market insight describes how music distributors are competing to offer music-streaming services. It illustrates how Spotify stole a march on Apple's iTunes service by developing a technologically superior approach to music distribution (streaming versus digital downloading). The case also illustrates the difficulties inherent in designing and offering a new service when technological standards and business models are still in flux.

Related Topics

service design; technological generations; diffusion of innovation; customer value; beta testing

1 **Why do you think Apple has come so late to the music-streaming market?**

2 **What does Spotify need to do to retain its market leadership?**

3 **How do you think music distribution might develop in the future? What service developments might take place?**

If organizations are to improve the effectiveness of their service development processes, service development researchers point towards the need for them to:

- leverage their employees' skills, resources, and experiences in the new service development process;

- develop more customer-oriented services; and

- undertake an interdisciplinary approach to service development, bringing together marketing, operations, and innovation staff (Papastathopoulou and Hultink, 2012).

The Process of Adoption

The process by which individuals accept and use new propositions is referred to as adoption (Rogers, 1983). The different stages in the **process of adoption** are sequential and are characterized by the different factors that are involved at each stage (for example the media used by each individual). The process starts with people gaining awareness of a proposition as it moves through various stages of adoption before a purchase is eventually made. Figure 8.6 sets out the various stages in the process of adoption.

In the *knowledge* stage, consumers become aware of the new proposition. They have little information and have yet to develop any particular attitudes towards the product. Indeed, at this stage, consumers are not interested in finding out any more information.

The *persuasion* stage is characterized by consumers becoming aware that the innovation may be of use in solving a potential problem. Consumers become sufficiently motivated to find out more about the proposition's characteristics, including its features, price, and availability.

In the *decision* stage, individuals develop an attitude toward the proposition and reach a decision about whether the innovation will meet their needs. If this is positive, they will experiment with the innovation.

During the *implementation* stage, users try the innovation for the first time. Sales promotions often offer samples to allow individuals to test the product without any undue risk. Individuals accept or reject an innovation on the basis of their experience of the trial. Consider, for example,

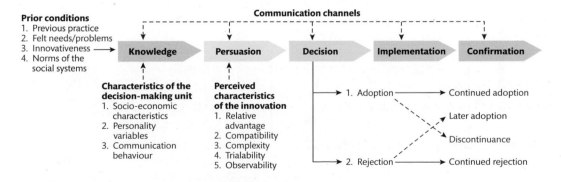

Figure 8.6

Stages in the innovation decision process of adoption

Source: Reprinted from Rogers (1983) with the permission of the Free Press, © 1962, 1971, 1983 by the Free Press.

the way in which manufacturers work with supermarkets or duty-free airport retailers to encourage people to sample their food and drink products.

The final *confirmation* stage is signalled when an individual successfully purchases the proposition on a regular basis without the help of the sales promotion or other incentives.

The model in Figure 8.6 assumes that the adoption stages occur in a predictable sequence, but this is not always the case. Rejection of the innovation can occur at any point—even during implementation and the very early phases of the confirmation stage. Generally, mass communications are more effective in the earlier phases of the adoption process for propositions that buyers are actively interested in and more interpersonal forms are more appropriate in later stages—especially implementation and confirmation.

Diffusion Theory

Consumers may have both functional and emotional motives when purchasing, but customers adopt new propositions differently. Their different attitudes to risk, and their levels of education, experience, and needs, mean that different groups of customers adopt new propositions at varying speeds. The rate at which a market adopts an innovation is referred to as the **process of diffusion** (Rogers, 1962). According to Rogers (1962), there are five categories of adopter, as shown in Figure 8.7:

■ **Innovators**—This group, which constitutes 2.5 per cent of the buying population, is important because it kick-starts the adoption process. These people like new ideas, and are often well educated, young, confident, and financially strong. They are more likely to take risks associated with new propositions. However, being an innovator in one category, such as buying a new model smartphone, does not mean that a person will be an innovator in another category, such as buying an electric car. Innovative attitudes and behaviour can be specific to only one or two areas of interest.

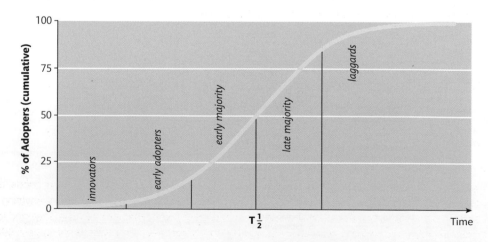

Figure 8.7

The process of diffusion

Source: Rogers (1962): fig. 5.1 © 1955, 2003 by Everett M. Rogers © 1962, 1971, 1983 by the Free Press.

- **Early adopters**—This group, comprising 13.5 per cent of the market, is characterized by a high percentage of opinion leaders. These people are very important for speeding up the adoption process. Consequently, marketing communications need to be targeted at these people, who, in turn, will stimulate word-of-mouth communications to spread information. Although early adopters prefer to let innovators take all the risks, they enjoy being at the leading edge of innovation, tend to be younger than any other group, and are above average in education. Other than innovators, this group reads more publications and consults more salespeople than all others.

- **Early majority**—This group, which forms 34 per cent of the market, is more risk-averse than the previous two groups. Individuals require reassurance that the offering works and has been proved in the market. They are above average in terms of age, education, social status, and income. Unlike the early adopters, they tend to wait for prices to fall, prefer more informal sources of information, and are often prompted into purchase by other people who have already purchased.

- **Late majority**—A similar size to the previous group (34 per cent), the late majority are sceptical of new ideas and adopt new offerings only because of social or economic factors. They read few publications and are below average in terms of education, social status, and income.

- **Laggards**—This group of people, comprising 16 per cent of the buying population, are suspicious of all new ideas and their opinions are very hard to change. Laggards have the lowest income, social status, and education of all the groups, and take a long time to adopt an innovation, if they ever adopt it at all.

According to Gatignon and Robertson (1985), the rate of diffusion is a function of the speed at which sales occur, the pattern of diffusion (as expressed in the shape of the curve), and the size of the market. This means that diffusion does not occur at a constant or predictable speed; rather, it may be fast or slow. One of the tasks of marketing communications is to speed up the process, so that the return on the investment necessary to develop the innovation is achieved as quickly and as efficiently as possible.

Marketing managers need to ensure that they consider diffusion groups when attempting to understand and predict the diffusion process for innovations. It is likely that a promotional campaign targeted at innovators and the early majority, and geared towards stimulating word-of-mouth communications, will be more successful as a result.

Chapter Summary

To consolidate your learning, the key points from this chapter are summarized here:

- **Explain the different levels of a proposition.**

  A proposition encompasses all the tangible and intangible attributes related not only to physical goods, but also to services, ideas, people, places, experiences, and even a mix of these various elements. Anything that can be offered for use and consumption in exchange for money or some other form of value is referred to as a proposition. Unlike products, services are considered to be processes. Propositions encompass three levels: the core proposition, consisting of the real core benefit or service (for example bottled water is thirst-quenching); the embodied proposition, consisting of the physical good or delivered service that provides the expected benefit (for example the packaging); and the augmented proposition, consisting of the embodied offering plus all those other factors that are necessary to support the purchase and any post-purchase activities (for example the exclusivity associated with Voss bottled water and its Norwegian heritage).

■ **Identify and describe the various types of physical proposition and explain particular concepts relating to the management of products, including the product life cycle.**

Consumer and business products are classified in different ways, but both classifications are related to the way in which customers use them. Consumer products are bought to satisfy personal and family needs, and industrial and business products are bought either as a part of the business's operations or to make other products for resale. To meet the needs of different target markets, most organizations offer a range of products and services, which are grouped together in terms of product lines and product mix. Products are thought to move through a sequential pattern of development, referred to as the product life cycle. It consists of five distinct stages: development; birth; growth; maturity; and decline. Each stage of the cycle represents a different set of market circumstances and customer expectations that need to be met with different strategies.

■ **Explain the relationship between product and service offerings, and describe the product–service spectrum.**

A service is any act or performance offered by one party to another that is essentially intangible. Consumption of the service does not result in any transfer of ownership, even though the service process may be attached to a physical product. There is a spectrum of product–service combinations. At one extreme, there are pure products with no services, such as grocery products. At the other end of the spectrum are pure services, for which there is no tangible product support, such as education and dentistry. In between, there is a mixture of product–service arrangements. The product–service spectrum recognizes that many products combine physical goods with a service element.

■ **Explore the processes and issues associated with innovating new propositions.**

The development of new propositions is complex and high risk, so organizations usually adopt a procedural approach. The procedure consists of several phases that enable progress to be monitored, test trials to be conducted, and the results analysed before there is any commitment to the market. The development of new services follows a similar staged process, whereby additional services are added to a core product until a point is reached at which the service and the core product are integrated into a bundled offering. This is known as servitization.

■ **Describe how new propositions are adopted by markets.**

The processes of adoption and diffusion explain the way in which individuals adopt new propositions and the rate at which a market adopts an innovation. The process by which individuals accept and use new propositions is referred to as adoption. The different stages in the adoption process are sequential and are characterized by the different factors that are involved at each stage. The rate at which a market adopts an innovation differs according to an individual's propensity for risk and is referred to as the process of diffusion.

 # Review Questions

1 Draw the spectrum of product–service combinations and briefly explain its main characteristics.
2 Identify the three levels that make up a proposition.
3 Describe the three types of convenience good and find examples to illustrate each one.
4 What are the six types of business product?
5 What is the product life cycle and what key characteristics make up each of its stages?

6 How do the essential characteristics of services affect the marketing of services?

7 What are the main stages associated with the development of new physical propositions?

8 What is servitization?

9 Name four companies that have used the servitization approach and explain how.

10 Why is knowledge about the process of adoption useful to marketers?

 ## Discussion Questions

1 Having read Case Insight 8.1, how should Cheil UK develop its client Samsung's omni-channel offering to bring together Samsung's customers' experiences both online and offline?

2 Describe the three elements of a proposition for the following:

   A A live football match at the stadium of Spanish football club Real Madrid

   B A can of Diet Coke purchased from a vending machine in a train station

   C A watercooler system from Aquaid for use in offices

3 Prepare a brief report in which you explain the nature of the product life cycle for a grocery brand of your choice. Consider how it might be used to improve your brand's marketing activities and, from this, highlight any difficulties that might arise when using the product life cycle to develop strategies.

4 Consider three offerings that you bought recently. For each of them, determine what kind of adopter you were and how you were influenced to purchase the offering that you bought. (*Hint*: Use Roger's theory of diffusion.)

 Visit the online resources and complete the Multiple-Choice Questions to assess your knowledge of Chapter 8.

 ## Glossary

accessory equipment goods goods that support the key operational processes and activities of the organization.

beta testing the stage at which software is made available on a website to allow users to test its functionality after it has gone through a development phase and to allow any necessary modification before full commercialization.

built-in obsolescence when a manufacturer develops a product so that it deliberately requires replacement, aiming to enhance sales and/or profitability.

capital equipment goods those goods, such as buildings, heavy plant, and factory equipment, that are necessary to build or assemble products.

co-creation the process of developing a proposition of value to a customer by incorporating their input and that of other stakeholders into its design, development and/or delivery.

content marketing the marketing process for the creation and dissemination of narrative (non-product) content to attract and engage a specific target audience to encourage a particular marketing action (for example sales).

convenience products non-durable goods or services, often bought with little pre-purchase thought or consideration.

co-production the process of involving customers and stakeholders in the development and delivery of the proposition; differs slightly from co-creation in that customers and stakeholders are involved earlier, at the design stage.

digital value the means by which digital processes and systems can be used to provide customers with enhanced product and service value.

distributors organizations that buy goods and services, often from a limited range of manufacturers, and normally sell them to retailers or resellers.

durable goods goods bought infrequently, which are used repeatedly and involve a reasonably high level of consumer risk.

early adopters a group of people in the process of diffusion who enjoy being at the leading edge of innovation and who buy into new products at an early stage.

early majority a group of people in the process of diffusion who require reassurance that a product works and has been proven in the market before they are prepared to buy it.

extensive problem-solving occurs when consumers give a great deal of attention and care to a purchase decision of which they have no previous or similar product purchase experience.

freemium a business model incorporating the offer of a free basic service, together with a paid-for enhanced service.

innovators a group of people in the process of diffusion who like new ideas and who are most likely to take risks associated with new products.

laggards a group of people in the process of diffusion who are suspicious of all new ideas and whose opinions are very hard to change.

late majority a group of people in the process of diffusion who are sceptical of new ideas and who adopt new products only because of social or economic factors.

limited problem-solving occurs when consumers have some product and purchase familiarity.

maintenance, repair, and operating (MRO) goods those goods, other than raw materials, that are necessary to ensure that the organization is able to continue functioning; often referred to as consumables.

non-durable goods low-priced products that are bought frequently, used only once, and incur low levels of purchase risk.

offerings things produced for sale.

process of adoption the process through which individuals accept and use new products; comprises different sequential stages characterized by different factors.

process of diffusion the rate at which a market adopts an innovation (Rogers, 1962), within which there are five categories of adopters: innovators; early adopters; early majority; late majority; and laggards.

product anything that is capable of satisfying customer needs.

product life cycle the pathway a product assumes over its lifetime, in which there are said to be five main stages: development; birth; growth; maturity; and decline.

proposition a product or service that represents a promise made to customers and stakeholders.

pure-play a company that focuses exclusively on one offering or operates only on the Internet.

routinized response behaviour a form of purchase behaviour that occurs when consumers have suitable product and purchase experience and they perceive low risk.

service any act or performance offered by one party to another that is essentially intangible and consumption of which does not result in any transfer of ownership.

service-dominant logic (SDL) an approach that asserts that organizations, markets, and society are concerned fundamentally with the exchange of services based on the application of knowledge and skills; rejects the notion of dualism between goods and services marketing, arguing that all offerings provide a service.

servitization the practice of integrating bundles of products and services in which the services are an integral part of the core product.

shopping product a type of consumer product that is bought relatively infrequently and requires consumers to update their knowledge prior to purchase.

speciality product the type of consumer product that is bought very infrequently, is very expensive, and represents very high risk.

stock-outs occasions on which an organization no longer has a particular offering in its inventory and that item is no available for customers to purchase, thus losing the organization potential revenue.

tangibility possessing the characteristics of something that is physical—that is, it can be touched and it has form or physical presence.

test marketing a stage in the new product development process, undertaken with a sample of customers or in a specified geographical area, to judge customers' reactions prior to a national launch.

unsought product a good that a customer would not normally purchase, either because they are

unaware of it or have no desire to purchase it, but under certain circumstances (usually fear or danger) they are required to purchase it, for example funeral services, insurance, and first aid kits.

References

Ala-Kurikka, S. (2015). Lifespan of consumer electronics is getting shorter, study finds. *The Guardian*, 3 March. Retrieve from: https://www.theguardian.com/environment/2015/mar/03/lifespan-of-consumer-electronics-is-getting-shorter-study-finds (accessed 13 October 2018).

Anon. (2011). Chanel No.5: The story behind the classic perfume. *BBC News*, 29 May. Retrieve from: https://www.bbc.co.uk/news/world-13565155 (accessed 13 October 2018).

Anon. (2015a). History of advertising: No. 132—the world's most expensive TV commercial. *Campaign*, 14 May. Retrieve from: https://www.campaignlive.co.uk/article/history-advertising-no-132-worlds-expensive-tv-commercial/1346688 (accessed 13 October 2018).

Anon. (2015b). The music business. *The Economist*, 13 June, 76.

Anon. (2017). Vinyl gets its groove back. *The Economist*, 20 May, 66.

Anon. (2018). Feed the beast. *Curseforge*. Retrieve from: https://www.feed-the-beast.com/ (accessed 13 October 2018).

Anon. (n.d.). Buckler beer on the Dutch market. *Institute of Brilliant Failures*. Retrieve from: https://www.briljantemislukkingen.nl/en/2012/02/buckler-beer-on-the-dutch-market/ (accessed 13 October 2018).

Armitage, J. (2015). How Airbus' bet on big went awry. *The Independent*, 15 August, 49.

Ausick, P. (2014). Will more seats help the Airbus A380 pay back its development cost? *24/7 Wall St*, 24 September. Retrieve from: https://247wallst.com/aerospace-defense/2014/09/24/will-more-seats-help-the-airbus-a380-pay-back-its-development-cost/ (accessed 13 October 2018).

Ausick, P. (2015). What does Boeing 787 Dreamliner cost? *24/7 Wall St*, 26 July. Retrieve from: https://247wallst.com/aerospace-defense/2015/07/26/what-does-boeing-787-dreamliner-cost/ (accessed 13 October 2018).

Briggs, F. (2014). Boxwood insights puts ASOS operating model under the spotlight. *Retail Times*, 12 December. Retrieve from: https://www.retailtimes.co.uk/retail-times-exclusive-boxwood-insights-puts-asos-operating-model-spotlight/ (accessed 13 October 2018).

Chaffey, D., Mayer, R., Johnston, K., and Ellis-Chadwick, F. (2009). *Internet Marketing* (4th edn). Harlow: FT/Prentice Hall.

Chenze, E. (2015). Apple Music for Android Beta invites to start rolling out soon. *Techweez*, 29 September. Retrieve from: https://www.techweez.com/2015/09/29/apple-music-android-beta-betabound/ (accessed 13 October 2018).

Christman, E. (2017). Spotify's losses more than double to $581m, revenues rise to $3b. *Billboard*, 15 July. Retrieve from: https://www.billboard.com/articles/business/7833686/spotify-2016-losses-financial-results-revenue (accessed 13 October 2018).

Clark, N. (2009). Knowing when to swing the axe. *Marketing*, February, 30–1.

Connell, A. (2016). Happy birthday Coco: here are the most iconic Chanel No.5 ads ever. *Stylecaster*. Retrieve from: https://stylecaster.com/beauty/vintage-chanel-no-5-ads/ (accessed 13 October 2018).

de Brentani, U. (1991). Success factors in developing new business services. *European Journal of Marketing*, 25(2), 33–59.

Drucker, P.F. (1985). The discipline of innovation. *Harvard Business Review*, 63(3), 67–72.

Edelman, D.C. (2010). Four ways to get more value from digital marketing. *McKinsey Quarterly*, March. Retrieve from: https://www.mckinsey.com/business-functions/marketing-and-sales/our-insights/four-ways-to-get-more-value-from-digital-marketing (accessed 13 October 2018).

Edgett, S. (1994). The traits of successful new service development. *Journal of Services Marketing*, 8(3), 40–9.

Edmond-Sargeant, T. (2014). The 5 most popular perfumes of all time. *The Richest*, 29 June. Retrieve from: https://www.therichest.com/rich-list/most-popular/the-5-most-popular-perfumes-of-all-time/ (accessed 13 October 2018).

Edvardsson, B., Kristensson, P., Magnusson, P., and Sundström, E. (2012). Customer integration within service development: a review of methods and an analysis of in situ and ex situ contributions. *Technovation*, 32(7), 419–29.

Etherington, D. (2014). Microsoft has acquired Minecraft for $2.5 billion. *Tech Crunch*. Retrieve from: https://techcrunch.com/2014/09/15/microsoft-has-acquired-minecraft/ (accessed 13 October 2018).

Gatignon, H., and Robertson, T.S. (1985). A propositional inventory for new diffusion research. *Journal of Consumer Research*, 11(4), 849–67.

Glass, S. (2012). What were they thinking? The chips that sent us to the loo. *Fast Company*, 17 January. Retrieve from: https://www.fastcompany.com/1809002/what-were-they-thinking-chips-sent-us-running-loo (accessed 13 October 2018).

Govindarajan, V., and Srinivas, S. (2013). The innovation mindset in action: 3M Corporation. *Harvard Business Review*, 6 August. Retrieve from: https://hbr.org/2013/08/the-innovation-mindset-in-acti-3 (accessed 13 October 2018).

Griffin, A., and Page, A.L. (1993). An interim report on measuring product development success and failure. *Journal of Product Innovation Management*, 10(4), 291–308.

Grönroos, C. (2009). Marketing as promise management: regaining customer management for marketing. *Journal of Business and Industrial Marketing*, 24(5–6), 351–9.

Hepher, T. (2018). Emirates hands Airbus A380 superjumbo a lifeline with $16 billion order. *Reuters*, 18 January. Retrieve from: https://www.reuters.com/article/us-airbus-emirates/emirates-hands-airbus-a380-superjumbo-a-lifeline-with-16-billion-order-idUSKBN1F71KJ (accessed 13 October 2018).

Hise, R.T., O'Neal, L., Parasuraman, A., and McNeal, J.U. (1990). Marketing/R&D interaction in new product development: implications for new product success rates. *Journal of Product Innovation Management*, 7(2), 142–55.

Holbrook, M.B., and Hirschman, E.C. (1982). The experiential aspects of consumption: consumer fantasies, feelings, and fun. *Journal of Consumer Research*, 9(2), 132–40.

IFPI (International Federation of the Phonographic Industry) (2017). *Global Music Report 2017*. Retrieve from: http://www.ifpi.org/downloads/GMR2017.pdf (accessed 13 October 2018).

Johnston, C. (2017). Why big brand perfumes may be losing their allure. *BBC News*, 4 October. Retrieve from: https://www.bbc.co.uk/news/business-41339121 (accessed 13 October 2018).

Jones, B. (2017). How long are these leading Android devices built to last for? *PSafeBlog,* 3 June. Retrieve from: https://www.psafe.com/en/blog/how-long-android-phones-last/ (accessed 13 October 2018).

Leistén, J., and Nilsson, M. (2009). Crossing the chasm: launching and re-launching in the Swedish mobile phone industry. Bachelor's dissertation, Jönköping International Business School. Retrieve from: https://www.diva-portal.org/smash/record.jsf?pid=diva2%3A158025&dswid=-3234 (accessed 13 October 2018).

Ljubisavljevic, M. (2016). Psychology of perfumes. *Scentbird*, 24 June. Retrieve from: https://www.scentbird.com/blog/psychology-perfumes/ (accessed 13 October 2018).

Maiberg, E. (2014). Minecraft's terms and conditions to clarify meaning of trolling. *Gamespot*, 2 March. Retrieve from: https://www.gamespot.com/articles/minecraft-s-terms-and-conditions-to-clarify-meaning-of-trolling/1100-6418047/ (accessed 13 October 2018).

Makuch, E. (2014). Minecraft passes 100 million registered users, 14.3 million sales on PC. *Gamespot*, 26 February. Retrieve from: https://www.gamespot.com/articles/minecraft-passes-100-million-registered-users-14-3-million-sales-on-pc/1100-6417972/ (accessed 13 October 2018).

Möller, K., Rajala, R., and Westerlund, M. (2008). Service innovation myopia? A new recipe for client/provider value creation. *California Management Review*, 50(3), 31–48.

Moon, Y. (2005). Break free from the product life cycle. *Harvard Business Review*, 83(5), 86–94.

Moore, G.A. (2014). *Crossing the Chasm: Marketing and Selling Disruptive Products to Mainstream Customers*. New York: HarperBusiness.

Narayanan, A., Padhi, A., and Williams, J. (2012). Designing products for value. *McKinsey Quarterly*, October. Retrieve from: https://www.mckinsey.com/insights/innovation/designing_products_for_value (accessed 13 October 2018).

Nobel, C. (2011). Clay Christensen's milkshake marketing. *Harvard Business School Working Knowledge Blog*, 14 February. Retrieve from: https://hbswk.hbs.edu/item/clay-christensens-milkshake-marketing (accessed 13 October 2018).

O'Shaughnessy, J., and O'Shaughnessy, N.J. (2009). The service-dominant perspective: a backward step? *European Journal of Marketing*, 43(5–6), 784–93.

Ozer, M. (2003). Process implications of the use of the Internet in new product development: a conceptual analysis. *Industrial Marketing Management*, 32(6), 517–30.

Page, H. (2018). New transaction. *Impact*, January, 50–4.

Papastathopoulou, P., and Hultink, E.J. (2012). New service development: an analysis of 27 years of research. *Journal of Product Innovation Management*, 29(5), 705–14.

Parnell, B.-A. (2012). Offical: Sony and Ericsson are divorced. *The Register*, 16 February. Retrieve from: https://www.theregister.co.uk/2012/02/16/sony_ericsson_divorce_final/ (accessed 13 October 2018).

Plé, L., and Chumpitaz Cáceres, R. (2010). Not always co-creation: introducing interactional co-destruction of value in service-dominant logic. *Journal of Services Marketing*, 24(6), 430–7.

Reuters (2017). A quick guide to Apple Music, Spotify, and more top music streaming services. *Fortune*, 11 September. Retrieve from: http://fortune.com/2017/09/11/spotify-apple-music-tidal-streaming/ (accessed 13 October 2018).

Roberts, G. (2015). Sinclair C5: Sir Clive Sinclair's one-seat wonder celebrates 30 years since its launch. *Mirror*, 5 January. Retrieve from: https://www.mirror.co.uk/news/uk-news/sinclair-c5-sir-clive-sinclairs-4920067 (accessed 13 October 2018).

Robinson, T., Clarke-Hill, C.M., and Clarkson, R. (2002). Differentiation through service: a perspective from the commodity chemicals sector. *Service Industries Journal*, 22(3), 149–66.

Rodionova, Z. (2018). Pretty in pink: Nestle now makes a PINK KitKat—but you'll have to travel pretty far to get it. *The Sun*, 18 January. Retrieve from: https://www.thesun.co.uk/money/5369550/nestle-now-makes-a-pink-chocolate-kitkat-but-youll-have-to-travel-pretty-far-to-get-it/ (accessed 13 October 2018).

Rogers, E.M. (1962). *Diffusion of Innovations*. New York: Free Press.

Rogers, E.M. (1983). *Diffusion of Innovations* (3rd edn). New York: Free Press.

Sexton, P. (2015). And now the streaming screaming starts as Apple declares war on Spotify. *The Sunday Times*, 14 June, 3.

Shelton, R. (2009). Integrating product and service innovation. *Research Technology Management*, 52(3), 38–44.

Statista (2018). Number of active players of Minecraft worldwide as of February 2017 (in millions). Retrieve from: https://www.statista.com/statistics/680139/minecraft-active-players-worldwide/ (accessed 13 October 2018).

Tynan, C., and McKechnie, S. (2009). Experience marketing: a review and reassessment. *Journal of Marketing Management*, 25(5–6), 501–17.

Vargo, S.L., and Lusch, R.F. (2004). Evolving to a new dominant logic for marketing. *Journal of Marketing*, 68(1), 1–17.

Vargo, S.L., and Lusch, R.F. (2016). Institutions and axioms: an extension and update of service-dominant logic. *Journal of the Academy of Marketing Science*, 44(1), 5–23.

Vellequette, L.P. (2017). Midsize coupe is next for Alfa. *Automotive News*, 18 September. Retrieve from: http://www.autonews.com/article/20170918/OEM04/170919779/alfa-romeo-future-product (accessed 13 October 2018).

Witt, S. (2015). Kicking and streaming. *Financial Times*, 13–14 June, 1–2.

Woolfson, D. (2017). Moderation on trend as sales of low and no-alcohol beer soars. *The Grocer*, 23 August. Retrieve from: https://www.thegrocer.co.uk/stores/consumer-trends/moderation-on-trend-as-sales-of-low-and-no-alcohol-beer-soars/556762.article (accessed 13 October 2018).

Chapter 9
Price and Customer Value Decisions

Learning Outcomes

After reading this chapter, you will be able to:

▶ Explain the concept of price elasticity of demand

▶ Define price, and understand its relationship with costs, quality, and value

▶ Describe how customers perceive price

▶ Understand pricing strategies and how to price new offerings

▶ Explain cost-, competitor-, demand-, and value-oriented approaches to pricing

▶ Explain how pricing operates in the business-to-business setting

Case Insight 9.1
Simply Business

Market Insight 9.1
Sugar Tax: Paying Sweetly?

Market Insight 9.2
Price Discount Illusions

Market Insight 9.3
Masstige Pricing at MED

Market Insight 9.4
Electrical Price Promises

Market Insight 9.5
Stripe: Revolutionizing Online Payments

Case Insight 9.1
Simply Business

Founded in 2005, Simply Business is an online insurance broker. We speak to Philip Williams, director of strategy and pricing, to find out more about how the company has developed its pricing strategy.

Simply Business has grown from a team of six, gathered in a room near Tower Bridge in London, to become one of the UK's largest insurance providers to small and medium-sized enterprises (SMEs). It provides cover for about 360,000 small businesses in the UK for liability insurance lines (employers' liability, professional indemnity, public/products liability) in addition to specialty landlord insurance. Its simple and fast online quote process allows customers to receive quotes and buy from a range of different insurance companies simultaneously, providing an instantly comparable, and ordered, panel of prices.

We are proud of our technological capability, seeing ourselves as a tech business, first and foremost, which happens to operate as an insurance brokerage. Our main competitors in the online SME insurance market include Hiscox, Direct Line for Business, AXA, and Towergate, but our market is constantly developing. The online market has grown by about 20 per cent year on year. Of the 5.8 million businesses in the UK, 5.1 million are classified as SMEs, but these businesses usually buy their insurance through local high-street brokers. This is changing, especially at the microbusiness end, as customers get used to comparing and buying their personal insurance online. Four large price-comparison websites have grown in the UK to dominate personal insurance (Compare the Market, Money Supermarket, GoCompare, and Confused.com). Whilst price comparison for home and motor insurance is now well established, the comparison sites have not ventured into the less homogeneous and smaller SME insurance market. Simply Business moved into this vacuum and formed strategic partnerships with two of the large aggregators (Money Supermarket and GoCompare) to develop a **white-labelled product** price-comparison portal.

Since a management buyout in 2013, we have continued to grow revenues by around 25 per cent year on year. We have won numerous awards including, in 2015 and 2016, the number one spot in the '*Sunday Times* Best Company to Work for' awards. To develop our unique proposition, we felt that we needed to extend our control over the value chain. Therefore not only do we provide a platform for customers to compare business insurance rates, but also we have obtained delegated authority from our panel of around 20 insurance providers to bind policies on their behalf. So we handle all customer interactions, including payment, and have agreement to handle all but the largest claims without the need for the insurers to become involved.

The traditional approach to setting prices in the business insurance market has been to use the cost-plus method. Insurers set a risk rate for each customer based on the details provided by the customer within a proposal form (for example postcode, turnover, number of staff). A base cost is determined using these details, before adding additional loads for expenses, reinsurance, and broker commission. Broker commission is typically negotiated between each broker and insurer on a broker-by-broker basis. Those brokers able to provide higher volumes of business, or those who can provide superior quality clients (through unique selection processes or route to market), are best able to negotiate higher levels of commission.

Whilst this strategy and business model is straightforward, for us at Simply Business it was based on two negatives as far as customer value was concerned. A price comparison using the standard methodology would show customers an unfair

Case Insight 9.1

continued

picture, with business insurance prices with lower costs before commission appearing below prices with higher costs (as a result of a higher negotiated commission level). From a customer viewpoint, we knew it would be difficult to justify to our customers why the commission we received from different insurers should be different.

Second, control of customer volumes is difficult to manage because any commission change must be negotiated with a supplier. This is easily manageable in an offline environment, but more difficult in an online world with significantly increased volumes and increased customer price-sensitivity driven by ease and access to competition. So we used our scale to negotiate a flexible commission structure with our insurance providers. This has allowed Simply Business to move towards a demand-oriented pricing approach and to standardize commissions on quotes, presenting a fair comparison to customers with no incentive for Simply Business to sell one product over another. This

transparent approach reflects our brand, which focuses on honesty and simplicity.

One extra difficulty is that all prices quoted for customers are generated specifically for that individual or business and tailored to their requirements and different customers have different price-sensitivities. We wanted to respond to some customers' requirements for price discounts, but it would be too onerous to negotiate with each of our suppliers for each quotation. We also knew that we could not afford to discount all our customers' policies across the board.

The question that arose was: how could Simply Business develop a system that offered tailored policies, including discounts, to those customers who were more price-sensitive?

 Visit the **online resources** to watch a video interview with Philip Williams in which he explains what Simply Business did.

Introduction

When did you last buy something you thought was really expensive? Was it worth the **price** you paid? Did you wonder if others would consider it expensive too? When is a price expensive and when is it not? How do companies set prices? What procedures do they use? Since price wars are self-defeating, why do companies start them or respond to them in the first place? These are just some of the questions we set out to consider in this chapter.

Our understanding of pricing and costing has developed from accounting practice. Economics has also contributed to our understanding of pricing through models of supply and demand, operating at an aggregate level (that is, across all customers in an industry). Psychology contributes greatly to our understanding of customers' perceptions of prices. Marketing, as a field, integrates all of these components to provide a better understanding of how the firm sets price to achieve higher profits and maintain satisfied customers. Pricing is the most difficult aspect of the marketing mix to comprehend because an offering's price is linked to the cost of the many different **components** that make up a particular proposition. The marketing manager rarely controls the costs and prices of a particular offering, and usually refers to the accounting and finance department, or the marketing/financial controller, to set prices.

In this chapter, we provide insight into how customers respond to price changes—what economists call the **price elasticity** of demand, which is an indication of the **value** they perceive in a particular price. We define price, quality, costs, and value, and outline the relationship between them. We provide insights into how customers perceive and learn about prices—a necessary step prior to evaluating them and their fairness, which impacts on customers' willingness to pay. We describe the four main approaches to pricing, based on evaluating costs and adding a margin, copying competitors' prices, basing prices on demand, and pricing according to perceived customer value. We also consider the two principal means by which to price a new proposition, based on skim pricing and market penetration pricing. Finally, we consider what pricing tactics are used in the business-to-business (B2B) setting.

The Price Elasticity of Demand

The concept of the price elasticity of demand was first developed in the field of economics, but it is a very useful concept in marketing. It provides us with an understanding of how demand shifts with changes in price. Such information is useful, but the data needed to determine price elasticities requires detailed research of price and quantity changes over time. Price elasticity is affected by both brand and category characteristics, as well as by general economic conditions, including such factors as time, product category, brand (manufacturer versus own-label), stage of product life cycle, country, household disposable income, and inflation rates (Bijmolt, van Heerde, and Pieters, 2005).

In some categories, for example cigarettes as opposed to washing powder, changes in price (whether positive or negative) lead to smaller changes in demand. For instance, a 10 per cent increase in cigarette prices might lead to only a 2 per cent decrease in quantity sold; conversely, a 10 per cent increase in washing powder prices might lead to a 20 per cent decrease in sales. In this case, we say that washing powder is the more price-elastic offering.

We define price elasticity as the percentage change in quantity demanded as a proportion of the percentage change in price. We can express this as:

$$\text{Price elasticity of demand} =$$

$$\eta \text{ (pronounced } eta) = \frac{\text{Percentage change in quantity demanded}}{\text{Percentage change in price}}$$

When the price of an offering rises or falls, the quantity demanded falls or rises. When the percentage change in price is positive (negative), the percentage change in quantity demanded is negative (positive). Consequently, the price elasticity of demand is always negative. The price elasticity of demand for most marketed goods is somewhere between −9 and −1. In a **meta-analysis** of a set of 1,851 price elasticities, based on 81 studies, the average price elasticity was found to be −2.62 (Bijmolt et al., 2005). In other words, for these goods (including **consumer durables** and other types of product), a 10 per cent increase in price would produce an average 26.2 per cent decrease in quantity demanded. This is an average across offerings. Individual products and services can vary greatly from this average.

Generally, we can refer to three main extremes of price elasticity, as follows.

- In the case of *unit price elasticity of demand* ($\eta = -1$), a 10 per cent increase (decrease) in price produces a 10 per cent decrease (increase) in quantity demanded.

Market Insight 9.1

continued

Related Topics

pricing; cost-plus pricing; price elasticity of demand; advertising elasticity of demand; price perception

1 What decision would you make if you were the chief executive officer (CEO) of Coca-Cola in the UK?

2 What other data might help you to make a decision? Why do you say this?

3 To offset the likely drop in demand when the tax is imposed, do you think it would make sense to advertise more? Why do you say this?

Proposition Costs

To price properly, we need to know what the offering costs us to make, produce, or buy. Cost represents the total money, time, and resources sacrificed to produce or acquire an offering. For example, the costs incurred to produce the Burger King child's cheeseburger meal includes the costs of heat and light in the restaurant, of advertising and sales promotion costs, of rent or of the mortgage interest accrued from owning the restaurant, of management and staffing, and of the franchise fees paid to Burger King's central headquarters to cover training, management, and marketing. There are costs associated with the distribution of the product components to and from farms and other catering suppliers to the restaurants. There are the costs of acquiring and maintaining computer and purchasing systems, and the costs of the packaging, bags, and any extras, such as the BK® crown, and other gifts and toys.

Typically, a firm determines what its fixed costs are and what its variable costs are for each proposition. These items vary for individual industries. Table 9.1 provides a general indication of what is included. Fixed costs do not vary according to the number of units of goods made or services sold and are independent of sales volume. In a Burger King restaurant, fixed costs are the cost of heating and lighting, rent, and staffing costs. In contrast, variable costs depend on the number of units of goods made or services sold. For example, with the production of Burger King cheeseburger meals, when sales and demand decrease, fewer raw goods such as cheeseburger ingredients, product packaging, and novelty items such as toys are required, so less spending on raw materials is necessary. Conversely, when sales increase, more raw materials are used and spending rises.

The Relationship between Pricing and Proposition Costs

The relationship between price and costs is important because costs should be substantially less than the price assigned to a proposition; otherwise the firm will not sell sufficient units to obtain sufficient revenues to cover costs and make long-term profits. Total revenue can be calculated as:

$$\text{Total revenue} = \text{Volume sold} \times \text{Unit price}$$

Table 9.1 Examples of fixed and variable costs

Fixed costs	Variable costs
Manufacturing plant and equipment	Equipment servicing costs
Office buildings	Energy costs
Cars and other vehicles	Mileage allowances
Salaries	Overtime and bonus payments
Professional service fees (e.g. legal, architectural)	Professional services fees (e.g. legal) in a business with a strong regulatory regime (e.g. pharmaceuticals)

Profit can be expressed as:

$$\text{Profit} = \text{Total revenue} - \text{Total costs}$$

The price at which a proposition is set is important because increases in price have a disproportionately positive effect on profits and decreases in price have a disproportionately negative effect on profits. For example, in one study, it was identified that:

- a 1 per cent improvement in price achieves an 8.7 per cent improvement in operating profit;

- a 1 per cent improvement in variable costs achieves only a 5.9 per cent improvement in operating profit;

- a 1 per cent improvement in volume sales achieves a 2.8 per cent improvement in operating profit; and

- a 1 per cent improvement in fixed costs achieves only a 1.8 per cent improvement in operating profits (Baker, Marn, and Zawada, 2010: 5).

Until recently, organizations have had fairly rudimentary methods of assessing the effectiveness of their pricing decisions, but changes in computing power and the availability of data now allows companies to simulate thousands of 'what if' pricing scenarios to predict likely demand and profit levels (Michard, 2016). Whenever possible, then, we should aim to increase prices. However, deciding how to price a proposition is complex and customers seldom want to pay more. Consider Burger King again. A firm like Burger King might well have 100 products on any one restaurant menu in any one country (including meals, individual burgers, ice creams, drinks, salads, **secret menus**, etc.). If we bear in mind that different countries have different menus to incorporate local tastes (for example the 480¥ Premium Kuro Burger® in Japan, where the product is served in a black bun, and the Fish Royale® available in Turkey for ₺25 and available throughout much of the Middle East as Hammour Royale®), we can envisage that, worldwide, Burger King must have an enormous menu of products, despite the appearance of standardization. But how do we cost and price each individual product? The first step is to determine costs, but, in any one restaurant, how do we allocate fixed costs such as heat and light, rent and tax, to each of the individual offerings sold? Once we've allocated the fixed costs, we need to determine variable costs for each offering. Once we've allocated fixed costs and determined the variable costs associated with an offering, we set its initial price. But costs of components, such as heat and light, and other costs change constantly. How do we determine whether we need to change our prices on an item after we've set them because of changes in component costs? After all, we can't keep changing prices every time a component cost changes. So at what point do we change a product offering's price?

To increase the accuracy of the cost data, we need to spend more time collecting and analysing it. Determining costs is an exercise in which we trade off accuracy against the benefits and costs of data collection, storage, and processing (Babad and Balachandran, 1993). Determining costs and prices is more difficult when organizations are split into separate profit centres selling on to other divisions within the same company—especially when these adopt inefficient **transfer pricing** mechanisms (Ward, 1993). For example, Airbus, the airline company owned by the European Aeronautic Defence and Space Company (EADS), assembles its planes using parts made in several European countries. When these parts are made by the respective divisions, they are sold on, using a transfer pricing process, to the main holding company, which assembles the plane from its component parts. But it's not only costs that matter; we might also observe changes in demand for our offerings as customers' desires change. In setting pricing levels, we should also consider customers' price perceptions.

Customer Perceptions of Price, Quality, and Value

Marketers are concerned with how individuals react to the way in which offerings are priced, questioning how consumers perceive prices and why they perceive them as they do. Here, we consider individual perceptions of proposition quality and value, and their relationship to customer response to prices.

Proposition Quality

Quality is important in setting proposition pricing levels. Quality can be defined as 'the standard of something as measured against other things of a similar kind; the degree of excellence of something; a distinctive attribute or characteristic possessed by someone or something' (Oxford Dictionaries, 2016b). In this context, the quality of goods and services relates to standards to which that offering satisfies needs. For example, a very high-quality car (such as the Aston Martin DB11 or the Porsche Panamera) will satisfy both an aesthetic need for aerodynamic beauty and an ego-driven and/or functional need for high-performance road-handling, speed, and power. But quality is not a single standard in an offering; rather, it encompasses many standards because there are many levels at which our needs might or might not be satisfied.

Quality is multifaceted (that is, comprising different functional and non-functional needs) and multilayered (that is, comprising degrees of satisfaction). Because each person has their own definition of quality, we prefer to talk of **perceived quality**. For example, some might be very dissatisfied and others highly satisfied with even the same offering.

The Relationship between Quality and Pricing Levels

There is an assumption that as price increases, so does quality, and that, in general, price reflects quality (see Research Insight 9.1). However, research has demonstrated that there is only a weak relationship between price and perceived quality, although this is category-dependent (Gerstner, 1985). For example, 'snob' consumers in the fashion clothing and fragrance sectors assume that higher prices reflect higher-quality garments and fragrances (Amaldoss and Jain, 2005; Yeoman and McMahon-Beattie, 2006). The idea that price indicates quality (perceived quality) is based on an assumption that prices are objectively determined by market forces. In truth, people within firms set prices, often dispassionately, to try to obtain the maximum profit possible. Various studies to determine whether or not price bears a relation to quality found that a general relationship between price and perceived quality does not exist (Gerstner, 1985; Zeithaml, 1988), except for in the case of wine and fragrance (Zeithaml, 1988). Völckner and Hofmann (2007) conducted a meta-analysis of studies investigating the price–perceived quality relationship published between 1989 and 2006, and found that the price effect on perceived quality had decreased. Interestingly, they also found that the price–perceived quality relationship is stronger in studies that investigate higher-priced products and use samples from European countries, but is weaker for services, durable goods, and respondents who are familiar with the offering.

However, a study designed to understand the relationship between price and quality when price information is available online (Boyle and Lathrop, 2009) found that US consumers believe that higher prices correspond to higher quality for consumer durables (for example cars, televisions), but are less likely to perceive this with non-durables (for example foodstuffs).

The Relationship between Perceived Value, Product Quality, and Pricing Levels

Value is defined as:

> the regard that something is held to deserve; importance, worth, or usefulness of something; principles or standards of behaviour; one's judgement of what is important in life; the numerical amount denoted by an algebraic term; a magnitude, quantity, or number.
>
> (Oxford Dictionaries, 2016c)

Research Insight 9.1

To take your learning further, you might wish to read this influential paper:

Völckner, F., and Hofmann, J. (2007). The price–perceived quality relationship: a meta-analytic review and assessment of its determinants. *Marketing Letters*, 18(3), 181–96.

This article uses a meta-analytic approach to evaluate various studies performed between 1989 and 2006 to provide evidence that there is an increasingly weakening relationship between price and perceived quality.

 Visit the online resources to read the abstract and access the full paper.

There are differing views on how it should be calculated. In marketing terms, value refers to the quality of what we get for what we pay. It is often expressed as:

$$\text{Value} = \frac{\text{quality}}{\text{price}} = \text{quality rating per unit of currency}$$

A related version of this equation replaces quality with 'benefits'—that is, those benefits obtained from buying an offering—and price with 'costs'. This approach to quantifying value indicates that to increase a customer's perception of the value of an offering, we must either lower the price or increase the quality (and this can be hard to measure).

Note that, mathematically, the equation works only when we pay something—that is, more than 0p (otherwise we divide by 0, which is mathematically undefined). So this equation could not be used to determine the value we place on an item we are given (even though this item might have some residual value and could potentially be resold on eBay or Amazon Exchange). This example also illustrates the difference between inherent value (what you could get for it if it were resold) and value in exchange (what you are prepared to pay for it). Therefore, in some ways, the intuitive definition in the equation is a simplistic conception of value. It also suffers because quality is not always well defined: is it a rating, or is quality the customer's perceived **reference price** for the offering given its benefits? If this is the case, then any calculated figure for 'value' greater than 1 indicates a good deal, less than 1, a bad deal, and equal to 1, a satisfactory deal.

This brings us to the following equation suggested by Leszinski and Marn (1997), consultants at McKinsey, to calculate the value to the customer:

$$\text{Value} = \text{Perceived benefits} - \text{Perceived price}$$

In this equation, the customer perceives positive value if the perceived benefits (a proxy for quality) outweigh the price paid for those benefits. Usefully, if the price paid is 0 (that is, an item is given away), the value to the customer is the value of the perceived benefits (which makes sense), and if there are no benefits, the value is the negative value of the price paid. When the benefits of an offering are reduced, the value is also seen to be reduced if customers notice the difference in offerings. An example of this occurred when Cadbury reduced the number of chocolate fingers in its traditional pack from 24, weighing 125 g, to 22, weighing 114 g, with an increase in price from around £1.19 in 2014 to around £1.43 in 2015 (Hayward, 2015), changing the cost of each chocolate finger from 4.96p to 6.5p (for a marginally lighter chocolate finger at 5.18 g compared with 5.21 g). In our view, then, this last equation is the best way of expressing the relationship between price and value.

Influences on Customer Price Perceptions

A Framework for Price Perception Formation

How we perceive prices as customers can be summarized in a theoretical framework (see Figure 9.1). Here, price perceptions are based on a variety of antecedents. Once we see a price, we make a judgement. This judgement is a newly formed price perception, which affects our willingness to pay, which in turn affects our purchase behaviour. Price perceptions are affected by prior beliefs, prior knowledge of reference prices, prior experiences with the offering or brand under consideration, price consciousness (that is, how aware we are of prices), our own price sensitivities (how much extra we are prepared to pay for something), customer characteristics, and cultural factors. We compare the price we see with internal reference prices

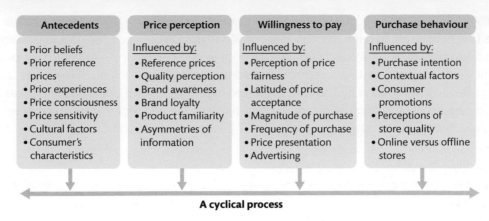

Figure 9.1

A framework for price perception formation

Source: Mendoza and Baines (2012).

(price knowledge gained from experience) and external reference prices (what others tell us prices should be, perhaps through price comparison websites). Reference prices are price bands against which customers judge the purchase price of offerings. Reference prices can be viewed as predictive price expectations based on prior experience with those offerings or gained through word of mouth.

Price perception formation is influenced by exposure to reference prices (internal and external), quality perceptions, brand awareness, brand loyalty, product familiarity, memory of prices (paid previously and seen previously), and asymmetries of information (the extent to which the customer does not know various factors about the offerings). Price perceptions affect customers' willingness to pay. Willingness to pay is influenced by perceptions of the fairness of prices set, latitude of price acceptance (customers appear willing to accept a price within a range of prices, suggesting a 'price zone of tolerance'), magnitude (absolute price) and frequency of purchase, price presentation (how prices are presented might produce different levels of willingness to pay), and advertising.

Actual purchase behaviour is influenced by purchase intention, contextual factors (for example store format, location, timing, and stock-out situations), promotions (for example in-store and external promotions), perceptions of store quality, and whether or not the customer is online or in-store, partly because it is much easier to comparison shop online than it is in-store. However, price perception formation is a dynamic process. In other words, the framework indicates that once the purchase behaviour occurs, there is a recalibration of the customer's price perception because new purchase experiences and new information provide the stimulus for that recalibration. Therefore the process is cyclical. Next, we consider key elements within the price perception process—that is, willingness to pay, price consciousness, and **pricing cues**.

Willingness to Pay

In an online consumer survey of price perceptions in the United States (Sheth, Sisodia, and Barbulescu, 2006), around half of the respondents (53 per cent) had strongly negative perceptions of the price of replacement razor cartridges and prescription drugs, and a quarter of respondents (27 per cent) regarded airline pricing negatively. This indicates that we memorize certain prices for some items, and when companies deviate from those prices, we perceive them as unfair. A key question is: why do some consumers see one proposition's price as fair and others don't? If we are to price an offering according to customer needs, we should understand which customers think a particular price is a fair price to pay, or what they expect to pay, or what they think others would pay. For example, Superdrug in the UK was forced to review its 'sexist' pricing after an investigation by *The Times* revealed that women were being charged more than men on certain offerings such as razors. In some retailers, the gender price surplus that women were expected to pay for similar products was 37 per cent (Hipwell and Ellson, 2016).

Price Consciousness

In addition to deciding whether a price is fair or what customers expect to pay, we also need to know whether customers are conscious of prices in a particular category. Most people do not have a good knowledge of prices. Think of your parents or a friend significantly older than you: do they know the monthly subscription price for streaming music tracks? Do you know the price of a good-quality dining table or £200,000 worth of life insurance cover? As an industrial buyer, how much should you pay for the installation and servicing of a new human resources (HR) system, perhaps Oracle's PeopleSoft application, designed to keep records for 5,000 staff? These examples indicate that our price experience contributes to what we know about reference prices. Our experience is limited to previous actual or considered purchases. There are certain groups of grocery items that supermarket shoppers are more likely to know and it is these items that supermarkets frequently discount, and advertise, to attract shoppers, rather than other lesser known items, the prices of which may be raised. Items including bread, milk, and baked beans are discounted because shoppers assume that if these items are discounted, other items must be discounted. So if people do not know the reference prices of particular offerings, how can they determine their fairness? In the world of contactless payment cards, consumers are increasingly less likely to remember prices as they 'swipe and go', meaning that they are also likely to spend more (Poulter, 2018). In the UK, supermarkets have come under pressure to pay farmers more for their produce because it has emerged that many supermarket chains have been paying the farmers less than the cost of production, meaning that many farmers have been forced to sell at a loss, and the public have seen this as unfair (Neville, 2015).

Pricing Cues

Estimating reference prices is subject to seasonality for some items, including flowers, fruit, and vegetables (particularly exotic varieties such as orchids from Thailand or tulips from Holland); for others, quality and size of items are not universal across companies' offerings, product designs vary over time, and customers might not purchase some offerings frequently (Anderson and Simester, 2003).

When customers assess prices, they estimate value using pricing cues because they do not always know the true cost and price of the item that they are purchasing. Pricing cues include things such as sale signs, odd-number pricing, the purchase context, and price bundling and rebates:

■ *Sale signs* act as cues, indicating the availability of a bargain. This seduces the customer to buy, suggesting that an item is desirable and may not be available if it's not bought quickly enough. The sale sign uses scarcity as a persuasive device because the scarcer we perceive an offering to be, the more we want it (Cialdini, 1993)—sometimes, regardless of whether we need it.

- Another pricing cue is the use of *odd-number pricing*—that is, prices that end in the figure 9. Have you ever wondered why the Nintendo Wii U you bought was, say, US$299, or £229, or SEK2,999? Why not simply round it up to $300, £230, or SEK3,000? According to Anderson and Simester (2003), raising the price of a woman's dress in a national mail-order catalogue from $34 to $39 increased demand by 33 per cent, but demand remained unchanged when the price was raised to $44! The question is why did the increase in demand take place when there was a higher price? It is unlikely that demand would have increased if the item were priced at $38. The reason is that we perceive the first price as relative to a reference price of £30 (which is £34 rounded down to the nearest unit of 10) and more expensive, whereas the second price of $39 we perceive as cheaper than a reference price of $40 (that is, $39 rounded up to the nearest 10). (See Market Insight 9.2.)

- *Purchase context* is another key factor. Our perception of risk is greater if we are continually reminded of it than if we consider it only at the point of purchase. For example, gyms use the technique of charging a monthly fee, even though they often demand an annual membership agreement, for precisely this reason. In fact, a monthly price (instead of an annual, semi-annual, or quarterly charge) drives a higher level of gym attendance because customers are more regularly reminded of their purchase. So the way you set your price not only influences demand, but also drives consumption (Gourville and Soman, 2002). Research on **price anchoring** shows that if we are exposed to higher-priced items first, our reference prices are anchored at the higher level, whereas if we are exposed to lower prices, they are anchored at the lower level (Smith and Nagle, 1995). Therefore it makes sense to redesign catalogues to include more expensive items in the earlier pages (Nunes and Boatwright, 2001) or, in an online store, to show the most expensive items on a page first by default (even though the customer should be able to sort them afterwards as desired). Location also has an impact on price perceptions. For example, we will pay more for a can of Coca-Cola from a hotel minibar than from the hotel bar or a supermarket, indicating the context-specific nature of price perception.

Visit the **online resources** and complete Internet Activity 9.1 to learn more about the impact that the purchase context (for example time of day, week, online versus telephone booking, etc.) has on the pricing of budget airline services.

Price Bundling and Rebates

Marketers highlight their prices to customers by bundling other products and services into an offering to make the price look more reasonable. For example, magazines frequently bundle gifts in with the magazine to make it appear more attractive—a practice known as **pure price bundling**. Sunday newspapers (in the UK, France, Thailand, Sweden) often contain numerous supplements (for example fashion, entertainment, property) to make the newspaper appear to be better value for money. New cars are sold with three years' warranty on parts so that customers know they won't have to pay for any repairs within the warranty period. Fast food restaurants have meal deal offers whereby you can buy a burger, fries, and a drink at a cheaper price than buying all the items individually (so-called **mixed price bundling**).

Price bundling does not always mean that the company needs to give the customer other items; rather, we might simply be offered a rebate—that is, given money back.

Market Insight 9.2
Price Discount Illusions

Consider a situation in which you are in an airport duty-free environment. Let's assume that the several outlets are all selling high-quality Belgian chocolates. In two different stores, you are offered different promotional offers. In both outlets, the original price of, say, the Godiva Gold collection box of 14 chocolates is £15.99 for 165 g. Your choice of promotional offers is 25 per cent extra free in one shop versus 25 per cent off the price in another. Which shop is selling the better offer or is this simply the same offer? Make your choice now before reading on.

Now consider that you are browsing the website of British online fashion and beauty store ASOS. You are looking to buy a particular branded jacket. Let's say it's a Parka London jacket. Its original price was £285. However, you remember that it has been discounted twice, first by 20 per cent and then by a further 25 per cent. Let's assume that, for some reason, you can't see the final price. Would you prefer to take this double-discount deal or the one where the jacket was discounted once by 40 per cent? Make your choice now before reading on.

If we revisit the Godiva chocolate offer, the 25 per cent extra free means we get 206 g for £15.99, which is equivalent to 7.75p per gram. The 25 per cent discount means that we get 165 g for £11.99, which is equivalent to 7.27p per gram. So the better deal is the price discount and price discounting by 25 per cent is not the same as offering 25 per cent extra free.

On the jacket offer, given that the original price was £285, a 20 per cent first discount followed by a further 25 per cent discount would mean a final price of £171. A one-off discount of 40 per cent would mean a final price of £171. In other words, the two discounts are exactly the same.

Sources: Chen et al. (2012); https://www.godivachocolates.co.uk/gifts; https://www.asos.com

Theory into Practice

This market insight describes how difficult it is to perceive the value in different prices, and how apparently similar offers can be different and apparently different offers can be the same. Marketers frequently use the psychology of consumer price perception when setting prices.

Related Topics

perception; sales promotion; consumer behaviour; reference pricing; willingness to pay

1 Did you get both answers correct? If you did, your arithmetic is excellent and you need not worry about misreading prices. If not, how will this knowledge affect your shopping behaviour?

2 When was the last time you bought a discounted offering? What did you buy and why?

3 What offerings are most frequently discounted and what offerings are seldom discounted?

Credit card companies offer cashback schemes on money spent on their credit cards as a proportion of the total amount spent. For example, Amex Platinum offers 5 per cent introductory cashback and then 1.25 per cent cashback on purchases thereafter, with an annual fee.

Pricing Approaches

Price setting depends on various factors, including how price affects demand, how sales revenue is linked to price, how cost is linked to price, and how investment costs are linked to price (Doyle, 2000). Price setting also depends on how sales revenue relates to price. Raising prices tends to increase revenue up to a point, but then further increases in unit price produce declining increases in revenue. The relationship between price and sales revenue follows a bell curve (see Figure 9.2).

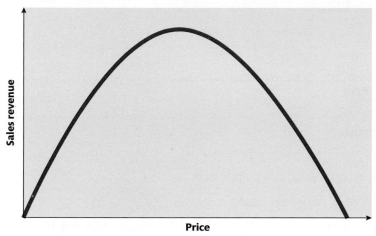

Figure 9.2
How price relates to sales revenue

Costs vary with price in a linear fashion because higher prices reduce volume sales, producing lower total costs (see Figure 9.3). Investment costs, including both **working capital** and **fixed capital** (cost of plant and machinery etc.), also affect prices, with lower prices tending to require higher sales volume targets, with correspondingly higher levels of investment. Investments are made at fixed intervals (for example on a six-monthly basis), with investment costs dropping compared with price increases (and sales volumes decreases). The relationship between investment and price looks like a downward staircase (see Figure 9.4).

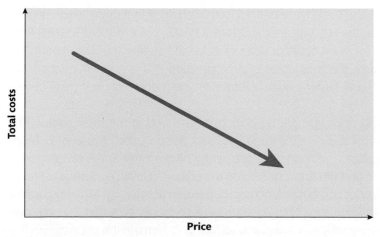

Figure 9.3
How price relates to total costs

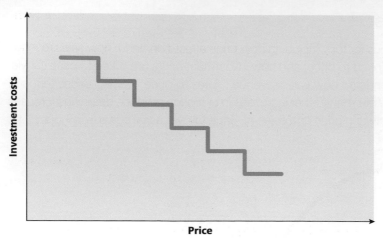

Figure 9.4

How price relates to investment costs

Broadly, there are four types of underlying pricing approach:

■ the *cost-oriented* approach (that is, prices set based on costs);

■ the *demand-oriented* approach (that is, prices set based on price sensitivity and demand);

■ the *competitor-oriented* approach (that is, prices set based on competitors' prices); and

■ the *value-oriented* approach (that is, prices based on what customers believe to offer value).

When setting prices, an organization might use a combination of these. For example, identifying the costs and trying to work out potential demand before setting a price is a common approach. We consider each of these pricing approaches in more detail next.

The Cost-Oriented Approach

The cost-oriented approach advances the idea that the most important element of pricing is the cost of the component resources that constitute the offering. It can be used for services, in a business-to-business (B2B) context, or in a product context. The marketer sells output at the highest price possible, regardless of the buyer's preferences or costs. If that price is high enough compared with the seller's costs, the firm earns a profit and survives. If not, either the seller finds a way of increasing the price or lowering costs or both, or it doesn't survive (Lockley, 1949). The cost-oriented approach considers the total costs of a proposition in the pricing equation, but does not take into account non-cost factors, such as brand image, degree of prestige in ownership, or effort expended.

One approach to determining price is mark-up pricing, often used in the retail sector. This method operates on the basis of a set percentage mark-up. When used, the cost-oriented method leads to the use of list prices, with single prices set for all customers. We simply add to the cost a mark-up of X per cent and the total constitutes the price. In British supermarket retailing, the mark-up is around 6–8 per cent, but in American supermarket retailing, it is often around 4 per cent or less. Mark-ups on wine served in restaurants are typically between 200 per cent and 300 per cent. The cost-oriented approach requires us first to determine the price we set that just covers our costs. This is known as breakeven pricing. It represents the point at which our total costs and our total revenues are exactly equal.

To exemplify the concept of mark-up pricing further, we might use the example of a computer company selling high-quality laptop computers costing £1,000 per unit to manufacture. Suppose that the computer company uses the mark-up pricing method, adding 66.7 per cent. The final price set can be calculated as:

$$\text{Sales price}(£) = (\text{mark-up}^* \times \text{cost}) + \text{cost} = (0.67 \times 1,000) + 1,000 = £1,670$$

(Note that mark-up is expressed as a decimal between 0 and 1—that is, we divide mark-up percentage by 100 to get a mark-up figure.)

It is important to note that the gross profit margin (that is, that proportion of the revenue which is profit) is not the same as the mark-up percentage (which is a proportion of cost). The gross profit margin in the preceding example can be calculated as:

$$\text{Gross margin}(\%) = (\text{mark-up/sales price}) \times 100 = (670/1,670) \times 100 = 40.11\%$$

If we consider that, in a supply chain, there is typically more than one customer interaction, as we move along the supply chain each partner takes their share, adding to the costs and the final selling price. A toy (for example a teddy bear) bought by a UK importer from a Chinese toy manufacturer based in Hong Kong, typically 'free on board' (which means that all costs after shipping are borne by the importer), brought to the UK, warehoused, stored, financed, and eventually sold at £5.90 (in cases of 12), may well have cost around £4.50 to that importer. The eventual retail price would probably be around the £10 retail price point—that is, £9.99. The mark-up (MU) here for the retailer can be calculated as:

$$\text{MU}(\%) = [(\text{sales price/cost}) - 1] \times 100 = [(£9.99/£5.90) - 1] \times 100 = 69\%$$

The mark-up for the importer is much lower, at 31 per cent—that is, (£5.90/£4.50) − 1] × 100.

However, the importer may well buy a container of the teddy bears, comprising, say, 4,800 individual bears (400 boxes, each containing 12 units), and sell these over the three months between September and November for the Christmas retail season. The retailer, by contrast, may sell only six boxes of 12 during the period October–December, so the retailer has to make a higher profit on a smaller volume with a wider range of items to give the customer some choice.

The cost-oriented approach does mean that we have to use a mark-up pricing approach. In some industries, prices are based on fixed formulae, set with a supplier's costs in mind. For example, in the ethical prescription pharmaceutical industry in France, Italy, and Spain, government-fixed formulae have tended to dictate prices, with limited scope for pharmaceutical manufacturers to negotiate, whereas in the UK and Germany, the tradition has been for the country's national health authorities not to fix individual product prices, but to set an overall level of profitability with which the pharmaceutical manufacturer must agree, based on a submission of its costs (Attridge, 2003). In the UK, however, there is increasing recognition that the current pharmaceutical pricing system, the Pharmaceutical Price Regulation Scheme (PPRS), is inadequate for containing costs and incentivizing innovation (Latif, 2013).

The Demand-Oriented Approach

With the demand-oriented approach to pricing, the firm sets prices according to how much customers will pay. This approach is prevalent in marketing services, but again could be used in B2B or consumer marketing contexts (see Market Insight 9.3). Airline companies use this approach, with customers paying different amounts for seats with varying levels of service attached. Most airline companies offer three types of cabin service, for example first class, business class, and economy class, with varying benefits according to the price paid based on the seat pitch (and availability as a bed), the entertainment package, the quality of the meal options, the availability and quality of airport lounges, transportation to and from the airport, the in-flight service offered, and the experience through immigration and security. Other benefits are available through membership and loyalty schemes, including premier access through immigration lanes, instant seat upgrades, and priority seats. Low-cost carriers in Europe, such as Ryanair, Norwegian, easyJet, and Germanwings, operate fairly sophisticated yield management approaches via online booking systems. These set prices to ensure that planes operate at full capacity by charging increasing amounts as the purchase date gets closer to the travel date, flying on particular days of the week, and managing the price at which different service classes are sold. Tickets are usually priced cheaply initially to increase demand (and generally priced substantially less than the legacy airline carriers such as British Airways, SAS, or Air France). There is a general perception among passengers that Asian airlines offer the best service for the price charged, with European airlines perceived as not particularly satisfying and US airlines as very unsatisfying, as illustrated in Figure 9.5 (Anon., 2016b). In another consumption setting, a pub in Stockton in the northeast of England, offered a pint of beer at the beginning of the New Year starting at £1.55 from 9 a.m., with the cost of the drink increasing by the hour in the morning, alongside the advert, 'The earlier you are in, the cheaper the drink!' Unsurprisingly, the promotion drew the ire of campaign groups seeking to reduce alcohol drinking (Jeeves, 2018).

Companies operating a demand pricing policy should be wary of overcharging their customers, particularly where customers' requests are urgent. Examples include emergency purchases, such as funeral services. When companies do set charges that are perceived to be

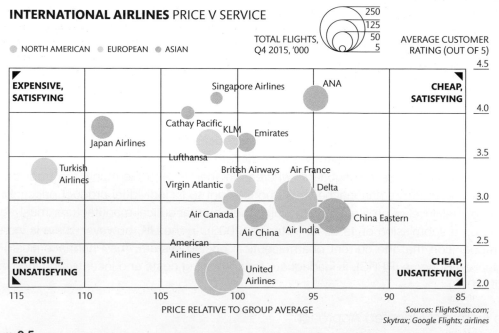

Figure 9.5

International airlines: price versus service

Source: From *1843 Magazine* © 2016 The Economist Newspaper Limited. All rights reserved.

Market Insight 9.3
Masstige Pricing at MED

MED priced its lingerie and swimwear higher internationally than domestically, with great success
Source: Photo courtesy of Chris Liassides.

MED is a luxurious swimwear, underwear, and eyewear label that has been serving the Greek market for more than 25 years. It is a successful masstige (that is, mass–prestige) brand following a fully vertically integrated business model. Like many Greek firms, it has been affected by the country's sovereign debt crisis, which has seen the country's economic output contract by 26 per cent. MED produces its masstige swimwear and eyewear in-house, although the production of its eyewear lines is fully outsourced. Primarily operating in Greece, MED employs more than 300 people and has 30 retail stores, but also distributes its product lines through some other 150 stores in Greece and abroad (primarily in Germany and Cyprus) through wholesalers.

Seeing the sales of the company plunging, chief executive officer (CEO) Efthimis Hatzivasileiou had to revise the company's strategy. He changed the marketing strategy by expansion abroad and primarily by introducing differentiated pricing. The head designer of the company proceeded to create a less expensive underwear line (selling at prices 30–40 per cent less than those of its competitors). This action boosted sales and revenues by 14 per cent in just two months after the new product launch.

The company exploited two new markets: by opening a store in Cannes, France, taking advantage of the tourists that visit all year round (with prices set twice as high as in Greece); and by establishing a new store in a mall selling exclusive brands in Istanbul in Turkey, with prices set 30 per cent higher than in Greece. These initiatives further increased revenues, but the strategic decision that really helped the company to thrive was its implementation of a differentiated pricing strategy. The MED stores on islands in the Aegean, such as the cosmopolitan island of Mykonos, have created a buying trend in underwear and the swimwear product lines, and have increased brand awareness both domestically and internationally. The retail prices here were set almost 30 per cent higher than elsewhere, enabling the company to be perceived as a luxury brand. The brand received a further boost when it was worn by international celebrities including television and films stars, such as Eva Longoria, who purchased the products while holidaying on the island (effectively granting the company unpaid celebrity endorsement). This was the best promotion the company could have received.

MED had dared to implement differentiated pricing, acted quickly, and smartly took the market by storm. The company enjoyed growth of 8 per cent in 2017 (with estimated growth at 12 per cent in 2018), despite the adverse conditions of the economy and the market, establishing itself as a leader in the underwear and swimwear category, while obtaining market shares in companies that were less fortunate.

Sources: Kolitsopoulou (2017); Smith (2017); https://shop.med.com.gr/en-gb/about

Market Insight 9.3
continued

Theory into Practice

The market insight illustrates that companies can yield very positive and promising results when choosing the most appropriate pricing strategy. Differentiated pricing, as used in this case, is the strategy of selling the same product to different customers at different prices. It first requires a full analysis of the business environment, as well as an indication that customers are willing to pay the prices set before implementation. A secondary insight from the case is that small and medium-sized enterprises (SMEs) can adopt any pricing strategy considered appropriate for larger companies by adapting it to their own needs and capabilities.

Related Topics

marketing strategy; international expansion; differential pricing

1 Why do you think it was possible for MED to sell its products at higher prices in Cannes?

2 Do you think buyers in Cannes would be concerned that the product they bought was much cheaper in Greece? Why do you say this?

3 Can you think of an example of a company that uses a **differential pricing** strategy? How does its strategy compare with that used by MED?

This market insight was kindly contributed by Chris Liassides, University of Sheffield, International Faculty, CITY College.

unfair, they are liable to claims of **price gouging**. For example, in 2015 and under former CEO Martin Shkreli, Turing Pharmaceuticals raised the price of anti-infection drug Daraprim by 5,555 per cent, from US$13.50 to $750 (Crow, 2015)—although it later reduced the price for hospitals by 50 per cent after a media backlash (Constantinides and Rahman, 2015).

The Competitor-Oriented Approach

Companies can also set prices based on competitors' prices, also known as the going rate, or 'me too' pricing. This approach is used in B2B, services, and consumer marketing contexts. The advantage of this approach is that when your prices are lower than those of the competition, customers are more likely to purchase from you, provided that they know your prices are lower.

Price guarantee schemes such as that outlined in Market Insight 9.4 seek to provide customers with the peace of mind of knowing that the price paid is competitive. In reality, such schemes are expensive to operate, requiring continuous monitoring of the full range of competitors' prices and a strong focus on cost control. However, it is worth considering that adopting a competitor-oriented pricing strategy can lead to price wars (see Research Insight 9.2).

Visit the **online resources** and complete Internet Activity 9.2 to learn more about how John Lewis brings the 'Never Knowingly Undersold' promise to life in its advertising.

Market Insight 9.4
Electrical Price Promises

Online-only retailer of electrical goods AO seeks to be the leading retailer in Europe, and currently operates in the UK, Germany, and the Netherlands. With around 2,500 employees, AO saw gross sales of just over £700 million in 2017. What is unique about AO is that it cares not only about selling existing products, but also about recycling old products. AO's approach is to offer an everyday low price and a price promise, rather than to offer discounts, because it believes this is a better alternative than price discounting with which to build consumer trust and perceptions of value.

AO's price-match promise stipulates that if a customer finds a cheaper product from any other UK retailer (online or instore), it will match that price and refund the difference. The price-match promise is valid on the day on which the customer orders a product and up to seven days afterwards. Given that other retailers are also offering competitive prices and price matching,

AO seeks to differentiate itself based on the quality of its service—especially its in-house logistics capability. Delivery of items is also an important consideration for consumers when buying bulky products like fridges and cookers.

AO's competitor, Curry's, also offers a price promise scheme, matching against AO.com, Argos, Asda, John Lewis, Tesco, and even Amazon. Curry's offers to match any price the competitors offer on the sale of the particular item under consideration and they make it particularly easy to compare competitors prices by means of an app available on Google Play called 'Compare prices Curry's PC World'.

Sources: Chahal (2015); AO (2017); https://www.currys.co.uk/gbuk/price-promise-1023-theme.html; https://ao.com/help-and-advice/help-with-my-order/price-match-promise

Theory into Practice

This market insight outlines how two highly popular electrical retailers seek to compete against each other and other competitors by running a price guarantee scheme—that is, each guarantees that its prices cannot be beaten by anyone else. There is a question of how many consumers actually bother to check

competitors' prices and then claim the refund, but that's not really the point; for most companies, the point is to build trust with the consumer by offering the price match—which is available if they want to use it—to make the purchase decision an easier one to make.

Related Topics

price guarantee; price promise; price promotions; retailing

1 What data does AO need to determine whether or not to pay out on a customer's claim under the price promise scheme?

2 Do you think the cost of collecting the competitor pricing data, as Curry's would

have to do for its app, is justified for its price promotion commercially? Why do you say that?

3 What other companies are you aware of that offer price promise schemes? How are they similar to or different from those outlined above?

Price wars occur when competitors' pricing policies are overly focused on competitors, rather than customers, when price is pushed downwards, and when pricing results in interactions between competitors that lead to unsustainable prices. For example, in 2003,

Research Insight 9.2

To take your learning further, you might wish to read this influential paper:

Reinemoeller, P. (2014). How to win a price war. *Sloan Management Review*, 55(3), 15–17.

This article, based on a study of Albert Hejn in the Netherlands, explains that companies can win price wars by leveraging five strategic capabilities—that is, the ability to:

- affirm the need for a price war;
- carefully select an appropriate battlefield using advanced analytics capabilities;
- pick a single target competitor;
- stay under the radar (by targeting former customers rather than explicitly poaching new customers); and
- align revenues with reformed cost structures.

 Visit the online resources to read the abstract and access the full paper.

when Dutch supermarket retailer Albert Hejn slashed its prices in response to competition from Aldi and Lidl, the resulting battle saw an 8.2 per cent reduction in food prices, costing Dutch supermarkets €900 million (£700 million) and 30,000 jobs in a single year (van Heerde, Gijsbrechts, and Pauwels, 2008; Blackhurst, 2014)—although, by 2005, after the price war had ended, Albert Hejn managed to regain lost market share to become market leader again (Reinemoeller, 2014). In 2017, Amazon set the stage for a price war with Walmart in the United States when it dropped prices at its newly acquired grocery retailer, Whole Foods Market (Helmore, 2017).

In a review of more than 1,000 examples, researchers found that price wars could be averted if companies responded to market-based, firm-based, product-based, and consumer-based early warning signals (van Heerde et al., 2008). So, some firms, under certain circumstances and within certain industries, are more susceptible to price wars than others (see Table 9.2).

Calculating and anticipating competitor response is important when setting prices and responding to competitors' price cuts. We should analyse consumer responses when a competitor starts to cut prices, but if purchase behaviour changes only modestly or temporarily, other marketing mix elements (for example promotion, distribution, or product differentiation) may be more likely to win back customers (van Heerde et al., 2008).

We do not always have to respond to a price war with a price cut. Instead, we might promote increased service quality (Rust, Danaher, and Varki, 2000) or customer value improvements more generally.

The Value-Oriented Approach

Even in the consumer durables category (for example furniture, **white goods**, carpets), in which we might expect customers to be less price-sensitive, firms have long practised pricing

Table 9.2 Circumstances under which price wars are more or less likely to occur

Circumstances under which price wars are more likely to occur

- As market entry occurs and an entrant gains, or is expected to gain, a sizeable market position
- When an industry possesses excess production capacity—which stimulates the intensity of the price war
- When markets have marginal or negative growth prospects
- Where market power within an industry is highly concentrated
- Where barriers to exit are greater (meaning that it's difficult to leave an industry, e.g. because of high investment costs)
- Where financial conditions of at least one firm in the industry worsen or as a firm approaches bankruptcy
- Where the offering concerned is of strategic importance to the company
- When an offering is more like a commodity and so does not command a price premium
- When firms introduce very similar offerings to one another
- When there is little brand loyalty in evidence from customers
- When customers are more highly price-sensitive—which also increases the intensity of the price war

Circumstances under which price wars are less likely to occur

- Where one or more firms have established a reputation for strong and tough responses to past price wars
- Where markets have intermediate levels of market power concentration (so neither suppliers nor buyers are dominant in a market)

approaches with customers' considerations in mind (Foxall, 1972). We term this the value-oriented approach to pricing, because prices are set on the basis of buyers' perceptions of specific product or service attribute values rather than on the basis of costs or competitors' prices. This approach can be used in B2B, services, and consumer contexts.

We no longer live in an era in which offerings are priced at what people can afford, because people are generally much wealthier now than they were 30 or more years ago. Resources are more plentiful and consumers have much of what they need. So they are more interested in obtaining value from the offerings they buy. With value-based pricing, the pricing process begins with the customer, determining what value they derive from the offering and then determining price, rather than the opposite approach used in cost-oriented pricing, whereby costs are determined first and then the price is set.

In value-based pricing, deciding what is of value to the customer is determined using customer research. The result may be that the company does not necessarily offer a cheaper price. In fact, it could mean a higher-priced offering. If that offering is to represent true value to the customer, they must feel that it has more benefits than equivalent offerings. A recent study of 1, 812 pricing professionals demonstrated that a value-based pricing strategy is positively linked to firm performance, whereas a cost-based approach is not (Liozu and Hinterhuber, 2013). A good example of a brand using this approach is L'Oréal, which has advertised its products using spokesmodels for a long time, for example South Korean model Soo-Joo Park, British pop sensation and television personality Cheryl, Chinese model Xiao Wen Ju, Dutch model Lara Stone, Australian actor Naomi Watts, and Hungarian model Barbara Palvin, among many others, on the basis that we should use their products 'because we're worth it'.

Xiao Wen Ju, Lara Stone, and Luma Grothe for L'Oréal: because they're worth it
Source: Courtesy of The Advertising Archives.

Research indicates that brands that generate revenues over and above those obtained by an own-label or generic version of the offering also generate revenue premiums, which acts as a useful measure of **brand equity** (Ailawadi, Lehmann, and Neslin, 2003). Brand equity is important, because it contributes to company valuations when they are sold, acquired, or merged. Companies increasingly focus on generating price premiums. Nevertheless, a price premium is useless if it's perceived to be unfair. When setting value-based prices, it is important to consider the following questions (Anderson, Wouters, and van Rossum, 2010):

1 What is the market strategy for the segment? What does the supplier want to accomplish?

2 What is the differential value that customers are likely to perceive—that is, the value between this offering and the next best alternative, assuming that the differential value can be verified with the customer's own data?

3 What is the price of the next-best alternative?

4 What is the cost of the supplier's offering?

5 What pricing tactics will be used initially (for example price discounting)?

6 What is the customer's expectation of a 'fair' price? (Refer back to Market Insight 9.2.)

Pricing Strategies and Objectives

Whilst companies might use a variety of pricing approaches to set their prices over the long term, they also need to understand how they might set their prices in the shorter term. Companies tend to establish their pricing strategy based around what their pricing objectives are. The four main pricing strategies are as follows:

- *Premium pricing* focuses on pricing an offering to indicate its distinctiveness in the marketplace. For example, Aston Martin prices the DB11 in this way, at around £150,000 (see Chapter 13).

- *Penetration pricing* refers to setting the price low relative to the competition to gain market share. Amazon has adopted this approach to build its now substantial customer base. This strategy is frequently used for new proposition launches.

- *Economy pricing* involves setting the prices at a bare minimum to attract price-sensitive customers. Supermarkets often use this approach with their everyday low pricing approach (for example Walmart in the United States, Aldi all over Europe, and Jumbo in the Netherlands).

- *Price skimming* occurs when the price is initially set high and then lowered in sequential steps. Apple iPhone adopted this strategy, for example. This strategy is frequently used for the launch of new offerings.

Companies' pricing objectives may relate to other objectives, for example to maximize profit, or to achieve a satisfactory level of profits or sales, or achieve a particular return on investment. Companies may price to generate cash flow, offering discounts for quick payment. A firm's pricing objectives could be marketing-based, for example pricing to achieve a particular market share (so-called market penetration pricing) or to position the brand so that it is perceived to be of a certain quality. Sometimes, companies price their propositions simply to survive, for example pricing to discourage new competitors from entering the market by lowering prices to maintain sales volumes whenever competitors lower their prices. Alternatively, a company might price to avoid price wars, maintaining prices at levels similar to its competitors—so-called competitor-oriented pricing. Finally, a company may price to achieve certain social goals (for example a pharmaceutical company pricing a drug to ensure maximum reach in a highly disease-afflicted country). The important consideration is whether or not the pricing objective is reasonable and measurable. Often, companies pursue different pricing objectives simultaneously and some pricing objectives may be incompatible with each other. For example, pricing to increase cash flow by offering quick payment discounts is not compatible with maximizing profitability. However, it is compatible with obtaining a satisfactory profitability, as long as the discounts offered are not greater than the cost of the offerings sold.

Launch Pricing

When launching new offerings, organizations tend to adopt one of two classic pricing strategies. In the first approach, they charge a lower price in the hope of generating a large volume of sales and recouping their research and development (R&D) investment that way (hence penetration pricing). With the second approach, they charge an initially high price and reduce the price over time, recouping the cost of the R&D investment from sales to the group of customers who are prepared to pay the higher price (hence price skimming the market).

Figure 9.6 shows both market penetration and market skimming price strategies, as well as their hypothetical impact on quantity demanded (Q1 and Q2, respectively). For any given demand curve, the market skimming price offers a higher unit price than the market penetration price. The actual amount sold at each of these unit prices depends on the price elasticity of demand and a more inelastic demand curve would give greater revenue from a market skimming price than a market penetration price, because the quantity sold would not be very different between the two prices. On average, the market skimming price is likely to yield a lower quantity of offerings sold than the market penetration price.

Skim pricing is a fairly standard approach for high-tech offerings or those offerings that require substantial R&D investment initially (such as games consoles and prescription pharmaceuticals). For example, Microsoft dropped the price for its Xbox One machine, bringing the official base price to US$299 in 2016, having opened with a launch price of $500 (Thier, 2016). The skim pricing approach is particularly appropriate:

- when companies need to recover their R&D investment quickly;
- when demand is likely to be price inelastic;
- where there is an unknown elasticity of demand, since it is safer to offer a higher price and then lower it than to offer a lower price and try to increase it;
- where there are high barriers to entry within the market;
- where there are few economies of scale or experience; and
- where product life cycles are expected to be short (Dean, 1950; Doyle, 2000).

The market penetration pricing approach is used for fast-moving consumer goods (FMCGs) and consumer durables, where the new offering introduced is not demonstrably different

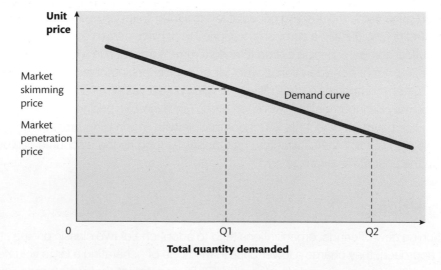

Figure 9.6

Launch pricing strategies

Source: Adapted from Burnett (2002). Reproduced with the kind permission of the author, John Burnett.

from existing formulations. So, if a car manufacturer introduces a new coupé, relatively similar to its previous model, which has no new features and is not significantly better than competing models, it might use the market penetration pricing strategy. Items aimed at capturing price-sensitive customers might use this approach. Nissan stated that it would use this pricing approach with the launch of the Datsun Redi GO model in India in 2016, which was to be priced at between ₹2.5 lakh and ₹4 lakh (Vijayraghvan, 2015). In a recessionary environment, customers are particularly sensitive to the value they receive when purchasing consumer or B2B offerings (see Research Insight 9.3). The penetration approach is more effective where:

- there is a strong threat of competition;

- the offering is likely to exhibit a high price elasticity of demand in the short term;

- there are substantial savings to be made from volume production;

- there are low barriers to entry;

- product life cycles are expected to be long; and

- there are economies of scale and experience to take advantage of (Dean, 1950; Doyle, 2000).

Research Insight 9.3

To take your learning further, you might wish to read this influential paper:

Van Heerde, H.J., Gijsenberg, M.J., Dekimpe, M.G., and Steenkamp, J.-B.E.M. (2013). Price and advertising effectiveness over the business cycle. *Journal of Marketing Research*, **50(2), 177–93.**

This article considers whether or not marketing activity (specifically, pricing and advertising) is affected by the economic cycle (for example an expanding economy versus contracting economy). The authors estimate short- and long-term advertising and price elasticities for 150 brands across 36 consumer packaged goods categories, using 18 years of monthly UK data from 1993 to 2010. They conclude that, during economic contractions, consumers are less responsive to advertising and react more strongly to price reductions. Generally, the authors suggest reallocation of marketing expenditure from advertising to price discounting, but only if the firm's objective is to maintain sales (as opposed to profit maximization). There are differential effects for categories, and even brands within categories, for example advertising elasticity is high (that is, more advertising creates more sales) during a contraction for food brands, but not for beverages. For premium mass brands, advertising during a recession can lead to greater willingness to pay and reductions in price sensitivity (that is, people will pay more). Interestingly, the authors also find that consumer packaged goods firms tend to do less well in an expanding economy because consumers shift spending to out-of-home spending, but return to in-home spending during a contraction.

 Visit the **online resources** to read the abstract and access the full paper.

Pricing Management

In the information era, marketing information systems (MkIS), database artificial intelligence, and Internet-enabled technologies have all changed how companies make pricing decisions. Pricing strategies such as 'real-time' or 'dynamic' pricing have increasingly been developed in both consumer and B2B markets, sometimes through online price-comparison sites, online auctions, and companies' own websites, because prices can be changed easily. For example, Amazon updates its price list every 10 minutes based on constant data analysis (Anon., 2016c). Dynamic pricing even allows changes at the customer level (Grewal et al., 2011). In the UK in 2018, Tesco, Sainsbury's, and Morrisons were all working on 'surge pricing'—a process that allows them to raise or cut the price of groceries depending on demand, and to reflect these changed prices on electronic price tags (Ellson, 2018).

Visit the **online resources** and follow the web links to visit Kelkoo, Price Runner, Touslesprix. com, Beslist.nl, and Preis Suchmaschine—all examples of online price-comparison decision aids in different European countries.

Comparison sites have developed large customer databases covering all types of offering, including complex services, such as gas and electricity supply, insurance, mobile phone packages, and travel, as well as standard offerings, such as cars and breakdown cover. Marketers are working in an increasingly price-transparent environment and they should recognize that pricing is a capability at which some companies are better than others. Those companies that are excellent at pricing manage their costs and price complexity well, and offer sustainability and innovation in pricing approaches (Hinterhuber and Liozu, 2012). Online retailers are recognizing that it's not only the price that matters, but also how easy it is to pay online, because a more efficient payment process can lead to more time shopping (see Market Insight 9.5).

Pricing Tactics

In reality, when setting prices, an organization trades off the different approaches by considering all the following factors:

- *Competition*—How much are competitors charging for similar offerings?

- *Cost*—How much do the individual components that make up our offering cost?

- *Demand*—How much of this product or service will we sell at what price?

- *Value*—What components of the offering does the customer value and how much are they prepared to pay for them?

Although we outlined that four main pricing approaches can be used to determine prices earlier (that is, cost-, demand-, competitor- and value-oriented, or some combination of these), and four main pricing strategies in the long term (premium, penetration, economy, price skimming), in fact there are also many different possible pricing tactics within these approaches and strategies in the short term that could be used, including the following:

- *List pricing* occurs when a single price is set for an offering, for example hotels charging what they call 'rack rates' for hotel conferencing facilities, combining residential accommodation for a set number of delegates with daytime accommodation for a conference room, refreshments, and lunch.

- *Loss-leader pricing* involves setting the price at a level lower than the actual cost incurred to produce it. This approach is often used in supermarkets on popular price-sensitive items (for example best-selling novels) to entice customers into store. The loss incurred is made up by increasing the prices of other less price-sensitive items or it is absorbed as a short-term promotional cost.

Market Insight 9.5
Stripe: Revolutionizing Online Payments

Fintech (that is, financial technology), start-ups, and scaling companies are identified as key drivers in the international financial services sector. One example of this is a start-up called Stripe, recently valued at US$5 billion. Stripe was founded in 2011 by two Irish brothers, Patrick and John Collison, to simplify the online payments process. Until recently, the payment sector for the credit card and banking industry had been based on 1980s business models in which the costs of inefficiencies were passed on to merchants and small businesses.

stripe

Simple logo; pain-free payment transactions
Source: Courtesy of Stripe.

Stripe, frequently considered a rival to PayPal, provides processing services for online and mobile transactions. Essentially, the company provides a suite of application programming interfaces (APIs) that allow businesses to integrate payment-processing technologies into mobile apps and services, thereby facilitating credit card payments, bank transfers, and bitcoin transactions. One of Stripe's unique selling points is that it makes the digital payment process via smartphones and websites 'so pain-free it's practically invisible', without the need for integration with third-party payment service providers such as PayPal. This seamless experience entices customers to stay longer on a merchant's website, while also reducing the time taken to make

a payment. As a result, this encourages customer retention.

Recently, Stripe has revised its service to facilitate payments in more than 130 currencies, thereby massively extending its market reach. In addition, Stripe's latest service, 'Stripe Connect', allows merchants to change their business models (such as their pricing strategy or their target market) at any time—a key requirement for today's fluid, rapidly changing business environment. For example, transportation companies are often required to quickly pivot to address regulatory changes in the markets in which they operate, or companies might want to quickly grow a market share in a new sector, after which they can adapt their business model once their position as a leading provider is established.

The Stripe payment model is similar to that of its competitors, such as PayPal, but Stripe charges a flat rate in each country of operation. For example, in Europe, for every successful charge on a credit card, it costs 1.4% + 25c; for cards from non-European countries, it costs 2.9% + 25c. This amount decreases based on volume. In addition, although PayPal follows the same basic fee structure and boasts of providing payment for transactions faster than Stripe (that is, within one business day), its pricing includes a number of service fees on top of its flat rate. Stripe presents another competitive advantage in terms of data portability, meaning that, unlike its competitors, Stripe facilitates the migration of customer credit card data in a secure and payment card industry (PCI) compliant manner.

Sources: Newenham (2014); IFS Ireland (2015); Perez (2015); https://stripe.com/ie/pricing

Market Insight 9.5
continued

Theory into Practice

This market insight shows how an Irish company achieved exponential growth by revolutionizing the online payments process. By offering a flat rate per credit card transaction, as opposed to monthly fees, Stripe made it easy—particularly for small businesses—to develop an online payments facility and process payments from many countries (since Stripe charges only a modest exchange rate). Paypal, Stripe's major rival, has since acquired Braintree, a payment processing company that uses a similar business model to Stripe. The market insight therefore illustrates both the importance of having a clear pricing strategy and how an easy payment process can generate greater amounts of business for an organization.

Related Topics

pricing; online retailing

1 If a company is considering Stripe versus PayPal, what might drive its final decision? (*Hint*: Search both companies' payment approaches online.)

2 What approach to pricing is Stripe using at present? In your answer, describe how Stripe uses marketing cues to persuade customers that its rates are good value compared with those of its competitors.

3 As a consumer, if you are making a payment online, what pricing tactics, if any, influence your decision to stay longer on a merchant's website?

This market insight was kindly contributed by Dr Ethel Claffey, Waterford Institute of Technology, Ireland.

- *Promotional pricing* sees companies temporarily reduce their prices below the standard price to raise brand awareness and to encourage trial. Such approaches incorporate the use of loss leaders, sales discounts, cash rebates, low-interest financing (for example car manufacturers offering 0 per cent interest-free financing deals), and other price-based promotional incentives. For example, in late 2015, French hypermarket chain Leclerc advertised and offered Epson printers at a price of €44.99—down from €54.99—for a fixed ten-day period, with the tagline '*Chez E. Leclerc, vous savez que vous achetez moins cher*' ('At E. Leclerc, you know you are buying cheaper').

- *Segmentation pricing* involves setting prices for different groups of customers. For example, Unilever's ice cream is offered as various different ice-cream products at differing levels of quality and price, ranging from super-premium (for example Ben & Jerry's ice cream, available in cinemas) to economy offerings (for example standard vanilla ice cream available in supermarkets). Economists call this approach **price discrimination**.

- *Customer-centric pricing*, as suggested by Cross and Dixit (2005), involves companies taking advantage of customer segments by measuring their value perceptions, measuring the value created, and designing a unique bundle of products and services to cater to the value requirements of each segment, then continually assessing the impact this has on company profitability, taking advantage of up-selling (that is, offering a customer a more expensive offering in the same category) and cross-selling (that is, selling other different offerings to the same customer).

- The *pay-what-you-want approach to pricing*, used by street music artists, allows customers to pay whatever they want. It has also occasionally been used in publishing, for example music publishing, when Radiohead released their album *In Rainbows* in 2007 (Anon., 2012), and in book/game publishing by Humble Bundle, which allows customers to also donate part of the fee to a charity (Baddeley, 2015). Under certain circumstances, customers may pay more using this scheme than if companies had set the price (Kim, Natter, and Spann, 2009), although others have argued that it works only for promotions and is, in the long run, a 'dangerous pricing technique' (Leatherdale, 2015), offering 'slim pickings' (Harford, 2013). It tends to work best where an offering has a low marginal cost, when there is a fair-minded consumer, where an offering could be sold at a wide range of prices, in a competitive marketplace, and where there is a strong relationship between buyer and seller (Shan, 2015).

Business-to-Business Pricing

Business-to-business markets sell offerings to other businesses. They differ from consumer markets because buyers are professionally trained procurement executives, often with qualifications from professional institutes, such as the UK's Chartered Institute of Purchasing and Supply (CIPS), the Australian Association of Procurement and Contract Management (AAPCM), or Silf, the Swedish Purchasing and Logistic Association. Their function is often highly technical, even for apparently simple offerings. For example, to produce a pen, a manufacturer might buy the pens in Italy, packaging and printing from China, refills from Germany, and the final product assembly in Bulgaria.

In the B2B context, the discussion of price takes place between the buyer and the seller in an atmosphere in which both are trying to make the best commercial decision for their organizations. The seller wants to maximize profit (by getting a high price), and the buyer wants to procure at a low price to lower costs and maximize their profits. Their task is to resolve their mutual needs in a win–win situation. From the seller's perspective, there are numerous pricing tactics that can be adopted, including the following:

- *Geographical pricing* sees prices based on customer location (for example pharmaceutical companies selling their prescription drugs at different prices in different countries). This might include free on board (FOB) factory prices whereby the price represents the cost of the goods and the buyer must pay for all transport costs incurred. Free on board destination pricing refers to the situation in which the manufacturer agrees to cover the cost of shipping to the destination, but not transport costs incurred on arrival at the port (air or sea).

- *Negotiated pricing* sees prices set according to specific agreements between a company and its clients or customers (for example in professional services, such as architectural or structural engineering). This approach occurs where a sale is complex and consultative, although sales representatives should not concede on price too quickly before properly understanding a client's needs (Rackham, 2001).

- *Discount pricing* sees companies reducing the price on the basis that a customer commits to buying a large volume of that offering now or in the future, or is prepared to pay for it quickly. Large retailers work on the discount principle when buying for their stores. Their mighty procurement budgets and long experience ensure that they can buy at cheaper prices from their suppliers and so lower their costs. Note that, when price is discounted, we disproportionately reduce the operating profit (Baker et al., 2010).

- *Value-in-use pricing* focuses attention on customer perceptions of the attributes of offerings and away from cost-oriented approaches. It prices offerings based on what the customer is prepared to pay for the individual benefits received from that proposition, so the company must first ascertain what benefit components the customer perceives to be important, quantify those benefit values, determine the price equivalence of value, rate competitive and alternative products to provide a benchmark for price determination, quantify the value in use (that is, the value in using its product vis-à-vis its competitors' products), and only then is the price actually fixed (Christopher, 1982). This approach is particularly used for industrial propositions.

- *Relationship pricing* seeks to understand customers' needs before pricing the offering around those needs to generate a long-term relationship. This means offering excellent financial terms, credit or more lenient time periods for payment, or discounts based on future sales revenue or the risk involved in the purchase.

- *Pay-what-you-want (PWYW) pricing* allows customers to pay whatever they want for an offering. For example, legal services firm CMS Cameron McKenna has offered PWYW pricing to its corporate clients (Hollander, 2010). However, one new restaurant offering PWYW pricing in Guiyang, China, lost 100,000 RMB (about US$15,000 at that time) in one week despite positive customer evaluations of the food and service. This type of pricing works best for last-minute sales to fill empty capacity, where the customer has a previous relationship with the business, or when the earnings are given to charity (Dholakia, 2017).

- *Transfer pricing* occurs in large organizations where considerable internal dealing between different company divisions occurs, often across national boundaries. Prices may be set at commercial rates, on the basis of negotiated prices between divisions, or using a cost-based approach, depending on whether the division is a cost or profit centre. Internal dealings can sometimes mean that the final offering is overpriced for a given customer. Airbus Industries, the European aircraft manufacturer owned by the European Aeronautic Defence and Space Company (EADS), adopts this approach when constructing its planes built from components made in different countries.

- With *economic value to the customer (EVC) pricing*, a company prices an offering according to its perceived value by the purchasing organization (that is, total profit generated *less* the costs paid), typically by means of comparison with a reference or market-leading offering, taking into consideration not only the actual purchase price of the offering, but also the start-up and post-purchase costs, to give an overall indication of how much better its pricing structure is compared with that of a competitor. The final price is then set based on a negotiation between the buyer and seller over the difference in value and how likely this value is to be achieved. This kind of pricing approach might be used by a large consultancy solutions company, such as IBM, when it sells its system solutions.

- With *tendering and bid pricing*, organizations invite other organizations to bid for the right to deliver a particular job or task (a tender) and to name their own price. This approach is used heavily within the public sector. The difficulty arises in that organizations do not always provide a budgetary range to allow bidders an idea of what price would be accepted. The manager should know the profitability of their bid when determining the price, and should aim to discover the winning bidder's name and price on lost jobs where possible (Walker, 1967). Where the winning bidder sets their bid price so low that they win an unprofitable contract that they are nonetheless duty-bound to deliver, this is known as the **winner's curse**.

 # Chapter Summary

To consolidate your learning, the key points from this chapter are summarized here:

- **Explain the concept of price elasticity of demand.**

  Price elasticity of demand allows us to determine how the quantity of an offering relates to the price at which it is offered. Inelastic propositions are defined as such because increases or decreases in price produce relatively smaller decreases or increases in sales volumes, whereas elastic offerings have larger similar effects. Understanding price elasticity helps us to devise demand-oriented pricing mechanisms.

- **Define price, and understand its relationship with costs, quality, and value.**

  Price, costs, quality, and value are all interrelated. *Price* is what an offering is sold for and *cost* is what it is bought for. When value is added to a proposition, the price that can be obtained exceeds the cost. Price and cost are often confused, and are assumed erroneously to be the same thing. They are not. *Quality* is a measure of how well an offering satisfies the need for which it is designed to cater. *Value* is best described either as a function of the quality of an offering as a proportion of the price paid or the perceived benefits *less* the perceived price.

- **Describe how customers perceive price.**

  Understanding how customers and consumers perceive pricing helps when setting prices. Customers have an idea of reference prices based on what they ought to pay for an offering, what others would pay, or what they would like to pay. Their knowledge of actual prices is limited to well-known and frequently bought and advertised offerings. Consequently, customers tend to rely on price cues such as odd-number pricing, sale signs, the purchase context, and price bundles when deciding whether or not value exists in a particular proposition.

- **Understand pricing strategies and how to price new offerings.**

  There are four main pricing strategies, comprising premium pricing (pricing an offering to indicate its distinctiveness in the marketplace), penetration pricing (pricing low relative to the competition to gain market share), economy pricing (pricing at the bare minimum to attract price-sensitive customers), and price skimming (setting the price high initially and then lowering it in sequential steps). The two classic approaches to pricing new offerings are market skimming and market penetration pricing. The former is favoured when a company needs to recover its R&D investment quickly, when customers are price-insensitive or of unknown price sensitivity, when product life cycles are short (see Chapter 8), and when barriers to entry to competitors are high. The latter is favoured otherwise.

- **Explain cost-, competitor-, demand-, and value-oriented approaches to pricing.**

  There are a variety of different pricing policies that can be used, depending on whether we are pricing a consumer, service, or B2B offering. They tend to be cost-oriented (based on what we paid for it and what mark-up we intend to add), competitor-oriented (the so-called going rate, or based on the price at which competitors sell an offering), demand-oriented (based on how much of an offering can be sold at what price), or value-oriented (what attributes of the offering are of benefit to the customer and what will they pay for them).

■ **Explain how pricing operates in the business-to-business setting.**

A variety of pricing tactics are used in the B2B setting, including geographical, negotiated, discount, value-in-use, relationship, pay-what-you-want, transfer, economic value to the customer, and bid pricing. Business-to-business pricing differs in that buyers are frequently expert in purchasing for their organizations. They are likely to pay particular attention to the value that they derive from the offering.

 # Review Questions

1　Define price, cost, quality, and value, and how they relate to each other.

2　Explain the concept of price elasticity of demand, giving examples of offerings that are both price-elastic and price-inelastic.

3　What are pricing cues?

4　How does odd-number pricing work?

5　What are the four main pricing strategies?

6　When might you use price skimming as a pricing approach?

7　When might you use penetration pricing?

8　Name four B2B pricing tactics.

9　Under what circumstances does the pay-what-you-want pricing approach work best?

10　How does pricing operate in tender and bidding processes?

 # Discussion Questions

1　Having read Case Insight 9.1, how would you advise Simply Business to develop a pricing system that offers tailored policies, including discounts, to those customers who are more price-sensitive?

2　What pricing policy would you advise in each of the following scenarios when setting the price? (State the assumptions under which you are working when you decide on each.)

　A　The senior manager at Northrop Grumman, a US defence manufacturer, wants to set the price for a medium-range integrated air and defence missile programme he's selling to Poland, so it can defend itself against perceived external threats and aggression and maintain its national security.

　B　The product manager at American car maker Ford wants to set the price range for the updated Ford Mustang GT in the UK, launched in 2018.

　C　The manager at Bird & Bird, a well-known large legal services firm in Denmark, has been commissioned by a medium-sized import–export company, with turnover of €20 million, to complete some work in relation to a recent company acquisition. What further information would the manager require to price such work and what pricing approaches could you offer?

3 How would you go about determining the price sensitivity of your customers in the following scenarios?

A You are a hotel marketing manager and you want your hotels to operate at full capacity throughout the week, including weekends and weekdays.

B You are the pricing manager for a corporate legal services firm and you want to utilize all your lawyers up to 80 per cent of capacity (leaving the other 20 per cent for business development and administration).

C You are the financial director for an airline company and you want your planes to operate at 80 per cent capacity during the off-peak season.

Visit the online resources and complete the Multiple-Choice Questions to assess your knowledge of Chapter 9.

Glossary

advertising elasticity a measure of how responsive the demand for offerings is in relation to changes in advertising expenditure (that is, how effective an advertising campaign is in generating new sales).

brand equity the revenues generated from consumers' perception of the brand rather than from the product itself.

components part of something larger (for example an engine as part of a car, or the casing, ink, and packaging as parts of a pen).

consumer durables manufactured consumer products that are relatively long-lasting (for example cars or computers), as opposed to non-durables (for example foodstuffs).

differential pricing the process of maximizing profit by selling different groups of customers the same product at different prices.

fixed capital the cost of plant, equipment, and machinery owned by a business.

meta-analysis where the results of multiple similar studies are combined and analysed statistically to draw more valid and reliable conclusions about particular relationships within the larger dataset.

mixed price bundling when a product or service is offered together with another typically complementary product or service, which is also available separately, to make the original product or service seem more attractive (for example a mobile phone package sold with text messages and international call packages included in the price).

perceived quality a relative subjective measure; a term used because there is no truly objective absolute measure of product or service quality.

price the amount that the customer has to pay to receive a good or service.

price anchoring a cognitive bias whereby we have a tendency to rely heavily on information first offered to us rather than that collected later.

price discrimination occurs where the price of a good or service is set differently for certain groups of people.

price elasticity the percentage change in volume demanded as a proportion of the percentage change in price, usually expressed as a negative number; a score close to 0 indicates that a product or service price change has little impact on quantity demanded, whereas a score of −1 indicates that a product or service price change effects an equal percentage quantity change and a value above −1 indicates a disproportionately higher change in quantity demanded as a result of a percentage price change.

price gouging occurs when a seller sets the price of a good or service at a level far higher than is considered reasonable.

pricing cues proxy measures used by customers to estimate the reference price of a product or service, such as quality, styling, packaging, sale signs, and odd-number endings.

pure price bundling when a product or service is offered together with another typically complementary product or service, which is not available separately, to make the original product or service seem more attractive (for example a CD attached to a music magazine).

reference price the price band against which customers make a judgement about the purchase price of goods and services.

secret menus many fast-food outlets have menus that are not displayed, but which can be requested, for example Burger King's mustard Whopper® and Frings (fries with onion rings), among numerous other items.

showrooming visiting a shop to see an offering, then buying it cheaper online.

transfer pricing typically occurs in large organizations and represents the pricing approach used when one unit of a company sells to another unit within the same company.

value the regard that something is held to be worth, typically, although not always, in financial terms.

webrooming researching a product online, but then buying it in-store.

white goods large electrical goods used in residences, typically, but not necessarily, white in colour (for example refrigerators, washing machines).

white-labelled product an offering developed by one organization that other organizations rebrand and market as if it were their own.

winner's curse situation in the bidding process in commercial markets whereby a company ends up submitting a bid at a price that is unprofitable or not very profitable simply to win the contract.

working capital in accounting terms, a company's short-term financial efficiency and is the difference between its current assets (what it owns) and its current liabilities (what it owes).

References

Ailawadi, K., Lehmann, D.R., and Neslin, S.A. (2003). Revenue premium as an outcome measure of brand equity. *Journal of Marketing*, 67(4), 1–17.

Amaldoss, W., and Jain, S. (2005). Pricing of conspicuous goods: a competitive analysis of social effects. *Journal of Marketing Research*, 42(1), 30–42.

Anderson, E., and Simester, D. (2003). Mind your pricing cues. *Harvard Business Review*, 81(9), 96–103.

Anderson, J.C., Wouters, M., and van Rossum, W. (2010). Why the highest price isn't the best price. *Sloan Management Review*, 51(2), 69–76.

Andreyeva, T., Long, M.W., and Brownell, K.D. (2010). The impact of food prices on consumption: a systematic review of research on the price elasticity of demand for food. *American Journal of Public Health*, 100(2), 216–22.

Anon. (2012). Paying what you want: conscience versus commerce. *The Economist*, 5 May. Retrieve from: https://www.economist.com/finance-and-economics/2012/05/05/conscience-v-commerce (accessed 13 October 2018).

Anon. (2015). Taking sugary drinks: stopping slurping. *The Economist*, 26 November. Retrieve from: https://www.economist.com/news/finance-and-economics/21679259-taxes-fizzy-drinks-seem-work-intended-stopping-slurping (accessed 13 October 2018).

Anon. (2016a). A tax on sugar: pricier pop. *The Economist*, 19 March. Retrieve from: https://www.economist.com/news/britain/21694993-levy-drinks-may-change-recipes-not-waistlines-britain-gets-new-tax-sugary-drinks (accessed 13 October 2018).

Anon. (2016b). International airlines: price vs service. *The Economist 1843*, April–May, 141.

Anon. (2016c). Flexible figures. *The Economist*, 30 January, 64.

AO (2017). *Building for Growth: Annual Report and Accounts 2017*. Retrieve from: https://ao.com/corporate/wp-content/uploads/2017/06/AO_AR2017_200617-final.pdf (accessed 13 October 2018).

Attridge, J. (2003). A single European market for pharmaceuticals: could less regulation and more negotiation be the answer? *European Business Journal*, 15(3), 122–43.

Babad, Y.M., and Balachandran, B.V. (1993). Cost driver optimisation in activity-based costing. *Accounting Review*, 68(3), 563–75.

Baddeley, A. (2015). When 'pay what you want' means 'don't pay at all'. *The Guardian*, 26 April. Retrieve from: https://www.theguardian.com/books/2015/apr/26/when-pay-what-want-means-dont-pay-online-bookshop (accessed 13 October 2018).

Baker, W.L., Marn, M.V., and Zawada, C.C. (2010). *The Price Advantage* (2nd edn). Hoboken, NJ: John Wiley.

Bijmolt, T.H.A., van Heerde, H.J., and Pieters, R.G.M. (2005). New empirical generalisations on the determinants of price elasticity. *Journal of Marketing Research*, 42(2), 141–56.

Blackhurst, C. (2014). Check out the Dutch for supermarket price wars. *Evening Standard*, 2 October, 47.

Boyle, P.J., and Lathrop, E.S. (2009). Are consumers' perceptions of price–quality relationships well-calibrated? *International Journal of Consumer Studies*, 33(1), 58–63.

Burnett, J. (2002). *Core Concepts in Marketing*. Chichester: John Wiley.

Chahal, M. (2015). Brands battle over best approach to pricing. *Marketing Week*, 8 October. Retrieve from: https://www.marketingweek.com/2015/10/08/brands-battle-over-best-approach-to-pricing/ (accessed 13 October 2018).

Chen, H., Marmorstein, H., Tsiros, M., and Rao, R.R. (2012). When more is less: the impact of base value neglect on consumer preferences for bonus packs over price discounts. *Journal of Marketing*, 76(4), 64–77.

Christopher, M. (1982). Value-in-use pricing. *European Journal of Marketing*, 16(5), 35–46.

Cialdini, R.B. (1993). *Influence: The Psychology of Persuasion*. New York: Quill William Morrow.

Colchero, M.A., Salgado, J.C., Unar-Munguía, M., Hernández-Ávila, M., and Rivera-Dommarco, J.A. (2015). Price elasticity of the demand for sugar-sweetened beverages and soft drinks in Mexico. *Economics and Human Biology*, 19, 129–37.

Constantinides, A., and Rahman, K. (2015). Pharmaceutical entrepreneur who jacked up AIDS pill price by 5000% says he should have charged even more. *Mail Online*, 5 December. Retrieve from: https://www.dailymail.co.uk/news/article-3347441/Martin-Shkreli-said-raised-price-Daraprim-more.html (accessed 13 October 2018).

Cross, R.G., and Dixit, A. (2005). Customer-centric pricing: the surprising secret for profitability. *Business Horizons*, 48(6), 483–91.

Crow, D. (2015). A provocateur in the pharma wars. *Financial Times*, 26–27 September, 3.

Dean, J. (1950). Pricing policies for new products. *Harvard Business Review*, 28(6), 45–53.

Dholakia, U. (2017). When does pay what you want pricing work? *Psychology Today*, 5 March. Retrieve from: https://www.psychologytoday.com/blog/the-science-behind-behavior/201703/when-does-pay-what-you-want-pricing-work (accessed 13 October 2018).

Dolan, R.J., and Simon, H. (1997). *Power Pricing: How Managing Price Transforms the Bottom Line*. New York: Free Press.

Donnelly, L. (2016). Sugar tax in Mexico cuts sales of sugary drinks by 12 per cent. *The Telegraph*, 6 January. Retrieve from: https://www.telegraph.co.uk/news/health/news/12085408/Children-aged-five-eating-own-weight-in-sugar-every-year.html (accessed 13 October 2018).

Doyle, P. (2000). *Value-Based Marketing: Marketing Strategies for Corporate Growth and Shareholder Value*. Chichester: John Wiley.

Duffy, M. (1999). The influence of advertising on the pattern of food consumption in the UK. *International Journal of Advertising*, 18(2), 131–68.

Ellson, A. (2018). Supermarket prices to rise as you shop. *The Times*, 26 June, 21.

Foxall, G. (1972). A descriptive theory of pricing for marketing. *European Journal of Marketing*, 6(3), 190–4.

Gerstner, E. (1985). Do higher prices signal higher quality? *Journal of Marketing Research*, 22(2), 209–15.

Gourville, J., and Soman, D. (2002). Pricing and the psychology of consumption. *Harvard Business Review*, 80(9), 90–6.

Grewal, D., Ailawadi, K.L., Gauri, D., Hall, K., Kopalle, P., and Robertson, J.R. (2011). Innovations in retail pricing and promotions. *Journal of Retailing*, 87(S1), S43–52.

Harford, T. (2013). Pay-what-you-want pricing: play tag with price tags. *Financial Times*, 16 August. Retrieve from: https://www.ft.com/cms/s/2/fd79cc8e-0467-11e3-a8d6-00144feab7de.html (accessed 13 October 2018).

Hayward, S. (2015). So this is what Cadbury thinks of biscuit lovers. *Sunday Mirror*, 12 April, 24.

Helmore, E. (2017). Amazon primed for price war with rival Walmart. *The Guardian*, 25 August, 29.

Hinterhuber, A., and Liozu, S. (2012). Is it time to rethink your pricing strategy? *Sloan Management Review*, 53(4), 76.

Hipwell, D., and Ellson, A. (2016). Superdrug takes razor to sexist pricing. *The Times*, 5 February, 21.

Hollander, G. (2010). Camerons invites legal clients to pay what they want for legal work. *The Lawyer*, 5 August. Retrieve from: https://www.thelawyer.com/camerons-invites-clients-to-pay-what-they-want-for-legal-work/1005236.article (accessed 13 October 2018).

IFS Ireland (2015). *IFS 2020: A Strategy for Ireland's International Financial Services Sector 2015–2020*. Retrieve from: https://finance.gov.ie/wp-content/uploads/2017/05/IFS2020-Strategic-Plan.pdf (accessed 13 October 2018).

Jeeves, P. (2018). Landlord under fire for bargain breakfast-time pints in 'January sale'. *Daily Express*, 6 January, 29.

Kannan, P.K. (2014). The future of pricing in the digital era. In: L. Moutinho, E. Bigné, and A.K. Manrai (eds), *The Routledge Companion to the Future of Marketing*, Abingdon: Routledge, 282–95.

Kim, J-Y., Natter, M., and Spann, M. (2009). Pay what you want: a new participatory pricing mechanism. *Journal of Marketing*, 73(1), 44–58.

Kolitsopoulou, M. (2017). Eva Longoria–Pepe Baston: exclusive pictures from their holidays in Greece. *Like.com.cy*, 20 September. Retrieve from: https://like.philenews.com/eva-longkoria-pepe-baston-apoklistikes-ikones-apo-tis-diakopes-tous-stin-ellada/ (accessed 13 October 2018).

Latif, A. (2013). Value-based pricing. *The Lancet: Policy Matters*, 16 August. Retrieve from: https://ukpolicymatters.thelancet.com/value-based-pricing/ (accessed 13 October 2018).

Lavin, R., and Timpson, H. (2013). *Exploring the Acceptability of a Tax on Sugar-Sweetened Beverages: Brief Evidence Review*. Centre for Public Health, Liverpool John Moores University, April. Retrieve from: http://www.

cph.org.uk/wp-content/uploads/2013/11/SSB-Evidence-Review_Apr-2013-2.pdf (accessed 13 October 2018).

Leatherdale, D. (2015). Do pay-what-you-want pricing strategies work? *BBC News*, 22 July. Retrieve from: https://www.bbc.co.uk/news/uk-england-33609867 (accessed 13 October 2018).

Leszinski, R., and Marn, M.V. (1997). Setting value, not price. *McKinsey Quarterly*, February. Retrieve from: https://www.mckinsey.com/business-functions/marketing-and-sales/our-insights/setting-value-not-price (accessed 13 October 2018).

Liozu, S.M., and Hinterhuber, A. (2013). Pricing orientation, pricing capabilities, and firm performance. *Management Decision*, 51(3), 594–614.

Lockley, L.C. (1949). Theories of pricing in marketing. *Journal of Marketing*, 13(3), 364–7.

Mendoza, J., and Baines, P. (2012). Towards a consumer price perception formation framework: a systematic review. Presented at: Australia and New Zealand Marketing Academy Conference (ANZMAC) 2012, Adelaide, Australia, 3–6 December.

Michard, Q. (2016). Why brands should be using data analytics to inform pricing strategy. *Impact*, January, 68–9.

Neville, S. (2015). Supermarkets surrender to farmers after milk price protest. *The Independent*, 15 August, 46.

Newenham, P. (2014). Irish founded payments start-up Stripe now valued at $3.5bn. *Irish Times*, 2 December. Retrieve from: https://www.irishtimes.com/business/technology/irish-founded-payments-start-up-stripe-now-valued-at-3-5-billion-1.2023112 (accessed 13 October 2018).

Nunes, J.C., and Boatwright, P. (2001). Pricey encounters. *Harvard Business Review*, July–August. Retrieve from: https://hbr.org/2001/07/pricey-encounters (accessed 24 September 2018).

Oxford Dictionaries (2016a). Price. Retrieve from: http://oxforddictionaries.com/definition/english/price?q=price (accessed 13 October 2018).

Oxford Dictionaries (2016b). Quality. Retrieve from: http://oxforddictionaries.com/definition/english/quality?q=quality (accessed 13 October 2018).

Oxford Dictionaries (2016c). Value. Retrieve from: http://oxforddictionaries.com/definition/english/value?q=value (accessed 13 October 2018).

Perez, S. (2015). Stripe's new product helps marketplaces go global more quickly. *Techcrunch.com*, 23 March. Retrieve from: https://techcrunch.com/2015/03/23/stripes-new-product-helps-marketplaces-go-global-more-quickly/#.uxlor18:sOTB (accessed 13 October 2018).

PHE (Public Health England) (2015). *Sugar Reduction: The Evidence for Action*. Retrieve from: https://assets.publishing.service.gov.uk/government/uploads/system/uploads/attachment_data/file/470179/Sugar_reduction_The_evidence_for_action.pdf (accessed 13 October 2018).

Pindych, R.S., and Rubinfeld, D.C. (2005). *Microeconomics* (6th edn). Upper Saddle River, NJ: Pearson Prentice Hall.

Poulter, S. (2018). Contactless cards leave us clueless on everyday prices. *Daily Mail*, 28 February, 31.

Rackham, N. (2001). Winning the price war. *Sales and Marketing Management*, 253(11), 26.

Reinemoeller, P. (2014). How to win a price war. *Sloan Management Review*, 55(3), 15–17.

Rust, R.T., Danaher, P.J., and Varki, S. (2000). Using service quality data for competitive marketing decisions. *International Journal of Service Industry Management*, 11(5), 438–69.

Shan, C. (2015). Where can the 'pay-what-you-want' model succeed? *Quora*, 2 June. Retrieve from: https://www.quora.com/Where-can-the-pay-what-you-want-model-succeed (accessed 13 October 2018).

Sheth, J.N., Sisodia, R.S., and Barbulescu, A. (2006). The image of marketing. In: J.N. Sheth and R.S. Sisodia (eds), *Does Marketing Need Reform*? New York: M.E. Sharpe, 26–36.

Smith, G.E., and Nagle, T.T. (1995). Frames of reference and buyer's perceptions of value. *California Management Review*, 38(1), 98–116.

Smith, H. (2017). Greek debt crisis: 'People can't see any light at the end of the tunnel'. *The Guardian*, 30 July. Retrieve from: https://www.theguardian.com/world/2017/jul/30/greek-debt-crisis-people-cant-see-any-light-at-the-end-of-any-tunnel (accessed 13 October 2018).

Thier, D. (2016). Microsoft just dropped the Xbox One price again. *Forbes*, 18 March. Retrieve from: https://www.forbes.com/sites/davidthier/2016/03/18/microsoft-just-dropped-the-xbox-one-price-again/#3527d83920f1 (accessed 13 October 2018).

van Heerde, H.J., Gijsbrechts, E., and Pauwels, K. (2008). Winners and losers in a major price war. *Journal of Marketing Research*, 45(5), 499–518.

van Heerde, H.J., Gijsenberg, M.J., Dekimpe, M.G., and Steenkamp, J-B.E.M. (2013). Price and advertising effectiveness over the business cycle. *Journal of Marketing Research*, 50(2), 177–93.

Vijayraghvan, S. (2015). Upcoming cars in India: new hatchbacks under ₹4 Lakh. *carandbike*, 3 December. Retrieve from: https://auto.ndtv.com/news/upcoming-cars-in-india-new-hatchbacks-under-rs-4-lakh-720235 (accessed 13 October 2018).

Völckner, F., and Hofmann, J. (2007). The price-perceived quality relationship: a meta-analytic review and assessment of its determinants. *Marketing Letters*, 18(3), 181–96.

Walker, A.W. (1967). How to price industrial products. *Harvard Business Review*, 45(5), 125–32.

Ward, K. (1993). Gaining a marketing advantage through the strategic use of transfer pricing. *Journal of Marketing Management*, 9, 245–53.

Yeoman, I., and McMahon-Beattie, U. (2006). Luxury markets and premium pricing. *Journal of Revenue and Pricing Management*, 4(4), 319–28.

Zeithaml, V.A. (1988). Consumer perceptions of price, quality and value: a means–end model and synthesis of evidence. *Journal of Marketing*, 52(3), 2–22.

Chapter 10
Principles of Marketing Communications

Learning Outcomes

After reading this chapter, you will be able to:

▶ Define and describe the nature, purpose, and scope of marketing communications

▶ Explain three models of communication and describe how personal influences can enhance the effectiveness of marketing communication activities

▶ Understand the models used to explain how marketing communications and advertising work

▶ Understand the role of marketing communications in marketing

▶ Describe the different steps in the strategic marketing communications planning process

▶ Describe what culture is and explain how it can impact on the use of marketing communications

Case Insight 10.1
Åkestam Holst

How can marketing communications stay relevant for consumers increasingly avoiding marketing messages? We speak to Petronella Panérus, chief executive officer (CEO) at the advertising agency Åkestam Holst, to find out how the agency works with clients to ensure that the advertising they create is relevant to consumers' everyday life.

In 2017, Swedish advertising agency Åkestam Holst was named International Agency of the Year by US industry magazine Ad Week. The same year, the agency received numerous awards for its creative work, including a Grand Prix in the Innovation category in the Cannes Lions—quite an achievement for a Swedish advertising agency with only 70 employees. The strength of the agency lies in its innovative work, relationships with clients, and the internal culture, says CEO Petronella Panérus.

Åkestam Holst was founded in 1998 with the intention of being a different type of advertising agency. Our core product is offering clients creative solutions that help to ensure that their brands and products become known, liked, and bought, but it was clear from the start that this agency should balance employee satisfaction and well-being with such creative success. This means that we have always put an emphasis on promoting a welcoming and supportive office culture.

Today, we have a strong track record of promoting diversity and equality in our workforce. This culture has been the foundation for our success. If we are to make ads for many different target groups, we have to make sure that several different perspectives are represented in the work groups of our agency.

The foundation for all our work is deep business understanding and research-based communication insights. We complement our business insights with a profound interest in, and ability to understand, human driving forces and behaviours. On top, we add creative talent and an extreme willingness to make things different, better, more interesting. For the people and for the world. We never stand still and always embrace change.

The importance of understanding different realities is highlighted in our work for IKEA. Under the concept 'Where Life Happens', the campaign highlights everyday situations in a matter-of-fact tone. In one campaign, a newly divorced dad decorates his son's bedroom to be identical to the room he has in his mother's house. In another, a single mom struggles with a house full of messy teens. In a digital campaign, we also renamed several IKEA products after frequently Googled problems that those products solve. Under the headline 'Retail Therapy', this campaign received attention around the world. In all these examples, we have used real-life situations to connect IKEA with its customers.

In 2018 and onwards, we will continue to evolve our long-standing experiment with producing world-class advertising from within an agency culture that values respect, diversity, and equality. We are determined to contribute to doing good in the communications that we create. Hard work, talent, customer focus, and a great agency culture is, and has always been, the foundation. In the future, we will put a special focus on pushing ourselves to think more long term, to create ideas that last and create value over time, and to take responsibility for how our work impacts society.

What competences will an advertising agency such as Åkestam Holst need to develop to make advertising that is fit for everyday life in the future?

 Visit the online resources to watch a video interview with Petronella Panérus in which she explains what Åkestam Holst did.

Introduction

Have you ever wondered how organizations such as IKEA manage to communicate effectively with so many different people and organizations? Well, this is the first of two chapters that explain how this can be accomplished through the use of marketing communications. This chapter introduces and explains what marketing communications is and how it can be planned. The following chapter considers the configuration of the marketing communications mix.

Marketing communications is about developing messages that target audiences can understand and act on. The purpose of this chapter is to introduce some of the fundamental ideas and concepts associated with such communications. To achieve this, the chapter commences with a definition of marketing communications. We then proceed by discussing the scope and functions of marketing communications, which includes a consideration of communications theory. This is important because it provides a basis on which to appreciate the different ways in which marketing communications are used. Communications theory specifies the scope of the subject and provides a framework within which to appreciate the various communications activities undertaken by organizations. We then present the principles by which marketing messages are communicated and consider how marketing communications might work. The chapter concludes with an overview of what culture is and how it can impact on marketing communications.

This chapter is intended to help you understand some of the fundamental ideas associated with planned marketing communications. It sets out the broad scope of marketing communications and enables you to appreciate the diversity of this fascinating subject. The tools and media used by marketing communications are an important aspect of this topic, and Chapter 11 is devoted to a fuller examination of each of them.

Defining Marketing Communications

Marketing communications can be defined as a management process by means of which an organization attempts to engage with its various audiences. By conveying messages that are of significant value, the organization encourages audiences to offer attitudinal and behavioural responses (Fill, 2013).

There are three main aspects associated with this definition, as follows:

- *Engagement*—What are the audience's communications needs and is it possible to engage with them on their terms, using one-way, two-way, or dialogic communications?

- *Audiences*—Which specific audience(s) do we need to communicate with, and what are their various behaviour and information-processing needs?

- *Responses*—What are the desired outcomes of the communication process? Are they based on changes in perception, values, and beliefs, or are changes in behaviour required?

Engagement deals with the way in which communication influences its audiences (see 'How Marketing Communications Works'). What to expect in terms of engagement is largely dependent on the decisions made with regard to the target audience and target responses for different marketing communication activities (see 'Planning Marketing Communications').

The Scope of Marketing Communications

As discussed in Chapter 1, promotion is one of the 4Ps of the marketing mix and focuses on the communication of a proposition to its target market. Marketing communications is a more contemporary term for promotion. It is used to communicate the elements of an organization's offerings to target audiences. The offer might refer to a product, a service, or the organization itself as it tries to build its reputation.

Marketing communications can be considered from a number of perspectives. Although it is an activity used by organizations with varying degrees of sophistication, it is mainly concerned with the way in which audiences are encouraged to perceive an organization and/or its offerings. Therefore it should be regarded as an audience-centred activity. Fundamentally, marketing communications comprises three elements—that is, a set of tools, media, and messages. The five common tools are advertising, sales promotion, **personal selling**, direct marketing, and public relations (PR). In addition, a range of media, such as television, radio, press, and the Internet, are used to convey different messages to target audiences (covered in more detail in Chapter 11).

Still, these tools, media, and messages are not the only sources of information for consumers; there is also implicit and important communication through the other elements of the marketing mix (for example a high price symbolizing high quality), as well as unplanned or unintended experiences (for example empty stock shelves or accidents leading to negative perceptions) in relation to the offer.

Figure 10.1 highlights the breadth and complexity of managing marketing communications. Our focus in this chapter will be on planned marketing communications (Duncan and Moriarty, 1998). This component is really important because it has the potential not only to present offers in the best possible way, but also to influence people's expectations about both product and service experiences. (See Market Insight 10.1 for an example of marketing communications, which draws on a range of media.)

Visit the **online resources** and follow the web link to the European Association of Communication Agencies (EACA) to learn more about advertising, media, and sales promotion activities across Europe.

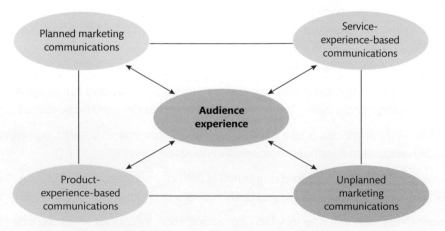

Figure 10.1

The scope of marketing communications

Source: Hughes and Fill (2007). Adapted with the kind permission of Emerald Group Publishing Limited and Westburn Publishers.

Market Insight 10.1
On the Watch for a New Kind of Watch

In September 2014, Apple CEO Tim Cook announced the company's first original product since the introduction of the iPad in 2010: the Apple Watch. With this product, Apple stepped into a new territory for the company. In the words of Cook: 'We've never sold anything as a company that people could try on before.'

Marketing communications played a large role in the launch of the Apple Watch
Source: © Anna Hoychuk/Shutterstock.com.

The watch had been much awaited and news of its arrival spread quickly. The announcement was followed by a long period of anticipation, because the watch did not become available to consumers until late April 2015.

Throughout this period, Apple shared information about the product and its design on its website, as well as in different interactions with the press. For example, it was highlighted that the watch would come in three different forms: the Apple Watch Sport, in polished or black stainless steel; the standard Apple Watch, in grey or silver anodized aluminium; and the luxury Watch Edition, available in rose or yellow. Consumers were told that prices would start at US$349, with luxury watches priced around $10,000. Information about pre-orders and availability at Apple stores (to which initial sales were restricted) was shared both online and offline.

To conquer the marketplace, Apple also launched its advertising campaign for the release with a 12-page insert in the March issue of *Vogue*. This outlet was selected based on the insight that, to succeed, the Apple Watch must have an appeal not only as a gadget, but also as a fashion statement.

Apple does not share data about sales for specific products, but stated that 2015 sales of the Apple Watch were up against the company's internal forecasts. According to estimates, the Apple Watch accounted for at least 50 per cent of all smartwatch sales in 2015.

Sources: Williams (2014); Moynihan (2015); Pierce (2015).

Theory into Practice

Although the 4Ps of marketing all convey important information about a product or service on offer, marketing communications typically refers to planned communication (that is, promotion).

Marketing communications played a large role in the launch of the Apple Watch. The design (product), the pricing (price), and the distribution (place) all conveyed information about the intended positioning of the new product, but Cook's public announcement of the watch, the way in which information about the product, price, and place of the coming launch was shared, and the advertising campaign used to support the launch are examples of marketing communications.

The type of media used in marketing communication can be categorized as paid-for, owned, and earned media (POEM) (see Chapter 11). The event could be considered part of a strategy to gain earned media, the sharing of information was mainly through Apple's own media, and the advertising campaign an example of bought media.

Market Insight 10.1

continued

Related Topics

new product development; pricing; distribution; advertising

1 How successful would you say that the launch was? What role in that success would you attribute to marketing communications?

2 In what way do design, pricing, and distribution influence perceptions of the Apple Watch?

3 Why did Apple choose *Vogue* as an important media vehicle for the launch?

How Marketing Communications Works

Ideas about how advertising, then promotion, and now marketing communications works have been a constant source of investigation, endeavour, and conceptual speculation. To suggest that a firm conclusion has been reached would be untrue. However, particular ideas have stood out and have played a more influential role in shaping our ideas about this fascinating topic. Some of these are presented here. Before considering the specific theories about how *marketing* communication works, however, we will take a closer look at communication theory. This is important because it provides a foundation on which to base our understanding of marketing communications.

Communication Theory

Communication theory is important because it helps to explain how and why certain marketing communication activities take place. Communication is the process by which individuals share meaning. Thus it is necessary for participants to be able to interpret the meanings embedded in the messages they receive and then, as far as the sender is concerned, to be able to respond coherently. The act of responding is important, because it completes an episode in the communication process. Communication that travels only from the sender to the receiver is essentially a one-way process and the full communication process remains incomplete. This **linear model** of communication is shown in Figure 10.2.

When Marabou displays its chocolate bars on a poster in the Stockholm Metro, the person standing on the platform can read that poster and understand it, and may even be entertained by it. However, the person does not have any immediate opportunity to respond to the ad in such a way that Marabou can hear, understand, and act on their comments and feelings. When that same ad is presented on a website, or a sales promotion representative offers that same person a chunk of Marabou milk chocolate in a supermarket, there are opportunities for the company to hear, record, and even respond to the comments that the person makes. This form

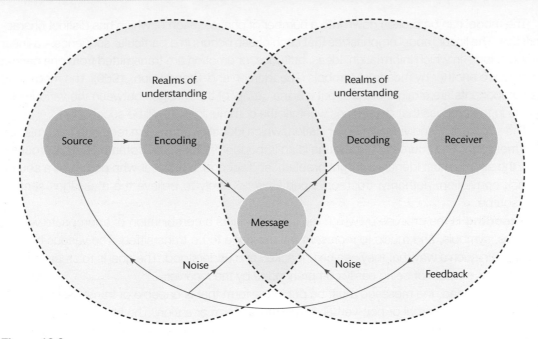

Figure 10.2

A linear model of communications

Source: Based on Schramm (1955); Shannon and Weaver (1962).

of communication travels from a sender (Marabou's representative) to a receiver (the person in the supermarket) and back again. It is referred to as a two-way communication and represents a complete communication episode.

Visit the **online resources** and follow the web link to the International Association of Business Communicators (IABC), a business network that aims to improve the effectiveness of marketing communications among communication professionals.

These basic models form the basis of this introduction to communication theory. It is important that those involved in managing and delivering marketing communications understand these processes and the associated complexities. By understanding the communication process, they are more likely to achieve their objective of sharing meaning with each member of their target audience. This not only helps to create opportunities to interact with their audiences, but also encourages some people to develop a **dialogue**—the richest and most meaningful form of communication.

Understanding the way in which communication works provides a framework within which we can better understand not only the way in which marketing communications works, but also how it can be used effectively by organizations. Three main models or interpretations of how communication works are considered here: the linear model; the two-step model; and the interaction model.

The Linear Model of Communication

The linear model of communication, first developed by Wilbur Schramm (1955), is regarded as the basic model of mass communications. The key components of this model are set out in Figure 10.2.

The model can be broken down into a number of phases, each of which has distinct characteristics. The linear model emphasizes that each phase occurs in a particular sequence—a linear progression—in which information, ideas, attitudes, or emotion are transmitted from one person or group to another by means of symbols (Theodorson and Theodorson, 1969). The model and its components are straightforward, but it is the quality of the linkages between the various elements in the process that determines whether the communication will be successful.

The source is an individual or organization, which identifies a problem requiring transmission of a message. The source of a message is an important factor in the communication process: first, the source must identify the right problem; and second, a receiver who perceives a source to lack conviction, authority, trust, or expertise is not likely to believe the messages sent by that source.

Encoding is the process by which the source selects a combination of appropriate words, pictures, symbols, and music to represent the message to be transmitted. The various bits are 'packed' in such a way that they can be unpacked and understood. The goal is to create a message that is capable of being easily comprehended by the receiver.

Once encoded, the message must be put into a form that is capable of transmission. It may be oral or written, verbal or non-verbal, in a symbolic form or a sign. The channel is the means by which the message is transmitted from the source to the receiver. These channels may be personal or non-personal. The former involves face-to-face contact and word-of-mouth communications, which can be extremely influential. Non-personal channels are characterized by mass-media advertising, which can reach large audiences. Ads placed in newspapers are typical of this approach. Whatever the format chosen, the source must be sure that what is being put into the message is what they want to be decoded by the receiver.

Once the receiver—an individual or organization—has seen, heard, smelt, or read the message, they decode it. In effect, they are 'unpacking' the various components of the message—that is, starting to make sense of it and give it meaning. The more clearly the message is encoded, the easier it is to unpack and comprehend what the source intended to convey when it constructed the message. Thus **decoding** is that part of the communication process in which **receivers** give meaning to a message.

Once the message is understood, receivers provide a set of reactions, referred to as a response. These reactions may vary from an emotional response, based on a set of feelings and thoughts about the message, to a behavioural or action response.

Feedback is another part of the response process. It is important to know not only that the message has been received, but also that it has been correctly decoded and the right meaning attributed. However, while feedback is an essential aspect of a successful communication event, feedback through mass media channels is generally difficult to obtain, mainly because of the inherent time delay involved in the feedback process. However, feedback through personal selling can be instantaneous, through explicit means such as questioning, raising objections, or signing an order form. For the mass-media advertiser, the process can be vague and prone to misinterpretation. If a suitable feedback system is not in place, the source will be unaware that the communication has been unsuccessful and is liable to continue wasting resources. This represents inefficient and ineffective marketing communications.

Noise is concerned with those influences that distort information and, in turn, make it difficult for the receiver to correctly decode and interpret the message as intended by the source. So if a telephone rings, or someone rustles sweet papers during a sensitive part of a film screened in a cinema, the receiver is distracted from the message.

The final component in the linear model concerns the 'realm of understanding'. This is an important element in the communication process because it recognizes that successful communications are more likely to be achieved if the source and the receiver understand each other. This understanding concerns attitudes, perceptions, behaviour, and experience—the values that both parties bring to the communication process. Effective communication is more likely when there is some common ground—that is, a realm of understanding between the source and receiver. (To learn more about 'realms of understanding' in the context of marketing communications, please see Research Insight 10.1.)

One of the problems associated with the linear model of communication is that it ignores the impact that other people can have on the communication process. People are not passive; they actively use information—and the views and actions of other people can impact on the way in which information is sent, received, processed, and given meaning. One of the other difficulties with the linear model is that it is based on communication through mass media.

This model was developed at a time when first radio, and then television, with only a few channels, were the only media available. Today, there are hundreds of television channels, and audiences use the Internet, mobile phones, and an increasing array of digital equipment to manage their work, leisure, and entertainment. Increasing numbers of people engage with interactive-based communications and, in circumstances such as online gaming, organizations and individuals can be involved in real dialogue. Therefore the linear model is no longer entirely appropriate.

The Two-Step Model of Communication

One interpretation of the linear model is that it is a one-step explanation. Information is directed and shot at prospective audiences, rather like a bullet being propelled from a gun. However, we know that people can have a significant impact on the communication process and hence the **two-step model**, sometimes referred to as the influencer model, goes some way towards reflecting their influence (see Figure 10.3).

Research Insight 10.1

To take your learning further, you might wish to read this influential paper:

Friestad, M., and Wright, P. (1994). The persuasion knowledge model: how people cope with persuasion attempts. *Journal of Consumer Research*, 21(1), 1–31.

This article provides a useful framework for the 'realms of understanding' surrounding marketing communications. More specifically, it discusses how consumer understanding of what marketers are trying to achieve ('persuasion knowledge') influences reactions to different types of marketing communication. The insights that the authors offer have proved very useful in understanding reactions to new forms of marketing communications, such as social media sponsorships and branded content.

 Visit the online resources to read the abstract and access the full paper.

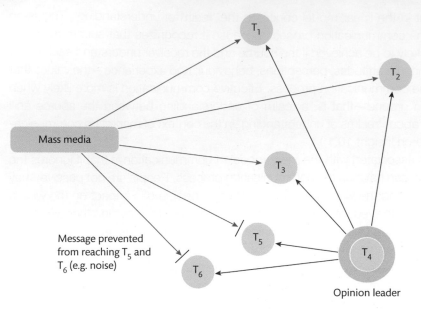

Figure 10.3

The two-step model of communications

Source: *Marketing Communications* (6th edn) Fill, C. (2013). Reproduced with the kind permission of Pearson Education Limited.
© Pearson Education Limited 2013.

The two-step model compensates for the linear, or one-step, model because it recognizes the importance of personal influences when informing and persuading audiences to think or behave in particular ways. This model depicts information flowing via various media channels to particular types of person to whom other members of the audience refer for information and guidance. There are two main types of influencer: one is referred to as an opinion leader; the other, as an opinion former. The first is simply an ordinary person who has a heightened interest in a particular topic; the second is involved professionally in the topic of interest. These are discussed in more detail later in this chapter, but they both have enormous potential to influence audiences. This may be because messages from personal influencers provide reinforcement and message credibility, or because this is the only way of reaching the end-user audience.

The Interaction Model of Communications

The **interaction model** of communication is similar to the two-step model, with one important difference: in this model, the parties are seen to interact among themselves and communication flows among all the members in what is regarded as a communication network (see Figure 10.4). Mass media are therefore not the only source of communication.

Unlike the linear model, in which messages flow from the source to the receiver through a channel, the interaction model recognizes that messages can flow through various channels, and that people can influence the direction and impact of a message. It is not necessarily one-way, but interactive communication that typifies much of contemporary communications. Often, marketing communication campaigns set out to create audience participation, for example through engagement, such as liking or sharing in social media. The interaction that such campaigns create among people, sometimes referring to the sender only indirectly, is a good demonstration of the interaction model in practice.

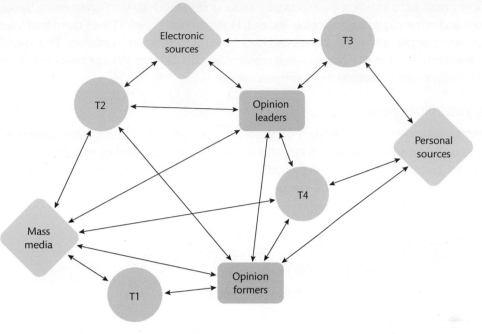

Figure 10.4
An interaction model

Interaction is an integral part of the communication process. Think of a conversation with a friend: the face-to-face, oral-based, and visual-based communication enables both of you to consider what the other is saying and to react in whatever way is appropriate. Mass communication does not facilitate this interactional element and therefore the linear model might be regarded as an incomplete form of the pure communication process.

Interaction is about actions that lead to a response and much attention is now given to the interaction that occurs between people. However, care needs to be taken because the content associated with an interactional event might be based on an argument, a statement of opinion, or a mere casual social encounter. What is important here is interaction that leads to mutual understanding. This type of interaction concerns 'relationship specific knowledge' (Ballantyne, 2004)—that is, the interaction is about information that is relevant to both parties. Once this is established, increased levels of trust develop between the participants, so that, eventually, a dialogue emerges between communication partners. Therefore interactivity is a prelude to dialogue—the highest or purest form of communication.

Dialogue occurs through reasoning, which requires both listening and adaptation skills. Dialogue is concerned with the development of knowledge that is specific to the parties involved and can be referred to as 'learning together' (Ballantyne, 2004: 119). The development of digital technologies has been instrumental in enabling organizations to provide increased interaction opportunities with their customers and other audiences. For example, think of the number of times when watching Sky television that you are prompted to press the red button to get more information. Many news programmes now encourage viewers to tweet, phone, or email comments, opinions, and pictures about particular issues, in an attempt to get audiences to express their views about a subject and, in doing so, promote access to, and interaction with, the programme. Whereas, at one time, interaction occurred only really through personal selling, it is now possible to interact, and so build mutual understanding, with consumers through the Internet and other digital technologies. Indeed, Hoffman and Novak (1996) claim that interactivity between people is now supplemented by interactivity between machines. This means that the interaction—or indeed dialogue—that previously occurred through machines can now occur with the equipment facilitating the communication.

Personal Influencers

As mentioned earlier, two main types of personal influencer can be recognized: **opinion leaders** and **opinion formers**. In addition, social media has led to **word of mouth** among regular consumers becoming even more influential. These different types of personal influencer are now discussed in turn (see also Market Insight 10.2).

Market Insight 10.2
Becoming a YouTube Superstar

Felix Kjelberg, better known by his online alias 'PewDiePie', is an online influencer
Source: Wikimedia Commons.

In April 2010, Felix Kjellberg—then a 21-year-old Swedish engineering student—created a new account on YouTube. For some time, he had been posting videos of himself playing video games on YouTube, but, having forgotten the password to the initial account, he was forced to set up a new one: PewDiePie. Little did he know that this account was going to change his life.

Kjellberg's videos turned out to be very popular. In fact, Kjellberg's foul-mouthed videos have dominated YouTube over the past years. Many attribute his success to the attention he pays to his fans. Kjellberg spends a lot of time talking about them, answering

their questions in the YouTube comments section, and forming a community of 'bros'.

In 2011, Kjellberg dropped out of university to devote more time to his YouTube channel; in 2012, it had more than 1 million subscribers. Since then, Kjellberg has broken numerous records on YouTube. For example, his PewDiePie channel grew from 12 million subscribers in August 2013 to more than 20 million in January 2014. In September 2015, PewDiePie was the world's largest independent YouTube channel, with 10.1 billion total views and 39.3 million total subscribers. By January 2016, the channel had more than 11 billion views and close to 42 million subscribers.

In 2017, however, Kjellberg lost the spot as the leading influencer on YouTube. His earnings dropped from US$15 million in 2016 to $11.5 million in 2017, largely as a result of criticism prompted by videos including racist language and anti-Semitic imagery. These videos led many marketers to blacklist Kjellberg, and YouTube removed him from its preferred programme and cancelled his show *Scare PewDiePie*.

Sources: Rosengren (2012); Tamburro (2014); Kosoff and Jacobs (2015); Berg (2017).

Market Insight 10.2
continued

Theory into Practice

The two-step model of communications recognizes the importance of personal influences when informing and persuading audiences to think or behave in particular ways. There are two main types of influencer: an opinion leader is an ordinary person who has a heightened interest in a particular topic; an opinion former is involved professionally in the topic of interest. Many YouTubers start out small. After a while, as their following increases, they become important opinion leaders. Those who become really big, such as Kjellsson aka PewDiePie, then move on to become opinion formers.

Related Topics
social media; digital marketing; user-generated content

1 **At what stage would you say that Kjellberg moved from opinion leader to opinion former? Or do you think it's impossible to say?**

2 **Visit the PewDiePie YouTube channel. To what extent is Kjellberg's communication with his followers based on interaction and dialogue?**

3 **Even though Kjellberg has built his career on foul-mouthed videos, in 2017 his remarks led several marketers and media platforms to end collaborations with him. Why?**

Opinion Leaders

Studies of American voting and purchase behaviour conducted by Katz and Lazarsfeld (1955) led them to conclude that some individuals were more predisposed than others towards receiving information and then reprocessing it to influence others. They found that these individuals had the capacity to be more persuasive than information received directly from the mass media. They called these people opinion leaders and one of the defining characteristics that the researchers identified is that these people belong to the same peer group as the people whom they influence—that is, they are not distant or removed.

It has been reported in subsequent research that opinion leaders have a greater exposure to relevant media and, as a result, have more knowledge of, or familiarity and involvement with, a certain category of offering than others. Non-leaders, or **opinion followers**, turn to opinion leaders for advice and information about offerings they are interested in. Opinion leaders are also more gregarious and self-confident than non-leaders, and are more confident of their role as influencers (Chan and Misra, 1990). Therefore it is not surprising that many marketing communication strategies are targeted at influencing opinion leaders, because they will, in turn, influence others. For example, watch manufacturer Daniel Wellington has built its business around

Insaf Bennis, fashion blogger from Sparkles in Paris, showcases her Daniel Wellington watch
Source: © Edward Berthelot/Getty.

collaborations with social media influencers, such as successfully sending free watches to selected influencers, so that they can showcase them to their followers.

This approach has also been used to convey specific information and help to educate large target audiences through television and radio programmes. For example, in the UK, television programmes such as *Coronation Street*, *Eastenders*, and *Emmerdale*, and radio programmes such as *The Archers*, have been used as opinion-leadership vehicles to bring to attention to, and open up debates about, many controversial social issues, such as contraception, abortion, drug use and abuse, and serious illness and mental health concerns.

Opinion Formers

The other main type of independent personal influencer is the opinion former. They are not part of the same peer group as the people they influence; rather, their defining characteristic is that they exert personal influence because their profession, authority, education, or status is associated with the object of the communication process. They provide information and advice as part of the formal expertise they are perceived to hold. For example, shop assistants in music equipment shops are often experienced musicians in their own right. An aspiring musician seeking to buy their first proper guitar will often consult these perceived 'experts' about guitar brands, styles, models, and associated equipment, such as amplifiers. In the same way, doctors carry such conviction that they can influence the rate at which medicines are consumed. Drug manufacturers, such as GlaxoSmithKline and Pfizer, often launch new drugs by enlisting the support of eminent professors, consultants, or doctors who are recognized by others in the profession as experts. These opinion formers are invited to lead symposia and associated events, and in so doing build credibility and activity around the new proposition.

Organizations target their marketing communications at opinion leaders and formers to penetrate the market more quickly than relying on communicating directly with the target audience. However, in addition to these forms of influence, reference needs to be made to spokespersons. There are some potential problems that advertisers need to be aware of when considering the use of celebrities. First, does the celebrity fit the image of the brand, and will the celebrity be acceptable to the target audience both now and in the long run? If the lifestyle of the celebrity changes, what impact will the changes have on the target audience and their attitude towards the brand? For example, well-publicized allegations about the behaviours of supermodel Kate Moss led her to lose several sponsorship and brand endorsement contracts (such as H&M and Burberry)—although it is alleged that her overall income actually increased as a result of the negative publicity and sales of her Topshop brand soared.

Market Insight 10.3
Celebrity Endorsements Gone Wrong

Using celebrities in marketing is a strategy that dates back more than 200 years. The first known celebrity might have been Josiah Wedgwood, who styled himself 'Potter to Her Majesty' Queen Charlotte (wife of King George III, at the turn of the nineteenth century), and who named part of his product range 'Queen's Ware'. With the rise of social media, the use of celebrities in marketing communications has proliferated. Celebrities such as Katy Perry, Justin Bieber, and Beyoncé have more social media followers than many countries have inhabitants. In addition, a new breed of celebrity, such as Chiara Ferragni, Lilly Singh, and Brian Kelly, has entered the marketing world. Often referred to as social media influencers, these celebrities have a devoted following who consider them to be close friends, and who rely on their advice and recommendations on anything from beauty and fashion, to eating and interior design, to gaming and tech advice (to name a few).

Although celebrity endorsements have great potential in terms of adding visibility, credibility, and interest to a brand, there are several pitfalls in working with celebrities and influencers. These have to do with both the way in which the collaboration is conducted and the types of association the celebrity or influencer evokes, based on past or future behaviours. A brand that has experienced this first hand is Pepsi.

In 2017, Pepsi launched a new campaign based on a collaboration with model Kendall Jenner. In an effort to connect with contemporary culture, a commercial

was released in which Jenner offers a Pepsi to a police officer in the middle of a street protest. The commercial was immediately critiqued for trying to capitalize on the protests against police use of force against Black Americans. In less than 24 hours, critical posts on social media led Pepsi to withdraw the commercial and end the campaign. It also issued an apology, stating:

> Pepsi was trying to project a global message of unity, peace and understanding. Clearly we missed the mark, and we apologize. We did not intend to make light of any serious issue. We are removing the content and halting any further rollout. We also apologize for putting Kendall Jenner in this position.

However, this was not the first time Pepsi had experienced turmoil based on its collaborations with celebrities. The brand has a long history of celebrity endorsements and attached controversies. For example, in 1989, the company withdrew a commercial featuring Madonna as a consequence of her video for 'Like a Prayer', in which she was depicted kissing a black saint, which was widely criticized at the time—and even declared a blasphemy by the Vatican. Although the specific scene was not part of the Pepsi commercial, the controversy around Madonna was deemed too unfavourable for the brand to continue airing its ad.

Sources: Colliander and Dahlén (2011); Anon. (2015); Escalas and Bettman (2017); Kaufman (2017); Turner and Kaplan (2018).

Market Insight 10.3
continued

Theory into Practice

The value of celebrity endorsement in marketing has traditionally been explained by theories of source credibility. More specifically, celebrities have been found to increase attention to advertising and enhance persuasion as a result of their attractiveness, credibility, and/or likeability. More recent studies also show that the value of celebrities lies in their role as cultural resources to which consumers can refer when constructing their own identities. For social media influencers, the level of para-social interaction has also been found to explain the positive effects of using celebrities as senders of a marketing message.

Related Topics

celebrity endorsements; social media; source effects

1 **Look up the Kendall Jenner Pepsi commercial on YouTube. What changes would you suggest to make it more in tune with contemporary society?**

2 **Look up the Madonna 'Like a Prayer' video on YouTube. Almost 30 years have passed since it caused controversy; would it would be seen as controversial today?**

3 **What can marketers do to avoid the potential pitfalls when working with celebrities and influencers?**

The second problem concerns the impact that the celebrity has relative to the brand: there is a danger that the receiver will remember the celebrity, but not the message or the brand. The celebrity becomes the proposition, rather than the product being advertised. (To learn more about celebrity endorsements, please see Market Insight 10.3.)

All of the models of communication discussed have a role to play in marketing communications. Mass-media communication, in the form of broadcast television and radio, is still used by organizations to reach large audiences. Two-step and interaction forms of communication are used to reach smaller, specific target audiences and to enable a range of people to contribute to the process. Interaction and dialogue are higher levels of communication, and are increasingly used to generate personal communication with individual customers. The skill that marketing practitioners must acquire is knowing when to move from linear, to two-step, to interaction, and then dialogue-based marketing communications.

Word of Mouth

Word-of-mouth communication does not involve any payment for media, because communication is freely given through conversation. Word-of-mouth communication can be defined as 'interpersonal communication regarding products or services where the receiver regards the communicator as impartial' (Stokes and Lomax, 2002: 350).

Personal influence within the communication process is important. This is because customers perceive word-of-mouth recommendations as objective and unbiased. In comparison with advertising messages, word-of-mouth communications are more robust (Berkman and Gilson, 1986). Word-of-mouth messages are used either as information inputs prior to purchase or as a support and reinforcement of a consumer's own purchasing decisions.

People like to talk about their product (service) experiences. The main stimulus for behaviour is that the offering in question gave them either particular pleasure or particular *dis*pleasure. These motivations to discuss experiences vary between individuals and with the intensity of the motivation at any one particular moment. Consider, for example, the first of your friends to buy the newest version of iPhone: they will undoubtedly be happy to share their point of view on what the model has to offer in comparison to previous ones. These points of view can be both positive and negative. Today, organizations actively manage word-of-mouth communications to generate positive comments and as a way of differentiating themselves in the market. Viral marketing and social media mentions are electronic versions of the spoken endorsement of an offering. Often using humorous messages, games, video clips, and screensavers, information can be targeted at key individuals, who then voluntarily pass the message to friends and colleagues, and in so doing endorse and bestow much valued credibility upon the message. Both online and offline word of mouth is becoming increasingly important if marketing communications is to have its desired impact (Keller and Fay, 2012; Baxendale, MacDonald, and Wilson, 2015).

For many organizations, it is important to direct messages at individuals who are predisposed to discussing its content, because it is likely that they will propel word-of-mouth recommendations. Therefore the target of certain campaigns is not necessarily the target market, but opinion leaders within target markets—that is, those individuals who are most likely to volunteer their positive opinions about the offering and who, potentially, have some influence over people in their peer group (see Research Insight 10.2).

 Visit the **online resources** and complete Internet Activity 10.1 to learn more about the importance of word of mouth in contemporary advertising.

 ## Research Insight 10.2

To take your learning further, you might wish to read this influential paper:

Baxendale, S., MacDonald, E.K., and Wilson, H.N. (2015). The impact of different touchpoints on brand consideration. *Journal of Retailing*, 91(2), 235–53.

This is an interesting article that uses a novel methodology to track the impact of marketing communications and other brand touchpoints on brand consideration. By investigating the impact of marketing communications, word of mouth, and 'earned' touchpoints simultaneously, the authors are able to pinpoint their relative value.

 Visit the online resources to read the abstract and access the full paper.

Marketing Communication Theory

As mentioned earlier, there is no coherent theory or model explaining how marketing communications or advertising works. The first important idea about how advertising works was based on how the personal selling process works. Developed by Strong (1925), the **AIDA** model—referring to the need first to create *awareness*, then to generate *interest* and to drive *desire*, from which *action* (a sale) emerges—has become extremely well known and is used by many practitioners. As a broad interpretation of the sales process, the model is generally correct, but it fails to provide insight into the depths of how advertising works.

Thirty-six years later, Lavidge and Steiner (1961) presented a model based on what is referred to as the **hierarchy of effects (HoE)** approach. Similar in nature to AIDA, it assumes that a prospect must pass through a series of steps before a purchase will be made. It is assumed—correctly—that advertising cannot generate an immediate sale because there are a series of thought processes that need to be fulfilled prior to action. These steps are represented in Figure 10.5.

These models have become known as hierarchy of effects (HoE) models, simply because the effects (on audiences) are thought to occur in a top-down sequence. Some of the attractions of these HoE models and frameworks are that they are straightforward, simple, easy to understand, and (if creating advertising materials) provide a helpful broad template for the development and evaluation of campaigns.

However, although attractive, this sequential approach has several drawbacks. People do not always process information nor do they always purchase offerings following a series of sequential steps. This logical progression is not reflected in reality when, for example, an impulse purchase is followed by an emotional feeling towards a brand. There are also questions about what actually constitutes adequate levels of awareness, comprehension, and conviction. How can it be known which stage the majority of the target audience has reached at any one point in time and is this purchase sequence applicable to all consumers for all purchases?

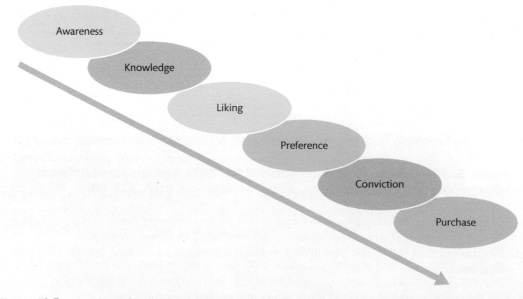

Figure 10.5
Stages in the hierarchy of effects model

The Strong and Weak Theories of Advertising

So if advertising cannot be assumed to work in only one particular way, what other explanations exist? Of the various models put forward, two stand out: the **strong theory** of advertising (Jones, 1991); and the **weak theory** of advertising (Ehrenberg, 1974).

The Strong Theory of Advertising

According to Jones (1991), advertising has a strong effect because it can persuade people to buy an offering that they have not previously purchased. Advertising can also generate long-run purchase behaviour. The strong theory proposes that advertising is capable of increasing sales for a brand and for the **product class**. These upward shifts are achieved through the use of manipulative and psychological techniques, which are deployed against largely passive consumers who—perhaps because of apathy—are either generally incapable of processing information intelligently, or have little or no motivation to become involved.

This interpretation is a persuasion view and corresponds very well to the HoE models referred to earlier. Persuasion occurs by moving buyers towards a purchase by easing them through a series of steps, prompted by timely and suitable promotional messages. It seems that this approach correlates closely with new offerings for which new buying behaviours are required.

The strong theory has close affiliation with an advertising style that is proposition-oriented, in which features and benefits are outlined clearly for audiences, and pack shots are considered important.

The Weak Theory of Advertising

Contrary to the strong perspective, the weak theory proposes that a consumer's brand choices are driven by purchasing habit rather than by exposure to promotional messages. One of the more prominent researchers in this area was Ehrenberg (1974), who believed that advertising represents a weak force. He believed that advertising has little impact on persuading consumers to buy offerings, mainly because consumers process information actively, not passively.

Ehrenberg proposed that the awareness–trial–reinforcement (**ATR**) framework is a more appropriate interpretation of how advertising works. Both Jones and Ehrenberg agree that *awareness* is required before any purchase can be made, although the elapsed time between awareness and action may be very short or very long. Out of the mass of people exposed to a message, a few will be sufficiently intrigued to want to try an offering—that is, to *trial* it (the next phase). *Reinforcement* follows, to maintain awareness and provide reassurance to help customers to repeat the pattern of thinking and behaviour. Advertising's role is to breed brand familiarity and identification (Ehrenberg, 1997).

According to the weak theory, advertising is employed as a defence, to retain customers and to increase brand usage. Advertising is used to reinforce existing attitudes, not necessarily to drastically change them. This means that when people say that they 'are not influenced by advertising', they are, in the main, correct.

Both the strong and weak theories of advertising are important because they are equally right and equally wrong. The answer to the question 'How does advertising work?' lies somewhere between the two and is dependent on the context. For advertising to work, involvement is likely to be high and so here the strong theory is the most applicable. However, the vast majority of product-purchase decisions generate low involvement and so decision-making is likely to be driven by habit. Here, advertising's role is to maintain a brand's awareness with the purchase cycle, so the weak theory is most applicable.

Visit the **online resources** and complete Internet Activity 10.2 to learn more about the strong and weak theories of advertising.

A Composite Approach

Most of the frameworks presented so far have their roots in advertising. If we are to establish a model that explains how marketing communications works, a different perspective is required—one that draws on the key parts of all the models. This is possible because the three key components of the attitude construct lie within these different models. Attitudes have been regarded as an important aspect of marketing communications activities and advertising is thought to be capable of influencing the development of positive attitudes towards brands (see also Chapter 2).

The three stages of attitude formation are that we *learn* something (the cognitive or learning component), *feel* something (an affective or emotional component), and then *do* something based on our attitudes (a behavioural or conative component). So, in many situations, we learn something, feel something towards a brand, and then proceed to buy or not to buy. These stages are set out in Figure 10.6.

The HoE models and the strong theory contain this sequential approach of learn–feel–do. However, we do not always pass through this particular sequence, and the weak theory places greater emphasis on familiarity and reminding (awareness) than on the other components. So, if we look at Figure 10.7, we can see that these components have been worked into a circular format. This means that, when using marketing communications, it is not necessary to follow each component sequentially; rather, the focus can be on what the audience requires—whether that is the learning, feeling, or acting components, as determined by the audience. In other words, for marketing communications to be audience-centred, we should develop campaigns based on the overriding need of the audience at any one time—that is, their need to learn, feel, or behave in particular ways.

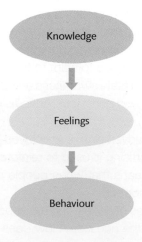

Figure 10.6
Attitude construct: linear

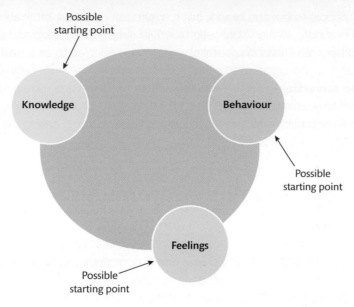

Figure 10.7
Attitude construct: circular

Learn

Where learning is the priority, the overall goal should be to inform or educate the target audience. If the offering is new, it will be important to make the target audience aware of the offering's existence and to inform them of the brand's key attributes and benefits. This is a common use for advertising because it has the capacity to reach both large and targeted audiences. Other than making them aware of the offering's existence, additional tasks include showing the target audience the ways in which a brand is superior to competitive offerings—perhaps demonstrating how an offering works, and educating the audience about when and in what circumstances they should use it.

Feel

Once the audience is aware of a brand and knows something about how it might be useful to them, it is important that they develop a positive attitude towards the brand. This can be achieved by imbuing the brand with a set of emotional values that it is thought will appeal and be of interest to the audience. These values need to be repeated in subsequent communications to reinforce the brand attitudes.

Marketing communications should be used to involve and immerse people in a brand. So, for example, advertising or brand placement within films and music videos will help to show how it fits in with a desirable set of values and lifestyles. Use of suitable music, characters that reflect the values of either the current target audience or an aspirational group, a tone of voice, colours, and images all help to create a particular emotional disposition and understanding about what the brand represents or stands for. Indeed, for some people, advertising works only at this emotional level and the cognitive approach is irrelevant.

Do

Most organizations find that, to be successful, they need to use a much broader set of tools and that the goal is to change the behaviour of the target audience. This behavioural change may be about getting people to buy the brand, but it may often be about motivating them to visit a website, call for a brochure, fill in an application form, or simply visit a shop and sample the brand free of cost and other risk. This behavioural change is also referred to as a **call to action**.

When the accent is on using marketing communications to drive behaviour and action, **direct-response advertising** can be effective. Often, television ads have a telephone number or website address to enable such responses. However, sales promotion, direct marketing, and personal selling are particularly effective at influencing behaviour and calling the audience to act.

The Role of Marketing Communications in Marketing

Marketing communications are used to achieve one of two principal goals. The first concerns the development of brand values (that is, feelings, emotions, and beliefs about a brand or organization). Brand communication seeks to make us think positively about a brand, and helps us to remember and develop positive brand attitudes in the hope that, when we are ready to buy that type of offering again, we will buy brand X because we feel positively about it.

The alternative and more contemporary goal is to use communications to make us behave in particular ways. Rather than spend lots of money developing worthy and positive attitudes towards brands, the view of many today is that we should use this money to encourage people to behave differently. This might be through buying the offering, or driving people to visit a website, request a brochure, or make a telephone call. This is called behaviour change and is driven by using messages that provide audiences with a reason to act—what is referred to as a call to action.

So communications can be used, on the one hand, to develop brand feelings and, on the other, to change or manage the behaviour of the target audience. These are not mutually exclusive. For example, many television advertisements are referred to as direct-response ads because they not only attempt to create brand values, but also carry a website address, telephone number, or details of a special offer (sales promotion). In other words, the two goals are mixed in a hybrid approach.

The success of marketing communication depends on the extent to which messages engage their audiences. These audiences can be seen to fall into three main groups, as follows:

- *Customers*—These may be consumers or end-user organizations.

- *Channel members*—Each organization is part of a network of other organizations, such as suppliers, retailers, wholesalers, value-added resellers, distributors, and other retailers, who join together, often freely, to make the offering available to end users.

- *General stakeholders*—This refers to organizations and people who either influence or are influenced by the organization. These may be shareholders, the financial community, trade unions, employees, the local community, or others.

Therefore marketing communications involves not only customers, but also a range of other stakeholders. It can be used to reach consumers as well as business audiences (see Research Insight 10.3 for more about the role of marketing communications in building relationships). Market Insight 10.4 illustrates a marketing communications campaign aiming to engage stakeholders by connecting with the feminist movement.

Research Insight 10.3

To take your learning further, you might wish to read this influential paper:

Duncan, T., and Moriarty, S. (1998). A communication-based marketing model for managing relationships. *Journal of Marketing*, 62(2), 1–13.

This is one of the most important academic articles in the field of marketing communications. It was pivotal because it drove the transition from a functional perspective of integrated marketing communications to a perspective that emphasized its role within relationship marketing.

 Visit the online resources to read the abstract and access the full paper.

Market Insight 10.4
Advertising 'Like a Girl'

Ever heard of 'femvertising'? The term initially gained traction in 2014, when a US-based lifestyle site called SheKnows, in collaboration with industry newspaper *Advertising Week*, hosted a panel discussing portrayals of women and girls in advertising. Although female empowerment has been part of advertising executions dating back to the 1960s, if not longer, the panel was a sign of a renewed interest in the topic.

Starting with Dove's campaign 'Evolution' in 2006, the panel was a response to a renewed interest in a different type of portrayal of women and girls that challenges (female) gender stereotypes and empowers women. Since then, femvertising (that is, advertising that challenges traditional female advertising stereotypes) has gained traction. In January 2018, the term generated 49,900 hits on Google, including major media outlets such as CNN, *The Guardian*, and *Huffington Post*. By then, several campaigns using femvertising appeals had become highly successful. Well-known examples include P&G/Always and its 'Like a Girl' campaign (initially for the US market, but later launched globally), P&G's 'Touch the Pickle' (India), Pantene's 'Labels against Women' (the Philippines), Under Armour's 'I Will What I Want' (the United States), and Sport England's 'This Girl Can' (the UK). Many of these campaigns have also gone viral and demonstrated impressive results, leading industry media

to proclaim that 'gender sells' and that marketers can now 'cash in on feminism'. Interestingly, however, many of the marketers behind these campaigns also highlight how they have not necessarily focused on brands and sales objectives, but rather have regarded the campaigns as a part of the brand's sustainability efforts, with objectives related to fostering a more balanced view of female ideals in society.

Sources: Dahlén and Rosengren (2016); Åkestam (2017); Åkestam, Rosengren, and Dahlén (2017).

Procter & Gamble's Always feminine hygiene brand uses a femvertising approach to empower women
Source: Image courtesy of The Advertising Archives.

Market Insight 10.4

continued

Theory into Practice

The femvertising movement focuses on promoting non-stereotypical portrayals of women and girls in advertising. As highlighted in this market insight, industry press has tended to focus on the effects on brands and sales when discussing these efforts. This means that they focus on the marketing communication tasks captured by the DRIP framework.

Many marketers, however, talk about femvertising in terms of the effects it might have on societal ideals and self-perceptions of female consumers. These effects are often referred to as the extended or social effects of advertising and are related more to the sustainability efforts of brands.

Related Topics

advertising appeals; female consumers; corporate social responsibility (CSR)

1 **Look up the 'Like a Girl' campaign on YouTube. How does it differ from other commercials you have seen for products targeting female consumers?**

2 **Female advertising stereotypes are not the only stereotypes that are currently being challenged in advertising; a similar trend can be seen, for**

example, **in terms of portrayals of age, sexuality, and race. What examples of non-traditional advertising stereotypes have you seen?**

3 **What would you say are the marketer's responsibilities when it comes to the portrayals of women and girls that they choose to use in their advertising?**

Marketing Communications Tasks

Digitalization has had a large impact on marketing communications. Over the past decade, there have been some sizeable changes to the way in which the marketing communications industry is structured. One of the most important of these has been the emergence of a number of powerful and dominant industry groups, such as WPP and News Corporation, whose business interests span cross-media ownership, content development, and delivery on a global scale. The changing industry structure is a response to several variables—particularly, developments in technology, the configuration of the communications mix and media used by organizations, and the way in which client-side managers are expected to operate. These changes mean that marketing communication in general, and advertising in particular, is in constant flux (see Chapters 11 and 12).

Despite these constant changes, the task of marketing communications has remained the same. Fundamentally, marketing communications can be used to engage audiences by undertaking one of four main tasks, referred to by Fill (2002) as the **DRIP** model, that is (and in no particular order) communications can be used to *differentiate* brands and organizations; to *reinforce* brand memories and expectations; to *inform* (that is, to make aware or educate audiences); and finally to *persuade* them to do things or to behave in particular ways. See Table 10.1 for an explanation of each.

 Visit the **online resources** and complete Internet Activity 10.3 to learn more about the way in which fashion house Burberry uses marketing communications.

These tasks are not mutually exclusive; indeed, campaigns might be designed to target two or three of them. For example, the launch of a new brand will require that audiences be informed, made aware of its existence, and enabled to understand how it is different from competitor brands. A brand that is well established might try to reach lapsed customers by reminding them of its key features and benefits, and offering them an incentive (persuasion) to buy again. For example, M&S's website Style and Living is a digital magazine designed to showcase what is new in Marks & Spencer's stores, and to give fashion and style advice. However, it features only offerings available at M&S. The website is an integral part of the company's communication mix and is used, among many other activities, to engage customers with the brand and drive readers into the store to shop.

Table 10.1 The DRIP tasks for marketing communications

Marketing communication task	Explanation
Differentiate	In many markets, there is little to separate brands (e.g. mineral water, coffee, printers). In these cases, it is the images created by marketing communications that help to *differentiate* one brand from another and position them so that consumers develop positive attitudes and make purchasing decisions.
Reinforce	Communications may be used to *remind* people of a need they might have or of the benefits of past transactions, with a view to convincing them that they should enter into a similar exchange. In addition, it is possible to provide *reassurance* or comfort either immediately prior to an exchange or, more commonly, post purchase. This is important because it helps to retain current customers and improve profitability. This approach to business is much more cost-effective than constantly striving to lure new customers.
Inform	One of the most common uses of marketing communications is to *inform*, i.e. to make potential customers aware of the features and benefits of an organization's offering. In addition, marketing communications can be used to educate audiences—to show them how to use an offering or what to do in particular situations.
Persuade	Communication may attempt to *persuade* current and potential customers of the desirability of entering into an exchange relationship.

Source: Fill (2002).

Planning Marketing Communications

Management's task is to formulate and implement a communications strategy that blends the right mix of tools and media to deliver the right messages, in the right place, at the right time, for the right audience. Strategically, the main decisions have to do with defining the appropriate target audience and setting the right objectives. To accomplish this, there are inevitably a series of issues that need to be addressed before decisions can be made. These issues embrace a range of activities, such as developing strategy in the light of both audience and brand characteristics, agreeing communication objectives, and then formulating, implementing, and evaluating marketing communications strategies and plans, many of which need to be integrated—an important topic itself in contemporary marketing communications. Developing the right message and the configuration of the right mix of tools and media are more tactical decisions, and will be covered in greater detail in Chapter 11.

To understand what a marketing communications plan should achieve, it is helpful to appreciate the principal tasks facing marketing communications managers, as follows:

- Who should receive the messages?

- What should the messages say?

- What image of the organization or brand are receivers expected to retain?

- How much is to be spent establishing this new image?

- How are the messages to be delivered?

- What actions should the receivers take?

- How do we control the whole process once implemented?

- What was achieved?

For many reasons, planning is an essential management activity, and if planned marketing communications are to be developed in an orderly and efficient way, the use of a suitable framework is necessary. A framework for integrated marketing communications plans is presented in Figure 10.8.

The marketing communications planning framework (MCPF) provides a visual guide to what needs to be achieved and brings together the various elements in a logical sequence of activities. As with all hierarchical planning models, each level of decision-making is built on information generated at a previous level in the model. Another advantage of using the MCPF is that it provides a checklist of activities that need to be considered. The MCPF represents a sequence of decisions that marketing managers undertake when preparing, implementing, and evaluating communication strategies and plans. This framework reflects a deliberate, or planned, approach to strategic marketing communications.

In practice, marketing communications planning is not always developed as a linear process, as depicted in this framework. Indeed, many marketing communications decisions are made outside any recognizable framework, because some organizations approach the process as an integrative—sometimes spontaneous—activity. However, the MCPF approach presented here is intended to highlight the tasks to be achieved, the way in which they relate to one another, and the order in which they should be accomplished.

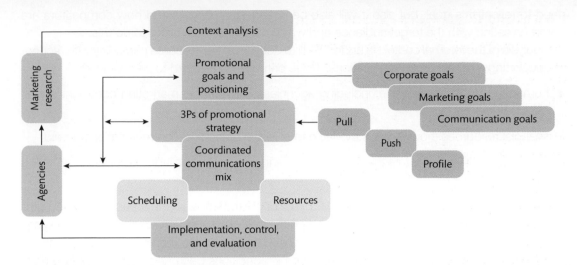

Figure 10.8

The marketing communications planning framework

Source: Marketing Communications (6th edn) Fill, C. (2013). Reproduced with the kind permission of Pearson Education Limited. © Pearson Education Limited 2013.

The Elements of the Marketing Communications Planning Framework

A marketing communications plan should be developed for each level of communications activity, from strategy to individual tactical aspects of a campaign. The difference between them is the level of detail that is included.

Context Analysis

The marketing plan is the bedrock of context analysis. This will already have been prepared and contains important information about the target segments, business and marketing goals, competitors, and timescales in which the goals are to be achieved. The context analysis needs to elaborate and build on this information to provide the detail, so that the plan can be developed and justified.

The first and vital step is to analyse the context in which marketing communications activities are to occur. Unlike a situation analysis used in general planning models, context analysis should be communications-oriented and should use the marketing plan as a foundation. There are four main components of the communications context analysis: customer; business; internal; and external contexts.

Understanding the *customer* context requires information and market research data about the target audiences specified in the marketing plan. Here, detailed information is necessary about their needs, perceptions, motivation, attitudes, and decision-making characteristics relative to the proposition category (or issue). In addition, information about the media and the people they use for information about the category needs to be determined.

Understanding the *business* context in general, and the marketing communications environment in particular, is also important, because these influence what has to be achieved. If the marketing strategy specifies growth through market penetration, then not only will messages need to reflect this goal, but also it will also be important to understand how competitors are communicating with the target audience and which media they are using to do this.

Analysis of the *internal* context is undertaken to determine the resource capability with respect to supporting marketing communications. Three principal areas need to be reviewed:

■ human resources (are people, including agencies, with suitable marketing communications skills available?);

■ financial resources (how much is available to invest in marketing communications?); and

■ technological resources (are the right systems and processes available to support marketing communications?).

The final area to be reviewed is the wider *external* context. Similar to the areas considered during the strategic analysis, emphasis is placed on the political, economic, societal, technological, legal, and ecological (PESTLE) conditions. However, the impact on marketing communications needs to be emphasized. For example, if economic conditions become tough, people will have lower levels of disposable income; hence sales promotions, promotional offers, and extended credit terms become more attractive in this context.

Context analysis provides the rationale for the rest of the plan. It is from this analysis that the marketing objectives (from the marketing plan) and the marketing communications objectives are derived. The type, form, and style of the message are rooted in the characteristics of the target audience, and the media selected to convey messages should be based on the nature of the tasks, the media preferences and habits of the audience, and the resources available.

Marketing Communications Objectives

Having performed a context analysis, the next step is to define marketing communication objectives. Many organizations assume that their marketing communications goals are the same as their sales targets—but they are wrong. There are so many elements contributing to sales, such as competitor pricing, product attributes, and distributor policies, that making marketing communications solely responsible for sales is naive and unrealistic. Ideally, marketing communications objectives should consist of three main elements, as follows:

■ *Corporate* objectives are derived from the business or marketing plan. They refer to the mission and the business area that the organization believes it should be in.

■ *Marketing* objectives are derived from the marketing plan and are sales-oriented. These might be market share, sales revenues, volumes, return on investment (ROI), and other profitability indicators.

■ *Communications* objectives are derived from the context analysis and refer to levels of awareness, perception, comprehension/knowledge, attitudes, and overall degree of preference for a brand. The choice of communications goal depends on the tasks that need to be accomplished.

These three elements constitute the overall set of marketing communications objectives. They should be set out in **SMART** terminology—that is, each should be specific, measurable, achievable, realistic, and timed. Thus, at this point in the planning process, the brand's positioning intentions are developed and these should be related to the market, the customers, or a product dimension (see also Chapter 6). The justification for this will have been identified in the context analysis.

Marketing Communications Strategy

The marketing communications strategy is derived from the objectives and context analysis. There are three types of strategy: *pull*, for the end-user markets; *push*, for the trade and channel intermediaries; and *profile*, designed to reach all significant stakeholders. The DRIP framework can be used to elaborate the relevant strategy to be pursued. For example, if a new brand is being launched, the first task will be to *inform* and *differentiate* the brand for members of the trade, before using a pull strategy to *inform* and *differentiate* the brand for the target end-user customers. For example, UK retailer John Lewis has developed a reputation for a series of highly emotional and well-executed campaigns in the lead-up to Christmas. In its 2015 campaign, the television ads used little-known Norwegian artist Aurora's cover of Oasis's 'Half the World Away' to such effect that the song subsequently made its way onto the official UK charts.

An organization wishing to signal a change of strategy and/or a change of name following a merger or acquisition may choose to use a profile strategy, the primary task of which will be to inform about the name change. An organization experiencing declining sales may choose to remind customers of a need or it may choose to improve sales through persuasion.

Traditionally, pull strategies in the grocery sector have been based on delivering mass-media advertising supported by below-the-line communications—most notably, sales promotions delivered in-store and through direct mail and email to registered customers (for example Tesco Clubcard customers). The decision to use a pull strategy should be supported by a core message that will try to differentiate (position), remind or reassure, inform, or persuade the audience to think, feel, or behave in a particular way. This approach can be interpreted as a pull/remind or pull/position communication strategy, because this describes the audience and direction of the strategy and also clarifies what the strategy seeks to achieve.

A push strategy should be treated in a similar way. The need to consider the core message is paramount because it conveys information about the essence of the strategy. Push/inform, push/position, or push/key accounts/discount might be examples of possible terminology.

Although these three strategies are represented here as individual entities, they are often used as a 'cluster'. For example, the launch of a new toothpaste brand will involve a push strategy to get the product on the shelves of the key supermarkets and independent retailers. The strategy will focus on building retailer acceptance of the new brand and positioning it for them as profitable. The goal is to get the toothpaste on the retailers' shelves. To achieve this, personal selling, supported by trade sales promotions, will be the main marketing communications tools. Hence a push strategy alone would be insufficient to persuade a retailer to stock a new brand; the promise of an accompanying pull strategy, aimed at creating brand awareness and customer excitement, needs to be made, accompanied by appropriate PR activities and any initial sales promotions necessary to motivate consumers to change their brand preference. The next step is to create particular brand associations and thereby position the brand in the minds of the target consumer audience. Messages may be primarily informational or emotional, but will endeavour to convey a brand promise. This may be accompanied or followed by the use of incentives to encourage consumers to trial the product. To support the brand, customer care lines and a website, as well as a buyer reference point, will need to be put in place to provide credibility.

Communications Method

The communications method part of the plan includes a number of activities. A creative message needs to be developed for each specified target audience in the strategy. This should be based on the positioning requirements and will often be developed by an outside communications agency. Simultaneously, it is necessary to formulate the right mix of communication tools to reach each particular audience. The right media mix needs to be determined, both online and offline, and again media experts will most probably undertake this task. Here, integration is regarded as an important feature of the communication mix. This is covered more in detail in Chapter 11.

The Schedule

The next step is to schedule the way in which the campaign is to be delivered. Events and activities should be scheduled according to the goals and the strategic thrust. So, if it is necessary to communicate with the trade prior to a public launch, those activities tied into the push strategy should be scheduled prior to those calculated to support the pull strategy. Similarly, if awareness is a goal, then (funds permitting) it may be best first to use television and poster ads offline, plus banners and search engine ads online, before using sales promotions (unless sampling is used), direct marketing, point of purchase, and personal selling.

Resources

The resources necessary to support the plan need to be determined. These refer not only to the financial resources, but also to the quality of available marketing expertise. This means that the right sort of marketing knowledge may not be present internally and may have to be recruited. For example, if a customer relationship management (CRM) initiative is being launched, it will be important to have people with knowledge and skills related to running CRM programmes. With regard to external skills, it is necessary that the current communications agencies are capable of delivering the creative and media plan. This is an important part of the plan that is often avoided or simply forgotten. Software project planning tools, simple spreadsheets, or Gantt charts can be used not only to schedule the campaign, but also to chart the resources relating to the actual and budgeted costs of using the selected tools and media.

Control and Evaluation

Once launched, campaigns should be monitored. This is to ensure that if there is any major deviation from the plan, opportunities exist to get back on track as soon as possible. In addition, all marketing communications plans should be evaluated. There are numerous methods of evaluating the individual performance of the tools and the media used, but perhaps the most important measures concern the achievement of the communication objectives.

Feedback

The marketing communications planning process is completed when feedback is provided. Not only information regarding the overall outcome of a campaign should be considered, but also individual aspects of the activity. For example, the performance of the individual tools used within the campaign, whether sufficient resources were invested, the appropriateness of the strategy in the first place, whether any problems were encountered during implementation, and the relative ease with which the objectives were accomplished are aspects that need to be fed back to all internal and external parties associated with the planning process.

This feedback is vitally important because it provides information for the context analysis that anchors the next campaign. Information fed back in a formal and systematic manner constitutes an opportunity for organizations to learn from their previous campaign activities—a point often overlooked and neglected.

Cultural Aspects of Marketing Communications

Marketing communications has the potential to influence more than only customers. Indeed, a wide range of other stakeholders, such as suppliers, employees, religious and faith groups, trade unions, and local communities, can be targeted.

The tools, media, and messages used by organizations influence, and are influenced by, the culture and environment in which they operate. Culture and related belief systems are significant factors in the way in which organizations choose to communicate in the different areas and regions in which they operate. For example, communications based on the strong theory of advertising are observed more frequently in North America, whereas examples of the weak theory are quite prevalent in Europe.

In this final part of the chapter, consideration is given to some of the cultural issues associated with marketing communications (see Market Insight 10.5 for an example).

Culture

Culture refers to the values, beliefs, ideas, customs, actions, and symbols that are learnt by members of particular societies. Marketing communications should be an audience-centred activity, whether those audiences are located domestically or anywhere around the globe. Because there are so many international, regional, and local communities, each with cultural variances, the development of marketing communications for these audiences must be based on a sound understanding of their culture.

Culture is important because it provides individuals within a society with a sense of identity and an understanding of what is deemed to be acceptable behaviour. According to Hollensen (2007), it is commonly agreed that culture has three key characteristics—that is, it is learned, interrelated, and shared. See Table 10.2 for a fuller account of these variables.

Table 10.2 Characteristics of culture

Cultural characteristic	Explanation
Learned	Culture is not innate or instinctual; otherwise, everyone would behave in the same way. Human beings across the world do not behave uniformly or predictably, and they learn values and behaviours that are shared with common groups. Thus different cultures exist and there are boundaries within cultures, framing behaviours and lifestyles.
Interrelated	There are deep connections between different elements within a culture. Thus family, religion, business/work, and social status are interlinked.
Shared	Cultural values are passed through family, religion, education, and the media. This progression of values enables culture to be passed from generation to generation. This is important because it provides consistency, stability, and direction for social behaviour and beliefs.

Source: Hollensen (2007).

Market Insight 10.5
Advertising, Arabic Style

Cultural values are an important consideration for brands in the Middle East, especially when advertising to Muslim consumers. While each country has its own guidelines to regulate advertising messages and to prevent offensive products and services from being promoted, brands need to take cultural values into consideration when developing advertising for Muslim consumers across the region.

In many Middle Eastern countries, advertising alcohol or gambling is forbidden, and there are other cultural taboos of which brands need to be aware. In Saudi Arabia, for example, for women, the custom is to wear black if they leave the house and showing dogs in the house or pigs in any advertising is not allowed. Serving food with the left hand is also considered a cultural taboo and so advertising must be sensitive to this.

Culture dictates that any form of marketing communications should be respectful of the Islamic faith and show respect for women and the elderly. Advertising messages should be fair and truthful, and hence avoid being critical of competitive brands.

Heritage is also seen to be an important part of Middle Eastern culture. Many brands choose to reflect cultural aspects in their advertising campaigns and draw heavily on the cultural heritage of the country in their communications strategy. It is not unusual for advertising in the Gulf States to include images of traditional sailing vessels (dhows) or camels to represent their trading heritage. Arabic language and calligraphy are other devices used by brands to show an appreciation of cultural heritage.

Family plays a central role in Middle Eastern culture and the family is often a focus of advertising. In 2014, PepsiCo ran a campaign in the Middle East called 'Ramadan Reunions', which was based on getting families together for the month of Ramadan. Because Ramadan is traditionally seen as a month of gatherings, this emotional campaign sought to draw on the importance of family bonds among Muslim consumers. Similarly, in 2014, Johnson's Baby developed a campaign called 'Grandparents' Frame', which distributed digital picture frames to grandparents in the Middle East, allowing them to receive images of their grandchildren living abroad. The campaign demonstrates the importance of family in the Middle East and highlights how powerful marketing communications can be when it taps into the cultural values of the consumer.

Sources: Otterman (2007); Traboulsi and Guidère (2009); Impact BBDO (2014a, 2014b).

Bridging the gap between grandparents and their grandchildren in the Middle East
Source: © Johnson & Johnson.

Theory into Practice

Given that marketing communications is an audience-centred activity, it is important to keep in mind that audiences are part of a cultural context, which will influence how they interpret the messages used. When working with marketing communications on a global scale, marketers must bear in mind how both legal and cultural requirements may differ. As highlighted in this market insight, both PepsiCo and Johnson & Johnson have adjusted their advertising in the Middle East to align with these requirements.

Market Insight 10.5
continued

Related Topics

consumer decision-making; international marketing; culture; advertising

1 **What cultural values are most important for marketers to consider in your own country?**

2 **What would be the key holidays for advertisers to consider in your own country?**

3 **What role do older people typically play in advertising in your own country?**

This market insight was kindly contributed by Dr Sarah Turnbull, University of Portsmouth, UK.

These boundaries between cultures are not fixed or rigid, which would suggest that cultures are static; rather, they evolve and change as members of a society adjust to new technologies, government policies, changing values, and demographic changes, to mention but a few dynamic variables. Unsurprisingly, therefore, brands and symbols used to represent brands have different meanings as they are interpreted in the light of the prevailing culture.

Culture consists of various layers. Hollensen (2010) refers to a nest of cultures, with one inside another—a structure similar to a 'Russian doll' (see Figure 10.9). Here, it can be imagined that a buyer in one country and a seller in another will be faced with several layers of culture, all inter-related and all influencing an individual's behaviour.

- *National culture* sets out the cultural concepts and the legislative framework governing the way in which business is undertaken.

- *Industry/business culture* refers to the fact that particular business sectors adopt a way of doing business within a competitive framework. The shipping business, for example, will have its own way of conducting itself based on its own heritage. As a result, all participants know what is expected and understand the rules of the game.

- *Organizational culture* refers not only to the overall culture within an organization, but also the various subcultures that can emerge, each of which will also have a system of shared values, beliefs, meanings, and behaviours.

- *Individual culture* arises because each individual is affected by, and learns from, the various cultural levels.

Marketing communications, at both formal and informal levels, need to assimilate these different cultural considerations to ensure that they understand and respond to an individual's behaviour, and the ways in which culture will impact on that individual's (or organization's, in a business-to-business context) decision-making processes and procedures. In many markets (for example mineral water, coffee, printers), there is little to separate brands. In these cases, it is the images created by marketing communications that help to differentiate one brand from another and

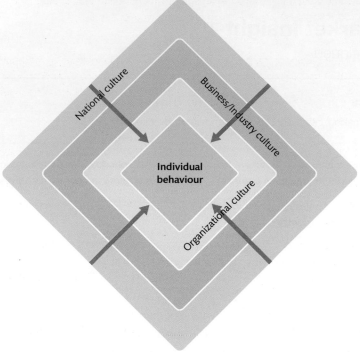

Figure 10.9

Layers of culture

Source: *Global Marketing: A Decision-Oriented Approach* (5th edn), Hollensen, S. (2010). Pearson Education Limited.

position them so that consumers develop positive attitudes and make purchasing decisions. The way in which different societies perceive these same brands is a reflection of the cultural drivers that frame people's perceptions.

 # Chapter Summary

To consolidate your learning, the key points from this chapter are summarized here:

■ **Describe the nature, purpose, and scope of marketing communications.**

Marketing communications is a management process by means of which an organization attempts to engage with its various audiences. Marketing communications—or promotion, as it was originally called—is one of the 4Ps of the marketing mix. It is used to communicate an organization's offer relating to products, services, or the overall organization. In broad terms, this management activity consists of several components: the communications experienced by audiences relating to their use of products and the consumption of services; the communications arising from unplanned or unintended experiences; and planned marketing communications.

■ **Explain the three models of communication and describe how personal influences can enhance the effectiveness of marketing communication activities.**

The linear, or one-way, model of communication is the traditional mass-media interpretation of how communication works. The two-step model incorporates the influence of other people into the communication process, whereas the interaction model explains how communication flows not only between sender and receiver, but also throughout a network of people. Interaction is about actions that lead to a response and—most importantly, in an age of interactive communication—interactivity is a prelude to dialogue, which is the highest or purest form of communication.

- **Understand the models used to explain how marketing communications and advertising work.**

  Marketing communication models have evolved from sequential communication models such as AIDA and the HoE models. A circular model of the attitude construct supports our understanding of the tasks of marketing communication—namely, to inform audiences, to create feelings and a value associated with offerings, and to drive behaviour.

- **Understand the role of marketing communications in marketing.**

  The role of marketing communications is to engage audiences and there are four main tasks that it can be used to complete. These tasks are summarized in the mnemonic DRIP—that is, to differentiate a brand, to reinforce a perception or behaviour, to inform audiences, and to persuade audiences to behave in particular ways. Several of these tasks can be undertaken simultaneously within a campaign.

- **Describe the different steps in the strategic marketing communications planning process.**

  Management's task is to formulate and implement a communications strategy that blends the right mix of tools and media to deliver the right messages, in the right place, at the right time, for the right audience. The marketing communications planning framework (MCPF) identifies the following key steps in this process: context analysis; marketing communications objectives; marketing communications strategy; communications method; scheduling; resources; control and evaluation; and feedback.

- **Describe what culture is and explain how it can impact on the use of marketing communications.**

  Culture refers to the values, beliefs, ideas, customs, actions, and symbols that members of particular societies learn. Culture is important because it provides individuals within a society with a sense of identity and an understanding of what is deemed to be acceptable behaviour. Culture is learnt, the elements are interrelated, and culture is shared among members of a society or group. Organizations that practise marketing communications in international environments have to be fully aware of the cultural dimensions associated with each of their markets. In addition, they need to consider whether it is better to adopt a standardized approach and use the same unmodified campaigns across all markets, or to adapt campaigns to meet the needs of local markets.

 Review Questions

1. What role does marketing communication (formerly, promotion) play in the marketing mix?
2. What is the linear model of communication and what are each of its main elements?
3. Make brief notes outlining the meaning of interaction and how dialogue can develop.
4. What are the main differences between opinion leaders and opinion formers?
5. What is a hierarchy of effects (HoE) model?
6. What are the strong and weak theories of advertising?
7. Why is the circular interpretation of the attitude construct better than the linear form?
8. Explain the key role of marketing communications and find examples to illustrate the meaning of each element within the DRIP framework.
9. What is the relation between corporate objectives, marketing objectives, and communications objectives?
10. Hollensen (2010) argues that culture is made up of three elements and four layers. Name them.

Discussion Questions

1 Having read Case Insight 10.1, why do you think Åkestam Holst sees both its focus on business and consumer insights and its internal culture as key success factors in creating advertising?

2 Consider the key market exchange characteristics that will favour the use of linear, or one-way, communication and then repeat the exercise with respect to interaction communication. Discuss the differences and find examples to illustrate these conditions.

3 Day Birger et Mikkelsen is a leading Danish fashion retailer, providing a range of fashion clothing for young people aged 18–35. As a marketing assistant, you have just returned from a conference at which the role of personal influencers was highlighted. You now wish to convey your new knowledge to your manager. Prepare a brief report in which you explain the nature of opinion leaders and opinion formers, as well as consumer word of mouth in general, and discuss how Day Birger et Mikkelsen might use them to improve its marketing communications. Using at least three examples, make it clear who you think might be good opinion formers for Day Birger et Mikkelsen.

4 To what extent should organizations operating an advertising standardization policy consider the culture of the countries in which they are operating?

Visit the online resources and complete the Multiple-Choice Questions to assess your knowledge of Chapter 10.

Glossary

AIDA deriving from awareness, interest, desire, and action (that is, a sale), a hierarchy of effects (HoE), or sequential, model used to explain how advertising works.

ATR deriving from awareness–trial–reinforcement, a framework developed by Ehrenberg (1974) to explain how advertising works.

call to action a part of a marketing communication message that explicitly requests that the receiver act in a particular way.

decoding that part of the communication process in which receivers unpack the various components of the message, and begin to make sense of the message and give it meaning.

dialogue the development of knowledge that occurs when all parties to a communication event listen, adapt, and reason with one another about a specific topic.

direct-response advertising advertising that contains a mechanism, such as a telephone

number, website address, email or postal address, designed to encourage viewers to respond immediately to the ad; most commonly used on television.

DRIP deriving from differentiate, reinforce, inform, and persuade, a mnemonic with which to remember the four primary tasks that marketing communications can be expected to accomplish.

encoding that part of the communication process in which the sender selects a combination of appropriate words, pictures, symbols, and music to represent a message to be transmitted.

feedback that part of the communication process in which receivers offer responses.

hierarchy of effects (HoE) general sequential models used to explain how advertising works; popular in the 1960s–80s, these models provided a template that encouraged the development and use of communication objectives.

interaction model a model in which the flow of communication messages leads to mutual understanding about a specific topic.

linear model (also known as one-way communications) a communication model in which communication travels only from the sender to the receiver and the full communication process remains incomplete.

noise those influences that distort information in the communication process and, in turn, make it difficult for the receiver to decode and interpret a message correctly.

opinion followers those people who turn to opinion leaders and formers for advice and information about products and services they are interested in purchasing or using.

opinion formers those people who exert personal influence because their profession, authority, education, or status associates them with the object of the communication process; not part of the same peer group as the people whom they influence.

opinion leaders those people who are predisposed to receiving information and then reprocessing it to influence others; belong to the same peer group as—that is, are not distant or removed from—the people whom they influence.

personal selling the use of interpersonal communications with the aim of encouraging people to purchase particular products and services, for personal gain and reward.

product class a broad category referring to various types of related product, for example cat food, shampoo, or cars.

receivers individuals or organizations who have seen, heard, smelt, or read a message.

SMART deriving from specific, measurable, achievable, realistic, and timed, an approach used to write effective objectives.

strong theory a persuasion-based theory of advertising aiming to explain how it works.

two-step model (also known as two-way communications) a communication model that reflects a receiver's response to a message.

weak theory a theory of advertising that suggests it is a weak force and works only by reminding people of preferred brands.

word of mouth a form of communication founded on interpersonal messages regarding products or services sought or consumed in which the receiver regards the communicator as impartial and credible, because they are not attempting to sell products or services.

References

Åkestam, N. (2017). Understanding advertising stereotypes. Doctoral dissertations. Stockholm School of Economics. Retrieve from: https://www.hhs.se/contentassets/85ded4ca9b574ab6ba846a5f82975067/sse-phd-diss-2017-nina-akestam_final2articles_lowres.pdf (accessed 13 October 2018).

Åkestam, N., Rosengren, S., and Dahlén, M. (2017). Advertising 'like a girl': toward a better understanding of 'femvertising' and its effects. *Psychology and Marketing*, 34(8), 795–806.

Anon. (2015). History of advertising: No.129—Josiah Wedgwood's Queen's Ware. *Campaign*, 23 April. Retrieve from: https://www.campaignlive.co.uk/article/history-advertising-no-129-josiah-wedgwoods-queens-ware/1343726 (accessed 13 October 2018).

Ballantyne, D. (2004). Dialogue and its role in the development of relationship specific knowledge. *Journal of Business and Industrial Marketing*, 19(2), 114–23.

Baxendale, S., MacDonald, E.K., and Wilson, H.N. (2015). The impact of different touchpoints on brand consideration. *Journal of Retailing*, 91(2), 235–53.

Berg, M. (2017). The highest-paid YouTube stars 2017: Gamer DanTDM takes the crown with $16.5 million, *Forbes*, 16 December. Retrieve from: https://www.forbes.com/sites/maddieberg/2017/12/07/the-highest-paid-youtube-stars-2017-gamer-dantdm-takes-the-crown-with-16-5-million/#2143e7561397 (accessed 13 October 2018).

Berkman, H., and Gilson, C. (1986). *Consumer Behavior: Concepts and Strategies*. Boston, MA: Kent.

Chan, K.K., and Misra, S. (1990). Characteristics of the opinion leader: a new dimension. *Journal of Advertising*, 19(3), 53–60.

Colliander, J., and Dahlén, M. (2011). Following the fashionable friend: the power of social media. *Journal of Advertising Research*, 51(1), 313–20.

Dahlén, M., and Rosengren, S. (2016). If advertising won't die, what will it be? Towards a new definition of advertising. *Journal of Advertising*, 45(3), 334–45.

Duncan, T., and Moriarty, S. (1998). A communication-based marketing model for managing relationships. *Journal of Marketing*, 62(2), 1–13.

Ehrenberg, A.S.C. (1974). Repetitive advertising and the consumer. *Journal of Advertising Research*, 14(2), 25–34.

Ehrenberg, A.S.C. (1997). How do consumers come to buy a new brand?' *Admap*, March, 20–4.

Escalas, J.E., and Bettman, J. (2017). Connecting with celebrities: how consumers appropriate celebrity meanings for a sense of belonging. *Journal of Advertising*, 46(2), 297–308.

Fill, C. (2002). *Marketing Communications: Contexts, Strategies and Applications* (3rd edn). Harlow: FT/Prentice Hall.

Fill, C. (2013). *Marketing Communications: Brands, Experiences and Participation* (6th edn). Harlow: FT/Prentice Hall.

Friestad, M., and Wright, P. (1994). The persuasion knowledge model: how people cope with persuasion attempts. *Journal of Consumer Research*, 21(1), 1–31.

Hoffman, D.L., and Novak, P.T. (1996). Marketing in hypermedia computer-mediated environments: conceptual foundations. *Journal of Marketing*, 60(3), 50–68.

Hollensen, S. (2007). *Global Marketing: A Decision-Oriented Approach* (4th edn). London: Pearson Education.

Hollensen, S. (2010). *Global Marketing: A Decision-Oriented Approach* (5th edn). Harlow: FT/Prentice Hall.

Hughes, G., and Fill, C. (2007). Redefining the nature and format of the marketing communications mix. *Marketing Review*, 7(1), 45–57.

Impact BBDO (2014a). Johnson's Baby: grandparents frame. Retrieve from: http://impactbbdo.com/#!&pageid=0&subsection=2&itemid=27 (accessed 13 October 2018).

Impact BBDO (2014b). PepsiCo: Ramadan reunions. Retrieve from: http://impactbbdo.com/#!&pageid=0&subsection=7&itemid=51 (accessed 13 October 2018).

Jones, J.P. (1991). Over-promise and under-delivery. *Marketing and Research Today*, 19(40), 195–203.

Katz, E., and Lazarsfeld, P.F. (1955). *Personal Influence: The Part Played by People in the Flow of Mass Communication*. Glencoe, IL: Free Press.

Kaufman, G. (2017). Madonna mocks Kendall Jenner Pepsi ad fiasco by recalling her own Cola controversy, *Billboard*, 6 April. Retrieve from: https://www.billboard.com/articles/columns/pop/7752245/madonna-mocks-kendall-jenner-pepsi-ad (accessed 13 October 2018).

Keller, E., and Fay, B. (2012). Word-of-mouth advocacy: a new key to advertising effectiveness. *Journal of Advertising Research*, 52(4), 459–64.

Kosoff, M., and Jacobs, H. (2015). The 15 most popular YouTubers in the world. *Business Insider*, 18 September. Retrieve from: https://uk.businessinsider.com/the-most-popular-youtuber-stars-in-the-world?r=US&IR=T (accessed 13 October 2018).

Lavidge, R.J., and Steiner, G.A. (1961). A model for predictive measurements of advertising effectiveness. *Journal of Marketing*, 25(6), 59–62.

Moynihan, T. (2015). Yes, there's a market for that $10,000 Apple watch. *Wired*, 3 September. Retrieve from: https://www.wired.com/2015/03/yes-theres-market-10000-apple-watch/ (accessed 13 October 2018).

Otterman, S. (2007). Does the veiled look sell? Egyptian advertisers grapple with the hijab. *Arab Media and Society*, 21 May. Retrieve from: https://www.arabmediasociety.com/does-the-veiled-look-sell-egyptian-advertisers-grapple-with-the-hijab/ (accessed 13 October 2018).

Pierce, D. (2015). iPhone killer: the secret history of the Apple watch. *Wired*, May. Retrieve from: https://www.wired.com/2015/04/the-apple-watch/ (accessed 13 October 2018).

Rosengren, L. (2012). Han hoppade av Chalmers—blev heltidskändis på Youtube. *IDG.se*, 19 November. Retrieve from: https://cio.idg.se/2.1782/1.477094/han-hoppade-av-chalmers—blev-heltidskandis-pa-youtube (accessed 13 October 2018).

Schramm, W. (1955). How communication works. In W. Schramm (ed.), *The Process and Effects of Mass Communications*, Urbana, IL: University of Illinois Press, 3–26.

Shannon, C., and Weaver, W. (1962). *The Mathematical Theory of Communication*. Urbana, IL: University of Illinois Press.

Stokes, D., and Lomax, W. (2002). Taking control of word-of-mouth marketing: the case of an entrepreneurial hotelier. *Journal of Small Business and Enterprise Development*, 9(4), 349–57.

Strong, E.K. (1925). *The Psychology of Selling*. New York: McGraw-Hill.

Tamburro, P. (2014). PewDiePie's $7.4 million salary actually highlights YouTube's low wages. *Mandatory*, 8 July. Retrieve from: http://www.mandatory.com/fun/875679-pewdiepies-7-4-million-salary-actually-highlights-youtubes-low-wages (accessed 13 October 2018).

Theodorson, S.A., and Theodorson, G.R. (1969). *A Modern Dictionary of Sociology*. New York: Cromwell.

Traboulsi, S., and Guidère, M. (2009). Tell me which country you live in, I'll tell you which ad to broadcast. *The Observers*, 20 July. Retrieve from: http://observers.france24.com/en/20090720-tell-which-country-you-live--tell-you-which-ad-broadcast-saudi-arabia-advertising-rules (accessed 13 October 2018).

Turner, N., and Kaplan, J. (2018). PepsiCo looks to bounce back from Kendall Jenner debacle with retro ads, *Bloomberg News*, 11 January. Retrieve from: https://www.bloomberg.com/news/articles/2018-01-11/pepsico-looks-to-bounce-back-from-jenner-debacle-with-retro-ads (accessed 13 October 2018).

Williams, R. (2014). Apple launches iPhone 6, 6 Plus and Apple Watch. *The Telegraph*, 9 September. Retrieve from: https://www.telegraph.co.uk/technology/apple/11086000/Apple-launches-iPhone-6-6-Plus-and-Apple-Watch.html (accessed 13 October 2018).

Chapter 11

Configuring the Marketing Communications Mix

Learning Outcomes

After reading this chapter, you will be able to:

▶ Describe the role and configuration of the marketing communications mix

▶ Explain the characteristics of each of the primary tools, messages, and media

▶ Set out the criteria that should be used to select the right communications mix

▶ Discuss the changing marketing communications landscape

▶ Consider the principles and issues associated with integrated marketing communications

Case Insight 11.1
Adnams

Market Insight 11.1
Variable Mixes

Market Insight 11.2
What's in a Name?

Market Insight 11.3
Damart Modernizes Its Welcome Programme

Market Insight 11.4
EY Uses Art to Distinguish Itself

Market Insight 11.5
Super Bowl Advertising: More than Meets the Eye

Case Insight 11.1
Adnams

The Adnams brand, founded in 1872, in Southwold, Suffolk, England, is synonymous with beer and, since 2010, now gin, vodka, and whisky too. The company also owns and manages a number of pubs, inns, and retail stores. We speak to Emma Hibbert, marketing director, to find out how the beer at the heart of the brand has been, and continues to be, promoted.

In a traditional market such as the brewing industry, Adnams' 'Beer from the Coast' campaign in 2003 disrupted the advertising model. At the time, all advertising for beer products included (usually) a man and always a photograph of a pint. Adnams worked with advertising agency Campbell Doyle Dye (which, before it closed, was known for its flair in digital and below-the-line campaigns) to create its campaign using book illustrator Chris Wormell's linocut images to showcase beer in an engaging and subtler way. For example, along a row of beach groynes (that is, a series of man-made barriers to stop coastal erosion), one of the barnacles would be an Adnams bottle top. The campaign won awards, and was even made into artwork and sold to fans. It can still often be found on walls and coffee mugs 15 years later.

Our communication campaigns have definitely changed in format since then and over the years. Ten years ago, we made a strategic shift from above-the-line campaigns (for example television, radio, print advertising) to experiential marketing (which focuses on helping consumers to experience the brand directly), usually with a heavy link to digital marketing. We have tended to use sponsorship and events to get our 'brand in hand', to generate content for social media, and to develop more meaningful conversations with Adnams' fans. In order of importance, our communications would tend to look something like:

1   digital marketing;

2   experiential marketing;

3   public relations (PR);

4   sales promotion;

5   advertising;

6   direct marketing (excluding digital); and

7   personal selling.

More recently, we were successful with our #showmetheghostship campaign, which ran across our digital channels. We even projected a 2-minute film onto the walls of the brewery, supporting this by showing the film on YouTube (see https://www.youtube.com/watch?v=CcGflliD7ws&feature=youtu.be or type in 'the return of the ghost ship' and select Adnams Southwold). We also hosted Twitter competitions and developed a host of other online content. The idea was to shift our 'Ghost Ship' beer product from its position as a seasonal Halloween beer to year-round bestseller—and it worked. Adnams Ghost Ship continued to grow well in our heartland. However, our ambitions rose as we next saw an opportunity to grow volumes both nationally and specifically in London. To do this, we decided to partner in two major national events by sponsoring them. We decided we would develop integrated campaigns to exploit the sponsorships and to increase our brand awareness, to improve rate of sale, and to recruit Adnams fans. The campaign was to be run in pubs, on packs, in our shops, and online. The events would add the experiential element by allowing us to get 'brand in hand'.

The question for Adnams was: how could it run an *integrated* marketing communications campaign?

 Visit the online resources to watch a video interview with Emma Hibbert in which she explains what Adnams did.

Introduction

What 'touchpoints' do you have with your mobile phone provider? These might be email, telephone, text messaging (SMS), Twitter, direct mail items and/or personal correspondence? What about television ads, web pages, articles and ads in magazines, posters, and perhaps news items that generate general brand awareness? Organizations use a variety of tools, **media**, and messages to engage their audiences. Collectively, these are referred to as the **marketing communications mix**—a set of five tools, as well as a variety of media and messages, all of which can be used in various combinations and with different degrees of intensity to communicate successfully with target audiences.

The five principal marketing communications tools are **advertising**, **sales promotion**, **public relations (PR)**, **direct marketing**, and **personal selling**. In addition, 'the media' are used primarily, but not exclusively, to deliver advertising messages to target audiences. Although the word 'medium' (plural, *media*) refers in the marketing context to any mechanism or device that can carry a message, we typically use the phrase 'the media' to refer to paid-for media, processes, and systems that are owned by third parties, such as the News Corporation (which owns *The Sun* and *The Sunday Times* newspapers, as well as the BSkyB TV platform), Condé Nast (which owns *Tatler*, *Vanity Fair*, and *Vogue* magazines, among others), Singapore Press Holdings (which owns the *Business Times* in Singapore), and Time Warner Inc. (a leading media and entertainment company, whose business interests span interactive services, cable systems, television and film entertainment, television networks, and publishing). These organizations rent out time and space to client organizations so that they can send their messages and make content available to engage various audiences. The list of available paid-for media is expanding, but it is possible to identify six key classes: broadcast; print; outdoor; in-store; digital; and other (which includes both cinema and ambient media). All of these are explored in this chapter.

On completing this chapter, you should understand the main characteristics associated with the principal tools, messages, and media that make up the marketing communications mix. Readers should also appreciate that, by reconfiguring the mix, it is possible to achieve different goals. Finally, you will come to recognize that a more efficient and effective outcome can be accomplished through an integrated approach to marketing communications.

The Role of the Marketing Communications Mix

The marketing communications mix consists of five main tools, four forms of messages or content, and three types of media. These are depicted in Figure 11.1 and each is explored later in this chapter.

Traditionally, organizations were able to use a fairly predictable and stable range of tools and media. Advertising was used to build awareness and brand values, sales promotions were used to stimulate demand, PR conveyed goodwill messages about organizations, and personal selling was seen as a means of getting orders, particularly in the business-to-business (B2B) market. However, there have been some major changes in the environment and in the way in which organizations communicate with their target audiences. Digital technology has given rise to a raft of different media and opportunities for advertisers to reach their audiences. We now have access to hundreds of commercial television and radio channels; cinemas show multiple films at

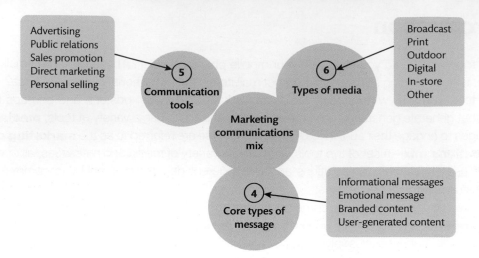

Figure 11.1

The elements of the marketing communications mix

multiplex sites; and the Internet has transformed the way in which we communicate, educate, inform, and entertain ourselves.

This expansion of the media is referred to as **media fragmentation**. At the same time, people have developed a whole host of new ways of spending their leisure time; they are no longer restricted to a few media. This expansion of an audiences' choice of media is referred to as **audience fragmentation**. So although the range and type of media has expanded, the size of audiences that each medium commands has generally shrunk. In addition, the recent rise in the use of ad-blocking software by consumers has further complicated the task of managing the marketing communications mix.

The Internet enables opportunities to engage consumers at different points in their day and at different stages in their purchase decision-making journeys. Many organizations have found that the principles through which particular tools work offline do not necessarily apply in an interactive environment.

For organizations, one of the key challenges is to find the right mix of tools, messages, and media that enable them to reach and engage with their target audiences effectively and economically. To do this, they have had to revise and redevelop their marketing communications mixes (see Market Insight 11.1). For example, in the 1990s, there was a dramatic rise in the use of **direct-response media** as direct marketing emerged as a new and powerful tool. Since then, the use of the Internet and digital technologies has enabled an increasing variety of interactive forms of communication in which the receiver has far greater responsibility for their part in the communication process and is encouraged to interact with the sender. As a result of these changes, many organizations are redistributing their investments in favour of digital or interactive media (see Chapter 12).

Visit the **online resources** and complete Internet Activity 11.1 to learn more about how Toyota uses an interactive website to inform its target audience about a complex proposition, the Hybrid Synergy Drive.

This has shifted the role of the media. Previously, the emphasis of a mix was to enable and persuade customers to buy products and services in the short term. Today, although a

Market Insight 11.1
Variable Mixes

Benadryl

Hayfever suffers can be affected by different types of grass and tree pollen at virtually any time of the year. The unpredictability of pollen counts led market-leading brand Benadryl to raise its brand profile within the allergy market by means of the BENADRYL® Social Pollen Count, which involved Benadryl's own interactive map and the sponsorship of part of the Met Office site. The goal was to help sufferers to fight hay fever. Using daily updates of official Met Office data and encouraging hayfever sufferers to report local pollen levels, Benadryl was able to show other sufferers across the UK what the pollen count was in different areas. It was also able to direct people to nearby stockists of the BENADRYL® product range.

Benadryl engaged in a communications campaign aimed at building a map of the levels of pollen: very valuable information for its customers
Source: Courtesy of Johnson and Johnson

The LEGO Movie

To celebrate the release of *The LEGO Movie*, an entire television ad break made of LEGO® was broadcast on Sunday 9 February 2014 during *Dancing on Ice*. Four recent UK television ads—for the British Heart Foundation, Confused.com, BT, and Premier Inn—were re-created, frame by frame and brick by brick, in LEGO.

People were helped to connect to *The LEGO Movie* (not only LEGO) because the ads were separated by five different 2-second 'stings' featuring characters

from the film and *The LEGO Movie* logo. The break ended with a 40-second trailer for the film. The entire break was also simultaneously released in full on YouTube to ensure that those who missed it could see it and catch up with the social media conversation. The ads were never shown again on television, but were used in cinemas before screenings of *The Lego Movie*.

Volvo Trucks

To change driver perceptions and raise awareness of the launch of a new range of heavy-duty Volvo trucks, a viral marketing campaign was produced, featuring a series of live test videos. Each video showcased different new technical aspects, such as the trucks' stability (with a tightrope walker), and the reliability and strength of the front towing hooks (hoisting a truck 20 metres above the water in Gothenburg harbour, with the president of Volvo Trucks standing on the front panel). Others included a video demonstrating the trucks' ground clearance (by driving 'over' one of Volvo's technicians buried up to his neck in sand) and a truck manoeuvring through tight streets in Pamplona in Spain, chased by furious bulls, to demonstrate agility and speed.

One video featured actor Jean-Claude Van Damme performing spectacular splits, balanced on the wing mirrors of two reversing Volvo FM trucks. This showcased the precision of the dynamic steering, which enabled the truck drivers to maintain exactly the distance between them and the same speed while travelling in reverse.

The videos were posted on YouTube and Facebook channels, whilst the use of PR and tailored press information made sure that they were distributed online to the news media and bloggers to amplify the story.

Sources: Carter (2014); Ridley (2014); Anon (2015a); https://www.benadryl.co.uk/social-pollen-count; https://www.metoffice.gov.uk/health/public/pollen-forecast

Market Insight 11.1
continued

Theory into Practice

These three campaigns demonstrate different ways of configuring the marketing communications mix. The Benadryl campaign shows how an established consumer brand used sponsorship and interactive media. This campaign actively involved people and, through participation, was able to associate itself with an authoritative and trusted body (the Met Office).

The LEGO® Ad Break campaign used television, cinema, and social media, with PR providing support and credible information for use by news organizations. This is a more traditional approach, although the single use of one large ad break is unusual.

The Volvo Trucks campaign is also unusual because it is convention in B2B marketing to use significant print advertising, heavy media relations, and, in some cases, sponsorship. The use of viral marketing represented recognition that decision-making in this market now involves a variety of stakeholders, including several influencers such as drivers, families, and friends. The campaign conveys factual information about product attributes by engaging emotional executions. The success of the viral content and its amplification across the Internet is also partly the result of good use of PR, as well as social media.

Related Topics

corporate advertising; creativity; word of mouth; opinion leaders; opinion formers

1 **Describe the key elements of the message in each of the three campaigns.**

2 **How do the media used for these campaigns enable their messages to reach target audiences?**

3 **Which of these three campaigns impresses you most? Why?**

short-term focus still prevails for many firms, goals such as developing understanding and preference, reminding and reassuring customers, and building brand value have become accepted as important aspects of marketing communications. Binet and Field (2013) have shown that this longer-term brand-building perspective is a more profitable approach than a short-term direct-response focus on sales.

It is now expected that marketing communications, and the mix of tools, messages, and media used, needs to become an integral part of an organization's overall communications and relationship management strategy. Above all else, the marketing communications mix should be an audience-centred activity. An increasing number of organizations are trying to use the mix more efficiently, to coordinate what they say and when they say it, and to develop relationships not only with key customers, but also with key suppliers and other important stakeholders. Today, therefore, an increasing number of organizations are reformulating and integrating the mix to encourage customer retention, not only acquisition.

Selecting the Right Tools

One of the challenges facing marketing communications managers is how to select the right mix of tools for each communication task. Although the tools can be seen as independent entities, each with its own skills and attributes, a truly effective communication mix occurs when tools complement each other and work as an interactive unit. Only by appreciating their characteristics is it really possible to achieve an optimal mix.

Advertising

The role of advertising has always been based on the notion of clients renting media time or space to place product or brand messages to engage and influence audiences. Unfortunately, many forms of marketing communications are invariably seen by the public as advertising—a confusion that embraces PR and publicity, **sponsorship**, **brand placement**, and wider media-based activities.

Advertising was once formally understood to be a non-personal form of communication, in which a clearly identifiable sponsor pays for a message to be transmitted through media. There are several issues associated with this definition, however, and in an attempt to update the definition, Richards and Curran (2002: 74) suggested that advertising might be said to be 'a paid, mediated form of communication from an identifiable source, designed to persuade the receiver to take some action, now or in the future'. Since then, the nature of advertising and the different forms of engagement have, of course, evolved with changing technology, economic development, and shifting societal and cultural values. Dahlén and Rosengren (2016) have identified three particular dynamics that they believe need to be incorporated within any contemporary definition of advertising: (new) media and formats; (new) 'consumer' behaviours related to advertising; and the extended effects of advertising (see Research Insight 11.1).

Today, it can be argued that advertising is not only about paid media, that it does not always seek only to persuade audiences, and that the source need be neither identifiable nor non-personal.

Research Insight 11.1

To take your learning further, you might wish to read this influential paper:

Dahlén, M., and Rosengren, S. (2016). If advertising won't die, what will it be? Towards a new definition of advertising. *Journal of Advertising*, **45(3), 334–45.**

This article provides a timely and interesting consideration of the way in which advertising has been and should be defined, within an academic context. Taking into account a range of issues and developments, the authors propose a new definition that they believe is a better fit for purpose.

 Visit the **online resources** to read the abstract and access the full paper.

Sales Promotion

Sales promotions offer a direct inducement or an incentive to encourage customers to buy an offering. These inducements can be targeted at consumers, distributors, agents, and members of the sales force. Sales promotions are concerned with offering customers additional value to induce an immediate sale. These sales might well have taken place without the presence of an incentive; it is simply that the inducement brings the time of the sale forward. The key forms of sales promotion are sampling, coupons, deals, premiums, contests and sweepstakes, and, in the trade, various forms of allowance.

Public Relations

Public relations is used to influence the way in which an organization is perceived by various groups of stakeholders, such as employees, the public, supplying organizations, and the media. Public relations does not require the purchase of airtime or space in media vehicles, such as television magazines or online. These types of message are low cost and are perceived to be extremely credible. Public relations attempts to integrate its own policies with the interests of stakeholders, and it formulates and executes a programme of action to develop mutual goodwill and understanding.

Different types of PR can be identified, but the main approach is referred to as 'media relations' and consists of press releases, conferences, and events. Other forms of PR include lobbying, investor relations, and corporate advertising. Two further activities, sponsorship and **crisis communications**, are discussed later in this chapter. Through the use of PR, relationships can be developed that, in the long run, are considered to be in the interests of all parties.

Direct Marketing

The primary role of direct marketing is to drive a response and shape the behaviour of the target audience with regard to a brand. This is achieved by sending personalized and customized messages, often requesting a 'call to action', designed to provoke a change in the audience's behaviour.

Direct marketing is used to create and sustain a personal and intermediary-free communication with customers, potential customers, and other significant stakeholders. In most cases, this is a media-based activity and offers great scope for the collection and utilization of pertinent and measurable data. Some of the principal techniques are direct mail, telemarketing, email, and, increasingly, Internet-based communications such as 'Search'. One of the key benefits of direct marketing is that there is limited communication wastage. The precision associated with target marketing means that messages are sent to, received by, processed by, and responded to by members of the target audience and no others. This is unlike advertising, whereby messages often reach some people who are not targets and are unlikely to be involved with the brand.

 Visit the **online resources** and follow the web links to the Federation of European Direct and Interactive Marketing Association (FEDMA) and the Institute of Promotional Marketing (IPM) to learn more about the communication tools of direct marketing and sales promotions.

Personal Selling

Personal selling involves interpersonal communication through which information is provided, positive feelings developed, and behaviour stimulated. Personal selling is an activity undertaken by an individual representing an organization, or collectively in the form of a sales force. It is a highly potent form of communication simply because messages can be adapted to meet the requirements of both parties. Objections can be overcome, information can be provided in the context of the buyer's environment, and the conviction and power of demonstration can be brought to the buyer when requested.

An overview of each of the tools highlights a number of characteristics that they share—that is, the degree to which a tool and the message conveyed are controllable, the credibility of the message conveyed, the associated costs, the degree to which a target audience is dispersed, and the DRIP tasks that marketing communications are required to accomplish (see Chapter 10). These five elements can serve as a starting point when selecting the right marketing communications mix and each is considered in turn.

Table 11.1 provides a summary of the relative strengths of each of the tools of the communications mix against these criteria. However, although depicted individually, the elements of the mix should be regarded as a set of complementary instruments, each potentially stronger when it draws on the potential of the others. The tools are, to a limited extent, partially interchangeable and different tools should be used in different circumstances to meet different objectives. For example, in a business context, personal selling will be the predominant tool, whereas in a consumer market context, advertising has traditionally reigned supreme.

What is clear is that the nature, configuration, and use of what was once called the promotional mix have changed. No longer can the traditional groupings of tools be assumed to be the most effective forms of communication; the role of the media in the communication process is now much more significant than it was previously. The arrival and development of digital media expands opportunities for people and organizations to converse globally, personally, more speedily, and factually. Word-of-mouth communication also plays a more significant part in contemporary communications, especially because communications-literate consumers are increasingly sceptical of the messages conveyed by many organizations.

Table 11.1 The relative strength of the tools of the marketing communication mix

	Advertising	Sales promotion	Public relations (PR)	Direct marketing	Personal selling
Level of control	Medium	High	Low	High	Medium
Level of cost	High	Medium	Low	Medium	High
Level of credibility	Low	Medium	High	Medium	Medium
Level of dispersion (consumer)	Low	Medium	High	High	Medium
Level of dispersion (B2B)	Medium	High	High	Medium	High
Primary DRIP tasks	Differentiating; informing	Persuading	Differentiating; informing	Persuading; reinforcing	Persuading

Marketing Communications Messages

Our consideration of communication theory in Chapter 10 confirms the importance of communicating the right message that can be understood and responded to in context. From a receiver's perspective, the process of decoding and giving meaning to messages is affected by the volume and quality of information received, and the judgement they make about the methods and how well the message is communicated. We also know that, if messages are to be processed successfully, they should reflect a balance between the need for information and the need for pleasure or enjoyment in consuming the message. We can identify four main forms of message content that are not independent entities: informational messages; emotional messages; **user-generated content (UGC)**; and **branded content**.

Informational Messages

Messages can be categorized as either proposition-oriented and rational or customer-oriented and based on feelings and emotions. As a general, but not universal, guideline, when audiences experience high involvement (see Chapter 2), the emphasis of a message should be on the information content, with the key attributes and the associated benefits emphasized. For example, ad campaigns for charities (such as Greenpeace, Oxfam) or financial services (Allianz, Banco do Brasil, Aviva), and government campaigns for health, tax, and other state services, normally make a statement about the product ingredients and deliver a rational reason why the target should behave in a particular way. Informational messages are also more common for products that fulfil functional needs (such as toothpaste or insurance).

Emotional Messages

When audiences experience low involvement, messages should attempt to gain an emotional response. For example, ads for fashion, cosmetics, fast food, and soft drinks often engage audiences through the use of fear, humour, animation, and storytelling. The use of celebrity endorsers and peer-to-peer word of mouth can also amplify these messages. Emotional messages are also more common for products that fulfil hedonic needs (such as lipstick or holidays).

There are, of course, many situations in which buyers need both rational and emotional messages to make purchasing decisions. These include cars, smartphones, dentistry, energy suppliers, and apps, to name a few.

The presentation of messages should reflect the degree to which factual information or emotional content is required for a message to engage an audience—namely, to command attention and then be processed. There are numerous presentational or executional techniques and Table 11.2 outlines some of the more commonly used appeals.

 Visit the **online resources** and complete Internet Activity 11.2 to learn more about how Bacardi uses product demonstration and a digital media format (.mp3) to inform target audiences how to make a Bacardi Mojito.

User-Generated Content

The development of social media has enabled individuals to communicate with organizations, communities, friends, and family. The content of the message can be about brands, experiences, or events, and is developed and shared by individuals. This is referred to as user-generated

Table 11.2 Information and emotional appeals

Information-based messages

Factual	Messages provide rational logical information and are presented in a straightforward, 'no frills' manner.
Slice of life	Uses people who are similar to the target audience presented in scenes that the target audience can readily associate with and understand. For example, washing powder brands are often presented by stereotypical 'housewives', who are seen discussing the brand in a kitchen.
Demonstration	Brands are presented in a problem-solving context. So people with headaches are seen to be in pain, but then take brand X, which resolves the problem.
Comparative	In this approach, brand X is compared favourably, in terms of two or three main attributes, with a leading competitor.

Emotion-based messages

Fear	Products are shown either to relieve danger or ill-health through usage (e.g. toothpaste), or to dispel the fear of social rejection (e.g. anti-dandruff shampoos) or to discourage behaviour (anti-smoking ads).
Humour	The use of humour can draw attention, stimulate interest, and place audiences in a positive mood.
Animation	Used to reach children and as a way of communicating potentially boring and uninteresting offerings (gas/electricity, insurance) to adults.
Sex	Excellent for getting the attention of the target audience, but unless the offering is related (e.g. perfume, clothing), these ads generally do not work.
Music	Good for getting attention and differentiating between brands.
Fantasy and surrealism	Used increasingly to provide a point of differentiation and brand intrigue (e.g. Cadbury's chocolate, Coca-Cola).

content (UGC) and can be seen in action at, for example, YouTube, Snapchat, Flickr, and Twitter. Kaplan and Haenlein (2010) consider UGC to refer to all of the ways in which people make use of social media—that is, the various forms of media content that are publicly available and created by end users.

There are three main elements that characterize UGC:

■ the content is freely accessible to the public—that is, it should be published either on an open website or on a social networking site accessible to a selected group of people;

■ the material demonstrates creativity; and

- the material should be amateur in nature, in the sense that it has not been created by an agency or professional organization.

Although there have been instances of commercial involvement in UGC, the very nature of this type of content takes the communication initiative away from organizations. As a result, marketers are listening to and observing consumers through UGC. As a consequence, many are finding out the different meanings consumers attribute to brands, which helps the marketers with brand development and helps them to reposition brands.

Some companies also invite consumers to offer content (ads), thereby utilizing crowdsourcing (see Chapter 12 and Market Insight 11.2) as a way of engaging with their audiences.

Market Insight 11.2
What's in a Name?

Companies and other organizations have sought to engage their customers and the general public by inviting them to crowdsource a broad range of aspects. One type of crowdsourcing involves open calls for naming an object, or even an animal.

One of the most famous examples is Greenpeace's attempt to name a specific humpback whale that was being tracked by satellite as part of the organization's Great Whale Trail Expedition in 2007. The aim was to raise awareness about the Japanese Fisheries Agency's hunting of humpback whales. The unusual name 'Mister Splashy Pants' gained the attention of several online communities, who subsequently campaigned to increase the number of votes for this particular name. Greenpeace was initially taken aback because neither the name nor the way in which the online communities were backing it represented what Greenpeace had envisioned. It did, however, embrace the result and the whale was indeed named Mister Splashy Pants. This unusual name helped Greenpeace to gather enough public attention and impact to convince the Japanese government to abandon the hunt.

An unexpected name that goes against the initial wishes of the hosting organization may therefore turn out to be a blessing. Rather less popular might be ignoring the winning name of a crowdsourcing campaign. A recent example of this is the attempt to name a £200 million polar research ship in the UK. Despite the huge popularity of the winning submission 'Boaty McBoatface', the ship was instead named RRS *Sir David Attenborough*—an option that came fourth in the public vote. A concession was made: the winning

name is instead used for the submersibles aboard the vessel. Following mixed reactions among the general public to the decision to overrule the result of the vote, members of the House of Commons Science and Technology Committee opened up a debate on whether the process was a success or failure (as the committee chair described it, a 'triumph of public engagement or a PR disaster').

The boat that had a lucky escape
Source: © Rolls-Royce. By Permission of the Natural Environment Research Council.

Regardless, the Boaty McBoatface debacle came to such international awareness that it has spawned a sequence of imitators: a racehorse named Horsey McHorseface; a Megabus interdeck coach in the UK now called Mega McMegaface; and an MTR Express train in Sweden now bearing the name Trainy McTrainface. All of these crowdsourcing campaigns owe their public interest and attention to Boaty McBoatface.

Sources: Fuchs, Prandelli, and Schreier (2010); Liljedal (2016)

Market Insight 11.2
continued

Theory into Practice

Crowdsourcing is a way of engaging consumers and citizens in a brand or cause by inviting them to participate in previously closed processes. In the examples in the market insight, the act of suggesting and selecting a name is enough to create a sense of ownership of the result, for as long as it is in line with the wishes of the participants. Similarly, non-participating consumers' or citizens' views of the hosting organization are also affected by crowdsourcing. Here too the results are generally positive—especially for tasks deemed simple, such as naming an object.

Related Topics

public relations; digital marketing; social media marketing; co-creation; content marketing

1 **What motivations do people have to engage in crowdsourcing alternatives?**

2 **Imagine you were to evaluate the naming campaign of RRS *Sir David Attenborough*. Would you consider it a 'triumph of public engagement or a PR disaster'? On which factors would you base your evaluation?**

3 **In the future, how should companies and other organizations go about crowdsourcing campaigns to minimize the risks of failure?**

This market insight was kindly contributed by Dr Karina T. Liljedal, Stockholm School of Economics, Sweden.

Branded Content

Branded content refers to the use of entertainment material that features a single company or brand. The recent growth in the use of branded content rests with a drive to realize the potential that 'owned' media offers. Branded content can enable conversations, particularly in social media, and this serves to raise a brand's profile and its credibility.

One of the earliest forms of branded content is customer publishing. Under this model, organizations develop magazines with articles and content considered to be of interest to their customers. The magazine includes references to, even articles and stories about, the sponsoring brand. The development and distribution of these magazines to the brand's customer base is a paid media operation.

Today, consumers use a variety of platforms and devices, so there is a need to develop content for use across the web, mobile, email, video, social media, and apps. This provides an opportunity to integrate material and allows customers to form a coherent or interconnected experience with a brand. Native advertising—a term which refers to any paid advertising that takes the specific form and appearance of editorial content from the publisher or context in which it is conveyed (Wojdynski and Evans, 2016)—is one way of achieving such integration.

Examples of native advertising include fashion and beauty ads in *Glamour* and *Vanity Fair*, and ads from sports equipment manufacturers within related magazines and websites, but also 'in-stream' ads and those used in Twitter, LinkedIn Sponsored Updates, Facebook News Feed, and Buzzfeed.

Branded content is sometimes created as part of a company's content marketing operations, which focuses on the creation and dissemination of content around a brand that does not overtly attempt to sell products and services. The goal is to provide audiences with valuable information that enhances understanding and knowledge. Content marketing is examined in more detail in Chapter 12.

The Media

Once a client has decided to use a particular message, decisions need to be made about how and when it is conveyed to engage target audiences. There is a huge and expanding range of media available, and making sure that the right mix of media channels is selected is becoming increasingly challenging. Table 11.3 gives a general list of media in the UK, set out by classification, type, and vehicle. Some media are owned by a client organization, for example its website or the signage outside a building. However, these media do not enable messages to reach a very large or targeted audience nor do they allow for specific proposition-oriented messages to be conveyed to particular target audiences. In most circumstances, therefore, client organizations need to use media owned by others and to pay a fee for renting the space and time to convey their messages. In the next section, we consider the terminology and the role of the media; we then examine digital media and, finally, the principles of direct response media.

The development of digital media has had a profound impact on the way in which client organizations communicate with their audiences. Generally, the trend has been to reduce the amount of traditional media used and increase the amount of digital online and mobile media. For example, major fast-moving consumer goods (FMCG) companies Procter & Gamble and Unilever have reduced the amount they spend on television and increased their digital investments. The main impact of this has been to improve the effectiveness of their campaigns, because the combination of television and digital media drives superior performance compared with using the two media independently (Whitehouse, 2014).

 Visit the **online resources** and complete Internet Activity 11.3 to learn more about the differing media that was used for Ray-Ban's 'Neverhide' campaign.

An Overview of Each Class of Media

Using the classification presented in Table 11.3, the following section provides a brief description of each class of media.

Broadcast

Advertisers use broadcast media (television and radio) because they can reach mass audiences with their messages at a relatively low cost per target reached. Broadcast media

Table 11.3 Summary classification of the main forms of UK media

Class	Type	Vehicles
Broadcast	TV	*Coronation Street*, *X Factor*
	Radio	Classic FM, Capital Radio
Print	Newspapers	*Sunday Times*, *Mirror*, *Daily Telegraph*
	Magazines:	
	Consumer	*Cosmopolitan*, *Woman*
	Business	*The Grocer*, *Plumbing News*
Out-of-home	Billboards	96-, 48-, and 6-sheet
	Street furniture	Adshel
	Transit	Underground stations, airport buildings, taxis, hot-air balloons
Digital media	Internet, social media, auctions, billboards, apps	Websites, email, Facebook, Instagram, Twitter, eBay, Clear Channel, Google Play
In-store	Point of purchase	Bins, signs and displays, gondolas, slatwalls
	Packaging	Coca-Cola contour bottle
Other	Cinema	Pearl & Dean
	Exhibitions and events	Ideal Home, Motor Show
	Product placement	Films, TV, books
	Ambient	Litter bins, golf tees, petrol pumps, washrooms
	Guerilla	Flyposting

Source: Marketing Communications (6th edn) Fill, C. (2013). Reproduced with the kind permission of Pearson Education Limited. © Pearson Education Limited 2013.

allow advertisers to add visual and/or sound dimensions to their messages. This helps them to demonstrate the benefits of using a particular offering, and can bring life and energy to an advertiser's message. Television uses sight, sound, and movement, whereas radio can use only its audio capacity to convey meaning. Both media have the potential to tell stories and to appeal to people's emotions when transmitting a message. These are dimensions that the print media find difficult to achieve effectively within an advertiser's time and cost parameters.

Print

Newspapers and magazines are the two main media in the print media class; others include custom magazines and directories. Print is very effective at delivering messages to target audiences because it allows explanation in a way that is not possible with most other media. This may be in the form of either a picture or a photograph demonstrating how an offering should be used. Alternatively, the written word can be used to argue why an offering should be chosen, and to detail the advantages and benefits that consumption will provide for the user.

Out-of-Home

Out-of-home (OOH), or outdoor, media consist of three main formats: street furniture (such as bus shelters); billboards (which consist primarily of 96-, 48-, and 6-sheet poster sites); and transit (which includes buses, taxis, and the London Underground). The key characteristic associated with OOH media is that they are observed by their target audiences at locations away from home and they are normally used to support messages that are transmitted through primary media—namely, broadcast and print. Outdoor media can therefore be seen as secondary, but important, support media for a complementary and effective media mix.

Digital

Generally, most traditional media provide one-way communications, whereby information passes from a source to a receiver, but there is little opportunity for feedback, let alone interaction. Digital media enable two-way interactive communication, with information flowing back to the source and again to the receiver, as each participant adapts their message to meet the requirements of their audience. For example, banner ads can provoke a click, which takes the receiver to a new website, where the source presents new information and the receiver makes choices and responds to questions (for example registers at the site), and the source again provides fresh information. Indeed, the identity of the source and receiver becomes blurred in this type of communication.

These interactions are conducted at high speed and low cost, and usually with great clarity. People drive these interactions at a speed that is convenient to them; they are not driven by others. Space (or time) within traditional media is limited, so costs rise as demand for the limited space or time increases. Conversely, because space is unlimited on the Internet, costs per contact fall as more visitors are received.

In-Store

There are two main forms of in-store media: point-of-purchase (POP) displays; and **packaging**. Retailers control the former and manufacturers, the latter. The primary objective of using in-store media is to get the attention of shoppers and to stimulate them to make purchases. The content of messages can be controlled easily by both retailers and manufacturers. In addition, the timing and the exact placement of in-store messages can be equally well controlled. There are a number of POP techniques, but the most frequently used are window displays, floor and wall racks used to display merchandise, posters, and information cards, plus counter and checkout displays. Packaging has to protect and preserve products, but it also has a significant communication role and is a means of influencing brand choice decisions.

Other

Two main media can be identified: cinema and ambient. Cinema advertising has all the advantages of television-based messages, such as high-quality audio and visual dimensions, which combine to provide high impact. However, the vast majority of cinema visitors are people aged 18–35, so if an advertiser wishes to reach different age segments, or perhaps a national audience, not only will cinema be inappropriate, but also the costs will be much higher than those for television. Ambient media are regarded as OOH media that fail to fit any of the established outdoor categories.

Ambient media can be classified according to a variety of factors. These include posters (typically found in washrooms); distribution (for example ads on tickets and carrier bags); digital media (in the form of video and LCD screens); sponsorships (as in golf holes and petrol pump nozzles); and aerials (in the form of balloons, blimps, and towed banners).

The Changing Role of the Media

The continuing proliferation of the media has led to an increasingly complex media landscape. This makes decisions about which combination of media channels should be used more challenging. It should be recognized, however, that digital media has enabled more accurate, more realistic, and faster campaign measurement.

The idea that 'digital' defines a particular media format is redundant because digital technologies can be applied to most classes of media that we identified earlier. For example, digital OOH technology has become so technologically advanced that digital billboards can be altered in seconds to generate trending messages. In addition, automated (programmatic) media buying enables the display of contextual ads that display only those messages that reflect surrounding conditions, such as the temperature or location. Out-of-home can also send push messages directly to the phones of people in the vicinity (Lepitak, 2015).

To reflect these changes, practitioners use a media classification known as POEM—that is, paid-for, owned, and earned media (see Table 11.4). The classification reflects the increasing scope of contemporary media and the range of media opportunities to engage audiences. It assumes that media is not only about paid-for media and embraces all items that can be used to convey brand-oriented messages, regardless of whether a payment is necessary (see Market Insight 11.3 and Research Insight 11.2).

Using Media for Brand Building or Direct Response

For a long time, commercial media have been used to convey messages designed to develop consumers' attitudes and feelings towards brands. This is referred to as an attitudinal response and concerns building a brand over the longer term. Today, many messages are designed to provoke audiences into responding, either physically, cognitively, or emotionally. This is referred to as a behavioural (direct) response, which concerns activation and is essentially a short-term activity. It therefore follows that attitude and behaviourally oriented communications require different media.

Table 11.4 POEM: a classification of the media by source

Type of media		Explanation
P	Paid-for	Advertising traditionally requires that media time and space are rented from a media owner in order to convey messages and reach target audiences. The selection of the media mix is planned, predetermined, and measured in terms of probable size of audience, costs, and scheduling.
O	Owned	Organizations have a range of assets that they can use to convey messages to audiences, and through which they can develop conversations. Ownership means that there are no rental costs, as with paid-for media. For example, a brand name or product display on a building, a telephone number or URL on a vehicle, or the use of the company website and its links to other sites do not incur usage fees.
E	Earned	Earned media refers to comments and conversations, both offline and online, in social media, in the news, or through face-to-face communications, about a brand or organization. These comments can be negative or positive, but the media carrying them are diverse and can be referred to as 'unplanned', although many campaigns seek to stimulate strong word-of-mouth communications through earned media.

Source: Marketing Communications (7th edn). Fill, C. and Turnbull, S. (2016). Pearson Education Limited. © Pearson Education Limited 2016.

Research Insight 11.2

To take your learning further, you might wish to read this influential paper:

Rosario, A.B., Sotgiu, F., De Valck, K., and Bijmolt, T.H.A (2016). The effect of electronic word of mouth on sales: a meta-analytic review of platform, product, and metric factors. *Journal of Marketing Research*, 53(3), 297–318.

In this article, the authors conduct a meta-analysis of previous research on the effects of electronic word of mouth (eWOM) on sales. Based on 96 studies covering 40 platforms and 26 product categories, they find that, on average, eWOM is positively correlated with sales (0.091), but also that its effectiveness differs across platform, product, and metric factors.

 Visit the **online resources** to read the abstract and access the full paper.

Direct-response media are characterized by the provision of a contact mechanism, such as a telephone number or web address, and increasingly through search activities on the Internet. These mechanisms enable receivers to respond to messages. Direct mail, search, telemarketing, and door-to-door activities are the main direct-response media, because they allow more personal, direct, and evaluative means of reaching precisely targeted customers. However, in reality, any type of media can be used simply by attaching a telephone number, website address, mailing address, or response card.

Market Insight 11.3
Damart Modernizes Its Welcome Programme

Damart, a French clothing company, operates in the UK, Belgium, Luxembourg, Switzerland, and the United States, and also through partnerships in Australia, Cyprus, and Spain, distributing its products to more than 10 million customers worldwide.

Damart supports its future through strategic marketing
Source: © ricochet64/Shutterstock.com.

Damart UK started to update its direct response campaigns targeted at new customers because of a desire to modernize its welcome programme to reflect the changes in recruited customers' preferences. Previously, first-time ordering customers were entered into an intensive welcome campaign. This involved sending them a catalogue every two weeks for a 26-week period. After this, they entered a more traditionally modelled customer mailing plan.

This approach generated a high level of second orders from customers. Unfortunately, it also brought a high level of customer attrition as newly recruited customers

requested to be removed from the company's marketing programmes.

It was clear that this method was not appropriate and a new communications approach was needed. Rather than focus on direct-response campaigns based solely on transactions, a new mix was developed to build relationships over the longer term and hence to realize higher lifetime customer value.

Any fresh approach required a more informed understanding of the new customers, which could then be used to reconfigure the communications mix to influence their subsequent orders. For example, if a customer's first order was placed on the web, Damart wanted to know the source of their order: was it an online ad, from a media insert, or an off-the-page magazine ad? Where a new customer could be identified as 'pure web and email', subsequent customer communications could then be channelled through the web via improved personalization in marketing emails.

If a new customer had responded to a heavily discounted offer, analysis could reveal whether a full-price order might be obtained from a main catalogue or this customer will simply have an overall lower lifetime value. If the latter were the case, then Damart could reduce its initial investment in marketing communications.

By driving new customers to order online, Damart was able to reduce the operational costs associated with processing offline orders and expose forms of cross-selling not available via mail order. It also meant that the company could invest more in web activities, including search.

Market Insight 11.3
continued

Theory into Practice

At one level, Damart's move represents a significant strategic marketing shift. The previous approach was largely sales-driven and was geared to moving stock. This is an inside–out view, whereby sales represent the dominant perspective. The shift to a more complex multichannel approach was in part a recognition of the need to put customers first—a marketing orientation. The new communication mix represented an outside–in perspective, which is more likely to bring long-term success.

At another level, the change in the configuration of the communication mix at Damart signalled a move away from a purely response-based behavioural goal towards building brand value over time. This links with the work of Binet and Field (2013), who found that the optimal balance of a communication mix was 60:40—that is, 60 per cent of the mix designed to build a brand and 40 per cent geared to driving an immediate response.

Related Topics

message appeals; budgeting; communications strategy

1 To what extent does the shift in the balance of the mix represent a brand nearing maturity rather than any other factor? What role might social media play in developing this brand?

2 Should organizations such as Damart be concerned about upsetting or irritating a few customers when a campaign successfully drives sales?

3 Visit the site of another fashion retailer and decide whether its mix is configured to drive brand response or to build brand associations. Give your reasons.

This market insight was kindly contributed by Leon Savidis, business analyst, Damart.

Table 11.5 sets out the main media used within direct-response marketing. Direct-response media also allow clients the opportunity to measure the volume, frequency, and value of audience responses. This enables them to determine which direct-response media work best and so helps them become more efficient, as well as more effective. Direct-response television (DRTV) is attractive to service providers such as those in financial services, charities, and tourism, but grocery brands are increasingly using this format. The growth in video advertising reflects the involvement of people in their online and mobile activities.

In addition, television, mobile, and online media are complementary. Consumers often research an offering online only after watching a television ad.

Visit the **online resources** and follow the web link to the Radio Advertising Bureau (RAB) to learn more about the role and importance of radio in today's fragmented media landscape.

Table 11.5 Direct-response (DR) media formats

Types of DR media	Explanation
Digital media	The use of the Internet, email, viral marketing, blogging, and social networking sites now represents the major form of interactive and direct-marketing opportunities. In particular, 'search' enables brands to be reached by audiences who can then be converted into customers.
Telemarketing	The telephone provides interaction, flexibility, immediate feedback, and the opportunity to overcome objections, all within the same communication event. Telemarketing also allows organizations to undertake separate marketing research, which is both highly measurable and accountable in that the effectiveness can be verified continuously, while call rates, contacts reached, and the number and quality of positive and negative responses are easily recorded and monitored.
Carelines	Carelines and contact centres enable customers to complain about a product performance and related experiences, to seek product-related advice, to make suggestions regarding product or packaging development, and to comment about an action or development concerning the brand as a whole.
Radio and TV	Television has much greater potential than radio as a direct-response mechanism because it can provide a visual dimension. Nearly half of all TV ads carry a response mechanism.
Print	There are two main forms of direct-response advertising through the printed media: catalogues; and magazines and newspapers. Consumer direct print ads sometimes offer an incentive and are designed explicitly to drive customers to a website, where transactions can be completed without reference to retailers, dealers, or other intermediaries.
Door-to-door	Although the content and quality can be controlled in the same way, door-to-door response rates are lower than direct mail because of the lack of a personal address mechanism. Door-to-door can be much cheaper than direct mail because there are no postage charges to be accounted for.

One aspect that is crucial to the success of a direct-response campaign is not the number of responses, but the conversion of leads into sales. This means that the infrastructure to support these activities must be thought through and implemented; otherwise, the work and resources invested at the visible level will be wasted if customers cannot get the information they require when they respond.

To conclude this section, we ask an important question: how much of a firm's media budget should be directed towards brand-building activities and how much should be generating short-term responses? The answer rests with an understanding of the campaign goals and media characteristics. Those media with a broad reach, such as television, radio, OOH, and other traditional display media, as well as online display, are best for brand building. Those channels that enable tight targeting, such as search, telemarketing, email, and classified media, are more appropriate for short-term selling to narrow audiences. Extensive research by Binet and Field (2013) shows that, on average, a 60:40 brand building–response split appears to maximize efficiency and effectiveness.

Other Promotional Methods and Approaches

In addition to the primary elements mentioned earlier, there are numerous other instruments that organizations can use to reach their audiences. These can be regarded as secondary tools that are used to support the primary mix, although they can be used in their own right as stand-alone methods of communications. Some of these other instruments are briefly considered here.

Sponsorship is normally associated with PR, but it has strong associations with advertising. Now considered an important discipline in its own right, sponsorship can be defined as 'a commercial activity whereby one party permits another an opportunity to exploit an association with a target audience in return for funds, services, or resources' (Fill, 2009: 599). Sports, arts, and programme sponsorship are the principal types, designed to generate awareness and brand associations, and to cut through the clutter of commercial messages. Some sponsorship arrangements are being used to actively demonstrate a firm's business credentials (see Market Insight 11.4). For example, logistics company DHL sponsors the Red Bull Air Race. In addition to the normal exposure and associations, DHL also provides transportation services. So, by moving planes, fuel, and broadcast equipment, the brand is able to demonstrate its functional expertise and tell stories about these activities (Anon., 2015b).

Sponsorship gets your brand noticed
Source: © Grekov/123RF.com.

Market Insight 11.4
EY Uses Art to Distinguish Itself

In an attempt to distinguish itself in a crowded B2B marketplace, professional services firm EY (formerly known as Ernst & Young) has been sponsoring art for over 20 years. It claims that this strategy helps to single it out as both different and interesting.

One of its high-profile sponsorships is the EY Tate Arts Partnership, a six-year partnership extending from 2013 to 2019, which so far has resulted in EY sponsoring four exhibitions at Tate Modern, Tate Britain, and many of the Plus Tate partners around the country (with three more to come by 2019). EY's corporate memberships at the British Museum, the National Gallery, the Royal Academy, Tate Liverpool, Tate St Ives, and the V&A extend the reach of the firm's involvement in art.

EY ensures that its target audience is fully aware of the partnership by means of a series of multichannel marketing activities. This includes holding many private client events at the galleries, such as early-morning tours, receptions, dinners, family art workshops, and evening viewings. The EY name and logo also appear on all materials for the exhibitions, giving the brand huge exposure.

Art is an integral element of the company culture. Apart from its own art collection of more than 350 pieces, the firm's arts club, which has nearly 2,500 members, organizes social events and trips to places of significant interest. Employees receive art guide training, which can entitle them to act as guides at client events. All employees have complimentary access to the galleries, members' rooms, and internal arts competitions, and there are discounts on events and access to private views.

EY have also sponsored several leading sports events, including the Rugby World Cup, the Ryder Cup, and the Commonwealth Games.

Sources: McGreal (2015); https://www.ey.com

Art is an integral element of the company culture at EY
Source: Courtesy of EY.

Theory into Practice

Sponsorship involves two main parties: a sponsor and a sponsored organization. The success of any sponsorship can be considered in terms of the degree of fit between these two parties. This level of fitness in turn helps to determine the relative effectiveness of the relationship and hence the success of the sponsorship.

Sponsorship can be considered in terms of the use of association. By being seen to be associated with an established, credible, and knowledgeable entity such as Tate, EY can expect to inherit and be seen to share

similar associations. In much the same way, Tate seeks to benefit from being seen to be associated with EY.

Sponsorship represents a form of collaborative communication, in the sense that two (or more) parties work together so that one is able to reach the other's audience. These associations are considered to offer mutual value to the parties concerned. Sponsorship can be considered in terms of a network of actors (media agencies, different audiences, event organizers) rather than only the sponsor and sponsored. This expands the realm of interaction and introduces a wider range of issues.

Market Insight 11.4
continued

Related Topics

relationship marketing; network analysis; corporate advertising; emotional intensity

1 Why might EY focus its sponsorship and its culture on art?

2 What might be the key associations that EY wants to make through its involvement with prestigious sports events?

3 How might EY's sponsorship lead to a crisis?

Brand placement is another form of sponsorship and represents a relationship between film/television producers and managers of brands. Through this arrangement and for a fee, brand managers are able to present their brands 'naturally' within a film or entertainment event. Such placement is designed to increase brand awareness, to develop positive brand attitudes, and to (potentially) lead to purchase activity. Similarly, collaborations with social media influencers can also be seen as a form of brand placement.

Packaging provides an important form of communication that is critical at the point of sale. Packaging can be an integral part of a brand's story. For example, Heinz's 'Get Well Soup' campaign enabled people to give a can of soup to someone not feeling well and hence reinforced the brand's nurturing position. Greater customization and personalization of packaging has been enabled through digital printing.

'Get Well Soup': Heinz and some clever packaging
Source: © urbanbuzz/Shutterstock.com.

Field marketing is about providing support for the sales force and merchandising personnel. One of the tasks is concerned with getting free samples of a product into the hands of potential customers; another is to create an interaction between the brand and a new customer; yet another is to create a personal and memorable brand experience for potential customers.

Exhibitions are held for both consumer and B2B markets. Organizations benefit from meeting their current and potential customers, developing relationships, demonstrating products, building industry-wide credibility, placing and taking orders, generating leads, and gathering market information. For customers, exhibitions enable them to meet new or potential suppliers, to find out about new offerings and leading-edge brands, and to bring themselves up to date with market developments. In B2B markets, exhibitions and trade shows can be an integral element of the marketing communications mix. Meeting friends, customers, suppliers, competitors, and prospective customers is an important sociological and ritualistic event in the communications calendar for many companies.

Viral marketing is based on the credibility and reach associated with word-of-mouth communications. Porter and Golan (2006: 33) refer to viral marketing in terms of how information is communicated and suggest that it commonly involves the 'unpaid peer-to-peer communication of provocative content originating from an identified sponsor using the Internet to persuade or influence an audience to pass along the content to others'. Numerous definitions have been proposed, but, according to van der Lans and colleagues (2010), viral marketing concerns the mutual sharing and spread of marketing-relevant information, initially distributed deliberately by marketers to stimulate and capitalize on word-of-mouth behaviours.

Crisis communications have become increasingly necessary as the incidence of crises has increased. This appears to be as a result of an increasing number of simple managerial mistakes, incorrect decision-making, technology failures, and uncontrollable events in the external environment. For example, both TalkTalk and AshleyMadison.com have had to communicate with their stakeholders to try to restore customer and media confidence following the loss of customer data to computer hackers.

Organizations are encouraged to plan for crisis events so that they can respond quickly using planned communications. Using websites, social media, and mobile technologies, managers of an afflicted organization can post up-to-date information quickly, and through video and news media it can attempt to reassure communities by explaining events honestly, demonstrating concern, and sympathizing with any affected groups, before explaining what is being done to rectify the situation.

There are many other, largely digital media, methods of communicating with target audiences, including mobile communications, text messaging (that is, short message service, or SMS), blogging, and podcasting, to name a few. These are all considered in Chapter 12.

The Changing Marketing Communications Landscape

Lately, there have been some major changes to the way in which the marketing communications industry is structured. One of the most important of these has been the emergence of a number of powerful and dominant industry groups, such as WPP and the News Corporation, whose business interests span cross-media ownership, content development, and delivery. The changing industry structure is a response to several variables—particularly, developments in technology, the reconfiguration of the communications mix, and, in particular, the media used by organizations and the way in which client-side managers are expected to operate—that is, to drive short-term sales results.

There can be no doubt that technology has had a dramatic impact on the communications industry. As a result, the way in which organizations configure the communications mix has changed considerably. The sales force was the dominant tool of the mix used by organizations operating in B2B markets. Many organizations in B2B markets have slashed the size of their sales forces, partly to cut costs, but also to use technology more efficiently and to allow the sales force to focus on their main activity—namely, to build and maintain viable customer relationships. However, their use of digital marketing communications has yet to reach its full potential (Karjaluoto, Mustonen, and Ulkuniemi, 2015).

Today, the use of sponsorship, direct and event marketing, and online, mobile, and digitally driven interactive media is growing at the expense of offline mass media advertising and sales promotions in consumer markets. In addition, there are multichannel digital opportunities to reach audiences. As a result, one strategy has been to build content that can be deployed across different channels. For example, *The Guardian* newspaper's advertising strategies are structured around the distribution of rich content through different channels throughout a working day. In the morning, brief content is moved through mobile channels as commuters use smartphones during their commute to work. At lunchtime, content is switched to desktops, when social media is updated, and in the evening, when audiences relax, there is a change to the use of tablets so that they can digest richer content.

A key area of change within the media concerns the use of content. Traditionally, content is provided by a client organization, which uses the media to interrupt and transfer its message to its target audience—usually, a mass audience. Advancements in digital media and changes in consumer behaviour now enable audiences not only to generate their own content, but also to discuss and consider the opinions and attitudes of others. This means that advertisers no longer have control over what is said about their brands, who says it, and when. The rise of online communities and social networking sites, blogging, wikis, and Rich Site Summary (RSS) feeds enable users to create content and to become more involved with a brand.

Recently, there have been substantial changes in the digital media landscape. These include the development of automated ad buying, convergence, and increasing levels of ad avoidance and use of ad-blockers.

Automation

The automation of the media planning, buying, and selling process is referred to as programmatic. The conventional media planning approach to buying ad space and time involves media planners purchasing television and radio programmes or space (magazines, newspapers, and billboards) on behalf of their clients, whose messages then interrupt the target audiences' reading and viewing activities.

Programmatic is about systems that automatically buy audiences, wherever they appear, according to particular predetermined parameters. A subsection of programmatic is real-time bidding (RTB), an auction dimension. This approach allows advertisers to automatically present ads to specific online or mobile audiences that reflect their browsing behaviour.

Convergence

Convergence means a 'bringing together'—in this case, of media and various technologies. This can be seen in marketing communications in various ways, including content served over a number of devices used by consumers, different technologies packaged as one entity (for example Sky selling broadband), and new platforms such as television through games consoles.

This movement represents a threat to traditional media owners. For example, newspaper publishers experience declining readership as people get their news at different times of the day from a variety of digital news platforms through various devices. In turn, this can be seen as an opportunity by reformatting content and distributing it across different digital platforms, and so attracting different advertisers.

Digital media owners such as Google, Apple, Facebook, Amazon, and Netflix are all seeking cut-through, some creating new platforms such as Amazon Prime. Others see collaboration as a viable strategy, as demonstrated by the BBC, C4, Five, and BT working together to create YouView—a mini set-top box that allows viewers to watch the UK's Freeview channels and catch-up television from the BBC, ITV, and other major channels.

Ad Avoidance

Finally, the changes in the way in which ads are presented through the media, and the rise of digital media in particular, has led to an increased use of ad-blockers. This software screens out and prevents the presentation of ads. This raises questions about the longer-term effectiveness of online and mobile advertising, about the role of content in apps, and about privacy, as well as the ethics and morality of advertising to audiences who are largely disinclined to engage with advertising. When Apple released iOS 9, the operating system enabled ad-blocking and deep linking in apps. Part of the motivation was to enable iPhone users to have a cleaner and faster web experience (Ghosh, 2015). One of the questions raised by this development, however, is that if mobile advertising becomes ineffective, how will content be paid for in the future?

Integrated Marketing Communications

So far in this chapter we have looked briefly at the five main tools of marketing communications, ideas about how messages should be developed, and how the media landscape is evolving. For these to work most effectively and most efficiently, however, it makes sense to integrate them so that they work as a unit. In so doing, they will have a greater overall impact. This bringing together is referred to as **integrated marketing communications (IMC)**.

Integrated marketing communications has become a popular approach with both clients and communications agencies. Ideas about IMC originated in the early 1990s. At first, it was regarded as a means of orchestrating the tools of the marketing communications mix, so that audiences perceive a single consistent unified message whenever they have contact with a brand. Duncan and Everett (1993) referred to this new, largely media-oriented, approach as 'orchestration', 'whole egg', and 'seamless' communication.

Integrated marketing communications can be considered from both a tactical and strategic perspective. The former is well understood and practised, but the latter is less well developed (Kerr and Patti, 2015).

The tactical perspective can be observed in the following levels of integration, identified by the Institute of Practitioners in Advertising (IPA):

- *Advertising-led* campaigns are united by 'look and feel'. Referred to as the 'matching luggage' concept, unification is often achieved visually through an icon (a celebrity, logo, or brand identifier) deployed across all tools and media.

- *Brand-led orchestration* campaigns are built on the tangible brand concept associated with a specific need-state, occasion, tightly defined target audience, or a specific 'point of market entry' upon which to focus the activity and the channel orchestration.

- *Participation-led integration* campaigns are based on the use of digital media designed to integrate brands into people's lives through conversation, and brand and audience interaction (Cox, 2011).

At a strategic level, Luxton, Reid, and Mavondo (2015) consider IMC to be part of a firm's overall capability, which contributes to brand performance. This is achieved by enabling the development and implementation of IMC campaigns that result in positive brand-related market performance and improved financial outcomes. Kerr and Patti (2015) developed a measure of strategic integration that evaluates organizational proficiency and diagnoses the integration of IMC campaigns. This has yet to be operationalized.

For a period soon after IMC was first considered, numerous definitions emerged as the concept was explored. Since then, Duncan (2002), Grönroos (2004), Kitchen and colleagues (2004), and Kliatchko (2008) have provided various definitions and valuable insights into IMC. Although there have been fewer definitions advanced in recent years, there is still little agreement about what constitutes and defines IMC (Reinold and Tropp, 2012).

Given this vagueness, in this book IMC is used to denote both a strategic and tactical approach to the planned management of an organization's communications. Integrated marketing communications require that organizations coordinate their various strategies, resources, and messages to enable meaningful engagement with audiences. The main purposes are to develop a clear positioning and to encourage stakeholder relationships that are of mutual value (Fill and Turnbull, 2016). Embedded within this definition are links with both business-level and marketing strategies, as well as confirmation of the importance of the coherent use of resources and messages. What should also be evident is that IMC can be used to support the development and maintenance of effective relationships—a point made first by Duncan and Moriarty (1998), and then by both Grönroos (2004) and Ballantyne (2004).

One quite common use of an integrated approach can be seen in the use of the tools: rather than using advertising, PR, sales promotions, personal selling, and direct marketing separately, it is better to use them in a coordinated manner (see Market Insight 11.5). So organizations often use advertising or sales promotion to create awareness, then involve PR to provoke media comment, and then reinforce these messages through direct marketing or personal selling. The Internet can also be incorporated to encourage comment, interest, and involvement in a brand, yet still convey the same message in a consistent way. Mobile communications are used to reach audiences to reinforce messages and to persuade targets to behave in particular ways, wherever they are. The evolution of digital media poses problems for IMC and for planning marketing communications activities. Some of these issues concern campaign metrics and measurement, budgeting, brand control, and content development (Winer, 2009).

Market Insight 11.5
Super Bowl Advertising: More than Meets the Eye

On the first Sunday of February every year, more than 110 million Americans (and many others worldwide) gather in front of their televisions to watch the Super Bowl—the final game in the American National Football League (NFL). However, viewers' excitement is not only about the game; the Super Bowl experience also includes a spectacular halftime show—and lots of advertising.

In 2018, marketers wanting to advertise during the Super Bowl paid around US$5 million for 30 seconds— that is, $166,667 per second.

The price tag of Super Bowl commercials is often widely discussed in industry and, every year, voices are raised about the soundness of putting so much money into buying a spot. Often, this discussion fails to consider the fact that the Super Bowl offers a context in which people actually *want* to see advertising: several studies have shown that a large proportion of viewers are more interested in the commercials than the actual game.

The discussion also fails to recognize that the 30-second spot during the Super Bowl is often partnered with other types of activity—both before and after the actual event. Commercials are pre-launched on YouTube, discussed in media, and followed up by public votes for best commercial after the actual event. What's more, many Super Bowl advertisers combine the events with different types of point-of-purchase display and packaging activities.

Sources: Rosengren and Dahlén (2015); Rosengren (2017)

Theory into Practice

The commercials run during the Super Bowl are examples of advertising, but they are typically part of an IMC campaign relying on several marketing tools, including PR (pre-announcements and exclusive accounts of what will happen targeted at news and social media) and advertising in social media (paid placements of the actual commercials and/or related content), as well as different types of in-store promotion.

There is no unifying IMC theory, but it is clear that most Super Bowl advertisers plan and manage their activities with an integrated approach. They clearly attempt to bring the various elements of the mix together so that one reinforces the other and, ultimately, brand resonance is improved.

Related Topics

Advertising; mass media; public relations (PR); social media; sports

1 **Look up the most recent Super Bowl commercials online and watch between three and five of them. What kind of messages are used? Why do you think that is?**

2 **Pick one of the commercials and search for more information about the campaign of which** it was part. What other communication tools and media were used?

3 **What were the integrating elements for this campaign?**

Integrated marketing communications has emerged for many reasons, but the two main ones concern customers and costs. First, organizations began to realize that their customers were more likely to understand a single message, delivered through various sources, than to try to appreciate a series of different messages transmitted through different tools and a variety of media. Therefore IMC is concerned with harmonizing the messages conveyed so that audiences perceive a consistent set of meanings within the messages they receive, through all touchpoints.

The second reason concerns costs: as organizations seek to lower their costs, it is becoming clear that it is far more cost-effective to send a single message, using a limited number of agencies and other resources, than to develop several messages through a number of different agencies.

At first glance, IMC might appear to be a practical and logical development that should benefit all concerned with an organization's marketing communications. However, there are issues concerning the concept, including what should be integrated, over and above the tools, media, and messages. For example, what about the impact of employees on a brand, and other elements of the marketing mix, as well as the structure, systems, processes, and procedures necessary to deliver IMC consistently through time? There is some debate about the nature and contribution IMC can make to an organization, if only because there is no main theory to underpin the concept (Cornelissen, 2003) (see Research Insight 11.3).

Research Insight 11.3

To take your learning further, you might wish to read this influential paper:

Ots, M., and Nyilasy, G. (2015). Integrated marketing communications (IMC): why does it fail? *Journal of Advertising Research*, 55(2), 132–45.

This article provides an interesting view of IMC's implementation as a reason for its failure. The authors identify four aspects of IMC implementation dysfunction: miscommunication; compartmentalization; loss of trust; and decontextualization.

 Visit the online resources to read the abstract and access the full paper.

Although IMC has yet to become an established marketing theory, the original ideas inherent in the overall approach are intuitively appealing and appear to be of value. However, what is integration to one person may simply be coordination and good practice to another, and, until there is a theoretical base on which to build IMC, the term will continue to be misused, misunderstood, and interpreted in a variety of ways.

Chapter Summary

To consolidate your learning, the key points from this chapter are summarized here:

■ **Describe the role and configuration of the marketing communications mix.**

Organizations use the marketing communications mix to convey messages and to engage their various audiences. The mix consists of five tools, four main forms of messages or content, and three forms of media. These elements are mixed and adapted to meet the needs of the target audience and the context in which marketing communications operate. Tools and media are not the same: the former are methods or techniques; the latter are the channels through which the messages are conveyed to the target audience.

■ **Explain the characteristics of each of the primary tools, messages, and media.**

Each of the tools—that is, advertising, sales promotion, public relations (PR), direct marketing, and personal selling—communicates messages in different ways and achieves different outcomes. Media can be classified according to whether they are paid, owned, or earned. Each medium has a set of characteristics that enable it to convey messages in particular ways to and with target audiences. Messages are a balance of informational and emotional content. Some content can be branded, whilst some can be generated by users.

■ **Set out the criteria that should be used to select the right communications mix.**

Using a set of criteria can help to simplify the complex and difficult process of selecting the right marketing communications mix. There are five key criteria—namely, the degree of control over a message, the credibility of the message conveyed, the costs of using a tool, the degree to which a target audience is dispersed, and the task that marketing communications is required to accomplish.

■ **Discuss the changing marketing communications landscape.**

Advancements in digital media and changes in consumer behaviour now enable audiences not only to generate their own content but also to discuss and consider the opinions and attitudes of others. This means that advertisers no longer have control over what is said about their brands, who says it, and when. The rise of online communities and social networking sites, blogging, wikis, and RSS feeds enables users to create content and become more involved with a brand. Recently, there have been substantial changes in the digital media landscape. These include the development of automated ad buying, convergence, and increasing levels of ad avoidance and the use of ad-blockers.

■ **Consider the principles and issues associated with integrated marketing communications.**

Rather than use advertising, PR, sales promotions, personal selling, and direct marketing separately, integrated marketing communications (IMC) is concerned with working with these tools (and media) as a coordinated whole. So organizations often use advertising to create awareness, then involve PR to provoke media comment and sales promotion to create trial, and then reinforce these messages by means of direct marketing or personal selling to persuade audiences. The Internet can also be incorporated to encourage comment, interest, and involvement in a brand, yet still convey the same message. Mobile communications are used to reach audiences to reinforce messages and to persuade audiences to behave in particular ways, wherever they are.

Review Questions

1 Make brief notes about the nature and role of the marketing communications mix and explain how the configuration has changed.

2 Write a definition for advertising, PR, and one other tool from the mix. Identify the key differences.

3 Why do organizations like to use direct-response media?

4 How does media fragmentation affect audiences?

5 What five criteria can be used to select the right mix of communication tools?

6 Make a list of the four main message formats and find an example to illustrate each one.

7 Write brief notes explaining the differences between informational and emotional messages.

8 Write a list that categorizes the media. Identify a media vehicle that represents each type of medium.

9 To what extent are online, mobile, and digital media likely to replace the use of traditional media?

10 What are the principles of integrated marketing communications?

 Discussion Questions

1 Having read Case Insight 11.1, how could you advise Adnams to run an IMC campaign? (*Hint*: Consider on-pack and in-pub promotions targeted at the trade and consumers, PR, social media and experiential marketing, and event sponsorship in your mix.)

2 Select an organization you are familiar with or for which you would like to work. Visit its website and try to determine its use of the marketing communications tools, messages, and media. How could its mix be improved?

3 Select an organization in the consumer technology industry or one for which you would like to work. Visit its website and look at its ad archive and read the press releases. Determine its approach to marketing communications. Now visit the website for its main competitor and determine its marketing communications. Discuss the similarities and differences.

4 Zylog is based in Denmark and manufactures and distributes a range of consumer electronic equipment. Ennike Christensen, Zylog's new marketing manager, has indicated that she wants to introduce an integrated approach to the firm's marketing communications. However, Zylog does not have any experience of IMC and the company's current communications agency, Red Spider, has started to become concerned that it may lose the Zylog account. Discuss the situation facing Zylog and suggest ways in which it might acquire the expertise it needs—then discuss ways in which Red Spider might acquire an IMC capability.

 Visit the online resources and complete the Multiple-Choice Questions to assess your knowledge of Chapter 11.

 Glossary

advertising a form of non-personal communication, by an identified sponsor, transmitted through the use of paid-for media.

audience fragmentation the disintegration of large media audiences into many smaller audiences, caused by the development of alternative forms of entertainment that people can experience, which means that, to reach large numbers of people in a target market, companies need to use a variety of media, not rely on only a few mass-media channels.

brand placement the planned and deliberate use of brands within films, television, and other entertainment vehicles, with a view to developing awareness and brand values.

branded content entertainment material, delivered through paid-for or owned media, which features a single company or product/ service brand.

crisis communications a part of PR, used to protect and defend a brand (individual or organization) when its reputation is damaged or threatened.

direct marketing a marketing communications tool that uses non-personal media to create and sustain a personal and intermediary-free communication with customers, potential customers, and other significant stakeholders; in most cases, a media-based activity.

direct-response media media that carry advertising messages enabling audiences to respond immediately; most commonly used in print, banner ads, and on television (known as DRTV).

exhibitions events at which groups of sellers meet collectively with the key purpose of attracting buyers.

field marketing a marketing communications activity concerned with providing support for the sales force and merchandising personnel.

integrated marketing communications (IMC) an approach associated with the coordinated development and delivery of a consistent marketing communications message(s) with a target audience.

marketing communications mix a set of five tools, a variety of media, and messages that can be used in various combinations, and with different degrees of intensity, to communicate with specific audiences.

media (plural of medium) facilities used by companies to convey or deliver messages to target audiences.

media fragmentation the splintering of a few mainstream media channels into a multitude of media and channel formats.

packaging protects contents and communicates key rational and emotional information about a brand.

personal selling the use of interpersonal communications aimed at encouraging people to make a purchase for personal gain and reward.

public relations (PR) a non-personal form of communication used by companies to build trust, goodwill, interest, and ultimately relationships with a range of stakeholders.

sales promotion a communications tool that adds value to a product or service, with the goal of encouraging people to buy now rather than at some point in the future.

sponsorship a marketing communications activity whereby one party permits another an opportunity to exploit an association with a target audience in return for funds, services, or resources.

user-generated content (UGC) content made publicly available over the Internet that reflects a certain amount of creative effort and which is created by users, not professionals.

viral marketing the unpaid peer-to-peer communication of often provocative content, originating from an identified sponsor, using the Internet to persuade or influence an audience to pass along the content to others.

References

Anon. (2015a). Case study: Volvo trucks live test series—the best of digital marketing. *Best Marketing*. Retrieve from: http://www.best-marketing.eu/case-study-volvo-trucks-live-test-series/ (accessed 13 October 2018).

Anon. (2015b). DHL turns sponsorship into 'active ads'. *Warc*, 10 November. Retrieve from: https://www.warc.com/newsandopinion/news/dhl_turns_sponsorship_into_active_ads/35692 (accessed 13 October 2018).

Ballantyne, D. (2004). Dialogue and its role in the development of relationship-specific knowledge. *Journal of Business and Industrial Marketing*, 19(2), 114–23.

Binet, L., and Field, P. (2013). *The Long and Short of It*. London: IPA.

Carter, M. (2014). How Volvo trucks pulled off an epic split and a game-changing campaign. *Fast Company*, 18 June. Retrieve from: https://www.fastcompany.com/3031654/how-volvo-trucks-pulled-off-an-epic-split-and-a-game-changing-campaign (accessed 13 October 2018).

Cornelissen, J.P. (2003). Change, continuity and progress: the concept of integrated marketing communications and marketing communications practice. *Journal of Strategic Marketing*, 11(4), 217–34.

Cox, K. (2011). *New Models of Marketing Effectiveness: From Integration to Orchestration*. London: Institute for Practitioners in Advertising/World Advertising Research Centre.

Dahlén, M., and Rosengren, S. (2016). If advertising won't die, what will it be? Towards a new definition of advertising. *Journal of Advertising*, 45(3), 334–45.

Duncan, T. (2002). *IMC: Using Advertising and Promotion to Build Brands*. New York: McGraw-Hill.

Duncan, T., and Everett, S. (1993). Client perceptions of integrated marketing communications. *Journal of Advertising Research*, 3(3), 30–9.

Duncan, T., and Moriarty, S. (1998). A communication-based marketing model for managing relationships. *Journal of Marketing*, 62(2), 1–13.

Fill, C. (2009). *Marketing Communications: Interactivity, Communications and Content* (5th edn). Essex: Prentice Hall.

Fill, C. (2013). *Marketing Communications: Brands, Experience and Participation* (6th edn). Harlow: FT/Prentice Hall.

Fill, C., and Turnbull, S. (2016). *Marketing Communications: Discovery, Creation and Conversations* (7th edn). Harlow: Pearson Education.

Fuchs, C., Prandelli, E., and Schreier, M. (2010). The psychological effects of empowerment strategies on consumers' product demand. *Journal of Marketing*, 74(1), 65–79.

Ghosh, S. (2015). Apple's iOS 9 forces a dramatic rethink for mobile marketing. *Marketing Magazine*, 1 September. Retrieve from: http://www.marketingmagazine.co.uk/article/1362246/apples-ios-9-forces-dramatic-rethink-mobile-marketing (accessed 13 October 2018).

Grönroos, C. (2004). The relationship marketing process: communication, interaction, dialogue, value. *Journal of Business and Industrial Marketing*, 19(2), 99–113.

Kaplan, A.M., and Haenlein, M. (2010). Users of the world, unite! The challenges and opportunities of social media. *Business Horizons*, 53(1), 59–68.

Karjaluoto, H., Mustonen, N., and Ulkuniemi, P. (2015). The role of digital channels in industrial marketing communications. *Journal of Business and Industrial Marketing*, 30(6), 703–10.

Kerr, G., and Patti, C. (2015). Strategic IMC: from abstract concept to marketing management tool. *Journal of Marketing Communications*, 21(5), 317–39.

Kitchen, P., Brignell, J., Li, T., and Spickett Jones, G. (2004). The emergence of IMC: a theoretical perspective. *Journal of Advertising Research*, 44(1), 19–30.

Kliatchko, J. (2008). Revisiting the IMC construct: a revised definition and four pillars. *International Journal of Advertising*, 27(1), 133–60.

Lepitak, S. (2015). It's about the here and now. *The Drum*, 22 June. Retrieve from: https://www.thedrum.com/news/2015/06/22/it-s-about-here-and-now-jean-charles-decaux-transforming-our-cities-digital-out-home (accessed 13 October 2018).

Liljedal, K. (2016). The effects of advertising consumer co-created new products: a brand alliance-framework model can predict perceptions about co-created brands and their creators. *Journal of Advertising Research*, 56(1), 53–63.

Luxton, S., Reid, M., and Mavondo, F. (2015). Integrated marketing communication capability and brand performance. *Journal of Advertising*, 44(1), 37–46.

McGreal, J. (2015). Campaign of the month: EY. *B2B Marketing*, June. Retrieve from: https://www.b2bmarketing.net/en-gb/resources/features/campaign-month-ey (accessed 13 October 2018).

Ots, M., and Nyilasy, G. (2015). Integrated marketing communications (IMC): why does it fail? *Journal of Advertising Research*, 55(2), 132–45.

Porter, L., and Golan, G.J. (2006). From subservient chickens to brawny men: a comparison of viral advertising to TV advertising. *Journal of Interactive Advertising*, 6(2), 30–8.

Reinold, T., and Tropp, J. (2012). Integrated marketing communications: how can we measure its effectiveness? *Journal of Marketing Communications*, 18(2), 113–32.

Richards, J.I., and Curran, C.M. (2002). Oracles on 'advertising': searching for a definition. *Journal of Advertising*, 31(2), 63–77.

Ridley, L. (2014). Watch 'groundbreaking' Lego ad break by PHD. *Campaign*, 10 February. Retrieve from: https://www.campaignlive.co.uk/article/watch-groundbreaking-lego-ad-break-phd/1230530#k3XwhqoVTjhwSBkB.99 (accessed 13 October 2018).

Rosario, A.B., Sotgiu, F., De Valck, K., and Bijmolt, T.H.A. (2016). The effect of electronic word of mouth on sales: a meta-analytic review of platform, product, and metric factors, *Journal of Marketing Research*, 53(3), 297–318.

Rosengren, S. (2017). Det här kan svensk reklam lära av Super Bowl, *Resumé*, 1 February. Retrieve from: https://www.resume.se/nyheter/artiklar/2017/02/07/sara-rosengren-det-kan-svensk-reklam-lara-av-super-bowl/ (accessed 13 October 2018).

Rosengren, S., and Dahlén, M. (2015). Exploring advertising equity: how a brand's past advertising may affect consumer willingness to approach its future ads. *Journal of Advertising*, 44(1), 1–13.

van der Lans, R., van Bruggen, G., Eliashberg, J., and Wierenga, B. (2010). A viral branching model for predicting the spread of electronic word-of-mouth. *Marketing Science*, 29(2), 348–65.

Whitehouse, L. (2014). P&G continues to make big increases in its advertising spend. *CosmeticDesign.com*, 24 July. Retrieve from: https://www.cosmeticsdesign.com/Business-Financial/P-G-continues-to-make-big-increases-in-its-advertising-spend (accessed 13 October 2018).

Winer, R.S. (2009). New communications approaches in marketing: issues and research directions. *Journal of Interactive Marketing*, 23(2), 108–17.

Wojdynski, B.W., and Evans, N.J. (2016). Going native: effects of disclosure position and language on the recognition and evaluation of online native advertising. *Journal of Advertising*, 45(2), 157–68.

Chapter 12
Digital and Social Media Marketing

Learning Outcomes

After reading this chapter, you will be able to:

▸ Define digital marketing and social media marketing

▸ Explain how digitalization is transforming marketing practice

▸ Discuss key techniques in digital marketing and social media marketing

▸ Review how practitioners measure the effectiveness of social media marketing

▸ Discuss crowdsourcing and explain how it can be harnessed for marketing

Case Insight 12.1
Spotify

Market Insight 12.1
Who's in Charge?

Market Insight 12.2
Play It Forward

Market Insight 12.3
What's in a Click?

Market Insight 12.4
Searching the Amazon

Market Insight 12.5
The World in Your Pocket

Case Insight 12.1
Spotify

What role do social media play and how should organizations incorporate it into their communication campaigns? We talk to Chug Abramowitz, vice president of global customer service and social media at Spotify, to find out more.

Spotify's dream is to make all of the world's music available instantly to everyone.

Our streaming service launched in Sweden in 2008 and, as of 2017, we were available in 61 markets, with more than 159 million active users. Of these, more than 70 million are paid users. Today, Spotify brings you the right music for every moment—on computers, mobiles, tablets, home entertainment systems, cars, gaming consoles, and more.

Social media has been an important part of Spotify's growth in two ways. The marketing team has worked with agencies to create social media campaigns that engage customers and attract them to the Spotify brand, while the customer support team has monitored social media channels and used them as tools to help dissatisfied customers.

We've noticed that the customer support social media team is more effective than our agencies at customer engagement. The agencies are typically less in tune with what Spotify actually stands for and our tone. And while customer service is primarily about reacting to customers' concerns and praise, our reactions help to build the Spotify brand.

For example, after solving someone's issues, our customer support social team regularly replies by drafting a message in a playlist. Jelena Woehr, a satisfied customer, shared her experience online of a playlist in which the titles of the songs spelled out a message 'Jelena/You Are Awesome/Thanks a Lot/For These Words/It Helps Me/Impress/The Management'. The list quickly went viral.

We call these RAKs, which stands for Random Acts of Kindness. This is our way of doing something special for our customers that highlights music and our product in a very Spotify way. Our internal support advisers came up with RAKs, which is why I think they nail our tone of voice so well.

My focus now is to devise a strategy that incorporates the spot-on tone our social media support team has in our marketing campaigns. Most likely, campaigns will continue to be agency-created, but they will have to be filtered through the lens of our in-house social media crew. We also need to be better at using what we already have internally, in terms of both our content and our people. At Spotify, we create tons of content and we're not maximizing its value. Why have an agency make content when internal teams are developing materials that espouse Spotify's brand at its core? On top of that, Spotify's employees love music and go to gigs every week. We're missing an engagement opportunity with tremendous potential to show who we are and our entire company's love of music.

It's clear that social media offers so many possibilities, especially to a brand like Spotify that's centred on music, an integral part of most people's lives. Social media offers the potential to show a company's passion for what it does and nobody is fully taking advantage of that yet. There are many brands out there doing interesting things here and there, but no one has been able to put it all together on a consistent basis. We're going to be the ones who do it.

Case Insight 12.1
continued

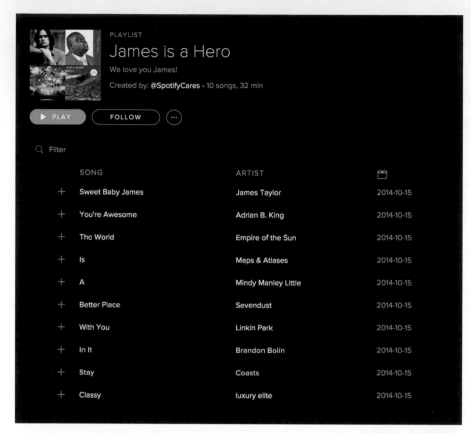

Another example of Spotify's use of playlists as Random Acts of Kindness (RAK)
Source: Courtesy of Spotify.

To move forward, the company says that the first thing it needs to figure out is: how can Spotify combine its customer support's great engagement, evident in interactions such as its RAKs, with the type of advance planning and scale needed for marketing campaigns?

 Visit the **online resources** to watch a video interview with Chug Abramowitz in which he explains what Spotify did.

Introduction

Consider, for a moment, your own personal use of digital technology and social media. How often do you go online? What device do you use? And what do you use it for? Now consider, for a moment, how you used digital technology and social media five years ago. How often did you go online? Using what devices? Doing what?

It is most likely that you will notice that your behaviours have changed rather dramatically in the past five years. Devices such as the iPhone and the iPad, now an integral part of many people's everyday lives, were first introduced to the market as recently as 2007 and 2010, respectively. The same is true for many of the services and apps we use. Airbnb (founded in 2008), Spotify (founded in 2006), and Uber (founded in 2009), which have used digital technology to transform how we travel, listen to music, and move around cities, all began their international expansions in the 2010s. Similarly, Instagram was launched in 2010, Snapchat in 2011, and Tinder in 2012.

Today, many of the social interactions and information exchanges in which we engage are facilitated by digital and social media technologies enabled by Internet technology. By December 2017, Internet penetration stood at 35.2 per cent in Africa, 48.1 per cent in Asia, 85.2 per cent in Europe, 64.5 per cent in the Middle East, 95 per cent in North America, 67 per cent in Latin America/Caribbean, and 68.9 per cent in Oceania/Australia (Internet World Stats, 2017). With increasing broadband penetration (increasingly via mobile devices), the adoption of digital and social media marketing techniques is vital. Apps, blogs, microblogs, social networking sites, wikis, and other multimedia sharing services have become commonplace. The technological development is rapidly changing the way in which consumers behave and marketers need to adapt accordingly. This has led to a 'digital transformation of marketing' over the past 15–20 years (Lamberton and Stephen, 2016). As people change how they communicate, the marketing profession has turned to digital and social media marketing to complement, and sometimes replace, traditional marketing channels and activities. However, digitalization is not only altering consumer expectations of their interaction with organizations online; it is also changing marketing in all forms.

Digitalization enables a shift in consumer behaviours that transforms expectations and interactions between consumers and marketers beyond the digital touchpoints being used. Digital and social media affect the very core of marketing, because they can be used to both anticipate and satisfy needs through mutually beneficial exchanges. Whereas **digital marketing** has typically focused on using digital and social media platforms to communicate (for example through search engine marketing and corporate websites) and satisfy needs (for example online retailing and digital products), companies are also increasingly turning to them as a tool for market insights (for example big data and social media monitoring), meaning that they are also used for understanding and anticipating needs.

Throughout the rest of this chapter, we will focus on digital marketing and social media marketing as tools with which we can communicate and interact with consumers. First, we define digital and social media marketing, and we track their evolution. We will then move on to discuss key areas of digital marketing communications: Internet advertising, search marketing, email marketing, social media marketing, content marketing, and **mobile marketing**. We then define crowdsourcing and explain how it is used in marketing. Finally, we review some wider considerations in the development of digital marketing strategy.

Digital Marketing

Digital marketing is the management and execution of marketing using digital electronic technologies and channels (for example Internet, email, digital television, wireless media) and digital data about user/customer characteristics and behaviour. It is an established, and increasingly important, subfield of marketing brought about by advancements in digital media technologies and digital media environments. Digital marketing extends beyond Internet marketing, which is one form of digital marketing specific to the use of Internet-only technologies (for example email, intranet, extranets), in that it makes use of a range of different electronic technologies and channels, such as mobile telephony, digital display advertising, and the Internet of Things.

A variety of terms related to digital marketing are used, including e-marketing, Internet marketing, direct marketing, interactive marketing, mobile marketing, and social media marketing, among many others. Although these terms are sometimes incorrectly used interchangeably, each has its own specific meaning (see Table 12.1). Increasingly, 'digital marketing' is being used as an umbrella term, whereas the others are used to describe specific subsets of digital marketing activities, such as Internet ('Internet marketing'), social media ('social media marketing'), or mobile ('mobile marketing'), or types of direct ('direct marketing') or interactive ('interactive marketing') communication with consumers. Sometimes, social marketing is used as a synonym for social media marketing. This is incorrect, because social marketing is an established term referring to the use of marketing to influence the behaviour of a target audience in which the benefits of the

Table 12.1 Defining digital marketing terms

Term	Definition
Digital marketing	Management and execution of marketing using digital electronic technologies and channels (e.g. web, email, digital TV, wireless media) and digital data about user/customer characteristics and behaviour.
Direct marketing	'A specific form of marketing that attempts to send its communications direct to consumers using addressable media such as post, Internet, email, and telephone and text messaging' (Harris, 2009: 70).
Interactive marketing	Marketing that moves away from a transaction-based effort to a conversation (i.e. two-way dialogue) and can be described as a situation or mechanism through which marketers and customers (e.g. stakeholders) interact, usually in real time. Not all interactive marketing is electronic (e.g. face-to-face sales).
e-marketing	Process of marketing accomplished or facilitated through the use of electronic devices, applications, tools, technologies, platforms, and/or systems. It is not limited to one specific type or category of electronic technology (e.g. Internet, TV), but includes both older analogue and developing digital electronic technologies.
Internet marketing	Process of marketing accomplished or facilitated via the use of Internet technologies (e.g. web, email, intranet, extranet).
Mobile marketing	'A set of practices that enable organizations to communicate and engage with their audience in an interactive and relevant manner through and with any mobile device or network' (MMA, 2009).
Social marketing	'[Marketing] designed to influence the behaviour of a target audience in which the benefits of the behaviour are intended by the marketer to accrue primarily to the audience or to the society in general and not to the marketer' (AMA, 2015).
Social media marketing	A form of digital marketing that describes the use of the social web and social media (e.g. social networks, online communities, blogs, wikis) or any online collaborative technology for marketing activities.

behaviour are intended by the marketer to accrue primarily to the audience or to society in general and not to the marketer. Social media marketing is increasingly being used by, for example, non-profit and public organizations to achieve such social benefits. Thus the terms are not synonyms.

Visit the **online resources** and follow the web link to the eMarketer website for a comprehensive source of information on marketing in a digital world.

An important feature of digital marketing is that it is continuously changing. Initially, the Internet played a key role in the digitalization of marketing. Over the past couple of years, social media and mobile have driven its development, and we are now seeing how artificial intelligence, automation, and voice search are increasingly impacting on digital marketing (DeMers, 2017).

Social Media Marketing

The term 'social media' refers to a group of Internet-based applications that allow the creation and exchange of content between people. This includes a wide range of online word-of-mouth forums, including blogs, company-sponsored discussion boards, and chat rooms, as well as consumer-to-consumer messaging services, consumer product or service rating websites and forums, Internet discussion boards and forums, moblogs (sites containing digital audio, images, movies, or photographs), and social networking websites (Mangold and Faulds, 2009). Table 12.2 lists the most used social media networks.

Table 12.2 Top 10 social media networks in 2018 (based on active users)

Social network	Users (million)
Facebook	2,167
YouTube	1,500
WhatsApp	1,300
Facebook Messenger	1,300
WeChat	980
QQ	843
Instagram	800
Tumblr	794
QXone	568
Sina Weibo	376

Source: Statista (2018a).

Social media has had a major impact on marketing. In fact, many argue that it has turned marketing practice upside down. This argument is primarily based on two main changes. The first change has to do with power. Social media enables users to generate, share, and comment on content at their own discretion (van den Bulte and Wuyts, 2007). Content in social media is co-created by consumers rather than (as in traditional offline media) primarily created by media companies and marketers. The proliferation of **user-generated content (UGC)**—that is, content made available over the Internet that reflects creative effort and is created outside professional routine and practices (Wunsch-Vincent and Vickery, 2007), such as **review sites** (for example Epinions.com, Tripadvisor.com, and reviews on Amazon.com) and widely shared first-hand feedback about consumer experiences (for example through a picture and comment on Instagram)—means that consumers have become increasingly influential. Social media allow consumers to share their experiences with each other at their own discretion, making service and product quality assessments widely available, and thereby shifting power from marketers to consumers.

The second shift has to do with *control.* Whereas marketers have traditionally been in charge of the messages they communicate, this is no longer the case. In a social media environment, consumers not only are able to create and modify content to pertain to their needs, and to share this content with consumers, companies, or third parties, but also have a voice in reacting to product offers and marketing that they do or do not like. As an example, the choice of (very thin or objectified) models used by fashion retailers in their advertisements is frequently debated and questioned in social media (examples include H&M and American Apparel), forcing the retailers to rethink the way in which they cast models in all their marketing communications. With social media come higher transparency and less control for marketers in terms of how their communications are received and passed on.

The changing power and control over communication clearly shows how social media marketing is not about mass marketing, but about facilitating *conversations* around the organization, the brand, or an individual. Engaging in these digital conversations requires trust and transparency, and involves authentic engagement in a real two-way dialogue (see Market Insight 12.1).

Market Insight 12.1
Who's in Charge?

In the past 15 years or so, social media has evolved from a debating ground for the initiated few to become a conversational arena for the masses. Nowhere is this more evident than when it comes to discussions about purchases, companies, and brands. Customers taking their negative experiences online cause headaches for many marketing executives. Social media conversations, even in a company's own social media channels, are difficult to control, and if they are handled poorly, they can spin out of control and become issues in their own right. Moreover, the public nature of social media

conversations makes such failings available to everyone for a very long time.

One example is the case of US retailer Target and Mike Melgaard. Mr Melgaard, upon surfing Facebook one night, discovered that Target had removed gender-based labels on its toys. Anticipating outraged reactions from his more conservative American compatriots (with whom he does not agree on this issue), he quickly set up a fake Facebook account called 'Ask for Help', and included a profile picture similar to that of Target's own bullseye logo. Mr Melgaard then began commenting

Market Insight 12.1
continued

on the many negative posts that were soon piling up on Target's Facebook page as if he were an actual Target customer service representative. Over the course of 16 hours, Mr Melgaard gave humorous and slightly obnoxious replies to almost 50 posts before his fake account was shut down. One of Mr Melgaard's comments included a response to a negative post, which began 'I know this means little to Target, but I am tired of all this political correctness . . .' Mr Melgaard replied: 'Actually Gary, it means NOTHING to us that you feel this way. Have a great day!'

Target, when queried about the incident, offered a neutral statement that it is committed to customer

service for everyone and that Mr Melgaard clearly did not represent the company. A few days later, however, Target quietly endorsed Mr Melgaard's actions by posting a picture of two toy trolls on its Facebook page, captioned, 'Remember when trolls were the kings of the world? Woo hoo! They're back and only at Target stores.' The photo generated more than 30,000 likes. Mr Melgaard, under his own name this time, commented on the photo, saying: 'Target. Seriously You are AWESOME.' That comment alone generated more than 2,500 likes.

Sources: Colliander and Wien (2013); Nudd (2015a, 2015b).

Theory into Practice

As we have seen, social media has fundamentally changed marketing, the two key changes being shifts in power and control. The shift in power occurs because social media enables consumers to generate, share, and comment on content at their own discretion. What's more, such consumer-generated content is easily and widely shared, thereby shifting power from marketers to consumers. In terms of control, social media enables consumers to voice any concerns that they have with regard to a brand, its offering, and its marketing. This leaves little room for error. Taken together, this means that marketers have to adapt to a role as a 'host',

whose main purpose is not to control, but to facilitate conversations around the brand, regardless of whether what is being said is good or bad.

In Target's case, the shift in power and control is evident in the behaviours and comments of both Mr Melgaard and the consumers opposing the gender-neutral toy assortment. Target reacts to the conversation as a host, clarifying the different roles of consumers taking part. After discussion has gone silent, it also finds a way of rejuvenating it by subtly commenting on what happened.

Related Topics

digital marketing; social media marketing; co-creation; content marketing; customer service

1 **Visit Target's website. In your opinion, what segment does Target consider its main target audience? Among that audience, do you think Target benefited from Mr Melgaard's actions?**

2 **What do you make of Target's strategy to cope with the situation? Could it or should it have done something differently?**

3 **How do you think Target's decision to quietly endorse Mr Melgaard's actions affected this incident and its core business?**

This market insight was kindly contributed by Dr Jonas Colliander, Stockholm School of Economics, Sweden.

Thus the development of social media marketing is not only impacting on where managers spend their budgets, but also challenging how they communicate, share information, interact, and create (or produce) an offering. When anybody on the Internet can create, comment on, or share information about what companies, brands, organizations, or people do, what they represent, and how they work, those companies, brands, organizations, and people no longer have power or control over how they are perceived in the marketplace. Marketers increasingly have to find strategies to share such control, be it through the use of hashtags that help to co-create meaning around brands and campaigns, or by means of viral campaigns that consumers pass on and share with each other. Marketing activities related to social media are discussed further later in the chapter (see 'Social Media Marketing Communications' and 'Crowdsourcing').

Visit the **online resources** and complete Internet Activity 12.1 to learn more about how EY (formerly Ernst & Young) uses Twitter to maintain an ongoing real dialogue with its followers.

How Digitalization Is Transforming Marketing

The changing nature of the socio-technical environment means that many marketing executives must reconsider how brand management and marketing activities more generally need to change to suit the digital environment. Not only do digital channels operate differently from traditional ones, but also the consumer behaviours that they shape will affect behaviours in traditional media.

It is also important to remember that digital marketing does not exist in a silo, independent of other marketing principles (for example pricing, distribution, or customer service). Integrating digital marketing into marketing research (see Chapter 3), marketing communications plans (see Chapter 11), and channel distribution plans (see Chapter 12) requires detailed consideration if it is to be effective, not least because the digital environment is not simply another channel, but a channel in which consumers often behave differently. Therefore digital marketing should be considered more widely because digital media allows consumers to interact with other consumers, quite often outside the control of the organization around which they might be interacting.

Thus digital technology has the potential to transform marketing at its core. In fact, it is transforming business. According to a study by McKinsey & Co., companies that are integrating digital technology into their business perform significantly better financially than those that are not (Alldredge, Newaskar, and Ungerman, 2015). The same study identifies the following key characteristics for such digitally advanced companies:

■ *Strategy*—Ninety per cent of online leaders have digital initiatives fully integrated into their strategic planning process, not added as a bolt-on. They avoid getting bogged down in overplanning and instead focus on testing the viability of a market, product, or segment in near real time—through limited releases, small campaigns to compare markets, and prototyping with early adopters.

■ *Culture*—While 84 per cent of companies indicate that their culture is risk-averse, companies such as Amazon and Google embrace a different mentality. Instead of waiting for perfection, digital leaders adopt a fail–fast-forward mindset. They push a simple product into the market, gauge interest, collect customer feedback, and iterate. There is an emphasis on failing often and succeeding early.

Research Insight 12.1

To take your learning further, you might wish to read this influential paper:

Lamberton, C., and Stephen, A.T. (2016). A thematic exploration of digital, social media, and mobile marketing: research evolution from 2000 to 2015 and an agenda for future inquiry. *Journal of Marketing*, 80(6), 146–72.

This article provides an overview of the evolution of academic research on digital, social, and mobile marketing. More specifically, it tracks the changes in academic research perspectives over time and provides future research directions for the field.

 Visit the **online resources** to read the abstract and access the full paper.

- *Organization*—Leading companies use non-traditional organizational structures, digital talent acquisition, and management to execute their digital vision. Sixty-five per cent of digital leaders have an aggregated digital budget and sufficient budget allocation to scale their digital initiatives.

- *Capabilities*—Digital leaders make decisions based on data and build capabilities that connect people, processes, and technology across all channels that engage with consumers. Eighty per cent of digital leaders effectively invest in their digital information technology (IT) infrastructure to support growth. That means moving beyond model building to implementing processes that can mobilize relevant internal and external resources to take action quickly.

It is thus clear that mastering digital marketing is becoming vital to succeed in the contemporary marketplace, and that such mastery means integrating digital technology and media into all corporate activities. For clarity, we will continue this chapter by discussing digital *marketing communications*. However, it should be noted that, in practice, marketing activities related to understanding consumers (see Chapters 2 and 3) and satisfying their needs (see Chapter 14) are increasingly interrelated and, to fully reap the benefits of digital and social media marketing, they should be managed such that they reinforce each other. (See Research Insight 12.1 to learn more about the developments in research on digital, social media, and mobile marketing.)

Digital Marketing Communications

Investments in digital marketing communications are growing rapidly. Focus is primarily on communication using Internet-only technologies (for example web, email, intranet, extranet), which are accessed using desktops, laptops, mobile devices, and/or tablets, but different types of digital display and tracking device are also increasingly being used to market products and brands.

Not all digital marketing communications fit with a traditional definition of advertising as paid placements. Because consumers are actively searching for and sharing information on the Internet, marketers need to make sure that information is easily accessed and shared, meaning that the brand's own online channels and the potential of its content to be passed on is becoming increasingly important. Whereas traditional media are easily divided into formats based on the underlying logic, this is not the case for digital marketing communications. The borders between paid-for ('advertising') media, earned media ('publicity' and 'word of mouth'), and own media (for example websites, profiles on social media, emails) are blurry and hard to establish. For example, the IKEA films described in Market Insight 12.2 reached consumers in several ways: they were used in paid-for placements (for example display ads on newspaper websites), made shareable for newspapers, bloggers, and consumers to pass on to their readers or friends (for example on social media), and published on IKEA's own channels (for example website, YouTube channel). Typically, the different aspects of a digital marketing communication campaign are tightly linked and hard to disentangle.

Market Insight 12.2
Play It Forward

In November 2015, IKEA launched a new play collection named Lattjo, which includes a variety of games, musical instruments, and toys featuring new characters inspired by insects, roots, animals, and vegetation. The mission of the Lattjo collection is to encourage people, both young and old, to play more.

'We know that the world wants and needs more play. In our research we've seen that 50 per cent of all adults want to find their inner child, and that both children and parents want to play more together', says Maria Thörn, range manager at Children's IKEA.

This insight is based on thorough research. Overall, IKEA has conducted interviews with nearly 30,000 parents and children from 12 countries. The results clearly show that parents want to spend quality time with their children, but find it difficult to carve out playtime. Over half of the parents surveyed also said that play can include the use of smartphones, tablets, game consoles, and computers. Based on these concerns, the Lattjo collection was designed to remove barriers to play and to connect online and offline play.

With a long tradition of offering playful experiences for children in their stores, the Lattjo collection is the first effort to make Children's IKEA digital. In addition to the physical product, the collection includes a 'play

IKEA's Lattjo collection sets out to inspire young and old to play together
Source: Used with the permission of Inter IKEA Systems B.V.

together when apart' app. Through the app, children and adults can enjoy social play even if they are not physically in the same place. All the games depend on collaboration and togetherness: the more people play together, the more togetherness points they get.

The launch of the Lattjo collection was built around more than 25 animated short films, created by DreamWorks Studios. These animated stories celebrate and expand the imaginative worlds of the Lattjo characters in playful 2D and stop-motion

Market Insight 12.2
continued

animation. The video series utilizes DreamWorks Animation's storytelling expertise to bring the collection to life.

'Working with our world-class storytellers, this content series is a celebration of imagination and play that we hope surprises and delights viewers as they meet these characters in the coming months', said Brian Robinson, global head of creative design and development at DreamWorks Animation.

Sources: Budds (2015); Madov (2015); Miller (2015).

Theory into Practice

The growth of digital technologies is changing not only consumer behaviour, but also business itself. Successful marketing in a digital world requires digital marketing to be integrated into marketing research, as well as marketing communications and channels for distribution plans. However, digital marketing should be considered and adapted more widely than as only a new communication or distribution channel; rather, it can help to create new business opportunities and enable new relationships (and thereby insights) both with and between consumers.

The launch of Lattjo shows that IKEA has embraced digitization. The physical products are complemented by digital games that encourage social play around them (the app). A digital campaign built around carefully created films complements the in-store launch and all aspects of the launch are social.

Related Topics

digital marketing; social media marketing; content marketing; new product development

Visit IKEA's website and look for the Lattjo collection. Then visit IKEA's YouTube channel and watch the Lattjo films.

1 How has IKEA adapted its offering to an increasingly digital environment?

2 How has IKEA adapted its offering to an increasingly social environment?

3 What key learning do you think IKEA will take away from the Lattjo launch? How might it use this in developing other parts of the IKEA offering in the future?

We will now discuss some of the most frequently used digital marketing communications activities in more detail.

Internet Advertising Communications

Internet advertising refers to a form of marketing communication that uses the Internet for the purpose of advertising, regardless of what device is being used to access it. Typically, it involves marketers paying media owners to carry the marketers' messages on the owners' websites.

Payment is impression-based (for example cost-per-thousand, or CPM, pricing), performance-based (for example cost per click, sale, lead, acquisition, or application), or straight revenue share (for example percentage commission paid upon sale). The aim of Internet advertising is to increase website traffic and/or encourage product trial, purchase, and repeat purchase activity (Cheng et al., 2009), and ad format and payment should be adapted accordingly.

A list of different Internet ad formats and their definitions is given in Table 12.3.

Table 12.3 Types of Internet advertising format

Ad format	Description
Banner advertising	Advertiser pays an online company for space on one or more of the online company's pages to display a static or linked banner or logo.
Sponsorship	Advertiser pays for custom content and/or experiences, which may or may not include ad elements such as display advertising, brand logos, advertorial, or pre-roll video.
Search	Advertisers pay fees to online companies to list and/or link their company site domain name to a specific search word or phrase (includes paid search revenues). Search categories include paid listings, contextual search, paid inclusion, and site optimization.
Lead generation	Advertisers pay fees to online companies that refer qualified potential customers (e.g. auto dealers that pay a fee in exchange for receiving a qualified purchase inquiry online) or provide consumer information (demographic, contact, behavioural) where the consumer opts in to being contacted by a marketer (email, post, telephone, fax). These processes are priced on a performance basis (e.g. cost per action, lead, or enquiry), and can include user applications (e.g. for a credit card), surveys, contests (e.g. sweepstakes), or registrations.
Classifieds and auctions	Advertisers pay fees to online companies to list specific products or services (e.g. online job boards and employment listings, real estate listings, automotive listings, auction-based listings, Yellow Pages).
Rich media	Display-related ads that integrate some component of streaming interactivity. Rich media ads often include Flash or Java script, but not content, and can allow users to view and interact with products or services (e.g. scrolling or clicking within the ad opens a multimedia product description, expansion, animation, video, or 'virtual test-drive' within the ad).
Digital video advertising	Advertising that appears before, during, or after digital video content in a video player (i.e. pre-roll, mid-roll, or post-roll video ads). Digital video ads include TV commercials online and can appear in streaming content or in downloadable video. Display-related ads on a page (not in a player) that contains video are categorized as rich media ads.

> **Table 12.3 continued**
>
> | Ad format | Description |
> | --- | --- |
> | Mobile advertising | Advertising tailored to and delivered through wireless mobile devices such as smartphones, feature phones (e.g. lower-end mobile phones capable of accessing mobile content), and media tablets. Typically taking the form of static or rich media display ads, text messaging ads, search ads, or audio/video spots, such advertising generally appears within mobile websites (e.g. websites optimized for viewing on mobile devices); mobile apps; text messaging services (i.e. SMS, MMS); or mobile search results (i.e. 411 listings, directories, mobile-optimized search engines).

 Mobile advertising formats include search; display (banner ads, digital video, digital audio, sponsorships, and rich media); and other advertising served to mobile devices. |
> | Digital audio | Refers to partially or entirely advertising supported audio programming available to consumers on a streaming basis, delivered via the wired and mobile Internet. |
> | Social media advertising | Advertising delivered on social platforms, including social networking and social gaming websites and apps, across all device types, including desktop, laptop, smartphone, and tablet. |
> | Email | Banner ads, links, or advertiser sponsorships that appear in email newsletters, email marketing campaigns, and other commercial email communications. This includes both ads within an email or the entire email itself. |
>
> *Source*: IAB/PwC (2017).

Major considerations when using Internet advertising include the following:

- *Cost*—Internet adverts are still relatively cheap compared with traditional advertising.

- *Timeliness*—Internet adverts can be updated at any time with minimal cost.

- *Format*—Internet adverts are richer, using text, audio, graphics, and animation. In addition, games, entertainment, and promotions can be incorporated.

- *Personalization*—Internet adverts can be interactive and targeted to specific interest groups and/or individuals.

- *Location-based*—By using wireless technology and geo-location technology (such as the Global Positioning System, or GPS), Internet advertising can be targeted to consumers wherever they are (for example near a restaurant or theatre).

- *Intrusive*—Some Internet advertising formats (for example pop-ups) are seen as intrusive and suffer more consumer complaints than other formats.

Recent developments in Internet advertising focus on programmatic buying, in which advertising is planned, analysed, and optimized via demand-side software interfaces and algorithms.

Recently, there has also been a lot of controversy with regard to online advertising. First, reports of exposure to online advertising have been found to have been inflated. This is as a result of the automated systems used to account for exposure not being able to distinguish actual viewers from automated viewers ('bot traffic'). It is estimated that advertisers will have lost the equivalent of over US$50 million per day in 2018 and that this figure will continue to rise (Greiner, 2017). Second, the use of ad-blocking software (that is, software that blocks advertising content from appearing on websites) is growing rapidly. In 2017, estimates were that 30.1 per cent of the US Internet users were equipped with ad-blockers (Anon., 2017). (See Market Insight 12.3 to learn more about the challenges of measuring online advertising.)

Market Insight 12.3
What's in a Click?

Marketing departments are increasingly using the many opportunities of digital media to measure marketing impact—but the fact that something can be measured does not mean that it is a relevant figure that can tell us something useful. An example of one such metric is click-through rate (CTR), which is the ratio of number of clicks per visitor.

In the early days of the Internet, the CTR was quite high on average, because consumers were curious about digital ads. Measuring CTR gained ground as a result of the fact that it is a universal measure with a clear standard that can easily be measured, communicated, and understood, as well as being a measure closely linked to purchase. At the same time, many companies, such as Google, profited from the CTR metric and hence promoted it even more.

Unfortunately, the CTR does not measure the average effect on the target audience resulting from ad exposure. It has also been shown that many clicks are, in fact, mistakes. Findings also show that who clicks on the ad is not proportionate across all visitors of the site: visitors who click tend in general to be younger and have below-average incomes.

In contrast to what many people believe, it will still be necessary to collect the classic brand-equity metrics, even in a time in which we can measure behaviour online. In fact, by 2003, research had already shown that clicks were a bad measure of the effectiveness of a banner because of difficulties in attribution—that is, knowing what exposure has led to what outcome. Often, there is a long time delay between exposure and actual behaviour. The connection between the classic brand equity measurements and CTR has actually been shown to be very low—sometimes even negative. Thus, many times, these digital metrics must be complemented with a survey if a marketer is to see the full result of the exposure.

Even when only behavioural variables can be collected, for example when no survey can be distributed, there are better metrics to focus on than CTR. For example, industry data shows that the correlation between CTR and actual conversion is 0.01 (an extremely low correlation, since the scale stretches from 0 to 1), whereas the correlation between **mouse-over** and actual conversion is 0.49 (a much higher level of correlation).

When only including directly behavioural measures, the brand runs the risk of focusing too much on actions that are very close to a purchase, forgetting the importance of long-term branding.

Sources: Drèze and Hussherr (2003); Modig and Söndergaard (2018).

Theory into Practice

A key facet of digital platforms is measurability. However, it is important to keep in mind that the measures being used are connected to the objectives of the marketing campaign. Accurate measures that match marketing objectives are key to an accurate understanding of what the effects of a campaign actually are.

Market Insight 12.3
continued

Related Topics

digital marketing; search marketing; consumer information search

1 **Consider the different marketing communication objectives discussed in Chapter 10. Which objectives would you say could be accurately assessed in terms of CTR?**

2 **Google provides benchmarks for CTR in different industries. Search to find the latest benchmarks for CTR in display and search advertising.**

3 **Why do you think CTR is typically higher for search advertising compared to display advertising?**

4 **CTR varies somewhat between industries. How and why do you think this is?**

This market insight was kindly contributed by Dr Erik Modig and Martin Söndergaard, Stockholm School of Economics, Sweden.

 Visit the **online resources** and follow the web link to the Interactive Advertising Bureau (IAB) to learn more about developments and standards for Internet advertising activities (including those relating to programmatic buying, bot traffic, and ad blocking).

Search Marketing Communications

The growth in digital content available through the Internet has given rise to a number of interactive decision aids used to help users to locate data, information, and/or an organization's digital objects (for example pictures, videos). The main two types of decision aid are a **search directory** (that is, a web directory) and a **search engine**, but increasingly voice services such as Apple's Siri or Amazon's Alexa are moving into this field (DeMers, 2017).

A search directory is a human-edited database of information. It lists websites by category and subcategory, with categorization usually based on the whole website, rather than one page or a set of keywords. Search directories often allow site owners to submit their site directly for inclusion and editors review submissions for fitness. Given its large scope, Amazon could also be considered to offer a search directory for shopping.

In contrast, a search engine operates algorithmically, or uses a mixture of algorithmic and human input, to collect, index, store, and retrieve information on the web (for example, web pages, images, information, and other types of files), making this information available to users in a manageable and meaningful way in response to a search query. Information is retrieved by a web crawler (also known as a spider), which is an automated web browser that follows every link on the site, analysing how it should be indexed using words extracted from page and file titles, headings, or special fields called meta tags. The indexed data are then stored in an index database for use in later queries. When a user enters a query into a search engine (typically using keywords), the engine examines its index and provides a listing of the best-matching web pages, according to its criteria, on search engine result pages (SERPs). There are only a few dominant search engines in the market, Google leading the global market share rankings with

87.1 per cent, followed by Bing (5.8 per cent), Yahoo! (3.0 per cent), and Chinese Baidu (0.9 per cent) (Statista, 2017).

Search engines have evolved significantly over the years. Whereas searches in the early years of the Internet focused on keywords, today's semantic analysis ensures that they also take into account previous search behaviour and knowledge about the context in which the search is being made (for example when, where, how, and who). An example of contextual adaption is local searches, whereby search results are adapted to the location in which the search is undertaken.

Given its central role in consumer online behaviour, it is not surprising that search is central to most digital marketing strategies. In 2016, 48 per cent of all Internet advertising investments were in search, with about half of the investments going to desktop and half to mobile search (IAB/PwC, 2017). Search—often referred to as search engine marketing (SEM)—is one of the main forms of Internet advertising. Its aim is to promote websites by increasing their visibility in SERPs. Methods include paid listings, contextual search, **paid inclusion**, and search optimization:

■ *Paid listings*, or **pay per click (PPC)**, refers to payments made for clicks on text links that appear at the top or side of search results for specific keywords. The more a marketer pays, the higher the position it gets. Marketers pay only when a user clicks on the text link. Paid listings typically mean that the advertisers bid on keywords or phrases relevant to their target market in return for sponsored or paid search engine listings to drive traffic to a website. The search engine ranks ads on the basis of a competitive auction and other related criteria (for example popularity, quality). Google AdWords, Yahoo! Search Marketing, and Bing Ads are the three largest ad-network operators, with all three operating under a bid-based model.

■ *Contextual search* is a form of targeted advertising, with advertisements (for example banners, pop-ups) appearing on websites. The advertisements themselves are selected and served by automated systems based on the content displayed to the user. A **contextual advertising** system scans the text of a website for keywords and returns advertisements to the web page based on what the user is viewing. Google AdSense was the first major contextual advertising program. Payments are typically made for only clicks on text links that appear in an article based on the context of the content rather than a user-submitted keyword.

■ *Paid inclusion* occurs when a search engine company charges fees related to inclusion of websites in its search index. Some organizations mix paid inclusion with organic listings (for example Yahoo!), whereas others do not allow paid inclusion to be listed within organic lists (for example Google and Ask.com). Payments are made to guarantee that a marketer's URL is indexed by a search engine (that is, it is not paid only for clicks, as in paid listings).

■ *Site optimization* occurs when a website's structure and content is improved to maximize its listing in organic search engine results pages using relevant keywords or search phrases. Payments are made to optimize a site to improve the site's ranking in SERPs. Increasingly, there is recognition that search engine optimization (SEO) and social media are interlinked. By gaining a massive amount of social shares, you're not only boosting your SEO signals and your site visibility, but also creating content with value for your customer base.

All of these search marketing methods allow marketers to match users with content according to their interests. Search engines and directories take a different approach, but one thing unites them: search marketing is one of the most cost-effective methods of digital marketing. However, although search is still by far the largest online ad format, it is declining slightly in importance as digital marketers look increasingly to shift budget into mobile and social channels. (To learn more about Amazon's investment in becoming a leading search engine for online shopping, see Market Insight 12.4.)

Market Insight 12.4
Searching the Amazon

Search is a key behaviour online and Google is the go-to place for search—or is it? In 2015, 44 per cent of US consumers stated that they head directly to Amazon when searching for products, up from 30 per cent in 2012. In comparison, 34 per cent go straight to a search engine such as Google, Yahoo, and Bing.

Whereas Google has done its part in making product discovery and search intuitive, convenient, and seamless, Amazon now seems ready to step in and take over. Almost half of US consumers bypass search engines and other websites in favour of Amazon when on a shopping mission. This means that the search bar is increasingly becoming a key asset in Amazon's user experience.

Enabling search not only allows consumers to find the products they are looking for, but also enables Amazon to collect valuable data on consumer searches and relate that data to actual sales. On-site search queries are clear expressions of user intent. Coupled with reviews from the millions of Amazon customers who have left appraisals on the website, the data is invaluable, and Amazon continually leverages it to intelligently promote products across its website.

Amazon's advanced algorithmic recommendation capability accurately predicts intent and suggests products better than any other website. Now, Amazon is using its shopping pattern data to get advantages offline as well. In November 2015, Amazon opened its first

bricks-and-mortar bookstore in Seattle, Washington. Seattle was chosen as the company's first physical bookstore because it is close to Amazon's headquarters and because Seattle is a top market for readers.

The assortment in Amazon's physical store has been selected using data on online shopping patterns
Source: © SEA STOCK/Shutterstock.com

In opening a bookstore, Amazon is betting that the vast store of data it generates from shopping patterns on its website will give it advantages in its retail location that other bookstores cannot match and that using this data to pick titles that will most appeal to Seattle shoppers will allow Amazon to succeed where others have not.

Sources: Greene (2015); Leggatt (2015); B. Johnson (2015).

Theory into Practice

The vast amount of digital content available through the Internet has given rise to a number of interactive decision aids used to help web users to find what they are looking for. The main two decision aids are search directories (web directories) and search engines. Increasingly, search results are adapting semantic

analysis whereby they take into account contextual factors (for example who is searching, for what, at what time, and using what device) to come up with relevant results. Alongside search giant Google, retailers such as Amazon are also working hard to facilitate search and to monetize the data that it generates.

Market Insight 12.4
continued

Related Topics

digital marketing; search marketing; retailing; marketing channels

Visit Amazon's website and search for a product you are interested in.

1 What options for finding the product do you have? How useful is the directory? How useful is the search engine?

2 What type of contextual information does Amazon seem to use to guide the results that are presented?

3 How do the search results you get on Amazon differ from what you would get using Google, Bing, or Yahoo!?

Email Marketing Communications

Email is one of the most frequently used digital marketing tools. Given that companies themselves run many email marketing activities, based on customer relationship management (CRM) systems and mailing lists, the lead-generation category listed in Table 12.3 covers only parts of all email marketing activities.

Email, when used properly, goes beyond simply sending a sales message; it also helps to create trust, retain customers, build customer referrals, and generate revenues. What's more, email marketing tends to be appreciated by consumers. For example, 63 per cent of UK office workers reported that they preferred to receive brand communications this way compared with 6 per cent preferring to be reached by social media and 5 per cent, by a mobile app (Anon., 2015).

Importantly, with email marketing, the communicator sends the message only to those who have agreed to receive messages. Such permission-based email marketing is a highly cost-effective form of digital marketing (Cheng et al., 2009). As a marketing tool, it is easy to use and costs little to send. However, costs can be higher when personalizing messages and where a database must be developed or purchased. Nevertheless, email can reach millions of willing prospects within minutes. Unsolicited emails, which clog email servers and use up much-needed Internet bandwidth, are referred to as **spam**.

In designing a successful email campaign, marketers need to think carefully about the target audience and their willingness to receive emails. Under European legislation, list members must have clearly opted in to receiving such emails and they must be offered the opportunity to opt out (that is, unsubscribe) each time they receive an email. It will be good practice to allow list members to choose what type of email offerings they are interested in receiving (for example newsletters, discount offers, and specific updates), and, as far as possible, emails should be personalized. Using an email system that allows tracking and reporting on all elements of the campaign (including opens, clicks, pass along, unsubscribe, and bounce-backs) allows marketers to closely test and monitor different email marketing strategies in terms of when and how often to send them, as well as what to offer, what to write, and what to highlight. The insights gained from such data-mining exercises can be invaluable. For example, a large-scale study of more than 1 billion emails over a two-year period showed that people are 38 per cent more likely to click and 47 per cent more likely to convert when they are presented with an offer of a percentage discount rather than a cash discount (O'Brien, 2015). According to the same study, short subject lines (of 6–10 words), visual and personalized messages, and clear calls to action are key to a successful email marketing communication.

Social Media Marketing Communications

Social media marketing describes the use of the social web and social media (for example social networks, online communities, blogs, wikis) or any online collaborative technology for marketing activities (for example sales, public relations, research, distribution, customer service). Social media marketing includes both the creation and curation of corporate or brand profiles and content on social media and advertising. Social media advertising (SMA) refers to advertising delivered on social platforms, including social networking and social gaming websites and apps, across all device types.

Marketers are increasingly investing in social networks (for example Facebook, LinkedIn, QQ in China); video-sharing sites (for example YouTube); image-sharing sites (Flickr, Pinterest); blogging platforms (WordPress); and microblogs (Twitter) for marketing purposes. According to the 2018 Chief Marketing Officer (CMO) survey, 12.1 per cent of marketing budgets are invested in social media and this share is expected to grow to 20.5 per cent in the next five years (Moorman, 2018). The same survey also shows that the top reasons for using social media is to raise brand awareness and brand building (45 per cent), followed by customer acquisition (33 per cent).

It is important to keep in mind that social media come in many different variations and that social media marketing strategies need to be adjusted to the type of consumer engagement taking place on the specific platform being used (Voorveld et al., 2018). The social web does not make conversations happen; it simply supports them. By understanding how social media supports conversations, businesses can open up interactions with individuals and communities. For example, companies respond to customer care queries and concerns using Twitter and Facebook, share brand-related behind-the-scenes imagery on Instagram and Pinterest, and promote time-limited offers on Snapchat (see Research Insight 12.2). Mangold and Faulds (2009) outlined some examples of marketing activities that can stimulate conversations, including:

- networking platforms, such as Sephora's Beauty Insiders, Nike +;

- blogs and social media tools to engage customers—because customers like to give feedback on a broad range of issues (see 'Content Marketing Communications');

- using both Internet and traditional promotional tools to engage customers;

- supplying information on, for example, correct or alternative product usage;

- offering exclusivity—because people like to feel special;

- designing offerings from the perspective of consumers' desired self-images and with talking points to make advocacy easier, for example US budget airline JetBlue's offer of leather seats and televisions to its customers;

- demonstrating support for causes that people value; and

- creating memorable stories.

Research Insight 12.2

To take your learning further, you might wish to read this influential paper:

Voorveld, H., van Noor, G., Muntiga, D.G., and Bronner, F. (2018). Engagement with social media and social media advertising: the differentiating role of platform type. *Journal of Advertising*, 47(1), 38–54.

This article examines how consumers' engagement with social media platforms drives engagement with advertising embedded in these platforms. The findings show that engagement is highly context-specific, suggesting that social media advertising will have to be adapted to the specifics of the platform being used. In fact, the authors argue that there is no such thing as 'social media' advertising.

 Visit the online resources to read the abstract and access the full paper.

One example of the last—creating memorable stories—is UK food and beverage company inno-cent, which outlines the story of the foundation of the firm on its website. The story has it that three friends set up a stall to sell smoothies at a London music festival. A sign above the stall read, 'Should we give up our jobs to make these smoothies?', and people were asked to throw their empties into one of two bins marked either 'Yes' or 'No'. Needless to say, 'Yes' won.

Paid media placements online and offline have been found to be important for getting conversations going (Niederhoffer et al., 2007; Keller and Fay, 2012). The UK is estimated to be the largest market in Europe for social media advertising, with total investments reaching approximately US$1.7 billion in 2016; with $475 million and $427 million, respectively, Germany and France rank second and third (Statista, 2018b).

The options available for social media advertising differ between different social media platforms. They are also constantly changing.

 Visit the **online resources** and undertake Internet Activity 12.2 around advertising options on different social media platforms.

Evaluating Social Media Marketing Communications

Although marketers agree that social media marketing is a key to success in the contemporary marketplace, many marketers are still struggling in terms of how to evaluate these activities. Estimates show that only around 20–25 per cent of CMOs feel that they are able to prove the impact of social media investments quantitatively and as many as 30–40 per cent are still unable show the impact of their investments (Moorman, 2018). This clearly shows that engaging in social communities provides several opportunities for marketers, but it can also be a challenge.

Because social media is increasingly used as part of the marketing manager's planning (for both communications and research), there is an increasing need to understand whether what marketers are doing in social media is working or not. Web activity is amazingly measurable, because web users leave traces of their presence and activity on the various sites they visit.

However, the process of measuring social media effectiveness requires a systematic approach. Based on interviews with experiences social media marketers, Keegan and Rowley (2017) suggest the following framework for evaluating social media:

1 Start out by setting campaign objectives. This means identifying specific and clear evaluation objectives that are aligned with marketing objectives and overall business goals.

2 Identify key performance indicators (KPIs) that fit with the objectives set. This step involves identifying the most appropriate performance indicators that fit with the overall campaign objectives set in step 1.

3 Identify metrics to be used to assess the selected KPIs. Table 12.4 lists commonly used social media measures that are typically easily available to marketers and which can be used to assess the success of the campaign. Which one(s) you should use depends on the conclusions you drew in steps 1 and 2.

Table 12.4 **Common social media measures used by marketers**

Measure

Hits/visits/page views

Number of followers and friends

Repeat visits

Conversion rates (from visitor to buyer)

Buzz indicators (mentions, shares)

Sales levels

Online products/service ratings

Customer acquisition costs

Net promoter score

Revenue per customer

Text analysis ratings

Customer retention costs

Abandoned shopping carts

Profits per customer

Source: Moorman (2014).

4 Collect and monitor the previously identified metrics and KPIs from relevant social media channels. Here, there is typically room to monitor and make adjustments in the execution of the campaign in real time.

5 Report results. This step includes compilation of the KPIs and metrics into a presentable format in which the overall campaign performance is assessed. Often, benchmarks are needed, in terms of previous performance or industry standards in terms of KPIs, to allow the marketer to draw conclusions.

6 Make a decision based on the insights gained. Based on the report, the performance of the campaign can be assessed and conclusions for future iterations or campaigns can be drawn. This also makes it possible to ascertain what changes are necessary to meet the benchmark targets or if benchmarks should be updated.

This framework can be applied either to social media campaigns run for limited time or to more continuous social media efforts (such as a Facebook page, Instagram account, or YouTube channel) and evaluations can be made on daily, weekly, monthly, and/or quarterly basis.

Content Marketing Communications

Content marketing is an approach to marketing communication in which brands create and disseminate content to consumers with the intention that the content will generate interest, engage consumers, and influence behaviour (Stephen, Sciandra, and Inman, 2015). Although branded content has been around for more than 100 years (with one of the pioneering examples being the *Guide Michelin*, which included restaurant recommendations to get French car owners to drive more and thus increase their need for Michelin tyres), this marketing activity has accelerated in the digital space.

Most of the digital marketing communication activities discussed so far rely on consumers actively deciding to take part in marketing. For example, search marketing requires consumers to actively click on a link and social media marketing relies on consumers actively engaging (liking, sharing, co-creating) content created by brands. This means that brands are under increasing pressure to create online content that consumers value; hence marketers are paying increasing attention to creating online content that can benefit their target audiences, and they are doing so by adapting traditional journalism and publishing techniques. These activities are often referred to as content marketing. Although the appropriate definition of content marketing is debated (Neff, 2015), there is little doubt that these practices are important for marketers. Global content marketing investments reached US$212.2 billion in 2016 (PQ Media, 2017). In addition, strategies to direct the target audience towards the content need to be in place—most commonly, via search marketing, promotions, and advertising. Whereas content marketing investments have traditionally been more common in business-to-business (B2B) marketing, growth rates in consumer marketing are expected to be higher than in B2B, making the share of investments between the two perfectly balanced by 2019 (PQ Media, 2017).

The intention of content marketing is to create content that has value for the receiver (for example by being useful, educational, or entertaining in and of itself), thereby pulling the consumer toward the brand (see Research Insight 12.3). There are numerous ways of creating such value. Whereas consumer content marketing typically has focused on entertainment and information, and B2B on knowledge and competence (for an overview of the most commonly

Research Insight 12.3

To take your learning further, you might wish to read this influential paper:

Rosengren, S., and Dahlén, M. (2015). Exploring advertising equity: how a brand's past advertising may affect consumer willingness to approach its future ads. *Journal of Advertising*, 44(1), 1–13.

This article investigates what drives consumer's willingness to pay attention to advertising. Based on empirical studies of more than 1,700 consumers and 100 brands across more than 12 different product categories, it shows how adding value in advertising is vital to succeeding in digital environments in which consumers are increasingly in charge of their own media consumption.

 Visit the online resources to read the abstract and access the full paper.

Table 12.5 Top B2B content marketing tactics 2015

Rank	Tactic	Use
1	Social media post	95%
2	Case studies	77%
3	Videos	72%
4	E-books/White Papers	71%
5	Infographics	65%

Source: Murton Beets and Handley (2018).

---

used content marketing tactics among B2B firms, see Table 12.5), these borders are blurring. For example, Volvo Trucks, which offers heavy-duty trucks to a professional audience, has been very successful in a content-centred campaign focusing on entertaining and spectacular online videos (see Market Insight 11.1 in Chapter 11), while Red Bull has transformed its content operations into a fully fledged media house (Red Bull Media House) specializing in high-quality coverage of extreme sports. Thus there is plenty of opportunity to provide value—sometimes referred to as 'advertising equity' (Rosengren and Dahlén, 2015)—in a way that can be mutually beneficial for the brand and the receiver.

Successful content marketing depends on a marketer being able to balance the needs of the brand and the needs of the receiver. Typically, this requires taking contextual aspects, such as the timing and the place (for example social media or paid platform), of the communication into account. For example, research shows that, for social media branded content to be influential in persuading consumers to engage in desirable ways (for example by clicking a link or spreading word of mouth), marketers must design content that is *not* highly persuasion-oriented. What's more, the social media content needs to be adapted to consumer behaviour on the platform being used. For example, on Facebook, the most successful content is relevant to the brand, but does not have an ad-like tone or a clear message; hence this content should not use 'hard sell', or even 'soft sell', but rather open space up in which consumers can make sense of the content themselves. This is particularly important when the audience comprises mostly core consumers, since they are somewhat less forgiving of, and more sensitive to, pushy messages (Stephen et al., 2015).

Mobile Marketing Communications

Mobile marketing refers the set of practices that enables organizations to communicate and engage interactively with their audiences by means of any mobile device or network (MMA, 2009). With the added benefits of store-and-send technology giving the option of message storage, mobile marketing is quick and inexpensive, and reaches markets wherever they are, despite limitations in message content.

In 2016, mobile marketing accounted for more than half of all Internet advertising revenues in the United States (IAB/PwC, 2017). According to the 2018 CMO survey, marketers invested 7 per cent of their marketing budgets in media in 2017 and expected this share to grow to 13.5 per cent in the following three years (Moorman, 2018). Investments in mobile are through both paid-for media (mobile advertising) and the development of own media, such as apps. Mobile is the fastest growing digital medium. In 2011–16, the compound average growth rate for mobile advertising in the United States has been 16 per cent (IAB/PwC, 2017). Similar growth rates can be found in Europe.

Just as with traditional online advertising, mobile advertising relies on several different ad formats, with display and search advertising being the largest (see Table 12.6). The growth of mobile marketing is driven by consumer adaption of smartphones. Increasingly, we can access digital technologies, share information, socialize online, and play games on the move. The number of mobile Internet users has grown exponentially as the wireless infrastructure and mobile devices required to support the mobile Internet have evolved. As an illustration, Swedish smartphone penetration has grown from 27 per cent in 2011 to 85 per cent in 2017 (Statista, 2018c).

Current changes in behaviours clearly show that mobile is taking over more and more of consumer online searches, and that marketers need to consider how to stay relevant and accessible at different stages in the consumer decision process. Increasingly, the use of smartphone apps is becoming the default mechanism for such searches. These apps use a combination of barcode scanning and location-based services to provide relevant information, for example showing only stores near the consumer when they are carrying out a price comparison. Thus these apps are suited to delivering context-specific, and hence more relevant, information to consumers. Mobile search also enables the convergence of online and offline, for example by enabling barcode scanning. From a consumer perspective, app usability depends on five factors—that

Ad format	Description	Share of mobile ad investments*
Display	Banner ads, digital video, digital audio, sponsorships, and rich media advertising served to mobile devices	38%
Search	Advertisers pay fees to online companies to list and/or link their company site domain name to a specific search word or phrase (includes paid search revenues)	47%
	Search categories include: paid listings; contextual search; paid inclusion; site optimization	
Video	N/A	11%
Other formats	N/A	4%

Table 12.6 **Types of mobile advertising format**

* Based on US ad spend in 2016.
Source: IAB/PwC (2017).

is, user-friendliness, personalization, speed, fun, and omnipresence (the ability to be used anywhere) (Baek and Yoo, 2018).

Depending on factors such as context, product category, user experience, and availability of (other) information, consumers' mobile search behaviours focus on different types of information. Daurer and colleagues (2015) investigated consumer searches via an app that enables product searches based on barcodes. The results show that access to more types of information—especially product-related information—reduces search on price information. This suggests that availability of information content can lower price-sensitivity in mobile search. They also found that mobile search does not necessarily occur at the point of purchase; consumers carry out mobile search in many situations other than shopping (for example while consuming the product), suggesting that companies need to adapt their marketing beyond the point of purchase. In addition, geographic travel (mobility); the availability of specific types of product information; and contextual factors (for example economic surroundings, competition, and weather) influence search intensity.

Location-based marketing has long been expected to be the next big thing in mobile advertising. However, adaptation has been slow and location-based marketing still makes up just a small part of total mobile investments. In part, this may be explained by technological problems that result in location-based assessments having low accuracy. Thus location-based marketing is expected to pick up pace in the next few years as the accuracy of mobile technologies improves (L. Johnson, 2015) (see Market Insight 12.5).

Consumers are increasingly searching for information about products through various digital platforms and devices—but is this the case for all products?

Market Insight 12.5
The World in Your Pocket

Smartphones have dramatically changed the way in which people interact with each other and marketers. Mobile devices provide consumers with entertainment and functionality anywhere at any time. For marketers, these devices offer vast opportunities to interact, but technology sometimes tends to lead us astray. In 2018, hot topics for mobile marketers included the Internet of Things (IoT), chatbots, intelligent agents (IAs), and artificial intelligence (AI), all of which are expected to take mobile to the next level. Top mobile marketers include the British Broadcasting Corporation (BBC), for its *Dr Who* campaign, and Gordon's Gin, which used location tagging and a National Rail application programming interface (API) to offer delayed rail passengers a gin and tonic.

However, there might be room for caution. Forrester, a leading research and advisory firm specializing in business and technology, reports that marketers need to first master the basics of mobile before homing in on new technologies. They conclude that marketers often (wrongly) think that, having developed mobile apps and responsive websites, they can move on to exciting new technologies. In a study, Forrester found that 53 per cent of the surveyed marketers are still not using mobile to transform their overall customer experience and hence are not getting the full potential of mobile. To change this, Forrester recommends that marketers involve top management in crafting a mobile strategy.

Sources: Kurzer (2018); Digital Marketing Institute (n.d.).

Theory into Practice

Mobile marketing is rapidly becoming core in digital marketing. The smartphone enables links between digital and physical environments and, as such, it has great potential as a tool to integrate customer experience between channels. Still, technologies and possibilities need to be aligned with consumers' behaviours and needs if they are to fulfil this potential.

Related Topics

digital marketing; consumer behaviours, customer experience, technology adaptation

1 **What innovative technologies used by marketers have you encountered on your smartphone?**

2 **To what extent do you use your smartphone in making purchase decisions?**

3 **How does your use of smartphone vary depending on whether you are considering purchasing groceries, fashion, or insurance?**

Visit the **online resources** and undertake Internet Activity 12.3 to find out more about online and offline search.

Crowdsourcing

The previous discussion has concerned social media, technologies, and marketing, and how marketing is increasingly being co-created with consumers; we will now consider how marketers make use of social media to interact and co-create with communities through the technique of crowdsourcing. Crowdsourcing is used increasingly in marketing and can be defined as follows:

> Crowdsourcing represents the act of a company or institution taking a function once performed by employees and outsourcing it to an undefined (and generally large) network of people in the form of an open call. This can take the form of peer-production (when the job is performed collaboratively), but is also often undertaken by sole individuals. The crucial prerequisite is the use of the open call format and the large network of potential labourers.

> (Howe, 2006: 5)

Crowdsourcing can be used in marketing in different ways, with different requirements for the role of the crowd, the end goal, how the crowd is remunerated, and the size and diversity of the crowd necessary for the task. However, it is probably most helpful to think of it as used in four main categories: for routine activities; for content; for creative activities; and for funding (see Table 12.7).

Table 12.7 Forms of crowdsourcing (CS)

Consideration	CS of routine activities	CS of content	CS of creative activities	CS of funds
Role of the crowd	Provision of time; ability to process information	Provision of content (especially information)	Provision of solutions, ideas, and knowledge	Provision of monetary resources
Goal	Division of labour (integrative)	Division of labour (integrative)	Winner takes all (selective)	Raise money
Remuneration	Micropayments	Micropayments or volunteer	Micro- to high payments	Equity/loan/ reward
Size of the crowd	Very important	Very important	Of little importance	Very important
Diversity of the crowd	Not important	Very important	Very important	Not important
Commercial examples	reCAPTCHA	iStockphoto; openstreetmap	InnoCentive; Wilogo	FundedByMe

Source: Adapted from Burger-Helmchen and Pénin (2011).

One example of the crowdsourcing of *routine activities* was in the development of reCAPT-CHA—CAPTCHA derived from 'Completely Automated Public Turing test to tell Computers and Humans Apart'. The initiative for this was to digitize books by supplying websites with CAPTCHA protection from bots attempting to access restricted sites. The CAPTCHA test requires users to retype images of words not recognized by optical character recognition (OCR) machines and, in so doing, it helps to digitize books scanned into the Internet archive and the archives of the *New York Times*.

iStockphoto and openstreetmap are good examples of companies that crowdsourced *content*.

Companies that have used crowdsourcing for *creative activities* include InnoCentive and Wilogo, which use crowdsourcing mechanisms for research and development (R&D) projects and to produce logo designs, respectively.

When it comes to crowdsourced *funding*—that is, crowdfunding—there are several different websites offering this opportunity. According to a recent report from one of them, the success of crowdfunding campaigns is highly contingent on social media sharing, as well as the accuracy and reliability of market assessments and financial forecasts (Lundquist and Gromek, 2015).

Crowdsourcing is becoming increasingly ubiquitous in marketing as organizations seek to use it to reduce their marketing costs, reduce the time required to undertake a particular task, find and use resources (skills, labour, money) that do not exist in-house, obtain information and market intelligence, design new products and services, and design promotional material. One of the key considerations when setting up a crowdsourcing task is how to motivate the crowd to take part. One common rule of thumb suggests that 90 per cent of visitors to the site will consume the content (see the task); 9 per cent will partially engage (read the task, consider taking part or request further information); and 1 per cent will fully engage (for example provide a submission). Table 12.8 cites some examples of early users of crowdsourcing in marketing.

Legal and Ethical Considerations

The rise in digital resources, and their increasing use for marketing activities, is accompanied by complications and changes to legislation and regulated business practices. The legal, ethical, and regulatory issues that marketers need to consider include the following:

- *Jurisdiction*—Where does digital marketing activity take place? Commercial law is based on transactions within national boundaries, but digital marketing exposes both individual organizations and the community to information, transactions, and social activity outside these boundaries.

- *Ownership*—Who owns the content we create and share? Copyright law is a national issue and copyright law (what can and cannot be used without the originator's permission) differs from one country to another. Some countries do not have copyright or intellectual property protection, and so ideas, designs, etc. sent to those countries can be taken and used without the agreement of the copyright holder. The value of copyright is also being questioned with the increase in user-generated and **co-created content**, as well as the rise of the Creative Commons (CC) free licence system.

Table 12.8 Pioneer and early users of crowdsourcing

Organization	Date of first use	Details
Threadless	2000	Began selling T-shirts with designs developed and rated by its user community, instead of expensive designers, in an ongoing competition process. Winning designers received US$2,000 prize money and a $500 voucher to spend at Threadless. Submitters of winning slogans received $500 prize money.
iStockphoto	2000	Sells royalty-free stock images, media, and design elements using material sourced online from a crowd of largely amateur artists, designers, and photographers. Contributors receive a percentage of the purchase price when their images are downloaded. A smaller group of contributors screen new applicants and maintain the image database, earning a higher percentage from work downloaded.
InnoCentive	2001	Began life as a spin-off company from US pharmaceutical giant Eli Lilly. InnoCentive works by posting online research and development (R&D) and scientific challenges for its crowd of users to solve. Winning contributors are paid a large financial incentive and InnoCentive takes a fee for hosting the challenge.
LEGO®	2012	Developed its product innovation platform LEGO® Cuusoo, released initially in beta version, to invite users to submit LEGO product ideas and get them rated by other users. Any idea that receives 10,000 votes is considered by the LEGO product review board for production. If a user's LEGO idea is chosen, the submitting user receives a 1 per cent royalty on total net sales of that product. Initial ideas receiving more than 10,000 votes have included the Exo Suit and the *Back to the Future*™ Time Machine (Kronsberg, 2012).
Flippin' Burgers	2012	This gourmet hamburger restaurant in Stockholm, Sweden, has not only been ranked the greatest burger restaurant outside America (Santana, 2014), but also has crowdfunding to thank for its existence. Before it opened, Flippin' Burgers was launched on the crowdfunding site fundedbyme.se to test demand and to gather capital. In two months, 178 people donated a combined total of SEK36,000 based on a promise that they would, at some time in the future, be able to try a hamburger that didn't yet exist from a restaurant that didn't yet exist.
Volvo Cars	2015	Instead of buying expensive ad time during the US Superbowl, Volvo decided to hijack the car brands that did. To this end, consumers were given the opportunity to nominate someone they deemed deserving of a Volvo XC60 every time any car spot aired during the live event. All they had to do was tweet using the hashtag #VolvoContest. In four hours, Volvo received 50,000 tweets with the programme hashtag (the most of any automotive brand) (Buss, 2015).

- *Permissions*—Do we have the right permissions to upload and share content? Privacy legislation is also national or regional, and the right of an individual or organization to use information is subject to this legislation.

- *Security*—How secure are the data and information we share? Information and transaction security and protection from fraud and identity theft is another area of increasing change. Legislation varies from country to country and region to region, with further differences evident in the laws that govern and protect consumer and business interests, such as distance selling regulations and consumer protection (e-commerce) regulations.

- *Accessibility*—Does everyone who wants access have access? Disability and discrimination legislation also requires consideration. As more services and marketing information is being shared digitally, the right to access and usability for all becomes an important agenda item for the dissemination of information and services.

Since May 2018, digital resources dealing with personal data have been regulated under the European Union's General Data Protection Regulation (GDPR). To deal with the issue of jurisdiction, the GDPR applies to all companies processing the personal data of data subjects residing in the Union, regardless of the company's location. The GDPR also regulates the ownership, permissions, security, and accessibility of such data. For more information about the GDPR, see Chapter 3.

 Visit the **online resources** and complete Internet Activity 12.4 to learn more about consumer privacy concerns.

 # Chapter Summary

To consolidate your learning, the key points from this chapter are summarized here:

- **Define digital marketing and social media marketing.**

    Digital marketing is the management and execution of marketing using digital technologies and channels (for example email, digital television, Internet) to reach markets in a timely, relevant, personal, interactive, and cost-efficient manner. It is related to, but distinct from, e-marketing, direct marketing, and interactive marketing. Social media marketing is a form of digital marketing that uses social networking sites to produce content that users will share and which will in turn create exposure of the brand to customers and thereby increase or reinforce its customer base.

- **Explain how digitalization is transforming marketing practice.**

    The growth of digital technologies is not only changing consumer behaviours, but also changing business itself. Successful marketing in a digital world requires digital marketing to be integrated into marketing research, products, and services, as well as marketing communication and channel distribution plans. Thus digital marketing should be considered and adapted more widely than simply as a new communication or distribution channel. It can help to create new business opportunities and enable new relationships (and thereby insights) with and between consumers.

■ **Discuss key techniques in digital marketing and social media marketing.**

Key techniques in digital marketing include Internet advertising, search marketing, email marketing, social media marketing, content marketing, and mobile marketing. Characteristic of digital marketing, especially that through social media, is that marketers need to give up some control and power to consumers. Marketers must share control over their brands with their online users; users will co-create content and generate their own content; customers will develop their own communities to which marketers should seek to contribute rather than usurp. It is about dialogue, conversation, and listening, rather than monologue and transmitting.

■ **Review how practitioners measure the effectiveness of social media marketing.**

To measure the effectiveness of a social media campaign, marketers should follow a seven-step process: identify a set of appropriate social media metrics; review the social media campaign objectives; map the campaign by highlighting links to brand-generated content, consumer-generated content, consumer-fortified content, and exposure to content(ed) consumers; choose the criteria and tools of measurement; establish a benchmark; undertake the campaign; and measure it frequently.

■ **Discuss crowdsourcing and explain how it can be harnessed for marketing.**

Crowdsourcing is the process of outsourcing a task or group of tasks to a generally large 'crowd' of people. It can be used in marketing to outsource routine activities, to obtain content (for example Volvo's Twitter campaign), or to obtain creative input (for example LEGO® and new product development). It can also be used as a way of gaining access to financial resources (for example Flippin' Burger and its funding of a restaurant).

 Review Questions

1 Define how digital marketing differs from interactive and Internet marketing.

2 How is digitalization transforming marketing practice?

3 What is social media marketing and why do marketers use it?

4 How can you measure the effectiveness of social media marketing?

5 What is content marketing and why do marketers use it?

6 How is the growth of mobile devices (for example smartphones) impacting on marketing?

7 What marketing activities can crowdsourcing support?

 Discussion Questions

1 Having read Case Insight 12.1 at the beginning of this chapter, how could Spotify use social media to support its service and build customer loyalty?

2 Do you think that digital resources are redefining marketing?

3 Why are many marketers having difficulties adapting to a situation in which they have to share control and power over a brand with consumers?

4 Privacy and ownership of digital information is increasingly challenged. When participating on Facebook, I think I control my own data and information—but do I? Discuss.

Visit the online resources and complete the Multiple-Choice Questions to assess your knowledge of Chapter 12.

Glossary

co-created content content resulting from the interaction of two or more parties to create content or applications.

contextual advertising a form of targeted advertising on websites whereby advertisements are selected and served by automated systems based on the content displayed to the user.

cookies pieces of data or records transmitted by a webserver to a client computer—that is, small text files found on your hard drive that allow information about your web activity patterns to be stored in your browser.

digital marketing the process of marketing accomplished or facilitated through the application of electronic devices, appliances, tools, techniques, technologies, and/or systems.

mobile marketing the set of practices that enable organizations to communicate and engage with their audience in an interactive and relevant manner through any mobile device or network.

mouse-over an event—such as a pop-up window or description box—triggered as a result of a cursor, controlled by a mouse, being hovered over a particular location on a graphical user interface.

paid inclusion method of ensuring that a website is included in a search engine's natural listings.

pay per click (PPC) method of advertising that uses sponsored search engine listings to drive traffic to a website whereby the advertiser bids for search terms and the search engine ranks ads based on a competitive auction, as well as other factors.

review site a website on which reviews can be posted about people, businesses, products, or services, such as Epinions.com, Tripadvisor.com, and reviews on Amazon.com.

search directory a database of information maintained by human editors, which lists websites by category and subcategory, usually based on the whole website rather than one page or a set of keywords.

search engine operates algorithmically, or using a mixture of algorithmic and human input, to collect, index, store, and retrieve information on the web and make it available to users in a manageable and meaningful way in response to a search query.

spam unsolicited email—the junk mail of the twenty-first century—which clogs email servers and uses up much-needed bandwidth on the Internet.

user-generated content (UGC) content made publicly available over the Internet that reflects a certain amount of creative effort and is created by amateur users, not professionals.

References

Alldredge, K., Newaskar, P., and Ungerman, K. (2015). The digital future of consumer-packaged-goods companies. *McKinsey Insights*, October. Retrieve from: https://www.mckinsey.com/insights/consumer_and_retail/the_digital_future_of_consumer_packaged_goods_companies (accessed 13 October 2018).

AMA (American Marketing Association) (2015). Social marketing. Retrieve from: https://marketing-dictionary.org/s/social-marketing/ (accessed 13 October 2018).

Anon. (2015). People prefer email for brand outreach in the UK. *E-marketer*, 9 October. Retrieve from: https://www.emarketer.com/Article/People-Prefer-Email-Brand-Outreach-UK/1013083 (accessed 13 October 2018).

Anon. (2017). As ad blocker use grows, publishers face new challenges. *E-marketer*, 26 June. Retrieve from: https://www.emarketer.com/Article/Ad-Blocker-Use-Grows-Publishers-Face-New-Challenges/1016076 (accessed 13 October 2018).

Baek, T.H., and Yoo, C.Y. (2018). Branded app usability: conceptualization, measurement, and prediction of consumer loyalty. *Journal of Advertising*, 47(1), 70–82.

Budds, D. (2015). How IKEA is defining the state of play (with a little help from DreamWorks). *Fast Company*, 23 October. Retrieve from: https://www.fastcompany.com/3052589/how-ikea-is-defining-the-state-of-play-with-a-little-help-from-dreamworks (accessed 13 October 2018).

Burger-Helmchen, T., and Pénin, J. (2011). Crowdsourcing: definition, enjeux, typologie [Crowdsourcing: definition, stakes, typology]. *Revue Management et Avenir*, 41(1), 254–69.

Buss, D. (2015). Volvo wins its Super Bowl contest: 5 questions with EVP Bodil Eriksson. *Brandchannel*. 3 February. Retrieve from: https://brandchannel.com/2015/02/03/volvo-wins-its-super-bowl-contest-5-questions-with-evp-bodil-eriksson/ (accessed 13 October 2018).

Cheng, J.M.-S., Blankson, C., Wang, E.S.-T., and Chen, L.S.-L. (2009). Consumer attitudes and interactive digital advertising. *International Journal of Advertising*, 28(3), 501–25.

Colliander, J., and Wien, A. (2013). Trash talk rebuffed: what can we learn from the phenomenon of consumers defending companies criticized in online communities? *European Journal of Marketing*, 47(10), 1733–57.

Daurer, S., Molitor, D., Spann, M., and Manchanda, P. (2015). Consumer search behavior on the mobile Internet: an empirical analysis. Marketing Science Institute Working Paper No. 15–111. Retrieve from: https://papers.ssrn.com/sol3/papers.cfm?abstract_id=2603242 (accessed 22 July 2016).

DeMers, J. (2017). The technology trends that will dominate 2018. *Forbes*, 30 December. Retrieve from: https://www.forbes.com/sites/jaysondemers/2017/12/30/7-technology-trends-that-will-dominate-2018/#288c967457d7 (accessed 13 October 2018).

Digital Marketing Institute (n.d.). 5 best mobile campaigns of 2017. Retrieve from: https://digitalmarketinginstitute.com/blog/2017-12-18-5-best-mobile-campaigns-of-2017 (accessed 13 October 2018).

Drèze, X., and Hussherr, F.X. (2003). Internet advertising: is anybody watching? *Journal of Interactive Marketing*, 17(4), 8–23.

Greene, J. (2015). Amazon opening its first real bookstore—at U-Village. *Seattle Times*, 2 November. Retrieve from: https://www.seattletimes.com/business/amazon/amazon-opens-first-bricks-and-mortar-bookstore-at-u-village/ (accessed 13 October 2018).

Greiner, A. (2017). Invasion of the ad fraud super bots. *Forbes*, 30 November. Retrieve from: https://www.forbes.com/sites/forbestechcouncil/2017/11/30/invasion-of-the-ad-fraud-super-bots/#4451bbab7996 (accessed 13 October 2018).

Harris, P. (2009). *Penguin Dictionary of Marketing*. London: Penguin Books.

Howe, J. (2006). The rise of crowdsourcing. *Wired*, 1 June. Retrieve from: https://www.wired.com/wired/archive/14.06/crowds.html (accessed 13 October 2018).

IAB/PwC (2017). *IAB Internet Advertising Revenue Report: 2016 Full Year Results*. Retrieve from: https://www.iab.com/wp-content/uploads/2016/04/IAB_Internet_Advertising_Revenue_Report_FY_2016.pdf (accessed 13 October 2018).

Internet World Stats (2017). Internet usage statistics: the Internet big picture. Retrieve from: https://www.internetworldstats.com/stats.htm (accessed 13 October 2018).

Johnson, B. (2015). The evolution of search on Amazon. *Digital Commerce 360*, 11 June. Retrieve from: https://www.digitalcommerce360.com/2015/06/11/evolution-search-amazon/ (accessed 13 October 2018).

Johnson, L. (2015). Are marketers finally getting the hang of location-based mobile ads? *Adweek*, 28 September. Retrieve from: https://www.adweek.com/news/technology/are-marketers-finally-getting-hang-location-based-mobile-ads-167212 (accessed 13 October 2018).

Keegan, B.J., and Rowley, J. (2017). Evaluation and decision making in social media marketing. *Management Decision*, 55(1), 15–31.

Keller, E., and Fay, B. (2012). Word-of-mouth advocacy: a new key to advertising effectiveness. *Journal of Advertising Research*, 52(4), 459–64.

Kronsberg, M. (2012). How Lego's great adventure in geek-sourcing snapped into place and boosted the brand. *Fast Company*, 2 February. Retrieve from: https://www.fastcompany.com/1812959/how-legos-great-adventure-geek-sourcing-snapped-place-and-boosted-brand (accessed 13 October 2018).

Kurzer, R. (2018). Majority of mobile marketers plan to increase video spend in 2018. *Marketing Land*, 1 March. Retrieve from: https://marketingland.com/majority-mobile-marketers-plan-increase-video-spend-year-youappi-survey-says-235241 (accessed 13 October 2018).

Lamberton, C., and Stephen, A.T. (2016). A thematic exploration of digital, social media, and mobile marketing: research evolution from 2000 to 2015 and an agenda for future inquiry. *Journal of Marketing*, 80(6), 146–72.

Leggatt, H. (2015). Amazon the go-to place for consumers to search for products. *BizReport*, 9 October. Retrieve from: https://www.bizreport.com/2015/10/amazon-the-go-to-place-for-consumers-to-search-for-products.html (accessed 13 October 2018).

Lundquist, A., and Gromek, M. (2015). Successful equity crowdfunding campaigns: a Nordic review. *Fundedbyme.com*, 7 July. Retrieve from: https://www.slideshare.net/MichalGromek/successful-equity-crowdfunding-campaigns3 (accessed 13 October 2018).

Madov, N. (2015). DreamWorks creates a magical world for IKEA's new line of toys. *AdAge*, 21 October. Retrieve from: https://adage.com/creativity/work/ikea-welcome-to-the-world-of-lattjo/43838 (accessed 13 October 2018).

Mangold, W.G., and Faulds, D.J. (2009). Social media: the new hybrid element of the promotion mix. *Business Horizons*, 52(4), 357–65.

Miller, M.J. (2015). Play it forward: IKEA taps DreamWorks to bring Lattjo games to life. *Brandchannel*, 26 October. Retrieve from: https://www.brandchannel.com/2015/10/26/ikea-dreamworks-lattjo-102615/ (accessed 13 October 2018).

MMA (Mobile Marketing Association) (2009). Mobile marketing. Retrieve from: https://www.mmaglobal.com/wiki/mobile-marketing (accessed 13 October 2018).

Modig, E., and Söndergaard, M. (2018). Managing digital media investments. In: P. Anderson, S. Movin, M. Mähring, R. Teigland, and K. Wennberg (eds), *Managing Digital Transformation*, Stockholm: Stockholm School of Economics Institute for Research, 133–52.

Moorman, C. (2014). *CMO Survey Report: Highlights and Insights*. Retrieve from: https://cmosurvey.org/files/2014/09/The_CMO_Survey-Highlights_and_Insights-Aug-2014.pdf (accessed 13 October 2018).

Moorman, C. (2018). *CMO Survey Report: Highlights and Insights*. Retrieve from: https://cmosurvey.org/wp-content/uploads/sites/15/2018/02/The_CMO_Survey-Highights_and_Insights_Report-Feb-2018.pdf (accessed 13 October 2018).

Murton Beets, L., and Handley, A. (2018). *B2B Content Marketing: 2018 Benchmarks, Budgets, and Trends*. Retrieve from: https://contentmarketinginstitute.com/wp-content/uploads/2017/12/2018_B2C_Research_Final.pdf (accessed 13 October 2018).

Neff, J. (2015). Is it content or is it advertising? *AdAge*, 12 October. Retrieve from: https://adage.com/article/ad-age-research/content-advertising/300858/ (accessed 13 October 2018).

Niederhoffer, K., Mooth, R., Wiesenfeld, D., and Gordon, J. (2007). The origin and impact of CPG new-product buzz: emerging trends and implications. *Journal of Advertising Research*, 47(4), 420–6.

Nudd, T. (2015a). Man poses as target on Facebook, trolls haters of its gender-neutral move with epic replies. *Adweek*, 13 August. Retrieve from: https://www.adweek.com/adfreak/man-poses-target-facebook-trolls-haters-its-gender-neutral-move-epic-replies-166364 (accessed 13 October 2018).

Nudd, T. (2015b). Target loved the guy who trolled its haters, judging by this genius Facebook post. *Adweek*, 14 August. Retrieve from: https://www.adweek.com/adfreak/target-loved-guy-who-trolled-its-haters-judging-genius-facebook-post-166408 (accessed 13 October 2018).

O'Brien, M. (2015). How to construct the perfect marketing email. *ClickZ*, 22 October. Retrieve from: https://www.clickz.com/clickz/news/2431283/how-to-construct-the-perfect-marketing-email (accessed 13 October 2018).

PQ Media (2017). *Global Content Marketing Forecast 2017*. Retrieve from: https://www.pqmedia.com/product/global-content-marketing-forecast-2017/ (accessed 13 October 2018).

Rosengren, S., and Dahlén, M. (2015). Exploring advertising equity: how a brand's past advertising may affect consumer willingness to approach its future ads. *Journal of Advertising*, 44(1), 1–13.

Santana, F. (2014). The 10 greatest burger places outside America. *Daily Meal*, 27 September. Retrieve from: https://www.thedailymeal.com/10-greatest-burger-places-outside-america (accessed 13 October 2018).

Statista (2017). Worldwide market share of leading search engines from January 2010 to October 2017. Retrieve from: https://www.statista.com/statistics/216573/worldwide-market-share-of-search-engines/ (accessed 13 October 2018).

Statista (2018a). Most famous social network sites worldwide as of January 2018, ranked by number of active users (in millions). Retrieve from: https://www.statista.com/statistics/272014/global-social-networks-ranked-by-number-of-users/ (accessed 13 October 2018).

Statista (2018b). Social media advertising revenue in selected countries in Europe in 2018 (in million US dollars). Retrieve from: https://www.statista.com/statistics/461963/social-media-advertising-revenue-countries-digital-market-outlook-europe/ (accessed 13 October 2018).

Statista (2018c). Share of individuals who had access to a smartphone at home in Sweden from 2011 to 2017. Retrieve from: https://www.statista.com/statistics/543474/sweden-smartphone-user-penetration/ (accessed 13 October 2018).

Stephen, A.T., Sciandra, M.R., and Inman, J.J. (2015). The effects of content characteristics on consumer engagement with branded social media content on Facebook. Marketing Science Institute Working Paper No. 15-110. Retrieve from: http://msi.org/reports/the-effects-of-content-characteristics-on-consumer-engagement-with-branded/ (accessed 22 July 2016).

Vallone, J. (2011). Crowdsourcing could predict terror strikes, gasoline prices. *Investors' Business Daily*, 29 August, 5.

van den Bulte, C., and Wuyts, S. (2007). *Social Networks and Marketing*. Boston, MA: Marketing Science Institute.

Voorveld, H., van Noor, G., Muntiga, D.G., and Bronner, F. (2018). Engagement with social media and social media advertising: the differentiating role of platform type. *Journal of Advertising*, 47(1), 38–54.

Wunsch-Vincent, S., and Vickery, G. (2007). *Participative Web: User-Created Content—Report of the Working Party on the Information Economy*. Organisation for Economic Co-operation and Development Doc. DSTI/ICCP/EI(2006)7/FINAL. Retrieve from: https://www.oecd.org/internet/interneteconomy/38393115.pdf (accessed 13 October 2018).

Chapter 13
Branding Decisions

Learning Outcomes

After reading this chapter, you will be able to:

▶ Explain the characteristics and principal types of brand and branding

▶ Discuss ways in which brands work through associations and personalities

▶ Examine how branding has evolved, utilizing relational and co-creation perspectives

▶ Explain how brands can be built

▶ Describe the principal issues associated with branding in services, business-to-business, internal, and global contexts

▶ Explore the issues and activities associated with brand equity, and demonstrate why branding is important to marketing managers

Case Insight 13.1
Aston Martin

The Aston Martin brand, founded in 1913, is synonymous with hand-crafted luxury, peerless beauty, incredible performance, and international motorsport glory. We speak to Simon Sproule, director of global marketing and communications, to find out how the brand is promoted in China.

Aston Martin's brand projects: Power. Beauty. Soul. We see this as more than a tagline. It's about the mission for the company. Naturally, these words describe the attributes of our cars, but we bring more than a beautiful car to our customers. As with all products in the luxury market, they are a discretionary purchase and are bought for a variety of reasons. The common denominator, however, is the emotional connection our cars have with customers, and the physical product and values of the company/brand. With an Aston Martin, you join an exclusive club with only just over 80,000 members. This is the total number of cars produced in our history. By contrast, our large mainstream competitors will produce that many cars in three days!

The Aston Martin brand also stands for beautiful hand-crafted cars, evident in every aspect of the product and, for our customers, when they visit the factory in Gaydon, Warwickshire, and see the cars being made. Iconic Hollywood British spy character James Bond has become a brand attribute for Aston Martin through the 50-year association that started with the DB5 in Goldfinger. However, for our customers in new and emerging markets such as China, James Bond may not have the same cultural resonance as it does in the UK. For those new customers to Aston Martin, we stand for the best of British style and elegance, combined with the power of our V8 and V12 engines. In essence, we are the quintessential British GT car and more. We describe our branding approach as the 'Goldilocks strategy'—getting the balance between exclusivity and accessibility 'just right'. Although we are selling a luxury product to 1 per cent of the world's population, we have a massive popular following: 6.5 million Facebook fans and more than 1 million fans on Instagram. We need to be constantly mindful that the respect granted to our brand from our fans

is an important motivator for our customers buying an Aston Martin. The simplest way of describing this is to imagine being stuck in heavy traffic at a busy intersection: our customers tell us that they always get let out of a junction . . . which, in the most basic way, speaks to the respect and affection people have for our cars. So our brand strategy is to balance the aspirational nature of the company and its products, but at the same time be friendly and accessible to all.

To implement our branding strategy, we combine high technology—we are in the process of implementing Salesforce to run our customer engagement—and a very personal touch. Buying an Aston Martin is not only about the cars, but also about becoming part of a family in which you feel welcomed and valued. Like the majority of auto makers, we operate a franchise business, with dealers handling the majority of the sales and service interface. That said, our customers also seek a direct relationship with the 'factory', and we encourage and embrace those relationships. I spend time with customers every week! To convey the brand values to target customers, we are moving towards storytelling driven by content and experiences. We invest relatively little in conventional advertising, preferring to engage our customer and fans with interesting and cool content. We want to encourage customers to spend time with us, visit the factory, and attend events and motor races. The most convincing way to sell an Aston Martin is a test drive.

The question for Aston Martin was: how should it go about raising brand awareness and brand familiarity in China, an important emerging market?

 Visit the online resources to watch a video interview with Simon Sproule in which he explains what Aston Martin did.

Introduction

Our world is full of **brands**, from soap powders and soft drinks, to airlines and financial services—even musicians, sports and film stars, buildings, cities and destinations, and social networks. Brands are configured in all shapes, sizes, and entities. So there are a huge variety of branding opportunities and, as Case Insight 13.1 notes, people form associations with brands—but what exactly is a brand? How are brands developed? Who really creates them? What exactly is the nature of these relationships? Why are they significant? These are the key questions we explore in this chapter.

Branding is a process by which manufacturers and retailers help customers to differentiate between various offerings. Brand names provide information about content, taste, durability, quality, price, and performance, without requiring the buyer to undertake time-consuming comparison tests with similar offerings or other risk-reduction approaches to purchase decisions. We saw in Chapter 6 that a comprehensive segmentation strategy involves targeting and positioning. Positioning is concerned with the processes associated with creating and altering the perceptions consumers have about a firm's products or brands (Crawford, 1985). In other words, **brand positioning** is not about a brand's physicality; rather, it is about the place the brand occupies in a consumer's mind (Ries and Trout, 1972). Brand positioning is a strategic activity used to differentiate and distinguish a brand, so that a consumer not only remembers the brand, but also understands it. Branding and positioning are interrelated (Tudor and Negricea, 2012). A credible position cannot be sustained without a strong brand and a brand cannot be developed or preserved without an audience that perceives its justifiable position in terms of performance.

In addition to the largely transactional positioning strategies set out in Chapter 6, some brands attempt to position themselves as relational brands. The aim is to attract relationship-oriented buyers—that is, people who, as Crosby (2012: 10) indicates, appreciate and seek 'recognition, appreciation, personalization, customization, exceptional customer service, fairness, reciprocity, information sharing, honesty/trustworthiness, cooperative problem solving and harmonious interactions' with their chosen brands. Successful brands such as Aston Martin, Apple, and Airbnb represent customer promises and shape their expectations. When expectations and experiences of the brand in use match the promise, brand performance is accomplished. Successful brands tend to be innovators and deliver consistently on their promises. This serves to reinforce the positioning and credibility of the promise.

Successful brands can therefore be said to capture three core brand elements: promises, positioning, and performance. These are depicted at Figure 13.1 as the three brand Ps (3BPs). At the core of this concept is communication, which enables a promise to be known (brand awareness), positions the brand correctly (brand attitude), and delivers brand performance (brand response). And increasingly consumers are actively participating in the branding process by co-creating meaning, for example through social media.

What Is a Brand?

A brand can be distinguished from its proposition or unbranded commodity counterparts by the perceptions and feelings that consumers have about its attributes and performance. Bottled water, for example, is essentially a commodity, but brands such as Highland Spring, Aqua Falls,

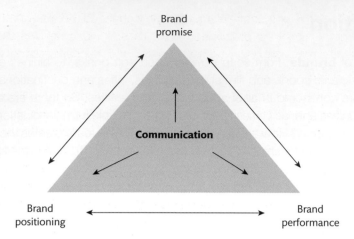

Figure 13.1

The triangulation of the 3BPs

Source: Marketing Communications (7th edn) Fill, C. and Turnball, S. (2016). Reproduced with the kind permission of Pearson Education Limited. © Pearson Education Limited 2016.

and Crystal Clear have all developed their offerings with imagery that serves to enhance customer feelings and emotions about the actual water in the packaging. Ultimately, a brand resides in the mind of the consumer (Achenbaum, 1993).

Brands are products and services that have added value. This value has been deliberately designed and presented to augment a product with associations that are recognized by, and are meaningful to, their customers. Although marketing managers have to create, sustain, protect, and develop the identity of the brands for which they are responsible, it is customer perception, the use of the various senses that help to fashion images of these brands, and the meaning and value that customers give to the brand that are important. Thus both managers and customers are involved in the branding process.

Although brands are generally considered important, there is a lack of common definition of the term. De Chernatony and dall'Olmo Riley (1998), for example, identified 12 types of brand definition. One of the more common is that a brand is a name, symbol, words, or mark that identifies and distinguishes a proposition or company from its competitors. However, this definition focuses only on the identification of products through a brand; in practice, brands consist of much more than these identification elements. As Aaker (2014: 1) remarks, 'far more than a name or a logo it is an organization's promise to a customer to deliver what a brand stands for . . . in terms of functional benefits but also emotional, self-expressive and social benefits'. Brands make promises to customers in a way that differentiates the offered products or services from competing alternatives. From this, then, it can be concluded that a brand comprises both brand awareness (identification) and brand attitude or brand knowledge (differentiation) as defining elements (Keller, 1998; Rossiter, 2014). The latter is also often referred to in terms of **brand associations**.

Brands have characters—personalities, even—that set them apart from the competition in the minds of consumers. To develop character, it is important to understand that brands are constructed of two main types of attribute: intrinsic and extrinsic:

- **Intrinsic attributes** are the functional characteristics of a proposition, such as its shape, performance, and physical capacity. If any of these intrinsic attributes were to be changed, this would directly alter the proposition.

- **Extrinsic attributes** refer to those elements that, if changed, do not alter the material functioning and performance of the proposition itself. These include devices such as the brand name, marketing communications, packaging, price, and mechanisms that enable consumers to form associations that give meaning to the brand.

Buyers often use the extrinsic attributes to help them to distinguish one brand from another, because, in certain categories, it is difficult for them to make decisions based on the intrinsic attributes alone. For example, many financial companies develop brands because their propositions are very complex, and many consumers are reluctant or unable to take the time and effort necessary to understand them. By developing a single brand, firms such as Prudential and Zurich have tried to establish high levels of trust and reliance in their insurance brands, which can help to reduce customers' perceived risk and speed up the decision-making process.

Why Brand?

Brands represent opportunities for both consumers and organizations (manufacturers and retailers) to buy and sell products and services easily, more efficiently, and relatively quickly. We will now consider the benefits from each perspective.

Consumers like brands because they:

- help people to identify their preferred offerings;

- reduce levels of perceived risk and, in doing so, improve the quality of the shopping experience;

- help people to gauge the quality of the product, service, or experience;

- reduce the amount of time that must be spent making proposition-based decisions and hence decrease the time that must be spent shopping around;

- provide psychological reassurance or reward, especially for offerings bought on an occasional basis; and

- inform consumers about the source of an offering (country or company).

Brands helps customers to identify the offerings they prefer to use to satisfy their needs and wants. Equally, brands help them to avoid the offerings that they dislike, either as a result of previous use, or because of other image associations or other psychological reasoning.

Consumers experience a range of perceived risks when buying different offerings. These include financial risks ('Can I afford this?'), social risks ('What will other people think about me going to this bar?'), or functional risks ('Will this smartphone work?'). Branding helps to reduce these risks, so that buyers can proceed with a purchase without fear or uncertainty. Strong brands encapsulate a range of values that communicate safety and purchase security.

In markets unknown to a buyer or in which there is technical complexity (for example computing, financial services), consumers use brands to make judgements about the quality of an offering. This, in turn, helps consumers to save shopping time and, again, helps to reduce the amount of risk they experience.

Perhaps above all other factors, brands help consumers to develop relationships based on respect and trust, as exemplified by Aston Martin in Case Insight 13.1. Strong brands are normally well trusted; annual surveys often announce that Apple, British Airways, and Kellogg's are among the most trusted brands. Such surveys also declare those brands that are least trusted by consumers and these announcements often trigger, or at least coincide with, falling sales and reducing market share. Creating trust is important, because it enables consumers to buy with confidence.

Visit the **online resources** and follow the web link to the branding articles on the website of the American Marketing Association (AMA).

Manufacturers and retailers use brands because they:

- can increase the financial valuation of companies;
- enable premium pricing;
- help to differentiate one proposition from competitive offerings;
- can deter competitors from entering the market;
- encourage cross-selling to other brands owned by the manufacturer;
- help to develop customer trust, loyalty/retention, and repeat-purchase buyer behaviour;
- help in the development and use of integrated marketing communications;
- contribute to corporate identity programmes; and
- provide some legal protection.

Branding is an important way in which manufacturers can differentiate their brands in crowded marketplaces. This enables buyers to recognize the brand quickly and make fast, unhindered purchase decisions. One of the brand owner's goals is to create strong brand loyalty to the extent that customers always seek out that brand, and are primed to accept cross-product promotions and **brand extensions**.

With its shaped glasses and sophisticated packaging, Stella Artois positions itself as a premium brand
Source: © Denis Michaliov/123RF.com.

Perhaps one of the strongest motivations for branding is that it can allow manufacturers to set premium prices. Brands such as Andrex, Stella Artois, and L'Oréal charge a premium price, often around 25–35 per cent higher than the average price in their respective product categories. Premium prices allow brand managers to reinvest in brand development and, in some markets, this is important if the brand is to remain competitive. However, it should not be assumed that the establishment of a brand will lead automatically to success; many brands fail, sometimes because a firm does not invest in a brand at the level required, or because management has not recognized or accepted the need to change, adapt, or reposition its brands when market preferences have moved on. (See Market Insight 13.1 for an example of a how a luxury brand repositioned itself after losing its lustre.)

The greater the number of product-based brands, the greater an organization's motivation to develop a corporate brand. Organizations such as Aviva and Johnson & Johnson use an umbrella branding approach. This requires that they need to invest heavily in only one brand, rather than in each and every product-based brand. This approach is not applicable to all sectors, although in business-to-business (B2B) markets, in which there is product complexity, corporate branding is an effective way of communicating and focusing on a few core brand values.

 Visit the **online resources** and complete Internet Activity 13.1 to learn more about how major organizations perceive the importance of branding and their brands.

How Brands Work: Associations and Personalities

The development of successful brands requires customers to be able to make appropriate brand-related associations. Normally, these should be based on utilitarian functional issues, as well as on emotions and feelings towards a brand.

Clayton and Heo (2011) refer to brand image, perceived quality, and brand attitude as the main dimensions of brand associations, citing work by Aaker (1991), Keller (1993), and Low and Lamb (2000) in this area. Keller (1993) believes that brand associations themselves are made up of the physical and non-physical attributes and benefits aligned with attitudes to create a brand image in the mind of the consumer. In fact, many brands are deliberately imbued with human characteristics, to the point at which they are identified as having **brand personalities**. For example, Timberland is 'rugged', Victoria's Secret is 'glamorous', Virgin is associated with 'youthfulness' and 'rebelliousness', and management consultancies such as PricewaterhouseCoopers (PwC) seek to be seen as 'successful', 'accomplished', and 'influential'.

Marketing communications play an important role in communicating the essence of a brand's personality. By developing positive emotional links with a brand, consumers can find reassurance within their brand purchases. The development of brand personalities means that marketing managers can position their brands using emotional attributes and hence develop stronger consumer–brand relationships (Ahmad and Thyagaraj, 2014). These associations and images may sometimes enable consumers to construe a psychosocial meaning associated with a particular brand. The idea that consumers might search for brands with a personality that complements their self-concept is not new (McCracken, 1986). Belk (1988) suggested that brands offer a means of self-expression, whether this is in terms of who they want to be (their desired self), who they strive to be (their ideal self), or who they think they should be (their ought self). Brands therefore provide a way in which individuals can indicate to others their preferred personality, as they relate to these 'self' concepts.

Market Insight 13.1
Restitching a Heritage Brand

What is the one thing that Jude Law, Jay Z, Winston Churchill, and Prince Charles all have in common?

They have all had suits made on Savile Row.

Savile Row tailors have been making suits for the smart set since the late eighteenth century. Consequently, Savile Row tailors are some of the best in the world. The term 'Savile Row' has long been synonymous with high-quality bespoke suits and shirts.

Although Savile Row tailors continue to provide suits to their customers, they seem to have lost their relevance and connection with consumers—especially middle-class and younger consumers. Several establishments that had a rich history and boasted famous clients closed as a result of poor financial performance during the middle of the twentieth century. Indeed, one famous Italian designer described Savile Row as a 'comedy, a melodrama lost in the past'.

Savile Row, Mayfair, central London, UK
Source: © Alan Kean/Shutterstock.com.

Establishments on Savile Row started the process of modernization during the 1960s, but significant steps were made during the early 1990s by three entrepreneurial designers, Richard James, Ozwald Boateng, and Timothy Everest, who took innovative steps to connect with those consumers more used to reasonable-quality, mass-produced suits. For example, some tailors placed more emphasis on made-to-measure suits, at price points between £1,500 and £2,000. When buying made-to-measure suits, such consumers will typically have the traditional personal consultation sessions with Savile Row tailors; however, to reduce costs, they will usually be offered fewer types of cloth and pattern to choose from, or the production will be outsourced to foreign factories.

This new generation of tailors are more marketing-savvy. Other than dignitaries, who are still an important source of endorsement, they connect with consumers through non-traditional elites, such as film stars, sports personalities, and artists or musicians. In addition, they promote themselves in targeted publications, including *GQ* and *Vanity Fair*.

Some Savile Row tailors can be offputting to consumers not used to this type of atmosphere and ambience. Creating a more relaxed environment and experience has become another priority for store managers. Some tailors have made their environments more consumer-friendly by modernizing their storefront displays, redesigning interior spaces, and creating a more contemporary feel. Known as the New Bespoke Movement, in this way Savile Row tailors have reconnected with modern consumers from home and aboard, regained their influence in the global fashion industry, and contributed to expanding the UK's economy and image.

Sources: Sheth, Newman, and Gross, (1991); Sweeney and Soutar (2001); Jacobs (2012); Armstrong (2015); Peng and Chen (2017).

Market Insight 13.1
continued

Theory into Practice

Consumption value has been the focus of marketers' attention since the late 1980s. It is a key influencer of consumers' purchase decisions because it considers the benefits that consumers receive from an offering and the sacrifices they make to obtain it (Sheth et al., 1991; Sweeney and Soutar, 2001). According to Sweeney and Soutar (2001), consumption value includes emotional value; social value; financial value (that is, price or value for money); and functional value (that is, performance and/or quality). Because luxury products tend to have a premium quality, a recognizable style, and high hedonism, in addition to an increased cost, Peng and Chen (2017) suggest that marketers need to promote these offerings based on their functional value, financial value, hedonic value, and symbolic or expressive value.

Related Topics

experiential marketing; luxury consumption; segmentation and targeting; customization; international marketing

1 **What are the advantages and disadvantages of using spokespeople from a diverse range of professions as endorsers?**

2 **What other British industries have a rich heritage and the potential for brand revival?**

3 **If you were a Savile Row tailor, how would you emphasize your offering's value better? (Hint: Think about functional value, financial value, emotional value, and symbolic value.)**

This market insight was kindly contributed by Dr Norman Peng, University of Westminster, UK.

This emotional and symbolic approach is intended to provide consumers with additional reasons to engage with a brand beyond the normal functional characteristics a brand offers, which are often easily copied by competitors (Keller, 1998). To be able to measure brand personality, Aaker (1997) developed the **Brand Personality Scale**, which consists of five main dimensions of psychosocial meaning and 42 personality traits. The dimensions are:

- sincerity (wholesome, honest, down-to-earth);

- excitement (exciting, imaginative, daring);

- competence (intelligent, confident);

- sophistication (charming, glamorous, smooth); and

- ruggedness (strong, masculine).

These are depicted in Figure 13.2.

These psychosocial dimensions have subsequently become enshrined as dimensions of brand personality. Aaker (1997) developed a five-point framework around these dimensions, which has been used frequently and cited many times by academics and marketing practitioners.

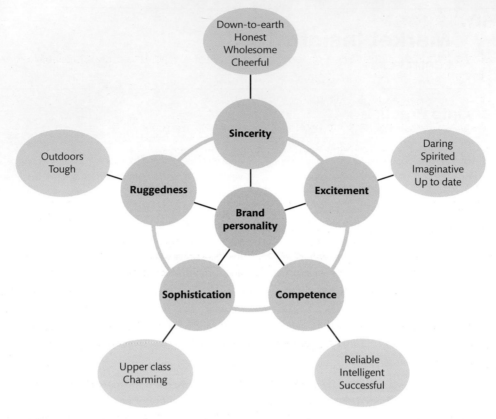

Figure 13.2

Five dimensions of psychosocial meaning

Source: Reprinted with permission from J. Aaker (1997) 'Dimensions of brand personality', Journal of Marketing Research 34 (August), 347–56, published by the American Marketing Association.

For example, various studies have found that consumers choose brands that reflect their own personality (Linville and Carlston, 1994; Phau and Lau, 2001). They prefer brands that project a personality that is consistent with their self-concepts. As Arora and Stoner (2009: 273) indicate, 'brand personality provides a form of identity for consumers that expresses symbolic meaning for themselves and for others'. Brand personality can therefore be construed as a means of creating and maintaining consumer loyalty, if only because this aspect is difficult for competitors to copy.

Customers assign a level of trust to the brands they encounter. Preferred brands signify a high level of trust and indicate that the brand promise is delivered; hence marketing managers need to ensure that they do not harm or reduce the perceived levels of trust in their brands. Indeed, action should be taken to enhance trust. One way of achieving this is to use labels and logos to represent a brand's values, associations, and source. For example, many brands use the 'footprint' symbol to refer to the amount of carbon dioxide associated within a brand's supply chain, while all Apple products are signified, and identified, by the fruit with a bite removed and UK meat products carry a red tractor symbol. According to the National Farmers' Union (NFU), the red tractor logo indicates that the meat was produced to exacting standards of food safety, kindness to animals, and environmental protection. Thus the brand is intended to reassure customers about the origin and quality of the meat.

Brand Names

Choosing a name for a brand is a critical foundation stone, because it should ideally allow the brand to be:

- easily recalled, spelled, and spoken;
- strategically consistent with the organization's branding policies;
- indicative of the offering's major benefits and characteristics;
- distinctive;
- meaningful to the customer; and
- capable of registration and protection.

Sometimes, social pressure, or even a crisis, can stimulate a change of name. For example, Philip Morris changed the overall company name to Altria Group following sustained attacks about its cigarette and tobacco products. Although changing the name alone does not stop the cause of the crisis, it can trigger a change in culture, values, and approach. Name changes can also be a consequence of new business models being explored, such as Google and luxury handbag manufacturer Coach changing their corporate brand names to Alphabet and Tapestry, respectively. Both of these examples were driven by the company wanting to explore new business opportunities (Danzinger, 2017), while letting the more well-known name remain a brand name connected to a specific offering.

Brand names need to transfer easily across markets, and if they are to do this successfully, it helps if customers can not only pronounce the name, but also recall it unaided. Short names, such as LEGO®, Mars, Sony, Flash, or Shell, have this strength. One of the reasons why high-profile grocery brands are advertised so frequently is to create brand name awareness, so that when a UK customer thinks of pet food, they think of Felix or Winalot. Customers are unlikely to accept names that are difficult to spell or are difficult to pronounce. Problems can also arise as a result of interpretation issues. For example, the launch of Puffs tissues in Germany might have been easier if management had known that Puff means 'brothel' in German.

Brand names should have some internal strategic consistency and be compatible with the organization's overall positioning. Ford Transit, Virgin Atlantic, and Cadbury Dairy Milk are names that reflect a policy that the company name always prefixes the product brand names. Some brand names incorporate a combination of words, numbers, or initials. The portable 'sat nav' TomTom GO 510/610 and Canon's EOS 700D DSLR digital camera, for example, use names that do not inform about the functionality, but use a combination of words and numbers to reflect the parent company, product line to which they belong, and a hint of their technological content. A brand's functional benefit can also be incorporated within a name, because this helps to convey its distinctive qualities. Deodorant brands such as Sure and Right Guard use this approach, although Lynx has relied on imagery plus fragrance and dryness.

Most brands do not have sufficient financial resources to be advertised on television or in mainstream media; hence it is not possible to convey brand values through imagery and brand advertising. For these brands, it is important that the name of the brand reflects the functionality of the offering itself, for example No More Nails super-adhesive and Snap-on interchangeable tools. For these brands, packaging and merchandising is important to communicate with customers in-store.

Increasingly, brands are being developed through the use of social media. This is essentially about people talking, either spontaneously to one another, through blogs, or through formal or informal communities, about brands that they have experienced in some way (see 'Brand Co-creation').

 Visit the **online resources** and complete Internet Activity 13.2 to learn more about generating brand names.

Types of Brand

There are three main types of brand—that is, manufacturer, distributor, and generic.

Manufacturer Brands

In many markets and especially the fast-moving consumer goods (FMCG) sector, retailers influence the way in which a product is displayed and presented to customers. As a result, manufacturers try to create brand recognition and name recall by means of their marketing communications activities with end users. The goal is to help customers to identify the producer of a particular brand at the point of purchase. For example, Persil, Heinz, Cadbury, and Coca-Cola are strong **manufacturer brands**; they are promoted heavily, and customers develop preferences based on performance, experience, communications, and availability. So, when customers are shopping, they use the images they have of various manufacturers, combined with their own experience, to seek out their preferred brands. Retailers who choose not to stock certain major manufacturer brands run the risk of losing customers.

Distributor (or Private Label) Brands

The various organizations that make up the marketing channel often choose to create a distinct identity for themselves. The term **distributor brand**, or 'private label brand', refers to the identities and images developed by the wholesalers, distributors, dealers, and retailers who make up the marketing channel. Wholesalers, such as Nurdin & Peacock, and retailers, such as Argos, Gap, Sainsbury's, and Amazon, have all created strong brands of their own (see Market Insight 13.2).

The private label strategy potentially offers advantages to the manufacturer, which can use excess capacity to manufacture such brands, as well as to retailers, who can earn a higher margin than they can with manufacturers' branded goods and, at the same time, develop strong store images. Retailers have the additional cost of promotional initiatives, necessary in the absence of a manufacturer's support. Some manufacturers, such as Kellogg's, refuse to make products for distributors to brand, although others (Cereal Partners) are happy to supply a variety of competitors.

Occasionally, conflict emerges, especially when a distributor brand displays characteristics that are very similar to the manufacturer's market-leader brand. Coca-Cola defended its brand when it was alleged that the packaging of Sainsbury's new cola drink was too similar to Coca-Cola's own established design.

Generic Brands

Generic brands are sold without any promotional materials or any means of identifying the company, with the packaging displaying only information required by law. The only form of identification is the relevant product category, for example plain flour. Because it is not necessary

---

Market Insight 13.2
Owning the Brand

Over the last few decades, distributor brands have become an important element of the retail business. In 2016, the market share of distributor brands reached an all-time high in Germany, Italy, the Netherlands, Belgium, Poland, Austria, Sweden, Norway, and Denmark. In many European markets, the share of distributor brands reaches 30–40 per cent. In the UK and Germany, distributor brands' market share is, on average, a staggering 45 per cent.

One sector in which the shift to distributor branding is moving quickly is apparel. Although fast-fashion retailers such as H&M and Zara have long relied on their own brands, the fashion apparel industry is largely dominated by manufacturer brands such as luxury fashion houses Dior and Gucci, sportswear giants Nike and Adidas, or lifestyle brands Burberry and Ralph Lauren.

Until now, that is. In the United States, Amazon, Walmart, and Target are investing heavily in their own fashion brands. In Europe, the same can be said for Asos, Zalando, and even low-price supermarket chain Lidl, which launched its own 40-piece collection in collaboration with supermodel Heidi Klum in 2017.

Arguments favouring distributor brands typically focus on millennial consumers being less interested in brands and the trend towards apparel shopping moving online. As consumers increasingly shop apparel online, the

logic for choosing a specific item is changing. Online searches rarely start with the brand; rather, they tend to focus on the product needed. When consumers search generic product categories online, the hits typically show pictures of different alternatives levelling the playing field between manufacturer and distributor brands. However, the argument against distributor brands taking over considers that consumers still want to try on fashion apparel before buying, as well as the fact that buying fashion offerings is (often) as much about experience and identity as finding a good deal.

Sources: Boyle (2017); Nielsen/PLMA (2017).

Supermodel Heidi Klum—not your typical model for a distributor brand, until now
Source: © Shakeyjon/Alamy Stock Photo.

Theory into Practice

Distributor brands provide retailers with higher margins than manufacturer brands and hence have a positive effect on retailer profitability. In addition, distributor brands offer retailers an opportunity to differentiate their selections from those of their competitors. When

offering products that customers like under their own brands, retailers offer something unique that potentially helps build loyalty among their customers. Given these advantages, it is not surprising that both online and offline retailers invest in private-label branding.

Market Insight 13.2

continued

Related Topics

branding; consumer behaviour; fashion; retailing

1 Visit Amazon's website and check out the distributor brands offered in its fashion assortment. How easy is it to determine whether a product is a manufacturer, distributor, or generic brand?

2 Visit Zalando's website and check out the distributor brands offered in its fashion

assortment. How easy is it to determine whether a product is a manufacturer, distributor, or generic brand?

3 What differences do you see between the distributor brands offered by Amazon and Zalando? How does this relate to their respective strategies?

to pay for promotional support, these brands are sold at prices that are substantially below the price of normal brands. However, although they were briefly successful in the 1990s, their popularity has declined, and manufacturers now see no reason to produce these 'white carton' products. Only firms in the pharmaceutical sector use this type of brand.

Branding Strategies

An overall branding strategy can provide direction, consistency, and brand integrity within an organization's portfolio of brands. This provides the basis of the brand architecture. There are three core brand strategies—that is, individual, family, and corporate.

Individual Branding

Once referred to as a multibrand policy, individual branding requires each product offered by an organization to be branded independently of all the others. Grocery brands offered by Unilever (for example Knorr, Cif, and Dove) and Procter & Gamble (for example Fairy, Crest, and Head & Shoulders) typify this approach.

One of the advantages of this approach is that it is easy to target specific segments and to enter new markets with separate names. If a brand fails or becomes subject to negative media attention, the other brands are not likely to be damaged. However, there is a high financial cost because each brand needs to have its own promotional programme and associated support.

Family Branding

Once referred to as a multiproduct brand policy, family branding requires that all the products use the organization's name, either entirely or in part. Microsoft, Heinz, and Kellogg's all incorporate the company name, because they hope that customer trust will develop across all brands.

For these types of brand, promotional investment need not be as high. This is because there will always be a halo effect across all the brands when one is communicated and brand experience will stimulate word of mouth following usage. A prime example of this is Google, which has pursued a family brand strategy with Google Adwords, Google Maps, and Google Scholar, to name but a few. What's more impressive is that Google's shattering achievements have been accomplished in just ten years and with minimal advertising spend.

Line family branding is a derivative policy whereby a family branding policy is followed for all products within a single line. Bosch is a technology company operating in the automotive, industry, and home markets. Many of its products are branded Bosch, but it uses line family branding for its Blaupunkt and Qualcast brands in its car entertainment and garden products divisions.

Corporate Branding

Many retail brands adopt a single umbrella brand, based on the name of the organization. This name is then used at all locations, and is a way of identifying the brand and providing a form of consistent differentiation and a form of recognition, whether on the high street or online. Major supermarkets such as Tesco in the UK, Carrefour in France, and ASDA Walmart use this branding strategy to attract and help to retain customers.

Corporate branding strategies are also used extensively in business markets, such as IBM, Cisco, and Caterpillar, and in consumer markets in which there is technical complexity, such as financial services. Companies such as HSBC and Prudential adopt a single-name strategy. One of the advantages of this approach is that promotional investments are limited to one brand. However, the risk is similar to that of family branding, in that damage to one offering or operational area can cause problems across the organization. For example, when the British Broadcasting Corporation (BBC) experienced editorial problems with its Newsnight programme, which resulted in extensive and persistent negative media coverage, not only did the director-general decide to resign, but also questions were asked about declining trust in and reputation of the BBC as a whole.

 Visit the **online resources** and follow the web link to learn more about IBM's corporate brand.

How to Build Brands

The development of successful brands is critical to an organization's success. This requires marketers to achieve three essential branding activities: to enable identification and differentiation; to maintain consistency; and to communicate the existence and attributes to customers and other marketing channel audiences (Pennington and Ball, 2009).

According to Keller (2016), successful brand building is best accomplished by considering the brand-building process as a sequence of steps:

1 Enable customers to identify with the brand and help them to make associations with a specific product class or customer need.

2 Establish what the brand means by linking various tangible and intangible brand associations.

3 Encourage customer responses based around brand-related judgement and feelings.

4 Foster an active relationship between customers and the brand.

Figure 13.3 depicts the rational steps on the left-hand side, with the emotional counterpart shown on the right-hand side. In the centre are six blocks that make up a pyramid, echoing these rational and emotional steps. To achieve a successful brand, or brand resonance, Keller (2016) argues that a foundation is necessary and that these building blocks need to be developed systematically.

To further understand the terminology, we can apply this brand pyramid to a shampoo brand as an example:

- Brand salience—How easily and often do customers think of the shampoo brand when thinking about hair care brands or when shopping?

- Brand performance—How well do customers believe the shampoo brand cleans and conditions their hair?

- Brand imagery—This describes the extrinsic properties of the shampoo (its colour, packaging, product consistency, associations) and the level to which these satisfy customers' psychological or social needs.

- Brand judgements—These focus on customers' own personal opinions and evaluations about the shampoo.

- Brand feelings—This refers to customers' emotional responses and reactions with respect to the shampoo brand when prompted by communications, by friends, or when washing their hair.

- Brand resonance—This speaks of the nature of the relationship that customers have with the shampoo brand and the extent to which they feel loyal to the brand.

Brand resonance is most likely to result when marketers create proper salience, as well as breadth and depth of awareness. From this position, 'points of parity' and 'points of difference' need to be established, so that positive judgements and feelings can be made that appeal to both the head and the heart, respectively. (To learn more about branding as an academic topic, see Research Insight 13.1.)

 Visit the **online resources** and follow the web link to learn more about Keller's brand equity model.

Branding Perspectives

So far, we have assumed a largely managerial perspective with regard to the concept of brand. However, there are other approaches to understanding brands and what they represent. These draw on sociological, psychological, and socio-cultural interpretations about brands and their consumption. We consider two important perspectives. The first considers relational issues, and how people are believed to interact with brands and develop relationships through repeated consumption; the second reflects contemporary issues about co-creation and **customer branding**, which reverses the managerially driven view that brands are only a product of marketers.

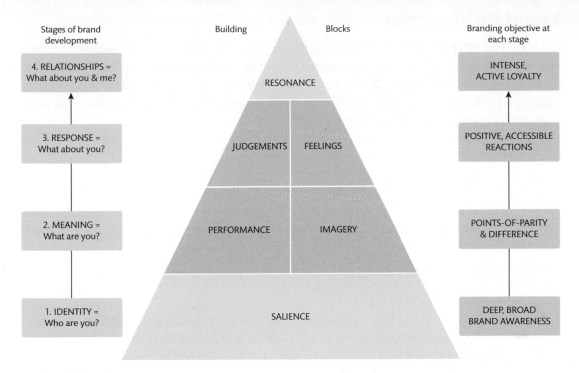

Figure 13.3

Brand pyramid: building blocks

Source: Keller, K.L., 'Building strong brands in a modern marketing communications environment', *Journal of Marketing Communications*, July 2009, Taylor & Francis. Reprinted by permission of the publisher (Taylor & Francis Ltd, https://www.tandf.co.uk/journals).

 Research Insight 13.1

To take your learning further, you might wish to read this influential paper:

Keller, K.L. (2016). Reflections on customer-based brand equity: perspectives, progress, and priorities. *AMS Review*, 6(1–2), 1–16.

In 1993, Kevin Lane Keller published an article on brand equity in the *Journal of Marketing* that had a major impact on the development of branding research and practice, and which informed much of his later thinking on brand building. In this 2016 article, Keller looks back at the development of branding as an academic field in the 25 years that have followed publication of his 1993 paper and outlines those areas that remain in need of additional research.

 Visit the **online resources** to read the abstract and access the full paper.

Brand Relationships

Although branding has its roots in identification and differentiation, this perspective considers that a 'brand-mark is a relational asset whose value to the firm is contingent on past, present and future interactions with various firm stakeholders' (Ballantyne and Aitken, 2007: 366). Fournier (1998) was one of the first researchers to introduce and utilize relationship theory to understand the roles that brands play in the lives of consumers.

Originally, relationship marketing was considered to be most relevant in inter-organizational relationships. Here, the management of relationships between buying and selling organizations is considered valid and appropriate—more so than in the relationship between an organization and a consumer. Fournier changed this when she explored ideas about consumers who think about brands as if they were human characters—that is, the personification of brands. She also found that consumers accept attempts by marketers to personalize brands (for example through advertising), which suggests the potential for interaction and relationships. She identified six facets that characterize the quality of brand relationship: love and passion; a connection between the brand and self; a high degree of interdependence; a high level of commitment; intimacy; and a positive evaluation of brand quality.

Fournier believes that it is important to understand consumer–brand relationships and that, by understanding how consumers interact with brands and the meaning that brands represent to people through consumption, marketing theory and practice can be advanced. She argues that it is necessary to consider the broad context of consumers' lives to understand the role and relationship that brands play in them. In addition, meaningful consumer–brand relationships can be observed when the brand represents the key dimension 'perceived ego significance'. Fournier stresses the importance of understanding what consumers do with brands that adds meaning to their lives (see Market Insight 13.3). (To learn more about brand relationships, see Research Insight 13.2.)

Perhaps the most important finding of Fournier's research concerns the meaning that consumers attribute to brands and how it differs from meanings intended by brand managers. This contribution has been developed in many areas, including in B2B markets in which it is now

Research Insight 13.2

To take your learning further, you might wish to read this influential paper:

Fournier, S. (1998). Consumers and their brands: developing relationship theory in consumer research. *Journal of Consumer Research*, 24(4), 343–73.

This seminal article has been characterized as a modern classic as a result of its significant contribution to our understanding of marketing and consumer research. The author discusses the need to incorporate relationship marketing theory with branding and explores the types of relationship that people form with brands.

 Visit the online resources to read the abstract and access the full paper.

Market Insight 13.3
Musicians Dying for Success

Michael Jackson, Whitney Houston, Bob Marley, and Amy Winehouse are all highly regarded music icons whose personal brands have thrived since their deaths. Although their reputations probably would not have been prolonged if fans were not so emotionally affected by news of their deaths, posthumous branding activities have significantly contributed to their longevity. New memorabilia, merchandise, and re-releases by marketers and estate holders, as well as releases of previously unknown material, have become a regular way of keeping the interest in deceased musicians alive.

The importance of emotional impact on consumption is well understood. We can see how emotion impacts buying decisions when a music artist dies. For example, the news about Michael Jackson's death in June 2009 spread rapidly—and was rapidly followed by a huge surge in sales of his back catalogue, as well as his Greatest Hits album topping the charts that same month.

The success of musicians who have passed away is not restricted to the time of death. For example, in December 2017, a Whitney Houston compilation called 'I Wish You Love: More from The Bodyguard' entered the Billboard R&B Album chart, five years after her death in 2012. This compilation was part of a set of activities marking the 25th anniversary of Houston's acting debut in the film The Bodyguard.

In fact, once they are dead, the value of a musician's portfolio often rises. Generally, the artist can release no more new material, making what already exists even more valuable. Often, copyright ownership passes onto the next of kin, who, if they act sufficiently quickly, can turn the late artist into a posthumous iconic brand. Bob Marley's family was quick to exploit his musical stature with T-shirts, mugs, and lighters—even naming a strain of cannabis after the Rastafarian icon.

The grief felt by Amy Winehouse's fans following her death was accompanied by a surge of interest in her music
Source: © Dutourdumonde Photography/Shutterstock.

Similarly, Amy Winehouse's download sales increased to 1.15 million in the United States in the year following her death in 2011, compared with 170,000 downloads earlier that year. Four years later, a documentary commemorating her life and a book written by her father were released, making US$1.5 million for the Amy Winehouse Charity Foundation.

Sources: Anon. (2009); Caulfield (2012); Adebayo (2014); Anderson (2017).

Theory into Practice

Just as brands can be imbued with human-like characteristics, humans can become brands. These brands have the potential to live on long after the person themselves has passed away. The potential value of brand relationships is clearly visible in this market insight. The rush to purchase music when a musician dies can be considered a way of extending that brand relationship across time. It is the emotional and symbolic value that is transferred, rather than the functional value of the music. The successful propagation of music and memorabilia after a musician's death can be attributed to an understanding of the unique relationship values that the musician represented and the meanings they (continue to) provide to fans.

Market Insight 13.3
continued

Related Topics

brand personality; brand meanings; relationships

1 How might the deaths of David Bowie and Prince be reflected not only in music sales, but also in other areas of culture and society?

2 What do you consider the main differences between a human as a brand and a brand as a human?

3 Make a list of other brand-related situations in which the termination of the brand has led to increased or delayed sales.

This market insight was kindly contributed by Naomi Ramage, former student, Buckinghamshire New University.

recognized that both sellers (suppliers) and buyers (their customers) and other stakeholders co-create brand meanings. As Ballantyne and Aitken (2007) state, this indicates that brand meanings are socially constructed.

The increasing use of user-generated content (UGC) in the form of blogs, tweets, wikis, and social networks now enables consumers to assume a greater role in defining what a brand means to them—something that they now share with their friends, family, and contacts, rather than with the organization itself. This means that both managers and customers are involved in the branding process. The control of brands used to reside with brand owners; today, this influence has shifted to consumers as they redefine what brands mean to them, how they differentiate among similar offerings, and the way in which they associate certain attributes or feelings and emotions with particular brands.

However, as Bengtsson (2003) argues, there is doubt about whether consumers really want a relationship with brands—or even whether they do have a relationship with them. His doubt concerns whether relationship theory is appropriate when examining the way in which consumers interact with brands.

Another relational perspective on brands is offered by de Lencastre and Côrte-Real (2010), who believe a brand to be a sign and use **semiotics** (that is, the science of signs) to create a model that considers the different components of the relationships among them. They attempt to integrate the multiple facets of the brand concept and, in doing so, define three main brand dimensions: the identity sign itself; the marketing object to which the sign refers; and the market response to the sign. One of the points they make is that brands today are largely regarded as socio-cultural concepts in which relational and community issues replace the former power-based managerial perspective whereby brand managers assumed control over a brand.

 Visit the **online resources** and follow web links to learn more about brand semiotics.

Brand Co-creation

The managerial perspective assumes that marketers develop and manage brands, while individual consumers are passive and can influence only their own brand meaning or perception of a brand.

In recent years, this perspective and process has been challenged by increasing evidence that customers can create brands. In customer branding, the customer attaches a name, term, or other feature that enables them to identify one seller's good or service as distinct from those of other sellers (AMA, 2012). This is commonly referred to as co-creation (see Chapter 12). Although many indicate that this is not a recent phenomenon, France, Merrilees, and Miller (2015: 6) point out that there is still no exact understanding of the co-creation construct and that there is 'some confusion in the literature, especially in the area of brand co-creation and brand engagement'.

Pennington and Ball (2009: 455) define customer branding as 'a process in which a customer, or customers, define, label, and seek to purchase a subset of an otherwise undifferentiated or unbranded product. The customer can be anywhere along the value chain, including intermediate and end-user customers.'

In conventional branding processes, a business is able to influence external stakeholders and customers through promises of value creation, and internally as means of employee branding and organizational identity. Where there is customer branding, the organization surrenders control of the brand's ability to convey these and other messages to customers and employees (Pennington and Ball, 2009).

In conventional branding activities, communication about a brand flows from the marketer to the consumer. In co-creation contexts, it is the customer who knows what they want, badges it, and requests it by means of the badge they have provided or by means of some other characteristic that others will recognize. In other words, in customer branding, the flow is reversed.

Pennington and Ball (2009) identify three key conditions that need to be met for customer branding to occur:

1 there must be a variety of offerings in the market;

2 the delivery and quality of offerings must be acceptable; and

3 customers must be able to obtain a reliable and satisfactory alternative from within the marketing channel.

For them, 'for the customer to expend the effort to take over branding activities that the marketer is not performing, the customer must show certain needs, perceptions and abilities' (Pennington and Ball, 2009: 459).

In addition to customer branding, customers can co-create in different ways, most of which are rooted in brand value. France and colleagues (2015) refer to co-creation in the context of exchanges with and experiences of a brand, influencing customer perception of a brand, customer-generated advertising, new product development, social media, and word of mouth (see Market Insight 13.4).

Ideas about brand co-creation are not confined to product or service offerings. For example, Juntunen (2012) found that a range of stakeholders, not only customers, is involved in corporate brand co-creation. These stakeholders include employees, relatives, friends, university researchers, students, employees and managers of other companies, advertising agencies, financiers,

Market Insight 13.4
The Mashing of Peppa Pig

Peppa Pig is a popular character in a British-made children's cartoon—the star of a television series targeted at preschool children, aged between 2 and 6. Peppa is a sweet, but cheeky, anthropomorphic female pig who lives with her little brother George, and her parents, Mummy Pig and Daddy Pig. The gentle narrative revolves around family life and everyday experiences.

More than 200 episodes have been aired and the show is distributed in 180 countries. Significantly, Peppa Pig has more than 73 licences and endorses a number of products, such as cake mixes, ice lollies, and porridge.

The show has spurred the production of character merchandise, including toys and plush collectables, books, DVDs, apps, and clothing. Significantly, in 2010, the show made £200 million from merchandising in the UK alone. What's more, in 2012, the brand expanded to major territories including the United States, Australia, Spain, Russia, and the Benelux countries (that is, Belgium, the Netherlands, and Luxembourg), and Peppa Pig is set for continued international expansion into Asia and Latin America. Peppa Pig also has an enviable presence on Facebook and Twitter, and in the wider blogosphere, boasting many unofficial fan pages, in addition to the official company ones. The animation company hosts live stage productions in which the public can meet Peppa and her posse of family and friends. There is even a theme park in Hampshire, which is becoming a popular family destination. It is clear that 'Peppa Pig' can be considered a household name and a brand in its own right.

Peppa Pig has attracted the attention of a range of other content-creating animators. However, these concentrate on making absurd disingenuous mash-ups—that is, combinations of disparate bits of digital video, audio, text, and graphics, refashioned into something new, and then uploaded to YouTube. Peppa Pig has been mashed up and parodied in a variety of ways, including dancing 'Gangnam Style', doing the Harlem Shake, or trying her hand as a nightclub disc

jockey. On another level, she can be seen listening to explicit voiceovers of various episodes, as well as killing herself and others ('Peppa Pig dies . . . haha'). The bizarre scenarios made available for viewing are seemingly endless.

Peppa Pig is a popular cartoon character, yet is subject to mash-ups and parody in numerous bizarre scenarios
Source: © tanuha2001/Shutterstock.

Although these YouTube mash-ups represent a threat, research indicates that they have not tarnished the brand. There is strong disdain for their creators, and most are condemned for exploiting what is widely regarded as an innocent and upstanding brand. The brand is considered a victim—one that has fallen prey to 'pathetic' and 'sad' creators.

Interviews with the mash-up creators revealed that there was no definitive motive behind their creation of these controversial videos. Although motivations were varied, three broad categories were identified:

- creativity ('I love making these videos for my own pleasure; it is strangely entertaining, it is fun');

- social capital (a genuine sense of gratification out of pleasing others); and

- aversion (a deep-seated hatred of the brand or pigs).

Source: Wilkinson and Patterson (2013).

Market Insight 13.4
continued

Theory into Practice

The Internet has generated an 'architecture of participation' that has led to consumer empowerment on a level previously unimaginable. These co-creators appear to consider themselves to be brand co-owners, rather than passive recipients of company-created brand messages. Mash-ups are amateur productions that present parodies ranging from playful imitations through to clear intentions to criticize a brand. They represent brand co-creation. Mash-up makers construct new narratives around brands so that their own existence can be acknowledged. YouTube, as the name suggests, says much more about the content creator than about the actual content of any videos that mash-up makers upload.

Related Topics

branding; differentiation; positioning; participation

1 **Which other brands have you seen similar mash-ups for?**

2 **What similarities and/or differences can you see between the brands you identified in those other brands and Peppa Pig?**

3 **What other examples of brand co-creation can you think of?**

This market insight was kindly contributed by Professor Anthony Patterson, University of Liverpool.

---

lawyers, and graphic designers, as well as customers. She revealed that stakeholders engage in various sub-processes of corporate brand co-creation even before a company is formed (Kollmann and Suckow, 2007). These include inventing the corporate name before a company is established, developing a new corporate name, updating the logo and communications material, and developing the proposition and the business after establishment of the company.

 Visit the **online resources** and complete Internet Activity 13.3 to learn more about the Peppa Pig brand.

Brand Preference or Relevance

Conventional brand strategies are based on competition for **brand preference**. According to Aaker (2012: 44), this is about 'my brand being better than yours', and requires making sure that customers prefer your brand of fruit juice rather than your competitors' brands. This is achieved by innovations that lead to claims based on 'faster, cheaper, better', resulting in a more attractive, reliable, or less costly brand promise. Inevitably, however, competitors respond very quickly, nullifying any short-term gains.

Unfortunately, preference strategies have little impact, because the evidence shows there is little or no shift in sales or market share. This is mainly as a result of brand and market inertia. Brand preference competition works if the goal is customer retention, but, as Aaker (2012: 44) states, 'it can lead to price and margin erosion and a decline into irrelevance'.

An alternative—although rarely used—strategy is to compete on the basis of being the most relevant brand. The key is to create offerings that have particular characteristics that are so attractive to a segment that any competitive offering that does not have the desirable characteristic will be rejected. These defining characteristics can be considered 'must haves', and may comprise benefits related to personality, organizational values, social programs, self-expressive benefits, or community benefits (Aaker, 2012). Aaker (2012) refers to innovations such as SalesForce.com, which advocated for cloud computing; Cirque du Soleil, which reinvented the circus; and Kevlar, the branded ingredient that created a new subcategory in the body armour market.

Competing through **brand relevance** can generate real growth and is far more effective than the 'faster, cheaper, better' strategies. It requires innovations that lead to the creation of new categories or subcategories, all of which reflect changes in the market and involve substantial risk and new business models.

Sector Branding

Brands work in different ways according to the prevailing environment. Here, we consider branding within services, B2B, internal, and global contexts.

Service Brands

The development of brand strategies for services is important simply because the intangible nature of services (see Chapter 15) requires that customers be helped to understand the value associated with a service offering. Essentially, a brand provides a snapshot of the value and position offered by a service. Brands convey information about the standard of service and, in doing so, seek to achieve two main goals. First, brands seek to reduce the uncertainty associated with the purchase of services—especially when there are no tangible elements on which to base purchase decisions. Consider the complexity and risk associated with buying financial services, such as insurance, pensions, and savings products. Developing strong brands enables these risks to be rolled up into a single identity that is familiar and trusted. For example, Virgin Money is a relative newcomer to the financial services market, but is already well established and growing quickly. The use of sampling and free trials is another popular approach to reducing risk in service-based purchases.

The second goal is to reduce the amount of time people spend searching for a particular service, especially when they are unfamiliar with a particular market or category. When travelling, many visitors to a city will stay at hotels such as Marriott, Travelodge, Holiday Inn, or Hilton because the brands say something about the standard of service that they can expect. Branding shapes customer expectations and can provide a quick answer to a purchase decision. Advertising can also be used to help to make the benefits of a service tangible, rather than the features, which can be limited or boring, or both. Credit cards often promote the feature of a 0 per cent balance transfer, but they also demonstrate the benefits by showing holidays, electrical goods, or fashion items bought as a result of using the credit card.

Good services branding involves the use of logos and symbols, as well as straplines and slogans. These can also help to make the intangible more tangible by relating to some of the core benefits a brand offers. Many service providers use their physical facilities to shape the environment so that customers feel at ease and are attracted into the service process. Booms and Bitner (1981) termed this the **servicescape**, and refer to the need to consider customer expectations and their emotional states. Branding the environment using signs, colours, clothing, and other physical items can provide recall of previous use of the service provider and also influence customer expectations. Consider the environment and overall design of fast-food restaurants such as McDonald's and Burger King. These servicescapes are designed and replicated in high streets across the globe, are easily recognized, and convey information about the type of food offered and the standard of service. Empirical research by Harris and Ezeh (2008) reinforces the view that restaurant managers should actively manage their servicescapes (see Chapter 15).

The emotional dimension of service brands has grown in significance as it becomes increasingly difficult to establish and maintain functional differentiation. By means of marketing communications, brands seek to develop trust and a positive attachment and identification with a brand's values. This can lead to an emotional preference for a brand and so establish a form of competitive advantage that is difficult to copy. Just as the ownership of prestige brands, such as designer fashion brands, trainers, cars, and watches, can be used to convey status, so ownership (and display) of many prestige service brands can convey similar status and position. Examples of this include travelling first class, using platinum credit cards, and being a member of certain clubs or societies.

Finally, not all services are able to develop strong brands; they simply do not have the resources, or the inclination. However, communications should still be an important part of those services' marketing. Those delivering services in which the credence properties are dominant and customers are unable to distinguish the quality of service can emphasize their professionalism by displaying certificates and diplomas, by having a long list of professional qualifications on their business cards, and by referring in their sales literature and websites to the number and types of client with which they have worked.

To conclude this section, we present a comment made by services marketing practitioners responding to a research survey undertaken by Marquardt, Golicic, and Davis (2011: 54) — that is, that 'the most effective means of building brand meaning for business-to-business services is to promote superior, deeper, and richer customer experiences'. The significance of brand meaning and its link to customer experience is important. We consider customer experience marketing in Chapter 15.

Branding in Business-to-Business Markets

The benefits that can accrue from branding in B2B marketing are no different from those that accrue in consumer markets. Some argue that branding in business markets is not appropriate or necessary, but this view is no longer widely held (Kuhn, Alpert, and Pope, 2008). However, there are some specific B2B context branding issues that can be distilled into four main dimensions: functional and product use benefits; emotional benefits; self-expressive benefits; and relational benefits. These are set out in Table 13.1.

Many people assert that business markets have been slow to develop brands and that B2B product-based branding is a relatively underdeveloped area (Mudambi, 2002). In support of this view, Roper and Davies (2010) remark on the scarcity of true business brands. However, many believe that branding in a B2B context is very often corporate, rather than product, branding and, more importantly, that branding can influence business purchasing decisions.

Table 13.1 Benefits derived from branding

Brand benefit	B2B example
Functional	Product performance and high quality associations
	Superior service and support associations
	Specific application and/or location advantages
Emotional	Improved confidence and trust resulting from a reduction in uncertainty
Self-expressive	Buyer-related personal and professional satisfaction
Relational	Larger and stronger networks and collaboration opportunities

There could be many reasons for this underdeveloped use of branding, one of which may be the nature of organizational decision-making processes and associated group activities. Mudambi (2002) concludes that branding is not of equal significance to all organizational buyers nor is it important in all B2B buying situations. Bendixen, Bukasa, and Abratt (2004) and Zablah, Brown, and Donthu (2010) find that delivery, price, and the services offered are consistently more important to buyers than a brand name.

As a counter-argument, both Michell, King, and Reast (2001) and Lennartz and colleagues (2015) suggest that branding is widely used by B2B organizations. This is primarily because product and corporate branding can be important contributors to successful performance, and is, in part, a reflection of the increasing awareness of the importance of relationships within business markets. For example, a partnership might develop whereby the brand provides reassurance, among other things, for a buyer, who in turn supports the brand, on a regular or even frequent basis, and pays the brand's price premium. As a result, business brands not only provide solutions on a continuous basis for certain customers, but also may become integral to a long-term relationship. The launch of Celanese Corporation's 'The chemistry inside innovation' was intended to unify the Celanese portfolio, including its associated brands, and was designed to convey its capabilities and diverse products (Claye, Myer, and Timelin, 2014).

Lindgreen, Beverland, and Farrelly (2010) observe that organizational buyers make decisions using emotional benefits and self-expressive benefits (such as personal and professional satisfaction) in addition to the functional elements. Indeed, work by Roper and Davies (2010: 584) provides timely empirical evidence that B2B brands can have a demonstrable personality, and that 'industrial brands can benefit from the concept of brand image and personality'. (For an illustration of B2B branding, see Market Insight 13.5.)

Visit the **online resources** and follow the web links to read Sarin (2014) and to learn more about the Structura brand, as well as about Sintex.

To develop business brands, three core elements need to be managed: symbolic devices; communication; and behaviour. Together, these might be considered to be the branding mix. In corporate reputation management, these elements are referred to as the identity mix (Birkigt and Stadler, 1986). All organizations use symbolism to signal who they are and what they stand

Market Insight 13.5
Sintex Is the Name

Sintex Industries is an Indian-based holding company engaged in the manufacture of plastic products and textile manufacturing. The early growth of the company was marked by a series of product failures based around a plastic moulding unit designed to manufacture plastic cans to carry cotton slivers in the textile industry. These were not marketed and further experiments also ended in failure. This forced the owners to consider other possible end uses that might have substantial market potential. This led to the development of black plastic water tanks in the late 1970s.

At the time, there were other very small and geographically fragmented manufacturers of water containers, but it was a commodity market. The owners decided to name their water tanks Sintex, using sin from the plastic sintering process and tex from the word 'textiles'. Most water tanks sit on residential and commercial property roofs in India, and the visual prominence of the word Sintex provides a constant free brand reminder to the community. In addition, Sintex spends 70 per cent of its communication budget on mass media—mainly press and popular magazines. Its involvement in trade fairs and exhibitions accounts for 7 per cent, outdoor only 3 per cent, and dealers' meetings and other promotional activities account for the remaining 20 per cent. The Sintex website provides company details and information about its various products. The website is perceived to be a strong brand-building tool. Overall, Sintex spends less than 1.5 per cent of sales on communications.

Part of the brand's success has been attributed to the emphasis placed on innovation. Sintex has developed solutions for the housing sanitation, power, and education sectors, and wishes to be known as a 'thinking company'—that is, one that produces innovative products designed to save the environment, rather than one that merely produces plastic products.

From a simple beginning, Sintex has become the surrogate brand for all plastic water tanks in India, has seized approximately 45 per cent of the market, and now operates in nine other countries across four continents.

Source: Sarin (2014); https://www.superbrandsindia.com/; https://in.reuters.com/finance/

Theory into Practice

Sintex capitalized on a market opportunity within a commodity market. Its subsequent growth and success can be explained in terms of the added value that its simple branding activities brought to the different B2B markets in which it chose to operate. However, simply developing a brand does not bring long-term success, and it was its development of brand values through innovation that drove both consumer and dealer demand for Sintex.

Although the market insight does not tell us, it is highly probable that Sintex was able to charge a premium price and hence derive a better margin than its competitors. This resource was invested in innovation of new products and continued the growth of the company.

Related Topics

brand names; relationships; B2B branding

1 **To what extent should Sintex's success be attributed to its being the first to brand in a commodity market?**

2 **How vulnerable might Sintex be to a global water container brand entering the Indian market?**

3 **How might Sintex's communications evolve as it becomes increasingly regarded as a 'thinking company'?**

for. Logos, company names, straplines, colours, architecture, design, workwear, and delivery vehicles are all symbols. Communication can be considered in terms of management communication (internal and external), organization communication (public relations, or PR), and marketing communication. These need to be integrated around a central theme or strategic platform. The behaviour of employees and managers—not only with one another, but also with external stakeholders—is often overlooked in the branding and reputation management process. One of the key tasks is to align employees' values with the organization's values, and this requires training, communication, and attention by management. Some of the issues associated with internal branding are discussed later in this chapter.

Lennartz and colleagues (2015) found that, to build B2B brands, above all else core brand strength is driven through brand associations, with 'sustainability and corporate governance', as well as 'innovation and expertise', across all countries and industries. In addition, perceptions of product and distribution performance are major factors when building and sustaining B2B brands.

Of importance in B2B markets, but not as critical as in consumer markets, are communications, according to Lennartz and colleagues (2015). Organizations must develop modern integrated communications programmes targeted at all of their key stakeholder groups. Stakeholders demand transparency, accountability, and instant—often online—access to news, developments, research, and networks. This means that inconsistent or misleading information must be avoided. In addition, the leading contributors to the strength of a corporate brand are seen to be their products and services, followed by a strong management team, internal communications, PR, social accountability, change management, and the personal reputation of the chief executive officer (CEO).

Mudambi (2002) suggests that there are three types, or clusters, of B2B customer based upon the way in which they each perceive the importance of branding in the organizational purchase decision process. These are set out in Table 13.2.

Communications for the low-interest cluster need to stimulate interest in the offering and associated purchase decision, perhaps by using testimonials and mini-cases highlighting the experiences of customers in similar purchase situations.

Table 13.2 B2B customer clusters

Cluster name	Characteristics
Highly tangible	Require messages that stress quantifiable and objective benefits of the product and company
Brand-receptive	Require messages that emphasize the support of a well-established and highly reputable manufacturer; should stress the emotional and self-expressive benefits
Low-interest	More likely to respond to brand-based communications that highlight the importance of the purchase decision, and which are supported with processes and procedures that assist the ordering systems

Source: Adapted from Mudambi (2002).

Internal Branding

Employees are an integral part of a brand, if only because they interact with customers and other stakeholders. Lennartz and colleagues (2015: 133) reinforce this when they say that the contact between employees and customers is crucial for driving brand strength, which means that a firm's brand success depends 'significantly on the interactions between firms and customers throughout the selling process'. Employees deliver the functional aspects of an organization's offering and they also deliver the emotional dimensions, particularly in service environments. Through interaction with these two elements, long-term relationships between sellers and buyers can develop. Both scholars and practitioners rightly emphasize the need to integrate internal audiences in brand development (Rosengren and Bondesson, 2017).

This process whereby employees are encouraged to communicate with stakeholders so that organizations ensure that customers realize what is promised is referred to as 'living the brand'. Welch and Jackson (2007) considered some of the issues associated with internal communication. They suggest that internal corporate communication refers to communication between an organization's strategic managers and its internal stakeholders, with the purpose of promoting commitment to the organization, a sense of belonging (to the organization), awareness of its changing environment, and understanding of its evolving goals.

The success of many corporate and service brands is founded on the strength of the internal dimension. The greater the degree to which staff believe and uphold the values, mission, and vision of an organization, the more likely it is that reputation and performance goals will be achieved. Slowly, more energy is being put into the internal aspect of B2B marketing activities.

Global Branding

Brands can be considered in terms of the markets they operate in—sometimes referred to as **brand scope**. Brand scope can involve operating in local and domestic markets, in selected foreign markets, and across a range of international markets. Townsend, Cavusgil, and Baba (2010) provided a useful typology of brands (see Table 13.3).

The scope or reach of a brand is a result of decisions to enter different geographical regions to achieve particular goals. As organizations extend their scope, so their branding and marketing strategies must adapt to influence local cultures and customer needs. However, global branding is characterized by a consistency of marketing strategies—a transfer of the same strategy across all markets, as practised by IBM, AT&T, and China Mobile.

One of the most influential advocates of global branding was Theodore Levitt, whose work on globalization we considered in Chapter 7. Levitt (1983) argued that a global market for uniform products and services requires transnational organizations to standardize their products, packaging, and communications to achieve a common positioning that would be effective across cultures. Growth was to be achieved by selling standardized products all over the world (Holt, Quelch, and Taylor, 2004). However, there are few pure examples of this practice, because even 'global' brands such as McDonald's and Coca-Cola adjust their propositions to suit some local market needs.

The way in which an organization manages its brands and associated products with respect to one another is known as a brand portfolio. According to Townsend and colleagues (2010), citing Douglas, Craig, and Nijssen (2001), it seems as though global branding has become more significant, based on observations that organizations are focusing on core brands and implementing brand portfolio structures to encourage brand consistency across international

---

Table 13.3 A hierarchy of brand scope

Brand scope	Criteria and characteristics	Examples
Domestic	A brand with a presence only in the home market and managed locally	White Stuff Timothy Taylor Thornton's William Hill
International	Sold across a few country markets and managed largely by the home market, often using local agents in international markets Positioning, identity, image, and distinguishing characteristics (including attributes, associations, and identifiers of the brand) virtually identical to the home market	Eddie Stobart Ideal Standard
Multidomestic	Sold across multiple country markets and managed through decentralized management, with local control Positioning, identity, image, and distinguishing characteristics (including attributes, associations, and identifiers of the brand) vary across markets	Ferrero Samsung Philips Diageo GM Caterpillar
Global	Sold across multiple country markets, with distribution located in three major developed continents; centralized brand management coordinates local execution Core essence of the brand remains unchanged; positioning, identity, image, and distinguishing characteristics (including attributes, associations, and identifiers) maintain high degree of consistency across worldwide markets	Coca-Cola McDonald's IBM Apple Google

Source: Adapted from Townsend et al. (2010).

---

markets. However, because different brands within a portfolio are targeted at different market segments, including different geographical markets, it is not unusual for global companies such as Samsung and Toyota to carry international brands within the portfolio.

In addition to the economics of globalization, there are prestige and status advantages associated with global brands, which also manifest themselves in terms of improving **brand equity** (Johansson and Ronkainen, 2005), higher quality, prestige, and intention to purchase (Steenkamp, Batra, and Alden, 2003).

Whatever its merits, the purity of the global brand concept has not been entirely realized because issues of adaptation to local market needs, including social and cultural issues, have led to a need to achieve a balance between these two extremes. For example, Coca-Cola adapts the taste to meet the needs of local markets, even across Europe. So, because the consumption of different offerings naturally varies across countries (for example chocolate, milk, coffee, cars), it is not surprising that we find manufacturers and producers varying their marketing strategies. What this means is that marketers need to determine which elements can be standardized (for example products, name, packaging, service) and which need to be adapted (typically language, communications, and voiceovers) to meet local needs.

Brand Equity

The importance of brands, and thus their value, varies across countries and product categories (see Research Insight 13.3). Brand equity is a measure of the value and strength of a brand. It is an assessment of a brand's wealth, sometimes referred to as goodwill. Financially, brands consist of their physical assets plus a sum that represents their reputation or goodwill, with the latter far exceeding the former. When Michel Kors paid US$2.12 billion for Italian fashion brand Gianni Versace in 2018, the price was high in relation to the current financials of the company, indicating that Michel Kors was willing to pay a premium for the brand (Danzinger, 2018).

Brand equity is considered important because of the increasing interest in measuring the return on marketing investments and pressure by various stakeholders to value brands for balance-sheet purposes. A brand with strong equity is more likely to be able to preserve its customer loyalty and to fend off competitor attacks.

There are two main views about how brand equity should be valued—that is, the financial perspective and the marketing perspective (Lasser, Mittal, and Sharma, 1995). The financial perspective is founded on consideration of a brand's asset value, which is based on the net value of all the cash the brand is expected to generate over its lifetime. The marketing perspective is based on the images, beliefs, and core associations that consumers have about and with particular brands, and the degree of loyalty or retention a brand is able to sustain. Market

Research Insight 13.3

To take your learning further, you might wish to read this influential paper:

Fischer, M., Völckner, F., and Sattler, H. (2010). How important are brands? A cross-category, cross-country study. *Journal of Marketing Research*, 47(5), 823–39.

This article investigates the importance of brands across different product categories and countries. The results show that the importance of brands is higher in the United States than in Asia and Europe. In terms of product categories, the importance of brands is found to differ between countries. The importance of brands in different contexts is likely to vary over time. The article offers a framework for assessing brand importance at a given point in time, and thus can be used to guide brand investments across products and geographical markets.

 Visit the online resources to read the abstract and access the full paper.

awareness, penetration, involvement, attitudes, and purchase intervals (frequency) are typical measures in this regard. However, Feldwick (1996) suggests that there are three aspects of brand equity:

- brand value, based on a financial and accounting base;

- brand strength, measuring the strength of a consumer's attachment to a brand; and

- brand description, represented by the specific attitudes customers have towards a brand.

Brand equity is strongly related to marketing and brand strategy because this type of measurement can help to focus management on brand development. However, there is little agreement about what should be measured or how and when it should be measured. Ambler and Vakratsas (1998) argue that organizations should not seek a single set of measures simply because of the varying circumstances and contextual factors that impinge on brand performance. In reality, however, the measures used by most firms share many common elements.

Stahl and colleagues (2012) researched the relationship between brand equity and customer lifetime value (CLV), which is composed of customer acquisition, retention, and profitability. They found that brand equity has a 'predictable and meaningful impact on CLV' (Stahl et al., 2012: 59). They conclude that brand equity is a multidimensional concept, because the components of brand equity exert different effects on acquisition, retention, and profit. Most interestingly, they suggest that brand management and customer management should be integrated so that they work together in organizations and are not siloed.

 # Chapter Summary

To consolidate your learning, the key points from this chapter are summarized here:

- **Explain the characteristics and principal types of brand and branding.**

   Brands are products and services that have added value. Brands help customers to identify and differentiate between the various offerings. There are three main types of brand—that is, manufacturer, distributor, and generic.

- **Discuss ways in which brands work through associations and personalities.**

   Brands are capable of triggering associations in the minds of consumers. These associations may sometimes enable consumers to construe a psychosocial meaning associated with a particular brand. This psychosocial element can be measured in terms of the associations consumers make across five key dimensions: sincerity; excitement; competence; sophistication; and ruggedness. Brand personality provides a form of identity for consumers that expresses symbolic meaning for themselves and for others.

- **Examine how branding has evolved, utilizing relational and co-creation perspectives.**

   Definitions and types of brand have evolved and emerged as potentially powerful socio-cultural concepts in which relational and community issues replace the former managerial perspective involving senders and receivers, and the control of one party over another. A co-created brand or customer branding can be seen when a customer attaches a name, term, or other feature that enables them to identify one seller's goods or service as distinct from those of other sellers.

■ **Explain how brands can be built.**

Keller's brand pyramid consists of several building blocks and brands are built through a series of steps. The first enables customers to identify with the brand and helps them to make associations with a specific product, class, or customer need. The second step establishes what the brand means by linking various tangible and intangible brand associations. The third step encourages customer responses based around brand-related judgements and feelings. The final step is about fostering an active relationship between customers and the brand.

■ **Describe the principal issues associated with branding in services, business-to-business, internal, and global contexts.**

Branding is important in various sectors. These include services, because the intangibility of services requires that customers be helped to understand the value associated with a service offering. In business markets, branding is increasingly regarded as important because research shows that buyers make decisions based on emotional benefits and self-expressive benefits, not only on utilitarian elements. Employees are an integral part of a customer's brand experience and the management of global brands requires there to be brand consistency across all markets.

■ **Explore the issues and activities associated with brand equity, and demonstrate why branding is important to marketing managers.**

Brand equity is a measure of the value of a brand. It is an assessment of a brand's wealth, sometimes referred to as goodwill. Financially, brands consist of their physical assets plus a sum that represents their reputation or goodwill, with the latter far exceeding the former. There are two main views about how brand equity should be valued—namely, the financial and marketing perspectives.

 Review Questions

1 What is the difference between intrinsic and extrinsic attributes?
2 Why is branding important to consumers and to organizations?
3 What are the main types of brand?
4 Why is it necessary to consider the broad context of consumers' lives to understand the role and relationship that brands play in them?
5 What are Aaker's five dimensions of brand personality?
6 When Ballantyne and Aitken (2007) argue that brand meanings are socially constructed, what do they mean?
7 Draw Keller's brand pyramid and name the individual building blocks.
8 What is the difference between preference and relevance brand strategies?
9 Write brief notes explaining the two main perspectives on brand equity.

 Discussion Questions

1 Having read Case Insight 13.1 at the beginning of this chapter, how would you advise Aston Martin to develop brand awareness and brand familiarity in the Chinese market?

2   When Ingrid Stevenson was appointed brand manager for a range of well-established fruit juices, one of her first tasks was to understand the market and how consumers related to the brand. How might an understanding of Aaker's Brand Personality Scale help her in this task?

3   To what extent are ideas about co-creation and socially constructed meaning relevant to B2B brands?

4   British celebrity chef Jamie Oliver owns and runs a series of high-profile restaurants. He is opening restaurants worldwide, stars in his own ground-breaking chef/food-based television programmes, and has a number of books and other business interests. Discuss the view that celebrities cannot be brands because they do not meet the common brand criteria.

Visit the online resources and complete the Multiple-Choice Questions to assess your knowledge of Chapter 13.

Glossary

brand a multidimensional and emotional construct, with many definitions; typically refers to the added value a product or service is granted in consumers' minds when identified as different from other products.

brand associations the physical and non-physical product attributes and benefits aligned with attitudes that consumers use to create an image of a brand.

brand equity a measure of the value and strength of a brand; an assessment of a brand's wealth, sometimes referred to as goodwill.

brand extension the use of an established brand name to lever entry into a new market or when launching a new product.

brand personalities the associations and images that enable consumers to construe a psychosocial meaning associated with a particular brand.

Brand Personality Scale a set of dimensions used to measure brand personality, developed by Aacker (1997).

brand positioning a strategic activity aiming to differentiate and distinguish a brand.

brand preference a customer's tendency to choose one brand over that of a competitor.

brand relevance the extent to which a brand has characteristics that are so attractive that any competitive brand without the desirable characteristic is rejected.

brand scope the range of international markets in which a brand operates.

customer branding the name, term, or other feature devised by customers that enables them to identify otherwise undifferentiated or unbranded products.

distributor brand a brand developed by a wholesaler, distributor, dealer, or retailer within the distribution channel; sometimes referred to as a private label brand.

extrinsic attributes those elements that, if changed, do not alter the material functioning and performance of the product itself.

generic brands brands sold without any promotional materials or any means of identifying the company.

intrinsic attributes the functional characteristics of a product, such as its shape, performance, and physical capacity.

manufacturer brand a brand created and sustained by a producer to encourage consumer awareness, recognition, and purchase.

semiotics the science of signs.

servicescape the set of stimuli that impact upon customers in a service environment, similar to the atmospherics present in a retail environment.

References

Aaker, D.A. (1991). *Managing Brand Equity*. New York: Free Press.

Aaker, D.A. (2012). Win the brand relevance battle and then build competitor barriers. *California Management Review*, 54(2), 43–57.

Aaker, D.A. (2014). *Aaker on Branding*. New York: Morgan James.

Aaker, J. (1997). Dimensions of brand personality. *Journal of Marketing Research*, 34(3), 347–56.

Achenbaum, A.A. (1993). The mismanagement of brand equity. Presented at: ARF Fifth Annual Advertising and Promotion Workshop, 1 February.

Adebayo, D. (2014). Bob Marley's legacy is going up in cannabis smoke. *The Guardian*, 20 November. Retrieve from: https://www.theguardian.com/commentisfree/2014/nov/20/bob-marley-legacy-cannabis-smoke-reggae-dopeheads (accessed 13 October 2018).

Ahmad, A., and Thyagaraj, K.S. (2014). Brand personality and brand equity research: past developments and future directions. *IUP Journal of Brand Management*, 11(3), 19–56.

AMA (American Marketing Association) (2012). *Branding*. Retrieve from: https://www.ama.org/resources/pages/dictionary.aspx?dLetter=B (accessed 13 October 2018).

Ambler, T., and Vakratsas, D. (1998). Why not let the agency decide the advertising? *Market Leader*, 1, 32–7.

Anderson, T. (2017). Whitney Houston's 'Bodyguard' redux debuts on charts after American Music Awards tribute, *Billboard*, 1 December. Retrieve from: https://www.billboard.com/articles/columns/chart-beat/8054883/whitney-houston-bodyguard-reissue-debuts-american-music-awards-tribute (accessed 13 October 2018).

Anon. (2009). Michael Jackson set to be number one in charts following his death. *The Telegraph*, 27 June. Retrieve from: https://www.telegraph.co.uk/news/worldnews/5662997/Michael-Jackson-set-to-be-number-one-in-charts-following-his-death.html (accessed 13 October 2018).

Armstrong, A. (2015). Savile Row given a modern and exotic splash of technicolour as Chinese billionaire moves in. *The Telegraph*, 13 June. Retrieve from: https://www.telegraph.co.uk/finance/newsbysector/retailandconsumer/11670781/Savile-Row-measures-up-for-a-new-age-as-Chinese-billionaire-william-fung-moves-in.html (accessed 13 October 2018).

Arora, R., and Stoner, C. (2009). A mixed method approach to understanding brand personality. *Journal of Product and Brand Management*, 18(4), 272–83.

Ballantyne, D., and Aitken, R. (2007). Branding in B2B markets: the service-dominant logic. *Journal of Business and Industrial Marketing*, 22(6), 363–71.

Belk, R. (1988). Possessions and the extended self. *Journal of Consumer Research*, 15(2), 139–68.

Bendixen, M., Bukasa, K.A., and Abratt, R. (2004). Brand equity in the business-to-business market. *Industrial Marketing Management*, 33(5), 371–80.

Bengtsson, A. (2003). Towards a critique of brand relationships. *Advances in Consumer Research*, 30, 154–8.

Birkigt, K., and Stadler, M.M. (1986). *Corporate Identity: Grundlagen, Funktionen, Fallspielen*. Landsberg am Lech: Verlag Moderne Industrie.

Booms, B.H., and Bitner, M.J. (1981). Marketing strategies and organization structure for service firms. In: J.H. Donnelly and W.R. George (eds), *The Marketing of Services*, Chicago, IL: American Marketing Association, 47–51.

Boyle, M. (2017). The retail apocalypse is fueled by no-name clothes. *Bloomberg Businessweek*, 11 December. Retrieve from: https://www.bloomberg.com/news/articles/2017-12-11/the-retail-apocalypse-is-fueled-by-no-name-clothes (accessed 13 October 2018).

Caulfield, K. (2012). Amy Winehouse's death led to surge in sales, chart moves. *Billboard*, 23 July. Retrieve from: https://www.billboard.com/articles/news/480976/amy-winehouses-death-led-to-surge-in-sales-chart-moves (accessed 13 October 2018).

Claye, A., Myer, T., and Timelin, B. (2014). The brand beyond the brands. *McKinsey & Company*, May. Retrieve from: https://www.mckinsey.com/business-functions/marketing-and-sales/our-insights/the-brand-behind-the-brands (accessed 13 October 2018).

Clayton, M., and Heo, J. (2011). Effects of promotional-based advertising on brand associations. *Journal of Product and Brand Management*, 20(4), 309–15.

Crawford, M.C. (1985). A new positioning typology. Journal of Product Innovation Management, 2(4), 243–53.

Crosby, L.A. (2012). Relational brands. *Marketing Management*, 21(2), 10–11.

Danzinger, P.N. (2017). Coach becomes tapestry: will a new name change its fortunes? *Forbes*, 13 October. Retrieve from: https://www.forbes.com/sites/pamdanziger/2017/10/13/coach-becomes-tapestry-will-a-new-name-change-its-fortune/ (accessed 13 October 2018).

Danzinger, P.N. (2018). Why fashioning Michael Kors' new Capri Holdings after LVMH is a bad idea. *Forbes*, 6 October. Retrieve from: https://www.forbes.com/sites/pamdanziger/2018/10/06/on-the-versace-acquisition-and-why-fashioning-kors-capri-after-lvmh-is-a-bad-idea/#46ebd1625793 (accessed 13 October 2018).

de Chernatony, L., and dall'Olmo Riley, F. (1998). Defining a brand: beyond the literature with experts' interpretations. *Journal of Marketing Management*, 14(4–5), 417–43.

de Lencastre, P., and Côrte-Real, A. (2010). One, two, three: a practical brand anatomy. *Brand Management*, 17(6), 399–412.

Douglas, S.P., Craig, C.S., and Nijssen, E.J. (2001). Integrating branding strategy across markets: building international brand architecture. *Journal of International Marketing*, 9(2), 97–114.

Feldwick, P. (1996). What is brand equity anyway, and how do you measure it? *Journal of Marketing Research*, 38(2), 85–104.

Fill, C., and Turnball, S. (2016). *Marketing Communications* (7th edn). London: Pearson Education.

Fischer, M., Völckner, F., and Sattler, H. (2010). How important are brands? A cross-category, cross-country study. *Journal of Marketing Research*, 47(5), 823–39.

Fournier, S. (1998). Consumers and their brands: developing relationship theory in consumer research. *Journal of Consumer Research*, 24(4), 343–73.

France, C., Merrilees, B., and Miller, D. (2015). Customer brand co-creation: a conceptual model. *Marketing Intelligence and Planning*, 33(6), 848–64.

Harris, L.C., and Ezeh, C. (2008). Servicescape and loyalty intentions: an empirical investigation. *European Journal of Marketing*, 42(3–4), 390–422.

Holt, D.B., Quelch, J.A., and Taylor, E.L. (2004). How global brands compete. *Harvard Business Review*, 82(9), 68–81.

Jacobs, E. (2012). A cut above in a downturn. *Financial Times*, 26 April. Retrieve from: https://www.ft.com/content/8ecadcdc-8944-11e1-85af-00144feab49a (accessed 13 October 2018).

Johansson, J.K., and Ronkainen, I.A. (2005). The esteem of global brands. *Brand Management*, 1(5), 339–54.

Juntunen, M. (2012). Co-creating corporate brands in start-ups. *Marketing Intelligence and Planning*, 30(2), 230–49.

Keller, K.L. (1993). Conceptualizing, measuring, and managing customer-based brand equity. *Journal of Marketing*, 57(1), 1–22.

Keller, K.L. (1998). *Strategic Brand Management: Building, Measuring, and Managing Brand Equity*. Upper Saddle River, NJ: Prentice Hall.

Keller, K.L. (2009). Building strong brands in a modern marketing communications environment. *Journal of Marketing Communications*, 15(2–3), 139–55.

Keller, K.L. (2016). Reflections on customer-based brand equity: perspectives, progress, and priorities. *AMS Review*, 6(1–2), 1–16.

Kollmann, T., and Suckow, C. (2007). The corporate brand naming process in the net economy. *Qualitative Market Research*, 10(4), 349–61.

Kuhn, K.-A.L., Alpert, F., and Pope, N.K.L. (2008). An application of Keller's brand equity model in a B2B context. *Qualitative Market Research*, 11(1), 40–58.

Lasser, W., Mittal, B., and Sharma, A. (1995). Measuring customer-based brand equity. *Journal of Consumer Marketing*, 12(4), 11–19.

Lennartz, E., Fischer, M., Krafft, M., and Peters, K. (2015). Drivers of B2B brand strength: insights from an international study across industries. *Schmalenbach Business Review*, 67(1), 114–37.

Levitt, T. (1983). The globalization of markets. *Harvard Business Review*, May. Retrieve from: https://hbr.org/1983/05/the-globalization-of-markets (accessed 13 October 2018).

Lindgreen, A., Beverland, M.B., and Farrelly, F. (2010). From strategy to tactics: building, implementing, and managing brand equity in business markets. *Industrial Marketing Management*, 39(8), 1223–5.

Linville, P., and Carlston, D.E. (1994). Social cognition of the self. In P.G. Devine, D.L. Hamilton, and T.M. Ostrom (eds), *Social Cognition: Impact on Social Psychology*, San Diego, CA: Academic Press, 143–93.

Low, G.S., and Lamb, C.W. (2000). The measurement and dimensionality of brand associations. *Journal of Product and Brand Management*, 9(6), 350–68.

Marquardt, A.J., Golicic, S.L., and Davis, D.F. (2011). B2B services branding in the logistics services industry. *Journal of Services Marketing*, 25(1), 47–57.

McCracken, G. (1986). Culture and consumption: a theoretical account of the structure and movement of the cultural meaning of consumer goods. *Journal of Consumer Research*, 13(1), 71–84.

Michell, P., King, J., and Reast, J. (2001). Brand values related to industrial products. *Industrial Marketing Management*, 30(5), 415–25.

Mudambi, S. (2002). Branding importance in business-to-business markets: three buyer clusters. *Industrial Marketing Management*, 31(6), 525–33.

Nielsen/PLMA (2017). *Annual International Private Label Yearbook*. Retrieve from: https://www.plmainternational.com/international-private-label-yearbook (accessed 13 October 2018).

Peng, N., and Chen, A. (2017). Examining consumers' intentions to dine at luxury restaurants while traveling. *International Journal of Hospitality Management*, 71, 59–67.

Pennington, J.R., and Ball, D.A. (2009). Customer branding of commodity products: the customer-developed brand. *Brand Management*, 16(7), 455–67.

Phau, I., and Lau, K.C. (2001). Brand personality and consumer self-expression: single or dual carriageway? *Journal of Brand Management*, 8(6), 428–44.

Ries, A., and Trout, J. (1972). The positioning era cometh. *Advertising Age*, 24 April, 35–8.

Roper, S., and Davies, G. (2010). Business-to-business branding: external and internal satisfiers and the role of training quality. *European Journal of Marketing*, 44(5), 567–90.

Rosengren, S., and Bondesson. N. (2017). How organizational identification among retail employees is affected by advertising, *Journal of Retailing and Consumer Services*, 38, 204–9.

Rossiter, J.R. (2014). Branding explained: defining and measuring brand awareness and brand attitude. *Journal of Brand Management*, 21(7–8), 533–40.

Sarin, S. (2014). Relevance and creation of strong brands for B2B markets. *Vikalpa*, 39(4), 91–100.

Sheth, J.N., Newman, B.I., and Gross, B.L. (1991). Why we buy what we buy: a theory of consumption values. *Journal of Business*, 22(2), 159–70.

Stahl, F., Heitmann, M., Lehmann, D.R., and Neslin, S.A. (2012). The impact of brand equity on customer acquisition, retention and profit margin. *Journal of Marketing*, 76(4), 44–63.

Steenkamp, J.E., Batra, R., and Alden, D.L. (2003). How perceived brand globalness creates brand value. *Journal of International Business Studies*, 34(1), 53–65.

Sweeney, J.C., and Soutar, G.N. (2001). Consumer perceived value: the development of a multiple item scale. *Journal of Retailing*, 77(1), 203–20.

Townsend, J.D., Cavusgil, S.T., and Baba, M.L. (2010). Global integration of brands and new product development at General Motors. *Journal of Product Innovation Management*, 27(1), 49–65.

Tudor, E., and Negricea, I.C. (2012). Brand positioning: a marketing resource and an effective tool for small and medium enterprises. *Journal of Knowledge Management, Economics and Information Technology*, 11(1), 182–90.

Welch, M., and Jackson, P.R. (2007). Rethinking internal communication: a stakeholder approach. *Corporate Communications*, 12(2), 177–98.

Wilkinson, C., and Patterson, A. (2014). Peppa Piggy in the middle of marketers and mashup makers: a netnography of absurd animation on YouTube. In: S. Brown and S. Ponsonby-McCabe (eds), *Brand Mascots and Other Marketing Animals*, London: Routledge, 123–40.

Zablah, A.R., Brown, B.P., and Donthu, N. (2010). The relative importance of brands in modified rebuy purchase situations. *International Journal of Research in Marketing*, 27(3), 248–60.

Part 4
Principles of Customer Management

Chapter 14
Channels, Supply Chains, and Retailing

Learning Outcomes

After reading this chapter, you will be able to:

▶ Describe the nature and characteristics of a marketing channel

▶ Explain the different types of intermediary and their roles in the marketing channel

▶ Understand the different marketing channel structures and their core characteristics

▶ Explain the factors that influence the design and structure of marketing channels

▶ Describe the main elements that constitute supply chain management

▶ Consider the role and function of retailers in the marketing channel

Case Insight 14.1
Åhléns

Market Insight 14.1
Channelling Motorbikes

Market Insight 14.2
Packaged Goods Companies Look Online

Market Insight 14.3
Fashioning a Circular Supply Chain

Market Insight 14.4
Enhancing Channel Experiences

Market Insight 14.5
Retail App-reciation

Case Insight 14.1
Åhléns

As shopper behaviour turns increasingly digital, established retailers have to adapt their channel strategies. We talk to Lotta Bjurhult, business developer retail operations at Åhléns, Sweden's largest department store chain, to find out what it takes to add an online channel to an existing network of department stores.

Åhléns is Sweden's leading department store chain. You could say that we hold a position similar to John Lewis in the UK or Karstadt in Germany. In 2015, we had a turnover of about SEK5 billion, employed some 3,000 people, and served a total of 65 million visitors in our 70 department stores located throughout Sweden. Our customer base is very loyal, with more than 2.2 million club members who shop, on average, 8.5 times a year at our stores.

Our mission is to offer carefully selected, priceworthy, and sustainable solutions that we believe can satisfy people's requirements in a simple, inspiring, and accessible way. As with most department stores, we offer a broad assortment of products and provide a wide array of customer service facilities for store customers. In our department stores, customers are offered a carefully considered collection of selected brands and proprietary labels all under one roof. Our customers are able to browse among an inspiring assortment of value-for-money products within home styling and interior design, fashion, beauty, foodstuffs, and entertainment.

Adding an online channel to an existing department store operation is complex. The challenge is to keep the overall experience of Åhléns, which is very much centred on the in-store shopping experience, while simultaneously adapting it to an online setting. Customers consider Åhléns to be one department store: they don't care if they buy something offline or online. In developing our online offer, we have looked at a range of issues.

In terms of assortment, we have used statistics on what customers are already buying online as a starting point. We have also considered what products are

A key challenge for Åhléns is translating the in-store shopping experience online
Source: Courtesy of Åhléns.

currently not available in all our local department stores. At the end of 2016, our online channel will hold around 50,000 different products, which means that it will offer a larger assortment than most of our physical department stores, but will be equal in size to our larger department stores in Uppsala and Malmö. Over time, we are aiming to provide the same assortment online as we do in our flagship store Åhléns City Stockholm.

We have also developed a tailor-made information technology (IT) system to support the online channel. In creating our online store, we have gone through and developed all our internal processes—starting with how we relate to suppliers and vendors, through where to stock and how to deliver products, as well as to the role of physical store employees. Going online exposes any weaknesses you might have in your business operations. If something is not really working in a physical store, there are store employees who can fix it. And things such as payments and returns, which are

Case Insight 14.1

continued

quite easily managed in a physical department store, become a lot trickier online.

Another key consideration for us has been how to engage store employees and make them embrace the online channel as part of the overall value proposition of Åhléns. The online channel has profound and long-lasting effects on the role they play in creating a high-quality customer experience.

One of my key tasks has been to ensure that in-store employees and customer service embrace the online channel and make it part of the experience offered to

our customers every day. This is essential if we are to offer our customers a seamless experience.

Key questions for Åhléns have been: what roles should store employees play in integrating the offline and online channels? What activities are needed to ensure their support for a new online channel?

 Visit the online resources to watch a video interview with Lotta Bjurhult in which she explains what Åhléns did.

Introduction

Have you ever considered the journey that a bottle of water, a computer, or a bag of potatoes might take from its source (manufacturer or producer) to be available for you to purchase at the point you prefer? In many cases, this journey can be complex, involving transactions between many organizations, countries, and people.

The organizations involved with any one journey are collectively termed a distribution channel or **marketing channel**. These are chains of organizations that are concerned with the management of the processes and activities involved in creating and moving products from producers and manufacturers to end users. Each organization adds something of value before passing it to the next, and it is this interaction that provides mutual advantage (Kotler and Keller, 2009) and underpins the concept of channel marketing.

Each of the various organizations electing to interact with others performs a specific role in the chain of activities. Some act as manufacturers; some, as agents; others may be distributors, dealers, value-added resellers, wholesalers, or retailers. Whatever the role, it is normally specific and geared to refining, adding value, and moving a product closer to the end user. This interaction requires coordination if participating organizations are to achieve their goals and make available final products and services that represent superior value to the channel's end users, especially when there are multichannel activities (Ailawadi and Farris, 2017).

In this chapter, we consider three main elements. The first concerns the management of the intangible aspects, or issues of ownership, control, and flows of communication between the parties responsible for making an offering accessible to target customers, commonly referred to as marketing channel management.

The second element concerns the management of the tangible or physical aspects of moving a product from the producer to the end user. This must be undertaken so that a customer can freely access an offering, and so that the final act of the buying process is as convenient and easy as possible. This is part of supply chain management, which includes the logistics associated with moving products closer to end users.

The third and final element is about **retailing**—a critical element of the way in which consumers access the products they desire.

Channel Management

Europe's largest clothing maker and retailer Inditex has seen its clothing sales rise consistently in recent years because it adds new stock to its fashion stores (for example Zara, Pull&Bear, and Massimo Dutti) twice a week, keeping the stock fresh and up to date with the latest fashion trends. It achieves this by manufacturing over 50 per cent of its stock in Spain or Portugal. Although this is more costly in terms of production, Inditex can get new designs into European and American stores twice as quickly as it would if it were to have to wait for delivery of stock manufactured in Asia. This shows that, by managing its marketing channels, Inditex has improved its overall business performance.

If we consider the skills Inditex needs to design and assemble a range of garments, to source the materials, and to manufacture, package, and then distribute the final fashion garments to its stores and other customers globally, we can see that a major set of complex operations are required. For many organizations, trying to undertake all these operations is beyond their skillset or core activity. For all organizations, there is a substantial risk associated with producing too many or too few, too soon or too late for the target market. There are risks associated with changing buyer behaviours, and with storage, finance, and competitors' actions, to name but a few of the critical variables.

By collaborating with other organizations that have the necessary skills and expertise, firms can reduce these uncertainties. Working with organizations that can create customer demand or access, and manage specialist financial issues, storage, or transportation, adds value and develops competitive advantage. For example, to reach the 600,000 rural villages in India, Samsung partnered with the Indian Farmers Fertiliser Cooperative Ltd to sell its handsets. With this new marketing channel, Samsung can now reach over 90 per cent of villages in India.

Collectively, organizations that combine to enable offerings to reach end users quickly and efficiently constitute a marketing channel—sometimes referred to as a distribution channel. Organizations that combine to reduce risk and uncertainty do so by exchanging offerings that are of value to others in the channel. Therefore marketing channels enable organizations to share or reduce uncertainty. By reducing the uncertainty experienced by all members in a channel, each is in a better position to concentrate on other tasks.

How Channels Help to Reduce Uncertainty

Marketing channels enable different types of uncertainty to be decreased in several ways (Fill and McKee, 2012). These include reducing the complexity, increasing value and competitive advantage, routinization, and providing specialization.

Reducing Complexity

If it were to contact them directly, the number of transactions and the frequency of contact a producer might have with each individual end user would be so high that the process would be unprofitable. This volume of activity can be seen in Figure 14.1.

If an intermediary is introduced into the process, the number of transactions falls drastically, as demonstrated in Figure 14.2. The fall in the number of transactions indicates not only that are costs reduced, but also that producers are better placed to redirect their attention towards the needs of intermediaries. This allows them to focus on their core activities—that is, production or manufacturing. In much the same way, end users receive improved individual support from channel intermediaries in comparison with that which they would be likely to get from a producer. For example, a local farmer could focus on growing a particular crop and cultivating cattle, and then ship the produce in large quantities to a wholesaler, who then takes over the responsibly of selling and distributing the produce to retailers, who in turn sell them on to consumers.

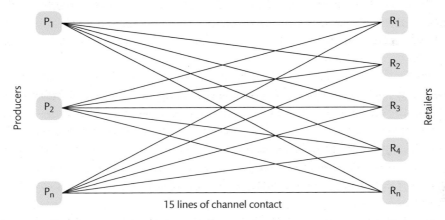

Figure 14.1
The complexity of channel exchanges without intermediaries

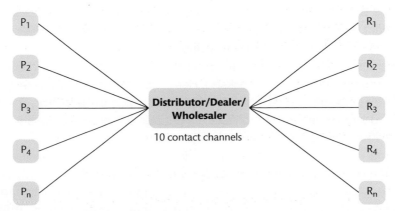

Figure 14.2
The impact of intermediaries on channel exchanges

Increasing Value and Competitive Advantage

By using intermediaries, producers can reduce purchase risk—that is, the uncertainty that customers might reject the offering. Intermediaries, rather than producers, have the skills and core competencies necessary to meet end users' requirements, for example retailing. By improving the overall value that customers perceive in an offering relative to competing products and customer experience, it is possible to develop competitive advantage. For example, individuals might not value the produce (for example strawberries) grown by a farmer so much that they are willing to drive out to the farm to buy it, but when offered the strawberries by a retailer those same individuals may see the produce as a relevant addition to other items they might be buying as part of their shopping trip.

Routinization

Performance risk can be reduced by improving transaction efficiency. Standardizing, or 'routinizing', the transaction process—perhaps by regulating order sizes, automating operations, and managing delivery cycles and payment frequencies—allows distribution costs to be reduced. For the local farmer, selling produce to a wholesaler provides the opportunity to routinize transactions in relation to, for example, size, delivery time, and payments compared to selling them directly to end users who might have a wide variety of preferences in terms how much, when, and how they want to buy.

Specialization

By providing specialist training services, maintenance, installation, bespoke deliveries, or credit facilities, intermediaries can develop a service that has real value to other channel members or end users. Value can also be improved for customers by helping them to locate the offerings they want. Intermediaries can provide these specialist resources, whereas producers are not normally interested or able to do so. This is because they prefer to produce large quantities of a small range of goods. Unfortunately, end users want only a limited quantity of a wide variety of goods.

Intermediaries provide a solution by bringing together and sorting out all the goods produced by different manufacturers in the category. They then represent these goods in quantities and formats that enable end users to buy the quantities they wish, as frequently as they prefer. This is referred to as sorting and smoothing. Table 14.1 provides an explanation of these forms of specialization.

Intermediaries provide other utility-based benefits. For example, they assist end users by bringing a product produced a long distance away to a more convenient location for purchase and consumption—that is, they offer **place utility**.

They also help the end user because the product might be manufactured during the week, but purchased and consumed at the weekend. Here, manufacturing, purchase, and consumption occur at different points in time, and intermediaries provide **time utility**.

Immediate product availability through retailers enables ownership to pass to the consumer within a short period of time—that is, **ownership utility**.

Finally, intermediaries can also provide information about the product to aid sales and usage. The Internet has led to the development of a new type of intermediary: an information intermediary (for example Expedia, Google). Here, the key role is to manage information to improve the efficiency and effectiveness of the distribution channel—that is, **information utility**.

There are some disadvantages to the use of intermediaries. For example, as the number of intermediaries in a channel increases, a lack of product control can develop. Some manufacturers

Table 14.1 Aspects of sorting and smoothing

Aspect	Explanation
Sorting out	Grading products into different sizes, qualities, or grades (e.g. potatoes, eggs or fruit)
Accumulation	Bringing together different products from different producers to provide a wider category choice
Allocation	Often referred to as breaking bulk (by wholesalers), this involves disaggregating bulk deliveries into smaller lot sizes that customers are able (and prefer) to buy
Assorting	Assembling different collections of goods/services thought to be of value to the customer (retailers and consumers)

Source: Fill and McKee (2012). Used with kind permission.

are unable to influence intermediaries in terms of in-store merchandising, placement, and even pricing. Furthermore, intermediaries might be susceptible to competitor inducements, such as trade promotions. For many manufacturers and producers, intermediaries often become a market in their own right, and developing and sustaining a relationship with them can require considerable time, money, and personnel.

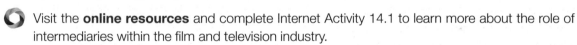 Visit the **online resources** and complete Internet Activity 14.1 to learn more about the role of intermediaries within the film and television industry.

Types of Intermediary

Having seen that intermediaries play a significant role in marketing channels, we now need to consider the different types of intermediary. There are, of course, a number of such, each fulfilling different roles and providing various forms of specialization. Some of the more common ones are as follows:

- An *agent or broker* acts as the intermediary between the seller of an offering and buyers, bringing them together without taking ownership of the offering. These intermediaries have the legal authority to act on behalf of the manufacturer and typically make money through commissions. For example, fish and seafood agents typically help fisheries to sell their catches to wholesalers and authors typically use international agents when selling rights to their books on the international market.

- A *merchant* undertakes the same actions as an agent, but takes ownership of a product.

- *Distributors or dealers* distribute the product. They offer value through services associated with selling inventory, credit, and aftersales service. Often used in business-to-business (B2B) markets, they can also be found dealing directly with consumers, for example automobile distributors. (See Market Insight 14.1 for a view of Honda's dealers and distributors.)

- A *franchisee* holds a contract to supply and market an offering to the requirements or blueprint of the franchisor, the owner of the original offering. The contract might cover many aspects of the design of the offering, such as marketing, product assortment, or service delivery.

Market Insight 14.1
Channelling Motorbikes

Honda sells more than 12 million motorcycles each year in the Asia–Oceania region alone, and the management of its distribution networks is a vital element in maintaining customer access and satisfaction. Honda produces a wide range of motorcycles, ranging from the 50cc class to the 1,800cc class, and is the largest manufacturer of motorcycles in the world in terms of annual units of production. In the region, Honda's motorcycles are produced at sites in Japan, Indonesia, the Philippines, Pakistan, and India.

In Japan, sales of Honda motorcycles (and automobiles and power products) are made through different distribution networks. Honda's products are sold to consumers primarily through independent retail dealers and motorcycles are distributed through more than 11,500 outlets, including approximately 1,400 authorized dealerships. These authorized dealerships sell all Honda's Japanese motorcycle models, not only selected models.

Most of Honda's overseas sales are made through its main sales subsidiaries, which distribute Honda's products to local wholesalers and retail dealers. In Indonesia, Honda has recently developed its dealer network of 4,000 dealers and service shops to support sales and provide excellent aftersales service. In the United States, Honda's wholly owned subsidiary markets Honda's motorcycle products through a sales network of approximately 1,260 independent local dealers. Many of these motorcycle dealers also sell other Honda products.

In Europe, subsidiaries of the company in the UK, Germany, France, Belgium, the Netherlands, Spain, Switzerland, Austria, Italy, and other European

Honda uses simulators to enable riders to practise riding, receive risk awareness training, and experience the brand
Source: © Bloomberg/Getty.

countries distribute Honda's motorcycles through approximately 1,600 independent local dealers.

One core element of Honda's dealer strategy, worldwide, is its comprehensive '4S' support system, which covers sales, service, spare parts, and safety. For example, Honda provided its dealers in Thailand, Indonesia, Vietnam, and India with an easy-to-use riding simulator, called Riding Trainer, by means of which riders can receive risk awareness training and riding practice, and of course develop engagement with the Honda brand.

Recently, a fifth 'S' has been added: 'second-hand' (or used) business. In Thailand, for example, the second-hand motorcycle business has been deliberately strengthened as a means of developing business. The strategy encourages potential motorcycle owners and those ready for an upgrade to purchase pre-owned Honda models, drawing this segment into the brand.

Source: https://www.honda.com/

Market Insight 14.1
continued

Theory into Practice

This market insight demonstrates the variety and complexity of Honda's marketing channels. The design of a marketing channel depends partly on the context, culture, and level of economic development in a country or region. In other words, no one channel design can fit every situation.

The level of control and degree to which Honda, as a manufacturer, can control the marketing activities associated with its motorbikes varies considerably. Honda's control over the marketing channel is enhanced by the establishment of authorized dealerships and, in the United States, by wholly owned subsidiaries. At the other end of the spectrum are independent local dealers, whom Honda has attempted to influence and retain through the use of simulators. This, in turn, helps to attract and retain customers.

Related Topics

intermediaries; channel structures; channel relationships

1 **Why does Honda set up subsidiary organizations in each overseas region or country?**

2 **What do you think are the benefits of the '5S' support system?**

3 **What might affect Honda's dealer network (marketing channel) in the future?**

The uniformity of differing branches of McDonald's and KFC is an indication of franchisee contracts; however, franchise agreements are not used only in the fast food or product sectors:

- A *wholesaler* stocks goods before the next level of distribution and takes both legal title and physical possession of the goods. In consumer markets, wholesalers do not usually deal with the consumer, but with other intermediaries (for example retailers). In B2B markets, sales are made directly to consumers. Examples include Costco Wholesalers in the United States and Makro in Europe.

- *Retailers* sell directly to consumers and may purchase directly from manufacturers or deal with wholesalers. This is dependent on their purchasing power and the volume purchased. Leading retailers include Walmart, Marks & Spencer, Carrefour, and electronics retailers such as Media-Saturn and Zalando.

- *Infomediaries* are Internet-based organizations, such as Google and Pricerunner, designed to provide information to channel members, including end users.

Visit the **online resources** and follow the web link to the European Franchise Association (EFA) to learn more about business franchise collaboration activities across Europe.

Managing Marketing Channels

There are two main issues associated with the management of marketing channels: the design of the channel, its structure and activities; and the relationships between channel members. These are considered in turn.

Channel Design

The design of an appropriate channel—that is, its structure, length, and the membership and their roles—varies according to context. For example, the channels necessary to support a new product or organization start-up are different from those required when modifying an existing structure to adapt to changing market conditions. The channel design decision process requires three key decisions:

- the *distribution intensity decision*—that is, the level of purchase convenience required by the different customer segments to be served;

- the *channel configuration decision*—that is, the number and type of intermediaries necessary to deliver products to the optimum number of sales outlets; and

- the *multichannel decision*—that is, the number of different types of channel to be used.

This helps us to determine what is the most effective and efficient way of getting the offering to the customer.

Key Considerations

When designing distribution channels, we need to consider a variety of factors to ensure that the channel suits the organization's objectives. Three broad elements need to be considered, as follows:

- *Economics* requires us to recognize where costs are being incurred and profits being made in a channel to maximize our return on investment.

- *Coverage* is about maximizing the offering's availability in the market for the customer, satisfying the desire to have the offering available to the largest number of customers, in as many locations as possible, at the widest range of times.

- *Control* refers to achieving the optimum distribution costs without losing decision-making authority over the offering—that is, how it is priced, promoted, and delivered in the distribution channel.

Sometimes, by covering a wide range of delivery times and locations by means of intermediaries, organizations sacrifice some control in decision-making. Intermediaries start changing the price, image, and display as they seek to maximize sales of a whole range of products. Think about the positions of HTC, Huawei, Samsung, and Apple. To get the maximum number of customers using their mobile phone handsets, they need to have the maximum number of retailers and mobile phone networks promoting and selling their phones. However, the same networks and retailers also sell the handsets of their competitors. As the retailers and networks compete to sign up customers, they push for lower prices, or they demand advertising subsidies to help them to sell the phones. So Samsung and LG may discover that their phones are being sold at very low prices, and that their brand images are being compromised by retailers

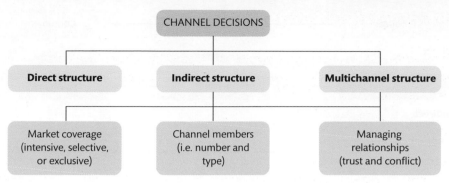

Figure 14.3
Distribution channel strategy decisions

and networks who are desperately seeking to maximize their own sales. What happens if LG reduces the number of retailers or networks it deals with to increase control over its marketing mix? The danger, of course, is that its competitors will gain market share by continuing to deal with these retailers and networks. In contrast, Apple has specific policies on what distributors can and cannot discount on products like the iPhone. All face a trade-off between economics, coverage, and control.

Visit the **online resources** and follow the web links to the Institute of Supply Chain Management (ISM) and the Chartered Institute of Purchasing and Supply (CIPS) to learn more about the profession and activities of managing the distribution and supply chain.

Distribution Channel Strategy

When devising a distribution channel strategy, several key decisions need to be made to serve customers and to establish and maintain appropriate buyer–seller relationships. These are summarized in Figure 14.3. The first decision is selecting how the channel will be structured. If the channel requires intermediaries, we need to consider the type of market coverage we want, the number and type of intermediaries to use, and how we should manage the relationships between members in the channel. These choices are important because they can affect the benefits provided to customers.

Channel Structure

Distribution channels can be structured in a number of ways. There are three main configurations involving producers, intermediaries, and customers: direct channels; indirect channels; or multichannel structures. A **direct channel structure** involves selling directly to end users with little involvement from other organizations, while an **indirect channel structure** uses intermediaries and a **multichannel structure** combines both. These are presented in Figure 14.4.

We now consider the advantages and disadvantages of each of type of channel structure.

Direct Channel Structure

In a direct channel structure, the producer uses strategies to reach end users directly rather than dealing through an intermediary (an agent, broker, retailer, or wholesaler) (see Figure

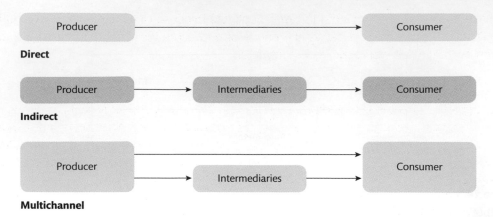

Figure 14.4
Distribution channel structure

14.4). Have you ever been to a farmers' market and purchased produce directly from a farmer, or downloaded music from the site of a local band? These are examples of direct distribution. The advantages of this structure are that the producer or manufacturer maintains control over its product and profitability, and builds strong customer relationships. However, this structure is not suitable for all products. It is ideally suited to those products that require significant customization, technical expertise, or commitment on behalf of the producer to complete a sale (Parker, Bridson, and Evans, 2006) — although electronic technologies such as the Internet have enabled a greater number of product manufacturers to reach customers directly.

Efficiency within the direct channel structure can be improved in the following ways:

- *By processing orders and distributing the offering electronically directly to customers* — Adobe Reader is free universal software manufactured by Adobe Systems Inc. that enables users to read and share electronic documents. To increase the cost-efficiency of delivery, the organization employs a direct structure via the Internet, providing digital delivery, installation, and customer support.

- *Supporting the physical distribution of the product offering directly to customers* — One of the best-known examples of this is Dell Computer Corporation's system. Dell sells computer equipment through its own website, using telesales for product ordering, and database technology for order processing, tracking, and inventory and delivery management. The organization also distributes its products through its own delivery and installation staff.

The disadvantages of a direct channel structure typically include the large amount of capital and resources required to reach customers. This means that there are virtually no economies of scale. Manufacturers might also suffer from offering a low variety of offerings, which may not meet the needs of buyers. This is especially apparent in consumer markets, such as fast-moving consumer goods (FMCGs). Imagine having to shop for bread, milk, and a soft drink at three differing retail outlets owned by each product manufacturer. Few consumers today would purchase their offerings from individual manufacturers because of the inconvenience and time costs involved. Thus retailers satisfy the needs of end users for variety—something a direct channel of distribution would not necessarily fulfil.

Indirect Channel Structure

Indirect channel structures enable producers to concentrate on the skills and processes necessary to make offerings, and use one or more intermediaries for distribution. For example, Procter & Gamble (P&G) focuses its resources and expertise on developing new types of FMCG, whereas the core retailing activity of Sainsbury's is to make P&G's products (and those of P&G's competitors) available to consumers.

Multichannel Structure

An increasing number of organizations adopt a hybrid or multichannel structure to distribute goods and services (Ailawadi and Farris, 2017). Here, the producer controls some marketing channels and intermediaries control others. For example, many airlines sell their tickets directly to consumers through the Internet, but also rely on travel agents. Consider the options for the purchase of a mobile device. This could occur directly from the Samsung website, from a service provider such as EE, or perhaps at Tesco, while picking up some bread and milk. Samsung, Lenovo, and LG Electronics use service providers, electronic retailers, and wholesale discount clubs alongside their own direct Internet and telesales channels to market and deliver their mobile phone handsets.

The benefits of a multichannel structure include the following:

- *Increased reach*—By utilizing existing direct networks and the relationships of intermediaries, the provider can reach a wider target audience.

- *Producer control*—Producers have greater control over prices, communication, and can reach customers directly.

- *Greater compliance*—Adherence to channel rules is more likely when producers use multiple intermediaries and are not perceived to be a (direct channel) competitor.

- *Optimized margins*—Producers can improve margins from the direct channel element and increase their bargaining power as they become less dependent on intermediaries.

- *Improved market insight*—By developing relationships with their direct customers, producers can derive a better understanding of their needs and market issues.

The use of multichannel strategies has been encouraged by the growth of the Internet, which has increased the efficiency with which consumers and manufacturers can interact. At the same time, technologies are increasing the efficiency of information exchange between producers and intermediaries, for example through electronic data interchange (EDI) and extranets. However, the sharing of profits among channel members can be a source of conflict, especially when intermediaries perceive the producer to be a competitor, as well as a supplier. This structure may also confuse and alienate customers who are unsure about which channel they should use. (For more about the challenges of using multiple channels, see Research Insight 14.1 and Market Insight 14.2.)

Research Insight 14.1

To take your learning further, you might wish to read this influential paper:

Ailawadi, K.L., and Farris, P.W. (2017). Managing multi- and omni-channel distribution: metrics and research directions. *Journal of Retailing*, 93(1), 120–35.

In this article, the authors present a framework for managing distribution in increasingly complex channel structures. In doing so, they point towards important questions that contemporary marketers are grappling with in terms of distribution channels and also summarize the metrics that are relevant to each element of the framework.

    Visit the online resources to read the abstract and access the full paper.

Market Insight 14.2
Packaged Goods Companies Look Online

The impact of e-commerce has been significant in many markets, but the consumer packaged goods (CPG) market has, until recently, avoided any major disruption. Traditionally, CPGs have been distributed through independent retailers and supermarkets, using distributors and strategically placed distribution centres. Online sales accounted for less than 1 per cent of total sales in packaged food and approximately 3 per cent in non-food in 2013.

Since then, there have been several innovative experiments in e-commerce in the CPG sector. A

Reorder your favourite products with the touch of a button

Source: © 2018 Amazon.com, Inc. or its affiliates.

Market Insight 14.2

continued

number of regional grocers have piloted various 'click and collect' operations whereby products are purchased online and picked up in stores. Perhaps one of the most significant moves has been the trend towards major CPG companies strengthening their digital channel strategies by working with Amazon and other key digital players. One of the primary approaches has been to locate teams of digital and functional specialists at Amazon, then, through investment, to develop co-marketing activities with Amazon.

Amazon has tested Amazon Pantry, which lets its Prime users fill a box with selections of more than 2,000 products and ship them for a small fee. Prime Now offers delivery to the home within one or two hours and

the Dash Button—an Internet-connected device placed anywhere in the home—provides a one-touch way of ordering refills.

In September 2016, supermarket retailer Sainsbury's began the process of integrating high-street digital retailer Argos into its business. Sainsbury's purchased Argos to compete more effectively and better adapt to changes in the retailing environment. It was also felt that there were several synergies between the two organizations that could be developed.

Sources: Alldredge and Ungerman (2015); Alldredge, Newaskar, and Ungerman (2015); Armstrong (2016); Sheffield (2016).

Theory into Practice

The traditional marketing channels in the consumer packaged goods (CPG) market are determined largely by market size. Manufacturers distribute their goods directly to large supermarket customers via distribution points and warehouses. Ownership moves from the producer to the retailer. Smaller customers, who buy smaller volumes, buy branded products from distributors, such as wholesalers, who then sell them to retailers. In this case, ownership moves with the product.

The development of online channels means that manufacturers have direct access to end users—in this case, consumers. This lowers many of the **supply chain** costs, but, because of the small number of units involved in any one transaction, distribution costs can raise prices. This can be partially alleviated through click-and-collect arrangements.

Related Topics

co-branding; collaboration; channel intensity

1 What might be the forces driving CPG companies to develop e-commerce?

2 Outline the advantages and disadvantages of using an online channel for packaged goods.

3 Now that Sainsbury's has bought Argos, who might it consider to be its main competitor?

Channel Intensity

Sometimes referred to as channel coverage, channel intensity refers to the number and dispersion of outlets an end user can use to buy a particular offering. This decision concerns the level of convenience customers expect and suppliers need to provide to be competitive. The wider the coverage, the greater the number of intermediaries, which leads to higher costs associated with the management control of the intermediaries.

A decision to introduce a new channel refers to the addition of a new set of internal or external channel entities to the firm's existing channel system. This could be a decision to establish its own retail stores or to provide an online e-commerce shopping facility. For example, Homburg, Vollmayr, and Hahn (2014) refer to China Unicom, which started to sell its telecommunication services in consumer electronics retail stores, such as Suning, in addition to its own specialized telecommunications stores. Although the new channel offered a lower level of customer service than China Unicom's own stores, it carried a wider product variety and broader assortment, enabling customers to purchase different kinds of electronic products and related services in one store.

There are three levels of channel intensity—that is, intense, selective, and exclusive (see Figure 14.5).

Intensive distribution involves placing an offering in as many outlets or locations as possible. It is used most commonly for offerings that consumers are unlikely to search for and which they purchase on the basis of convenience or impulse, such as magazines, soft drinks, or confectionery. However, retailers have increased control over the extent to which distribution is intensive. For example, a manufacturer of a new brand of yoghurt might want its new brand put on the shelves of all supermarkets; however, owing to limited shelf space, the retailers might limit their assortment to the leading brands of yoghurt.

Selective distribution occurs when a limited number of outlets are used. This is because, when customers are actively involved with a purchase and experience moderate to high levels of perceived risk, they are prepared to seek out appropriate suppliers. Those that best match their overall requirements are successful. Producers determine and control which intermediaries are to deliver the required products and level of services. Electrical equipment, furniture, clothing, and jewellery are categories in which selective distribution is appropriate.

Sometimes, an organization might use an intensive distribution to increase awareness of its brand when entering a new market, but then move to a more selective strategy to improve control over quality and to manage costs and price.

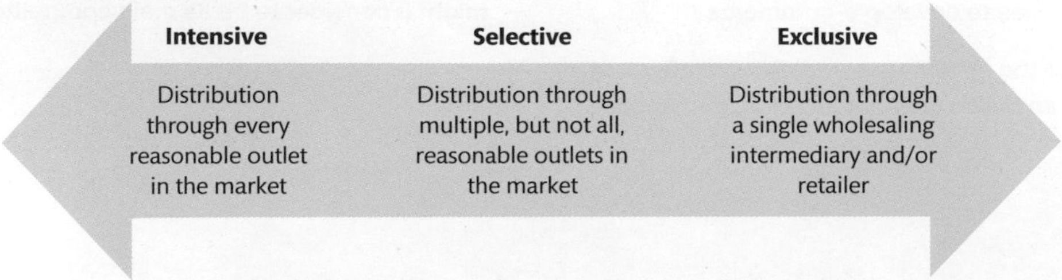

Intensive	Selective	Exclusive
Distribution through every reasonable outlet in the market	Distribution through multiple, but not all, reasonable outlets in the market	Distribution through a single wholesaling intermediary and/or retailer

Figure 14.5
Intensity of distribution continuum

Exclusive distribution occurs when intermediaries are given exclusive rights to market an offering within a defined 'territory'. This is useful where significant support is required from the intermediary, and hence the exclusivity is 'payback' for their investment and support. For example, high-prestige goods such as Ferrari sports cars and designer fashion apparel such as Chanel and Gucci adopt this type of distribution intensity.

If an offering requires complex servicing arrangements or tight control, then the exclusive form of distribution may be best. The threat of price competition is also diminished, because it would be inconsistent with the positioning strategy these offerings normally adopt.

Nearly all distribution through the Internet is intensive because of the massive reach of the web. Even the smallest manufacturer can advertise and sell worldwide, using the same courier services as major firms to deliver its offerings.

The decision about the number of intermediaries is often driven by cost considerations. The costs of intensive distribution are higher because of the number of outlets that must be served. The implications of these three distribution strategies are summarized in Table 14.2.

Disintermediation and Re-intermediation

Disintermediation concerns a reduction in the number or strength of intermediaries required in a marketing channel. More specifically, it refers to a situation in which market intermediaries are either displaced or eliminated, and manufacturers and buyers trade directly with each other without the presence of agents (Tay and Chelliah, 2011). There has been an active debate about

Table 14.2 Intensity of channel coverage

Characteristics	Exclusive	Selective	Intensive
Objectives	Strong image channel control and loyalty; price stability	Moderate market coverage; solid image; some channel control and loyalty	Widespread market coverage; channel acceptance; volume sales
Channel members	Few in number; well-established reputable stores	Moderate in number; well-established better stores	Many in number; all types of outlet
Customers	Few in number; trendsetters; willing to travel to store; brand-loyal	Moderate in number; brand-conscious; somewhat willing to travel to store	Many in number; convenience-oriented
Marketing emphasis	Personal selling; pleasant shopping conditions; good service	Promotional mix; pleasant shopping conditions; good service	Mass advertising; nearby location; items in stock
Examples	Automobiles; designer clothes; caviar	Furniture; clothing; watches	Groceries; household products; magazines

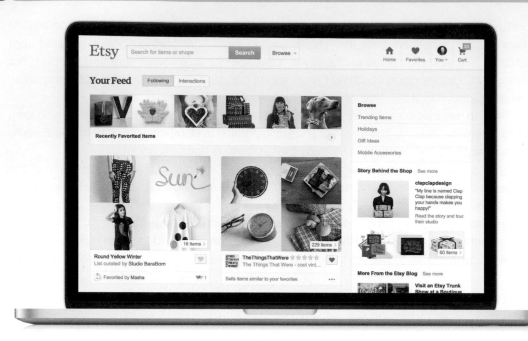

Sites like Etsy put manufacturers in direct contact with their customers
Source: © Etsy.com.

whether the rate of disintermediation is increasing, but it is clear that online technologies and virtual marketplaces have enabled buyers and sellers to find each other and to conduct business efficiently across both B2B (for example Virtual Chop Exchange for electronics, ChemConnect for chemicals) and consumer (for example eBay, Etsy) sectors.

The assumption underlying increasing disintermediation is that if producers could reach their customers directly, they would no longer need intermediaries—or at least they would not need so many of them. The technical possibility of reducing the number of intermediaries doesn't affect only 'bricks and mortar' intermediaries, but also electronic intermediaries. In Amazon's case, for example, more consumers could skip the intermediary and buy books online directly from publishers. Some publishers and printers have been disintermediated, with authors now selling e-books directly to the consumer. Where disintermediation does occur, it is strongly dependent on the nature of the offerings distributed.

Although there are significant numbers of customers who like buying directly, many customers value and prefer the role of traditional intermediaries, such as bricks-and-mortar retailers, for certain purchases. In fact, such is the value of some intermediaries to both customers and producers that there has been a trend towards **re-intermediation** (Anderson and Anderson, 2002)—that is, the introduction of additional intermediaries into the distribution channel. In fact, digitalization seems to have led to a kind of re-intermediation opening up for new types of intermediary, such as price comparison websites that add value by lowering search costs and reducing information asymmetry, thereby supporting consumers in making a product choice (Laffey and Gandy, 2009). Examples of such intermediaries are Mysupermarket and

Research Insight 14.2

To take your learning further, you might wish to read this influential paper:

Chakravarty, A., Kumar, A., and Grewal, R. (2014). Customer orientation structure for Internet-based business-to-business platform firms. *Journal of Marketing*, 78(5), 1–23.

This article develops a two-dimensional conceptualization of customer orientation for Internet-based B2B platforms, aiming to understand the unique challenges of platforms offering a triadic exchange system involving a seller side, a buyer side, and the intermediary platform. It thus reflects the premise that this type of intermediary must satisfy the needs of both buyers and sellers, both of whom are customers of the platform.

 Visit the online resources to read the abstract and access the full paper.

Pricerunner. Internet-based B2B platforms are also examples of such intermediaries (see Research Insight 14.2).

Managing Relationships in the Channel

An important managerial issue concerns channel relationships. Because channels are open social systems (Katz and Kahn, 1978), some level of conflict between channel members is inevitable. Conflict follows a breakdown in the levels of cooperation between channel partners (Shipley and Egan, 1992) and may well affect channel performance. Gaski (1984: 11) defined channel conflict as 'the perception on the part of a channel member that its goal attainment is being impeded by another, with stress or tension the result'.

Channel conflict may involve intermediaries on the same level (tier), for example between retailers or between agents (**horizontal conflict**). It may also occur between members on different levels (tiers), for example involving a producer, wholesaler, and a retailer (**vertical conflict**).

If strategies to prevent or avoid conflict have failed, it is necessary to resolve the conflict that erupts. The strategies depicted in Table 14.3 vary from selfishness/stubbornness and a refusal to work with other members, through cooperation and compromise, to a strategy that seeks to accommodate all of the views of other parties, even to the extent of jeopardizing one's own position. The prevailing corporate culture, attitude towards risk, and the sense of power that exists within coalitions shapes the chosen strategy.

 Visit the **online resources** and follow the web links to read about the conflict that has arisen in the UK supermarket industry.

Table 14.3 Conflict resolution strategies	
Strategy	**Explanation**
Accommodation	Modify expectations to incorporate requirements of others
Argument	A considered attempt to convince others of the correctness of your position
Avoidance	Removal from the point of conflict
Compromise	Meet the requirements of others halfway
Cooperation	Mutual reconciliation through cooperation
Instrumentality	Agree minimal requirements to secure short-term agreement
Self-seeking	Seek agreement on own terms or refuse further cooperation

Source: Fill and McKee (2012). Used with kind permission.

Grey Marketing

The unauthorized sale of new branded products diverted from authorized distribution channels, or imported into a country for sale without the consent or knowledge of the manufacturer, is referred to as **grey marketing** and is a source of channel conflict. Very often, this is accompanied by a cut in prices. Grey marketing is common in several different product categories, ranging from designer handbags and make-up, through electronics and automobiles, to prescription drugs. This activity is not necessarily illegal, but could fall foul of licensing agreements or trade regulations. Sometimes referred to as parallel importation, this can concern the purchase of a product in one country at a considerable discount and its resale in another at a far higher price. Differences in exchange rates can stimulate this activity, as experienced by Chinese shoppers in search of luxury items. As the value of the euro fell in 2015, many Chinese shoppers travelled to Europe to buy the same products at a much lower price. This affected the luxury brands, which lost out on high-margin sales in China and Hong Kong (Stefan, 2015). In recent years, online grey marketing has also grown rapidly, making it an important consideration for many brands (Zhao, Zhao, and Deng, 2016).

Supply Chain Management

The second major issue associated with marketing channels concerns the movement of parts, supplies, and finished products through a chain of suppliers involved in providing raw materials (upstream), through the assembly and manufacturing stages, to distribution to end users (downstream). This linkage is referred to as a supply chain and the process is commonly referred to as supply chain management (SCM). The phrase supersedes the previous terms 'logistics' and, before that, 'physical distribution'. Melnyk and colleagues (2009) believe that SCM is about the creation of value—a value chain—across of all the activities associated with distribution.

Integrated SCM refers to the business processes associated with the movement of parts, raw materials, work-in-progress, and finished goods. Unlike marketing channels, which are concerned with the management of customer behaviour, finished goods, and inter-organizational relationships, the goal of SCM is to improve efficiency and effectiveness with regard to the physical movement of products. Supply chain management is essentially about the management of all the business activities necessary to get the right product, in the right place, for the right customer to access in a timely and convenient way (Fill and McKee, 2012). Supply chain management is changing rapidly and developments in artificial intelligence, block-chain technology, and the Internet of Things are expected to impact supply chain management profoundly in the coming years (WEF, 2018).

Supply chain management comprises four main activities: **fulfilment**; **transportation**; **stock management**; and **warehousing**. Brewer and Speh (2000) argue that it is more apt to say that SCM seeks to accomplish four main goals—that is, waste reduction, time compression, flexible response, and unit cost reduction. These are explained in Table 14.4.

By achieving these four goals, the organization can improve the efficiency of its supply chain and, as a result, end users will experience improved levels of channel performance. Figure 14.6 shows these activities and goals brought together to promote superior supply chain performance.

Table 14.4 Supply chain management goals

Goal	Explanation
Waste reduction	By reducing the level of duplicated and excess stock in the chain, it becomes possible to harmonize operations between organizations to achieve new levels of uniformity and standardization.
Time compression	Reducing the order-to-delivery cycle time improves efficiency and customer service outputs. A faster cycle indicates a smoother and more efficient operation and associated processes. Faster times mean less stock, faster cash flow, and higher levels of service output.
Flexible response	By managing the order-processing elements (size, time, configuration, handling), specific customer requirements can be met without causing them inconvenience and contributes to efficiency and service delivery.
Unit cost reduction	By understanding the level of service output that is required by the end-user customers, it becomes possible to minimize the costs involved in delivering to that required standard.

Source: Fill and McKee (2012); adapted from Brewer and Speh (2000).

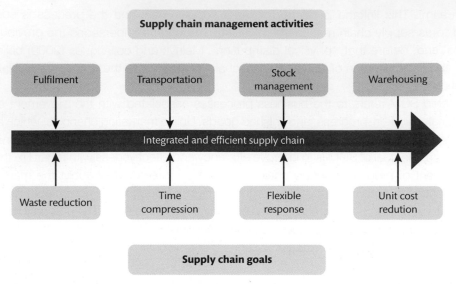

Figure 14.6

Developing high-performance supply chains

Management of ASDA Walmart's supply chain is based on computerized scanning to inform suppliers very quickly of which products need delivery and in what quantities. More recent developments in electronic technologies, such as radio frequency identification (RFID) tags, are improving the efficiency and effectiveness with which supply chain activities are managed. Increasingly, supply chain efforts are also aiming to create more sustainable flows, for example by seeking to build circular supply chains that enable the reuse and recycling of materials (Genovese et al., 2017). For more about this, see Market Insight 14.3.

Market Insight 14.3
Fashioning a Circular Supply Chain

Filippa K. is a medium-sized Swedish fashion brand, known for its minimalist and timeless designs that last for many years. Recently, Filippa K. has led the way in creating a more sustainable fashion industry.

One avenue through which it aims to promote sustainability is by redesigning a formerly linear supply chain to accommodate circular material flows.

Linear systems emerged from fast-fashioning the industry, leading fashion brands to use cheaper, lower-quality raw materials in their production. The materials are typically used for the first time (virgin materials), are mixed materials (which therefore cannot be recycled), and are of a lower quality (making them unfit for second-life use). The best-case scenario is that these

Would Filippa K's sustainability credentials tempt you in-store?

Source: © Iain Masterton/Alamy Stock Photo.

Market Insight 14.3
continued

types of material can be recycled to become lower-purpose products (known as down-cycling), such as plastic pellets or fillings in car seats, but typically they get disposed in landfills at the end of their lifetime.

Circular material flows, however, aim at reusing materials. This requires, for instance, reducing the use of virgin raw materials, increasing the use of recycled materials, and the production of mono-material products that make recycling and upcycling efficient and affordable, as well as designing products for easy repair and establishing systems that allow the product to have a second life.

Filippa K. is devoted to transforming its material flows to fit a circular economy business model. It has consequently launched the project '4Rs':

- *Reduce* aims at minimizing waste in the design stage of the clothes.

- *Repair* encourages the consumer to mend their clothes either themselves or by returning them to Filippa K. for mending.

- *Reuse* involves making part of the collection available for lease and supports a Stockholm-based second-hand store.

- *Recycle* targets the collection of worn-out Filippa K. clothes by rewarding customers with a 15 per cent discount on future purchases.

Filippa K. has identified the composition of material as key to achieving circularity. To ensure circular material flows, Filippa K is committed to long-term supply chain partnerships, some of which have been under contract since the early 1990s. Recently, the company has started a comprehensive transparency initiative, which is crucial for controlling more circular material flows. Unfortunately, however, Filippa K. experiences difficulties in convincing its suppliers to be part of the transparency initiative, because its small size gives the company little purchasing power in relation to large fabric suppliers.

Sources: Svensson (2007); Filippa K. (2017); Genovese et al. (2017).

Theory into Practice

Supply chain management is concerned with the value creation processes associated with physical distribution of goods. With the increasing scarcity of resources, companies have started to employ more circular supply chain designs that will close the loop between production and consumption. By moving discussions of waste reduction upstream in the supply chain, new approaches can be found. Still, most companies are embedded in linear supply chain systems, which are difficult and expensive to transform. Lack of suitable business partners who can offer circular supply chains is one of several reasons why the shift from linear to circular is not always easy.

Related Topics

supply chain; recycling; circular business models; sustainability

1 **Given that most current supply chain partners are part of a linear system, how can Filippa K. keep its long-term business relationship strategy, but still achieve a more circular supply chain?**

2 **In your opinion, what aspects in achieving circularity seem the most important: design, production, or consumption?**

3 **Visit Filippa K.'s website. How well are different aspects of its circular supply chains conveyed?**

This market insight was kindly contributed by Tina Sendlhofer, PhD candidate at the Stockholm School of Economics, Sweden.

Cost control is a core SCM activity given that about 15 per cent of an average product's price is accounted for in shipping and transport costs alone. IKEA can sell its furniture 20% cheaper than competitors as it buys it ready for assembly, thereby saving on transport and inventory costs. The Benetton distribution centre in Italy is run largely by robots, delivering numerous goods to 120 countries within 12 days. Benetton also uses just-in-time (JIT) manufacturing, with some garments manufactured in neutral colours and then dyed to order, with very fast turnaround to suit customer requirements. However, beyond lowering costs, many organizations are increasing their focus on managing activities, in order to improve customer service, meet the explosion in product variety, and harness the improvements in information and communication technologies (ICT).

Fulfilment

Fulfilment, or materials handling, is about locating and picking stock, and packing and securing it, before shipping the selected items or bundle to the next channel member. The increasing use of specialist software, IT, and equipment helps to manage a range of fulfilment activities. Intra-warehouse stock movement needs to be minimized, while inter-warehouse movement is optimized (Fill and McKee, 2012). Automated emails are sent out to customers following an online purchase of, for example, music from iTunes, a book from Amazon, or a train ticket. Accuracy and speed of billing and invoicing customers is also vitally important—especially for customer relationships.

In the retailing sector, order-processing technologies provide quick-response programmes to help to manage a retailer's replenishment of stock from suppliers. Kmart uses this kind of system, with EDI/extranets to transmit daily records of sales to suppliers, who analyse the information, create an order, and send it back to Kmart. Once in Kmart's system, the order is treated as though Kmart created it itself. Many technologies also speed up the billing cycle. For example, General Electric operates a computer-based system that, on receipt of a customer order, checks the customer's credit rating, as well as whether and where the items are in stock. The computer then issues an order to ship, bills the customer, updates the inventory records, sends a production order for new stock, and sends a message back to the salesperson that the customer's order is on the way—all in less than 15 seconds. The hospitality industry also uses order-processing technology to improve service delivery efficiency. Fast-food outlets such as McDonald's and KFC have long recorded food orders through telecommunications systems, transmitting them to food preparation areas, with orders fulfilled within a matter of minutes, improving customer satisfaction in service delivery.

Transportation and Delivery

Transportation is considered to be the most important activity within SCM. Transportation involves the physical movement of products using, for example, road, rail, air, pipeline, and shipping. Sometimes, transportation is simply seen as a way of supplying tangible goods, but it can also be as relevant to many service organizations and to the delivery of electronic (or digital) products. Consultants, IT companies, and health organizations have to move staff around, incurring transport and accommodation costs. Management of transport usually involves making decisions between one or more transportation methods and ensuring vehicle capacity. Transportation methods also include electronic delivery modes such as electronic vending machines, the telephone, the Internet, or EDI.

Physical Delivery

Information and communication technologies have improved physical product delivery. For example, where freight moves, the size of typical shipments and the time periods within which goods must be delivered have changed, with significant economic benefits to all transportation activities. Systems for transportation now include in-vehicle navigation and route guidance solutions to help to manage transport fleets, track shipments, and optimize transportation, and businesses are experimenting with autonomous vehicles and drone deliveries (WEF, 2018). Amazon's tracking system assigns a tracking number and, using proprietary software, provides information to customers in real time about where the package or shipment is located, improving customer experience.

Electronic Delivery

As early as the introduction of the television, radio, or even the telephone, electronic technologies have been used to deliver products. Because of product digitization, producers of music, games, video, or software are typically unconstrained by the needs of physical distribution, and this has increased with the development of the Internet. Organizations such as travel agents, banks, and insurance companies, which have traditionally relied on customers coming to a branch or agency, have quickly moved to using automated teller machines (ATMs), mobile telecommunications, and the Internet to reach more customers. The Internet has clearly added to the capacity of these electronic distribution channels, so that huge numbers of customers now bank, trade stocks, and arrange insurance and travel through electronic channels—particularly mobile phones.

Stock Management

Stock or inventory management involves trying to balance responsiveness to customer needs with the resources required to store stock. The management of both finished and unfinished goods can be critical to many organizations. For example, a balance needs to be achieved between the number of finished goods to be available when customers need it (known as speculation) against a store of unfinished goods that can be assembled at a later date or when the stock of finished goods runs low (known as postponement).

Carrying too little stock might jeopardize customer service levels, whilst carrying too much can be expensive and adds to working capital. Imagine the cost of storing all the books Amazon has listed for sale, or all the fashion items in the spring ready for summer demand. With JIT systems, producers and retailers carry only small inventories of merchandise—often only enough for a few days' operations. New stock arrives exactly when it is needed, rather than being stored. ASDA Walmart and even Burger King use these systems to track sales to service their outlets worldwide, automatically replenishing their ingredients according to product sales.

Zero-inventory, or JIT, production is ideal for many organizations, because it minimizes the use of resources that are often tied up in stock that doesn't sell. This must be balanced against the risk of not having the products available when customers want them.

Warehousing and Materials Handling

Supply chains involved with the exchange of goods usually require storage facilities for the periods between production, transportation, and purchase/consumption. For example, books, dry goods such as sugar and canned goods, and even clothing require some level of storage between the time they leave the producer or manufacturer and that at which they are required to be delivered to end users.

Decisions involving the location, size, design, and operating systems used in warehouses are important because they can impact on the performance of others in the supply chain.

Producers using distributors will require a relatively small number of warehouses, as the distributors take ownership and physical possession of stock. A higher number of warehouses are required in channels in which agents and manufacturers' representatives are preferred, because these intermediaries do not take ownership or physical possession. Organizations must decide on how many and what type of 'warehouses' it needs, as well as where they should be located. The type of warehouse is dependent on the type of product—that is, tangible, digital, or perishable.

Visit the **online resources** and use the web link to read about how a major retailer has had to redesign and update its warehousing to cope with online sales.

Warehousing Tangible Goods

For the storage of tangible goods, such as FMCGs, an organization can use either **storage warehouses** or **distribution centres**. Storage warehouses store goods for moderate to long periods (that is, they have long shelf lives), whereas distribution centres are designed to move goods, rather than only to store them. For products that are highly perishable with a short shelf life, such as fruit and vegetables, distribution centres are more appropriate. Grocery chains such as Woolworths in Australia and Tesco in the UK use large cold-store distribution centres to move perishable items such as fruit and vegetables to their various retail outlets. Storage centres are more appropriate for products with long shelf lives or which might require stockpiling to meet seasonal demands.

Warehousing Digital 'Products'

Electronic warehousing systems, or database systems, are increasingly being used for the storage of products (or product components) that can be digitized. These systems can be searched or browsed electronically, providing the user with immediate electronic delivery options. For example, emerald-library.com, ABI-Inform, and ScienceDirect are electronic databases accessible through the web that store a vast array of documents electronically to facilitate customers' search for information. In addition, many organizations use data warehousing facilities whereby product information, or even actual products, are stored in digital form awaiting distribution. For example, Amazon Kindle allows books to be downloaded and read immediately rather than having physical books shipped to the reader.

Retailing

Retailing encompasses all the activities directly related to the sale of products and services to consumers for personal use. Retailers differ from wholesalers, who distribute the product to businesses, not consumers. Whether they are large retailers, such as Lotte (South Korea), Extra (Brazil), or Carrefour (France), or one of the thousands of small owner-run retailers in India, all retailers provide a downstream link between producers and end users.

Retailers help to reduce the uncertainty experienced by other intermediaries in the channel, such as wholesalers and manufacturers. They do so by taking small quantities of stock on a regular basis, promoting cash flows, and providing demand for their products and services.

Retailers provide consumers with access to products. As such, it is very important to find out what consumers actually want from a retailer if they are to deliver value. Convenience and time utility is the primary concern for most consumers, with people increasingly being 'leisure time poor' and keen to trade shopping time for more leisure time (Seiders, Berry, and Gresham, 2000). Consequently, convenience drives most innovations in retailing, for example the development of supermarkets, department stores, shopping malls, the web, and self-scanning kiosks. As noted by Seiders and colleagues (2000), from a customer's perspective, convenience means speed and ease in acquiring a product, and it consists of four key elements:

- *access*—that is, being easy to reach;

- *search*—that is, enabling customers to easily identify what they want;

- *possession*—that is, being easily obtained; and

- *transaction*—that is, ease of purchase and return of products.

These elements are outlined in more detail in Table 14.5.

Table 14.5 Retailing convenience: a customer's perspective

Element	Description
Access convenience	■ The speed and ease with which consumers can reach or engage with a retailer ■ Influenced by factors such as location, availability, hours of operation, parking, proximity to other outlets, as well as telephone, mail, and Internet ■ Convenience does not exist without access
Search convenience	■ The speed and ease with which consumers identify and select products they wish to buy ■ Influenced by factors such as product focus, intelligent outlet design and layout (servicescape), knowledgeable staff, interactive systems, product displays, packaging and signage, etc. ■ Convenience in search means efficiently moving through the shopping experience
Possession convenience	■ The speed and ease with which consumers can obtain desired products ■ Influenced by having merchandise in stock and available on a timely basis ■ Obtaining the product is the final objective when shopping, which makes possession convenience critical. The Internet scores highly for search convenience, yet is generally low in terms of possession convenience
Transaction convenience	■ The speed and ease with which consumers can effect and amend transactions before and after the purchase ■ Influenced by factors before and after the actual purchase, such as trying on, waiting lines, and returns. Well-designed service systems can mitigate the peaks and troughs in store traffic as with the use of in-store traffic counters ■ Transaction convenience is a significant issue on the Internet, with pure Internet retailers having problems with returns and customers not prepared to pay for shipping and handling costs

Source: © 2000 from MIT Sloan Management Review/Massachusetts Institute of Technology. All rights reserved. Distributed by Tribune Content Agency.

Types of Retailer

There are numerous types of retailer. These can be classified according to the marketing strategy employed (that is, product, price, and service) and the store presence (that is, store or non-store retailing).

Marketing Strategy

Major types of retailer can be classified according to the marketing strategies employed, paying particular attention to three specific elements: product assortment; price level; and customer service. Table 14.6, although not exhaustive, provides a useful summary of these elements across the differing types of retailing channel.

Table 14.6 Marketing strategy and retail store classification

Type of retail store	Product assortment	Pricing	Customer service	Example
Department	Very broad and deep, with layout and presentation of products critical	Minimize price competition	Wide array and good quality	David Jones; Debenhams; Harrods
Discount	Broad and shallow	Low price positioning	Few customer service options	Poundstretcher;, Dollar Dazzlers; Poundland
Convenience	Narrow and shallow	High prices	Avoid price competition	Co-op; 7-Eleven
Limited line	Narrow and deep	Traditional— avoids price competition New kinds—low prices	Vary by type	Bicycle stores; sports stores
Speciality	Very narrow and deep	Avoids price competition	Standard; extensive in some	Running shops; bridal boutiques
Category killer	Narrow and very deep	Low prices	Few to moderate	Officeworks; IKEA
Supermarket	Broad and deep	Some are low price; others avoid price disadvantages	Few and self-service	Tesco plc (UK); Woolworths Ltd (Australia); Carrefour (Europe)
Superstores	Very broad and very deep	Low prices	Few and self-service	Tesco Extra; Walmart

The types of retailing establishment can be distinguished as follows:

- *Department stores*—These are large-scale retailing organizations that offer a very broad and deep assortment of products (both hard and soft goods) and provide a wide array of customer service facilities for store customers. For example, Debenhams has a wide array of products, including home furnishings, foods, cosmetics, clothing, books, and furniture, and also provides variety within each category (including brand, feature variety). Debenhams, like many department stores, provides a wide array of customer service facilities to rationalize higher prices and minimize price competition. Value-added services include wedding registries, clothing alterations, shoe repairs, lay-by facilities, home delivery, and installation.

- *Discount retailers*—This type of retailer is positioned based on low prices combined with the reduced costs of doing business. The key characteristics here involve a broad, but shallow, assortment of products, low prices, and very few customer services. For example, Matalan in the UK, Kmart in Australia, and Target in the United States all carry a broad array of soft goods, such as apparel, combined with hard goods, such as appliances and home furnishings. To keep prices down, the retailers negotiate extensively with suppliers to ensure low merchandise costs.

- *Limited line retailers*—This type of retailer has a narrow, but deep, product assortment and customer services vary from store to store. Clothing retailers, butchers, baked goods, and furniture stores that specialize in a small number of related product categories are all examples. The breadth of product variety differs across limited line stores, and a store may choose to concentrate on several related product lines (for example shoes and clothing accessories), a single product line (for example shoes), or a specific part of one product line (for example sports shoes). Examples include bookstores, jewellers, athletic footwear stores, dress shops, newsagents, etc.

- *Category killer stores*—As the name suggests, these retailers are designed to kill off the competition and are characterized by a narrow, but very deep, assortment of products, low prices, and few-to-moderate customer services. Successful examples include IKEA in home furnishings, Office Works in office supplies, and B&Q in hardware.

- *Supermarkets*—Founded in the 1930s, these are large self-service retailing environments offering a wide variety of differing merchandise to a large consumer base. Tesco Extra in the UK stocks products ranging from clothing, hardware, music, groceries, and dairy products to soft furnishings. Operating largely on a self-service basis, with minimum customer service and centralized register and transactional terminals, supermarkets provide the benefits of a wide product assortment in a single location, offering convenience and variety. Today, supermarkets are the dominant institution for food retailing.

- *Convenience stores, or corner shops*—These offer a range of grocery and household items that cater for convenience and the last-minute purchase needs of consumers. Key characteristics include long opening times (for example 24 hours a day, seven days a week, or 24/7), being family-run, and belonging to a trading group. Examples include 7-Eleven, Spar, and the Co-op.

Store Presence

We can further categorize retailers according to their presence—either store or non-store retailing. Most retailing occurs through fixed stores, with existing operators having 'sunk' investment into a physical building and equipment. The physical location of a store is seen as a source of competitive advantage, providing crucial entry barriers to competitors. Several characteristics make store retailing unique from the customer viewpoint. The retail environment provides the sensation of touch, feel, and smell, which is very important for many product categories, such as clothing, books, and perfumes (see Market Insight 14.4). Furthermore, customers can interact and seek advice with in-store staff. Once a product is selected and a purchase made, customers can walk out of the store with the merchandise in hand.

Market Insight 14.4
Enhancing Channel Experiences

The rise of digital and mobile marketing and the growth of online shopping has put pressure on retailers to reconsider and improve their in-store customer experience. One of the approaches has been to involve music in retail environments, which has been found to encourage customers to stay longer and spend a little more than when there is no music. Sales can also be improved by matching the music with the products being sold. This is referred to as directional audio. For example, research has shown that sales of French wine increase when French music is played and, likewise, sales of German wine increased when German music was played. In a similar study in Sweden, shoppers bought 10 per cent more organic products when they could hear the sound of farm animals, with a narrator talking about the various benefits of organic products.

Changes in the luxury retail market have forced retailers to adapt and enhance the in-store experience. Many luxury consumers have been found to be less interested in accumulating possessions and much more interested in the buying (shopping) experience. One of these involves the use of in-store sales associates to assist luxury customers in their purchase decisions. Whilst the use of personal shoppers in luxury stores is well established, stores such as Bebe, Zara, and Anthropologie now offer personal styling services in-store.

The role of play within retail stores is becoming an important feature in the drive to create meaningful experiences. Hamleys launched its largest European store in Moscow with a central design feature to provide opportunities for customers of all ages to play. Nine different zones, which include an enchanted forest to explore, a motor city with a go-kart track, and a safari section, make the store feel more like a theme park than a pure retail outlet. Each zone is designed to stimulate the senses, and it achieves this by mixing interactive attractions and entertainment.

US clothing and footwear brand Vans opened 'The House of Vans' in the tunnels under Waterloo Station. It offered London's only permanent indoor skate park, as well as an art gallery, live music venue, and cinema, with events and exhibitions that are changed regularly. The informality of the environment enables brand relationships to develop through soft interaction.

The House of Vans is based in the tunnels under Waterloo Station and is London's only permanent indoor skate park
Source: Courtesy of House of Vans London.

Car manufacturer Audi has developed 'Audi City in London'. This environment encourages visitors to explore and configure their ideal car using touchscreens and multisensory displays. 'The Lexus Intersect' space focuses on the whole Lexus lifestyle, not only cars. By focusing on a range of topics, from food to fashion, Lexus has positioned itself as a cultural hub more than a showroom.

Sources: Anon. (2014); Regan (2015); Sorin (2015).

Market Insight 14.4
continued

Theory into Practice

What is evident in these retail examples of customer experience is the search for a position that helps a retailer to differentiate its brand in such a way that it can provide competitive advantage. What may be an issue, however, is whether these types of experience provide an advantage that is sustainable: competitors can easily replicate providing touchscreens and multisensory displays and hence what was once a memorable experience may become an expectation of all such experiences.

A further issue concerns customer perceived value. A one-off visit may provide a memorable experience, but how many visits before the thrill wears off and the value is negated? How much time can consumers afford to spend experiencing a brand in these ways, and if the answer is 'not very much', then what is the long-term value of providing these experiences? Will customers revert to an online store? (More ideas about experience marketing are considered in Chapter 16.)

Related Topics

purchase decision-making; information processing; branding

1 **How might a fashion retailer provide a memorable in-store experience?**

2 **Identify those types of retailer that may be more dependent than others on the value-added activities of the marketing channel.**

3 **Go to the websites of a department store (such as John Lewis) and a supermarket. How do they compare? Are there any retailing similarities?**

In contrast, retailing can also involve non-store retailers. These are retail transactions that occur away from a fixed store location. Examples include automatic vending machines, direct selling, and, most notably, online retailing. Direct selling is one of the oldest retailing methods, and is the personal contact between a salesperson and a consumer at a location away from a retailing environment. These activities include door-to-door canvassing and party plans, where sales presentations are made within a home to a party of guests. Examples include cosmetics companies such as Avon, Nutri-Metics skincare, and Amway household products. **Telemarketing** or telesales is another form of non-store retailing whereby purchase occurs over the telephone.

Another form of non-store retailing is the **electronic kiosk**. These are placed in shopping centres (or malls) to assist the retailing experience. These computer-based retailing environments offer increased self-service opportunities, a wide array of products, and a large amount of data and information to help the customer to make a decision. Automatic vending machines provide product access 24/7. Products distributed through vending machines are normally convenient and typically low priced, and include cigarettes, soft drinks, hot beverages, condoms, newspapers, and magazines. We also see the wide adoption of ATMs to facilitate the delivery of financial retailing services.

Research Insight 14.3

To take your learning further, you might wish to read this influential paper:

Mallapragada, G., Chandukala, S.R., and Liu, Q. (2016). Exploring the effects of 'what' (product) and 'where' (website) characteristics on online shopping behavior. *Journal of Marketing*, 80(2), 21–38.

In this article, the authors explore online shopping behaviour by investigating the impact of various characteristics on the basket value of an online transaction, after incorporating the role of other aspects of the browsing process, including page views and visit duration. Their results indicate various product and website strategies for online retailers.

 Visit the **online resources** to read the abstract and access the full paper.

Another form of non-store retailing is the online store. The key consumer categories on the Internet are travel, clothes, groceries, and consumer electronics. Mallapragada, Chandukala, and Liu (2016) point out that online retailers have a strategic interest in the basket value of an online shopping transaction. This is because the delivery costs associated with an online purchase can amount to 50 per cent of a firm's operating costs and so impact directly on their profits. This is unlike traditional stores, who are mostly interested in total sales. Thus these researchers suggest that online shopping can be considered as a two-stage process. The first is a browsing stage, which requires consumers to spend time visiting several web pages (page views) and which may lead to a purchase decision; the second stage, purchase, involves the completion of the financial transaction. However, these two stages mask several complexities, involving what it is that is being purchased, the product or service, and where it is being purchased—namely, the website. Online stores are thus interested in ensuring that browsing is converted into sales (that is, the conversion rate), as well as driving the basket size for each transaction. (To learn more about online retailing, see Research Insight 14.3.)

The shopping behaviour of contemporary consumers, however, tends to reflect a mix of online and offline channels (Voorveld et al., 2016). This is reflected in the practice of 'showrooming', whereby consumers use their smartphones in-store to compare prices, get the opinions of family and friends through social media, and then negotiate the purchasing process (MacKenzie, Meyer, and Noble, 2013), as well as the practice of 'webrooming', which occurs when consumers research products online, but then complete their purchase in a bricks-and-mortar store (Adler, 2014). From a retailer's perspective, understanding and managing consumer movements between channels is thus increasingly important (Rosengren et al., 2017). Market Insight 14.5 offers an illustration of the way in which smartphone apps can be used by retailers to facilitate such movements.

 Visit the **online resources** and complete Internet Activity 14.2 to learn more about the variety of Internet retailing sites and the importance of delivery information for the music sector.

Market Insight 14.5
Retail App-reciation

As shopper behaviour is coming increasingly digital, retailers are making efforts to bring digital elements in-store. Many of these efforts centre on the smartphone and apps. Mobile apps offer many benefits for the retailer. They can provide data on which customer is shopping where and when. They also enable tailored offers and inspiration to be sent to the customer both inside and outside the physical store. However, getting shoppers interested in apps has proved to be quite a challenge, in terms of both the value offered to shoppers through apps and getting shoppers to actually download and use them.

As an example, when restaurant chain McDonald's launched its mobile app in 2015, it quickly received low ratings among customers in terms of the value it added. In fact, the app took the bottom place among all major restaurant chains' apps in terms of ratings. While apps from competitors such as Starbucks and Chipotle offered payment solutions, loyalty programmes, rewards, and more, the McDonald's app was limited to nutrition information, coupons, and a coffee loyalty programme. Additionally, the McDonald's app required

its users to have their location setting on to unlock deals, which was not the standard on all phones at the time, causing many to miss out on deals. Despite this, the McDonald's app quickly became one of the most downloaded food and drinks apps in the United States.

Others retailers face the reverse problem. ICA AB, the largest grocery retailer chain in the Nordic Countries, has consistently received relatively high ratings of its app ever since the launch in 2012. The app contains sophisticated personalized offers tied to its loyalty programme, recipes, shopping lists, and maps of the stores to find specific products. All app content is synchronized with weekly flyers, the shopper's personal account on the retailer website, and in-store stand-alone coupon terminals—a truly seamless experience. However, despite all these functions, less than 1 per cent of shoppers are actively using the app while they are in the store, even though a large fraction of shoppers used their smartphone for other activities, such as social media. In ICA's case, the problem is to get customers to try the app in the first place.

Sources: Ericsson (2017); Grewal et al. (2017).

Theory into Practice

Whereas retailers have traditionally been categorized in terms of their physical store presence (as illustrated by the use of store versus non-store as a way of describing retail), digitalization is moving retail offers into what is typically called omni-channel retailing. As illustrated in this market insight, smartphones and

apps provide a way of linking online and digital offers, and there are many ways in which they might have a positive impact on instore experiences. Still, in spite of apps having been around for quite some time, the advantages of apps to retailers seems to be clearer than the advantages of apps to shoppers.

Related Topics

customer behaviour; digital marketing; relationship marketing; big data; services

1 **Look in your own smartphone. What retailer apps have you downloaded (if any)? Consider why you downloaded them and what types of customer value they offer for you.**

2 **What do you think is the biggest barrier to getting customers to try a retailer app? Does it differ between customer segments?**

3 **What is a good metric for a successful retailer app (for example number of downloads, number of active users, user ratings/satisfaction)? Might different metrics be beneficial for different strategic purposes?**

This market insight was kindly contributed by Carl-Philip Ahlbom, PhD candidate at the Stockholm School of Economics, Sweden.

Chapter Summary

To consolidate your learning, the key points from this chapter are summarized here:

- **Describe the nature and characteristics of a marketing channel.**

  Marketing channels are chains of organizations that are concerned with the management of the processes and activities involved in creating and moving particular offerings from producers and manufacturers to end users (customers). Marketing channels enable different types of uncertainty to be lowered by reducing complexity, increasing value and competitive advantage, offering routinization, and/or providing specialization.

- **Explain the different types of intermediary and their roles in the marketing channel.**

  An intermediary is an independent organization that operates as a link between producers and consumers or industrial users. There are several different types of intermediary, including agents, merchants, distributors, franchises, wholesalers, and retailers. The main role of intermediaries is to reduce the uncertainty experienced by producers and manufacturers, and to promote efficiency. The key difference between the various intermediaries is that not all of them take legal title or physical possession of a product.

- **Understand the different marketing channel structures and their core characteristics.**

  There are three main channel structures: direct, indirect, and multichannel. A direct channel structure involves selling directly to end users; an indirect channel structure involves using intermediaries; a multichannel structure involves both. At the simplest level, direct channels offer maximum control, but do not always reach all of the target market. Indirect channels can maximize coverage, but often at the expense of control. This is because intermediaries start adapting the marketing mix and demand a share of the profits in return for their involvement. Multichannel strategies often result in greater channel conflict because intermediaries perceive the manufacturer to be a competitor.

- **Explain the factors that influence the design and structure of marketing channels.**

  When establishing or adapting marketing channels, it is necessary to consider the type of market coverage that is required, the number and type of intermediaries to use, and how the relationships between channel members are to be managed. These choices are important because they can affect the value that is ultimately provided to customers.

- **Describe the main elements that constitute supply chain management.**

  Supply chain management concerns the various suppliers involved in providing raw materials (upstream), those that assemble and manufacture products, and those that distribute finished products to end users (downstream). It embraces four main activities—fulfilment, transportation, stock management, and warehousing—which also subsume other important activities, such as order processing and purchasing. Although these are not traditionally marketing management decisions, it is important to understand that they require a marketing focus and marketing insight.

- **Consider the role and function of retailers in the marketing channel.**

  Retailing concerns all activities directly related to the sale of goods and services to consumers for personal and non-business use. Retailers provide consumers with access to products and help to reduce the uncertainty experienced by other intermediaries in the channel, such as wholesalers and manufacturers. This is achieved by taking small quantities of stock on a regular basis, promoting cash flows, and providing demand for their products and services. The different types of retailing establishment can be classified according to two key characteristics: the marketing strategy (that is, product, price, and service); and the store presence (that is, store or non-store retailing).

Review Questions

1 What do we mean by 'marketing channel management'?

2 Why do organizations use intermediaries?

3 Why are economics, coverage, and control important when making marketing channel decisions?

4 What are the key elements of a channel strategy?

5 What are the advantages and disadvantages of the three different channel structures?

6 What are the advantages of using an exclusive, rather than an intensive, marketing channel strategy?

7 Why is supply chain management of increasing importance to marketers?

8 What are some of the reasons for channel conflict?

9 Identify six types of retailer.

10 What does the term 'non-store retailing' mean? Identify the main types.

 # Discussion Questions

1 Having read Case Insight 14.1, what do you see as the main challenges for Åhléns in developing its online offer? How would you advise Åhléns to deal with them?

2 Discuss the importance of intermediaries. In your discussion, outline the benefits and limitations of three types of intermediary.

3 Convenience has become a critical issue in marketing channel decisions. Assess the arguments for and against focusing on convenience, from a customer's perspective.

4 What sort of marketing channels do you believe might be most relevant in the following markets in the year 2020? Identify the three most relevant for each of the product categories:

A Music and video
B Home entertainment software (for example video games)
C Business application software
D Engineering consulting advice (say, on mining or construction applications)
E Financial services
F Shampoo
G Personal services (for example hairdressing, beauty therapies)

 Visit the online resources and complete the Multiple-Choice Questions to assess your knowledge of Chapter 14.

Glossary

direct channel structure a distribution structure whereby the product moves directly from the producer to the end user.

disintermediation a reduction in the number or strength of intermediaries that are required in a marketing channel.

distribution centre a facility designed to move goods, rather than to store them.

electronic kiosk machine placed in a shopping centre (mall) to assist the retailing experience; mediated by hypermedia web-based interfaces, these computer-based retailing environments offer consumers increased self-service opportunity, wide product assortment, and large amounts of data and information aiding decision-making.

exclusive distribution a distribution agreement whereby intermediaries are given exclusive rights to market the good or service within a defined 'territory' and hence only a limited number of intermediaries are used.

fulfilment those activities associated with locating and picking stock, packing, and shipping the selected items to the next channel member.

grey marketing the unauthorized sale of new branded products diverted from authorized distribution channels or imported into a country for sale without the consent or knowledge of the manufacturer.

horizontal conflict conflict that may arise between members of a channel on the same level of distribution.

indirect channel structure a distribution structure whereby the product goes from the producer through an intermediary, or a series of intermediaries such as a wholesaler, retailer, franchisee, agent, or broker, to the end user.

information utility the extent to which information about the product offering is provided before and after sales, which can further provide information about those purchasing it.

intensive distribution a distribution structure whereby a product or service is placed in as many outlets or locations as possible to maximize the opportunity for customers to find and buy it.

marketing channel (also known as a distribution channel) an organized network of agencies and organizations that together perform all the activities required to link producers and manufacturers with consumers, purchasers, and users to distribute product offerings.

multichannel structure a distribution structure whereby multiple sales channels provide a variety of customer touchpoints.

ownership utility the extent to which goods are available immediately from the intermediaries' stocks and hence ownership passes to the purchaser.

place utility the extent to which the location of an offering enables its more convenient purchase and consumption.

re-intermediation an increase in the number or strength of intermediaries that are required in a marketing channel.

retailing (also known as the retail trade) the activities directly related to the sale of goods and services to the end-consumer for personal and non-business use.

selective distribution a distribution structure whereby where some, but not all, available outlets for the good or service are used.

stock management the management of the balance between the anticipated number of finished goods required by customers and a sufficient store of unfinished goods that can be assembled at a later date or when the stock of finished goods runs low.

storage warehouses facilities that store goods for moderate to long periods of time.

supply chain the value chain formed when organizations are linked in the supply and distribution of a product or service.

telemarketing (also known as telesales) a form of non-store retailing whereby purchase occurs over the telephone.

time utility the extent to which the manufacture, purchase, and consumption of a product or service might occur at differing points in time.

transportation the physical movement of products using, for example, road, rail, air, pipeline, and shipping.

vertical conflict conflict that may arise between sequential members in a distribution network, such as producers, distributors, and retailers, over such matters as carrying a particular range or price increases.

warehousing facilities used to store tangible goods for the periods between production, transportation, and purchase/consumption.

References

Adler, E. (2014). Reverse showrooming: bricks-and-mortar retailers fight back. *Business Insider UK*, 13 July. Retrieve from: http://uk.businessinsider.com/reverse-showrooming-bricks-and-mortar-retailers-fight-back-2-2014-2?r%20=%20US (accessed 13 October 2018).

Ailawadi, K.L. and Farris, P.W. (2017). Managing multi- and omni-channel distribution: metrics and research directions. *Journal of Retailing*, 93(1), 120–35.

Alldredge, K., and Ungerman, K. (2015). Cohabiting with your e-commerce partners. *McKinsey Insights*, June. Retrieve from: https://www.mckinsey.com/insights/marketing_sales/cohabiting_with_your_ecommerce_partners (accessed 13 October 2018).

Alldredge, K., Newaskar, P., and Ungerman, K. (2015). The digital future of consumer-packaged-goods companies. *McKinsey Insights*, October. Retrieve from: https://www.mckinsey.com/insights/consumer_and_retail/the_digital_future_of_consumer_packaged_goods_companies (accessed 13 October 2018).

Anderson, E., and Anderson, R. (2002). The new e-commerce intermediaries. *MIT Sloan Management Review*, 43(4), 53–62.

Anon. (2014). How to create immersive in-store experiences with directional audio. *Retail Customer Experience*, 18 September. Retrieve from https://www.retailcustomerexperience.com/articles/how-to-create-immersive-in-store-experiences-with-directional-audio/ (accessed 13 October 2018).

Armstrong, A. (2016). Sainsbury's bid could spell break up of Home Retail. *The Telegraph*, 5 January. Retrieve from: https://www.telegraph.co.uk/finance/12082535/Sainsburys-makes-bid-approach-for-Argos-owner.html (accessed 13 October 2018).

Brewer, P.C., and Speh, T.W. (2000). Using the balanced scorecard to measure supply chain performance. *Journal of Business Logistics*, 21(1), 75–95.

Chakravarty, A., Kumar, A., and Grewal, R. (2014). Customer orientation structure for Internet-based business-to-business platform firms. *Journal of Marketing*, 78(5), 1–23.

Ericsson (2017). *Ericsson Mobility Report November 2017*. Retrieve from: https://www.ericsson.com/en/mobility-report/reports/november-2017 (accessed 24 September 2018).

Filippa K. (2017). *Sustainability Report 2016*. Retrieve from: https://www.filippa-k.com/media/wysiwyg/filippa-k-world/sustainability/reports/Filippa-K-Sustainability-Report-2016.pdf (accessed 13 October 2018).

Fill, C., and McKee, S. (2012). *Business Marketing*. Oxford: Goodfellow.

Gaski, J.F. (1984). The theory of power and conflict in channels of distribution. *Journal of Marketing*, 48(3), 9–29.

Genovese, A., Acquaye, A.A., Figueroa, A., and Koh, S.L. (2017). Sustainable supply chain management and the transition towards a circular economy: evidence and some applications. *Omega*, 66, 344–57.

Homburg, C., Vollmayr, J., and Hahn, A. (2014). Firm value creation through major channel expansions: evidence from an event study in the United States, Germany, and China. *Journal of Marketing*, 78(3), 38–61.

Katz, D., and Kahn, R.L. (1978). *The Social Psychology of Organisation* (2nd edn). New York: John Wiley.

Kotler, P., and Keller, K. (2009). *Marketing Management*. Englewood Cliffs, NJ: Prentice Hall.

Laffey, D., and Gandy, A. (2009). Comparison websites in UK retail financial services. *Journal of Financial Services Marketing*, 14(2), 173–86.

MacKenzie, B., Meyer, C., and Noble, S. (2013). How retailers can keep up with consumers. *McKinsey Insights*, October. Retrieve from: https://www.mckinsey.com/industries/retail/our-insights/how-retailers-can-keep-up-with-consumers (accessed 13 October 2018).

Mallapragada, G., Chandukala, S.R., and Liu, Q. (2016). Exploring the effects of 'what' (product) and 'where' (website) characteristics on online shopping behavior. *Journal of Marketing*, 80(2), 21–38.

Melnyk, S.A., Lummus, R.R., Vokurka, R.J., Burns, L.J., and Sandor, J. (2009). Mapping the future of supply chain management: a Delphi study. *International Journal of Production Research*, 47(16), 4629–53.

Parker, M., Bridson, K., and Evans, J. (2006). Motivations for developing direct trade relationships. *International*

Journal of Retail and Distribution Management, 34(2), 121–34.

Regan, J. (2015). The art of play is becoming serious business for retailers. *The Guardian*, 28 May. Retrieve from: https://www.theguardian.com/media-network/2015/may/28/play-retail-experiences-brands-marketing (accessed 13 October 2018).

Rosengren, S., Lange, F., Hernant, M., and Blom, A. (2017). Catering to the digital consumer: from multichannel to omnichannel retailing. In: P. Andersson, S. Movin, M. Mähring, R. Teigland, and K. Wennberg (eds), *Managing Digital Transformation*, Stockholm: Stockholm School of Economics Institute for Research, 97–114.

Seiders, K., Berry, L.L., and Gresham, L.G. (2000). Attention retailers! How convenient is your convenience strategy? *Sloan Management Review*, 41(3), 79–89.

Sheffield, H. (2016). Sainsbury's reveals Argos owner Home Retail Group rejected takeover bid. *The Independent*, 6 January. Retrieve from: https://www.independent.co.uk/news/business/news/sainsburys-reveals-argos-owner-home-retail-group-turned-down-takeover-bid-a6797306.html (accessed 13 October 2018).

Shipley, D., and Egan, C. (1992). Power, conflict and cooperation in brewer–tenant distribution channels. *International Journal of Service Industry Management*, 3(4), 44–62.

Sorin, K. (2015). Evolving retail expectations require enhanced experiences in-store: report. *Luxury Daily*, 2 July. Retrieve from: https://www.luxurydaily.com/ evolving-retail-expectations-require-enhanced-experiences-in-store-report/ (accessed 13 October 2018).

Stefan (2015). Why are fashion brands worried about a weak euro and Chinese tourists? *China Ready News*, 30 June. Retrieve from: https://chinareadynews.com/2928/why-are-fashion-brands-worried-about-a-weak-euro-and-chinese-tourists/ (accessed 13 October 2018).

Svensson, G. (2007). Aspects of sustainable supply chain management (SSCM): conceptual framework and empirical example. *Supply Chain Management*, 12(4), 262–6.

Tay, K.B., and Chelliah, J. (2011). Disintermediation of traditional chemical intermediary roles in the electronic business-to-business (e-B2B) exchange world. *Journal of Strategic Information Systems*, 20(3), 217–31.

Voorveld, H.A.M., Smit, E.G., Neijens, P.C., and Bronner, A.E. (2016). Consumers' cross-channels use in online and offline purchases: an analysis of cross-media and cross-channel behaviors between products. *Journal of Advertising Research*, 56(4), 385–400.

WEF (World Economic Forum). (2018). Digitalization of supply chains. Retrieve from: https://toplink.weforum.org/knowledge/insight/a1Gb0000000pTDoEAM/explore/dimension/a1Gb0000005Qya0EAC/summary (accessed 13 October 2018).

Zhao, K., Zhao, X., and Deng, J. (2016). An empirical investigation of online gray markets. *Journal of Retailing*, 92(4), 397–410.

Chapter 15
Services and Relationship Marketing

Learning Outcomes

After reading this chapter, you will be able to:

▶ Explain the nature and characteristics of services

▶ Describe what is meant by the terms 'service processes' and 'service encounters', and the principles associated with measuring service quality

▶ Outline the principles of relationship marketing, and consider the merits of customer retention and loyalty programmes

▶ Understand the concepts of trust, commitment, and customer satisfaction, and explain how they are interlinked

▶ Explain the term 'customer experiences', the dimensions associated with it, how it has evolved, and how it might be measured

▶ Explain the term 'customer engagement' and the strategies marketers use to increase it

Case Insight 15.1
Withers Worldwide

Founded in London in 1896, Withers Worldwide has global revenues of over US$200 million, 163 partners, more than 1,000 employees, and clients in more than 80 countries, and has acted for 42 per cent of the top 100 *Sunday Times* Rich List and 20 per cent of the top 100 of the *Forbes* Rich List. We speak to Laura Boyle, head of EU marketing and business development, to explore how Withers works to improve the quality of its client relationships.

Predicting the global nature of private capital, Withers set out over a decade ago, from its origins as a London-based firm, to do something that law firms had not done before: to develop a genuinely international offering for global wealth. Choosing global centres of private wealth, the firm strives to ensure that we match our clients' evolving needs. We are now the largest law firm focused on the needs of private wealth in the world, with 18 offices across the United States, Europe, Asia Pacific, and the Caribbean. Until recently, other law firms focused on this market have operated from a domestic base.

As a professional services organization, making sure that our employees understand our strategy and brand is paramount, because they liaise with our clients and embody the customer experience. Keeping everyone informed on developments has been challenging, given our rapid expansion. In addition to the usual internal communications, such as newsletters, intranet, and leadership briefings, we have developed 'Withers TV'—television screens placed in prominent places in our offices. They share daily news updates about clients and our people, so that everyone is in the best position to feel part of the Withers Worldwide brand and knows how to talk about it externally. This supports more personal communications too—for example with annual general meeting (AGM) sessions for all staff. We run standardized inductions for new joiners and each team is assigned a business development manager, who acts like a key account manager for them as internal clients, connecting them to central strategy, the brand, and our best practice approach.

The variability of our service offering worldwide is a real benefit to our clients; it is how we deliver tailored services. We need to have lawyers, with associated legal

support, operating in different areas of specialism and at differing levels of experience to deliver a comprehensive service, priced in the best way for clients. Any conversation with a prospective client first considers what their needs are and then we calibrate the input of senior partner time required, together with the support needed from more junior lawyers and paralegals.

We avoid potential issues around variance in service quality through our marketing function, which incorporates client relationship management (CRM) specialists. We seek feedback from our clients, but also from those who refer work to us and who recommend us to their clients. Our learning and development team delivers a global employee training programme, ensuring that, as we grow and acquire new teams of lawyers, they are brought into the Withers 'way of working'. We also work hard to ensure that our collective and accumulated knowledge is shared across all offices by running a global precedent system.

The problem we had as an organization focused on the way in which we sought client feedback. We had always focused on the trusted adviser, client–lawyer, relationship, which involved personal and tailored requests for feedback. But while we had a good idea of where we were doing well and where one-off problems existed, we had no central view of how clients perceived our service quality.

The following question arose for Withers: how should it develop a more comprehensive system to evaluate the quality of how clients experienced its service offering?

Visit the online resources to watch a video interview with Laura Boyle in which she explains what Withers did.

Introduction

The service sector represents a very large component of many countries' gross domestic product (GDP) (see Chapter 4). It is also a major component of the exports of many countries, including countries such as the United States, UK, China, India, Ireland, and the Netherlands, to name a few of the largest (World Bank, 2017). But have you ever considered how marketing a service might be different from marketing a product? Service businesses have specific characteristics that differentiate them from manufactured products. The range of services on offer (to organizations and consumers) is enormous, and we consume services in nearly all areas of our work, business, home, and leisure activities. In this chapter, we review what makes services so unique and how marketers can manage them effectively. After discussing services marketing, our attention turns to the evaluation of relationships in marketing. We study why companies wish to build long-term relationships with their customers and the different strategies they employ. Both these two areas—the study of services and the importance of marketing relationships—are consistent with a fundamental switch in marketing towards a service-dominant logic (SDL) (see also Chapters 1 and 8). As will be seen in this chapter, current marketing theory and practice goes beyond the management of individual transactions to focus on the development of engaging relationships with customers and other stakeholders, aimed at creating value for all those involved.

The Unique Characteristics of Services

As discussed earlier, the services sector can be very diverse. Table 15.1 indicates the variety of sectors and some of the areas in which we consume different types of service.

To begin with, however, it is necessary to define what a service is, so that we can determine what binds the services offered in all the sectors listed in Table 15.1, so that we can use a common approach to marketing them. As with many topics, there is no firm agreement, but for our purposes the following definition, derived from a number of authors, will be used:

> A service is any act or performance offered by one party to another that is essentially intangible. Consumption of the service does not result in any transfer of ownership even though the service process may be attached to a physical product.

Much of this definition is derived from the work of Grönroos (1990), who considered a range of definitions and interpretations. Most scholars agree that services are characterized by five distinct characteristics, as depicted in Figure 15.1—that is, **intangibility**, **perishability**, **variability**, **inseparability**, and a lack of **ownership**. These are important aspects that shape the way in which marketers design, deliver, and evaluate the marketing of services.

Intangibility

The purchase of products involves the use of most of our senses. We can touch, see, smell, hear, or even taste products before we buy them, let alone use them. When purchasing a tablet or smartphone, it is possible to see the physical product and its various attributes, such as size and colour, to test the functionality, to feel the weight, and to touch it. These are important purchasing decision cues, and even if the equipment fails to work properly, it is possible to take it back for a replacement. However, if a decision is made to buy additional insurance or support, this will

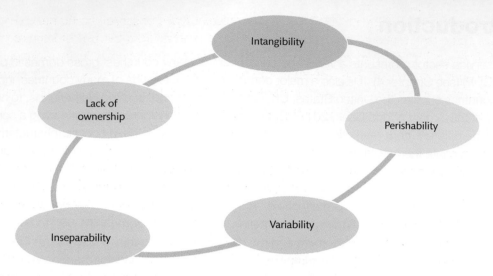

Figure 15.1

The five core characteristics of services

Table 15.1 Service sectors

Sector	Examples
Business	Financial; airlines; hotels; solicitors; lawyers
Manufacturing	Finance and accountants; computer operators; administrators; trainers
Retail	Sales personnel; cashiers; customer support advisers
Institutions	Hospitals; education; museums; charities; churches
Government	Legal system; prisons; military; customs and excise; police

be itemized on the receipt, but cannot be touched, tasted, seen, heard, or smelt. Services are intangible, and they are delivered and experienced only post-purchase.

Intangibility does not mean that customers buy services without using their senses; rather, it means that they use substitute cues to help them to make these purchasing decisions and to reduce the uncertainty because they cannot touch, see, smell, or hear the service. People make judgements based on a range of quality-related cues. These cues serve to make the intangible service tangible. Two types of cue can be identified: intrinsic and extrinsic (Olson and Jacoby, 1972):

- *Intrinsic* cues are drawn directly from the 'service product' itself and are regarded as difficult to change.

- *Extrinsic* cues are said to surround the 'service product' and can be changed relatively easily.

Brady, Bourdeau, and Heskel (2005) found that different types of service brand need different types of cue. Financial and investment-based brands prosper from the use of intrinsic cues, which stress objective information sources, such as a strong reputation, industry rankings, and favourable media reviews. The reverse is true of services that have a more tangible element, such as hotels and transport services. In these circumstances, more subjective communication, such as advertising and referrals through word of mouth, is more influential.

Perishability

A bottle of shampoo on a supermarket shelf benefits from a number of opportunities to be sold and consumed. When the store closes and opens again the following day, the bottle is still available to be sold and it remains available until it is purchased or until it reaches its expiry date. This is not the case with services. Once a train pulls out of a station, or an aeroplane takes off, or a film starts, those seats are lost and can never be sold. This is referred to as perishability and is an important aspect of services marketing. Services are manufactured and consumed simultaneously; they cannot be stored either prior to or after the **service encounter**.

The reason why these seats remain empty reflects variations in demand. This may be a result of changes in the wider environment and may follow easily predictable patterns of behaviour, for example family holiday travel. One of the tasks of service marketers is to ensure that the number of empty seats and lost-forever revenue is minimized. In cases of predictable demand, service managers can vary the level of service capacity—for example with a longer train, a bigger aircraft, or extra screenings of a film (multiplex facilities). However, demand may vary unpredictably, in which case service managers are challenged to provide varying levels of service capacity at short notice.

One of the main ways in which demand patterns can be influenced is through differential pricing (see Chapter 9). By lowering prices to attract custom during quieter times and raising prices when demand is at its highest, demand can be levelled and marginal revenues increased. Hotel and transport reservation systems have become very sophisticated, making it easier to manage demand and improve efficiency, as well, of course, as customer service. Some football clubs categorize matches according to the prestige or ranking of the opposition and adjust prices to fill the stadium. In addition to differential pricing, extra services can be introduced to divert demand. Hotels offer specialist breaks, such as golfing or fishing weekends, and mini-vacations, to attract people outside the holiday season. Leisure parks offer family discounts and bundle free rides into prices to stimulate demand.

Variability

As already noted, an important characteristic of services is that they are produced and consumed by people, simultaneously, as a single event. It is therefore exceedingly difficult to standardize the delivery of services for even the same customer on consecutive occasions. It is also difficult to deliver services so that they always meet the brand promise, especially because these promises often serve to frame customer service expectations. If demand increases unexpectedly and there is insufficient capacity to deal with the excess number of customers, service breakdown may occur. A flood of customers at a restaurant may extend the waiting times of those customers already seated who have ordered their meals, or too many train passengers may mean that there are not enough seats. In both these cases, it is not possible to provide a service level that can be consistently reproduced.

A different way of looking at variability is to consider a theatre. The show may be doing well and the lead actors performing to critical acclaim. However, the actual performance that each actor delivers each night will be slightly different. This change may be subtle, such as a change in the tone of voice or an inflexion, and will pass by relatively unnoticed. At the other extreme, some actors go out of their way to make their performances very different. It is alleged that actor Jane Horrocks once remarked that, during her performance of a certain play, she deliberately changed each evening's show to relieve her boredom.

There has been substantial criticism of some organizations that, in an effort to lower costs, have relocated some or all of their call centre operations offshore. These strategies sometimes fail, because the new provider has insufficient training, insufficient local or product knowledge, or in some cases simply cannot be understood. This type of service experience will vary among customers and for each customer. The resulting fall in customer satisfaction can lead to increased numbers of customers defecting to competitors.

The variability of services does not mean that planning is a worthless activity. By anticipating situations in which service breakdown might occur, service managers can mitigate the potential for harm. For example, entertainment can be provided for queues at cinemas or theme parks to change the customers' perception of the length of the time it takes to experience the service (that is, the film or ride).

Inseparability

As established previously, products can be built, distributed, stored, and eventually consumed at a time specified by the ultimate end user. Services, however, are consumed at the point at which they are produced. In other words, **service delivery** cannot be separated or split out of service provision or service consumption.

This event in which delivery coincides with consumption means not only that customers come into contact with the service providers, but also that there must be interaction between the two parties. This interaction is of particular importance not only to the quality of service production, but also to the experience enjoyed by the customer. So, to extend the earlier theatre example, the play itself may provide suitable entertainment, but the experience may be considerably enhanced if the lead—Jane Horrocks, Judi Dench, or Scarlett Johansson—actually performs rather than has the night off because she is unwell. Alternatively, private doctors may develop a strong reputation and, if there is an increase in demand beyond manageable levels, pricing can be used to reduce or reschedule demand for their services.

These service experiences highlight service delivery both as a mass service experience (the play) and as a solo experience (the doctor). The differences between the two impact on the nature of the interaction process. In the mass service experience, the other members of the audience have the opportunity to influence a customer's perceived quality of the experience. Audiences create atmosphere and this may be positively or negatively charged. A good production can involve audiences in a play and keep them focused for the entire performance; a poor performance can frustrate audiences, leading some members to walk out and hence influence the perception that others have of the performance and their experience of the play.

Interaction within the solo experience (doctor–patient) allows the service provider to exercise greater control, if only because they can manage the immediate context within which the interaction occurs and not be unduly influenced by wider environmental issues. Opportunities exist for flexibility and adaptation as the service delivery unfolds. For example, a check-in operator for an airline operates within a particular context, is not influenced by other major events during the interaction, and can adapt tone of voice, body language, and overall approach to meet the needs of particular travellers.

One final aspect of variability concerns the influence arising from the mixture of customers present during the service delivery. If there is a broad mix of customers, service delivery may be affected because the needs of different groups have to be attended to by the service provider. Such a mixture may dilute the impact of the service actually delivered.

Lack of Ownership

The final characteristic associated with services marketing arises naturally from the other features: services cannot be owned, because nothing is transferred during the interaction or delivery experience. Although a legal transaction often occurs with a service, there is no physical transfer of ownership as there is when a product is purchased. The seat in a theatre, train, plane, or ferry is rented on a temporary basis in exchange for a fee. The terms associated with the rental of the seat determine the time and use or experience to which the seat can be put. However, the seat remains the property of the theatre owner, rail operator, airline, and ferry company, respectively, because it needs to be available for renting to other people for further experiences.

One last point concerns **loyalty** schemes, such as frequent flyer programmes and membership clubs, whereby the service provider actively promotes a sense of ownership. By creating customer involvement and participation, even though there is nothing to actually own, customers can develop an attitude based around their perceived right to be a part of the service provider.

 Visit the **online resources** and follow the web link to the British Bankers Association (BBA) to learn more about how it supports its financial services member organizations worldwide.

While the characteristics discussed above have proven useful to describe some key differences between products and services, they are not always applicable (Moeller, 2010). For example, while inseparability and perishability are typical features of many service experiences, thanks to digital technologies it is now possible to widely distribute services that formerly needed to be created on one specific occasion and in one specific location. It is therefore possible to teach a class via Skype and to record such a performance, so that it can be used later. This means that a service (that is, teaching) can be, at least in some cases, both separable and not perishable. Similarly, it is hard to argue that all services are intangible. Imagine you are taking your car to a garage to repair a dent to its exterior. Your primary judgement of the service will likely depend on whether the physical damage has been repaired expertly such that you are now the newly proud owner of a dent-free car! Rather than consider the five core characteristics of services (that is, intangibility, inseparability, variability, perishability, and lack of ownership) as definite prescriptions for how to undertake services marketing, we should instead consider them as general guidelines that apply, alone or in combination, in many situations. Their effective importance should, however, be considered critically in each case.

Service Processes

An important feature of services is that they are essentially processes. A process is a series of sequential actions that leads to a predetermined outcome. So a simple process might be the steps necessary to visit a dentist, whereas a complex process might be the actions necessary to manage passengers on a two-week luxury cruise. Importantly, customers are often involved in these processes. Service marketing strategy should therefore be based on insight into the ways in which customers interact or contact a service. The form and nature of the customer encounter are of fundamental importance.

A service encounter is best understood as a period of time during which a customer interacts directly with a service (Shostack, 1985). These interactions may be short and encompass all the actions necessary to complete the service experience. Alternatively, they may be protracted, involve several encounters, several representatives of the service provider, and indeed several locations if the service experience is to be completed. Whatever their length, the quality of a service encounter impacts on perceived service value, which, in turn, influences customer satisfaction (Gil, Berenguer, and Cervera, 2008).

Originally, the term 'encounter' was used to describe the personal interaction between a service provider and customers. A more contemporary interpretation needs to include all those interactions that occur through people and their equipment and machines, with the people and equipment belonging to the service provider (Glyn and Lehtinen, 1995), as set out in Market Insight 15.1. As a result, three levels of customer contact can be observed, as follows:

- In *high-contact services*, customers visit the service facility, so that they are personally involved throughout the service delivery process, for example in retail branch banking and higher education.

- In *medium-contact services*, customers visit the service facility, but do not remain for the duration of the service delivery, for example in consulting services, and delivering and collecting items to be repaired.

- *Low-contact services* require little or no personal contact, for example software repairs, and television and radio entertainment.

If processes are an integral part of the operations performed by service organizations, in the general sense, what are they processing? Lovelock, Vandermerwe, and Lewis (1999) present a categorization into four different processes: people processing; possession processing; mental stimulus processing; and information processing.

People Processing

In people processing, people have to physically present themselves so that they become immersed within the **service process**. This involves spending varying amounts of time actively cooperating with the service operation. So people taking a train have to physically go to the station and get on a train, and then spend time getting to their destination. People undergoing dentistry work will have made an appointment prior to attending the dentist's surgery, and they will sit in the chair, open their mouths, and cooperate with the dentist's various requests. They have physically become involved in the service process offered by their dentist.

From a marketing perspective, consideration of the process and the outcomes arising from participation in the service process can lead to ideas about what benefits are being created and what non-financial costs are incurred as a result of the service operation. In the dentistry example, a comfortable chair, background music, non-threatening or neutral-to-warm decor, and a pleasant manner can be of help.

Possession Processing

Just as people have to go to the service operation for people processing, so objects have to become involved in possession processing. Possessions such as kitchen gadgets, gardens, cars, and computers are liable to break down or need maintenance. Cleaning, storing, repairing, couriering, installation, and removal services are other typical possession-processing activities.

In these situations, people will either take an item to the service provider or invite someone in to undertake the necessary work. In possession processing, the level of customer involvement

Market Insight 15.1
Contactless: Speedy and Efficient Service Encounters

Whether it is Hong Kong, Auckland, Amsterdam, or London, the huge numbers of people travelling by trains, buses, trams, ferries, and metro systems introduce service problems not only in terms of seating capacity and general comfort, but also in terms of the time and queues associated with purchasing travel tickets and enabling people to keep moving. At peak times, queuing for tickets can be frustrating and cause enormous delays.

Ticket offices provide people with an opportunity to discuss their requirements on an interpersonal basis with a member of staff. However, this is an expensive and, at times, time-poor use of resources. There are many people who know what (ticket) they need and self-service ticket machines are a way of providing a service for people who do not want or need a personal service encounter. An enormous number of people make the same journey each day. In much the same way, airlines use e-ticketing and on-airport self-check-in solutions, such as **electronic kiosks**, and off-airport self-check-in through kiosk, web, and mobile apps.

In London, travellers can wave a prepaid Oyster card a few centimetres from a point-of-sale terminal on entry and exit from the bus, Tube, tram, DLR, London Overground, and National Rail services, and a price for the journey is debited from the card. In 2014, Transport for London (TfL) added the facility for contactless card payments. Contactless payments work in the same way as the Oyster card, allowing customers to use their debit cards to pay an adult-rate fare for their journey. Used in this way, near-field communication (NFC) technology spares travellers the time they would otherwise spend topping up their Oyster balances,

simply because fares are charged directly to their payment card accounts. The system also calculates the lowest possible fare, ensuring that commuters are charged at the weekly, rather than the daily, rate.

In Hong Kong, the Octopus card is based on a smartcard that also incorporates NFC technology. This enables two devices to exchange data when they are adjacent. Here, the 'wave and pay' card is used not only for transport and ticketing services, but also for a whole range of purchases, including supermarkets, restaurants, gift shops, and even hospitals and cinemas.

The NFC chip technology can be embedded in a variety of products, such as watches, key chains, ornaments, and, of course, smartphones.

Sources: Oates (2009); Laja (2012); Curtis (2014).

Oyster cards are prepaid and use wireless technology, allowing customers of the London transport network to get in and out of stations quickly
Source: iStock.com/mikeinlondon.

Market Insight 15.1
continued

Theory into Practice

One way of interpreting service encounters is through uncertainty reduction theory. A service provider and user will interact to better understand each other and hence reduce the uncertainty that exists between the parties at the outset of their relationship. Through communication, a reduction in uncertainty occurs that drives trust and transaction frequency.

Another interpretation involves role theory. This holds that people are social actors whose behaviour, or performance, has been learned relative to the different positions they occupy.

Related to this interpretation is script theory. This holds that a script contains information about a role that is to be performed. Deviation from the script leads to disorientation.

In the examples outlined in this market insight, the role of the service provider is clear and the contactless payment system serves to develop the roles so that service receivers are less likely to deviate from their script. This, in turn, should encourage further interaction and use of the service, with increasingly less uncertainty and disorientation.

Related Topics

service processes; service quality management; relationship marketing; customer experiences

1 **How would you classify 'wave and pay' as a form of service encounter with transport systems?**

2 **How might business-to-business (B2B) marketers make use of 'wave and pay'?**

3 **How might a symbol or logo that indicates that a card uses contactless technology assist in the marketing of this service?**

---

is limited compared with that in people processing. In most cases, the sequence of activities is as follows:

1. For an object to be attended to, a telephone call is often required to fix an appointment.

2. The item then either needs to be taken to the service provider or the customer must wait for an attendant to visit.

3. A brief explaining the problem/task/solution is given and the work is completed.

4. The customer then returns at an agreed time and location to pay and take away the renewed item.

This detachment from the service process enables people to focus on other tasks. The key difference here is that the quality of the service is not dependent on the presence of the owner or representative of the possession while the service operation takes place.

Mental Stimulus Processing

Mental stimulus processing tries to shape attitudes or behaviour. To achieve this, these services have to be oriented to people's minds and hence the phrase mental stimulus processing. Examples of these types of service include education, entertainment, professional advice, and news. In all of these, people have to become involved mentally in the service interaction and give their time if they are to experience the benefits of this type of service.

Service delivery can be through one of two locations. Services can be created in a location that is distant from the receiver, in which case media channels are used to deliver the service; alternatively, services can be delivered and consumed at the point at which they originate—that is, in a studio, theatre, or hall. One of the key differences here is the form and nature of the audience experience: the theatre experience is likely to be much richer than the distant format. Digital technology has enabled opportunities for increased amounts of interactive communication, even though the experience will be different from the original. In the same way, online or e-learning in its purest form has not yet become an established format, perhaps because learners need to spend some of their learning time in interaction with their co-learners and in the presence of a tutor. As examples, consider Open University's use of summer schools and the increasing success of blended learning programmes.

Information Processing

The final type of service concerns the huge arena of information processing, the most intangible of all the services. Transformed by advances in technology in general, and computers in particular, information processing has become quicker, more accurate, and more frequent. The use of technology is important, but we should not exclude people, because individuals have a huge capacity to process information. Banking, insurance services, entertainment, and news all represent examples of service areas that rely on information-processing activities.

One key issue that organizations need to consider concerns the degree to which employees should become involved in the delivery of information processing services. Organizations could deliberately route customers away from people processing by reducing the number of clerks and counters, and towards information processing by pushing online and automated teller machine (ATM) operations. easyJet reduces costs by making it difficult for customers to telephone the company and seek advice from staff. Its approach is to drive people to its website and to answer customer queries with the frequently asked questions (FAQs) found there.

Key Dimensions of Services Marketing

The marketing of services can be improved by understanding how customers evaluate service performance. This gives rise to the question: how do customers judge the quality of a bank's services, or those of an airline? This is potentially very difficult, because complex services such as surgery or stockbroking have few tangible clues based on which a customer can make a judgement about whether the service was extremely good, good, satisfactory, poor, or a disgrace.

Zeithaml (1981) developed a framework categorizing different services, which, in turn, influence the degree to which market offerings can be evaluated and identified three main properties, as follows:

- *Search* properties are those elements that help customers to evaluate an offering prior to purchase. As already mentioned, physical products tend to have high search attributes, which serve to reduce customer risk and increase purchase confidence.

- *Experience* properties do not enable evaluation prior to purchase. Sporting events, holidays, and live entertainment can be imagined, they can be explained, and they can be illustrated, but only through the experience of the performance or the feel of sitting in an audience of 100,000 people can a customer evaluate the service experience.

- *Credence* properties relate to those service characteristics that customers find difficult to evaluate even after purchase and consumption. Zeithaml (1981) refers to complex surgery and legal services to demonstrate the point.

As demonstrated earlier, most physical goods are high in search properties. Services, however, reflect the strength of experience and credence characteristics that, in turn, highlight their intangibility and their variability.

Many organizations recognize the importance and complexities associated with the marketing of services. As a result, they often develop and plan their marketing activities in such a way that they help and reassure their customers prior to, during, and after purchase. The services triangle (see Figure 15.2) is a marketing framework that summarizes these complexities. The model suggests that success in services marketing depends on three sets of relationships: customers' relationship with the firm; customers' interaction with the employees who deliver the service; and the employees' ongoing **commitment** to the company (Bitner, 1995). Managers need to consider three types of marketing to deal with such relationships effectively: external marketing; interactive marketing; and internal marketing.

To explain the differences between these three, let's consider a traditional service business such as a restaurant:

- External marketing relates to the offering that makes the restaurant attractive to customers: a nice and enticing menu, reasonable prices, and a good location.

- Interactive marketing concerns the relationship between staff and customers, for example how effectively employees can deal with customers' requests and whether they are able to provide an excellent experience.

- Internal marketing requires offering a good experience to staff, so that good employees can be attracted and retained over time.

Service marketing thus needs these three type of activities working together to achieve financial success.

Understanding service encounters, customer satisfaction, and associated service measurement techniques, however, fails to lead to an understanding beyond the moment of truth—that is, the point at which the service is actioned. Understanding and measuring the experience that customers take away as a result of an interaction is much more pertinent and insightful.

Measuring Service Quality and Performance

Measuring the quality of a service encounter with a financial institution such as Withers Worldwide (see Case Insight 15.1) and other organizations has become a major factor in the management

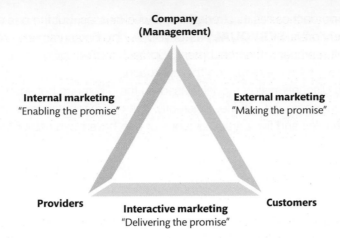

Figure 15.2
The services marketing triangle
Source: Adapted from Bitner (1995).

of service-based organizations. **Service quality** is based on the idea that customer expectations of the service they will receive shape their perception of the actual service encounter. In essence, therefore, customers compare perceived service with expected service.

So if the perceived service meets, or even exceeds, expectations, customers are deemed to be satisfied and are much more likely to return at some point in the future. However, if the perceived service falls below what was expected, they are more likely to feel disappointed and are unlikely to return.

To help organizations to manage and provide a consistent level of service, various models have been proposed. Primarily, these have been based on performance measures, disconfirmation (the gap between expected and perceived service encounter), and importance–performance ideas (Palmer, 2005) (see Table 15.2).

Table 15.2 Three approaches to service quality measurement

Contact level	Explanation
Performance measures	Derived from the manufacturing sector, this approach simply asks customers to rate the performance of a service encounter. SERVPERF is the standard measurement technique.
Disconfirmation	This approach is based on the difference between what is expected from a service and what is delivered, as perceived by the customer. SERVQUAL is the standard measurement technique.
Importance– performance	This seeks to compare the performance of the different elements that make up a service with the customer's perception of the relative importance of these elements. Importance–performance analysis (IPA) is the standard measurement technique.

Each of these approaches has its strengths and weaknesses, but the one approach that has received most attention is **SERVQUAL**, as developed by Parasuraman, Zeithaml, and Berry (1988). For some, it represents the benchmark approach to managing service quality. (See also Research Insight 15.1 for more details on this approach.)

SERVQUAL is a disconfirmation model, based on the difference between the expected services and the actual perceived service. Inherently, this approach assumes that there is a gap between these variables and five particular types of gap have been established across service industries, as follows:

- *GAP 1—The gap between the customer's expectations and management perception* By not understanding customer needs correctly, management directs resources into inappropriate areas. For example, train service operators may think that customers want places in which to store bags, whereas they actually want a seat in a comfortable, safe environment.

- *GAP 2—The gap between management perception and service quality specification* In this case, management perceive customer wants correctly, but fail to set a performance standard and/or fail to clarify it, or set a standard that is not realistic and hence is unachievable. For example, the train operator understands customers' desire for a comfortable seat, but fails to specify how many should be provided relative to the anticipated number of travellers on each route.

- *GAP 3—The gap between service quality specifications and service delivery* In this situation, the service delivery does not match the specification for the service. This may be as a result of human error, poor training, or a failure in the technology necessary to deliver parts of a service. For example, the trolley buffet service on a train may be perceived as poor because the trolley operator was impolite (perhaps because they had not received suitable training), or because the train company's supplier had not delivered the sandwiches on time.

- *GAP 4—The gap between service delivery and external communications* The service promise presented in advertisements, on the website, and in sales literature helps to set customer

Research Insight 15.1

To take your learning further, you might wish to read this influential paper:

Parasuraman, A., Zeithaml, V., and Berry, L.L. (1988). SERVQUAL: a multiple-item scale for measuring consumer perceptions of service quality. *Journal of Retailing*, 64(1), 5–37.

This is a classic article, structured in five sections, which describes the development of SERVQUAL, the multiple-item scale for measuring service quality. It also includes an interesting discussion regarding the scale's properties and its potential applications. Slightly adapted to the specific context, these items can be used to obtain reliable service-quality evaluations and to determine the aspects of the offering in highest need of improvement.

  Visit the online resources to read the abstract and access the full paper.

expectations. If these promises are not realized in service delivery practice, customers become dissatisfied. For example, if an advertisement shows the interior of a train with comfortable seats and plenty of space, yet a customer boards a train only to find a lack of space and hard seating, the external communications have misled customers and distorted their view of what might be realistically expected.

- *GAP 5—The gap between perceived service and expected service*   This gap arises because customers misunderstand the service quality relative to what they expect. This may be as a result of one or more of the previous gaps. For example, a customer might assume that the lack of information when a train comes to a standstill for an unexpectedly long period of time is a consequence of ignorance or because 'they never tell us anything'. In reality, this silence may be a failure of the internal communication system.

Using this 'gaps' approach, five different dimensions of service quality have been established:

- *reliability*—that is, the accuracy and dependability of repeated performances of service delivery;

- *responsiveness*—that is, the ability and willingness of staff to provide prompt service;

- *assurance*—that is, the courtesy, confidence, and competence of employees;

- *empathy*—that is, the ease and individualized care shown towards customers; and

- *tangibles*—that is, the appearance of employees, the physical location, and any facilities and equipment, as well as the communication materials.

The SERVQUAL model consists of a questionnaire comprising 22 items based on these dimensions. When completed by customers, it provides management with opportunities to correct areas in which service performance is perceived to be less than satisfactory and to learn from, and congratulate, people about the more successful components.

Although SERVQUAL has been used extensively, there are some problems associated with it, including the different dimensions customers use to assess quality, which varies according to each situation. In addition, there are statistical inconsistencies associated with measuring differences and the scoring techniques, and reliability issues associated with asking customers about their expectations after they have consumed a service (Gabbott and Hogg, 1998). Finally, ideas about measuring satisfaction are being overtaken as understanding about **customer experience** becomes more widely known. This is explored further at the end of this chapter.

The Principles of Relationship Marketing

Our attention now turns to ideas about **relationship marketing**. First, we look at some foundational ideas about the exchanges that occur between a pair of buyers and sellers. Two main types can be identified: **market (or discrete) exchanges** and **collaborative exchanges** (see also Chapters 1 and 14).

Market (or discrete) exchanges occur where there is no prior history of exchange and no future exchanges are expected between a buyer and a seller. In these transactions, the primary focus is on the product and price. Often referred to as transactional marketing, the '4Ps' approach to the marketing mix variables (that is, the marketing management school of thought) is used to guide and construct transactional behaviour. Buyers are considered to be passive and sellers, active, in these short-term exchanges.

However, the assumption that buyers are passive was soon challenged by the notion that, in reality, buyers are active problem-solvers seeking solutions that are both efficient and effective. Research into business markets identified that, in practice, purchasing is not about a single discrete event; rather, it is about a stream of activities between two organizations. These activities are sometimes referred to as episodes. Typically, these may be price negotiations, meetings at exhibitions, or a buying decision, but they all take place within the overall context of a relationship. This framed the relationship marketing school of thought, in which the buyer–seller relationship was the central element of analysis. This meant that the focus was no longer the product, or even the individual buying or selling firm, but the relationship and its particular characteristics over time.

Therefore relationship marketing is based on the principle that there is a history of exchanges and an expectation that there will be exchanges in the future. Furthermore, the perspective is long term, envisaging a form of loyalty or continued attachment by the buyer to the seller. Price, as the key controlling mechanism, is replaced by customer service and quality of interaction between the two organizations. The exchange is termed collaborative because the focus is on both organizations seeking to achieve their goals in a mutually rewarding way and not at the expense of one another.

See Table 15.3 for a more comprehensive list of fundamental differences between transactional and collaborative marketing.

Although market exchanges focus on products and prices, there is still a relational component, if only because interaction requires a basic relationship between parties for the transaction to be completed (Macneil, 1980).

Table 15.3 Characteristics of market and collaborative exchanges

Attribute	Market exchange	Collaborative exchange
Length of relationship	Short-term Abrupt end	Long-term Continuous process
Relational expectations	Conflicts of goals Immediate payment No future problems (there is no future)	Conflicts of interest Deferred payment Future problems expected to be overcome by joint commitment
Communication	Low frequency of communication Formal communication predominates	Frequent communication Informal communication predominates
Cooperation	No joint cooperation	Joint cooperative projects
Responsibilities	Distinct responsibilities Defined obligations	Shared responsibilities Shared obligations

Dwyer, Schurr, and Oh (1987) refer to relationship marketing as an approach that encompasses a wide range of relationships not only with customers, but also with suppliers, regulators, government, competitors, employees, and others. From this, relationship marketing might be regarded as all marketing activities associated with the management of successful relational exchanges.

Theron, Terblanche, and Boshoff (2013), among others, recognize that the role of collaboration in relationship marketing is important. However, many organizations maintain a variety of relationships with their different customers and suppliers, some highly collaborative and some market-oriented—or, as Spekman and Carroway (2005: 1) suggest, 'where they make sense'.

 Visit the **online resources** and follow the web link to the Association for the Advancement of Relationship Marketing (AARM) to learn more about continuing professional development in relationship marketing.

The Customer Relationship Life Cycle

Relationship cost theory identified benefits associated with stable and mutually rewarding relationships. Such customers avoided costly switching costs associated with finding new suppliers, whereas suppliers experienced reduced quality costs, incurred when adapting to the needs of new customers.

Reichheld and Sasser (1990) identified an important association between a small (for example 5 per cent) increase in **customer retention** and a large (for example 60 per cent) improvement in profitability. So a long-term relationship leads to lower relationship costs and higher profits. It is on the basis of this simple, yet crucial, principle that many organizations develop and run loyalty programmes (see Research Insight 15.2).

 ## Research Insight 15.2

To take your learning further, you might wish to read this influential paper:

Reichheld, F.F., and Sasser, E.W. (1990). Zero defections: quality comes to services. *Harvard Business Review*, 68(5), 105–11.

Often quoted by other authors and researchers, this article reported that a small increase in the number of retained customers can have a disproportionately large increase in profitability, a finding which has helped to propel a wealth of research and interest in relationship marketing. By definition, loyal customers are less likely to switch, and therefore incur lower sales and service costs. They also help, through word of mouth, to recruit new customers, so the net result is that they all contribute to higher profits. Although the specific loyalty gains might have changed since the time the research was conducted, the analysis is an important reminder of how crucial customer loyalty is for the profitability of any business.

 Visit the online resources to read the abstract and access the full paper.

By undertaking a customer profitability analysis, it is possible to identify those segments that are worth developing. This enables the construction of a portfolio of relationships, from which it is possible to identify relationships that have the potential to provide mutually rewarding benefits. This then provides a third dimension of the customer dynamic—namely, **customer development**.

Understanding the economics associated with relationship stability and profitability uncovers three main stages within customer relationships: **customer acquisition**; customer development; and customer retention. This suggests similarities to the phases or stages of development associated with the concept of the product life cycle.

Taking this idea one step further allows us to develop a **customer relationship life cycle**. This consists of four main stages—namely, customer acquisition, customer development, customer retention, and finally **customer decline** or termination (see Table 15.4).

Just as different strategies can be applied to different phases of the product life cycle, so it is possible to observe that customers have different requirements as a relationship evolves. These requirements are reflected in the intensity of the relationship and, of course, the level of intensity will vary through time. Figure 15.3 illustrates the customer relationship life cycle.

Table 15.4 Stages in the customer life cycle

Stage	Explanation
Acquisition	There are three main events. First, both buyers and sellers search for a suitable match. Second, once a suitable partner has been found, there is a period of initiation, or 'settling in', during which both parties seek out information about the other before any transaction occurs. The third phase is characterized by socialization. Once a transaction occurs, the buyer and seller start to become more familiar with each other, and gradually begin to reveal more information about themselves.
Development	Sellers encourage buyers to purchase increased quantities, to try other products, to engage with other added value services, and to vary delivery times and quantities. The number and value of transactions increase as both buyer and seller begin to understand each other's requirements and goals in greater detail. During this stage, sellers also develop a better understanding of the wider array of their buyers' stakeholder relationships. This can have a significant influence on the nature of the supplier's relationship with the buyer, often indicating the depth to which the relationship aspires.
Retention	The relationship becomes stabilized, typified by greater levels of trust and commitment between the partners. This facilitates increased cross-buying and product experimentation, joint projects, and product development. Suppliers often provide customer loyalty schemes to increase the volume and value of products and services bought, and to lock in their customers by creating relationship exit barriers.
Decline	Relationships can become destabilized and uncertainty between partners can develop. There are many reasons for this, including purchasing agreements and loyalty programmes that are not sufficiently attractive to lock in customers, as well as changes in the wider environment such as legislative, climatic, or economic developments. Customer recovery strategies are required at the first sign a relationship is waning.

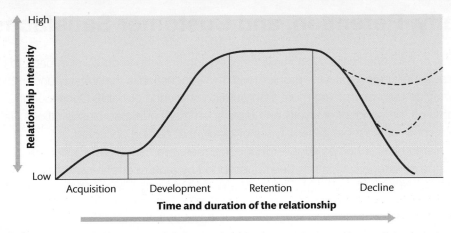

Figure 15.3

The customer relationship life cycle

Key to this concept is the differing level of relationship intensity that determines each stage. Bruhn (2002) suggests that there are three primary indicators that make up this intensity dimension—that is, the psychological intensity, behavioural intensity, and economic intensity indicators—and these are depicted in Figure 15.4:

■ The *psychological intensity* indicators are based on a customer's judgement about the quality of the relationship and the extent to which they **trust**, and are committed to, the seller or supplying organization. These are important foundations for establishing and maintaining ongoing and mutually rewarding two-way relationships. These are explored in more detail later in this chapter.

■ *Behavioural intensity* indicators refer to the manner and scope of a customer's search for information, including word-of-mouth communication, as well as their purchasing behaviour.

■ *Economic intensity* indicators refer to both the profit contribution and the lifetime value a customer represents.

These three indicators signal the intensity of a relationship. They vary through time and help to explain the characteristics associated with each of the relationship stages.

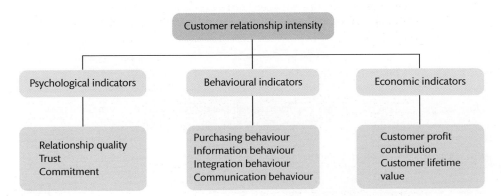

Figure 15.4

Indicators of customer relationship intensity

Source: *Relationship Marketing: Management of Customer Relationships*, Bruhn, M. (2002). Pearson Education Limited.

Loyalty, Retention, and Customer Satisfaction

The customer relationship life cycle implies that customers who keep coming back to buy from a particular supplier are loyal. One problem with this suggestion is that what is understood to be 'loyalty' may actually be nothing more than pure convenience or habit. Consequently, scholars have examined the concept of loyalty and developed more nuanced classifications. Table 15.5 represents some of the more general types of loyalty that can be observed.

These hierarchical schemes suggest that consumers are capable of varying degrees of loyalty. This type of categorization has been questioned by a number of researchers. Fournier and Yao (1997) doubt the validity of such approaches, and Baldinger and Rubinson (1996) support the idea that consumers work within an evoked set and switch between brands. This view is supported on the grounds that many consumers display elements of curiosity in their purchase habits, enjoy variety, and are happy to switch brands as a result of marketing communication activities and product experiences.

At one level, loyalty can be seen to be about increasing sales volume—that is, fostering loyal purchase behaviour. However, high levels of repeat purchase are not necessarily an adequate measure of loyalty, because there may be a number of situational factors determining purchase behaviour, such as brand availability (Dick and Basu, 1994). At whichever level of loyalty, customer retention is paramount and neither behavioural nor attitudinal measures alone are adequate indicators of true loyalty. O'Malley (1998) suggests that a combination of the two is of greater use, and that the twin parameters of relative attitudes (to alternatives) and patronage behaviour (the recency, frequency, and monetary model), as suggested by Dick and Basu (1994), offer more accurate indicators of loyalty when used together.

This expansion in the number of loyalty programmes led Capizzi, Ferguson, and Cuthbertson (2004) to suggest that five clear trends within the loyalty market can be identified. These are set out in Table 15.6. These trends suggest that successful sales promotions schemes will be those that enable members to perceive significant value linked to their continued association with a scheme. That value will be driven by schemes run by groups of complementary brands, which use technology to understand customer dynamics and communications that complement their

Table 15.5 Types of loyalty

Type	Explanation
Emotional loyalty	This is a true form of loyalty, and is driven by personal identification with real or perceived values and benefits.
Price loyalty	This type of loyalty is driven by rational economic behaviour and the main motivations are cautious management of money or financial necessity.
Incentivized loyalty	This refers to promiscuous buyers with no one favourite brand, who demonstrate through repeat experience the value of becoming loyal.
Monopoly loyalty	This class of loyalty arises where a consumer has no purchase choice owing to a national monopoly. This is not a true form of loyalty.

Table 15.6 Five loyalty trends

Trend	Explanation
Ubiquity	For example, the proliferation of loyalty programmes in most mature markets, in which many members have little interest other than in the functionality of points collection.
Coalition	Schemes are run by a number of different organizations to share costs, information, and branding (e.g. Nectar, Star Alliance) and appear to be the dominant industry model.
Imagination	Opportunities to exploit technologies and niche markets will depend on creativity and imagination if a company is to acquire customer data to feed into the loyalty system.
Wow	To overcome consumer lethargy and boredom with loyalty schemes, in the future many rewards will be experiential, emotional, and unique in an attempt to appeal to life stage and aspirational lifestyle goals—i.e. to 'wow' the customer.
Analysis	To be competitive, the use of customer data analytics and business intelligence is becoming critical, if only to feed customer relationship management (CRM) programs. It is essential to collect and analyse customer information effectively.

Source: Adapted from Capizzi et al. (2004).

preferred values. The medium-term goal might be that these schemes should reflect customers' different relationship needs and recognize the different loyalty levels desired by different people. Market Insight 15.2 describes the main loyalty schemes used by airlines (but see Market Insight 15.4, later in the chapter, which offers a reminder that relationship marketing goes well beyond loyalty schemes and discusses the ability to create strong bonds with customers without a loyalty card).

 Visit the **online resources** and complete Internet Activity 15.1 to learn more about how to increase customer loyalty.

Relationship Trust, Commitment, and Satisfaction

It is difficult to find a definition of trust on which everyone agrees, because many authors fail to specify clearly what they mean when using it (Cousins and Stanwix, 2001). There is, however, a general consensus that trust is an element associated with personal, intra-organizational, and inter-organizational relationships, and is necessary for their continuation. Gambetta (1988) argues that trust is a means of reducing uncertainty so that effective relationships can develop.

Cousins and Stanwix (2001) also suggest that although trust is a word used to explain how relationships work, it often refers to ideas concerning risk, power, and dependency, and these propositions are used interchangeably. From their research on vehicle manufacturers, it emerges that B2B relationships are about the creation of mutual business advantage and the degree of confidence that one organization has in another.

Market Insight 15.2
Alliances in the Sky

As costs have increased and competition intensified, airlines around the world have formed strategic alliances. These collaborative schemes require members to share routes, facilities such as executive lounges, and, of course, customers. Three main alliances have emerged:

- The oneworld® Alliance consists of 15 airlines, including Qantas, American Airlines, and British Airways, and together they fly to more than 150 countries.

- The Star Alliance has 26 member airlines, including Air China, Singapore Airlines, and United, and flies to more than 1,269 airports in 193 countries.

- The SkyTeam has 20 members, including Air France, Delta Airways, and China Airlines, and collectively they serve 1,064 destinations.

The use of loyalty schemes in the airline industry is well established. These enable airlines to add value and help to brand their propositions by decommoditizing their services and offerings. Frequent flyer programmes (FFPs) are now regarded as a key part of an alliance's success. Each airline within an alliance has its own loyalty programme, with its own procedures and complexities. In addition to these, alliances offer a single alternative loyalty programme, which is integrated with the home airline's primary loyalty programme. Alliance schemes have several membership tiers, based on usage. The membership tiers in the oneworld® Alliance are branded Emerald, Sapphire, and Ruby. In the Star Alliance, there are two

premium levels, Silver and Gold, whilst SkyTeam offers SkyTeam Elite and Elite Plus.

These schemes offer seamless travel, better usage of amenities at airports, and—through compatible loyalty schemes and code-sharing—the transference of frequent flyer miles from various alliance-based carriers, which helps to build customer loyalty to the alliance rather than to an airline.

Sources: https://www.cheapflights.co.uk/travel-tips/airline-alliances/; https://www.oneworld.com/ffp/my-oneworld-tier-status; https://www.staralliance.com/en/recognition

The oneworld® alliance consists of 15 of the world's leading airlines and approximately 30 affiliated carriers. Frequent flyers with the partner airlines earn and redeem points on eligible oneworld flights.
Source: © EQRoy/Shutterstock.com.

Theory into Practice

Alliances occur when two or more organizations seek mutual collaboration that is deemed beneficial. This means that organizational goals and external opportunities jointly determine the formation of alliances. Such coalitions are formed to share costs, customer and market information, and branding. The question of which organizations link to which other organizations is based on whether or not they have a mutual fit of resources. Successful matching requires that an organization holding a valued resource must seek something that the approaching organization can provide in return.

Networks, such as those formed in airline alliances, are considered to be a set of firms that coordinate their activities to fulfil different roles and add different competencies. These are recognized as being important to the strategic success of businesses, especially in business-to-business (B2B) markets. Such coalitions can impact on the relationship with customers, since the firms are likely to be sharing resources in their go-to-market strategy.

Market Insight 15.2
continued

Related Topics
relationship marketing; trust and commitment; loyalty schemes; customer retention

1 Do you think that operating both an airline and an alliance loyalty scheme is a good use of resources? Justify your view.

2 How might smartphone manufacturers retain customers?

3 Some organizations choose not to offer loyalty schemes, preferring to offer low prices. To what extent does this offer customers better value?

Trust involves judgements about reliability and integrity, and is concerned with the degree of confidence that one party to a relationship has that another will fulfil its obligations and responsibilities. The presence of trust in a relationship is important because it reduces both the threat of opportunism and the possibility of conflict, which in turn increases the probability of buyer satisfaction. It has been claimed that the three major outcomes from the development of relationship trust are satisfaction, reduced **perceived risk**, and continuity (Pavlou, 2002):

- *Satisfaction* is defined as meeting customer expectations (see 'Measuring Service Quality and Performance').

- *Perceived risk* is concerned with the expectation of loss and therefore is tied closely to organizational performance. Trust that a seller will not take advantage of the imbalance of information between buyer and seller effectively reduces risk.

- *Continuity* is related to business volumes, necessary in online B2B marketplaces, and the development of both online and offline enduring relationships. Trust is associated with continuity and therefore, when present, it is indicative of long-term relationships.

Trust within a consumer context is important because it can reduce uncertainty. Financial institutions such as RBS, UBS, and HSBC have lost considerable amounts of consumer trust as a result of their illegal behaviour, including the London interbank offered rate (Libor) fixing scandal, cynical charges (such as payment protection insurance, or PPI), and questionable investments (see Chapter 18). Strong brands provide sufficient information for consumers to make calculated purchase decisions in the absence of full knowledge. In a sense, consumers transfer their responsibility for brand decision-making, and hence brand performance, to the brand itself. Through regular brand purchases, habits, or 'routinized response behaviour', develop. This is important not only because complex decision-making is simplified, but also because the amount of communication necessary to assist and provoke purchase is considerably reduced.

Commitment is important because it implies a desire that a relationship continues and is strengthened because it is of value. Morgan and Hunt (1994) proposed that commitment and trust are fundamental in explanations of the benefits of relationship marketing (see Figure 15.5). These two variables connect the causes of relationship marketing to its consequences. In other words, the authors believe that the positive consequences associated with the development of a relationship (for example the increase in cooperation) can be explained by the increase in trust and commitment towards the partner.

According to the commitment–trust model, the greater the losses anticipated through the termination of a relationship, the greater the commitment expressed by the exchange partners. When relationship partners share similar values, commitment increases. Morgan and Hunt (1994) proposed that building a relationship based on trust and commitment can give rise to a number of benefits. Some of these are developing a set of shared values, reducing costs when the relationship finishes, and increasing profitability as a greater number of customers are retained because of the inherent value and satisfaction they experience. Cooperation arises from a relationship driven by high levels of both trust and commitment.

Ryssel, Ritter, and Gemunden (2004: 203) recognize that trust (and commitment) has a 'significant impact on the creation of value and conclude that value creation is a function of the atmosphere of a relationship rather than the technology employed'. Trust and commitment are concepts that are central to relationship marketing.

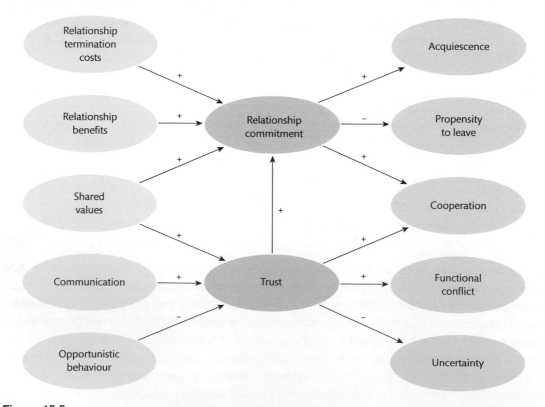

Figure 15.5

The commitment–trust model of relationship marketing

Source: Reprinted with permission from R.M. Morgan and S.D. Hunt (1994), 'The commitment–trust theory of relationship marketing', *Journal of Marketing*, 58(July), 20–38, published by the American Marketing Association.

Customer Satisfaction

A natural outcome from building trust and developing commitment is the establishment of customer satisfaction. This is seen as important because satisfaction is thought to be positively related to customer retention, which in turn leads to an improved return on investment and hence profitability. Unsurprisingly, many organizations seek to improve levels of customer satisfaction, with the intention of strengthening customer relationships and driving higher levels of retention and loyalty (Ravald and Grönroos, 1996). So the simple equation is build trust, drive satisfaction, improve retention, and increase profits.

However, customer satisfaction is not driven by trust alone; customer expectations also play an important role and help to shape a customer's perception of product or service performance. Customers compare performance against their expectations and, through this process, feel a sense of customer satisfaction or dissatisfaction. More recent ideas suggest that the **perceived value** of a relationship can be more important than trust when building customer satisfaction (Ulaga and Eggert, 2005). If customer expectations are met, customer satisfaction is achieved. If Withers Worldwide can exceed the expectations of its customers, both parties will be delighted (see Case Insight 15.1). If expectations are not met, customers will be said to be dissatisfied.

It generally follows that satisfied customers are more likely to remain loyal. This simplistic interpretation can be misleading, however, because satisfaction does not always imply loyalty (Mittal and Lassar, 1998); what may be seen as loyalty may be nothing more than convenience, or even inertia, and dissatisfaction need not result in brand desertion (O'Malley, 1998).

The following elements contribute to customer satisfaction and are therefore within the marketer's purview to exploit in pursuit of building customer loyalty:

- *the core product or service*—that is, the bundle of attributes, features, and benefits that must reach competitive levels if a relationship is to develop;

- *support services and systems*—that is, the quality of services and systems used to support the core product or service;

- *technical performance*—that is, the synchronization of the core product or service with the support infrastructure to deliver on the promise;

- *the elements of customer interaction*—that is, the quality of customer care demonstrated through face-to-face and technology-mediated communications; and

- *the affective dimensions of services*—that is, the subtle and non-core interactions that say something about how the organization feels about the customer (Cumby and Barnes, 1998).

This is a more useful insight into what it is that drives customer satisfaction, because it incorporates a wide range of factors and recognizes the importance of personal contact. Customer satisfaction and the quality of customer relationships are related, in differing ways, among differing people and contexts. However, one factor that is common to both is the perceived value of the interaction between parties.

Customer Experiences

The idea that providing a superior customer service might help in the (repeat) purchase decision process is something that several organizations, including Withers Worldwide (see Case Insight 15.1), now appreciate. For a long time, it was assumed that product quality and pricing were sufficient differentiators. However, product quality is no longer a viable means of establishing competitive advantage, simply because of shortening life cycles and evolving technologies. Service, although difficult to deliver in a consistent way, is very difficult to replicate and has become an important aspect of customer management.

Although generating customer satisfaction is important, it provides an incomplete picture. Of greater interest is customer experience. As Prahalad and Ramaswamy (2004a: 137), cited by Iyanna, Bosangit, and Mohd-Any (2012), suggest, the literature on value is no longer embedded in goods and services, or indeed relationships, but 'is now centered in the experiences of consumers'. Customer value is regarded by an increasing number of academics and practitioners as the central marketing activity (Iyanna et al., 2012), and that value is now central to customers' experiences. The implications for marketing are clearly put by Meyer and Schwager (2007: 118) when they say that 'customer experience encompasses every aspect of a company's offering—the quality of customer care, of course, but also advertising, packaging, product and service features, ease of use, and reliability'.

The importance and significance of customer experience to both individuals and society was first established by Pine and Gilmore (1998) when they referred to the 'experience economy'—a term frequently used by authors and researchers in this area (see Market Insight 15.3). Chang and Horng (2010) suggest that themed restaurants, such as Starbucks and the Hard Rock Café, are prime examples of good companies generating excellent customer experiences. These brands are not only about the consumption of coffee, but also present a situation or environment in which the consumption of services occurs and relationships are developed, thereby providing a meaningful or valuable customer experience. Ismail and colleagues (2011) refer to the trend towards creating unique experiences for customers with a view to developing a competitive advantage—something that must be sustainable, particularly for those in the service sector, because replication is very difficult.

There are some similarities between many of these definitions. For example, customer experience is seen to be an individual event, and concerns emotional reactions following direct and indirect interaction with an organization. It is also related to events prior to, during, or after consumption. Perhaps one crucial point is that it is not possible for two people to have or to share the same experience (Pine and Gilmore, 1998). As a result, the task of managing and measuring customer experiences is inherently complex.

To help to disentangle some of this complexity, Pine and Gilmore (1998) derive four distinct realms of experience, based on two dimensions: a customer's participation in an experience (weak/passive or active/strong); and an individual's connection with the environment of the experience or environmental relationship (from absorption/weak to immersion/strong).

The four realms that emerge from these dimensions are as follows:

- The *educational* realm emerges when an individual learns and enhances their skills and knowledge as a result of the events unfolding before them (Pine and Gilmore, 1999; Oh, Fiorie, and Jeoung, 2007).

- The *entertainment* realm occurs when an individual views a performance, listens to music, or reads for pleasure. The experience is absorbed passively (Pine and Gilmore, 1999).

- The *aesthetic* realm occurs when an individual passively appreciates an event or environment, but leaves without affecting or altering the nature of that environment (Pine and Gilmore, 1999; Oh et al., 2007).

Market Insight 15.3
Co-creating the Zoo Experience

Zoological parks invest heavily in their services and attractions every year. To keep up with the competition and to keep surprising returning guests, millions of euros are spent on new attractions, landscaping, restaurants, and merchandising. Deciding on these investments relies on the positioning of the brand, but also on research and assumptions about the needs of different types of guest.

Over the course of a day, zoo guests will be in contact with staff members at restaurants and outlets, but they will also visit various exhibits, animal habitats, and often shows or playgrounds. We refer to this sequence of activities as the customer journey. Different types of guest will have different customer journeys. Depending on their preferences and expectations, guests will evaluate the day as positive or negative, leading to recommendations to others and/or the intention to revisit in the future. Understanding the purpose of the zoo visit from the perspective of the guests is pivotal in the decision-making around new investments and in marketing communication.

In 2013, GaiaZOO in the Netherlands, with more than 500,000 visitors a year, wanted to get a better understanding of the experiential value it offers to its visitors, to help it to decide on future investments. To understand the experiential value of a visit and to predict the impact of investments in this area,

experiential value research was undertaken on the experience needs of visitors. As a result, four main visitor experience segments were identified, including:

1 the zoo as an enjoyable place for kids—these visitors go to a zoo to entertain their children;

2 the zoo as a place to be outdoors—these visitors enjoy the physical activity of walking through a natural environment;

3 the zoo as a place to be in contact with nature—these visitors want to observe the aesthetic quality of the flora and fauna; and

4 the zoo as a place to be together—these visitors are at the zoo to spend time with their loved ones and to create shared memories.

Visitors from each segment were then asked to rate their experience. GaiaZOO was rated as excellent by visitor types 1 and 3, whereas visitor types 2 and 4 were less happy. GaiaZOO was advised to invest in shows and restaurant facilities for type 4 visitors, whereas for type 2 new self-guided tours were developed to positively influence their experiences. These investments were prioritized over investments in new playgrounds, edutainment, and new habitats for new animals (type 1 and 3 visitors).

Source: Smit and Melissen (2018).

Theory into Practice

This market insight describes how, in this case, zoological parks are switching from a company-centric approach to value creation to a customer-centric process of value (co-)creation by segmenting customers on the basis of the customer journey. This customer-centric approach to service and experience design is relatively new in many service-oriented businesses. In academia, the new paradigm of

customer-centricity has received a lot of attention from authors such as Pine and Gilmore (1999) on the experience economy, Prahalad and Ramaswamy (2004b) on experience co-creation, and Vargo and Lusch (2004, 2008) on service-dominant logic (SDL) and the idea of all propositions being a bundle of 'service' benefits.

Market Insight 15.3

continued

Related Topics

new service development; new product development; branding; innovation; nature of services; customer experiences; service encounters

1 **Can you describe your customer journey at your educational institute today? Which service encounters and service environments have you been in?**

2 **If your educational institute had designed the service of being educated in a customer-centred way, what would change immediately?**

3 **Compare the service of Amazon.com to the service provided by your local supermarket. What are the differences and similarities in the experiential value each creates for you?**

This market insight was kindly contributed by Bert Smit, NHTV University of Applied Sciences, Netherlands.

- The *escapist* realm occurs when individuals become completely immersed in their environment and actively participate, so that they affect actual performances or occurrences in the environment (Pine and Gilmore, 1999; Oh et al., 2007).

Before exploring the characteristics and issues associated with customer experience, it is helpful to consider how the concept is defined. Although there have been several attempts in this regard, there has been little consensus. Some of the more notable definitions are set out in Table 15.7.

This approach has subsequently led to research that focuses on the ways in which experiences are produced, narrated, and mediated (Lofgren, 2008).

Various authors have contributed to what might be the key dimensions of customer experience. Of these, Nysveen and Pedersen (2014) used the dimensions highlighted by Brakus, Schmitt, and Zarantonello (2009)—namely, sensory, affective, intellectual, and behavioural—and added a further relational dimension, as determined by Nysveen, Pedersen, and Skard (2013):

- the *sensory* dimension refers to the extent to which a brand appeals to, and makes impressions on, a consumer's senses;

- the *affective* dimension refers to how strongly a brand induces consumer feelings and emotions;

- the *intellectual* (or *cognitive*) dimension speaks of how much a brand stimulates a consumer's curiosity, thinking, and problem-solving;

- the *behavioural* dimension measures how strongly a brand engages consumers in physical activities; and

- the *relational* dimension refers to how well an experience creates value for customers by driving social engagement, providing a social identity and a sense of belonging.

Table 15.7 Definitions of experience

Source	Definitions
Csikszentmihalyi (1977: 36)	The individual is experiencing flow when they have 'a unified flowing from one moment to the next, in which [they are] in control of [their] actions and in which there is little distinction between self and environment, between stimulus and response, between past, present and future'.
Holbrook and Hirschman (1982), cited in Carù and Cova (2008)	Experience is defined as a personal occurrence, often with important emotional significance, founded on the interaction with stimuli, which are the products or services consumed.
Carbone and Haeckel (1994: 8)	'The take-away impression formed by people's encounters with products, services, and businesses, a perception produced when humans consolidate sensory information.'
Schmitt (1999: 60)	From a customer perspective: 'Experiences involve the entire living being. They often result from direct observation and/or participating in the event—whether they are real, dreamlike or virtual.'
Shaw and Ivens (2002: 6)	'An interaction between an organization and a customer. It is a blend of an organization's physical performance, the senses stimulated and emotions evoked, each intuitively measured against customer experience across all moments of contact.'
Gentile et al. (2007: 397)	'The customer experience originates from a set of interactions between a customer and a product, a company, or part of its organization, which provoke a reaction. This experience is strictly individual and implies the customer's involvement at different levels (rational, emotional, sensorial, physical and spiritual). Its evaluation depends on the comparison between a customer's expectations and the stimuli coming from the interaction with the company and its offering in correspondence of the different moments of contacts or touch-points.'
Brakus et al. (2009: 53)	'[S]ubjective, internal consumer responses (sensations, feelings, and cognitions) and behavioural responses evoked by brand related stimuli that are part of a brand's design and identity, packaging, communications, and environments.'
Ismail et al. (2011: 208)	'Emotions provoked, sensations felt, knowledge gained and skills acquired through active involvement with the firm before, during, and after consumption.'

Source: Adapted from Ismail et al. (2011).

Market Insight 15.4
Mercadona: Loyalty without the Card

Mercadona is a market leader in the Spanish retail sector, and it offers a unique and unconventional example of how firms can successfully manage customer loyalty without necessarily following the dominant trends in their industry. Founded in 1977, this family-owned discount-supermarket began as a small butcher's shop in Valencia. Now, with 1,622 stores throughout Spain, Mercadona is the most profitable retailer in Spain, supplying products to 5.1 million households and accounting for about 24 per cent of total market value. Carrefour, its nearest rival, has a market share of approximatley 9 per cent. One of the most striking facts about Mercadona is that, unlike its competitors, it does not have a loyalty programme to reward customers with incentives on their purchases. Nevertheless, it has a strategy able to foster customer loyalty, interaction, and long-term engagement.

Mercadona is the most profitable retailer in Spain
Source: Er nun wieder/Wikimedia Commons (CC BY-SA 3.0).

There are three prongs to Mercadona's relationship marketing strategy. First, Mercadona focuses on understanding customers' needs and stimulating customer feedback through a number of touchpoints, including extremely friendly and motivated salespeole who are constantly listening to the consumer. Based on such feedback, Mercadona decided to cut its prices by 15 per cent during the recent economic crisis to avoid losing customers and even reduced the number of items on shelves to make it easier for consumers to find their favorite products. In 2011, Mercadona developed a powerful research tool, the Co-Innovation Labs, with the aim of testing and improving products or developing new solutions. Co-innovation Labs are spaces in which customers participate in research projects and consume their groceries, while interacting with, and being observed by, professionals from the company.

A second focus is on working closely with a limited number (about 120) of integrated supplier-manufacturers with whom Mercadona signs long-term agreements. Close collaboration allows Mercadona to achieve (a) high quality of products sourced, (b) low prices, and (c) flexibility in responding to a volatile market environment.

A third area of focus is the development of high-quality private-label brands that are real favorites in many Spanish households. Brands such as Hacendado, Bosque Verde, Deliplus, and Compy are consistently ranked #1 by customers in terms of value for money and are up to 40 per cent cheaper than the products of Mercadona's main competitors.

Sources: Institut Cerdá (2016); Valero (2016); García (2017).

Theory into Practice

While loyalty programmes can improve the relationship with consumers and generate useful insights for marketers, the case of Mercadona shows that relationship marketing can also be based on solid service processes and a superior service offering. In other words, while a loyalty card can be useful in improving customer retention and deepening customers' engagement with a brand, there is much more to relationship marketing than only a loyalty programme. Having a comprehensive marketing strategy that produces customer satisfaction, positive customer experiences in store, and emotional attachment to the brand is far more important than having a loyalty scheme. Mercadona shows that companies become customer-centric by redesigning their marketing strategy and operations, not simply by having a loyalty card.

Market Insight 15.4

continued

Related Topics

relationship marketing; loyalty programmes; services; business models in retail

1 **What, in your opinion, are Mercadona's key marketing levers to build strong relationships with customers?**

2 **What are the advantages of having strong private-label brands for retailers? How do these brands contribute to a retailer's relationship marketing strategy?**

3 **Mercadona implements an 'always low price' model (see Chapter 9). Do you think this strategy is consistent with the principles of relationship marketing? Why, or why not?**

This market insight was kindly contributed by Professor Victoria Labajo González, Universidad Pontificia Comillas, Spain.

From their research, Nysveen and Pedersen (2014) validated the importance of all these dimensions. However, they stressed the significance of the relational dimension and its strong positive influence on both brand satisfaction and brand loyalty. Market Insight 15.4 discusses the case of Mercadona, the leading grocery retailer in Spain. Its strength on the relational component of customer experience means that it does not need to have a loyalty card—something very atypical in the retail industry.

 Visit the **online resources** and follow the web links to see how the Customer Experience Professionals Association (CXPA) supports the industry.

Experience Quality

Earlier in the chapter (see 'Measuring Service Quality and Performance'), we considered SERVQUAL, the leading approach to measuring service quality. Although SERVQUAL has many benefits and is used extensively, it is not suitable for measuring **experience quality**. SERVQUAL does provide a measure of customer satisfaction, but, as Maklan and Klaus (2011) argue, it largely focuses upon customers' assessment of the service process and human interactions.

Building on earlier research into the quality of life experience by Csikszentmihalyi and LeFevre (1989), Chang and Horng (2010: 2403) define experience quality as 'how customers emotionally evaluate their experiences as they participate in consumption activities'. Chang and Horng (2010: 2404) are keen to point out that the evaluation of experience quality is not only about emotions, but also about putting more emphasis on the emotional nature of experience quality, which can 'reveal more of the characteristics of experience that underlie contemporary experience marketing'. Thus they conceptualize experience quality as a customer's emotional judgement about their total experience and they identify five dimensions for the construct: the physical surroundings; the service providers; other customers; customers' companions; and the customers themselves. Chang and Horng (2010) also refer to four sub-dimensions of the physical surroundings—that is, atmosphere, concentration, imagination, and surprise—and suggest that the dimension of 'customer themselves' has two sub-dimensions—that is, cognitive learning and having fun. Their study concludes that the development of 'elaborate physical surroundings to elicit positive customers' emotional perceptions of experience quality is significant for experience design. Customers are commonly more impressed with service settings with atmosphere' (Chang and Horng, 2010: 2415).

Following their review of the literature, Chahal and Dutta (2014) also suggest that there are five dimensions associated with outstanding customer experience. For these authors, however, these dimensions are: sensory experience (*sense*); affective experience (*feel*); creative cognitive experience (*think*); physical experience, behaviours and lifestyles (*act*); and social identity experience (*relate*). This model is illustrated in Figure 15.6.

Chahal and Dutta (2014) recognize customer experience as a central aspect of contemporary marketing, from both academic and practitioner perspectives. They also acknowledge the lack of the empirical research that would help to consolidate ideas and underpin suitable managerial advice. However, their model is useful because it serves to bring together some of the central issues associated with understanding and developing customer experiences.

Visit the **online resources** and follow the web links to explore more about customer experience.

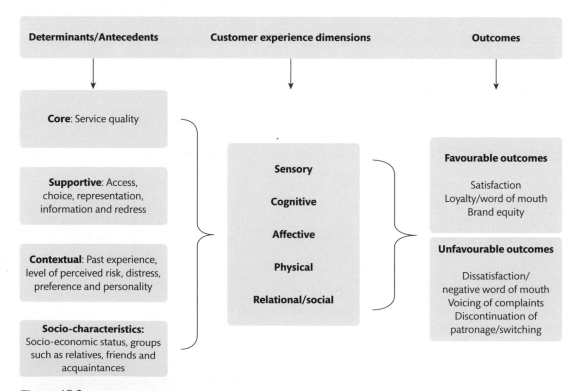

Figure 15.6

A proposed customer experience model

Source: Chahal, H., and Dutta, K. (2014). 'Conceptualising customer experiences: Significant research propositions', *Marketing Review*, 14(4), 361–81. Reproduced by permission of Westburn Publishers Ltd.

Customer Engagement

While the concept of experience focuses on a deeper understanding of the interactions between the company and its customers, marketers are also concerned with the level of **customer engagement**. Pansari and Kumar (2017) define 'engagement' as the level of customers' contribution to the company through both direct and indirect activities. *Direct* contributions refer to product or service purchases; *indirect* contributions comprise a range of activities that are crucial for firms, especially in today's interconnected world—that is, referring customers to the firm, influencing customers through positive online and offline activities, and offering feedback to the firm so that it can continuously improve its products.

The 'Up for Whatever' campaign, devised by Bud Light and described in Market Insight 15.5, is a clear example of a marketing activity aimed specifically at maximizing indirect benefits by means of an event that energizes current advocates of the brand and offers them a platform to influence others and generate positive media coverage. Digital technologies offer especially powerful tools to reinforce the direct and indirect contributions of customers to the firm. Researchers identify four different types of tools that firms can use to grow the level of customer engagement (Harmeling et al., 2017):

- *Amplificative* tools, such as retweets or share buttons, increase the presence of the brand within the customer's existing networks.

- *Connective* tools help to link customers to other customers or to the brand. Examples include tagging and following on social media, online virtual communities, and newsletters.

- *Feedback* tools help to generate useful insights that the firm can use to improve its offering and include text boxes, surveys, and polls/ratings that can be collected from customers.

- Finally, *creative* tools facilitate the exchange of ideas and the creation of new offerings. For example, for more than a decade computer manufacturer Dell has been using its ideastorm.com as a platform to collect ideas for potential improvements and innovations from users and information technology (IT) professionals.

It is important to recognize the relationships between experience and customer engagement. Most scholars agree that positive experience is a precursor to higher levels of customer engagement (Van Doorn et al., 2010; Pansari and Kumar, 2017). Specifically, customer engagement tends to be higher when customers are strongly satisfied by the offering, can identify with the brand, and experience strong positive emotions towards the brand (Van Doorn et al., 2010; Pansari and Kumar, 2017). While satisfaction is mostly caused by a cognitive evaluation, customer engagement is greatly enhanced by emotional attachment to the brand. (To find out more about customer engagement, read the article summarized in Research Insight 15.3.)

Market Insight 15.5
Doing Customer Engagement: Experiences from Start-ups and Market Leaders

How do you boost customer engagement in practice? One example was Bud Light's 'Up for Whatever' campaign, aimed at strengthening the brand's connection with millennial consumers in the United States. The strategy comprised a television campaign, which kicked off with a viral advert during the 2014 Super Bowl, and thousands of events across the United States. The final event was a weekend-long branded party in Crested Butte, Colorado. Bud, one of the brands owned by global beer giant AB Inbev, selected 1,000 customers over a period of almost a year. More than 100,000 people auditioned live or on social media in 2015 and the company ran a series of successful trade promotions.

The company specifically targeted individuals with large social networks and the willingness to share. The customers were invited to participate free of charge in the Up for Whatever event, which was hosted in several US locations over the years. Each event comprised a 'town' built specifically for the event, themed around Bud Light and named 'Whatever, USA'. The events, hosted during the weekend, were streamed on social media, with the objective of generating interest in the campaign and attracting the next round of potential invitees, who would become brand ambassadors for the brand.

Guests attend the welcome parade at Bud Light's Whatever, USA in Catalina Island, California, where Bud Light invited 1,000 consumers to a weekend full of unexpected concerts, classes, adventures, and more
Source: © Mark Davis/Getty.

The campaign generated significant impact and won several awards. In only its first year (2014), the 1,000 attendees posted on social media 37,000 pieces of content that were accessed by a total of 15 million people on Facebook and Twitter. By the time the campaign ended, usage among millennials had grown by 39 per cent.

However, customer engagement is also a useful strategy for smaller companies with limited resources. An interesting example is sneaker brand Pompeii. The company was founded in 2014 by five undergraduate students in Spain, with a tiny capital of €18,000. They aimed to sell casual, yet stylish, trainers to a millennial target market. The company sells more than 70,000 pairs of trainers a year around Europe. Some 85 per cent of their sales come from Instagram, where the brand currently has more than 152,000 followers. Considering its limited resources, customer engagement was always a key strategy. Before the launch, the company shared on its social media accounts draft designs and mock-ups of its trainers to generate interest. Pompeii also uses limited sales, selling trainers for a limited period of time and/or in pop-up stores that open for only one day every month. These strategies created a sense of scarcity and exclusivity, and the feeling of uniqueness among prospect customers.

Customer engagement is also built by involving customers in the innovation process. Pompeii asks consumers to vote on new models, frequently asks for feedback on its Instagram posts, and encourages consumers to share their ideas. Pompeii also creates one-off engagement initiatives to promote brand interactions with its followers. For example, online games allow customers to earn discounts. The brand also organizes fun activities such as competitions across its social sites or special events in its pop-up stores. For Halloween, for example, Pompeii created a pop-up store named 'Cemetery Shop' in which the only way to get discounts or to buy a pair of 'limited edition' trainers was to lie in a casket dressed as Count Dracula. Pompeii communicated the promotion through catchy videos on Instagram and Facebook. The whole event was broadcast on Pompeii's social media accounts.

Sources: Nudd (2014); Monllos (2015); Anon. (2017); Bargueño (2017).

Market Insight 15.5
continued

Theory into Practice

This market insight offers examples of practical strategies that help to create customer engagement. From a behavioral perspective, customer engagement is defined by the frequency by which community members use social media to interact with the marketing generated content. This market insight demonstrates the power of brand content to create interest and strengthen relationships with the brand.

Related Topics

customer engagement; brand community; branding relationships; relationship marketing; loyalty; marketing communications

1 **Engagement is based on creating genuine interest among consumers in the content generated by the brand. What do you think are the challenges that this strategy poses to marketers?**

2 **Would you say that engagement can be achieved regardless of the type of product and industry? Explain your arguments.**

3 **What indicators would you use to measure the effectiveness of a marketing campaign aimed at promoting consumer engagement with a brand?**

This market insight was kindly contributed by Professor Carmen Abril, IE Business School, Spain.

Research Insight 15.3

To take your learning further, you might wish to read this influential paper:

Pansari, A., and Kumar, V. (2017). Customer engagement: the construct, antecedents, and consequences. *Journal of the Academy of Marketing Science*, 45(3), 294–311.

This recent article is destined to become a marketing classic because it conceptualizes customer engagement and examines its potential consequences for companies. It aims to start academic debates on this topic, offering a set of theoretical propositions that can be examined in future empirical investigations of this construct. For companies, the article identifies drivers of engagement and contingent factors that reinforce its outcomes. Managers can consider these crucial variables and evaluate their current performance in terms of these indicators, as well as devise marketing programmes able to increase customer engagement. The key message of the article is that engagement is driven by a mixture of customer satisfaction and positive emotions towards the brand. The authors also present a customer engagement matrix based on high or low levels of these two variables. Strategies are offered for each of the four categories identified.

  Visit the online resources to read the abstract and access the full paper.

Chapter Summary

To consolidate your learning, the key points from this chapter are summarized below:

- **Explain the nature and characteristics of services.**

  Unlike products, services are considered to be processes, and products and services have different distinguishing characteristics. These are based around their intangibility (that is, you can touch a product, but not a service); perishability (that is, products can be stored, but you cannot store a service); variability (that is, each time a service is delivered, it is different, but products can be identical); inseparability (that is, services are produced and consumed simultaneously); and a lack of ownership (that is, you cannot take legal possession of a service). These are important because they shape the way in which marketers design, develop, deliver, and evaluate the marketing of services.

- **Describe what is meant by the terms 'service processes' and 'service encounters', and the principles associated with measuring service quality.**

  A process is a series of sequential actions that leads to predetermined outcomes. Four main service process categories can be identified: people; possession; mental stimulus; and information processing. A service encounter is best understood as a period of time during which a customer interacts directly with a service (Shostack, 1985). There are three levels of customer contact: high-contact services; medium-contact services; and low-contact services. As more services are introduced, so opportunities for service variability and service failure also develop. Service quality is based on the idea that a customer's expectations of the service they will receive shape their perception of the actual service encounter. In essence, customers compare perceived service with expected service. SERVQUAL is one model commonly used to measure service quality. It is a disconfirmation model, and is based on the difference between the expected service and the actual perceived service.

- **Outline the principles of relationship marketing, and consider the merits of customer retention and loyalty programmes.**

  Relationship marketing is based on the premise that retained customers are more profitable than customers based on transactional marketing. Loyalty is an important concept within relationship marketing and different customers represent different levels of value to organizations. There are also different forms of loyalty (for example behavioural and attitudinal) and different marketing strategies are required to reach each of them.

- **Understand the concepts of trust, commitment, and customer satisfaction, and explain how they are interlinked.**

  There are several key concepts associated with the management of customer relationships. The main ones are trust, commitment, and satisfaction. These are interrelated, and the management of customer relationships should be based on the principles of reducing the influence of power and the incidence of conflict to build customer trust, gain customer commitment, and, through satisfaction, generate loyalty and retention. This approach should increase the perceived value of the relationship for all parties.

- **Explain the term 'customer experiences', the dimensions associated with it, how it has evolved, and how it might be measured.**

  Customers experience an emotional transition and response through interactions with an organization and its offerings. This individuality of experience implies that there are different types or levels of experience, such as rational, emotional, sensorial, physical, and spiritual. The development of customer experience marketing has been built on evolving ideas concerning service encounters, perceived value, relationship marketing, and customer satisfaction.

■ Explain the term 'customer engagement' and the strategies marketers use to increase it.

Building strong bonds with customers is also important because it allows us to obtain indirect benefits from customers' engagement with the brand. Critically, engaged customers recruit new customers for the brand, influence the opinions of other consumers, and provide useful feedback for organizations. Companies therefore need to plan events and campaigns that allow them to develop customer engagement and maximize its benefits for the firm.

 # Review Questions

1 Identify the essential characteristics of services and make brief notes explaining how they affect the marketing of services.

2 What are the main types of service process? Identify their key characteristics.

3 Explain the term 'service encounter'.

4 How does an understanding of the relevant search, experience, and credence properties of a service influence the way in which it is marketed?

5 Name the five dimensions of service quality and explain their key characteristics.

6 What are the key differences between transactional marketing and relationship marketing?

7 Why is trust an important aspect of relationship marketing?

8 To what extent does the concept of relationship intensity assist our understanding of relationship marketing?

9 Make notes for a short presentation in which you explain the term 'customer experience' and track its evolution.

10 What dimensions are used by Csikszentmihalyi and LeFevre (1989) to measure experience quality?

11 Think of a popular service brand and develop a marketing campaign aimed at increasing customer engagement for this company.

 # Discussion Questions

1 Having read Case Insight 15.1, how would you advise Withers Worldwide about how best to evaluate the quality of its service offering?

2 Westcliffe & Sons makes a range of fruit juice drinks. Its business falls into two main segments: consumers; and business users, such as local councils and catering companies. Recent sales figures suggest that orders from some catering companies are down on previous years and some have stopped buying from Westcliffe altogether. The marketing director has reported that he cannot understand the reason for the decline in business because product quality and prices are very competitive. Advise the marketing director about the key issues he should consider and discuss how the company should re-establish itself with the catering companies.

3 Consider the view that loose, or arm's-length, B2B customer relationships can be just as productive as those that are intense and close.

Visit the online resources and complete the Multiple-Choice Questions to assess your knowledge of Chapter 15.

Glossary

collaborative exchanges a series of transactions between a buyer and seller in which the relationship is the main focus.

commitment a desire that a relationship should continue.

customer acquisition the search for and settling in of new customers.

customer decline a stage in a buyer–seller relationship that is unstable and during which the relationship weakens.

customer development a period during which buyers and sellers become more familiar with each other's propositions and needs.

customer engagement the total of a consumer's direct contributions (that is, purchases) and indirect contributions (that is, referral, influence, and feedback) to a company; develops when a customer is satisfied and feels intense positive emotions towards a company or brand.

customer experience the individual feelings and emotions felt during interactions with an organization and its offerings.

customer relationship life cycle the four main stages associated with managing customer relationships—namely, customer acquisition, development, retention, and decline or termination.

customer retention a stage in a buyer–seller relationship that is stable and holds the strongest levels of trust and commitment.

electronic kiosk a computer terminal located within a retail environment that provides individuals with information about products and services.

experience quality the emotional evaluation by customers of their experiences as they participate in consumption activities.

inseparability a characteristic of a service—namely, its instantaneous production and consumption.

intangibility a characteristic of a service—namely, that it does not have physical attributes and so cannot be perceived by the senses (that is, cannot be tasted, seen, touched, smelt, or possessed).

loyalty the extent to which a customer supports a particular brand, possibly through repeat purchases.

market (or discrete) exchanges a type of transaction between a buyer and seller in which the main focus is on the product and price.

ownership possession of and control over goods.

perceived risk the real and imagined uncertainties that customers consider when purchasing products and services.

perceived value the 'net satisfaction' derived from consuming and using a product, not only the costs involved in obtaining it.

perishability a characteristic of a service—namely, the fact that spare or unused capacity cannot be stored for use at some point in the future.

relationship marketing marketing activities associated with the management of successful relational (collaborative) exchanges.

service delivery the means through which services are experienced by customers.

service encounter an event that occurs during which a customer interacts directly with a service.

service process a series of sequential actions that lead to the delivery of a predetermined service.

service quality the extent to which customer expectations of a service are met in an actual service encounter.

SERVQUAL a model that measures the difference between the expected service and the actual perceived service.

trust the extent to which one party to a relationship is confident in the reliability and integrity of the other, and that each will fulfil its obligations and responsibilities.

variability a characteristic of a service—namely, the amount of diversity allowed in each step of service provision.

References

Anon. (2017). Pompeii crea Cemetery Shop y 70 zapatillas para los más arriesgados. *MarketingDirecto.com*, 29 October. Retrieve from: https://www.marketingdirecto.com/anunciantes-general/anunciantes/pompeii-crea-cemetery-shop-70-zapatillas-los-mas-arriesgados (accessed 13 October 2018).

Baldinger, A., and Rubinson, J. (1996). Brand loyalty: the link between attitude and behaviour. *Journal of Advertising Research*, 36(6), 22–34.

Bargueño, M.A. (2017). El último milagro de la moda española: las zapatillas de 50 euros que arrasan entre los jóvenes. *El Pais*, 6 July. Retrieve from: https://elpais.com/elpais/2017/07/05/icon/1499256782_740357.html (accessed 13 October 2018).

Bitner, M.J. (1995). Building service relationships: it's all about promises. *Journal of the Academy of Marketing Science*, 23(4), 246–51.

Brady, M.K., Bourdeau, B.L., and Heskel, J. (2005). The importance of brand cues in intangible service industries: an application to investment services. *Journal of Services Marketing*, 19(6), 401–10.

Brakus, J.J., Schmitt, B.H., and Zarantonello, L. (2009). Brand experience: what is it? How is it measured? Does it affect loyalty? *Journal of Marketing*, 73(3), 52–68.

Bruhn, M. (2002). *Relationship Marketing: Management of Customer Relationships*. Harlow: FT/Prentice Hall.

Capizzi, M., Ferguson, R., and Cuthbertson, R. (2004). Loyalty trends for the 21st century. *Journal of Targeting Measurement and Analysis for Marketing*, 12(3), 199–212.

Carbone, L.P., and Haeckel, S.H. (1994). Engineering customer experiences. *Marketing Management*, 3(3), 8–19.

Carù, A., and Cova, B. (2008). Small versus big stories in framing consumption experiences. *Qualitative Market Research*, 11(2), 166–76.

Chahal, H., and Dutta, K. (2014). Conceptualising customer experiences: significant research propositions. *Marketing Review*, 14(4), 361–81.

Chang, T.-C., and Horng, S.-C. (2010). Conceptualizing and measuring experience quality: the customer's perspective. *Service Industries Journal*, 30(14), 2401–19.

Cousins, P.D., and Stanwix, E. (2001). It's only a matter of confidence! A comparison of relationship management between Japanese and UK non-owned vehicle manufacturers. *International Journal of Operations and Production Management*, 21(9), 1160–80.

Csikszentmihalyi, M. (1977). *Beyond Boredom and Anxiety*. San Francisco: Jossey-Bass.

Csikszentmihalyi, M., and LeFevre, J. (1989). Optimal experience in work and leisure. *Journal of Personality and Social Psychology*, 56(5), 815–22.

Cumby, J.A., and Barnes, J. (1998). How customers are made to feel: the role of affective reactions in driving customer satisfaction. *Customer Relationship Management*, 1(1), 54–63.

Curtis, S. (2014). Transport for London goes contactless. *The Telegraph*, 15 September. Retrieve from: https://www.telegraph.co.uk/technology/news/11096354/Transport-for-London-goes-contactless.html (accessed 13 October 2018).

Dick, A.S., and Basu, K. (1994). Customer loyalty: toward an integrated framework. *Journal of the Academy of Marketing Science*, 22(2), 99–113.

Dwyer, R.F., Schurr, P.H., and Oh, S. (1987). Developing buyer–seller relationships. *Journal of Marketing*, 51(2), 11–27.

Fournier, S., and Yao, J.L. (1997). Reviving brand loyalty: a reconceptualisation within the framework of consumer–brand relationships. *International Journal of Research in Marketing*, 14(5), 451–72.

Gabbott, M., and Hogg, G. (1998). *Consumers and Services*. Chichester: John Wiley.

Gambetta, D. (1988). *Trust: Making and Breaking Co-operative Relations*. New York: Blackwell.

García, F. (2017). Tendencias en la distribución 2017. *Kantar World Panel*, 18 September. Retrieve from: https://www.kantarworldpanel.com/es/Noticias/Tendencias-en-la-distribucion-2017 (accessed 13 October 2018).

Gentile, C., Spiller, N., and Noci, G. (2007). How to sustain the customer experience: an overview of experience components that co-create value with the customer. *European Management Journal*, 25(5), 395–410.

Gil, I., Berenguer, G., and Cervera, A. (2008). The roles of service encounters, service value, and job satisfaction in business relationships. *Industrial Marketing Management*, 37(8), 921–39.

Glyn, W.J., and Lehtinen, U. (1995). The concept of exchange: interactive approaches in services marketing. In: W.J. Glyn and J.G. Barnes (eds), *Understanding Services Management*, Chichester: John Wiley, 89–118.

Grönroos, C. (1990). *Service Management and Marketing: Managing the Moment of Truth in Service Competition*. Lexington, MA: Lexington Books.

Harmeling, C.M., Moffett, J.W., Arnold, M.J., and Carlson, B.D. (2017). Toward a theory of customer engagement marketing. *Journal of the Academy of Marketing Science*, 45(3), 312–35.

Holbrook, M.B., and Hirschman, E.C. (1982). The experiential aspects of consumption: consumer fantasies, feelings, and fun. *Journal of Consumer Research*, 9(2), 132–40.

Institut Cerdá (2016). *El Valor de la Inovación Conjunta*. Retrieve from: https://info.mercadona.es/document/es/el-valor-de-la-innovacion-conjunta.pdf (accessed 13 October 2018).

Ismail, A.R., Melewar, T.C., Lim, L., and Woodside, A. (2011). Customer experiences with brands: literature review and research directions. *Marketing Review*, 11(3), 205–25.

Iyanna, S., Bosangit, C., and Mohd-Any, A.A. (2012). Value evaluation of customer experience using consumer generated content. *International Journal of Management and Marketing Research*, 5(2), 89–102.

Laja, S. (2012). Transport for London's contactless tickets roll out behind schedule. *Government Computing*, 22 May. Retrieve from: https://www.governmentcomputing.com/news/2012/may/22/contactless-tickets-tfl-delay-wave-pay (accessed 13 October 2018).

Lofgren, O. (2008). The secret lives of tourists: delays, disappointments and daydreams. *Scandinavian Journal of Hospitality and Tourism*, 8(1), 85–101.

Lovelock, C., Vandermerwe, S., and Lewis, B. (1999). *Services Marketing: A European Perspective*. Harlow: FT/Prentice Hall.

Macneil, I.R. (1980). *The New Social Contract*. New Haven, CT: Yale University Press.

Maklan, S., and Klaus, P. (2011) Customer experience: are we measuring the right things? *International Journal of Market Research*, 53(6), 771–92.

Meyer, C., and Schwager, A. (2007). Understanding customer experience. *Harvard Business Review*, February. Retrieve from: https://hbr.org/2007/02/understanding-customer-experience (accessed 13 October 2018).

Mittal, B., and Lassar, W.M. (1998). Why do consumers switch? The dynamics of satisfaction versus loyalty. *Journal of Services Marketing*, 12(3), 177–94.

Moeller, S. (2010). Characteristics of services: a new approach uncovers their value. *Journal of Services Marketing*, 24(5), 359–68.

Monllos, K. (2015). Welcome to Whatever, USA, Bud Light's big party for a few fans. *Adweek*, 29 May. Retrieve: https://www.adweek.com/brand-marketing/welcome-whatever-usa-bud-lights-big-party-few-fans-165045/ (accessed 13 October 2018).

Morgan, R.M., and Hunt, S.D. (1994). The commitment–trust theory of relationship marketing. *Journal of Marketing*, 58(3), 20–38.

Nudd, T. (2014). Bud Light on secretly creating its own party town: 'this is content marketing on steroids'. *Adweek*, 6 August. Retrieve from: https://www.adweek.com/brand-marketing/bud-light-secretly-creating-its-own-party-town-content-marketing-steroids-159322/ (accessed 13 October 2018).

Nysveen, H., and Pedersen, P.I. (2014). Influences of co-creation on brand experience. *International Journal of Market Research*, 56(6), 807–32.

Nysveen, H., Pedersen, E.E., and Skard, S. (2013). Brand experiences in service organizations: exploring the individual effects of brand experience dimensions. *Journal of Brand Management*, 20(5), 404–23.

O'Malley, L. (1998). Can loyalty schemes really build loyalty? *Marketing Intelligence and Planning*, 16(1), 47–55.

Oates, J. (2009). Westminster readies 'wave and pay' parking meters. *The Register*, 29 October. Retrieve from: https://www.theregister.co.uk/2009/10/29/westminster_parking_scheme/ (accessed 13 October 2018).

Oh, H., Fiorie, A.M., and Jeoung, M. (2007). Measuring experience economy concepts: tourism applications. *Journal of Travel Research*, 46(2), 119–32.

Olson, J.C., and Jacoby, J. (1972). Cue utilization in the quality perception process. In: M. Venkatesan (ed.), *Proceedings of the Third Annual Conference of the Association for Consumer Research*. Provo, UT: Association for Consumer Research, 167–79.

Palmer, A. (2005). *Services Marketing*. Maidenhead: McGraw Hill.

Pansari, A., and Kumar, V. (2017). Customer engagement: the construct, antecedents, and consequences. *Journal of the Academy of Marketing Science*, 45(3), 294–311.

Parasuraman, A., Zeithaml, V., and Berry, L.L. (1988). SERVQUAL: a multiple-item scale for measuring consumer perceptions of service quality. *Journal of Retailing*, 64(1), 5–37.

Pavlou, P.A. (2002). Institution-based trust in interorganisational exchange relationships: the role of online B2B marketplaces on trust formation. *Journal of Strategic Information Systems*, 11(3–4), 215–43.

Pine, B.J., and Gilmore, J.H. (1998). Welcome to the experience economy. *Harvard Business Review*, 76(4), 97–105.

Pine, B.J., and Gilmore, J.H. (1999). *The Experience Economy: Work Is Theatre and Every Business a Stage*. Boston: MA: Harvard Business School Press.

Prahalad, C.K., and Ramaswamy, V. (2004a). *The Future of Competition: Co-creating Unique Value with Customers*. Boston, MA: Harvard Business School Press.

Prahalad, C.K., and Ramaswamy, V. (2004b). Co-creation experiences: the next practice in value creation. *Journal of Interactive Marketing*, 18(3), 5–14.

Ravald, A., and Grönroos, C. (1996). The value concept and relationship marketing. *European Journal of Marketing*, 30(2), 19–33.

Reichheld, F.F., and Sasser, E.W. (1990). Zero defections: quality comes to services. *Harvard Business Review*, 68(5), 105–11.

Ryssel, R., Ritter, T., and Gemunden, H.G. (2004). The impact of information technology deployment on trust, commitment and value creation in business relationships. *Journal of Business and Industrial Marketing*, 19(3), 197–207.

Schmitt, B.H. (1999). *Experiential Marketing*. New York: Free Press.

Shaw, C., and Ivens, J. (2002). *Building Great Customer Experiences*. New York: Palgrave Macmillan.

Shostack, G.L. (1985). Planning the service encounter. In: J.A. Czepiel, M.R. Solomon, and C.F. Surprenant (eds), *The Service Encounter*, Lexington, MA: Lexington Books, 243–54.

Smit, B., and Melissen, F. (2018). *Sustainable Customer Experience Design. Co-creating Experiences in Event, Tourism and Hospitality.* London: Routledge.

Spekman, R.E., and Carroway, R. (2005). Making the transition to collaborative buyer–seller relationships: an emerging framework. *Industrial Marketing Management*, 35(1), 10–19.

Theron, E., Terblanche, N.S., and Boshoff, C. (2013). Building long-term marketing relationships: new perspectives on B2B financial services. *South African Journal of Business Management*, 44(4), 33–45.

Ulaga, W., and Eggert, A. (2005). Relationship value in business markets: the construct and its dimensions. *Journal of Business-to-Business Marketing*, 12(1), 73–99.

Valero, M. (2016). Mercadona es la cadena más rentable por metro cuadrado: triplica en ventas a DIA. *El Confidencial*, 11 January. Retrieve from: https://www.elconfidencial.com/empresas/2016-11-01/mercadona-carrefour-dia-hipercor-supermercados-rentabilidad_1283153/ (accessed 13 October 2018).

Van Doorn, J., Lemon, K.N., Mittal, V., Nass, S., Pick, D., Pirner, P., and Verhoef, P.C. (2010). Customer engagement behavior: theoretical foundations and research directions. *Journal of Service Research*, 13(3), 253–66.

Vargo, S.L., and Lusch, R.F. (2004). Evolving to a new dominant logic for marketing. *Journal of Marketing*, 68(1), 1–17.

Vargo, S.L., and Lusch, R.F. (2008). Service-dominant logic: continuing the evolution. *Journal of the Academy of Marketing Science*, 36(1), 1–10.

World Bank (2017). Service exports (BoP, US$). *World Bank Data*. Retrieve from: https://data.worldbank.org/indicator/BX.GSR.NFSV.CD?view=chart (accessed 13 October 2018).

Zeithaml, V.A. (1981). How consumer evaluation processes differ between goods and services. In: C. Lovelock (ed.) (1991), *Marketing of Services*, Chicago, IL: American Marketing, 39–47.

Chapter 16

Business-to-Business Marketing

Learning Outcomes

After reading this chapter, you will be able to:

▶ Explain the main characteristics of business markets and understand the different types of organizational customer

▶ Describe the different types of offering that are bought and sold in business markets

▶ Set out the main processes and stages associated with organizational buying and purchasing

▶ Explain what business-to-business marketing is and the marketing issues associated with professional services firms

▶ Understand the principles of key account management

Case Insight 16.1
Grant Thornton UK LLP

Market Insight 16.1
Translating the World: TRSB Style

Market Insight 16.2
Marketing the Big League

Market Insight 16.3
KPMG Engages through Social Media

Market Insight 16.4
Groupon: KAM Gone Wrong

Case Insight 16.1
Grant Thornton UK LLP

Grant Thornton UK LLP is part of Grant Thornton International Limited (GTIL), one of the world's leading independent advisory, tax, and audit firms. In the UK, Grant Thornton traces its origins to Thornton and Thornton in Oxford in 1904. It grew through many mergers and, by 1980, had formed an alliance with US firm Alexander Grant & Co. One year later, a new international organization, GTIL, was set up. We speak to Anne Blackie, head of bids and strategic accounts at Grant Thornton UK, to find out how the firm manages its client relationships.

Working in both the private and public sectors, Grant Thornton provides audit, tax, and advisory services to more than 22,000 clients. Our clients range from large corporates (FTSE350 and equivalent), mid-market, small and medium-sized enterprises (SMEs), start-ups, and individuals. Our go-to-market approach is through nine industry channels, such as financial services and business support services, and other channels such as intermediaries (banks, lawyers, and private equity). One characteristic that a number of clients share is that they are dynamic growing organizations.

As a professional services firm, we sell the experience and expertise of our people. Building relationships with our clients is key to our propositions, and the theme that runs through our diverse client and supplier base is that we focus on building trusted, sustainable relationships that deliver value. Depending on the organization and its complexity, our relationships can be one to one, one to many, or many to many. For example, for our larger clients, we will have a number of different relationships across that organization and an account manager who manages the account, while for a smaller organization the relationship is more likely to be one to one with the finance director or chief executive officer (CEO). More recently, we also have developed community-based relationships via programmes such as Growth 365, which brings together like-minded CEOs. This has been particularly successful and, through a very targeted approach, we now have a well-established community that

is continuing to grow. With our suppliers, we have outsourced services ranging from catering and office facilities to marketing, working with niche agencies on the promotion of specific projects.

For us, the key to successful client relationships is understanding the client and the market or environment they work in, so that we can spot trends quickly. Marketing has to be relevant, insightful, and attention-grabbing, since our audiences are often from the **C-Suite**. And ensuring that we follow up is a key part of the business development process. We regularly review what worked well and respond quickly when necessary. To identify new market opportunities, we get feedback from clients, targets, and marketplace advisers, we watch developments in other industries, we undertake **horizon scanning**, and we use technology and data analysis to identify trends.

We segment our clients in terms of complexity and size. For example, large banking clients are typically more complex in their structure and we are more likely to provide them with a number of different services across their business than we would a smaller SME. These larger, more complex clients tend to have dedicated account managers and are part of our strategic accounts programme.

Feedback from clients indicates that the reason they choose us is because of our client relationship skills, our understanding of their needs, our experience/expertise, and the insight we share with them. We focus on

Case Insight 16.1
continued

building relationships with organizations right from the targeting stage, to build trust with the buyers prior to going into a formal buying process. Such relationship-building means that we understand our clients' needs, so can articulate a better value client proposition and help the client to find the right solution for them.

Building relationships like these takes time (typically, 12–24 months). One of the challenges we have is that we spend a lot of time building a relationship with a key individual, getting to know them, and understanding what's important to them—and that individual then leaves or moves on to another part of

the organization. So all the work we have done has to be started again with a new individual and that can take us back 12 months.

The question for Grant Thornton is: how can it ensure that such churn does not damage its strategic relationships and the proposition it has developed when key individuals in those firms move elsewhere?

 Visit the online resources to watch a video interview with Anne Blackie in which she explains what Grant Thornton did.

Introduction

For many of us, marketing is concerned with consumer products, meaning those that we buy and consume on a regular basis. There is, however, another (colossal) market hidden from our daily view of the world: the business market. **Business-to-business (B2B) marketing** concerns the marketing of the huge range of offerings bought and sold between organizations in this market.

Some of the characteristics of B2B marketing are different from those associated with **consumer marketing**. There are numerous reasons for these differences and the way in which they impact varies among organizations. In this chapter, we explore the nature and impact of these characteristics. We highlight the main types of B2B organization, learn about the different types of B2B offering, and develop an understanding about the way in which organizations make buying decisions, who makes them, and how this affects their purchasing strategies.

The traditional perception of business marketing activity is that it concerns salespeople selling products with services attached (Leigh and Marshall, 2001). In many ways, this used to be true, but now that much customer ordering is online, the role of the sales department has shifted. Now, salespeople focus on managing relationships, increasing customer productivity, and closing deals (Rocco and Bush, 2016).

Many B2B firms are also servitizing their products (see Chapters 1 and 15), meaning that they are hiring out or leasing their products, usually with an enhanced service component, instead of selling them outright. For example, elevator (lift) company Otis offers a remote elevator monitoring (REM®) service that detects problems with its lifts and automatically makes a maintenance service call. Research by Storbacka and colleagues (2009) shows, first, that sales is increasingly about process, rather than a series of separate transactions carried out by a specific function.

Consequently, sales is much more relational than it used to be. Additionally, the sales function now involves close working links between sales and operations—especially because sales is increasingly linked to information gathering, processing, and interpretation, resource mobilization, and delivery. This makes sales much more cross-functional than it was previously. Finally, Storbacka and colleagues (2009) observe an increasing emphasis on customer issues and on sales metrics, suggesting that the sales function has shifted from an operational activity to become more strategic.

A key part of B2B marketing is associated with managing the relationships that develop between organizations and those representing them. Managing customers is vitally important, and one task is to identify and manage those customers who are important to the organization's success. Research has identified that when sales representatives for a business-to-business firm leave, it can lead to a 13.2–17.6 per cent loss in annual sales (Shi et al., 2017). Keeping hold of major accounts is referred to as key account management. We examine this important topic later in this chapter. Although the chapter focuses on the distinctive characteristics of B2B marketing, we conclude with a reflection of the similarities that exist between B2B and consumer marketing.

What Is Business-to-Business Marketing?

Just imagine the complexity associated with the design and construction of the International Space Station, the new Elizabeth Line on the London underground (which opens in 2019), the new mega-city NEOM to be built on the Red Sea coast in Saudi Arabia (opening in 2022), or the Hålogaland Bridge in Norway. Specifying, negotiating, buying and selling, building, delivering and storing, and then replacing parts and materials as they are used can involve a vast network of organizations, large and small. The operational task alone is enormous, and the value of the materials, components, labour, and energy involved far exceeds consumer spending in either the soap, beauty, or confectionery markets. The B2B market really is huge.

To make a car, a manufacturer tries to create value by buying a range of finished and part-finished items, assembling them, and distributing the completed cars to dealers, who sell them on to consumers or businesses (fleet buyers). The array of parts and finished items that the manufacturer buys involves a large number of suppliers. This is how the business market operates; the actions undertaken by a supplier of a brake system to influence the car manufacturer to select that system (rather than a competitor's) constitute B2B marketing.

Some B2B suppliers seek to manage not only relationships with their direct customers (buyers), but also those relating to their customers' customers (sometimes referred to as end users). This approach provides valuable market information, creates product preferences among these indirect customers, and drives derived demand. For example, network equipment company Cisco supplies systems to service providers, but in addition approaches the service providers' customers to learn about their requirements (Homburg, Wilczek, and Hahn, 2014).

In a number of ways, B2B marketing is fundamentally different from consumer goods or services marketing because organizational buyers do not consume the offerings themselves. Unlike consumer markets, in which offerings are consumed individually, invariably by the people who buy them, the essence of business markets is that organizations, not individual people, undertake the act of purchase.

Research Insight 16.1

To take your learning further, you might wish to read this influential paper:

Achrol, R.S. (1997). Changes in the theory of interorganizational relations in marketing: toward a network paradigm. *Journal of the Academy of Marketing Science*, 25(1), 56–71.

Achrol sets out how the then-established vertically integrated multidivisional type of organization started to be replaced by new forms of network organization consisting of large numbers of functionally specialized firms tied together in cooperative exchange relationships. He considers four main types, the variables involved, the economic rationale, and the types of coordination and control mechanism necessary for organizations to adapt to the new environment.

 Visit the online resources to read the abstract and access the full paper.

Far larger than the consumer market, the business market comprises many types and sizes of organization. Each organization interacts with a selection of others, and they form relationships of varying significance and duration. This web of interaction is referred to as a network (see also Chapter 1 and Research Insight 16.1). Although organizations are often structurally and legally independent entities, a key characteristic is that they are also interdependent—that is, they have to work with other organizations, to varying degrees, to achieve their goals.

The Characteristics of Business Markets

Business markets are characterized by a number of distinct factors, but the main ones are the nature of demand, the buying processes, international dimensions, and—perhaps most importantly—the relationships that develop between organizations in the process of buying and selling. These are shown in Figure 16.1 and each is examined next.

The Nature of Demand

There are three key aspects of demand in business markets: derivation; variance; and elasticity. Demand in business markets is ultimately derived from consumers (Gummesson and Polese, 2009). Consider, for example, the demand for building trains. When Banverket, the Swedish Railway Administration, and Canadian firm Bombardier Transportation considered developing a 'Green Train', the goal was to develop a new generation of high-speed, super-efficient trains to meet the special technical and traffic requirements in the Nordic countries. Part of the project team's calculation was to estimate the number of people likely to make train journeys and what they would be prepared to pay. Even though each train is the result of hundreds of organizations

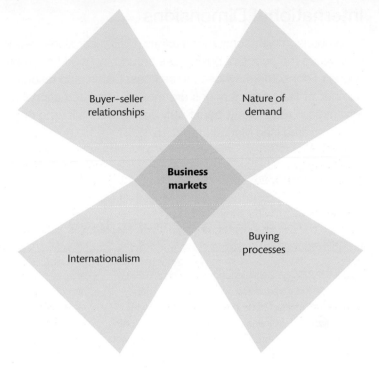

Figure 16.1
Key characteristics of business markets

interacting, it is the train's passengers (consumers) who actually stimulate demand for the construction of such trains.

Demand is variable because consumer preferences and behaviour fluctuate. For example, the demand for rail journeys usually declines following a major train accident or a significant fare increase; it also increases in response to petrol price rises and calls for consumers to be more environmentally aware. The subsequent impact will be felt by rail operators, support services, train manufacturers, and the whole array of suppliers and subcontractors in the market—all of which suggests that organizations need to monitor and anticipate demand.

Demand is essentially inelastic (see Chapter 9). If suppliers raise their prices, most manufacturers will try to absorb the increases into their own cost structures either to avoid letting their customers down in the short term or because they are tied into fixed-price contracts. Incorporating these price increases, at least over the short-to-medium term, means that there is price inelasticity. In the medium term, manufacturers can eliminate the original parts, redesign the proposition, or search for new suppliers.

The Buying Processes

Organizations' buying processes differ in a number ways from those of consumers. These differences are a reflection of the potentially high financial value associated with B2B transactions, the product complexity, the typically high value of individual orders, and the nature of risk and uncertainty. As a result, organizations have developed specific buying processes and procedures involving large numbers of people. The group of people involved in organizational purchasing processes is referred to as a **decision-making unit (DMU)**. The types of purchase that they make are classified as **buyclasses**. The circumstances in which they buy are called **buyphases**. Full details of these processes are outlined later in the chapter (see 'The Processes of Decision-Making Units').

International Dimensions

In comparison with consumer markets, B2B marketing is easier to conduct internationally. This is because the needs of businesses around the world are more similar to one another than the needs of consumers, whose preferences, tastes, and resources vary. As a result, an increasing number of B2B organizations are moving into international markets. This is often enabled by advances in technology, particularly via the web, allowing organizations to cover a greater geographical area (see Market Insight 16.1).

Market Insight 16.1
Translating the World: TRSB Style

Traductions Serge Bélair Inc, now known as TRSB, is a professional translation and localization agency founded in the late 1980s in Montréal, Canada, by Serge Bélair. Fast forward 30 years and TRSB is one of North America's foremost translation agencies, with a team of more than 200 professionals. The company translates into more than 100 languages for a large client base spread across four continents. Over a quarter of the company's sales come from outside Canada. Interestingly, with less than 0.5 per cent of the world population, Canada held 10 per cent of the global translation market in 2013—around half of which is held by firms located in the French-speaking province of Québec. TRSB faces much competition in Canada, not least because the Québécois market is so attractive. There is a considerable amount of translation undertaken in Canada from English to French and French to English, given that the Canadian Official Languages Act 1969 (as amended) gives English and French equal status.

Common Sense Advisory, a market research firm, suggests that the global translation market is growing at an annual rate of around 7 per cent and was worth around US$43 billion in 2017, when TRSB was the 14th largest provider in North America. Competitors included the UK's SDL, America's TransPerfect and Lionbridge, and Switzerland's Star Group.

Part of TRSB's success lies in its use of technology. Via a portal, clients can gain immediate access to their translation project data, request translations, change and track orders, manage review processes, create workload, expenditure, and service-level agreement (SLA) reports, and manage a project audit trail. If a client wants it to do so, the portal will also integrate with the client's own e-procurement systems. To make its translation more efficient, TRSB uses computer-aided translation techniques. This means that when clients need to use previously translated material, they can, and do not have to pay for it twice.

Sources: Turcotte (2013); Turgeon, Lavoie, and Bergeron St-Onge (2017); https://www.trsb.com/en/about-trsb/the-company/; http://www.trsb.com/en/category/media/; https://www.trsb.com/en/technology/portal/

Theory into Practice

This market insight illustrates how the unique cultural and historical circumstances of Montréal in Canada have set the conditions for the development of local translation services. One of those translation services, TRSB, has managed to develop a global operation, because it recognized that the services required by governments, investment companies, banks, and so on, in other countries were similar to those required by clients in Canada. TRSB achieved global expansion by means of export, making good use of technology to transcend geographic boundaries.

Market Insight 16.1
continued

Related Topics

B2B marketing; e-procurement; international marketing; branding; export; services marketing

1 Who would be in the DMU for translation services in client companies?

2 What value do you think TRSB creates for its B2B clients?

3 Would the portal that TRSB has developed be detrimental to the development of client relationships in an industry based on intercultural communication?

In comparison with consumer markets, B2B organizations display a lower variety of product functionality and performance. This is partly because trading associations around the world have agreed standards relating to content and performance, such as standardized electric socket types, or the digital video broadcasting (DVB) standard for digital television used in countries including Australia, South Africa, India, and those in Europe. Having agreed standards means that the buying and selling of products and services, wherever the supplier and buyer are located, becomes a relatively simple process and the trading environment can be well regulated and controlled. Many industries (for example the steel, plastic, chemicals, and paper industries) have commonly agreed standards aiming to facilitate inter-organizational exchange processes. In consumer markets, however, there are numerous issues concerning consumer culture and values, and the need to adapt propositions and promotional activities to meet various colour, ingredient, stylistic, buying process, packaging, and language requirements.

 Visit the **online resources** and follow the web link to the Association for B2B Agencies (ABBA) to learn more about B2B organizations.

Relationships

If there is one characteristic that separates business marketing from consumer marketing, it is the importance of relationships. In consumer markets, the low **perceived value** of the offerings and the competitive nature of the market, which makes product substitution relatively easy, make relationships between manufacturers and consumers relatively more difficult to establish. In business marketing, the interaction between buyers, sellers, and other stakeholders is of major significance. The development and maintenance of relationships between buying and selling organizations is pivotal to success. Interdependence, collaboration, and in some cases partnership in the development, supply, and support of products and services is considered a core element of B2B marketing. Strong inter-organizational relationships are referred to as **embedded ties**. Noordhoff and colleagues (2011) refer to these as a close and reciprocal relationship between a customer firm and a supplier firm. Embedded ties improve relational and

Research Insight 16.2

To take your learning further, you might wish to read this influential paper:

Dwyer, R.F., Schurr, P.H., and Oh, S. (1987). Developing buyer–seller relationships. *Journal of Marketing*, **51(2), 11–27.**

This article is one of the most cited in the subject area. Its popularity is based on the critical observation that buyer–seller exchanges are not discrete activities or events, but a part of ongoing relationships. The authors present a framework for developing buyer–seller relationships that links into marketing strategy.

   Visit the online resources to read the abstract and access the full paper.

business performance outcomes because they facilitate the transfer of complex, sensitive, and even tacit knowledge between partners (Reagans and McEvily, 2003), and they improve innovation. In the same way, damage to these ties can be a reason to terminate a business relationship (Schreiner, 2015).

The importance of relationships in B2B marketing should not be underestimated (see Research Insight 16.2). More information on relationship issues and concepts can be found in Chapters 14 and 15.

Types of Organizational Customer

Once known as industrial marketing, B2B marketing has come to recognize the involvement of a range of other, non-industrial, suppliers, agents, and participants. The government, the non-profit sector, and charities and institutions in most countries are responsible for a huge level of B2B activity. Consider the huge range of pharmaceutical and medical supplies offerings necessary to support the healthcare sector, as well as the products and infrastructure necessary to maintain prison services and the armed forces. All of these represent a major slice of B2B activity.

It is possible to categorize organizations by their size (by revenue or number of employees)—that is, as large, medium, and small organizations. Macfarlane (2002) refers to global and national organizations, the public sector, SMEs, and small offices/home offices (SOHOs). However, this approach is too general, and fails to accommodate different buyer needs and purchasing procedures. In Table 16.1, we outline the principal characteristics of broad types of B2B organization: commercial; government; and institutional.

All of these types of B2B organization buy other companies' offerings. The types of marketing activity used to encourage repeat exchanges between these various types of organization can be considerable. However, one strategy common to all three has been to develop relationships by means of cooperation and collaboration.

Table 16.1 Key types of business organization

Type of organization		Key characteristics
Commercial	Distributors (wholesalers, value-added resellers, retailers, and distributors/dealers)	Not only do they smooth the progress of products through the marketing channel, but also they should add value to them by providing storage (through distribution centres), services (such as training), or financial support (such as credit facilities).
	Original equipment manufacturers (OEMs)	Refers to one company relabelling a product and incorporating it within a different product to sell it under the company's own brand name, offering its own warranty, support, and licensing. For example, Toyota may have a contract with a headlight manufacturer to supply Toyota with a certain quantity of headlight assemblies. Toyota is the OEM, because it builds these headlight assemblies into its different cars and sells the car as a Toyota, without identifying the manufacturer of the headlight assembly.
	Users	Organizations that purchase goods and services, which are then consumed as part of their production and manufacturing processes. Therefore users are not identified in the final product offering, but do contribute to its production. Toyota will purchase many support materials (e.g. machine tools, electrical manufacturing equipment, vending machines, office furniture, and stationery). None of these can be identified within the cars they produce.
	Retailers	Need to purchase goods to resell them, just as do other organizations. However, the buying processes are not always as complex or as intricate as those normally associated with organizational buying and the group of people who make purchase decisions, i.e. the DMU. Suppliers need to understand their retailers and their markets.
Government		The value of the business undertaken by governments is very high. Health, policing, education, transport, environmental protection, and national defence and security are a few of the areas that require public investment. Many of the larger projects that concern governments and associated ministries are large and complex, and involve a huge number of stakeholders. Although bound by similar constraints to those of commercial purchasing procedures and guidelines, buyers in the public sector are also affected by political constraints, including budgets, regulation, and trade bloc directives (e.g. the EU, Mercosur).
Institutions		Include not-for-profit organizations such as churches and charities, community-based organizations such as housing associations, and government-related organizations such as hospitals, schools, museums, libraries, and universities. Characteristically, institutions tend to form large buying groups. Through collaboration, the group is able to negotiate greatly reduced prices and much larger discounts, usually related to bulk purchases.

Table 16.2 Types of business goods and service

Type of goods	Explanation
Input goods Raw materials, semi-manufactured parts, and finished goods	Input goods have been subjected to different levels of processing (raw materials, semi-manufactured parts, and finished goods), and so they lose their individual identities and become part of the finished item.
Equipment goods Otherwise known as capital or investment goods	These are necessary for manufacturing and operations to take place. Land and buildings, computer systems, and machine tools are all necessary to support the production process, but they cannot be identified in the finished proposition.
Supply goods Otherwise known as maintenance, repair, and operating (MRO) materials	These goods and services are 'consumables' because they are necessary to keep production processes and the organization running. For example, lubricants, paints, screws, and cleaning materials may all be necessary to maintain a firm's operations. Computer or IT servicing is necessary to maintain operations and to avoid down time, whilst accounting audits are a legal requirement.

Type of Business Goods and Service

Just as there are a variety of types of organization in the business sector, so too the offerings are equally varied and complex. Table 16.2 sets out the three principal business types of goods and service.

Most organizations, at various points in their development, have to decide whether to make or supply their own propositions or to buy them in from outsourced providers. This 'make or buy' decision can have long-term effects not only on the strategic and operational aspects of an organization, but also on the purchasing function and its role within an organization.

Outsourcing has become more popular with a wide range of organizations. As a result, companies have adapted their purchasing behaviours accordingly, impacting on their business marketing practices. The development of 'lean management' techniques has enabled organizations to concentrate on their core processes and to outsource all other activities. As organizations become 'leaner', they dramatically reduce their use of resources and the importance of purchasing increases (Towne, 2010).

Visit the **online resources** and complete Internet Activity 16.1 to learn more about how the Internet is used to market computing software to business customers.

Organizational Buying Behaviour

Organizations need to appreciate customers' particular behaviours, purchasing systems, people, and policies if they are to effect suitable marketing and selling strategies. This section builds on the introduction to buyer processes outlined earlier and the information about

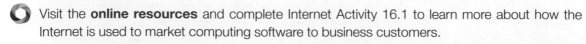

organizational market segmentation introduced in Chapter 6. It considers some of the key issues associated with the way in which organizations purchase the offerings necessary to achieve their corporate goals.

Two definitions of **organizational buying behaviour (OBB)** reveal important aspects of this subject. First, Webster and Wind (1972: 2) defined organizational buying as 'the decision making process by which formal organizations establish the need for purchased products and services and identify, evaluate and choose among alternative brands and suppliers'. This adopts a buying organization's perspective and highlights how OBB involves numerous processes, rather than being a single static one-off event. There are a number of stages, or phases, associated with procurement, each often requiring a key decision to be made.

Organizational buying behaviour concerns purchasing an offering to solve organizational needs, for example H&M's announcement in 2017 of new investment in its supply chain by bringing production to Europe and investing heavily in automation, to remedy the fact that its supply chain lead times were double those of rival Zara (Sit, 2017). Organizational buying behaviour can be seen as more of an exercise of muddling through the buying problem rather than working through a well-planned, goal-oriented process, largely because the organizational buying decision involves critical decision points and evolving information requirements (Makkonen, Olkkonen, and Halinen, 2012).

Organizational buying behaviour is concerned with three key issues:

- the functions and processes that buyers move through when purchasing products for use in business markets;

- strategy, where purchasing is designed to assist value creation and competitive advantage, and to influence supply chain activities; and

- the network of relationships that organizations belong to when purchasing, in that the placement of orders and contracts between organizations can confirm a current trading relationship, initiate a new set of relationships, or signal the demise of a relationship.

What should be clear is that OBB is not only about the purchase of other companies' offerings, but also the strategic development of the organization, creating value, and the management of inter-organizational relationships, all of which are key issues in B2B marketing. These issues overlap with each other and are not discrete items.

Hollyoake (2009) argues that business marketing is increasingly about managing buyers' experiences and interactions. This involves creating expectations—often referred to as the brand promise—and then delivering propositions against these promises. It is important that a customer's evaluation of their experience is beyond that which they expected. Hollyoake (2009) develops these ideas into 'ease of doing business' as a measure of the supplier–customer relationship and suggests that customer experiences are based on four pillars: trust; interdependence; integrity; and communication. These ideas are explored in Chapters 14 and 15.

Grönroos (2009) develops these principles about customers' expectations into a new perspective on (business) marketing, which he refers to as **promise management**. These ideas are rooted in the value-creation process. Firms are involved in developing and delivering value propositions (promises). Value propositions are realized only when an offering is consumed by customers; value creation, when experienced by customers, can be termed value fulfilment.

Decision-Making Units

The purchasing process is the means by which organizations create value. It is an integral part of an organization's value at some future point. Although organizations usually designate a 'buyer' as responsible for the purchase of a range of offerings, in reality numerous people are usually involved in the purchasing process. This group of people is referred to as either the decision-making unit (DMU) or the buying centre. In many circumstances, these informal groupings of people align in varying ways to contribute to the decision-making process. Some procurement projects—usually those of major significance or value—require a group of people to be put together formally. This group has responsibility for overseeing and completing the purchase of a stipulated item or offerings. Consider, for example, the buying team at Boeing, who help the organization to produce planes by buying engines from Rolls-Royce, tyres from Michelin Aircraft Tires, and engineering solutions from Novator AB, among many other suppliers.

The Characteristics of Decision-Making Units

Decision-making units vary in composition and size according to the nature of each individual purchasing task. Webster and Wind (1972) identified the following people who undertake different roles within buying centres, as illustrated in Figure 16.2:

- **Initiators** start the whole process by requesting an item for purchase. They may also assume other roles within the DMU or wider organization.

- **Users** use the product once it is acquired. They also evaluate its performance. Users may initiate the purchase process, but are sometimes also involved in the specification process. Their role is continuous, although this may vary from the highly involved to the peripheral.

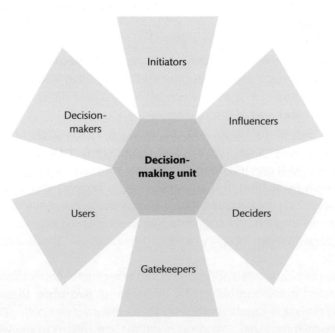

Figure 16.2

Membership of the decision-making unit

Source: Fill and McKee (2012). Reproduced with the kind permission of Goodfellow Publishers.

- **Influencers** often help to establish the technical specifications for the proposed purchase and help to evaluate potential suppliers' alternative offerings. This group might comprise consultants hired to complete a particular project. For example, an office furniture manufacturer will regard office managers as key decision-makers, but understand that specifiers, such as office designers and architects, also influence that office manager's decision about furniture.

- **Deciders** (also known as key decision-makers, or KDMs) are those who make purchasing decisions and they are the most difficult to identify. This is because they may not have formal authority to make a purchase decision, yet are sufficiently influential internally that their decision carries the most weight. In repeat buying activities, the buyer may also be the decider. However, it is normal practice for a senior manager to authorize expenditure decisions involving sums over certain financial limits.

- **Buyers**, or purchasing managers, select suppliers and manage the process whereby the required offerings are procured. Buyers may not decide which offering is to be purchased, but they influence the framework within which the decision is made. They will formally undertake the process whereby offerings are purchased once a decision has been made to procure them. For example, they may be formal buyers and may kick-start the purchase of a type of lubricant because the stock figures have fallen to a threshold level that indicates that current supplies will be exhausted within a certain number of weeks. They will therefore assume the roles of both initiator and buyer.

- **Gatekeepers** have the potential to control the type and flow of information to the organization and the members of the DMU. These gatekeepers may be personal or other assistants or secretaries, technical personnel, or telephone switchboard operators.

The size and form of the buying centre is not static; rather, it can vary according to the complexity of the offering being considered for purchase and the degree of risk each decision is perceived to carry for the organization. Different roles are required and adopted as the nature of the buying task changes with each new purchase situation (Bonoma, 1982). All of the roles outlined might be carried out by one individual for certain decisions. It is vital for seller organizations to identify members of the buying centre, and to target and refine their messages to meet the needs of each member of the centre.

Membership of the DMU is far from fixed and this fluidity poses problems for selling organizations simply because it is not always possible to identify key members or shifts in policy or requirements. Spekman and Gronhaug (1986) suggest that the DMU can reach across numerous different functional roles and that any number of individuals might participate or exert influence over the process at any particular time. Within this context, how DMU members behave is governed by the interpersonal relationships between the centre's members.

The Processes of Decision-Making Units

Organizational buying decisions vary based on the nature of the offering, the frequency and the relative value of purchases, their strategic impact (if any), and the type of supplier relationship. These, and many other factors, are potentially significant to individual buying organizations. There are three main types of buying situation. Referred to by Robinson, Faris, and Wind (1967) as buyclasses, these are **new task**, **modified rebuy**, and **straight rebuy**. These situations are summarized in Table 16.3.

> **Table 16.3 Main characteristics of the buyclasses**
>
> | Buyclass | Degree of familiarity with the problem | Information requirements | Alternative solutions |
> |---|---|---|---|
> | New buy | The problem is fresh to the decision-makers | A great deal of information is required | Alternative solutions are unknown; all are considered new |
> | Modified rebuy | The requirement is not new, but is different from previous situations | More information is required but past experience is of use | Buying decision needs new solutions |
> | Rebuy | The problem is identical to previous experiences | Little or no information is required | Alternative solutions not sought or required |
>
> Source: *Marketing Communications* (7th edn), Fill, C. and Turnbull, S. (2016). Reproduced with the kind permission of Pearson Education Limited. © Pearson Education Limited (2016).

New Task

As the name implies, in a new task the organization is faced with a first-time buying situation. Risk tends to be high at this point because there is little collective experience of the offering being purchased (the 'solution') or the relevant suppliers. As a result of these factors, if the solution purchased is a complex one, there may be a large number of DMU participants. Each participant requires a lot of information, and a relatively long period of time is needed for the information to be assimilated and a decision to be made.

Modified Rebuy

Having purchased a solution previously, uncertainty is reduced, but not eliminated, so the organization may request through their buyer(s) that certain modifications be made to future purchases, for example adjustments to the specification of the solution, further negotiation on price levels, or perhaps an arrangement for alternative delivery patterns. Fewer people are involved in the decision-making process for a modified rebuy than in the new task situation.

Straight Rebuy

In the straight rebuy situation, the purchasing department reorders on a routine basis, very often working from an approved supplier list. Offerings repurchased in this situation may be solutions that an organization consumes to keep operating (for example office stationery), or low-value materials used within the operational value-added part of the organization (for example the manufacturing processes), or low-value services (for example maintenance contracts). No other people are involved with the procurement exercise until suppliers try to change the decision-making environment. For example, a new supplier may provide a potentially better offer and this could stimulate the emergence of a modified rebuy situation.

Straight rebuy presents the classic conditions for the use of automatic reordering systems, allowing costs to be reduced, managerial time redirected to other projects, and the relationship between buyer and seller embedded within a stronger framework. One possible difficulty with automatic reordering systems is that both parties may perceive the procurement system to be a significant exit barrier if conditions change and this may deter them from offering flexibility or restrict opportunities to develop the relationship.

The use of electronic purchasing systems at the straight rebuy stage has, however, enabled organizations to empower employees to make purchases, although control still resides with purchasing managers. Employees can buy directly online from a catalogue list of authorized suppliers. The benefits are that employees are more involved, the purchasing process speeds up, costs are reduced, and purchasing managers can spend more time with other higher priority activities.

 Visit the **online resources** and follow the web link to Electronic Commerce Europe, the biggest online trade network in the world, for more information on the use of electronic B2B purchasing.

Buyphases

Organizational buying behaviour consists of a series of sequential activities through which organizations proceed when making purchasing decisions. Robinson and colleagues (1967) refer to these as buying stages, or buyphases. The following sequence of buyphases is particular to the new task situation just described; many of these buyphases are ignored or compressed according to the complexity of the offering and when either a modified rebuy or straight rebuy situation is encountered.

Need/Problem Recognition

The need/problem recognition phase is about the identification of a gap between the benefits an organization is experiencing now and the benefits it would like to have. For example, when a new offering is to be produced, there is an obvious gap between having the necessary materials and components and being out of stock and unable to build. The first decision is therefore about how to close this gap. There are two broad options for the organization—that is, whether it should outsource the whole, or parts, of the production process, or build or make the offering itself. Once the need has been recognized and the gap identified, that decision must be taken—and we will assume, in the rest of this section, that the organization has decided to build the offering itself.

Product Specification

As a result of identifying a problem and the size of the gap, influencers and users can determine the desired characteristics of the solution needed to resolve the problem. This may take the form of either a general functional description, or a much more detailed analysis and the creation of a detailed technical specification for a particular proposition. What sort of photocopier is required? What is it expected to achieve? How many documents should it copy per minute? Is a collator or tray required? What associated services will be required (for example warranty, maintenance)? This is an important part of the process, because if it is executed properly, it will narrow the supplier search and save on the costs associated with evaluation prior to a final decision. The results of the functional and detailed specifications are often combined within a purchase order specification.

Supplier and Proposition Search

At the supplier and proposition search stage, the buyer actively seeks suppliers who can supply the necessary solution(s). There are two main issues at this point: will the solution match the specification and the required performance standards; and will the potential supplier meet the other organizational requirements, such as experience, reputation, accreditation, and credit rating? In most circumstances, organizations review the market and their internal sources of information, then arrive at a decision based on rational criteria.

Wherever possible, organizations work to reduce uncertainty and risk. By working with other organizations that it knows, of which it has direct experience, and which can be trusted, the organization can reduce risk and uncertainty. This highlights another reason why many organizations prefer to operate within established networks that can provide support and advice when needed, rather than to operate individually (see Market Insight 16.2).

Market Insight 16.2
Marketing the Big League

The sports industry within which leagues and teams participate is characterized by multiple primary B2B relationships. These occur between the teams and their owners, those who own the league, corporate sponsors, various media groups, and any governing bodies. In addition, there are the business-to-consumer relationships that teams have with their supporters.

In February 2015, the English Premier League governing body awarded the live television broadcast rights for 168 matches, across three football seasons ending in 2019, to two main media groups, Sky and BT Sport. The sale of these rights raised more than £5 billion, to be distributed amongst Premier League clubs and also to be used to support grass-roots football.

The sale of broadcast rights is one of several transactions that participant teams benefit from as a league member. Sports leagues, such as UK football's Premier League, Italy's Serie A, Spain's La Liga, Holland's Eredivisie, or Sweden's Allsvenskan, all create value that teams acting individually would not be able to generate. This is because sport leagues drive team cooperation to make the league attractive to its various stakeholders. This causes teams to be mutually dependent on each other, yet at the same time they have to be competitive to win the league. Team supporters and sports fans, however, have a widening choice of entertainment options, meaning that leagues can compete in a broader entertainment market.

The sale of live television broadcast rights by the English Premier League drives substantial income for football clubs
Source: © Krivosheev Vitaly/Shutterstock.com.

Professional sports leagues can operate across local, national, and international markets, and the sale of game broadcast rights is a key league activity. At an individual team level, the sale of admissions and concessions at home games, stadium leasing and naming rights, shirt sponsorship, and ancillary merchandise and event sales constitute critical revenue generators. These activities, plus those necessary to sustain a team's operations, all involve a wide range of organizations.

Sources: Mason (1999); Benijts, Lagae, and Vanclooster (2011); de Menezes (2015).

Market Insight 16.2
continued

Theory into Practice

The teams in a league constitute an interactive network, which can be considered using network theory. Participants strive to add value for the league and, in doing so, they create multiple B2B relationships. The Premier League can be interpreted as a marketing channel network. This is a type of marketing channel structure characterized by the performance of the teams and their relationships with intermediaries—in this case, the various organizers, such as sponsors and the media—and a focal organization—here, the league or the sport's governing body.

The interaction and relationships that develop among these teams and in the name of a league enable stability, strong relationships, value creation, and the facilitation of B2B marketing.

Related Topics

B2B marketing; transaction and collaborative exchanges; business relationships; channel design and structure; value creation

1 **Think of a sports industry with which you are familiar and make a list of the different stakeholders and the relationships that might exist within it.**

2 **Identify the ways in which individual sports teams can create value that benefits their league.**

3 **How might changes in the environment impact the relationships within sports leagues?**

Evaluation of Proposals

Depending on the complexity and value of the potential order(s), the proposal is a vital part of the process and should be prepared professionally. The proposals from the shortlisted organizations are reviewed in light of two main criteria: the purchase order specification; and the evaluation of the supplying organization. If the potential supplier is already part of the network, little search and review time is needed. If the proposed supplier is not part of the network, a review may be necessary to establish whether it will be appropriate (in terms of price, delivery, and service), as well as whether there is the potential for a long-term relationship or whether this is a single purchase that is unlikely to be repeated.

Supplier Selection

The DMU will normally undertake a supplier analysis and use a variety of decision criteria, according to the particular type of item sought. A further useful perspective is to view supplier organizations as a continuum, ranging from reliance on a single source to the use of a wide variety of suppliers for the same offering. Jackson (1985) proposed that organizations might buy an offering from a range of different suppliers to maintain a range of multiple sources (a practice within many government departments). She labelled this approach 'always a share', because several suppliers are given the opportunity to share the business available to the buying centre. The major disadvantage is that this approach fails to drive cost as low as possible, because the discounts derived from volume sales are not achieved. The advantage to the buying centre is that a relatively small investment is required and little risk is entailed via this strategy.

At the other end of the continuum are organizations that use a single-source supplier. All purchases are made from the single source until circumstances change to such a degree that the buyer's needs are no longer being satisfied. Jackson (1985) referred to these organizations as 'lost for good', because once they have developed a relationship with a new supplier, they are lost for good to the original supplier. An increasing number of organizations are choosing to enter alliances with a limited number of suppliers, or even a single source. The objective is to build a long-term relationship, to work together to build quality, and to help each other to achieve their goals. For example, outsourcing manufacturing activities for non-core activities has increased considerably.

Evaluation

Next, the order is written against the selected supplier, which is then monitored and evaluated against diverse criteria such as responsiveness to enquiries, modifications to the specification, and timing of delivery. When the offering is delivered, it may reach the stated specification, but fail to satisfy the original need. In this case, the specification needs to be rewritten before any future orders are placed.

Developments in the environment can impact on organizational buyers and change both the nature of decisions and the way in which they are made. For example, the decision to purchase new plant and machinery requires consideration of the future cash flows that will be generated by the capital item. Many people will be involved in the decision and the time necessary for consultation may mean that other parts of the decision-making process are completed simultaneously.

 Visit the **online resources** and complete Internet Activity 16.2 to learn about the seven buying phases that organizations go through when purchasing industrial goods and services.

Buygrids

When the buyphases are linked to the buyclasses, a buygrid is determined, as illustrated in Table 16.4.

The buygrid serves to illustrate the relationships between buyphases and buyclasses. It is important because it highlights the need to focus on buying situations or contexts, rather than on offerings. Even though this approach was developed over 40 years ago, it remains an important foundation for this topic.

According to the buyphase model, buyers make decisions rationally and sequentially, but this does not entirely mesh with practical experience. For example, such a long and complex process is not evident in every buying situation, which will differ according to the kinds of offerings bought, the experience and resources available to organizations, and the prevailing culture. In other words, there are many variables influencing organizational buying behaviour.

Many B2B marketing concepts were developed in the pre-Internet era and tend to concentrate on dyadic (that is, two-party) relationships—namely, the interchange between buyers and sellers. In many cases, this is still true and relevant. However, the development of e-commerce platforms and other digital marketplace exchanges, such as auction sites, introduces

Buyphases	Buyclasses		
	New task	**Modified rebuy**	**Straight rebuy**
Problem recognition	Yes	Possibly	No
General need description	Yes	Possibly	No
Product specification	Yes	Yes	Yes
Supplier search	Yes	Possibly	No
Supplier selection	Yes	Possibly	No
Order process specification	Yes	Possibly	No
Performance review	Yes	Yes	Yes

Table 16.4 The buygrid framework

a third dimension which suggests that, in some circumstances, B2B relationships should be considered a triadic (that is, three-party) relationship system—namely, seller–platform–buyer. For Chakravarty, Kumar, and Grewal (2014), this means that, in some e-commerce settings, the platform firm should adopt a customer orientation towards both the seller and buyer firms that they seek to attract and maintain within a relationship.

Purchasing in Organizations

All organizations have to buy a variety of other companies' offerings to operate normally and achieve their performance targets. What we have set out so far are the general principles, types, and categories associated with organizational buying. However, the way in which organizations buy these offerings varies considerably and does not always fit neatly with the categories presented here. For many organizations, professional purchasing is not only an important (if not critical) feature, but also an integral part of their overall operations and strategic orientation (Ryals and Rogers, 2006; Pressey, Tzokas, and Winklhofer, 2007).

In the past, an organization's purchasing activities could be characterized as an 'order-delivery response function'. Purchasing departments signed orders and the right deliveries were made at the right place at the right time, then invoiced correctly. The goal was to play off one supplier against another and, as a result, to reduce costs and improve short-term profits. Purchasing departments were an isolated function within organizations—a necessary, but uninteresting, aspect of organizational performance.

This perspective changed towards the end of 1990s. Now, organizations reduce the number of their suppliers, sometimes to only one, and **strategic procurement** (as it is often termed) is used to negotiate with suppliers on a cooperative basis to help to build long-term relationships. Purchasing has become an integral and strategic part of an organization's operations, and managing a smaller number of suppliers can improve performance considerably. For example, Senn, Thoma, and Yip (2013: 27) reported that Airbus had reduced its supplier portfolio by 80 per cent, from 3,000 to 500.

One of the main reasons for this changed approach was research that showed that business performance improves when organizations adopt a collaborative, rather than adversarial, approach to purchasing and account management (Swinder and Seshadri, 2001). Integral to this approach is the use of information systems, which, according to Rodríguez-Escobar and González-Benito (2015), are tools for streamlining and simplifying the way in which the purchasing task is undertaken. For example, information technology (IT) can enhance the implementation of various purchasing practices that improve the quality, cost, flexibility, or reliability of supply. This leads to an overall improvement in purchasing performance, benefiting both supplier and buyer.

However, there are several other related issues that have changed the role of purchasing—namely, customer sophistication, increasing competition, digital technology, branding, and various strategic issues.

Customer Sophistication

Owing to increasing customer sophistication, organizations are trying to differentiate their offerings and become more specialized. Organizational purchasing has to follow this movement and also become more specialized; otherwise, the organization will become increasingly ineffective in meeting customer needs.

Increasing Competition

With increasing competition, margins have been eroded. As a result, more attention has been paid to internal costs and operations. By influencing the purchasing costs and managerial costs associated with dealing with multiple suppliers, the profitability of the organization can be directly impacted. Consequently, the importance of purchasing polices, processes, and procedures within organizations has increased.

Digital Technology

The impact of digital technology has been felt across all functions within organizations. Digital marketing refers to the use of all kinds of digital tools, including social media, and encompasses various integrated elements, platforms, and tools that facilitate social interaction. In a B2B context, these instruments allow companies to develop interaction and dialogue between businesses and customer networks with a view to securing stronger relationships, increased cooperation, and opportunities for co-creation.

Social media presents a major opportunity for the development of inter-organizational relationships. Research has shown that social media can be used at different stages in the sales process (Schultz, Shwepker, and Good, 2012). It can be used in the early stages of a customer relationship, at which awareness, lead building, and prospecting take place, and to maintain business relationships with established customers. Twitter and LinkedIn are used for referral requests to influence potential prospects.

However, the numbers of companies using social media is relatively small, and it is seldom used for business purposes by managers and senior managers (Keinänen and Kuivalainen, 2015). This might be because many senior managers do not use social media within a workplace setting because they do not see it bringing them benefits. It is also because a large number of B2B firms still use linear, or one-directional, communications, such as email marketing and newsletters (Järvinen et al., 2012). Since Järvinen and colleagues (2012) published, the use of social media has increased, but it may still be used primarily by younger salespeople who have migrated their personal skills into their work context, rather than those who have been specifically trained by organizations to use social media within their role (see Market Insight 16.3 later in the chapter).

Branding

Despite the view that business brands are important assets that can enhance customer trust, branding remains a greatly underutilized resource within business marketing. There are outliers, such as Google, Cisco, Oracle, Intel, and IBM, all of whom realized the importance of B2B branding between 1992 and 2006 (Seyedghorban, Matanda, and LaPlaca, 2016). Lennartz and colleagues (2015) and Wiersema (2012) both acknowledge that branding has tremendous potential and is of growing importance within business markets. Indeed, the role of branding within this context appears to be gaining momentum at a time when digital marketing has gained a stronger presence. In a digital interactive environment, the brand should be considered to be the platform for all of a B2B company's actions. In addition, branding in industrial contexts provides a means of enabling the integration of different functions—an important requirement in B2B organizations (Sisko, Lipiäinen, and Karjaluoto, 2015). (For more on branding within business markets, see Chapter 13.)

Strategic Issues

There are several strategic issues related to the purchasing activities undertaken by organizations. First is the 'make or buy' decision: should organizations make and/or assemble products for resale, or outsource or buy in particular products, parts, services, or sub-assemblies and concentrate on what are referred to as core activities or competences?

Second, the benefits that arise through closer cooperation with suppliers, as well as the increasing influence of buyer–seller relationships and 'joint value creation', have inevitably led to a tighter, more professional, and integrated purchasing function.

The third strategy-related issue concerns the degree to which the purchasing function is integrated into the organization. New IT systems have raised the level of potential integration of purchasing and operations to the extent at which the competitive strength of the organization is enhanced (Hemsworth, Sánchez-Rodríguez, and Bidgood, 2008).

As if to highlight the variation in approaches to purchasing behaviour, Svahn and Westerlund (2009) identify six principal purchasing strategies that organizations may use, as follows:

■ The *price minimizer* purchasing strategy sees a buyer increase their efficiency, seeking the lowest priced offering. To help them to achieve this, the buyer actively promotes competition among several potential suppliers.

■ A *bargainer* purchasing strategy means that a buyer aims to achieve operational efficiency through long-term collaboration with a selected supplier (Håkansson and Snehota, 1995).

■ The *clockwiser* purchasing strategy refers to network relationships that function predictably and precisely, just as a clock works. Here, the goal is strict efficiency, achieved through the vigilant integration of production-based integrated control systems and IT, and the careful coordination of the value activities performed by each supply network partner (Glenn and Wheeler, 2004).

- The *adaptator* purchasing strategy focuses on adapting the manufacturing processes between the exchange parties. This can arise during the purchase of one major product or service, when the seller is required to accommodate its offering to the particular needs of the buyer.

- The *projector* purchasing strategy occurs between buyers and sellers who are development partners. It can arise during projects when partners develop their offerings in collaboration, after which the joint development project is completed and the parties continue the development work independently. As an example of this strategy, consider the collaboration between Nokia and Skype. These major players in the information and communication technologies (ICT) industry joined their development efforts to develop a radically novel type of mobile phone that utilized Voice over Internet Protocol (VoIP) to create a free calling system.

- The *updater* purchasing strategy is based on collaboration in research and development (R&D). Here, collaboration between partners is continuous and the nature of the relationship is not dyadic, but a supply network. This collaboration is intentional, as demonstrated by Intel and various manufacturers of personal computers (PCs), which produce updated versions as a result of constant co-development.

Developing a Customer Portfolio Matrix

Companies have an assortment of customers, many of whom vary in terms of their values and contribution to the supplier. These customers constitute a portfolio and, although a large portfolio might sound attractive, many organizations actively seek to reduce their numbers of customers, aiming instead to increase their efficiency and profitability. For example, Senn and colleagues (2013: 27) refer to 'Tetra Pak, the Swedish–Swiss processing and packaging solutions company, [which] earns roughly half of its revenues from a portfolio of 50 key customers'.

The six core strategies mentioned earlier reflect the complexity and the variety of purchasing activities undertaken by buying organizations. Most supplying organizations have a mixture of different types of customer or account. Each account varies in terms of frequency of purchase, types of product and service bought, prices paid, delivery cycles, time taken to pay, level of support required, purchasing strategies, and many other factors. These variables reflect the strength of the relationship between buyer and seller, and they impact on the profitability that each account represents to the seller.

It makes sense to categorize customers to determine their relative profitability. This, in turn, enables sellers to allocate resources to customers according to their potential to deliver profits in the future. One useful approach, known as a **customer (or account) portfolio matrix**, brings together the potential attractiveness and the current strength of the relationship between seller and buyer (see Figure 16.3).

The *relationship* dimension incorporates the strengths from a customer's perspective relative to competitors. For example, a strong relationship is indicative of two organizations working closely together, whereas a weak relationship suggests that they have little interest in each other. *Customer attractiveness* refers to total revenue spend, average rate of growth, and the opportunities a buyer represents to the seller in terms of profit potential. These calculations can be complicated and involve a measure of management judgement. For clarity, these scales are presented as high or low, strong or weak. However, they should be considered as a continuum

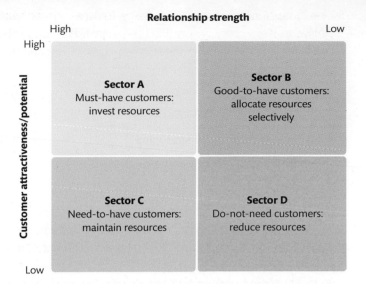

Figure 16.3
Customer portfolio matrix

and accounts can be positioned on the matrix not only within a sector, but also at a particular position within a sector. As a result, strategies can be formulated to move accounts to different positions, which, in turn, necessitate the use of different resources:

- In sector A, *must-have* customers enjoy a close business relationship and are also attractive in terms of their profit potential. Many of these customers are assigned **key account** status (see 'Key Account Management'), but all represent investment opportunities and resources should be allocated to develop them all.

- In sector B, *good-to-have* customers are essentially prospects, because although they are highly attractive, their relationship with the seller is currently weak. In this situation, marketing resources should be allocated on a selective basis proportional to the value that each prospect represents—that is, high investment for good prospects and low for the others.

- In sector C, relationships with customers are strong, but customers do not offer strong potential; hence these *need-to-have* customers are important only because they provide steady background business that is marginally profitable, so resources need to be maintained. Where it is identified that some of these customers are supported by a relatively large sales team, significant cost savings can be achieved relatively quickly.

- There is little reason to invest in the *do-not-need* customers in sector D. Relationships with these customers are weak and, because they are relatively unattractive in terms of profit potential, many of these customers should be let go—that is, released to competitors. These customers represent a net drain on the selling organization, and hence customers in this sector should receive little support, and resources subsequently freed up should be directed to customers in sectors A and B.

One of the benefits of developing a customer portfolio matrix is that it becomes easier to allocate sales channels to customers. Multichannel marketing decisions are important and should be rooted within the customer portfolio matrix. A range of channel strategies that relate to the channel needs of business customers and to any end-user target consumer segments can be

| Personal selling & KAM | Telemarketing | Direct mail | Print & sales literature | Web site/ Mobile | Social media | e-commerce |

Personal contact and face-to-face interaction

Electronic contact and faceless interaction

Figure 16.4
A spectrum of multichannel strategies

identified (Payne and Frow, 2004). These can be considered to be part of a spectrum. At one end, channels can consist of a dedicated, personal key account manager (highly personalized sales channel); at the other end, the channel can be purely electronic, with no personal contact at all. In the middle, there will be a range of different combinations of personal and electronic channels (see Figure 16.4).

In reality, most business customers will use a mixture of online and offline resources wherever possible and according to their specific needs. It is important for selling organizations to identify and allocate the most appropriate set of channels for their customers, based on the business potential each customer represents. These channels can be changed as the intensity of a customer relationship and their attractiveness develops over time.

Professional Services Marketing

Professional services firms (PSFs) can be distinguished as an independent type of organization. They provide services to all other organizations and can be found in many sectors, including engineering, architecture, IT and software, and management consultancy and financial services companies such as PricewaterhouseCoopers (PwC), Deloitte, KPMG, and EY (formerly Ernst & Young). They offer extremely complex and customized services that are created and delivered by highly qualified personnel (Reid, 2008). Professional services firms possess an authority that is granted by the community in which they operate. For example, accounting firms delineate international accounting standards, which in turn impact financial markets. They are governed by ethical codes and exhibit a professional culture (Thakor and Kumar, 2000).

According to Gummesson (1978), a professional service is provided by qualified people, is advisory, focuses on problem-solving, and is an assignment from the buyer to the seller. Typical services include management, accounting, law, engineering, surveying, and medicine, and are often referred to as 'knowledge engines for business' (Lorsch and Tierney, 2002: 14).

Greenwood and colleagues (2005: 661) define PSFs as 'those whose primary assets are a highly educated (professional) workforce and whose outputs are intangible services encoded with complex knowledge'. They use this understanding to identify two characteristic dependencies that serve to segregate PSFs from goods-producing organizations. The first concerns a client's dependency on the PSF as a result of the imbalance of information held by the two parties; the second concerns the dependency on its professional workforce and the high levels of mobility necessary to generate the PSF's output (see Market Insight 16.3).

Market Insight 16.3
KPMG Engages through Social Media

KPMG is one of the world's largest professional services companies, and its High Growth Technology (HGT) Group was established to build strong and meaningful relationships with entrepreneurs and founders of tech start-ups. The goal was to become the 'go to' professional services provider for the tech sector.

To raise awareness of the HGT Group among relevant companies, and to establish thought leadership and drive traffic, a mobile-optimized microsite and social media strategy was activated, supported by an ongoing programme of content. It was important to ensure that the HGT Group's social identity was separate from that of the corporate part of KPMG. It was important to grow new follower communities.

New material, including video, blog posts, and infographics, was posted on a weekly basis, feeding the social media strategy. This approach was designed to encourage repeat visits and to demonstrate the breadth and credibility of the HGT Group proposition.

Social media was a critical activity because the tech start-up community is active on social media, and uses these channels to stay informed and to connect with like-minded people and companies. Twitter was identified as the main social channel, supported by Instagram. A dedicated Twitter profile was set up for audience acquisition, direct posting, and fostering relationships with media, influencers, and the business community in and around Tech City (a technology district located in East London).

Interestingly, KPMG's agency not only assumed the role of site editor responsible for the creation and management of the site content, which included editorial, video, blog posts, and infographics, but also ran social media training workshops for all KPMG HGT Group members. This helped them to get the most from their own use of Twitter and LinkedIn for networking, and to extend the reach of HGT Group content.

Sources: https://www.b2bmarketing.net; http://www. kpmgtechgrowth.co.uk; http://www.thecroc.com/case-study/kpmg-start-ups-tech/

Theory into Practice

KPMG aimed at being both a key influencer and valued partner to tech start-ups in this sector. The credentials for a successful influencer involve being credible, trustworthy, and being seen to behave with integrity. By linking up via social media, KPMG sought to drive word-of-mouth communication and encourage the spread of positive comments regarding its services. Over time, both forms of dependency can be observed with KPMG. The first dependency concerns a start-up's dependency on KPMG because of the information the PSF holds; the second concerns a start-up's dependency on KPMG in terms of its professional workforce and mobility.

KPMG's attempt to build meaningful long-term relationships with start-ups can be best understood in terms of the key mediating variables (KMV) model (Morgan and Hunt, 1994). Morgan and Hunt (1994) demonstrated that the presence of both commitment and trust leads to cooperative behaviour, customer satisfaction, and ultimately successful relationship marketing. They argue that building a relationship based on trust and commitment leads to major benefits: the development of a set of shared values; reduced costs when the relationship finishes; and increased profitability because a greater number of end users are retained as a consequence of the inherent value and satisfaction they experience.

Market Insight 16.3
continued

Related Topics

word-of-mouth communication; relationship trust; endorsement; opinion formers; opinion leaders

1 What value might potential clients perceive, through social media, of working with a large PSF such as KPMG?

2 To what extent do PSFs influence industry standards and regulations? When might there be an ethical issue as a result of the part PSFs play in this?

3 Find two PSFs in the same industry and consider their brand identities and their reputation. What are the differences and similarities?

An important question concerns what it is that characterizes a PSF. Greenwood and colleagues (2005) identify two core characteristics. The first is that the outputs of PSFs are intangible and are normally applications of complex knowledge, which makes it difficult for customers to compare and evaluate the relative competence of suppliers, and makes clients dependent on the professionals delivering these services.

The second defining characteristic concerns the engine of this knowledge. This is generated within a highly educated workforce—professionals who are qualified and skilled at customizing complex knowledge to different client situations. Professional services firms have to attract and retain qualified people who can develop close ties with each client.

These two core characteristics shape the marketing strategies of PSFs. To simplify the outputs into understandable units of information and so convince clients of its superior competence, a PSF will strive to develop a superior reputation. To ensure that its workforce delivers complex knowledge and fosters client relationships, it is necessary for the PSF to attract and retain suitable professionals.

As Greenwood and colleagues (2005) acknowledge, herein lies an interesting and self-fulfilling cycle of activities. The quest for suitable professionals is assisted by the development of corporate reputation, because the latter helps the PSF to attract the best recruits. A strong reputation can also lower marketing costs because clients seek out higher-status firms (Podolny, 1994). Strong brand names allow organizations to charge premium fees (Krishnan and Schauer, 2000).

Professional services firms—especially the larger multinational consultancies—invariably adopt relational marketing strategies designed to retain, rather than acquire, clients (see Case Insight 16.1, for example). According to Reid (2008), marketing activities are then geared towards generating a financial return and building a business network. However, it is the quality of the client relationship that is critical, and that relationship quality can be both formal (for example evidenced in project briefings) and informal (for example social). This in turn requires a range of technical and interpersonal skills, and the organization must have a clear brand vision and identity that is internalized by the professional workforce.

For PSFs, the key to successful marketing is the development of a strong reputation, and this involves the creation and maintenance of a corporate brand. Marquardt, Golicic, and Davis

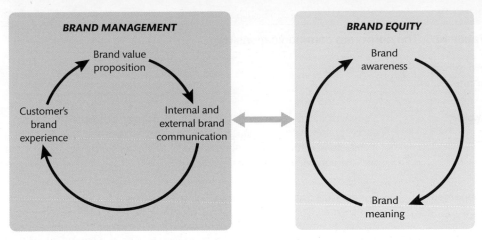

Figure 16.5
The B2B service brand process
Source: Marquardt et al. (2011).

(2011) have developed a service brand process model (see Figure 16.5). This is useful because it identifies three brand management components:

■ the need to develop a compelling brand value proposition, or promise;

■ the use of internal and external communications to inform and influence stakeholders—particularly clients—about the brand; and

■ customers' experiences with the brand and the realization of the brand promise.

These components are directly affected by interactions with the professional workforce (Berry, 2000). Indeed, there is general agreement that the development of a strong corporate reputation has to be founded on a workforce that embodies, and identifies with, the mission and values of the organization (Roper and Davies, 2010). The issue of customer experience is examined in Chapter 15. Collectively, these managerial components impact on the development of brand equity, which Marquardt and colleagues (2011) see as a composite of brand awareness and brand meaning.

Corporate Social Responsibility

Organizations communicate with one another through application of a **corporate communications mix**. The mix provides a series of cues by means of which stakeholders develop impressions about an organization. It can be considered to be composed of five main elements—that is, symbolic, management, marketing, organizational, and behavioural communications (see Table 16.5).

Through the use of the different elements of corporate communications, organizations seek to build strategies that differentiate the firm. Berry (2000: 131) argues that there is 'a conscious effort to be different, a conscious effort to carve out a distinct brand personality'. He also argues

> **Table 16.5 The corporate communications mix**
>
> | Form of corporate communication | Explanation |
> |---|---|
> | **Symbolic** | Communications concerning the visual aspects of an organization. These encompass names, letterheads, logos, signage, emblems, colour schemes, architecture, and the overall appearance of all the design aspects associated with the company. |
> | **Management** | Communications by managers who have a responsibility for the deployment of resources. These communications may be directed at internal or external audiences. |
> | **Marketing** | Communications designed to engage customer-oriented audiences with regard to the promotion of an organization's products and services. |
> | **Organizational** | Communications aimed at a range of stakeholders, not just customers, that are designed to build identification, commitment, and relationships with an organization, and are not sales oriented. |
> | **Behavioural** | Communications that emanate from the interactions, decisions, tone of voice, and overall empathy between employees and with others outside the organization. |
>
> *Source*: Fill (2013). Based on Birkigt and Stadler (1986) *and* van Riel and Fombrun (2007). Reprinted with the kind permission of Pearson Education.

that organizations need to represent something that is important to their customers. In the PSF sector, this is represented by superior knowledge—the one critical element with which clients want to be associated and that they use to compare propositions.

An important use of the mix is the development of corporate social responsibility (CSR), which is considered to be of strategic importance for organizations (Homburg, Stierl, and Bornemann, 2013). A key aim of CSR, according to Bhattacharya, Korschun, and Sen (2009), is the creation of mutually beneficial relationships with stakeholders over the long term.

Homburg and colleagues (2013) identify two facets of CSR. The first is *business practice CSR*, targeted at the primary stakeholders. These are normally considered to be those employees and customers who are involved with a firm's core business operations and with whom there is market exchange. The second facet concerns *philanthropic CSR*, which is targeted at secondary stakeholders—that is, those external to a firm's core business operations. These are essentially community and non-profit organizations, and the goal is to stimulate philanthropic engagement.

Research by Homburg and colleagues (2013) found that business practice CSR can increase trust in a supplier, while philanthropic CSR can improve customer–company identification. Part of their conclusion was that managers should be proactive in their use of CSR issues in their business strategy, that they should engage in CSR continually, and that they should communicate their CSR efforts transparently.

Key Account Management (KAM)

It is common knowledge that not all customers represent the same potential and profitability. However, it is quite common for a small number of customers to contribute a disproportionately large part of an organization's income and profitability. As a result, these customers often become essential to the firm's survival, so it is not surprising that, as Sharma and Evanschitzky (2016: 3) report, 'key accounts receive special treatment, with directed additional resources, compared with other sales accounts'.

The term 'key accounts' has become the established way of referring to those customers who are considered to be strategically important. A key account might offer the supply-side company opportunities to learn about new markets or types of customer. It might provide access to new and valuable resources, offer involvement with other key organizations, or simply be symbolically valuable in terms of influence, power, and stature. Size alone is not sufficient for key account status.

The underlying principle of relationship marketing in business markets requires that the focus should shift from short-term transactional exchanges to longer-term and collaborative relationships. The fundamental purpose of KAM is to create strategic alliances with key accounts through the development of long-term relationships (Tzempelikos and Gounaris, 2013). Establishing key accounts and the supporting infrastructure represents a significant investment for organizations and an opportunity cost.

 Visit the **online resources** and complete Internet Activity 16.3 to learn more about the use of **sales force automation (SFA)** applications to aid the management of key client accounts.

So why have so many organizations established and formalized their key account strategies? There are many reasons, some of which are particular to each organization; however, the main ones relate to changes in the competitive environment and in industry structure.

Changes in the Competitive Environment

In an increasingly complex and competitive environment, in which product life cycles appear to be shortening and differentiation difficult to sustain, the need to find new ways of enhancing business performance has intensified. One of the ways of achieving this is to provide a range of services that are tailored to meet each customer's needs.

Many types of service can be customized, for example training and development programmes, extranets, customer-driven delivery routes and timings, product support, and customer service lines. However, it is through the provision of value-added services that relationships are often developed and maintained. Establishing key accounts is a natural extension of providing particular services for key customers: not only does this enhance the profile of these customers, both internally and externally, but it also helps to focus resources on particular customers and their individual needs.

Changes in Industry Structure

Many organizations have centralized their purchasing activities—a move driven by two main factors. First is the amount of industry consolidation, a process whereby a few organizations grow larger by merging or acquiring their competitors, so that the industry is concentrated around a small number of large organizations. Industry consolidation has increased substantially in recent years. Second, in industries in which consolidation has not been significant, many organizations have moved towards centralizing their purchasing departments, processes, and functions as a means of achieving cost savings, improving effectiveness and efficiencies, and in so doing improving profits. ABB Sweden is a global corporation operating in a variety of industry segments, including power generation, pulp and paper, water, and chemicals. Brehmer and Rehme (2009) evaluate the way in which ABB Sweden used three different approaches to key account programmes, recognizing sales opportunities, customer demands, and a need to be more customer-focused.

The result of both of these actions is that there are a smaller number of purchasing units responsible for a larger proportion of business. For business marketers and suppliers generally, these trends towards industrial concentration and purchasing centralization mean that competition is increased and marketing strategies need to be much more customer-specific. Key account programmes are used with the deliberate intention of building relationships, often achieved by influencing levels of trust and commitment to generate more business.

However, in relationships between manufacturers and retailers (for example the grocery business), the presence of a key account relationship does not appear to have any significant benefit on the amount of resources allocated to the supplier's products (Verbeke, Bagozzi, and Farris, 2006).

Key Account Relationship Cycles

Key accounts do not only appear and flourish; they are the result of careful management, nurturing, and time. Key accounts represent a particular strength of relationship and, as with good wine, need time to develop to reach full potential (see Market Insight 16.4). Consequently, each key account will, at any one moment, be at a particular stage of relationship development (Millman and Wilson, 1995).

Key accounts can be plotted through various stages of a **KAM development cycle**. One such cycle is shown in Table 16.6. The time between stages is not fixed, and varies according to the nature and circumstances of the parties involved. The stages can be negotiated quickly, in some cases, or negotiations may become protracted. The titles of each of the stages reflect the relationship status of both parties rather than of the selling company (for example preferred supplier) or buying company (for example prospect).

Managing Key Accounts

Key account managers provide the main link between employer and key account customers. They provide a route through which information flows—preferably in both directions. They must be capable of dealing with organizations in which buying decisions can be both protracted and delayed (Sharma, 1997), and quick and demanding. However, key account managers do not operate alone and are not the sole point of contact between organizations; normally, there are a number of levels of interaction between the two organizations, to the extent that there could be 'an entire team dedicated to providing services and support to the key account' (Ojasalo, 2001: 109). Therefore key account managers assume responsibility for all points of contact within the customer organization.

The value that a customer derives from a particular offering will have a significant influence on the level of attention given by the buyer to the supplier's programme. Furthermore, the level to which an organization uses centralized buying procedures will also impact on the effectiveness of a KAM programme. Key account managers' behaviours differ from those in field sales roles in relation to internal management, adaptability to customers, and planning, but align in relation to

Market Insight 16.4
Groupon: KAM Gone Wrong

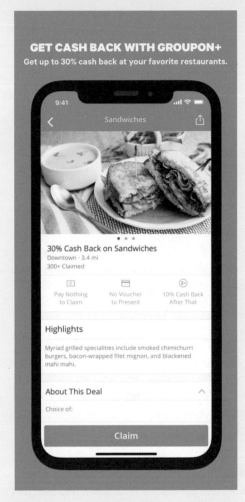

Cashback at restaurants is just one of many deals the Groupon app offers

Source: © Groupon.

Since its inception in 2008, Groupon has become a global e-commerce leader, offering consumers a vast marketplace of unbeatable local deals all over the world. The UK deals market was worth an estimated £6 billion by 2011. Groupon, with an estimated 100 million customers worldwide at that time, was worth US$13 billion. By putting a twist on the boring old coupon, Groupon created a powerful direct marketing platform. Bricks-and-mortar-businesses with limited marketing budgets or a lack of skill in advertising online could profit from broadcasting their offerings on the Groupon website, and hence tap into the company's huge database of subscribers globally. The classic deal worked on the basis that the merchant offered a 50 per cent discount, after which the merchant and Groupon split the rest of the revenue. After fees and discounts, a merchant would generate around 23p in each £1 of the original price, but this would be money well spent if it were to generate new customers. Consequently, consumers won by gaining the chance to find hidden shopping and leisure gems in their locales, at bargain prices. Local businesses ('merchants', in Groupon jargon) benefited from exposure to an untapped and widely inaccessible online target audience, attracting new customers to their businesses.

Nevertheless, horror stories began to surface of dissatisfied merchants whose businesses were capsizing under unexpectedly large hordes of voucher holders, because Groupon's salesforce had not consulted with them properly. From the German subsidiary, many of the company's key accounts (merchants forming the so-called dream partners list, such as renowned restaurants, retailers, or spas) raised their concerns about key account managers' business practices. Complaints were made about false promises made, specifically not capping the agreed maximum number of deals available on the Groupon website, which was intended to ensure that merchants did not run the risk of being overwhelmed by voucher holders. One merchant went so far as to accuse Groupon's key account management team of deliberately making up contracts between merchants and Groupon because of a fear of getting sacked in the wake of a growing 'hire and fire' mentality amongst Groupon Germany's Berlin-based management. As a consequence, sales slumped in the following months in virtually all markets. In 2013, Groupon's stock price fell and the company's value dropped to $3 billion.

To recover, Groupon developed a series of self-service websites—mobile and tablet enhancements—to make it easier for valued merchants to create and manage their own Groupon marketing campaigns for their businesses across any of their devices, wherever they are located.

Market Insight 16.4
continued

Branded the 'Groupon Merchant Centre', merchants use the app to cap their deals, monitor campaign performance, share feedback via social media, and get in touch with Groupon's customer service centre whenever needed. Having learned from their earlier mistakes, Groupon now provides value-added services in its business model, hoping to re-establish, develop, and maintain long-term relationships with key merchants and its growing base of 52.7 million customers worldwide by the end of 2016.

The changes made seemed to have worked: Groupon claims category-leading customer satisfaction ratings and a net promoter score of 72, rating it alongside some of the world's best-known brands.

Sources: Morgan and Hunt (1994); Bice (2012); Kaczmarek (2012); Kaczmarek and Wohlert (2012); Tzempelikos and Gounaris (2015); Sheppard (2017); https://investor.groupon.com/financials/annual-reports-and-proxy-statements/default.aspx; https://www.groupon.de/

Theory into Practice

If relationships with key account partners of a firm are not properly developed and nurtured, solely emphasizing a transactional approach to B2B relationships can have a detrimental effect upon the whole business in profit terms (Tzempelikos and Gounaris, 2015). To reach an interdependent and integrated relationship with key accounts, the supplying firm needs to establish trust and commitment (Morgan and Hunt, 1994), by adding extra services such as the Groupon Merchant Centre, to demonstrate recognition of each other's mutual importance. Being transparent about sharing sensitive information, as well as giving a firm's most valued customers the chance to participate in joint problem-solving, makes the retention of committed (long-term) profitable relationships with key partners more likely.

Related Topics

key account management; relationship trust; relationship failure; KAM development cycle

1 Why do you think Groupon failed to consider merchants' ability to fulfil customers' voucher deals?

2 What should Groupon have done to ensure that merchants using its platform were not inundated with more business than they could handle?

3 How do you think this incident would affect trust and commitment between Groupon and its merchants?

This market insight was kindly contributed by Julius Stephan, Aston University, UK.

goal orientation, network embeddedness, and strategic priorities. In addition, many companies treat KAM as a sales initiative rather than as a business-wide change management programme (Davies and Ryals, 2013).

Abratt and Kelly (2002) found six factors that were of particular importance when establishing a KAM programme—that is, key account manager suitability, understanding of the client's business, commitment to the partnership, delivering value, trust, and the proper implementation and understanding of the KAM concept.

Table 16.6 Key account management development stages

Development stages within a cycle	Explanation
Exploratory	Suppliers identify and isolate those customer accounts that have key account potential.
Basic	In this transactional period, exchanges are used by both parties to test each other as potential long-term partners.
Cooperative	An increasing number of people from both parties become involved in the relationship.
Interdependent	This stage involves mutual recognition of each other's importance. Very often, single-supplier status is conferred.
Integrated	Both parties share sensitive information and undertake joint problem-solving. The relationship is regarded as a single entity.
Disintegrated	The termination or readjustment of the relationship can occur at any time.

In addition to the interpersonal relationships that exist between the customer's contact person and the supplier's key account manager, there are also inter-organizational relationships that may concern system and policy issues (see Research Insight 16.3). These will vary in strength and some may not be compatible with the tasks facing the key account manager.

Research Insight 16.3

To take your learning further, you might wish to read this influential paper:

Workman Jr, J.P., Homburg, C., and Jensen, O. (2003). Intraorganizational determinants of key account management effectiveness. *Journal of the Academy of Marketing Science*, **31(1), 3–21.**

In this article, the authors investigate what dimensions of the KAM approach affect KAM effectiveness, concluding that these include the KAM team's *esprit de corps* (that is, pride and sense of loyalty to the team), marketing and sales resource access, activity intensity, activity proactiveness, and top management involvement. Conversely, formalizing the KAM approach is negatively related to performance. The authors also found that factors such as top management involvement and KAM team *esprit de corps* mattered more than formalization of the approach. The surprising conclusion is therefore that formalizing the approach to key account management may lead to bureaucracy and inflexibility in responding to the key account clients' demands.

 Visit the online resources to read the abstract and access the full paper.

Chapter Summary

To consolidate your learning, the key points from this chapter are summarized here:

■ **Explain the main characteristics of business markets and understand the different types of organizational customer.**

Business markets are characterized by four main factors: the nature of demand; the buying processes; international dimensions; and the relationships that develop between organizations. A range of organizations make up business markets; and these can be classified as commercial, government, and institutional. These organizations buy products and services to make goods for resale to their customers, but they also consume items that are required to keep their offices and manufacturing units functioning.

■ **Describe the different types of offering that are bought and sold in business markets.**

Products and services bought and sold through business markets are categorized as input goods, equipment goods, and supply goods.

■ **Set out the main processes and stages associated with organizational buying and purchasing.**

Organizational buying behaviour can be understood as a group buying activity in which a number of people with differing roles make purchasing decisions that affect the organization and the achievement of its objectives. Buying decisions can be understood in terms of different types of decision (buyclasses) and different stages (buyphases).

■ **Explain what business-to-business marketing is and the marketing issues associated with professional services firms.**

Business-to-business marketing is concerned with the identification and satisfaction of business customers' needs. This requires that all stakeholders benefit from the business relationship and associated transactions. Customers derive satisfaction by purchasing offerings that they perceive as providing them and/or their organizations with particular value. Professional services firms focus on developing their reputation as the main means of differentiation.

■ **Understand the principles of key account management.**

Some suppliers refer to some of their strategically important customers as 'key accounts'. Relationships with these customers move through various stages known as key account management development cycles. Each stage is marked by particular characteristics, and part of the role of the key account manager is to ensure that all contact between the supplier and the customer builds on strengthening the inter-organizational relationship.

Review Questions

1. Make notes setting out the essential purpose of B2B marketing.
2. What are the key characteristics associated with B2B markets?
3. What are the different types of organization that make up the business market?
4. Name four of the different types of person who make up a decision-making unit.
5. Distinguish clearly between buyphases and buyclasses.
6. What is the customer portfolio matrix?
7. What are key accounts and why are they important?

8 What are the different phases associated with key account development cycles?

9 How might social media be of help to professional services firms?

10 What are the main characteristics of the B2B corporate communications mix?

 Discussion Questions

1 Having read Case Insight 16.1, how should Grant Thornton ensure that changes in its customer relationships (for example when individual clients move elsewhere) within clients' designated key accounts do not damage those relationships and the propositions it has developed for the client?

2 What are the main characteristics of business marketing and what differences are there, if any, when you compare these with the main characteristics of consumer marketing?

3 Wirebelt Ltd has been developing a conveyor belt designed to meet new government-driven hygiene standards. The problem in many manufacturing, packaging, and assembly plants is that floors underneath conveyor belts can become wet and hence may present a danger to people working around the equipment. The new belt has a trough incorporated into it, which runs along its entire length. Spillages feed into the trough, where collection sumps and filters remove the excess liquids before they overflow to the floor (see https://www.wirebelt.co.uk/company-info/improve-hygiene-standards). Make brief notes advising Wirebelt's marketing manager about marketing the new conveyor.

Visit the online resources and complete the Multiple-Choice Questions to assess your knowledge of Chapter 16.

 Glossary

business-to-business (B2B) marketing the marketing of products and services that are bought and sold between organizations.

buyclasses the different types of buying situation faced by organizations.

buyers (also known as purchasing managers) individuals within organizations who select suppliers and manage the process whereby the required products are procured.

buying centre *see* **decision-making unit**

buyphases the series of sequential activities or stages through which organizations proceed when making purchasing decisions.

consumer marketing the marketing of products and services that are bought by consumers.

corporate communications mix the particular configuration of the symbolic, management,

marketing, organizational, and behavioural elements of communications.

C-Suite the range of top-level executives whose title includes the word 'chief', for example chief executive officer (CEO), chief financial officer (CFO), chief marketing officer (CMO), etc.

customer (or account) portfolio matrix a 2 × 2 grid used to reflect the strength of the relationships between a buyer and seller, and the profitability that each account represents to the seller.

deciders people who make organizational purchasing decisions; often very difficult to identify.

decision-making unit (DMU) a group of people who make purchasing decisions on behalf of an organization.

embedded ties strong, close, and mutually rewarding relationships between firms.

gatekeepers people who control the type and flow of information into an organization, in particular to members of the DMU.

horizon scanning (also known as environmental scanning) the process whereby firms gather, analyse, and disseminate external information to support organizational decision-making in support of the organization's strategic objectives.

influencers people who help to set the technical specifications for a proposed purchase and assist the evaluation of alternative offerings by potential suppliers.

initiators people who start the organizational buying decision process.

key account a business customer who is strategically significant and with whom a supplier wishes to build a long-lasting relationship.

key account management (KAM) development cycle the stages through which an organization passes as it develops a relationship with a key account customer.

modified rebuy the organizational processes associated with the infrequent purchase of products and services.

new task the organizational processes associated with buying a product or service for the first time.

organizational buying behaviour (OBB) the characteristics, issues, and processes associated with the behaviour of producers,

resellers, government units, and institutions when purchasing goods and services.

perceived value the 'net satisfaction' derived from consuming and using a product, not only the costs involved in obtaining it.

professional services firms (PSFs) organizations that deliver highly complex and customized services that are created and delivered by highly qualified personnel.

promise management the process of enabling an organization to make and keep promises to customers by meeting the expectations that have been created by those promises.

sales force automation (SFA) occurs when firms computerize routine tasks or adopt technological tools to improve the efficiency or precision of sales force activities.

straight rebuy the organizational processes associated with the routine reordering of goods and services, often from an approved list of suppliers.

strategic procurement an approach used to negotiate with suppliers on a cooperative basis to help to build long-term relationships.

users people or groups who use business products and services once they have been acquired and who then evaluate the performance of the businesses, products and services.

References

Abratt, R., and Kelly, P.M. (2002). Perceptions of a successful key account management program. *Industrial Marketing Management*, 31(5), 467–76.

Achrol, R.S. (1997). Changes in the theory of interorganizational relations in marketing: toward a network paradigm. *Journal of the Academy of Marketing Science*, 25(1), 56–71.

Benijts, T., Lagae, W., and Vanclooster, B. (2011). The influence of sport leagues on the business-to-business marketing of teams: the case of professional road cycling. *Journal of Business and Industrial Marketing*, 26(8), 602–13.

Berry, L.L. (2000). Cultivating service brand equity. *Journal of the Academy of Marketing Science*, 28(1), 128–37.

Bhattacharya, C.B., Korschun, D., and Sen, S. (2009). Strengthening stakeholder–company relationships through mutually beneficial corporate social responsibility initiatives. *Journal of Business Ethics*, 85(2), 257–72.

Bice, B. (2012). Groupon isn't a good deal for businesses. *CNBC*, 20 September. Retrieve from: https://www.cnbc.com/id/49092709 (accessed 13 October 2018).

Birkigt, K., and Stadler, M.M. (1986). *Corporate Identity, Grundlagen, Funktionen, Fallspielen.* Landsberg am Lech: Verlag Moderne Industrie.

Bonoma, T.V. (1982). Major sales: who really does the buying? *Harvard Business Review*, 60(3), 111–18.

Brehmer, P.-O., and Rehme, J. (2009). Proactive and reactive: drivers for key account management programmes. *European Journal of Marketing*, 43(7–8), 961–84.

Chakravarty, A., Kumar, A., and Grewal, R. (2014). Customer orientation structure for Internet-based business-to-business platform firms. *Journal of Marketing*, 78(5), 1–23.

Davies, I.A., and Ryals, L.J. (2013). Attitudes and behaviours of key account managers: are they really any different to senior sales professionals? *Industrial Marketing Management*, 42(6), 919–31.

de Menezes, J. (2015). Premier League broadcast rights set to be sold for record £4.4bn deal as clubs continue to reap the financial rewards of the top flight. *The Independent*, 10 February. Retrieve from: https://www.independent.co.uk/sport/football/news-and-comment/premier-league-broadcast-rights-set-to-be-sold-for-record-44bn-deal-as-clubs-continue-to-reap-the-financial-rewards-of-the-top-flight-10035695.html (accessed 13 October 2018).

Dwyer, R.F., Schurr, P.H., and Oh, S. (1987). Developing buyer–seller relationships. *Journal of Marketing*, 51(2), 11–27.

Fill, C. (2013). *Marketing Communications: Brands, Experiences and Participation* (6th edn). Harlow: FT/Prentice Hall.

Fill, C., and McKee, S. (2012). *Business Marketing*. Oxford: Goodfellow.

Fill, C., and Turnbull, S. (2016). *Marketing Communications: Discovery, Creation, and Conversations* (7th edn). Harlow: FT/Prentice Hall.

Glenn, R.R., and Wheeler, A.R. (2004). A new framework for supply chain manager selection: three hurdles to competitive advantage. *Journal of Marketing Channels*, 11(4), 89–103.

Greenwood, R., Li, S.X., Prakash, R., and Deephouse D.L. (2005). Reputation, diversification, and organizational explanations of performance in professional service firms. *Organization Science*, 16(6), 661–73.

Grönroos, C. (2009). Marketing as promise management: regaining customer management for marketing. *Journal of Business and Industrial Marketing*, 24(5–6), 351–9.

Gummesson, E. (1978). Towards a theory of professional services marketing. *Industrial Marketing Management*, 7(2), 89–95.

Gummesson, E., and Polese, F. (2009). B2B is not an island! *Journal of Business and Industrial Marketing*, 24(5–6), 337–50.

Håkansson, H., and Snehota, I. (1995). *Developing Relationships in Business Networks*. London: Routledge.

Hemsworth, D., Sánchez-Rodríguez, C., and Bidgood, B. (2008). A structural analysis of the impact of quality management practices in purchasing on purchasing and business performance. *Total Quality Management and Business Excellence*, 19(1–2), 151–64.

Hollyoake, M. (2009). The four pillars: developing a bonded business-to-business customer experience. *Database Marketing and Customer Strategy Management*, 16(2), 132–58.

Homburg, C., Stierl, M., and Bornemann, T. (2013). Corporate social responsibility in business-to-business markets: how organizational customers account for supplier corporate social responsibility engagement. *Journal of Marketing,* 77(6), 54–72.

Homburg, C., Wilczek, H., and Hahn, A. (2014). Looking beyond the horizon: how to approach the customers' customers in business-to-business markets. *Journal of Marketing*, 78(5), 58–77.

Jackson, B. (1985). Build customer relationships that last. *Harvard Business Review*, 63(6), 120–8.

Järvinen, J., Tolänen, A., Karjaluoto, H., and Jayawardhena, C. (2012). Digital and social media marketing usage in B2B industrial section. *Marketing Management Journal*, 22(2), 102–17.

Kaczmarek, J. (2012). Wann kommt die Grouponkalypse? Leak Tiefenanalyse. Ghomorra auf der Mitarbeiterseite, Sodom bei den Haendlern? *Gruenderzene*, 20 April. Retrieve from: https://www.gruenderszene.de/allgemein/grouponkalypse-gomorrha (accessed 13 October 2018).

Kaczmarek, J., and Wohlert, N.-V. (2012). Groupon-Gomorrha? *Gruenderszene*, 17 February. Retrieve from: https://www.gruenderszene.de/news/groupon-gomorrha-leak (accessed 13 October 2018).

Keinänen, H., and Kuivalainen, O. (2015). Antecedents of social media B2B use in industrial marketing context: customers' view. *Journal of Business and Industrial Marketing*, 30(6), 711–22.

Krishnan, J., and Schauer, P.C. (2000). The differentiation of quality among auditors: evidence from the not-for-profit sector. *Auditing*, 19(2), 9–25.

Leigh, T.W., and Marshall, G.W. (2001). Research priorities in sales strategy and performance. *Journal of Personal Selling and Sales Management*, 21(2), 83–93.

Lennartz, E., Fischer, M., Krafft, M., and Peters, K. (2015). Drivers of B2B brand strength: insights from an international study across industries. *Schmalenbach Business Review*, 67(1), 114–37.

Lorsch, J.W., and Tierney, T.J. (2002). *Aligning the Stars*. Boston, MA: Harvard Business School Press.

Macfarlane, P. (2002). Structuring and measuring the size of business markets. *International Journal of Market Research*, 44(1), 7–31.

Makkonen, H., Olkkonen, R., and Halinen, A. (2012). Organizational buying as muddling through: a practice–theory approach. *Journal of Business Research*, 65(6), 773–80.

Marquardt, A.J., Golicic, S.L., and Davis, D.F. (2011). B2B services branding in the logistics services industry. *Journal of Services Marketing*, 25(1), 47–57.

Mason, D.S. (1999). What is the sports product and who buys it? The marketing of professional sports leagues. *European Journal of Marketing*, 33(3–4), 402–18.

Millman, T., and Wilson, K. (1995). From key account selling to key account management. *Journal of Marketing Practice: Applied Marketing Science*, 1(1), 9–21.

Morgan, R.M., and Hunt, S.D. (1994). The commitment–trust theory of relationship marketing. *Journal of Marketing*, 58(3), 20–38.

Noordhoff, C.S., Kyriakopoulos, K., Moorman, C., Pauwels, P., and Dellaert, B.G.C. (2011). The bright side and dark side of embedded ties in business-to-business innovation. *Journal of Marketing*, 75(5), 34–52.

Ojasalo, J. (2001). Key account management at company and individual levels in business-to-business relationships. *Journal of Business and Industrial Marketing*, 16(3), 199–220.

Payne, A., and Frow, P. (2004). The role of multi-channel integration in customer relationship management. *Industrial Marketing Management*, 33(6), 527–38.

Podolny, J.M. (1994). Market uncertainty and the social character of economic exchange. *Administrative Science Quarterly*, 39(33), 458–83.

Pressey, A., Tzokas, N., and Winklhofer, H. (2007). Strategic purchasing and the evaluation of 'problem' key supply relationships. What do key suppliers need to know? *Journal of Business and Industrial Marketing*, 22(5), 282–94.

Reagans, R., and McEvily, B. (2003). Network structure and knowledge transfer: the effects of cohesion and range. *Administrative Science Quarterly*, 48(2), 240–67.

Reid, M. (2008). Contemporary marketing in professional services. *Journal of Services Marketing*, 22(5), 374–84.

Robinson, P.J., Faris, C.W., and Wind, Y. (1967). *Industrial Buying and Creative Marketing*. Boston, MA: Allyn & Bacon.

Rocco, R.A., and Bush, A.J. (2016). Exploring buyer–seller dyadic perceptions of technology and relationships: implications for Sales 2.0. *Journal of Research in Interactive Marketing*, 10(1), 1–22.

Rodríguez-Escobar, J.A., and González-Benito, J. (2015). The role of information technology in purchasing function. *Journal of Business and Industrial Marketing*, 30(5), 498–510.

Roper, S., and Davies, G. (2010). Business to business branding: external and internal satisfiers and the role of training quality. *European Journal of Marketing*, 44(5), 567–90.

Ryals, L.J., and Rogers, B. (2006). Holding up the mirror: the impact of strategic procurement practices on account management. *Business Horizons*, 49(1), 41–50.

Schreiner, A. (2015). Triadic analysis of business relationships ending: a case study of a dyad and a third actor. *Journal of Business and Industrial Marketing*, 30(8), 891–905.

Schultz, R., Shwepker, C.H., and Good, D.J. (2012). An exploratory study of social media in business-to-business selling: salesperson characteristics, activities and performance. *Marketing Management Journal*, 22(2), 76–89.

Senn, C., Thoma, A., and Yip, G.S. (2013). Customer-centric leadership: how to manage strategic customers as assets in B2B markets. *California Management Review*, 55(3), 27–59.

Seyedghorban, Z., Matanda, M.J., and LaPlaca, P. (2016). Advancing theory and knowledge in the business-to-business branding literature. *Journal of Business Research*, 69(8), 2664–77.

Sharma, A. (1997). Who prefers key account management program? An investigation of business buying behaviour and buying firm characteristics. *Journal of Personal Selling and Sales Management*, 17(4), 27–39.

Sharma, A., and Evanschitzky, H. (2016). Returns on key accounts. Do the results justify the expenditures? *Journal of Business and Industrial Marketing*, 31(2), 174–82.

Sheppard, E. (2017). How small business owners fell out of love with deal websites. *The Guardian*, 5 January. Retrieve from: https://www.theguardian.com/small-business-network/2017/jan/05/how-small-business-owners-fell-out-of-love-with-deal-websites (accessed 13 October 2018).

Shi, H., Sridhar, S., Grewal, R., and Lilien, G. (2017). Sales representative departures and customer reassignment strategies in business-to-business markets. *Journal of Marketing*, 81(2), 25–44.

Sisko, H., Lipiäinen, M., and Karjaluoto, H. (2015). Industrial branding in the digital age. *Journal of Business and Industrial Marketing*, 30(6), 733–41.

Sit, S.-S. (2017). H&M overhauls supply chain to compete with Zara. *Supply Management*, 3 April. Retrieve from: https://www.cips.org/supply-management/news/2017/april/hm-to-overhaul-supply-chain-to-compete-with-zara/ (accessed 13 October 2018).

Spekman, R.E., and Gronhaug, K. (1986). Conceptual and methodological issues in buying centre research. *European Journal of Marketing*, 20(7), 50–63.

Storbacka, K., Ryals, L., Davies, I.A., and Nenonen, S. (2009). The changing role of sales: viewing sales as a strategic, cross-functional process. *European Journal of Marketing*, 43(7–8), 890–906.

Svahn, S., and Westerlund, M. (2009). Purchasing strategies in supply relationships. *Journal of Business and Industrial Marketing*, 24(3–4), 173–81.

Swinder, J., and Seshadri, S. (2001). The influence of purchasing strategies on performance. *Journal of Business and Industrial Marketing*, 16(4), 294–306.

Thakor, M.V., and Kumar, A. (2000). What is a professional service? A conceptual review and bi-national investigation. *Journal of Services Marketing*, 14(1), 63–82.

Towne, J. (2010). Lean transformations: planning a 'lean' health care makeover. *Health Facilities Management*, 1 October. Retrieve from: https://www.hfmmagazine.com/articles/1121-lean-transformations (accessed 13 October 2018).

Turcotte, C. (2013). Un monde à traduire. *Le Devoir*, 21 January. Retrieve from: https://www.ledevoir.com/economie/actualites-economiques/368839/un-monde-a-traduire (accessed 13 October 2018).

Turgeon, N., Lavoie, A., and Bergeron St-Onge, J. (2017). TRSB (A): strengthening a service brand in business to business (B2B) marketing. *International Journal of Case Studies in Management*, 15(2). Retrieve from: https://education.hec.ca/centredecas/app/en/case/6201?frtok=361 (accessed 13 October 2018).

Tzempelikos, N., and Gounaris, S. (2013). Approaching key account management from a long-term perspective. *Journal of Strategic Marketing*, 21(2), 179–98.

Tzempelikos, N., and Gounaris, S. (2015). Linking key account management practices to performance outcomes. *Industrial Marketing Management*, 45, 22–34.

van Riel, C.B.M., and Fombrun, C.J. (2007). *Essentials of Corporate Communication*. London: Routledge.

Verbeke, W., Bagozzi, R.P., and Farris, P. (2006). The role of key account programs, trust, and brand strength on resource allocation in the channel of distribution. *European Journal of Marketing*, 40(5–6), 520–32.

Webster, F.E., and Wind, Y. (1972). *Organizational Buying Behaviour*. Englewood Cliffs, NJ: Prentice Hall.

Wiersema, F. (2012). *The B2B Agenda: The Current State of B2B Marketing and a Look Ahead*. University Park, PA: Institute for the Study of Business Markets.

Workman Jr, J.P., Homburg, C., and Jensen, O. (2003). Intraorganizational determinants of key account management effectiveness. *Journal of the Academy of Marketing Science*, 31(1), 3–21.

Part 5
The Social Impacts of Marketing

Chapter 17

Not-for-Profit and Social Marketing

Learning Outcomes

After reading this chapter, you will be able to:

▸ List some key characteristics of not-for-profit organizations

▸ Explain why not-for-profit organizations do not always value their customers

▸ Analyse stakeholders and develop appropriate engagement strategies

▸ Describe and assess cause marketing campaigns

▸ Understand how marketing is used in social and political marketing campaigns

Case Insight 17.1
City of London Police

Market Insight 17.1
Red Nose Day: Coming to America

Market Insight 17.2
Whetting Appetites for Welsh Water

Market Insight 17.3
Shell Develops Room to Breathe

Market Insight 17.4
Midwife or Marketer?

Market Insight 17.5
No Means No! Get It!

Case Insight 17.1
City of London Police

Founded in 1839, the City of London Police (CoLP) police London's 'Square Mile' financial district, with a national responsibility for fraud and economic crime. Because they also police many high-profile public events, they also focus on the prevention of terrorism and crime. We speak to Superintendent Helen Isaac to find out how the CoLP uses social marketing to support law enforcement.

The Force's core mission statement is 'to uphold the law fairly and firmly; preventing crime and anti-social behaviour; keeping the peace; protecting and reassuring the community; investigating crime and bringing offenders to justice'. No other place has the unique blend of tourism, range of businesses, and resident population that the City of London enjoys, where all this diversity is condensed into 1.6 km². Our community comprises the 9,000 residents of the City, the 300,000 who travel into the City to work every day, and businesses large and small, in addition to the many famous multinational financial corporations. We also serve the Corporation of London, our local authority (and police authority) for the Square Mile. The Home Office provides us with our 'core grant' and other funding streams for specialist responsibilities, and a number of trade bodies provide extra funding.

The City is a global powerhouse attracting hordes of tourists because of the many iconic locations within the Square Mile. Any act of terrorism here would have a potentially highly damaging impact on the UK economy and on the confidence of our community to keep them safe. To counter this threat, the City introduced the 'ring of steel'—a security and surveillance cordon—in the mid-1990s, following the bombings of Bishopsgate and St Mary Axe by the Provisional Irish Republican Army (IRA), both of which caused severe disruption and damage in the City and resulted in death and injury. This security measure was designed to deter large vehicle-borne devices being brought into the City (the main terrorist threat identified), but since the bombings of 7 July 2005 ('7/7'), the terrorist threat has changed.

One key element of policing is communication with local communities and other stakeholders. Although we use many of the same communication channels that a brand would, our campaigns are rooted in providing

a service to the public, not selling. We exist to keep people safe and we measure ourselves accordingly. Our measures of success focus around social considerations, including public perceptions of safety and confidence in the CoLP to keep the public safe.

The general public can sometimes see policing as reactive, with police responding after a crime has been committed. But we designed Project Servator as a proactive strategic approach to policing, incorporating unpredictable and highly visible CoLP deployments, involving a wide range of assets including specially trained officers, supported and amplified by community engagement, and media and public relations (PR) to help to disrupt hostile reconnaissance and wider criminality, whilst reassuring and engaging the public. Servator is principally a counter-terrorism operation, but its wider intention is to impress upon terrorists and other criminals that the City's police presence is unpredictable, while simultaneously reassuring the general public around public safety fears. Project Servator is about working with the public as partners in being vigilant and reporting suspicious activity. Our partnership with the community is crucial; they are our eyes and ears.

Given the dual target audience for its communication, the CoLP had a seemingly impossible task: how was it to design a social marketing campaign (including message and media mix) that would deter terrorists and criminals more generally, but simultaneously reassure the general public and encourage them to report suspicious activity?

 Visit the online resources to watch a video interview with Helen Isaac in which she explains what the CoLP did.

Introduction

Over the last 50 years, the role of marketing in not-for-profit organizations has grown substantially as these types of organization have begun to realize how marketing can help them to develop a strong understanding of customers and other **stakeholders**. But have you ever wondered whether or not the techniques we use in commercial marketing are relevant in a not-for-profit, in which the remit is not to enrich shareholders? Are the principles behind marketing not incompatible with the mission of a charity? Are there any differences in how we use marketing techniques in a social environment, for example when governments use marketing to reduce drink driving, or to increase fruit-and-vegetable consumption to five or six portions a day, or to increase voter registration? In this chapter, we answer some of these questions.

So far, our attention has centred on commercial organizations intent on making profits. However, other types of organization—that is, those that operate in the not-for-profit sector—do not seek to maximize profit. Kotler and Levy (1969) pioneered the ground-breaking application of marketing to not-for-profit enterprises. In the twenty-first century, marketing is readily used by local government, churches, museums, charities, universities, political parties, zoos, public hospitals, and many others, all of which operate without profit as their central goal. However, the view is no longer whether or not marketing should be undertaken by not-for-profits, but how it should be applied (Wright, Chew, and Hines, 2012). There are also organizations that can be characterized as somewhere between charity and commercial enterprise (for example cooperatives). Facebook's chief executive officer (CEO) Mark Zuckerberg and his wife Priscilla Chan announced in 2015 that they would donate 99 per cent of the Facebook shares they then held (then worth US$45 billion) to the Chan Zuckerberg Initiative, a private company, which will itself donate money to various charitable causes (Brandom, 2015).

Despite the similarities between not-for-profit and commercial marketing highlighted by Kotler and Levy (1969) (see Research Insight 17.1), there are some key differences in how marketing is used—particularly in relation to marketing communications. These key differences are as follows (Rothschild, 1979):

- *Proposition*—With not-for-profit offerings, the unique selling proposition is weaker—that is, there are weaker direct benefits. For example, giving to charity provides us with a sense of 'doing good', but this feeling may not be sufficient to induce many people to give. For social marketing, the proposition relates to the audience benefit gained from undertaking a specific desired behaviour (LeFebvre, 2011), for example that *not* drinking and driving saves lives.

- *Price*—This has different connotations in not-for-profit situations. For example, in a social marketing context, what is the price when **demarketing** (that is, reducing the demand for) the use of illicit recreational drugs such as cocaine? Is it the potential physical harm that could arise from not stopping using a particular drug, or the damage it could do to the user's relationships with friends and family, for example? In social marketing, therefore, 'price' can be perceived as the incentives and costs of (not) taking up a particular desired behaviour (LeFebvre, 2011). The incentive to stop using cocaine, for example, relates to the removal of psychological and physiological problems, such as mood swings and the risk of heart-related conditions, whereas the cost might relate to the momentary loss of self-confidence or the feeling of having fun (Jones, Baines, and Welsh, 2014). In relation to charities, the amount donated is often left to the discretion of the donor (although suggestion of specific amounts tends to be more effective) and is largely determined by the donor, rather than being specified as in a commercial transaction.

- *Involvement*—We speak of high and low involvement in commercial situations regarding how consumers learn more about an offering during the purchasing process. The involvement in not-for-profit situations displays more extreme tendencies: people often either really engage with a charity (for example Oxfam, Médecins sans Frontières) or a political party (for example Freedom Party in Austria, or Sweden's Feminist Initiative) or social cause (such as People for the Ethical Treatment of Animals, or PETA, and Greenpeace) or exhibit strong reactions against it.

- *Segmentation*—In the not-for-profit environment, it is often important to develop a campaign that drives behaviour in all targets rather than a specific segment, as in commercial markets. For example, a health promotion campaign might wish to encourage *all* adults to eat five portions of fruit and vegetables a day, although there may well be subgroups who need specific targeted messages (for example young children).

Another key difference in the marketing of not-for-profit organizations is the need to check the marketing strategy against the environment, the available resources, and—uniquely—against the organization's social values (Hatten, 1982). In the latter case, the social values of the organization impact not only on why the organization exists, but also on how it goes about its marketing activities, including fundraising, promotional programmes, and operational programme developments. In the UK, major charities such as Oxfam and the British Red Cross came under considerable pressure when they used an outsourced telemarketing firm employing predatory fundraising techniques, targeting vulnerable people who were confused or even terminally ill. Unsurprisingly, they dropped these techniques shortly after a media furore (Weaver, 2015).

Table 17.1 outlines the mission statements for various not-for-profit organizations. For commercial organizations, the mission statement usually focuses on being 'best in market' and consequently achieving high levels of profit; in the not-for-profit sector, mission statements focus on causes. The *raison d'être* of a not-for-profit is to solve a particular societal problem. Of course, if a charity were ever truly to solve a problem (for example if a cancer charity were to find a cure), it might cease to operate—or it might simply amend its mission. Like any other organization, a charity interacts with its environment and must stay relevant within the context that it operates if it is to attract funding.

Research Insight 17.1

To take your learning further, you might wish to read this influential paper:

Kotler, P., and Levy, S.J. (1969). Broadening the concept of marketing. *Journal of Marketing*, 33(1), 10–15.

In this seminal article, the authors proposed that marketing techniques and concepts, as typified by the 4Ps, could be applied to non-business organizations and could be applied to the marketing of organizations, persons, and ideas. It provoked considerable debate, with some writers suggesting that the concept of marketing had been broadened too far.

 Visit the online resources to read the abstract and access the full paper.

Table 17.1 A selection of mission statements from not-for-profit organizations

Organization	Mission statement
The Louvre (France)	'To adapt to the diverse nature of [its] public, the Louvre continually strives for greater accessibility. To this end, its initiatives include the progressive widespread use of labeling in two or even three languages to describe the 38,000 artworks exhibited; the revamped numbering of exhibition rooms; the development of a new, more user-friendly floor plan; and the fostering of art education. In addition, the Louvre website . . . offers various visitor tips on planning a visit, gaining in-depth knowledge, and teaching art history to children. Not content merely to receive visitors, the Louvre often engages in public outreach, in France in particular. The opening . . . of the Louvre Lens in northern France is a case in point. . . . In keeping with the universal scope of its vocation, the Louvre enjoys relations with over 75 countries. Its activities serve to strengthen its bonds with its collections' countries of origin, to gain a better understanding of overseas visitors, and to reach out to those who are unable to travel to Paris.'
Emirates Red Crescent	**Our Motto:** Life care. **Our Vision:** Leadership and excellence in humanitarian work. **Our Mission:** Mobilizing human power to support the vulnerable. **Our Role:** The Authority works to support the official authorities in peacetime and wartime, in accordance with the provisions of Article (26) of the First Geneva Convention of 1949. **In PeaceTime:** Organizing awareness programs, first aid, protection and control of epidemics, paying attention to the social issues, and providing humanitarian assistance for vulnerable, needy people and victims of accidents and disasters. **In WarTime:** Transferring and treating the wounded and assisting prisoners in the scope of the Geneva Conventions. Provide first aid and relief to the victims. Protection of civilians and sheltering the displaced and homeless. Search for missing persons and reunion of separated families.'
Civil Nuclear Constabulary (UK)	'With over 1000 highly trained Police Officers and Police Staff, the CNC is a specialist armed police service dedicated to protecting the civil nuclear industry. We protect 14 civil nuclear sites across England, Scotland and Wales, safeguard nuclear material in transit and play a key role in national security. The civil nuclear industry includes nuclear research and provides nuclear energy to millions of people. To protect such an important commodity, as well as the public, the Civil Nuclear Constabulary (CNC) and Civil Nuclear Police Authority (CNPA) were established on 1 April 2005. The CNPA is CNC's governing authority and reports into the Department of Energy and Climate Change. It is their job to ensure that we police effectively and efficiently while being responsive to the needs and priorities of the stakeholders we serve. **Ambition** To be recognised as the leading UK authority on the armed protection of civil nuclear facilities and material in transit.

Table 17.1 continued

	Mission
	In partnership with the civil nuclear industry, national security agencies and regulatory bodies the CNC will deter any attacker whose intent is the theft or sabotage of nuclear material whether static or in transit. If an attack occurs CNC will defend that material and deny access to it. If material is seized or high consequence facilities compromised the CNC will recover control of the facility and regain custody of the material.'
China Charity Federation (CCF, China)	'The goals of CCF [established in 1994] are to uphold the spirit of humanitarianism and the Chinese tradition to help people in poverty as well as people in difficulties. There are over 387 affiliates of CCF throughout China.
	Since its establishment, CCF has maintained its goals of extending charitable work in various fields and increasing public awareness of the great difficulties faced by many members of our society. . . .
	. . . Our projects include the following areas, which have great influence on all aspects of our society: disaster relief, poverty relief, care of seniors and orphans, education assistance, medical assistance and helping the disabled. So far, through extensive fundraising activities, CCF has raised more than ¥60 billion [about £1.37 billion in 2018], both in cash and in kind.'
SIDA (Sweden)	'SIDA is a government agency working on behalf of the Swedish parliament and government, with the mission to reduce poverty in the world. Through our work and in cooperation with others, we contribute to implementing Sweden's Policy for Global Development (PGU).
	We implement the Swedish development policy that aims to enable people living in poverty to improve their lives. Another part of our mission is reform cooperation with Eastern Europe. The third part of our assignment is to distribute humanitarian aid to people in need of assistance.
	We carry out enhanced development cooperation with a total of 36 countries in Africa, Asia, Europe and Latin America. Our selection of cooperation countries are based on political decisions made by the Swedish government.'

Note: In some cases, the wording may differ slightly from that on the organization's website. Changes have been made to correct the English and to abridge the wording, where necessary.

Sources: https://www.louvre.fr/en/missions-projects; https://www.rcuae.ae/en/about.aspx#course and https://www.rcuae.ae/en/about.aspx#role; http://www.cnc.jobs/about/; https://www.chinacharityfederation.org/English/NewsContent/121/1280.html; https://www.sida.se/English/About-us/Our-mission/

The Key Characteristics of Not-for-Profit Organizations

The main characteristics impacting on marketing are the existence of multiple stakeholders, the degree of transparency expected when working to pursue the organization's mission and in dealing with its finances, the presence of multiple objectives in business and social terms, a different orientation compared with commercial organizations, and, finally, different customer perceptions (see Figure 17.1). We consider each of these characteristics in what follows.

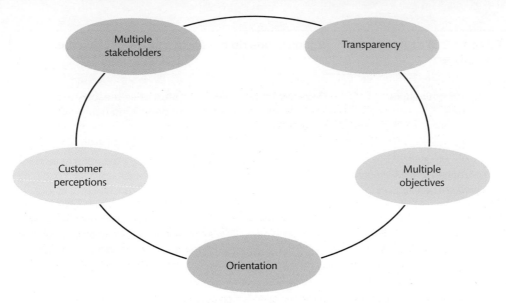

Figure 17.1
Key characteristics of not-for-profit organizations

Multiple Stakeholders

Although for-profit or private-sector organizations interact with a range of stakeholders to achieve their business goals, their focus is on customers and shareholders. What differs about not-for-profit organizations is their concern for a wider group of stakeholders. Stakeholders are groups with whom the organization has a relationship and which impact on the operations of the organization. This includes shareholders (or trustees), regulatory bodies, other charity or not-for-profit partners, supply chain partners, employees, and customers. In private companies, revenue is distributed from customers to shareholders; it is initially converted into profits by the organization and shareholders are rewarded with a dividend as a share of the profits earned. Companies also have stakeholders, but those stakeholders have less influence on how the organization's profits are distributed.

Not-for-profits provide an offering, but their customers or end users seldom pay the full costs incurred by the organization to provide them. Many not-for-profits rely on stakeholders to finance the organization's operations. Instead of revenue from customers being used to reward shareholders, there are usually no profits to be redistributed because those who fund the organization do not require a return on their resource provision. For example, local council taxes, Lottery funding for special projects, and business rates are three of the main sources of income that fund city councils in the UK, and some selected councils receive central government funding. Charities are supported by individual and corporate donations. Museums may rely on a mixture of grants, lottery allocations, entrance fees, and individual donations and bequests. Universities rely on a mixture of government research and teaching grants, learner tuition fees, individual and corporate donations, and fees from businesses for corporate services.

Because they serve multiple stakeholders, not-for-profits do not always value their beneficiary customers (that is, those who receive their charitable services) as well as they should and they sometimes fail to explain sufficiently to donors (that is, supporter customers) how

Table 17.2 Why not-for-profit organizations do not always seem to value their customers

Reasons for not valuing beneficiaries	Reasons for not valuing supporters	Interactive reasons for undervaluing customers
Many not-for-profits exist in a monopolistic situation, which potentially engenders an arrogant culture towards beneficiaries.	Donors claim to be approached too often for donations and do not feel sufficiently appreciated.	Dealing with multiple stakeholders can cause inter-group tension when one group's call on resources takes precedence over others. For example, a high-value donor for a university might want their donation to be used in a way that is different from that envisaged by the management of the university.
Demand far outstrips supply, creating problems in delivering a consistent quality of service.	Volunteer service workers can often feel undervalued and under-supported.	
There may be a lack of market segmentation for beneficiaries. Research into beneficiary customers' needs is not common because funds available are seen as better used for funding operations.		

donations will be used. The difficulties arising when seeking to satisfy multiple stakeholder groups are outlined in Table 17.2, which considers beneficiary and supporter customers, and explains why charities sometimes fail to satisfy—and may undervalue—these groups of customers (Bruce, 1995).

Not-for-profits should determine which of the different stakeholders have the most interest in their activities and the most power to affect their organization's performance. One common method used to distinguish between the interests and power of stakeholders is the stakeholder mapping matrix, outlined in Figure 17.2. The matrix can be used to identify four types of stakeholder, based on the high or low levels of interest that they have in an organization and the level of power they exert over it:

- Those with high levels of interest and power (group A) are key stakeholders, which need to be continuously engaged. They might be funding bodies or powerful regulators, for example.

- Those with high interest, but low levels of power (group B), for example individual donors to charities, should be informed about that charity's activities to maintain their interest.

- Group C represents those organizations with high power, but low interest. It is important for the not-for-profit to increase information flow to these organizations to increase their interest, so that they can exert their power in the not-for-profit's favour (as a funding body might), or alternatively to keep them satisfied if they intend to exert their power against the not-for-profit (as a regulator might).

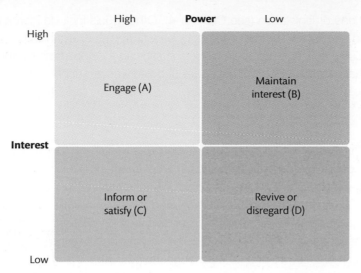

Figure 17.2
The stakeholder mapping matrix
Source: Scholes (2001).

■ Finally, an organization's relationships with those stakeholders who have little power or interest should either be disregarded or revived (group D).

The use of public money and donations in not-for-profit organizations requires their source and allocation to be understood, audited, and tracked. Public scrutiny or transparency of funding is a feature that distinguishes these organizations from their private-sector counterparts. For donations to continue to flow, not-for-profit organizations should demonstrate trust, integrity, and honesty. For example, UK charities are governed by regulatory requirements that require them to provide greater information on how they are governed compared with their commercial counterparts. Charities' executive teams are overseen by boards of trustees—often unpaid volunteers who are senior and experienced people who have some interest in running the organization. In parallel, the executive teams of private or public limited companies are overseen by paid executive and non-executive directors.

Private-sector organizations declare the minimum financial information required—just enough to comply with government disclosure requirements. By comparison, not-for-profit organizations provide considerable detail of their internal procedures and processes. This is because they do not want to be judged as financially incompetent, and they want to avoid adverse media coverage and the negative perceptions that would follow.

Multiple Objectives

In manufacturing and other sectors, profit is a central overriding goal. Investment decisions are often based on the likely rate of return and resources are allocated according to the contribution (to profit) they will make. Profit provides a relatively easy measure of success. As the name suggests, in the not-for-profit sector, profit is not the central overriding goal. Not-for-profit organizations have a range of goals—a multiple set of tasks that they seek to achieve. These include generating awareness, motivating people to be volunteers, distributing information, contacting customers, raising funds, allocating grants, and **lobbying** members of Parliament (MPs) for changes in regulations or legislation (see Chapter 4). Other goals include increasing their geographical spread to reach new people who might benefit from the organization's activities and campaigning to focus media attention on a particular issue. In the non-profit sector, performance measurement is challenging, because a wider set of objectives are used.

Orientation

As a general rule, rather than manufacturing, distributing, and selling a physical product, not-for-profit organizations deliver a service. Developing a market orientation (see Chapter 1) is important, because the stronger the market orientation, the stronger the organization's market performance, particularly for smaller charities (Seymour, Gilbert, and Kolsaker, 2006). How the not-for-profit generates income can impact upon the organization's market orientation. In a study of Australian not-for-profits, it was found that poorly operating charities can improve their organizational performance by becoming more market-oriented, although the motivations and beliefs of employees in this sector present unique managerial challenges (Chad, Motion, and Kyriazis, 2013).

Not-for-profit organizations need to create positive awareness about their cause or activities. The principal focus of the organization is to motivate and encourage people to become involved and identify with the aims of the organization, which might lead on to financial contributions and/ or volunteering support (for example by working in a charity's shop, or by contributing financial, marketing, or other professional services expertise).

Raising funds is an ongoing critical activity in the not-for-profit sector. The payment handed over by a customer to a charity does not operate in the same way as the payment by a customer for a banking service at the point of receiving the service. Raising funds for a charity requires people or donors to contribute money, so the expectations of not-for-profit customers are different from those of commercial firms. This leads to a greater focus on engaging supporters to become part of, and identify with, the ethos of the not-for-profit organization rather than simply being a customer.

Customers' Perceptions

Customers of private-sector organizations realize that, in exchange for an offering, they are contributing to the profits of the organization with which they are dealing: customers have a choice, and organizations compete to get their attention and money. In the not-for-profit sector, customers do not always have a choice: donors are free to give to one charity rather than another, or not to give anything at all. In the public sector, choice is limited, although governments do try to provide some choice (for example in school provision or choice of hospital for surgery in many countries). In reality, however, there is little practical opportunity for the public to choose among different public services in the same way as they can in the private sector. For example, services provided by some local councils, such as meal services for the elderly and infirm, or by all councils, such as magistrates' courts, or building regulations and planning, are effectively single source; there is no choice or alternative supplier. In these cases, pressure to deliver a superior level of service interaction can often be based on an individual's own sense of duty and integrity, rather than on any formal organizational service policy and training.

Visit the **online resources** and follow the web link to the National Council of Non-profit Associations (NCNA) to learn more about the challenges and developments facing non-profit organizations.

Types of Not-for-Profit Organization

We can classify four main types of not-for-profit organization: charities; the **social enterprise** sector; the public sector; and political parties and campaigning organizations. How each of these organizations uses marketing is considered next.

Charities

The increasing success experienced by many charities has resulted from improved commercial professionalism and the adoption of commercial approaches from the private sector, together with greater collaboration with the private sector through **cause marketing** activities. However, there has also been a simultaneous increase in the number of charities in the marketplace. This means that there is greater competition as more charities chase a finite number of donor contributions.

Cancer Research UK raised £8 million in one week on the back of the #nomakeupselfie meme—a campaign it didn't start

Source: © Cancer Research UK (2014).

The act of making a donation to a charitable organization is the culmination of a decision-making process involving a wide range of variables. Attitude to the cause, personal involvement or related experience, and trust that the charity will use the funds appropriately are critical to encouraging donations. Consequently, charities seek to develop empathy with potential donors and to build trust on the basis of which an initial transaction or donation can be made. Traditionally, the acquisition of a new donor is relatively expensive compared with the low costs associated with the collection of monthly standing orders and direct debits. Costs are minimized when repeat donations occur, so charities, just like private-sector organizations, practise relationship marketing principles (see Chapter 15).

However, charities are recognizing the power of the social media to generate significant increases in fundraising revenue quickly. Cancer Research UK (CRUK) raised £8 million in one week alone in 2014, when a young mother from Staffordshire in England set up a 'No Make-Up for Cancer Awareness' Facebook page, encouraging people to submit a photo of themselves wearing no make-up, to tag it #nomakeupselfie, and to donate £3 to CRUK (Duncan, 2014). Once CRUK realized just how many people were taking notice of the campaign, it sent out the following tweet: 'Many are asking—we didn't start #nomakeupselfie #cancerawareness trend. We like the sentiment!' This tweet generated so many retweets that CRUK then generated a text-message donation number and tweeted this on Facebook, Twitter, Instagram, and Google+ (Eccles, 2014).

The process of giving is based on a strong emotional involvement with the objectives of the charity. This means that charities try to communicate through messages that invoke an emotional response in their target donors. In the case of marketing foster care, research has found that positive emotional appeals are more persuasive than negative emotional appeals (Randle et al., 2016). Charities need to provide people with a rationale—a reason to give money (see Market Insight 17.1).

Market Insight 17.1
Red Nose Day: Coming to America

Red Nose Day, first run in the UK in 1988, was set up by charity Comic Relief to tackle poverty via a biennial **telethon** held in March. Co-founded by comedian Sir Lenny Henry and screenwriter and producer/film director Richard Curtis of *Love Actually* fame, by 2015 the event had helped Comic Relief to raise more than £1 billion worldwide.

Comic Relief partners with the British Broadcasting Corporation (BBC) to produce a live television event, featuring stunts and acts by renowned comedians, and other entertainment programmes, to encourage people to give generously to the cause of alleviating poverty. What has particularly strengthened the reach of the fundraising activity is its partnership with corporates. Early partners included BT (British Telecom), which provides the call centres to take people's donations; Sainsbury's, which sells a variety of Red Nose

merchandise; and Oxfam, which also sells the Red Noses in its charity shops and online. Since the early days, the number of corporate partners has significantly increased. The marketers of washing powder brand, Persil, raised £350,000 in 2001 and achieved a 25 per cent increase in sales during the promotion period. British Airways (BA) became a first-class partner with Comic Relief in 2010, launching its Flying Start programme encouraging passengers to donate their small (foreign) change for the cause, from which BA has since raised more than £17 million. For Red Nose Day 2015, among other partners Mars took part by donating 5p from each special Red Nose Day bag of Maltesers sold, while Unilever donated 8p per special pack of PG Tips teabags sold. In 2017, Pepsico (via its Walkers Snacks brand) teamed up with Sainsbury's over a three-week promotional period to offer 500 customers who

Market Insight 17.1

continued

bought a six-pack of crisps the opportunity to win £50 off their next shop and a £50 donation to Comic Relief.

Red Nose Day is, however, not limited to the UK. Comic Relief has granted international licences to organizations around the world, including in China, Belgium, Finland, Germany, Iceland, and the United States.

In the United States, which holds Red Nose Day events annually, the first event took place in 2015, culminating in a three-hour live primetime television special on NBC, featuring celebrities from across the entertainment industry. US corporate partners in 2015 included Walgreens—the US pharmacy chain owned by Walgreens Boots Alliance—which acts as the exclusive retailer of Red Nose merchandise, confectioner M&M's, and NBC itself. In 2016, Walgreens donated 50 cents for each US$1 nose purchased and 10 per cent of the ticket price for other Red Nose merchandise, raising more than $20 million.

It seems that partnering with Red Nose Day is a laughing matter.

Sources: Gray (2003); Farey-Jones (2015); Roderick (2017); Walgreens (2017); Comic Relief (n.d.).

'Monkey' with a Red Nose makeover on promotional packs of PG Tips
Source: © Paul Daniels/Shutterstock.com.

Theory into Practice

This market insight describes how companies have partnered with a UK charity with global reach in an attempt to alleviate poverty. Red Nose Day allows companies to develop their social responsibility programmes by using a cause marketing campaign. Because the programme has a global reach, companies in individual country markets can benefit from wider consumer awareness and interest. Corporate benefits for cause marketing campaigns generally include improvements in corporate reputation, improved sales, and improved employee satisfaction.

Related Topics

cause marketing; social responsibility; sales promotion

1 Do you think Red Nose Day will be more or less successful in raising funds in the United States compared with the UK? Why, or why not?

2 What are the likely business benefits of partnering with Red Nose Day for US companies Walgreens, NBC, and M&M's, respectively?

3 How important is it that a company promotes not only a cause, but also the fact that the company is undertaking the initiative in the first place?

Charities also try to raise funds by working in partnership with commercial organizations in cause marketing campaigns. According to Kotler (2000), companies differentiate themselves by sponsoring popular social causes to win the public's favour. Such an approach, termed cause marketing, is a useful way of developing a positive brand image for the private company because it builds not only customer loyalty, but also employee respect. The charity gains vital income from this partnership. The American Marketing Association (AMA, 2018) defines cause-related marketing (now more commonly known as simply cause marketing) as a:

> Promotional strategy that links a company's sales campaign directly to a non-profit organization. Generally includes an offer by the sponsor to make a donation to the cause with (the) purchase of its product or service. Unlike philanthropy, money spent on cause marketing is a business expense, not a donation, and is expected to show a return on investment.

This type of campaign associates a company's sales with the mission or campaign of a not-for-profit organization and includes a promise to make a donation for each unit bought. However, cooperation between the two organizations takes many forms. Traditionally, these schemes are based on sales promotions, whereby a donation to the charity is made as a percentage of sales. Yorkshire Water, a regional utility, won the 2017 Business Charity Awards in the UK for its cause marketing programme 'Big Wish for Ethiopia', run in association with WaterAid and aiming to deliver safe water, sanitation, and hygiene education to those without it. Every time one of its customers signs up to pay their water bill by direct debit, Yorkshire Water makes a donation to WaterAid—and it raised more than £731,000 in a 12-month period (Yorkshire Water, 2017).

Cause marketing is an increasingly attractive proposition for organizations. Several reports have found that a very large proportion of consumers (more than 85 per cent) agree that when price and quality are equal, they are more likely to buy an offering associated with a 'cause' or good deed. Therefore companies are increasingly likely to differentiate themselves by co-opting social causes (Kotler, 2000). Other relationships, such as those between pharmaceutical companies and medicine distribution charities, are based on the company providing free product and technical knowledge ('gifts in kind'). A good example of a global cause marketing campaign is Kellogg's 'Breakfast for Better Days' initiative, which

The winning campaign at the 2017 Business Charity Awards, UK
Source: By permission of Yorkshire Water.

has provided 1.9 billion servings of cereal for people in need and aims to provide 3 billion servings in the future by donating 2.5 billion servings of food, expanding breakfast programmes to reach 2 million children, supporting the livelihoods of 500,000 farmers, involving employers in 45,000 volunteer days, and engaging 300 million people to help with the whole effort (Kellogg's, 2018).

 Visit the **online resources** and complete Internet Activity 17.1 to learn more about cause marketing.

Cause marketing can affect consumers' overall attitude towards the sponsoring company or brand, as well as their cognitive knowledge of the brand (that is, what they know). Cause marketing campaigns are more effective when they are used over time and when there is a strong fit between the brand and the cause (Till and Nowak, 2000). The perceived fit between the company and the cause is important to the effectiveness of the campaign. Nevertheless, there are risks to be considered for the not-for-profit organization. The charitable organization's most important asset is its name; because cause marketing is a business transaction, it is subject to contract and hence there is a risk that the charity could suffer reputational damage (Gifford, 1999). Cause marketing should be used as part of a wider corporate social responsibility (CSR) strategy (Steckstor, 2012). To reduce the risk, charities should not sell their association at less than what it is really worth. They should also obtain the fee up front and control all uses of their name (Gifford, 1999).

Social Enterprises

A new form of organization has emerged, with a format and purpose that has captured the imagination of many different people, including people in commercial business, people working in the social sector, volunteers, academics, and leading political parties. In the UK, the government considers a social enterprise to be an enterprise that 'is a business with primarily social objectives whose surpluses are principally reinvested for that purpose in the business or in the community, rather than being driven by the need to maximize profit for shareholders and owners' (BIS, 2011: 2). Social enterprises blend social objectives with commercial reality. There is a drive to make a profit, but any surplus might be reinvested into the enterprise and not redistributed as a reward to owners. In the UK, Fairtrade schemes, Welsh Water (Glas Cymru—see Market Insight 17.2), Jamie Oliver's Fifteen, the Co-operative Group, charities, and even farmers' markets are all examples of social enterprise organizations. Elsewhere, examples include Groupe SOS in France, which offers products and services to the disadvantaged and socially excluded, Specialisterne in Denmark, which specializes in software testing and employs mainly people with Asperger's, an autistic spectrum disorder, and Solvatten in Sweden, which provides clean and hot water for households using the power of the sun. One long-standing social enterprise in the United States is food company Newman's Own, set up by late Hollywood actor Paul Newman in 1982. It gives away all of its after-tax profits and, by the end of 2017, the organization had paid more than US$495 million to charitable causes worldwide.

 Visit the **online resources** and follow the web link to the Newman's Own website to learn more about this inspiring social enterprise.

Fifteen is a social enterprise set up by celebrity chef Jamie Oliver to train disadvantaged young people to work in the hospitality industry, with restaurants in London, Cornwall, and Amsterdam

Source: © David Bathurst Photography.

Market Insight 17.2
Whetting Appetites for Welsh Water

The UK water industry was taken out of public ownership (that is, privatized) in 1989. In subsequent years, Welsh Water Authority, a utility company providing water and sewerage services to more than 3 million people in Wales and adjoining parts of England, acquired an electricity business and became saddled with debt. It was eventually taken over by US utility company Western Power Distribution (WPD). In 2001, Glas Cymru, a not-for-profit company limited by guarantee, was set up to raise the money to buy the water company assets off WPD (Glas Cymru paid £1), to pay off the debt through what was then the largest corporate bond issue in UK corporate history, at £1.9 billion, and to remove shareholders. It remains the UK's first and only not-for-profit utility company—but working for customers and stakeholders instead of shareholders has not dented its financial performance. It was named the best water and sewerage company in England and Wales by UK water regulator Ofwat in 2003.

By 2011, the company had achieved the best credit rating in the UK water sector. A study by Cardiff University found that the company generated more than £1 billion for the Welsh economy annually, generating more than £1.56 for every £1 invested in it. By 2016, its 15th anniversary, the company had invested £4.5 billion in water and wastewater services, returned more than £300 million in 'customer dividends' (effectively, rebates on fees charged), helped 50,000 customers who were struggling financially to pay their bills, and come second in Ofwat's customer satisfaction survey in 2015–16 for the second year running.

Market Insight 17.2
continued

In 2016, the company launched a branding campaign to promote its unique not-for-profit status and summer customer consultation programme over future investment decisions. Roger Pride, managing director at Heavenly, the agency running the campaign for Welsh Water, talked of how Welsh Water was putting people, not pipes, at the centre of the campaign. In summer 2017, the company launched another 'world first' innovation: a Welsh bilingual chatbot to gauge the views of its 3 million customers on issues such as upgrading of its water and sewerage networks, and on climate change, in its 'have your say' consultation conducted on Facebook Messenger and its own website.

Sources: Glas Cymru (2016); Heavenly (2016); Newing (2016); Stewart (2017).

Theory into Practice

This market insight outlines how a water utility company transformed itself from a failing for-profit into a dynamic and innovative not-for-profit company. Over several stages of its evolution, the company has carefully consulted its customers. It thrives by being highly customer-oriented—particularly by consulting its customers about issues ranging from the company's remit, through its investment decisions, to its operating principles—but also by returning any surplus funds, after investment decisions are taken, to its customers in the form of 'customer dividends'. Whilst consultation helps to increase customer satisfaction, providing rebates also generates customer loyalty.

Related Topics

social entrepreneurship; customer dividends, stakeholder marketing, customer consultations

1 **How sustainable do you think this social enterprise is in the long term?**

2 **How do you think Welsh Water is using marketing techniques differently compared to traditional water companies?**

3 **Take a look at the website of Swedish social enterprise Solvatten (https://solvatten.org/). How does its business model compare with that of Glas Cymru?**

However, social enterprises are not restricted in format. The sector is very diverse and includes public limited companies (PLCs), community enterprises, cooperatives, housing associations, charities, and leisure and development trusts, among others. All of these can adopt social enterprise values. Companies, and their wealthy owners, also frequently donate to charitable causes. Examples include Google, Microsoft, Pepsico, and Shell (see Market Insight 17.3). All have active corporate philanthropy programmes with gift-matching programmes whereby the company will match the amounts that its employees donate to charity (Weinger, 2015). Indeed, Porter has long argued that companies should be more philanthropic because there is a long-term strategic opportunity in being so (Porter and Kramer, 2002) (see Research Insight 17.2).

Research Insight 17.2

To take your learning further, you might wish to read this influential paper:

Porter, M.E., and Kramer, M.R. (2002). The competitive advantage of corporate philanthropy. *Harvard Business Review*, 80(12), 56–68.

In this highly cited article, the authors argue that firms must look beyond the public relations (PR) value of their social contributions; rather, the key to successful philanthropy is to focus giving on the context in which the firm operates. They explain how Cisco Systems set up the Cisco Networking Academy to train computer network administrators to alleviate a potential constraint on the company's growth—that is, lack of available trained employees. Interestingly, the authors argue that philanthropy can be the most cost-effective way in which a company can improve its competitive context, given that, under these circumstances, companies can leverage the efforts and resources of not-for-profit organizations and other institutions to make systemic changes.

 Visit the online resources to read the abstract and access the full paper.

Market Insight 17.3
Shell Develops Room to Breathe

A good example of a social marketing campaign is that launched in India by Shell Foundation (SF), the Anglo-Dutch oil-and-gas major's charitable foundation. The company has long been trying to develop a market for a more efficient cookstove, which reduces fuel usage, poisonous emissions, and cooking time—but to no, or perhaps only limited, avail. Since 2007, SF has partnered with US social enterprise Envirofit International to produce a range of clean, efficient, and affordable cookstoves. In late 2008, SF launched the 'Room to Breathe' campaign in Shimoga, Karnataka, India. The aim was to raise awareness of the benefits of the new improved cookstoves, principally because around 70 per cent of residents are impacted by the indoor air pollution caused by existing dirty cookstoves. The campaign's aim was to raise awareness in the local population (of 1.6 million), to sell 58,000 cookstoves, and to achieve a metric of campaign spend per additional stove sold of US $5.75. It is important to note that all previous attempts by cookstove manufacturers focused on the health and environmental benefits of the improved cookstoves had failed. The new campaign promoted the cookstoves using billboard and wall paintings, a van campaign,

Clean cookstoves reduce smoke and toxic emissions, and offer economic and environmental benefits
Source: Envirofit International/Jessica Alderman.

sustained activist householders (typically, women operating using a network marketing approach), and using word of mouth amongst Anganwadi workers (government health workers in the villages) and, in the latter stages of the campaign, through a microfinance initiative (with Grameen Koata), which allowed villagers to buy a stove and repay the cost in instalments (that is, hire purchase).

Market Insight 17.3
continued

Envirofit's cookstoves retailed at ₹1,399 (£15.69/€17.64). Other cookstoves promoted through the 'Room to Breathe' programme included Prakti's single pot (₹750 or £8.41/€9.46), double pot (₹1,100 or £12.34/€13.87), and First Energy's Oarja Plus (₹1,250 or £14.02/€15.76). Such prices, whilst competitive, were beyond the reach of many Indians living in the region.

The campaign enjoyed some success. It ran between October 2009 and July 2012, hit 300,000 people, raised awareness in the population above the 30 per cent target, but sold only 11,447 improved cookstoves—way below the target of 58,000. The total cost of the campaign was US$350,000. Lessons learned by SF and its partners were that having a great product, which was good for people's health and made economic sense, was insufficient in itself because people were not aware of the product and its benefits, and were suspicious of the new technology. However, the benefits for those who switched were

clear. Women perceived that it caused them to cough less, meant less cleaning and saved time, was healthier (particularly for children), and did not impact on the taste of the food cooked. Men said that they liked the stove because it saved money and time, because the food retained a smoky taste, because the cookstove was easier to carry, and because the fuel it used was cheaper. However, 55 per cent of people thought that the cookstove was too expensive, 21 per cent did not know how to operate it, and 18 per cent did not trust it to deliver the benefits promised.

The campaign achieved the most success in its final phase, through the microfinance initiative with Grameen Koata, when promotional activities were combined with loans to buy the cookstoves. This approach ultimately brought the cost of the campaign down to $4 per stove—a level that could then be built into the $30 stove loan.

Source: Bishop, Pursnani, and Sumpter (2013).

Theory into Practice

This market insight describes how the not-for-profit foundation of an oil-and-gas major sought to develop the market, with partners, for a new form of cooker, which would have significant health benefits and would cost users less in maintenance and running costs. It also demonstrates how difficult it can be to persuade people to adopt new products or new behaviours and how suspicious people can be of those new products or new suggested behaviours, even when the product

or behaviour is better for them. The case particularly highlights the importance of developing an appropriate pricing strategy when targeting people on very limited incomes and how important the provision of credit can be in such situations. Finally, the case demonstrates the importance of developing a set of objectives that are carefully measured to evaluate whether or not a social marketing campaign has been successful.

Related Topics

social marketing; marketing metrics; awareness; advertising

1 Why do you think it was so difficult to change the behaviour of the target audience—that is, Indians living in Shimoga in Karnataka, India?

2 Why do you think Shell Foundation decided to develop this campaign?

3 What are the risks of developing a campaign like this for (a) stove manufacturers and (b) Shell Foundation?

The Public Sector

The term 'public sector' covers a range of activities around the provision of services by local and central government, and by government agencies. These services are concerned with satisfying social needs and benefiting society. In many countries, the public sector has developed on the back of ideas embedded within the concept of the welfare state, although many of these countries have privatized their telecommunications, water, gas, and electricity provision. The types of service provided are founded on the principle of improving the quality of people's lives.

Public-sector organizations operate in industrial, governmental, consumer, and societal markets, and their marketing activities are driven by a complex web of stakeholder relationships. Marketing in the public sector is governed by three main forces: social; economic; and political. The interaction of these forces within an increasingly uncertain and unstable environment makes the provision of customer choice of service more problematic.

Internal marketing is crucial in these organizations. Rather than refer to buyers and sellers, the public-sector approach is based around providers and users. One distinguishing characteristic of the public sector concerns the political tensions that arise between the various stakeholder groups. For example, the conflict between central and local government is crucial, and perceptions of who is responsible for taxation and why tax rates rise faster than inflation reflect the power imbalance between the participants.

Governments use marketing for a variety of reasons, including as a complement to law enforcement (as Case Insight 17.1 demonstrates) and to help to promote services to support companies with their export business, as well as 'to bring about societal change or improvement' (LeFebvre, 2011: 57). Social marketing interventions can be highly effective in achieving behavioural change in target audiences across a variety of social settings (Stead et al., 2007). Visual messages are more effective than text messages in conveying an anti-smoking message, according to a study of French consumers (Gallopel-Morvan et al., 2009). Demarketing is often used to demarket behaviours—for example to encourage people *not* to use drugs, *not* to smoke, *not* to drink drive, or *not* to avoid paying their vehicle tax.

'Allo, 'allo, 'allo, what's that then? British Transport Police and Network Rail use advertising to encourage the reporting of unattended items
Source: Courtesy of the Department for Transport.

DVLA's 'we can always spot an untaxed car' ad campaign
Source: Driver & Vehicle Licensing Agency (UK), photographer Garry Simpson.

An example of a demarketing campaign (see also Market Insight 17.4) is that run by the Thai Health Promotion Foundation to stigmatize the giving of alcohol as a New Year gift since 2008, reducing it from 30.5 per cent of gifts to 9 per cent in the last nine years. In Thailand, 22,356 people were killed in road accidents in 2016, of which half involved alcohol consumption, according to the World Health Foundation. The campaign is called *Hai Lao Taokap Chaeng*, meaning 'giving liquor as a gift is to put a curse on the receiver, resulting in their injury or death' (Charoensuthipan, 2017). A key success factor in social marketing is to have a proper understanding of the causality of the target audience's behaviour—that is, why they are behaving as they are now and what might cause them to adopt a different behaviour (Wymer, 2011). The Thai campaign works because it links the giving of alcohol as a gift with injury or death, but it also ties into Thai superstition that a violent death results in the creation of an angry ghost (Anon., 2015a).

Market Insight 17.4
Midwife or Marketer?

Smoking during pregnancy remains common in the UK. Despite the documented dangers, around 10 per cent of pregnant women smoke. Evidence from midwives suggests that this figure is understated, with actual rates in the population at 16 per cent. This is supported by studies showing that self-reporting by pregnant women is unreliable, often because women feel shame to admit they are still smoking.

Smoking in pregnancy is a significant health problem. It increases the risk of miscarriage, low birth weight, stillbirth, and antenatal depression. There is an association between pre-term birth weight and mortality rates in the first four weeks after birth, low birth weight and coronary heart disease in adulthood, as well as a risk of miscarriage and sudden infant death syndrome (SIDS). Smoking during pregnancy is the single most modifiable risk factor for adverse outcomes in pregnancy, contributing to 40 per cent of all infant deaths.

Organizations responsible for public health now embrace marketing to encourage healthy behaviours in pregnant women. A range of interventions offered to promote smoking cessation in pregnancy include community and

Market Insight 17.4
continued

individual-level programmes. Marketing designed to reduce a particular behaviour is known as demarketing. Nottinghamshire County Primary Care Trust (PCT) applied a number of social marketing techniques such as clearly defining the behaviour it sought to promote, conducting research to generate insight, applying behaviour change theory, and identifying the barriers to behavioural change. Using these techniques, the PCT recognized the need to carefully segment audiences to help it to achieve local smoking cessation targets. The PCT's Tobacco Control Team (TCT), responsible for promoting smoking cessation overall, decided that pregnant women represented a key segment because health interventions amongst pregnant women impact the health of their baby; women influence the smoking habits of their partners, parents, friends, and other relatives; and if the pregnant woman quits, the generational cycle of smoking may be broken. The TCT produced a series of DVDs based on the self-told stories of successful quitters—one of whom was a pregnant woman.

Midwives are at the front line of the PCT's efforts to reduce smoking in pregnancy. Although they face a considerable challenge from the marketing activities of tobacco manufacturers, they gain an advantage from being able to intervene at the individual level—a *segment of one* not always available to commercial marketers. This allows midwives to gain specific insight into the individual's life, motivations, fears, and resources, and the things they value. Often, this is at a level of insight that traditional research cannot produce. Using this insight, alongside the DVD success story, midwives delivered individual-level interventions in clinical and home settings across Nottinghamshire. These interventions proved to be highly cost-effective methods designed to encourage smoking cessation.

Note: The Nottinghamshire County PCT has now been replaced by six local clinical commissioning groups (CCGs).

Sources: Bauld (2008); ONS (2016); POST (2016); ASH (2017).

Theory into Practice

This market insight shows how public health organizations can use commercial marketing methods to design individual and insightful marketing messages for the social good. It demonstrates how using success stories to inform and influence behaviour such as smoking cessation in pregnant smokers is potentially a cost-effective way of communicating directly to specific social groups. A secondary insight from the case is that marketing tools can be applied in non-business

settings and that customer value can be understood in terms other than price (the value in this case being the health benefits that result in not smoking in the unborn child versus the cost of compliance with the message of not smoking, which might include addiction pangs, irritability etc.). The insight shows how social marketers can often work at the individual level to produce targeted interventions that, in aggregate, provide a wide benefit at the general level.

Related Topics
social marketing; segmentation; social groups; consumer behaviour; demarketing

1 What do you consider to be the main marketing challenges in reducing the smoking rate amongst pregnant women?

2 Can you think of any ethical problems in demarketing tobacco use among pregnant women?

3 Explain what you see as the main differences and similarities between social marketing and commercial marketing.

This market insight was kindly contributed by Dr Seamus Allison, Nottingham Business School, and Claire Allison, Sherwood Forest Hospitals NHS Foundation Trust.

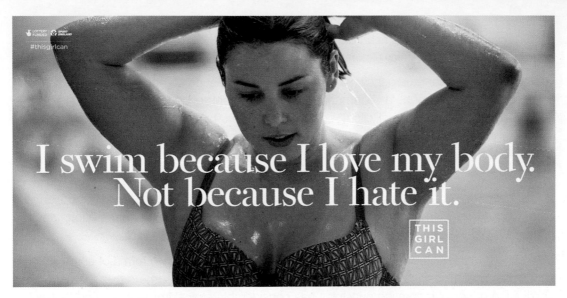

Sport England's 'This Girl Can' campaign, designed to improve women's self-motivation
Source: Courtesy of Sport England.

Social marketing can also be used to promote healthy behaviours. For example, Sport England's award-winning 'This Girl Can' campaign was designed to improve the participation of women in sport and exercise activities. The Brazilian Ministry of Health ran a campaign hijacking Tinder and Hornet (two dating apps) to promote a safer sex message by creating a series of fake profiles of people stating a lack of interest in using condoms. Those who swiped right on these profiles were shown a strong warning of the danger of unprotected sex (Toor, 2015).

The idea that marketing techniques could be used in this way was first discussed by Kotler and Zaltman (1971). One example was when the Crown Prince of Thailand, wearing a 'Bike for Mom' T-shirt and in a bid to rehabilitate his image, led thousands of cyclists through the streets of Bangkok to celebrate his mother Queen Sirikit's birthday (Associated Press in Bangkok, 2015).

There is debate over the extent to which advertising, for example, can really change people's views and behaviour on social issues. There is also debate over whether or not advertising should be used by the public sector at all in certain circumstances. An ineffective—and certainly inappropriate—example of public-sector advertising was when road signs were installed in Treviso, Italy, in 2010, bearing the words *attenzione prostitute* ('Beware, prostitutes!'), warning motorists and pedestrians of the presence of sex workers, but without making the purpose of the warning clear (Anon., 2015b).

Nevertheless, most social marketing campaigns are clear-cut—designed to advance social causes to the benefit of a particular audience by changing social attitudes and behaviours. Social marketing campaigns are typically, but not exclusively, run by public-sector organizations, including examples such as the following:

- Government health departments commonly encourage healthy eating (for example the Danish six-a-day campaign to encourage people to eat more fruit and vegetables), exercising, stopping smoking and other addictive behaviours, or road safety.

- British Heart Foundation (BHF) ran the 'Rock up in Red' campaign to raise money to support research into beating heart disease—a campaign previously backed by model and actor Rosie Huntington-Whiteley (Anon., 2013a).

- The police or other emergency services use social marketing campaigns to reduce undesirable behaviour, either as an alternative or a complement to law enforcement. For example, the City of London Police, Police Scotland, and others have used handbills and posters to inform the general public about their 'Project Servator' crime-reduction security operations (see Case Insight 17.1), and social marketing communications including cinema advertising were used as part of the Wales Arson Reduction Strategy (JAG, 2011).

Visit the **online resources** and follow the web link to the Healthcare Communication and Marketing Association, Inc. (HCMA), to learn more about marketing communications and the healthcare profession.

Marketing has the potential to improve mass public communication in terms of ensuring message receipt and positive processing of the message. However, some argue that wholesale application of social marketing principles has considerable ethical implications and that public oversight bodies should regulate social marketing techniques (Laczniak, Lusch, and Murphy, 1979). In the People's Republic of China (PRC), film companies have been praised by state media for launching a new era of 'main melody' **propaganda** films, promoting the Communist Party line and building youthful patriotism. One example is *Wolf Warrior 2*, about a Chinese soldier in Africa who saves locals and his compatriots from American mercenaries, which grossed ¥5.7 billion (£650 million) in 2015 (Anon., 2017).

One question arising is this: when might social marketing be propagandist? Some argue that social marketing and social propaganda are distinctly different, but related, fields (O'Shaughnessy, 1996). A useful distinction is that while social marketing is based on audience wants, identified through audience research, propaganda is a one-way evangelizing communication (that is, the propagandist is convinced of the message's own rightness; seeks to convince the target, often coercively; and uses research only as a means of increasing the propaganda's effectiveness). Propaganda typically uses language aimed at either uniting or instilling grievances in minority groups.

The idea that marketing can be used to counter negative social ideas, or grievances, has a long pedigree. In 1942—that is, during the Second World War—Edward Bernays, grandfather of the PR industry and nephew of Austrian psychoanalyst Sigmund Freud, wrote a far-sighted article on how the United States should use marketing and PR techniques to help people to 'see' the true alternative between democracy and fascism, and democracy and Nazism. In the present day, governments around the world are increasingly seeking to develop public communications programmes to counter the narrative of terror groups such as so-called Islamic State (also known as ISIS or Daesh) and Al-Qaeda. These include campaigns to urge law-abiding citizens to report suspicious activity (such as that organized by the City of London Police, outlined in Case Insight 17.1) and the 'If you see something, say something'™ campaign launched by the US Department of Homeland Security in 2010. Others have launched social marketing counter-terrorism campaigns independently of government, such as that produced by a former Islamist extremist who created the Abdullah-X cartoon aiming to stop British Muslims from leaving the UK to join Daesh in Syria (Simpson, 2014). (See Research Insight 17.3 for a useful article on how to design behavioural intervention campaigns.)

Visit the **online resources** and follow the web link to the US Department of Homeland Security's website to learn more about how it uses marketing communications to counter terrorism.

Research Insight 17.3

To take your learning further, you might wish to read this influential paper:

Michie, S., van Stralen, M.M., and West, R. (2011). The behaviour change wheel: a new method for characterizing and designing behaviour change interventions. *Implementation Science*, 6(1), 42–53.

In this highly readable article, the authors undertake a systematic literature review to identify frameworks for behaviour change interventions. They synthesize a new framework, based on 19 identified extant behaviour change intervention frameworks, which they call the COM-B system. The COM-B system explains how behavioural change should be analysed from the perspective of the *capabilities*, *opportunities*, and *motivations* that target audiences have to change their *behaviour*. The analysis then leads to nine intervention functions—that is, education, persuasion, incentivization, coercion, training, enablement, modelling, environmental restructuring, and restrictions.

 Visit the online resources to read the abstract and access the full paper.

Political Parties and Campaigning Organizations

The use of marketing by political parties and third-party interest groups has increased since the development of television and mass-media broadcasting worldwide around the 1950s. Scientific methods of assessing market and public opinion have transformed how political campaigns are run. Charities and other campaigning organizations use marketing techniques to influence legislation and public opinion by means of lobbying techniques. With the development of globalized industries, the interplay between marketing and politics has increased further, and so companies use marketing methods associated with political campaigning to influence legislators and regulators (for example in the European Parliament, on Capitol Hill in Washington, DC, and at World Trade talks). Regulators seek to influence legislation associated with these markets.

Political parties use marketing to exchange political influence (for example legislative change or amendment) for political support (for example votes, petitions, donations, volunteering). Political marketing can be seen as a marketing–propaganda hybrid—that is, as mixing marketing and propaganda. This is particularly the case, but not exclusively so, in the United States, where **negative campaigning** is rife (O'Shaughnessy, 1990), 30-second and 15-second advertising spots commonly being used to launch malicious attacks on political opponents. One example of a negative campaign was that aimed at Mitt Romney by Barack Obama in the 2012 US presidential campaign, which leveraged undercover video to position Romney as an uncaring elitist on the basis that, in a closed session with his supporters, he had described the 47 per cent intending to vote for Obama as 'victims' looking for handouts (Joyella, 2016).

In representative democracies, political parties use marketing to provide citizens and voters with information on current plans for running the country (that is, their manifestos). In the process, parties seek to improve social cohesion, democratic participation, and citizen belongingness. The recent use of political marketing in post-war democracies worldwide appears to have co-occurred with a decline in political participation. Whether or not the two effects are related is difficult to determine. Citizens do seem to be increasingly disengaged from political parties. Some argue that marketing in politics has been overused, thereby damaging public trust; however, the truth is more likely that marketing techniques can be used to promote a poor party or candidate just as they can be used to market an excellent party or candidate. In politics, it is difficult to determine between the two until the party enters power. The disaffection and disappointment that citizens and voters then feel can fuel later disengagement. In that sense, politics is a **credence service** (see Chapter 15). In many countries around the world, there are different legal requirements for political advertising compared with commercial advertising. In the UK, political advertising regulations allow the comparison of political parties and adverts as long as they are 'decent' and in 'good taste'. In 2001, the BBC refused to air a party-political broadcast by the Pro-Life Alliance Party because it contained graphic footage of an abortion (House of Lords, 2003). It is more difficult to determine that a political advert must be truthful, however, because politics is often a matter of opinion and judgement. In contrast, advertising claims for commercial products must always adhere to the guidelines on taste, decency, and truthfulness. (For more on the ethics of political advertising, see Chapter 18.)

Most political marketing campaigns (corporate or party political) have historically been undertaken by specialized marketing and PR agencies on an ad hoc basis, although political parties and multinational corporations are increasingly conducting their political marketing activity in-house. In the United States, political consultants are more specialized, undertaking work in such areas as polling, petition management, fundraising, strategy, media buying, advertising, public affairs, **grass-roots lobbying**, law, donor list maintenance, online campaigning, and campaign software consulting. The Internet and social media have become important areas for generating campaign finance and grass-roots support. Social media have become the battleground of political campaigning efforts in elections around the world.

As with the use of marketing for social campaigning, its input into politics is cause for concern in many who think that politics should not adopt such techniques. Marketing has played a strong role in revolutions against Soviet-allied governments in Serbia, Georgia, and the Ukraine, where American political consultants advised opposition parties that deployed 'revolutionary symbols and slogans' to encourage activists to take to the streets (Sussman and Krader, 2008). Facebook was used to generate support for the 'We are all Khaled Said' campaign, helping to bring down the Egyptian government in 2011 (Ghonim, 2012). Twitter played a role in generating public support in various revolutions, including in Moldova in 2009 during civil unrest around the election result in which the Communist Party of Moldova (PCRM) allegedly fixed its majority (Mungiu-Pippidi and Munteanu, 2009), and in Iran during student protests in 2009–10, also over disputed election results (Grossman, 2009). Russia is alleged to have sought to influence the US presidential election campaign of 2016, spending around US$100,000 on adverts from false sources on Facebook and Twitter (Solon, 2017). Given marketing's ability to influence the general public, the question arises: what is and what is not a legitimate use of marketing in the political sphere?

Under certain circumstances, it is possible to influence the political environment, and therefore the political agenda (see Chapter 4), in favour of an organization's strategy. Charities and not-for-profit organizations frequently focus on campaigning to change legislation or government policy agendas (a process known as lobbying or public affairs). The organization Purpose.com in the United States has had considerable success working with companies such as Google and Audi, and organizations such as the Bill & Melinda Gates Foundation, aiming to build mass movements online to support particular causes. For example, when Audi entered the Indian car market, part of its entry strategy involved designing and promoting clean water machines (Anon., 2013b).

Lobbying or public affairs campaigns often use stunts to obtain media publicity to influence public opinion and, in turn, influence parliamentary opinion in the countries concerned. For example, PETA campaigns for animal rights globally. It organized a protest with AnimaNaturalis during the 'Running of the Bulls' event in Pamplona, Spain, recruiting activists to pose topless with signs such as 'Stop bullfights!' and circulating a petition demanding that the Spanish prime minister outlaw animal cruelty during such events (PETA, 2017). Publicity is important in pressure group campaigning. Typically, pressure groups try to advance policy change despite government opposition; on other occasions, they try to change social behaviour more generally. In Cairo, for example, the Imprint Movement took out ads in a bid to stop the harassment of women on the Metro (Anon., 2015c) (see also Market Insight 17.5). The publicity serves to highlight the cause and to bring supporters from the general public, who can then volunteer their time or support, or provide donations in the same way as they would with a charity.

Market Insight 17.5
No Means No! Get It!

In recent years, Sweden has emerged as the poster child for progressive values on issues as diverse as social welfare, gender equality, and the environment. Indeed, such values are at the heart of its national identity, which influences not only domestic policy, but also a highly effective form of public diplomacy. After a century of social democracy, there is widespread adherence to the principle of collective action and high levels of public trust in the institutions of government, which have allowed consecutive administrations to pursue social agendas for a longer term than might otherwise have been the case. And, in those instances in which legal compliance might be seen as too 'heavy-handed', Sweden has also allowed state-sponsored social marketing campaigns to successfully steer voluntary behavioural change in areas such as alcohol consumption, smoking, clean energy, and sexual attitudes.

But social marketing is not solely the preserve of governments; there are a multitude of not-for-profit organizations seeking to influence societal and/ or subgroup behaviour, and these are increasingly turning to commercial marketing approaches for inspiration. One such organization, FATTA, an advocacy group formed to tackle the issue of sexual violence and to demand an amendment to Swedish rape legislation, has—through an approach based on brand co-creation—cultivated a powerful, and growing,

political consumer tribe. Formed by two feminist artists and culture and music groups—Crossing Borders and Femtastic—FATTA initially mobilized support from existing memberships. However, the objective from the outset was to reach beyond the traditional audience for such messages (as well as beyond the highbrow debate columns of national newspapers) and, utilizing hip-hop music, street art, and culture, to directly engage a powerful youth audience across the country.

FATTA's aim to force legislative change for a consent law presents numerous difficulties for policymakers, but should be viewed against a backdrop of powerful social attitudes towards sexual violence specifically, and gender equality more generally, in Sweden. In the period following its launch, FATTA built on its physical community engagement activities with a significant social media presence. Membership numbers grew rapidly and traditional media outlets began to show interest in the organization. Importantly, from the group's perspective, rape cases began to receive more media attention at this time and created many opportunities for discussing the case for a consent law. This, in turn, placed a burden on the target stakeholder group, policymakers, who were quickly pushed into a defensive position on the issue. FATTA stepped up its efforts to engage more men in the movement with the FATTA MAN launch.

Sources: Anon. (2018); https://www.fatta.nu

Market Insight 17.5

continued

Theory into Practice

This market insight describes how a pressure group, FATTA, used social marketing techniques to successfully press the case for, and achieve, a change in Sweden's rape law in 2018 to require consent between adults indulging in sexual relations. The insight shows how FATTA used marketing techniques to develop a social movement to press for legislative change, effectively developing a grass-roots lobbying strategy.

Related Topics

social media marketing; stakeholder analysis; grass-roots lobbying; public affairs

1 Do you think social marketing techniques should be used to change rape legislation? Why, or why not?

2 Given the strength of feeling around this issue, does it matter how FATTA uses marketing techniques to promote its cause?

3 Should any and all pressure groups be allowed to use social marketing techniques to effect behaviour change? What topics might be 'out of bounds'?

This market insight was kindly contributed by Dr Ian Richardson, Stockholm University, with support from Maja Magnusson, Cecilia Granström, and Hanna Kretz.

Chapter Summary

To consolidate your learning, the key points from this chapter are summarized here:

■ **List some of the key characteristics of not-for-profit organizations.**

Not-for-profit organizations are differentiated from their commercial counterparts in numerous ways. Not-for-profit organizations tend to have multiple stakeholders and, because there are no shareholders, any profit earned is reinvested in the organization. Because not-for-profit organizations do not distribute funds to shareholders and are social enterprises, public-sector organizations, or charities, there is a need for transparency in determining how these organizations operate, because they are claiming to act for the common good. Accordingly, they have multiple objectives, rather than a simple profit motivation. Historically, not-for-profit organizations have not been strongly market-oriented, but this is changing as they become more experienced in marketing. Customers' perceptions of not-for-profit organizations differ from those of their commercial counterparts because the not-for-profit typically has a unique mission and set of values, as well as a non-financial organizational purpose.

■ **Explain why not-for-profit organizations do not always value their customers.**

Not-for-profit organizations frequently do not value their beneficiary customers because they exist in a monopolistic situation, because demand far outstrips supply, because a lack of market segmentation activity exists, and because research into customer needs is not seen as a priority for expenditure and investment. Not-for-profit organizations frequently also undervalue supporter customers because, typically, they approach them to solicit funds too often and do not sufficiently appreciate customers when they do donate. Moreover, volunteer service workers who generously give their time can often feel undervalued. Because not-for-profit organizations have multiple stakeholders, problems can arise between these groups that need resolution, but which can often lead to customers feeling undervalued as those tensions are resolved.

■ **Analyse stakeholders and develop appropriate engagement strategies.**

A common way of analysing stakeholders is by mapping them on a power–interest matrix to identify four types based on the level of interest they display in an organization and the level of power they exert. Those with high levels of interest and power (group A) are key stakeholders in need of continuous engagement. Those with high interest, but low levels of power (group B), should be informed about the organization's activities to maintain their interest. Group C represents those organizations with high power, but low interest. Here, it is important either to increase information flow to these organizations to increase their interest, so that they can exert their power in the not-for-profit's favour, or alternatively to keep them satisfied if they intend to exert their power against the not-for-profit. Finally, an organization's relationships with those stakeholders who have little power or interest (Group D) should either be disregarded or revived.

■ **Describe and assess cause marketing campaigns.**

A cause marketing campaign occurs when companies and non-profit organizations form marketing alliances. Often, these marketing campaigns are focused on sales promotions developed for mutual benefit whereby the purchase of a commercial offering is linked to donations to a charitable third-party organization. Such campaigns tend to work best where there is a strong strategic fit between the commercial organization and the not-for-profit organization, particularly in relation to the audiences targeted and when the campaign runs over the longer term.

■ **Understand how marketing is used in social and political marketing campaigns.**

Over nearly 50 years, we have embraced the use of marketing for social and political causes. Marketing is commonly used in government social marketing campaigns to drive positive behavioural change and to improve citizens' well-being around such causes as encouraging populations to eat healthily, not to use drugs or smoke, and not to drink and drive, for example. However, we might question whether or not government should have this role and the ethics of using marketing in social and political campaigning. The use of marketing techniques in election campaigns has a long pedigree and is now common in most countries (democratic or otherwise) worldwide. In this scenario, marketing is used to understand the electorate's wants or needs and to provide them with a set of party policies and leaders that suit those needs. In addition to the use of marketing by government to influence society, and by political parties to gain support and votes, marketing is used by third-party organizations (for example pressure groups) to drive legislative change in lobbying campaigns—particularly by courting publicity and the media's support more generally.

 Review Questions

1 What key differences exist in marketing communications for not-for-profit versus for-profit organizations?

2 How do not-for-profit organizations differ from commercial organizations in marketing terms?

3 Why do not-for-profit organizations not always value their beneficiaries?

4 Why do not-for-profit organizations not always value their donors?

5 What axes are used on a stakeholder analysis matrix?

6 How is marketing used to raise funds for charitable organizations?

7 What is cause marketing?

8 How do we assess cause marketing programmes?

9 What is social marketing and what is its purpose?

10 How do public-sector organizations use social marketing techniques?

 Discussion Questions

1 Having read Case Insight 17.1 on the City of London Police, how would you use marketing and PR techniques for the following purposes?

A To deter terrorists and criminals more generally

B To encourage the general public to report suspicious activity and unattended items, and to remain vigilant at all times

2 Working in small groups, select three different not-for-profit organizations and consider the following:

A How do their 'propositions' differ from each other?

B What is the nature of 'place' (from the 4Ps) for each organization?

C What is the nature of customer involvement for each proposition?

D How can the audiences for these not-for-profit offerings be segmented, if at all?

3 Use Google Search to identify how social marketing campaigns are run in your own country, if at all, in the following areas:

A The police service

B Health promotion campaigns, such as reducing smoking and alcohol consumption and increasing vegetable consumption

C Road safety awareness

 Visit the online resources and complete the Multiple-Choice Questions to assess your knowledge of Chapter 17.

 Glossary

cause marketing a campaign in which a company is linked to a charity or social cause with the express intention of building its own customer goodwill, providing the charity with an increase in resource and the company with either a concomitant increase in sales of its product/ service or a reputational dividend.

credence service a service delivered by professionals that is difficult to evaluate beforehand because of its technical nature.

demarketing the use of marketing techniques to discourage, as opposed to encourage, demand for a particular proposition.

grass-roots lobbying the targeting of the general public using marketing communications techniques to persuade them to support the case for legislative or regulatory change, often by asking those members of the public to contact their MPs or other political actors directly to press the case.

lobbying the process employed by companies, charities, and third-party interest groups to develop and build relationships with regulatory and political bodies to influence legislation in their favour or to advance a particular cause.

negative campaigning campaigning in which marketing communications techniques are used to present opposing candidates or parties in a bad light so as to win electoral advantage.

propaganda a technique used by a communicating party expressing opinions or activities to influence the opinions or activities of a receiving party and to direct them towards a predetermined agenda drawn up by the communicating party, often using psychological and symbolic manipulations.

social enterprise a business whose primary objectives are essentially social and whose surpluses are reinvested for that purpose in the business or in the community, rather than dispersed to the owners.

stakeholders people with an interest (a 'stake') in the levels of profit an organization achieves, its environmental impact, and its ethical conduct in society.

telethon a portmanteau word combining 'television' and 'marathon' to refer to a long television event, usually held for purposes of fundraising.

 # References

AMA (American Marketing Association) (2018). Cause marketing. Retrieve from: https://www.ama.org/resources/Pages/Dictionary.aspx?dLetter=C (accessed 13 October 2018).

Anon. (2013a). Rosie Huntington-Whiteley backs British heart charity's campaign. *Express*, 11 January. Retrieve from: https://www.express.co.uk/celebrity-news/370187/Rosie-Huntington-Whiteley-backs-British-heart-charity-s-campaign (accessed 13 October 2018).

Anon. (2013b). The business of campaigning: profit with purpose. *The Economist*, 26 January, 60.

Anon. (2015a). Thailand: a culture rooted in superstition, black magic and ghosts. *Malay Mail Online*, 2 February. Retrieve from: http://www.themalaymailonline.com/features/article/thailand-a-culture-rooted-in-superstition-black-magic-and-ghosts#Wo63UtWVxs8zDY57.97 (accessed 13 October 2018).

Anon. (2015b). Prostitute sign confuses motorists. *The Telegraph*, 2 April. Retrieve from: https://www.telegraph.co.uk/news/newstopics/howaboutthat/7547224/Prostitutes-sign-confuses-motorists.html (accessed 13 October 2018).

Anon. (2015c). Sexual harassment in Egypt: slapping back. *The Economist*, 21 November, 57.

Anon. (2017). Happy bunny: how the private sector is helping China to modernise propaganda. *The Economist*, 2 December, 56.

Anon. (2018). Sweden approves new law recognising sex without consent as rape. *BBC News*, 24 May. Retrieve from: https://www.bbc.co.uk/news/world-europe-44230786 (accessed 13 October 2018).

ASH (Action on Smoking and Health) (2017). Smoking in Pregnancy Challenge Group media release: smoking during pregnancy rates. Press release, 15 June. Retrieve from: http://ash.org.uk/media-and-news/press-releases-media-and-news/smoking-in-pregnancy-challenge-group-media-release-smoking-during-pregnancy-rates/ (accessed 13 October 2018).

Associated Press in Bangkok (2015). Thailand celebrates queen's birthday with bicycle ride. *The Guardian*, 16 August. Retrieve from: https://www.theguardian.com/world/2015/aug/16/thailand-queens-birthday-bike-for-mom-bangkok-queen-sirikit (accessed 13 October 2018).

Bauld, L. (2008). Reaching smokers: how can we encourage more people to use effective treatment? *Addiction*, 103(6), 1007–8.

Bernays. E. (1942). The marketing of national policies: a study of war propaganda. *Journal of Marketing*, 6(3), 236–45.

BIS (Department for Business, Innovation and Skills) (2011). *A Guide to Legal Forms for Social Enterprise*, November. Retrieve from: https://assets.publishing.service.gov.uk/government/uploads/system/uploads/attachment_data/file/31677/11-1400-guide-legal-forms-for-social-enterprise.pdf (accessed 13 October 2018).

Bishop, S., Pursnani, P., and Sumpter, C. (2013). *Social Marketing in India*. Retrieve from: https://www.shellfoundation.org/ShellFoundation.org_new/media/Shell-Foundation-Reports/shell_founation_social_marketing_in_india.pdf (accessed 13 October 2018).

Brandom, R. (2015). Mark Zuckerberg and Priscilla Chan to donate 99 percent of their Facebook fortune.

The Verge, 1 December. Retrieve from: https://www.theverge.com/2015/12/1/9831554/mark-zuckerberg-charity-45-billion (accessed 13 October 2018).

Bruce, I. (1995). Do not-for-profits value their customers and their needs? *International Marketing Review*, 12(4), 77–84.

Chad, P., Motion, J., and Kyriazis, E. (2013). A Praxis framework for implementing market orientation into charities. *Journal of Nonprofit and Public Sector Marketing*, 25(1), 28–55.

Charoensuthipan, P. (2017). Anti-alcohol drive 'a success'. *Bangkok Post*, 28 December, 4.

Comic Relief (n.d.). The history of Comic Relief. Retrieve from: https://www.comicrelief.com/about-comic-relief/history (accessed 13 October 2018).

Duncan, A. (2014). Still wondering who kick-started the #nomakeupselfie craze? Creator revealed to be teenage mum from Stoke-on-Trent. *Metro*, 25 March. Retrieve from: https://metro.co.uk/2014/03/25/still-wondering-who-kick-started-the-nomakeupselfie-craze-creator-revealed-to-be-a-teenage-mum-from-stoke-on-trent-4678163/ (accessed 13 October 2018).

Eccles, A. (2014). How Cancer Research UK raised £8m from a campaign they didn't start. *CharityComms*, 26 March. Retrieve from: https://www.charitycomms.org.uk/articles/how-cancer-research-uk-raised-8m-from-a-campaign-they-didn-t-start (accessed 13 October 2018).

Farey-Jones, D. (2015). Comic Relief 2015: how brands are supporting the cause. *Campaign*, 4 February. Retrieve from: https://www.campaignlive.co.uk/article/comic-relief-2015-brands-supporting-cause/1332261 (accessed 13 October 2018).

Gallopel-Morvan, K., Gabriel, P., Le Gall-Elly, M., Rieunier, S., and Urien, B. (2009). The use of visual warnings in social marketing: the case of tobacco. *Journal of Business Research*, 64(1), 7–11.

Ghonim, W. (2012). *Revolution 2.0*. London: Fourth Estate.

Gifford, G. (1999). Cause-related marketing: ten rules to protect your non-profit assets. *Nonprofit World*, 17(4), 11–13.

Glas Cymru (2016). Glas Cymru celebrates 15th anniversary. Press release, 11 May. Retrieve from: https://www.dwrcymru.com/en/Media-Centre/News-Summary/2016/05/Glas-Cymru-celebrates-15th-anniversary.aspx (accessed 13 October 2018).

Gray, R. (2003). Corporate social responsibility: partnerships fuel Comic Relief 2003. *Campaign*, 13 March. Retrieve from: https://www.campaignlive.co.uk/article/corporate-social-responsibility-partnerships-fuel-comic-relief-2003/173907 (accessed 13 October 2018).

Grossman, L. (2009). Iran protests: Twitter, the medium of the movement. *Time Magazine*, 17 June. Retrieve from: http://content.time.com/time/world/article/0,8599,1905125,00.html (accessed 13 October 2018).

Hatten, M.L. (1982). Strategic management in not-for-profit organisations. *Strategic Management Journal*, 3, 89–104.

Heavenly (2016). Heavenly launches Welsh Water's first ever brand campaign. Press release, 12 July. Retrieve from: https://heavenly.co.uk/brand-agency-news/welsh-water-launches-first-ever-brand-campaign/ (accessed 13 October 2018).

House of Lords (2003). Judgments: *Regina v. British Broadcasting Corporation (Appellants) ex parte Pro-Life Alliance (Respondents)*. Retrieve from: https://www.publications.parliament.uk/pa/ld200203/ldjudgmt/jd030515/bbc-3.htm (accessed 13 October 2018).

JAG (Joint Arson Group) (2011). *Wales Arson Reduction Strategy: A Review by the Joint Arson Group*, November. Retrieve from: http://www.nwales-fireservice.org.uk/media/64363/wars_review_final_nov_2011.pdf (accessed 13 October 2018).

Jones, N., Baines, P., and Welsh, S. (2014). Counter-marketing in a wicked problem context: the case of cocaine. In: N. Bradley and J. Blythe (eds), *Demarketing*, Abingdon: Routledge, 44–66.

Joyella, M. (2016). 10 iconic presidential campaign ads that changed political advertising. *Adweek*, 31 July. Retrieve from: https://www.adweek.com/tv-video/10-iconic-presidential-campaign-ads-changed-political-advertising-172600/ (accessed 13 October 2018).

Kellogg's (2018). Open for breakfast! Retrieve from: https://www.openforbreakfast.com/en_US/content/giving-back/breakfast-better-days.html (accessed 13 October 2018).

Kotler, P. (2000). Future markets. *Executive Excellence*, 17(2), 6.

Kotler, P., and Levy, S.J. (1969). Broadening the concept of marketing. *Journal of Marketing*, 33(1), 10–15.

Kotler, P., and Zaltman, G. (1971). Social marketing: an approach to planned social change. *Journal of Marketing*, 35(3), 3–12.

Laczniak, G.R., Lusch, R.F., and Murphy, P.E. (1979). Social marketing: its ethical dimensions. *Journal of Marketing*, 43(2), 29–36.

LeFebvre, R.C. (2011). An integrative model for social marketing. *Journal of Social Marketing*, 1(1), 54–72.

Michie, S., van Stralen, M.M., and West, R. (2011). The behaviour change wheel: a new method for characterizing and designing behaviour change interventions. *Implementation Science*, 6(1), 42–53.

Mungiu-Pippidi, A., and Munteanu, I. (2009). Moldova's 'Twitter Revolution'. *Journal of Democracy*, 20(3), 136–42.

Newing, R. (2016). Case study: Welsh Water. *Financial Times*, 8 November. Retrieve from: https://www.ft.com/content/837994d6-6f28-11db-ab7b-0000779e2340 (accessed 13 October 2018).

O'Shaughnessy, N. (1990). *The Phenomenon of Political Marketing*. London: Macmillan.

O'Shaughnessy, N. (1996). Social propaganda and social marketing: a critical difference? *European Journal of Marketing*, 30(10–11), 62–75.

ONS (Office for National Statistics) (2017). Adult smoking habits in Great Britain. Dataset release, 3 July. Retrieve from: https://www.ons.gov.uk/peoplepopulationandcommunity/healthandsocialcare/drugusealcoholandsmoking/datasets/adultsmokinghabitsingreatbritain (accessed 13 October 2018).

PETA (People for the Ethical Treatment of Animals) (2017). PETA activists fill sky with 'blood' to protest torture of bulls in Pamplona. *PetaUK Blog*, 5 July. Retrieve from: https://www.peta.org.uk/blog/peta-activists-fill-sky-blood-protest-torture-bulls-pamplona/ (accessed 13 October 2018).

Porter, M.E., and Kramer, M.R. (2002). The competitive advantage of corporate philanthropy. *Harvard Business Review*, 80(12), 56–68.

POST (Parliamentary Office of Science and Technology) (2016). Infant mortality and stillbirth in the UK. *PostNote*, May. Retrieve from: https://researchbriefings.parliament.uk/ResearchBriefing/Summary/POST-PN-0527#fullreport (accessed 13 October 2018).

Randle, M., Miller, L., Stirling, J., and Dolnicar, S. (2016). Framing advertisements to elicit positive emotions and attract foster carers. *Journal of Advertising Research*, 56(4), 456–69.

Roderick, L. (2017). What brands are doing for Comic Relief's Red Nose Day. *Marketing Week*, 24 March. Retrieve from: https://www.marketingweek.com/2017/03/24/comic-relief-red-nose-day/ (accessed 13 October 2018).

Rothschild, M.L. (1979). Marketing communications in non-business situations or why it's so hard to sell brotherhood like soap. *Journal of Marketing*, 43(2), 11–20.

Scholes, K. (2001). Stakeholder mapping: a practical tool for public sector managers. In: G. Johnson and K. Scholes (eds), *Exploring Public Sector Strategy*, London: FT/Prentice Hall, 165–84.

Seymour, T., Gilbert, D., and Kolsaker, A. (2006). Aspects of market orientation of English and Welsh charities. *Journal of Nonprofit and Public Sector Marketing*, 16(1–2), 151–69.

Simpson, J. (2014). Abdullah-X: the new cartoon made by former extremist aimed at stopping Britain's young Muslims from leaving for Syria. *The Independent*, 14 July. Retrieve from: https://www.independent.co.uk/news/uk/home-news/abdullah-x-the-new-cartoon-made-by-former-extremist-aimed-at-stopping-britain-s-young-muslims-from-9604967.html (accessed 13 October 2018).

Solon, O. (2017). Facebook says likely Russia-based group paid for political ads during US election. *The Guardian*, 7 September. Retrieve from: https://www.theguardian.com/technology/2017/sep/06/facebook-political-ads-russia-us-election-trump-clinton (accessed 13 October 2018).

Stead, M., Gordon, R., Angus, K., and McDermott, L. (2007). A systematic review of social marketing effectiveness. *Health Education*, 107(2), 126–91.

Steckstor, D. (2012). *The Effects of Cause-Related Marketing on Customers' Attitudes and Buying Behavior*. New York: Gabler Verlag.

Stewart, T. (2017). Welsh Water introduces 'world first' bilingual chatbot. *Mobile Marketing*, 24 August. Retrieve from: https://mobilemarketingmagazine.com/welsh-water-bilingual-chatbot-facebook-messenger (accessed 13 October 2018).

Sussman, G., and Krader, S. (2008). Template revolutions: marketing US regime change in Eastern Europe. *Westminster Papers in Communication and Culture*, 5(3), 91–112.

Till, B.D., and Nowak, L.I. (2000). Toward effective use of cause-related marketing alliances. *Journal of Product and Brand Management*, 9(7), 472–84.

Toor, A. (2015). Swipe right on these fake Tinder profiles for a warning about AIDS. *The Verge*, 11 February. Retrieve from: https://www.theverge.com/2015/2/11/8017933/fake-tinder-profiles-aids-awareness-campaign-brazil (accessed 13 October 2018).

Walgreens (2017). Walgreens inspires 'noses on' across America to support third annual Red Nose Day in the US. Press release, 17 April. Retrieve from: https://news.walgreens.com/press-releases/general-news/noses-on-walgreens-welcomes-red-nose-day-back-to-america-as-the-exclusive-retailer-of-the-new-sparkle-red-nose.htm (accessed 13 October 2018).

Weaver, M. (2015). Watchdog to investigate charities' 'boiler room' tactics. *The Guardian*, 7 July. Retrieve from: https://www.theguardian.com/money/2015/jul/07/watchdog-investigate-charities-boiler-room-tactics-pressuring-vulnerable-people (accessed 13 October 2018).

Weinger, A. (2015). 5 companies doing corporate philanthropy right. *Triplepundit*, 9 March. Retrieve from: https://www.triplepundit.com/2015/03/5-companies-corporate-philanthropy-right/ (accessed 13 October 2018).

Wright, G., Chew, C., and Hines, A. (2012). The relevance and efficacy of marketing in public and non-profit service management. *Public Management Review*, 14(4), 433–50.

Wymer, W. (2011). Developing more effective social marketing strategies. *Journal of Social Marketing*, 1(1), 17–31.

Yorkshire Water (2017). Yorkshire Water scoops national CSR award. Press release, 26 May. Retrieve from: https://www.yorkshirewater.com/about-us/newsroom-media/business-charity-award-2017 (accessed 13 October 2018).

Chapter 18
Marketing, Society, Sustainability, and Ethics

Learning Outcomes

After reading this chapter, you will be able to:

▶ Assess the negative impact that marketing has on society

▶ Define sustainable marketing and its implications for marketing practice

▶ Define stakeholder marketing and its role in corporate social responsibility initiatives

▶ Define marketing ethics

▶ Explain the common ethical norms applied in marketing

▶ Describe the role of ethics in marketing decision-making

▶ Understand how ethical breaches occur in marketing mix programmes

Case Insight 18.1
One Bag Habit

Market Insight 18.1
Collaborative Consumption Surely Glitters . . . But Is It Gold?

Market Insight 18.2
Surviving a Food Scandal

Market Insight 18.3
Volkswagen: Up in Smoke?

Market Insight 18.4
Forex Fixing

Market Insight 18.5
Drug Money in China

Case Insight 18.1
One Bag Habit

Many sustainability initiatives require new thinking and new partners. Sometimes, they require a collaboration with your competitors. We talk to Anna-Karin Dahlberg, corporate sustainability manager, Lindex; Felicia Reuterswürd, sustainability manager, H&M Sweden; and Fredrika Klarén, sustainability manager, KappAhl, to understand the challenges involved in working on initiatives targeted at stimulating more sustainable consumption behaviours together with your closest competitors.

Responsible consumption and production have been identified as one of the United Nations' Sustainable Development Goals (SDGs) under Agenda 2030. Another goal focuses on the importance of partnerships in achieving sustainability goals. An example of one such partnership is the One Bag Habit initiative, which brings together Swedish mass fashion retailers H&M, KappAhl, and Lindex, and aims to change shopper behaviours related to shopping bag usage. The initiative had two main goals: to reduce the number of bags used by customers; and to spread awareness about the environmental effects of bags.

'In fashion retailing,' we have often worked together on sustainability initiatives related to manufacturing and supply chain,' says Anna-Karin Dahlberg of Lindex, 'but joining forces at the point of purchase in our stores is something different. And it is an important step to take. Engaging consumers around sustainability is typically quite difficult, but crucial if we are to change the industry to become more sustainable.'

'When we decided to come together in this initiative, plastic bags had been on the sustainability agenda for quite some time,' says Fredrika Klarén of KappAhl, 'but neither regulators nor the actors in the retail industry seemed to be able to move forward. In December 2016, we decided to come together to change our customers' behaviours in relation to all bags regardless of material.'

'We realized that, to achieve real change, we needed to act jointly', explains Felicia Reuterswürd of H&M. 'If one of us changed it would not be enough. To change consumer behaviours at the core, efforts by one retailer will not suffice.'

The initiative was launched on 1 June 2017. In a joint statement, the three retailers said of the initiative:

Our vision is that the One Bag Habit should contribute to a more rapid development of sustainable consumption in terms of bags. We want to spread awareness of the negative environmental impact of bags and urge other retailers to join the initiative.

The initiative is based on an agreement that customers should always pay for shopping bags and that the revenues gained by selling bags should be donated to causes promoting sustainable development. So far, the initiative has been a success. In its first year, 17 Swedish retailers joined, leading to a major impact on the market as a whole. For H&M, the use of plastic bags in Swedish stores was down 51 per cent in the first six months of the initiative. Similarly, approximately 70 per cent of KappAhl's customers chose not to use a bag for their shopping. One Bag Habit has also spread to other markets, because KappAhl and Lindex have implemented it in all markets in which they operate stores.

'There are several reasons why the One Bag Habit worked,' says Fredrika Klarén, 'but one important aspect is the simplicity of the concept. Sustainability initiatives are often complex and hard to communicate.

In One Bag Habit we managed to create a concept that was easy to understand and buy into, both for our store employees and for our customers.'

'Another key factor is that we separated the revenue flow from bags from the revenues for the retailers', continues Felicia Reuterswärd. 'All revenues from sales of bags are to be donated to a predefined sustainable development cause, which makes it easy for both customers and store employees to endorse the One Bag Habit.'

'Because we have implemented One Bag Habit in several different markets, we can see that the customer reactions vary', says Anna-Karin Dahlberg. 'We also notice that the effects of the initiative are greater in markets when we are not alone.'

Having seen the advantages of working together, the three are confident that collaboration is the way forward for future initiatives targeted at sustainable consumption—but collaborating with your competitors in customer-facing activities is a balancing act. A key challenge, looking forward, is how to determine which sustainability initiatives to pursue independently and which to pursue jointly.

The dilemma for Anna-Karin Dahlberg, Felicia Reuterswärd, and Fredrika Klarén, in setting the agenda for future collaboration building on the insights gained from their participation in the One Bag Habit initiative, is: which sustainability initiatives targeted at sustainable consumption will require them to continue to collaborate with each other or with competitors and which should they pursue independently?

 Visit the online resources to watch a video interview with Anna-Karin Dahlberg, Felicia Reuterswärd, and Fredrika Klarén, in which they explain what they did.

Introduction

What is critical marketing and what is **sustainable marketing**? Why are banks reconsidering their ethical policies? When are advertising and marketing communications coercive? When should companies give back to their communities? What is 'good' marketing behaviour and what is 'bad' marketing behaviour? Are **corporate social responsibility (CSR)** initiatives a good idea or are they used only cynically to further organizational interests? These are the sorts of question considered in this chapter.

We begin by looking at critical marketing, considering the practices it critiques through the lens of unsustainable marketing. We discuss marketing's shift towards sustainable economic development and the sub-discipline of sustainable marketing, defining and explaining its implications for marketing practice. We discuss the topic of ethics, before applying ethical principles to the marketing context. We outline how ethical situations impact on the marketing decision-making process. Four main ethical approaches to marketing decision-making are also considered, while ethical situations arising in product, promotion, price, and place (distribution) programmes are also explained. We consider ethical issues in international marketing—that is, whether or not different cultures should have different moral rules—and, finally, we discuss the important topic of bribery as an aberrant element of sales management or lobbying processes.

An understanding of **marketing ethics** is critical to making marketing practice more sustainable. But it is also important that we, as practitioners, understand the ethical, legal, and social dimensions of marketing decision-making to develop the analytical skills for considering ethical problems when they arise; otherwise, ethical problems can wreak substantial reputational damage on an organization, threatening its very existence and certainly its leaders' careers.

Unsustainable Marketing: The Critical 'Turn'

Some argue that **capitalism** is under siege, given that it is a major cause of social, environmental, and economic problems (Porter and Kramer, 2011). We agree that not all marketing's contributions to society are good; consequently, there is a need to develop a critical approach to understanding marketing practice. To truly understand the discipline, we need to study both mainstream and critical marketing, given their interdependence (Shankar, 2009). Critical marketing analysis helps in 'problematizing hitherto uncontentious marketing areas to reveal underlying institutional and theoretical dysfunctionalities' (Saren, 2011: 95). A critical approach to marketing suggests that we consider:

- the need to (re-)evaluate marketing activities, categories, and frameworks, and to improve them so that marketing operates in a desirable manner within society;

- the extent to which marketing knowledge is developed based on our contemporary social world—for example the extent to which current marketing knowledge is Western-centric (and especially focused on practice and research conducted in the United States)—and the implications this might have for the rest of the world;

- how the historical and cultural conditions in which we operate, as consumers and as students of marketing, impact on how we see marketing as a discipline; and

- how marketing can benefit from other intellectual perspectives, for example social anthropology, social psychology, linguistics, philosophy, and sociology (Burton, 2001).

Some key topics in critical marketing include the notion of marketing as manipulation, commodity fetishism, and the nature of need versus choice (Tadajewski, 2010). We consider each of these topics next.

Marketing as Manipulation

Since its inception, marketing has been charged with the notion that it serves itself, rather than consumers, and that it supports the capitalist, rather than the labouring, classes. Packard (1960) critiqued marketing by explaining that it beguiled its target audiences, often covertly, and frequently without people even understanding that they were being manipulated.

Marketers and public relations (PR) officers certainly do frame their communications to make them more persuasive. **Framing** is the action of marketers presenting persuasive communication and audiences interpreting that communication to assimilate it into their existing understanding (Scheufele and Tewksbury, 2007). The framing takes place in relation to situations (for example by highlighting sales promotions available for a fixed time only); attributes (for example by highlighting usage features of, say, a mobile phone); choices (for example by showing a potential car buyer options across the range); actions (for example buy now, pay later schemes); issues (for example Asda explaining why it boycotted the 2015 UK Black Friday sales promotion); responsibilities (for example Save the Children explaining why children in Indonesia or the Yemen need help, so that it can solicit donations); and news (for example Volkswagen explaining why its chief executive was replaced after the emissions scandal) (Hallahan, 1999) (see also Market Insight 18.3, later in the chapter).

The problem arises when framing becomes 'spin', because then marketing promotion becomes corporate propaganda. For example, some photographic tricks to make food offerings look great in print adverts include using motor oil as syrup or honey, or glue or shampoo as milk in cereals. For hotels and resorts, photos are frequently doctored to remove unwanted elements or a wide-angle lens is used to make scenes look expansive. In the United States, whilst ads are generally fairly trusted, ads for diet offerings, financial services, and prescription drugs are far less so (Anon., 2014a).

 Visit the **online resources** and complete Internet Activity 18.1 to learn more about manipulative practices in marketing.

Commodity Fetishism

As a critical perspective derived from Marxist economic theory, commodity fetishism proposes that society is overly dominated by consumption and hence fetishizes it (that is, places supreme importance on it). Marx (1867 [1990]) suggested that, prior to industrialization, goods were produced for their use-value. A producer manufactured a product for a user and exchanged it with the customer. After industrialization, the social relationship between producer and user changed. Marx argued that workers were exploited for their labour, because they became removed from the product they produced and were paid a piece rate rather than a share of the financial return generated as a result of their labour. In the process, the commodity produced acquired exchange-value, becoming tradable with other commodities within the capitalist market system, benefiting the capitalist (that is, the investor). Marx felt that the rigid pursuit of capitalism was so doctrinal that it represented a religious ideology. Commodities produced as a result of capitalist endeavour took on a religious aura, worshipped by those seduced by their perceived value (Sherover, 1979). The idea that we are worshipping consumption triggers the question of whether marketers meet our wants or our needs—or neither.

Need and Choice

The received wisdom is that marketing works to meet the needs of customers and consumers. However, Alvesson (1994), coming from outside the marketing discipline, rejects this notion. He argues that people in affluent societies seek more without gaining any further long-term satisfaction from such consumption, because much of the consumption is superficial anyway, and because appealing to people's fantasies and highlighting their imperfections (to encourage them to reduce these feelings of inadequacy by buying a particular offering) leads to narcissistic tendencies. Inherently, the notion that more choice is good in itself has been challenged (Newman, 2001). Further, some customers are persuaded and manipulated into purchasing offerings that they do not want or which are unfit for their requirements. For example, financial services companies in the UK commonly mis-sold payment protection insurance (PPI). By 2015, British banks had had to put aside £27 billion for extra administration and to settle customers' compensation to cover the claims of 16.5 million people, with a further 5.5 million still to claim (Treanor, 2015).

Ultimately, the aggregate marketing system (Wilkie and Moore, 1999; see also Chapter 1) distributes anything, including harmful products such as alcohol, tobacco, and gambling services. If prostitution and drugs, such as cannabis, were made legal in the UK, the aggregate marketing system would distribute them. It already does this in the Netherlands, for example, where they are not criminalized. The aggregate marketing system is amoral (as opposed to immoral)—that is, not designed to harm as such, but designed without any care as to whether it harms or not.

The system is made moral only by the decisions taken by governments and other institutional actors in regulating the aggregate marketing system.

However, illegal offerings can be marketed in almost the same way as legal offerings. This occurs via the 'dark web' (also called **cryptomarkets**) in which illegal offerings, such as drugs, forged passports, guns, stolen credit card details, and other ill-gotten gains, are traded (Franklin, 2013). Previous websites have included DarkMarket and Silk Road, both of which were closed by law enforcement officials. Interestingly, whilst previous dark markets worked reasonably well as trading platforms between criminal parties, contemporary cryptomarkets have closed down relatively quickly because site owners have taken customers' money after an initial period of trading. They have therefore been operating more like scam sites (Greenberg, 2016).

Of particular concern are those situations in which one group is unfairly disadvantaged over another, or in which one group exerts its power over another. Fairtrade is an example of a movement established to counter this by ensuring that, in the coffee market, for example, shippers, roasters, and retailers pay fair prices to the supplying farmers, who are mostly located in developing countries such as Kenya and Colombia.

Some other controversial issues include the following:

- Is the price paid by companies or organizations in wealthier countries for supplies obtained in poorer countries fair? Major multinational corporations, for example Nike and Gap, have been caught exploiting labour in foreign countries to produce expensive branded goods (Ellis et al., 2010: 219). The moral dilemma, and the resultant consumer backlash, has in part led to companies taking steps to eliminate such practices from their supply chain.

Paying for products imported from overseas: are you prepared to pay more to give farmers and labourers a fair deal?

Source: © Tracing Tea/Shutterstock.com.

■ To what extent should the cultural propositions and ideas of one country be marketed in preference to those of another? This is known as cultural imperialism and marketers are starting to consider its implications. China, for example, has blocked Twitter, Facebook, and Google, preferring instead to set up its own search engine (Baidu), microblogging site (Weibo), and social networking site (QQ), and this has implications for the flow of information.

■ How much should we consume of any one offering? When should governments step in to limit consumption? In Sweden, alcohol retailing is run by state alcohol monopoly Systembolaget to ensure that public health is not adversely impacted by over-consumption. In the UK, in 2015, police chiefs urged retailers to abandon Black Friday—American-led promotional activity whereby a sales event is held on the fourth Friday of November (the day after Thanksgiving)—after the 2014 flash sale caused 'scenes of chaos', with shoppers literally fighting each other and clambering over each other to bag the best deals (Clarke-Billings, 2015).

■ Are some producers or buyer groups more powerful than others and what impact, if any, does this have on society? For example, for many years, producers have been using intrusive ads (automatic video, pop-up ads) to raise awareness of their offerings, but ad-blocking software such as that offered by Germany's Eyeo is now commonly available (Anon., 2015b).

Argos offered many heavily discounted Black Friday deals in 2015, suggesting that bargain hunters browse its website between 3 and 4 a.m., to avoid online queues
Source: Courtesy of Argos.

This makes it difficult for some legitimate organizations, such as publishers (for example the UK's *The Guardian*), to make their business models work, since they provide free content on the basis that they can raise revenue from advertising to the readership.

■ Does the shift from customer research to customer surveillance benefit customers? For example, retailers are using mannequins integrated with facial recognition software of the type used by law enforcement agencies in an effort to track the age, gender, and race of their customers as they pass through or by a store. Depending on whether or not, and how, these data are stored (and the purposes for which they are used), such an approach has serious ethical implications (Clark, 2012).

These examples illustrate imbalances in power structures between consumers, producers, retailers, and other actors. The question that arises for marketers is: how should these relationships be structured to ensure that they are fair to all concerned?

Although companies are increasingly recognizing the negative impacts they can have on society (known as **externalities**), many are also increasingly trying to contribute positively to societal development through CSR programmes.

Sustainable Marketing

Supporters of sustainable marketing accept the limitations of marketing philosophy and acknowledge the need to impose regulatory constraints on marketing (van Dam and Apeldoorn, 1996), particularly concerning its impact on the environment. Sustainable economic development—that is, development that meets the needs of current generations without imposing constraints on the needs of future generations—was first proposed at a United Nations Conference in Stockholm in 1972 (WCED, 1987). To understand why a policy on sustainable development is necessary, consider the following two examples of companies having catastrophic environmental impacts:

■ In 2010, more than 200 million gallons of oil were spilled into the Gulf of Mexico after a BP oil rig explosion that killed 11 people. The resulting oil spill affected 1,000 miles of shoreline, killing thousands of birds, at least 153 dolphins, and other local wildlife. The disaster caused BP to initially lose half of its share value and total costs (including fines, compensation, legal fees, and other costs) for the disaster stood at US$53.8 billion in 2015 (Bryant, 2011; Anon., 2015a).

■ In 2011, three former executives at Tokyo Electric Power (Tepco) were charged with professional negligence contributing to death and injury from the meltdown in 2011 at the Fukushima Daiichi nuclear plant (McCurry, 2016). The meltdown was caused after a magnitude 9 earthquake caused a massive tsunami, flooding the nuclear reactors. The men were charged with failing to take measures to defend the plant, despite knowing the risks. More than 300,000 people were made homeless and 20,000 were killed as a result of the earthquake and the tsunami across Japan (Conca, 2015).

Sustainability concerns, however, do not apply only to environmental issues; questionable marketing practices can lead to significant social harm even when catastrophic environmental consequences are not at stake. Consider the scandal that engulfed American bank Wells Fargo in 2017. Because of unreasonable pressure from management demanding constant revenue increases, many employees of the bank started creating fake bank accounts and new credit cards (Egan, 2016). Customers who had never requested such products in the first place could then be charged fees on these unsolicited products. Misbehaviour was so widespread that the bank uncovered at least 3.5 million fake bank and credit card accounts (Egan, 2017).

Sustainable marketers thus attempt to broaden sustainable development to the practice of marketing beyond simple economic development. This introduces the following maxims, known as the 3Es of sustainable marketing:

1 *Ecological*—Marketing should not negatively impact upon the environment.

2 *Equitable*—Marketing should not allow or promote inequitable social practices.

3 *Economic*—Marketing should encourage long-term economic development as opposed to short-term economic development.

Sustainable marketing has been said to be the 'third age' of green marketing (Peattie, 2001). In the 'first age', ecological green marketing (*c*.1960s–70s) was concerned with automobile, oil, and agrichemical companies, which encountered environmental problems in the production process. The 'second age', environmental green marketing (*c*.1980s), saw the development of green consumers—that is, people who purchased offerings to avoid negative environmental impacts (for example cosmetic products that had not been tested on animals). But green marketing was too heavily focused on the purchasing element of consumption (Peattie and Crane, 2005), perhaps because the sustainability debate did not consider the business-to-business (B2B) dimension sufficiently.

The third age of green marketing is sustainable green marketing. Sustainable marketers focus on positioning, stimulating demand for recycled and remanufactured products and build-to-order offerings, as well as consider supply chain management issues such as enabling materials recovery from end users, designing offerings to enable their dismantlement, enabling **reverse logistics** for recycling and remanufactured offerings, and reducing supply by offering build-to-order offerings (Sharma et al., 2010). In the third age, companies also need to lengthen the time horizons across which they achieve investment returns and require emphasis on the full costs of purchase, rather than simply the price paid. Proposition development activities should fully consider, equitably, inputs and cooperation from all members of the supply chain. Companies need to adopt environmental auditing methods (to include costs for disposal, as well as development, delivery, and consumption) and organizations may actually discourage consumption in certain cases (Bridges and Wilhelm, 2008)—or at least encourage more mindful consumption and temperance, rather than acquisitive, repetitive, or aspirational over-consumption behaviour (Sheth, Sethia, and Srinivas, 2011). For example, in 2013, Coca-Cola launched a worldwide campaign on obesity (partnering in the UK until 2015 with StreetGames, a sport participation charity) by introducing smaller bottles (375 ml) and displaying detailed calorie content on the pack (Mintel, 2013). But the company has not always been consistent: in 2012, it was said to have used more water than around a quarter of the world's population—that is, 79 billion gallons to dilute its syrup and an extra 8 trillion gallons in other elements of production (Gwyther, 2015). In 2014, The Body Shop—to maintain its own strict policy against animal testing—removed all products from duty-free shelves in airports in China after consumer watchdog Choice revealed that the Chinese government had conducted post-market testing of Body Shop products on animals (Davidson, 2014).

Such longer-term thinking led to the development of what is known as the **circular economy**. For example, Vodafone runs a 'Red Hot' deal whereby a customer leases a phone and returns the old one for an upgrade. Airbnb, founded only in 2008, but valued at US$25.5 billion in 2015 and $38 billion by 2018, is another example of a company encouraging the sharing, swapping, and renting of possessions (that is, **collaborative consumption**) in the spare-room business (Alba, 2015; Trefis Team, 2018). (For more information on collaborative consumption and its positive and negative societal consequences, read Market Insight 18.1.)

Market Insight 18.1
Collaborative Consumption Surely Glitters . . . But Is It Gold?

Collaborative consumption is one of the disruptive trends of the present century. Collaborative consumption refers to markets in which consumers exchange products or other offerings among themselves. Collaborative consumption frequently relies on digital devices and electronic marketplaces or platforms, as in the case of popular brands such as Airbnb, Uber, Couchsurfing, Freecycle, or Blablacar. Users perform the role of producer, that of consumer, or both. The exchange may adopt many forms, such as renting, lending, swapping, reselling, or donating. The exchanges are not professional—that is, producers in these markets do not rely on the income to make a living. Yet the distinction blurs in practice: on Airbnb, there are professional hosts with several listings, or private owners who have their homes managed by professional agencies. Collaborative consumption has been also termed crowd-capitalism, because these markets emerge on a distributed network of peers. Platforms rely on peer control to avert any frauds or malpractice. In many of these markets, companies create the marketplace in which consumers interact and exchange. Companies may either act merely as matchmakers, providing no further services, or they may perform other services and charge a fee accordingly.

Collaborative consumption creates value in three ways. Economically, it increases choice, provides more affordable and convenient alternatives, helps consumers to maintain material welfare when liquidity is limited, and becomes a source of extra cash (without providing other benefits associated with traditional employment). Second, it enhances trust and bonding among otherwise unknown others, thus increasing social capital. Environmentally, it facilitates the use of underutilized assets and avoids waste. One report by the European Parliament estimated the potential economic gain linked with a better use of otherwise underused capacity to be €572 billion in annual consumption across the (then) EU-28.

However, collaborative consumption also destroys value. First, many of these exchanges are not taxable, which reduces income for the state, having further consequences on society's welfare. Second, social capital may not be created if users exchange only with other users similar to them or people whom they would have met anyway. Furthermore, recent studies suggest that some consumer segments lacking technological skills are excluded from these markets. Studies in the United States have found evidence of racial discrimination in home-sharing: hosts are less likely to accept Black Americans as guests. Thus collaborative consumption may lead to greater marginalization and social exclusion. Another unsolved social problem is how consumers' rights can be protected and enforced in these markets and what the responsibilities of the marketplace are. Finally, what scholars call rebound effects may offset any environmental gains offered by collaborative consumption. For instance, if people travel more by car because car sharing is a cheap alternative to public transport, emissions may increase, rather than be reduced. There may be other negative, more systemic, effects. To illustrate, the legitimacy of home-sharing is being threatened by mounting evidence of the relationship between an increase in home-sharing availability and excessive tourism, which creates housing shortages and rising prices for locals, and noise and pollution for long-term residents. Thus private individuals are getting more income, but the community is worse off.

Sources: Goudin (2016); Ranchordas, Gedeon, and Zurek (2016); Schor (2016); Edelman, Luca, and Svirsky (2017); Sundararajan (2017).

Market Insight 18.1
continued

Theory into Practice

This market insight illustrates a traditional conundrum in sustainability: the management of positive and negative externalities created by market innovations. It also helps to explain the coincidence of self-regulation and traditional state regulation in corporate and citizens' control. From a critical point of view, this leads us to discuss whether these platforms, which were allegedly created by socially and environmentally oriented entrepreneurs, have ended up being business-as-usual with all of the usual potential impacts on stakeholders.

Related Topics

stakeholder view of the firm; value creation; social business; consumers' rights

1 If you have not yet done so, spend some time on different collaborative consumption platforms. How are these platforms designed to build trust? How does the community self-regulate?

2 There is a dark side to collaborative consumption and the sharing economy. How are stakeholders impacted by the activity of major players? What can be done (if anything) to minimize negative externalities while ensuring the delivery of social, economic, and environmental value?

3 Do you think that collaborative consumption is a sustainable way of constructing markets or is it simply business-as-usual?

This market insight was kindly contributed by Dr Carmen Valor, Universidad Pontificia Comillas, Spain.

Corporate Social Responsibility and Stakeholder Marketing

Corporate social responsibility initiatives are increasingly common. Most companies publish annual CSR or sustainability reports. Governments and supranational organizations actively encourage CSR initiatives (for example the UN Global Compact project). Corporate social responsibility practitioners and academics continue to try to demonstrate the commercial effectiveness of CSR programmes to explain why being 'good' translates into being profitable.

Despite any obvious return, businesspeople and companies have long given to charity. Famous cases include the John Paul Getty Foundation in the United States (built on oil industry profits), which funds art and social projects, and Anglo American, the mining conglomerate, which provides welfare support in Africa for its employees living with HIV/AIDS. In 2014, Mars launched a campaign named 'Choose GALAXY® (RED). Make lives better', whereby donations from special packs of GALAXY® chocolate helped to provide more than 3 million days' worth of life-saving medication to help to prevent the transmission of HIV from mothers to their babies in Ghana.

The rationale for developing CSR initiatives, irrespective of their financial contribution, is based around the following ideas (Buchholz, 1991: 19):

- Corporations have responsibilities going beyond the production of their offerings at a profit.

- These responsibilities involve helping to solve important social problems, especially those that the corporation helped to create.

- Corporations have a broader constituency of stakeholders than shareholders alone.

- The impacts of corporations go beyond simple marketplace transactions.

- Corporations serve a wider range of human values, not captured solely by a focus on economic values.

A central theme of CSR is that corporations have a responsibility to society that goes beyond pursuing profit (Martin, 2002). Intercontinental Hotels Group (IHG) illustrates this by running three core programmes:

- the IHG Green Engage System, allowing individual hotels to track their carbon footprints;

- the IHG Academy, in which locals from a hotel's community can work; and

- IHG Shelter in a Storm, a fundraising programme allowing IHG to come to the aid of employees or guests, such as when Crowne Plaza Kathmandu allowed 1,000 people to sleep in the ballroom when an earthquake struck in Nepal (Basford, 2015).

Marketers have echoed this focus on CSR and some have called for the need to introduce the concept of **stakeholder marketing**. Stakeholder marketing explicitly recognizes the important role played by a multiplicity of stakeholders (for example employees, suppliers, government, media, publics) in generating positive outcomes for the organization and for society at large (Hult et al., 2011).

There are two aspects to the implementation of stakeholder marketing. The first is recognizing marketing's important role in engaging with stakeholders meaningfully to define suitable CSR programmes (see Research Insight 18.1 for a specific analysis of this point). The second relates to the importance of managing stakeholders' relationships to achieve superior performance. In other words, actively managing relationships with many stakeholders is a specific capability of the firm, since these relationships are strategic resources to be leveraged to achieve a competitive advantage (Kull, Mena, and Korschun, 2016). Think of a pharmaceutical company developing a new drug treatment. Success in this context will depend on a large network of stakeholders: regulators need to approve the drug; doctors will recommend it; insurance companies might need to be involved and offer coverage; nurses might teach patients how to use the new drug. Advocacy groups or the media might also play important role in covering the launch and supporting the adoption of the new medicine. Value in stakeholder marketing is created by the network of stakeholders and not only by the firm (Hillebrand, Driessen, and Koll, 2015). Companies need to be able to engage with all stakeholders, and if they are to do so meaningfully, they need to recognize and meet those stakeholders' expectations (Maignan, Ferrell, and Ferrell, 2005; Hillebrand et al., 2015). From this point of view, therefore, CSR is necessary for a firm's success because it nurtures the ability to act in harmony with a firm's relevant stakeholders. However, when CSR is not designed on the basis of stakeholder feedback, it can be seen as a 'gentle soap for washing dirty hands' (Debeljak, Krkac, and Bušljeta Banks, 2011: 12). Indeed, it is often used by companies in industries regarded as unsustainable (for

Research Insight 18.1

To take your learning further, you might wish to read this influential paper:

Maignan, I., Ferrell, O.C., and Ferrell, L. (2005). A stakeholder model for implementing social responsibility in marketing. *European Journal of Marketing*, **39(9–10), 956–77.**

This is a highly cited and readable article providing a managerial framework to help marketers to orient towards stakeholders' needs when designing CSR programmes. The authors base their advice on the observation that stakeholders are central to marketing activity and that the important role of stakeholders is recognized by the definition of 'marketing' given by the American Marketing Association (AMA).

Given the importance of stakeholders, the authors provide a series of eight steps outlining how to implement CSR:

1 discover organizational norms and values;

2 identify stakeholders;

3 identify stakeholder issues;

4 assess the meaning of CSR;

5 audit current practices;

6 implement CSR initiatives;

7 promote CSR; and

8 gather stakeholder feedback.

 Visit the online resources to read the abstract and access the full paper.

example oil and gas, tobacco, alcohol) because managers believe that it is a way in which they can improve their companies' otherwise poor environmental credentials (Cai, Jo, and Pan, 2011). Research suggests, however, that these efforts are likely to be unsuccessful because stakeholders are very sensitive to the motives that underpin CSR activities and react negatively when companies are seen as engaging in CSR for selfish, or 'strategic', motives (Vlachos et al., 2009).

Ethics and Marketing

Ethics, a sub-discipline of philosophy more than 2,000 years old, can be defined as 'the branch of knowledge that deals with moral principles' (Oxford Dictionaries, 2016). Ethics can be divided into the following types:

- *Normative ethics* is concerned with the rational enquiry into standards of right and wrong (that is, norms), good or bad, with respect to character and conduct, which ought to be accepted by a class of individuals.

- *Social or religious ethics* are concerned with what is right and wrong, good and bad, with respect to character and conduct. It does not claim to be established merely on the basis of rational enquiry and instead makes an implicit claim to general allegiance to something (for example God, Allah, the Buddha).

- *Positive morality* is a body of knowledge generally adhered to by a social group of individuals, concerning what is right and wrong, good and bad, with respect to character and conduct.

- *Descriptive ethics* are concerned with the study of the system of beliefs and practices of a social group from the perspective of being outside that group.

- *Meta-ethics* is a form of philosophical enquiry that treats ethical concepts and belief systems as objects of philosophical enquiry in themselves.

Considering morality in marketing gives rise to the question: how should a 'good' marketer behave? As we discuss next, this question has a complex answer. Since there are both prescriptive and descriptive components of ethics, we define marketing ethics as the analysis and application of moral principles to marketing decision-making and the outcomes of these decisions (see Research Insight 18.2).

Ethical Norms in Marketing Decision-Making

Norms are suggestions about how we *should* behave. Professional marketing organizations have a code of professional practice that requires members to behave and act in a certain manner, as do many companies and organizations. For example, the American Marketing Association (AMA) requires its members to:

1 Do no harm. This means consciously avoiding harmful actions or omissions by embodying high ethical standards and adhering to all applicable laws and regulations in the choices we make.

2 Foster trust in the marketing system. This means striving for good faith and fair dealing so as to contribute toward the efficacy of the exchange process as well as avoiding deception in product design, pricing, communication, and delivery of distribution.

3 Embrace ethical values. This means building relationships and enhancing consumer confidence in the integrity of marketing by affirming these core values: honesty; responsibility; fairness; respect; transparency; and citizenship. AMA (2018)

In ethics, norms typically comprise five general approaches: **deontological ethics**; **teleological ethics**; **managerial egoism**; **utilitarianism**; and **virtue ethics** (see Table 18.1). We outline each approach next, with examples to help you to understand the differences.

Research Insight 18.2

To take your learning further, you might wish to read this influential paper:

Hunt, S.D., and Vitell, S. (2006). The general theory of marketing ethics: a revision and three questions. *Journal of Macromarketing*, 26(2), 143–53.

This article builds upon the authors' 1986 paper—one of the most highly cited in marketing ethics—which defined the study of marketing ethics (Hunt and Vitell, 1986). This 2006 article suggests that the original 1986 theory required revision because the model was applicable in any ethical decision-making situation, not only in business and management contexts, and required empirical testing. The authors argue that ethical judgements lead to intentions and hence to behaviour. Our intentions to act ethically, however, can be based on two different types of motivation, based on two main traditions in ethics. On the one hand, ethical decisions can be based on a set of rules or principles (that is, deontological ethics); on the other, ethical choices can be based on the perceived positive consequences of an action (that is, teleological ethics). Which of these two is preferred will depend on contextual and personal factors.

 Visit the **online resources** to read the abstract and access the full paper.

Table 18.1 The main normative approaches to ethical decision-making

Ethical approach	Explanation
Deontological ethics	An ethical approach whereby the rightness or wrongness of an action or decision is not judged to be based exclusively on the consequences of that action or decision
Teleological ethics	An ethical approach whereby the rightness or wrongness of an action is determined by its consequences
Managerial egoism	An ethical approach recognizing that a manager ought to act in their own best interests and that an action is right if it benefits the manager undertaking that action
Utilitarianism	An ethical approach developed by English philosopher Jeremy Bentham suggesting that an action is right if—and only if—it conforms to the principle of utility, whereby utility (i.e. pleasure, happiness, or welfare) is maximized and pain or unhappiness is minimized, more than any alternative
Virtue ethics	A form of ethical approach associated with Aristotle, stressing the importance of developing virtuous principles, 'right' character, and the pursuit of a virtuous life

Deontological Ethics

Deontological ethics proposes that the rightness of an action is not determined by the consequences of that action (Mautner, 1999); rather, deontological ethics emphasizes the importance of codes of ethics, such as those outlined by the Market Research Society (MRS), governing market research in the UK, or by ESOMAR, the world association for market research. Deontological approaches propose that we have not only a moral duty to ensure customer satisfaction via the finished offering, but also a duty to ensure integrity in how the offering is produced and marketed. (See Market Insight 18.2 for cases of ethical concern in food processing.)

Market Insight 18.2
Surviving a Food Scandal

With an annual revenue of £3.1 billion in 2016 and employing more than 23,000 people, 2 Sisters Food Group provides approximately a third of the poultry that is consumed in the UK. However, in September 2017, video evidence from *The Guardian* and ITV showed employees at the West Bromwich plant relabelling meat products to change the date on which the animal was butchered. Images showed meat being dropped onto the floor and then put back among other food products, and there were instances in which food that had been returned by supermarkets was repackaged and sent out again. Not only could this have serious consequences in terms of hygiene and safety, but mislabelling would also negatively impact any food recall processes. Following the report, major supermarkets, including Marks & Spencer, Lidl, and Aldi, announced that they had stopped buying 2 Sisters products.

2 Sisters immediately issued a statement to the public in which it said that although the Food Standards Agency (FSA) had visited the plant on a daily basis since the video evidence surfaced and had found no obvious violations to food safety requirements, the company had begun its own internal investigation into the allegations and found that there were some cases in which quality levels were not met. As a result of these findings, the company stopped production and required all employees to undergo retraining on various aspects of food safety. During this time, workers were paid in full. The company also stressed that production

would resume only when it was happy that retraining had been successfully completed.

There are, of course, stringent requirements that must be adhered to regarding food safety, laid out in the UK in the Food Safety Act 1990, which led many people to question how such behaviour could go unnoticed. The scandal at 2 Sisters follows the infamous horsemeat scandal of 2013, whereby horsemeat was found to have entered the supply chain and been sold as beef to thousands of unsuspecting customers. And in 2017 some 700,000 eggs contaminated with potentially harmful pesticides were found to have been distributed and made available for sale in four major supermarkets.

Research has shown that such instances of corporate social *ir*responsibility can spark consumer backlash and have devastating consequences for a company's reputation. Trust is perhaps the most important part of a relationship between a customer and brand; once this has been broken, it is very difficult to recover. Research indicates that, after such a scandal has occurred, customers must perceive that the company has taken appropriate action to rectify the situation if they are to continue being loyal to the brand. By immediately taking responsibility for the issues and conducting its own investigation into the claims, 2 Sisters Food Group instantly began to rebuild trust with both the public and supermarkets. Similarly, the response from supermarkets to cease

Market Insight 18.2
continued

trading with the group upon learning about the scandal reinforced the trust between them and their customers. The best type of communication during a scandal depends, however, on the specific circumstances. In March 2018, 2 Sisters Food Group was still struggling to recover its earlier position in the marketplace and job cuts were expected in a number of its factories.

Sources: Antonetti and Maklan (2016); The Economist (2016); Goodley (2017); Roberts (2017); Anon. (2017).

Theory into Practice

This market insight offers an example of how a corporate crisis or scandal unfolds and presents the marketing implications in a B2B context. Once a scandal is communicated, existing relationships with customers and other key stakeholders are potentially threatened. At this stage, the firm tries to implement a suitable response that includes both a communication strategy and practical actions to deal with the problem raised. The entire future of a crisis-stricken organization can hinge on this attempt to manage the scandal and its negative consequences.

Related Topics

corporate social responsibility; stakeholder marketing; supply chain management

1 **Did 2 Sisters Food Group respond correctly to the video evidence and what could it have done differently?**

2 **How do scandals such as this, regarding food safety, affect public attitudes towards the brand and the product? How would they affect perceptions of the industry (beyond the firms directly involved)?**

3 **What are the different stakeholders damaged (directly and indirectly) by this scandal? How might 2 Sisters Food Group attempt to recover their trust?**

This market insight was kindly contributed by Rachael Millard, PhD candidate, Queen Mary University of London (UK).

Teleological Ethics

Teleological ethics proposes that the rightness of an action depends on the value of the consequences (Mautner, 1999). An organization is acting morally if it does not intend harm to come from its actions, but harm is caused by accident anyway, or if its behaviour is 'bad', but 'good' consequences result, for example paying a warlord 'tax' to continue operations in a developing country as Firestone did in Liberia in 1992 (Taddonio, 2014).

Managerial Egoism

The rationale for egoism is the pursuit of one's own interests, or self-interest. We assume that the interests of marketing managers align with the interests of owners or directors of the organization (but they might not). The ethical principle of managerial egoism is to maximize shareholder value, or stakeholder value for a non-profit organization. If managers maximize their own self-interest (in a free market), economic welfare is maximized for all, according to Adam Smith (1776). Adopting the managerial egoist principle, we conclude that companies should shape their marketing programmes in a way that maximizes shareholder or stake-holder value. However, markets are amoral and the free market mechanism does not work to promote ethical decisions; rather, it works to supply the optimal amount of offerings in a society.

Utilitarianism

Utilitarianism, developed by English philosopher Jeremy Bentham, proposes that an action is right if, and only if, its performance is more productive of pleasure or happiness or wel-fare, or more preventive of pain or unhappiness, than alternatives (Mautner, 1999). Utilitarian arguments are concerned with an action's consequences. Ethical arguments proposed by marketers are typically utilitarian. Marketing itself could be argued to be utilitarian, because it is often concerned with satisfying consumer needs and wants at the market level (Nantel and Weeks, 1996). Utilitarianism advocates maximizing the benefits of a certain action for the largest possible number of people—that is, what philosophers refer to as 'the greater good for the greatest number of people' (Mautner, 1999). The problem is that the maximization of one group's utility may lead to the minimization of another's. To evaluate the utility associated with a particular decision, we must determine the 'costs' and 'benefits', which are extremely dif-ficult to quantify. For example, where an offering may save lives, such as with life-saving drugs or health treatments, the losers may pay with their lives and the gainers survive—particularly where that offering is in scarce supply. An (extreme) example of utilitarianism is the rationing of supplies, as occurs in wartime, and as occurred with electricity supply in Chile in 1999, with petrol in Iran and diesel in China in 2007, and with an extension of rationing to diesel in Iran in 2012.

Virtue Ethics

Previous normative ethical theories—that is, managerial egoist, utilitarian, and deontological—provide marketers with decision-making approaches that inform their choice between alterna-tive courses of 'right' action. In direct contrast, virtue ethics stresses the development of virtuous principles, with 'right' character, and the pursuit of a virtuous life. This branch of ethics is associ-ated principally with Aristotle (Mautner, 1999). Virtue ethics proposes the development of good character, suggesting that we aim to develop the virtuous organization. Murphy (1999) argues that virtue ethics offers a suitable framework for international marketing because it is compatible both with Western moral traditions and the Eastern philosophical tradition of Confucianism. But what virtues should organizations develop?

Many organizations claim to be virtuous. The values statements of pharmaceutical and oil and gas companies often emphasize 'integrity'. UK supermarket Tesco artificially inflated its earnings by £250 million (by delaying payments to suppliers), which, when exposed, wiped £2 billion off its market value and precipitated an SFO investigation (Wearden, 2014; Butler, 2016). But in its 2013 Tesco and Society Report, Tesco claimed that its plan was to 'use our scale for good' and to 'trade responsibly' (Tesco, 2013).

So what exactly are virtuous principles and how are they operationalized? Aristotle, in *Nicomachean Ethics*, defines virtue as general dispositions that will determine how people will feel and act in specific circumstances (Mautner, 1999). He defines 11 virtues—namely, bravery, self-control, generosity, magnificence, self-respect, balanced ambition, gentleness, friendliness, truthfulness, wittiness, and justice. Although a company does not have a character in the same way as a person does, its employees do. We can therefore consider how these virtues *might* relate to a company. For example, generosity might relate to the development of CSR or corporate philanthropy programmes, or incentives for employees and channel partners.

Table 18.2 outlines each virtue and how it might be applied to organizations.

Visit the **online resources** and complete Internet Activity 18.2 to learn more about National Australia Bank, which topped the list of the world's most ethical companies in 2016.

Table 18.2 Moral virtues applied to companies

Moral virtue	Application in business and marketing
Bravery, valour	In relation to innovation/new proposition development and long-term, as opposed to short-term, goal-setting
Self-control in respect of bodily pleasure	Not given to excessive pricing or profit-taking
Generosity	Development of CSR/philanthropy, or in terms of discounted offerings or other incentives given to employees/others
Magnificence	Aiming to build a large enterprise with a well-defined mission that serves its stakeholders well
Self-respect or pride	Openly communicating to stakeholders the good and bad news associated with a company's operations
Having some ambition, but not in excess	Competitive, but not at all costs and not combative within an industry
Gentleness or good temper	Takes a balanced approach to dealings with stakeholder relations, e.g. industrial relations, consumer boycotts
Friendliness	The will to join forces with competitors in the same industry where necessary, e.g. for purposes of self-regulation, to develop industry standards, and for an exemplary approach to customer service and satisfaction

Table 18.2 continued	
Truthfulness	In relation to financial integrity and other stakeholder communications
Wittiness	Taken to mean intelligence and a company's ability to redefine the 'rules of the game' without taking itself too seriously
Justice	Auditing one's own ethical approaches and initiating reward/ punishment when in breach

The Ethical Decision-Making Process

Having defined five main ways of analysing how organizations should behave, we now consider how they make ethical decisions. Initially, managers must perceive an ethical dilemma to exist before entering the ethical decision-making process (Hunt and Vitell, 2006). If no ethical dilemma is perceived, no consideration of alternative action can take place. Further, deciding whether a situation has ethical content is culturally specific: some cultures perceive ethical breaches more easily than others. However, there are also some universal standards. For example, bribery is universally condemned and almost all countries have laws making bribery of public officials illegal, yet it still happens in practice (see 'Bribery', later in the chapter).

Early attempts to devise frameworks modelling how to act ethically involved asking a series of reflective questions (Laczniak and Murphy, 1993):

■ Does the contemplated action violate the law? (Legal test)

■ Is this action contrary to widely accepted moral obligations? (Duties test)

■ Does the proposed action violate any other special obligations that stem from the type of marketing organization in focus? (Special obligations test)

■ Is the intent of the contemplated action harmful? (Motives test)

■ Is it likely that any major damage to people or organizations will result from the contemplated action? (Consequences test)

■ Is there a satisfactory alternative action that produces equal or greater benefits to the parties affected than the proposed action? (Utilitarian test)

■ Does the contemplated action infringe on property rights, privacy rights, or the inalienable rights of the consumer? (Rights test)

■ Does the proposed action leave another person or group less well off? Is this person or group already a member of a relatively underprivileged class? (Justice test)

An elaborate model of ethical decision-making is illustrated in Figure 18.1. The authors cite five key issues for ethical consideration: **bid rigging**; price collusion; bribery; falsifying research data; and advertising deception.

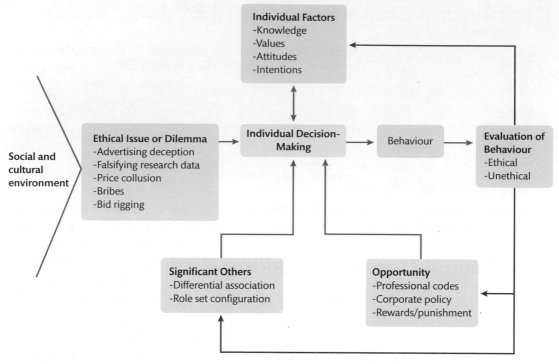

Figure 18.1

A contingency model of ethical decision-making in a marketing organization

Source: Reprinted with permission from *Journal of Marketing*, published by the American Marketing Association, Ferrell and Gresham, 1985, 49(3), 87–96.

In bid rigging, subcontractors might collude to agree in advance who will win a bid, with some submitting bids with overly expensive pricing, to ensure selection of the preconceived competitor. Alternatively, companies might not even submit a bid so another company can successfully win the contract. **Collusion** occurs when companies collaborate on submitting bids for some competitions, but not others. With price collusion, companies either conspire to set prices or limit production, which has similar effects.

How a person in an organization responds to situations with ethical content depends on their social and cultural environment. Although bribery is illegal worldwide, it remains more prevalent in some countries than others. How an employee makes a decision on an ethical issue is affected by their own knowledge, cultural background, values, and attitudes, and whether or not the company has a corporate ethics policy and guidelines on rewards or punishment for ethical and unethical behaviour.

A person's ethical decision-making also depends on how they interact with others (that is, their reference group). Association with others behaving unethically, combined with the opportunity to be involved in such behaviour oneself, is a major predictor of unethical behaviour (Ferrell and Gresham, 1985). Therefore the behaviour of superiors determines how employees behave and is the most important factor influencing ethical/unethical decisions.

Next, we consider how ethics impacts on the marketing mix.

Distribution Management and Ethics

Distribution and production policy can have major ethical dimensions. Ethical breaches in distribution management occur when, for example, companies collude over production quotas, abuse their monopoly status, or overcharge or exploit supply chain partners. The following are some examples of companies and situations in which ethical breaches have occurred:

- *Collusion*—The best-known and most tolerated global example of production collusion is that which takes place in the oil industry, through the Organization of Oil-Exporting Countries (OPEC), which co-manages oil production quotas in countries such as Nigeria, Saudi Arabia, Iran, Venezuela, and elsewhere.

- *Abuse of monopoly status*—Google abused its monopoly power in the search engine market 'in ways that harmed Internet users and competitors' according to a US Federal Trade Commission (FTC) report in 2012, but the FTC backed off from suing it because it thought Google would be a tough case to prosecute (Pagliery, 2015). The accusation was that Google's own products and services would be favoured in the search engine's results, which would limit unfairly access to the market for relevant competitors. The European Commission fined Microsoft €561 million for failing to adhere to previous EU anti-monopoly judgments regarding Microsoft's dominance of the browser market with Internet Explorer (Halfacree, 2013). Microsoft used to bundle Internet Explorer within its operating system, without offering customers an initial choice to opt for a competitor's web browser.

- *Exploitation of supply chain partners*—In France, the Châtel Act stops supermarkets selling at below-cost prices (which damage supply chain partners' margins) and is aimed at increasing competition in the sector. All discounts and services provided by the distributor to the supplier now require stipulation up front in an annual agreement (Boutin and Guerrero, 2008). In the UK, supermarkets have been shamed into paying dairy farmers a fair price for milk after the price paid by consumers at supermarket tills dropped below the price of production. One supermarket in the north of England, Booths, paying 33p a litre against the national average of 24p a litre, saw a 5 per cent increase in sales during the first four weeks of a price increase for its Fair Milk brand (Ruddick, 2015).

Promotion and Ethics

There arc many advertising issues prompting ethical consideration, for example shock and sexual appeals in advertising, the labelling of consumer products, the use of propaganda and advertising in political campaigns, and marketing to children, each of which is considered next.

The Use of Sexual and Shock Appeals

Advertisers use emotional appeals to capture attention. We are persuaded by them because we are less likely to consider objections about why we might not agree with the message. For Baudrillard (2005), all advertising has an erotic element to it, because it seduces us into buying something. But the ethical question arises where sexual themes are used explicitly (for example naked or semi-naked models) and depending on the circumstances. Italian fashion brand Diesel has famously used sexual appeals, advertising on dating apps Tinder and Grindr and on adult website Pornhub (Allwood, 2016). In fact, Pornhub became its top referral website following the advertising deal (Maytom, 2016). A good example of a highly successful and long-running campaign that used sexual appeal in a humorous way in some of its executions was the 'Got Milk?' campaign run for the California Milk Processor Board by Goodby Silvstein and Partners between 1995 and 2014.

Critics argue that sex appeals exploit women, and sometimes men, as sex objects. The fashion industry has decided not to use models aged 16 or younger, but it does use, and encourages, models to become dangerously thin. In 2013, Israel was the world's first country to ban the use of female models whose body mass index (BMI) was less than 18.5 (Bannerman, 2015). Others argue that sexual advertising appeals can be appropriate, depending on the offering (for example perfume)—but for what other offerings is it appropriate, in what countries, to what degree, and targeted at people of what age? Interestingly, one cross-cultural study found that young Chinese consumers hold similar attitudes towards the use of sex appeals in advertising as US consumers and even more favourable attitudes than Australian consumers (Liu, Cheng, and Li, 2009). Consumers generally prefer mildly erotic ads to non-erotic ads. When erotica is used in cause-related advertising, for example, one study found it to be received more favourably if it is congruent with the cause and to be received favourably more by women than by men (Pope, Voges, and Brown, 2004).

Shock advertising appeals can also create controversy. Charities often use hard-hitting guilt appeal messages to raise funds for suffering children. Less commonly, Slater+Gordon, a British law firm, used a shock appeal with the tagline 'Going through a divorce? Call us, before your ex does', causing upset on social media. But the firm argued that such an approach was necessary to raise awareness of the firm's services in a sector in which clients generally have a weak understanding of what solicitors actually offer, including mediation for couples (McAlister, 2015).

Shockingly humorous advert from British law firm Slater+Gordon created a firestorm on social media, raising awareness of legal services in an area not renowned for advertising
Source: Courtesy of Slater+Gordon, https://www.slatergordon.co.uk

Product Labelling

The key ethical issue with product labelling is whether or not labels mislead the buying public. Proper labelling is important in the food, pharmaceutical, and cosmetic industries, because we consume and absorb these offerings into our bodies. Food products—and particularly meat products in Europe and elsewhere—are required to demonstrate their country of origin. For Europe's Muslims, whether or not food products are labelled **halal** is important. A food product needs to meet certain requirements to be considered halal. Products that contain alcohol or pork meat cannot be labelled halal. This labelling also requires specific production practices, because Muslims believe that animals should be slaughtered according to the custom of cutting the animal's throat while it is alive and then draining its blood. Some animal rights groups condemn the practice, and Sweden, Norway, Iceland, Switzerland, and Poland have all banned 'ritual slaughter' despite the fact that it is allowed under EU law (Hasan, 2012). Similar dietary regulations apply also to other religions. For example, **kosher** foods follow Jewish dietary regulations, which include, among other norms, rules on 'ritual slaughter' of animals.

Unscrupulous companies do circumvent product labelling rules by importing food products from one country, processing them in another, and claiming that they come from the country in which they are processed. However, guidelines on label advertising claims in the UK are covered under Trading Standards, which investigates misleading packaging and labelling on behalf of the consumer.

Propaganda and Political Advertising

In many countries, political advertising is exempt from the rules and regulations associated with traditional advertising. As a consequence, it can be highly negative, making vitriolic statements aiming to damage the credibility of other candidates and parties. In the UK, political advertising on billboards, in cinemas, and in magazines is exempt from the advertising rules set by the Advertising Standards Authority (ASA).

Unlike their commercial counterparts, political parties are not expected to be truthful—that is, to validate their claims. Therefore the ethical question is: *should* politicians be exempt from the rules and regulations associated with traditional marketing activity, when many of the adverts used can be so negative?

Concerns related to political campaigning and propaganda have intensified in 2018 following media reports of how operatives associated with Donald Trump's 2016 presidential campaign tracked the Facebook profiles of millions of consumers to deliver targeted messages appealing to individuals' fears (Cadwalladr, 2018; see also Chapter 6). There are two issues that are relevant for marketing ethics here. The first pertains to the potential misuse of private data, which was allegedly shared in violation of Facebook's own code of conduct (see Research Insight 18.3). The second, perhaps more systemic, concern relates to the idea that the widespread use of micro-targeting (that is, the targeting of specific political messages to single individuals), which was also successfully implemented by the Obama campaign in 2012, might lead to a more fragmented society. Being able to deliver different messages to different people might relieve politicians of the burden to develop a broad, unifying message, with the consequence that multiple, independent, and perhaps irreconcilable worldviews can be fostered within a single political community (Jamieson, 2013; Summers, 2018). (See Market Insight 6.2, in an earlier chapter.)

Research Insight 18.3

To take your learning further, you might wish to read this influential paper:

Martin, K.D., and Murphy, P.E. (2017). The role of data privacy in marketing. *Journal of the Academy of Marketing Science*, 45(2), 135–55.

This recent article maps and summarizes the field of study on marketing and data privacy. It offers an overview of current knowledge in this area and identifies several important research questions that need to be tackled in the future. The article also reviews differences among companies' approaches to the management of privacy issues. The authors question current practice and show how consumers actually see certain practices that are currently common (for example the use of cookies and other techniques to track their online activity) as a cause for concern. One contention advanced in this article is that firms who are committed to protect the privacy of their customers will be rewarded with improved trust and loyalty in the long term.

 Visit the **online resources** to read the abstract and access the full paper.

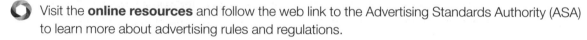 Visit the **online resources** and follow the web link to the Advertising Standards Authority (ASA) to learn more about advertising rules and regulations.

However, political advertising is not only undertaken by political parties; other campaigning organizations also use its general approach (see also Chapter 16). For example, marketing tools and techniques are used by terror groups such as Al-Qaeda, which pioneered the use of propaganda videos online to promote the cause of suicide bombing through Qatari television station Al Jazeera and on the Internet (O'Shaughnessy and Baines, 2009). More recently, so-called Islamic State (also known as ISIS or Daesh) has made extensive use of social media in the West to disseminate violent propaganda, aimed particularly at disaffected Muslims and Muslim converts, to promote their murderous cause and suicide bombing, which they depict as martyrdom (Jones et al., 2015). It is critical to realize that an understanding of marketing and PR provides users with the means of persuading huge groups of people. The question then arises as to whether it is legitimate for governments and special interest groups (including terrorists) to use these means to persuade citizens and electorates about their causes. The problem, of course, is that terror groups seldom take notice of any law and their ethical conduct is usually suspect.

Finally, companies also sometimes develop overt political messages and campaign stances (see Chapter 16). Ben & Jerry's, the ice cream brand now owned by Unilever, has also campaigned on socio-political issues, announcing on social media that it is 'open to creating a cannabis-infused ice-cream', and urging consumers to sign an online petition to tackle climate change at the UN summit in Paris in 2015 (Anon., 2015c).

Marketing to Children

Academics frequently comment on whether or not children should be targeted for advertising, given their immature views of time, money, and identity. Researchers have found evidence that children are explicitly targeted in promotional campaigns and that parents are concerned by this:

- Children are more exposed to marketing than ever before and parents increasingly feel that they are losing control of the marketing directed at their children.

- Parents are particularly concerned about the marketing channels used to target children directly (for example the Internet, mobile phones, social media, and advergames).

- Inappropriate marketing to children damages the brand, making it less likely that marketers will get past the parent as gatekeeper.

- More appropriate marketing methods are informative and help parents to feel more in control.

- Consumers are willing to support companies that communicate with children in a responsible way.

- Marketers, especially advertisers, should use the means of communication appropriately, and should educate parents and children alike on newer and less traditional communication media (Daniels and Holmes, 2005).

One example of a company under pressure for its promotion to children is McDonald's, whose offerings are designed to appeal particularly to children via the use of licensed characters and celebrity endorsement. Child obesity is regarded as a major problem in many countries (for example Australasia, the UK, the European Union generally, and the United States). While inactive lifestyles and lack of exercise play a part, the problem is exacerbated by advertising fast food to children—and fast food retailers have come under increasing pressure to make their menus healthier.

Products and Ethics

Companies must follow strict guidelines on product quality. Where consumers have concerns about a particular company's product quality, they can inform a government body, which will then be charged with looking into the case on the consumer's or customer's behalf. For instance, the Swedish Consumer Agency (*Konsumentverket*), Dubai Central Laboratory, and Ireland's Competition and Consumer Protection Commission (CCPC) all perform this role. Most countries charge organizations with enforcing minimum levels of product quality. The same degree of protection for enforcing services quality does not exist, probably because it is more difficult to monitor service quality, decide on minimum service standards, and determine whether or not breaches have been made. Agencies often provide consumer information. In some countries, product quality standards are supervised directly by governmental authorities. For example, in France, a unit within the Ministry for the Economy and Finance is responsible for protecting consumer rights and enforcing product quality standards.

Visit the **online resources** and follow the web links to the various consumer agencies and government fair trading bodies to learn more about the regulations and guidelines that organizations must follow to ensure the health and safety of consumers and the conduct of fair business practice.

Breaches in product quality can be extremely serious, and can lead to serious injury or even death—particularly in the food industry. For this reason, countries have separate official bodies charged with enforcing food safety guidelines, for example the US Food and Drug Administration (FDA), the UK's Food Standards Agency (FSA), France's Agence nationale chargée de la sécurité sanitaire de l'alimentation, de l'environnement et du travail (Anses), and the binational Food Standards Australia and New Zealand (FSANZ), which covers both territories.

A recent example of a defective product causing not only injury and inconvenience, but death, occurred when General Motors (GM) failed to promptly recall cars with a faulty ignition switch despite allegedly uncovering the problem up to a decade previously. As many as 124 deaths were the result and, in 2014, GM paid US$900 million in criminal damages and eventually recalled 800,000 cars (Smithers, 2016). In 2015, another car manufacturer, Volkswagen, announced a product recall after it was found to have installed software allowing it to falsify emission reports to pass safety tests, affecting up to 11 million vehicles (Bryant and Sharman, 2015; see also Market Insight 18.3).

Market Insight 18.3
Volkswagen: Up in Smoke?

On 11 September 2015, Volkswagen Group announced to the world's media that it was again the most sustainable automaker in the world's leading sustainability rankings. It had even depicted its engineers as angelic in ads aired during the US Super Bowl in 2014. However, the company's celebrations were short-lived: exactly seven days later, the US Environmental Protection Agency (EPA) stunned the global business community by accusing Volkswagen of illegally using 'cheat devices' to evade clean air standards for six years between 2009 and 2014. The scandal affected 11 million cars worldwide, 1.2 million of which were in the UK. After the accusations were made, Volkswagen chief executive officer (CEO) Martin Winterkorn resigned when media investigators uncovered systematic abuses within the company taking place over many years, involving managers at all levels of the organization.

Previously, Volkswagen had been viewed as a global leader in CSR. Its annual report was packed full of descriptions of projects it backed and the charities it supported. It was viewed as a thought leader on social issues and a change agent for improving society. Globally, it was ranked as the best company in the world for its CSR work. In the wake of this controversy, critics have begun to question the whole concept of CSR. Some commentators have suggested that CSR has become a 'dangerous racket', because it 'allow[s]

Since Volkswagen installed 'cheat devices' in its diesel cars, the VW brand has no longer been squeaky clean
Source: © villorejo/Shutterstock.com.

companies to parade their virtue and look good while internal standards are allowed to slip'. The scandal has also led many commentators to conclude that Volkswagen was **greenwashing** (that is, promoting environmental initiatives, but actually operating in a way that is damaging to the environment) and was more focused on doing the occasional good deed or project rather than on embedding good deeds within its core company values.

Volkswagen offered to fix the models affected and started the recall in January 2016. Estimated fines could be as much as US$45 billion in the United States alone, based on the civil charges filed by the US

Market Insight 18.3
continued

Department of Justice (DoJ), although the company is likely to pay only a fraction of that sum. Volkswagen is facing investigations in many other countries, as well as lawsuits from motorists. Only time will tell whether Volkswagen will survive the scandal and the associated loss of customer trust, bouncing back from this devastating blow to its 'angelic' brand image.

Sources: Hardyment (2015); Izzo (2015); Kaye (2015); Lynn (2015); Marshall (2015); Paton (2015); Tovey (2016).

Theory into Practice

This market insight illustrates how employees within Volkswagen, an apparent leader in CSR, displayed shockingly unethical, and illegal, behaviour in engineering 'defeat devices', allowing Volkswagen to cheat stringent emissions tests to gain access to various large automotive markets. Whilst the company did eventually accept responsibility for the cheating, its CEO had to resign as a consequence, and the company is set to pay billions of dollars in fines, lawsuits, and compensation payments. In the UK, the company's share of the overall car market plunged from 9.4 per cent to 7.2 per cent in the months immediately after the emission scandal. The United States' EPA, and other country regulators, will now have to work out what the cost to society is as a result of the higher levels of noxious chemicals that have been released into the atmosphere over a six-year period. As an aside, the case also illustrates the importance of having strong regulatory bodies for both the testing of products (the EPA) and the enforcement of punishment for contraventions of the law (the DoJ).

Related Topics

corporate deception; product standards

1. **Given the recent scandal, should Volkswagen abandon its CSR efforts?**

2. **Who is to blame for the emissions scandal at Volkswagen—the CEO, senior engineers who signed off on this, or all employees who were involved?**

3. **How have other companies refocused their efforts and recovered from the negative fallout of similar scandals?** (*Hint:* Consider GM and its faulty ignition switches, or Toyota's instant acceleration problem.)

This market insight was kindly contributed by Marie O'Dwyer, Waterford Institute of Technology, Republic of Ireland.

However, determining when to recall products is a difficult ethical problem. Often—and particularly with food products—the **precautionary principle** operates. For example, Tulip Food Company, operating in Denmark and Sweden, recalled its Danish deli food products in 2014 despite the fact that the traces of listeria found were minuscule (Herriman, 2014). Where a risk of injury is likely, a product should certainly be recalled—namely, when:

- a serious consumer illness or injury is caused by product contamination;
- there are similar complaints of illness or injury that apply to a specific product;

- a design or manufacturing failure could result in potential harm to consumers; and/or

- there is defective product labelling that could result in potential harm to consumers or a product has been tampered with.

Pricing and Ethics

The main ethical concern in pricing is fairness. Key considerations concern **price gouging**, whereby prices are set far higher than is considered reasonable, **price discrimination**, whereby prices are set for different groups of people, and price collusion, whereby competitors work together to set prices to the detriment of consumers and competitors. Price gouging occurs when companies operate a demand-pricing formula (see Chapter 9) where demand is very high, leading the companies to charge customers high prices. One shocking example is that of Turing Pharmaceuticals, which raised the price of a life-saving drug from US$13.50 to $750, putting lives at risk in the name of profit and creating a media furore (McCoy and Bomey, 2015).

Price discrimination involves setting different prices for different groups of people—that is, price discrimination is linked to market segmentation (see Chapter 6). It is not necessarily an unethical practice as such, but is more questionable where there is no difference in the offer and the price remains the only difference. Price discrimination is commonplace. For example, signs at tourist sites in different countries often show the price for foreigners versus the cost for domestic nationals. For example, the price for international visitors to visit the Taj Mahal in India has sometimes been 25 times that of the cost for Indian nationals.

Price discrimination also commonly occurs on airlines. For example, easyJet and Ryanair use **yield management** systems to sell airline tickets, with different prices charged depending on time of booking. Women's haircuts are often more expensive than men's, although it *may* be that the service provided is more attentive and takes longer. And until new EU rules were introduced in 2012, women could obtain up to 40 per cent cheaper car insurance than men in the UK (King, 2012). This is still possible in the United States, where equalizing legislation has not been introduced, and women are said to tend to drive more safely than men (that is, be involved in fewer accidents), get fewer speeding tickets, and be less likely to be charged with driving under the influence (esurance, 2016). Price discrimination also occurs when customers haggle (Kimes and Wirtz, 2003). **Haggling** is more common in some markets than others (for example buying a home or a car in Europe), and in some countries than others (for example Middle Eastern and Southeast Asian countries).

Another ethical issue in pricing arises when companies collude to set prices (see also Market Insight 18.4). Many well-known companies have been fined for this. In 2016, the European Commission fined Mitsubishi Electric and Hitachi €137.8 million for fixing the prices of car alternators and starters between 2004 and 2010. Denso, the world's second-largest maker of car parts, avoided a fine by informing on the cartel (Anon., 2016). Price collusion is regarded as unethical because it results in unfair, and higher, charges to customers and it stifles innovation because competitors do not need to develop better offerings—and that means that consumers do not benefit from improvements in quality and performance.

Market Insight 18.4
Forex Fixing

Between 2009 and 2013, the global banking industry was fined more than £166 billion in settlement fees and provisions for bad behaviour including fixing the London interbank offered rate (Libor); currency market manipulation; breaching sanctions on Iran, Sudan, and Cuba; money laundering for Mexican drug cartels; abusive mortgage practices in the United States; and mis-selling of payment protection insurance (PPI) in the UK. That's quite a list of dodgy dealing.

Consider foreign exchange (forex) currency market manipulation. This occurred between 2007 and 2013 in a market totalling an estimated £3.3 trillion a day, 41 per cent of which came through the City of London. Fines imposed by the UK's Financial Conduct Authority (FCA) and numerous regulators in the United States on various international banks, including Barclays and Royal Bank of Scotland (RBS), totalled £6.3 billion. Barclays was fined £1.5 billion by five regulators, including £284 million by the FCA. Barclays, RBS, and HSBC also agreed to pay out £600 million to settle a US investor class-action lawsuit related to the fixing of forex markets. Investor claims are also likely to be submitted in London, a much larger market than the United States, meaning that the banks face legal costs running into further billions.

But what did the banks do to deserve these fines and lawsuits? The answer is that their employees rigged the market by colluding with other traders in closed-membership online chatrooms (with names such as 'The Bandits Club' and 'The Cartel'), sharing confidential client currency order information that allowed them to submit large currency orders simultaneously during the time at which the benchmark price is set. This is the price that many customers request to settle deals and it is calculated within the 30 seconds of trading either side of 4 p.m. GMT (known as the 'fix' time). If, just before these big trades occur, the traders also buy some currency on their own trading account using the bank's money (knowing that the currency price will, say, go up because of their client's large currency orders), they can then sell the currency after the large trade has taken place and make a hefty profit (since they bought the currency at a lower exchange rate than the rate at which they later sell it). If several currency traders collude, they are more likely to affect 'the fix' and to a larger degree to their advantage.

Despite the apparent evidence, in 2016 the UK's Serious Fraud Office (SFO) closed the criminal investigation into forex fixing, deciding that there was no serious prospect of getting a conviction under English law. Losers include the banks themselves (because of the fines imposed), the banks' clients because of slight skews in the market, and the financial system itself because public trust is further undermined.

Sources: Goodley (2014); Kollewe, Treanor, and Hickey (2014); Augar (2015); Treanor and Rushe (2015); Trotman (2015); Treanor (2016).

Theory into Practice

The market insight illustrates the sheer scale of fines and compensation that large global banks have had to pay as a result of their employees' unethical behaviour. Some bank employees, who were sacked for their conduct as part of the regulatory settlements, showed no respect whatsoever for the wider forex system, acting purely in their own interests (in pursuit of higher profits for the bank and bonuses for themselves). No normative ethical framework (that is, utilitarian, deontological, teleological, virtue ethics), other than a managerial egoist approach (what is in the trader's interest is in the best interests of everyone), can justify the traders' forex-fixing actions. But even the managerial egoist approach, which assumes that managers' interests are linked to shareholders' interests, fails to justify the actions in the longer term, given that the banks eventually received stringent fines (thereby reducing shareholder value).

Market Insight 18.4
continued

Related Topics
corporate social responsibility; critical marketing

1 Why do you think global banks have been mired in so many scandals?

2 Barclays has developed an ethical code of conduct, known as The Barclays Way. Do you think such a policy will help to ensure that a

scandal like forex fixing never happens to the bank again? Why, or why not?

3 Look up the ethical policies of two other global banks on their websites. How are they similar and how do they differ?

Universalism or Cultural Relativism in Marketing Ethics

Some cultures are less likely than others to perceive ethical dilemmas. Ethicists say that different groups of people see ethical situations from two perspectives. From one perspective, universal ethical codes of practice should exist because there are things that are simply 'wrong', no matter what the colour or creed of the people concerned (for example murder, bribery, extortion). This is termed *universalism*. The opposite argument, termed *cultural relativism*, suggests that different groups consider ethical situations (for example gifts, corporate entertainment) from varied viewpoints and that there is nothing wrong with this. The debate in international marketing ethics concerns itself with this dichotomy between cultural relativism and ethical universalism.

How should a director of a Western company ensure that local managers do not use bribery to gain access to particular markets? This question arose when French industrial company Alstom paid more than US$75 million in bribes to government officials in Indonesia, Saudi Arabia, Egypt, Taiwan, and the Bahamas, attracting a $773.2 million fine from the US Department of Justice in late 2014 (Chon, 2014). The excuse was that if its managers did not agree to the bribes, competitors would, and they would win the business. From a cultural relativist perspective, such a practice is ethically unacceptable except where bribery might lead to a greater good—say, widespread distribution of health-giving pharmaceuticals—whereas the universalist perspective suggests that bribery is a fundamental ethical breach regardless of the circumstances. A study concerning American–Thai differences showed that American marketers were more likely than Thai marketers to perceive unethical marketing behaviours to be serious (Marta and Singhapakdi, 2005). A study of Thai managers suggested that one approach that might improve their ethical decision-making would be to encourage idealism—that is, the degree to which individuals 'assume that desirable consequences can, with the "right" action, always be obtained' (Singhapakdi, Salyachivin et al., 2000: 273)—rather than relativism, whereby people reject universal moral rules (Forsyth, 1980). Building on idealism, Singhapakdi, Marta, and colleagues (2000) also found a strong positive relationship between a marketer's religiousness and their degree of idealism—that is, that the more religious someone is, the more likely they are to hold universal ethical principles.

In a study of marketing ethics in Korea, Kim and Chun (2003) found that Koreans perceived the hierarchy of seriousness of ethical problems as follows:

1 bribery;

2 unfair price increases;

3 exaggerated advertising; and

4 sexual discrimination.

They found that younger Koreans were less likely to perceive situations as having ethical content, whereas older people perceived less ethical content in bribery situations.

Bribery

Transparency International publishes a Corrupt Perceptions Index to indicate the perceived level of public-sector corruption in different countries around the world. In 2017, New Zealand, Denmark, Finland, Norway, and Switzerland were the least corrupt governments, whilst the worst perceived offenders were Somalia, South Sudan, Syria, Afghanistan, Yemen, and Sudan (Transparency International, 2018). From an analysis of 427 international bribery cases by the **Organisation for Economic Co-operation and Development (OECD)**, the most common offending industries from which bribes originated included companies from the extraction (oil and mining), construction, transportation, information and communication, and manufacturing sectors (Kottasova, 2014). Companies in these industries have a greater need for ethical training, confidential helplines, and robust whistleblowing procedures to allow employees to highlight ethical breaches to senior managers without fear of penalty.

Where bribery occurs, it is used either to influence potentially adverse legislative programmes (that is, for lobbying purposes) or to obtain favourable contracts at another company's expense (that is, for sales purposes). Many countries' bribery acts are extraterritorial—that is, personnel can be charged for their activities in other countries. To comply with the UK Bribery Act 2010, for example, British companies must put in place procedures to deter employees from paying bribes (see Market Insight 18.5).

Market Insight 18.5
Drug Money in China

In 2014, GlaxoSmithKline (GSK) was fined 元3 billion (£297 million) by Chinese authorities after it was found to have bribed doctors and hospitals to promote its drugs. Numerous GSK senior executives were given suspended jail sentences and deported from the country. The company was said to have made US$150 million in illegal profits as a result of the bribery. The scale and duration of the 15-month investigation at

Market Insight 18.5

continued

GSK led to a huge increase in whistleblowers' reports in China, from 48 in 2013 to 652 in 2014, and a considerable drop in Chinese drug sales. In a survey conducted for a white paper by Charney Research, 35 per cent of companies operating in China had paid bribes or given gifts simply to stay in business. Bribery also differed by region, being more prevalent in Beijing than Shanghai, and much less prevalent in the north and west of the country. The corruption problem is so bad that nine in ten companies regard it as a plague on doing business.

GlaxoSmithKline now has an anti-bribery and corruption (ABAC) policy statement that reads:

> We do not, directly or through a third party, promise, offer, make, authorise, solicit or accept any financial or other advantage, to or from anyone to obtain or retain business, or secure an improper advantage in the conduct of business. This rule applies regardless of whether they are *government officials* or work in a private sector entity.

Financial or other advantage covers anything of value, including cash, gifts, services, job offers, loans, travel expenses, entertainment, or hospitality.

We prohibit all facilitation payments as they are bribes. These payments are unofficial, improper, small payments or gifts offered or made to government officials to secure or expedite a routine or necessary action to which we are legally entitled.

ABAC Programme elements

- Our leadership and managers lead by example, ensuring our Staff and relevant third parties are aware of the ethical significance and critical role of our ABAC principles and standards.

- We perform a comprehensive risk assessment to determine the company's exposure to bribery and corruption risk. The risk assessment is reviewed and updated regularly to reflect changes in our risk profile.

- The ABAC principles and standards established in this policy are developed and supported by a number of periodically reviewed corporate written standards which constitute our ABAC controls, policies and procedures.

- We provide mandatory periodic ABAC training to our Staff and relevant third parties in accordance with their roles, responsibilities, and the risks they face.

- We perform risk-based due diligence prior to engaging any third party or undertaking a business development transaction and ensure appropriate contractual clauses and monitoring controls are put in place as described in the relevant written standards.

- Our dedicated ABAC website and regular communications ensure ABAC awareness and support are available across the company.

Sources: Anon. (2014b); Kollewe (2014); GlaxoSmithKline (2016); Levick (2015); Roland (2015).

Theory into Practice

The market insight illustrates how senior executives of a major UK multinational pharmaceutical manufacturer were found guilty by public authorities of bribery in China. The case reveals the difficulty of doing business in a country in which bribery of public officials is systematic, varied, and expected, but also when the Chinese president has initiated a strong focus on anti-corruption and Western governments are prosecuting companies using extra-territorial laws such as the US Foreign Corrupt Practices Act of 1977 and, in the UK, the Bribery Act 2010.

Market Insight 18.5
continued

Related Topics
deontological ethics; ethical codes of conduct

1 Do you think the GSK ABAC statement stops the company's employees and contractors from offering bribes to public officials in every part of the world, including China? Why, or why not?

2 Is it always unethical to pay bribes when doing business? Can you envisage any circumstance in which it might be ethical to do so?

3 What other major Western companies are you aware of that have been charged with bribery in China recently? Why do you think bribery is so commonplace in China?

Chapter Summary

To consolidate your learning, the key points from this chapter are summarized here:

■ **Assess the negative impact that marketing has on society.**

The critical marketing perspective suggests that marketing impacts negatively on society. The perspective calls for the (re-)evaluation of marketing activities, categories, and frameworks to improve them, so that marketing can operate in a more desirable manner within society. It critiques the nature of marketing knowledge and questions in whose interests existing frameworks, approaches, and techniques operate.

■ **Define sustainable marketing and its implications for marketing practice.**

Sustainable marketing has been termed the 'third age' of green marketing, and it is concerned with ecological, equitable, and economic impacts of marketing practice. Sustainable marketers seek to meet the needs of existing generations, whilst not compromising the ability of future marketers to meet those of future generations. Consequently, companies are re-imagining marketing practices, for example by recovering the costs of investment financing over longer payback periods, by emphasizing the full costs of purchase to customers, by considering all members of the supply chain and ensuring that they are paid equitably, and by demarketing consumption to vulnerable groups or those who are overconsuming.

■ **Define stakeholder marketing and its role in corporate social responsibility initiatives.**

Stakeholder marketing comprises marketing activities undertaken in a system of interaction with different stakeholders and aimed at generating value for all stakeholders involved, both internal and external to the organization. Stakeholder marketing is important for an organization's ability to develop successful CSR programmes that demonstrate a concern for social and/or environmental issues. By implementing stakeholder marketing, an organization ensures that its CSR engagements are relevant to the concerns of its stakeholders.

- **Define marketing ethics.**

  Marketing ethics is concerned with how marketers go about the marketing process. In particular, it is the application of moral principles to decision-making in marketing and the consideration of the outcomes of those decisions.

- **Explain the common ethical norms applied in marketing.**

  Marketing ethics can be divided into normative and descriptive branches, distinguishing between how we *ought* to act and how people *actually behave* when making marketing decisions. The five main normative approaches to marketing decision-making are: deontological ethics (doing 'the right thing' because it's the right thing to do); teleological ethics (the right thing to do is the thing with the right consequences); managerial egoism (doing the right thing because it's the best thing to do for ourselves); utilitarianism (doing the right thing for the largest number of people); and virtue ethics (doing the right thing for everyone).

- **Describe the role of ethics in marketing decision-making.**

  Models of marketing decision-making outline the importance of the ethical content of a situation and the importance of 'significant others', employees' values, and the ethical training given by a company in line with its own ethical policy. Hunt and Vitell's (2006) model of marketing decision-making stresses the importance of considering what is the *right* thing to do (deontological norms) and what are the *right* intended outcomes for us to follow (teleological norms).

- **Understand how ethical breaches occur in marketing mix programmes.**

  Ethical breaches occur in all aspects of an organization's marketing activity, including pricing, promotion, product, and place (distribution) policies. Ethical breaches are often made by employees who may or may not be following company ethical guidelines and codes of conduct appropriately.

 # Review Questions

1 Name the key concepts in critical marketing.
2 How will sustainable marketing impact on marketing practice?
3 How will stakeholder marketing impact on marketing practice?
4 What do we mean by ethics in marketing?
5 What role does ethics in marketing play in the marketing decision-making process?
6 What are key ethical considerations when pricing offerings?
7 What are key ethical considerations when promoting offerings?
8 What are key ethical considerations when distributing offerings?
9 What are key ethical concerns when developing the product offering?
10 What is bribery?

Discussion Questions

1 Having read Case Insight 18.1, what do you think are the most important issues to consider when determining whether to work together with competitors to address sustainability challenges?

2 Consider Reckitt Benckiser's condom product Durex, designed to reduce the proportion of people sustaining sexually transmitted diseases (STDs) and women experiencing unwanted pregnancies. Assuming that this is legally permitted, would it be appropriate for the company to promote condom usage to (a) children below the age of consent (for example 16 years old in the UK) and (b) countries in which conservative religious views are prevalent? (*Hint:* you might need to re-read the section on normative ethics.) Discuss this ethical problem using the following approaches:

   A Managerial egoism—that is, the principle of managerial self-interest
   B Utilitarianism—that is, the principle of the greater good for the greater number of people
   C Deontological ethics—that is, the principle of duty-based ethics

3 Consider whether or not it is unethical to act in the following ways in the following circumstances:

   A You are a salesperson working for a South African construction company trying to secure a road-building contract in Nigeria. You know that if you do not pay a 'commission' to the public official in charge of tendering for the project, you will not win the contract. Should you pay the 'commission' or do you have other options?
   B You are a Dubai-based banker. A potential new client in Dubai insists on taking you to a very exclusive restaurant at the Burj al Arab to discuss a loan she requires to purchase a new building for her rapidly expanding business. Should you accept?
   C You are a farmer supplying a large chain supermarket in Copenhagen with selected prime cuts of meat products. The supermarket requests an upfront 'listing' fee of 170,000 Danish Krone before it can accept you as a supplier; you can then expect high-value orders of millions of Krone. Should you pay the 'listing fee'? What other courses of action do you have?

Visit the online resources and complete the Multiple-Choice Questions to assess your knowledge of Chapter 18.

 # Glossary

bid rigging when organizations conspire to determine which company or companies should win a particular contract.

capitalism the political system in which private (as opposed to governmental) capital and wealth is the predominant means of producing and distributing goods.

circular economy an alternative to a traditional linear economy (make–use–dispose) in which we keep resources in use for as long as possible, extract the maximum value from them whilst in use, and then recover and regenerate products

and materials at the end of each service life (WRAP, 2016).

collaborative consumption the trend towards the sharing, swapping, and renting of possessions.

collusion when a group of competitor companies conspires to control the market, often at the expense of the consumer or customer and typically in relation to price fixing.

corporate social responsibility (CSR) typically, a programme of social and/or environmental activities undertaken by a company on behalf of one or more of its stakeholders to develop sustainable business operations, foster goodwill, and develop the company's corporate reputation.

cryptomarkets hidden online marketplaces in which people buy illicit offerings, often using anonymous web browsers and untraceable currency forms for payment.

deontological ethics a form of ethical approach whereby the rightness or wrongness of an action or decision is not judged to be exclusively based on the consequences of that action or decision.

externalities negative impacts that arise as a result of economic development, for example on the environment, to society, etc.

framing the dual action whereby communicators present ideas and concepts, and members of an audience interpret those concepts by assimilating them into their pre-existing cognitive schema.

greenwashing occurs when an organization's rhetoric concerning the promotion of its environmental impacts (based on its offering or organizational practices) is not backed up in practice—that is, it makes misleading claims about how environmentally friendly it is.

haggling when a customer argues with a supplier, usually a retailer, over the price to be paid for a good or service and is successful in obtaining a discount.

halal a term referring to what is permissible under Sharia law and most typically used in Western societies when referring to permissible foodstuffs; halal food must not contain alcohol, blood or its by-products, or the meat of an omnivore or carnivore; where the food is from an animal, a Muslim must have pronounced the name of Allah before slaughtering the animal.

kosher a term referring to those food products permitted under Jewish dietary regulations—that is, according to the extensive list of forbidden animals found in the Torah, which includes pigs, several birds, and most animals that crawl (although some foods have been subject to interpretation and debate within Jewish communities).

managerial egoism a form of ethical approach whereby a manager is said to be bound to act in their own best interests and an action is said to be right if it benefits the manager undertaking that action.

marketing ethics the analysis and application of moral principles to marketing decision-making and the outcomes of these decisions.

Organisation for Economic Co-operation and Development (OECD) a grouping of 34 countries that exists to promote the economic and social well-being of people worldwide.

precautionary principle the principle that, when the risk of a threat to the environment or human health exists, it is better to put in place measures to mitigate that risk than not to do so, even if there is no scientific evidence for a cause–effect relationship for the threat implied by the risk.

price discrimination occurs where the price of a good or service is set differently for certain groups of people.

price gouging occurs when a seller sets the price of a good or service at a level far higher than is considered reasonable.

reverse logistics the process of returning goods in a physical distribution channel, for example a flow from customer to manufacturer via a retailer (say, for repair or replacement).

stakeholder marketing marketing activities undertaken in a system of interaction with different stakeholders and aimed at generating value for all stakeholders involved, both internal and external to the organization.

sustainable marketing marketing activities undertaken to meet the wants and/or needs of present customers without comprising the wants and/or needs of future customers, particularly in relation to negative environmental impacts on society.

teleological ethics a form of ethical approach whereby the rightness or wrongness of an action or decision is judged primarily based on the intentions of the decision-maker.

utilitarianism an ethical approach originally developed by English philosopher and social reformer Jeremy Bentham, which postulates that an action is right if, and only if, it conforms to the principle of utility, whereby utility (pleasure, happiness, or welfare) is maximized, or pain or unhappiness minimized, more than any alternative.

virtue ethics principally associated with Aristotle, a branch of ethics that stresses the importance of developing virtuous principles, with 'right' character, and the pursuit of a virtuous life.

yield management a system for maximizing the profit generated from activities, which carefully manages price to ensure full utilization of capacity, while balancing supply and demand factors.

References

Alba, D. (2015). Airbnb confirms $1.5bn funding round, now valued at $25.5bn. *Wired*, 17 July. Retrieve from: https://www.wired.com/2015/12/airbnb-confirms-1-5-billion-funding-round-now-valued-at-25-5-billion/ (accessed 13 October 2018).

Allwood, E.H. (2016). Why Diesel is about to start advertising on Pornhub. *Dazed*, 9 January. Retrieve from: http://www.dazeddigital.com/fashion/article/29089/1/why-diesel-is-about-to-start-advertising-on-pornhub (accessed 13 October 2018).

Alvesson, M. (1994). Critical theory and consumer marketing. *Scandinavian Journal of Marketing*, 10(3), 291–313.

AMA (American Marketing Association) (2018). *Statement of Ethics*. Retrieve from: https://www.ama.org/AboutAMA/Pages/Statement-of-Ethics.aspx (accessed 13 October 2018).

Anon. (2014a). The art of deceptive advertising: from brown shoe polish on burgers to hairspray for brighter ingredients, how commercials trick us into buying their products. *Mail Online*, 11 June. Retrieve from: https://www.dailymail.co.uk/femail/article-2655351/The-art-deceptive-advertising-From-brown-shoe-polish-burgers-hairspray-brighter-ingredients-commercials-trick-buying-products.html (accessed 13 October 2018).

Anon. (2014b). GlaxoSmithKline fined $490m by China for bribery. *BBC News*, 19 September. Retrieve from: https://www.bbc.co.uk/news/business-29274822 (accessed 13 October 2018).

Anon. (2015a). BP and Deepwater Horizon: a costly mistake. *The Economist*, 2 July. Retrieve from: https://www.economist.com/news/business-and-finance/21656847-costly-mistake (accessed 13 October 2018).

Anon. (2015b). Online advertising: block shock. *The Economist*, 6 June, 60.

Anon. (2015c). We get the scoop on whether Ben & Jerry's licks rival ice-cream brands on social media. *Marketing*, July, 21.

Anon. (2016). Car parts price-fixing fines for Hitachi and Mitsubishi Electric. *BBC News*, 27 January. Retrieve from: https://www.bbc.co.uk/news/business-35419762 (accessed 13 October 2018).

Anon. (2017). Updated statement to the *Guardian*/ITV investigation. *2 Sisters Food Group*, 1 October. Retrieve from: https://www.2sfg.com/news/archive/2017/updated-statement-to-the-guardianitv-investigation/ (accessed 13 October 2018).

Antonetti, P., and Maklan, S. (2016). An extended model of moral outrage at corporate social irresponsibility. *Journal of Business Ethics*, 135(3), 429–44.

Augar, P. (2015). How the forex scandal happened. *BBC News*, 20 May. Retrieve from: https://www.bbc.co.uk/news/business-30003693 (accessed 13 October 2018).

Bannerman, L. (2015). I won't lose weight, says angry model. *The Times, 16 October, 3.*

Basford, L. (2015). Corporate responsibility. *The Marketer*, July–August, 30–3.

Baudrillard, J. (2005). *The System of Objects* (trans. James Benedict). London: Verso Books.

Boutin, X., and Guerrero, G. (2008). The 'Loi Galland' and French consumer prices. *Conjoncture in France*, June. Retrieve from: https://www.insee.fr/en/indicateurs/analys_conj/archives/june2008_d1.pdf (accessed 13 October 2018).

Bridges, C.M., and Wilhelm, W.B. (2008). Going beyond green: the 'why' and 'how' of integrating sustainability into the marketing curriculum. *Journal of Marketing Education*, 30(1), 33–46.

Bryant, B. (2011). Deepwater Horizon and the Gulf oil spill: the key questions answered. *The Guardian*, 20 April. Retrieve from: https://www.theguardian.com/environment/2011/apr/20/deepwater-horizon-key-questions-answered (accessed 13 October 2018).

Bryant, C., and Sharman, A. (2015). Martin Winterkorn resigns as VW boss over emissions scandal. *Financial Times*, 23 September. Retrieve from: https://www.ft.com/content/d2288862-61d1-11e5-97e9-7f0bf5e7177b (accessed 13 October 2018).

Buchholz, R.A. (1991). Corporate responsibility and the good society: from economics to ecology: factors which influence corporate policy decisions. *Business Horizons*, 34(4), 19–31.

Burton, D. (2001). Critical marketing theory: the blueprint? *European Journal of Marketing*, 35(5–6), 722–43.

Butler, S. (2016). Tesco delayed payments to suppliers to boost profits, watchdog finds. *The Guardian*, 26 January. Retrieve from: https://www.theguardian.com/business/2016/jan/26/tesco-ordered-change-deal-suppliers (accessed 13 October 2018).

Cadwalladr, C. (2018). 'I made Steve Bannon's psychological warfare tool': meet the data war whistleblower. *The Guardian*, 18 March. Retrieve from: https://www.theguardian.com/news/2018/mar/17/data-war-whistleblower-christopher-wylie-faceook-nix-bannon-trump (accessed 13 October 2018).

Cai, Y., Jo, H., and Pan, C. (2011). Doing well while doing bad? CSR in controversial industry sectors. *Journal of Business Ethics*, 108(4), 467–80.

Chon, G. (2014). Alstom to pay record $772m for bribery. *Financial Times*, 22 December. Retrieve from: https://www.ft.com/content/0a8989c6-8934-11e4-9b7f-00144feabdc0 (accessed 13 October 2018).

Clark, L. (2012). Mannequins are spying on shoppers for market analysis. *Wired*, 23 November. Retrieve from: https://www.wired.co.uk/article/mannequin-spies-on-customers (accessed 13 October 2018).

Clarke-Billings, L. (2015). Police chiefs urge stores to cancel Black Friday as Asda abandons flash sale. *The Telegraph*, 11 November. Retrieve from: https://www.telegraph.co.uk/news/shopping-and-consumer-news/11985589/Asda-we-will-not-be-part-of-Black-Friday-this-year.html (accessed 13 October 2018).

Conca, J. (2015). The Fukushima disaster wasn't disastrous because of the radiation. *Forbes*, 16 March. Retrieve from: https://www.forbes.com/sites/jamesconca/2015/03/16/the-fukushima-disaster-wasnt-very-disastrous/#4d68476951e7 (accessed 13 October 2018).

Daniels, J., and Holmes, C. (2005). *Responsible Marketing to Children: Exploring the Impact on Adults' Attitudes and Behaviour*. London: Business in the Community.

Davidson, H. (2014). Body Shop removes all its products from Chinese duty-free stores. *The Guardian*, 12 March. Retrieve from: https://www.theguardian.com/world/2014/mar/12/body-shop-removes-products-from-chinese-duty-free-stores (accessed 13 October 2018).

Debeljak, J., Krkac, K., and Bušljeta Banks, I. (2011). Acquiring CSR practices: from deception to authenticity. *Social Responsibility Journal*, 7(1), 5–22.

Edelman, B., Luca, M., and Svirsky, D. (2017). Racial discrimination in the sharing economy: evidence from a field experiment. *American Economic Journal: Applied Economics*, 9(2), 1–22.

Egan, M. (2016). 5,300 Wells Fargo employees fired over 2 million phony accounts. *CNN Money*, 9 September. Retrieve from: https://money.cnn.com/2016/09/08/investing/wells-fargo-created-phony-accounts-bank-fees/index.html (accessed 13 October 2018).

Egan, M. (2017). Wells Fargo uncovers up to 1.4 million more fake accounts. *CNN Money*, 31 August. Retrieve from: https://money.cnn.com/2017/08/31/investing/wells-fargo-fake-accounts/index.html (accessed 13 October 2018).

Ellis, N., Fitchett, J., Higgins, M., Jack, G., Lim, M., Saren, M., and Tadajewski, M. (2010). *Marketing: A Critical Textbook*. London: Sage.

esurance (2016). Why women pay less for car insurance. Retrieve from: https://www.esurance.com/info/car/why-women-pay-less-for-car-insurance (accessed 13 October 2018).

Ferrell, O.C., and Gresham, L.G. (1985). A contingency framework for understanding ethical decision making in marketing. *Journal of Marketing*, 49(3), 87–96.

Forsyth, D.R. (1980). A taxonomy of ethical ideologies. *Journal of Personality and Social Psychology*, 39(1), 175–84.

Franklin, O. (2013). Unravelling the dark web. *GQ (British)*, February, 184–9.

GlaxoSmithKline (2016). *Anti-Bribery and Corruption Policy*, 22 December. Retrieve from: https://www.gsk.com/media/2976/anti-bribery-and-corruption-policy-v11.pdf (accessed 13 October 2018).

Goodley, S. (2014). The foreign exchange trader: 'the closer you get to 4pm, the less the risk'. *The Guardian*, 12 March. Retrieve from: https://www.theguardian.com/business/2014/mar/12/forex-trader-closer-4pm-less-risk (accessed 13 October 2018).

Goodley S. (2017). Scandal-hit 2 Sisters suspends chicken production at West Midlands plant. *The Guardian*, 1 October. Retrieve from: https://www.theguardian.com/business/2017/oct/01/scandal-hit-2-sisters-suspends-chicken-production-at-west-midlands-plant (accessed 13 October 2018).

Goudin, P. (2016). The cost of non-Europe in the sharing economy: economic, social and legal challenges and opportunities. Retrieve from: http://www.europarl.europa.eu/RegData/etudes/STUD/2016/558777/EPRS_STU(2016)558777_EN.pdf (accessed 13 October 2018).

Greenberg, A. (2016). The Silk Road's dark-web dream is dead. *Wired*, 14 January. Retrieve from: https://www.wired.com/2016/01/the-silk-roads-dark-web-dream-is-dead/ (accessed 13 October 2018).

Gwyther, M. (2015). The real thing: ain't what it used to be. *Management Today*, March, 42–3, 45–6.

Halfacree, G. (2013). Microsoft hit with €561m fine. *Bit-Tech*, 7 March. Retrieve from: https://www.bit-tech.net/news/bits/2013/03/07/microsoft-eu-fine/1 (accessed 13 October 2018).

Hallahan, K. (1999). Seven models of framing: implications for public relations. *Journal of Public Relations Research*, 11(3), 205–42.

Hardyment, R. (2015). CSR after the Volkswagen scandal. *TriplePundit*, 28 October. Retrieve from: https://www.triplepundit.com/2015/10/csr-volkswagen-scandal/ (accessed 13 October 2018).

Hasan, M. (2012). Mehdi Hasan on the not-so hidden fear behind halal hysteria. *New Statesman*, 9 May. Retrieve from: https://www.newstatesman.com/politics/politics/2012/05/halal-hysteria (accessed 13 October 2018).

Herriman, R. (2014). Deli meat sold in Sweden recalled due to listeria. *Outbreak News Today*, 23 August. Retrieve from: https://outbreaknewstoday.com/deli-meat-sold-in-sweden-recalled-due-to-listeria-36588/ (accessed 13 October 2018).

Hillebrand, B., Driessen, P.H., and Koll, O. (2015). Stakeholder marketing: theoretical foundations and required capabilities. *Journal of the Academy of Marketing Science*, 43(4), 411–28.

Hult, G.T.M., Mena, J.A., Ferrell, O.C., and Ferrell, L. (2011). Stakeholder marketing: a definition and conceptual framework. *AMS Review*, 1(1), 44–65.

Hunt, S.D., and Vitell, S.J. (1986). A general theory of marketing ethics. *Journal of Macromarketing*, 6(1), 5–16.

Hunt, S.D., and Vitell, S.J. (2006). The general theory of marketing ethics: a revision and three questions. *Journal of Macromarketing*, 26(2), 143–53.

Izzo, J. (2015). VW scandal a growing-up time for the CSR movement. *Sustainable Brands*, 7 October. Retrieve from: https://www.sustainablebrands.com/news_and_views/marketing_comms/dr_john_izzo/vw_scandal_growing-_time_csr_movement (accessed 13 October 2018).

Jamieson, K.H. (2013). Messages, micro-targeting, and new media technologies. *The Forum*, 11(3): 429–35.

Jones, N., Baines, P., Craig, R., Tunnicliffe, I., and O'Shaughnessy, N.J. (2015). The Islamist cyberpropaganda threat and its counter-terrorism policy implications. In: J.L. Richet (ed.), *Cybersecurity Policies and Strategies for Cyberwarfare Prevention*, Hershey, PA: IGI Global, 341–66.

Kaye, L. (2015). VW scandal exposes what has gone awry with 'CSR'. *TriplePundit*, 23 February. Retrieve from: https://www.triplepundit.com/2015/09/vw-scandal-exposes-what-is-has-gone-awry-with-csr/ (accessed 13 October 2018).

Kim, S.Y., and Chun, S.Y. (2003). A study of marketing ethics in Korea: what do Koreans care about? *International Journal of Management*, 20(3), 377–83.

Kimes, S.E., and Wirtz, J. (2003). Has revenue management become acceptable? Findings from an international study on the perceived fairness of rate fences. *Journal of Service Research*, 6(2), 125–35.

King, M. (2012). Women count cost of car insurance as EU gender rules come into force. *The Guardian*, 21 December. Retrieve from: https://www.guardian.co.uk/money/2012/dec/21/women-car-insurance-eu (accessed 13 October 2018).

Kollewe, J. (2014). GlaxoSmithKline affirms policy of anti-corruption amid 14% profits fall. *The Guardian*, 23 July. Retrieve from: https://www.theguardian.com/business/2014/jul/23/glaxosmithkline-andrew-witty-anti-corruption-profits-fall (accessed 13 October 2018).

Kollewe, J., Treanor, J., and Hickey, S. (2014). Banks pay out £166bn over six years: a history of banking misdeeds and fines. *The Guardian*, 12 November. Retrieve from: https://www.theguardian.com/business/2014/nov/12/banks-fined-200bn-six-years-history-banking-penalties-libor-forex (accessed 13 October 2018).

Kottasova, I. (2014). World's most corrupt industries. *CNN Money*, 3 December. Retrieve from: https://money.cnn.com/2014/12/02/news/bribery-foreign-corruption/ (accessed 13 October 2018).

Kull, A.J., Mena, J.A., and Korschun, D. (2016). A resource-based view of stakeholder marketing. *Journal of Business Research*, 69(12), 5553–60.

Laczniak, G.R., and Murphy, P.E. (1993). *Ethical Marketing Decisions: The Higher Road.* Englewood Cliffs, NJ: Prentice Hall.

Levick, R. (2015). New data: bribery is often 'an unspoken rule' in China. *Forbes*, 21 January. Retrieve from: https://www.forbes.com/sites/richardlevick/2015/01/21/new-data-bribery-is-often-an-unspoken-rule-in-china/#451e19ec45fc (accessed 13 October 2018).

Liu, F., Cheng, H., and Li, J. (2009). Consumer responses to sex appeal advertising: a cross-cultural study. *International Marketing Review*, 26(4–5), 501–20.

Lynn, M. (2015). Corporate social responsibility has become a racket—and a dangerous one. *The Telegraph*, 28 September. Retrieve from: https://www.telegraph.co.uk/finance/newsbysector/industry/11896546/Corporate-Social-Responsibility-has-become-a-racket-and-a-dangerous-one.html (accessed 13 October 2018).

Maignan, I., Ferrell, O.C., and Ferrell, L. (2005). A stakeholder model for implementing social responsibility in marketing. *European Journal of Marketing*, 39(9–10), 956–77.

Marshall, J. (2015). The VW scandal: huge consequences, simple ethics lessons, ominous implications. *Ethics Alarms*, 27 September. Retrieve from: https://ethicsalarms.com/2015/09/27/the-vw-scandal-huge-consequences-simple-ethics-lessons-ominous-implications/ (accessed 13 October 2018).

Marta, J.K.M., and Singhapakdi, A. (2005). Comparing Thai and US businesspeople: perceived intensity of unethical marketing practices, corporate ethical values and perceived importance of ethics. *International Marketing Review*, 22(5), 562–77.

Martin, K.D., and Murphy, P.E. (2017). The role of data privacy in marketing. *Journal of the Academy of Marketing Science*, 45(2), 135–55.

Martin, R.L. (2002). The virtue matrix: calculating the return on corporate responsibility. *Harvard Business Review*, 80(3), 5–11.

Marx, K. (1867 [1990]). *Capital: Critique of Political Economy*, Vol. 1. London: Penguin.

Mautner, T. (ed.) (1999). *Penguin Dictionary of Philosophy*. London: Penguin.

Maytom, T. (2016). Pornhub becomes Diesel's top referral website following ad deal. *Mobile Marketing*, 21 March. Retrieve from: https://mobilemarketingmagazine.com/pornhub-becomes-diesels-top-referral-site-following-ad-deal/ (accessed 13 October 2018).

McAlister, A. (2015). Call us before your ex does . . . , *Slater+Gordon Blog*, 19 November. Retrieve from: https://www.slatergordon.co.uk/media-centre/blog/2015/11/call-us-before-your-ex-does/ (accessed 13 October 2018).

McCoy, K., and Bomey, N. (2015). Shkreli resigns as Turing CEO. *USA Today*, 18 December. Retrieve from: https://www.usatoday.com/story/money/2015/12/18/martin-shkreli-turing-pharmaceuticals/77557514/ (accessed 13 October 2018).

McCurry, J. (2016). Former Tepco bosses charged over Fukushima meltdown. *The Guardian*, 29 February. Retrieve from: https://www.theguardian.com/environment/2016/feb/29/former-tepco-bosses-charged-fukushima (accessed 13 October 2018).

Mintel (2013). Coca-Cola brings anti-obesity push to the UK, 11 April. Retrieve from: https://www.mintel.com (accessed 13 October 2018).

Murphy, P.E. (1999). Character and virtue ethics in international marketing: an agenda for managers, researchers and educators. *Journal of Business Ethics*, 18(1), 107–24.

Nantel, J., and Weeks, W.A. (1996). Marketing ethics: is there more to it than the utilitarian approach? *European Journal of Marketing*, 30(5), 9–19.

Newman, K. (2001). The sorcerer's apprentice? Alchemy, seduction and confusion in modern marketing. *International Journal of Advertising*, 20(4), 409–29.

O'Shaughnessy, N.J., and Baines, P. (2009). The selling of terror: the symbolisations and positioning of jihad. *Marketing Theory*, 9(2), 227–41.

Oxford Dictionaries (2016). Ethics. Retrieve from: https://en.oxforddictionaries.com/definition/ethics (accessed 13 October 2018).

Packard, V.O. (1960). *The Hidden Persuaders.* Harmondsworth: Penguin Books.

Pagliery, J. (2015). Google abused its monopoly power, FTC experts found. *CNN Money*, 20 March. Retrieve from: https://money.cnn.com/2015/03/19/technology/google-monopoly-ftc/ (accessed 13 October 2018).

Paton, G. (2015). Buyers shun Volkswagen after diesel test scandal. *The Times, 5 December, 49.*

Peattie, K. (2001). Towards sustainability: the third age of green marketing. *Marketing Review*, 2(2), 129–46.

Peattie, K., and Crane, A. (2005). Green marketing: legend, myth, farce or prophesy? *Qualitative Market Research*, 8(4), 357–70.

Pope, N.K.L., Voges, K.E., and Brown, M.R. (2004). The effect of provocation in the form of mild erotica on attitude to the ad and corporate image: differences between cause-related and product-based advertising. *Journal of Advertising*, 33(1), 69–82.

Porter, M.E., and Kramer, M.R. (2011). Creating shared value. *Harvard Business Review*, January–February. Retrieve from: https://hbr.org/2011/01/the-big-idea-creating-shared-value (accessed 13 October 2018).

Ranchordas, S., Gedeon, Z., and Zurek, K. (2016). Home-sharing in the digital economy: the cases of Brussels, Stockholm, and Budapest. Retrieve from: http://ec.europa.eu/docsroom/documents/16950/attachments/1/translations/en/renditions/native (accessed 13 October 2018).

Roberts, R. (2017). Eggs recall: 700,000 distributed in UK contaminated with Fipronil pesticide. *The Independent*, 10 August. Retrieve from: https://www.independent.co.uk/news/uk/home-news/eggs-recall-uk-pesticide-fipronil-contaminated-germany-lidl-aldi-netherlands-a7886041.html (accessed 13 October 2018).

Roland, D. (2015). GlaxoSmithKline bribery scandal led to 13-fold increase in China whistleblower reports. *The Telegraph*, 26 February. Retrieve from: https://www.telegraph.co.uk/finance/newsbysector/pharmaceuticalsandchemicals/11438063/GlaxoSmithKline-bribery-scandal-led-to-13-fold-increase-in-China-whistleblower-reports.html (accessed 13 October 2018).

Ruddick, G. (2015). Retailer admits 'duty' to farmers. *The Guardian,* 17 August, 21.

Saren, M. (2011). Critical marketing: theoretical underpinnings. In: G. Hastings, K. Angus, and C. Bryant (eds), *The Sage Handbook of Social Marketing*, London: Sage, 95–107.

Scheufele, D.A., and Tewksbury, D. (2007). Framing, agenda setting and priming: the evolution of three media effects models. *Journal of Communication*, 57(1), 9–20.

Shankar, A. (2009). Reframing critical marketing. *Journal of Marketing Management*, 25(7–8), 681–96.

Sharma, A., Gopalkrishnan, I.R., Mehotra, A., and Krishnan, R. (2010). Sustainability and business-to-business marketing: a framework and implications. *Industrial Marketing Management*, 39(2), 330–41.

Sherover, E. (1979). The virtue of poverty: Marx's transformation of Hegel's concept of the poor. *Canadian Journal of Political and Social Theory*, 3(1), 53–66.

Sheth, J.N., Sethia, N.K., and Srinivas, S. (2011). Mindful consumption: a customer-centric approach to sustainability. *Journal of the Academy of Marketing Science*, 39(1), 21–39.

Singhapakdi, A., Marta, J.K., Rallapalli, K.C., and Rao, C.P. (2000). Towards an understanding of religiousness and marketing ethics: an empirical study. *Journal of Business Ethics*, 27(4), 305–19.

Singhapakdi, A., Salyachivin, S., Virakul, B., and Veerayangkur, V. (2000). Some important factors underlying ethical decision-making of managers in Thailand. *Journal of Business Ethics*, 27(3), 271–84.

Smith, A. (1776). *The Wealth of Nations.* London: Penguin, 1982.

Smithers, R. (2016). Product recalls hit all-time high fuelled by car and food scandals. *The Guardian*, 14 March. Retrieve from: https://www.theguardian.com/money/2016/mar/14/product-recalls-hit-all-time-high-fuelled-by-car-and-food-scandals (accessed 13 October 2018).

Summers, T. (2018). Facebook is killing democracy with its personality profiling data, *The Conversation*, 21 March. Retrieve from: https://theconversation.com/facebook-is-killing-democracy-with-its-personality-profiling-data-93611 (accessed 13 October 2018).

Sundararajan, A. (2017). The collaborative economy: socioeconomic, regulatory and policy issues. Retrieve from: http://www.europarl.europa.eu/RegData/etudes/IDAN/2017/595360/IPOL_IDA(2017)595360_EN.pdf (accessed 13 October 2018).

Tadajewski, M. (2010). Towards a history of critical marketing studies. *Journal of Marketing Management*, 26(9–10), 773–824.

Taddonio, P. (2014). How we uncovered Firestone's deal with Charles Taylor. *PBS Frontline*, 18 November. Retrieve from: https://www.pbs.org/wgbh/frontline/

article/how-we-uncovered-firestones-deal-with-charles-taylor/ (accessed 13 October 2018).

Tesco (2013). *What Matters Now: Using Our Scale for Good—Tesco and Society Report 2013*. Retrieve from: https://www.tescoplc.com/files/pdf/reports/tesco_and_society_2013_ipad.pdf (accessed 13 October 2018).

Tovey, A. (2016). VW accounts delay 'may signal bigger costs from emissions scandal'. *The Telegraph*, 16 February. Retrieve from: https://www.telegraph.co.uk/finance/newsbysector/industry/12160427/VW-accounts-delay-may-signal-bigger-costs-from-emissions-scandal.html (accessed 13 October 2018).

Transparency International (2018). *Corrupt Perceptions Index 2017*. Retrieve from: https://www.transparency.org/news/feature/corruption_perceptions_index_2017 (accessed 13 October 2018).

Treanor, J. (2015). FCA unable to estimate future PPI cost to banks. *The Guardian*, 26 November. Retrieve from: https://www.theguardian.com/money/2015/nov/26/fca-unable-to-estimate-future-ppi-cost-to-banks (accessed 13 October 2018).

Treanor, J. (2016). SFO ends foreign exchange fraud inquiry with no charges brought. *The Guardian*, 15 March. Retrieve from: https://www.theguardian.com/law/2016/mar/15/sfo-serious-fraud-office-foreign-exchange-inquiry-forex-rigging (accessed 13 October 2018).

Treanor, J., and Rushe, D. (2015). Banks hit by record fine for rigging forex markets. *The Guardian*, 20 May. Retrieve from: https://www.theguardian.com/business/2015/may/20/banks-hit-by-record-57bn-fine-for-rigging-forex-markets (accessed 13 October 2018).

Trefis Team (2018). As a rare profitable unicorn, Airbnb appears to be worth at least $38 billion. *Forbes*, 11 May. Retrieve from: https://www.forbes.com/sites/greatspeculations/2018/05/11/as-a-rare-profitable-unicorn-airbnb-appears-to-be-worth-at-least-38-billion/#508b61d2741e (accessed 13 October 2018).

Trotman, A. (2015). UK investors could start forex lawsuits after banking trio settle for $1bn in US. *The Telegraph*, 22 October. Retrieve from: https://www.telegraph.co.uk/finance/financial-crime/11949515/UK-investors-could-start-forex-lawsuits-after-banking-trio-settle-for-1bn-in-US.html (accessed 13 October 2018).

van Dam, Y.K., and Apeldoorn, P.A.C. (1996). Sustainable marketing. *Journal of Macromarketing*, 16(2), 45–56.

Vlachos, P.A., Tsamakos, A., Vrechopoulos, A.P., and Avramidis, P.K. (2009). Corporate social responsibility: attributions, loyalty, and the mediating role of trust. *Journal of the Academy of Marketing Science*, 37(2), 170–80.

WCED (World Commission on Environment and Development) (1987). *Our Common Future: The Brundtland Report*. Oxford: Oxford University Press.

Wearden, G. (2014). £2bn wiped off Tesco's value as profit overstating scandal sends shares sliding—as it happened. *The Guardian*, 22 September. Retrieve from: https://www.theguardian.com/business/live/2014/sep/22/tesco-launches-inquiry-after-overstating-profit-forecasts-by-250m-business-live (accessed 13 October 2018).

Wilkie, W.L., and Moore, E.S. (1999). Marketing's contributions to society. *Journal of Marketing*, 63(3–4), 198–218.

WRAP (Waste and Resources Action Programme) (2016). WRAP and the circular economy. Retrieve from: http://www.wrap.org.uk/content/wrap-and-the-circular-economy (accessed 13 October 2018).

Index